EUROPE in 1715 after the Treaties of Utrecht & Rastadt

0   100   200   300   400
SCALE OF MILES

Hapsburg Dominions
Piedmont (House of Savoy)
Prussia
Hanover (House of Brunswick)
Bavaria and the Palatinate
Venice
Boundary of the Empire

Stockholm

St. Petersburg

RUSSIA

BALTIC SEA

POLAND

Königsberg

Thorn

Warsaw

Breslau

Lublin

RUSSIA

MOLDAVIA

Budapest

HUNGARY

Temesvar

WALLACHIA

BLACK SEA

BOSNIA

SERVIA

TURKISH   EMPIRE

Constantinople

SEA

(apal)

Athens

Smyrna

MOREA

RHODES

CYPRUS

WONG

BY WILL DURANT

The Story of Philosophy
Transition
The Pleasure of Philosophy
Adventures in Genius

BY WILL AND ARIEL DURANT

THE STORY OF CIVILIZATION

1. *Our Oriental Heritage*
2. *The Life of Greece*
3. *Caesar and Christ*
4. *The Age of Faith*
5. *The Renaissance*
6. *The Reformation*
7. *The Age of Reason Begins*
8. *The Age of Louis XIV*
9. *The Age of Voltaire*
10. *Rousseau and Revolution*
11. *The Age of Napoleon*

The Lessons of History
Interpretation of Life
A Dual Autobiography

THE AGE OF VOLTAIRE

A History of Civilization in Western Europe from 1715 to 1756, with Special Emphasis on the Conflict between Religion and Philosophy

by

Will and Ariel Durant

MJF BOOKS
NEW YORK

Published by MJF Books
Fine Communications
POB 0930
Planetarium Station
New York, NY 10024-0540

Copyright © 1965 by Will and Ariel Durant
Copyright Renewed © 1992 by Monica Mihell

Library of Congress Catalog Card Number 92-82064
ISBN 1-56731-020-6

This edition published by arrangement with Simon & Schuster Inc. This edition
is identical to that published by Simon & Schuster Inc.

Manufactured in the United States of America

MJF Books and the MJF colophon are trademarks of Fine Creative Media, Inc.

10 9 8 7 6 5 4 3 2 1

TO OUR BELOVED
GRANDSON
JIM

Apology

BLAME for the length of this volume must rest with authors fascinated to exuberant prolixity by the central theme—that pervasive and continuing conflict between religion and science-plus-philosophy which became a living drama in the eighteenth century, and which has resulted in the secret secularism of our times. How did it come about that a major part of the educated classes in Europe and America has lost faith in the theology that for fifteen centuries gave supernatural sanctions and supports to the precarious and uncongenial moral code upon which Western civilization has been based? What will be the effects—in morals, literature, and politics —of this silent but fundamental transformation?

The scale of treatment in each volume has grown with the increasing number of past events and personalities still alive in their influence and interest today. This and the multiplicity of topics—all aspects of civilization in Western Europe from 1715 to 1756—may offer some excuse for the proliferation of the tale. So *The Age of Voltaire* has burst its seams, and spills over into a contemplated Part X, *Rousseau and Revolution*, which will carry the story to 1789. This will look at the transformation of the world map by the Seven Years' War; the later years of Louis XV, 1756–74; the epoch of Johnson and Reynolds in England; the development of the Industrial Revolution; the flowering of German literature from Lessing to Goethe, of German philosophy from Herder to Kant, of German music from Gluck to Mozart; the collapse of feudalism in the France of Louis XVI; and the history of those peripheral nations—Sweden, Denmark, Poland, Russia, Turkey, Italy, Portugal, Spain—which have been deferred from this volume partly to save space, and as not directly involved (except through the papacy) in the great debate between reason and faith. This final volume will consider the later phases of that debate in the revolt of Rousseau against rationalism, and the heroic effort of Immanuel Kant to save the Christian theology through the Christian ethic. The perspective of the age of Voltaire will be completed in that Part X of *The Story of Civilization*. The epilogue to the present volume reviews the case for religion; the epilogue to *Rousseau and Revolution*, surveying all ten volumes, will face the culminating question: What are the lessons of history?

We have tried to reflect reality by combining history and biography. The experiment will legitimately invite criticism, but it carries out the aim of "integral history." Events and personalities go hand in hand through time, regardless of which were causes and which were effects; history speaks in

vii

events, but through individuals. This volume is not a biography of Voltaire; it uses his wandering and agitated life as connective tissue between nations and generations, and it accepts him as the most significant and illustrative figure of the period between the death of Louis XIV and the fall of the Bastille. Which, of all the men and women of that turbulent era, is more vividly remembered, more often read, more alive in influence today, than Voltaire? "Voltaire," said Georg Brandes, "summarizes a century."[1] "*Le vrai roi du dix-huitième siècle*," said Victor Cousin, "*c'est Voltaire.*"[2] Let us follow that living flame through his century.

The manuscript has had the advantage of being read by Dr. Theodore Bester-man, Director of the Institut et Musée Voltaire in Geneva; we thank him for his patience, and for opening to us his great collection of Voltaireana. He found one serious error in our text, but otherwise voted us "a very high degree of ac-curacy." Doubtless some errors still remain. We shall welcome all corrections that are tempered with mercy.

Our warm appreciation to Sarah and Harry Kaufman for their help in classify-ing the material, and to our grandson, James Easton, for revising the chapter on the history of science. Our daughter Ethel not only typed the manuscript but improved it by her suggestions. And we have had again the benefit of expert and scholarly editing of the text, the notes, and the index by Mrs. Vera Schneider.

NOTES ON THE USE OF THIS BOOK

1. Dates of birth and death will be found in the Index.

2. Voltaire reckoned a 50 per cent depreciation of French currency between 1640 and 1750.[3] The general reader may use the following rough equivalents, as between 1750 and 1965, in terms of the currency of the United States of America:

crown, $6.25	guilder, $5.25	penny, $.10
ducat, $6.25	guinea, $26.25	pound, $25.00
écu, $3.75	gulden, $5.25	shilling, $1.25
florin, $6.25	livre, $1.25	sou, $.0625
franc, $1.25	louis d'or, $25.00	thaler, $4.00
	mark, $16.67	

3. The location of works of art, when not indicated in the text, will usually be found in the Notes. In allocating such works, the name of the city will imply its leading gallery, as follows:

Amsterdam—Rijksmuseum	Edinburgh—National Gallery
Berlin—Staatsmuseum	Frankfurt—Städelsches Kunstinstitut
Bologna—Accademia di Belle Arti	Geneva—Musée d'Art et d'Histoire
Budapest—Museum of Fine Arts	The Hague—Mauritshuis
Chicago—Art Institute	Kansas City—Nelson Gallery
Cincinnati—Art Institute	Leningrad—Hermitage
Cleveland—Museum of Art	London—National Gallery
Detroit—Institute of Art	Madrid—Prado
Dresden—Gemälde-Galerie	Milan—Brera
Dulwich—College Gallery	Naples—Museo Nazionale

New York—Metropolitan Museum of
    Art
Paris—Louvre

San Marino, Calif.—Henry E. Hunt-
    ington Art Gallery
Vienna—Kunsthistorisches Museum
Washington—National Gallery

4. Passages in reduced type are especially dull and recondite, and are not essential to the general picture of the age.

Table of Contents

PROLOGUE

BOOK I: ENGLAND: 1714–56

BOOK II: FRANCE: 1723–56

BOOK IV: THE ADVANCEMENT OF LEARNING
1715–89

BOOK V: THE ATTACK UPON CHRISTIANITY
1730–74

List of Illustrations

THE page numbers in the captions refer to a discussion in the text of the subject or the artist, and sometimes both.

PROLOGUE

CHAPTER I

France: The Regency

1715–23

I. THE YOUNG VOLTAIRE: 1694–1715

HE was not yet Voltaire; till his release from the Bastille in 1718 he was
François Marie Arouet. He was born in Paris on November 21, 1694,
and became its distilled essence till 1778. His presumptive father, François
Arouet, was an affluent attorney, acquainted with the poet Boileau and the
courtesan Ninon de Lenclos, whose wills he wrote, and with the dramatist
Pierre Corneille, whom he described as "the most boring mortal" he had
ever met.[1] The mother, Marie Marguerite Daumard, was of slightly noble
lineage, daughter of an official of the Parlement, and sister of the comptroller general of the royal guard; through them she had access to the court
of Louis XIV. Her vivacity and sprightly wit made her home a minor salon.
Voltaire thought she possessed all the intellect in his parentage, as his father
had all the financial skill; the son absorbed both of these gifts into his heritage. She died at the age of forty, when he was seven. Of her five children
the eldest was Armand, who adhered zealously to the Jansenist theology
and the patrimonial property. François Marie, the youngest child, was so
sickly in his first year that no one believed he could survive. He continued
till his eighty-fourth year to expect and announce his early death.

Among the friends of the family were several abbés. This title, meaning
father, was given to any secular ecclesiastic, whether or not he was an ordained priest. Many abbés, while continuing to wear ecclesiastical dress,
became men of the world and shone in society; several were prominently
at home in irreverent circles; some lived up to their title literally but clandestinely. The Abbé de Châteauneuf was the last lover of Ninon de Lenclos
and the first teacher of Voltaire. He was a man of wide culture and broad
views; he passed on to his pupil the paganism of Ninon and the skepticism
of Montaigne. According to an old but questioned story, he introduced to
the boy a mock epic, *La Moïsade*, which was circulating in secret manuscripts; its theme was that religion, aside from belief in a Supreme Being,
was a device used by rulers to keep the ruled in order and awe.[2]

Voltaire's education proceeded when his abbé tutor took him on a visit
to Ninon. The famous hetaera was then (1704) eighty-four years old.
François found her "dry as a mummy," but still full of the milk of woman's

kindness. "It pleased her," he later recalled, "to put me in her will; she left me two thousand francs to buy books with."[3] She died soon afterward.

To balance this diet he was entered, age ten, as a resident student at the Jesuit College of Louis-le-Grand on the Left Bank of Paris. It was reputed the best school in France. Among its two thousand pupils were such sons of the nobility as could bear an education; in his seven years there Voltaire made many of the aristocratic friends with whom he maintained an easy familiarity throughout his life. He received a good training in the classics, in literature, and especially in drama; he acted in plays presented there, and, aged twelve, wrote a play himself. He did well in his studies, won many prizes, and delighted and alarmed his teachers. He expressed disbelief in hell, and called heaven "the great dormitory of the world."[4] One of his teachers sadly predicted that this young wit would become the standard-bearer of French deism—i.e., a religion that discarded nearly all theology except belief in God. They endured him with their customary patience, and he reciprocated by retaining, through all his heresies, a warm respect and gratitude for the Jesuits who had disciplined his intellect to clarity and order. He wrote, when he was fifty-two:

> I was educated for seven years by men who took unrewarded and indefatigable pains to form the minds and morals of youth. . . . They inspired in me a taste for literature, and sentiments which will be a consolation to me to the end of my life. Nothing will ever efface from my heart the memory of Father Porée, who is equally dear to all who have studied under him. Never did a man make study and virtue so pleasant. . . . I had the good fortune to be formed by more than one Jesuit of the character of Father Porée. What did I see during the seven years that I was with the Jesuits? The most industrious, frugal, regulated life; all their hours divided between the care they took of us and the exercises of their austere profession. I call to witness the thousands educated by them, as I was; there is not one who would belie my words.[5]

After graduation François proposed to make literature his profession, but his father, warning him that authorship was an open sesame to destitution, insisted on his studying law. For three years François, as he put it, "studied the laws of Theodosius and Justinian in order to know the practice of Paris." He resented "the profusion of useless things with which they wished to load my brain; my motto is, TO THE POINT."[6] Instead of absorbing himself in pandects and precedents he cultivated the society of some skeptical epicureans who met in the Temple—the remains of an old monastery of the Knights Templar in Paris. Their chief was Philippe de Vendôme, grand prior of France, who had enormous ecclesiastical revenues and little religious belief. With him were the Abbés Servien, de Bussy, and de Chaulieu, the Marquis de La Fare, the Prince de Conti, and other notables of easy income and gay life. The Abbé de Chaulieu proclaimed that wine and women were the most delectable boons granted to man by a wise and beneficent Nature.[7] Voltaire adjusted himself without effort to this regimen, and shocked his father by staying out with such revelers till the then ungodly hour of 10 P.M.

Presumably at the father's request, Voltaire was appointed page to the French ambassador at The Hague (1713). All the world knows how the excitable youth fell in love with Olympe Dunoyer, pursued her with poetry, and promised her eternal adoration. "Never love equaled mine," he wrote to her, "for never was there a person better worthy of love than you."[8] The ambassador notified Arouet *père* that François was not made for diplomacy. The father summoned his son home, disinherited him, and threatened to ship him off to the West Indies. François, from Paris, wrote to "Pimpette" that if she did not come to him he would kill himself. Being wiser by two years and one sex, she answered that he had better make his peace with his father and become a good lawyer. He received paternal pardon on condition that he enter a law office and reside with the lawyer. He agreed. Pimpette married a count. It was apparently Voltaire's last romance of passion. He was as high-strung as any poet, he was all nerves and sensitivity, but he was not strongly sexed; he was to have a famous liaison, but it would be far less an attraction of bodies than a mating of minds. His energy flowed out through his pen. Already at the age of twenty-five he wrote to the Marquise de Mimeure: "Friendship is a thousand times more precious than love. It seems to me that I am in no degree made for passion. I find something a bit ridiculous in love . . . I have made up my mind to renounce it forever."[9]

On September 1, 1715, Louis XIV died, to the great relief of Protestant Europe and Catholic France. It was the end of a reign and an age: a reign of seventy-two years, an age—*le grand siècle*—that had begun in the glory of martial triumphs, the brilliance of literary masterpieces, the splendor of baroque art, and had ended in the decay of arts and letters, the exhaustion and impoverishment of the people, the defeat and humiliation of France. Everyone turned with hope and doubt to the government that was to succeed the magnificent and unmourned King.

II. THE STRUGGLE FOR THE REGENCY: 1715

There was a new king, Louis XV, great-grandson of Louis XIV, but he was only five years old. He had lost his grandfather, his father, his mother,

his brothers, his sisters, his great-grandfather last of all. Who would be regent for him?

Two dauphins had preceded Le Roi Soleil to death: his son Louis, who
had died in 1711, and his grandson, the Duke of Burgundy, who had died
in 1712. Another grandson had been accepted as Philip V of Spain, on condition of renouncing all rights to the throne of France. Two of the old King's
illegitimate sons survived him; he had legitimized them, and had decreed
that in default of princes of the royal blood, they should inherit his crown.
The elder of them, Louis Auguste, Duc du Maine, now forty-five, was an
amiable weakling whose consciousness of his club foot intensified his shy-
ness and timidity; he might well have been content with the luxury and
ease of his 900,000-livre estate at Sceaux (just outside of Paris), had not
his ambitious wife prodded him to compete for the regency. The Duchesse
du Maine never forgot that she was the granddaughter of the Great Condé;
she maintained an almost royal court at Sceaux, where she patronized artists and poets (including Voltaire), and gathered about her a gay and faithful entourage as a prelude and springboard to sovereignty. She had some
charms. She was immaculate in body and garb, so short and slim that she
could have been taken for a girl; she had wit and cleverness, a good classical education, a ready tongue, an inexhaustible and exhausting vivacity. She
was sure that under her thumb her husband would make a delightful regent. She had prevailed sufficiently with the forces about the dying King
to have drawn from him (August 12, 1715) a will that left to the Duc du
Maine control of the young Louis' person, education, and household troops,
and a place on the Council of Regency. However, a codicil (August 25)
to that will named, as president of the Council, Philippe II, Duc
d'Orléans.

Philippe was the son of the old King's androgynous brother Philippe I
("Monsieur") by a second wife, the robust and realistic Charlotte Elisabeth,
Princess Palatine. The youth's education had been entrusted to an abbé
whom both Saint-Simon's *Memoirs* and Duclos' *Secret Memoirs of the Regency* describe as a *cloaca maxima* of vices. The son of a provincial apothecary, Guillaume Dubois studied hard, earned his living by tutoring,
married, then left his wife, with her consent, to enter the Collège Saint-
Michel at Paris, where he paid his tuition by zealously performing menial
tasks. Graduating, he accepted a position as aide to Saint-Laurent, officer
of the household to "Monsieur." He took the tonsure and minor orders,
apparently forgetting his wife. When Saint-Laurent died Dubois was made
tutor to the future Regent. According to the rarely impartial Duclos, "the
Abbé felt that he would soon be despised by his pupil if he did not corrupt
him; he left nothing undone to accomplish this end, and unfortunately was

but too successful."[10] Saint-Simon, who hated unpedigreed talent, enjoyed himself describing Dubois:

> A little, pitiful, wizened, herring-gutted man in a flaxen wig, with a weazel's face brightened by some intellect. In familiar terms, he was a regular scamp. All the vices unceasingly fought within him for supremacy, so that a continual uproar filled his mind. Avarice, debauchery, ambition were his gods; perfidy, flattery, footlicking his means of action; complete impiety was his religion; and he held the opinion, as a great principle, that probity and honesty are chimeras with which people deck themselves, but which have no existence. . . . He had wit, learning, knowledge of the world, and much desire to please and insinuate himself, but all was spoiled by an odor of falsehood which escaped in spite of him through every pore of his body. . . . Wicked, . . . treacherous, and ungrateful, expert in the blackest villainies, terribly brazen when detected. He desired everything, envied everything, and wished to seize everything.[11]

Saint-Simon was close to Philippe's family, and must not be rashly contradicted; we must add, however, that this abbé was a good scholar, an able aide, a wise and successful diplomat, and that Philippe, knowing the man well, remained faithful to him to the end.

The pupil, perhaps already botched by his paternal ancestry, took readily to his tutor's instructions, and bettered them in mind and vice. He delighted his teacher by his tenacious memory, his intellectual acumen, his penetrating wit, his understanding and appreciation of literature and art. Dubois secured Fontenelle to ground the youth in science, and Homberg to initiate him into chemistry; later Philippe, like Charles II of England and Voltaire at Cirey, was to have his own laboratory, and seek in chemical experiments some respite from adultery. He painted tolerably, played the lyre, engraved illustrations for books, and collected art with the most discriminating taste. In none of these fields did he dig deeply; his interests were too varied, and his amusements had an option on his time. He was quite devoid of religious belief; even in public he "affected a scandalous impiety."[12] In this and in his sexual license he gave a symbol and impetus to his country and century.

Like most of us he was a confusion of characters. He lied with ease and sly delight at need or whim; he spent millions of francs, drawn from an impoverished people, on his personal pleasures and pursuits; however, he was generous and kindly, affable and tolerant, "naturally good, humane, and compassionate" (said Saint-Simon[13]), and more faithful to his friends than to his mistresses. He drank himself drunk as a nightly ritual before going to bed.[14] When his mother reproved him he answered her, "From six o'clock in the morning till night I am subjected to prolonged and fatiguing labor; if I did not amuse myself after that, I could not bear it; I should die of melancholy."[15]

Perhaps his sexual redundancies had some excuse in the abortion of his first love. He developed a passionate attachment to Mlle. de Séry, a high-born maid of honor to his mother. He wrote poetry for her, sang to her, visited her twice a day, and wished to marry her. Louis XIV frowned, and powerfully recommended his bastard daughter, the Duchesse de Blois. Philippe obeyed (1692), but continued his attentions to Mlle. de Séry so zealously that she bore him a son. The angry monarch banished her from Paris. Philippe sent her many livres, but tried, with brief success, to be faithful to his wife. She gave him a daughter, the future Duchesse de Berry, who became his dearest love and bitterest tragedy.

The death of his father (1701) gave Philippe the ducal title and family wealth, with no other obligation but to enjoy his life in peace and risk it in war. He had already fought bravely against the first Grand Alliance (1692–97), receiving some major wounds; now he won further distinction by his reckless gallantry in the War of the Spanish Succession (1702–13). Surviving, he rewarded himself with a feast of tarts. Through all his sins, and except in his impieties, he maintained a charm of manners and a refinement and courtesy of speech reminiscent of the Sun King's idyllic youth.

Only when all direct heirs to the throne had been removed by death or treaty did it occur to Philippe that he might claim the regency. Gossip accused him of having poisoned the princes of the blood to clear his way to sovereignty, but posterity has agreed with Louis XIV in rejecting this calumny. Several groups began to think of him as a lesser evil than the Duc and Duchesse du Maine. French Protestants who had under duress accepted conversion to Catholicism prayed for his accession to the regency as a man notably inclined to toleration; so did the Jansenists, suffering under royal persecution and papal bulls; so did the *esprits forts*, or freethinkers, who were delighted with the idea of a freethinker ruling France; so did the Parisian populace, tired of the late King's tardy austerities; so did George I of England, who offered him financial aid, which Philippe refused. Above all, the "nobility of the sword"—the titled families that had been reduced from their ancient power by Richelieu and Louis XIV to become dependent parasites of the court—hoped through Philippe to avenge itself against the royal insult of subjection to bastards in rule and to tradesmen in administration. Saint-Simon, himself among the highest-ranking nobles, urged Philippe to abandon his idleness and debauchery, and fight for his right to the regency.

Philippe cared more for pleasure than for power, and might have preferred to be left alone. But now, prodded by his friends, he spurred himself
to a flurry of action. He or they, under the Duc du Maine's nose, bought
the support of the royal household troops. They won political and military
notables with promises of office, and coddled the Parlement with hopes of
former privileges renewed. On September 2, 1715—the very day after
Louis XIV's death—Philippe summoned the Paris Parlement, the leaders
of the nobility, and the chief officials of the state to the Palais de Justice.
The Duc du Maine came hoping to receive the regency, but the audacity,
mendacity, and eloquence of the Duc d'Orléans outplayed him. "I shall
never," Philippe promised, "have any other purpose but to relieve the
people, to re-establish good order in the finances, to maintain peace at
home and abroad, and to restore unity and tranquillity to the Church.
Therein I shall be aided by the wise representations of this august assembly,
and I hereby ask for them in anticipation";[16] i.e., he offered to restore to
the Parlement that "right of remonstrance" (against royal edicts) which
the late King had denied and ignored. This adroit move carried the day;
the Parlement almost unanimously declared Philippe regent, and gave him
full control of the Council. The Duc du Maine protested that these arrangements contravened the dead King's will, and that under such conditions he could no longer be answerable for the boy King's person, and
must ask to be relieved of that duty. Philippe and the Parlement took him at
his word, and Maine, furious but helpless, retired to Sceaux and the tirades
of his wife. Philippe d'Orléans, aged forty-two, became for eight years
regent of France.

III. BOOM AND CRASH: 1716-20

His first task was to restore financial order and stability to the state. He
inherited a bankrupt government, with a debt of 2,400,000,000 livres; to
which was added a floating debt of 590 million livres in the form of *billets
d'état*—royal promissory notes circulating in the nation, and now worth
hardly a third of their face value. The net receipts of the government for
1715 were 69 million livres; its expenses, 147 million. Most of the revenue
expected in 1716 had been spent in advance.[17]

Saint-Simon advised a flat declaration of bankruptcy. Duc Adrien Maurice
de Noailles protested. The Regent compromised with some intermediate
measures of economy and reform. The army was reduced to 25,000 men; dis-
charged soldiers were exempted from taxes for six years; those with eight
children were permanently exempt. The taille, the gabelle, the capitation,
and other taxes were reduced; abuses in their collection were denounced,

and some were remedied. Hundreds of dispensable governmental office-holders were dismissed—2,400 in Paris alone. A Chambre de Justice was established (March, 1716) before which all those financiers, merchants, munitions manufacturers, and others were summoned on suspicion of having defrauded the government. Here Noailles, accustomed to military measures, instituted a veritable terror; those who would reveal their fellow defaulters were promised lenience; informers were promised a fifth of all funds recovered by their help; the penalty of death was decreed against interference with informers; confiscation of property and condemnation to the galleys for life were prescribed for those who gave false testimony about their finances. Some convicted persons were hanged; some were put into pillories before a rejoicing populace; a few financiers, hopeless of clearing themselves, committed suicide. The results were not commensurate with the methods. Most of the guilty bought exemption from examination or conviction by bribing the officials of the Chamber, or the friends of the Regent, or his mistresses. Corruption ran to the point where, instead of the guilty offering bribes, the courtiers solicited them. A financier having been fined 1,200,000 livres, a courtier promised to have the fine forgiven for a fee of 300,000 livres. "My dear Count," said the financier, "you come too late; I have just concluded a similar arrangement with your wife for half that sum."[18] The edict that dissolved the Chambre de Justice (March, 1717) declared, with a candor rare in governments, that "corruption was so widely spread that almost all classes were infected with it, so that just punishments could not be laid upon so great a number of guilty persons without dangerously disturbing commerce, public order, and the state." The net profit to the government, when the inquisition was ended, was some seventy million francs.[19]

Disappointed with these results, the Regent gave ear to a remarkable Scot who offered him a new system of finance. John Law, born to an Edinburgh banker in 1671, studied banking in London, saw the opening of the Bank of England in 1694, fought a duel over a love affair, killed his rival, and fled to the Continent with a death sentence on his head. He was handsome, affable, mathematical; he speculated successfully in foreign exchange, and his capacity for calculating and remembering the combinations of cards helped him to butter his bread in divers lands. He watched the working of the banks at Amsterdam, Hamburg, Venice, and Genoa. In Amsterdam especially he felt the magic of the credit system, by which a bank issued paper money to many times the gold value of its reserves, putting ten gulden to work on the security of one, and so stimulating, facilitating, and multiplying industrial and commerical activities; and there he saw how, with a bank that businessmen could trust, transactions might be effected by a mere shifting of bank balances, without the nuisance of carrying or exchanging silver or gold. He wondered why such a national bank and credit system could not be established in France. He conceived what was later called his *Système*.

His central conception was to increase the employment of men and materials by issuing paper money, on the credit of the state, to twice the value of the national reserves in silver, gold, and land; and by lowering the rate of interest, so encouraging businessmen to borrow money for new enterprises and methods in industry and commerce. In this way money would create business, business would increase employment and production, the national revenues and reserves would rise, more money could be issued, and the beneficent spiral would expand. If the public, instead of hoarding the precious metals, could be induced, by interest payments, to deposit its savings in a national bank, these savings could be added to the reserves, and additional currency could be issued; idle money would be put to work, and the prosperity of the country would be advanced.

In 1708 Law expounded his ideas to the French government; Louis XIV rejected them. When Philippe d'Orléans became regent, Law proposed to redeem with his System the bankrupt finances of France. He inquired why it was that only France, Spain, and Portugal, among the leading states of Europe, were still without national banks, and why it was that France, with a soil so fruitful and men so clever, was nevertheless lying prostrate in economic stagnation. Philippe agreed to let him establish, as a private venture, a Banque Générale (1716). It accepted deposits, paid interest, made loans, and issued bank notes—for ten, a hundred, and a thousand francs—whose steady value, tied to a fixed weight of silver, soon made them a preferred medium of exchange. These notes constituted the first regular paper money, and Law's bank, with its provincial branches, set up the first organized credit system in France. In April, 1717, the notes of the bank were made receivable for taxes.

In September Law advanced to a more adventurous stage of his ideas. He secured from the Regent a concession to a new Compagnie d'Occident for the exploitation of the whole Mississippi basin, then under French control. He sold to the public 200,000 shares in this Company of the West at 500 livres per share; it was a high price, but three quarters of the payment could be made in *billets d'état*—government notes—at their face value, which was thrice their actual worth. Glad of this opportunity to exchange depreciated paper for shares in a profit-promising enterprise, the public soon took up all the shares. With swelling optimism Law instructed his bank to buy the royal tobacco monopoly, and all French companies handling foreign trade; these he combined with the Compagnie d'Occident in a Compagnie des Indes, which was to monopolize all foreign commerce. A socialism of external trade seemed to some businessmen to presage a socialism of internal production and distribution; opposition to Law began to form.

On December 4, 1718, Law's bank was reconstituted as the Banque Royale; its notes were declared legal tender, and it was given almost full control of the nation's finances. He issued new stock in the Compagnie des Indes at 550 livres the share; it was soon subscribed. Expectation of high returns raised the public estimate of the shares' worth; they were exchanged at an ever-increasing price in a wave of speculation, until they were quoted at 5,000 livres, nine or ten times their face value. Lady Mary Wortley Montagu, passing through Paris in 1718, smiled at the sight of France submitting its economic life to a Briton. Law himself allowed his imagination to distance his judgment. The new Banque Royale not only took charge of the Mint and all tax collections; it took over the national debt by giving a share in the Compagnie des Indes in exchange for 5,000 livres' face value in government obligations; in this way, he thought, passive capital would become active in his varied enterprises. He further endangered the solvency of the Banque by making a gift of 24,00 shares to the Regent.

Despite these rash ventures, public confidence in him was unimpaired, public enthusiasm for the Compagnie rose, buyers bid higher and higher for its shares. Counterfeiters added to the furor by throwing false share certificates upon the market. The narrow, dirty Rue Quincampoix, where the System had its offices, was for two years the Wall Street of Paris. Buyers and sellers of all classes, duchesses and prostitutes, Parisians, provincials, foreigners, gathered there in numbers and excitement mounted day by day. Some were trampled to death in the crush, or were run down by the carriages of the aristocracy. Old Maréchal de Villars, riding by, stopped to lecture the crowd for its fanatic greed. Tiny stalls in the little street fetched higher rentals per month than houses had brought in twenty years. Residents complained that the noise was unbearable. Still the buyers shouted their competing offers; the price of a share rose almost daily, sometimes hourly; at the end of 1719 some were sold for 12,000 livres each; by that time the market value of all outstanding shares was eighty times greater than the worth of all the known gold and silver in France.[20] Since only ten per cent of its face value had to be paid for a share, turnovers were rapid, and fortunes were made in a day. A banker made 100 million livres, a hotel waiter thirty million.[21] Now for the first time men heard the word *millionaire*.[22]

Law was the man of the hour. In 1720 he was made comptroller general of finances. Highflown lords and ladies fluttered in his anteroom, seeking his advice in money matters or his support in court intrigues. "I myself," Voltaire would recall, "saw him pass through the galleries of the Palais-Royal followed by dukes and peers, marshals of France, bishops of the Church."[23] A duchess humbly kissed his hand.

He was not visibly spoiled by the apparent triumph of his ideas, or by the exaltation of his personal power; indeed, he was alarmed by the exaggerated value that public avidity had placed upon the shares of the company.[24] He took no advantage of his position to swell his own wealth. Saint-Simon, who opposed the System, declared:

> There was neither avarice nor roguery in his composition. He was a gentle, good, respectable man, whom excess of credit and fortune had not spoiled, and whose deportment, equipage, table, and furniture could not scandalize anyone. He suffered with singular patience and constancy all vexations excited by his operations, until toward the last . . . he became quick and bad-tempered.

Some of the nobility frowned upon him as an alien and a Protestant, and noted that he and his English wife, though they seemed devoted to each other, were not legally married. To reduce this hostility Law accepted French citizenship and the Roman Catholic faith.

He used his power to spur the prosperity of his adopted country. He reduced taxes and put an end to their clumsy and corrupt collection by private agencies. He showed for the masses a sympathy unusual in financiers. He broke up, for cultivation by the peasantry, large estates held by the Church or by corporations; he went so far as to propose, soon after being made comptroller general, that the Church be compelled to sell all the property it had acquired since 1600—that is, half of all its French possessions.[25] He anticipated Turgot by abolishing duties on the movement of food and goods within France. He organized the building or repair of roads, bridges, and canals. He brought in skilled artisans from abroad to establish new industries; he encouraged industrial expansion by lowering the rate of interest on loans; French enterprises increased sixty per cent in the two years (1719–20) of his ascendancy. He revived and multiplied the merchant marine by expanding trade with Asia, Africa, and America; French ships engaged in foreign trade numbered sixteen in March, 1719, three hundred in June, 1720; French foreign commerce, under Law, reached again the zenith it had touched under Colbert. He persuaded French nobles to finance the production of coffee and tobacco in Louisiana, and himself financed the development of the Arkansas River area. In 1718 New Orleans was founded, and took the Regent's family name.

Despite the many-sided efforts of Law and Philippe, the American enterprise did not prosper. Much of the Mississippi Valley was still unconquered wilderness. Every effort was made to settle the region with French colonists. Law offered dowries and 450 acres to emigrating families. When emigration proved less attractive than speculation, prisoners, vagabonds, and prostitutes were deported to Louisiana, and young men and women (like the Manon Lescaut of Prévost's novel) were pressed into the venture by stratagem or force. Such victims were so badly fed that many of them died on the way. Edicts of May, 1720, stopped this barbarous impressment. In the colony itself poor equipment, bad management, and rebellion hampered economic improvement, and made the earnings of the "Mississippi Company" (as the people called it) far less than speculation had presumed. Hopes of gold or precious stones to be mined from the colonial soil proved illusory, though Law himself had entertained that dream.

News of these difficulties must have reached France. The cleverest of the speculators judged that the shares of the company had touched their peak, and that it was now time to sell. They made great profits by selling promptly; thousands of others, equally greedy but poorer in information or judgment, were ruined by selling too late. In December, 1719, the selling became more eager and competitive than the buying. Within a month the Duc de Bourbon disposed of his shares for twenty million livres; the Prince de Conti sold his for fourteen million; three wagons were needed to cart away the gold that Law did not dare refuse the Prince for his bank notes and company shares.[26] A Prussian speculator unloaded his holdings and departed with thirty million livres in gold. Others cashed their shares to buy land, houses, jewelry, and other articles whose worth rested on the solid base of human need or vanity. The financiers who had been punished by the Chamber of Justice revenged themselves by cashing their notes and sending the gold out of France. Law tried to stop the drain of gold from the treasury by securing from the Regent edicts forbidding the public to hold, trade, or export the precious metals, and requiring the surrender of all gold and silver above the value of five hundred francs to the Banque Royale. Agents of the bank were empowered to enter homes and search for hidden precious metal; even Louis XIV had never ventured upon such an invasion of privacy. "Many people," according to Saint-Simon, "hid their money with so much secrecy that, dying without being able to say where they had put it, their little treasures remained buried and lost to their heirs."[27]

As the price of shares continued to decline, Law tried to bolster it by offering 9,000 livres (in paper money) per share; but the consequent increase in bank notes lowered their value and raised the price of goods. By May, 1720, prices had risen one hundred per cent, wages seventy-five per cent, as compared with 1716; by July a pair of silk stockings brought forty livres. A panic of inflation set in; men rushed to exchange paper currency and stock certificates for goods; so the Duc de La Force amassed candles, and the Maréchal d'Estrées piled up stores of coffee and chocolate. To check this flight from money to goods, Law announced (May 21) a fifty per cent reduction in the official value of bank notes and company shares. It was a serious error—perhaps due to pressure from the frightened Regent, who himself felt the pressure of Law's noble and clerical foes.[28] Philippe tried to ease the crisis by restoring all his company shares to the bank.[29]

Nevertheless, the wave of selling continued. In July the bank was compelled to suspend payment on any of its notes above ten francs. Holders of the notes besieged the bank, clamoring for the redemption of their paper in silver or gold. In Paris the crowd was so great that ten women were trampled to death in the confusion; later three of the corpses were carried in an angry procession beneath the windows of the Regent. The people, whose mad speculation had caused the collapse of the System, held Law responsible for all difficulties. Attempts were made to seize and kill him; these failing, his coach was smashed to pieces in the courtyard of the Palais-Royal. Repeated riots expressed the feeling of the public that it had been deceived by financial tricks, and that the upper classes had profited at the expense of the community. Parlement joined in the attacks upon Law; Philippe banished it to Pontoise (July 20); the people defended the Parlement.

In August the shares of the Mississippi Company, which at their peak had reached 12,000 livres, fell to 2,000, and the bank notes dropped to ten per cent of their original worth. In October the news leaked out—and spread from mouth to mouth—that the Regent, during the prosperity of the Banque Royale, had drawn from it notes to the total face value of three billion francs, of which a large part had been consumed in lavish gifts to friends and mistresses. About the same time a cashier of the bank absconded to Prussia with an enormous quantity of its gold. The shares of the Mississippi Company fell to 200 livres. In December the Regent abolished the bank, dismissed Law, and recalled the Parlement. On the fourteenth, Law left France with his son. He had sunk his own fortune into the Compagnie des Indes, and shared the fate of most shareholders; he had deposited no funds abroad; now he took with him only two thousand livres and a few mediocre gems. At Brussels he received from Peter the Great an invitation to come and take charge of Russia's finances; he refused. He retired to Venice, was joined by his wife and daughter, lived in obscurity and poverty, and died there in 1729.

The principles upon which he had established his bank were theoretically sound; they would have made France solvent and prosperous had it not been for the incredible avidity of speculators and the extravagance of the Regent. Law's own accounts, on examination, were found to be without fault. Temporarily the French economy was left apparently in ruins: shareholders and noteholders were demanding impossible payment, the circulation of money was almost paralyzed, industry was hesitating, foreign commerce was becalmed, prices were beyond the capacity of the people to pay. The Regent summoned the brothers Paris to make some order out of the chaos. They called in all bank notes and redeemed their diverse categories with liens on the national revenue, at a loss of sixteen to ninety-five per cent to the holders. The public, its fury exhausted, submitted patiently to this practical bankruptcy.

Something remained from the debacle. Agriculture benefited from the rise in the value of its products and the depreciation of the currency. Industry, stimulated by low interest and high prices, recovered rapidly; new enterprises appeared everywhere. Internal trade profited from the reduction of internal tolls; commerce, when the chaos subsided, resumed its extension overseas. The middle classes, in whom the pursuit of gain was natural and necessary, emerged unscathed and enlarged. Financiers multiplied in number and power. The nobility gained by paying its debts in cheapened currency, but lost face by having shown, in the fever of speculation, a concupiscence as blatant as in any class. The Regency remained tarnished with its faithlessness to its financial obligations and its continued luxury amid widespread disaster. An anonymous critic complained that "it will take centuries to eradicate the evil which Law is responsible for in having accustomed the people to ease and luxury, in having made them discontented with their condition, in having raised the price of food and manual labor, and in making all classes of tradespeople look for exorbitant profits."[30] But that same commercial spirit stimulated the economy and the intellect of France, while lowering the moral tone of French society. By 1722 the French economy had recovered sufficiently to let the Regent return, with the easy conscience of a government, to his wonted ways of kindly rule and generous adultery.

IV. THE REGENT

His German mother had warned him to check his amiability. "It is better to be kind than harsh," she told him, "but justice consists in punishing as well as rewarding; and it is certain that he who does not make Frenchmen fear him will soon fear them, for they despise those who do not intimidate them."[31] Philippe, molded by Montaigne, admired English liberty, and spoke optimistically about having subjects who would not obey him blindly, but would be intelligent enough to let him explain to them the reasons for his laws. He symbolized the spirit of his regime by abandoning Versailles and coming to live in the Palais-Royal, in the heart and fever of Paris. He disliked the ceremonies and publicity of court life, and put them behind him. For further ease and privacy he arranged that the young

King should live not at Versailles but in the château of suburban Vincennes. Far from poisoning the boy, as gossip alleged, Philippe showed him every kindness and all due subordination, so that Louis XV preserved throughout his life a grateful remembrance of the care which the Regent had lavished upon him.[32]

Two days after Louis XIV had been buried, Philippe ordered the release from the Bastille of all prisoners except those known to have been guilty of serious crimes against society. Hundreds of these men had been imprisoned by secret letters (*lettres de cachet*) of the late King; most of them were Jansenists accused only of religious nonconformity; others had been incarcerated so long that no one, not even themselves, knew the cause. One man, arrested thirty-five years before, had never been brought to trial or told the reason of his confinement; released in his old age, he found himself bewildered by freedom; he did not know a soul in Paris, and had not a sou; he begged, and was allowed, to remain in the Bastille to the end of his life.

The dead King's confessor, Michel Le Tellier, who had hounded the Jansenists, was banished from Paris. The Regent advised the opposing factions in the Church to quiet their disputes. He winked an eye at clandestine Protestants, and appointed several of them to administrative posts. He wished to renew the liberal Edict of Nantes, but the Jesuits and the Jansenists united in denouncing such toleration, and his minister Dubois, angling for a cardinal's hat, dissuaded him.[33] "The justice refused to the Protestants by the two factions in the Church was won for them only by philosophy."[34] The Regent was a Voltairean before Voltaire. He had no perceptible religious belief; under the pious Louis XIV he had read Rabelais in church;[35] now he allowed Voltaire, Fontenelle, and Montesquieu to publish books that only a few years before would have been banned from France as imperiling Christian belief.

Politically, and even when he sent Voltaire to the Bastille, Philippe was a liberal and enlightened ruler. He explained his ordinances to the people in terms so moderate and sincere that Michelet saw in them a herald of the Constituent Assembly of 1789.[36] Offices were filled with able men regardless of their enmity to the Regent himself; one who had threatened him with assassination was made chief of the Council of Finance.[37] Philippe, by nature epicurean, remained a stoic till 5 P.M.; till then, says Saint-Simon, "he devoted himself exclusively to public business, reception of ministers, councils, etc., never dining during the day, but taking chocolate between two and three o'clock, when everybody was allowed to enter his room . . . His familiarity and his readiness of access extremely pleased people, but were much abused."[38] "Of all the race of Henry IV"—that is, of all the Bourbons—said Voltaire, "Philippe d'Orléans resembled that monarch the most in his courage, goodness of heart, openness, gaiety, affability, and freedom of access, and with an understanding better cultivated."[39] He disconcerted ambassadors and councilors by the range of his knowledge, the penetration of his mind, the wisdom of his judgment.[40] But he shared the weakness of philosophers—the ability and willingness to see so many sides to a subject that time was absorbed in discussion, and decisive action was deferred.

Liberal though he was, he would not tolerate any abridgment of the traditional royal authority. When Parlement, availing itself of the privilege of remonstrance which he had promised it, refused to register some of his decrees (i.e., to enter them among the recognized laws of the land), he summoned it (August 25, 1718) to a famous *lit de justice*—a session at which the King, seated on a "bed" of judgment, exercised his sovereignty to compel the registration of a royal edict. The 153 magistrates, solemn in their scarlet robes, walked on foot to the Tuileries. The young King, following Philippe's instructions, ordered them—and they proceeded—to register the Regent's decrees. Since the Duc and Duchesse du Maine had continued to oppose him in council and by intrigues, he took the occasion to deprive the royal bastards of their status as princes of the blood. The legitimate dukes were restored to their former precedence and rights, to the delight of the Duc de Saint-Simon, to whom this was the greatest achievement of the Regency, and the noblest moment of his *Mémoires*.

The Duchesse du Maine did not accept defeat. She financed some of the wits who pricked the Regent with lampoons. He tolerated these barbs with the patience of St. Sebastian, excepting, as we shall see, the *Philippiques* and the *J'ai-vus* ("I-have-seens") attributed to Voltaire. In December, 1718, the Duchess entered into a conspiracy with Cellamare, the Spanish ambassador, with Alberoni, the Spanish premier, and with Cardinal Melchior de Polignac to overthrow the Regent and make Philip V of Spain king of France, with the Duc du Maine as his chief minister. The conspiracy was discovered, the ambassador was dismissed, the Duke and Duchess were sent to separate prisons, from which they were released in 1721. The Duke claimed ignorance of the plot. The Duchess resumed her court and intrigues at Sceaux.

Amid these harassments, and within the limits of tradition and his character, Philippe undertook some moderate reforms. More roads were built during his brief tenure than in Louis XIV's half century. He saved millions of francs by abandoning Marly and Versailles, and keeping a numerically modest court. Many of Law's innovations survived in a more economical and merciful collection of taxes, and the dismissal of taxgatherers accused of corruption or waste. Philippe contemplated a graduated income tax: he tried it in Normandy, in Paris, and at La Rochelle; it lapsed with his premature death. He did his best to keep France out of war; he demobilized thousands of troops, and settled them on uncultivated land; he housed the remaining soldiers in barracks instead of quartering them upon the people. With generous vision he opened the University of Paris and the Bibliothèque Royale to all qualified students without charge; the state paid their tuition.[41] He supported with public funds the Académie Royale des Sciences, the Académie Royale des Inscriptions et Belles-Lettres, the Académie Royale de l'Architecture; he financed the publication of learned works; he established in the Louvre an Académie des Arts Mécaniques to promote invention and the industrial arts.[42] He gave pensions to artists, scholars, and savants, provided rooms for them in the royal palaces, and loved to talk with these men about their diverse pursuits. His measures and reforms fell short of full fruition partly because of the incubus of debt and the collapse of Law's financial revolution, and partly through the Regent's own physical and moral defects.

It is one of the pitiful tragedies in the history of France that this man with so many virtues of mind and heart was sullied and weakened with the debauchery of his class and time. Son of a sexual invert, tutored by an ecclesiastical rake, he grew up almost devoid of restraint in sexual indulgence. "He would have had virtues," said Duclos, "if one could have them without principles."[43] Forced to marry an illegitimate daughter of Louis XIV, and finding no love or comfort in his wife, he took to frequent drunkenness, and to such a concatenation of mistresses as no ruler has equaled outside of Islamic seraglios. He chose his male friends among roisterers whom he called *roués*, who spent fortunes in venery and furnished their homes with costly art and sexual stimulants.[44] In the Palais-Royal, or in his villa at St.-Cloud, Philippe joined his friends—mostly young nobles, but also some cultivated Englishmen like Lords Stair and Stanhope—in *petits soupers* where cultured women like Mme. du Deffand mingled with actresses, divas, and mistresses in providing feminine stimulation to male wit. Says Saint-Simon, with possibly some sanctimonious coloration:

> At these parties the character of everyone was passed in review, ministers and favorites like the rest, with a liberty which was unbridled license. The gallantries past and present of the court and the town, all the old stories, disputes, jokes, absurdities, were raked up; nobody was spared; M. le Duc d'Orléans had his say like the rest. But very rarely did these discourses make the slightest impression upon him. The company drank as much as they could, inflamed themselves, said the filthiest things without stint, uttered impieties with emulation; and when they had made a good deal of noise and were very drunk, they went to bed to recommence the same game the next day.[45]

Philippe's restless, uprooted spirit expressed itself in the brief tenure of his concubines. They rarely reigned beyond a month, but the superseded ones bided their time till it came their turn again. His valets, even his friends, brought him ever new candidates. Women of high rank, like the Comtesse de Parabère, adventuresses like Mme. de Tencin, singers and dancers from the opera, models of perfect beauty like Mme. de Sabran (whose "noble bearing" and "figure finest in the world" agitated even the virtuous Saint-Simon), gave themselves to the Regent for a spell of royalty, or for pensions, subsidies, jewelry; and he lavished gifts upon them from his own income or the ailing treasury. Careless though he was, he never allowed these women to elicit state secrets from him, or to discuss state affairs; when Mme. de Sabran tried to, he made her look at herself in a mirror, and asked her, "Can one talk business to such a pretty face? I shouldn't like it at all."[46] Her sway ended soon afterward.

This same paragon of promiscuity loved his mother, visited her twice daily, and meekly bore her sorrowful reprimands. He did not love his wife, but he gave her attentions and courtesy, and found time to have five children by her. He loved his children, grieved when his youngest daughter took to a nunnery, and let no day pass without visiting, in the Luxembourg Palace, his oldest daughter, whose life was almost as sad a scandal as his own.

Her marriage with Charles, Duc de Berry, soon became an oscillation of war and truce. Having caught him in alien arms, she agreed to smile upon his infidelities if he would condone her own; a contemporary chronicle adds that "they undertook to protect each other."[47] Granddaughter of "Monsieur le Sodomite," and scion of a Bavarian family with insanity in its blood, she found stability of mind or morals beyond her power; and her consciousness of her faults heated a haughty temper that alarmed all who entered her life. She took full advantage of her derivation, rode through Paris like a queen, and kept at the Luxembourg a luxurious ménage, sometimes with eight hundred servants.[48] When her husband died (1714) she entertained a succession of lovers. She shocked everyone by her drunkenness and debauchery, indecent language, and scornful pride; and her fits of piety alternated with skeptical sallies against religion.

She seems never to have loved anyone so much as her father, nor he anyone so much as her. She shared his intelligence, sensitivity, and wit along with his morals, and her beauty in youth rivaled that of his choicest mistresses. The gossip of Paris, having no heart and knowing no law, accused them of incest; for good measure it added that he had committed incest with all three of his daughters.[49] Probably some of these rumors were set afloat by the circle of Mme. du Maine.[50] Saint-Simon, closest to the situation, rejected them as base cruelties; Philippe himself never bothered to deny them. His complete freedom from jealousy of his daughter's lovers,[51] and her lack of jealousy of his mistresses[52] hardly accord with the possessive character of love.[53]

Only one man could detach her from her father—Captain Rion of her palace guard, who so entranced her with his masculinity that she became his slave. In 1719 she shut herself in at the Luxembourg with a few attendants, and gave birth to the captain's daughter. Soon afterward she secretly married him. She begged her father to let her announce this marriage; he refused; her love for him turned into a mad resentment. She fell sick, neglected herself, developed an alarming fever, and died, aged twenty-four, of a purgative administered by her doctor (July 21, 1719). An autopsy revealed some malformations in her brain. No bishop would consent to officiate at her funeral, and Philippe was humbly grateful when the monks of St.-Denis allowed her remains to be deposited in the royal vaults of their abbey church. Her mother rejoiced at her daughter's death; her father buried himself in the emptiness of power.

V. SOCIETY UNDER THE REGENCY

The growth of wealth in France between the Edict of Nantes (1598) and its Revocation (1685), the urbanization of life, and the decline of religious belief after the religious wars and the Jansenist disputes, had produced in the nobility a relaxation of morals symbolized by Louis XIV in the youth of his reign. The marriage of the King to Mme. de Maintenon (1685), his conversion to monogamy and morality, and the sobering effect of military disasters, had compelled his court to change at least its external ways; and the self-reforms of the clergy had for a generation checked the weakening of the Church. The freethinkers had censored their own publications, and the epicureans had kept their revels from public view. But when the stern and repentant King was succeeded by the skeptical, licentious, and tolerant Regent, these restraints fell away, and the resentment of suppressed instincts broke out in a wave of irreligion and self-indulgence similar to the sensual riot of English society in Restoration England after a generation of Puritan ascendancy (1642-60). Immorality was now a badge of liberation and sophistication; "debauchery became a kind of etiquette."[54]

Christianity was in decline long before the *Encyclopédie* attacked it, even before Voltaire first aimed at it the darts of his pen. Dupuy in 1717 complained of the large number of materialists in Paris.[55] "Today," said Massillon in 1718, "ungodliness almost lends an air of distinction and glory; it is a merit that gives access to the great, . . . that procures for obscure men the privilege of familiarity with the people's prince."[56] That prince's mother, shortly before her death in 1722, wrote: "I do not believe that there are in Paris, either among ecclesiastics or people of the world, one hundred persons who have a true Christian faith and really believe in our Saviour; and this makes me tremble."[57] Few of the younger generation thought of going from Catholicism to Protestantism; they went to atheism, which was much safer. The Cafés Procope and Gradot, like the Temple, were the rendezvous of unbelieving wits.

If irreligion shared in releasing moral laxity in the upper class, poverty co-operated with the natural lawlessness of men in producing moral chaos among the lower strata of Paris. The learned Lacroix calculated that "the dangerous characters, beggars, vagabonds, thieves, swindlers of every description, formed perhaps a sixth of the people";[58] and we may assume that among the urban poor, as among the rich, adultery tempered toil. Crime of all sorts flourished, from pickpockets in Paris to brigands on the roads. Paris had an organized police, but this could not keep up with crime, and sometimes contented itself with a part of the spoils.[59] In 1721 the Ministry of War at last succeeded in arresting Cartouche, the Jack Sheppard of France, and rounded up five hundred members of his band, which had made the highways unsafe even for kings. Only the peasantry and the middle classes sustained the moral stability of French life.

But in the nobility at Paris, in the floating gentry of the town, in the addicts of literature or art, in the financiers and the *abbés commendataires*, the moral precepts seemed quite forgotten, and Christianity was remembered only for a Sunday social hour. The double standard, which had sought to protect the inheritance of property by making the infidelity of the wife a far graver offense than that of the husband, was left behind when the wife came to Paris or Versailles; there the wife who confined her favors to her husband was considered old-fashioned; there women rivaled the men in tying and untying knots. Marriage was accepted to preserve the family, its possessions, and its name; but beyond that no fidelity was demanded, by the mores of the time and class, from either the husband or the wife.[60] In the Middle Ages marriage had been counted on to lead to love; now marriage as seldom led to love as love to marriage; and even in adultery there was little pretense of love. Here and there, however, a faithful couple shone as a brave exception amid the kaleidoscopic crowd: the Duke and Duchess of Saint-Simon, the Count and Countess of Toulouse, M. and Mme. de Luynes, M. and Mme. de Pontchartrain, M. and Mme. de Belle-Isle. Many reckless wives graduated into subdued and exemplary grandmothers. Some, their charms worn out with circulation, retired to comfortable convents, and distributed charity and wisdom.

One of the most enterprising women of the Regency was Claudine Alexandrine de Tencin. She bounced out of a nunnery at the age of thirty-two into a giddy progression of liaisons. She had excuses: her father was a successful philanderer as well as president of the Parlement of Grenoble; her mother was a flighty coquette; and Claudine herself was conscious of a beauty that itched to be sold. Her older sister Mme. de Grolée was only less promiscuous; in her deathbed confession at the age of eighty-seven she explained, "I was young, I was pretty; men told me so and I believed them; guess at the rest."[61] Claudine's older brother Pierre took holy orders, and made his way through many women to a cardinal's hat and the archbishopric of Lyons. To save a dowry Claudine's father entered her into a convent at Montfleury. There she fretted in reluctant piety for sixteen years. In 1713, aged thirty-two, she escaped, and hid in the room of the Chevalier Destouches, an artillery officer, with whose aid she became (1717) the mother of the philosopher d'Alembert. Not foreseeing the *Encyclopédie* in this infant, she exposed him on the steps of the Church of St.-Jean-le-Rond in Paris. She passed on to Matthew Prior and Lord Bolingbroke and Marc René de Voyer d'Argenson, and then flung herself—allegedly after posing as a nude statue[62]—into the arms of the Regent himself. Her stay there was brief; she tried to transmute her caresses into a benefice for her beloved brother; Philippe replied that he did not like wenches who talked business between sheets;[63] he ordered his doors closed to her. She picked herself up and conquered Dubois. We shall meet her again.

Amid this moral flux some women of Paris carried on the distinctive French virtue of assembling titles, intellect, and beauty in salons. The most polished society in the capital gathered in the architectural splendor of the Hôtel de Sully; there came statesmen, financiers, poets—Fontenelle in his silent sixties, Voltaire in his brash twenties. A more lighthearted group met at the Hôtel de Bouillon, which Lesage immortalized in an angry moment: invited to read there his play *Turcaret*, and arriving late, he was haughtily reproved by the Duchess, "You have made us lose an hour"; he replied, "I will make you gain twice the time," and left the house.[64] We have noted the salon of Mme. du Maine at Sceaux. Marguerite Jeanne Cordier de Launay, who was to be Baronne de Staal, served the Duchess as lady in waiting, and wrote bright *Mémoires* (published in 1755) describing the comedies, conceits, *fêtes-de-nuit*, and masquerades that left scant room for conversation amid *les divertissements de Sceaux*.

But conversation dominated the salon that Anne Thérèse de Courcelles, Marquise de Lambert, held in the Hôtel de Nevers (now the Bibliothèque Nationale). Rich but austere, she continued into the riotous Regency the staid and stately manners of Louis XIV's declining years. She discouraged cardplaying, chess, even music; she was all for intellect. Like the Marquise du Châtelet, she was interested in science and philosophy, and sometimes (says Voltaire) she talked above her own head; but the head was pretty and titled, which made any metaphysic effervesce. Every Tuesday she enter-

tained scientists and aristocrats; every Wednesday, writers, artists, and
scholars, including Fontenelle, Montesquieu, and Marivaux. At her gatherings savants gave lectures, authors read their forthcoming books, and literary reputations were made; from that *bureau d'esprit*, or ministry of mind,
this generous and ambitious hostess waged a score of successful campaigns
to get her protégés into the French Academy. She was one of the hundreds
of gracious, cultured, civilized women who make the history of France the
most fascinating story in the world.

VI. WATTEAU AND THE ARTS

A revolution in art mirrored the change in politics and morals. After the
collapse of Louis XIV's imperialistic policy in the War of the Spanish Succession (1702–13), the spirit of France turned from the gore of glory to the
pleasures of peace. The mood of the time found no need for new churches,
more use for city mansions like the Hôtel Matignon and the Palais-Bourbon
(1721–22). Excepting such architectural immensities, dwellings and rooms
became smaller now, but their decoration was more delicate and refined.
Baroque began to pass into rococo:* i.e., the style of irregular forms and
abundant ornament took a turn toward an almost brittle elegance, running
to playful and incalculable fantasy. The delight in exquisite finish, bright
colors, and surprising evolutions of design became a mark of the *style
Régence*. The classical orders disappeared under a frolic of dainty curves,
corners were concealed, moldings were lavishly carved. Sculpture abandoned the Olympian grandeur of Versailles for smaller forms of graceful
movement and emotional appeal. Furniture shunned right angles and
straight lines, and aimed at comfort rather than dignity. Now came the
siège à deux, the armchair built for two, designed for friends and lovers resenting the pathos of distance. Charles Cressent, chief cabinetmaker to the
Regent, established the Regency style with chairs, tables, desks, and bureaus
brilliant with mother-of-pearl marquetry and gay with conscious loveliness.

Philippe himself, in person, manners, and tastes, symbolized the transition
to rococo. When he moved the government from Versailles to Paris he
brought art down from the classic sobriety of Louis XIV to the lighter
spirit of the capital, and he directed the wealth of the bourgeoisie to the
patronage of art. He was patron *ex officio* and *par excellence;* he was rich
in his own right, and paid handsomely. His taste was not for grandeur or
massive display, nor for the traditional pictorial themes of religion, legend,

---

* Probably from *rocaille*, a term used in seventeenth-century France for the construction or
decoration of grottoes with rocks and shells.

or history, but for minor masterpieces of perfect workmanship tempting the fingers and opening the eyes, like jeweled caskets, silver vessels, golden bowls, fanciful *chinoiseries*, and paintings of luscious women dressed in nature by Rubens or Titian, or swaying in Veronese's gorgeous robes. His art collection in the Palais-Royal was thrown open to all responsible visitors; it would have rivaled any collection had it not been for his mistresses, who asked and received. Artists came to his rooms to study and copy, and Philippe went to their studios to watch and learn. To Charles Antoine Coypel, his *premier peintre*, he spoke with characteristic courtesy and modesty: "I am happy and proud, monsieur, to receive your advice, and to avail myself of your lessons."[65] He would have been a highly civilized man had he not suffered from thirst and an uncontrollable appreciation of beauty.

The quality of the age expressed itself most clearly in painting. Liberated by the Regent and their new patrons, artists like Watteau, Pater, Lancret, and Lemoyne discarded the rules that Le Brun had laid down in the Académie Royale des Beaux-Arts. They responded willingly to the demand for pictures that would reflect the Regent's appetite for beauty and pleasure, the vivacious grace of Regency women, the warm colors of Regency furniture and drapes, the gay parties in the Bois de Boulogne, the games and masquerades of the court at Sceaux, the fluid morals of actors, actresses, prima donnas, and danseuses. The pagan mythology replaced the grim stories of somber saints; strange figures from China, Turkey, Persia, or India let the released mind roam freely through exotic dreams; idyllic pastorals supplanted heroic "histories"; portraits of purchasers superseded the exploits of kings.

Some painters already famous under Louis XIV continued to flourish in the Regency. Antoine Coypel, after adorning Versailles in the correct style of the old court, painted in the Palais-Royal ladies in alluring *négligé*. Nicolas de Largillière, already fifty-nine when the Grand Monarque died, carried on for thirty years more; he hangs in pride and wig, with wife and daughter, in the inexhaustible Louvre. Alexandre François Desportes, who died at eighty-two in 1743, was now painting spacious landscapes, like the *Paysage d'Île de France* in the Musée de Compiègne. François Lemoyne, who killed himself at forty-nine (1737), decorated the Church of St.-Sulpice piously, then warmed the Salon d' Hercule at Versailles with voluptuous forms that would be inherited by Boucher. And Claude Gillot, designer of scenery and costumes for the stage, engraver of landscapes and theatrical tableaux, introduced that style of *fêtes champêtres* which we associate with his pupil Antoine Watteau.

Antoine was a Fleming, born to a tiler in Valenciennes (1684). Flemish influences first molded him—the paintings of Rubens, Ostade, and Teniers, and the teaching of a local painter, Jacques Gérin. When Gérin died (1702), Watteau advanced to Paris, penniless. He earned his bread by assisting a scene painter, then by working in a factory that turned out small portraits and devotional pictures wholesale. His wages were three francs a week plus enough food to keep him alive and let him develop tuberculosis. Another fever burned in him—the hunger for greatness and fame. He gave his evenings and holidays to drawing persons and places from nature. One of these sketches struck the eye and fancy of Gillot, who was painting panels for the Comédie-Italienne; he invited Watteau to join him. Antoine came, and fell in love with the actors; he painted incidents from their hectic lives, their reckless shifting loves, their games and picnics, their voluble panic when Mme. de Maintenon, offended by their satire, restricted them to pantomime. Watteau captured the pathos of their instability, the comical expressions of their faces, the folds of their strange costumes; and he gave these pictures a gleaming texture that may have stirred some jealousy in Gillot. In any case master and pupil quarreled and parted, and Antoine moved to the studio of Claude Audran in the Luxembourg. There he studied with awe Rubens' pictorial apotheosis of Marie de Médicis; and in the gardens he found vistas of trees and clouds that lured his pencil or brush.

Those were bitter years when French boys were being hurried off to one battlefield after another in the long War of the Spanish Succession. Their immolation was duly prefaced by patriotic parades and pathetic farewells; Watteau described them in *The Departure of the Troops* with such delicacy of feeling and technique that Audran in turn took alarm at being surpassed. Hoping to win the Prix de Rome, Antoine entered the competition offered by the Académie Royale de Peinture et de Sculpture in 1709; he won only the second prize, but the Academy enrolled him as a member in 1712. After many minor efforts, he reached the crest of his curve with *The Embarkation for Cythera* (1717), now one of the choicest treasures of the Louvre. All Paris applauded it; the delighted Regent made him an official painter to the King, and the Duchesse de Berry commissioned him to decorate her Château La Muette. He worked feverishly, as if knowing that he had only four more years to live. Antoine Crozat, who rivaled Philippe himself as a patron of art, offered Watteau board and bed in his commodious *hôtel*; there the younger Antoine studied the finest collection yet gathered by a private citizen. For Crozat he painted four decorative panels, *The Seasons*. Soon dissatisfied with luxury, he moved from place to place, even to London (1719); but coal dust and fog drove him back to Paris, where he lived for a time with the art dealer Gersaint. For him Antoine painted, in eight mornings, two sides of a signboard showing fashionable Parisians examining pictures in a shop; over the casual realism the delicate folds of a woman's dress cast the shimmering light characteristic of Watteau. Daily his consumptive cough grew worse. Hoping that rural air would help him, he took a house in Nogent, near Vincennes. There, in the arms of Gersaint and the Church, he died (July 18, 1721), aged thirty-seven.

His long illness infected his character and his art. Slender and ailing, nervous and diffident, easily tired, seldom smiling and rarely gay, he kept his sorrow out of his art, and painted life as his wishes saw it—a panorama of lively actors and lissome women, an ode to wistful joy. Too frail for sensuality, he maintained amid the license of the Regency a decency of morals which was reflected in the temper of his work. He painted a few nudes, but they held no fleshly lure; for the rest his women wore radiant costumes tiptoeing through the vestibules of love. His brush fluctuated between the vicissitudes of actors, the rituals of courtship, and the kaleidoscope of the sky. He clothed *L'Indifférent*[66] in the costliest, laciest raiment he could imagine. He pictured *The French Comedians*[67] in a dramatic scene, and caught the Italian actor Giuseppe Baletti as *Gilles* the clown[68] in a brown study and white pantaloons. He surprised *A Guitar Player*[69] in a mood of amorous melancholy, and saw *A Music Party*[70] entranced by a lute. He placed his figures against dreamy backgrounds of playful fountains, swaying trees, and gliding clouds, with here and there a pagan statue echoing Poussin, as in *La Fête d'Amour*[71] or *Les Champs-Élysées*.[72] He loved women from a timid distance, with all the longing of one too weak to woo; and he was moved not so much by cozy contours as by the luster of their hair and the sinuous flow of their robes. Upon their garments he cast all the wizardry of his colors, as if knowing that by such raiment woman had become the mystery engendering, besides mankind, half the wit and poetry and adoration of the world.

So he poured his spirit into his most famous picture, *L'Embarquement pour Cythère*, in which graceful women, succumbing to male agitation, embark with their courtiers for the isle where Venus, it was said, had a temple, and had emerged, dripping with beauty, from the sea. Here the men almost outshine the ladies in the splendor of their dress; but what charmed the Academy was the overhanging grandeur of the trees, and the distant island's snowy crest tinged with the sun and touching clouds. Watteau liked this subtle theme so well that he painted it in three variations. And Paris responded by choosing Watteau to carry the colors of the Regency, to celebrate the pleasures of life in a regime that would die as soon as it had spent its youth. He became by official title the *peintre des fêtes galantes*, the painter of urban lovers picnicking pastorally in a tranquil countryside, mingling Eros and Pan in the sole religion of the age. A breath of melancholy passes over these seemingly carefree scenes; these pliant sylphs could not be so tender if they had not known some suffering, or could not guess the brevity of adoration. This is the quality of Watteau—the delicate rendering of perfect moments that must pass.

He died too soon to savor his fame. After he was gone connoisseurs discovered his drawings, and some preferred them to his paintings, for here the chalk or pencil had achieved a finesse of detail in hands and hair, a subtlety of nuance in eyes and pose and flirting fan, that the oils had never quite revealed.[73] The women of Paris became especially fond of themselves as seen in the dead artist's longing; the beau monde dressed itself à la Watteau, walked and lounged à la Watteau, adorned its boudoirs and salons as these had been in the shapes and colors of his vision. The *style Watteau* entered into the design of furniture, into the rural motifs of decoration and the airy arabesques of rococo. Artists like Lancret and Pater took over Watteau's specialty, and pictured *fêtes champêtres, conversations galantes,* musicales in the park, dances on the green, declarations of love's eternity. Half the painting of France through the next one hundred years was a memory of Watteau. His influence continued through Boucher to Fragonard to Delacroix to Renoir, and the Impressionists found in his technique suggestive foreshadowings of their theories of light and shade and mood. He was, as the captivated Goncourts said, "the great poet of the eighteenth century."[74]

VII. AUTHORS

Under the easy morals and tolerance of the Regency literature prospered, and heresy found a footing that it never lost again. Theaters and the opera recovered from the frowns of the late King and Mme. de Maintenon; Philippe, or some of his household, attended the Opéra, the Opéra-Comique, the Théâtre-Français, or the Théâtre des Italiens almost every evening. The Théâtre-Français, while preserving Corneille, Racine, and Molière, opened its stage to fresh plays like Voltaire's *Oedipe,* in which the voice of a new and rebel age was heard.

Barring Voltaire, the greatest writers of this period were conservatives molded under the Grand Monarque. Alain René Lesage, born in 1668, belonged in spirit and style to the seventeenth century, though he lived till 1747. Educated by the Jesuits at Vannes, he came to Paris and studied law —his mistress paying his tuition fees.[75] After sufficient service to a tax collector to make him hate financiers, he undertook to support his wife and children by writing books; he might have starved had not a kindly abbé pensioned him with six hundred livres per year. He translated some plays from the Spanish, and Avellaneda's continuation of *Don Quixote.* Inspired by Vélez de Guevara's *El diablo cojuelo (The Lame Devil),* he struck a happy vein with *Le Diable boiteux* (1707), which pictured an impish demon, Asmodeus, perching on a pinnacle in Paris, lifting roofs at will with his magic wand, and revealing to his friend the private lives and unlicensed loves of the unsuspecting residents. The result was a rollicking disclosure of the sordid schemes, hypocrisies, vices, and devices of humanity. One lady, surprised by her husband in bed with his valet, solves a dozen problems at once by crying out that she is being raped; the husband kills the valet, the lady saves both her virtue and her life, and dead men tell no tales. Nearly everyone rushed to buy or borrow the book, delighted to see *other* people exposed; "two seigneurs of the court," said the *Journal de Verdun* for December, 1707, "fought, sword in hand, in Barbin's shop, to get the last copy of the second edition."[76] Sainte-Beuve found almost an epitome of the age in the remark of Asmodeus about a brother demon with whom he had quarreled: "We embraced, and since then we are mortal enemies."[77]

Two years later Lesage reached almost the level of Molière with a comedy satirizing the financiers. Some of these had advance news of *Turcaret*, and tried to prevent its performance; a story, probably legendary, pictured them offering the author 100,000 francs to withdraw the play;[78] the Dauphin, son of Louis XIV, ordered it produced. Turcaret is a contractor-merchant-moneylender who lives in luxury amid the destitution of war. He is generous only to his mistress, who bleeds him as sedulously as he bleeds the people. "I marvel at the course of human life," says the valet Frontin; "we pluck a coquette; the coquette devours a man of affairs; the man of affairs pillages others; and all this makes the most diverting chain of knaveries imaginable."[79]

Perhaps the satire here is unfair and is edged with revenge. In the most famous of eighteenth-century French novels Lesage succeeded in depicting a more complex character, and with greater objectivity. Following Spanish models again, *The Adventures of Gil Blas de Santillane* moves in picaresque style through a world of banditry, drinking bouts, abductions, seductions, and politics, in which cleverness is the supreme virtue and success pardons all. Gil begins as an innocent youth, tender with ideals and love of mankind, but credulous, talkative, and vain. He is captured by robbers, joins them, learns their arts and ways, graduates from them to the Spanish court, and serves the Duke of Lerma as aide and pander. "Before I was about the court my nature was compassionate and charitable; but tenderness of heart is an unfashionable frailty there, and mine became harder than any flint. Here was an admirable school to correct the romantic sensibilities of friendship."[80] He turns his back upon his parents, and refuses to help them. His luck fails, he is imprisoned, he resolves to reform; he is released, retires to the country, marries, and tries to be a good citizen. Finding this an intolerable bore, he returns to the court and its code. He is knighted, marries again, and is surprised by the virtue of his wife and by his happiness in her children, of whom "I devoutly believe myself the father."[81]

Gil Blas became the favorite novel of French readers until Hugo's *Les Misérables* (1862) challenged its size and supremacy. Lesage loved his book so well that he spread it over twenty years of his life. The first two volumes appeared in 1715, the third in 1724, the fourth in 1735; and, as in Cervantes' *Don Quixote*, the last was as good as the first. He financed his old age by writing little comedies for the popular Théâtre de la Foire (Theater of the Fair); and in 1738 he issued another novel, *Le Bachelier de Salamanque*, padding the book with unacknowledged pilferings in the manner of the time. He had become almost deaf at forty, but could hear with a trumpet; lucky man, who could close his ears at will, as we close our eyes. Toward the end of his life he lost the use of his faculties "except in the middle of the day," so that, said his friends, "his mind seemed to rise and set with the sun."[82] He died in 1747, in his eightieth year.

Lesage's *Gil Blas* finds fewer readers today than the *Mémoires* of Louis de Rouvroy, Duc de Saint-Simon. No one loves the Duke now, for he lacked the modest man's ability to conceal his vanity. He never forgot that he was one of the *ducs et pairs* of France, ranking in grandeur only after the royal family itself; he never forgave Louis XIV for preferring bourgeois competence to noble mediocrity in the administration of the government, nor for putting the royal bastards ahead of the "dukes and peers" in the ritual of the court and succession to the throne. On September 1, 1715, he tells us,

> I learned the death of the King upon awakening. Immediately afterward, I went to pay my respects to the new monarch. . . . I went thence to M. le Duc d'Orléans; I reminded him of a promise he had given me, that he would allow the dukes to keep their hats on when their votes were asked for.[83]

He loved the Regent sincerely, served him in the Council of State, admonished him to moderation in mistresses, and comforted him in bereavements and defeats. Close to events for fifty years, he began in 1694 to record them—from the standpoint of his class—from his own birth in 1675 to the Regent's death in 1723. He himself survived till 1755 into an uncongenial age. The Marquise de Créqui set him down as "an old sick crow, burning with envy and devoured by vanity."[84] But she was writing memoirs, too, and could not stomach his obstinate continuance.

The garrulous Duke was always biased, often unjust in his judgments, occasionally careless of chronology,[85] sometimes consciously incorrect in his report;[86] he ignored everything but politics, and lost himself, now and then, in bootless gossip about the aristocracy; but his twenty volumes are a detailed and precious record by an observant and penetrating eye and a fluent pen; they enable us to see Mme. de Maintenon, Fénelon, Philippe d' Orléans, and Saint-Simon almost as vividly as Bourrienne allows us to see Napoleon. To give his prejudices freedom, he tried to keep his memoirs secret, and forbade their publication within a century of his death. None of them reached print till 1781, many of them not before 1830. Of all the memoirs that illuminate the history of France these stand unrivaled at the top.

VIII. THE INCREDIBLE CARDINAL

If we were to believe Saint-Simon, the most inspiring maxims of our youth were contradicted by the career of Guillaume Dubois. He had all the vices, and every success except *succès d'estime*. Hear Saint-Simon again on his fellow councilor:

> His intellect was of the most ordinary kind; his knowledge the most commonplace; his capacity nil; his exterior that of a ferret, of a pedant; his conversation disagreeable, broken, always uncertain; his falsehood written upon his features. . . . Nothing was sacred to him. . . . He had a declared contempt for faith, promises, honor, probity, truth; took pleasure in laughing at all these things; was equally voluptuous and ambitious. . . . With all this he was soft, cringing, supple, a flatterer, a false admirer, taking all shapes with the greatest facility. . . . His judgment . . . was involuntarily crooked. . . . With such defects it is surprising that the only man he was able to seduce was M. le Duc d'Orléans, who had so much intelligence, such a well-balanced mind, and so much clear and rapid perception of character[87]

—which should have led the acidulous author to doubt the perspicacity of his jealousy. We must confess, however, that Duclos agrees with Saint-Simon.[88]

Dubois was in his sixtieth year when the Regency gave him power. He was a bit dilapidated, having survived several venereal diseases,[89] but he was able to entertain Mme. de Tencin when she fell out of Philippe's arms. In any case he must have had some intellectual acumen, for he managed foreign affairs reasonably well. He took a fat bribe from Britain to do what he thought was good for France. The Whigs in England and Emperor Charles VI in Austria were plotting to repudiate the Treaty of Utrecht and renew the war against France. Philip V, not content with the throne of Spain, was itching to be king of France, and thought an entente with England would clear his way. If England, Spain, Austria, and the Austrian Netherlands ("Belgium") should unite in another Grand Alliance, the old circumvallation of France would rise again, and all the policies and victories of Richelieu and Louis XIV would be annulled. To forestall such a union Dubois and Philippe signed an accord with England and the United Provinces ("Holland") on January 4, 1717. This was a boon to France, to the European balance of power, and to Britain; for if France and Spain had come under one head their combined fleets would have challenged England's control of the seas. It was also a boon to the new and insecure Hanoverian monarchy in England, since France was now pledged to give no further aid to the Stuart claimants to the English crown.

The Spanish government was outwitted, and was not pleased. Its ruling minister, Alberoni, joined in the plot of Cellamare and the Duchesse du Maine to overthrow the Regent and make Philip V king of France. Dubois unearthed the conspiracy, and persuaded the reluctant Philippe to follow England in declaring war against Spain (1718). The Treaty of The Hague (1720) ended this conflict. To consolidate the peace, Dubois arranged the mating of Philip's daughter to Louis XV, and of Philippe's daughters to Philip's sons. The marriages were contracted on the frontier island of Bidassoa (January 9, 1722), and were celebrated with an auto-da-fé.[90] As the Infanta María Ana Victoria was only three years old, it would be some time before Louis XV could elicit from her an heir to the throne; if in this interim the young King should die, the Regent would become king of France, and Dubois would be his perpetual minister.

He climbed subtly step by step. In 1720 he was made archbishop of Cambrai; by the humor of history a Protestant king, George I, asked the skeptical Regent to persuade the Pope to give Dubois this famous archiepiscopal see, recently ennobled by Fénelon; and the bishops of France, including the saintly Massillon, joined in the ceremonies conferring this dignity upon a man whom many Frenchmen considered an epitome of sin. Dubois felt himself inadequately rewarded for his services to France. He used French money to promote to the papacy a candidate pledged to send him a red hat. Innocent XIII sadly kept the promise, and the Archbishop became Cardinal Dubois (July 16, 1721). A year later he was made principal minister of the realm, with a salary of 100,000 livres. As he had an income of 120,000 livres from his archbishopric, and 204,000 from seven abbeys, and 100,000 as superintendent of the post, and an English pension reckoned by Saint-Simon at 960,000, Dubois now had an annual income of some 1,500,000 livres.[91] His only worry was that his wife, who was still alive, might refuse his bribes, reveal her existence, and invalidate his ecclesiastical dignities.[92]

Time caught up with him. On February 5, 1723, Louis XV came of age, and the Regency ended. Still only thirteen, the King, enjoying life at Versailles, asked Philippe to continue to govern the kingdom, and Dubois remained Philippe's principal aide. But on August 1 the Cardinal's bladder burst, and suddenly, loaded with livres, he was dead. Philippe took over the administration, but with him too time had run out. Surfeited with women, stupefied with drink, losing his sight, losing even his good manners, he bore in semiconsciousness the contumely of a regime that had begun with almost universal good will and was ending in official abasement and public contempt. The doctors warned him that his mode of life was killing him. He did not care. He had drunk the wine of life too greedily, and had reached the dregs. He died of an apoplectic fit, December 2, 1723, falling into the arms of his mistress pro tem. He was forty-nine years old.

Philippe d'Orléans does not impress us as a bad man, despite the gamut of his sins. He had the vices of the flesh rather than of the soul: he was a spendthrift, a drunkard, and a lecher, but he was not selfish, cruel, or mean. He was a man of mercy, brave and kind. He won a kingdom by a gamble, and gave it away with light heart and open hand. His wealth provided him with every opportunity, his power offered him no discipline. It is a pitiful sight—a man brilliant in mind, liberal in views, struggling to repair the damage done to France by the bigotry of the Great King, letting noble purposes drown in meaningless intoxication, and losing love in a maelstrom of debauchery.

Morally, the Regency was the most shameful period in the history of France. Religion, beneficent in the villages, disgraced itself at the top by anointing men like Dubois and Tencin with high honors, so losing the respect of the emancipated intellect. The French mind enjoyed comparative freedom, but used it not to spread a humane and tolerant intelligence so much as to loose human instincts from the social control necessary to civilization; skepticism forgot Epicurus, and became epicurean. Government was corrupt, but it preserved peace long enough to let France recover from a devastating reign of grandeur and war. The "System" of Law collapsed in bankruptcy, but it gave a powerful stimulus to the French economy. Those eight years saw the spread of free education, and the liberation of art and literature from royal tutelage and domination; they were the years of *The Embarkation for Cythera*, of *Gil Blas*, of *Oedipe*, of Montesquieu's *Lettres persanes*. The Regency sent Voltaire to the Bastille, but it gave him such freedom and toleration as he would never know again in France even in the hour of his triumph and his death.

IX. VOLTAIRE AND THE BASTILLE: 1715–26

A characteristic passage in Saint-Simon describes a young upstart who made much noise during the Regency:

Arouet, son of a notary who was employed by my father and me until his death, was exiled ... to Tulle at this time [1716] for some verses very satirical and very impudent. I should not amuse myself by writing down such a trifle if this same Arouet, having become a great poet and academician under the name of Voltaire, had not also become ... a manner of personage in the republic of letters, and even achieved a sort of importance among certain people.[93]

This young upstart, now twenty-one, described himself as "thin, long, and fleshless, without buttocks."[94] Perhaps because of this disability, he pranced from one host or hostess to another, welcomed even in lordly circles for his sparkling verse and ready wit, imbibing and effusing heresy, and playing the gallant. Shining especially at Sceaux, he pleased the Duchesse du Maine by satirizing the Regent. When Philippe reduced by a half the horses in the royal stables, Arouet quipped that he would have done better to dismiss half the asses that crowded his Highness's court. Worse yet, he seems to have set afloat some lines on the morals of the Duchesse de Berry. Voltaire denied authorship, but those lines were later published in his *Works*. He kept up this strategy of denial almost to the end of his life, as a forgivable protection against a threatening censorship. The Regent could pardon lampoons of himself, for they were often undeserved; but he was deeply hurt by squibs on his daughter, for they were mostly true. On May 5, 1716, he issued an order that "the Sieur Arouet, the son, be sent to Tulle"—a town three hundred miles south of Paris, famed for its odorous tanneries, not yet for the delicate fabric that later took its name. Arouet's father persuaded the Regent to change the place of exile from Tulle to Sully-sur-Loire, a hundred miles from the capital. Arouet went, and was received as a house guest by the current Duc de Sully, descendant of Henry IV's great minister.

He enjoyed there everything but liberty. Soon he addressed a verse "Épître à M. le duc d'Orléans," protesting his innocence, and begging release. It was granted; and by the end of the year he was back in Paris, fluttering and rhyming, sometimes obscenely, often superficially, always cleverly. Consequently any able satire running anonymously along café tables was ascribed to him. Early in 1717 an especially pointed diatribe appeared, in which each sentence began with *J'ai vu*—"I have seen." For example:

I have seen the Bastille and a thousand other prisons filled with brave
    citizens, faithful subjects.
I have seen the people wretched under a rigorous servitude.
I have seen the soldiery perishing of hunger, thirst ... and rage.
I have seen a devil in the guise of a woman ... ruling the kingdom. ...
I have seen Port-Royal demolished. ...

I have seen—and this includes all—a Jesuit adored. . . .
I have seen these evils, and I am not yet twenty years old.[95]

Obviously these verses referred to Louis XIV and Mme. de Maintenon, and they must have been written by a Jansenist foe of the Jesuits, rather than by an impious skeptic who still had a kindly beat in his heart for the Society of Jesus. The real author was A. L. Le Brun, who later begged Voltaire's forgiveness for having let him bear the blame.[96] But gossip lauded Arouet for the poem; literary gatherings importuned him to recite it, and no one (except the author) believed his denials. Reports to the Regent accused him not only of the *J'ai-vus* but also—and apparently with justice—of a Latin inscription, *"Puero regnante . . ."*—"A boy [Louis XV] reigning; a man notorious for poisoning and incest ruling; . . . public faith violated [failure of Law's bank]; . . . the country sacrificed to the hope of a crown; an inheritance basely anticipated; France about to perish."[97] On May 16, 1717, a *lettre de cachet* directed "that Sieur Arouet be arrested and taken to the Bastille." The poet was surprised in his rooms, and was allowed to take with him nothing but the clothes he wore.

He had no time to bid adieu to his current mistress, Suzanne de Livry; his friend Lefèvre de Genonville took his place on her bosom; Arouet pardoned them philosophically—"We must put up with these bagatelles."[98] A few years later Lefèvre died, and Voltaire wrote to his memory verses that may exemplify the young rebel's talent for gracious poetry, and the tender sentiments always deeper in him than his doubts:

> *Il te souvient du temps, et l'aimable Égérie,*
> *Dans les beaux jours de notre vie,*
> *Nous nous aimions tous trois. La raison, la folie,*
> *L'amour, l'enchantement des plus tendres erreurs,*
> > *Tout réunissait nos trois coeurs.*
> > *Que nous étions heureux! même cette indigence,*
> > *Triste compagne des beaux jours,*
> *Ne put de notre joie empoisonner le cours.*
> *Jeunes, gais, satisfaits, sans soins, sans prévoyance,*
> *Aux douceurs du présent bornant tous nos désirs,*
> *Quel besoin avions-nous d'une vaine abondance?*
> *Nous possédions bien mieux, nous avions les plaisirs.*[99]*

---

* "He remembers you, and the lovely Egeria [Suzanne], in the fair days of our life, when we loved one another, all three. Reason, folly, love, the enchantment of tender errors, all bound our three hearts in one. How happy we were then! Even poverty, that sad companion of happy days, could not poison the stream of our joy. Young, gay, content, without care, without a thought for the future, limiting all our desires to our present delights—what need had we of useless abundance? We had something far better; we had happiness."

Suzanne married the wealthy Marquis de Gouvernet, and refused to admit Voltaire when he called at her home. He consoled himself with the thought that "all the diamonds and pearls that deck her now are not worth one of her kisses in the old days."[100] He did not see her again until, fifty-one years later, he came back to Paris to die; then, aged eighty-three, he made it a point to visit the widowed Marquise, aged eighty-four. There was a devil in this Voltaire, but also the kindest heart in the world.

He did not find the Bastille intolerable. He was allowed to send—and pay—for books, furniture, linen, a nightcap, and perfume; he often dined with the governor, played billiards and bowling with prisoners and guards; and he wrote *La Henriade*. The *Iliad* was among the books he had sent for; why should he not rival Homer? And why limit epics to legends? There, in living history, was Henry IV, gay, bold, heroic, lecherous, tolerant, generous; why could not that adventurous, tragic life be fit for epic poetry? The prisoner was not allowed writing paper, for this in his hands could be a deadly weapon; so he wrote the first half of his epic between the lines of printed books.

He was released on April 11, 1718, but was forbidden to stay in Paris. From Châtenay, near Sceaux, he wrote letters to the Regent, begging forgiveness; again the Regent relented, and on October 12 issued permission to "le Sieur Arouet de Voltaire to come to Paris whenever he pleases."[101]

But when and how had he come to that new name? Apparently about the time of this imprisonment in the Bastille. We find it first in the edict just cited. Some[102] have thought it an anagram for AROUET L[e] J[eune], taking U as V and J as I. The Marquise de Créqui[103] ascribed it to Veautaire, a small farm near Paris; Voltaire had inherited this from a cousin; it conveyed no seigneurial rights, but Arouet, like Balzac, took the seigneurial *de* by right of genius, and signed himself, as in the dedication to his first play, "Arouet de Voltaire." Soon he would need only one name to identify himself anywhere in Europe.

That play, *Oedipe*, was an event in the literary history of France. It was stark insolence in a lad of twenty-four to challenge not only Corneille, who had staged his *Oedipe* in 1659, but Sophocles too, whose *Oedipus Tyrannus* had appeared 330 B.C. Moreover, this was a tale of incest, and might be taken as reflecting upon the relations of the Regent with his daughter—precisely the issue on which Arouet had been imprisoned. The Duchesse du Maine, at whose court the poet had conceived his play, interpreted it so, and rejoiced. With his usual audacity, Voltaire asked the Regent might he dedicate the piece to him; the Regent demurred, but permitted dedication to his mother. The première was announced for November 18, 1718. Two factions formed among the playgoers of Paris—those supporting the Regent, and those favoring the Duchesse du Maine; it was expected that their duel of hisses and cheers would make a farce of the performance. But the clever author had inserted lines to please one faction, other lines to please the other. The Regent's party was appeased by a passage describing how King Laius (like Philippe) dismissed the costly palace guard; the Jesuits were gratified to see how well their pupil had profited from the dramas they had staged at the Collège Louis-le-Grand; but the freethinkers hailed enthusiastically two lines, in the first scene of Act IV, that were to become the theme song of Voltaire's life:

> *Nos prêtres ne sont pas ce qu'un vain peuple pense;*
> *Notre crédulité fait toute leur science*

—"Our priests are not what a silly populace supposes; all their learning consists in our credulity." Each faction applauded in turn, and in the end the drama was greeted with unanimous approval. According to an old tradition Voltaire's father, approaching death, came to the first night still breathing anger against his worthless and disreputable son, but wept with pride at the splendor of the poetry and the triumph of the play.

Oedipe had an unprecedented run of forty-five days. Even Corneille's nephew, the aging Fontenelle, praised it, though he suggested to Voltaire that some of the verses were "too strong and full of fire." The brash youth replied with an ungracious *double-entendre*: "To correct myself I shall read your *Pastorales*."[104] Paris insisted on identifying the incestuous Oedipus with the Regent, and Jocasta with his daughter. Facing the gossip bravely, the Duchesse de Berry attended several performances. The Regent had the play produced at his palace theater, and welcomed the author to his court.

A few months later a scandalmongering poet, hiding under anonymity, issued *Les Philippiques*, diatribes in which Philippe was accused of planning to poison the young King and usurp the throne. Voltaire was widely suspected of authorship; he protested his innocence, but he had lied so flagrantly in similar cases that now only the author believed him. Philippe gave him the benefit of the doubt, and merely advised him to absent himself from Parisian felicity a while. He went back to the Château de Sully (May, 1719). After a year he was allowed to return to the capital. There he was for a time a darling of the aristocracy.

Convinced that money was the philosopher's stone, he put his sharp wits to the problems and tricks of finance. He cultivated bankers, and was well rewarded for helping the brothers Paris to secure contracts to supply provisions and munitions to the army;[105] our hero was a war profiteer. He stayed out of Law's System, invested judiciously, lent money at interest. In 1722 his father died, and after some resolute litigation Voltaire inherited an annuity of 4,250 francs. In that same year he received from the Regent a pension of 2,000 livres. He was now a rich man; soon he would be a millionaire. We must not think of him as a revolutionist, except in religion.

Fortunately for his education, his second drama, *Artémire*, failed (February 15, 1720). He ran from his box onto the stage, and argued with the audience on the merits of the piece; they applauded his speech but kept their thumbs down; after eight performances he withdrew the play. Later in that year he read part of *La Henriade* at a gathering; there were some criticisms; in a Virgilian gesture he threw the manuscript into the fire; Hénault snatched the sheets from the flame, and compared himself to Augustus rescuing the *Aeneid*; Voltaire, he said, now owed him an epic and "a nice pair of sleeve ruffles."[106] The poet easily recovered his pride when the Regent himself listened to a reading from the poem. Wherever he went he read some part of it. In 1723 he visited Lord Bolingbroke and his French wife at their villa, La Source, near Orléans; they assured him that his epic surpassed "all poetical works which have appeared in France."[107] He pretended to doubt it.

Meanwhile he exchanged philosophies with the titled skeptic, and heard of the deists who were bedeviling Christianity in Britain. He began to suspect that England had advanced beyond France in science and philosophy. But he had come to Bolingbroke's heresies before meeting him or reading the English deists. In 1722 he accepted the invitation of the Comtesse Marie de Rupelmonde to accompany her to the Netherlands. She was a widow, aged thirty-eight, and intellectual, but she was beautiful. He, aged twenty-eight, accepted. At Brussels he met a rival poet, Jean Baptiste Rousseau, who praised *Oedipe* but chided Voltaire for impiety. Seldom able to bear criticism patiently, Voltaire remarked about Rousseau's "Ode to Posterity," "Do you know, my master, that I do not believe this ode will ever reach its address?"[108] They continued to snap at each other till Rousseau's death. As Voltaire and his Countess continued on their way to Holland, she revealed her religious doubts to him, and asked him for his own views. Bubbling with verse, he replied in a famous *Épître à Uranie*, which was not published till 1732, and not acknowledged by Voltaire till forty years afterward. Every sensitive Christian youth will recognize in it a stage in his own development.

> *Tu veux donc, belle Uranie,*
> *Qu'érigé par ton ordre en Lucrèce nouveau,*
> *Devant toi, d'une main hardie,*
> *Aux superstitions j'arrache le bandeau;*
> *Que j'expose à tes yeux le dangereux tableau*
> *Des mensonges sacrés dont la terre est remplie,*
> *Et que ma philosophie*

T'apprenne à mépriser les horreurs du tombeau,
Et les terreurs de l'autre vie.*

The poet proceeds with "respectful step." "I wish to love God, I seek in him my father"; but what kind of God does the Christian theology offer? "A tyrant whom we should hate. He created men in 'his own image,' only to make them vile; he gave us sinful hearts to have the right to punish us; he made us love pleasure, so that he might torment us with frightful pains . . . eternal." He had hardly given us birth when he thought of destroying us. He ordered the water to engulf the earth. He sent his son to atone for our sins; Christ died, but apparently in vain, for we are told that we are still stained with the crime of Adam and Eve; and the Son of God, so acclaimed for mercy, is represented as waiting vengefully to plunge most of us into hell, including all those countless people who never heard of him. "I do not recognize in this disgraceful picture the God whom I must adore; I should dishonor him by such insult and homage." And yet he feels the nobility and the living inspiration in the Christian concept of the Saviour:

> Behold this Christ, powerful and glorious, . . . trampling death under his triumphant feet, and emerging victorious from the gates of hell. His example is holy, his morality is divine. He consoles in secret the hearts that he illumines; in the greatest misfortunes he gives them support; and if he bases his doctrine on an illusion, it is still a blessing to be deceived with him.

In conclusion the poet invites Uranie to make up her own mind on religion, in full trust that God, who "has placed natural religion in your heart, will not resent a simple and candid spirit. Believe that before his throne, in all times, in all places, the soul of the just man is precious; believe that the modest Buddhist monk, the kindly Moslem dervish, find more grace in his eyes than a pitiless [predestinarian] Jansenist or an ambitious pope."

Back in Paris Voltaire settled down in the Hôtel de Bernières on the Rue de Beaune and the present Quai Voltaire (1723). In November he went to a gathering of notables in the Château de Maisons (nine miles from Paris), where the greatest actress of the age, Adrienne Lecouvreur, was to read his new play, *Mariamne*. But before that ceremony could take place he came down with smallpox, which in those days killed a high percentage of its hosts. He made his will, confessed, and awaited death. The other guests

---

* "You wish, then, lovely Urania [a name for Aphrodite], that, raised at your command into a new Lucretius, I should before you, with bold hand, tear the veil from superstitions; that I should expose to your eyes the dangerous tableau of holy lies with which the earth is filled, and that my philosophy should teach you to despise the horrors of the tomb and the terrors of the other life."

fled, but the Marquis de Maisons called in Dr. Gervais from Paris. "Instead of the cordials usually given in this disease, he made me drink two hundred pints of lemonade."[109] The two hundred pints, more or probably less, "saved my life." It was many months before he recovered his health; indeed, from that time onward he treated himself as an invalid, nursing the fitful life of the frail body that had to house his consuming fire.

In 1724 *La Henriade* began secretly to circulate among the intelligentsia. It was a political broadcast on an epic scale. Taking the Massacre of St. Bartholomew as a text, it traced religious crimes through the ages: mothers offering their children to be burned on the altars of Moloch; Agamemnon preparing to sacrifice his daughter to the gods for a little breeze; Christians persecuted by Romans, heretics by Christians, fanatics "invoking the Lord while slaughtering their brothers"; devotees inspired to kill French kings. The poem lauded Elizabeth for helping Henry of Navarre. It described the battle of Ivry, the clemency of Henry, his liaison with Gabrielle d'Estrées, his siege of Paris. It approved his conversion to Catholicism, but it criticized the papacy as a power "inflexible to the conquered, complaisant to conquerors, ready, as interest dictates, either to absolve or to condemn."

Voltaire had hoped that *La Henriade* would be accepted as the national epic of France, but Catholicism was too dear to his countrymen to let them receive the poem as the epos of their soul. And its faults leaped to the scholarly eye. The obvious imitations of Homer and Virgil—in the battle scenes, in the visit of the hero to hell, in the intrusion of personified abstractions, after the manner of Homeric deities, into the action—sacrificed the charms of invention and originality; and though the style made good prose, it lacked the illuminating imagery of verse. The author, drunk with printer's ink, had no suspicion of this. He wrote to Thieriot: "Epic poetry is my forte, or I am much deceived."[110] He was much deceived.

Even so, the plaudits seemed to justify him. A French critic pronounced it superior to the *Aeneid*, and Frederick the Great thought that "a man without prejudice will prefer *La Henriade* to the poem of Homer."[111] The first edition was soon disposed of; a pirated edition was published in Holland and exported into France; the police banned the book; everyone bought it. It was translated into seven languages; we shall see it making a stir in England. It played a part in reviving the popularity of Henry IV. It made France ashamed of its religious wars, and critical of the theologies that had inflamed men to such ferocity.

Now for a time Voltaire enjoyed fame and fortune unalloyed. He was recognized as the greatest living poet in France. He was received at the court of Louis XV; the Queen wept over his plays, and gave him 1,500 livres from her privy purse (1725). He wrote a dozen letters complaining and boasting of his life as a courtier. He talked in a tone of easy familiarity with lords, noble or ignoble. Doubtless he talked too much, which is the easiest thing in the world. One night at the opera (December, 1725) the Chevalier de Rohan-Chabot, hearing him hold forth in the lobby, asked him, with a very superior air, *"Monsieur de Voltaire, Monsieur Arouet—comment vous appelez-vous?* [what really is your name?]" We do not know what the poet replied. Two days later they met at the Comédie-Française; Rohan repeated his question. Voltaire's rejoinder is diversely reported; in one account he answered, "One who does not trail after a great name, but knows how to honor that which he has";[112] in another version he retorted, "My name begins with me, yours ends with you."[113] The noble lord raised his cane to strike; the poet made a move to draw his sword. Adrienne Lecouvreur, who was present, had the wit to faint; a truce was called.

On February 4 Voltaire was lunching at the house of the Duc de Sully when a message came that someone wished to see him at the palace gate. He went. Six ruffians pounced upon him and beat him mercifully. Rohan, directing the operation from his carriage, cautioned them, "Don't strike his head; something good may come out of that."[114] Voltaire rushed back to the house, and asked Sully's aid in taking legal action against Rohan; Sully refused. The poet retired to a suburb, where he practiced swordsmanship. Then he appeared at Versailles, resolved to demand "satisfaction" from the Chevalier. The law made dueling a capital crime. A royal order bade the police watch him. Rohan refused to meet him. That night, to the relief of everyone concerned, the police arrested the poet, and he found himself again in the Bastille. "The family of the prisoner," reported the lieutenant general of the Paris police, "applauded unanimously . . . the wisdom of an order which kept the young man from committing some new folly."[115] Voltaire wrote to the authorities defending his conduct, and offering to go in voluntary exile to England if released. He was treated as before, with every comfort and consideration.

His proposal was accepted; after fifteen days he was freed, but a guard was ordered to see him to Calais. Members of the government gave him letters of introduction and recommendation to prominent Englishmen, and the Queen continued to pay his pension. At Calais he was entertained by friends while waiting for the next boat to sail. On May 10 he embarked, armed with books for the study of English, and not unwilling to see the country in which, he had heard, men and minds were free. Let us see.

BOOK I

ENGLAND

1714–56

CHAPTER II

The People

1714–56

THE England that Voltaire found was a nation enjoying a quarter century of relative peace after a generation of costly victories over France; a nation now mistress of the seas, therefore of commerce, therefore of money; holding the lever and balance of power over Continental governments; proudly triumphant over a Stuart dynasty that had sought to make it Catholic, and over Hanoverian kings who were the servants of Parliament's swelling purse. This was the England that had just won world preeminence in science through Newton, that had just produced the unintentionally revolutionary Locke, that was undermining Christianity with deism, that would substitute Alexander Pope for all the pontiffs of Rome, that would soon watch uncomfortably the devastating operations of David Hume. It was the England that Hogarth loved and excoriated in engravings, the England where Handel found home and audience and outshone all the Bachs as the *maestro dei maestri* of the age. And here, in this "fortress built by Nature for herself against infection, . . . this blessed plot, . . . this England,"[1] the Industrial Revolution began to transform everything but man.

I. PRELUDE TO THE INDUSTRIAL REVOLUTION

1. The Sustainers

Defoe, traversing England in 1722, drew a patriotic picture of "the most flourishing and opulent country in the world," of green fields and overflowing crops, of pastures rambled by golden fleece, of lush grass turning into plump kine, of peasants roistering in rural sports, squires organizing peasants, nobles organizing squires, lordly manors giving law and discipline to villages, and now and then, refuge to poets and philosophers.[2] Word peddlers tend to idealize the countryside, if they are exempt from its harassments, boredom, insects, and toil.

Rural life in the England of 1715 was very much as it had been for a thousand years. Each village—almost each household—was a self-contained economic unit, growing its own food, making its own clothing, cutting its timber for building and fuel from the adjacent woods. Each family baked its bread, hunted its venison, salted its meat, made its butter, jellies, and cheese. It spun and wove, and sewed; it tanned leather and cobbled shoes; it made most of its utensils, implements, and tools. So father, mother, and children found work and expression not only in the summer fields but in the long winter evenings; the home was a hub of industry as well as of agriculture. The wife was an honored mistress of many arts, from nursing her husband and rearing a dozen children to making frocks and brewing ale. She kept and dispensed the household medicines; she took care of the garden, the pigs, and the fowl. Marriage was a union of helpmates; the family was an economic as well as a social organism, and had thereby a solid reason and basis for its unity, multiplication, and permanence.

The peasants might have been content with the varied vitality of their homes if they had been allowed to preserve their ancient ways in the fields. They remembered when the landlord had permitted them, or their forebears, to graze their livestock on the manor's common fields, to fish freely in its streams, to cut wood in its forest; now, by a process begun in the sixteenth century, most of the "commons" had been enclosed by the owners, and the peasants found it hard to make ends meet. There was no serfdom left, and no formal feudal dues; but enterprising landlords, and city merchants investing in land, were farming on a larger scale, with more capital, better implements, greater skill, and wider markets than were available to yeomen tilling their narrow areas. Gregory King had reckoned some 180,000 such freeholders in the England of 1688. Voltaire, about 1730, reported "in England many peasants with 200,000 francs' worth of property, and who do not disdain to continue cultivating the earth that has enriched them, and in which they live free"; but this may have been propaganda for French stimulation. In any case, by 1750 the number of freeholders had declined.[3] The fatter landlords were buying up the thinner tracts; the small homestead, designed for family subsistence or local markets, was giving place to larger farms capable of profiting from improved methods and machines; the farmer was becoming a tenant or hired "hand." Moreover, the system of tillage predominant in England in 1715 divided the land of a village into different regions according to their fertility and accessibility; each farmer received one or more strips in the separate localities; co-operation was necessary, individual enterprise was balked, production lagged. The enclosers argued that large-scale operation under unified ownership increased agricultural production, facilitated sheep pasturage, and allowed a profitable output of wool; and doubtless they were right. Economic progress shut at least one eye to the human turmoil of displacement and transition.

It was chiefly on the expanded farms that agricultural technology advanced. The profit motive brought wastelands under cultivation, disciplined labor to greater efficiency, stimulated the invention of new tools and ways, promoted experiments in animal breeding, and sustained the toil of draining marshes, checking soil erosion, and clearing woods. Between 1696 and 1795 some two million acres were added to the cultivated area of England and Wales. In 1730

Charles Townshend introduced the four-course system of crop rotation instead of the wasteful plan of letting a third of the land lie fallow in each year: he planted wheat or oats in the first year, barley or oats in the second, clover, rye, vetches, rutabaga, and kale in the third, turnips in the fourth; then the sheep were brought in to eat the turnips or trample them into the ground, while their offal fertilized the soil; so the earth was prepared for a rich crop of wheat in the next year. His neighbors laughed at him, and called him Turnip Townshend, until a thirty per cent increase in his crops turned them to imitation. As Townshend was a viscount, other aristocrats followed him in improving their land; it became the fashion for an English lord to take a personal interest in agriculture, and the talk of the manors passed from hunting and dogs to turnips and manure.[4]

Jethro Tull was a lawyer; his health failing, he went back to his father's farm; his sharpened mind was fascinated by the miracle and profits of growth, but was repelled by the wasteful methods of tillage that he saw—farmers broadcasting nine or ten pounds of seed to an acre so carelessly "that two thirds of the ground was unplanted, and on the rest 'twas so thick that it did not prosper."[5] Traveling in France and Italy, he studied agricultural methods; returning, he bought a farm, and shocked his neighbors with inventions that doubled production. He began (c. 1730) by making a four-coultered plow that would uproot and bury weeds instead of merely shoving them aside. But his most decisive invention (c. 1733) was a horse-drawn drill mechanism that fed seed through notched funnels at a specific spacing and depth in two parallel rows, and then covered the seeds by a harrow attached to the drill. The machine saved seed and labor, and allowed the cultivation, aeration, irrigation, and weeding of the soil between the seeded rows. This apparently trivial change in sowing, and the improvement of the plow, shared in what came to be called the agricultural revolution, whose effects can be measured (even allowing for inflation) by the tenfold rise, during the eighteenth century, in the value of the lands where the new methods were used. The increased productivity of the soil enabled the farms to feed more workers in the towns, and made possible that growing urban population without which there could have been no Industrial Revolution.

Neither the peasants nor the town workers shared in the growing wealth. Peasant proprietors were squeezed out by large-scale competition; peasant laborers were paid as little as the fear of unemployment compelled them to accept. Hear the learned and high-caste Trevelyan:

> The social price paid for economic gain was a decline in the number of independent cultivators, and a rise in the number of landless laborers. To a large extent this was a necessary evil, and there would have been less harm in it if the increased dividend of the agricultural world had been fairly distributed. But while the landlord's rent, the parson's tithe, and the profits of [landowning] farmer and middleman all rose apace, the field laborer, deprived of his little rights in [the common] land and

his family's by-employment in industry, received no proper compensation in high wages, and in the Southern Counties too often sank into a
position of dependence and pauperism.[6]

The natural concentration of wealth was in some measure mitigated by
taxation and organized charity. The English rich, unlike the French nobles,
paid the larger part of the taxes that supported the government. The Poor
Laws, which had begun in 1536, required each parish to succor persons in
danger of starvation. The able-bodied unemployed were sent to workhouses, the disabled were committed to almshouses; the children were
bound out as apprentices to those willing to lodge and feed them for their
services. The expenses of the system were paid by a tax on the households
of the parish. A parliamentary committee reported that of all the children
born in workhouses, or those received in infancy, in the years 1763–65,
only seven per cent were alive in 1766.[7] It was a hard century.

2. Industry

The self-sufficient home of the countryside retarded, for good or ill,
the specialization of labor and the Industrial Revolution. Why should the
nascent capitalist finance a factory when he could have a hundred families
weave and spin for him under their own roofs and the automatic discipline
of competition? In the West Riding district of Yorkshire this domestic
industry produced 100,000 pieces of cloth for the market in 1740, and
140,000 pieces in 1750; as late as 1856 only half the woolen production of
Yorkshire came from factories, half still came from homes.[8] Nevertheless
those busy households were incipient factories: the head of the family
invited servants and outsiders to join in the work; additional rooms were
equipped with spinning wheels and looms. As these domestic operations increased in size, and the market widened through improved roads and control of the seas, domestic industry itself created a demand for better tools.
The first inventions were implements rather than machines; they could be
installed in homes, like Kay's flying shuttle; only when the inventors made
machines that required mechanical power did the factory system replace
domestic industry.

The transition was gradual; it took almost a century (1730–1830), and
perhaps "revolution" is too dramatic a term for so leisurely a change. The
break with the past was not so sharp as the romantification of history once
suggested. Industry was as old as civilization; invention had progressed at
a quickening pace since the thirteenth century; in Dante's Florence factories were as numerous as poets; in Rembrandt's Holland capitalists were
as numerous as artists. But taken in its progressive stages of steam, electric-

ity, oil, electronics, and atomic energy, the industrial transformation of the last two centuries (1760–1960), as compared with the rate of economic change in Europe before Columbus, constitutes a real revolution, basically transforming not only agriculture, transport, communication, and industry, but also politics, manners, morality, religion, philosophy, and art.

Many factors flowed together in compelling industrial change. The wars that followed the fall of Walpole's ministry (1742) intensified the urge to accelerate production and distribution. The growth of population, as a result of the rising food supply, offered a swelling domestic market for both agriculture and industry, and encouraged the making of better machines and roads. The machines required skills, which led to a specialization and division of labor promoting productivity. Huguenot and other immigrants brought to England their salvaged savings and their crafts; it was a Huguenot descendant who invented the first spinning machine (1738). The adoption of protective tariffs by Parliament (e.g., the "Calico Act" of 1721, prohibiting the use of imported printed calicos) narrowed foreign competition, and gave the English textile industry full control of the home market; while the growing influence of the merchants on legislation favored the extension of the British economy. In the middle and lower classes the Puritan tradition—soon to be reinforced by the Methodist movement—encouraged the virtues of industriousness, enterprise, and thrift; capital was accumulated, wealth was sanctioned, and the bourgeoisie seemed to enjoy the special grace of God.

Meanwhile the development of mining offered an expanding supply of coal as a fuel for industry. Wood had hitherto been the major fuel for homes and shops, but forests were being thinned to extinction; of sixty-nine great forests known to medieval England sixty-five had disappeared by the end of the eighteenth century.[9] Timber had to be imported from Scandinavia or America; it cost more and more, and demand arose for a cheaper fuel. But the mining of coal was still a primitive process; shafts were shallow, ventilation was crude; methane and carbonic-acid gas choked the miners; and the problem of pumping water out of the mines remained unsolved till the steam engines of Savery and Newcomen; indeed, this problem was the chief incentive to the development of such engines. Despite these difficulties the production of coal mounted and spread, so that by 1750 the coal burned in homes and factories was already darkening the London sky.[10]

The importance of coal for the Industrial Revolution lay especially in its use for smelting iron ore into purer, tougher, malleable iron by separating the metal from the minerals attached to it. Smelting required fusion, which required a high degree of heat; this, since the fourteenth century, had been produced by burning charcoal (i.e., charred wood) in blast furnaces supplied with heavy drafts of air; but now charcoal was becoming costlier through the falling supply of wood. In 1612 Simon Sturtevant recommended coal as smelter fuel; "Dud" Dudley claimed in 1619 that by these means he reduced the cost of smelting iron by one half; but his charcoal-using rivals united to drive him out of business. Finally (c. 1709) Abraham Darby I, settling at Coalbrookdale, where coal was plentiful, successfully and economically smelted iron ore by heating it with coke— i.e., coal "cooked," or burned, sufficiently to free it from its volatile elements. Coke itself had been known as far back as 1590. Abraham Darby II developed the use of coal or coke in smelting, and improved the blast furnace with bellows worked by a water wheel; soon he was able to outsell all other ironmasters in England. In 1728 the first English rolling mill was set up to pass iron between a succession of cylinders to compress it into desired forms. In 1740 Benjamin Huntsman invented the crucible process by which high-grade steel was produced through heating and purifying metal in clay pots. It was these developments in the marriage of coal with iron that made possible the machines of the Industrial Revolution.

3. Invention

The first half of the eighteenth century saw no spectacular acceleration of invention as compared with the two preceding centuries; and half a volume might be required to list the inventions that this age inherited from the past. As one example, the clock, so necessary in science, industry, and navigation, was almost perfected in the seventeenth century; by 1758 it reached a degree of accuracy (one minute's deviation in six hundred days) not surpassed till 1877.[11] The workers themselves, though often the source of inventions, discouraged them as threatening technological disemployment; so the hostility of labor compelled the abandonment of the first English sawmill (1663); not till 1767 was the attempt successfully renewed. Industrial invention was further retarded by poor roads; there was little incentive to increase production so long as the expansion of the market was hindered by difficulties of transport. Marine transportation, however, was improving; colonies, almost entirely agricultural, were avid customers for manufactured products; here was a rising stimulus to invention. The profit motive helped; Parliament granted patent rights for fourteen years. Foreign competition in the export trade provided another stimulus; so the textiles of India, produced by skilled but low-paid labor, spurred English manufacturers to economy of production through improved mechanical equipment. Hence it was in textile machinery that invention inaugurated the great change.

The first outstanding invention in textile production was John Kay's "flying shuttle" (1733); here might be dated the beginning of the Industrial Revolution. Previously, with minor exceptions, the width of the cloth to be woven had been limited to the stretch of the weaver's arms, for he had to throw the shuttle (the instrument that passed the threads of the woof through those of the warp) from one side of the loom with one hand and catch it with the other hand at the opposite side. Kay arranged a mechanism of wheels, hammers, and rods whereby a sharp tap of the hand would send the shuttle flying from one side to an automatic stop at any predetermined width, with a considerable saving of time. When he sought to install his invention at a mill in Colchester the weavers denounced him as trying to deprive them of their daily bread. He fled to Leeds (1738), and offered his patent to the cloth manufacturers for a fee; they took his invention, but withheld his royalties; he sued, and was ruined by legal costs. He went to his native Bury, but there the populace rose in a riot against him (1753), sacked his home, and threatened to kill him. One woman, however, greeted his machine with enthusiasm, crying, "Weel, weel! The warks o' God be wonderful, but the contrivance o' man bates Him at last!"[12] Kay found more acceptance in France, whose government adopted his invention and awarded him a pension. Not till 1760 did the flying shuttle surmount all opposition and pass into common use.

The textile industry was hampered by the fact that weavers could weave yarn faster than spinners could spin and supply it. Till 1738 spinning was done by hand, on wheels that still adorn homes idealizing the past. In that year Lewis Paul, son of a Huguenot immigrant, patented a spinning machine built apparently on lines suggested by John Wyatt: a system of rollers drew out the corded ropes of cotton or wool into threads of any desired fineness, and spun it on spindles, all with a minimum of toil. Paul and Wyatt sold the patent to Edward Cave, friend of Dr. Johnson. Cave set up five machines in a Northampton factory in 1742—the first of a long succession of spinning mills in old and New England.

Now that iron could be treated to make strong machines, and economic conditions called for large-scale production, the problem remained of finding some mechanical power to substitute cheaply for the muscles of men and the patience of women. The earliest solution was through water power. In a hundred countries the great water wheel, leisurely turning with the flow of streams, had from time unremembered moved pumps, bellows, rollers, hammers, even, since 1500, heavy iron machines. It continued to be the main source of mechanical energy through the eighteenth century; it survived into the twentieth; and the hydraulic installations of our time are water power transformed into portable electricity. The motive power of winds was not so reliable; comparatively little use was made of it in the calm lands of the south; but in northern latitudes the air currents were set to work turning windmills whose "sails" could be set into the "eye of the wind" by a hand-moved winch at the base. This clumsy and unsteady engine reached its zenith in the United Provinces in the eighteenth century, and then entered into its picturesque decline.

Meanwhile the inventors were striving to bring the steam engine to a profitable efficiency. It had already a long history, from Hero's steam-operated doors and toys in the third century A.D. through Jerome Cardan (1550), Giambattista della Porta (1601), Salomon de Caus (1615), Giovanni Branca (1629), the Marquis of Worcester (1663), Samuel Morland (1675), Christian Huygens (1680), Denis Papin (1681), and Thomas Savery (1698) to Thomas Newcomen's steam engine of 1712; this is a tale a thousand times told. Here again, at 1712, is a possible birth date for the Industrial Revolution; for Newcomen's "fire-engine" was equipped with piston, rocking beam, and safety valve, and was effectively applied to draining water from deep mines. It remained the basic model for steam-operated pumps for three quarters of a century.

4. Capital and Labor

As machines increased in size and cost, and required mechanical power for their operation, enterprising men found it profitable to replace domestic industry with factories that gathered men and machines into buildings located preferably near streams that could provide both energy and transportation. Factories, as we have seen, were no novelty; hundreds of them had existed in Elizabeth's England and Colbert's France. The "factory system"—if we define it as an industrial economy in which production is carried on *chiefly* in factories—hardly existed anywhere before the nineteenth century. But after the inventions of Kay and Paul textile factories began to take over more and more of the spinning and weaving that had been done in homes. In 1717 Thomas Lombe set up at Derby a textile factory 660 feet long, with three hundred workers operating 26,000 wheels. Soon other structures of like immensity rose at Stockport, Leek, Birmingham, Leominster, Northampton . . .

To buy and house machines, to secure raw materials, to hire labor and management, to transport and market the product, required capital. The capitalist—the provider or manager of capital—was also an ancient phenomenon; but as the demand for capital increased, the men who would take the risk of providing it rose in economic importance and political power. The guilds, still theoretically governing most European industry, resisted the capitalistic reorganization of production and distribution. But the guild system was predicated on handicrafts rather than machines; it was equipped to supply local needs rather than a national, much less an international, market; it could not meet the rising demands of armies, cities, and colonies; it was hampered by fidelity to traditional methods and norms; and it was deteriorating into a coterie of masters exploiting apprentices and journeymen. The capitalist was better able to organize quantity production and distant distribution; he had learned the subtle art of making money breed money; and he was favored by a Parliament eager for industrial capacity to supply far-ranging commerce and wars.

As factories and capitalism spread, the relation of the worker to his work was transformed. He no longer owned the tools of his trade, nor did he fix the hours and conditions of his toil. He had only a minor share in determining the rate of his earnings or the quality of his product. His shop was no longer the vestibule of his home; his industry was no longer a part of his family life. His work was no longer the proud fashioning of an article through all its stages; it became, by the division of labor that would so impress Adam Smith, the impersonal and tedious repetition of some part of a process whose finished product no longer expressed his artistry; he ceased to be an artisan, and became a "hand." His wages were set by the hunger of men competing for jobs against women and children. As a miner he received, on the average, one shilling sixpence a day; as a building laborer, two shillings; as a plumber, three shillings; these rates varied little between 1700 and 1770.[13] A male weaver, toward 1750, was paid six shillings per week; a woman weaver, five shillings sixpence; a child, two shillings sixpence. Women spinners received from two to five shillings per week; girls six to twelve years old earned one shilling to one shilling sixpence.[14] Prices, however, were low, and remained stable till 1760.[15] Sometimes an allowance was added for bread and beer at work, and most miners received free coal.

Employers contended that their workmen merited no more, being addicted to laziness, drink, unreliability, and irreligion. The only way to make workers temperate and industrious, argued an employer (1739), was to "lay them under the necessity of laboring all the time they can spare from rest and sleep in order to procure the common necessaries of life."[16] "The poor," said a writer in 1714, "have nothing to stir them up to be serviceable but their wants, which it is prudence to relieve, but folly to cure."[17] Eleven to thirteen hours constituted the normal working day, six days a week; the long stretch was relieved by an hour and a half for meals; but those who lingered unduly over their meals forfeited a quarter of a day's pay.[18] Employers complained that their workmen stopped work to attend fairs, prize fights, hangings, or wakes. To protect themselves against these and other irregularities the employers liked to have a pool of unemployed workers in the neighborhood, upon which they could draw in emergency or in times of quickened demand.[19] When times were slack, workers could be laid off and left to live on the credit of the local tradesmen.

Slowly a dependent proletariat formed in the towns. An old law of Edward VI forbade working-class combinations, and this prohibition was renewed by Parliament in 1720. But the journeymen—i.e., day laborers—continued to organize, and appealed to Parliament for better wages; these journeymen's associations—not the guilds—became the forerunners of the trade-union movement that took form in England at the end of the eighteenth century. In 1756, on an appeal from the textile workers of Gloucestershire, the House of Commons ordered the justices of the peace to maintain the legal minimum wage, and to prevent wage cutting in the industry; but a year later this order was withdrawn, and Parliament adopted the policy of letting the supply and demand of labor fix wages.[20] The age of "free enterprise" and *laissez-faire* had begun.

5. Transport and Trade

The development of the economy depended upon improvements in communication and transport. England had an advantage in her coastline and rivers; half the population lived within reasonable access to the sea, and could use it to carry goods; rivers ran far inland, providing natural waterways. But the condition of England's roads was a constant sore in English life. Their soil was soft, their ruts were hard and deep in winter, many of them were turned into streams by spring or summer rains, or into sinks of mud so tenacious that carriages had to be exhumed by supplementary teams of horses or oxen, and foot travelers had to take to neighboring fields or woods. Only after Bonnie Prince Charlie had led his rebel Scots as far south as Derby in 1745, because the state of the highways thwarted the royal forces sent against him, did the government undertake, for military purposes, to build a system of turnpikes "proper for the passage of troops, horses, and carriages at all times of the year"[21] (1751). Robbers, however, still haunted the roads, and the cost of transport was high.

Those who could afford it traveled on horseback or by private carriage. On long trips they could hire fresh horses at "posts" (i.e., positions) en route; there were such "post houses" all over Western Europe. The word *post* came to be applied to the transmission of mail because at such points the mail carriers could deliver or pick up mail and change horses; by this system they could cover 120 miles per day. Even so, Chesterfield complained (1749) that "our letters go, at best, so irregularly, and so often miscarry totally."[22] He thought it "uncommon diligence" that a letter from Verona reached London in eight days. Most travel was by stagecoach, drawn by two or four horses with driver and armed guard on the outside, and six passengers swaying within. Coaches left London on a regular schedule two or three mornings a week for the major towns of south England; they averaged seven miles an hour, and took six days between London and Newcastle.

Hampered by roads, internal trade remained picturesquely primitive. The wholesale merchant usually accompanied the pack horses that carried his goods from town to town; and peddlers hawked their wares from house to house. Shops were distinguished from dwellings chiefly by colorful signs; goods were kept inside, and ordinarily there was no window display. Almost every store was a general store; a "haberdasher" sold clothing, drugs, and ironware; the grocer was so called because he sold in gross; the "grocer" Henry Coward sold everything from sugar to nails. Each town had a market day, when, the skies permitting, merchants would expose samples of their wares. But the great centers of domestic commerce were the annual fairs held in London, Lynn, Boston, Gainsborough, Beverley, and, above all, Stourbridge. There, every August and September, a veritable city took form, with its own administration, police, and courts; nearly all products of English industry could be found there, and manufacturers from all over the island met to compare prices, qualities, and woes.

Foreign commerce was expanding, for Britain ruled the waves. Exports more than doubled in value and quantity in the first half of the century; tonnage of vessels leaving English ports rose from 317,000 in 1700 to 661,000 in 1751 to 1,405,000 in 1787.[23] Liverpool doubled its size and docks every twenty years. Imports came from a hundred lands to tickle the fancies or stomachs of the rich, or to adorn milady's dressing table with captivating toiletries. The East India Company made such profits by buying cheap in India and selling dear in Europe that it lured fifteen dukes or earls, twelve countesses, eighty-two knights, and twenty-six clergymen and physicians into the roster of its shareholders.[24] The aristocracy did not in England turn up its nose at commerce as it did in France, but helped to finance it, and shared in its prosperity. Middle-class Voltaire was delighted to find English nobles taking an active interest in trade. "It is only because the English have taken to trade," he told France in 1734, "that London has outgrown Paris both as to size and as to the number of its inhabitants, and that England can have two hundred men-of-war and subsidize allied kings."[25]

The great merchants were now rivaling the old landowning aristocracy in riches and power, determining foreign relations, fomenting and financing wars for markets, resources, and trade routes. The merchants who managed the English trade in sugar, tobacco, and slaves controlled the life of Bristol; the shippers ruled Liverpool, the coal owners dominated Newcastle. The wealth of the merchant Sir Josiah Child, who held £50,000 of stock in the East India Company, equaled that of many lords; his gardens at Wanstead were among the famous sights of England. "In most countries of Europe," wrote Hume in 1748, "family—i.e., hereditary—riches, marked with titles and symbols from the sovereign, are the chief source of distinction. In England more regard is paid to present opulence."[26] A considerable osmosis went on between the upper and middle classes: the daughters of rich merchants married the sons of the landed nobility, the sons of merchants bought estates from impoverished aristocrats, the gentry went into trade and law and administration. Aristocracy was passing into plutocracy; money was replacing birth as a title to power.

6. Money

European bankers were now providing nearly all financial services. They received deposits, protected these from fire and theft, arranged payments between depositors by merely transferring from the account of one to that of another, and issued bank notes redeemable in gold or silver on demand. Since not all noteholders were expected to ask for such redemption at the same time, the banks could issue notes up to five or ten times the value of their mutual reserves. The circulation of money, so multiplied, provided additional capital for business enterprise, and shared in expanding the European economy. Bankers stimulated industry by lending money on the security of land, buildings, materials, or simply on trust in a person's responsibility. Commerce was eased with letters of exchange or credit, which enabled capital to travel by mere transfer of bank paper, even across hostile frontiers.

Joint-stock companies were formed in England, as in Holland, Italy, and France. Promoters—then called "projecters"—organized industrial or commercial associations, issued shares, and promised dividends; stock or share certificates could be transferred from one person to another; and for that purpose a stock exchange had been established in London in 1698. The early eighteenth century saw a brisk development of speculation in company shares, with "stock jobbers" who manipulated the rise and fall of market values. Defoe in 1719 described such a manipulator:

> If Sir Josiah Child had a mind to buy, the first thing he did was to commission his brokers to look sour, shake their heads, suggest bad news from India; . . . and perhaps they would actually sell for ten, perhaps twenty, thousand pound. Immediately the Exchange . . . was full of sellers; nobody would buy a shilling, till perhaps the stock would fall six, seven, eight, ten per cent, sometimes more. Then the cunning

jobber had another set of them employed . . . to buy, but with privacy and caution, till by selling ten thousand pound at four or five per cent loss, he would buy a hundred thousand pound stock at ten or twelve per cent under price; and in a few weeks, by just the contrary method, set them all a-buying, and then sell them their own stock again at ten or twelve per cent profit.[27]

Almost as soon as stock exchanges opened, the eagerness of the public for unearned increment raised waves of speculation and deflation. The inflation and collapse of the "South Sea Bubble" in England followed in unusual concord the rise and fall of John Law's "Mississippi Bubble" in France. Sensitive to complaints by Bolingbroke, Swift, and others that the national debt — £52,000,000 in 1714—laid upon the state a ruinous annual charge of £3,-500,000 interest, the government conceived a plan to transfer £31,000,000 of the debt to the South Sea Company. This had been formed in 1711 with a grant of monopoly in English trade with Spanish colonies in America and the Pacific isles. The holders of government notes were invited to exchange them for stock in the company. King George I became its governor and every effort was made to spread the belief that its monopoly charter promised high profits. The apparent success of Law's "System" in contemporary France infected England with a similar fever of speculation. Within six days of the company's offer to accept government notes in payment for shares, two thirds of the noteholders accepted the proposal. Many others bought shares, which in a month rose from £77 to £123.5 (1719). To ensure continued governmental co-operation, the company directors voted large gifts of stock to members of the ministry, and to two mistresses of the King.[28] Robert Walpole, not yet minister, warned the House of Commons against the scheme as "pernicious . . . stockjobbing"; the project, he said, was "to raise artificially the value of the stock, by exciting and keeping up a general infatuation, and by promising dividends out of funds which would not be adequate to the purpose." He predicted, with remarkable accuracy, that the project would fail, and that if it were allowed to involve the general public its failure would entail a general and dangerous discontent.[29] He argued that at least some limit should be placed upon the rise of the company's stock. The House refused to heed his warning. On April 7, 1720, both houses of Parliament approved the proposals of the company.

On April 12 the company issued new stock at £300 a share; this was subscribed for at once. On April 21, flush with the government's payment of interest on the government notes now held by the company, it announced that it would pay a summer dividend of ten per cent. It took advantage of the enthusiasm aroused by this announcement to float a further issue of shares at £400 (April 23); this was taken up in a few hours. The rush to purchase shares raised their price to £550 on May 28, and to £890 on June

2; in July a new issue was sold at £1,000 a share. The whole fashionable world came to subscribe: dukes, clergymen, politicians, musicians, poets; Exchange Alley became the scene of such excited competition in buying as could be found only in the Rue Quincampoix in Paris at almost the same time; the nature of man revealed itself across frontiers. Shares were bargained for in taverns, coffeehouses, and milliners' shops; each night men and women calculated how rich they had become, and how much richer they might be if they had bought sooner or more.

Public money was so eager for speculation that eighty-six minor issues were floated. Stock was sold in companies formed to transmute metals into silver, to erect hospitals for bastard children, to extract oil from radishes, to create perpetual motion, to import jackasses from Spain. One promoter announced "a company for carrying on an undertaking of great advantage, but nobody to know what it is" until later; he received a thousand subscriptions of £2 each by midday, and disappeared in the afternoon.[30]

The excesses of these smaller "bubbles" (for so the time called them) began the reaction against the South Sea enterprise. Walpole and others renewed their warnings and sold their shares. On June 11 the King outlawed all stock issues except by companies licensed by Parliament. Most of the lesser ventures soon collapsed, and their failure cooled the fever of speculation. Word spread that the Spanish government was severely restricting the trade of the company in the American settlements. In July news came that Law's "Mississippi Bubble" had burst in Paris. Sir John Blount and other directors of the South Sea Company secretly sold their shares at great profit. During all of August the stock declined, until on September 2 it was quoted at £700.

The rush to sell now became a stampede; the approaches to Exchange Alley were crowded to suffocation. The shares fell to £570, to £400, to £150, to £135 (September 29). Hundreds of English families lost their savings in the crash. Stories of ruin and suicide ran the rounds.[31] Banks that had lent money on the security of the South Sea Company share certificates went into bankruptcy. Public meetings throughout England demanded the punishment of the directors, but absolved the public of vanity and greed. The King hurried back from Hanover, and summoned Parliament. The treasurer of the company fled to France, taking with him many of the records that would have incriminated the directors. In January, 1721, a parliamentary committee, examining the books of the company, found "a scene of iniquity and corruption" [32] startling even in that age when legislation by corruption of Parliament seemed part of the constitution of England. Apparently the directors had spent £574,000 in bribing leaders of the government.

Some members of Parliament called for drastic penalties; one proposed that the guilty directors should be sewn in a sack and thrown alive into the Thames.[33] The debate rose to such warmth that members challenged one another to duels; one member suffered a hypertension crisis, and died the next day. Directors and government ministers were summoned to trial before the House. John Aislabie, chancellor of the exchequer, was sentenced to the Tower; the estates of the directors—including Edward Gibbon, grandfather of the historian—were confiscated, leaving them some ten per cent of their fortunes. It was noted that Sir John Blount, who had been a prime organizer of the company, and among the first to sell his shares, was a man "of a most religious deportment," who had "constantly declaimed against the thievery and corruption of the age" and the avarice of the rich.[34]

Robert Walpole, whose predictions had been justified by the event, counseled moderation in the vengefulness of the reaction, and mitigated the collapse of the company by persuading the Bank of England and the East India Company to absorb some £18,000,000 of the troubled stock. Sufficient reserves were found in the South Sea Company to allow an early payment of thirty-three per cent to its shareholders. Shorn of its privileges and its glamour, but making money on the sale of slaves, the company continued to exist, in waning vitality, till 1853.

II. ASPECTS OF LONDON

Venturesome statisticians estimate the population of Europe at some 100 millions in 1650, some 140 millions in 1750. Voltaire in 1750 reckoned the population of France at twenty millions, of Germany and Austria at twenty-two, of Great Britain and Ireland at ten, of European Russia at ten, of Spain and Portugal at eight, of Poland at six, and he allotted three millions each to European Turkey, Sweden, Denmark (plus Norway), and the United Provinces.[35] A German jurist thought that the increase in northern Europe was largely due to the transfer of monks and nuns from celibacy to parentage by the Protestant Reformation, and urged that "a statue be erected to Luther as the preserver of the species";[36] but we must not exaggerate the continence of medieval monks. The increase in population was probably due to improvements in agriculture and transport augmenting the supply and distribution of food, and advances in sanitation and medical treatment reducing the death rate in infants and adults. England and Wales, which may have had no more than three millions population in 1500, appear to have had four millions in 1600, six in 1700, nine in 1800.[37] Nearly all the increase went to the towns, nourishing and nourished by industry and trade. By 1740 London prided itself on some 725,000 inhabitants; it was now the most populous city on the globe; Defoe in 1722 condemned it as "overgrown."[38] Paris came next with 675,000 in 1750; then Amsterdam,

Vienna, Naples, Palermo, Rome. London was ten times more populous than Bristol, which was the second-largest English city, and eighteen times more than Norwich, the third-largest. Metropolitan centers were gathering the controls of the nation's economic life, and were turning the labor and products of fields and mines and shops into the subtle profits of finance.

London was well situated to grow with English commerce and colonies. Oceangoing vessels could sail up the Thames, and though (till 1794) the docks could not berth them, an army of profane longshoremen, using a swarm of three hundred lighters, was available to transfer goods from ship to shore or other ships; so London became an animated entrepôt for the re-export, to the Continent, of imports from overseas. The riverside was not as tidy as we find it now; it was alive with lusty longshoremen, sex-starved sailors, and women loose in dress and code, foul in person and speech, living in hovels and taverns, and rivaling the seamen in drunkenness and violence.[39] The river itself was picturesque with a motley of vessels ranging from fishing smacks to massive men-of-war, while little ferries plied the stream. The King, the Lord Mayor, and some notables maintained elaborate barges, and used them to go up the river to Windsor or other palaces. Till 1750 London Bridge remained the only way of crossing on foot from the northern to the southern side of the city, but in that year Westminster Bridge was completed, and in 1757 London Bridge was freed from its burden of houses and stores. Antonio Canaletto, the Venetian painter who visited London in 1746 and 1751, was impressed by the scenes of vitality on the water, and left some famous pictures to show us the Thames as Pope and Johnson knew and loved it.

Johnson probably loved the streets of London even more, though they were as yet ill-lighted, ill-paved, and cleaned chiefly by the rains. In 1684 a system of street lighting had been established by setting up a candle lantern at every tenth house, but they were lit only on moonless nights, only till midnight, and only from Michaelmas (September 29) to Lady Day (March 25). In 1736 the city authorities voted to install fifteen thousand oil lamps throughout London, and to keep them lit from the setting to the rising of the sun; this was a gala event in the life of the capital, greatly improving the nocturnal safety of its streets.

Pavements, since the Great Fire of 1666, were mostly of small, round stones; this remained standard till the nineteenth century. In the middle of each street ran a gutter that received much refuse and sluiced off the rain. There were no curbs, but a line of posts railed off a six-foot pathway for pedestrians. The streets were noisy with carts, pack horses, hackney coaches, and private carriages, all drawn by horses with hoofs clattering against the paving stones; there were also peddlers—many of them women—hawking a hundred kinds of food or clothing; traveling artisans offering re-

pairs, drivers disputing, dogs barking, beggars soliciting, street singers bawl-
ing ballads, organs bouncing their melodies from wall to wall. The people
complained of but loved these noises, which were the vital medium of their
lives. Only the pickpockets and the prostitutes worked silently.

Houses began to receive street numbers in 1708. By 1750 most of them
had running water. Sanitation was improving. Every householder was required by law to keep the street walk clean before his property, and every
ward had a scavenger who organized the collection of waste. Toilets were
usually outhouses placed and screened off in the garden or yard. Some localities had sewers, but London had no general sewage system till 1865. Chim-
neys were cleaned by chimneysweeps who climbed them by pressing elbows and knees against the inner walls of brick or stone; this merciless
deformation of children continued till 1817.

A considerable part of the population was packed into slums filthy with
garbage and offal, breeding a hundred diseases.[40] In the Wapping and Lime-
house sections of London nearly every second inhabitant lived from hand
to mouth, depending on charity, theft, or prostitution to secure lodging and
food. Children ran barefoot, unwashed, and unkempt in the streets, clothed
in rags and schooled only in crime. In these slums men and women seldom
bothered to marry; sexual relations were a passing incident, a commodity
marketable without ceremony or law. There were hardly any churches
there, but beer shops and taverns abounded. Here too were the lairs of
thieves, pickpockets, highwaymen, and professional murderers. Many of the
criminals were organized in gangs. Watchmen who interfered with them
had their noses slit. One group, the "Mohocks," was wont to sally drunk
into the streets, prick passers-by with swords, make women stand on their
heads, and gouge out the eyes of unaccommodating victims. Less ferocious
gangsters contented themselves with breaking the windows of shops and
homes. "Thieves and robbers," Smollett reported in 1730, "were now become more desperate and savage than they had ever appeared since mankind
were civilized."[41] In 1744 the Lord Mayor and aldermen of London drew
up an address to the King in which they stated that "divers confederacies of
great numbers of evil-disposed persons, armed with bludgeons, pistols, cut-
lasses, and other dangerous weapons, infest not only the private lanes and
passages, but likewise the public streets and places of usual concourse, and
commit the most dangerous outrages upon the persons of your Majesty's
subjects."[42] Said Horace Walpole in 1752: "One is forced to travel even at
noon as if one were going to battle."[43]

The great metropolis, of course, was much more than this pullulation of
poverty and crime. It was also the city of Parliament and royal palaces, of a
thousand lawyers, merchants, journalists, poets, novelists, artists, musicians,
educators, clergymen, courtiers. As we proceed we must add to our vision

of eighteenth-century London the mansions, morals, and manners of the literate classes, the worshipers in the churches, the skeptics, scientists, and philosophers, the wits and belles and beaux of "society," the pleasure gardens of Vauxhall and Ranelagh, the promenaders in the parks and on the Mall, the regattas and festivals and barges on the Thames, the conversations in coffeehouses and clubs, the shops of craftsmen, clothiers, jewelers, the amusements of the home and the sports of the field, the crowds at cockfights, prize fights, puppet shows, theaters, and opera: only then will our perspective of London life be fair and reasonably complete, and allow us to feel history in all its phases pouring through the bodies and souls of two generations and 700,000 men.

III. SCHOOLS

In England, as elsewhere in this period, life began with a high percentage of infantile mortality: fifty-nine per cent of all children born in London died before reaching the age of five, sixty-four per cent before reaching ten.[44] Many babies were exposed at birth; of these the survivors were put out to nurse at public expense, and then were placed in workhouses. Carelessness of midwives and mothers resulted in a large number of physical deformities.

If the parents were poor, the child might receive no schooling whatever. There were "charity schools," which offered elementary education to both sexes and all classes without charge; but their total enrollment in 1759 was only 28,000, they excluded Dissenters, and they reached only a small fraction of the peasantry and hardly any of the urban poor. "The great majority of Englishmen," says an English authority, "went unlettered to their graves."[45] In the artisan class apprenticeship was considered the best education. For the middle-class child there were private schools, usually kept by "men broken down, bankrupt, or turned out of some other employment."[46] And there were "dames' schools," where humble schoolmistresses taught the three R's and much religion to boys and girls whose parents could pay. In all schools emphasis was laid upon teaching students to be content with their native rank, and to show proper subordination to the upper classes.

A small minority graduated into "grammar schools," where, for a modest fee that taught the teachers their humble place in the social scale, the boys could add a little Latin and Greek to their R's. Discipline was severe, class hours were long—six to eleven-thirty in the morning, and one to five-thirty in the afternoon. Much better in quality were the "public schools"—chiefly Eton, Westminster, Winchester, Shrewsbury, Harrow, and Rugby—where select youngsters, for some twenty-six pounds per year, could prepare for university, and lay up classical tags for future display. As these public schools admitted only Church of England boys, the Dissenters—Baptists, Presbyterians, Independents, Unitarians, Quakers, Congregationalists, Methodists—established academies for their youth.

Here, as befitted a middle-class clientele, less stress was laid upon the ancient classics, more upon modern languages, mathematics, history, geography, and navigation.

Dissenters were excluded from the universities. Most of the students there were from moneyed families; some poorer lads, however, received scholarships from philanthropic individuals or institutions, and some "servitors" or "sizars," like Newton, worked their way through the class-conscious halls. Both Oxford and Cambridge suffered stagnation in this period from conservatism in curriculum, methods, and ideas. Cambridge showed more willingness to enlarge scientific studies at the expense of the classics and theology; yet Chesterfield described Cambridge as "sunk into the lowest obscurity." Oxford clung to the old theology and the fallen Stuart dynasty, and allowed no visit from the crude Hanoverian kings. Adam Smith, a student at Oxford in 1745, said he had learned little there; Edward Gibbon, who studied there in 1752, denounced the dons as ignorant tipplers, and regretted the years he had wasted in the university. Many families preferred to engage private tutors.[47]

Girls received rudimentary instruction in village and charity schools—reading, writing, sewing, knitting, spinning, little arithmetic, much religion. Some girls were tutored, and a few, like Lady Mary Wortley Montagu, studied the classic languages and literatures surreptitiously. "My sex," said Lady Mary, "is usually forbid studies of this nature, and folly is reckoned so much our proper sphere we are sooner pardoned any excess of that, than the least pretensions to reading or good sense. . . . There is hardly a creature in the world . . . more liable to universal ridicule than a learned woman." She was inclined to suspect that men kept women ignorant in order the more inexpensively to seduce them.[48] If we may judge from the revenues of the King's mistresses, the women managed quite well without the classics, and needed no Ovid to instruct them in the game of love.

IV. MORALS

Premarital relations among women were probably less common then than today (1965), but prostitution flourished to an extent hardly known again till our time. A foreign observer reckoned them at fifty thousand in London. They were found at town taverns, roadside inns, city gardens, public dances, concerts, and theaters; in Exeter Street and the Strand they sat at windows to encourage hesitant trade. In Drury Lane, sang Gay in his *Trivia*,

> 'Tis she who nightly strolls with saunt'ring pace;
> No stubborn stays her yielding shape embrace;
> Beneath the lamp her tawdry ribbons glare,
> The new scour'd manteau, and the slattern air . . .
> With flatt'ring sounds she soothes the cred'lous ear:
> "My noble captain! charmer! love! my dear!"[49]

The law had no mercy on them. If found soliciting, they were taken to jail, whipped and pilloried. The *Grub Street Journal* for May 6, 1731, described the fate of one "madame":

> Yesterday the noted Mother Needham stood in the pillory in Park Place near St. James's Street, and was severely handled by the populace. She was so very ill that she lay along the pillory, notwithstanding which she was severely pelted, and it is thought she will die in a day or two.[50]

But only the most impoverished prostitutes reached the pillory. Usually they evaded the law by bribery, or their landlord bailed them out; and some guardians of the law, perhaps recognizing their former hostesses, felt a degree of sympathy for women whom the statutes punished for the promiscuity of men. Probably not ten males in a London hundred came virginal to the marriage bed. Vice was publicly denounced, virtue was privately scorned. John Cleland's *Memoirs of a Woman of Pleasure* (1749), later known as *Fanny Hill,* a concatenation of detailed seductions, was (and is) one of the most obscene and popular books of the century.

Some men banded together for mutual satisfaction. The *London Journal* for April 23 and 30, 1725, reported the arrest of seven homosexuals; on May 14 it recorded the hanging of three others for "sodomy." It added: "We learn that they [the police] have discovered twenty houses or clubs where sodomites meet; moreover, they have an eye on nocturnal assemblies where these monsters meet in great number." On July 7 the *Journal* noted the conviction of "Robert Whale and York Horner for having maintained in Westminster houses where they received amateurs of this detestable vice." On July 23 it announced that "Marguerite Clapp, convicted of keeping a house of assignation for the use of sodomites," had been "condemned to the pillory . . . , to pay a fine of ninety marks, and to spend two years in prison."[51]

We are told, on good authority, that "a very large proportion of the people [of London] lived in a state of illicit cohabitation without marriage."[52] Love marriages were rising in number, at least in the novels of Richardson and Fielding, but most marriages were still arranged by the parents after careful weighing of the bride's dowry against the bridegroom's actual or prospective income. An act of 1753 prohibited persons under twenty-one from marrying without the consent of their parents or guardians. As this law applied to England alone, many English elopers crossed the border into Scotland, where the parsons in the village of Gretna Green followed an easier rule. Further conveniences for eager lovers were provided by acquisitive clergymen who performed clandestine marriages in taverns, brothels, garrets, or other places in or near the Fleet (a street and the debtors' prison on it). Almost every tavern in that neighborhood had such a dominie ready, for a fee, to marry anyone without questions asked or license required. One such parson was reputed to have married six thousand couples per year. Marriages were entered upon in heat, and broken in thaw; thousands of women were deserted; sailors on shore for a day married, loved, and decamped. To end the evil Parliament decreed (1753) that no marriage in England, except between Quakers or Jews, should be valid unless performed by an Anglican priest in a parish church, after the publication of banns in that church for three successive Sundays; all violators of this statute were liable to deportation to the colonies.

Divorce was not allowed in England (before 1857) without a special act of Parliament,[53] and the cost of such a procedure made it a luxury of the rich. Adultery flourished in all but the middle classes, with Georges I and II giving a royal example. "Everybody in this society," Congreve had written in 1700, "was born with budding antlers";[54] and it was only less so in 1728, when Gay made Mrs. Peachum, in *The Beggar's Opera*, ask her husband about her daughter, "Why must our Polly, forsooth, differ from her sex, and love only her husband? . . . All men are thieves in love, and like a woman the better for being another man's property."[55] By and large, however, the morals of women were higher in England than in France; and in the middle classes, where the Puritan tradition was still strong, purity verged on prudery, and women might be such wives as men dream of—patient, industrious, and faithful. The double standard was imposed and accepted. Nice women heard much coarse speech and read Fielding and Smollett, but they were expected to blush alluringly, and to faint at a moment's notice.

In all classes woman was looked upon as naturally and irrevocably inferior to man. Even the proud and rebellious Lady Mary conceded this, though perhaps with her sharp tongue in her cheek:

> I am not now arguing for an equality of the sexes. I do not doubt God and nature have thrown us into an inferior rank; we are a lower part of the creation, we owe obedience and submission to the superior sex, and any woman who suffers her vanity and folly to deny this, rebels against the law of the Creator and indisputable order of nature.[56]

The Puritan interlude had brought woman down from her status under Elizabeth. One student judged that "about 1750, women in England had reached a new low level hardly in advance of their position in the twelfth century."[57]

Social, economic, and political morality were at nadir. Gambling, which had been discouraged by Queen Anne, was restored to royal grace by Georges I and II. A special officer, the groom porter, controlled gambling at the court. Cardplaying was the favorite amusement of rich and poor, seldom without stakes, often with cheating. It was not unusual for highborn wastrels to win or lose two hundred guineas at one sitting; the Duke of Devonshire gambled away an estate in one game; and Lord Chesterfield gambled recklessly between lectures to his son. Under George I gambling became a public passion to a degree probably never rivaled since. Gambling casinos were opened at White's Club, at Charing Cross, in Leicester Fields, in Golden Square, and in Bath. An engraving in Hogarth's *Rake's Progress* shows men and women gambling at White's, and paying no attention to an announcement that the building is on fire; the game must be fought to a decision.* George II forbade such organized gambling, but sanctioned the government lottery, which had been established in 1569 and which survived till 1826. Lottery tickets were sold to the public by every device of promotion; excitement was worked up to such a pitch that servants robbed their masters, clerks their employees, to get a stake in the game.[58]

Drinking was even more popular than gambling. Beer or ale was the national drink. The London male consumed a hundred gallons a year, or a quart per day, as safer and tastier than water. The damp climate created a demand for rum, punch, brandy, gin, cordials, whiskey; and wine was a favorite medicine. Taverns and liquor stores were everywhere; out of 7,066 houses in the parish of Holborn 1,350 sold liquor. Landowners—and therefore Parliament—smiled on the whiskey trade, since it opened an added market for their barley and wheat;[59] almost a third of the arable land of England was planted to barley. In the upper classes whiskey tended to replace wine as the repeated wars with France hindered the commerce with Bordeaux and Oporto, and the Dutch and the Germans brought in their preference for hard liquor. Here, as in gambling, the government set the pace: Harley, prime minister under Anne, was reported to have come drunk into the presence of the Queen; Bolingbroke sometimes sat up all night drinking; and Robert Walpole had been taught drunkenness by a father resolved not to be seen drunk by a sober son.[60]

When the passion for gin spread among the populace the government was disturbed. The spirits distilled in Britain rose from 527,000 gallons in 1684 to 5,394,000 gallons in 1735, with no comparable rise in population; on the contrary, physicians warned the government that gin drinking had rapidly increased the rate of mortality in London; and a Middlesex grand jury ascribed to that liquor much of the poverty and crime of the capital. Retailers of gin hung out signs promising to make their customers drunk for a penny, and offering them free beds of straw in the cellar.

The alarmed rulers tried prohibition by taxation. An act of Parliament in

---

* The famous club was burned down in 1733, but was soon restored.

1736 laid a duty of twenty shillings a gallon on gin, and required fifty pounds a year for license to sell it. The thirsting poor rose in violent riots. As Walpole had predicted, the prohibition led to smuggling, secret distilling, and clandestine trade. The number of gin shops rose to seventeen thousand, the distilled gallons to over seven million, and crime increased. The experiment was abandoned, the license fee was reduced to twenty pounds, the duty to a penny per gallon; the people rejoiced and drank. In 1751 a series of moderate and ingenious measures (such as making small debts to liquor dealers irrecoverable at law) effected a mild improvement.[61] The philosopher Berkeley illuminated the situation by denouncing the upper classes for the evil example they gave to the masses, and warning them that "a nation lighted up at both ends must soon be consumed."[62]

The moral level was low in business too. Great fortunes were derived from smuggling, piracy, and catching or selling slaves. Complaints arose that the water of the Thames was defiled by commercial as well as human waste, that wine was debased with cider and spirits of corn, that bread was adulterated with alum and chalk, that aging meats had their complexions freshened with chemicals dangerous to health and life. When attempts were made to check such practices, the patriots of business cried out for freedom and the right of "every man . . . to live in his own way without restraint."[63]

The government interfered with liberty, but chiefy to impress men into the armed services. When various financial inducements failed to man the navy, "press gangs" (from 1744 onward) were sent out by the state to snare, drug, or otherwise persuade men into his Majesty's ships. Intoxication was the easiest method, for in that condition a man could be led to sign away a year or more of his life. From the time they were so brought on board, said Admiral Vernon (1746), such men were "in effect condemned to death, since they are never allowed again to set foot on shore, but turned over from ship to ship . . . without any regard for the hardships they have undergone."[64] "No man," said Samuel Johnson, "will be a sailor who has contrivance enough to get himself into a jail. . . . The man in a jail has more room, better food, and commonly better company."[65] Sailors secured by impressment were usually weak in body and mind, but the rough discipline and ruthless selection by ordeal of fire and flogging (as described and doubtless exaggerated in Smollett's *Roderick Random*) made the survivors the toughest and proudest warriors on the sea.

Piracy was still winked at as a form of commerce, but it was in decline as navies grew stronger. The slave trade flourished; English, French, Dutch, and Portuguese ships competed for the privilege of selling African Negroes to American Christians. By the Treaty of Utrecht (1713) Spain had transferred from France to England the Asiento, the contract to supply the Spanish colonies annually with 4,800 slaves. Of the 74,000 slaves transported to America in the one year 1790, the French carried 20,000, the Dutch 4,000, the Danes 2,000, the Portuguese 10,000, and the British 38,000 —more than half the total.[66] "The English alone, at a low estimate," says an English authority, "carried over two million negroes to America in the period between 1680 and 1786."[67] Some Negro slaves were kept for service in English homes. The newspapers contained promises of rewards for the return of runaway slaves; one advertisement offered "a negro boy, about twelve years of age, . . . to be sold."[68] Slaves were sold at Paris till 1762, and even the popes had Turkish galley slaves from the sixteenth to the eighteenth century.[69] The Quakers began in 1727 a movement to end the British share in the slave trade; Steele and Pope supported them; the Methodists advanced the crusade; but the campaign for abolition made no substantial progress before 1772.

Political morality reflected the triumph of a hard commercial spirit. Hardly anything could be effected without bribery, and nearly every official had his price. Offices were sold, and votes in Parliament were bought like merchandise. M.P.s sold their franking privilege. Noble lords sold positions in their households,[70] and "obstructed attempts to check the purchase of nominations to Parliament, or of members of the Commons."[71] "Rotten boroughs," with a handful of inhabitants, sent to Parliament as many representatives as counties abounding in population and industry; "Old Sarum," with not a single resident, sent two delegates; and such boroughs were easily controlled by men of birth or wealth. Businessmen, seeking political influence commensurate with their economic power, bought nominations or nominees to Parliament for some £1,500 each.[72] All in all, this half century was the most corrupt and merciless in English history; and the historian finds it no simple matter to explain how, from the venality of that age, Britain has risen to such high repute for the integrity of its businessmen and its government.

Amid the debasement of morals and politics there were many touches of humanitarian sentiment. There were homes, however ill-kept, for the old, the disabled, and the poor. There were guilds in which masters were kindly fathers to their apprentices; there were families that sheltered and educated orphans; there were associations—"box clubs"—for mutual aid in evil days. There was an impressive example—the first in modern history—of international charity when England contributed £100,000 sterling to her economic ally, Portugal, for the relief of sufferers from the Lisbon earthquake of 1755.[73] Between 1700 and 1825 one hundred and fifty-four new hospitals and dispensaries were established in Britain, four in London in one generation (1700–45). Most of these institutions were financed by private subscription. The best of those set up in the first half of the eighteenth century was the Foundling Hospital, organized by Captain Thomas Coram. Hogarth painted him in 1740 as a gift to the hospital: rotund, white-haired, kindly, with the royal charter at his right hand, and a globe at his feet; for Coram had earned his fortune as a captain in the merchant marine. Retiring, he was shocked by the high infant mortality in London, and by the number of infants exposed or deserted by mothers with no funds to care for them or no father's name to give them. Coram persuaded highborn ladies to sign a petition for a foundling hospital; he secured a charter and two thousand pounds from George II; his appeal for contributions was met with unexpected generosity; the great Handel gave an organ and the now precious score of his *Messiah*, and directed concerts that raised ten thousand pounds. In 1739 the trustees commissioned Theodore Jacobsen to design a spacious group of buildings and grounds, which became one of the proudest sights of London.

V. CRIME AND PUNISHMENT

The people of eighteenth-century England were a tough breed, accustomed to hardship and violence, and capable of surviving anything except death. Two corporals fought each other with bare fists till both expired; two sergeants dueled till both suffered mortal wounds. A soldier who asked leave to marry an army prostitute was punished with a hundred lashes; he appeared the next day, his back all raw, before the same officer, and repeated his plea; this time it was granted. A drummer boasted that he had received 26,000 lashes in his fourteen years with the army; he received four thousand more in the one year 1727; he recovered cheerfully, and was soon reported as "hearty and well, and in no ways concerned."[74]

Brutal punishments, administered in public, encouraged public brutality. By a law repealed in 1790 a woman convicted of treason, or of murdering her husband, was to be burned alive, but custom allowed her to be strangled before burning.[75] Men guilty of treason were cut down from the gallows while still alive; their bowels were extracted and burned before their faces; they were then beheaded and quartered. Gallows were raised in every district of London, and on many of them the corpses were left for the nourishment of birds. A man might hang for half an hour before he died. It was usual, however, to dull the senses of the condemned with brandy; and the hangman, if well disposed, would pull on the dangling legs to hasten death.

The callousness of spectators and criminals gave hangings the character of a festival; people lined the road to see the condemned ride in the carts to

Tyburn; stalls and peddlers sold gin and gingerbread, nuts and apples, to the crowd; street singers sang ballads not quite so well as Captain Macheath in *The Beggar's Opera*. The public, never enthusiastic about laws or police-men, made heroes of criminals who carried off their exploits successfully, or, when captured, faced trial and death with scorn or smiles. Jack Shep-pard, "Rob Roy" (i.e., Robert Macgregor), Dick Turpin, Jonathan Wild, all flourished in this period. Jack, after almost daily robberies in or near London, was betrayed to the police by Jonathan Wild; he escaped, was re-arrested, escaped again, was caught in his cups, and was hanged, aged twenty-two, before a crowd of thousands that expected him to escape even with the noose around his neck. Defoe and Ainsworth told his story profitably, Sir James Thornhill painted his portrait. Turpin distributed money to mourners to follow his cart in state to the gallows; but what made him most famous was the fictitious account that Ainsworth wrote of Dick's breakneck ride from London to York. Likewise, Fielding's *Life of Mr. Jon-athan Wild the Great* has carried that scoundrel down the centuries. Most of that powerful satire is fiction, but it is no more interesting than the facts. Jonathan, like Janus, had a double face. He organized, managed, and ex-ploited thieves, bought their stolen goods at his own price, and betrayed them to the magistrates when his confederates rebelled. At the same time he opened a pretty office where he received people who had been robbed; he promised, for a substantial consideration, to get their goods or money re-turned to them; on the proceeds he maintained several mistresses, and lived in style for nearly fifteen years. But his prosperity outstripped his prudence; he was arrested as a dealer in stolen goods; and he was hanged to the joy of an enormous multitude (1725). He may have been part model for Mr. Peachum in *The Beggar's Opera*.

Lawlessness ran the social scale from the gentle pickpocket to the smug-gling merchant to the titled duelist. There were hundreds of duels, some in the open street, some in Hyde Park or Kensington Gardens, but most of them on the "Field of the Forty Footsteps" behind Montagu House (now the British Museum). They were seldom fatal, for pistols were clumsy, and few men could aim them accurately at thirty paces; probably many com-batants were careful to fire above the head; in any case reconciliation was normally achieved after the first drawing of blood. The duels were illegal, but were humored on the ground that they encouraged a cautious courtesy of speech. Arrests were rare except for fatalities; and if the survivor could show that he had followed the rules of the game he was released after a brief imprisonment.

In 1751 Fielding, then a magistrate, published *An Enquiry into the Causes of the Late Increase of Robbers, etc., with Some Proposals for Remedying the Growing Evil*. He ascribed the increase predominantly not to poverty but to the rise of "luxury" among the lower classes; the common people now had money enough to go to taverns, amusement parks, theaters, masquerade dances, and operas; and there they met persons adept in promiscuity and crime. The second cause, the great novelist thought, was an increase in the consumption of gin.

> Gin is the principal sustenance (if it may be so called) of more than an hundred thousand People in this Metropolis. Many of these wretches swallow Pints of this Poison within the Twenty-four Hours; the dreadful effects of which I have the misfortune every day to see and to smell, too.[76]

The third cause was gambling. The fourth was the incompetence of the law; it left the capture of criminals to watchmen

> chosen out of poor, old, decrepit people who, . . . armed only with a pole, which some of them are scarcely able to lift, are to secure the persons and houses of his Majesty's subjects from the attacks of gangs of young, bold, stout, desperate, and well-armed villains.[77]

Even if the watchman was not terrified by the violence of the robbers, he could be bribed; so could the constable to whom he reported; so could the magistrate to whom the constable brought a criminal. The policing of London was entrusted to 1,000 constables, 474 beadles, 747 watchmen. Between arrest and conviction lay 2,214 lawyers in London, some of them men of legal learning and reasonable integrity, some of them not quite so. Dr. Johnson said of a man who had just left the room that he "did not care to speak ill of any man behind his back, but he believed the gentleman was an attorney."[78]

Fielding did not agree with Coke that "the wisdom of all the wise men in the world, if they had all met together at one time, could not have equaled" the excellence of the English constitution. He would have admitted that that constitution, as Voltaire and Montesquieu had recently pointed out, had admirably arranged for the protection of the individual and his property from the tyranny of a king; he would have praised habeas corpus and trial by jury, and the great law schools in the Inns of Court. Certainly it was no small matter that an Englishman was free from arrest without legal warrant, from imprisonment without trial, from punishment without conviction by a jury of his peers; that he could not be taxed except by consent of Parliament; that he could assemble with his fellows provided he committed no disorder; that he might say what he pleased, short of sedition, libel, obscenity, and blasphemy. But the lawmakers of England had been so eager to protect the individual from the state that they had failed to protect society from the individual. The machinery of enforcement was breaking down before the spread and organization of crime.

The common law was administered by magistrates, or justices of the peace, whose decisions could be appealed to judges sitting in Westminster or traveling six months a year to hold assize courts in the county towns. These judges enjoyed life tenure, and displayed a reasonable level of integrity. Ecclesiastical courts survived, but they were limited to trying noncriminal cases involving only the clergy, or the validity of marriages, or the administration of wills. The Court of Admiralty had jurisdiction over exclusively maritime cases. Above these courts was the Court of Chancery, presided over by the lord chancellor. The supreme court of the land was Parliament itself, with the Commons trying commoners and the Lords trying peers. Equality before the law was still imperfect, for peers usually escaped punishment. The fourth Earl of Ferrers was executed in 1760 for killing his steward, but when the Duchess of Kingston was tried before the House of Lords in 1776 and was convicted of bigamy, she was freed with only the payment of fees. Latin remained the language of the courts till 1730, when English displaced it, paining Blackstone grievously.

In trials for capital felony (and most felonies were capital) the accused was allowed to hire counsel if he could afford one; the counsel might cross-examine the witnesses for the prosecution, but was not permitted to address the court; this was left to the prisoner, who, through weakness of body or mind, was in many cases incapable of presenting his defense. If he was acquitted he was returned to jail till he had paid all the fees exacted by the keepers for their services; before this regulation was revoked in 1774 there were several instances of acquitted men dying in jail. If convicted, the prisoner faced one of the severest penal codes in the history of law.

The code was an advance on the past, and on Continental procedures, in barring torture and punishment by the wheel, and it no longer split noses or cut off ears. Otherwise it had all the barbarity that sturdy Englishmen then considered necessary to control the natural lawlessness of mankind. When the penalty was flogging at the tail of a cart drawn through the streets, the executioner would sometimes receive an extra sum, collected from the spectators, to ply the thong with special vigor.[79] A prisoner who refused to plead on a capital charge was required by law to be laid naked on his back in a dark room, and weights of stone or iron were placed upon his breast till he was pressed or choked to death;[80] this law, however, was not enforced after 1721, and was repealed in 1772.

Throughout the eighteenth century acts of Parliament added to the number of crimes for which the statutory penalty was death. In 1689 there had been fifty such; by 1820 there were 160. Murder, treason, counterfeiting, arson, rape, sodomy, piracy, armed smuggling, forgery, destroying ships or setting them on fire, bankruptcy with concealment of assets, highway robbery, housebreaking, burglary of over forty shillings, shoplifting above five shillings, maiming or stealing cattle, shooting at a revenue officer, cutting down trees in an avenue or a park, setting fire to a cornfield, sending threatening letters, concealing the death of a husband or a child, taking part in a riot, shooting a rabbit, demolishing a turnpike gate, escaping from jail, committing sacrilege—all of these, and a hundred more, were, under the first three Georges, capital crimes. These laws reflected the resolve of Parliament to protect property. They may have been in some measure the result—and in part the cause—of popular lawlessness and brutality, and they may have helped to form the present law-abiding habits of the British people. The severity of the code was mitigated by the frequent refusal of judges or juries to convict, or by quashing the indictment on a technicality, or by arbitrarily fixing the value of a stolen article at less than the amount that would make the theft a capital crime. In time of war offenders might be pardoned on condition of joining the army or navy.

Lesser crimes were punished by imprisonment, the pillory, whipping, hard labor in houses of correction, or transportation to the colonies. By a law of 1718 convicted prisoners were sold to a contractor who shipped them, at his own expense, generally to Maryland or Virginia, and sold them, usually at auction, to tobacco planters for the term of their sentences. The condition of the prisoners en route resulted in a high percentage of deaths, and such enfeeblement of the remainder as to make them for a time incapable of labor. One contractor reckoned that he lost a seventh of his human cargo on an average voyage.[81] This traffic was ended only by the American War of Independence.

Such deportation was often preferred to imprisonment, for prisons were notorious for inhumanity and filth. On his entry the new arrival was put in irons, heavy or light according to his payment to the warden. His bed was straw. His food consisted of a pound of bread per day, unless he could arrange to supplement it with gifts from outside. Except in Newgate Prison little attempt was made to keep the prisons clean. Dirt and germs accumulated, infecting almost every prisoner with "jail fever"—often typhus or smallpox. Johnson thought that twenty-five per cent of the permanent prisoners died through "putrid fevers." The stench of foulness and disease was so strong that when a prisoner was brought to court the judges, jury, witnesses, and spectators took frequent sniffs of camphor, vinegar, or aromatic herbs to offset the smell. In May, 1750, a hundred prisoners from Newgate came to trial in the "Old Bailey," the chief criminal court of London. The fever they spread was so virulent that of the six judges who tried the case four died; of the jury and the minor officials, forty died; after this lesson the court ordered that thereafter all prisoners coming to trial should be washed with vinegar, and that sweet-smelling herbs should be placed in the prisoner's dock.[82]

A man sued for debt, judged guilty, and unable or unwilling to pay was committed to such a jail until he paid, or until his creditor withdrew the suit. The creditor was bound by law to pay fourpence a day toward the support of his prisoner; but if he failed to do this the debtor had no recourse but to sue him—which cost money. If, however, the prisoner could get funds from outside, he could bribe the warden and others to let him enjoy better bed and board, wider liberties, the comfort of his wife, even, now and then, a holiday in the city. A penniless debtor, if unable to pay for food, might slowly starve on the bread allowed him. Samuel Johnson calculated that of twenty thousand bankrupts imprisoned in an average year, five thousand died of privation within twelve months.[83] England had not found a milder way of protecting the rising business class from irresponsible borrowing or fraudulent bankruptcy.

Some mild protests were raised against the severity of the penal code. Johnson, no sentimentalist, pointed out in 1751 the danger in making so many crimes capital: "To equal robbery with murder is to . . . incite the commission of a greater crime to prevent the detection of a less."[84] The most powerful criticisms of prison administration appeared in the novels of Fielding and Smollett, and in the drawings of Hogarth. A modest amelioration was effected by James Oglethorpe, whose varied and energetic career shows the nobler side of John Bull. In 1714, aged eighteen, he left college to join the army of Prince Eugene of Savoy, and served in several actions against the Turks. Returning to England, he was elected to Parliament. A friend having been imprisoned for debt, and having died in jail of smallpox contracted there, Oglethorpe persuaded the Commons to appoint a committee—of which he was made head—to inquire into the conditions of the London prisons. The filth, disease, corruption, and oppression revealed by this investigation shocked for a moment the conscience of England. Some especially culpable wardens were dismissed, some new regulations mitigated old abuses; but most of the evils remained, and the actual reform of the prisons had to wait for John Howard and the final quarter of the eighteenth century. Oglethorpe turned to emigration as a means of reducing the pressure of poverty in England. In 1733 he founded the colony of Georgia; for a time he served as its governor; he forbade the importation of slaves, and welcomed the Moravians, and John Wesley, and Protestant refugees from Austria. Again in England and Parliament, he secured an act exempting the English Moravians from taking oaths or bearing arms. He became an intimate friend of Johnson, Goldsmith, and Burke, and lived to the age of eighty-nine. Pope crowned him with a couplet:

One driven by strong benevolence of soul
Shall fly like Oglethorpe from pole to pole.[85]

VI. MANNERS

The men who promenaded in the parks or on the Mall were still—as in Elizabethan or Restoration days—the more grandly dressed sex. Except at work or at home, they wore tilted three-cornered hats, often cocky with tassels, ribbons, or cockades. They bound their tresses with a pretty bow behind the neck, or covered their heads with a powdered wig. Their handsome coats, rustling about their knees, sported buttons designed to dazzle rather than to tie; and sleeves of rich brocade proclaimed income or class. Their fancy waistcoats sought the eye with their gaudy tints—yellow, orange, scarlet, pink, or blue—and dangled a watch fob of gold on a golden chain. Their shirts of fine linen were faced with frills, hiding flannel underwear. "Stocks" (cravats) of "lawn" (a fabric imported from Laon in France) were fitted snugly about their throats. Their breeches were fastened with buckles at the knees, three buttons at the waist, and three hidden in the fly. Their stockings were usually red, but would be of white silk at formal gatherings. Their shoes, in 1730, had to be red in toe and heel. Even with all this equipment the man of fashion felt naked without a sword. As the middle classes mounted, swords were replaced with canes, usually topped with some costly metal and finely carved; but since the streets were still dangerous, the cane often contained a sword. Umbrellas had entered the picture late in the seventeenth century, but did not become general till the end of the eighteenth. Specific costumes, of course, were required for riding in the park or with the hounds; and dandies ("Macaronis") clamored for attention with extremes of adornment or coloration. Another group ("Slovens") made a religion of careless manners and untidy clothes; they disheveled their hair with rebellious care, left their breeches unbuckled, and flaunted the mud on their shoes as declarations of independence and emblems of original thought.

Women, when on display, dressed as in our wondering youth, when the female structure was a breathless mystery costly to behold. Their fluffy skirts were generally inflated with hoops that lifted them lightly from step to step, and made a giddy revelation of sparkling ankles and prancing feet. Hoops, sometimes nine yards around, were ramparts, and stays were shields, so that the conquests of love required all the ardor of a knight piercing armor and scaling parapets; so much the better for poetry. The gloss and splendor of a woman's hair were partly lost in reinforced elevations so lofty that they had to be guarded against being ignited by chandeliers. Feminine faces were concealed by lotions, pastes, patches, powders, and adjustable eyebrows; and all the gems of the Orient were commandeered to adorn their hair and ears and neck and arms and dress and shoes. From her towering hat and scented curls to her silken and jeweled footwear the woman of fashion was dressed to kill any hesitation on the part of circumjacent males. By 1770 the arts of the toilette had reached such wizardry that Parliament, in a jovial mood, passed an act designed to protect the precipitous sex:

> That all women, of whatever age, rank, profession, or degree, whether virgins, maids, or widows, that shall, from and after such Act, impose upon, seduce, or betray into matrimony any of his Majesty's male subjects by the scents, paints, cosmetic washes, artificial teeth, false hair, Spanish wool, iron stays, hoops, high-heeled shoes, etc., shall incur the penalty of the law now enforced against witchcraft and like misdemeanours, and that the marriage, upon conviction, shall stand null and void.[86]

Sumptuary laws struggled to check conspicuous expenditure in dress, but custom required all loyal Britons to don a new outfit on the birthday of Queen Caroline, who at her coronation wore a costume costing £2,400,000 —mostly in borrowed gems.

Home was a place where one might discard the laborious accouterments of display; there one could dress in anything or less. Windows were not inquisitive, for their number was held down by a law that limited them to five and taxed any surplus as luxury. Interiors were dark and stuffy, and not designed for breathing. Lighting was by candles, usually not more than one at a time per family; the rich, however, brightened their rooms with gleaming chandeliers and with torches burning oil. In the mansions of the well-to-do, walls were paneled in oak, staircases were of massive wood and unshakable balustrades, fireplaces were marbles of majesty, chairs were padded with hair and upholstered in leather. Furniture was designed in heavy "Georgian" style, complex with carving and glaring with gilt. Toward 1720 mahogany was introduced from the West Indies; it was too hard for existing tools; sharper tools were made; and soon the new wood made the most brilliant pieces in English homes.

Houses were heated by burning coal in stoves or open grates, or wood in spacious hearths. London air was cloudy with smoke. Domestic cleanliness was made difficult but imperative by the ever-threatening dust and soot. The French rated their English enemies as next only to the Dutch in the grooming of their homes. Said Nicolas de Saussure in 1726:

> Not a week passes by but well kept houses are washed twice in the seven days, and that from top to bottom; and even every morning

most kitchens, staircases, and entrances are scrubbed. All furniture, and especially all kitchen utensils, are kept with the greatest cleanliness. Even the large hammers and the locks on the doors are rubbed and shine brightly.[87]

This despite the fact that soap was expensive and water limited. Bathrooms were a luxury of the few; most men and women bathed by standing and splashing in a tub.

Commoners spent most of their indoor and waking hours in the kitchen, courting the big stove; they ate there, chatted there, sometimes slept there, for the kitchens were immense. Dining rooms were for special occasions. In all ranks the main meal came after midday: in the middle classes at two or three o'clock, among the rich at five or six; then, as now, the more money you had, the longer you had to wait for dinner. In fashionable homes the women retired when eating was over, for then began male drinking, smoking, toasts, and tales. Dinners were substantial, but they were the city Briton's first food after breakfast and a light 11-A.M. "snack." Frenchmen were astonished at the amount of food an Englishman consumed at a sitting. Most of the diet in the upper and middle classes was meat; vegetables were negligible garniture. Heavy puddings were a favorite dessert. Tea drinking was universal, though tea cost ten shillings a pound. Supper at 9 P.M. rounded out the exploits of the day.

Most Englishmen hugged the safety of their homes at night, and amused themselves with conversation, drinking, quarreling, reading, music, dancing, chess, draughts (the American "checkers"), billiards, and cards. "Prithee," said Marlborough's Duchess, "don't talk to me about books. The only books I know are men and cards."[88] Bishops and parsons, even the prim Dissenting preachers, played, and philosophers too; Hume rarely went to bed without having a turn at whist (now "bridge"). In 1742 Edmond Hoyle systematized the laws of whist in a *Short Treatise,* after which, till 1864, the game had to be played "according to Hoyle." — Animal pets were a household necessity, not only dogs and cats, but, here and there, a monkey or two.[89] Almost every woman nursed flowers, and nearly every home had a garden.

Blest and harassed with rain, the English made garden design a national passion. Under Charles II English gardens followed French models—chiefly Versailles—in shaping formal gardens on geometrical lines, straight, rectangular, radial, or circular, with "picturesque vistas" and "perspectives" (these three words had entered the language in the seventeenth century), with trees, shrubbery, and hedges clipped to line, and classical statuary symmetrically placed. The amusement gardens at Vauxhall and Ranelagh were so laid out; we can sample this formal style today at Hampton Court. Though it accorded well with the neoclassical literature of the "Augustan

Age," Addison and Pope, the best exemplars of that age in print, rebelled against the formal garden, and cried out politely for a "natural garden" that would leave at least a part of nature's luxuriance unclipped and untamed, and would generate delighted surprises by preserving nature's incalculable irregularity. Chinese influences entered into the rebellion; pagodas replaced statues in some gardens; in his Kew gardens the Duke of Kent built a house for Confucius. The natural garden reflected the sentimental Thomson and Collins rather than the chaste Addison and the meticulous, trim and tidy Pope; it joined with the "poets of feeling" in a "Romantic" treble to a classical bass. Pope and Thomson agreed in praising the gardens designed on the "Stowe" estate of Richard Temple, Viscount Cobham. Charles Bridge-man had begun it on a formal design; William Kent and Lancelot "Capa-bility" Brown re-formed it in natural style; it became the talk of gardeners in England and France, and won the acclaim of Jean Jacques Rousseau.

Beyond the gardens lay the streams where oarsmen rowed and lazy anglers dreamed of snaring fish; and the woods where men shot pheasants, grouse, partridge, or wild fowl, or where scarlet huntsmen followed their dogs to the cornered fox or the exhausted hare. Less moneyed Britons amused themselves with cricket, tennis, fives ("handball"), bowling, horse racing, cockfighting, bear baiting, bull baiting, and boxing matches—be-tween women as well as between men. Prize fighters like Figg and Piper were the idols of every class, drawing immense crowds to the ringside. Till 1743 prize fighters fought with bare fists; boxing gloves were then intro-duced, but many years passed before these were accepted by the spectators as anything but an effeminate device unworthy of John Bull. Among the entertainments advertised in London in 1729–30 were "a mad bull to be dressed up with fireworks and turned loose" in a ring, "a dog to be dressed up with fireworks over him, a bear to be let loose at the same time, and a cat to be tied to the bull's tail."[90] In the game called "cock throwing" a cock was tied to a stake, and sticks were thrown at it from a distance till it died. The most popular cockfights were those in which as many as sixteen cocks were matched against another sixteen till all on one side were killed; then the victors were divided into opposing camps, and fought till all on one side were killed; and so on till all but one were dead. Counties, towns, and vil-lages pitted their cocks against one another with a noble patriotism, and an amiable writer hailed these sports as a moral equivalent for war.[91] Nearly all sports were accompanied by betting.

Those whose stomachs were not attuned to these spectacles could seek milder amusement at Vauxhall or Ranelagh, in whose shaded gardens they might, for a shilling, feel the comfort and security of crowds, if they kept their pockets guarded; there they could dance and masquerade, or sit under lanterned boughs, sip tea, and watch fashionable ladies and gallants, and the

FIG. 1—PORTRAIT AFTER NICOLAS DE LARGILLIÈRE: *Voltaire as a Young Man*. Château de Versailles

FIG. 2—MICHEL COR-
NEILLE: *Philippe
d'Orléans, Regent*. Châ-
teau de Versailles PAGE 6

FIG. 3—UNKNOWN ARTIST: *The Rue Quincampoix in 1718*. (Bettmann Archive) PAGE 12

Fɪɢ. 4.—*Regency Wall Paneling*. Château de Versailles

FIG. 5—ALLAN RAMSAY: *The Fourth Earl of Chesterfield.* National Portrait Gallery, London (Bettmann Archive)   PAGE 81

FIG. 6—PORTRAIT ATTRIBUTED TO JEAN MARC NATTIER: *Prince Charles Edward Stuart (The Young Pretender).* National Portrait Gallery, London (Bettmann Archive)   PAGE 109

FIG. 7—Antonio Canaletto: *View of the Thames from Richmond House.* The Good-
wood Estate (Bettmann Archive)   PAGE 60

FIG. 8.—ALLAN RAMSAY: *David Hume*.
Scottish National Portrait Gallery,
Edinburgh   PAGE 140

FIG. 9—W. HAMILTON: *John Wesley*.
National Gallery, London (Bettmann
Archive)   PAGE 128

FIG. 12—CHALK PORTRAIT ATTRIBUTED TO WILLIAM HOARE: *Alexander Pope*. National Portrait Gallery, London (Bettmann Archive)   PAGE 164

FIG. 13—PORTRAIT FROM THE STUDIO OF RICHARD BROMPTON: *William Pitt the Elder*. National Portrait Gallery, London (Bettmann Archive)   PAGE 113

FIG. 14—JOSEPH HIGHMORE: *Samuel Richardson*. National Portrait Gallery, London

FIG. 15—SIR GODFREY KNELLER: *Lady Mary Wortley Montagu.* Reproduced by permission of the Marquess of Bute and the Scottish National Portrait Gallery, Edinburgh

FIG. 16—ENGRAVING BASED ON
A SKETCH BY WILLIAM HO-
GARTH: *Henry Fielding*. (Bett-
mann Archive)   PAGE 193

FIG. 17—UNKNOWN ITALIAN ARTIST:
Tobias Smollett. National Portrait
Gallery, London (Bettmann Ar-
chive)   PAGE 199

FIG. 18—WILLIAM HOGARTH: Scene from *Marriage à la Mode*. Tate Gallery, London (Bettmann Archive)

FIG. 19—WILLIAM HOGARTH: *The Shrimp Girl*. National Gallery, London (Bettmann Archive)   PAGE 218

FIG. 20—WILLIAM HOGARTH: *Self-Portrait*. National Gallery, London (Bettmann Archive)   PAGE 217

FIG. 22—THOMAS HUDSON: *George Frederick Handel.* Staatsbibliothek, Hamburg (Bettmann Archive)

PAGE 226

FIG. 23—JACQUES ANDRÉ AVED: *Jean Philippe Rameau.* Musée Dijon (Bettmann Archive)   PAGE 295

FIG. 24—*The Tuileries Palace and Gardens*. From an engraving in the Albertina Museum, Vienna (Bettmann Archive)   PAGE 295

passing stars of the stage; they could gaze at fireworks or acrobats, hear popular music, dine in state, or seek adventure in lovers' lanes gratefully obscure. At Ranelagh, under the great Rotunda, they could lift themselves up to loftier music amid people of genteeler class. "Every night," wrote Horace Walpole in 1744, "I go to Ranelagh, which has totally beat Vauxhall. Nobody goes anywhere else; everybody goes there."[92] Vauxhall and Ranelagh were closed in winter; but then the rivers might freeze, and winter sports had their day. Once, at Christmas of 1739, even the Thames froze, and the Londoners showed their spirit by staging a carnival of dancing and dining on the ice; some enjoyed the thrill of driving by coach on the river from Lambeth to London Bridge.[93] Lastly there were the great fairs, where you met all the unpedigreed world, and enjoyed a variety of spectacles from peep shows to flying men.

Aside from some bluestockings, manners were rough and blasphemous. Hogarth will show us the life of the commonalty, but not their speech. Harlots and rakes, draymen and bargemen, soldiers and sailors, were masters of damnation and ribaldry, and the fishmongers at Billingsgate made their market immortal with their incomparable profanity. In the inns and taverns speech was less vivid but still coarsely free. Even in their homes the men alarmed the women with their stories, expletives, and toasts, and the ladies themselves were not above a hearty curse and a gay obscenity.

In the coffeehouses and clubs language took on more refinement. Steele, Swift, Fielding, Cowper, and Johnson wrote on conversation as a polite art. We picture the men in their jealously male gatherings, sampling their coffee or beer, gulping their liquor, smoking their pipes, arguing about arguments in Parliament, about Robert Walpole's vote buying, and the unseemly politics of those "French dogs" across the Channel. Laughter was deep in the belly and loud in the throat, despite the pleas of moralists like Shaftesbury and amoralists like Chesterfield that laughter should be left to the lowly and should simmer down to a smile.[94] Snuff-taking, first mentioned in 1589, had become a careful ritual in both sexes; like coffee, snuff (powdered tobacco) was supposed to have medicinal value: the sneezing it caused would clear the nasal passages, cure headache, colds, deafness, and sleepiness, soothe the nerves, and improve the brain. No man or woman of style was fully dressed without a snuffbox; and on that appendage the goldsmith, the jeweler, the enameler, and the miniaturist exercised their most delicate craft.

The three thousand coffeehouses in London were centers of reading as well as of talk. They took in newspapers and magazines, and circulated these among their customers; they provided pens, paper, and ink, accepted letters for mailing, and served as mailing addresses. Some coffee or chocolate houses, like White's, evolved in this period into exclusive clubs, where men could be sure to find only the company they preferred, and could gamble in privacy. By the end of the eighteenth century there were as many clubs as there had been coffeehouses at the beginning. Apparently the Freemasons began their English history as a club—the "Grand Lodge"—organized in London in 1717. The clubs encouraged drinking, gambling, and political intrigue, but they taught men at least half the art of conversation. The other half was missing, for the clubs were baccalaureate retreats; the finer courtesy and subtler wit required by the presence of women received no stimulus there. England was a man's land; women had little share in its cultural life; there were no salons; and when Lady Mary Montagu tried to establish one she was looked upon as an eccentric who did not know her place.[95]

In the upper classes women could ply their arts at receptions, dances, and musicales at the court or in their homes. The weekend in country houses was a gracious feature of English life, tarnished a bit by the high gratuities expected by the servants; the parting guest had to run the gantlet of valets, butlers, footmen, stewards, porters, maids, cooks, and other help standing in a double row at the door, while coachman and groom waited sternly outside. The reputed fidelity of British servants to their masters had scant reality in the first half of the eighteenth century; they were in many cases inattentive, insolent, rebellious, and changed domiciles readily for a better wage. Many of them robbed master, mistress, and guests when they could; they drank their master's wine, and donned their mistress' finery.

Next to acceptance at court, the crown of fashion was a stay at some watering place, to drink medicinal waters, or bathe with select bodies rather than in the promiscuous sea. Tunbridge was famous for its wells, but its clientele was indiscriminate. Epsom Wells offered music, morris dances, performing dogs, and purgative water, though its minerals had not yet been gathered into Epsom salts. Sea bathing was not popular, though Chesterfield noted some at Scarborough; but in 1753 Dr. Richard Russell's book *Of Glandular Consumption, and the Use of Sea-Water in Diseases of the Glands* sent a human wave to the shore, and coastal villages like Brighton, which had known only the humble families of fishermen, blossomed into bathing resorts.

The aristocracy preferred Bath. There, among the most distinguished of Britain's valetudinarians, one might drink—and bathe in—smelly waters touted to cure the ailments of the too-well-fed. The little spa had opened its first pump room in 1704, its first theater in 1707, and a year later the first of the "assembly rooms" celebrated in Fielding and Smollett. In 1755 the great Roman bath was discovered. John Wood and his son, as we shall see, remade the town in classical style. In 1705 "Beau" Nash, a lawyer and gamester, became the dictator of its social life. He forbade swords in places of public amusement, and succeeded in making duels—in Bath—disreputable.

He persuaded men to wear shoes instead of boots. He himself wore an immense white hat, and a coat with rich embroidery; he drove in a coach behind six horses that had to be gray; and he announced his coming with gay French horns. He improved the streets and buildings, laid out handsome gardens, provided music, and charmed all but a few with his geniality and wit. The English nobility flocked to his realm, for he gave them gaming tables as well as baths, and when laws were passed against gambling he invented new games of chance that bypassed the laws. Finally George II came, and Queen Caroline, and Prince Frederick Louis, and Bath was for a time a second court. The Earl of Chesterfield, who loved the town, would doubtless have applied to its elite the description that he gave of all courts, as places where "you must expect to meet with connections without friendship, enmities without hatred, honor without virtue, appearances saved and realities sacrificed; good manners with bad morals; and all vice and virtues so disguised that whoever has only reasoned upon both would know neither when he first met them at court."[96]

VII. CHESTERFIELD

Let us spend half an hour with this perceptive earl. He typified the English aristocracy of the age, except that he wrote a good book. His *Letters to His Son*, which it has been the fashion to depreciate, is a treasury of wisdom in sterling prose, a compact guide to the manners and ideals of his class, and an engaging revelation of a subtle and gracious intelligence.

At baptism (1694) he was Philip Dormer Stanhope, son of Philip Stanhope, third Earl of Chesterfield, and of Lady Elizabeth Savile, daughter of George Savile, Marquess of Halifax, the wily "Trimmer" of preceding reigns. His mother died in his childhood; his father neglected him; he was brought up by the Marchioness of Halifax. Under a private tutor he learned the classics and French uncommonly well, so that the culture of Rome and France in their maturity became part of his mind. He had a year at Cambridge, and set out in 1714 on the grand tour. At The Hague he gambled for heavy stakes; in Paris he sampled women with discriminating promiscuity. From Paris he wrote (December 7, 1714):

> I shall not give you my opinion of the French, because I am very often taken for one of them; and several have paid me the highest possible compliment they think it in their power to bestow, which is: "Sir, you are just like ourselves." I shall only tell you that I am insolent, I talk a great deal, I am very loud and peremptory, I sing and dance as I walk along; and, above all, I spend an immense sum on hair, powder, feathers, and white gloves.[97]

On his return to England he was appointed gentleman of the bedchamber to the current Prince of Wales (later George II). George I's favorite minister, James Stanhope, was Philip's relative. A borough was found for him to represent, and for eleven years he sat in Commons as a Whig. Becoming fourth Earl of Chesterfield on the death of his father (1726), he was transferred to the House of Lords, which he later called "the House of Incurables." Sent to The Hague as ambassador (1728), he managed his mission so well that he was rewarded with a knightly Garter and appointment as lord high steward. In 1732 a mistress, Mlle. du Bouchet, presented him with a son, Philip Stanhope, future recipient of the *Letters*. A year later he married the Countess of Walsingham, natural daughter of George I by the Duchess of Kendal. He may have expected her to bring him a royal dowry; she did not, and the marriage proved genteelly miserable.

He might have risen to higher place had he not opposed Walpole's bill for an excise tax on tobacco and wine. He helped to defeat the measure, and was soon dismissed from the government (1733). He labored for Walpole's fall, lost his health, retired to the Continent (1741), visited Voltaire in Brussels, associated with Fontenelle and Montesquieu in Paris. Back in England, he continued in opposition. The articles that he contributed as "Jeffrey Broadbottom" to a new journal, *Old England,* so pleased Sarah, Duchess of Marlborough, that she willed him twenty thousand pounds. In 1744 his "Broad Bottom" party won. He joined Pelham in the ministry, and was sent to The Hague to persuade the Dutch to join England in the War of the Austrian Succession. He accomplished this with tact and skill, and was advanced to the lord-lieutenancy of Ireland (1745). His one year in Ireland was the most successful in his career. He established schools and industries, cleansed the government of corruption and jobbery, administered affairs with competence and impartiality. He ended the persecution of Catholics, promoted several of them to office, and so earned the respect of the Catholic population that when the Young Pretender invaded England from Scotland, and England expected a simultaneous revolt in Ireland, the Irish refused to rise against Chesterfield.

He was brought back to London as secretary of state (1746). But now the master of delicacy and tact made a ruinous mistake: he paid court to the King's mistress rather than to the Queen, and Caroline succeeded in maneuvering his fall. In 1748 he abandoned public life, and retired to "my horse, my books, and my friends."[98] He was offered a dukedom by George II; he declined it. In 1751 he led the movement to adopt the Gregorian calendar, and bore the brunt of popular resentment against the "Popish theft" of eleven days from the English people. In 1755 he fell under Johnson's blunderbuss over the dedication to the *Dictionary;* we shall look at that fracas later on.

Meanwhile, since 1737, he had been writing letters to his son. His love for this by-product of his first embassy to Holland betrays the tenderness that he kept hidden from the public through most of his career. "From the time that you have had life," he told the youth, "it has been the principal and favorite object of mine to make you as perfect as the imperfections of human nature will allow."[99] He planned Philip's education not to make him a model Christian, but to prepare him for statesmanship and diplomacy. He began when the boy was five, with letters on classical mythology and history. Two years later he struck the note that was to recur so persistently in the correspondence:

> In my last I wrote concerning the politeness of people of fashion, such as are used to courts, the elegant part of mankind. Their politeness is easy and natural, and you must distinguish it from the civilities of inferior people and rustics, which are always constraining or troublesome. . . . A well-bred man shows a constant desire of pleasing, and takes care that his attentions be not troublesome. Few English are thoroughly polite; either they are shamefaced or impudent; whereas most French people are easy and polite in their manners. And as by the better half you are a little Frenchman, so I hope you will at least be *half* polite. You will be more distinguished in a country where politeness is not very common.[100]

So, when Philip was fourteen, his father sent him to Paris as the finishing school of manners, though quite aware that Paris would finish his morals too. The young man had to learn the ways of the world if he was to be useful to his government. The proper study of a statesman is man. After schooling Philip through tutors and letters in classic and literary lore, the Earl, who had such lore at his fingers' ends, steered him back from books to men.

> MY DEAR FRIEND: Very few celebrated negotiators have been eminent for their learning. . . . The late Duke of Marlborough, who was at least as able a negotiator as a general, was exceedingly ignorant of books but extremely knowing in men, whereas the learned Grotius appeared, both in Sweden and in France, to be a very bungling minister.[101]

If Philip proposed to enter government, he should, above all, study the governing classes, their background, morals, manners, aims, and means. He should read only the best literature, in order to acquire a good style of writing, for this too is part of the art of rule; and he should be acquainted with music and the arts; but God forbid that he should aspire to be an author or a musician.[102] He should study carefully the modern history of the European states, their kings and ministers, their laws and constitutions, their finances and diplomacy. He should read La Rochefoucauld and La Bruyère on the nature of man; they are cynical, but there would be no great mistake, at least in politics, in expecting every man to pursue his own interest as he sees it; let us suspect any politician who pretends anything else. Don't expect men to be reasonable; allow for their prejudices. "Our prejudices are our mistresses; reason is at best our wife, very often heard indeed, but seldom minded."[103] Learn to flatter, for only the greatest sages and saints are immune to flattery; but the higher you go, the more delicate and indirect your flattery must be. Study the genealogy of the most important families, for men are prouder of their pedigrees than of their virtues.[104] Make your court to women, chiefly to get their help; for even powerful statesmen are influenced by weak women, especially if these are not their wives.

In matters of sex Chesterfield's advice to his son amused the French and horrified the English. He thought a few liaisons were an excellent preparation for marriage and maturity. He merely insisted that Philip's mistresses should be women of good manners, so that they might refine him while sinning. He recommended Mme. du Pin because of her "good breeding and delicacy."[105] He instructed his son in the strategy of seduction. No refusal should be supinely accepted, for

> the most virtuous woman, far from being offended at a declaration of love, is flattered by it, if it is made in a polite and agreeable manner. . . . If she listens, and allows you to repeat your declaration, be persuaded that if you do not dare all the rest, she will laugh at you. . . . If you are not listened to the first time, try a second, a third, and a fourth. If the place is not already taken, depend upon it, it may be conquered.[106]

The Earl, having had no luck or taste in marriage, passed on to his son no very high opinion about women:

> I will, upon this subject, let you into certain *Arcana* that will be very useful to you to know, but which you must, with the utmost care, conceal and never seem to know. Women, then, are only children of a larger growth; they have an entertaining tattle, and sometimes wit; but for solid reasoning, good sense, I never knew in my life one that had, or who reasoned or acted consequentially for four-and-twenty hours together. . . . A man of sense only trifles with them, plays with them, humors and flatters them, . . . but he neither consults them about, nor trusts them with, serious matters, though he often makes them believe that he does both; which is the thing in the world that they are most proud of; for they love mightily to be dabbling in business (which, by the way, they always spoil). . . . No flattery is either too high or too low for them. They will greedily swallow

the highest, and gratefully accept the lowest; and you may safely flatter any woman from her understanding down to the exquisite taste of her fan. Women who are indisputably beautiful, or indisputably ugly, are best flattered on the score of their understanding.[107]

In France, said the Earl, it is necessary to flatter women with both assiduity and tact, for two reasons: they can make or break a man at court, and they can teach him the graces of life. It is by their grace of movement, manners, and speech, rather than by their beauty, that women maintain their lure; beauty without grace becomes invisible, but grace without beauty can still charm. "Women are the only refiners of the merit of men; it is true, they cannot add weight, but they polish and give luster to it."[108] The Earl cautioned his son against speaking ill of women; that would be trite, vulgar, foolish, and unfair; for women have done much less harm in this world than men. Besides, it is never wise to attack "whole bodies," classes, or groups; "individuals forgive, sometimes; but bodies and societies never do."[109]

Chesterfield never tired of inculcating good manners.

> Good manners are the settled medium of social, as specie is of commercial, life; returns are equally expected for both; and people will no more advance their civility to a bear than their money to a bankrupt.[110]

Here a good dancing master is helpful; he will at least teach us how to sit, stand, or walk with an economy of attention and energy. Being an aristocrat, the Earl called good manners "good breeding"; unconsciously, and perhaps rightly, he recognized how difficult it is to acquire good manners without being brought up in a family, and moving in a circle, that already has them. A "characteristic of a well-bred man is to converse with his inferiors without insolence, and with his superiors with respect and ease."[111] One must not take advantage of the accident of superiority.

> You cannot, and I am sure you do not, think yourself superior by nature to the Savoyard who cleans your room, or the footman who cleans your shoes; but you may rejoice, and with reason, at the difference that fortune has made in your favor. Enjoy those advantages, but without insulting those who are unfortunate enough to want them, or even doing anything unnecessarily that may remind them of that want. For my own part, I am more upon my guard as to my behavior to my servants, and others who are called my inferiors, than I am towards my equals: for fear of being suspected of that mean and ungenerous sentiment of desiring to make others feel that difference which fortune has, and perhaps too undeservedly, made between us.[112]

Good manners are of the mind as well of the body, and both kinds will be influenced by the company we keep.

> There are two sorts of good company: one, which is called the *beau monde*, and consists of the people who have the lead in courts, and in the gay parts of life; the other consists of those who are distinguished by some peculiar merit, or excel in some particular and valuable art or science. For my own part, I used to think myself in company as much above me when I was with Mr. Addison or Mr. Pope, as if I had been with all the princes in Europe.[113]

In either of these good companies it is advisable to keep a certain reserve: not to speak too much or too candidly; to be "dexterous enough to conceal a truth without telling a lie," and to appear frank while being reserved.

> Even where you are sure, seem rather doubtful; . . . and if you would convince others, seem open to conviction yourself. . . . Wear your learning, like your watch, in a private pocket, and do not pull it out . . . merely to show.[114] . . . Above all things, avoid speaking of yourself, if it be possible.[115]

Say nothing about religion; if you praise it, sophisticates will smile; if you condemn it the mature will mourn. You will profit by reading Voltaire's histories, but you will be on your guard against the *philosophes* who attack religion.

> You should by no means seem to approve, encourage, or applaud those libertine notions which strike at religions equally, and which are the poor threadbare topics of half-wits and minute philosophers. Even those who are silly enough to laugh at their jokes are still wise enough to distrust and detest their characters; for, putting moral virtues at their highest, and religion at the lowest, religion must still be allowed to be a collateral security, at least, to virtue, and every prudent man will sooner trust to two securities than to one. Whenever, therefore, you happen to be in company with these pretended *esprits forts*, or with thoughtless libertines who laugh at all religion to show their wit, . . . let no word or look of yours intimate the least approbation; on the contrary, let a silent gravity express your dislike; but enter not the subject, and decline such unprofitable and indecent controversies.[116]

In 1752 Chesterfield recognized in the attack upon religion the first stages of a social revolution. "I foresee that before the end of this century the trade of both king and priest will not be half so good a one as it has been."[117] And in 1753, two years after the appearance of the anticlerical *Encyclopédie*, he wrote to his son:

> The affairs of France . . . grow serious, and in my opinion will grow more and more so every day. The King is despised. . . . The French nation reasons freely, which they never did before, upon matters of religion and government, and begin to be *spregiudicati* [unprejudiced]; the officers do too; in short, all the symptoms, which I have ever met with in history previous to great changes and revolutions in government, now exist, and daily increase, in France.[118]

A delighted study of Chesterfield's eight hundred pages has given two readers a high opinion of his mind, if not of his morals. His English contemporaries, not having read his letters, tended too readily to classify him as a wit rather than a philosopher. They relished his remark, in the upper house, that "we, my lords, may thank Heaven that we have something better than our brains to depend upon."[119] They saw him gamble like any rake or fool, and they knew (what he confessed to his son) that he had not been a model of chastity. The irate Johnson described the *Letters* as inculcating "the morals of a whore and the manners of a dancing master."[120] This, like so many of the Great Cham's decrees, was somewhat one-sided; Chesterfield was teaching the youth the morals of his time and class, and the manners of the polite political world; we must bear in mind that he was grooming his son for diplomacy; and no diplomat dares to practice Christianity across frontiers.

Even so, much of the moral doctrine offered to Philip was excellent. "I have often told you in my former letters (and it is most certainly true) that the strictest and most scrupulous honor and virtue can alone make you esteemed and valued by mankind."[121] The advice about mistresses was probably an attempt to steer the boy away from promiscuity; note the warning: "As to running after women, the consequences of that vice are only the loss of one's nose, the total destruction of health, and, not infrequently, the being run through the body."[122] Johnson himself, in a forgiving moment, thought that "Lord Chesterfield's *Letters to His Son* might be made a very pretty book; take out the immorality, and it should be put into the hands of every young gentleman."[123] Perhaps the *Letters* inadequately inculcated honor, decency, courage, and fidelity, but it is not true that Chesterfield mistook wealth or place for virtue or wisdom. He lauded Milton, Newton, and Locke far above the politicians of the time. We have seen him cultivating the friendship of the best writers of his day. He had a warm appreciation of good literature, even if he was not fascinated by a dictionary. He himself wrote an English unsurpassed in contemporary prose: simple, vigorous, clear, with just enough lightness to float the burden of his thought. Despite his polyglot and classic range, he preferred the short and racy words of Anglo-Saxon speech. Voltaire ranked the *Letters* as "the best book on education ever written,"[124] and Sainte-Beuve called it "a rich book, not a page of which can be read without our having to remember some happy observation."[125]

If we judge a work by its immediate fruits, the *Letters* failed. Young Philip Stanhope never overcame his sluggish spirit, his careless habits, his awkward manner, his hesitating speech; after all those exhortations, he had, reported Fanny Burney, "as little good breeding as any man I met with."[126] Apparently some quirk of birth or circumstance nullified five pounds of precept. Philip suffered the handicap of having a rich parent and an assured and comfortable place; neither the fear of hunger nor the resentment of subordination stirred him to ambition or enterprise; as the frustrated father told him, he lacked "that *vivida vis animi*," that living force of soul, "which spurs and excites young men to please, to shine, to excel."[127] It is touching to see the aging Earl lavish so much sage counsel and paternal affection to so little result. "Be persuaded," he wrote when the boy was fourteen, "that I shall love you extremely while you deserve it, but not one moment longer";[128] however, his final letter to his son, twenty-two years afterward,[129] is warm with affection and solicitude. A month later Philip died in Paris (1768), aged thirty-six, leaving a widow and two sons. He had married without his father's knowledge, but Chesterfield had forgiven him; and now the Earl wrote to the bereaved wife letters that are models of courtesy and consideration.[130]

He himself, at that time, was frequently at Bath, incapacitated with gout and sadly deaf. "I crawl about this place upon my three legs, but am kept in countenance by my fellow crawlers; the last part of the Sphinx's riddle approaches, and I shall soon end, as I began, on all fours."[131] He interested himself in the education of his grandchildren; hope springs eternal in the aging breast. Returning to his estate at Blackheath, he took Voltaire's advice and cultivated his garden, proud of his melons and apples; he was content, he said, to "vegetate in company with them."[132] Voltaire wrote him consolatory letters, reminding him that a good digestion (which the Earl retained) was more conducive to pleasure than good ears. He faced the end with unfailing humor. Of himself and his friend Lord Tyrawley, also old and infirm, he said (perhaps recalling Fontenelle), "Tyrawley and I have been dead these two years, but we do not wish it to be known."[133] He died March 24, 1773, aged seventy-nine, unaware that his letters, whose publication he had forbidden, had been preserved and bequeathed by his son, and would, when printed in the following year, place him at once among the masters of worldly wisdom and English prose.

CHAPTER III

The Rulers

I. GEORGE I: 1714–27

THE English, as Voltaire and Montesquieu were soon to perceive, were much cleverer than the French in the matter of government. Having beheaded one sovereign and sent another scurrying in fright across the Channel, they now imported a king who had left his heart and mind in Germany, who took long leaves of absence in his native Hanover, and who could readily be ruled by a Parliament whose ways and language he could never understand.

The house of Hanover had its roots in medieval Germany, tracing its princely lineage through the dukes of Brunswick-Lüneburg to Henry the Lion (1129–95), and beyond him to his Welf, or Guelph, ancestry. Hanover itself became an electorate of the Holy Roman Empire in 1692. Its first Elector, Ernest Augustus, married Sophia, granddaughter of James I of England. After the death of Ernest his widow, by Parliament's Act of Settlement (1701), became heiress to the English throne.

Her son George Louis, second Elector of Hanover, clouded this happy heritage by an unhappy marriage. His wife, Sophia Dorothea, resented his infidelities, and planned elopement with Count Philipp von Königsmarck, handsome colonel of the guards. George discovered the plot; the Count was never heard of again, and was presumably put to death (1694). Sophia Dorothea was arrested and tried, her marriage was annulled, and she was imprisoned for the remaining thirty-two years of her life in the castle of Ahlden. She had borne to her husband a daughter who became the mother of Frederick the Great, and a son who became George II of England.

Sophia, Dowager Electress of Hanover, died in 1714, two months before the passing of Queen Anne; therefore she missed royalty, but her son was at once proclaimed George I of Great Britain and Ireland. On September 18 he reached England, beginning a new epoch in English history. He brought with him his son and daughter-in-law, a number of German aides, and two mistresses: Charlotte von Kielmannsegge, whom he made Countess of Darlington, and Countess Melusina von der Schulenburg, whom he made Duchess of Kendal and perhaps his wife. England might have accepted this arrangement as in accord with the morals of the time, but both ladies, to British eyes and purse, were ugly and costly. Melusina sold her influence for such fat sums that even Walpole, superintendent of corruption, complained; whereupon George asked had not Walpole himself received fees for his recommendations to office?[1]

In 1714 George I was fifty-four years old, tall and soldierly, a "plain, blunt man" who cared not a pfennig for books, but had shown his courage on more than one battlefield. Lady Mary Montagu called him "an honest blockhead,"[2] but he was not as dull as he seemed; and she admitted that "he was passively good-natured, and wished all mankind enjoyed quiet, if they would let him do so."[3] He could not be expected to feel at home in so unfamiliar an environment, so uncertain an employment. He had been hired by the British oligarchy to forestall a second Stuart restoration; he had no "divine right" or personal claim to the throne; he saw that these masterly Englishmen who ruled Parliament were bent on ruling him too; and he could scarcely forgive them for speaking English. He thought them inferior to his Hanoverian associates. He withdrew into the recesses of St. James's Palace, fled to Hanover almost annually, and did all that he could to divert English funds and policy to the protection of his beloved electorate.

To make matters worse, his own son hated him as a murderer. George Augustus, now Prince of Wales, denounced the continuing imprisonment of his mother, rebelled against the ascendancy and airs of the regal mistresses, quarreled with the King's ministers, and made his views so clear that his father excluded him from the palace. The Prince and his wife, Caroline, separated by royal order from their children, retired to form a rival court at Leicester House (1717). To them came Newton, Chesterfield, Hervey, Swift, Pope, and the livelier ladies of Vanity Fair, only to find the Prince even surlier and duller than the King.

This schism in the reigning family accorded more or less with the division of the ruling minority and the Parliament into Tories and Whigs. Voltaire estimated that some eight hundred men controlled municipal government, elections to Parliament, national legislation, administration, and the judiciary.[4] There was no longer any troublesome talk about democracy, such as had been raised by Cromwell's Independents and the Levellers. Voting for Parliament was limited to property owners—some 160,000 in this period[5]—and these normally accepted the candidate recommended by the local squire or lord.[6] Politicians were Tory or Whig according as they favored either the titled nobility or the gentry (lesser landowners) and the commercial interests. "Church of England men" followed the Tory line; Dissenters supported the Whigs. The Tories had opposed the subordination of the monarch to the Parliament; they clung, with the Established Church, to the theory of divine right in kings; in the last days of Queen Anne they had thought of recalling the exiled Stuarts to power; naturally, now that the house of Hanover was enthroned, they were displaced by the anti-Jacobite Whigs. Whereas heretofore the ministries had usually included men from both parties, George I called only Whigs to high office, and so established government by party through a cabinet. And since, not understanding English, he soon ceased to preside over cabinet meetings, the dominant member became "prime minister," and took over more and more of the functions and powers of the king.

The ministry was led for seven years by James Stanhope. One of his first and most popular acts was to restore John Churchill, Duke of Marlborough —who had been impeached by the Tories—to all his former offices, especially as captain general of the army. Returning from exile, the Duke retired to Blenheim Palace; there he suffered a long illness, and died on June 16, 1722. The nation, forgiving his acquisitions and remembering his uninterrupted victories, accepted Bolingbroke's verdict—"He was so great a man that I do not recollect whether he had any faults or not."[7] His widow, the Sarah Churchill who had for a decade ruled a queen, spent twenty-two years cherishing and defending his memory. When the Duke of Somerset asked her in marriage, she answered, "If I was young and handsome as I was, instead of old and faded as I am, and you could lay the empire of the world at my feet, you should never share the heart and hand that once belonged to John Churchill."[8] In 1743, a year before her death at eighty-four, she proposed to burn her early love letters, but reading them again she felt "I could not do it," and let them survive.[9] There must have been much good in a woman who could so faithfully love, and in a man who could win such devotion from so difficult a woman.

Bolingbroke replaced Marlborough in exile. Dismissed from the government by George I, threatened with impeachment for secretly negotiating with the fallen dynasty, hated by the Whigs and Dissenters whom he stung with his wit, and shunned by churchmen as a scorner of Christian theology, he fled to France (March, 1715), joined James III, became his secretary of stateless state, helped to organize a Jacobite rebellion in England, and proposed an invasion of England from France. Parliament declared him guilty of treason, confiscated his property, and condemned him to death.

The movement to restore the Stuarts almost toppled George I. The Tories, hating the Hanoverians as usurpers and boors; the common people of England, rooted in old loyalties, and secretly longing for the banished dynasty; the upper and lower classes of Scotland, proud of having given a Scottish king to England, and fretting under the Act of Union (1707) which had ended the Scottish Parliament—all were ready to abet an invasion by the youth whom Louis XIV had recognized as the only legitimate king of England.

James Francis Edward Stuart was now (1715) twenty-seven, though history knows him as "the Old Pretender." He had been brought up in France, and so steeped in the Catholic faith by monastic teachers and the sufferings of his father, James II, that he rejected Bolingbroke's plea that he should strengthen the Jacobite sentiment in England by promising conversion to Protestantism. How, Bolingbroke argued, could the Presbyterian Scots and the Tory Anglicans be roused to the support of a man bringing to their throne the religion that they had through a century of turmoil fought to overthrow? James was obdurate; he declared that he would rather be a throneless Catholic than a Protestant king. Bolingbroke, free from faith and principles, pronounced him fitter to be a monk than a king.[10] Meanwhile (August, 1714) Parliament had offered £100,000 for the capture of James III in case he should land on British soil.

A personal factor appeared to turn events to the Pretender's cause. John Erskine, Earl of Mar, had been secretary of state for Scotland in the final years of Queen Anne. Dismissed by George I, he laid plans for a Jacobite rising in England, then sailed to Scotland and called upon the Scots to join his standard of revolt (September 6, 1715). Several nobles rallied to him, raising his forces to six thousand foot and six hundred horses; but Edinburgh, Glasgow, and the southern Lowlands adhered to the Hanoverian. The British government decreed death for treason, and confiscation of property, against all rebels; it mobilized thirteen thousand men, and called six thousand more to the fleet; and it ordered the Duke of Argyll, commanding the garrisons at Edinburgh and Stirling, to suppress the rebellion. He met Mar's forces at Sheriffmuir (November 13, 1715) in an engagement from which neither side could claim a decisive victory. Another Scottish force of two thousand, instead of joining Mar, advanced recklessly to within thirty miles of Liverpool, vainly hoping to inspire and protect Jacobite uprisings in the English towns. At Preston a government army surrounded it and compelled its unconditional surrender (November 14).

James III must have known of these events before he sailed from Dunkirk on December 27. Bolingbroke had warned him that no Jacobite revolt would rise in England. The Pretender was carried on by faith in the divine legitimacy of his cause, plus 100,000 crowns from the French government, and thirty thousand from the Vatican. Landing in Scotland, he joined Mar's army at Perth, and made plans for a solemn coronation at Scone. But his taciturnity and melancholy countenance, and his complaint that he had been deceived about the extent of the rebellion, added nothing to the enthusiasm of the Scots; they complained in their turn that they never saw him smile, and rarely heard him speak;[11] moreover, he was shaking from the ague, and bore the northern winter hardly. Mar judged his troops unfit for battle; he ordered them to retreat to Montrose, and to burn all towns, villages, and crops in their wake as a measure to halt Argyll's pursuit. James lamented the destruction, and left money in part compensation for those whose property had suffered. Then, as Argyll's greatly superior army approached Montrose, James, Mar, and other leaders of the revolt fled precipitately to the coast, and took ship to France (February 4, 1716). Everywhere the rebel forces surrendered or dispersed.

Most of the prisoners were transported to servitude in the colonies; fifty-seven were executed, and a dozen Scottish nobles, now refugees in France, were marked for death if ever they returned. James had hoped that Philippe d'Orléans would send troops to his rescue in Scotland; but France was now contemplating an alliance with England, and urged James to leave French soil. He settled for a time at papal Avignon, and then in Rome.

Bolingbroke remained in France till 1723, and, knowing French well, made himself at home in the salons and among the philosophers. Clever in everything but politics, he bought shares in Law's System, and sold at great profit before the bubble burst. Having left his wife in England, he formed an almost honorable attachment with Marie Deschamps de Marcilly, the widowed Marquise de Villette. She was forty, he was thirty-eight. Like so many Frenchwomen, she had kept her charm even while losing some of her beauty; perhaps it was her grace, vivacity, and wit that drew him. He became her lover, and when Lady Bolingbroke died he married the Marquise and went to live with her at La Source. There, as we have seen, Voltaire visited him (1721). "I have found in this illustrious Englishman," reported the young philosopher, "all the erudition of his own nation, and all the politeness of ours."[12]

The suppression of the revolt had left a few nobles headless, but it had not reduced Jacobite sentiment in Britain. By the Triennial Acts of 1641 and 1694 no Parliament was to last over three years. Hence the first Parliament of George I faced in 1717 the prospect of an election in which a Tory and Jacobite majority might be returned. To guard against this the Parliament, by the Septennial Act of 1716, voted itself four additional years of life, and ruled that thereafter all Parliaments might continue for seven years. "This," said Marlborough's most brilliant descendant, "was the boldest and most complete assertion of Parliament's sovereignty that England had yet seen."[13] George I, also fearful of a Tory victory, approved the new law; in effect the Hanoverians had to abdicate in order to reign.

To further protect the new dynasty, Stanhope concluded with France and Holland (1717) a Triple Alliance that ended French support of Jacobite claims, and English support of Spain against France. In 1720 Spain signed a submissive peace, and George I could sit more securely, during his seven remaining years, on his alien throne. In 1726 his still imprisoned wife sent him a bitter letter, challenging him to meet her, within a year, at the judgment seat of God. Soon afterward she died of brain fever. Tradition represents a soothsayer as having predicted that George I would not outlive his wife by a year. In 1727 the King's health began to fail. In June he left England to visit his beloved Hanover. Near Osnabrück a folded paper was thrown into his carriage; it was a dying curse left him by his wife. Reading it, the King fell into a fit, and on June 11 he died.[14]

II. GEORGE II AND QUEEN CAROLINE

His son and enemy received the news as an unreasonably delayed act of justice on the part of Providence. When the Archbishop of Canterbury presented George Augustus with the late King's will, he stuffed it into his pocket, and he never let it be made public. Some said it was concealed because it proposed to put Hanover and England under separate heads; others claimed that it left to grandson Frederick Louis, to mistress or wife the Duchess of Kendal, and to his daughter the Queen of Prussia substantial sums that would thin the royal purse.[15] History does not know.

Like his father, George II was a good soldier. At twenty-five he had fought valiantly under Eugene and Marlborough at Audenaarde (1708); at sixty he was to lead his own troops to victory at Dettingen (1743). Often he carried the manners of the camp into the court, ranting irascibly; upon his ministers he lavished such terms as "scoundrels," "stinking blockheads," and "buffoons."[16] But he worked industriously at the king trade, spoke English correctly though with a thick Westphalian accent,[17] observed impatiently but carefully the limits placed upon his powers and income by Parliament, and for thirteen years firmly supported Robert Walpole in keeping John Bull solvent and peaceful. Like his father, he retired frequently to Hanover, to the delight of all concerned. Like his father, he quarreled with the Prince of Wales, for "it ran a little in the family," as Horace Walpole put it, "to hate the eldest son."[18] Like his father, he took mistresses, if only to be in the fashion; unlike his father, he dearly loved his wife.

Caroline, daughter of Margrave John Frederick of Brandenburg-Ansbach, had been brought up at the Charlottenburg court of George I's sister, Sophia Charlotte, first Queen of Prussia. There she had met Leibniz, had enjoyed the debates of philosophers, Jesuits, and Protestant divines, and had developed a scandalous degree of religious liberalism and tolerance. Charles VI, "Holy Roman" Emperor, offered her his hand and creed; she refused both, and married (1705) George Augustus, the "little red-faced"[19] Electoral Prince of Hanover; to him, with all his temper and hers, through all his mishaps and mistresses, she remained faithful and devoted to the end. George treated her harshly, and wrote her long letters about his liaisons; but he respected her mind and character enough to let her rule England (with

Walpole's help) in his long absences, and to let her guide his policies when he returned.

After her plump, fresh-colored youth she had no charms of body except lovely hands, and few graces of manner or speech, to hold her husband; however, he admired the architecture of her bust, and ordered her to expose it convincingly.[20] She grew stouter with each pregnancy, her face was scarred with smallpox, her voice was loud and guttural, she loved intrigue and power. But gradually the English began to like her hearty humor; they came to understand what sacrifice she was making of health and happiness to be a good wife and queen; and the intellect of England saw with surprise that this blunt Brandenburger had an appreciative mind and ear for the literature, science, philosophy, and music of the age.

Her court became almost a salon. There she welcomed Newton, Clarke, Berkeley, Butler, Pope, Chesterfield, Gay, and Lady Mary Montagu. She supported Lady Mary's initiative in vaccination. She saved a daughter of Milton from poverty; she supported Handel through all the changing moods of the public and the King. She contributed from her private purse the means to encourage young and needy talent;[21] she rescued the heretic Whiston with a pension; she secured religious liberty for the Scottish Jacobites. She arranged the appointment of Anglican bishops on the ground of their learning rather than their orthodoxy. She herself was a deist with a hesitant belief in immortality;[22] but she thought that the Established Church should be financed by the government as an aide to popular morality and calm.[23] "This princess," said Voltaire, "is certainly born for the encouragement of the arts, and for the good of the human race. . . . She is an amiable philosopher seated on a throne."[24]

She had enough philosophy to see, even in her last hour, the humor in life's tragedies. Suffering mortally from a rupture that she had long concealed from all but the King, she advised him, then fifty, to marry again after her death. His answer, sincere in his grief, revealed the time: "*Non, j'aurai des maîtresses* [No, I will have mistresses]." "*Ah, mon Dieu*," she exclaimed, "*cela n'empêche pas* [that will not interfere]!"[25] He mourned her loss with unwonted feeling: "I never yet saw a woman worthy to buckle her shoe."[26] Twenty-three years later, in pursuance of his will, her coffin in Westminster Abbey was opened so that his remains might lie by her side.

III. ROBERT WALPOLE

It was through her brave championship, against a pack of office-seeking, warmongering enemies, that Walpole was able to give England twenty years of prosperity and peace. He was no saint; he was probably the most corrupt minister that England has ever had, but he was also one of the best. In that corrupt age only through corruption could wisdom rule.

As the youngest son of an old Norfolk family, Robert had been intended for the Church, and at Eton, where he was the contemporary of his future foe, Bolingbroke, this was the object of his studies. But the death of his older brothers made him heir to the family fortune; and as the family controlled three electoral boroughs, he had no trouble in turning successfully from theology to politics. Aged twenty-five, he entered the House of Commons as a Whig (1701). His connections, money, quick intelligence, and mastery of administrative finance won him appointment as secretary of war (1708). In 1712 the victorious Tories unseated him, and sent him to the Tower on a charge of corruption; but as the smell of sterling had become so constant and ubiquitous as to produce olfactory insensibility, he was soon released, soon re-elected, soon in office as first lord of the treasury (1715). Political complications led him to resign in 1717. In 1720 the collapse of the South Sea Company, and the justification of his warnings, convinced even his enemies that he was the man best equipped to lead England back to financial stability. As again first lord of the treasury (1721), he stopped the panic, as we have seen, by putting the Bank of England behind the company's obligations; gradually the entire £7,000,000 owed by it to the public was repaid.[27] The grateful gamblers rewarded Walpole with twenty-two years of power.

The accession of George II briefly interrupted Walpole's ascendancy. The new King had sworn unforgiving hostility to all who had served his father; he dismissed Walpole, and asked Sir Spencer Compton to form a new ministry. But Compton soon displayed and acknowledged the inadequacy of his talents; Caroline advised her husband to recall Walpole, who clinched the argument by promising King and Queen a larger allowance; Sir Spencer gratefully accepted an earldom, and Walpole resumed his rule. To him first the title "prime minister" was applied, originally (as with *Christian*, *Puritan*, and *Methodist*) as a term of abuse. And he was the first chief minister to make 10 Downing Street his official home.

His character sheds some light on the art of political success. He had only a year at university, and was weak in the educational equipment usual in British prime ministers. There was little elegance in his manners or his speech. "When he ceased to talk politics," said Macaulay, "he could talk of nothing but women, and he dilated on his favorite theme with a freedom which shocked even that plain-spoken generation."[28] His son Horace did not hold it against him that he knew few books; "he knew mankind, not their writings; he consulted their interests, not their systems."[29] He had sufficient command of Latin to use it as his medium of communication with George I, for that king knew no English, and Walpole knew no German or

French. He had all the qualities of John Bull except pugnacity: he was stout, bluff, hearty, good-natured, practical; he enjoyed dinners and drink, but would work hard when called upon; and perhaps it was also like John Bull that he rattled his purse instead of his sword.

He had almost no morals. He lived for years in open adultery, showing little respect for the suave decorum of aristocratic vice. He jested with Queen Caroline on her husband's mistresses; after her death he advised her daughters to summon these maids of honor to distract the mind of the grieving King. He laughed at religion. When Caroline was dying he sent for the Archbishop of Canterbury. "Let this farce be played," he proposed; "the Archbishop will do it very well. You may bid him be as short as you wish. He will do the Queen no hurt, any more than any good, and it will satisfy all the wise and good fools, who will call us atheists if we don't pretend to be as great fools as they are."[30] He took no stock in noble motives or professions of unselfishness. Like Marlborough, he used public office to amass private wealth. He found political plums for his son Horace and other relatives. At a cost of £200,000 he built a magnificent mansion at his estate of Houghton, and adorned it with paintings valued by Horace at £40,000; he kept open house there for the entire county of Norfolk.[31] He was as generous as John Bull because (if we credit his enemies) he could not clearly distinguish between John Bull's funds and his own.

He used money to buy M.P.s as Richelieu had used it to buy armies, as Henri Quatre had used it to immobilize foes. Walpole employed it as a last resort, after all softer arguments had failed. The parliamentary corruption that had taken form under Charles II had reached the point where the House of Commons could be managed, for good or evil, only by massive lubrication. Walpole kept a secret reserve—even a special room—for the purchase of seats and votes and editors; it was alleged that he spent £50,000 annually in subsidizing periodicals to expound his point of view.[32] In 1725 he prompted George I to establish the Most Honorable Order of the Bath, to consist of the sovereign, a grand master, and thirty-six knights companions; to Walpole, as to Napoleon, it seemed more economical to rule men with ribbons than with currency.

He used these corrupt methods to maintain England in prosperity and calm. His ends did not justify his means, but they revealed the better side of his character. He was a man of good will, resolved to keep his country on an even keel despite all the commotions of party politics, the crosswinds of class interests, the chauvinistic cries for war. It was his motto, he said, *quieta* (or *tranquilla*) *non movere*—to let sleeping dogs lie; and though this left his rule undistinguished by conquests or reforms, he earned the commendation of the judicious. His enemies had to admit that he was not vindictive or unforgiving, and that he was more trustworthy, even more trusting, in his friendships than could have been expected of one so familiar with the baser aspects of mankind.[33] He had no far-flung schemes for glory, but he met each problem, as it arose, with such shrewdness, tolerance, and tact that England finally forgave him all his faults except his love of peace.

His economic legislation struck a compromise between the landowning gentry and the business class. He sought to reduce taxes on land, and supported extreme penalties for offenses against property. At the same time he welcomed the rise of capitalism. He favored merchants and manufacturers with export bounties and import dues, and seemed insensitive to the poverty of landless laborers in the villages and the growing proletariat in the towns; he appears to have felt that the maldistribution of wealth was an inevitable result of nature's maldistribution of ability. Excepting those bounties and dues, he advocated, long before the French physiocrats and Adam Smith, a policy of free trade; in a single year he reduced the duties on 106 articles of export, on thirty-eight articles of import; he removed many restraints on the commerce of the American colonies; and he argued that the English economy would prosper best under a minimum of state regulation. Time justified his view; the national wealth grew rapidly, however ill-distributed; governmental revenues rose; and by handling them with parsimony and efficiency Walpole won praise as "the best commercial minister the country ever produced."[34]

His most spectacular defeat came on his famous excise bill (1733). The smugglers of tobacco and wine were cheating the treasury of tariff dues, and burdening property with more than its share of taxes. To circumvent this form of private enterprise Walpole proposed an excise tax (a slice "cut out" for the government) to be levied on these articles wherever stored, and whenever sold, in England. Revenue officers ("excise men") were authorized to search any house at any time, and persons found hiding dutiable goods were subjected to fines or imprisonment. Everybody concerned in the importation, smuggling, sale, or consumption of tobacco or wine rose in protest. Walpole's opponents in the Commons denounced the tax, and the manner of its enforcement, as the arbitrary action of a tyrant, and a monstrous infringement of British liberty. "The members of Parliament," as Frederick the Great put the matter, "told Walpole that he could pay them for their ordinary mischief, but that this proposal was beyond the limits of their corruption"[35]—or perhaps they hoped to replace him in control of public funds. Pamphlets in thousands of copies reviled the minister in enthusiastic billingsgate. Crowds surged around Westminster Hall, burned effigies of Walpole in dozens of bonfires, and tried to lynch him as he left St. Stephen's Church; the nation was inflamed to the verge of revolution. Queen Caroline feared for the loyalty of the army, and trembled for the safety of the new dynasty. Walpole withdrew the measure, acknowledging defeat; and from that moment his power declined. His enemies gathered for the kill.

IV. BOLINGBROKE

They were many and diverse. One group, still Jacobite, plotted with the Old Pretender, and would soon thrill with the romance of young Bonnie Prince Charlie. One coterie danced around Frederick Louis, Prince of Wales, foe and heir to the King. Against the minister were the greatest English writers of the age—Swift, Pope, Fielding, Arbuthnot, Thomson, Akenside, Gay; they ridiculed his manners, exposed his morals, censured his policies, and reproached him for discontinuing that lavish aid to authors which had distinguished the government under William III and Queen Anne. The Tories, thirsting for the ichor of office, pulled strings, manipulated poets, and roused the winds of Parliament in their resolve to replace the ministerial Falstaff at the national trough. William Pulteney, Chesterfield, and the upcoming Pitt voiced their cause, and Bolingbroke defended it unrelentingly with his lethal pen.

Bolingbroke had received a royal pardon in 1723, allowing his return to England and his estates; but, by Walpole's influence, he was excluded from office and Parliament as a man of many treasons and dubious fidelity. He remained a power none the less. In his town house the intelligentsia of England gathered, fascinated by his handsome figure, his sophisticated wit, and the aura of his name. There and in his country home he traded barbs with Swift, heresies with Pope, and ballads with Gay; there he labored to weld hungry Tories and inadequately lubricated Whigs into a united opposition to Walpole; there he organized the staff and program of a magazine—called at first (1726) *The Country Gentleman* and then *The Craftsman*—which struck a blow, week after week for ten years, at everything that Walpole did or proposed to do. Bolingbroke himself wrote the most damaging articles, the most brilliant political prose of the age after the decline of Swift. A series of nineteen letters (1733–34)—*A Dissertation upon Parties*—was mockingly dedicated to Walpole. "Till I read [them]," Chesterfield wrote to his son, "I did not know all the extent and power of the English language."[36]

Bolingbroke's character was his defeat. His fine manners (which were his only code of morals) left him when his will was thwarted or his opinions were crossed. In June, 1735, he quarreled with Pulteney, nominal leader of the opposition, and returned in anger to France. There he settled with his Marquise near Fontainebleau, and salved his wounds with philosophy. His *Letters on the Study and Use of History* (written in 1735) described history as a vast laboratory in which events have made countless experiments with men, economics, and states; hence it is the best guide to the nature of man, and therefore to the interpretation of the present and the anticipation of the future. "History is philosophy teaching by examples. . . . We see men at their whole length in history."[37] We should "apply ourselves to it in a philosophical spirit," aiming not merely to comprehend causes, effects, and uniform sequences, but to conduct ourselves in ways that have heretofore proved most propitious to human development and happiness.[38] The difficulty in such studies is that "there are few histories without lies, and none without some mistakes. . . . The lying spirit has gone forth from ecclesiastical to other historians";[39] but the resolute student, by confronting liar with liar, may wriggle his way between them to the truth.

In 1736 Bolingbroke returned to the arena of politics with *Letters on the Spirit of Patriotism*, which attacked the corruption of Walpole's administration, and called for a new spirit of selfless devotion in English politics.

> Neither Montaigne in writing his *Essays*, nor Des Cartes in building new worlds, nor . . . Newton in discovering and establishing the true laws of nature on experiment and a sublime geometry, felt more intellectual joys than he feels who is a real patriot, who bends all the force of his understanding, and directs all his thoughts and actions, to the good of his country.[40]

His hope turned to the younger generation. Visiting England in 1738, he cultivated the friendship of Frederick Louis, Prince of Wales, who was now leading the opposition to Walpole. To Frederick's private secretary Bolingbroke now addressed his most famous production, *The Idea of a Patriot King*. Frederick died in 1751, but his son, the future George III, derived from these pages some articles of his political creed.[41] Essentially the essay was a plea for a benevolent monarchy, such as Voltaire and the *philosophes* were to dream of in the next generation. England—Bolingbroke argued—was now so debased that no one could save it except a king who should rise above faction and party, *even above Parliament*, take power into his own hands, repel and punish bribery, and rule as well as reign. But the patriot king would view his power not as a divine right but as a public trust, not as absolute but as limited by natural law, the liberties of his subjects, the freedom of the press, and the customs of the realm: and he would judge all issues according as they affected the prosperity and happiness of the people.[42] He would promote commerce as the chief source of a nation's wealth. He would, in Britain, strengthen the navy as the guardian of national independence and of the Continental balance of power.

The Idea of a Patriot King was an attempt to build, with displaced Tories and discontented Whigs, a new party of Tories dressed in Whig principles, renouncing Jacobitism, and seeking to reconcile land with commerce, empire with liberty, public service with private wealth.* When the essay was published (1749) it became the rallying cry of young enthusiasts who, as "the King's Friends," looked to the monarchy to cleanse the government of England. It formed the political philosophy of Samuel Johnson and both the elder and the younger Pitt. It inspired the liberal conservatism of Benjamin Disraeli, whose *Vindication of the English Constitution* (1835) hailed Bolingbroke as the father of Tory democracy, as the man whose "complete reorganization of the public mind laid the foundation for the future accession of the Tory party to power."[44] It was the Bolingbroke and Disraeli influence that remolded the defeated Tories into the progressive "Conservatives" of England today.

V. HOW TO GET INTO A WAR

Meanwhile Bolingbroke's propaganda shared with the bellicose spirit of a money-minded Parliament in ending Walpole's long ascendancy. Basing his tenure on tranquillity preserved, the cautious minister shied away from foreign entanglements, agreed with Cardinal Fleury—who was ruling France on similar principles—to maintain as long as possible the peace established by the Treaty of Utrecht, and, for the rest, left the management of external relations to his able brother Horatio. But the retention of Gibraltar by England, and the rivalry between England and Spain for control of America and the seas, begot increasing violence as the years progressed. Both George I and his minister Stanhope, in January and June, 1721, had assured Philip V of Spain that England would give up Gibraltar as soon as the finances of Britain and the temper of Parliament improved; but the British public refused to countenance such a surrender.[45] Let us follow now the English account of how England slipped into war; it will illustrate both the jingoism of the populace and the integrity of British historians.[46]

The South Sea Company, we are told, "grossly abused" the privilege accorded to England by Spain, of sending one trading ship per year to the Spanish possessions in the New World, and "a large illicit trade had sprung up," partly managed, partly connived at, by the company. Spain retaliated by boarding English vessels suspected of smuggling. Robert Jenkins alleged that in one such case (1731) he had lost an ear; he preserved it, displayed it in Britain, and cried out for revenge. The Spanish confiscated some English ships engaged in licit commerce, and kept English prisoners in irons; English privateers captured Spaniards and sold them as slaves in the British

---

* *Cf.* Lord Birkenhead's summary: "The Whigs went bathing, and Bolingbroke stole their clothes."[43]

colonies. Smuggling continued; the Spanish government protested; Walpole, reluctant to reduce the income of the struggling South Sea Company, temporized, though he dealt severely with smuggling along the English coasts. The English merchant class favored war, confident of naval superiority, secure against invasion, and hopeful of new markets and expanded trade. The people were excited with factual and fictitious tales of Spanish brutality; Englishmen who clamored for action were hailed as manly patriots, those who advised moderation were called lily-livered cowards. Jenkins showed Parliament his ear in a bottle (March, 1738), whereupon Pulteney, Pitt, and others of the opposition to Walpole made hot speeches about the honor of England.* In martial counterpoint the Spanish public denounced the English as heretical dogs, and swallowed a story that an English captain had made a noble Spaniard cut off and devour his own nose.

Both governments behaved sensibly. La Quadra, Spain's chief minister, issued for public consumption a hot letter to Walpole, but privately informed him that Spain would welcome a negotiated settlement. Defying popular uproar, the British government signed with Spain the Convention of the Pardo (January 14, 1739), in which both sides made concessions, and a commission was made to settle all outstanding grievances. Half the Spanish public accepted the convention; nearly all England rose in anger against it. The South Sea Company complained that the convention would severely limit its income and dividends; and the English ambassador at Madrid was also an agent of the company. Moreover, the Asiento by which Spain allowed England to supply Negro slaves to Spanish America expired on May 6, 1739, and Philip V refused to renew the contract.[49] Nevertheless, pursuing his pacific policy, Walpole recalled the British fleet from the Mediterranean; then, wrongly suspecting that Spain was signing a secret alliance with France, he revoked the order, and bade the fleet protect Gibraltar. La Quadra protested; Walpole, yielding to the martial mood of Parliament and people, broke off negotiations; and on October 19, 1739, England declared war against Spain. The public, still calling Walpole a coward, rejoiced, and throughout England church bells rang. Now James Thomson wrote his stirring ballad "Rule, Britannia!" pledging that "Britons never will be slaves."

Normally nothing so strengthens a government as a declaration of war, for then the loyal opposition muzzles its guns. But Walpole's ministry was an exception. His enemies rightly felt that his heart was not in marching armies or in squadrons belching fire; they blamed all military reverses on his mismanagement, and ascribed a naval success at Portobello (on the Isth-

---

* According to Horace Walpole, when Jenkins died he was found to have two perfectly sound ears. Burke spoke of "the fable of Jenkins' ears."[47] Another version attributed the amputation to a pirate, who was punished therefor by the Spanish government.[48]

mus of Panama) solely to the genius of Admiral Vernon, who was a member of the opposition. In February, 1741, Samuel Sandys proposed to Parliament that the King be advised to dismiss his chief minister. The motion was defeated, but only by Walpole's solicitation of Jacobite votes. He survived another year; nevertheless he realized that his time was up, and that the country wanted a change.

And he was exhausted. "He who in former years," his son wrote, "was asleep as soon as his head touched the pillow . . . now never sleeps above an hour without waking; and he who at dinner always forgot that he was minister, and was more gay and thoughtless than all his company, now sits without speaking, and with his eyes fixed, for an hour together."[50] New elections returned a Parliament overwhelmingly hostile; it defeated him in a minor matter, and on February 13, 1742, he resigned. Too old to face the tumult of the Commons, he easily persuaded George II to make him Earl of Orford, and as such he sank upward into the House of Lords. He had feathered his nest for his fall.

He died, after suffering stoically a long and painful illness, on March 18, 1745, aged sixty-eight. England bade goodbye to peace, and set out, with Pitt after Pitt, to conquer the world.

VI. IRELAND: 1714–56

Rarely in history has a nation been so oppressed as the Irish. Through repeated victories by English armies over native revolts, a code of laws had been set up that chained the Irish in body and soul. Their soil had been confiscated until only a handful of Catholic landowners remained, and nearly all of it was held by Protestants who treated their agricultural laborers as slaves. "The poor people in Ireland," said Chesterfield, "are used worse than Negroes by their lords and masters."[51] It was "not unusual in Ireland," said Lecky, "for great landed proprietors to have regular prisons in their houses for the summary punishment of the lower orders."[52] Many of the landlords lived in England, and spent there (Swift estimated) a third of the rents paid by Irish tenants.[53] The tenants—racked by rents paid to the landlord, by tithes paid to the Established Church which they hated, and by dues paid to their own priests—lived in mud hovels with leaky roofs, went half naked, and were often on the edge of starvation; Swift thought "the Irish tenants live worse than English beggars."[54] Those landlords who remained in Ireland, and the deputies of the absentees, drugged themselves against the barbarism and hostility of their surroundings with carousals of food and drink, extravagant hospitality, quarreling and dueling, and gambling for high stakes.

Having full power over Ireland, the British Parliament stifled any Irish industry that competed with England. We have seen elsewhere how an act of 1699 destroyed the nascent wool manufactures by forbidding the export of Irish woolens to any country whatever. In like manner such foreign commerce as Ireland had preserved amid political turmoil and military devastation was mercilessly throttled by English laws. Irish exports were saddled with export duties that cut them off from nearly all markets but England.[55] Many Irish had lived by raising cattle and exporting them to England; laws of 1665 and 1680 forbade the English importation of Irish cattle, sheep, or swine, of beef, mutton, bacon, or pork, even of butter or cheese. Ireland had exported her products to the English colonies; an act of 1663 required that, with a few exceptions, no European articles could be imported into English colonies except from England in English ships manned by Englishmen. The Irish merchant marine died. Said Swift: "The conveniency of ports and harbors, which nature bestowed so liberally on this kingdom, is of no more use to us than a beautiful prospect to a man shut up in a dungeon."[56]

Protestants as well as Catholics were harassed by England's legislation for her Irish subjects; and in one famous instance they joined the Catholics in overruling the British government. The export of money as rent to absentee landlords had by 1722 created a shortage of metal currency in Ireland. Walpole offered to relieve this by an issue of copper coins. The plan was reasonable, but was spotted with the usual corruption: the Duchess of Kendal was granted a patent to mint the new coinage; she sold it to William Wood, ironmaster, for £10,000; and to raise this sum plus his profit Wood proposed to coin £100,800 in halfpennies or farthings. As the total metal currency of Ireland was then only £400,000, the Irish protested that coppers would have to be used in payments as well as making change; that foreign accounts, including the rents of absentee landlords, would have to be paid in silver or bank notes; that the cheaper coins would drive the better ones into hoarding or export; and that soon Ireland would have nothing but troublesome coppers as its currency. To meet these complaints the British government agreed to reduce the new issue to £40,000, and it presented a report from Isaac Newton, master of the Mint, that Wood's halfpennies were quite as good in metallic content as the patent required, and much better than the coins inherited from earlier reigns.

At this juncture Jonathan Swift, Anglican dean of St. Patrick's Cathedral in Dublin, entered the argument by publishing a succession of letters under the pseudonym M. B. Drapier. With all the vehemence of his spirit and the resources of his invective, he attacked the new currency as an attempt to defraud the Irish people. He alleged that the coins sent to Newton for testing were specially minted, and that the vast majority of Wood's halfpennies were worth far less than their face value; and, indeed, some economists confirmed his claim by calculating that Ireland would sustain a loss of £60,480 by the issue as first proposed.[57] In the fourth letter Swift advanced to a powerful indictment of all English rule in Ireland, and laid down the principle that "all government without the consent of the governed is the very definition of slavery."[58] The Irish, including the majority of Protestants among them, responded eagerly to this bold note; ballads urging resistance to England were sung in the streets; and the English government, which had for centuries defied an entire people, now found itself in retreat before a single pen. It offered a reward of three hundred pounds for the apprehension of the author, but though hundreds knew that this was the gloomy Dean, no one dared take action against him. Nor would any Irishman face the anger of the people by accepting the new coins. Walpole acknowledged defeat, canceled the issue, and allowed Wood £24,000 compensation for his futile expenses and his vanished gains.

The structure of Irish politics made impossible any resistance to English domination except by mob action or individual violence. Since no one could hold office except by adherence to the Church of England, the Irish Parliament, after 1692, was composed entirely of Protestants,[59] and was now wholly subservient to England. In 1719 the English Parliament reaffirmed its paramount right to legislate for Ireland. Laws that in England protected parliamentary or individual liberty, like the Habeas Corpus Act and the Bill of Rights, were not extended to Ireland; the relative freedom of the press enjoyed in England had no existence in Ireland. The two parliaments resembled each other only in the corruption of their electors and their members. They differed again in the dominant influence of Anglican bishops in the Irish House of Lords.

The Established Church in Ireland included about a seventh of the population among its adherents, but it was supported by tithes taken from the peasantry, nearly all of whom were Catholics. A small proportion of the people followed the Presbyterian or other Dissenting creeds, and received a measure of toleration, short of eligibility to office. Catholics were excluded not only from office but from all the learned professions except medicine, and from nearly every avenue to higher education, wealth, or influence.[60] They were forbidden to purchase land, or to invest in mortgages on land, or to hold any long or valuable lease. They could not serve as jurors, except where Protestants were not available. They could not teach in schools; they could not vote for municipal or national offices; they could not validly marry a Protestant.[61] Their religious worship was permitted, if celebrated by a priest who had registered with the government and had taken the Oath of Abjuration disclaiming allegiance to the Stuart line; other priests were liable to imprisonment, but this law was seldom enforced after 1725; in 1732 a committee of the Irish Parliament reported that there were 1,445 priests in Ireland, 229 Catholic churches, 549 Catholic schools. After 1753 the zeal of the English abated, and the condition of the Catholics in Ireland improved.

The disorder of religious life shared with the poverty of the people and the hopelessness of social advancement in demoralizing Irish life. The ablest and bravest Catholics—who would have raised the level of Irish capacity, morality, and intelligence—emigrated to France or Spain or America. Many Irishmen sank into beggary or crime as an escape from starvation. Robber gangs hid in the countryside, smugglers and wreckers lurked near the shores, and some property owners kept as many as eighty bravos to do their bidding regardless of the law. Thousands of cattle and sheep were slaughtered by roving bands, apparently as acts of Catholic revenge upon Protestant landlords. It was difficult for a people to respect the laws passed by an Irish Parliament that often spoke of the Catholics—three quarters of the population—as "the common enemy."

There were some brighter elements in Irish life. The cheerful, easygoing, laughter-loving temper of the people survived through all their hardships; and their superstitions and legends surrounded their lives with magic and poetry without leading them to such violence as marked the witchcraft persecutions in Scotland and Germany. The Anglican clergy in Ireland included some fine scholars (e.g., Bishop Ussher of Armagh), a prominent philosopher (George Berkeley, bishop of Cloyne), and the greatest writer of English in the first quarter of the eighteenth century, Jonathan Swift, dean of St. Patrick's Cathedral. The Dublin Society, founded in 1731, labored to improve technology in agriculture and industry, to stimulate invention, and to encourage art. There were many cases of individual Protestants helping indigent Catholics, and of magistrates applying leniently the Draconian regulations of the penal code.

But by and large the Irish scene was one of the most shameful in history. A degrading poverty, a chaotic lawlessness, a nomadic pauperism, 34,000 beggars, countless thieves, an upper class living in drunken extravagance amid a starving peasantry, every crop failure bringing widespread starvation—"the old and sick," said Swift, "dying and rotting by cold and famine and filth and vermin"[62]—this terrible picture must find a place in our conception of man. After the long and bitter frost of 1739 came the desperate famine of 1740–41, in which, by one estimate, twenty per cent of the population perished, leaving many deserted villages. In the county of Kerry the number of taxpayers fell from 14,346 in 1733 to 9,372 in 1744. Berkeley calculated that "the nation probably will not recover this loss in a century."[63] He was wrong. Patiently the women bore children to replace the dead. Religious ardor declined among the Protestants as education spread; it increased among the Catholics as their religion identified itself with the struggle of the nation for freedom. The high birth rate favored by the Catholic Church, as her secret weapon against all opposition, soon countervailed the depredations of famine, pestilence, and war; by 1750 the population of Ireland had risen from approximately 2,000,000 in 1700 to some 2,370,000. In the long run the faith and fertility of the oppressed overcame the arms and greed of the conquerors.

VII. SCOTLAND: 1714–56

Why was the fate of Scotland so different from that of Ireland?

First of all, Scotland had never been conquered; on the contrary, it had given the English a Scottish king. Its Highland chieftains, still unsubdued, provided a fighting class that had led the Scots again and again in invasions of England. Its Lowland stock was Anglo-Saxon, basically of the same breed as the English. Its soil remained in resolute native hands. Its religion, like the Anglican, was a product of the Reformation, not a heritage from the medieval Church; and it united instead of dividing the nation. After the Act of Union (1707), Scotland shared in proportion to population in electing members of the now British—i.e., English-Welsh-Scottish—Parliament; it submitted to be ruled from London, but only after extorting commercial concessions that enriched the Scottish people. Every parish in Scotland tried to set up a school for its children, and four universities offered the best higher education then available in the British Isles. In the course of the eighteenth century this educational activity flowered into a "Scottish Enlightenment"—Hume, Hutcheson, Reid, Robertson, Adam Smith—that gave a heady pace to the English mind.

That bright fulfillment, however, had to be earned; fifty years passed before the fruits of the union matured. Scotland in 1714 was still basically feudal: each district, outside the cities, was ruled by a great noble through his vassal lairds, and the land was worked by a loyal and letterless tenant peasantry. But now the political union with England was rapidly undermining that structure. The nobles had dominated the Scottish Parliament; when that Parliament was ended the Scottish representatives in the British Parliament found themselves in an environment where the influence of trade and industry rivaled that of land; they adopted English ideas and technology; and by 1750 the manufacturers and merchants of Scotland were challenging the national leadership of the Argylls, the Atholls, the Hamiltons, and the Mars. The Jacobite adventure of 1745 was the last flare of Scottish feudal power; when it failed, the economic life of Scotland merged with the English economy, and the rule of the middle classes began. The union opened the English colonies to Scottish trade; in 1718 Glasgow launched the first Scottish vessel to cross the Atlantic; soon Scottish merchants were everywhere. Agricultural technology and urban sanitation improved; the death rate fell; population rose from 1,000,000 in 1700 to 1,652,000 at the close of the century. Edinburgh, with fifty thousand inhabitants, was in 1751 the third-largest city in Great Britain, surpassed only by London and Bristol.

The Presbyterian Kirk remained almost fanatically loyal to the Calvinist theology. Every Sunday the people walked—sometimes two or three miles—to churches sternly bare of ornament, and heard hours of preaching and prayer emphasizing the fatality of predestination and the terrors of hell. The Bible was the daily inspiration of every Scottish family; as late as 1763 Hume, in wry exaggeration, estimated two Bibles in Scotland to every man, woman, and child.[64] The preachers were men of little education but of sincere and moving piety; they lived in austere simplicity, and their example and precepts contributed forcefulness to the stability and integrity of the Scottish character. The elders and minister of each kirk watched sharply over the conduct and speech of the parishioners; they meted out penalties for swearing, slander, quarreling, witchcraft, fornication, adultery, any breach of the Sabbath, any deviation from their awful creed. The ministers condemned dancing, wedding festivities, and attendance at the theater. They still held trials for witchcraft, though executions for it were becoming rare. In 1727 a mother and daughter were convicted on such a charge; the daughter escaped, but the mother was burned to death in a barrel of pitch.[65] When the British Parliament (1736) repealed the law punishing witchcraft with death, the Scottish Presbytery denounced the repeal as violating the Bible's express command.[66]

Meanwhile the parish schools maintained by the Kirk, and the "burg schools" supported by the towns, prepared students for the universities. To Edinburgh, Aberdeen, St. Andrews, and Glasgow came eager young men from every class—from farms and workshops as well as from lairds' mansions and baronial halls. A zeal for knowledge animated them, and they bore any hardship in their quest. Many of them lived in cold attic rooms, and took their chief nourishment from a sack of oatmeal periodically carried in from the paternal farm. The professors too were stoics, rarely receiving over sixty pounds a year. In the universities hardly less than in the parish schools, theology was the core of the curriculum; but the classics were taught, and a little science; and the Scottish mind was touched by the secular thought of Europe. Francis Hutcheson, who held the chair of moral philosophy at Glasgow (1729–46), put aside dogmatic discussions, and based his ethics on natural grounds. Students and professors alike became tinged with the Arian heresy —that Christ, though divine, was not coequal or coeternal with God the Father. A Scottish author in 1714 mentioned "the great vogue, among our young gentry and students," of Hobbes and Spinoza.[67] Little coteries of youngsters intoxicated with emancipation formed clubs—the "Sulfur Society," the "Hell-fire," the "Demirip Dragoons"—proudly preaching atheism;[68] probably they mingled with Jacobite malcontents. For Scotland, outside of those merchant classes that were tied to the English economy, still thrilled to the memory of the Stuarts, and dreamed of the time when James III, or his son, would lead the Scots again across the border to restore a Scottish dynasty to the British throne.

VIII. BONNIE PRINCE CHARLIE: 1745

James III had exhausted himself in futile attempts to lead an expedition into England or Scotland. In 1719 he married Maria Clementina Sobieska, granddaughter of Poland's most famous king. It was an unhappy marriage, but it gave James a son whose lovely face and lively temper—going back perhaps to Mary Queen of Scots—were the pride and problem of his parents. England called Charles Edward Stuart "the Young Pretender"; Scotland called him "Bonnie Prince Charlie." Brought up in a discordant household, taught conflicting faiths by his Catholic and Protestant tutors, Charles grew up with an indifferent education, but with all the charms of athletic youth and all the ardor of a head itching for a crown. The Duke of Liria was thrilled by the lad's "great beauty," his merry brown eyes and light-brown hair; a bold rider, a good shot, a body six feet tall and made for war, a "mighty golfer," an accomplished musician, a graceful dancer—this, said the Duke, "is altogether the most ideal prince I have ever met."[69] Charles was conscious of his virtues, which made him now and then unmanageable. In 1734, still a boy of fourteen, he was allowed to sample war in the Spanish army at Gaeta; aroused by this baptism of fire, he could hardly wait for an opportunity to take England.

It seemed at hand when the British Parliament, overruling Walpole, opened hostilities with Spain (1739). Frederick the Great's attack on Silesia (1740) swelled into the War of the Austrian Succession; England sent its main army to the Continent; what better time could the Jacobites find to make another dash for the English throne? In Scotland they formed "the Association" (1739) pledged to that enterprise; they sent emissaries to England to stir up a Stuart revolution; they dispatched appeals to France for money, arms, and troops. Louis XV ordered seven ships of war and twenty-one troop transports to assemble at Brest and prepare to convey ten thousand men under Maréchal de Saxe from Dunkirk to England. In Italy Prince Charles anxiously awaited an invitation from Paris to join the expedition. No invitation came, but he left Rome on January 10, 1744, rode day and night to Frascati, Lerici, and Genoa, took ship to Antibes, and drove on madly to Paris. His aging father remained in Rome, and never saw him again. Charles was well received, and moderately financed, by the King. He went on to Gravelines, and waited impatiently for orders to sail with Maréchal de Saxe, who waited impatiently for the French fleet.

The winds and waves, as usual, declared for England. The French fleet, sailing from Brest (February 6), ran into a *"mer affreuse,"* a frightful sea, and *"toujours un vent,"* always a contrary wind. Ships collided, masts broke, all was in chaos when word came that an English squadron of fifty-two ships was approaching. The French fled back to Brest, but many of their vessels were lost, and the rest were badly hurt by the gale. With this discouraging news word reached France that the English Jacobites were disorganized and spiritless, and that no help could be expected from them if the French came. Louis informed Saxe that the invasion scheme must be abandoned. England, not yet formally at war with France, complained that the presence of Charles on French soil was a breach of treaty commitments. Charles, disguised, hid in Paris, vowing to his friends that he would invade England even if he had to go alone in an open boat. His father sent him a plea to avoid precipitate action, "which would end in your ruin, and that of all those who would join with you in it."[70] Meanwhile Charles' supporters intrigued against one another for influence and perquisities, and denounced one another to him, until he wrote in despair, "I am plagued out of my life" (November 16, 1744).[71]

Finally, despite all warnings, and without consulting the French court, he decided to "tempt my destiny" and "conquer or die." He sent agents to Scotland to rouse the clans; these were so little prepared that they thought of forbidding him to come. The English Jacobites, following Bolingbroke's lead, were seeking reconciliation with George II. Nevertheless Charles borrowed 180,000 livres, accepted the offer of two armed vessels, and sailed for Scotland (July 15, 1745). Near Land's End the little convoy was met by a British man-of-war; one of Charles's ships was so damaged that it returned to Brest. In the other he passed north to the west of England, and on August 3 he touched Scottish soil at Eriska, in the Outer Hebrides. A clan leader advised him to go home. "I *am* come home," answered the Prince. He was warned that on August 1 the British government had proclaimed a reward of 30,000 pounds to anyone who would bring him captive, alive or dead. Charles replied by dismissing the ship that had brought him, so cutting off his own retreat. On August 19 he raised his standard at Glenfinnan in the Highlands, and called all Jacobites to his aid.

Most clan leaders remained aloof; some professed followers plotted to betray him; half a dozen lords declared for him; of his two thousand men twelve hundred were Macdonalds and Camerons. Eluding government forces under Sir John Cope, Charles led his band south. On September 17 they entered Edinburgh, seized the guardhouse and the gates, and established their leader in the once royal palace of Holyrood, where Mary Stuart had argued with John Knox, and James VI and I had forgotten his mother. The

Prince, twenty-five years old, made an alluring picture in his Highland habit, with red velvet breeches, green velvet bonnet, and white cockade. Many a Scot, thinking that national glory had returned in this handsome reincarnation, knelt and kissed his hand, and all the ladies prayed and longed for him. He had hardly time to savor his reception when he learned that Cope was nearing Edinburgh with two thousand troops. On September 21 Charles led out his now three thousand men, met Cope's army at Prestonpans, routed it, took many captives, treated them humanely, and returned to Holyrood anointed with victory. Scotland seemed won.

At ease for a month, Charles requisitioned food and clothing for his soldiers, and welcomed the adhesion of additional clans. Louis XV sent him money and arms from France. On November 8 the happy Prince, on foot, crossed into England with 4,500 men; he besieged and captured Carlisle; he was welcomed in Manchester; he pressed on to Derby, hoping by his dramatic advance to rouse England to receive him as its legitimate king. He issued a proclamation vowing that Anglicans and Presbyterians should suffer no more hurt from him, a Roman Catholic, than they had received from George I, a Lutheran.[72] England did not believe him, and did not propose to begin anew the weary struggle of the younger faith against the old. Though hardly anyone in England rose against Charles, only a handful of English recruits came to his aid. The English Jacobites played safe.

George II had hastened back from Hanover to protect his threatened throne, and had ordered three English armies to converge at Derby. Charles was all for ignoring them and rushing on to London with his six thousand men, but his Scottish chieftains refused to follow him. They pointed out that each of the government armies was ten thousand strong, that these, in his rear, would harass and soon overwhelm him, and that the Jacobite rising which he had promised them was nowhere to be seen; they insisted on returning to Scotland, where they might raise more clans, and might receive reinforcements from France. Charles yielded, and led the sad retreat from Derby to Glasgow. At nearby Falkirk, with nine thousand men, he defeated an English force of ten thousand under Hawley (January 17, 1746). But it was a Pyrrhic victory. His army was weakened with losses and desertions; its supplies were running out; it was paid in oatmeal; its leaders were quarreling like clans. Again they advised retreat. The Prince pleaded for a stand; he saw nothing but disintegration and ruin in further retreat; why should they run away from an enemy no stronger than that which they had defeated? Again he yielded; but now he knew that he was beaten. The Scottish army turned back toward the Highlands. The pessimism of its leaders swept through the ranks; desertions ran into thousands; what remained was not so much an army as an undisciplined and disheartened crowd.

Meanwhile the main English force, under the Duke of Cumberland, entered Scotland, took control of the eastern coast, and received at Leith a reinforcement of five hundred Hessians brought by George II from Austria. With 8,800 men Cumberland marched north into Inverness county. There on Culloden Moor, April 16, 1746, Charles faced him with seven thousand men poorly armed, poorly fed, poorly led. They fought with Scottish courage, but they were shattered by Cumberland's superior artillery firing grapeshot—"bags of balls" (said a Scottish poet) that "hewed them down, aye, score by score, as grass does fall before the mower."[73] Charles rode about wildly, seeking to rally his retreating men, but they took to precipitate and individual flight. His aides forced him to withdraw from the battlefield by seizing the bridle of his horse. His spirit broken, he fled with a few friends, and wandered in hiding from one refuge to another, repeating, with glory departed, the tale of Charles II. At last (September 20) he found a vessel that took him back to France.

Cumberland pursued his routed foes with orders of "No quarter": every rebel Scot was to be killed on sight. Houses were searched; Scots found with arms were summarily shot; clans loyal to George II were let loose upon clans that had joined the revolt; hundreds of homes were burned down.[74] "Mild measures will not do," said the Duke; "all the good we have done is but a little bloodletting, which has only weakened the madness but not cured it."[75] And in truth the rebel clans tried again and again to renew the rebellion. For ten years more the Jacobites of Scotland sang and dreamed of past defeats and coming victories, until their faith was broken by the degeneration of their once bonnie Prince in Rome.

The Treaty of Aix-la-Chapelle (1748) between England and France required the expulsion of Charles from French soil. He refused to obey; he was forcibly evicted by French troops; he returned in disguise to Paris, even, in 1750, to London, seeking in vain to revive the Jacobite cause, promising in vain to abjure the Catholic faith.[76] Finally admitting defeat, he fell into such drunkenness and debauchery that all the major Catholic powers repudiated him. He died in Rome in 1788, aged sixty-eight. Voltaire, thirty years before, had already written a just epitaph upon the second Jacobite revolt:

> Thus [with the return of Charles to France in 1746] ended an adventure which in the times of knight-errantry might have proved fortunate, but could not be expected to succeed in an age when military discipline, artillery, and, above all, money, in the end determine everything.[77]

IX. THE RISE OF WILLIAM PITT: 1708–56

The fall of Walpole bequeathed England to a succession of minor ministries that floundered in political chaos and inconclusive wars. Lord Wilmington, as first lord of the treasury (1742–43), ruled at home while George II fought with theatrical but real heroism at Dettingen (June 27, 1743). "During all the battle," wrote Frederick the Great, "the King of England kept himself at the head of his Hanoverian battalion, his left foot behind, sword in hand and arm outstretched, very much like a master of fencing";[78] just the same he inspired his men by his bravery, while he modestly accepted the commands of his generals. The ministry of Henry Pelham (1743–54) led England back to peace, but it continued the technique of ruling by the purchase of votes in boroughs and Parliament. His brother, the Duke of Newcastle, kept a tariff of England's politicians, on which, for budgetary convenience, he listed the current market price of each man's soul.[79] The most lasting distinction of these two ministries is that they included the man who made the British Empire, and who stood out in his turbulent time as one of the most powerful characters in history.

William Pitt was born (1708) to money because his grandfather, Thomas Pitt, had made a vast fortune in India. Thomas himself was a man to be reckoned with. He took service as a sailor in a merchant vessel, settled in Bengal, and engaged in trade in "illicit" competition with the East India Company, to which Parliament had granted a monopoly. He was fined £1,000, continued to compete, brought the company to terms, joined it, and was for twelve years governor of Madras. By 1701 he was a man of sterling, rich enough to buy the famous "Pitt diamond" for £20,000, and clever enough to sell it to Philippe d'Orléans, Regent of France, for £135,000; now valued at £480,000, it is preserved among the state jewels of France in the Louvre as a brilliant witness to the depreciation of currencies. Thomas invested his gains in English realty, bought a seat in Parliament, and represented there, from 1710 to 1715, the "rotten borough" of Old Sarum. He devised his estate to Robert Pitt, his eldest son, who married Harriet Villiers, who gave him seven children, of whom William Pitt was the second son.

At Eton William protested against the discipline; he thought the fagging would break the spirit of the students; it did not break his. At Oxford he distinguished himself by suffering from gout at the age of eighteen. Hoping to shake off the ailment in a warmer climate, he left the university without a degree and traveled in France and Italy, but gout remained his cross through all his victories. Nevertheless he joined the army, served in it for four years, saw no battle, but came out with the conviction that war is the arbiter of history and the destiny of states. In 1735 his family, while keeping him relatively poor as a younger son, bought Old Sarum's votes for him, and he began his career in Parliament.

He soon made himself heard there, for he was the most effective orator that that forensic cavern has ever known. All the force of his passionate character went into his speeches, all his resolve to rise to power, to unseat Walpole, to dominate Parliament and the King, finally to remake Europe to his heart's desire. For those purposes he used logic, drama, imagination, enthusiasm, poetry, bombast, invective, sarcasm, satire, appeals to patriotism, to personal and national interest and glory. As the years progressed he developed his oratorical mastery until it embraced all the arts of a Demosthenes or a Cicero. He could lower his voice to a whisper, or raise it to an angry roar; he could sink an enemy with a phrase. He followed Demosthenes' rule and made action the life of speech; every line had its gesture, every feeling molded his hawklike face and glowed in his deep-set eyes, until his whole body came into play as if the word had been made flesh. He was the greatest actor that ever shunned the stage.

He was no saint. Ambition was the mast of his character and the wind in his sails; but it redeemed itself by embracing all England, and consumed itself in dragging England, willy-nilly, out over imperial seas to world supremacy. Feeling himself to be the voice of the state, beyond any Hanoverian gutturals or Walpolian bribes, he appropriated the ethic of governments—that all is good that advantages the state; if he used deception, calumny, intimidation, intrigue, ingratitude, perjury, treachery, these were tools of the statesman's trade, and were to be judged not by preachers but by kings. At nearly every step in his rise he turned his back upon a position that he had recently defended with all the sublimity of moral passion;[80] he seldom stopped to explain or apologize; he mounted all intent toward his goal; and his success—which was England's—sanctified his sins and haloed his head. Meanwhile there was something grand in his pride; he disdained to buy advancement with servility, he remained incorruptible amid corruption, and he attained his ends by the force of an uncompromising personality that would not be deterred.

He pursued Walpole as a peacemongering merchant too chicken-livered to risk war with Spain, and too subservient to a king who, said Pitt, showed an "absurd, ungrateful, and perfidious partiality for Hanover," and "considered England only as a province to a despicable electorate."[81] The ardent orator pursued his martial policy with such intensity that the Duchess of Marlborough, dying in 1744, left Pitt a legacy of ten thousand pounds, for Sarah had inherited her dead Duke's love of war. When Pelham came to office he asked the King to make Pitt secretary of war; George II, still burning with Pitt's fire, refused. Pelham persisted; he described Pitt as "the most able and useful man we have amongst us, truly honorable and strictly honest."[82] The King yielded, and in 1746 Pitt entered the ministry, first as joint vice-treasurer for Ireland, then as paymaster of the forces. This position had become by custom a mine of personal wealth: the paymaster took for himself one half of one per cent of all subsidies voted by Parliament to foreign princes; and he invested at interest—which he kept for himself—the large floating balance left with him for the payment of troops. Pitt refused to take anything more than his official salary; when the King of Sardinia pressed him to accept a gift equal to the usual deduction from his subsidy he declined it. England, which had long accounted such perquisites as a normal accommodation to the nature of man, applauded Pitt's anomalous integrity, and listened with eagerness to his pleas for a Britain that would bestride the world.

In June, 1755, without a declaration of war, hostilities between England and France broke out in America. In January, 1756, England signed a treaty with Prussia. In May France concluded a defensive alliance with Austria. In November Pitt, now secretary of state, became England's voice and arm in that Seven Years' War that would determine the map of Europe till the French Revolution.

CHAPTER IV

Religion and Philosophy

I. THE RELIGIOUS SITUATION

THE story of the eighteenth century in Western Europe had a double theme: the collapse of the old feudal regime, and the near-collapse of the Christian religion that had given it spiritual and social support. State and faith were bound together in mutual aid, and the fall of one seemed to involve the other in a common tragedy.

In both aspects of the great change England played the first act. On the political stage her Civil War of 1642–49 preceded by 147 years the French Revolution in deposing a feudal aristocracy and beheading a king. In the religious realm the deistic criticism of Christianity antedated by half a century the Voltairean campaign in France; the materialism of Hobbes preceded by a century the materialism of La Mettrie; Hume's *Treatise of Human Nature* (1739) and his essay "Of Miracles" (1748) antedated the attack of the French *philosophes* upon Christianity in the *Encyclopédie* (1751). Voltaire had learned his skepticism in France—partly from the English exile Bolingbroke—before coming to England; but his three years in England (1726–28) startled him with the sight of orthodoxy in decay, Catholicism humiliated, Protestantism breaking up into feeble sects, and deists challenging everything in Christianity except the belief in God—precisely the challenge that Voltaire would carry to France. "In France," said Voltaire, "I am looked upon as having too little religion; in England as having too much."[1]

Montesquieu, visiting England in 1731, reported, "There is no religion in England."[2] This was, of course, an exercise in striking hyperbole; at that very time John and Charles Wesley were founding the Methodist movement at Oxford. But Montesquieu, an aristocrat, moved mostly among lords and ladies of the peerage or the pen; and in these groups, he tells us, "if religion is spoken of, everybody laughs."[3] This too seems extreme; but hear Lord Hervey, who knew almost every man, woman, and deviate in the upper classes:

> This fable of Christianity . . . was now [1728] so exploded in England that any man of fashion or condition would have been almost as much ashamed to own himself a Christian as formerly he would

have been to profess himself none. Even the women who prided themselves at all on their understanding took care to let people know that
Christian prejudices were what they despised being bound by.[4]

In those exalted ranks or minds religion meant either the somnolence of
the Anglican communion or the "enthusiasm" of the Dissenting sects; and
Dr. Johnson would soon define enthusiasm as "a vain belief of private revelation"—literally a "god within." The Established Church had lost face and
influence by supporting the Stuarts against the Hanoverians and the triumphant Whigs; now it submitted to the state, and its clergy became humble
dependents of the ruling class. The country parson was the favorite butt
of literary satire or vulgar ridicule; Fielding honored the exceptions in
Parson Adams. Class distinctions prevailed in the churches; the rich had
special pews near the pulpit, the tradesmen sat behind them, the common
people sat or stood in the rear; and when the service was over, the commoners remained in their places while their superiors filed out in slow dignity.[5] In some London churches, when too many of the poor came to worship, the periwigged members fled, locking their pews behind them,[6] and
seeking fresher air.

Some Anglican bishops, like Butler, Berkeley, and Warburton, were men
of great learning, and two of these were of fine character; but most of the
upper clergy, maneuvering for promotion, played politics with the skeptics
and mistresses of the court, and consumed in luxury the revenues of many
parishes. Bishop Chandler, we are told, paid £9,000 for advancement from
Lichfield to Durham; Bishop Willis of Winchester, Archbishop Potter of
Canterbury, Bishops Gibson and Sherlock of London died "shamefully
rich," some of them worth £100,000.[7] Thackeray had no stomach for
them:

> I read that Lady Yarmouth [mistress of George II] sold a bishopric
> to a clergyman for £5,000. . . . Was he the only prelate of his time
> led up by such hands for consecration? As I peep into George II's St.
> James's, I see crowds of cassocks rustling up the back stairs of the
> ladies of the court; stealthy clergy slipping purses into their laps; that
> godless old King yawning under his canopy in his Chapel Royal as the
> chaplain before him is discoursing, [or] chattering in German . . . so
> loud that the clergyman . . . burst out crying in his pulpit because
> the defender of the faith and dispenser of bishoprics would not listen
> to him![8]

It was a sign of the times that the Established Church had become broadly
tolerant of different theologies and rituals among its members. Pitt described
it as "a Calvinist creed, a Popish liturgy, and an Arminian clergy"[9]—i.e., the

official doctrine was predestinarian, the ritual was semi–Roman Catholic, but a Latitudinarian spirit allowed Anglican ministers to reject Calvin's determinism and adopt the free-will teaching of the Dutch heretic Arminius. Toleration grew because faith declined. Heresies like Hume's, which would have startled seventeenth-century England, made now but a slight ripple on the stream of British thought. Hume himself described England as "settled into the most cool indifference with regard to religious matters that is to be found in any nation in the world."[10]

The letter of the law made the Anglican worship compulsory on all Englishmen. A man who absented himself from Sunday services was liable to a fine of a shilling for each truancy; and anyone who allowed such an absentee to live with him was subject to a fine of twenty pounds per month;[11] these laws, however, were seldom enforced. Again in law rather than practice, Catholic services were outlawed. A Catholic priest who performed any sacerdotal function was subject to life imprisonment. A like penalty discouraged any Catholic from keeping a school; and no parent might send his child abroad for a Catholic education, under penalty of £100 fine. Only those citizens who took the oaths of allegiance and supremacy (acknowledging the king of England to be head of the Church), and declared against transubstantiation, were eligible to buy or inherit land. Any Catholic who refused to take these oaths was excluded from civil or military office, from the practice of law, from bringing any action at law, and from living within ten miles of London; moreover, such a Catholic might at any time be banished from England, and be sentenced to death if he returned. Actually, however, under Georges I and II, Catholics regularly transmitted their property and their creed to their children; they could hear Mass unhindered in their chapels and homes; and many of them took the required oaths with a mental reservation.[12]

Nearly all ardent English Protestants were now in the sects dissenting from the Established Church. Voltaire laughed and rejoiced at their multiplicity: Independents (Puritans), Presbyterians, Baptists, Congregationalists, Quakers, Socinians (Unitarians). The Presbyterians, having lost political power, were becoming tolerant; they did not take predestination very seriously, and many of them were quietly content with a human Christ.[13] In 1719 an assembly of Presbyterian clergymen voted 73 to 69 that subscription to the orthodox doctrine of the Trinity should no longer be required of candidates for the ministry.[14] The Quakers were increasing not in number but in wealth; and as they rose in the social scale they became more reconciled to the ways and sins of men. A tendency to gloom infected nearly all Dissenters, even in prosperity; and while the upper classes made Sunday a day of frolic, the lower middle class—where Dissent was strongest —continued the "blue Sunday" of the Puritans. There, after morning prayers at home, the family went to the meetinghouse for a service that lasted two hours; back at home, the father read the Bible or pious books to his wife and children, who, as like as not, sat on cushions on the uncarpeted floor. Normally they went to services again in the afternoon and evening, prayed together, heard another sermon, and found some pleasure in singing sonorous hymns. No profane singing was allowed on that holy day, no card-playing, in general no amusement of any kind. Travel was to be avoided on the Sabbath, so allowing the highwaymen a day of rest.

Voltaire, reviewing the religious scene of England, found much in it to carry a lesson to a France where intolerance still ruled:

> Take a view of the Royal Exchange in London. . . . There the Jew, the Mohammedan, and the Christian transact business together as though they were all of the same religion, and give the name of Infidels to none but bankrupts; there the Presbyterian confides in the Anabaptist, and the Churchman depends upon the Quaker's word. At the breaking up of this . . . free assembly some withdraw to the synagogue, and others to take a glass. This man goes and is baptized in a great tub in the name of the Father, Son, and Holy Ghost; that man has his son's foreskin cut off, and causes a set of Hebrew words—to the meaning of which he himself is a total stranger—to be mumbled over the infant; others [Quakers] retire to their churches, and there wait the inspiration of heaven with their hats on; and all are satisfied.
>
> If one religion only were allowed in England, the government would very possibly become arbitrary; if there were but two, the people would cut one another's throats; but as there is such a multitude, they all live happy and in peace.[15]

II. THE DEISTIC CHALLENGE

Many factors worked together to undermine the Christian creed in England: the association of the Church with the rise and fall of political parties, the growth of wealth and the demands of pleasure in the upper classes, the internationalism of ideas through commerce and travel, the increasing acquaintance with non-Christian religions and peoples, the multiplication and mutual criticism of sects, the development of science, the growth of belief in natural causes and invariable laws, the historical and critical study of the Bible, the importation or translation of such epochal books as Bayle's *Dictionnaire* and Spinoza's *Tractatus theologico-politicus*, the abandonment (1694) of state censorship of the press, the rising prestige of reason, the new attempts of philosophy, in Bacon, Hobbes, and Locke, to give natural explanations of the world and man, and—summing up many of these factors—

the campaign of the deists to reduce Christianity to a belief in God and immortality.

That movement had begun with Lord Herbert of Cherbury's *De Veritate* in 1624; it had grown through the seventeenth and early eighteenth centuries with Charles Blount, John Toland, and Anthony Collins; now it proceeded with cumulative effect in Whiston, Woolston, Tindal, Middleton, Chubb, Annet, and Bolingbroke. William Whiston, who had succeeded Newton as Lucasian professor of mathematics at Cambridge, was dismissed from that post (1710) for expressing some doubts on the Trinity; he defended his Arianism in *Primitive Christianity Revived* (1712), and labored to show that Old Testament prophecies had no reference to Christ. When the defenders of Christianity abandoned the argument from prophecy, and based the divinity of Christ upon the miracles related in the New Testament, Thomas Woolston let loose his irreverent ebullience in *Six Discourses on the Miracles of Our Saviour* (1727–30). "Never," said Voltaire, "was Christianity so daringly assailed by any Christian."[16] Woolston argued that some of the miracles were incredible and others absurd. He found it especially unbelievable that Christ had cursed a fig tree for not producing figs so early in the year as Easter. He wondered what the English woolgrowers would have done to Jesus if he had sent a flock of their sheep to death as he had done with the Gadarene swine; they "would have made him swing for it," for English law made such an action a capital crime.[17] Woolston thought that the story of Christ's resurrection was an elaborate deception practiced by the Apostles upon their audiences. He covered all this with protestations that he remained a Christian "as sound as a rock." However, he dedicated each of his discourses to a different bishop with such condemnation of their pride and avarice that they indicted him for libel and blasphemy (1729). The court condemned him to pay a fine of a hundred pounds, and to give security for future good behavior. Unable to raise the required sums, he went to jail. Voltaire offered a third of the amount, the remainder was raised, and Woolston was freed. Doubtless the trial advertised the *Discourses;* they sold sixty thousand copies in a few years.[18] An anonymous *Life of Woolston* (1733) told how, when he was walking in St. George's Fields,

> a jolly young woman met him and accosted him in the following manner: . . . "You old rogue, are you not hanged yet?" To which Mr. Woolston answered: "Good woman, I know you not; pray, what have I done to offend you?" To which the woman replied: "You have writ against my Saviour; what would become of my poor sinful soul if it was not for my dear Saviour?—my Saviour who died for such wicked sinners as I am."[19]

The deistic propaganda reached its climax in Matthew Tindal, a fellow of All Souls' College, Oxford. After a quiet and respectable life, marked chiefly by conversions to and from Catholicism, he published at the age of seventy-three the first volume of *Christianity as Old as the Creation* (1730). At his death three years later he left the manuscript of a second volume, which fell into the hands of a bishop, who destroyed it. We may estimate the impact of Volume I from the 150 replies that sought to counter it; it was this book that called forth Bishop Butler's *Analogy of Religion* and Bishop Berkeley's *Alciphron.*

Tindal ranged with no tender mercy through all the fantasies of theology. He asked why God should have given his revelation to one small people, the Jews, had let it remain their exclusive possession for four thousand years, and then had sent his son to them with another revelation that after seventeen hundred years was still confined to a minority of the human race. What sort of god could this be who used such clumsy methods with such tardy and inadequate results? What ogre of a god was this who punished Adam and Eve for seeking knowledge, and then punished all their posterity merely for being born? We are told that the absurdities in the Bible are due to God's adapting his speech to the language and ideas of his hearers. What nonsense! Why could he not speak the simple truth to them intelligibly? Why should he have used priests as his intermediaries instead of speaking directly to every man's soul? Why should he have allowed his specially revealed religion to become an engine of persecution, terror, and strife, leaving men no better morally, after centuries of this dispensation, than before?—making them, indeed, more fierce and cruel than under the pagan cults! Is there not a finer morality in Confucius or Cicero than in the Christianity of history? The real revelation is in Nature herself, and in man's God-given reason; the real God is the God that Newton revealed, the designer of a marvelous world operating majestically according to invariable law; and the real morality is the life of reason in harmony with nature. "Whoever so regulates his natural appetites as will conduce most to the exercise of his reason, the health of his body, and the pleasures of his senses taken and considered together (since herein his happiness consists) may be certain he can never offend his Maker, who, as he governs all things according to their natures can't but expect his rational creatures should act according to their natures."[20] This is the true morality, this is the true Christianity, "as old as the creation."

Conyers Middleton carried on the attack from the historical angle. Graduating from Trinity College, Cambridge, he took holy orders, and, while dealing blow after blow at orthodox belief, continued the external practices of Christian worship. He wrote some of the best prose of his time, and his

Life of Cicero (1741), though it borrowed heavily from its predecessors, remains to this day an admirable biography. He pleased his fellow clergymen when he sent to England *Letters from Rome* (1729), showing in scholarly detail the residue of pagan rites in Catholic ritual—incense, holy water, relics, miracles, votive offerings and lights set up before sacred shrines, and the Pontifex Maximus of antiquity become the Supreme Pontiff of Rome. Protestant England applauded, but it soon discovered that Middleton's penchant for history could trouble Protestant as well as Catholic theology. When Daniel Waterland defended, against Tindal, the literal truth and inspiration of the Bible, Middleton in a *Letter to Dr. Waterland* (1731) warned the Protestant divines that to insist on all the legends of the Bible as actual history was suicidal; sooner or later the progress of knowledge would discredit such fables and compel Christian apologists to retreat shamefacedly to some more modest stand. Then Middleton resorted to an argument that betrayed the effect which his study of history had had upon his religious faith: even if Christian theology is incredible, a good citizen will support Christianity and the Christian Church as a bulwark of social order, providing admirable deterrents to the barbarism latent in mankind.[21]

Finally, Middleton issued his most substantial work, *A Free Inquiry into the Miraculous Powers Which Are Supposed to Have Existed in the Christian Church through Successive Ages* (1748)—a book that Hume later ranked as superior to his own contemporary essay "Of Miracles" (1748). He began by acknowledging the authority of the miracles ascribed in the canonical New Testament to Christ or his apostles; he proposed to show only that the miracles attributed to the Fathers, saints, and martyrs of the Church, after the first Christian century, were undeserving of belief; merely to relate those stories sufficed to reveal their absurdity. Some Fathers of the Church had sanctioned such tales while knowing them to be false; and Middleton quoted Mosheim, the learned ecclesiastical historian, as intimating his fear that "those who search with any attention into the writings of the greatest and most holy doctors of the fourth century will find them all, without exception, disposed to deceive and to lie whenever the interest of religion requires it."[22]

There were many defects in Middleton's book. He forgot that he too had recommended wholesale deception in support of Christianity, and he ignored the possibility that some strange experiences, like the exorcism of "diabolical possession," or St. Anthony's hearing the Devil at his door, were due to the power of suggestion or imagination, and may have seemed truly miraculous to those who honestly reported them. In any case the effect of the *Free Inquiry* was to throw back upon the miracles of the Old Testament, then of the New, the same methods of criticism that Middleton had applied to the patristic period; and his Catholic opponents were quite right in contending that his arguments would weaken the whole supernatural substructure of Christian belief. Perhaps Middleton had intended it so. But he kept his ecclesiastical preferments to the end.

The conversion of Bolingbroke to deism was a secret and a contagion in the aristocracy. In writings cautiously kept from publication during his life he directed his scornful invective against almost all philosophers except Bacon and Locke. He termed Plato the father of theological mendacity, St. Paul a fanatical visionary, Leibniz a "chimerical quack."[23] He called metaphysicians "learned lunatics," and described as "pneumatical [windy] madmen" all who thought soul and body distinct.[24] He laughed at the Old Testament as a farrago of nonsense and lies.[25] He professed belief in God, but rejected the remainder of the Christian creed. All knowledge is relative and uncertain. "We ought always to be unbelieving. . . . In religion, government, and philosophy we ought to distrust everything that is established."[26] He put behind him the last consolation of the skeptic—the belief in progress; all societies go through cycles "from generation to corruption, and from corruption to generation."[27]

In 1744 Bolingbroke inherited the family estate at Battersea, and left France to spend there the concluding years of his struggle against disease and despair. His former friends deserted him as his political influence fell and his temper rose. The death of his second wife (1750) ended his interest in human affairs; "I become every year more and more isolated in this world"[28]—the nemesis of selfishness. In 1751 he was seized with cancer spreading from the face. He dictated a pious will, but refused to let any clergyman attend him.[29] He died on December 12 after six months of agony, without hope for himself or mankind. Already the decline of religious belief was begetting the pessimism that would be the secret malady of the modern soul.

III. THE RELIGIOUS REBUTTAL

The defenders of Christianity did not meet the deistic attack in any spirit of resignation to defeat; on the contrary, they fought back with as hearty a vigor, as extensive a learning, as virulent a style as anything in Tindal, Middleton, or Bolingbroke. The weaker apologists, like Bishop Chandler of Lichfield and Bishop Newton of London, relied on trite arguments—that the Jews were fervently expecting a Messiah when Christ came, and that many Jewish prophecies had been fulfilled by his career; or, like Bishops Sherlock of London and Pearce of Rochester, they appealed to the multiple testimony for the resurrection of Christ. Sherlock and others insisted that the evidence for the Christian miracles was overwhelming, and sufficed to uphold the divinity of Christ and Christianity. To reject a well-attested event because it contradicts our experience, said Sherlock, is a very risky procedure; on the same basis the inhabitants of the tropics refused to believe in the reality of ice. When we assume that things cannot be otherwise than we have known them to be, "we outrun the information of our senses, and the conclusion stands on prejudice, not on reason."[30] Despite our wide but really narrow experience, we cannot be sure that a man may not rise from the dead. Consider how many marvels now accepted as routine events in our lives were once held to be inconceivable!

George Berkeley, who had made his mark in philosophy in the years 1709–13, sent from Rhode Island his contribution to the debate in *Alciphron, or The Minute Philosopher* (1733), a dialogue sparkling with bold thought and sprightly style. Alciphron describes himself as a freethinker who has progressed from Latitudinarianism to deism to atheism; now he rejects all religion as a deception practiced upon the people by priests and magistrates; he refuses to believe in anything but the senses, the passions, and the appetites. Euphranor, voicing Berkeley, warns the deists that their doctrine leads to atheism, and that atheism will lead to the collapse of morality. There may be a few good atheists, but will not their doctrine, if accepted by the masses, issue in libertinism and lawlessness? These skeptics of religion should be skeptics of science too, for many statements of scientists —as in higher mathematics—are quite beyond the evidence of our senses or the reach of our understanding. Certainly the doctrine of the Trinity is no more incomprehensible than the square root of minus one.

William Warburton was not the man to rest his faith or his ecclesiastical revenues upon so frail a base as Berkeley's surds. Trained as a lawyer, ordained an Anglican priest, he fought his way through the theological jungle with all the alert resourcefulness of the legal mind. Perhaps he was fitter for the army than for either the bar or the cloth; he relished battle, and could hardly sleep at night if he had not slain some adversary during the day. He described his life as "a warfare upon earth; that is to say, with bigots and libertines, against whom I have denounced eternal war, like Hannibal against Rome, at the altar."[31] His darts ranged far and wide, and when they ran out of foes they slaughtered friends. He gave succinct descriptions of his contemporaries: Johnson, a malign and insolent bully; Garrick, whose "sense, when he deviates into it, is more like nonsense"; Smollett, a "vagabond Scot" who "writes nonsense ten thousand strong"; Voltaire, a "scoundrel" wallowing in "the dirtiest sink of freethinking."[32]

His immense two-volume masterpiece appeared in 1737–41 as *The Divine Legation of Moses Demonstrated on the Principles of a Religious Deist*. Its argument was original and unique: The belief in a future state of reward and punishment is (as many deists agreed) indispensable to social order; but

Moses succeeded in organizing Jewish life to prosperity and morality without that belief; this miracle can be explained only by the divine guidance of Moses and the Jews; therefore the mission and laws of Moses were divine, and the Bible is the word of God. Warburton felt that this demonstration fell "very little short of mathematical certainty."[33] His theological colleagues were not quite happy over his view that God had guided the Jews through 613 laws and four thousand years without letting them know that their souls were immortal. But the lusty author had filled his pages with such learned disquisitions—on the nature of morality, on the necessary alliance of Church and state, on the mystery religions and rituals of antiquity, on the origin of writing, on the meaning of hieroglyphics, on Egyptian chronology, on the date of the Book of Job, and on the errors of freethinkers, antiquaries, scholars, historians, Socinians, Turks, and Jews—that all England gasped at the weight and reach of his erudition. Warburton advanced from battle to battle—against Crousaz, Theobald, Bolingbroke, Middleton, Wesley, Hume—to the lucrative and comfortable bishopric of Gloucester.

Joseph Butler was less tough of fiber but of finer grain: a man of great gentleness, modesty, and benevolence, who suffered deeply from his realization that the religion which had helped to wean European civilization from barbarism was facing a trial for its life. He was shocked by the popularity of Hobbesian materialism in the upper classes. When (1747) he was offered the archbishopric of Canterbury—the ecclesiastical primacy of England—he refused it on the ground that "it was too late for him to try to support a falling Church."[34] In 1751 he expressed his dismay at "the general decay of religion in this nation. . . . The influence of it is more and more wearing out in the minds of men. . . . The number of those who profess themselves unbelievers increases, and with their numbers their zeal."[35] As if he felt that a people might suffer a spiritual amnesia through the abandonment of its religious and moral heritage, he surprised his friend Dean Tucker by asking might not a nation, as well as an individual, go mad?

Nevertheless he gave his life to seeking an intellectual rehabilitation of Christian belief. When he was still a young priest of thirty-four he published *Fifteen Sermons* (1726), in which he modified Hobbes's pessimistic analysis of human nature by claiming that man, though in many ways naturally vicious, is also by nature a social and moral being, with an inborn sense of right and wrong. Butler argued that the nobler elements in the constitution of man owe their origin to God, whose voice they are; and on this basis he built a general theory of divine design as permeating the world. Caroline liked the argument, and in 1736 Butler was appointed "clerk of the closet" to the Queen.

In that year he issued what remained for a century the chief buttress of Christian argument against unbelief—*The Analogy of Religion, Natural and*

Revealed, to the Constitution and Course of Nature. The preface revealed the mood of the time:

> It is come, I know not how, to be taken for granted by many persons that Christianity is not so much as a subject of inquiry but that it is now at length discovered to be fictitious. And accordingly they treat it as if in the present age this were an agreed point among all people of discernment, and nothing remained but to set it up as a principal subject of mirth and ridicule, as it were by way of reprisals for its having so long interrupted the pleasures of the world.[36]

Intended as an answer to the deists, the *Analogy* assumed the existence of God. The "natural religion" of the deists had accepted the "God of Nature," the great designer and artificer of the world, but it had rejected, as quite incompatible with that lofty conception, the apparently unjust God of the Bible. Butler proposed to show that there are in nature as many signs of injustice and cruelty as in the Jehovah of the Old Testament; that there is no contradiction between the God of Nature and the God of Revelation; and that those who accepted the one deity should logically accept the other. The good clerk of the closet seems never to have dreamed that some hardy skeptics might conclude from his argument (as James Mill did) that neither of these two gods deserved to be worshiped by civilized men.

That both gods existed, and were one, Butler argued from probability. Our minds are imperfect, and subject to every manner of error; we can never have certainty, whether about God or about nature; it is enough to have probability; and probability supports the beliefs in God and immortality. The soul is clearly superior to the body, for the bodily organs are the tools and servants of the soul. The soul, as obviously the essence of man, need not perish with the body; probably, at death, it seeks other instruments in a higher stage. Is it not conformable to nature that an organism should be transformed from a lower to a finer form—as creeping things become winged ones, as the chrysalis changes into a butterfly? And another analogy makes it probable that in the life of the soul after the death of the body there will be rewards and punishments—always assuming the existence of God. For just as we punish criminals for their offenses against society, so does nature, in most cases, punish men for the evils they do; but since there are many instances in which vice meets with no evident penalty, and virtue no visible reward, in this life, it is incredible that God will not restore, in another life, a juster relationship between conduct and fate. Our conscience, or moral sense, could have come to us only from a just God.

Butler's arguments are now of interest chiefly as illustrating a stage in the evolution of the modern mind. As against the deists they had considerable point: those who accepted the evidence of divine design in nature had no reason to reject the Bible because of the cruel God revealed in the Old Testament, for the God of Nature is quite as cruel. It was a highly original way to defend Christianity; Butler apparently did not suspect that his argument might lead not to Christianity but to something more desperate than atheism—to Thomas Henry Huxley's conclusion that the ultimate forces in or behind the universe are unmoral, and run harshly counter to that sense of right and wrong upon which Butler, like Kant, based so much of his theology. In any case the *Analogy* marked an advance if only in its good temper; here was no *odium theologicum*, no unctuous vituperation, but an earnest attempt to be courteous even to those who seemed to be destroying the most precious hopes of mankind. Queen Caroline hailed the book as the best defense yet made of the Christian creed. Dying, she recommended Butler for ecclesiastical advancement; George II made him bishop of Bristol, then dean of St. Paul's, finally bishop of Durham. There Butler set an example to his peers by living simply, and giving much of his income to the poor.

His *Analogy* left so many openings to unbelief that many churchmen advised an end to debate, and preferred to rest their faith on religious needs and sentiments beyond the shafts of reason. So Henry Dodwell's *Christianity Not Founded on Argument* (1742) rejected reasoning in spiritual concerns; it is no guide to truth, much less to happiness, but is merely an enervating dance of pros and cons; no man ever builds his faith upon such fluid foundations. The arguments of Clarke, Warburton, Butler, and other Christian defenders, said Dodwell, had shaken more religious belief than they had reinforced; there might have been no atheism if the Boyle lecturers had not annually refuted it. Christ did not argue; he taught as one having authority. Look at any really religious person, and you will find an inner conviction, not an intellectual conclusion. For the simple soul faith must be an accepted tradition; for the mature spirit it must be a direct feeling of a supernatural reality.

William Law, after making his mark in controversy with the deists, was moved by reading Jakob Böhme to turn from argument to mysticism; and in this half century of triumphant materialism and cynicism he wrote of the inner presence and redeeming love of Christ as fervently and confidently as if he had been Thomas à Kempis reborn and unchanged. He sacrificed all worldly prospects by refusing to take the oath acknowledging George I to be the head of the English Church; he was deprived of his fellowship at Cambridge, and his degrees were revoked. He became tutor to Edward Gibbon's father, and remained with that family long enough to be remembered by the historian. "In our family," said the skeptic, "he left the reputation of a worthy and pious man who believed all he professed, and practiced all that he enjoined."[37] Johnson praised Law's *Serious Call to a Devout and*

Holy Life (1729) as "the finest piece of hortatory theology in any language."[38] Certainly its mysticism was healthier than that which loses itself in supernatural visions, celestial or infernal. "There is nothing that is supernatural," Law wrote, "in the whole system of our redemption. Every part of it has its ground in the workings and powers of nature, and all our redemption is only nature set right." Hell is not a place, but the condition of the disordered soul; heaven is not a place, it is "no foreign, separate, and imposed state," but the happiness of a soul in order and at peace.[39] And though Law was a faithful member of the Church of England, he dreamed of a regenerate and Protestant monasticism:

> If, therefore, persons of either sex, . . . desirous of perfection, should unite themselves into little societies, professing voluntary poverty, virginity, retirement, and devotion, that some might be relieved by their charities, and all be blessed with their prayers and benefited by their example; . . . such persons, . . . so far from being chargeable with any superstition or blind devotion, . . . might justly be said to restore that piety which was the boast and glory of the Church when its greatest saints were alive.[40]

Law's ideals and fine prose so moved Gibbon's aunt Hester Gibbon that she and a rich widow went to live near him in his native town of Kingscliffe, Northamptonshire, and devoted most of their income to charities under his supervision. He who had once been an eager scholar, loving learned and polite company, now found his happiness in distributing food, clothing, and homilies to the poor, the sick, and the bereaved. He carried his austerity to a condemnation of nearly all worldly pleasures; he renewed the Puritan campaign against the theater as the "house of the Devil," or at least "the porch of Hell."[41] The English character, and the temper of the times, proved inhospitable to Law's mysticism, and he seemed to be ending his life in a futile obscurity, when John Wesley came to sit at his feet.

IV. JOHN WESLEY: 1703–91

To understand his place in history we must remind ourselves again that when he and his brother Charles founded the Methodist movement at Oxford (1729) religion in England was at lower ebb than at any time in modern history. Not more than five or six members of the House of Commons went to church.[42] The Anglican clergy had so far accepted rationalism as to base nearly all their writings on reasoning. They seldom mentioned heaven or hell, and stressed social virtues rather than otherworldliness. An English sermon, as described by Voltaire, was a "solid but sometimes dry dissertation which a man reads to the people without gesture and without particular exaltation of the voice."[43] Religion was active and fervent only in the Dissenting sects of the middle class. The town workers were almost wholly ignored by the Anglican clergy; "there was a huge contingent, consisting of the lowest class, who were outside the reach of education or of religion, who had no religion, and had never been taught any";[44] they were abandoned to a poverty only dimly lightened by religious hope. It was against this background that John Wesley and George Whitefield effected a powerful revival of Puritan beliefs and ethics, and established the Methodist Church.

Wesley's ancestry was shot through with theology and rebellion. His great-grandfather, Bartholomew Westley, was ejected from his rectories in Dorset because he continued the Dissenting worship after the restoration of the Anglican Church to ecclesiastical monopoly in England. John's grandfather, John Westley, became a minister in Dorset, was imprisoned for refusing to use the Book of Common Prayer, was ejected from his rectory, and became a Dissenting pastor at Poole. John's father, Samuel Wesley, dropped the *t* from his name, worked his way through Oxford, abandoned Dissent, was ordained an Anglican priest, married Susanna Annesley (a preacher's daughter), and became rector of Epworth in Lincolnshire. Of his nineteen children eight died in infancy—illustrating the labors of women, the careless virility of clergymen, and the quality of medicine in eighteenth-century England. The father was a stern disciplinarian at home and in the pulpit; he brought up his children to fear a vengeful God, convicted one of his parishioners of adultery, and compelled her to walk through the street in a garment of repentance.[45] His wife rivaled him in strictness and piety. When her most famous son was twenty-nine she explained to him her philosophy of moral training:

> I insist upon conquering the will of children betimes, because this is the only strong and rational foundation of a religious education, without which both precept and example will be ineffectual. But when this is thoroughly done, then a child is capable of being governed by the reason and piety of its parents, till its own understanding comes to maturity. . . . When turned a year old they [her children] were taught to fear the rod and cry softly; by which means they escaped abundance of correction they might otherwise have had.[46]

The eldest of her sons, Samuel Wesley II, became a poet, a scholar, and an Anglican priest who deprecated the Methodism of his brothers. The eighteenth child was Charles Wesley, who powerfully seconded John's preaching with 6,500 hymns. John himself was the fifteenth, born at Epworth in 1703. When he was six the rectory burned down; he was left for lost amid the flames, but he appeared at a second-story window, and was rescued by a neighbor standing on the shoulders of another; thereafter he called himself "a brand plucked from the burning," and never overcame his vivid fear of hell. In his father's house any unexplained noise was interpreted as a supernatural presence, demonic or divine.

At eleven John was sent to Charterhouse "public" school, and at seventeen to Christ Church, Oxford. He overcame his poor health by resolute walking, riding, and swimming, and lived to be eighty-eight. He read widely, and kept careful notes and abstracts of his reading. He relished, above all other books, Jeremy Taylor's *Holy Living and Holy Dying*, and Thomas à Kempis' *Imitation of Christ*. Even in his college days he began—partly in cipher and shorthand—that *Journal* which is one of the classics of English literature and Protestant piety. In 1726 he was made a fellow of Lincoln College; in 1728 he was ordained an Anglican priest.

It was his brother Charles who first gathered at Oxford a little group of some fifteen students and teachers resolved to practice Christianity with methodical thoroughness. It was their enemies who in derision gave them the names "Holy Club" and "Methodists." They read together the Greek Testament and the classics; they fasted every Wednesday and Friday; they received the Lord's Supper every week; they visited prisoners and invalids to offer them comfort and religious hope; they accompanied condemned men to the scaffold. John Wesley came to the leadership of the group through his greater enthusiasm and devotion. He rose every day at four—a habit which he maintained into extreme old age. He planned methodically, every morning, the tasks allotted to each hour of the day. He lived on twenty-eight pounds a year, and distributed the remainder of his income in charity. He fasted so frequently that at one time he seemed to have ruined his health beyond repair. He made pilgrimages on foot to William Law to solicit his advice; Law's *Serious Call to a Devout and Holy Life* became his spiritual guide; from this book, his *Journal* records, "the light flowed in so mightily upon my soul that everything appeared in a new view.[47]

In 1735 he and Charles were invited by General Oglethorpe to accompany him as missionaries to Georgia. As their father had died, they consulted their mother. "If I had twenty sons," she told them, "I should rejoice if they were all so employed, though I should never see them more";[48] how shall we divested ones understand this devotion? The Holy Club adjourned *sine die*, and on October 14 John and Charles, with two other "Methodists," sailed on the *Simmonds* for Savannah. On board they were impressed by the cheerful piety of some Moravian Brethren who had left Germany to settle in America; when a severe storm buffeted the little vessel the Moravians showed no fear; they rivaled the tempest winds with their sturdy hymns; the Wesleys felt that this was a faith stronger than their own.

Arrived in Georgia (February 5, 1736), the brothers took different posts: Charles became secretary to Governor Oglethorpe, John became pastor to the new community, and occasional missionary to the neighboring Indians. At first he praised these as eager to receive the Gospel, but two years later he described them as "gluttons, thieves, dissemblers, liars, murderers of fathers, murderers of mothers, murderers of their own children"; we are told that he "was not a success with Indians."[49] The white population, which included hundreds of transported criminals, resented his Oxford accent, his masterful spirit, and his insistence on the strictest rules of ritual and discipline. For baptism he required total and triple immersion, and when a parent objected he refused to baptize the child. Still a "High Churchman of a very narrow type,"[50] he repulsed from the Communion table a man of respected life who confessed himself to be a Dissenter; he refused to read the funeral service over a colonist who had not renounced his Dissenting sect; he forbade the ladies of his congregation to wear rich dresses or gold ornaments; and he persuaded the governor to ban fishing and hunting on Sunday—the only day on which his parishioners had time to fish or hunt. He became enamored of Sophia Hopkey, the eighteen-year-old niece of Savannah's chief magistrate, but his Moravian friends disapproved of her. Tired of his hesitation, she married a Mr. Wilkinson. When she presented herself for Communion he refused her the Sacrament on the grounds that she had communicated only three times in the last three months, and had neglected to ask her pastor to announce the banns for her marriage. Her husband brought suit against him for defaming the wife's character; the court condemned Wesley's conduct as a suitor and his severities as a clergyman; he rejected its right to try him; popular feeling against him mounted. He fled to Charleston and embarked for England (December 22, 1737).

In London he renewed his austerities in the hope that they would restore his confidence. But Peter Böhler, a Moravian preacher en route to America, assured him that his faith was still inadequate; that no matter how perfect his morals might be, or how zealous his piety and ritual, he would remain in a state of damnation until, by a divine flash of illumination and conviction quite distinct from any process of reasoning, he should realize that Christ had died for *him*, and had expiated *his* sins; only after such conversion would a man be secure from sinning, and certain of salvation. Wesley commemorated in his *Journal* the *Magna Dies*, or Great Day, May 24, 1738, when this final conversion came to him:

> In the evening I went very unwillingly to a society in Aldersgate Street, where one was reading Luther's preface to the Epistle to the Romans. About a quarter before nine, while he was describing the change which God works in the heart through faith in Christ, I felt my heart strangely warmed. I felt I did trust in Christ, Christ alone,

for salvation; and an assurance was given me that He had taken away *my* sins, even *mine*, and saved me from the law of sin and death. I began to pray with all my might for those who had in a more especial manner despitely used me and persecuted me. I then testified openly to all there what I now first felt in my heart.[51]

In brief, he had recapitulated the evolution of Christianity from salvation by faith and works to salvation by faith alone (Luther) to salvation by a personal and divine illumination (the Quakers). Grateful to Böhler, Wesley crossed over to Germany in the summer of 1738, and spent several weeks in Herrnhut, the Saxon village where a colony of Moravian Brethren had been established on the estates of Count von Zinzendorf.

Meanwhile Charles Wesley, on his return to England, had experienced a similar conversion; in his more gentle way he had begun to preach to the prisoners in Newgate, and from every pulpit to which he was admitted. Still more important, a personality only less powerful than John Wesley was coming to the fore in the Methodist movement. George Whitefield was born to an innkeeper at Gloucester in 1714. For a year and more he served as a drawer of liquor for his father's guests. He worked his way through Pembroke College, Oxford, and was one of the first members of the Holy Club. He followed the Wesleys to Georgia in 1738, but returned to England in the fall of that year to be ordained an Anglican priest. Not satisfied with the opportunities given him in pulpits, and eager to bring the inspiration of his faith to the masses of the people, he began in February, 1739, to preach in the open fields near Bristol to coal miners who had seldom dared or cared to enter a church. His voice was so clear and strong that it could reach twenty thousand hearers, and his fervent oratory so moved these hardened and weary men that he could see (he tells us) "the white gutters made by their tears, which plentifully fell down their black cheeks."[52] The reputation of the new preacher, and the reports of his open-air preaching, stirred the imagination of England. Wherever Whitefield went, immense crowds gathered to hear him.

His preaching was unforgettable. He made no pretense to erudition, but he claimed to have talked intimately with God.[53] His language, said Wesley, inclined to be "luscious and amorous," using some startling images; so he spoke of Christ being "roasted, as it were, in the Father's wrath, and therefore fitly styled the Lamb of God."[54] Whitefield in the fields, like Pitt in Parliament, brought the arts of acting to his speech; he could weep at a moment's notice and apparently with sincere emotion; and he could make his simple auditors feel with immediate intensity the sense of sin, the terror of hell, and the love of Christ. Orators like Bolingbroke and Chesterfield, skeptics like Franklin and Hume, actors like Garrick, admitted his power. Welcomed everywhere, he made England, Wales, Scotland, Ireland, and

America his parish. Thirteen times he crossed the Atlantic, twelve times he traversed Scotland. It was not unusual for him to preach forty hours in a week. By the age of fifty he was worn out. Too late he reduced his program to "strict allowance"—that is, he preached only once each weekday, and only three times on Sunday. In 1769 he made his seventh visit to the colonies, and he died at Newburyport, Massachusetts, in the following year.

John Wesley, returning from Herrnhut, could not quite approve of Whitefield's hortatory style, and hesitated to follow his example of preaching under the sky. "Having been all my life (till very lately) so tenacious of every point relating to decency and order, . . . I should have thought the saving of souls almost a sin if it had not been done in a church."[55] He overcame his distaste, and took his message to the fields and streets; "I submitted to be more vile [common] in the highway" (April, 1739). His oratory was less passionate than Whitefield's, his language was that of a scholar and a gentleman, but he too spoke to the emotions of his audiences. He made the daily lives of simple folk seem to be part of a vast and noble drama in which their souls were the battleground of Satan and Christ; they moved with him into a world of portents and miracles; and they heard in him—as he claimed to be—the voice of God. And whereas Whitefield preached and then passed on, Wesley organized his followers into "little societies" in one town after another, and guided them to permanence. Their meetings recalled the agapes of the early Christians—feasts of religious joy and communal love; they confessed their sins to one another, submitted to scrutiny of their moral life, and joined in prayer and pious song. John had already composed or translated some stirring hymns, and Charles had begun his voluminous hymnology. In 1740 Charles wrote the most famous of his many beautiful hymns—"Jesus, Lover of My Soul."

In these fervent groups John Wesley trained lay preachers who carried on the new gospel when the leaders could not remain. Without ordination, without any fixed parishes, with or without a pulpit, these "helpers" spread over England, Scotland, and Wales, brought the fears and hopes of the Protestant theology to the working classes, and prepared for the revivalist visits of Wesley and Whitefield. Wesley himself traveled—on horseback, in coaches, or on foot—to the remotest corners of England, often sixty miles in a day, averaging four thousand miles a year for forty years. He preached at every opportunity: in jails to prisoners, in coaches to fellow passengers, in inns to wayfarers, on vessels crossing to Ireland or from port to port. At Epworth, being refused use of the pulpit which his father had held, he preached in the churchyard, standing on his father's tomb.

What did he preach? Essentially the Puritan creed that had seemed mortally stricken by the moral riot of the Stuart Restoration. He rejected (Whitefield accepted) predestination; following the Arminian wing of the

Established Church, he insisted that man had enough freedom of will to decide his own choice or refusal of divine grace. He repudiated all appeals to reason; religion, he felt, went beyond the reach of man-made logic, and depended upon divine inspiration and inward conviction; but he turned away from mysticism on the ground that it left everything to God and did not spur men to active goodness. He shared most of the superstitions of his class and time: he believed in ghosts, in the diabolical origin of strange noises, in the reality and criminality of witchcraft; to give up belief in witchcraft, he argued, is to give up belief in the Bible. He had no doubt about miracles; he thought they were happening every day among his followers. A headache, a painful tumor, a violent rupture, a broken leg were cured by his prayers or those of the Methodist societies; and he told of a Catholic girl who lost her sight whenever she read the Catholic Mass-book, but always recovered it when she read the New Testament. He accepted the accounts of women who claimed to have seen angels, Christ, heaven, or hell; and he recorded in his *Journal* a number of cases where adversaries of Methodism had been struck down by miraculous punishments.[56]

His preaching was so vivid that many individuals in his audiences were moved to hysteria and convulsions. The *Journal* tells of sinners who, hearing him, were overcome with physical pain and rolled in agony on the ground, while other believers knelt beside them and prayed for their deliverance from Satanic possession.[57] Wesley describes a meeting at Baldwin Street, London, in 1739:

> My voice could scarce be heard amidst the groanings of some and the cries of others. . . . A Quaker who stood by was not a little displeased . . . when he himself dropped down as if thunderstruck. The agony he was in was even terrible to behold. We besought God not to lay folly to his charge, and he soon lifted up his head and cried aloud: "Now I know that thou art a prophet of the Lord."[58]

An eyewitness quoted by Wesley describes a Methodist meeting at Everton in 1759:

> Some were shrieking, some roaring aloud. . . . The most general was a loud breathing, like that of people half strangled and gasping for life; and indeed almost all the cries were like those of human creatures dying in bitter anguish. Great numbers wept without any noise; others fell down as dead. . . . I stood upon the pew seat, as did a young man in the opposite pew, an able-bodied, fresh, healthy countryman; but in a moment, when he seemed to think of nothing else, down he dropt with a violence inconceivable. . . . I heard the stamping of his feet ready to break the boards, as he lay in strong convulsions at the bottom of the pew. . . . Almost all on whom God laid his hand

turned either very red or almost black. . . . A stranger, well-dressed, who stood facing me, fell backward to the wall, then forward on his knees, wringing his hands and roaring like a bull. . . . He rose and ran against the wall till Mr. Keeling and another held him. He screamed out, "Oh, what shall I do. What shall I do? Oh, for one drop of the blood of Christ!" As he spoke God set his soul at liberty; he knew his sins were blotted out, and the rapture he was in seemed too great for human nature to bear.[59]

Probably these hysterical outbreaks were caused by conditions affecting the victims before the Methodist meeting, and the hellfire sermon merely capped a climax beyond control. Wesley interpreted such seizures as Satanic possessions followed by divine cures. Sometimes, he thought, they brought no permanent good in conduct or character, but often, he felt, they cleansed the soul of sin, and inaugurated a new life.

The greatest success of Methodism was among the poor. The preachers themselves were men of modest learning, simple in their sentiments and speech; there was no barrier of class or culture between them and their audience. They brought their message of sin and repentance to peasants, miners, and criminals; and though they preached a faith that was based on fear rather than love, they gave to the letterless an ethical code that shared in the moral rehabilitation of England in the second half of the eighteenth century. It was the Puritan ethic against which our own time has moved into an extreme reaction. Wesley was hostile to almost all amusement. He allowed cardplaying, but thought it a sin to go to fairs, to wear jewelry or fine clothes, to attend a theater or to dance. In the school that he founded at Kingswood no time was allotted for play, for "he that plays when he is a child will play when he is a man."[60] But that Puritan ethic comported with the English character; it could be borne by strong men and patient women; and it gave to the working classes of England a proud sense of election and destiny that upheld them in poverty and made them hostile to any revolution that questioned Christianity. Conservatives later felt grateful to Wesley that he had saved the British poor from deism and free thought, and had turned their aspirations from social revolt to individual salvation, from an earthly utopia to a posthumous Paradise.[61]

Wesley himself inclined to conservatism in politics. He was ahead of his class in advocating some long-due reforms: he denounced the "rotten borough" system, the inequalities of representation in Parliament, the corrosive corruption of English politics, the inhumanity of slavery, the horrors of British jails. But he accepted the class structure of society as natural and just; he opposed any relaxation of the laws against Catholics, and in the revolt of the American colonies his sympathies were all with George III.

He remained an Anglican by creed, but he rejected the Anglican view that only a bishop in the Apostolic Succession could validly ordain a priest; he himself ordained ministers for Scotland and America. When he said "The world is my parish"[62] he proposed to preach wherever he wished, without episcopal permission or allocation; to that extent he seceded from the Established Church. But he exhorted his followers to attend Anglican services, to shun Dissenting assemblies and creeds, and to refrain from antagonizing the Anglican clergy. At first some Anglican pulpits were opened to Methodist ministers; but when Wesley's lay preachers assumed the right to administer the Sacrament, and Methodist doctrine reverted to the medieval emphasis on hell and the Puritan preoccupation with sin, the Anglican divines withdrew their support, as Erasmus had withdrawn from Luther; they preferred an orderly development, and excluded the Methodists from Anglican pulpits.

Persecution of the new sect came far less from the Established Church than from the simple commoners who could not tolerate new ways of preaching old ideas. In town after town the open-air preachers—like their later counterparts preaching a new social gospel—were assaulted by mobs happy to be cruel without fear and without reproach. At Monmouth a lay preacher was struck on the head by a rock, and died of the blow. At Wednesbury a crowd wrecked the homes of Methodists, abused their women, beat their men. When Wesley appeared it cried out for his blood, and applauded those who cudgeled him; he prayed aloud, and it let him go. At Bolton the house where he was preaching was invaded by an angry assemblage; amid a shower of stones, tiles, and eggs he continued his sermon to the end. At Devizes a water engine was turned upon the residence of Charles Wesley, and bulldogs were loosed upon his followers. At Exeter Whitefield was stoned almost to death. At Hoxton an ox was prodded into a Methodist congregation; at Pensford a bull, maddened by baiting, was driven full against the table at which John Wesley was preaching. The courage of the preachers appealed to the British character, and gained them tolerance and support.

Wesley was a little man five feet three inches tall, weighing 128 pounds. He was impressive in old age by his white hair, but already in middle age he arrested attention by his ascetic chiseled features and dominating eyes. He took it for granted that he was made to govern; his nervous energy and intellectual force put him naturally in the lead; his unquestioning self-confidence sometimes carried him to an arrogance that a Methodist bishop pronounced quite "overbearing."[63] He was not an easy man to get along with, for he thought and moved too fast for others to keep his pace. He married in 1751, having fallen in love, as we all do, with the nurse who tended him in illness. For two years his wife traveled with him on his hectic rounds; then her health and nerves broke down and she left him, as one might leap from an unmanageable steed. He attributed his health and vitality to his perpetual journeys on horseback or foot; perhaps we should add that oratory is an aerating exercise. In 1735 he became a vegetarian; a year later he and a friend decided to live on bread alone, to "try whether life might not as well be sustained by one sort as by variety of food. We . . . were never more vigorous and healthy than when we tasted nothing else";[64] but they soon relapsed into diversity.

What were the results of the Methodist preaching? In one generation religion, which had seemed to be dying under Anglican dignity and deist doubts, became a vibrant element in English life, subordinate only to politics and war. At Wesley's death (1791) his followers numbered 79,000 in England, 40,000 in North America; in 1957 there were 2,250,000 Methodists in Great Britain, 12,000,000 in the United States, 40,000,000 in the world.[65] Outside of its own membership it influenced other denominations; so, in the Anglican Church that rejected Methodism, Methodist ideals aroused the Evangelical movement in the later half of the eighteenth century, and may have entered into the Oxford movement of the nineteenth. Politically the results were a conservative resignation among the working classes till 1848. Morally Methodism improved personal conduct and family life among the poor, shared in reducing electoral and official corruption, shamed many of the master class out of frivolity and vice, and prepared the English revulsion against the trade in slaves. Culturally the movement was negative; it gave the people sacred songs, but it continued the Puritan hostility to art. From an intellectual point of view it was a step backward; it based its creed on fear, its ritual on emotion, and condemned reason as a snare. In the great conflict between faith and reason it placed all its hopes on faith; it put no trust in the progress of knowledge and science; it ignored or scorned the Enlightenment that was setting France on fire. It felt that the sole purpose and meaning of life were to escape everlasting damnation, and that the one thing needed for this end was faith in the redeeming death of Christ.

In January, 1790, aged eighty-six, Wesley wrote in his *Journal:* "I am now an old man, decayed from head to foot. My eyes are dim, my right hand shakes much, my mouth is hot and dry every morning, I have a lingering fever almost every day. . . . However, blessed be God, I do not slack my labor. I can preach and write still."[66] Two months later he began a speaking tour that lasted five months and took him through England and Scotland. A year later he died (March 2, 1791). If we judge greatness by influence he was, barring Pitt, the greatest Englishman of his times.

V. OF BEES AND MEN

Two minor figures stop us on our way to David Hume.

Bernard Mandeville was a London physician of French ancestry and Dutch birth, who published in 1705 a sixpenny ten-page pamphlet in rollicking verse, *The Grumbling Hive*. Its theme was a paradox: that the prosperity of the hive is due to the vices of the individual bees—to their selfish greed, reproductive ecstasy, and collective pugnacity. Applying the paradox to the human hive, the impish doctor held that the wealth and strength of the state depend not upon the virtues of its citizens but upon those vices which grumbling moralists foolishly condemn. For let us imagine what would happen if all acquisitiveness, vanity, dishonesty, and pugnacity were suddenly to end—if men and women ate only so much food as they required, wore only so much clothing as would suffice to protect them against the elements, never cheated or injured one another, never quarreled, always paid their debts, scorned luxuries, and were faithful to their mates. At once the whole society would come to a standstill: the lawyers would starve, the judges would be left without cases or bribes, doctors would waste away for lack of patients, winegrowers would go bankrupt, taverns would fail for lack of tipplers, millions of artisans producing fancy foods, ornaments, raiment, or houses would be thrown out of work, no one would want to be a soldier; soon the society would be conquered and enslaved.

The doggerel form of *The Grumbling Hive* debarred it from influence. Piqued, the vain, acquisitive, pugnacious doctor reissued it in 1714, and again in 1723, as *The Fable of the Bees*, repeatedly enlarged with prefaces, notes, and commentaries that expanded ten pages into two volumes. This time England and France listened, for these appendages constituted one of the most biting analyses of human nature ever written.

Mandeville took the third Earl of Shaftesbury as literally his *pièce de résistance*, for the Earl had interpreted human nature with optimistic eloquence, and had assumed in man an innate "sense of right and wrong . . . as natural to us as natural affection, and being a first principle in our constitution."[67] Pretty nonsense, answered Mandeville; human nature, before education and moral training, makes no distinction between virtue and vice, but is governed solely by self-interest. He agreed with the theologians that man is by nature "evil" [lawless]; but instead of threatening men with hell, he complimented them on the clever adaptation of individual vice to social good. So private prostitution protects public chastity;[68] the greed for products and services stimulates invention, supports manufactures and trade; great fortunes make possible philanthropy and massive art. While the theologians preached austerity Mandeville defended luxury, and argued that the desire for luxuries (i.e., anything but the bare necessities of life) is the root of industry and civilization; remove all luxury, and we would be savages again. While the moralists were supposed to condemn war, it was by the ability to wage war, said Mandeville, that a nation survived, for most states were beasts of prey.

He saw no morality in nature. Good and bad are words applicable to social or antisocial actions in man; but Nature herself pays no heed to our words or homilies; she defines virtue as any quality that makes for survival; and in our prejudiced terms the world of nature is a scene of voracity, lust, cruelty, slaughter, and meaningless waste. Yet out of that awful struggle, Mandeville thought, man had evolved language, social organization, and moral codes as instruments of social cohesion and collective survival. Praise and blame are not warranted by nature, but they are justified as means by which, appealing to man's vanity, fear, and pride, we may encourage in others forms of action advantageous to ourselves or the group.

Nearly everybody who heard of Mandeville berated him as a cynical materialist. Voltaire, however, agreed with him on the beneficence of luxuries, and the *laissez-faire* physiocrats of France applauded his view that if human greed is let alone it will make the wheels of industry hum. The whimsical doctor would probably have admitted that his paradox "Private vices are public goods" was largely a play upon words too loosely defined. "Vices" like acquisitiveness, amorousness, pugnacity, and pride were once "virtues" in the primitive struggle for existence; they became vices only when carried in society beyond social good; they became public benefits through being controlled by education, public opinion, religion, and law.

How different from this scandalous doctor was Francis Hutcheson! Born in Ireland of a Presbyterian minister, he diverged from the paternal groove and opened a private academy in Dublin. There, conscious of his obligation to turn young savages into citizens, he wrote an *Inquiry concerning Moral Good and Evil* (1725), in which he defined a good citizen as one that promoted the general good; and (anticipating verbatim utilitarian Bentham's formula) he described the general good as "the greatest happiness of the greatest number."[69] Promoted to the chair of moral philosophy in the University of Glasgow, he troubled the Presbytery by defending the right of private judgment, the legitimacy of pleasure, and "the ingenious arts of music, sculpture, painting, and even the manly diversions."[70] He did not share Mandeville's pessimistic conception of human nature. He admitted the faults and sins of men, their wild passions and violent crimes; "but the greatest part of their lives is employed in offices of natural affection, friendship, innocent self-love, or love of country." And he added a wholesome caution to historians:

Men are apt to let their imaginations run out upon all the robberies, piracies, murders, perjuries, frauds, massacres, assassinations they have ever either heard of, or read in history; thence concluding all mankind to be very wicked; as if a court of justice were the proper place for making an estimate of the morals of mankind, or an hospital of the healthfulness of a climate. Ought they not to consider that the number of honest citizens and farmers far surpasses that of all sorts of criminals in any state; . . . that it is the rarity of crimes, in comparision of innocent or good actions, which engages our attention to them, and makes them to be recorded in history; while incomparably more honest, generous domestic actions are overlooked, only because they are so common; as one great danger, or one month's sickness, shall become a frequently repeated story, during a long life of health and safety.[71]

Here was a healthy mind!

VI. DAVID HUME: 1711–76

1. The Young Philosopher

Hutcheson was a modest part of the "Scottish Enlightenment"; Hume was its greatest luminary. In his simple eight-page autobiography he tells us that he was born at Edinburgh April 26, 1711, "of a good family, both by father and mother; my father's family is a branch of the Earl of Home's or Hume's.* . . . My mother was daughter of Sir David Falconer, President of the College of Justice." The father died in 1712, leaving the estate to David's elder brother, John Home, and to David an income of eighty pounds a year—enough for survival on an abstemious regimen. The family, all Presbyterian, gave the boy a strong infusion of Calvinist theology, which remained as determinism in David's philosophy. Every Sunday morning he attended a church service three hours long, including two hours of preaching; every Sunday afternoon he returned to the kirk for an hour; to which were added morning prayers at home.[72] If David had any character in him he was bound to react into heresy.

At the age of twelve he entered the University of Edinburgh. After three years he left without a degree, resolved to give himself completely to literature and philosophy. At sixteen he wrote to a friend reproaching himself because

my peace of mind is not sufficiently confirmed by philosophy to withstand the blows of fortune. This greatness and elevation of soul

---

* A descendant of that earl was in 1964 prime minister of Great Britain. "Home" was and is pronounced "Hume."

is to be found only in study and contemplation. . . . You must allow
[me] to talk thus like a philosoper; 'tis a subject I think much on, and
could talk all day long of.[73]

Soon his religious faith faded away:

I found a certain boldness of temper growing on me, which was
not inclined to submit to any authority in these subjects [philosophy
and literature] . . . When I was about eighteen years of age there
seemed to be opened up a new scene of thought, which transported
me beyond measure, and made me, with an ardor natural to young
men, throw up every other pleasure or business to apply entirely to
it.[74]

He said later that "he never had entertained any belief in religion since he
began to read Locke and Clarke."[75] By the time he was seventeen he had
already planned a treatise on philosophy.

His relatives urged upon him that philosophy and eighty pounds a year
would give him but a meager existence; he must reconcile himself to making
money. Could he not study law? He tried for three painful years
(1726–29). His health broke down, and almost his spirit too; for a time he
lost his interest in ideas. "The law appeared nauseous to me";[76] he abandoned it, and returned to philosophy, with perhaps one deviation. Toward
the end of February, 1734, he left Edinburgh for London "to make a very
feeble trial for entering into a more active scene of life."[77] On March 5
Agnes Galbraith appeared before the Reverend George Home (David's
uncle), and confessed that she was with child. Brought before a session of
the kirk, she declared "that Mr. David Home . . . is the father." Doubting
her veracity, the session remitted her to the next meeting of the local
Presbytery; before this, on June 25, she repeated the accusation. According
to the minutes of the Presbytery of Chirnside,

the moderator . . . exhorted her to be ingenuous and confess if any
other person was guilty with her. . . . The Presbytery having considered the affair, and being informed that the said David Home was
gone out of the Kingdom, they remitted her to the Session of Chyrn-
side, to make satisfaction to the rules of the Church.[78]

This required that she should appear in sackcloth before the kirk, and be
exposed in the pillory on three Sundays. In 1739 Agnes was again convicted
of fornication.

After a stop in London Hume proceeded to Bristol, and took a position
in a merchant's office. "In a few months I found that scene totally unsuit-
able to me." He crossed over to France, where he could live more cheaply

than in England. For a while he stayed at Reims; then he moved to La Flèche (some 150 miles southwest of Paris), for the Jesuit college there had an extensive library. The canny Scot entered into cordial relations with the priests, and was allowed to use their books. One of the fathers described him in later perspective as "too full of himself; . . . his spirit more lively than solid, his imagination more luminous than profound, his heart too dissipated with material objects and spiritual self-idolatry to pierce into the sacred recesses of divine truths."[79]

In the shade of the Jesuits Hume composed the first two books of his skeptical masterpiece, *A Treatise of Human Nature*. In September, 1737, he returned to England bursting with manuscript. He had trouble with publishers, for in December he wrote to Henry Home: "I am at present castrating my work, that is, cutting out its noble parts, . . . endeavoring it shall give as little offense as possible."[80] The chief excisions were "reasonings concerning miracles"; these were stored away for use in safer days. The remainder, guaranteed to be unintelligible to antedeluvians, was published anonymously in two volumes in January, 1739, by John Noon of London. Hume sold the volumes outright for fifty pounds and twelve copies—not so bad a bargain for a book on logic and theory of knowledge by an unknown youth of twenty-seven. However, it was one of the peaks of modern philosophy.

2. Reason Deflated

The introductory "Advertisement" revealed Hume's confidence in his powers: he proposed to study human nature in understanding and passions, and, in a third volume forthcoming, in morals and politics. He proceeded to analyze "impression" (sensation), perception, memory, imagination, thought, reason, and belief. This investigation of how we come to *know* is fundamental, for the validity of science, philosophy, religion, and history depends upon the nature, origin, and reliability of knowledge. It is a difficult discipline, for it deals with abstract ideas rather than with concrete objects; and thought is the last thing that thought seeks to understand.

Hume begins by accepting as a starting point the empiricism of Locke: all ideas are ultimately derived from experience through impressions. These are external sensations like light, sound, heat, pressure, odors, taste, or internal sensations like stupor, hunger, pleasure, pain. A perception is a sensation interpreted; "noise" is a sensation, but "a knock at the door" is a perception. (Hume is not always precise or consistent in his use of these terms.) A man born blind or deaf has no *idea* of light or sound, because he has had no sensation of either. The ideas of space and time are derived from experience: the first is "the idea of visible or tangible points distributed in a certain order"; the second is the perception of sequence in our impressions.[81] Ideas differ from impressions only in the lesser "force and liveliness with which they strike upon the mind."[82] Belief "is nothing but a more vivid and intense conception of any idea; . . . it is something *felt* by the mind, which distinguishes the ideas of the judgment from the fictions of the imagination."[83]

In these definitions Hume seems to think of "the mind" as a real entity or agent experiencing, possessing, remembering, or judging impressions or ideas. As he proceeds, however, he denies the existence of any mind additional to the mental states—to the impression, perception, idea, feeling, or desire occupying consciousness at the moment.

> That which we call a *mind* is nothing but a heap or collection of different perceptions, united together by different relations, and supposed, though falsely, to be endowed with a perfect simplicity and identity. . . . For my part, when I enter most intimately into what I call *myself*, I always stumble on some particular perception or other, of heat or cold, light or shade, love or hatred, pain or pleasure. I never can catch *myself* at any time without a perception, and can never observe anything but the perception. When my perceptions are removed for any time, as by sound sleep, so long am I insensible of *myself*, and may truly be said not to exist. And were all my perceptions removed by death, and could I neither think, nor feel, nor see, nor love, nor hate, after the dissolution of my body, I should be entirely annihilated; nor do I conceive what is further requisite to make me a perfect nonentity. . . . Aside from some metaphysicians . . . I may venture to affirm of the rest of mankind that they are nothing but a bundle or collection of different perceptions, which succeed each other with inconceivable rapidity, and are in perpetual flux. . . . The successive perceptions . . . constitute the mind.[84]

So, at one blow from this brash youth, three philosophies fell: materialism, for (as Berkeley had shown) we never perceive "matter," and know nothing but our mental world of ideas and feelings; and spiritualism, for we never perceive a "spirit" additional to our particular and passing feelings and ideas; and immortality, for there is no "mind" to survive the transitory mental states. Berkeley had demolished materialism by reducing matter to mind; Hume compounded the destruction by reducing mind to ideas. Neither "matter" nor "mind" exists. Forgivably the wits of the time dismissed both philosophers with "No matter; never mind."

Freedom of will, in this dissolving view, is impossible: there is no mind to choose between ideas or responses; the succession of mental states is determined by the order of impressions, the association of ideas, and the alternation of desires; "will" is merely an idea flowing into action. Personal identity is the feeling of continuity when one mental state recalls previous mental states and relates them through the idea of cause.

But cause too is only an idea; we cannot show it to be an objective reality. When we perceive that A (e.g., flame) is regularly followed by B (heat), we conclude that A has caused B; but all that we have observed is a sequence of events, not a causal operation; we cannot know that B will always follow A. "All our reasonings concerning cause and effect are derived from nothing but custom."[85] The "laws of nature" that we talk of are merely sequences customary in our experience; they are not invariable and necessary connections in events; there is no guarantee that they will hold tomorrow. Science, therefore, is an accumulation of probabilities subject to change without notice. Metaphysics, if it pretends to be a system of truths about ultimate reality, is impossible, for we can know neither the "causes" behind sequences nor the "matter" behind sensations nor the "mind" allegedly behind the ideas. And so far as we base our belief in God on a chain of causes and effects supposedly leading back to a "Prime Mover Unmoved," we must abandon that Aristotelian sophistry. All things flow, and certainty is a dream.

After spreading devastation about him with the invincible Excalibur of his intellect, Hume pauses for a moment of modesty. "When I reflect on the natural fallibility of my judgment, I have less confidence in my opinions than when I consider the objects concerning which I reason."[86] He knows as well as we do that certainty is not necessary for life, nor for religion, nor even for science; that a high degree of probability suffices for crossing a street or building a cathedral, or saving our souls. In an appendix he admits that there might be, after all, a self behind ideas, a reality behind sensations, a causal connection behind persistent sequences. Theoretically he stands his ground: "I have not yet been so fortunate as to discover any very considerable mistakes in the reasonings delivered in the preceding volumes."[87] But in practice, he amiably confesses, he abandons his skepticism as soon as he drops his pen.

> Should it be asked me whether I sincerely assent to this argument which I have been to such pains to inculcate, and whether I be really one of those skeptics who hold that all is uncertain, . . . I should reply . . . that neither I nor any other person was ever sincerely and constantly of that opinion.[88] . . . I dine, I play backgammon, I converse and am merry with my friends; and when, after three or four hours' amusement, I would return to these speculations, they appear so cold and strained and ridiculous that I cannot find in my heart to enter into them any further.[89] . . . Thus the skeptic still continues to reason and believe, though he asserts that he cannot defend his rea-

son by reason; and by the same rule he must assent to the principle concerning the existence of body, though he cannot pretend, by any arguments of philosophy, to maintain its veracity."[90]

In the end Hume turns his back upon argument as a guide to life, and trusts to animal faith, to the belief, based upon custom, that reality is rational, permeated with causality. And by asserting that "belief is more properly an act of the sensitive than of the cognitive part of our natures,"[91] Hume, twenty-seven, holds out his hand to Jean Jacques Rousseau, twenty-six, in youth and theory, as he was destined to do later in friendship and tragedy. The cleverest reasoner in the Age of Reason not only impeached the causal principle of reason, he opened a door to the Romantic reaction that would depose reason and make feeling its god.

The second "book" and volume of the *Treatise* continues the dethronement of reason. Hume rejects the attempts of philosophers to build an ethic upon the control of passion by reason. By "passion" Hume means emotional desire. "In order to show the fallacy of all this philosophy, I shall endeavor to prove, first, that reason alone can never be a motive for any action of the will; and secondly, that it can never oppose passion in the direction [against the force] of the will."[92] "Nothing can oppose or retard the impulse of passion but a contrary impulse" (an echo of Spinoza?). To still further *épater les bourgeois*, Hume adds: "Reason is, and ought to be, the slave of the passions [the illuminating and co-ordinating instrument of desires], and can never pretend to any other office than to serve and obey them."[93]

He proceeds to a subtle analysis of the "passions"—chiefly love, hate, compassion, anger, ambition, envy, and pride. "The relation which produces most commonly the passion of pride is that of property."[94] All passions are based upon pleasure and pain; and ultimately our moral distinctions have the same secret source. "We tend to give the name of virtue to any quality in others that gives us pleasure by making for our advantage, and to give the name of vice to any human quality that gives us pain."[95] Even the concepts of beauty and ugliness are derived from pleasure and pain.

If we consider all the hypotheses which have been formed . . . to explain the difference betwixt beauty and deformity, we shall find that all of them resolve into this, that beauty is such an order and construction of parts as, either by the primary constitution of our nature [as in the beauty of the human body], by custom [as in admiring slenderness in women], or by caprice [as in the idealizing delusions of impeded desire], is fitted to give pleasure and satisfaction to the soul. . . . Pleasure and pain, therefore, are not only necessary attendants of beauty and deformity, but constitute their very essence.

. . . Beauty is nothing but a form which produces pleasure, as deformity is a structure of parts which conveys pain.[96]

Love between the sexes is compounded of this sense of beauty, plus "the bodily appetite for generation and a generous kindness and good will."[97]

In March, 1739, Hume returned to Edinburgh. He eagerly searched the journals for reviews of his two volumes, and suffered the consequences. "Never literary attempt was more unfortunate than my *Treatise of Human Nature*. It fell dead-born from the press, without reaching such distinction as even to excite a murmur among the zealots."[98] But when he wrote this in old age he had forgotten, perhaps through oblivescence of the disagreeable, that several reviews appeared within a year after the publication of his book. Nearly all of them complained that it was hard to understand, and that the author allowed his youth to show by frequent references to himself and to the epochal novelty of his ideas. "What is most offensive," said a typical censor, "is the confidence with which he delivers his paradoxes. Never has there been a Pyrrhonian more dogmatic. . . . The Lockes and Clarkes are often, in his eyes, but paltry and superficial reasoners in comparison with himself."[99]

Saddened but resolute, Hume prepared for the press the third volume of his *Treatise*, containing Book III, "Of Morals." It appeared on November 5, 1740. Its analysis of morality displeased the rationalists as much as the theologians. The rules of morality are not supernatural revelations, but neither are they the conclusions of reason, for "reason," Hume repeats, "has no influence on our passions or actions."[100] Our moral sense comes not from Heaven but from sympathy—fellow feeling with our fellow men; and this feeling is part of the social instinct by which, fearing isolation, we seek association with others. "Man's very first state and situation may justly be esteemed social"; a "state of nature" in which men lived without social organization "is to be regarded as a mere fiction";[101] society is as old as man. Being members of a group, men soon learned to commend actions advantageous—and to condemn actions injurious—to the community. Furthermore, the principle of sympathy inclined them to receive or imitate the opinions that they heard around them; in this way they acquired their standards and habits of praise and blame, and consciously or not they applied these judgments to their own conduct; this, and not the voice of God (as Rousseau and Kant were to imagine) is the origin of conscience. This law of sympathy, of communal attraction, is, says Hume, as universal and illuminating in the moral world as the law of gravitation in the material cosmos. "Thus, upon the whole," he concluded, "I am hopeful that nothing is wanting to an accurate proof of this system of ethics."[102]

Volume III attracted even less attention than Volumes I and II. As late as 1756 the remnants of the eleven hundred copies that constituted the first edition of the *Treatise* were still cluttering the publisher's shelves. Hume did not live to see a second edition.

3. Morals and Miracles

It was clear that he could not subsist by his pen. In 1744 he made an unsuccessful attempt to secure a professorship in the University of Edinburgh. Doubtless with some humiliation he accepted (April, 1745) a position as tutor to the young Marquis of Annandale at a fee of £300 a year. The Marquis went insane; Hume found that he was expected to be the keeper of a lunatic; there were quarrels; he was dismissed (April, 1746), and had to sue for his salary. For a year (1746-47) he served as secretary to General James St. Clair; the salary was good, the food was good, and in July, 1747, Hume returned to Edinburgh owning and weighing many more pounds than when he left. In 1748 the General re-engaged him, as secretary and aide-de-camp, on a mission to Turin; now David encased himself in a flaming scarlet uniform. James Caulfield (future Earl of Charlemont), then a student in Turin, was impressed by Hume's intellect and character, but dismayed by his flesh.

> The powers of physiognomy were baffled by his countenance . . .
> to discover the smallest trace of the faculties of his mind in the un-
> meaning features of his visage. His face was broad and fat, his mouth
> wide, and without any other expression than that of imbecility. . . .
> The corpulence of his whole person was far better fitted to communi-
> cate the idea of a turtle-eating alderman than that of a refined phi-
> losopher.[103]

The same Caulfield claims to have seen Hume (aged thirty-seven) on his knees before a married countess (aged twenty-four), professing his devotion and suffering the pangs of despised love; the lady dismissed his passion as "a natural operation of your system." According to the same reporter Hume fell into a fever and tried to kill himself, but was prevented by the servants. Another Scot relates that in his illness Hume "received Extreme Unction" from a Catholic priest. Hume, we are told, excused both gallantry and unction on the ground that "the organization of my brain was impaired, and I was as mad as any man in Bedlam."[104] In December, 1748, he retired to London and philosophy, having now raised his fortune to a thousand pounds.

Resolved to get another hearing for the ideas of the *Treatise*, he published in 1748 *An Enquiry concerning the Human Understanding*, and in 1751 *An Enquiry concerning the Principles of Morals*. In an "Advertisement" prefixed to a posthumous edition (1777) of these *Enquiries* he disclaimed the *Treatise* as a "juvenile work," and asked that "the following pieces may alone be regarded as containing his philosophical sentiments and principles."[105] Students of Hume have in general found more meat in the earlier than the later works; these cover the same ground in perhaps a less belligerent and incisive style, but they reach the same conclusions.

After repeating his skeptical analysis of reason, Hume offered, as Section X of the first *Enquiry*, that essay "Of Miracles" which the publisher had refused to print in the *Treatise*. He began with his usual self-assurance: "I flatter myself that I have discovered an argument . . . which, if just, will, with the wise and learned, be an everlasting check to all kinds of superstitious delusion, and consequently will be useful as long as the world endures." And then he let loose his most famous paragraphs:

> No testimony is sufficient to establish a miracle, unless the testimony be of such a kind that its falsehood would be more miraculous than the fact which it endeavors to establish. . . . When anyone tells me that he saw a dead man restored to life, I immediately consider with myself whether it be more probable that this person should either deceive or be deceived, or that the fact which he relates should really have happened. I weigh the one miracle against the other; and according to the superiority which I discover I . . . reject the greater miracle. There is not to be found in all history any miracle attested by a sufficient number of men, of such unquestioned good sense, education, and learning, as to secure us against all delusion in themselves; of such undoubted integrity as to place them beyond all suspicions of any design to deceive others; of such credit and reputation in the eyes of mankind as to have a great deal to lose in case of their being detected in any falsehood; and at the same time attesting facts performed in such a public manner, and in so celebrated a part of the world, as to render the detection unavoidable: all which circumstances are requisite to give us a full assurance in the testimony of men. . . .
>
> The maxim by which we commonly conduct ourselves in our reasonings is that the objects of which we have no experience resemble those of which we have; that what we have found to be most usual is always most probable; and that where there is an opposition of arguments, we ought to give the preference to such as are founded on the greatest number of past observations. . . . It forms a strong presumption against all supernatural and miraculous relations, that they are observed chiefly to abound among ignorant and barbarous nations. . . . It is strange . . . that such prodigious events never happen in our days. But it is nothing strange . . . that men should lie in all ages.[106]

Hume went on to allege other obstacles to Christian belief: the calm neutrality of nature as between man and his rivals on the earth; the prolific variety of evils in life and history; the apparent responsibility of God for Adam's sin, and for all sins, in a world where by Christian hypothesis nothing can happen without God's consent. To avoid the charge of atheism, Hume put into the mouth of "a friend who loves skeptical paradoxes," and whose principles "I can by no means approve," a defense of Epicurus' fancy that the gods exist, but pay no attention to mankind. The friend wonders why there cannot be an agreement between religion and philosophy not to molest each other, as he supposes there was in Hellenistic civilization:

> After the first alarm was over, which arose from the new paradoxes and principles of the philosophers, these teachers seem ever after, during the ages of antiquity, to have lived in great harmony with the established superstition, and to have made a fair partition of mankind between them: the former claiming all the learned and wise, the latter possessing all the vulgar and illiterate.[107]

What a way to offer a truce!

In 1749 Hume returned to Scotland to live with his brother and sister on their estate at Ninewells. Two years later John Home took a wife, and David moved to Edinburgh. Now he sent to the press the *Enquiry concerning the Principles of Morals* which he hoped would replace the third volume of the *Treatise*. He reaffirmed the derivation of the moral sense from sympathy or social feelings; he rejected the Socratic identification of virtue with intelligence, and emphatically repudiated La Rochefoucauld's notion that "altruistic" actions are egoistically motivated by the hope of pleasure from the social esteem they are expected to earn. The pleasure that we feel in such actions, said Hume, is not their cause but their accompaniment and result; the actions themselves are the operation of our social instincts.[108]

But the most noticeable feature of this second *Enquiry* is its elaboration of a utilitarian ethic. Twenty-three years after Hutcheson, thirty-eight years before Bentham, Hume defined virtue as "every quality of the mind which is useful or agreeable to the person himself or to others."[109] On this basis he justified the healthy pleasures of life as useful to the individual, and the double standard of morality as useful to society.

> The long and helpless infancy of men requires the combination of parents for the subsistence of their young; and that combination requires the virtue of chastity or fidelity to the marriage bed. . . . An infidelity of this nature is much more pernicious in women than in men. Hence the laws of chastity are much stricter over the one sex than over the other.[110]

Of this *Enquiry concerning the Principles of Morals* the fond author wrote: "In my own opinion (who ought not to judge on that subject), it is, of all my writings, . . . incomparably the best." He added: "It came unnoticed and unobserved into the world."[111]

4. Darwinism and Christianity

In 1751 he composed *Dialogues concerning Natural Religion*. Of all the productions of his Mephistophelean mood this is the most devastating and irreverent. Three persons converse: Demea, who defends orthodoxy, Cleanthes the deist, and Philo, who is transparently Hume. Demea argues that unless we posit some Supreme Intelligence behind phenomena, the world becomes unbearably unintelligible; but he admits that his God is quite incomprehensible to human reason.[112] Cleanthes reproaches Demea for trying to explain one unintelligibility with another; he prefers to prove God's existence by the evidences of design in nature. Philo laughs at both arguments. Reason, he claims, can never explain the world or prove God. "What peculiar privilege has this little agitation of the brain called thought, that we must make it the model of the whole universe?"[113] As for design, the adaptation of organs to purposes may have resulted not from divine guidance but from nature's slow and bungling experiments through thousands of years.[114] (Here is "natural selection" 1,800 years after Lucretius, 108 years before Darwin.) And even if we admit supernatural design, the imperfection of the adaptations and the myriad sufferings in the human and animal world reveal at best a god of limited powers and intelligence, or one quite indifferent to mankind. "Ultimately the life of a man is of no greater importance to the universe than the life of an oyster."[115]

> One would imagine that this grand production has not received the last hand of the maker, so little finished is every part, and so coarse are the strokes with which it is executed. Thus the winds . . . assist men in navigation; but how oft, rising up to tempests and hurricanes, do they become pernicious! Rains are necessary to nourish all the plants and animals of the earth; but how often are they defective! how often excessive! . . . There is nothing so advantageous in the universe but what frequently becomes pernicious by its excess or defeat; nor has nature guarded with the requisite accuracy against all disorders or confusion.[116]

Worse yet, there is not only disorder amid the order (if you view the world as designed), there is, amid the abounding life, an always futile struggle against death.

A perpetual war is kindled amongst all living creatures. Necessity, hunger, want, stimulate the strong and courageous; fear, anxiety, terror agitate the weak and infirm. The first entrance into life gives anguish to the newborn infant and to its wretched parent; weakness, impotence, distress attend every stage of that life, and it is at last finished in agony and horror. . . . Observe, too, . . . the curious artifices of nature, in order to embitter the life of every living being. . . . Consider that innumerable race of insects, which either are bred on the body of each animal, or flying about, infix their stings in him. . . . Every animal is surrounded with enemies, which incessantly seek his misery and destruction. . . . Man is the greatest enemy of man. Oppression, injustice, contempt, contumely, violence, sedition, war, calumny, treachery, fraud; by these they mutually torment each other.[117] . . .

Look around this universe. What an immense profusion of beings, animated and organized, sensible and active! You admire this prodigious variety and fecundity. But inspect a little more narrowly these living existences. . . . How hostile and destructive to each other! . . . The whole presents nothing but the idea of a blind nature, impregnated by a great vivifying principle, and pouring forth from her lap, without discernment or parental care, her maimed and abortive children.[118]

The conflicting evidences of good and evil in the world suggest to Philo a duality or multiplicity of competing gods, some of them "good," some "bad," and perhaps of diverse sex. He maliciously suggests that the world

was only the first rude essay of some infant deity, who afterwards abandoned it, ashamed of his lame performance; . . . or it is the production of old age and dotage in some superannuated deity, and, ever since his death, has run on at adventure, from the first impulse and active force which it received from him.[119]

As like as not the world, as the Brahmins asserted, "arose from an infinite spider, who spun this whole complicated mass from his bowels. . . . Why may not an orderly system be spun from the belly as well as the brain?"[120] So creation would be generation. Or conceivably "the world is an animal and the deity is the soul of the world, actuating it and actuated by it."[121] After all this badinage Philo comes back to design, and admits that "the cause or causes of order in the universe probably bear some analogy to human intelligence."[122] And he apologizes for his scandalous cosmologies:

I must confess that I am less cautious on the subject of natural religion than on any other. . . . You in particular, Cleanthes, with whom

I live in unreserved intimacy, you are sensible that notwithstanding
the freedom of my conversation, and my love of singular arguments,
no one has a deeper sense of religion impressed upon his mind, or pays
more profound adoration to the divine Being, as he discovers himself to
reason in the inexplicable contrivance and artifice of nature. A purpose,
an intention, or design strikes everywhere the most careless, the most
stupid thinker; and no man can be so hardened in absurd systems as at
all times to reject it.[123]

Despite this peace offering, Hume's friends pleaded with him not to publish the *Dialogues*. He yielded, and locked the manuscript in his desk; it did
not see print till 1779, three years after his death. But his fascination with
religion lured him back to the subject, and in 1757 he published *Four Dissertations*, of which one attempted a "Natural History of Religion." At his
publisher's insistence he withdrew two other essays, which were printed
when he was beyond fear and reproach: one on immortality, the other a
justification of suicide when a person has become a burden to his fellow
men.

The *Natural History* combines Hume's old interest in religion with his
new interest in history. He has passed beyond attacking old beliefs to in-
quiring how mankind came to adopt them. But he is not inclined to patient
research, even among the scanty materials then available on social origins;
he prefers to approach the problem by psychological analysis and deductive
reasoning. The mind of primitive man interpreted all causation on the analogy of his own volition and action: behind the works and forms of nature
—rivers, oceans, mountains, storms, pestilences, prodigies, etc.—he imagined
acts of will by hidden persons of supernatural power; hence polytheism
was the first form of religious belief. Since many forces or events were
harmful to man, fear had a large share in his myths and rituals; he personified and sought to propitiate these evil forces or demons. Perhaps (Hume
slyly suggests) Calvin's God was a demon, cruel, malicious, arbitrary, and
difficult to appease.[124] Since the good gods were conceived as like human
beings except in power and permanence, they were supposed to give aid
and comfort in return for gifts and flattery; hence the rituals of offerings,
sacrifices, adoration, and solicitous prayer. As social organization increased
in size and reach, and local rulers submitted to greater kings, the world of
divinities underwent a like transformation; an order of hierarchy and obedience was ascribed in imagination to the gods; monotheism grew out of polytheism, and while the populace still knelt to local deities or saints, cultured
men worshiped Zeus, Jupiter, God.

Unfortunately religion became more intolerant as it became more unified.
Polytheism had allowed many varieties of religious belief; monotheism demanded uniformity. Persecution spread, and the cry for orthodoxy became

"the most furious and implacable of all human passions."[125] Philosophy, which among the ancients had been left relatively free as the religion of the elite, was compelled to become the servant and apologist of the faith of the masses. In these monotheistic creeds—Judaism, Christianity, Mohammedanism—merit and "salvation" were more and more divorced from virtue and attached to ritual observance and unquestioning belief. In consequence educated persons became either martyrs or hypocrites; and as they rarely chose martyrdom, the life of man was tarnished with lip service and insincerity.

In less combative moods Hume condoned a measure of hypocrisy. When he was consulted as to whether a young clergyman who had lost his faith should remain in the Church and accept its preferments, David answered, Remain.

> Civil employments for men of letters can scarcely be found. . . . It is putting too great a respect on the vulgar and their superstition to pique oneself on sincerity with regard to them. Did ever one make it a point of honor to speak the truth to children or madmen? . . . The ecclesiastical profession only adds a little more to our innocent dissimulation, or rather simulation, without which it is impossible to pass through the world.[126]

5. Communism and Democracy

Tiring at last of debate on issues that on his own view were determined by feeling rather than by reason, Hume in his later years turned more and more to politics and history. In 1752 he published *Political Discourses*. He was surprised by its favorable reception. Britain was glad to forget the destructiveness of his theology in the conservatism of his politics.

He had some sympathy with aspirations toward a communistic equality:

> It must indeed be confessed that nature is so liberal to mankind that, were all her presents equally divided among the species, and improved by art and industry, every individual would enjoy all the necessaries, and even most of the comforts, of life. . . . It must also be confessed that wherever we depart from this equality we rob the poor of more satisfaction than we add to the rich, and that the slight gratification of a frivolous vanity in one individual frequently costs more than bread to many families and even provinces.

But he felt that human nature makes an egalitarian utopia impossible.

> Historians, and even common sense, may inform us that however precious these ideas of *perfect* equality may seem, they are really at bottom *impracticable*; and were they not so, would be extremely

pernicious to human society. Render possessions ever so equal, men's different degrees of art, care, and industry will immediately break that equality. Or if you check these virtues . . . the most rigorous inquisition is requisite to watch every inequality on its first appearance, and the most severe jurisdiction to punish and redress it. . . . So much authority must soon degenerate into tyranny.[127]

Democracy, like communism, received Hume's sympathetic rejection. It is, he thought, "a principle . . . noble in itself, . . . but belied by all experience, that the people are the origin of all just government."[128] He dismissed as childish the theory (soon to be revived by Rousseau) that government had originated in a "social contract" among the people or between people and ruler:

Almost all the governments which exist at present, or of which there remains any record in history, have been founded originally either on usurpation or conquest or both, without any pretense of a fair consent or voluntary subjection of the people. . . . It is probable that the first ascendant of man over multitudes began in a state of war. . . . The long continuance of that state, . . . common among savage tribes, inured the people to submission.[129]

In this way monarchy became the almost universal, the most lasting, and therefore presumably the most practical, form of government. "An hereditary prince, a nobility without vassals, a people voting by their representatives, form the best monarchy, aristocracy, and democracy."[130]

Besides disposing in advance of Rousseau, Hume used his lucid Addisonian style to discard in advance Montesquieu's theory of climate as a determinant of national character. In *Essays, Moral and Political*, whose second edition appeared almost simultaneously (1748) with *The Spirit of Laws*, Hume wrote: "As to physical causes I am inclined to doubt of their operation in this particular; nor do I think that men owe anything of their temper or genius to the air, food, or climate."[131] National character follows national boundaries rather than climatic zones; it is determined principally by laws, government, the structure of society, the occupations of the people, and the imitation of neighbors or superiors.

Under these local varieties human nature is basically the same in all times and climes; the same motives and instincts, made necessary by the demands of survival, produce in all ages and places essentially the same actions and results.

Ambition, avarice, self-love, vanity, friendship, generosity, public spirit: these passions, mixed in various degrees, and distributed through society, have been from the beginning of the world, and still are, the source of all the action and enterprises which have been observed among mankind. Would you know the sentiments, inclinations, and course of life of the Greeks and Romans? Study well the temper and actions of the French and English; you cannot be much mistaken in transferring to the former *most* of the observations which you have made with regard to the latter. Mankind are so much the same in all times and places that history informs us of nothing new or strange in this particular. Its chief use is only to discover the constant and universal principles of human nature, by showing men in all varieties of circumstances and situations, and furnishes us with materials from which we may form our observations and become acquainted with the regular springs of human action and behavior. These records of wars, intrigues, factions, and revolutions are so many collections of experiments, by which the political or moral philosopher fixes the principles of his science.[132]

In the *Political Discourses*, and in *Essays and Treatises on Various Subjects* (1753) Hume made substantial contributions to economic thought. He rejected the view of the French physiocrats that all taxes fall ultimately upon land; they fall at last, he believed, upon labor, for (here he echoes Locke) "everything in the world is purchased by labor."[133] Even before the Industrial Revolution had taken form he foresaw that the workers would "heighten their wages" by combination. He condemned the financing of governmental expenditures and enterprises by high taxes and frequent bond issues, and predicted that such fiscal measures would bring "free governments" to "the same state of servitude with all the nations that surround us."[134] Money is not wealth; to mint more of it than is needed for the convenience of commerce is to raise prices and hamper foreign trade. The false mercantile theory that still led European states to stress exports, block imports, and accumulate gold would deprive Europe of the international benefits derivable from the ability of each nation, through soil and climate and special skills, to produce specific goods at minimal cost and of optimal quality. He dared to pray,

> not only as a man but as a British subject, . . . for the flourishing commerce of Germany, Spain, Italy, and even France itself. I am at least certain that Great Britain and all those nations would flourish more did their sovereigns and ministers adopt such enlarged and benevolent sentiments towards each other. . . . The increase of riches and commerce in any one nation, instead of hurting, commonly promotes the riches and commerce of all its neighbors.[135]

These ideas, perhaps influenced by the *laissez-faire* physiocrats, influenced in their turn Hume's friend Adam Smith, played a part in developing a

British policy of free trade, and are finding fulfillment in Western Europe today.

6. History

In 1752, after a campaign of the orthodox party against him as an insolent infidel, Hume was elected keeper of the library of the Faculty of Advocates in Edinburgh. Despite the modest salary of forty pounds a year, the appointment meant much to him, for it made him master of thirty thousand volumes. It was through access to this library that he was able to write his *History of England.* In 1748 he had confessed to a friend: "I have long had an intention, in my riper years, of composing some history."[136] He called history "the great mistress of wisdom";[137] he hoped to discover in it the causes of the rise and fall of nations; besides,

> to see all the human race pass as it were in review before us, appearing in their true colors, without any of those disguises which, during their lifetime, so much perplexed the judgment of beholders—what spectacle can be imagined so magnificent, so various, so interesting? What amusement, either of the senses or of the imagination, can be compared with it?[138]

It is one of the glories of the eighteenth century that it produced within a generation three of the world's greatest historians: Voltaire, Hume, and Gibbon, all grounded in philosophy, seeking to reinterpret history in nontheological terms, and in the broadest perspective of the knowledge accumulated by their time. Gibbon never tired of praising Hume and acknowledging his influence; he valued Hume's praise of the initial volume of *The Decline and Fall of the Roman Empire* (1776) above any other commendation. Did Hume in turn owe much to Voltaire? He had reached and formulated his own philosophy as debtor to the English deists rather than to the French skeptics; the *Treatise of Human Nature* antedated all the major works of Voltaire, Diderot, and Montesquieu. But Hume's *History of England* (1754–62) may have owed something to Voltaire's *Age of Louis XIV* (1751), even to the *Essai sur les moeurs*, parts of which were printed in 1745 and 1755. All three of these historians agreed in exposing superstition, rejecting supernatural explanations, and identifying progress with the development of knowledge, manners, and arts.

Hume wrote his *History* backward. Its first volume (1754) covered the reigns of James I and Charles I—the years 1603–49; the second (1756) ran from 1649 to 1688; the third and fourth (1759), from 1485 to 1603; the fifth and sixth (1761), from the invasion of England by Julius Caesar to the accession of Henry VII in 1485.

The furor of criticism that fell upon the first volume surprised him. He believed that the domination of England by the Whigs since their importation of William III in 1688, and their fear of the Jacobite revolts of 1715 and 1745, had discolored English historiography with anti-Stuart passion; and he supposed that he was free from contrary predilections. "I thought that I was the only historian that had at once neglected present power, interest, and authority, and the cry of popular prejudice."[139] He forgot that he was a Scot, that Scotland was still secretly mourning her Bonnie Prince Charlie, and that the Scots, probably including Hume, had never forgiven England for killing the half-Scot Charles I and bringing in first a Dutchman and then a German to rule England, Scotland, and Wales. So, while admitting that Charles had overstretched the royal prerogative and deserved to be dethroned, he pictured Parliament as likewise overreaching its privilege and equally guilty of the Civil War. He admitted the right of the nation to depose a bad king, but he wished that no one had ever pushed that right to extremes; he feared the "fury and injustice of the people," and felt that the execution of the "mild and benign" Charles had dangerously loosened popular habits of respect for government. He scorned the Puritans as "sanctified hypocrites," who "polluted" their language with "mysterious jargon" and "interlaced their iniquities with prayers."[140] He dismissed the Commonwealth as a period of murderous piety, military tyranny, and social disorder, cured only by the Stuart Restoration. Voltaire, reviewing the *History*, thought Hume quite impartial:

> Mr. Hume . . . is neither pro-Parliament nor royalist, neither Anglican nor Presbyterian; he is simply judicial. . . . The fury of parties has for a long time deprived England of a good historian as well as of a good government. What a Tory wrote was disowned by the Whigs, who in their turn were given the lie by the Tories. . . . But in the new historian we find a mind superior to his materials; he speaks of weaknesses, blunders, cruelties as a physician speaks of epidemic diseases.[141]

British critics did not agree with Voltaire. They did not complain that Hume had seldom consulted original sources, but (he recalled) he

> was assailed by one cry of reproach, disapprobation, and even detestation: English, Scotch, and Irish, Whig and Tory, churchman and sectary, freethinker and religionist, patriot and courtier, united in their rage against the man who had presumed to shed a generous tear for the fate of Charles I and the Earl of Strafford; and after the first ebullitions of their fury were over, what was still more mortifying, the book seemed to sink into oblivion. Mr. Millar told me that in a twelvemonth he sold only forty-five copies of it.[142]

He was so discouraged that for a time he thought of moving, as in his youth, to some provincial town in France, where he could live under an assumed name. However, France and England were at war, and Volume II was nearly finished; he resolved to persevere. His prejudice grew from being opposed; in revising Volume I he made "above a hundred alterations," but, he tells us with all the puckish delight of a mountainous imp, "I have made all of them invariably to the Tory side."[143] Nevertheless the succeeding volumes had a good sale; the Tories now hailed him as their stout defender, and some Whigs admitted the charm of a style simple, clear, incisive, and direct, sometimes anticipating Gibbon's judicial dignity. The account of the dramatic conflict between Henry II and Thomas à Becket rivals Gibbon's narrative of the capture of Constantinople by the Turks. The cumulative impression made by the six volumes raised Hume's fame to its peak. In 1762 Boswell rated him as "the greatest writer in Britain"[144]— but Boswell was a Scot. In 1764 Voltaire modestly pronounced the book "perhaps the best history ever written in any language."[145] Gibbon and Macaulay have thrown it into the shade, and Macaulay has balanced its prejudice. We are not advised to read Hume's *History of England* today; its record of the facts has long since been improved upon; but one reader, who began it as a task, found it an illumination and a delight.

7. *The Old Philosopher*

In 1755 a movement was begun by some Scottish divines to indict Hume before the General Assembly of the Kirk on a charge of infidelity. Meanwhile the "Scottish Enlightenment" had generated a liberal movement among the young ministers, and they were able to prevent any open condemnation of the philosopher-historian; but ecclesiastical attacks upon him continued, stinging him again into meditating flight. His opportunity came when (1763) the Earl of Hertford invited him as deputy secretary on an embassy to France, and secured for him a pension of £200 a year for life.

He had long since admired French intellect, had been influenced by the earlier writers of the French *Illumination*, and had corresponded with Montesquieu and Voltaire. His works had received far more praise in France than in England. The Comtesse de Boufflers fell in love with him through print, wrote ingratiatingly to him, came to London to see him; he escaped her. But when he reached Paris she took him in tow, made him the lion of her salon, and struggled to arouse a manly passion in his breast; she found him too stabilized for amours. He was feted in one gathering after another; "no feast is complete without him," said Mme. d'Épinay. The aristocracy opened its arms to him; great ladies—even the ailing Pompadour—

fluttered about him. "I am convinced," he wrote, "that Louis XIV never, in any three weeks of his life, suffered so much flattery." He met Turgot, d'Alembert, d'Holbach, and Diderot; and Voltaire, from his distant throne at Ferney, called him "my St. David." The Earl of Hertford was astonished to find that his secretary was far more sought after and bowed to than himself. Horace Walpole resented all this, and some of the *philosophes*, growing jealous, made fun of Hume's corpulence. At one party, when Hume entered, d'Alembert, quoting the Fourth Gospel, remarked, "*Et verbum caro factum est*" (And the word was made flesh); whereupon a lady admirer is reported to have retorted, with incredible wit, "*Et verbum carum factum est*" (And the word was made lovable).[146] No wonder Hume, harassed in Edinburgh, unpopular in London, wrote: "There is a real satisfaction in living at Paris, from the great number of sensible, knowing, and polite company with which that city abounds."[147]

In November, 1765, a new British ambassador came, and Hume's appointment ended. He returned to Edinburgh, but in 1767 he accepted the post of undersecretary at the Foreign Office in London. It was in this period that he brought Rousseau into England, and had famous trouble with him there; this story must wait. In August, 1769, aged fifty-eight, he retired finally to Edinburgh, being now "very opulent (for I possessed a revenue of £1,000 a year), healthy, and though somewhat stricken in years, with the prospect of enjoying long my ease, and of seeing the increase of my reputation."[148]

His home on St. David Street became a salon, with Adam Smith, William Robertson, and other Scottish celebrities gathering about him as their acknowledged sovereign. They liked him not only for his mind. They saw that despite his iconoclastic reasoning he was amiable in discourse, cheerful of mood, moderate in controversy, tolerant of contrary views, not letting diversity of ideas abate the cordiality of his friendships. He seems (like Montaigne and Voltaire) to have valued friendship above love; "friendship is the chief joy of human life."[149] Yet he was popular with women, perhaps because he had no wife. He was a favorite guest in many homes; if his corpulence ruined the chairs,[150] his wit atoned for his weight. He suggested a tax on obesity, but expected that some "divines might pretend that the Church was in danger"; he blessed the memory of Julius Caesar for having preferred fat men. "Upon the whole," said Adam Smith, "I have always considered him . . . as approaching as nearly to the idea of a perfectly wise and virtuous man as perhaps the nature of human frailty will admit."[151]

If one must seek flaws in so amiable a character, or blind spots in so brilliant a mind, the hardest to forgive are the references to the "hideous hypothesis" of the "atheist" Spinoza,[152] which must have aimed at protective discoloration. Hume's psychology was the most penetrating of his time, but it did not quite account for the sense of personal identity; one mental state does not merely recall another, it may recall it as *mine*. The replacement of "cause" with "regular sequence" has required only a change of phrase; "regular sequence" is enough for science and philosophy; and the *History of England* still seeks to explain events by causes.[153] A skepticism that confessedly is abandoned in actual life must be wrong in theory, for practice is the final test of theory. And it is strange that while reducing cause to custom, and morality to sympathetic feeling, Hume gave so little weight to custom and feeling in his interpretation of religion, and showed such lack of sympathy for the persistent functions of religion in history. He was quite insensitive to the consolations of faith, the comfort it brought to souls shivering in the immensity of mystery, or the loneliness of grief, or the harsh fatality of defeat. The success of Wesley was history's answer to Hume.

Despite these cavils, we acknowledge again the cutting edge of Hume's catalytic mind. He was in himself the Enlightenment for the British Isles; there, except in political vision, he was essentially all that a dozen *philosophes* were for France. While feeling French influence deeply, he came to the ideas of the Enlightenment, and struck some of its most telling blows, before the *philosophes*—even before Voltaire—had bared their fangs against *l'infâme;* they owed as much to him as he to them. "I salute you," wrote Diderot, "I love you, I revere you."[154] In England he ended deism by challenging the capacity of reason to defend even the simplest fundamentals of religious faith; he carried the war not merely to the walls but to the citadel of the ancient creed. Gibbon was the offspring of Hume in philosophy, and his transcending disciple in history. In Germany the *Enquiry concerning the Human Understanding* woke Kant from his "dogmatic slumber" by apparently undermining all science, metaphysics, and theology through questioning the objectivity of cause. After reading the manuscript of Hamann's translation of the *Dialogues concerning Natural Religion*, Kant incorporated in the final preparation of his *Critique of Pure Reason* (1781) Hume's criticisms of the argument from design, and accounted them unanswerable.[155]

"May it be my fate, for my own sake and for that of all my friends," Hume wrote, "to stop short at the threshold of old age, and not to enter too far into that dismal region."[156] Fate took him at his word. Says his autobiography:

> In the spring of 1775 I was struck with a disorder in my bowels, which at first gave me no alarm, but has since, as I apprehend it, become

mortal and incurable. I now reckon upon a speedy dissolution. I have suffered very little pain from my disorder; and what is more strange, have, notwithstanding the great decline of my person, never suffered a moment's abatement of my spirits; insomuch that were I to name the period of my life which I should most choose to pass over again, I might be tempted to point to this later period. I possess the same ardor as ever in my study, and the same gaiety in company. I consider, besides, that a man of sixty-five, by dying, cuts off only a few years of infirmities.[157]

Diarrhea, the favorite vengeance of the gods upon the human great, conspired with internal hemorrhages to reduce him seventy pounds in that one year 1775. To the Comtesse de Boufflers he wrote: "I see death approaching gradually, without anxiety or regret. I salute you, with great affection and regard, for the last time."[158] He went to take the waters at Bath, but they proved useless against chronic ulcerated colitis. His mind remained calm and clear.

He returned to Edinburgh July 4, 1776, prepared to die "as fast as my enemies, if I have any, could wish, and as easily and cheerfully as my best friends could desire."[159] When he read, in Lucan's *Dialogues of the Dead*, the various excuses that the dying gave to Charon for not promptly boarding his boat to cross the Styx into eternity, he remarked that he could not find any excuse fit to his own case, except perhaps to plead: "Have a little patience, good Charon. . . . I have been endeavoring to open the eyes of the public. If I live a few years longer, I may have the satisfaction of seeing the downfall of some of the prevailing systems of superstition." But Charon answered: "You loitering rogue, that will not happen these many hundred years. Do you fancy that I will grant you a lease for so long a term? Get into the boat this instant!"[160]

Boswell, importunate and impertinent, insisted on putting the dying man to the question—did he not now believe in another life? Hume replied, "It is a most unreasonable fancy that we should exist forever." But, persisted Boswell, surely the thought of a future state is pleasing? "Not at all," answered Hume; "it is a very gloomy thought." Women came and begged him to believe; he diverted them with humor.[161]

He died quietly, "free from much pain" (said his doctor), on August 25, 1776. Despite a heavy rain a large crowd attended his burial. A voice was heard to remark, "He was an atheist." Another answered, "No matter, he was an honest man."[162]

CHAPTER V

Literature and the Stage

1714–56

I. THE REALM OF INK

ENGLAND was throbbing if not with literature at least with print. Not only had population grown, especially in the towns and above all in London, but literacy had spread as a necessity of commerce and industry and city life. The burgeoning bourgeoisie took to books as a distinction and a relief; women took to books and thereby gave audience and motives to Richardson and the novel. The reading public was further expanded by circulating libraries, of which the first on record was set up in 1740; soon there were twenty-two in London alone. The collective middle class began to replace the individual aristocrat as the patron of literature; so Johnson could flout Chesterfield. Government subsidies no longer—as formerly with Addison, Swift, and Defoe—commanded superior pens through political plums.

The bitter conflicts of Whigs and Tories, of Hanoverians and Jacobites, and the increasing involvement of England in Continental and colonial affairs whetted the appetite for news, and made the newspaper a force in British history. In 1714 there were eleven newspapers regularly published in London, most of them weekly; in 1733 there were seventeen, in 1776 fifty-three. Many of them were subsidized by political factions; for as demos raised its voice moneyed minorities bought newspapers to dictate its thoughts. Nearly all newspapers contained advertisements. *The Daily Advertiser*, founded in 1730, was at first given over entirely to advertisements; but soon, like our morning Leviathans, it added a fillip of news to bolster its circulation and raise its advertising fees. Some historic magazines were born in this period: *The Craftsman* (1726), Bolingbroke's scourge of Walpole; *The Grub Street Journal* (1730–37), the sharp tongue of Pope; *The Gentleman's Magazine* (1731), which gave Johnson a berth; and *The Edinburgh Review* (1755), which died only temporarily in 1756. Many English newspapers and journals are still alive after two hundred years of publication.

All these periodicals—daily, weekly, or monthly—gave the press a power that added something to the perils and vitality of British life. Robert Walpole, while forbidding the publication of parliamentary debates, allowed

journalists to attack him with all the virulence of eighteenth-century literature. Montesquieu, coming from censored France, marveled at the liberty
with which Grub Street pelted Downing Street with poisoned ink.[1] A
member of Parliament complained to the Commons in 1738 that

> the people of Great Britain are governed by a power that never was
> heard of, as a supreme authority, in any age or country before. This
> power, Sir, does not consist in the absolute will of the prince, in the
> direction of Parliament, in the strength of an army, in the influence of
> the clergy; it is the government of the press. The stuff which our weekly
> newspapers are filled with is received with greater reverence than Acts
> of Parliament; and the sentiments of these scribblers have more weight
> with the multitude than the opinion of the best politicians in the
> Kingdom.[2]

Printers worked with new fury to meet the widened demand. In London
there were 150, in all England three hundred; two of them in this age, William Caslon and John Baskerville, left their names on fonts of type. Printing, publishing, and bookselling were still in most cases united in the same
firm. One living firm, Longmans, was born in 1724. The word *publisher*
usually denoted the author; the man who brought out the book was the
bookseller. Some booksellers, like Johnson's father, carried their wares to
the fairs, or peddled them from town to town, opening a stall on market
days. Their charge for a bound volume varied from two to five shillings;
but a shilling in 1750 was worth approximately $1.25. Parliament had
passed a copyright act in 1710, which secured to an author or his assigns
the property rights to his book for fourteen years, with an extension to
twenty-eight years if he survived the first period. This law, however, protected him only in the United Kingdom; printers in Ireland and Holland
could publish piratical editions and (till 1739) sell them in England in competition with the bookseller who had paid for the book.

Under these conditions of risk the booksellers drove hard bargains with
authors. Usually the writer sold his copyright for a flat sum; if the volume
went unexpectedly well, the bookseller might give the author an added
sum, but this was not obligatory. For a book by a known author the fee
ranged from one hundred to two hundred pounds; Hume received the exceptionally high price of five hundred pounds per volume for his *History
of England*. An author might take subscriptions for his work, as Pope did
for his translation of the *Iliad;* usually in such cases the subscriber paid half
the purchase price in advance and the other half on delivery, and the author
paid the printer.

The great majority of authors lived in a galling poverty. Simon Ockley,
after working for a decade on his *History of the Saracens* (1708–57), had

to complete it in a debtors' prison; Richard Savage used to tramp the streets at night for lack of a lodging; Johnson was poor for thirty years before he became the sovereign of English letters. Grub (now Milton) Street was the historic habitat of "poetry and poverty" (Johnson's phrase), where hack writers—journalists, translators, compilers, proofreaders, magazine contributors, editors—sometimes slept three in a bed and dressed in a blanket for want of other clothes. This poverty was due not so much to the tightness of booksellers and the indifference of Walpole as to the unprecedented glutting of the literary market by mediocre talents underselling one another. The predominance of failures over successes in the "word business" shared with the divorce of literature from aristocratic patronage in debasing the social status of authors. At the same time when in France poets, philosophers, and historians were being welcomed into the fanciest homes and bosoms, in England—with two or three exceptions—they were excluded from "polite society" as unwashed bohemians. Perhaps that was why Congreve begged Voltaire not to class him as a writer. Alexander Pope challenged the prejudices of his time by claiming to be both a poet and a gentleman. By the latter word he meant a man of "gentle birth," not a man of gentle ways. On the contrary!

II. ALEXANDER POPE: 1688–1744

Johnson, who despised biographies that begin with a pedigree and end with a funeral, began his remarkable biography of Pope by telling us that "Alexander Pope was born in London May 22, 1688, of parents whose rank or status was never ascertained."[3] The father was a linen merchant who made a modest fortune and then retired to Binfield, near Windsor Forest. Both parents were Roman Catholics, and the year of Pope's birth was also the year when the dethronement of James II dashed the hopes of Catholics for the abatement of the anti-Catholic laws. The mother was especially gentle to the boy, who was her only child. He inherited from her a tendency to headaches, and from his father such curvature of the spine that he never grew beyond four and a half feet in height.

His early education was entrusted to Catholic priests, who made him proficient in Latin, and less so in Greek; other tutors taught him French and Italian. As his religion closed the universities and the professions to him, he continued his studies at home; and as his crooked figure and frail health handicapped him for active enterprise, his parents indulged his fondness for writing poetry. He tells us that

> As yet a child, nor yet a fool to fame,
> I lisp'd in numbers, for the numbers came.[4]

At twelve he had a glimpse of Dryden pontificating in Will's Coffeehouse; the sight stirred in him a wild desire for literary glory. At sixteen he composed some *Pastorals* which circulated in manuscript and won intoxicating praise; they were accepted for publication in 1709. Then, in 1711, in all the ripe wisdom of his twenty-three years, he astonished the wits of London with an *Essay on Criticism* in which—even while warning authors,

> A little learning is a dangerous thing;
> Drink deep, or taste not the Pierian spring[5]

of the Muses—he laid down with magisterial finality the rules of literary art. Here Horace's *Ars poetica* and Boileau's *Art poétique* were digested into 744 lines of good sense marvelously, often monosyllabically, phrased—

> What oft was thought, but ne'er so well expressed.[6]

The youth had a flair for epigram, for compressing reams of wisdom in a line, and rounding each idea with a rhyme. He took his versification from Dryden, but his theory from Boileau. Having leisure to file his verse, he readily accepted the classic counsel to perfect the form, to make the goblet more precious than its wine. Though still professing the Catholic faith, he adopted Boileau's doctrine that literature should be reason aptly dressed. Nature yes, but nature tamed by man; feeling yes, but chastened by intelligence. And what better guide could there be to such controlled and chiseled art than the practice of the ancient poets and orators, their resolution to be rational, and to make each part of every work an orderly element integrated into a harmonious whole? Here was the classic tradition, coming down through Italy and France, through Petrarch and Corneille, and now conquering England through Alexander Pope, as it seemed to Voltaire to have conquered Shakespeare through Addison's *Cato*, and as classic architecture, coming down through Palladio and Serlio, through Perrault and Wren, had overlaid or overridden Gothic fantasies and exaltation with sober pediments and calm colonnades. So was formed the young poet's concept of the classic mind functioning in an ideal critic:

> But where's the man, who counsel can bestow,
> Still pleased to teach, and yet not proud to know?
> Unbias'd or by favor or by spite;
> Not dully prepossessed, nor blindly right;
> Though learn'd, well-bred, and though well-bred, sincere;
> Modestly bold and humanly severe;
> Who to a friend his faults can freely show,
> And gladly praise the merits of a foe?

> Blest with a taste exact yet unconfined,
> A knowledge both of books and human kind;
> Gen'rous converse; a soul exempt from pride;
> And love to praise, with reason on his side?[7]

There were a few such critics ready to hail such verse and measured virtue from a lad of twenty-three; so Addison, who must have felt himself here described, offered the poet, in No. 253 of *The Spectator*, a precious acclaim soon to be forgotten in wordy wars. Another poet, John Dennis, author of the play *Appius and Virginia*, thought himself abused in Pope's uncautious lines,

> But Appius reddens at each word you speak,
> And stares, tremendous, with a threatening eye,
> Like some fierce tyrant in old tapestry,[8]

and countered with *Reflections, Critical and Satirical* (1711). He picked real flaws in Pope's thought and diction, and served them up in peppered sauce. He described Pope as an ugly hypocrite shaped like Cupid's bow or a hunchbacked toad, and congratulated him on not having been born in classic Greece, which would have exposed him at birth for his deformity.[9] Pope licked his wounds and bided his time.

He followed up his success by publishing *The Rape of the Lock* (1712). It was a frank imitation of Boileau's *Le Lutrin* (1674), but by general consent it excelled its original. Lord Robert Petre had expressed his enthusiasm for Mrs. Arabella Fermor by cutting off, and running off with, a lock of her lovely hair. A coolness ensued between raper and rapee. A Mr. Caryll suggested to Pope that Arabella's resentment might soften if the poet would tell the story in humorous verse and present the poem to her. It was so done and it so transpired; Mrs. Fermor forgave the lord, and consented to the publication of the poem. But then Pope, against the advice of Addison, enlarged and cluttered the lay with mock-heroic machinery of participating sylphs, salamanders, nymphs, and gnomes. This "light militia of the lower sky" fell in with the fancies of the time, and the amended *Rape* proved a success with everyone but Dennis. George Berkeley paused in his campaign against matter to compliment the author on the flexibility of his Muse. All the felicity of Pope's versification, and his inexhaustible mint of imagery and phrase make the poem sparkle like the gems in "Belinda's" hair. He describes with feminine learning the cosmetics with which a fairy arms the heroine for the wars of love, and he lists with sarcastic equivalents the vital issues of her day:

> Whether the nymph [Belinda-Arabella] shall break Diana's
>   law [of virginity],

> Or some frail china-jar receive a flaw;
> Or stain her honor, or her new brocade;
> Forget her prayers, or miss a masquerade;
> Or lose her heart, or necklace, at a ball . . .[10]

Belinda joins the gossip and gambling of titled company at Hampton Court, where

> At every word a reputation dies;[11]

and the poet marshals his artistry to recount a game of cards. Then, as Belinda bends to drink, the lusty baron snips her curl and steals away (this iambic flux is catching). Furious, she pursues and finds him, and throws a charge of snuff into his face;

> Sudden, with starting tears each eye o'erflows,
> And the high dome re-echoes to his nose.[12]

Meanwhile the gnomes, or sylphs, or salamanders themselves rape the lock and draw it, trailing clouds of glory, to the skies, where it becomes a comet outcoruscating Berenice's hair.

All this delighted the lords and ladies, the clubs and coffeehouses, of London; Pope found himself hailed as the cleverest poet in England; and all other poets became his foes. He added nothing to his fame with wearisome verses describing Windsor Forest (1713); nor did the Whigs, victorious in 1714, forget that in that poem he revealed his Catholic sympathies for the fallen dynasty.[13] But he recaptured his audience in 1717 by carving into couplets the fabled letters of Héloïse and Abélard. "Eloïsa," self-immured in a nunnery, bids the emasculated "Abelard" flaunt the laws of Church and state and come to her arms:

> Come, if thou dar'st, all charming as thou art!
> Oppose thyself to Heaven, dispute my heart;
> Come, with one glance of those deluding eyes
> Blot out each bright idea of the skies; . . .
> Snatch me, just mounting, from the bless'd abode;
> Assist the friends, and tear me from my God!

Then in another mood she tells him,

> No, fly me, far as pole from pole;
> Rise Alps between us! and whole oceans roll!
> Ah, come not, write not, think not once of me,
> Nor share one pang of all I felt for thee.[14]

Yet she trusts that in her dying hour he may come to her, not as a lover but as a priest:

> In sacred vestments may'st thou stand,
> The hallow'd taper trembling in thy hand,
> Present the cross before my lifted eye,
> Teach me at once, and learn of me, to die.[15]

Like almost every poet in those days Pope dreamed of writing an epic. He had begun one at the age of twelve. Later, studying Homer, the thought came to him that he might translate the *Iliad* into those "heroic couplets" that seemed to be almost his natural speech. He asked his friends about the idea; they approved. One of them, Jonathan Swift, introduced him to Harley, Bolingbroke, and other heads of government, hoping to get him a sustaining sinecure. Failing in this, he undertook to get subscriptions that would support the new Alexander prancing over Troy. Strategically placed between place seekers and ministry, Swift proclaimed that "the best poet in England was Mr. Pope, a Papist, who had begun a translation of Homer into English verse, for which he must have them all subscribe; for the author shall not begin to print till I have a thousand guineas for him!"[16] Pope proposed to render the *Iliad* in six volumes quarto, for six guineas ($180?) the set. Despite this lordly price the subscriptions were so many, and the enthusiasm so great, that Bernard Lintot, bookseller, agreed to pay Pope two hundred pounds for each volume, and to supply him gratuitously with copies for his subscribers. As the 575 subscribers took 654 sets, Pope earned £5,320 ($148,960?) for the *Iliad*. No author in England had yet received so handsome a sum. The first volume, containing four cantos, appeared in 1715. It encountered unexpected competition from the publication, on the same day, of a translation of Canto I by Thomas Tickell. Addison lauded Tickell's version, which Pope took to be really Addison's; he felt the simultaneous publication to be an unfriendly act, and added Addison to his foes.

If scholarship had been the only test, Pope's translation would have deserved little praise. He had only a modest knowledge of Greek; he had to engage scholastic help; he accomplished most of his task by collating earlier translations and rephrasing them in the iambic-pentameter couplets that were his special forte. Bentley, prince of then living Hellenists, judged the performance well: "A pretty poem, Mr. Pope, but you must not call it Homer."[17] The couplets and the drumbeat of their rhymes, the balanced phrases, clauses, and antitheses, halted the swift and surging style of the Greek hexameters. Nevertheless there was a marching grandeur, and a resource of language, in those marvelously sustained verses that carried them over Bentley's protests through the eighteenth into the nineteenth century as the favored translation of the *Iliad*. "The noblest version of poetry that the world has ever seen," said Johnson;[18] no other translation would ever equal it, said Gray.[19] So Britain judged until Keats looked into Chapman's Homer, and Wordsworth called down a plague upon the pompous artificial style that pleased so many in England's Augustan Age.

Pope's *Iliad* was published in 1715–20. Its success brought competing booksellers to his door. One of them begged him to edit Shakespeare's plays; he foolishly agreed, blind to the chasm that divided him from Shakespeare in mind and art. He toiled impatiently at the uncongenial task; the edition appeared in 1725, and was soon riddled as incompetent by Lewis Theobald, the best Shakespearean scholar of the day. Pope crucified him in *The Dunciad*.

Meanwhile Lintot persuaded him to translate the *Odyssey*, offering a hundred pounds for each of five volumes; and subscribers took 819 sets. But now, lacking the stimulus of youth and need, Pope tired of cutting couplets, and delegated half the work to two Cambridge scholars, who soon learned to counterfeit his style. He had forewarned subscribers that he would use aides; but in publishing his *Odyssey* (1725–26)—far inferior to his *Iliad*—he credited these assistants with five books of the twenty-four; actually they had translated twelve.[20] He paid them £770; he himself netted £3,500, rightly feeling that his name had sold the book. The two translations made him financially independent. Now, "thanks to Homer," he said, he could "live and thrive indebted to no prince or peer alive."[21]

In 1718 he bought a villa at Twickenham, with a garden of five acres sloping to the Thames. He designed the garden in "natural" style, avoiding the classical regularity that he practiced in his verse; "a tree," he said, "is a nobler object than a prince in his coronation robes."[22] From his house he had a tunnel dug under an intervening highway to emerge into the garden; this "grotto" he decorated fancifully with shells, crystals, coral, petrifacts, mirrors, and little obelisks. In that cool retreat he entertained many famous friends—Swift, Gay, Congreve, Bolingbroke, Arbuthnot, Lady Mary Wortley Montagu, Princess Caroline, and Voltaire. Lady Mary was his neighbor in what they both called "Twitnam"; Bolingbroke lived at Dawley, close by; London was only eleven miles away, by a pleasant boat ride on the Thames; and nearer still were the royal palaces at Richmond, Hampton Court, and Kew.

Dr. John Arbuthnot, whose *History of John Bull* (1712) had given England a personality and a name, joined Swift, Congreve, Gay, and Pope in the famous Scriblerus Club (1713–15), dedicated to ridiculing every kind of quackery and ineptitude. All their victims were added to the swelling roster of Pope's foes. With Lady Mary he had a half-real, half-literary romance that ended in bitter enmity. Swift sometimes stayed with him, as when publishing *Gulliver* (1726); the two exchanged misanthropies, and some letters that revealed the tenderness under their carapaces.[23] Pope's acquaintance with Bolingbroke began about 1713, and developed into a philosophical tutelage. Each paid the other fulsome compliments. "I really think," said Pope, "that there is something in that great man which looks as if it were placed here by mistake from some higher sphere"; and Bolingbroke, when Pope was dying, said, "I have known him these thirty years, and value myself more on this man's love"—whereat, we are told, his voice failed.[24]

There must have been something to love in this poet whom tradition, and sometimes his own pen, have pictured as quarrelsome, deceitful, mean, and vain. We should always remember that he was forgivably embittered by the daily humiliation of his physical disabilities. In early life he had been beautiful of face, and of pleasant temper; and his face always remained attractive, if only by the animation of his eyes. But as he grew up the curvature of his spine became more painfully pronounced. He described himself as "a lively little creature, with long legs and arms; a spider is no ill emblem of him; he has been taken at a distance for a small windmill."[25] (We are reminded of the pitiful Scarron.) At table, to be on a level with others, he had to be propped up on a raised seat like a child. He required almost constant attendance. He could not go to bed or get up without help; could not dress or undress himself; had difficulty in keeping himself clean. On rising he could scarce hold himself erect until his servant laced him in a bodice of stiff canvas. His legs were so thin that he wore three pairs of stockings to enlarge their size and keep them warm. He was so sensitive to cold that he wore "a kind of fur doublet" under a shirt of coarse warm linen. He rarely knew the zest of health. Lord Bathurst said of him that he had headaches four days a week, and was sick the other three. It is a marvel that Jonathan Richardson could have painted so presentable a portrait of Pope[26]—all alertness and sensitivity; but in the bust by Roubillac[27] we can see the tortured body torturing the mind.

It would be cruel to expect such a man to be even-tempered, complaisant, cheerful, or kind. Like any invalid he became irritable, demanding, and morose; he seldom came closer to laughter than a smile. Deprived of all physical charm, he comforted himself with pride of place and vanity of intellect. Like a weak or wounded animal, and as one of an oppressed minority, he developed cunning, evasion, and subtlety; he soon learned to lie, even to practice dishonesty with his friends. He flattered the aristocracy, but he scorned to write acquisitive dedications. He had the courage to refuse a pension offered him by a government that he despised.

We see some lovable qualities in his private life. Swift called him "the most dutiful son I have ever known or heard of."[28] His affection for his mother was the purest and most lasting sentiment of his troubled spirit; in her ninety-first year he wrote that her daily company made him insensitive to any lack of other domestic attachments. His sexual morals were better in practice than in speech; his frame was not adapted to fornication, but his tongue and pen could be licentious *ad nauseam*.[29] Even to the two women with whom he thought he was in love he wrote with a loose freedom that none but a trull would tolerate today. And yet one of these, Martha Blount, developed for the infirm poet a devotion that gossip mistook for a liaison. In 1730 he described her as "a friend . . . with whom I have spent three or four hours a day these fifteen years."[30] In his premature old age he became dependent upon her affection, and he bequeathed to her nearly all of his substantial estate.

Always conscious of his bodily defects, he felt with double keenness every word critical of his character or his poetry. It was an age pre-eminent in the vindictiveness of its literary wars; and Pope returned abuse with abuse sometimes unfit to print. In 1728 he gathered his foes and critics into the corral of his verse, and let loose upon them all the arrows of his wrath in his most powerful and disagreeable work. It was anonymous, but all literate London saw his signature in its style. Treading the rugged path of Dryden's *MacFlecknoe* (1682), Pope's *Dunciad* hailed the scribes of Grub Street as the leading dunces of the Court of Dullness, where Theobald is king. He mourned the death of Wren and Gay, and the Hiberniating exile of Swift, who was dying "like a poisoned rat in a hole"—i.e., Dublin Cathedral. For the rest he saw nothing about him but a venal and tasteless mediocrity. Theobald, Dennis, Blackmore, Osborne, Curll, Cibber, Oldmixon, Smedley, Arnall received in turn their meed of lashes, taunts, and filth—for the poet, perhaps as an attribute of impotence, had a flair for offal.[31]

In a later edition Pope, through the mouth of the poet Savage, told with pleasure how, on the date of first publication, a crowd of authors besieged the bookseller, threatening him with violence if he published the poem; how this made the public more avid for copies; how one edition after another was demanded and consumed; how the victims formed clubs to concert vengeance upon Pope, and destroyed him in effigy. Dennis' son came with a cudgel to beat Pope, but was diverted by Lord Bathurst; thereafter, for a while, Pope took with him on his walks two pistols and his great Dane. Several victims countered with pamphlets; Pope and his friends started (1730) *The Grub Street Journal* to continue the war. In 1742 he issued a fourth book of *The Dunciad*, in which, hungry for new enemies, he attacked the pedagogues and the freethinkers—who boast that

> We nobly take the high Priori Road,
> And reason downward till we doubt of God;
> Make Nature still encroach upon His plan,
> And shove Him off as far as e'er we can; . . .
> Or, at one bound o'erleaping all His laws,
> Make God man's image, man the final cause,
> Find virtue local, all relation scorn,
> See all in self, and but for self be born;
> Of nought so certain as our reason still,
> Of nought so doubtful as of soul and will.[32]

Obviously Pope had been delving into philosophy, and not only with Bolingbroke; Hume's dissolvent *Treatise of Human Nature* had appeared in 1739, three years before this Book IV of *The Dunciad*. There is some evidence that the Viscount had already transmitted to the poet the deism of Shaftesbury sharpened with the wisdom of the world.[33] Enough of satire and trivialities, said Bolingbroke; turn your Muse to divine philosophy. "Lord Bathurst," reported Joseph Warton, "repeatedly assured me that he had read the whole scheme of the *Essay [on Man]* in the handwriting of Bolingbroke, and drawn up in a series of propositions which Pope was to versify and illustrate."[34] Pope seems to have done this, even to using specific phrases of the lordly skeptic,[35] but he added some saving remnants of his Christian creed. So he issued his *Essay on Man:* Epistle I in February, 1733; Epistles II and III later in that year; Epistle IV in 1734. Soon it was translated into French, and a dozen Gauls hailed it as one of the most brilliant unions of poetry and philosophy ever composed.

Today it is remembered chiefly for lines that everyone knows; let us do Pope the justice to see them in the setting of his art and thought. He begins with an apostrophe to Bolingbroke:

> Awake, my St. John! leave all meaner things
> To low ambition and the pride of kings.
> Let us (since life can little more supply
> Than just to look about us and to die)
> Expatiate free o'er all this scene of man;
> A mighty maze! but not without a plan; . . .
> Together let us beat this ample field, . . .
> Laugh where we must, be candid where we can,
> But vindicate the ways of God to man.[36]

Here, of course, is a memory of Leibniz' *Theodicy* and Milton's *Paradise Lost*.[37] Pope proceeds to warn philosophers against hoping or pretending to understand—"Can a part contain the whole?" Let us be grateful that our reason is limited and our future unknown:

> The lamb thy riot dooms to bleed today,
> Had he thy reason, would he skip and play?
> Pleased to the last, he crops the flowery food,
> And licks the hand just raised to shed his blood.[38]

There is a secret pessimism here; hope can survive only through ignorance:

> Hope humbly, then; with trembling pinions soar;
> Wait the great teacher, Death, and God adore.
> What future bliss He gives not thee to know,
> But gives that hope to be thy blessing now.
> Hope springs eternal in the human breast,
> Man never Is, but always To be, blest.[39]

We cannot see the reason for the apparent injustices of life; we must recognize that nature is not made for man, that God must order all things for all things, not for man alone. Pope describes the "vast Chain of Being" between the lowest creatures through man and angel to God, and he keeps his faith in a divine order, however hidden from our ken:

> All Nature is but art, unknown to thee;
> All chance, direction which thou canst not see;
> All discord, harmony not understood;
> All partial evil, universal good;
> And, spite of pride, in erring reason's spite,
> One truth is clear, Whatever is, is right.[40]

The first lesson is intellectual humility. Then a magnificent remembrance of Pascal:

> Know then thyself, presume not God to scan;
> The proper study of mankind is man.
> Placed on this isthmus of a middle state,
> A being darkly wise, and rudely great, . . .
> Sole judge of truth, in endless error hurl'd:
> The glory, jest, and riddle of the world![41]

Within these human limits let us agree that "self-love, the spring of motion, act[ivate]s the soul," but also that reason must enter to give order and balance to our passions and save us from vice. For

> Vice is a monster of so frightful mien,
> As, to be hated, needs but to be seen;
> Yet seen too oft, familiar with her face,
> We first endure, then pity, then embrace.[42]

These passions, though they are all modes of self-love, are parts of the divine design, and may tend to an end good even to our blind vision. So the lust for the flesh continues the race, and mutual interest begot society. Social organization and religious belief are obvious boons, though kings and creeds have stained history with human blood.

> For forms of government let fools contest;
> Whate'er is best administered is best.
> For modes of faith let graceless zealots fight;
> His can't be wrong whose life is in the right.[43]

The fourth epistle of the *Essay on Man* examines happiness, and labors to equate it with virtue. If the good man suffers misfortunes, and the wicked sometimes prosper, it is because

> the Universal Cause
> Acts not by partial but by general laws;[44]

God ordains the whole, but leaves the parts to the laws of nature and to man's free will. Some of us mourn the inequality of possessions as a source of unhappiness; but class divisions are necessary to government;

> Order is Heaven's first law; and this confessed,
> Some are, and must be, greater than the rest.[45]

This is not as clear as a day in June, but what else could be said to (or by?) Viscount Bolingbroke? And despite the inequality of natural and acquired gifts, happiness is evenly distributed; the poor man is quite as happy as the king. Nor is the prosperous villain really happy; he hugs his gains but feels the world's contempt, while the just man, even in injustice, has a soul at peace.

What strikes us first in the *Essay on Man* is the unrivaled compactness of the style. "I chose verse," said Pope, "because I found I could express them |ideas| more shortly this way than in prose."[46] No one, not Shakespeare himself, equaled Pope in gathering infinite riches—at least considerable meaning—in a little room. Here in 652 couplets are more memorable lines than in any equal area of literature outside the New Testament. Pope knew his limits; he explicitly disclaimed originality of ideas; he proposed to rephrase a deistic and optimistic philosophy in syncopated art, and he succeeded. In this poem he laid aside his Catholic creed at least *pro tempore*. He kept God as a First Cause only, who exerts no "particular providence" to help the virtuous man from the wiles of the wicked. There are no miracles in this system, no God-given Scriptures, no falling Adam or atoning Christ; a vague hope of heaven, but no word of hell.

Many critics assailed the poem as versified humanism. "The proper study of mankind is man" defined one aspect of humanism, and seemed to scuttle all theology. When the *Essay* was translated into French it was pounced upon by a Swiss pastor, Jean Crousaz, who argued that Pope had left God off on a siding in a poem supposed to vindicate the ways of God to man. No other than the potent William Warburton came to Pope's defense against this alien attack; the poem, vouched the future bishop, was a work of impeccable Christian piety. To calm the clergy Pope published in 1738 a lovely hymn, "The Universal Prayer." The orthodox were not quite satisfied, but the storm died down. On the Continent the *Essay* was hailed with hyperboles; "in my opinion," Voltaire judged, "the finest, the most useful, the sublimest didactic poem that has ever been written in any language."[47]

In 1735 Pope prefaced a volume of satires with an "Epistle to Dr. Arbuthnot," defending his life and works, and dispatching further enemies. Here came the famous picture of Addison as "Atticus," and the murderous exposure of the ambisexual Lord Hervey, who had made the mistake of calling Pope "hard as thy heart, and as thy birth obscure."[48] Pope transfixed him as "Sporus" in lines that show the poet at his best and worst:

> What? that thing of silk,
> Sporus, that mere white curd of ass's milk?
> Satire or sense, alas! can Sporus feel,
> Who breaks a butterfly upon a wheel?
> Yet let me flap this bug with gilded wings,
> This painted child of dirt, that stinks and stings . . .
> Whether in florid impotence he speaks,
> And as the prompter breathes, the puppet squeaks;
> Or, at the ear of Eve, familiar toad,
> Half froth, half venom, spits himself abroad,
> In puns, or politics, or tales, or lies,
> Or spite, or smut, or rhymes, or blasphemies,
> His wit all seesaw, between that and this,
> Now high, now low, now master up, now miss,
> And he himself one vile antithesis.
> Amphibious thing! that acting either part,
> The trifling head, or the corrupted heart,
> Fop at the toilet, flatterer at the board,
> Now trips a lady, and now struts a lord.[49]

Pope was proud of his facility in such assassinations—

> Yes, I am proud; I must be proud to see
> Men, not afraid of God, afraid of me.[50]

He excused his bitterness on the ground that the age was threatened with the triumph of stupidity, and needed a scorpion to sting it into sense. But in 1743 he concluded that he had lost the battle; in his last revision of *The Dunciad* he painted a powerful picture—Donne's forebodings in Miltonic tones—of religion, morals, order, and art in universal darkness and decline. The Goddess of Dullness, enthroned, yawns upon a dying world:

> She comes! she comes! The sable throne behold
> Of night primeval and of Chaos old!
> Before her, fancy's gilded clouds decay,
> And all its varying rainbows die away. . . .
> As one by one, at dread Medea's strain,
> The sick'ning stars fade off th' ethereal plain; . . .
> Thus at her felt approach, and secret might,
> Art after art goes out, and all is night.
> See skulking Truth to her old cavern fled,
> Mountains of casuistry heaped o'er her head!
> Philosophy, that leaned on Heaven before,
> Shrinks to her second cause, and is no more.
> Physic [science] of metaphysic begs defense [against Hume?],
> And metaphysic calls for aid on Sense [Locke?]!
> See mystery to mathematics [Newton?] fly!
> In vain! they gaze, turn giddy, rave, and die.
> Religion blushing veils her sacred fires,
> And unawares morality expires. . . .
> Lo, thy dread empire, Chaos! is restored;
> Light dies before thy uncreating word;
> Thy hand, great Anarch, lets the curtain fall,
> And universal darkness buries all.[51]

Perhaps he mistook his own decomposition for the collapse of the cosmos. At the age of fifty-five he was already dying of old age. Dropsy made it difficult for him to walk, asthma made it painful for him to breathe. On May 6, 1744, he fell into delirium, from which he emerged at intervals; in one of these he expressed his confidence in life after death. A Catholic friend asked if he should call a priest; Pope answered, "I do not think it essential, but it will be very right, and I thank you for putting me in mind of it."[52] He died on May 30, "so placidly" (if we may believe Johnson) "that the attendants did not discern the exact time of his expiration." As a Catholic, he was ineligible for burial in Westminster Abbey; he was interred beside his father and mother in Twickenham.

Was he a gentleman? No; his vituperative hatreds shared in poisoning the literary air of England in the first half of the eighteenth century; his physical sufferings produced acrid acids, and deprived him of the strength that overflows in charity. Was he a genius? Of course: not in thought, which he borrowed, but in form, which he perfected in his genre. Thackeray called him "the greatest literary artist that the world has seen."[53] In felicity of speech, compression of expression, fertility of phrase, he was the paragon of his time. Even the French accepted him as the greatest poet of his generation; Voltaire looked up to him and imitated him, as in the *Discours sur l'homme*. For thirty years—longer than any other poet—he was the sovereign of English verse, and for thirty more he was the model of English bards till Wordsworth announced another age.

For us today, hurried with all our leisure, Pope's couplets, mechanically sliced, or rising and falling "like a seesaw,"[54] possess a *virtus dormitiva*, periodically arousing us with epigrams. Even the brilliant *Essay on Man* is poetry only in its feet and rhymes. Its workmanship is too visible; the artist has forgotten Horace's counsel to hide his art. He forgot, too, Horace's warning that the poet must himself have feeling before he can convey it; Pope felt, but mostly to scorn and revile. He lacked the sense of beauty for noble actions or feminine grace. His imagination was exhausted in finding correct, incisive, concentrated words for old ideas; it did not reach out to grasp the ideal forms that inspire great poets and philosophers. Only his hatreds gave him wings.

He remains the chief poetic symbol of England's "Augustan Age"—whose bounds might be defined by his life, 1688–1744. The growing familiarity of the British mind with the classics of Greece and Rome, and with the French drama of the *grand siècle;* the influence of aristocracy—of class dominating mass—in speech, manners, polite vocabulary, and gracious ease; the reaction of reason and realism after Elizabethan extravagance and Puritan converse with God; the passage of French norms to England with the Restoration; the new prestige of science and philosophy: all these collaborated to bring the prevalent forms of English poetry under the classic rules of Horace and Boileau. An age of criticism succeeded an age of imagination; whereas in Elizabethan England poetry invaded and colored prose, now in Augustan England prose degraded and discolored poetry. The impress of this "neoclassic" literature on the English language was good and bad: it gave it a new precision, clarity, and elegance; it forfeited the vitality, force, and warmth of Elizabethan speech. The old ebullience and individualism of character and expression yielded to a superimposed order that compelled conformity in life and form in literature. Youth became middle age.

This neoclassical style spoke for only a part of English life; it had no room for rebellion, sentiment, or idealizing love. Even during Pope's pontificate there were British poets who cried out against artificiality and logic, turned from reason to nature, and found a voice for feeling, wonder, imagination, brooding melancholy and grieving hope. At the peak of England's classic age the Romantic movement began.

III. THE VOICES OF FEELING

Neoclassic poetry contemplated hardly anything but the world of print. It saw Homer and Horace, Addison and Pope, more vividly than the men and women who passed in the streets, or the weather and landscapes that entered daily into human moods. But now literature again discovered what philosophers had so long argued, that *man* is a general and abstract notion; that only *men* exist, fondly individual and jealously real. Poets deepened themselves by touching the earth, by feeling and responding to fields, hills, sea, and sky, and by reaching down beneath ideas to the secret sentiments that speech less manifested than concealed. They shrugged off discourse, and resolved to sing; the lyric returned, the epic died away. The longing for supernatural comfort, for some mystic wonder enlarging life, survived the deistic attack on miracles, and sought increasingly, in medieval myths, Oriental romances, and Gothic forms, some escape from the harsh realities of this nether world.

Of course there had always been voices of feeling. Had not Steele's *Christian Hero* (1701) lauded old faith and kindly sentiment? Had not Shaftesbury's *Characteristics* (1711) centered human life on "passion" and "affection"? Would not the skeptic Hume and the economist Smith derive all morality from fellow feeling, sympathy? Nevertheless it was James Thomson who struck the first clear blow for "sensibility."

He was the son of a poor parson in the hills of Scotland. He went down to Edinburgh to study for the ministry, but was deterred by professorial condemnation of his diction as profanely poetical. He migrated to London, was robbed en route, approached starvation, and sold his poem *Winter* (1726) to buy a pair of shoes.[55] However, its dedication to Sir Spencer Compton brought him twenty guineas for his compliments; the English nobles were not as deaf or tight as Johnson thought. Thomson recalled the crunch of boots in the crust of snow, and how he had

> Heard the winds roar and the deep torrent burst,
> Or seen the deep-fermenting tempest brewed
> In the grim evening sky;

how he had watched from the shore the winds plow up the sea, turning "from its bottom the discolored deep," tearing ships from their anchorage, lifting them precariously upon one wave, pressing them down ominously beneath the next, flinging them upon "sharp rock or shoal insidious," and scattering them "in loose fragments . . . floating round." He pictured the peasant caught in a blizzard of blinding snow, sinking icy feet into deeper drifts as he struggles on, until he can lift his boots no more, and falls exhausted into a frozen death.

> Ah, little think the gay, licentious proud . . .
> How many feel, this very moment, death
> And all the sad variety of pain; . . .
> How many pine in want, and dungeon glooms,
> Shut from the common air and common use
> Of their own limbs; how many drink the cup
> Of baleful grief, or eat the bitter bread
> Of misery, sore pierced by wintry winds;
> How many shrink into the sordid hut
> Of cheerless poverty. . . .

Here was a new note of pity to shame Pall Mall and Downing Street, and a refreshing return to Milton's blank verse after what Thomson called the "little glittering prettiness" of Pope's rhymes.

Another year and patron saw Thomson's *Summer* through the press (1727), and in that year he joined, with a famous poem, in the cry for war with Spain:

> When Britain first at Heaven's command
>   Arose from out the azure main,
> This was the charter of her land,
>   And guardian angels sung this strain:
>   Rule, Britannia, rule the waves;
>   Britons never will be slaves.

From London he wandered for days and weeks into the countryside, absorbing with a poet's doubled senses "each rural sight, each rural sound"; loving the "smell of dairy" coming from the farms, thrilled by the sun triumphing after rain, or anticipating Keats's autumnal melancholy mood. So he published *Spring* in 1728, and, adding *Autumn* ("the envenomed leaf begins to curl"), united all four poems in *The Seasons* (1730). He was rewarded with a tour of the Continent as companion to Charles Talbot, son of the current Chancellor. Returning, he lived in ease and wrote poor poetry till the Chancellor died (1737). After another stay with poverty he was introduced to the Prince of Wales, who asked him about the state of his affairs; Thomson replied "that they were in a more poetical posture than formerly," and received a pension of a hundred pounds for his quip. Suddenly a cold caught on the Thames ended his life at the age of forty-eight.

The Seasons set a style in the minor verse of England, and found followers in France; there Jean François de Saint-Lambert, who stole Émilie from
Voltaire, composed *Les Saisons* (1769). While heroic couplets strutted
across the century, Edward Young, William Collins, William Shenstone,
Mark Akenside, and Thomas Gray widened the Romantic road to Wordsworth and Chatterton. Young, after writing gay nothings till sixty, feathered his celestial nest with *Night Thoughts on Life, Death, and Immortality* (1742–44). Voltaire dismissed this nocturnal emission as "a confused
mixture of bombast and obscure trivialities"; but perhaps that was because
Young had pricked him with an epigram:

> You are so witty, profligate, and thin,
> At once we think you Milton, Death, and sin.[56]

William Collins lived half as long as Young, and wrote twice as little and
as well. Evading a call to the ministry, he spent his last pennies polishing to
perfection the fifteen hundred lines he composed before he went mad and
died (1759), aged thirty-eight. Finer than his lauded "Ode to Evening" is
his epitaph for the British soldiers who had fallen in battle in 1745:

> How sleep the brave who sink to rest
> By all their country's wishes blest!
> When Spring, with dewy fingers cold,
> Returns to deck their hallow'd mold,
> She there shall dress a sweeter sod
> Than Fancy's feet have ever trod.
> By fairy hands their knell is rung,
> By forms unseen their dirge is sung;
> There Honor comes, a pilgrim gray,
> To bless the turf that wraps their clay;
> And Freedom shall awhile repair
> To dwell a weeping hermit there.

Most memorable among these poets of sensibility was the strange spirit
who gave our youthful melancholy many a tender phrase. Thomas Gray
was one of twelve children born to a London scrivener; eleven of them died
in infancy; Thomas survived that dangerous age only because his mother,
seeing him in convulsions, used her scissors to open his vein. At eleven he
went to Eton, where he began fateful friendships with Horace Walpole
and Richard West. Then to Cambridge, which he found "full of doleful
creatures" and dreary dons. He proposed to study law, but slipped into
entomology and poetry; eventually he became so learned in languages, sciences, and history that his verse was stifled with scholarship.

In 1739 he toured the Continent with Horace Walpole. Crossing the Alps in winter, he reported that "not a precipice, not a torrent, not a cliff but is pregnant with religion and poetry"; in 1740, writing from Rome, he introduced the word *picturesque* into the English language; even in 1755 Johnson's *Dictionary* knew it not. In Reggio Emilia he and Walpole quarreled; Horace had been too conscious of his pedigree, Thomas too proud of his poverty; a "mutual friend" betrayed to each of them the other's private opinion; they parted, and Gray went on alone to Venice, Grenoble, and London.

The death of his friend West (1742) at the age of twenty-six made him resent life. He retired to the home of an uncle at Stoke Poges; there, amid his continued studies, he wrote (1742) his "Ode on a Distant Prospect of Eton College." Looking from a safe remove upon those scholastic scenes, he thought of his friend so prematurely dead; and beyond the sports and gaiety of those youths he saw with morose vision their troubled destinies:

> These shall the fury Passions tear,
>   The vultures of the mind,
> Disdainful Anger, pallid Fear,
>   And Shame that skulks behind;
> Or pining Love shall waste their youth,
> Or Jealousy with rankling tooth
>   That inly gnaws the secret heart,
> And Envy wan, and faded Care,
> Grim-visaged comfortless Despair,
>   And Sorrow's piercing dart. . . .
>
> Lo! in the vale of years beneath,
>   A grisly troop are seen,
> The painful family of Death,
>   More hideous than their Queen.
> This racks the joints, this fires the veins,
> That every laboring sinew strains,
>   Those in the deeper vitals rage;
> Lo, Poverty, to fill the band,
> That numbs the soul with icy hand,
>   And slow-consuming Age.
>
> To each his sufferings; all are men,
>   Condemned alike to groan,
> The tender for another's pain,
>   The unfeeling for his own.
> Yet ah! why should they know their fate,
> Since sorrow never comes too late,
>   And happiness too swiftly flies?

Thought would destroy their paradise.
No more; where ignorance is bliss
'Tis folly to be wise.

Late in 1742 Gray returned to Cambridge to resume his studies. To Walpole, reconciled, he sent (1750) his "Elegy Written in a Country Churchyard." Walpole gave it some private circulation; a pirate publisher printed and garbled it; to protect his verse Gray let Dodsley issue a better, though still imperfect, version (1751). In this, one of the finest poems of the century, Gray clothed a romantic melancholy in chiseled classical form, replacing Pope's "clanging couplets" with quiet quatrains moving in melodious dignity to their somber end.

In 1753 his mother died; he wrote a tender epitaph, and buried himself in poetry. In an ode on "The Progress of Poesy" he hailed the passage of the Muses from Greece and Rome to "Albion"; he confessed his boyhood aspiration to rival Pindar, and begged of Poetry the gift of an "unconquerable mind." A still loftier ode, "The Bard," saw in the poets a redeeming feature of British life, exposing vice and tyranny. These two *Pindaric Odes*, published by Walpole's press at Strawberry Hill, were so artificial in form, so recondite in classical and medieval allusions, that only scholars could understand them. Gray wrapped his solitude in pride. "I would not have put another [explanatory] note to save the souls of all the owls in London. It is extremely well as it is—nobody understands me, and I am perfectly satisfied."[57] The owls were familiar with such whistling in the dark.

Morose in his room at Peterhouse, Cambridge, too poor and timid to marry, too sensitive for the scuffle of life, Gray became a melancholy introvert. Some undergraduates, resenting his distance and dignity, and knowing his fear of fire, startled him one night by shouting, under his window, that the hall was aflame. In his nightshirt, says a disputed story, he let himself out of the window and slid down a rope—into a tub of water placed by the pranksters to receive him.[58] In 1769 he toured the English lakes; in the *Journal* that he wrote (in a remarkably beautiful hand) he first made England realize the loveliness of that region. On another tour, at Malvern, he received a copy of *The Deserted Village;* "this man," he exclaimed, "is a poet." Then gout ended his travels, and soon afterward his life (1771).

For a time his reputation was extreme. By common consent, in 1757, he stood at the head of English poets; he was offered the laureateship, but declined. Cowper, passing over Milton, called Gray "the only poet since Shakespeare entitled to the character of sublime." Adam Smith, passing over Shakespeare, added: "Gray joins to the sublimity of Milton the elegance and harmony of Pope; and nothing is wanting to render him, perhaps, the first poet in the English language, but to have written a little more."[59] Johnson admired the "Elegy," but was learned enough to find a score of flaws in the odes; "Gray has a kind of strutting dignity, and is tall by walking on tiptoe. . . . I confess that I contemplate his poetry with less satisfaction than his life."[60]

We might justly invert that oracle. Gray's was an unhappy, unprepossessing life, from the quarrel with Walpole to the tale of a tub. Its noblest events were three or four poems that will remain for yet many generations among the most convincing arguments for the "progress of poesy" from Greece to Rome to Albion.

IV. THE STAGE

What were the London theaters doing in this half century? They were chiefly the Drury Lane and (from 1733) the Covent Garden; there were minor stages in Lincoln's Inn Fields and Goodman's Fields; the Haymarket had a Little Theatre for comedies, and His Majesty's Theatre for opera; altogether London had twice as many theaters as Paris. Performances began at 6 P.M. The audience had changed its character since Restoration days; "society" now withdrew from the theater to the opera. Favored or moneyed auditors still sat on the stage. The "pit" and galleries seated almost two thousand persons; there the middle class predominated, and determined by its applause the reception and quality of the plays; hence the rising competition of bourgeois with romantic themes. Women took all female parts, and many male hearts; now began the reign of famous actresses like Kitty Clive and Peg Woffington—whom Hogarth painted and Charles Reade novelized.

As the "first, great, ruling passion of actors," said Garrick, "is to eat,"[61] they preferred plays spiced with sex. Said Fielding's Parson Adams, "I never heard of any plays fit for a Christian to read but Addison's, and [Steele's] *The Conscious Lovers*"; however, Fielding himself produced bawdy comedies.[62] Voltaire described the theaters in England as "without decency." Sir John Barnard appealed to the House of Commons in 1735 for some check on the theaters, alleging that "the British nation . . . were now so extravagantly addicted to lewd and idle diversions . . . that it was astonishing to all Europe that Italian eunuchs and signoras should have set salaries equal to those of the Lords of the Treasury."[63] Nothing was done about immoral scenes and lines; but when Fielding and Gay made the theater a vehicle of political satire, attacking both Robert Walpole and George II, the minister, usually tolerant of opposition, carried through Parliament a Licensing Act (1737) directing the Lord Chamberlain to exercise more rigor in granting permission for dramatic representations.*

---

* This act, as modified in 1843, is still British law, but is very leniently enforced.

In the *Encyclopédie* Diderot went out of his way to praise a play, *The London Merchant*, produced in London in 1731. It interested Diderot because it marked the introduction of middle-class tragedy to the British stage. The French classic drama had established the principle that tragedy belonged to the aristocracy, and would lose caste and dignity if it descended to bourgeois scenes. George Lillo took a double risk: he brought tragic drama down to a tradesman's home, and he wrote in prose. Thorowgood, the honest merchant, upholds "the dignity of our profession," and trusts that "as the name of merchant never degrades the gentleman, so by no means does it exclude him." The plot is the ruin of a merchant's apprentice by a seductive courtesan; the theme is embroidered with moral exhortations, and is swathed in sentiment. It was applauded by a middle class glad to see its virtues and ideals presented on a British stage. Diderot welcomed and imitated it in his campaign to introduce *tragédie domestique et bourgeoise* to the French theater; Lessing adopted its tone in *Miss Sara Sampson* (1755). The middle classes were asserting themselves in literature as in politics.

In Scotland the dramatic pot was set to boiling by John Home, who offended his fellow clergymen by writing and producing (1756) *Douglas*, the most successful tragic drama of its time. John's cousin, David Hume, in a burst of enthusiasm hardly becoming a skeptic philosopher, hailed him as "a true disciple of Sophocles and Racine," who might "in time vindicate the English stage from the reproach of barbarism."[64] When Garrick refused the play Hume, Lord Kames (Henry Home), and the "Moderates" among the Scottish clergy arranged for its production in Edinburgh, and David acted as ticket seller. The event was a triumph for all Homes and Humes, and for the rest of Scotland, for Home had transformed an old Scottish ballad into a patriotic drama that brought tears of joy to Scottish eyes. We must except the Edinburgh Presbytery of the Kirk, which denounced Home as a disgrace to his cloth, and reminded him of "the opinion which the Christian Church has always entertained of stage plays and players as prejudicial to the interest of religion and morality."[65] Formal accusations were issued against Home and another minister, Alexander Carlyle, for attending the performance. David Hume, aflame with kinship, dedicated his *Four Dissertations* to his cousin, and wrote a hot indictment of intolerance. John resigned from the ministry, went to London, and saw his *Douglas* produced with Peg Woffington in the female lead (1757). There too it was a triumph; the Scots in London gathered to applaud it; and at the close of this London première a Scot called down from the gallery, "Ou, fie, lads, fot [what] think ye o' yir Willy Shakespeare now?"[66] The play, as dead today as Addison's *Cato*, kept the stage on and off for a generation. When Mrs. Siddons played it in Edinburgh in 1784, the General Assembly of the Kirk "was obliged to fix all its important business for the alternate days when she did not act."[67]

The most hilarious success of the London stage in this period was *The Beggar's Opera.* John Gay began as a merchant's apprentice, rose to be secretary to the Earl of Clarendon, and became one of the liveliest members of the Scriblerus Club. Pope described him as

> Of manners gentle, of affections mild;
> In wit a man; simplicity, a child;
> With native humor temp'ring virtuous rage,
> Form'd to delight at once and lash the age.[68]

Gay made his mark in 1716 with *Trivia, or The Art of Walking the Streets of London.* The clatter of wagon wheels on paving stones, the drivers urging their horses with whip and tongue, the "draggled damsel" bearing fish for Billingsgate, the serenity of "Pell Mell" with fragrant ladies leaning on the arms of beaux, the pedestrian weaving his way through a game of football filling the street, the gentle thieves who with "unfelt fingers make thy pocket light," and the burly "watchman who with friendly light will teach thy reeling steps to tread aright," and guide you to your door: *Trivia* still provides all this and more for those who would visualize the London of 1716.

In 1720 Gay's *Poems* were published by subscription, and brought him a thousand pounds; these he lost in the crash of the South Sea Company. Pope and others came to his aid, but in 1728 he lifted himself to renewed prosperity with *The Beggar's Opera.* The introduction presents the beggar, who presents his opera. This begins with a ballad sung by Peachum, who (like Jonathan Wild) pretends to serve the law by reporting thieves (when they refuse to serve him), but actually is a dealer in stolen goods. He calls himself an honest man because "all professions be-rogue one another," and are moved by the greed for gain. His affairs are muddled by the fact that his daughter Polly has fallen in love with, perhaps has married, the dashing, handsome highwayman Captain Macheath; this will interfere with the use of Polly's charms in managing buyers, sellers, and constables. Mrs. Peachum reassures him:

> Why must our Polly, forsooth, differ from her sex, and love only her husband, and why must our Polly's marriage, contrary to all observation, make her the less followed by other men? All men are thieves in love, and like a woman the better for being another's property.[69]

However, Mrs. Peachum warns her daughter:

> You know, Polly, I am not against your toying a trifle with a customer in the way of business, or to get out a secret or so; but if I find

that you have played the fool, and are married, you jade you, I'll cut your throat.

Polly excuses her marriage in a ballad:

> Can love be controlled by advice?
>   Will Cupid our mothers obey?
> Though my heart were as frozen as ice,
>   At his flame 'twould have melted away.
> When he kissed me, so closely he pressed,
>   'Twas so sweet that I must have complied;
> So I thought it both safest and best
>   To marry, for fear you should chide.[70]

Peachum rages; he is afraid that Macheath will kill him and his wife to inherit their fortune through Polly. He schemes to betray Macheath to the law and have him safely hanged. Macheath comes on the scene, comforts Polly with pressures, and assures her that henceforth he will be monogamous:

> My heart was so free
> It roved like the bee,
>   Till Polly my passion requited;
> I sipped each flower,
> I changed every hour,
>   But here every flower is united.

She begs him to swear that if transported he will take her with him. He swears: "Is there any power . . . that could tear me from thee? You might sooner tear a pension from a courtier, a fee from a lawyer, a pretty woman from a looking glass." And they join in a charming duet:

> HE.   Were I laid on Greenland's coast,
>   And in my arms embraced my lass,
>   Warm amidst eternal frost,
>   Too soon the half-year's night would pass.
> SHE. Were I sold on Indian soil,
>   Soon as the burning day was closed,
>   I could mock the sultry toil
>   When on my charmer's breast reposed.
> HE.   And I would love you all the day,
> SHE. Every night would kiss and play,
> HE.   If with me you'd fondly stray,
> SHE. Over the hills and far away.

She confides to him that her father plans to surrender him to the law, and sorrowfully she bids him hide for a while. He goes, but stops in a tavern to give his aides instructions for a robbery. When they are gone he dances and toys with the tavern tarts; Peachum has bribed them to betray him; while they fondle him they steal his pistols, then summon the constables; in the next scene he is in Newgate jail. There Polly and another of his wives contend for his person; they free him, but he is recaptured and is sent to the gallows. En route he comforts his ladies with a song:

> Then farewell, my love—dear charmers, adieu!
> Contented I die—'tis the better for you.
> Here ends all dispute for the rest of our lives,
> For this way, at once, I please all my wives.[71]

The beggar-author now appears, and prides himself on having made vice meet its due punishment, as in all proper plays. But an actor protests that "an opera must end happily" (how customs change!). The beggar yields, saves Macheath from one noose and gives him Polly as another; all dance around the couple, while the captain wonders has he met a fate worse than death.

Gay had had the luck to secure the services of Johann Pepusch, a German composer resident in England; Pepusch chose the music for Gay's ballads from old English airs; the result was irresistible. Despite the satire of corruption and hypocrisy, the audience at the première in Lincoln's Inn Fields Theatre (January 29, 1728) responded enthusiastically. The play ran for sixty-three consecutive nights, exceeding all precedents; it had long runs in the major towns of Britain; it still holds the stage on two continents, and has been made into one of the most delightful motion pictures of our time. The actress who played Polly became the toast of gay blades and the favorite of salons; her biography and her picture were sold in great number; her songs were painted on fans; she married a duke. But a High Churchman denounced Gay for making a highwayman his hero and letting him go unpunished. When Gay tried to produce a continuation under the title *Polly* the Lord Chamberlain refused to license it. Gay had *Polly* published; it sold so well, and the proceeds from *The Beggar's Opera* mounted so pleasantly, that (as a wit said) the play made Gay rich, and Rich, the manager, gay. Four years after his triumph colic carried the poet away.

V. THE NOVEL

The outstanding event in the literary history of this period was the rise of the modern novel. *Clarissa* and *Tom Jones* are more important historically than any English poem or play of the age. From 1740, as the scope of significant life broadened from the court to the people, and from actions to sentiments, the novel replaced the drama as the voice and mirror of England.

Stories were as old as writing. India had had her tales and fables; Judea had included in her literature such legends as those of Ruth, Esther, and Job; Hellenistic Greece and medieval Christendom had produced romances of adventure and love; Renaissance Italy had turned out thousands of *novelle* ("little novelties"), as in Boccaccio and Bandello; Renaissance Spain and Elizabethan England had written picaresque accounts of picturesque rogues; seventeenth-century France had weighted the world with love stories far longer than love. Lesage had spun out *Gil Blas;* Defoe had perfected the narrative of adventure to illustrate human courage; Swift had used a travelogue to excoriate mankind.

But were these productions novels in our present sense? They resembled eighteenth-century fiction in being imaginary narratives; some had the substance of indubitable length; some portrayed character with an effort at reality; but (perhaps excepting *Crusoe*) they lacked a plot that would unify events and characters in a developing whole. Mrs. Aphra Behn's *Oroonoko* (1688), the story of an African slave, had a unifying plot; so did Defoe's *Captain Singleton* (1720), *Moll Flanders* (1722), and *Roxana* (1724); but all these were still a string of episodes rather than a structural unity in which every part advances a unifying theme. When Richardson and Fielding seized this art of development, portrayed character growing through events, and made their novels picture the manners of an age, the modern novel was born.

1. Samuel Richardson: 1689–1761

The man who inaugurated the new novel was the son of a Derbyshire carpenter who moved to London soon after Samuel's birth. The family hoped to make him a clergyman, but was too poor to give him the requisite schooling; he managed, however, to do some preaching in his books. The circle in which he grew retained the Puritan morality. He was apprenticed to a printer, and his reputation for calligraphy enabled him to add to his income by composing letters for illiterate lovesick girls; this accident determined the epistolary form of his novels, and their extensive exploration of feminine psychology and sentiment. His industry and thrift served him well; he set up his own printing shop, married his ex-master's daughter (1721), and begot by her six children, of whom five died in infancy. She too died (1730), still young and loved, and these bereavements helped to form his rather somber mood. He married again, begot six more children, suffered more bereavements, and rose to be printer to the House of Commons. He was fifty years old before he published a book.

In 1739 two printer friends engaged him to write a little volume of sample letters as a guide for "those country readers who were unable to indite for themselves," and also as instruction in "how to think and act justly and prudently in the common concerns of human life."[72] While preparing this book—and here genius took hold of circumstance—Richardson conceived the idea of weaving a succession of letters into a love story that would illustrate a virgin's wise morality. The theme, chastity preserved through a long succession of temptations, may have been suggested by Marivaux's *Vie de Marianne* (1731–41). In any case Richardson, in November, 1740, set a milestone in English literature by issuing, in two volumes, *Pamela, or Virtue Rewarded, a Series of Familiar Letters from a Beautiful Young Damsel to Her Parents; now first published in order to cultivate the Principles of Virtue and Religion in the Minds of the Youth of Both Sexes*. The book went well, and Richardson added two more volumes in 1741, *Pamela in Her Exalted Condition*, telling of her virtues and wisdom after her marriage.

The first half of the story is still interesting, for we are never too old to be interested in seduction—though after a thousand pages even seduction becomes a bore. The stress on sentiment begins on the first page, where Pamela writes: "Oh, how my eyes run! Don't wonder to see the paper so blotted." She is a model of goodness, gentleness, and modesty. Sent out to "service" at sixteen, she remits to her parents the first money she earns, "for Providence will not let me want. . . . If I get more I am sure it is my duty, as it shall be my care, to love and cherish you both; for you have loved and cherished me when I could do nothing for myself."[73] The cautious parents refuse to use the money until they have assurance that it is not her bachelor employer's advance payment for Pamela's favors. They warn her that her beauty imperils her continence. "We fear—yes, my dear child, we *fear*—[lest] you should be too grateful, and reward him with that jewel, your virtue, which no riches . . . can make up to you." She promises to be chary, and adds: "Oh, how amiable a thing is doing good! It is all I envy great folks for." Her sentiments are admirable, though they lose some charm by being professed. In a culminating catastrophe her employer enters her bed without the proper preliminaries, and clasps her to his agitated bosom. She faints, and his program is disturbed. Recovering consciousness, "I put my hand to his mouth, and said, 'Oh, tell me, yet tell me not, what have I suffered in this distress?' "[74] He assures her that his intentions had miscarried. Appreciating the compliment of his desire, she gradually learns to love him; and the gradations by which her fear is shown turn-

ing to love are among the many subtle touches that support Richardson's
reputation as a psychologist. Nevertheless she resists all his sieges, and finally he breaks down and offers her marriage. Happy to have saved her
virtue and his soul, Pamela resolves to be a perfect English wife: to stay at
home, avoid grand parties, keep the household accounts carefully, distribute charity, make jellies, cookies, candies, and preserves, and be grateful
if her husband, descending the ladder of class, will give her now and then
the grace and benefit of his conversation. Richardson concludes Volume II
with a homily on the advantages of virtue in the bargaining of the sexes.
"The editor of these sheets will have his end if it [Pamela's virtue] inspires
a laudable emulation in the minds of any worthy persons, who may thereby
entitle themselves to the rewards, the praises, and the blessings by which
Pamela was so deservedly distinguished."

Some Englishmen, like the lusty Fielding, laughed, but thousands of
middle-class readers entered sympathetically into Pamela's throbs. The
clergy praised the book, glad to have found such reinforcements of their
sermons in a literature that had seemed sold to Beelzebub. Four editions of
Pamela were taken up in six months; naturally the publishers urged Richardson to dig further in the same rich vein. But he was not mercenary, and
besides, his health had begun to fail. He took his time, and proceeded with
his printing. It was not till 1747 that he sent forth the masterpiece that
brought all bourgeois Europe to his feet.

Clarissa, or The History of a Young Lady, two thousand pages long,
came out in seven volumes between November, 1747, and December, 1748.
Hurt by the charge that *Pamela* had shown virtue as merely a bargaining
strategy, and had pictured a reformed rake as a good husband, Richardson
undertook to show virtue as a divine gift to be rewarded in heaven, and
an unreformed rake as inevitably bound for an evil and shattering end. The
impetuous Lovelace, reputed a devil with women, seeks the hand of Clarissa
Harlowe. She distrusts him, but is insensibly fascinated by his reputation.
Her family forbids her to meet such a scoundrel; it closes its doors to him,
and offers her Mr. Solmes, a man of no vices and no character. She refuses.
To make her yield they scold her, torment her, lock her up. Lovelace hires
an aide to simulate an armed attack upon her by her relatives; to escape
them she allows him to abduct her to St. Albans. She is willing to marry
him, but he thinks this too desperate a venture. He writes to a friend:

> . . . Determined to marry I would be, were it not for this considera-
> tion, that once married, I am married for life.
>   That's the plague of it! Could a man do as the birds do, change
> [mates] every Valentine's Day, . . . there would be nothing at all in
> it. . . . Such a change would be a means of annihilating . . . four or
> five very atrocious capital sins: rape, vulgarly so called, adultery, and

fornication; nor would polygamy be panted after. Frequently it would prevent murders and dueling; hardly any such thing as jealousy (the causes of shocking violences) would be heard of. . . . Nor would there possibly be such a person as a barren woman. . . . Both sexes would bear with each other, in the view that they could help themselves in a few months. . . . The newspapers would be crowded with paragraphs . . . concerned to see *who and who's together*. Then would not the distinction be very pretty, Jack? as in flowers: such a gentleman, or such a lady, is an *annual*, such a one is a *perennial*.[75]

He tries to seduce Clarissa; she warns him that if he touches her she will kill herself. He keeps her in durance vile but genteel, during which she sends heartbroken letters to her confidante, Anna Howe. He invents one scheme after another to break through her defenses; she resists him, yet considers her honor irrevocably tarnished by her half-consenting to elope. She writes pitiful letters to her father begging him, not to forgive her, but to withdraw the curse which he has laid upon her, and which, she thinks, forever closes to her the gates of Paradise; he refuses. She falls into a wasting illness, in which her only support is her religious faith. Lovelace disappears into France, and is killed in a duel by Clarissa's uncle. At last her parents come offering forgiveness, and find her dead.

It is a simple story, too long drawn out on a single note to hold the attention of our hectic minds; but in eighteenth-century England it became a national issue; hundreds of readers, in the intervals of publication, wrote to Richardson imploring him not to let Clarissa die.[76] One father described his three daughters as having "at this moment each a separate volume [of *Clarissa*] in her hand; and all their eyes like a wet flower in April."[77] Lady Mary Wortley Montagu, as sophisticated as any Englishwoman of her time, took up the book as a concession to middle-class sentiment and the popular furor, but it offended her aristocratic taste:

> I was such an old fool as to weep over Clarissa Harlowe, like any milkmaid of sixteen over the ballad of the Lady's Fall. To say truth, the first volumes softened me by a near resemblance of my maiden days; but on the whole it is miserable stuff. . . . Clarissa follows the maxim of declaring all she thinks to all the people she sees, without reflecting that, in this mortal state of imperfection, fig leaves are as necessary for our minds as our bodies, and 'tis as indecent to show all we think as all we have.[78]

The women of England now importuned the triumphant Richardson to depict for them an ideal man, as he had, they thought, portrayed an ideal woman in *Pamela*. He hesitated before this ensnaring task, but he was goaded on by Fielding's satire of *Pamela* in *Joseph Andrews*, and Fielding's full-length portrait of a man in *Tom Jones*. So, between November, 1753, and March, 1754, he sent forth in seven volumes *The History of Sir Charles Grandison*. The blasé mood of our time finds it hard to understand why this third novel had as great a success as the other two; the twentieth-century reaction against Puritanism and the Mid-Victorian compromise has closed our hearts to pictures of ideal goodness, at least in the male; we have found good men, but none without redeeming faults. Richardson tried to embellish Sir Charles with some minor shortcomings, but we still resent the impassable distance between him and ourselves. Moreover, virtue loses charm when it is put on parade. Grandison barely escaped canonization.

Richardson was so intent on preaching that he allowed some flaws into his literary art. He was almost devoid of humor and wit. His attempt to tell a long story through letters involved him in many improbabilities (remembering such reams of conversation); but it allowed him to present the same events from a variety of views, and it gave the narrative an intimacy hardly possible in a less subjective form. It was quite in the custom of the time to write long and confiding letters to trusted relatives or friends. Furthermore, the epistolary method gave scope to Richardson's forte—the display of feminine character. There are faults here too: he knew men less than women, nobles less than commoners; and he seldom caught the variations, contradictions, and development in the soul. But a thousand details show his careful observation of human conduct. In these novels English psychological fiction was born, and the subjectivism that came to a fever in Rousseau.

Richardson took his success modestly. He continued his work as a printer, but he built himself a better home. He wrote long letters of advice to a wide circle of women, some of whom called him "dear Papa." In his later years he paid with nervous sensitivity and insomnia the price of concentrated thought and diffuse art. On July 4, 1761, he died of a paralytic stroke.

His international influence was greater than that of any other Englishman of his time except Wesley and the elder Pitt. At home he helped to mold the moral tone of Johnson's England, and to raise the morals of the court after George II. His ethical and literary legacy shared in forming Goldsmith's *Vicar of Wakefield* (1766) and Jane Austen's *Sense and Sensibility* (1811). In France he was considered without a rival in English fiction; "In no language whatsoever," said Rousseau, "has a novel the equal of *Clarissa*, or even approaching it, ever been written."[79] Richardson was translated by the Abbé Prévost; Voltaire dramatized *Pamela* in *Nanine;* Rousseau modeled *La Nouvelle Héloïse* on *Clarissa* in theme, form, and moral aim. Diderot rose to an ecstatic apostrophe in his *Éloge de Richardson* (1761); if, he said, he had to sell his library, he would keep, of all his books, only Homer, Euripides, Sophocles, and Richardson. In Germany Gellert translated and imitated *Pamela,* and wept over *Grandison;*[80] Klopstock went into raptures over *Clarissa;* Wieland based a play on *Grandison;* Germans made pilgrimages to Richardson's home.[81] In Italy Goldoni adapted *Pamela* to the stage.

No one reads Richardson today except through the compulsions of scholarship; we have no leisure to write such letters, much less to read them; and the moral code of an industrial and Darwinian age flees impatiently from Puritan cautions and restraints. But we know that these novels represented, far more than the poetry of Thomson, Collins, and Gray, the revolt of feeling against the worship of intellect and reason; and we recognize in Richardson the father—as in Rousseau the protagonist—of that Romantic movement which, toward the end of the century, would triumph over the classical artistry of Pope and the lusty realism of Fielding.

2. Henry Fielding: 1707–54

When he came upon London in 1727 everyone admired his tall figure, stalwart presence, handsome face, jolly speech, and open heart; here was a man equipped by nature to enjoy life in all its relish and disreputable reality. He had everything but money. Forced, as he put it, to be a hackney coachman or a hackney scribe, he harnessed himself to a pen, and buttered his bread with comedies and burlesques. His second cousin, Lady Mary Montagu, used her influence to have his play *Love in Several Masques* produced at the Drury Lane Theatre (1728); she went twice to see it, graciously conspicuous; and in 1732 she helped his *Modern Husband* to a good run. He persisted with one mediocre play after another, and struck a vein of good-natured satire in *The Tragedy of Tragedies, or The Life and Death of Tom Thumb the Great* (1731).

After four years' courtship he married Charlotte Cradock (1734). Soon she inherited £1,500, and Fielding retired with her to ease as a country gentleman. He fell in love with his wife; he described her uxoriously as the shyly beautiful Sophia Western and the infinitely patient Amelia Booth. Lady Bute assures us that "the glowing language he knew how to employ did no more than justice to the amiable qualities of the original, or to her beauty."[82]

In 1736 he was back in London, producing unmemorable plays. But in 1737 the Licensing Act laid restrictions upon the drama, and Fielding withdrew from the stage. He studied law, and was admitted to the bar (1740). The course of his life was diverted in that year by the appearance of Richardson's *Pamela.* All of Fielding's propensity to satire was provoked by the conscious virtues of the heroine and her creator. It was as a parody of *Pamela* that he began *The History of the Adventures of Joseph Andrews and His Friend Mr. Abraham Adams, Written in Imitation of the Manner of Cervantes* (1742). Joseph, who is introduced as Pamela's brother, is as pure and beautiful a youth as Pamela was a maiden. Like her he is repeatedly tempted by his employer, and resists; and like her he details in his letters the insidious attempts upon his virginity. His letter to Pamela is almost, not quite, Richardsonian:

DEAR SISTER PAMELA:
　　Hoping you are well, what news have I to tell you! . . . My mistress has fallen in love with me—that is, what great folks call falling in love—she has a mind to ruin me; but I hope I shall have more resolution and more grace than to part with my virtue to any lady on earth.
　　Mr. Adams hath often told me that chastity is as great a virtue in a man as in a woman. He says he never knew any more than his wife, and I shall endeavor to follow his example. Indeed, it is owing entirely to his excellent sermons and advice, together with your letters, that I have been able to resist a temptation which, he says, no man complies with but he repents in this world and is damned for it in the next. . . . What fine things are good advice and good examples! But I am glad she turned me out of the chamber as she did; for I had once almost forgotten every word Parson Adams had ever said to me.
　　I don't doubt, dear sister, but you will have grace to preserve your virtue against all trials; and I beg you earnestly to pray I may be enabled to preserve mine; for truly it is very severely attacked by more than one; but I hope I shall copy your example, and that of Joseph my namesake, and maintain my virtue against all temptation. . . .[83]

He succeeds, and remains a virgin till he marries the virgin Fanny. Pamela, lifted a social notch as wife of her rich employer, condemns Fanny for presuming to marry Joseph, whose social status has been raised by Pamela's genteel marriage. Richardson complained that Fielding had committed a "lewd and ungenerous engraftment" on *Pamela*.[84]

　　Fielding's appetite for satire was not sated by parodying Richardson; he burlesqued the *Iliad* by invoking the Muses and making his book an epic. His fount of humor bubbled over in the various characters that Joseph and Adams meet on their way, and especially the innkeeper Tow-wouse, who is surprised by Mrs. Tow-wouse *in flagrante delicto* with Betty the chambermaid, is forgiven, and "quietly and contentedly bore to be reminded of his transgressions . . . once or twice a day during the residue of his life." And since it was not in Fielding's nature to make a hero, and a whole novel, out of an impeccable youth, he soon lost interest in Joseph, and made Parson Adams the central figure of his book. This seemed an unlikely choice, for Adams was an honestly orthodox divine, who carried with him a manuscript of his sermons in search of a reckless publisher. But his creator endowed Adams with a strong pipe, a tough stomach, and a hard pair of fists; and though the parson is against war, he is a good fighter, and lays low a succession of scoundrels in the wake of his tale. He is by all odds the most lovable character in Fielding; and we share the author's pleasure in putting him through strange encounters with pigs, mud, and blood. Those of us who in youth were deeply moved by the Christian ideal must feel a warm affection for a clergyman who is utterly without guile and overflows with charity. Fielding contrasts him with the moneygrubbing Parson Trulliber, who was "one of the largest men you should see, and could have acted the part of Sir John Falstaff without stuffing."[85]

Flushed with success, Fielding issued in 1743 three volumes modestly entitled *Miscellanies*. Volume III contained a masterpiece of sustained irony in *The Life of Mr. Jonathan Wild the Great*. It was not a factual biography of the famous eighteenth-century Fagin; "my narrative is rather of such actions which he might have performed."[86] In its first form it was a hit at Sir Robert Walpole as a dealer in stolen votes; after Walpole's death it was reissued as a satire of "greatness" as usually rated and achieved. Most "great men," Fielding held, had done more harm than good to mankind; so Alexander was called "the Great" because, after "he had with fire and sword overrun a vast empire, had destroyed the lives of an immense number of innocent wretches, had scattered ruin and desolation like a whirlwind, we are told, as an act of his clemency, that he did not cut the throat of an old woman and ravish her daughters."[87] The thief should have an easier conscience than the "statesman," since his victims are fewer and his booty less.[88]

In the style of a political biography Fielding gives Jonathan a lofty ancestral tree, tracing his lineage to "Wolfstan Wild, who came over with Hengist." His mother "had a most marvelous glutinous quality attending her fingers."[89] From her Jonathan learned the art and ethics of thievery. His superior intelligence soon enabled him to organize a gang of brave youths dedicated to separating superfluous people from their superfluous goods or a meaningless life. He took the lion's share of their gains, and rid himself of disobedient subalterns by surrendering them to the forces of law and order. He failed to seduce the chased Laetitia, who preferred to be ruined by his assistant Fireblood, who "in a few minutes ravished this fair creature, or at least would have ravished her, if she had not by a timely compliance, prevented him."[90] Thereafter she married Wild. Two weeks later they indulge in "a dialogue matrimonial," wherein she explains her natural right to promiscuity; he calls her a bitch; they kiss and make up. He rises higher still and higher in the grandeur of his crimes, until his wife has the satisfaction of seeing him condemned to death. A clergyman attends him to the gallows; Wild picks his pocket en route, but gets only a cork-screw, for the dominie was a connoisseur of vintages. And "Jonathan Wild the Great, after all his mighty exploits was—what so few GREAT MEN can accomplish—hanged by the neck till he was dead."[91]

Toward the end of 1744 Fielding lost his wife; the event darkened his mood until he purged his grief by portraying her fondly, through the pathos of distance, as Sophia and Amelia. He was so grateful for the loyal devotion of his wife's maid, who remained to take care of his children, that in 1747 he married her. Meanwhile he suffered both in health and in income. He was rescued by appointment (1748) as justice of the peace for Westminster, and shortly thereafter for Middlesex. It was a laborious office, precariously paid by the fees of the litigants who came to his court in Bow Street. He called the aggregate three hundred pounds a year "the dirtiest money upon earth."[92]

During these troubled years, 1744–48, he must have been working on his greatest novel, for in February, 1749, it appeared in six volumes as *The History of Tom Jones, a Foundling*. The book was composed, he tells us, in "some thousands of hours" salvaged from law and hack writing; and no one could tell, from its robust humor and virile ethic, that these were years of grief and gout and thinning purse. Yet here were twelve hundred pages of what many consider the greatest English novel. Never before in English literature had a man been so fully and frankly described in body and mind, morals and character. Famous are the words of Thackeray introducing *Pendennis*:

> Since the author of *Tom Jones* was buried, no writer of fiction among us has been permitted to depict to his utmost power a MAN. We must drape him, and give him a certain conventional simper. Society will not tolerate the Natural in our Art. . . . You will not hear . . . what moves in the real world, what passes in society, in the clubs, colleges, mess-rooms—what is the life and talk of your sons.

Tom makes his debut as an illegitimate infant found in Mr. Allworthy's virtuous bed. Between this and Tom's concluding marriage Fielding squeezed a hundred episodes, apparently in picaresque and unconnected succession; but the reader is surprised, if he persists to the end, to find that nearly all those incidents were necessary to the skillfully woven plot, or to the exposition and development of the characters; the threads are unraveled, the knots are untied. Several of the personnel are idealized, like the almost Grandisonian Allworthy; some are too simplified, like the unfailingly despicable Blifil, or the Reverend Mr. Thwackum, the pedagogue "whose meditations were full of birch."[93] But many of them show the sap of life. Squire Western, of all things in this world, "held most dear . . . his guns, dogs and horses,"[94] then his bottle, then his incomparable daughter Sophia. Here is a Clarissa who knows her ways among the snares of men, a Pamela who snares her man without ado about his premarital experiments.

Tom is a little loose in the loins, but otherwise he is almost too good to survive. Adopted by Allworthy, schooled and thrashed by Thwackum, he grows into a sturdy manhood disturbed only by malicious reminders of his mysterious parentage. He robs an orchard and steals a duck, but his adoptive father forgives these pranks as in the best Shakespearean tradition. Sophia admires him from a chaste distance, but Tom, conscious of his illegitimacy, never dares to fall in love with a lady so remote from him in status and means. He contents himself with Molly Seagrim, the gamekeeper's daughter, and confesses himself as possibly the father of her child; he is much relieved to find that he is only one of several such possibilities. Sophia suffers when she learns of this liaison, but her admiration for Tom is only transiently cooled. He catches her in his arms as she falls from her horse while hunting; her blushes reveal her feeling for him; and now he loses no time losing his heart. Squire Western, however, has set his purse on marrying her to Mr. Blifil, who is the legitimate nephew and heir of the wealthy and childless Allworthy. Sophia refuses to marry this young hypocrite; the Squire insists; and the battle between father's will and daughter's tears saddens several volumes. Tom shies away, and lets himself be discovered in a grove with Molly in his arms; Sophie comes upon the scene, and faints. Tom is reluctantly dismissed by Allworthy, and begins those episodic travels without which Fielding, still apparented to Cervantes and Lesage, found it difficult to write a novel. His heart remains with the brokenhearted Sophia, but, thinking her forever lost to him, he slips into Mrs. Waters' bed. After many tribulations, and complications surpassing all belief, he is pardoned by Allworthy, replaces Blifil as heir, clears up matters with shy but forgiving Sophia, and is heartily welcomed as son-in-law by Squire Western, who a week before had been ready to slay him. The Squire is now all haste for consummation:

> "To her, boy, to her, go to her. . . . Is it all over? Hath she appointed the day, boy? What, shall it be tomorrow or the next day? I shan't be put off a minute longer than the next day. . . . Zoodikers! she'd have the wedding tonight with all her heart. Wouldst not, Sophy? . . . Where the devil's Allworthy? Harkee, Allworthy, I'll bet thee five pounds to a crown we have a boy tomorrow nine months."[95]

Not since Shakespeare had anyone depicted English life so abundantly or so frankly. It is not all there; we miss the tenderness, devotion, heroism, civilities, and pathos that can be found in any society. Fielding preferred the man of instinct to the man of thought. He scorned the bowdlerizers who in his time were trying to fumigate Chaucer and Shakespeare, and those poets and critics who supposed that serious literature should deal only with the upper class. He interpreted love between the sexes as physical love, and relegated other aspects of it to the world of delusion. He despised the money madness that he saw in every rank, and he abominated humbug and hypocrisy. He made short shrift of preachers; but he loved Parson Adams, and the only hero in *Amelia* is Dr. Harrison, an Anglican clergyman; Fielding himself preached at every opportunity.

After publishing *Tom Jones* he turned his pen for a while to the problems that he faced as a magistrate. His experience was bringing him daily into contact with London's violence and crime. He suggested methods of tightening the guard of public order and the administration of justice. Through his efforts, and those of his half brother Sir John Fielding, who succeeded him as magistrate in Bow Street, one of the gangs that had terrified London was broken up, and nearly all its members were hanged. An optimist reported in 1757 that "the reigning evil of street robberies has been almost wholly suppressed."[96]

Meanwhile (December, 1751) Henry had published his last novel, *Amelia*. He could not forget his first wife; he had forgotten any faults she may have had; now he raised a monument to her as the faultless mate of an improvident soldier. Captain Booth is kind, brave, and generous; he adores his Amelia; but he gambles himself into debt, and the book opens with him in jail. He takes a hundred pages to tell his story to another inmate, Miss Matthews; he expounds to her the beauty, modesty, fidelity, tenderness, and other perfections of his wife, and then accepts Miss Matthews' invitation to share her bed. He continues "a whole week in this criminal conversation."[97] In these and later prison scenes Fielding displays, with perhaps some exaggeration, the hypocrisies of men and women, the venality of constables and magistrates, the brutality of jailers. Here already are the debtors' prisons that will linger on for a century more to stir Dickens' ire. Justice Thrasher can tell a prisoner's guilt from his brogue. "Sirrah, your tongue betrays your guilt. You are an Irishman, and that is always sufficient evidence with me."[98] The number of villains rises with every chapter, until Amelia cries out to her pauperized children, "Forgive me for bringing you into the world."[99]

Amelia is Fielding's patient Griselda. She has her nose broken in an early chapter, but rhinoplasty repairs it, and she becomes again so beautiful that an attempt is made on her virtue in almost every alternate chapter. She admits her intellectual inferiority to her husband. She obeys him in everything, except that she refuses to go to a masquerade. She attends an oratorio by Handel, but hesitates to expose herself to the gaze of the philanderers in Vauxhall. When Booth returns to her after one of his escapades he finds her "performing the office of a cook with as much pleasure as a fine lady generally enjoys in dressing herself for a ball."[100] She receives a letter from the evil Miss Matthews betraying Booth's prison adultery; she destroys the letter, says nothing about it to her husband, and continues to love him through all his drinking, gambling, debts, and imprisonments; she sells her trinkets, then her clothing, to feed him and their children. She is discouraged less by his faults than by the cruelty of the men and institutions that enmesh him. Fielding, like Rousseau and Helvétius, supposed that most men are by nature good, but are corrupted by evil environments and bad laws. Thackeray thought Amelia "the most charming character in English fiction";[101] but perhaps she was only a husband's dream. In the end, of course, Amelia turns out to be an heiress; she and Booth retire to her estate, and Booth becomes a good man.

The conclusion is hardly justified by the premises: once a Booth always a Booth. Fielding tried to bring all the tangles of his plot to a happy unity, but here his sleight of hand is too obvious. The great novelist was tired, and he was sickened by his entourage of thieves and murderers. After completing *Amelia* he wrote: "I will trouble the world no more with any children of mine by the same Muse." In January, 1752, he started *The Covent Garden Journal*, contributed some vigorous articles, answered Smollett's criticism, took a shot at *Roderick Random*, and then, in November, he let the *Journal* die. The winter of 1753–54 was too much for his constitution, broken down by work, dropsy, jaundice, and asthma. He tried Bishop Berkeley's tar water, but the dropsy grew worse. His doctor recommended travel to a sunnier clime. In June, 1754, he sailed on the *Queen of Portugal* with his wife and daughter. En route he composed his *Journal of a Voyage to Lisbon*, one of his most amiable productions. He died in Lisbon October 8, 1754, and was buried there in the English cemetery.

What was his achievement? He established the realistic novel of manners; he described the life of the English middle classes more vividly than any historian has done; his books opened a world. He did not succeed so well with the upper classes; there, like Richardson, he had to be content with an outsider's view. He knew the body of his country's life better than its soul, and the body of love better than its spirit; the more delicate and subtle elements of the English character escaped him. Even so, he left his mark upon Smollett, Sterne, Dickens, and Thackeray; he was the father of them all.

3. Tobias Smollett: 1721–71

Smollett did not like him, for they competed for the same applause. The younger man was a Scot who agreed with Hume in regretting that England obstructed the way to France. His grandfather, however, had actively promoted the parliamentary union with England (1707), and had been a member of the united Parliament. His father died when Tobias was two years old, but the family financed the boy's education at Dumbarton Grammar School and Glasgow University, where he took premedical courses. Instead of completing work for his degree, he succumbed to the infection of authorship, and rushed off to London and Garrick with a worthless tragedy; Garrick refused it. Tobias, after a little starvation, signed as surgeon's mate on the battleship *Cumberland*, and sailed with it (1740) into the War of Jenkins' Ear. He took part in the bungled attack on Cartagena, off the Colombian coast. In Jamaica he left the service; there he met Nancy Lascelles, whom he married soon after his return (1744) to England. He took a house in Downing Street and practiced surgery; but the itch to write was too much for him, and his experiences in the navy demanded at least one recital. So in 1748 he published the most famous of his novels.

The Adventures of Roderick Random is the old picaresque romance of events strung upon a character. Smollett acknowledged no debt to Fielding, but much to Cervantes and Lesage. He was more interested in men and deeds than in books and words; he packed his story with incidents, gave it the stench of offal and the color of blood, and peopled it with characters reeking with personality and lusty speech. This is one of the first and best of a thousand English novels of the sea. But before being dragooned into the navy Roderick, like his creator, samples English inns and London morals. What have we not missed by not traveling in those eighteenth-century coaches and putting up in those inns!—such a gallery of conflicting egos, decaying soldiers, pimps and bawds, peddlers lugging their bundles and hiding their money, men turning over chamber pots in search of the wrong bed, women shrieking rape and quieted with coin, every poor soul pretending magnitude, and everyone swearing. Miss Jenny calls the peddler "you old cent per cent fornicator!" and asks the captain, "Damn you, sir, who are *you?* Who made *you* a captain, you pitiful, trencher-scraping, pimping curler? 'Sdeath! the army is come to a fine pass when such fellows as you get commissions."[102]

In London Roderick (who here = Smollett) becomes a "journeyman apothecary"—a druggist's assistant. He escapes marriage by finding his betrothed in bed with another man. "Heaven gave me patience and presence of mind to withdraw immediately, and I thanked my stars a thousand times for the happy discovery by which I resolved to profit so much as to abandon all thoughts of marriage for the future."[103] He contents himself with promiscuity, learns the ways and woes of streetwalkers, cures their infections, denounces the quacks that fleece them, and notes how the prostitute, "although often complained of as a nuisance, still escapes through her in-

terest with the justices, to whom she and all of her employment pay contributions quarterly for protection."[104]

Wrongly accused of theft, he loses his job, and falls into such destitution
that "I saw no resource but the army and navy." He is saved the torment
of deciding by a press gang that knocks him unconscious and drags him
aboard H. M. S. *Thunder*. He accepts his fate, and becomes surgeon's mate.
Only after a day at sea does he perceive that Captain Oakum is a half-
insane brute, who for economy's sake keeps sick sailors at work till they die.
Roderick fights at Cartagena; he is shipwrecked, swims ashore to Jamaica,
becomes footman to an old run-down poetess, falls "in love" with her niece
Narcissa, and "conceived hopes of one day enjoying this amiable creature."[105] And so the narrative runs on, in Smollett's breathless flow, in
paragraphs three pages long, in language simple, vigorous, and profane. In
London Roderick makes a new set of eccentric friends, including Miss
Melinda Goosetrap and Miss Biddy Gripewell. Then to Bath, with more
coach scenes; there he encounters sweet Narcissa, wins her love, loses her,
fights a duel. . . . He rejoins the navy as surgeon, sails to Guinea (where
his captain "buys" four hundred slaves to sell them in Paraguay "to great
advantage"), again to Jamaica, where he finds his long-lost, now moneyed
father; back to Europe; back to Narcissa; marriage; back to Scotland and
the paternal estate; Narcissa "begins to grow remarkably round in the
waist." As for Roderick,

> If there be such a thing as true happiness on earth, I enjoy it. The
> tempestuous transports of my passion are now settled and mellowed
> into endearing fondness and tranquillity of love, rooted by that intimate
> connection and interchange of hearts which nought but virtuous wed-
> lock can produce.

Roderick Random had a good sale. Smollett insisted now on publishing
his play, *The Regicide*, with a prefatory annihilation of those who had rejected it; throughout his career he gave his temper carte blanche to make
enemies. He went up to Aberdeen in 1750 and received the degree in medicine; but his personality impeded his practice, and he sank back into literature. In 1751 he brought forth *The Adventures of Peregrine Pickle*; here,
as in *Random*, the title invited the reader to a round of exciting incidents
in a wandering life; but now Smollett struck a vein of salty humor in his
most successful character. Commodore Trunnion is described as "a very
oddish kind of gentleman"; he has been "a great warrior in his time, and
lost an eye and a heel in the service";[106] he insists on telling, for the nth
time, how he bombarded a French man-of-war off Cape Finisterre. He
commands his servant Tom Piper to corroborate him; whereupon Tom
"opened his mouth like a gasping cod, and, with a cadence like that of the

east wind singing through a cranny," gave the required support. (Here, perhaps, Sterne took some hints for Uncle Toby and Corporal Trim.)

Smollett frolics through a boisterous account of how Mrs. Grizzle courts the Commodore, whose one-legged lieutenant, Jack Hatchway, begs him not to let her "bring him to under her stern," for "if once you are made fast to her poop, egad, she'll spank it away, and make every beam in your body crack with straining." The Commodore reassures him, "No man shall ever see Hawser Trunnion laying astern in the wake of e'er a b——h in Christendom."[107] Sundry stratagems, however, break down his chastity; he consents to "grapple"—i.e., marry; but he goes to the splicing "like a felon to execution, . . . as if every moment he dreaded the dissolution of Nature." He insists upon a hammock as a marriage bed; it breaks under the double load, but not before the lady "thought her great aim accomplished, and her authority secured against all the shocks of fortune." Nevertheless this navel engagement ends without issue, and Mrs. Trunnion falls back upon brandy and "the duties of religion, which she performed with a most rancorous severity."

Sir Walter Scott pictured Smollett in his forties as "eminently handsome, his features prepossessing, and, by the joint testimony of all his surviving friends, his conversation in the highest degree instructive and amusing."[108] By all accounts he was a man of hot temper and vivid speech. So he described Sir Charles Knowles as "an admiral without conduct, an engineer without knowledge, an officer without resolution, and a man without veracity."[109] The Admiral prosecuted him for libel, and Smollett suffered three months' imprisonment and a fine of a hundred pounds (1757). Along with his irascibility went many virtues: he was generous and humane, helped poor authors, and became, said Sir Walter, "a doting father and an affectionate husband."[110] His house in Lawrence Lane, Chelsea, was a rendezvous of minor scribes, who took his food if not his advice; some of them he organized into a corps of literary aides. He was one of the first prose writers (Dryden the first poet?) to make the booksellers support him in a condition befitting his genius. He earned sometimes six hundred pounds in a year, but he had to work hard for them. He wrote three more novels, two of them negligible; he persuaded Garrick to produce his play *The Reprisal*, which won success with its attacks upon France; he contributed pugnaciously to several magazines, and edited *The Briton* as a Tory mouthpiece. He translated *Gil Blas*, several works of Voltaire, and (with the help of an earlier version) *Don Quixote;* and he wrote—or presided over—a nine-volume *History of England* (1757–65). Certainly he used his "literary factory" of Grub Street hacks in compiling a *Universal History*, and an eight-volume *Present State of the Nations*.

By 1763, aged forty-two, he had paid with broken health for his eager life of adventure, work, brawls, and vocabulary. His physician advised him to consult a specialist, Dr. Fizes, at Montpellier. He went, and was told that his asthma, cough, and purulent expectoration indicated tuberculosis. Loath to return to England's verdant moisture, he remained on the Continent for two years, covering his costs by writing *Travels through France and Italy* (1766). Here, as in his novels, he showed his quick, sharp eye for the signs and mannerisms of individual and national character; but he peppered his description with candid vituperation. He told coachmen, fellow travelers, innkeepers, servants, and foreign patriots just what he thought of them; he challenged every bill, demolished French and Italian art, belabored Catholicism, and dismissed the French as acquisitive thieves who did not always coat their thefts with courtesy. Hear him:

> If a Frenchman is admitted into your family . . . the first return he makes for your civilities is to make love to your wife, if she is handsome; if not, to your sister, or daughter, or niece, . . . or grandmother. . . . If he is detected . . . he impudently declares that what he had done was no more than simple gallantry, considered in France as indispensable to good breeding.[111]

Smollett returned to England much improved in health. But in 1768 his ailments revived, and he sought a cure in Bath. He found its waters useless to him, and its damp air dangerous; in 1769 he was back in Italy. In a villa near Leghorn he wrote his last and best book, *The Expedition of Humphrey Clinker*, which Thackeray thought "the most laughable story that has ever been written since the goodly art of novel-writing began."[112] It is certainly the most pleasant and amiable of Smollett's books, if we can stomach a little scatology. Almost at the outset we meet Dr. L——n, who discourses on "good" or "bad" smells as purely subjective prejudices, "for that every person who pretended to nauseate the smell of another's excretions snuffed up his own with particular complacency; for the truth of which he appealed to all the ladies and gentlemen there present";[113] followed by a page or two of still more pungent illustrations. Having relieved himself of this morsel, Smollett went on to invent a jolly gamut of characters, who carry the narrative forward by their letters in the most incredible and delightful way. At their head is Matthew Bramble, an "old gentleman" and invincible bachelor who serves as Smollett's voice. He goes to Bath for health, but finds the stench of its waters more impressive than their curative power. He hates crowds, and once faints at their corporate odor. He cannot bear the polluted air of London, or its adulterated foods:

> The bread I eat in London is a deleterious paste, mixed up with chalk, alum, and bone ashes; insipid to the taste and destructive to the

constitution. The good people are not ignorant of this adulteration, but they prefer it to wholesome bread, because it is whiter. . . . Thus they sacrifice their taste and their health, . . . and the miller or the baker is obliged to poison them. . . . The same monstrous depravity appears in their veal, which is bleached by repeated bleedings, and other villain-ous arts, . . . so that a man might dine as comfortably on a fricassee of kidskin gloves. . . . You will hardly believe that they can be so mad as to boil their greens with brass half-pence in order to improve their color.[114]

So Matthew hurries back to his rural estate, where he can breathe and eat without risking his life. En route, after the story is one-fourth told, he picks up a poor, half-naked country lad, Humphrey Clinker; "his looks denoted famine, and the rags that he wore could hardly conceal what decency re-quires to be covered." This ragamuffin offers to drive the coach; but when he takes the high seat his aged breeches split, and Mrs. Tabitha Bramble (Matthew's sister) complains that Humphrey "had the impudence to shock her sight by showing his bare posteriors." Matthew clothes the boy, takes him into his service, and bears with him patiently even when the youth, having heard George Whitefield, becomes a Methodist preacher.

Another facet of the religious situation appears in Mr. H——t, whom Bramble meets in Scarborough, and who boasts of having conferred with Voltaire at Geneva "about giving the last blow to the Christian supersti-tion."[115] Another maverick, Captain Lismahago, enters the story at Durham —"a tall, meager figure, answering, with horse, to the description of Don Quixote mounted on Rozinante." He has lived among North American Indians, and he tells with relish how these roasted two French missionaries for saying that God had allowed his son "to enter the bowels of a woman, and be executed as a malefactor," and for pretending that they could "mul-tiply God *ad infinitum* by the help of a little flour and water." Lismahago "dwelt much upon the words *reason, philosophy,* and *contradiction in terms;* he bade defiance to the eternity of hell-fire; and even threw such squibs at the immortality of the soul as singed a little the whiskers of Mrs. Tabitha's faith."[116]

Smollett never saw *Humphrey Clinker* in print. On September 17, 1771, he died in his Italian villa, aged fifty, having made more enemies and cre-ated more vivacious characters than any other writer of his time. We miss in him the good nature, the healthy acceptance of life, and the painstaking construction of plot, that we find in Fielding; but there is a lusty vitality in Smollett, the tang and smell of Britain's towns and ships and middle class; and his simple episodic narrative flows on more freely and vividly, unim-peded by homilies. Characterization is less striking in Fielding, but more complex; Smollett is often content to accumulate mannerisms instead of exploring the contradictions, doubts, and tentatives that make a personality. This mode of individualization—by exaggerating some peculiarity as a leitmotiv in each person—passed down to Dickens, whose *Pickwick Papers* continued the tour that Matthew Bramble began.

Taken together, Richardson, Fielding, and Smollett describe mid-eighteenth-century England more fully and graphically than any or all the historians—who lose themselves in exceptions. Everything is here but that upper class which took from France her manners and her colonies. These novelists brought the middle classes triumphantly into literature, as Lillo brought them into drama, and Gay into opera, and Hogarth into art. They created the modern novel, and left it as a heritage unsurpassed.

VI. LADY MARY

So England familiarly called the most brilliant Englishwoman of her generation, who entered into the history of manners by striking at the conventions that imprisoned her sex, and who entered into the history of literature by writing letters that rival Mme. de Sévigné's.

She had a good start; she was granddaughter of Sir John Evelyn, and daughter of Evelyn Pierrepont, who, in the year of her birth (1689), was elected to Parliament, and soon thereafter succeeded to a rich estate as Earl of Kingston; hence his daughter was Lady Mary from her infancy. Her mother, Lady Mary Feilding (so she spelled it), had an earl for her father, and the novelist for her cousin. She died when our present heroine was only four. The father sent his children to be reared by his mother; when she passed away they returned to his luxurious country seat, Thoresby Park, in Nottinghamshire; and sometimes they lived in his town house in Piccadilly. He was especially fond of Mary, whom he nominated, aged eight, as toast of the year at the Kit-Cat Club; there she moved from lap to lap, and impishly displayed her wit. Helped by a governess, she educated herself in her father's library, spending there sometimes eight hours a day, absorbing French romances and English plays. She gathered some French and Italian, and taught herself Latin with Ovid's *Metamorphoses*. Addison, Steele, and Congreve frequented the house, encouraged her studies, and stirred her eager mind. We are told, on no authority but her own, that it was her knowledge of the Latin classics that won her the attention of Edward Wortley.

He was a grandson of Edward Montagu, first Earl of Sandwich; his father, Sidney Montagu, had taken the name Wortley on marrying an heiress of that name. Edward, when he met Mary (1708), was already, at thirty, a man of mark and great expectations; he had a university education, had been called to the bar at twenty-one, had won a seat in Parliament at twenty-seven. We do not know how her courtship of him began, but it made some progress, for on March 28, 1710, she wrote to him:

> Give me leave to say it (I know it sounds vain), I know how to make a man of sense happy; but then that man . . . must contribute something towards it himself. . . . This letter . . . is the first I ever writ to one of your sex, and shall be the last. You must never expect another.[117]

Her Fabian strategy prospered. When she fell ill of measles he sent her a note warmer than his wont: "I should be overjoyed to hear your Beauty is very much impaired, could I be pleased with anything that would give you displeasure, for it would lessen the number of Admirers."[118] Her reply carried the campaign a step onward: "You think, if you married me, I should be passionately fond of you for one month, and of somebody else the next; neither would happen. I can esteem, I can be a friend, but I don't know whether I can love."[119] This candor may have given him pause, for in November she wrote: "You say you are not yet determined; let me determine for you, and save you the trouble of writing again. Adieu forever! Make no answer!"[120] She wrote again in February, 1711, to tell him, "This is the last letter I shall send."[121] He resumed his advances, she retreated, and lured him into precipitate pursuit. Financial considerations intervened, and parental opposition. They planned elopement, though this meant that she could expect no dowry from her father. She gave Wortley an honest warning: "Reflect now for the last time in what manner you must take me. I shall come to you with only a nightgown and petticoat, and that is all you will get with me."[122] They met at an inn, and were married in August, 1712; henceforth she was Lady Mary Wortley Montagu. This last name she took as that of her husband's family line; but as he was the son of a second son, he continued to be called simply Edward Wortley.

Business and politics soon carried him to Durham and London, while he left her with very modest means in divers country houses to await the coming of her child. In April she joined Wortley in London, and there, in May, her first child was born. Her happiness was brief, for her husband went off to seek re-election, and soon she was complaining of her loneliness; she had looked for a romantic honeymoon, he looked for a seat in the new Parliament. His costly campaign failed, but he was appointed a junior commissioner. He rented a house near St. James's Palace, and there, in January, 1715, Lady Mary began her conquest of London.

She sampled the social whirl. She entertained on Mondays, went to the opera on Wednesdays, to the theater on Thursdays. She visited and was visited, fluttered about the court of George I, and nevertheless won favor

FIG. 25—HYACINTHE RIGAUD: *Louis XV at the Age of Six*. Château de Versailles (Bettmann Archive)

FIG. 26—MAURICE QUENTIN DE LA TOUR: *Louis XV*. Louvre, Paris (Bettmann Archive) PAGE 320

FIG. 27—HYACINTHE RIGAUD: *Cardinal Fleury*. Reproduced by permission of the Trustees of the Wallace Collection, London (Bettmann Archive) PAGE 269

FIG. 28—CARLE VANLOO: *Marie Leszczyńska*. Louvre, Paris (Bettmann Archive) PAGE 273

Fig. 29—François Boucher: *Madame de Pompadour*. Reproduced by permission of the Trustees of the Wallace Collection, London   PAGE 279

<small>Fig. 30—Maurice Quentin de La Tour: *Madame de Pompadour*. Louvre, Paris (Bettmann Archive)</small>

FIG. 31—JEAN MARC NATTIER: *Madame de Châteauroux*. Musée des Beaux-Arts, Mar-
seilles

Fig. 32—*Interior Decoration, Louis Quinze Style: Drawing Room in the Hôtel de Ludre*, Paris. From *French Art of the 18th Century*, Ed. Stéphane Faniel (New York: Simon and Schuster, 1957)   PAGE 304

FIG. 33—*Faïence Soup Tureen from Lunéville in Lorraine, Period of King Stanislas.* Nicolier Collection (reproduced from *French Art of the 18th Century*, ed. Faniel)

PAGE 305

FIG. 34—JACQUES CAFFIÉRI AND A. R. GAUDREAU: *Commode.* Reproduced by permission of the Trustees of the Wallace Collection, London (Bettmann Archive)   PAGE 304

Fig. 37—*Tapestry, Period of Louis XV.* Thiérard Collection (reproduced from *French Art of the 18th Century*, ed. Faniel)   PAGE 305

FIG. 35—*Andirons, Period of Louis XV*. Château de Versailles   PAGE 306

FIG. 36—*Mantel Clock, Period of Louis XV*.
Reproduced by permission of the Trustees of
the Wallace Collection, London   PAGE 306

FIG. 38—ROSLIN: *François Boucher.*
Château de Versailles   PAGE 313

FIG. 39—JEAN LAMOUR: *Iron Gates of the Place Stanislas*, Nancy. From Max Osborn,
Die Kunst des Rokoko (Berlin: Propyläen-Verlag, 1926)   PAGE 308

FIG. 40—FRANÇOIS BOUCHER: *The Luncheon* from *Italian Scenes* Tapestries. The Henry
E. Huntington Library and Art Gallery, San Marino, California   PAGE 315

FIG. 41—GUILLAUME COUSTOU I: *One of the Horses of Marly*, Place de la Concorde, Paris. Photograph courtesy of Roger Viollet (Bettmann Archive)   PAGE 308

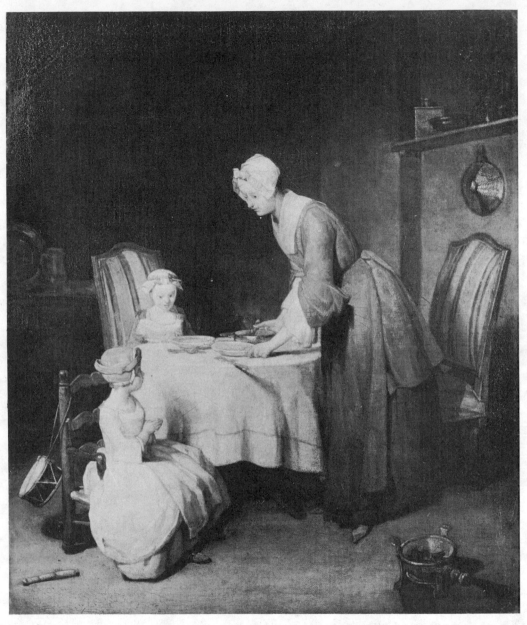

FIG. 42—JEAN BAPTISTE CHARDIN: *Le Bénédicité*. Louvre, Paris (Bettmann Archive)

FIG. 43—JEAN BAPTISTE CHARDIN: *The Artist's Second Wife*. Louvre, Paris (Bettmann Archive)   PAGE 318

FIG. 44—JEAN BAPTISTE CHARDIN: *Self-Portrait*. Louvre, Paris (Bettmann Archive)   PAGE 316

FIG. 45—FRANÇOIS BOUCHER: *The Rape of Europa.* Louvre, Paris (Bettmann Archive)

PAGE 314

with Princess Caroline. She cultivated the poets, and bandied wit with Pope and Gay. Pope was fascinated by her alert intelligence; he forgot for a moment his scorn of the subtler sex, applauded her efforts for the education of girls, and dedicated to her some hurried rhymes:

> In beauty or wit
> No mortal as yet
> To question your empire has dared;
> But men of discerning
> Have thought that in learning,
> To yield to a lady was hard.
>
> Impertinent schools
> With musty dull rules
> Have reading to females denied;
> So Papists refuse
> The Bible to use,
> Lest flocks be as wise as their guide
>
> 'Twas a woman at first
> (Indeed she was curs'd)
> In knowledge that tasted delight;
> And sages agree
> The laws should decree
> To the first possessor the right.
>
> Then bravely, fair dame,
> Resume the old claim,
> Which to your whole sex does belong;
> And let men receive
> From a second bright Eve
> The knowledge of right and of wrong.
>
> But if the first Eve
> Hard doom did receive
> When only one apple had she,
> What a punishment new
> Shall be found out for you,
> Who, tasting, have robbed the whole tree?[123]

Gay now composed an eclogue, "The Toilet," in which some London celebrities were satirized under transparent pseudonyms. Lady Mary took a hand in the game. With help from Gay and Pope, she wrote two eclogues whose cutting couplets rivaled theirs in elegance and pricking point. She did not publish these poems, but she allowed manuscript copies to pass among her friends. She now acquired the reputation of a female Pope, adept with pen and rhyme and wounds.

In December, 1715, she suffered a blow sharper than her darts. Small-pox, which had killed her brother, attacked her so severely that gossip talked of her death. She survived, but her face was pockmarked, her lashes had fallen out; only her brilliant black eyes remained of the beauty on which she had counted as a help to her husband's advancement. Wortley got his plum nevertheless; in April, 1716, he was appointed "ambassador extraordinary" to the court of Turkey. Lady Mary was delighted; she had dreamed of the East as the land of romance, and even with her husband along she might find romance in Constantinople or on the way. Pope, also touched with fantasy, wrote to her on July 1 a letter that elegantly skirted the precipice of love:

> If I thought I should not see you again, I would say some things here which I could not to your Person. For I would not have you die deceived in me, that is, go to Constantinople without knowing that I am, to some degree of Extravagance, as well as with the utmost Reason, Madam—

and then signed with the usual flourish of humble and obedient servitude.[124]

On August 1 Wortley, Mary, their three-year-old son, and a large retinue crossed to Holland. They passed down through Cologne to Regensburg, where they embarked on a houseboat which twelve oarsmen rowed past castled mountaintops. At Vienna she found a letter from Pope offering her his heart and assuring her

> not that I think everybody naked altogether so fine a sight as yourself and a few more would be. . . . You may easily imagine how desirous I must be of a correspondence with a person who had taught me, long ago, that it was as impossible to esteem at first sight as to love; and who has since ruined me for all the conversation of one sex, and almost all the friendship of the other. Books have lost their effect upon me, and I was convinced, since I saw you, that there is something more powerful than philosophy, and, since I heard you, that there is one alive wiser than all the sages.[125]

But he added the hope that she would be happy with her husband. She replied:

> Perhaps you'll laugh at me for thanking you very gravely for all the obliging concern you express for me. 'Tis certain that I may, if I please, take the fine things you say to me for wit and raillery, and, it may be, it would be taking them right. But I never in my life was half so well disposed to believe you in earnest.[126]

On February 3, 1717, Pope dispatched another declaration of profound affection, protesting against being considered "only her friend." These letters Mary kept to herself, happy to have stirred the ruins of the greatest living poet.

The party reached Constantinople in May. There Mary set about resolutely to learn Turkish; she progressed to the understanding and admiration of Turkish poetry; she adopted Turkish dress, visited harem ladies, and found them more civilized than the mistresses of George I. She observed the regular and successful practice of inoculation in Turkey as a preventive of smallpox; and she had her son inoculated by the English surgeon Dr. Maitland in Constantinople. Her letters from that city are as fascinating as any letters this side of Mme. de Sévigné, Horace Walpole, or Melchior Grimm. She did not wait to be told that they were literature; she wrote with that aspiration, and told her friends: "The last pleasure that fell my way was Mme. de Sévigné's letters; very pretty they are, but I assert, without the least vanity, that mine will be full as entertaining forty years hence. I advise you, therefore, to put none of them to the use of waste paper."[127]

Her correspondence with Pope continued. He begged her to take his protestations seriously, but his tone was a baffling mixture of playfulness and love. In his rakish imagination he conceived Turkey as a "land of jealousy, where the unhappy women converse with none but eunuchs, and where the very cucumbers are brought to them cut." And then, thinking sadly of his misshapenness, he added: "I am capable myself of following one I loved, not only to Constantinople, but to those parts of India where, they tell us, the women best like the ugliest fellows, . . . and look upon deformities as the signatures of divine favor." He will become a Mohammedan if she will, and will accompany her to Mecca; if sufficiently encouraged he will meet her in Lombardy, "the scene of those celebrated amours between the fairy princess and her dwarf."[128] When he learned that she was coming home he mounted to the semblance of ecstasy: "I write as if I were drunk; the pleasure I take in thinking of your return transports me beyond the bounds of common sense and decency. . . . Come, for God's sake, come, Lady Mary, come quickly!"[129]

Wortley's mission failed, and he was recalled to London. We get a sample of eighteenth-century travel in their departure from Constantinople on June 25, 1718, and their arrival in London on October 2. There Lady Mary resumed her life at court and with the wits, but Pope, now marching through Homer, was busy at Stanton Harcourt. In March, 1719, however, he moved to Twickenham, and in June, with his help, Wortley and Lady Mary found a home there, too, sold them by Sir Godfrey Kneller. Soon afterward Pope paid Kneller twenty guineas to paint her portrait for him.[130] It was well done, though Kneller was seventy-four. The hands were exquisite, the face almost as Oriental as the Turkish headdress; the lips sensually full, the eyes large, dark, and still entrancing—Gay celebrated them in

verses at this time. Pope hung the picture in his bedroom, and commemorated it in a poem which he sent to her:

> The playful smiles around the dimpled mouth,
> The happy air of majesty and truth; . . .
> The equal luster of the heavenly mind,
> Where every grace with every virtue's joined;
> Learning not vain, and wisdom not severe,
> With greatness easy, and with wit sincere . . .[131]

That year was her meridian, and the beginning of calamities. A French
visitor, Toussaint Rémond, left two thousand pounds with her to invest
at her discretion; on Pope's advice she bought South Sea Company stock;
it fell disastrously, reducing the two thousand to five hundred; when she so
reported to Rémond he accused her of stealing his funds (1721). In that
same year a smallpox epidemic threatened the life of the daughter born to
her in 1718; she sent for Dr. Maitland, who had returned from Constantinople, and had him inoculate the girl. We shall see later the effect of this
example on British medicine before Jenner.

Suddenly, in 1722, her friendship with Pope collapsed. As late as July
they saw each other so frequently that gossip flared in Twickenham. But
in September he began to write gallant epistles to Judith Cowper, in which,
for her comfort, he mentioned an obvious decline in "the brightest wit in
the world." Lady Mary claimed that Pope had made her a passionate declaration of love, and that he had never forgiven the levity with which she
had greeted this brave enterprise.[132] He held his peace for a while, but now
and then he pointed his occasional verse with barbs only transparently
disguised. When she wrote to a friend naming Swift, Pope, and Gay as
joint authors of a ballad that he thought was hers, he sent her a sharp reproof; and in the *Miscellanies* that he published in 1728 he printed this reproof with flagrant clarity:

> Such, Lady Mary, are your tricks;
> But since you hatch, pray own your chicks;
> You should be better skilled in nocks,
> Nor, like your capons, serve your cocks.[133]

In a poem called "Imitation" (1733) he referred to "furious Sappho . . .
p—x'd by her love"—i.e., infected with syphilis by a paramour.[134] According to Horace Walpole she threatened to have him whipped.

This obscene quarrel was added to the wreck of her marriage. Wortley,
resuming his place in Parliament, left her conspicuously neglected in
Twickenham. His father's death (1727) made him a very rich man; he

supplied her material wants, but left her to her own resources for love. Her son was proving himself a shiftless rascal. Her daughter, growing into an intelligent and well-mannered woman, was her only consolation. Lord Hervey tried to take the place of Pope in her life, but he was so constituted that he could not forgive her, or his wife, for being a woman. He must have known of Lady Mary's division of the human race into men, women, and Herveys.[135]

In 1736 an Italian meteor entered and altered her orbit. Francesco Algarotti, born in Venice in 1712, had already made some noise in science and belles-lettres. In 1735 he had been the house guest of Voltaire and Mme. du Châtelet at Cirey, where all three studied Newton. He came to London with letters of introduction from Voltaire, was received at court, met Hervey, and through him Lady Mary. She fell in love with him as never with Wortley, for her heart was empty, and he was handsome, brilliant, young; she trembled at the thought that she was forty-seven and he twenty-four. Her road to romance seemed cleared by the marriage of her daughter to the Earl of Bute (August, 1736). When she heard that Algarotti was returning to Italy she dispatched to him a letter of girlish passion:

> I no longer know in what manner to write you. My feelings are too lively; I should not be able either to explain or hide them. To bear with my letters you would have to be touched with an enthusiasm like mine. I see all its folly, without any possibility of correcting myself. The mere idea of seeing you has given me a transport to the point of melting away. What has become of that philosophic indifference which made the glory and tranquillity of my earlier days? I have lost it never to find it again; and should this passion be cured, I foresee nothing but a deadly ennui. Forgive the extravagance which you have caused, and come to see me.[136]

He came, and supped with her on the eve of his departure. Hervey had also invited him, and had been refused. Furious with jealousy, he wrote to Algarotti a bitter diatribe against Lady Mary, warning him that she was proclaiming to all London her Italian conquest with the boast *"Veni, vidi, vici."* Possibly, but her letters to Algarotti were not those of a conqueror.

> How timid one is when one loves! I fear to offend you in sending you this note, even though my intention is to give you pleasure. Indeed, I am so mad in all that concerns you that I am not sure of my own thoughts. . . . All that is certain is that I shall love you all my life long, despite your caprice and my reason.[137]

He did not answer this letter, nor a second, nor a third, though she spoke of suicide. A fourth letter drew a reply which came, she said, "in very good time to save the small remains of my understanding." She offered to follow him to Italy; he discouraged the idea, and for three years she nursed her passion in solitude. But in 1739 she persuaded her husband that she needed a trip to Italy. Having lost his love for her, he could behave like a gentleman. He saw her off when she left London, and agreed to send her a quarterly allowance of £245 from his own income, and to transmit to her the £150 annual income bequeathed her by her father. She traveled as quickly as she could to Venice, hoping to find Algarotti there; instead he went to Berlin (1740) to live with new-crowned Frederick II, who liked him this side of sodomy. Disconsolate, Mary took a house on the Grand Canal, established a salon, entertained literati and dignitaries, and received pleasant attentions from the Venetian aristocracy and government.

After a year in Venice she moved to Florence, where she stayed for two months at the Palazzo Ridolfi as the guest of Lord and Lady Pomfret. There Horace Walpole saw her, and he sent to H. S. Conway a tender description:

> Did I tell you Lady Mary Wortley is here? She laughs at my Lady Walpole [Horace's sister-in-law], scolds Lady Pomfret, and is laughed at by the whole town. Her dress, her avarice, and her impudence must amaze anyone that never heard her name. She wears a foul mob [a cap fastened under the chin] that does not cover her greasy black locks, that hang loose, never combed or curled; an old . . . blue wrapper that gapes open and discloses a canvas petticoat. Her face swelled violently on one side with the remains of a —— partly covered with a plaister, and partly with white paint. . . . She played pharaoh two or three times at Princess Craon's where she cheats horse and foot. She is really entertaining; I have been reading her works, which she lends out in manuscript; but they are too womanish; I like few of her performances.[138]

There was a basis in fact for this caricature: it was the custom in Italy for a woman in her own home to dress in loose and careless comfort; and doubtless Mary's face was badly pocked, but not certainly with syphilis.[139] It was quite usual for authors to lend their manuscripts to friends. Lady Mary had earned young Walpole's displeasure by befriending Molly Skerrett, who had earned his displeasure by becoming the second wife of his father. Probably Lady Mary was more than usually careless of her appearance now that Algarotti seemed hopelessly lost to her.

Then, learning that Algarotti was in Turin, she hurried thither, joined him (March, 1741), and lived with him for two months. But he treated her with coarseness and indifference; soon they quarreled and parted, he to Berlin, she to Genoa. There Walpole saw her again, enjoyed her hospitality, and addressed to her coach some venomous lines:

> O chaise, who art condemned to carry
> The rotten hide of Lady Mary,
> To Italy's last corner drive,
> And prithee set her down alive;
> Nor jumble off with jolts and blows
> The half she yet retains of nose.[140]

In 1760 she rejoiced to learn that her son-in-law had become a member of George III's Privy Council. On January 21, 1761, her husband died, leaving the bulk of his estate to his daughter, and £1,200 a year to his widow. Whether because his death removed some mysterious obstacle to her return, or her son-in-law's political prominence attracted her, Lady Mary, after twenty-one years of absence, returned to England (January, 1762).

She had only seven more months to live, and they were not happy. Her pursuit of Algarotti, and such reports as Horace Walpole's, had given her a bad name; and her daughter, though solicitous for her mother's health and comfort, did not enjoy her company. In June Lady Mary began to suffer from a tumor on the breast. She took calmly her doctor's confession that she had cancer; she said she had lived long enough. She died after months of pain (August 21, 1762).

One of her last requests was that her letters should be published to give her side of her story, and establish her title to remembrance. But she had entrusted her manuscripts to her daughter, and Lady Bute, now wife of the Prime Minister, did all she could to prevent their publication. However, the letters written from Turkey were clandestinely copied before being delivered to the daughter, and they were issued in 1763. Several editions were soon sold out. Johnson and Gibbon were among the delighted readers. The critics, who had been unmerciful to the author during her lifetime, were now extravagant in praising her correspondence. Smollett wrote that the letters were "never equaled by any letter-writer of any sex, age, or nation"; and Voltaire rated them as superior to Sévigné's.[141] Lady Bute, before she died in 1794, burned her mother's voluminous diary, but left the letters to the discretion of her eldest son. He allowed some of them to be printed in 1803; those to Algarotti remained secret until Byron persuaded John Murray to buy them from their Italian owner (1817). Not till 1861 was publication complete; and Lady Mary was recognized as sharing with Pope, Gray, Gay, Richardson, Fielding, Smollett, and Hume in making the literature of England the most varied, vibrant and influential of that virile age.

CHAPTER VI

Art and Music

1714–56

I. THE ARTISTS

SHINING brilliantly with its own light in literature and statesmanship, England was a humble satellite in music and art. The retardation in art had many causes. The gloomy skies could hardly be one of them, for skies gloomed in the Netherlands too, and yet Holland had as many artists as windmills. The Channel may have been a cause, shielding England from the arts as well as the wars of the Continent. Perhaps English talent was too absorbed in commerce and (after Walpole) in war. Protestantism might be blamed for the becalming of English art, for art grows on imagination, and Protestantism had banished imagination from art and dedicated it to literature and theology; but, again, Holland was Protestant. Probably the chief factor was the Puritan revolt and legacy: the execution of the art-loving Charles I, the dispersion of his art collection, and the recession of the English mind—barring Milton—during the chaotic Commonwealth. The Puritan influence bowed its head during the Restoration, but it returned with William III and the Hanoverians, and in Methodism it took a reinvigorated form. Beauty was again a sin.

There were some minor achievements in the minor arts. Fine soft-paste porcelain was produced in Chelsea (1755), imitating Meissen and Sèvres. Birmingham japanners made fortunes in lacquered ware; one of them, John Baskerville, grew rich enough to indulge in printing fine editions of English bards. Rococo curves in riotous fancy decorated books, fabrics, furniture, vessels, Sheffield silver, the Rotunda at Vauxhall Gardens, and some rooms in Chesterfield House and Strawberry Hill.

Sculptors were just beginning to be distinguished from masons. The leading sculptors in England were of foreign birth, though they usually became British citizens. Peter Schaemaekers came from Antwerp and joined Laurent Delvaux in carving the statue of the Duke of Buckingham and Normanby in Westminster Abbey. Greatest of these aliens was Louis Roubillac, son of a Lyonese banker. Coming to England in 1744, he was rapidly advanced as a protégé of the Walpoles. He executed the bust of Shakespeare now in the British Museum, and that of Handel now in the National Portrait Gallery. Queen Caroline favored him, sat for him, commissioned him to make busts of Boyle, Newton,

Locke, and other English worthies for her grotto at Richmond. Chesterfield, a man of taste, called Roubillac "the Pheidias of his day."[1] Roubillac died a bankrupt in 1762, after a life of devotion to his art.

Architecture was in a Palladian ecstasy. The rising wealth of upper classes prospering discontentedly under the Walpolian peace financed a thousand grand tours, during which British gentlemen imbibed a liking for Roman temples and Renaissance palaces. Venice was always on the itinerary; on the way the traveler stopped at Vicenza to admire Palladio's facades; and on their return they littered England with classical columns, architraves, and pediments. In 1715-25 Colin Campbell issued his *Vitruvius Britannicus*, which became the bible of the Palladians; William Kent (1727) and James Gibbs (1728) furthered the style with their architectural manuals. In 1716 Richard Boyle, third Earl of Burlington, printed a sumptuous edition of Palladio's texts, and in 1730 he published Palladio's restorations of ancient edifices. His own country house at Chiswick included a replica of Palladio's Villa Rotonda at Vicenza, with columned portico and central dome. Burlington was an openhanded patron of literature, music and art, friend of Berkeley and Handel, of Pope and Gay.

In 1719 he brought back with him from Rome a young architect, William Kent, who had won a papal prize for his paintings and was also an enthusiast for everything classical. Housed till his death in Burlington House (still, in its second incarnation, a center of English art), Kent became the most popular and versatile artist in England. He painted ceilings at Houghton, Stowe, and Kensington Palace; he designed furniture, dinner plate, mirrors, glass, a barge, and costumes for fashionable ladies; he carved the statue of Shakespeare in the Abbey; he was a leader in promoting the "natural" English garden; as an architect he built the Temple of Ancient Virtue in the Stowe gardens, Devonshire House in Piccadilly, the Horse Guards House in Whitehall, and the prodigious Holkham Hall in Norfolk.

In 1738 Lord Burlington submitted to the London City Council Kent's Palladian plan for Mansion House, residence of the lord mayor; a member objected that Palladio was a papist; Kent's design was rejected; George Dance the Elder, a Protestant, received the commission and acquitted himself well. But in that year the excavations began at Herculaneum; the discoveries there led to the unearthing of Pompeii (1748 f.); in 1753 Robert Wood published *The Ruins of Palmyra*, and in 1757 *The Ruins of Baalbek*; these revelations gave the classical campaign in England an irresistible verve, and put an end to the baroque exuberance that had flowered in Vanbrugh's palace for the Churchills, Blenheim. In 1748 Isaac Ware, another protégé of Burlington, built Chesterfield House in Curzon Street.

In their enthusiasm the Palladians forgot that classical architecture had been designed for Mediterranean skies, not for English winds and clouds. Colin Campbell was a special sinner in adopting Italian models without adapting them to English winters; his Mereworth Castle gave scant entry to the sun, and the Houghton Hall that he built for Robert Walpole sacrificed living space to majestic halls inviting icy drafts. James Gibbs, a disciple of Christopher Wren, used the classic style to fine effect in the Church of St. Mary-le-Strand in London (1714-17); its steeple is a lyric in stone. To the Church of St. Clement Dane, built by Wren, Gibbs added (1719) a steeple too lofty for its base, but still precariously beautiful. He capped his work in 1721 with the classic portico and Corinthian columns of St. Martin's-in-the-Fields, at Trafalgar Square, Finally in the Radcliffe Library (1737-47) he created a perfect harmony of columns and dome at Oxford.

The architectural splendor of Bath was due principally to John Wood. His dominating conception was to bind individual dwellings into a single mass; so he designed and began, and his son John ably completed, the massive "Royal Crescent"—thirty houses behind a united front of 114 Corinthian columns— severely but not irreparably damaged in the Second World War. Nearby Wood Senior and Junior built the "Circus" (1754-64), a handsome circle of residences faced by a continuous frieze and a three-tiered colonnade; here once lived the elder Pitt, Thomas Gainsborough, and Clive of India. For three sides of "Queen Square" Wood designed but never completed another series of homes united behind a palatial Renaissance façade. Much of this town-planning and -building program was financed by Ralph Allen, whom Fielding took as model for Squire Allworthy. For Allen the elder Wood raised a magnificent Palladian palace at Prior Park (1735-43), two miles outside Bath.

The poverty of Britain's masses was equaled by the splendor of her palaces. Allen's temple at Prior Park cost £240,000. A competitive craze inspired nobles and merchants to raise immense mansions for hospitality and display. According to Hervey, Robert Walpole earned the lasting enmity of Lord Townshend by building Houghton Hall on a still more lavish scale than Townshend's neighboring Raynham Park. Lord Lyttleton denounced this "epidemical madness" of palatial building; his wife, however, demanded a new palace, in Italian style; he yielded to her at the point of repetition and to the point of bankruptcy; when the palace was finished she left him for an Italian opera singer of uncertain sex. Soon England and even English Ireland were dotted with such show houses of the rich. Tours were organized, guidebooks were published, for visiting these lordly dwellings, their gardens, and their picture galleries. The fame of these edifices reached as far as Russia; Catherine the Great asked Josiah Wedgwood to make her an imperial table service decorated with views of English country seats.[2]

Most of the paintings in England were housed, and for the most part concealed, in these aristocratic homes; there were as yet no museums where pictures could be viewed by the general public. Patronage went chiefly to foreign artists, and almost entirely for portraits of notables who hoped to live on canvas while rotting in wood; there was no market for landscapes or "histories." When Carle Vanloo came to England in 1737 so many pedigreed faces clamored to be pictured that for several weeks after his arrival the train of carriages approaching his home rivaled that before a theater. Large sums were given to the man who kept the register of his engagements, as bribes to advance their appointments; else one might have to wait six weeks.[3]

The "Royal Society of Arts," founded in 1754, tried to stimulate native talent with competitions and exhibitions, but the demand for English art dallied for another generation. Joseph Highmore, a pupil of Kneller, secured a few purchasers by picturing scenes from *Pamela*,[4] and Thomas Hudson caught a fraction of Handel's vitality in the portrait that he painted in 1749.[5] Among Hudson's pupils was young Joshua Reynolds, "who," he predicted, "will never distinguish himself."[6] Sir James Thornhill had more foresight. He won success with portraits of Newton, Bentley, and Steele; he painted the inner cupola of St. Paul's, and ceilings at Greenwich Hospital and Blenheim Palace; and he achieved vicarious immortality by surrendering his daughter in marriage to the greatest English artist of the age.

II. WILLIAM HOGARTH: 1697–1764

His father was a schoolteacher plus literary hack, who apprenticed him in early youth to an engraver of arms. From this he passed to engraving on copper, and from this to making illustrations for books. In 1726 he prepared twelve large engravings for Butler's *Hudibras*. He joined Thornhill's art class, learned oil painting, and eloped with the master's daughter; Thornhill forgave him and engaged him as aide.

The illustrations that Hogarth made for *The Tempest, 2 Henry IV*, and *The Beggar's Opera* were vivid images: Miranda tender, Caliban coarse, Prospero kindly, Ariel strumming a lute in the air; Sir John Falstaff pontificating from his paunch; Captain Macheath in his irons and arias, still a hero to his wives. The coming satirist struck his distinctive vein in *The Sleeping Congregation*, for Hogarth hated all homilies except his own; while in *A Children's Party* he relished the fairest phase of English life. These pictures please us now, but drew no plaudits then.

He tried his hand at portrait painting, to indifferent results. The competition was severe. A dozen artists were making minor fortunes by flattering their sitters and dividing their tasks; they painted the head but delegated backgrounds and draperies to underpaid subordinates; "all this," said Hogarth, "is done at so easy a rate as enables the principal to get more money in a week than a man of the first professional talents can in three months."[7] He denounced the "phiz-mongers" who prettified the faces of their clients to feed their vanity and open their purses. As for himself he would portray his sitters with all their carbuncles, or not at all. When a distinctively simian noble sat for his picture Hogarth painted him with offensive honesty. The lord, never having seen himself as others saw him, refused to take the portrait. The artist sent him a message:

> Mr. Hogarth's dutiful respects to Lord ——. Finding that he does not mean to have the picture which was drawn for him, is informed again of Mr. Hogarth's need for the money. If, therefore, his Lordship does not send for it in three days, it will be disposed of, with the addition of a tail and some other little appendages, to Mr. Hare, the famous wild-beast man; Mr. Hogarth having given that gentleman a conditional promise of it for an exhibition picture . . .[8]

His Lordship paid.

Hogarth was confident that he could paint portraits as well as any man. When he was portraying Henry Fox (later Baron Holland) he told Horace Walpole that he had promised Fox, if he would sit as instructed, that he, Hogarth, would make as good a portrait of him as Rubens or Vandyck could have done;[9] which shocked Horace to the very core of his conventions. Many of Hogarth's male portraits may justify the distaste that Walpole expressed for them; the faces are too stereotyped, and some deserve his own scornful labeling of certain English portraits as "still life." We must except *Sir Thomas Coram*, already noted in commemorating the Foundling Hospital, which Coram founded and where he hangs; Hogarth caught the philanthropic nature in the smiling face, and the firm character in the closed hands. Generally the artist's brush was kinder to women than to men. The *Portrait of a Lady*[10] rivals Gainsborough; *A Lady in Brown*[11] has the strong features of a woman who has successfully mothered many children; and if *Miss Mary Edwards*[12] is slightly dead, it is brought to life by the—in Hogarth always present—dog. Finer are the group portraits, like *The Price Family*[13] and *The Graham Children;*[14] and better still *Hogarth's Servants,*[15] where every face is fondly limned in all its unduplicable character. Finest of all, of course, is *The Shrimp Girl*[16]—not a portrait but a hale man's memory of the young woman he had seen peddling shrimp from a basket balanced on her head; a girl free from all frills, not ashamed of the rags that robe her, looking out upon the world with the health of action ruddying her cheeks and brightening her eyes.

Hogarth left at least four portraits of himself. In 1745 he painted himself with his fat dog Trump.[17] In 1758 he showed himself at his easel: short, stout body, round and pudgy face, broad pug nose, blue eyes tired with fighting, lips tight with readiness to fight again. He was "a jovial, honest London citizen," in Thackeray's view, "a hearty, plain-spoken man, loving his laugh, his friends, his glass, his roast-beef of Old England."[18] He was hardly five feet tall, but he wore a sword[19] and took no nonsense from any man. Behind his defensive pugnacity was a warm heart, sometimes sentimental, forever pledged to war against hypocrisy and cruelty. He despised the lords whom he painted, he liked the simple Londoner who put on no airs. He brought the English masses into art; he pictured them in their sins and sufferings, in Bedlam, prison, debt, and heavy toil. He disliked the French as having corrupted England with finicky finery and aristocratic airs. He never forgot his being arrested for making sketches of Calais Gate; he took revenge by picturing the French as he had seen them there: rugged workmen, superstitious populace, and fat monk gazing in ecstasy upon a shoulder of beef.[20]

In his *Anecdotes* Hogarth told how the unprofitableness of his portraits turned him into the line that made his fame:

> I was unwilling to sink into a portrait manufacturer; and still ambitious of being singular [working independently], dropped all expectations of advantage from that source . . . As I could not bring myself to act like some of my brethren, and make it a sort of manufactory to be carried on by the help of background and drapery painters, it was not sufficiently profitable to pay the expenses my family required. I therefore turned my thoughts to painting and engraving modern moral subjects, a field not broken up in any country or any age.[21]

So in 1731 he painted six pictures which he called *A Harlot's Progress*; he engraved them on copper; from these engravings he made a series of prints which a year later were offered for sale. The girl arriving from the country is introduced to an itching gentleman by a persuasive procuress; the lass is a ready learner, and soon reaches an insolent prosperity. She is arrested not for prostitution but for theft; she does her stint in jail, beating hemp; she progresses quickly to disease and death, but she has the consolation of having a bevy of courtesans follow her funeral. Hogarth could easily have taken his characters from life; we have seen Mrs. Needham exposed in the pillory for prostitution, pelted by the populace, and dying of her injuries. (However, Colonel Charteris, twice accused of rape and twice condemned to death, was twice pardoned by the King, and died in state at his country seat.)[22] Hogarth was mistaken in thinking that he broke new ground in these genre prints; there had been many such in Renaissance Italy, in France, in the Netherlands, in Germany. But Hogarth now made an art and philosophy of "moral subjects." Like most moralists he was not himself immaculate; he had borne without horror the company of drunkards and prostitutes,[23] and his prints were designed first to make money and then, if possible, saints.

The *Harlot* prints sold well, appealing to twelve hundred subscribers and netting over a thousand pounds. Though pirated editions clipped the artist's coin, they drove the wolf from the door. The British public, which had no passion for paintings, took readily to these scenes of sin. Here was forbidden fruit, sterilized by morality but delightful none the less; here for a pittance one could make safe acquaintance with vice, and watch with satisfaction its proper punishment. With his earnings Hogarth could now feed his family; indeed, he took a home in fashionable Leicester Fields, and hung outside his door a golden head, indicating his profession as an artist. Later he bought a country house at Chiswick.

He painted some large pictures in the next few years, chiefly *Southwark Fair*—an English Brueghel—and a pretty group portrait, *The Edwards Family*. But in 1733 he returned to prints, and paralleled his *Harlot* with a series entitled *A Rake's Progress*. A giddy-pated youth suddenly inherits a rich estate; he abandons Oxford for London, enjoys taverns and wenches, squanders his money, is hauled off for debts, is rescued by his castoff mistress, recovers solvency by marrying an elderly lady with one eye but much money; he gambles away his new fortune at White's, is jailed again, and ends his career insane in "Bedlam" Hospital. It was a morality play in pictures easily understood and graphically presenting a segment of life. To guard the *Rake* prints from piracy, Hogarth campaigned for the legal protection of his rights. In 1735 Parliament passed "An Act for the Encouragement of the Arts of Designing, Engraving, Etching, etc."; this law, popularly known as "Hogarth's Act," gave him an equivalent of copyright on his prints. In 1745 he auctioned off the paintings from which he had engraved the *Harlot* and the *Rake*, and took in £427.

Solvent and confident, he made another foray into painting. "I entertained some hopes of succeeding in what the puffers in books call 'the great style of History painting.' "[24] In the decade from 1735 to 1745 he produced some excellent pictures which had to wait a century for appreciation. *The Distressed Poet*[25] is the old story of the impoverished author dunned for his rent while his wife knits fitfully and their cat sleeps in unconcerned content. *The Pool of Bethesda* attempted a Biblical scene, but Hogarth spiced it with a half-nude beauty full in the face of Christ. The artist was not immune to feminine flesh, and in the engraving *Strolling Actresses Dressing in a Barn* he gave it the added lure of clothing half removed. *The Good Samaritan*[26] comes close to the level of the "Old Masters." More appealing is a large painting, *David Garrick as Richard III*,[27] this was commissioned by a Mr. Duncombe, who paid for it two hundred pounds, the highest fee yet given to an English painter.

Nevertheless these works did not earn critical acclaim. Hogarth turned back (1745) to the satire of London life in engravings where the burin pointed a moral with a tale. In the first scene of *Marriage à la Mode* a bankrupt gouty earl contracts to marry his title and unwilling son to the unwilling daughter of an opulent alderman. The Earl displays the family pedigree as a tree on a scroll; the lawyer sprinkles blotting powder on the signatures; the bridegroom turns away from the bride, who lends an ear to her paramour; and two dogs monopolize the domestic peace. In the next scene the married couple are already at odds: the young lord has returned exhausted from an all-night adventure whose nature is signaled by a girl's lace cap protruding from his pocket; the young wife yawns after spending the night entertaining company with music, gambling, and small talk; again only the dog is happy. The third scene is Hogarth at his boldest: the lordly scoundrel brings his mistress to a quack doctor for an abortion. Scene four shows the wife having her hair dressed at her levee, or morning reception; her lover is with her, and she ignores the music played or sung by her guests, who include a deviate with curling papers in his hair. In the fifth scene her husband has caught her with her lover; the two men draw their swords; the husband is mortally wounded; the lover flees through the window; the wife is overcome with remorse; a constable appears at the door. In the final scene the young widow is dying; her father, removing a costly ring from her finger, salvages the last remnant of the fortune that he had paid for her title.

In 1751 Hogarth announced that he would sell at auction, at a given hour in his studio, the oil paintings that he had made for *Marriage à la Mode*; but he warned picture dealers to stay away. Only one person appeared, who bid £126 for the pictures and their frames. Hogarth let them go at this price, but privately raged at what he rated a shameful failure. In 1797 these paintings brought £1,381; today they are among the most highly prized possessions of London's National Gallery.

Meanwhile he had earned the ire of the King with *The March of the Guards toward Scotland* (1745). This was the year of Bonnie Prince Charlie's attempt to overthrow the Hanoverians. Hogarth pictured the Royal Guards assembling at Finchley, a suburb of London. A fifer and a drummer summon them; the soldiers accept their fate with the help of intoxication; they are a sorry-looking lot, fitter for a tavern carouse than for a rendezvous with heroic death. The artist had the painting shown to George II with request for permission to dedicate it to him. The King refused. "What?" he exclaimed. "A painter burlesque a soldier? He deserves to be picketed [imprisoned] for his insolence. Take his trumpery out of my sight!" Hogarth, says an uncertain story, dedicated the picture to Frederick the Great as "an encourager of arts and sciences."[28]

He resumed his satirical prints. In twelve plates entitled *Industry and Idleness* (1747) he traced the careers of two apprentices. Frank Goodchild works hard, reads good books, goes to church every Sunday, marries his master's daughter, gives alms to the poor, becomes sheriff, alderman, lord mayor of London. Tom Idle snores over his loom, reads wicked books like

Moll Flanders, drinks, gambles, picks pockets, is brought before Alderman Goodchild, who, weeping with mercy, condemns him to be hanged. Two engravings, *Gin Lane* and *Beer Street* (1751), contrasted the "dreadful consequences of gin-drinking" with the wholesome effects of beer. *The Four Stages of Cruelty* (1751) aimed, said the artist, "to correct that barbarous treatment of animals, the very sight of which renders the streets of our metropolis so distressing to every feeling mind. I am more proud of having been the author [of these prints] than I should be of having painted Raphael's Cartoons."[29] He aimed at fancier evils in *Four Prints of an Election* (1755–58), which attacked the corruption of English politics.

Taken merely as drawings, Hogarth's prints are crude in conception and execution, hasty and sketchy in detail. But he thought of himself as an author or playwright rather than an artist; he resembled his friend Fielding more than his favorite enemy, William Kent; he was presenting a picture of the age rather than displaying the techniques of art. "I have endeavored to treat my subject as a dramatic writer; my picture is my stage, and men and women my players, who by means of certain actions and gestures are to exhibit a dumb show."[30] As satires the prints are deliberate exaggerations; they stress an aspect and etch a point. They are more crowded with detail than a work of art should be; but every detail, except the inevitable dog, contributes to the theme. Taken all together, the prints allow us to see lower-middle-class London of the eighteenth century: the homes, taverns, Mall, Covent Garden, London Bridge, Cheapside, Bridewell, Bedlam, and the Fleet. It is not all of London, but what is there is shown with extraordinary vividness.

The art critics, collectors, and dealers of the time acknowledged neither Hogarth's ability as an artist nor his truth as a satirist. They charged him with picturing only the dregs of English life. They taunted him with having turned to popular prints through inability to paint successful portraits or historical scenes; and they condemned his drawing as careless and inaccurate. He retorted by denouncing the dealers as conspiring to praise their stock of Old Masters, while letting live artists starve:

> Unsanctioned by their authority and unascertained [not guaranteed] by tradition, the best preserved and highest finished picture . . . will not, at a public auction, produce five shillings; while a despicable, damaged, and repaired old canvas, sanctioned by their praise, shall be purchased at any price, and find a place in the noblest collections. All this is very well understood by the dealers.[31]

He refused to submit his judgment to such dealers or connoisseurs. He inveighed against the enslavement of English painters to the imitation of Vandyck or Lely or Kneller; even the giants of Italian art were nicknamed

"Black Masters" by him, as having cast a pall upon English painting by the black magic of their brown sauce. When a picture attributed to Correggio brought four hundred pounds at a London sale, he questioned the attribution and the value, and offered to paint as good a picture any time he liked. Challenged, he produced *Sigismunda* (1759)[32]—a good imitation of Correggio, with lace and finery and delicate hands and lovely face; but the eyes were too melancholy to please the prospective purchaser, who refused to pay the four hundred pounds that Hogarth asked for it. It was sold after his death for fifty-six pounds.

He gave another handle to his enemies by writing a book. On the palette in his portrait of himself and his dog (1745) he had traced a serpentine line which seemed to him to be the basic element of beautiful form. In a pedagogical treatise, *Analysis of Beauty* (1753), he defined this line as that formed by winding a wire in even progression around a cone. Such a line, he thought, was not only the secret of grace but also the movement of life. All this, to Hogarth's critics, seemed to be vapid moonshine.

Despite them he prospered. His prints were in almost every literate home, and their continuing sale gave him a steady income. In 1757, his *March of the Guards* having been forgotten, he was appointed "Serjeant Painter of all his Majesty's Works," which brought him an additional two hundred pounds a year. He could now afford new enemies. In 1762 he issued a print, *The Times*, which attacked Pitt, Wilkes, and others as warmongers. Wilkes replied in his journal, *The North Briton*, describing Hogarth as a vain and avaricious old man incapable of a "single idea of beauty." Hogarth retaliated by publishing a portrait of Wilkes as a squint-eyed monster. Wilkes's friend Churchill answered with a savage "Epistle to William Hogarth"; Hogarth issued a print showing Churchill as a bear. "The pleasure and pecuniary advantage which I derived from these two engravings," he wrote, "together with occasional riding on horseback, restored me to as much health as can be expected at my time of life."[33] But on October 26, 1764, he burst an artery and died.

He left no visible mark on the art of his time. In 1734 he opened a "life school" to train artists; it was merged in 1768 with the Royal Academy of Arts. Even the artists educated in his studio abandoned his realism for the fashionable idealism of Reynolds and Gainsborough. His influence was felt, however, in the field of caricature; there his humor and force passed down through Thomas Rowlandson to Isaac and George Cruikshank, and caricature became an art. Hogarth's present high repute as a painter began with Whistler's remark that Hogarth was "the only great English painter";[34] Whistler carefully excluded himself from the comparison. A less cautious judge ranked Hogarth, "taking him at his best," as "the supreme figure in eighteenth-century painting."[35] This estimate represents the current depreciation of Reynolds as a money-making beautifier of aristocrats. It is a mood that will pass. It is hard to rank Hogarth as an artist, because he was not only that; he was the voice of England angry at its own squalor and degradation; he rightly considered himself a social force. Fielding so understood him: "I almost dare affirm that those two works of his, which he calls *The Rake's* and *Harlot's Progress*, are calculated more to serve the cause of virtue . . . than all the folios of morality which have ever been written."[36] One thing is certain: he was the most English English artist that ever lived.

III. THE MUSICIANS

It is one of the puzzles of history why England, which has contributed so richly to economic and political development and theory, to literature, science, religion, and philosophy, has been relatively barren in the more complex forms of musical composition since the age of Elizabeth I. The passage from Catholicism may serve as a partial explanation: the new faiths offered less inducement to lofty musical productions; and though Lutheran ritual in Germany and the Anglican in England called for music, the severer forms of Protestantism in England and the Dutch Republic gave little encouragement to any music above the congregational hymn. The legends and liturgy of the Roman Church, often stressing the joys of faith, were replaced by somber predestinarian creeds stressing the fear of hell; and only Orpheus could sing in the face of hell. The madrigals of Elizabethan England died in the Puritan frost. The Restoration brought a merrier spirit from France, but after the death of Purcell a pall fell upon English music again.

Except for songs. These ranged from the corporate sonorities of glee clubs to the airy delicacy of lyrics from Shakespeare's plays. The word *glee* was the Anglo-Saxon *gleo*, meaning music; it did not necessarily imply joy. Usually it was applied to unaccompanied songs for three or more parts. Glee clubs flourished for a century, reaching their peak toward 1780 in the heyday of the chief composer of glees, Samuel Webbe. More beautiful were Thomas Arne's settings for Shakespeare's songs—"Blow, blow, thou winter wind," "Under the greenwood tree," and "Where the bee sucks, there suck I"; these are still heard in England. It was the melodious Arne who put to music Thomson's "Rule, Britannia!" Now, or earlier, some unknown patriot composed the national anthem of Britain, "God Save the King." So far as we know, this was first publicly sung in 1745, when news came that the forces loyal to George II had been defeated at Prestonpans by the Scots under the Young Pretender, and the Hanoverian dynasty seemed doomed. In its earliest known form (differing only slightly from the current words and melody), it asked God for victory over the Jacobite faction in English politics as well as over the Stuart army advancing from Scotland:

> God save our Lord the King,
> Long live our noble King [George II],
>   God save the King.
> Send him victorious,
> Happy and glorious,
> Long to reign over us;
>   God save the King.
>
> O Lord our God arise,
> Scatter his enemies,
>   And make them fall;
> Confound their politicks,
> Frustrate their knavish tricks,
> On him [now Thee] our hopes are fixed;
>   O save us all.[37]

The melody was adopted for varying periods by nineteen other countries for patriotic songs, including Germany, Switzerland, Denmark, and the United States of America, which in 1931 replaced "America" as national anthem by "The Star-Spangled Banner," sung to an unmanageable tune from an old English drinking song.

The popularity of exquisite songs in England shows a widespread musical taste. A harpsichord was in nearly every home except among the poor. Almost everyone played some instrument, and there were performers numerous enough to provide, for the Handel commemoration program of 1784 in Westminster Abbey, ninety-five violins, twenty-six violas, twenty-one violoncellos, fifteen double basses, six flutes, twenty-six oboes, twelve trumpets, twelve horns, six trombones, and four drums, plus a choir of fifty-nine sopranos, forty-eight altos, eighty-three tenors, and eighty-four basses—enough to make Handel tremble in his Abbey tomb. The clarinet was not admitted till later in the century. There were magnificent organs, and great organists like Maurice Greene, whose anthems and Te Deums—along with those of Handel and Boyce—were almost the only memorable church music of England in that age.

William Boyce, though his hearing was impaired in youth, rose to be master of the King's Band (i.e., orchestra) and organist in the Chapel Royal. He was the first maestro to conduct standing; Handel and other contemporaries conducted from the organ or harpsichord. Some of his anthems—especially "By the Waters of Babylon"—are still heard in Anglican churches; and English homes still hear at least two of his songs: "Hearts of Oak," which he wrote for one of

Garrick's pantomimes, and "Softly Rise, O Southern Breeze," an aria in the cantata *Solomon*. His symphonies sound weak and thin to our macerated ears.

The only excitement in the English musical world at the outset of the eighteenth century was the coming of opera. There had been such performances as far back as 1674, but opera took the English fancy only when, in 1702, Italian singers came from Rome. In 1708 a renowned *castrato*, Nicolini, shocked and charmed London with his soprano voice. Some other *castrati* came; England became accustomed to them, and went wild over Farinelli. By 1710 there were enough Italian singers in London to present there the first opera completely in their language. Many protests were raised against the invasion. Addison devoted the eighteenth number of *The Spectator* to it, proposing to

> deliver down to posterity a faithful account of the Italian opera. . . . Our great-grandchildren will be very curious to know the reason why their forefathers used to sit together like an audience of foreigners in their own country, to hear whole plays acted before them in a tongue which they did not understand.

He concluded from the plots that in opera "nothing is capable of being well set to music, that is not nonsense." He laughed at scenes where the hero made love in Italian and the heroine answered him in English—as if language mattered in such crises. He objected to lavish scenery—to actual sparrows flying about the stage, and Nicolini shivering in an open boat on a pasteboard sea.

Addison had a grudge: he had written the libretto for Thomas Clayton's English opera *Rosamond*, which had failed.[38] His blast (March 21, 1711) was probably set off by the première, on February 24, of an Italian opera, *Rinaldo*, at the Haymarket opera house. To complicate the insult, while the words were Italian the music was by a German recently arrived in England. To Addison's dismay the new opera was a great triumph: within three months it was produced fifteen times, always to packed houses; London danced to excerpts from its music, and sang its simpler arias.[39] So began the English phase of the most spectacular career in the history of music.

IV. HANDEL: 1685–1759[40]

1. Growth

The most famous composer of Johann Sebastian Bach's time was Georg Friedrich Handel.* He triumphed in Germany, he brought musical Italy

---

* In Germany he signed himself Händel; in Italy and England, Hendel.[41]

to his feet, he was the life and history of music in England for the first half of the eighteenth century. He took his supremacy for granted, and no one questioned him. He bestrode the world of music like a commanding colossus, weighing 250 pounds.

He was born in Halle, Upper Saxony, February 23, 1685, just twenty-six days before Johann Sebastian Bach, and eight months before Domenico Scarlatti. But whereas Bach and Scarlatti were baptized in music, fathered by famous composers, and reared to an obbligato of scales, Handel was born to parents indifferent to tones. His father was official surgeon at the court of Duke Johann Adolf of Saxe-Weissenfels; his mother was the daughter of a Lutheran minister. They frowned upon the boy's addiction to the organ and the harpsichord; but when the Duke, hearing him play, insisted that he should receive musical training, they allowed him to study with Friedrich Zachau, organist of the Liebfrauenkirche in Halle. Zachau was a devoted and painstaking teacher. By the age of eleven Georg was composing sonatas (six of these survive), and was so skilled an organist that Zachau and the resigned parents sent him to Berlin to perform before Sophia Charlotte, the cultured Electress of Brandenburg, soon to be queen of Prussia. When Georg returned to Halle (1697), he found that his father had just died. His mother survived till 1729.

In 1702 he entered the University of Halle, ostensibly to prepare for the practice of law. A month later the authorities at the Calvinist cathedral in Halle engaged him to replace their hard-drinking organist. After a year there the restless young genius, craving a wider sphere, pulled up all his Halle roots except his abiding love for his mother, and set out for Hamburg, where music was almost as popular as money. Hamburg had had an opera house since 1678. There Handel, aged eighteen, found a place as second violinist. He became friends with the twenty-two-year-old Johann Mattheson, the leading tenor at the opera and later the most famous musical critic of the eighteenth century. Together they made an expedition to Lübeck (August, 1703) to hear the aging Buxtehude play, and to explore the possibility of succeeding him as organist in the Marienkirche. They found that the successor must marry Buxtehude's daughter. They looked and came away.

Their friendship collapsed in a duel as absurd as in any play. On October 20, 1704, Mattheson produced and starred in his own opera, *Cleopatra*. It was a decided success, and was often repeated. In these performances Handel conducted orchestra and singers from the harpsichord. On some occasions Mattheson, drunk with glory, came down from the stage after dying as Antony, displaced his friend as conductor and harpsichordist, and shared happily in the final applause. On December 5 Handel refused to be so replaced. The friends expanded the opera with a warm dispute, and after the stage performance was over they proceeded to the public square, drew their swords, and fought to the plaudits of opera patrons and passers-by. Mattheson's weapon struck a metal button on Handel's coat, buckled, and broke. The tragedy became a comedy to all but the principals; they nursed their grievances until the director of the company accepted Handel's opera *Almira*, which required Mattheson in the tenor role. The success of the opera (January 8, 1705) made the enemies friends again.

Having forty-one arias in German and fifteen in Italian, *Almira* was so popular that it was repeated twenty times in seven weeks. Reinhard Keiser, who controlled the company and had composed most of its operas, turned jealous. The Hamburg opera declined in popularity, and for two years Handel lived at a reduced rate. Meanwhile Prince Giovan Gastone de' Medici, passing through Hamburg, had advised him to go to Italy, where everyone was mad about music, and waiters warbled *bel canto*. With two hundred ducats in his wallet, and a letter from Gastone to his brother Ferdinand, patron of opera in Florence, Handel dared the snows of the Alps in December, and reached Florence toward the end of 1706. Finding Ferdinand's pockets buttoned, he passed down to Rome. There, however, the opera house had been closed by Pope Innocent XII as a center of immorality. Handel played the organ in the Church of San Giovanni Laterano, and was acclaimed as a virtuoso; but as no one would produce his new opera, he returned to Florence. Gastone was now there, and pleaded for him; Ferdinand opened his purse, *Rodrigo* was staged; everyone was pleased; Ferdinand gave the young composer a hundred sequins ($300?) and a dinner service of porcelain. But Florence had no public opera house; Venice had sixteen. Handel went on to Venice.

It was the fall of 1707. The Queen of the Adriatic was under the spell of Alessandro Scarlatti, and was applauding his greatest opera, *Mitridate Eupatore;* there was no opening for a young German just beginning to learn the secrets of Italian melody. Handel studied Scarlatti's operas, and found a good friend in Alessandro's son. Story has it that when Handel, masked, played the harpsichord at a Venetian masquerade, Domenico Scarlatti exclaimed, "That is either the marvelous Saxon or the Devil."[42] The lasting friendship between the two greatest harpsichordists of the age is a moment of harmony amid the discords of history. Together they left Venice to older masters, and went off to Rome (January, 1708?).

This time Handel was better received. The news of *Rodrigo* had reached the capital; princes and cardinals opened their doors to him, more disturbed by his German accent than by his Lutheran faith. The Marchese di Ruspoli built a private theater in his palace to produce Handel's first oratorio, *La Risurrezione;* the music was a revelation in its power, complexity, and depth; soon all cultural Rome was talking about *"il gran Sassone,"* the tall and mighty Saxon. But his scores were more difficult than Italian performers liked. When Cardinal Pietro Ottoboni produced Handel's *Serenata* the music troubled Arcangelo Corelli, who played first violin and conducted the orchestra; he murmured politely, "*Caro Sassone*, this music is in the French style, which I do not understand."[43] Handel took the violin from Corelli's hands and played with his usual dash. Corelli forgave him.

Naples remained to be conquered. An unreliable tradition describes Handel, Corelli, and both the Scarlattis as traveling to that city together (June, 1708). Another dubious story ascribes a love affair to Handel there; but cautious history regrettably admits that it has no sound evidence of any love affair anywhere in Handel's life, except for his mother and music. It seems incredible that the man who could write such ardent arias had no flame of his own; perhaps expression dispersed its heat on the wings of song. So far as we know, the major event in this Neapolitan sojourn was Handel's meeting with Cardinal Vincenzo Grimani, Viceroy of Naples and scion of a rich Venetian family. He offered the composer the libretto of an opera on the old theme of Nero's mother. In three weeks Handel completed the work. Grimani arranged for its performance in the theater of his family at Venice; Handel hurried thither with the score.

The première of *Agrippina* (December 26, 1709) was the most exhilarating triumph that Handel had yet experienced. The generous Italians were not jealous that a German had beaten them at their own game, showing them splendors of harmony, audacities of modulation, devices of technique seldom achieved even by their favorite, Alessandro Scarlatti; they cried out, "*Viva il caro Sassone!*"[44] Part of the ovation went to the remarkable basso, Giuseppe Boschi, whose voice ranged smoothly over a gamut of twenty-nine notes.

Handel was now courted. Charles Montagu, Earl of Manchester, British ambassador at Venice, advised him to go to London; Prince Ernest Augustus, younger brother of Elector George Louis, offered him the post of *Kapellmeister* at Hanover. Venice was lovely, it breathed music, but how long could one eat out of one opera, and how long could you depend upon those temperamental Italians? At Hanover there would be fog and clouds and gutturals, but also a fine opera house, a steady salary, substantial German food; and he could ride off now and then to visit his mother at Halle. On June 15, 1710, age twenty-five, Handel was appointed *Kapellmeister* at Hanover, with an annual salary of fifteen hundred crowns, and permission for occasional absences. In the autumn of that year he asked and obtained permission to visit England, promising to return soon.

2. The Conquest of England

London opera was in trouble. An Italian company was singing there, with basso Boschi, his contralto wife, and male soprano Nicolini, whom Charles Burney, zealous historian of music, judged to be "the first truly great singer who has ever sung in our theater."[45] But both the Haymarket opera house (then called Her Majesty's Theatre) and the Drury Lane Theatre were in a rough section of the city, where pockets were picked and heads were broken; "society" hesitated to risk its wigs and purses there.

Hearing that Handel was in London, Aaron Hill, impresario, offered him a libretto drawn from Tasso's *Gerusalemme liberata*. Handel set to work with his massive energy, borrowed freely from his own compositions, and in a fortnight completed *Rinaldo*. Produced on February 24, 1711, it was repeated fourteen times to full houses before the end of the season on June 22. Addison and Steele attacked it, but London took to it, and sang its arias in the streets; two especially, "Lascia ch'io pianga" and "Cara sposa," touched sentimental chords, and can move us even today. John Walsh made fourteen hundred guineas by publishing the songs from *Rinaldo*; Handel wryly suggested that for the next opera Walsh should write the music and let him publish the score.[46] Soon this best of Handel's operas was produced in Dublin, Hamburg, and Naples. In London it held the stage for twenty years.

Sipping his success, Handel stretched his leave of absence to a year; then, reluctantly, he returned to Hanover (June, 1711). There he was not a lion in drawing rooms but a servant in the Elector's palace; the opera house was closed for the season; he composed *concerti grossi* and cantatas while his imagination soared in operas. In October, 1712, he asked leave for another "short" visit to England. The Elector indulged him, perhaps feeling that England was soon to be a Hanoverian appanage in any case. Handel reached London in November, and stayed forty-six years.

He brought with him a new opera, *Il Pastor Fido* (*The Faithful Shepherd*), whose pleasant overture still charms our air. It was produced on November 22, and failed. Stimulated rather than disheartened, he began at once on another theme, *Teseo* (*Theseus*). The première (January 10, 1713) was a triumph, but after the second night the manager absconded with the box office receipts. Another manager, John Heidegger, took over, carried *Teseo* to thirteen performances, and rewarded the unpaid composer by arranging a benefit for "Mr. Hendel," with the composer starring at the harpsichord. The Earl of Burlington, an enthusiastic auditor, invited Handel to make Burlington House his home; Handel accepted, was well lodged and too well fed, and met Pope, Gay, Kent, and other leaders in literature and art.

Good fortune crowded upon him. Queen Anne had longed for an end to the War of the Spanish Succession; it came with the Treaty of Utrecht; Handel pleased Anne with his "Utrecht Te Deum," and with a "Birthday Ode" for her anniversary; in these he showed that he had studied Purcell's choruses. The kindly Queen rewarded him with a pension of two hundred pounds. Comfortable and prosperous, he rested on his oars for a truant year.

On August 1, 1714, Anne died, and Elector George Louis of Hanover became George I of England. Handel looked with some apprehension upon this turn of events; he had in effect deserted Hanover, and might expect the royal shoulder to be cold. It was, but George held his peace. The Haymarket house was now renamed His Majesty's Theatre; the King felt obliged to patronize it; but it was playing the truant's *Rinaldo*. He went in disguise except for his accent, and enjoyed the performance. Meanwhile Handel had written another opera, *Amadigi di Gaula;* Heidegger produced it on May 25, 1715; George liked it. Soon thereafter the Italian violinist and composer Francesco Geminiani, being invited to perform at court, asked for Handel as the only harpsichordist in England who could fitly accompany him. He had his way; Handel outdid himself; the King forgave him, and raised his pension to four hundred pounds a year. Princess Caroline engaged him to teach her daughters, and added a pension of two hundred pounds. He was now the best-paid composer in Europe.

When George I left London (July 9, 1716) for a visit to Hanover he took Handel with him. The musician visited his mother at Halle, and began his periodic gifts of money to the impoverished widow of his old teacher Zachau. King and composer returned to London early in 1717. James Brydges, Earl of Carnarvon—later, Duke of Chandos—invited Handel to live at his sumptuous palace, Canons, in Middlesex, and to replace as its music master Dr. Johann Pepusch, who took delayed revenge by writing the music for *The Beggar's Opera*. There Handel composed *Suites de Pièces pour le Clavecin*—harpsichord fantasies in the style of Domenico Scarlatti and Couperin—some *concerti grossi*, twelve "Chandos Anthems," music for Gay's masque *Acis and Galatea*, and an opera, *Radamisto*.

But who would produce the opera? Attendance at His Majesty's Theatre had fallen off; Heidegger was nearing bankruptcy. To rescue him and opera a group of nobles and rich commoners formed (February, 1719) the Royal Academy of Music, financing it with fifty shares offered to the public at two hundred pounds each; George I took five shares. On February 21 a London weekly announced that "Mr. Hendel, a famous Master of Music, is gone beyond the sea, by order of His Majesty, to collect a company of the choicest singers in Europe for the Opera in the Haymarket."[47] Handel raided various companies in Germany, and visited his mother again. A few hours after he left Halle for England, Johann Sebastian Bach appeared in the town, having walked some twenty-five miles from Cöthen, and asked if he might see the great German who had conquered England. It was too late; the two masters never met.

On April 27, 1720, *Radamisto* was performed before the King, his mistress, and a house brilliant with titles and jewelry; pedigreed persons fought for admission; "several gentlemen," Mainwaring reported, "were turned back who had offered forty shillings for a seat in the gallery."[48] The English audience rivaled in its applause the Venetians who had acclaimed *Agrippina* eleven years before. Handel was again the hero of London.

Not quite. A rival group of music lovers, led by Handel's former patron the Earl of Burlington, preferred Giovanni Battista Bononcini. They persuaded the Royal Academy of Music to open its second season with Bononcini's opera *Astarto* (November 19, 1720); they secured for its leading role a male soprano now more adored than Nicolini; this "Senesino" (Francesco Bernardi), offensive in manners, captivating in voice, carried *Astarto* to triumph and a run of ten performances; Bononcini's admirers hailed him as superior to Handel. Neither composer was responsible for the war that now divided London's operatic public into hostile groups, but London, in this year of the bursting South Sea Bubble, was as excitable as Paris. The King and the Whigs favored Handel, the Prince of Wales and the Tories played up Bononcini, and the wits and pamphleteers crowded to the fray. Bononcini seemed to certify his supremacy with a new opera, *Crispo* (January, 1722), which was so successful that the Academy followed it with another Bononcini triumph, *Griselda*. When the great Marlborough died (June), Bononcini, not Handel, was chosen to compose the funeral anthem; and the Duke's daughter settled upon the Italian an annuity of five hundred pounds a year. It was Bononcini's year.

Handel fought back with *Ottone*, and a new soprano whom he lured from Italy by an unprecedented guarantee of two thousand pounds. Francesca Cuzzoni, as Horace Walpole saw her, "was short and squat, with a doughy cross face but fine complexion; was not a good actress; dressed ill; and was silly and fantastical";[49] but she warbled ravishingly. A contest of wills and tempers enlivened her rehearsals. "Madame," Handel told her, "I well know that you are a veritable female devil; but I myself, I will have you know, am Beelzebub, chief of the devils." When she insisted on singing an aria contrary to his instructions, he took hold of her and threatened to throw her out the window.[50] As the two thousand pounds would have followed her, she yielded. In the première (January 12, 1723) she sang so well that one enthusiast cried out from the gallery *in mediis rebus*, "Damme, she has a nest of nightingales in her belly."[51] Senesino rivaled her, and

Boschi's basso helped. On the second night seats sold for five pounds more. About this time John Gay wrote to Jonathan Swift:

> As for the reigning amusement of the town, it is entirely music; real fiddles, bass viols, and hautboys; not poetical harps, lyres, and reeds. There's nobody allowed to say *I sing* but an eunuch, or an Italian woman. Everybody now is grown as great a judge of music as they were, in your time, of poetry; and folks that could not distinguish one tone from another now daily dispute about the different styles of Handel, Bononcini, and Attilio [Ariosti]. . . . In London and Westminster, in all polite conversation, Senesino is daily voted the greatest man that ever lived.[52]

Again *in excelsis*, Handel bought a house in London (1723) and became a British citizen (1727). He continued till 1728 the operatic war. He combed history for subjects, and put Flavius, Caesar, Tamerlane, Scipio, Alexander, and Richard I on the stage; Bononcini countered with Astyanax, Erminia, Pharnaces, and Calpurnia; a third composer, Ariosti, set Coriolanus, Vespasian, Artaxerxes, and Darius to music; never had history been so harmonious. In 1726 the triune conflict took on added fire with the arrival of Faustina Bordoni, a mezzo-soprano who had already overcome Venice, Naples, and Vienna. She had not the tender and dulcet tones of Cuzzoni, but her voice was seconded by her face, her figure, and her grace. In *Alessandro* (May 5, 1726) Handel brought the two divas together, gave them the same number of solos, and carefully balanced them in a duet. For some evenings the audience applauded them both; then it divided; one part hissed while the other applauded; a new dimension was added to the tuneful war. On June 6, 1727, when the rival *prime donne* sang in Bononcini's *Astianatte*, the supporters of Cuzzoni broke out in a disgraceful pandemonium of hisses, boos, and roars when Bordoni tried to sing. A fight flared up in the pit and spread to the stage; the divas joined in it and tore at each other's hair; spectators joyfully smashed the scenery—all in the presence of the humiliated Caroline, Princess of Wales.

This *reductio ad absurdum* might of itself have killed Italian opera in England. The *coup de grâce* was struck by one of the gentlest spirits in London. On January 29, 1728, in Lincoln's Inn Fields Theatre, John Gay presented *The Beggar's Opera*. We have described its jolly, witty, ribald lyrics, but only those who have heard them sung to the music that Johann Pepusch composed or borrowed for them can understand why the theatergoing public turned almost en masse from Handel, Bononcini, and Ariosti to Pepusch, Polly, and Gay. Night after night for nine weeks *The Beggar's Opera* played to full houses, while the sirens and eunuchs at His Majesty's Theatre sang to empty seats. Moreover, Gay had satirized Italian opera;

he had made fun of the silly plots, the coloratura trills and ornaments of sopranos of either sex; he had taken thieves, beggars, and prostitutes as his dramatis personae instead of kings, nobles, virgins, and queens; and he of-fered English ballads as better songs than Italian arias. The public was de-lighted with words that it could understand, especially if the words were a bit risqué. Handel came back with more operas—*Siroe* and *Tolomeo, Re d'Egitto* (1728); they had fine moments but paid no bills. On June 5 the Royal Academy of Music declared bankruptcy and expired.

Handel did not admit defeat. Deserted by the nobles, who blamed him for their losses, he formed with Heidegger (June, 1728) the "New Acad-emy of Music," put into it ten thousand pounds—nearly all his savings—and received from the new King, George II, a pledge of a thousand a year in support. In February he set out on another Continental tour to recruit new talent, for Cuzzoni, Bordoni, Senesino, Nicolini, and Boschi had deserted his sinking ship and were trilling Venice. In their place Handel engaged new chanticleers and nightingales: Antonio Bernacchi, a male soprano, Annibale Fabri, tenor, Anna Maria Strada del Pò, soprano. On his way back he stopped to see his mother for the last time. She was now seventy-nine, blind and almost paralyzed. While he was in Halle he was visited by Wil-helm Friedemann Bach, who brought him an invitation to visit Leipzig, where the *Passion according to St. Matthew* had just received its first performance. Handel had to refuse. He had barely heard of Johann Sebas-tian Bach, and never dreamed that this man's fame would one day eclipse his own. He hurried back to London, picking up on the way the Hamburg basso Johann Riemenschneider.

The new cast appeared in *Lotario* on December 2, 1729, without suc-cess. He tried again on February 24 with *Partenope*, without success. Ber-nacchi and Riemenschneider were restored to the Continent; Senesino was recalled from Italy; with him and Strada del Pò, and a libretto by Meta-stasio, Handel's *Poro*—on which he had lavished some of his most moving arias—caught the ear of London (February 2, 1731). His Majesty's Thea-tre filled again. Two further operas, *Ezio* and *Sosarme*, were favorably received.

But the struggle to keep an English audience with Italian opera was be-coming ever more arduous; it appeared now to be a blind alley, in which physical and financial exhaustion was always around the corner. Handel had conquered England, but now England was apparently conquering him. His operas were too much alike, and were bound to wear thin. They were exalted by magnificent arias; but these were only tenuously related to the plot, they were in an unintelligible, however mellifluous, language, and many of them were composed for male sopranos, who were increasingly hard to find. Rigid rules and artistic jealousy governed the distribution of arias, and added to the artificiality of the tale. If Handel had continued on this Italian line he would hardly be remembered today. A series of accidents jolted him off his beaten track, and turned him into the field where he was to remain, even to our time, unsurpassed.

3. Defeat

On February 23, 1732, at the Crown and Anchor Tavern, Bernard Gates, to celebrate the composer's forty-seventh birthday, gave a private production of Handel's *Esther, an Oratorio*. It drew so profitable an audience that Gates repeated it twice—once for a private group, then (April 20) for the public; this was the first public performance of an oratorio in England. Princess Anne suggested that *Esther* should be presented at His Majesty's Theatre with costumes, scenery, and action; but the bishop of London protested against turning the Bible into opera. Handel made now one of the pivotal decisions of his career. He announced that he would produce *The Sacred Story of Esther* as "an Oratorio in English" at the Haymarket theater on May 2, but added that there would be "no action on the stage," and that the music was "to be disposed after the Manner of the Coronation Service"; so he distinguished oratorio from opera. He provided his own chorus and orchestra, and taught La Strada and other Italians to sing their solos in English. The royal family attended, and *Esther* bore five repetitions in its first month.

Another oratorio, *Acis and Galatea* (June 10), failed to please, and Handel turned back to opera. *Orlando* (January 27, 1733) had a good run; even so, the partnership with Heidegger faced bankruptcy. When Handel produced his third oratorio, *Deborah* (March 17), he tried to regain solvency by doubling the price of admission; an anonymous letter to *The Craftsman* denounced this measure, and called for a revolt against the domination of London's music by the "insolent, . . . imperious, and extravagant Mr. Hendel."[53] As Handel had won the patronage of the King, he automatically lost the good will of Frederick, Prince of Wales, son and foe of George II. Handel, whose manners often yielded to his temper, made the mistake of offending Frederick's drawing master, Joseph Goupy; Goupy took revenge by drawing a caricature of the composer as a monstrous glutton with the snout of a boar; copies of this were circulated through London, and added to Handel's misery. In the spring of 1733 the Prince of Wales encouraged his courtiers to form a rival company, the "Opera of the Nobility." It brought from Naples the most famous singing teacher of the age, Niccolò Porpora; lured Senesino from Handel and Cuzzoni from Italy; and on December 29, at the Lincoln's Inn Fields Theatre, it produced Porpora's

Arianna with great acclaim. Handel met this new challenge with an opera on a defiantly similar theme, *Arianna in Creta* (January 26, 1734); it too was well received. But at the end of the season his contract with Heidegger expired; Heidegger leased His Majesty's Theatre to the Opera of the Nobility; and Handel moved his company to John Rich's Covent Garden Theatre.

Porpora scored by calling upon the world's most renowned *castrato*, Carlo Broschi, known to all Europe as "Farinelli." On this man's singing we may dilate when we meet him in his native Bologna; here it need hardly be said that when (October 29) he joined Senesino and Cuzzoni in Porpora's *Artaserse* it was an event in the music history of England; the opera was repeated forty times during Farinelli's three-year stay. To compete with it Handel offered *Ariodante* (January 8, 1735), one of his finest operas, uniquely rich in its instrumental music; it earned ten performances in two months, and promised to make ends meet. But when Porpora produced *Polifemo* (February 1) with Farinelli in the leading role, the King, the Queen, and the court could not stay away; its run exceeded that of *Artaserse*, while Handel's *Alcina* (April 16) was soon playing to empty seats— though a suite from its score still appears on programs today. For half a year Handel retired from the battlefield to nurse his rheumatic pains with the waters of Tunbridge Wells.

On February 19, 1736, he returned to Covent Garden with an oratorio set to Dryden's "Alexander's Feast." A contemporary reported that the capacity audience of thirteen hundred received the oratorio with applause "such as had seldom been heard in London";[54] Handel was comforted with receipts of £450; but though he gave a stirring organ recital in the intermission the ode was too slight to bear more than four repetitions; and the desperate composer-impresario-conductor-virtuoso turned again to opera. On May 12 he offered *Atalanta* as a pastoral play celebrating the marriage of the Prince of Wales. He had summoned from Italy a new *castrato*, Gizziello (Gioacchino Conti), for the soprano role, and had distinguished the part with an aria, "Care selve," which is one of the most lovely and enduring of his songs. Frederick was so pleased that he transferred his patronage from Porpora's company to Handel's; but this victory was made sorrowful when the King, hearing of his son's move, canceled his annual subscription of a thousand pounds to Handel's enterprise.

Porpora gave up the battle in the spring of 1736. Handel filled his theater by alternating operas with oratorios, and adding to the cast of *Giustino* (February 16, 1737) "bears, fantastic animals, and dragons vomiting fire."[55] But the strain of his diverse responsibilities broke him down. In April he suffered a nervous collapse, and a stroke that for a time paralyzed his right arm. On May 18 he staged *Berenice*, the last of the operas that he wrote for his company. He closed his theater on June 1, owing many debts, and vowing to pay them all in full; he did. Ten days later the rival Opera of the Nobility disbanded, owing twelve thousand pounds. The great age of opera in England was over.

Handel's health was among the ruins. Rheumatism in his muscles, arthritis in his bones, gout in his extremities were capped in the summer of 1737 with a passing attack of insanity.[56] He left England to take the waters at Aachen. There, reported Sir John Hawkins,

> he submitted to such sweats, excited by the vapor baths, as astonished everyone. After a few essays of this kind, during which spirits seemed to rise rather than sink under an excessive perspiration, his disorder left him; and a few hours after . . . he went to the great church of the city, and got to the organ, on which he played in such a manner that men imputed his cure to a miracle.[57]

In November he returned to London, to solvency and honors. Heidegger had again engaged His Majesty's Theatre. He paid Handel a thousand pounds for two new operas; one of them, *Serse* (April 15, 1738) contained the famous "Largo," "Ombra mai fù." The lessee of Vauxhall Gardens paid Roubillac three hundred pounds for a statue showing the composer strumming a lyre; on May 2 this figure, ungainly in pose and stupid in expression, was unveiled in the Gardens with a musical entertainment. More pleasing to Handel must have been the benefit tendered him on March 28, bringing over a thousand pounds in receipts. Handel now paid off the more urgent of his creditors, one of whom was threatening to put him in the debtors' jail. Despite all honors, he was near the end of his financial rope. He could no longer look to Heidegger, who announced (May 24) that he had not received sufficient subscriptions to warrant his producing operas in 1738–39. Without a commission and without a company, Handel, aged fifty-three and shaken with ailments, entered upon his greatest period.

4. The Oratorios

This relatively modern form had grown out of medieval chorales representing events in Biblical history or the lives of the saints. St. Philip Neri had given the form its name by favoring it as a means of devotion and religious instruction in the *oratorio*, or prayer chapel, of the Fathers of the Oratory in Rome. Giacomo Carissimi and his pupil Alessandro Scarlatti developed the oratorio in Italy; Heinrich Schütz brought it from Italy into Germany; Reinhard Keiser raised the genre to high excellence before his death (1739). This was the heritage that in 1741 culminated in Handel's *Messiah*.

Part of Handel's success came from his adaptation of the form to English taste. He continued to choose the subjects of his oratorios from the Bible, but he gave them, now and then, a secular interest, as with the love theme in *Joseph and His Brethren* and in *Jephtha;* he emphasized the dramatic rather than the religious character, as in *Saul* and *Israel in Egypt;* and he used an entirely English text, only partly Biblical. It was in good part religious music, but it was independent of churches and liturgy; it was performed on a stage under secular auspices. Moreover, Handel used Biblical themes to symbolize English history: "Israel" stood for England; the Great Rebellion of 1642 and the Glorious Revolution of 1688 could be heard in the struggle of the Jews for liberation from Egyptian (Stuart) bondage and Hellenistic (Gallic) domination; the Chosen People was really the English nation, and the God of Israel was the same who had led the English people through trial to victory. Like the Puritans, Handel thought of God as the mighty Jehovah of the Old Testament, not as the forgiving Father of the New.[58] England felt this, and responded proudly to Handel's oratorios.

The ascent to the *Messiah* began with *Saul*, produced at His Majesty's Theatre January 16, 1739. "The solemn and majestic Dead March would alone immortalize this work."[59] But the audience was not accustomed to the oratorio form; *Saul* could sustain only six performances. With unbelievable energy Handel composed and presented (April 4) another masterwork, *Israel in Egypt*. Here he made the chorus the hero, the voice of a nation in birth, and wrote what many consider his supreme music.[60] It proved too vast and heavy for the current appetite, and Handel finished this historic season with new debts.

On October 23, 1739, England plunged into war with Spain for Jenkins' ear. Amid the turmoil Handel hired a small theater, and on the feast of the patron saint of musicians he offered his setting of Dryden's "Ode for St. Cecilia's Day" (November 22, 1739). Even in the cold and chaos of that wintry night London could not resist the bright melodious overture, the ethereal soprano aria in the third stanza, or the "soft complaining flute" and "warbling lute" in the fifth; while the "double double double beat of the thund'ring drum" accorded with the spirit of war that was rumbling through the streets. Handel took heart again, and tried an opera, *Imeneo* (1740), which failed; he tried another, *Deidamia* (1741); it too failed; and the tired giant retired for almost two years from the London musical scene.

These two years were his finest. On August 22, 1741, he began to compose the *Messiah*. The text was adapted by Charles Jennens from the books of Job, Psalms, Isaiah, Lamentations, Haggai, Zechariah, and Malachi in the Old Testament, and, in the New, the Gospels of Matthew, Luke, and John, the Epistles of Paul, and the Book of Revelation. The score was completed in twenty-three days; in some of these, he told a friend, "I did think I did see all Heaven before me, and the great God himself."[61] Having no early prospect of finding an audience for it, he went on to write another major oratorio, *Samson,* based on the *Samson Agonistes* of Milton. At an unknown date during these ecstasies he received an invitation to present some of his works in Dublin. The proposal seemed to come from an appreciative Providence; actually it came from William Cavendish, Duke of Devonshire, Lord Lieutenant of Ireland.

He reached Dublin November 17, 1741. He engaged the best singers he could find, including Susannah Maria Cibber, the accomplished daughter of Thomas Arne. Several charitable organizations arranged six concerts for him; these were so successful that a second series was presented. On March 27, 1742, two Dublin periodicals carried an announcement that

> for the relief of the Prisoners in the several Gaols, and for the support of Mercer's Hospital, . . . on Monday the 12th of April, will be performed, at the Musick Hall in Fishamble-street, *Mr. Hendel's new Grand Oratorio,* called the Messiah, in which the Gentlemen of the Choir of both cathedrals will assist, with some Concertos on the Organ by Mr. Hendel.[62]

Tickets were sold also for the rehearsal on April 8, which *Faulkner's Journal* reported as "performed so well that it . . . was allowed by the greatest Judges to be the finest Composition of Musick that ever was heard." To this was added a notice postponing the Monday performance to Tuesday, and requesting the ladies "please to come without Hoops, as it will greatly increase the Charity, by making room for more Company." A later item requested the men to come without their swords. In these ways the seating capacity of the Music Hall was raised from six hundred to seven hundred seats.

At last, on April 13, 1742, the most famous of all major musical compositions was presented. On April 17 three Dublin papers carried an identical review:

> On Tuesday last Mr. Hendel's Sacred Grand Oratorio, the Messiah, was performed. . . . The best Judges allowed it to be the most finished piece of musick. Words are wanting to express the exquisite Delight it afforded to the admiring crowded Audience. The Sublime, the Grand, and the Tender, adapted to the most elevated, majestic and moving Words, conspired to transport and charm the ravished Heart and Ear. It is but justice to Mr. Hendel that the world should know he

generously gave the money arising from this Grand Performance to be equally shared by the Society of relieving Prisoners, the Charitable Infirmary, and Mercer's Hospital, for which they will ever gratefully remember his Name.[63]

The *Messiah* was repeated in Dublin on June 3. It has been repeated a thousand times since; yet who has yet grown weary of those muted or majestic arias, with their subdued and gracious accompaniments—"He Shall Feed His Flock," "I Know That My Redeemer Liveth," "He Shall Be Exalted," "He Was Despised and Rejected"? When, at the Dublin première, Mrs. Cibber sang this last air, an Anglican clergyman cried out from the audience, "Woman, for this thy sins be forgiven thee!" All the depth and fervor of religious hope, all the tenderness of pious song, all the art and feeling of the composer came together to make these arias the supreme moments in modern music.

On August 13, replenished in spirit and purse, Handel left Dublin, resolved to conquer England again. He must have been comforted to find that Pope, in the fourth book of *The Dunciad* (1742), had gone out of his way to praise him:

> Strong in new arms, lo! giant Handel stands,
> Like bold Briareus, with a hundred hands [the orchestra]:
> To stir, to rouse, to shake the soul he comes,
> And Jove's own thunders follow Mars's drums.

So on February 18, 1743, at the Theatre Royal in Covent Garden, the rejuvenated composer presented his oratorio *Samson*. George II led London's elite to the première; the lovely overture pleased everyone but Horace Walpole, who was resolved *nil admirari;* the noble aria "O God of Hosts" was almost of *Messiah*nic splendor; *Samson*, like Samson, "brought down the house." But when, a month later (March 23), the *Messiah* itself was offered to London even the King, who then established a lasting custom by rising to his feet at the Hallelujah Chorus, could not lift the oratorio to acceptance. The clergy condemned the use of a theater for religious music; the nobility, still smarting from the failure of their opera company, stayed away. The *Messiah* was offered only three times in the next two years, then not again till 1749. In that year Handel, who was a philanthropist between bankruptcies, presented a handsome organ to the foundlings' hospital so dear to his friend Hogarth; and on May 1, 1750, he gave the first of many annual performances of the *Messiah* for the benefit of those lucky unfortunates.

On June 27, 1743, George II led his army to victory at Dettingen. When he returned to London the city greeted him with parades, illuminations, and music, and the Chapel Royal in the Palace of St. James resounded with the "Dettingen Te Deum" that Handel had composed for the occasion (November 27). It was a product of genius and scissors, for it contained passages pilfered from earlier and minor composers; but it was a miracle of agglutination. The King was pleased.

Encouraged by royal smiles, Handel renewed his efforts to recapture the ear of London. On February 10, 1744, he presented another oratorio, *Semele*. It contained the exquisite song "Where'er You Walk," which England and America still sing, but it could not exceed four performances. The nobles remained hostile; many titled ladies made a point of entertaining lavishly on the evenings scheduled for a concert by Handel; rowdies were hired to tear down his advertisements. On April 23, 1745, he canceled the eight concerts that he had announced; he closed his theater, and retired to Tunbridge Wells. Rumor had it that he was insane. "Poor Hendel," wrote the current Earl of Shaftesbury (October 24), "looks a little better. I hope he will recover completely, though his mind has been entirely deranged."[64]

The rumor may have erred, for Handel, now sixty years old, responded with all his powers to an invitation from the Prince of Wales to commemorate the victory of the Prince's younger brother, the Duke of Cumberland, over the Stuart forces at Culloden. Handel took as a symbolic subject Judas Maccabaeus' triumph (166–161 B.C.) over the Hellenizing schemes of Antiochus IV. The new oratorio was so well received (April 1, 1747) that it bore five repetitions in its first season. The Jews of London, grateful to see one of their national heroes so nobly celebrated, helped to swell the attendance, enabling Handel to present the oratorio forty times before his death. Grateful for this new support, he took most of his oratorio subjects henceforth from Jewish legend or history: *Alexander Balus, Joshua, Susanna, Solomon, Jephtha.* By contrast *Theodora*, a Christian theme, drew so small an audience that Handel ruefully remarked, "There was room enough to dance." Chesterfield left before the conclusion, excusing himself on the ground that he "did not wish to disturb the King in his privacy."[65]

5. Prometheus

The oratorios are but one species of the genus Handel. His polymorphous spirit turned with almost spontaneous accord to any of a dozen musical forms. Songs that still touch the chords of sentiment, keyboard pieces of exquisite delicacy, sonatas, suites, quartets, concertos, operas, oratorios, ballet music, odes, pastorals, cantatas, hymns, anthems, Te Deums, Passions —almost everything but the nascent symphony is there, rivaling the profuse immensity of Beethoven or Bach. The *Suites de Pièces pour le Clavecin* sound today, on the harpsichord, like the voices of happy children still un-acquainted with history. A second set of suites began with that prelude which Brahms frolicked with in "Variations and Fugue on a Theme of Handel."

Just as he had taken the oratorio from Carissimi and Keiser and brought it to its peak, so Handel took from Torelli and Corelli the *concerto grosso* —for two or more solo or duo instruments with a chamber orchestra. In Opus 6 he left twelve such *concerti grossi*, pitting two violins and a violon-cello against an ensemble of strings; some of them strike us as monotonous today, some come close to Bach's Brandenburg Concertos. There are also, in Handel, delightful concertos for a single solo instrument—harpsichord, organ, violin, viola, oboe, or harp. Those for keyboards were performed by Handel himself in preludes or interludes. Sometimes he left place in the concerto scores for what we should now call a cadenza, wherein the per-former could free his imagination and display his skill. Handel's improvisa-tions in such openings were the wonder of many days.

In July, 1717, George I arranged a royal "progress" in decorated barges on the Thames. The *Daily Courant* of July 19, 1717, reveals the scene:

> On Wednesday evening at about eight the King took water at Whitehall in an open barge, wherein were also the Duchess of New-castle, the Countess of Godolphin, Madam Kilmanseck, and the Earl of Orkney, and went up the river towards Chelsea. Many other barges with persons of quality attended, and so great a number of boats that the whole river in a manner was covered. A city company's barge was employed for the music, wherein were fifty instruments of all sorts, who played all the way from Lambeth . . . the finest symphonies, composed express for the occasion by Mr. Hendel, which his Majesty liked so well that he caused it to be played over three times in going and returning.[66]

This is the *Water Music* that is today the hardiest and most pleasant sur-vivor of Handel's instrumental compositions. Apparently there were origi-nally twenty-one movements—too many for modern auditors lacking barges and hours; generally we hear only six. Some are a bit tiresome in their melodious wandering; but most of them are healthy, joyous, sparkling music, as if flowing from a fountain to make a lullaby for royal mistresses. The *Water Music* is the oldest piece in today's orchestral repertoire.

A full generation later, for a second George, Handel dignified another outdoor occasion. To celebrate the Peace of Aix-la-Chapelle the govern-ment arranged a display of fireworks in the Green Park, and commissioned Handel to write the *Royal Fireworks Music*. When this was rehearsed in Vauxhall Gardens (April 21, 1749) twelve thousand persons paid the then considerable sum of two shillings each to hear it; so great was the congestion that traffic on the approach over London Bridge was held up for three hours—"probably the most stupendous tribute any composer ever received."[67] On April 27 half of London pushed its way into the Green Park; sixteen yards of its wall had to be torn down to let them enter in time. A "band" of a hundred musicians played Handel's music, and fireworks sparkled in the sky. A building erected for the occasion caught fire; the crowd panicked; many persons were injured; two died. All that remained of the festivity was Handel's music. Designed to commemorate a victorious war and to be heard at a distance, it is a blare of bravos and a din of drums, too noisy for an adagio ear; but one largo movement falls gratefully upon tired nerves.

England at last came to love the old German who had striven so hard to be an Englishman. He had failed, but he had tried, even to swearing in English. London had learned to forgive his massive corpulence, his broad face and swelling cheeks, his bow legs and heavy gait, his velvet scarlet greatcoat, his gold-knobbed cane, his proud and haughty air; after all his battles this man had the right to look like a conqueror, or at least a lord. His manners were rough, he disciplined his musicians with love and rage; he scolded his audience for talking at rehearsals; he threatened divas with violence. But he muffled his guns with humor. When Cuzzoni and Bordoni took to fisticuffs on the stage, he said calmly, "Let them fight it out"; and he accompanied their tantrums with a merry obbligato on the kettledrums.[68] When a singer threatened to jump upon the harpsichord because Handel's accompaniments attracted more attention than the singing, Handel asked him to name the date of this proposed performance, so that it might be advertised, for, he said, "more people will come to see you jump than to hear you sing."[69] His bon mots were as remarkable as Jonathan Swift's, but one had to know four languages to enjoy them.

In 1752 he began to lose his eyesight. While he was writing *Jephtha* his vision became so blurred that he had to stop. On the autograph manuscript in the British Museum are strange irregularities—"stems placed at some distance from the notes to which they belonged, and notes which had obviously lost their way."[70] At the foot of the page appears a line by the composer: "Have got so far, Wednesday, 13th February. Prevented from continuing because of my left eye." Ten days later he wrote on the margin: "The 23rd February, am a little better. Resumed work." Then he composed the music for the words "Our joy is lost in grief, . . . as day is lost in night."[71] On November 4 *The General Advertiser* reported: "Yesterday George Frederic Hendel, Esq., was couched [for cataract] by Wm. Bromfield, Esq., surgeon to her Royal Highness the Princess of Wales." The operation seemed successful, but on January 27, 1753, a London newspaper announced that "Mr. Hendel has at length, unhappily, quite lost his sight." Later reports indicate that he retained some vestiges of vision till his death.

He continued composing and conducting for seven years more. In six weeks (February 23 to April 6, 1759) he gave two performances of *Solomon*, one of *Samson*, two of *Judas Maccabaeus*, three of the *Messiah*. But on leaving the theater after the *Messiah* of April 6 he fainted, and had to be carried to his home. Regaining consciousness, he asked for one more week of life; "I want to die on Good Friday, in the hope of rejoining the good God, my sweet Lord and Saviour, on the day of His Resurrection."[72] He added to his will a codicil bequeathing a thousand pounds to the Society for the Support of Decayed Musicians and Their Families, and substantial bequests to thirteen friends, and "to my maidservants each one year's wages." He died on Holy Saturday, April 14, 1759. He was buried in Westminster Abbey on April 20, before "the greatest Concourse of People of all Ranks ever seen upon such or indeed upon any other Occasion."[73]

He left an unparalleled quantity of music: forty-six operas, thirty-two oratorios, seventy overtures, seventy-one cantatas, twenty-six *concerti grossi*, eighteen organ concertos, and so much else that the whole fills a hundred bulky volumes, almost equaling the works of Bach and Beethoven combined. Some of it was repetition, and some of it was theft, for Handel plagiarized, without acknowledgment, from at least twenty-nine authors to help him meet a deadline;[74] so the minuet in the overture to *Samson* was taken, so to say, *notatim* from Keiser's opera *Claudius*.[75]

It is difficult to estimate Handel, for only a small part of his *oeuvre* is offered to us today. The operas, except for some captivating arias, are beyond resurrection; they were adjusted to Italian modes that seem irrevocably gone; their extant scores are incomplete, and use symbols and abbreviations now largely unintelligible; they were written for orchestras of quite other constitution than ours, and for voices of a third sex quite different from the intermediate sexes of our time. The concertos remain, a happy hunting ground of forgotten treasures, and the *Water Music*, and the oratorios. But even the oratorios are "dated," having been written for embattled Englishmen and grateful Jews; those massive choruses and proliferated vowels require a musicological stomach for their digestion—though we should be glad to hear *Jephtha* and *Israel in Egypt* again. Musicians tell us that in the neglected oratorios there is a solemn grandeur, a sublimity of feeling, a power of conception, expression, and drama, a variety and skill in compositional technique, never again reached in the literature of that form. The *Messiah* survives its repetitions and dismemberments partly because it enshrines the central doctrines of Christianity, dear even to those who have shed them, but chiefly because its profound chants and triumphal choruses make it, all in all, the greatest single composition in the history of music.

England realized his greatness when he was gone. As the anniversary of his birth approached, the nobility, once hostile, joined with King and commoners to commemorate it with three days of his music. As his birth had fallen in 1684 by the English calendar, the first performance was given on May 26, 1784, in Westminster Abbey; the second and third on May 27 and 29. These having failed to meet the demand, two more were given in the Abbey on June 3 and 5. The singers numbered 274, the orchestra 251; now began the custom of making Handel overwhelmingly monumental. Similar immensities celebrated later Handel anniversaries, until in 1874 the number of performers swelled to 3,500. Burney, who heard one of these enormities, thought that the quantity of sound had not injured the quality of the music.[76] In any case these were the most massive commemorations that any musician has ever received. Now that they have subsided it may be possible to hear Handel's music again.

V. VOLTAIRE IN ENGLAND: 1726–28

There was a young Frenchman, in the England of 1726, who was to prove far more important than Handel in the history of the eighteenth century. Voltaire touched English shores at Greenwich, near London, on May 10 or 11. His first impression was enthusiastic. It was the week of the Greenwich Fair; the Thames was almost covered with boats and stately sails; the King was coming downstream in a decorated barge, preceded by a band. On shore men and women moved proudly on prancing horses; on foot were scores of pretty girls, dressed for a holiday. Voltaire, thirty-two, was stirred by their graceful figures, demure modesty, and rosy cheeks. He forgot them when he reached London and found that the banker on whose funds he had a letter of exchange for twenty thousand francs had declared bankruptcy. He was rescued by Everard Falkener, a merchant whom he had met in France; for some months he stayed at this generous Briton's estate at Wandsworth, a suburb of London. George I, hearing of Voltaire's contretemps, sent him a hundred guineas.

He had letters of introduction from Horatio Walpole, British ambassador to France, to many celebrities; sooner or later he met nearly everyone of any prominence in English letters or politics. He was received by Robert Walpole, prime minister; by the Duke of Newcastle; by Sarah, Duchess of Marlborough; by George Augustus and Caroline, Prince and Princess of Wales; and finally by the King, who gave him a valuable watch, which

Voltaire sent as a peace offering to his father. He visited "mylord and my-lady Bolingbroke," and "found their affection still the same."[77] In August he made a flying trip to France, still eager to fight Rohan, but probably to regulate his financial affairs. For three months he lived—part of the time with Swift—as guest of the third Earl of Peterborough. For another three months he enjoyed at Eastbury Manor the hospitality of Bubb Dodington, corrupt politician but kindly Maecenas to Fielding, Thomson, and Young. Voltaire met the two poets there, and read them with no profit. He set himself resolutely to learn the language; by the end of 1726 he was writing letters in English.[78] For the first months he confined himself to circles where French was understood; but nearly all men and women of consequence in English letters or politics knew French. The notebooks that he now filled were written in either language, and show that he learned the wicked words first.

He developed such an acquaintance with English literature as no French-man of note acquired again till Hippolyte Taine. He read Bolingbroke, but found the Viscount's pen less brilliant than his tongue; however, he may have taken from Bolingbroke's *Idea of a Patriot King* the belief that the best chance of social reform would be through an enlightened monarchy. He made his way through Swift's distilled hatreds, learned from him, per-haps, some arts of satire, and pronounced him "infinitely superior to Rabe-lais."[79] He read Milton, and pounced at once upon the fact that Satan was the real hero of *Paradise Lost*.[80] We have seen elsewhere his confused reac-tion to Shakespeare—admiration of the "amiable barbarian's" eloquence, "pearls" of sublimity or tenderness in an "enormous dunghill" of farces and vulgarities.[81] He imitated *Julius Caesar* in *La Mort de César*, and *Othello* in *Zaïre*. So *Gulliver's Travels* reappeared in *Micromégas*, and Pope's *Essay on Man* in the *Discours en vers sur l'homme*.

Soon after his arrival in England he went to see Pope. He was shocked by Pope's deformity and sufferings, amazed by Pope's sharpness of mind and phrase; he rated Pope's *Essay on Criticism* above Boileau's *Art po-étique*.[82] He visited the aging Congreve, and was piqued to find that the once great dramatist wished to be considered "not as an author but as a gentleman."[83] He learned with envy of the sinecures and pensions given to authors by English ministries before Walpole's, and contrasted this with the fate of France's leading poet, thrown into the Bastille for resenting a nobleman's slur.

From literature he passed to science, met members of the Royal Society, and began that study of Newton which would enable him later to replace Descartes with Newton in France. He was deeply impressed by the cere-monial funeral given to Newton by the elite of England, and noted how the Anglican clergy welcomed a scientist into Westminster Abbey. Though

he had become a deist before visiting England—had learned the art of doubt
from Rabelais, Montaigne, Gassendi, Fontenelle, and Bayle—he now derived corroboration from the deists of England—Toland, Woolston, Tindal,
Chubb, Collins, Middleton, and Bolingbroke; later his library would be
armed with their books. Stronger still was the influence of Locke, whom
Voltaire praised as the first to make a realistic study of the mind. He observed that very few of these insistent heretics had been imprisoned for
their views; he remarked the growth of religious toleration since 1689; he
thought there was no religious bigotry or fanaticism in England; even the
Quakers had subsided into comfortable businessmen. He visited one of
them, and was pleased to be told that Pennsylvania was a utopia without
classes, wars, or enemies.[84]

"How I love the English!" he later wrote to Mme. du Deffand. "How I
love these people who say what they think!"[85] And again:

> See what the laws of England have achieved: they have restored to
> every man his natural rights, from which nearly all monarchies have
> despoiled him. These rights are: full freedom of person and property;
> to speak to the nation through his pen; to be judged in criminal matters
> by a jury of free men; to be judged in any matter only according to
> precise laws; to profess in peace whatever religion he prefers, while
> abstaining from those employments to which only members of the
> Anglican Church are eligible.[86]

The last line shows that Voltaire recognized the limits of English freedom.
He knew that religious liberty was far from complete; and in his notebooks
he recorded the arrest of "Mr. Shipping" for derogatory remarks on the
King's speech.[87] Either house of Parliament could summon authors to trial
for unpleasant statements about M.P.s; the lord chamberlain could refuse
to license plays; Defoe had been pilloried for a sarcastic pamphlet. Nevertheless, Voltaire felt, the government of England, corrupt as it was, gave
the people a degree of liberty creatively stimulating in every area of life.

Here, for example, commerce was relatively free, not shackled by such
internal tolls as hobbled it in France. Businessmen were honored with high
posts in the administration; friend Falkener was soon to be made ambassador to Turkey. Voltaire the businessman liked the practicality of the English, their respect for facts, reality, utility, their simplicity of manners,
habits, and dress even in opulence. Above all he liked the English middle
class. He compared the English with their beer: froth at the top, dregs at
the bottom, but the middle excellent.[88] "If I were to follow my inclination,"
he wrote on August 12, 1726, "I would stay right here, for the sole purpose
of learning to think"; and in a burst of enthusiasm he invited Thieriot to

visit "a nation fond of their liberty, learned, witty, despising life and death, a nation of philosophers."[89]

This love affair with England was clouded for a while by the suspicion, in Pope and others, that Voltaire was acting as a spy on his Tory friends for the Walpole ministry.[90] The suspicion proved unjust and was soon rejected, and Voltaire won considerable popularity among the aristocracy, and the intelligentsia of London. When he decided to publish *La Henriade* in England, nearly all literate circles, beginning with George I, Princess Caroline, and the rival courts, sent in subscriptions; Swift solicited, or commanded, a number of these. When the poem appeared (1728) it was dedicated to Caroline, now Queen, with an incidental bouquet to George II, who responded with a gift of four hundred pounds and an invitation to royal suppers. Three editions were sold out in three weeks, despite the princely price of three guineas per copy; from this English edition Voltaire estimated his receipts at 150,000 francs. He used part of the money to help several Frenchmen in England;[91] the remainder he invested so wisely that he later judged this windfall to have been the origin of his wealth. He never ceased to be grateful to England.

He owed to it, above all, an immense stimulation of mind and maturing of thought. When he returned from exile he brought Newton and Locke in his baggage; he spent part of his next twenty years introducing them to France. He brought also the English deists, who supplied him with some of the ammunition that he was to use in his war against *l'infâme*. As England under Charles II had learned good and evil from the France of Louis XIV, so the France of Louis XV was to learn from the England of 1680–1760. Nor was Voltaire the only medium of exchange in this generation; Montesquieu, Maupertuis, Prévost, Buffon, Raynal, Morellet, Lalande, Helvétius, Rousseau also came to England; and others who did not come learned enough English to become carriers of English ideas. Voltaire later summed up the debt in a letter to Helvétius:

> We have borrowed, from the English, annuities, . . . sinking funds, the construction and maneuvering of ships, the laws of gravitation, . . . the seven primary colors, and inoculation. Imperceptibly we shall acquire from them their noble freedom of thought, and their profound contempt for the petty trifling of the schools.[92]

Nevertheless he was lonesome for France. England was ale, but France was wine. He repeatedly begged permission to return. Apparently it was granted on the mild condition that he avoid Paris for forty days. We do not know when he left England; probably in the fall of 1728. In March, 1729, he was in St.-Germain-en-Laye; on April 9 he was in Paris, chastened but indestructible, bursting with ideas, and itching to transform the world.

BOOK II

FRANCE

1723–56

CHAPTER VII

The People and the State

THE France that Voltaire returned to in 1728 had some nineteen millions population, divided into three *états* (states, or classes): the clergy, the nobility, and the *tiers état* (Third Estate), all the rest. We must look at each "state" carefully if we would understand the Revolution.

I. THE NOBILITY

The territorial seigneurs who derived their titles from the land they owned (approximately a fourth of the soil) called themselves *la noblesse d'épée,* the nobility of the sword. Their chief duty was to organize, and lead the defense of, their seigniory, their region, their country, and their king. In the first half of the eighteenth century they headed some eighty thousand families comprising 400,000 souls.[1] They were divided into jealous ranks. At their top stood the offspring and nephews of the reigning king. Below these were the *pairs,* or peers, of France: princes of the blood (lineal descendants of previous kings); seven bishops; fifty dukes. Then came lesser dukes, then marquises, then counts, viscounts, barons, chevaliers . . . Various ceremonial privileges distinguished the several grades; so there were tragic disputes over the right to walk under parasols in the Corpus Christi procession, or to sit in the presence of the king.

Within the *noblesse d'épée* a minority tracing its titles and possessions through many generations designated itself *la noblesse de race,* and looked down upon those nobles who owed their titles to the ennoblement of recent ancestors or themselves under Louis XIII or Louis XIV. Some of these new titles had been conferred as reward for services to the state in war, administration, or finance; some had been sold for as little as six thousand livres by the late needy Grand Monarque; in this way, said Voltaire, "a huge number of citizens—bankers, surgeons, merchants, clerks, and servants of princes—obtained patents of nobility."[2] Certain governmental offices, such as chancellor or chief justice, automatically ennobled their holders. Under Louis XV any commoner could achieve nobility by buying for 120,000 livres appointment as a secretary of state; under Louis XVI there would be nine hundred such imaginary secretaries. Or one could buy a title by buying a nobleman's estate. By 1789 probably ninety-five per cent of all nobles were of middle-class origin.[3]

Among these the majority had arrived at exaltation by studying law and becoming judicial or administrative magistrates. In this number were the members of the thirteen *parlements* that served as law courts in the greater cities of France. As a magistrate was allowed to transmit his office to his son, a new hereditary aristocracy took form—*la noblésse de robe*, the nobility of the gown. In the judiciary, as in the clergy, the gown was half the authority. Overwhelming in their scarlet robes, massive mantles, frilled sleeves, powdered wigs, and plumaged hats, the members of the *parlements* ranked just below the bishops and the territorial nobility. But as some magistrates, through their legal fees, became richer than most pedigreed landholders, the barriers between the *noblesse d'épée* and the *noblesse de robe* broke down, and by 1789 there was an almost complete amalgamation of the two nobilities. The class thus formed was then so numerous and powerful that the King did not dare oppose it, and only the Jacqueries of the Revolution could overthrow its costly privileges.

Many of the old nobility were impoverished by careless or absentee management of their domains, or by unprogressive agricultural methods, or by exhaustion of the soil, or by depreciation of the currency in which they received tenant rents or feudal dues; and as nobles were not supposed to engage in commerce or industry, the growth of manufactures and trade developed a money economy in which one might own much land and still be poor. In some districts of France there were hundreds of nobles as indigent as the peasantry.[4] But a large minority of nobles enjoyed and dissipated great fortunes. The Marquis de Villette had an annual income of 150,000 livres, the Duc de Chevreuse 400,000, the Duc de Bouillon 500,000. To make their lives more tolerable most nobles were exempt, except in emergency, from direct taxation. Kings feared to tax them lest they demand the summoning of a States-General; such a meeting of the three *états* might exact some control over the monarch as the price of voting subsidies. "Every year," said de Tocqueville, "the inequality of taxation separated classes, . . . sparing the rich and burdening the poor."[5] In 1749 an income tax of five per cent was levied on the nobles, but they prided themselves on evading it.

Before the seventeenth century the landed nobility had served economic and administrative, as well as military, functions. However their property had been acquired, the seigneurs organized the division and cultivation of the soil, either through serfdom or through leasing parcels to tenants; they provided law and order, trial, adjudication, and punishment; they maintained the local school, hospital, and charity. On hundreds of seigniories the feudal lord had performed these functions as well as the natural selfishness of men allowed, and the peasants, recognizing his usefulness, gave him obedience and respect, sometimes even affection.

Two main factors changed this feudal relationship: the appointment of intendants by and after Cardinal Richelieu, and the transformation of the major seigneurs into courtiers by Louis XIV. The intendants were middle-class bureaucrats sent by the king to govern the thirty-two districts into which France was divided for administration. Usually they were men of ability and good will, though they were not all Turgots. They improved the sanitation, lighting, and embellishment of the towns; they reorganized the finances; they dammed rivers to irrigate the soil, or diked them to prevent floods; they gave France in this century a magnificent network of roads then unequaled elsewhere in the world, and began to line them with the trees that shade and adorn them today.[6] Soon their greater diligence and competence displaced the territorial lords from regional rule. To accelerate this centralizing replacement, Louis XIV invited the seigneurs to attend him at court; there he gave them lowly offices glorified with exalted titles and intoxicating ribbons; they lost touch with local affairs while drawing from their manors the revenues needed to maintain their palaces and equipages in Paris or Versailles; they clung to their feudal rights after abandoning their feudal tasks. Their loss of administrative functions, in both the economy and the government, opened them to the charge that they were dispensable parasites on the body of France.

II. THE CLERGY

The Catholic Church was an essential and omnipresent force in the government. The number of her clergy in France has been estimated at 260,000 in 1667,[7] 420,000 in 1715,[8] 194,000 in 1762;[9] these figures are guesses, but we may assume a decline of some thirty per cent during the eighteenth century, despite an increase in the population. Lacroix calculated that in 1763 France had eighteen archbishops, 109 bishops, 40,000 priests, 50,000 *vicaires* (assistant priests), 27,000 priors or chaplains, 12,000 canons regular, 20,000 clerks, and 100,000 monks, friars and nuns.[10] Of 740 monasteries 625 were *in commendam*—i.e., they were governed by assistant abbots on behalf of absentee abbots who received the title and half or two thirds of the revenue without being required to live an ecclesiastical life.

The higher clergy were practically a branch of the nobility. All bishops were appointed by the king, usually on nomination by the local seigneurs, and subject to papal consent. Titled families, to keep their property undivided by inheritance, secured bishoprics or abbacies for their younger sons; of 130 bishops in France in 1789 only one was a commoner.[11] Such scions of old stock brought into the Church their habits of worldly luxury, sport, and pride. Prince Cardinal Édouard de Rohan had an alb bordered with point lace and valued at 100,000 livres, and his kitchen utensils were of massive silver.[12] Archbishop Dillon of Narbonne explained to Louis XVI why, after prohibiting the chase to his clergy, he himself continued to hunt: "Sire, my clergy's vices are their own; mine come from my ancestry."[13] The great age of French ecclesiastics—Bossuet, Fénelon, Bourdaloue —had passed; the epicurean riot of the Regency had freed men like Dubois and Tencin to rise in the hierarchy of the Church despite their achievements in both forms of venery. Many bishops lived most of the year in Versailles or Paris, joining in the gaiety and sophistication of the court. They kept one foot in each world.

Bishops and abbots had the rights and duties of seigneurs, even to providing a bull to service their peasants' cows.[14] Their vast domains, sometimes enclosing whole towns, were managed as feudal properties. Monasteries owned a great part of the city of Rennes, and most of the environing terrain.[15] In some communes the bishop appointed all judges and officials; so the Archbishop of Cambrai, suzerain over a region comprising 75,000 inhabitants, appointed all administrators in Cateau-Cambrésis, and half of those in Cambrai.[16] Serfdom survived longest on monastic estates;[17] the canons regular of St.-Claude, in the Jura, had twelve thousand serfs, and fervently resisted any reduction of feudal services.[18] The immunities and privileges of the Church were bound up with the existing social order, and made the ecclesiastical hierarchy the most conservative influence in France.

The Church annually collected, with some moderation and consideration, a tithe of every landholder's produce and cattle; but this *décime* was seldom an actual tenth; more often it was a twelfth, sometimes only a twentieth.[19] With this, and gifts, legacies, and the revenue from her realty, the Church maintained her parish priests in poverty and her bishops in luxury, she relieved the destitute, and educated and indoctrinated the young. Next to the king with his army, the Church was the strongest and richest power in France. She owned, by diverse estimates, from six to twenty per cent of the soil,[20] and a third of the wealth.[21] The bishop of Sens had a yearly income of 70,000 livres; the bishop of Beauvais, 90,000; the Archbishop of Rouen, 100,000; of Narbonne, 160,000; of Paris, 200,000; the Archbishop of Strasbourg had over a million a year.[22] The Abbey of Prémontré, near Laon. had a capital of 45 million livres. The 236 Dominican friars of Toulouse owned French property, colonial plantations, and Negro slaves, valued at many millions. The 1,672 monks of St.-Maur held property worth 24 million livres, earning eight million a year.

None of the Church's possessions or income was taxable, but periodically the higher clergy in national convocation voted a free donation to the state.

In 1773 this amounted to sixteen million livres for five years, which Voltaire reckoned to be a just proportion of the Church's income.[23] In 1749 J. B. Machault d'Arnouville, comptroller general of finances, proposed to replace this *don gratuit* by extending to the Church, as well as to all the laity, a direct annual tax of five per cent on all income. Fearing that this was a first step toward despoiling the Church to salvage the state, the clergy resisted with "an inflexible passion."[24] Machault proposed also to outlaw legacies to the Church without state sanction; to annul all religious establishments set up without royal approval since 1636; and to require all holders of ecclesiastical benefices to report their revenues to the government. An assembly of the clergy refused to obey these edicts, saying, "We will never consent that that which has heretofore been the gift of our love and respect should become the tribute of our obedience." Louis XV ordered the dissolution of the assembly, and his Council bade the intendants collect an initial levy of 7,500,000 livres on the property of the Church.

Voltaire sought to encourage Machault and the King by issuing a pamphlet, *Voix du sage et du peuple*, which urged the government to establish its authority over the Church, to prevent the Church from being a state within the state, and to trust to the philosophers of France to defend King and minister against all the forces of superstition.[25] But Louis XV saw no reason for believing that philosophy could win in a contest with religion. He knew that half his authority rested upon his anointment and coronation by the Church; thereafter, in the eyes of the masses, who could never come close enough to him to count his mistresses, he was the viceregent of God and spoke with divine authority. The spiritual terrors wielded by the clergy, enhanced by all the forces of tradition, habit, ceremony, vestments, and prestige, took the place of a thousand laws and a hundred thousand policemen in maintaining social order and public obedience. Could any government, without the support of supernatural hopes and fears, control the innate lawlessness of men? The King decided to yield to the bishops. He transferred Machault to another post, suppressed Voltaire's pamphlet, and accepted a *don gratuit* in lieu of a tax on ecclesiastical property.

The power of the Church rested ultimately on the success of the parish priest. If the people feared the mitered hierarchy, they loved the local curé, who shared their poverty and sometimes their agricultural toil. They grumbled when he collected the "tithe," but they realized that he was compelled to do it by his superiors, and that two thirds of it went to his bishop or some absentee beneficiary, while the parish church, as like as not, languished in a disrepair painful to piety. That beloved church was their town hall; there their village assemblies met under the presidency of the priest; in the parish register, as the witness of their patient continuity through the generations, were recorded their births, marriages, and deaths. The sound of the church bells was the noblest music to their ears; the ceremonies were their exalting drama; the stories of the saints were their treasured literature; the feasts of the Church calendar were their grateful holidays. They did not look upon the exhortations of the priest, or his instruction of their children, as a mythical indoctrination to support ecclesiastical authority, but as an indispensable aid to parental discipline and moral restraint, and as the revelation of a divine order that redeemed with eternal significance the dreary routine of their earthly lives. So precious was that faith that they could be inflamed to kill anyone who tried to take it from them. The peasant father and mother welcomed religion into the daily routine of their home, transmitted its legends to their children, and led them in evening prayer. The parish priest, loving them as they loved him, sided with them in the Revolution.

Monks, friars, and nuns were diminishing in number and growing in virtue[26] and wealth. They were rarely mendicant now, for they had found it wiser to elicit bequests from the dying as a fee for Paradise than to beg pennies in the villages. Some of their wealth overflowed into charity; many monasteries maintained hospitals and almshouses, and daily distributed food to the poor.[27] In 1789 many communities urged the Revolutionary government not to suppress the local monasteries, since these were the only charitable organizations in their region.[28] Nunneries performed several functions now otherwise served: they provided a refuge for widows, for women separated from their husbands, and for tired ladies who, like Mme. du Deffand, wished to live away from the turmoil of the world. The convents did not entirely renounce worldly pleasures, for the well-to-do used them as havens for surplus daughters, who might otherwise, by requiring marriage dowries, have lessened the patrimony of the sons; and these discarded virgins were not always inclined to austerity. The abbess of Origny had a coach and four, and entertained both sexes in her comfortable apartment; at Alix the nuns wore hoopskirts, and silk robes lined with ermine; at other nunneries they dined and danced with officers from nearby camps.[29] These were apparently sinless relaxations; many of the stories of conventual immorality in the eighteenth century were lurid exaggerations in the propaganda war of rival faiths. Instances of girls kept in convents against their will were now rare.[30]

The Jesuits had declined in power and prestige. Till 1762 they still controlled education, and provided influential confessors to King and Queen. But they had suffered from the eloquence of Pascal and the skeptics of the impious Regency, and were losing their long contest with the Jansenists. These Calvinistic Catholics had survived royal persecution and papal bulls; they were numerous in the business and artisan classes, and in law; they were nearing ascendancy in the Paris and other *parlements*. After the death of their ascetic theologian François de Pâris (1727), fervent sick Jansenists made pilgrimages to his tomb in the cemetery of St.-Médard; there they scourged themselves, and some fell into such cataleptic fits that they were called *convulsionnaires;* they groaned and wept, and prayed for cures, and several claimed to have been miraculously healed. After three years of these operations the authorities closed the cemeteries; as Voltaire put it, God was forbidden, by order of the King, to work any miracles there. The convulsions ceased, but the impressionable Parisians were inclined to credit the miracles, and in 1733 a journalist reported, with obvious exaggeration, that "the good town of Paris is Jansenist from top to bottom."[31] Many of the lower clergy, defying a royal edict of 1720, refused to sign the bull *Unigenitus* (1713), wherein Pope Innocent XIII had condemned 101 allegedly Jansenist propositions. The Archbishop of Paris ruled that the last sacrament should not be administered to anyone who had not confessed to a priest who had accepted the bull. The dispute shared in weakening the divided Church against the attacks of the *philosophes.*

Huguenots and other French Protestants were still outlawed, but small groups of them gathered clandestinely. Legally a French Protestant's wife was a concubine; her children were accounted illegitimate, and could not inherit property. Under Louis XV there were several outbreaks of persecution. In 1717 seventy-four Frenchmen caught in Protestant worship were sent to the galleys, and their women were jailed. An edict of 1724 decreed death for Protestant preachers; all persons attending a Protestant assemblage were to suffer confiscation of property, the men were to be condemned to the galleys, the women were to have their heads shaved and be shut up for life.[32] During the ministry of Cardinal Fleury this edict was only laxly enforced, but after his death it was revived at the request of Catholic bishops in southern France.[33] In 1749 the Parlement of Bordeaux ordered the separation of forty-six couples who had been married by Protestant rites. Children of parents who were suspected of Protestantism could be taken from them to be brought up in Catholic homes; we hear of a rich Huguenot spending 200,000 livres in bribing officials to let him keep his children.[34] Between 1744 and 1752 some six hundred Protestants were imprisoned, and eight hundred others were condemned to various penalties.[35] In 1752 the Protestant preacher Bénezet, twenty-six years old, was hanged at Montpellier. In that year Louis XV, under the influence of Mme. de Pompadour, ordered an end to these persecutions;[36] thereafter, especially in or near Paris, Protestants could escape penalties provided they attended a Catholic service once in the year.[37]

Despite the bigotry, worldliness, and will-to-power of their leaders, the French clergy included hundreds of men distinguished by laborious learning or devoted lives. Besides those bishops who squandered in Paris the tithes taken from the peasantry, there were others who came as close to sanctity as administrative duties would permit. Cardinal Louis Antoine de Noailles, archbishop of Paris, was a man of intelligence and nobility. Jean Baptiste Massillon, bishop of Clermont, was loved by the people despite the erudition of his sermons, which Voltaire liked to listen to at meals, if only for the beauty of their style. Gabriel de Caylus, bishop of Auxerre, gave all his wealth to the poor, sold his silver plate to feed the hungry, and then apologized to further suppliants, "My children, I have nothing left to give you."[38] Bishop François de Belsunce remained at his post in the terrible plague at Marseilles (1720), when a third of the population died and most doctors and magistrates fled. "Look at Belsunce," wrote Lemontey:

> all he possessed he has given; all who served him [his personal staff] are dead [from infection]; alone, in poverty, on foot, in the morning he penetrates into the most horrible den of misery, and in the evening he is found again in the midst of places bespattered with the dying; he quenches their thirst, he comforts them as a friend, . . . and in this field of death he gleans abandoned souls. The example of this prelate, who seeems to be invulnerable, animates with courageous emulation . . . the parish priests, the vicars, and the religious orders; not one deserts his colors; not one puts any bounds to his fatigue save with his life. Thus perished twenty-six Recollect friars, and eighteen Jesuits out of twenty-six. The Capuchins summoned their brethren from other provinces, and the latter rushed to martyrdom with the alacrity of the ancient Christians; out of fifty-five the epidemic slew forty-three. The conduct of the priests of the Oratory was, if possible, even more magnanimous.[39]

Let us remember, as we record the bitter conflict between religion and philosophy, and share the anger of the *philosophes* at stifling censorship and disgraceful superstition, that there was devotion as well as wealth in the hierarchy; dedication as well as poverty among the village priests; and, among the people, an abiding, indestructible love for a faith that gave some saving discipline to pride and passion, and brought a consoling vision to toilsome days.

III. THE THIRD ESTATE

1. The Peasantry

The "political economy" that Carlyle branded as the "dismal science" wondered whether the poor are poor because they are ignorant, or ignorant because they are poor. The question can be answered by contrasting the proud independence of the French *paysan* today with the degrading indigence of the French peasant in the first half of the eighteenth century.

His condition was improving in 1723 as compared with the extremity to which he had been reduced by the wars and exactions of Louis XIV. Subject to feudal dues and church tithes, he owned a rising proportion of the soil of France, varying from twenty per cent in Normandy and Brittany to fifty per cent in Languedoc and Limousin.[40] But the average holding of these small proprietors was so small—three to five acres—that they had to support their families by serving as hired hands on other farms. Most of the land was owned by the nobles, the clergy, or the king, and was tilled by tenants, by métayers (sharecroppers), or by day laborers under the discipline of a steward. Tenants paid the owner in money, produce, and service; métayers, in return for land, implements, and seed, paid the landlord half the crop.

Despite the growth of peasant proprietorship, there remained many survivals of feudalism. Only a small minority of proprietors—often as low as two per cent—held land in *franc-alleu*, i.e., free from feudal dues. All peasants except these "allodial" freeholders were required to give the local seigneur several days of labor yearly, enough to plow and plant his acres, reap his harvest, and stow his barns. They paid him a fee for fishing in the lakes or streams, and for pasturing their cattle in the fields, of his domain. (In Franche-Comté, Auvergne, and Brittany, until the Revolution, they paid him for permission to marry.[41]) They were obliged to use his mill, his bakehouse, his wine or oil presses, and no other, and to pay for each use. They paid the lord for every fireplace they had, every well they dug, every bridge they crossed on his terrain. (Some such taxes exist amongst us today in altered forms, as paid to the state.) Laws prohibited the lord and his companions from injuring the peasant's planting or animals while hunting, but these edicts were widely ignored, and the peasant was forbidden to shoot the seignorial pigeons nibbling on his crops.[42] Altogether, on a conservative estimate, fourteen per cent of the peasant's produce or income went to feudal dues; other estimates raise the proportion.[43]

In a few localities literal serfdom remained. A distinguished economic historian estimated that "the total number of serfs" in eighteenth-century France "did not exceed one million."[44] Their number declined, but there were still some 300,000 in 1789.[45] Such peasants were *adscripti glebae* — bound to the soil; they could not legally abandon, sell, or transfer their land, or change their dwelling place, without the lord's consent; and if they died without children living with them and ready to carry on the farm, the farm and its equipment reverted to the seigneur.

After paying his feudal dues and ecclesiastical tithes, the peasant had still to find money, or sell some of his produce or property, in order to meet the taxes laid upon him by the state. He alone paid the taille, or tax on poses-sessions. In addition he paid a gabelle, or tax on salt, and a *vingtième*—five per cent of income—laid upon every household head. Altogether he paid a third of his income to the landlord, the Church, and the state.[46] Tax collec-tors were authorized to enter, or force their way into, his cottage, search for hidden savings, and take away furniture to make up the sum allotted to the household as its share of the tax. And just as the peasant owed the lord labor as well as dues, so, after 1733, he was compelled to give to the state, annually, twelve to fifteen days of unpaid labor (*corvée*) for building or repairing bridges or roads. Imprisonment punished resistance or delay.

Since taxes rose with income and improvements, there was, among the peasantry, little incentive to invention or enterprise. Agricultural methods remained primitive in France as compared with those of contemporary Eng-land. The fallow system left each tract idle every third year, while England was introducing crop rotation. Intensive cultivation was almost unknown. Iron plows were rare, there were few animals on the farm, and little manure. The average holding was too small to allow the profitable use of machines.

The poverty of the French peasant shocked English travelers in this age. At every stop, wrote Lady Mary Montagu (1718), "while the post-horses are changed, the whole town comes out to beg, with such miserable starved faces, and thin tattered clothes, they need no other eloquence to persuade the wretchedness of their condition."[47] French observers gave no rosier picture until much later in the century. "In 1725," said Saint-Simon, "the people of Normandy live on the grass of the fields. The first king in Europe is great simply by being a king of beggars, . . . and by turning his kingdom into a vast hospital of dying people, from whom all is taken without a mur-mur."[48] And in 1740 Marquis René Louis d'Argenson calculated that "more Frenchmen had died of want in the last two years than had been killed in all the wars of Louis XIV."[49] "The clothing of the poor peasants," said Besnard, "and they were almost all poor, was . . . pitiful, for they had only one outfit for winter and summer. . . . Their single pair of shoes (very thin, and cleated with nails), which they procured at the time of their marriage, had to serve them the rest of their lives, or at least as long as the shoes lasted."[50] Voltaire estimated that two million French peasants wore wooden shoes in winter and went barefoot in summer, for high taxes on skins made shoes a luxury.[51] The peasant's dwelling was built of mud and roofed with thatch; usually it had but one room, low and ceilingless; in some parts of northern France, however, cottages were made stronger to bear the cold and winds of winter. The peasant's food consisted of soup, eggs, dairy products, and bread of rye or oats; meat and wheat bread were occasional dissipations.[52] In France, as elsewhere, those who fed the nation had the least to eat.

From this hard life the peasant found consolation in drunkenness and religion. Taverns were numerous, and home brews helped. Character was coarse, brutality was standard, violence flared between individuals, families, and villages. But within the family there was a strong though silent affection. Children were numerous, but death cut most of them down before maturity; there was hardly any increase in the population of France between 1715 and 1740. War, disease, and famine operated with Malthusian regularity.

2. The Proletariat

Still lower than the peasant in social status were domestic servants, who were so poor that few of them could afford to marry. A notch above the peasantry was the proletariat of the towns: the artisans in shops or factories, the carriers of goods and purveyors of services, the craftsmen who built or repaired. Most industry was still domestic, performed in rural cottages as well as in urban homes; merchants supplied the material, collected the products, and pocketed nearly all the profit. In the towns industry was largely in the guild stage, with masters, apprentices, and journeymen working under old rules by which the guild and the government fixed the hours and conditions of labor, the types, quality, and price of the product, and the limited permissible area of sale. These regulations made improvements difficult, excluded the stimulus of external competition, and shared with internal traffic tolls in retarding industrial development. The guilds had become an aristocracy of labor; fees for acceptance as masters ran as high as two thousand livres, and mastership tended to be hereditary.[53] Work in the shops began early, ended late; around Versailles the journeymen labored from as early as four in the morning till as late as eight at night;[54] but toil was less intense than in factories today, and the ecclesiastical festivals provided numerous holidays.

Most industry was "petty," employing only three or four "hands" outside the family. Even tanneries, glassworks, and dyeing establishments were small concerns. In Bordeaux the employees were only four times as numerous as the employers. The government, however, maintained some large plants—soap factories, the Gobelin tapestry works, and the porcelain industry at Sèvres. Mining was becoming a large operation as coal replaced wood for fuel. Protests were made about coal smoke poisoning the air, but industry then as now had its way, and in Paris, as in London, people breathed at the risk of their health. There were steelworks in Dauphiné, paper mills in Angoumois. Textile factories reached considerable size in the north; so Van Robais employed fifteen hundred persons in one mill at

Abbeville, and Van der Cruissen engaged three thousand men at Lille.[55] Such multiplication encouraged division and specialization of labor, and stimulated the invention of machinery for routine processes. The *Encyclopédie* of Diderot (1751 f.) contained descriptions and drawings of a surprising variety and complexity of mechanisms already introduced in French industry, seldom to proletarian applause. When the Jacquard loom was installed at Lyons the silk weavers smashed it to pieces in fear that it would throw them out of work.[56]

To encourage new industries the government, as in Elizabethan England, granted several monopolies, e.g., to the Van Robais family for the production of fine Dutch cloths; and it helped other projects with subsidies and interest-free loans. Over all industry the government exercised a rigorous regulation, inherited from Colbert. This system aroused a rising protest from manufacturers and merchants, who argued that the economy would expand and prosper if liberated from governmental interference. It was in voicing this claim that Vincent de Gournay, toward 1755, uttered the historic phrase "*Laissez faire*" (Let it alone), which in the next generation, with Quesnay and Turgot, would express the physiocrat plea for free enterprise and free trade.

The artisans too resented the regulations, which severely hampered their organization for better conditions and pay; but their chief grievance was that rural and factory labor was capturing the market from the guilds. By 1756 the manufacturers had reduced the artisans in the larger cities—and even the guild masters—to the condition of wage earners dependent upon the entrepreneurs.[57] Within the guilds the masters underpaid their journeymen, who periodically went on strike. Poverty in the towns was almost as great as in the villages. Crop failures brought the urban proletariat to famine and riot every few years; so at Toulouse in 1747, at Paris in 1751, at Toulouse in 1752.[58] Already, about 1729, Jean Meslier, the atheist priest, proposed to replace the existing system with a libertarian communism.[59]

By the middle of the century Paris, Rouen, Lille, Lyons, Bordeaux, Marseilles were teeming with *prolétaires*. Lyons for a time surpassed Paris as a manufacturing center. Thomas Gray, the English poet, described it in 1739 as the "second city of the kingdom in bigness and rank, its streets excessively narrow and nasty, the houses immensely high and large (25 rooms on a floor and 5 stories high), and swarming with inhabitants."[60] Paris was a turbulent hive of 800,000 souls, of whom 100,000 were servants and 20,000 were beggars; dismal slums and magnificent palaces; dark alleys and dirty streets behind fashionable promenades; art fronting destitution. Coaches, public cabs, and sedan chairs were engaged in vituperative collisions and traffic jams. Some thoroughfares had been paved since 1690; in 1742 Trésaquet paved roads with rolled stones (*chaussée empierrée et roulée*); but most of the streets were plain dirt, or laid with cobblestones fit for revolutionary barricades. Street lamps began to replace lanterns in 1745, but were lit only when the moon was not full. Street signs appeared in 1728, but there were no house numbers before the Revolution. Only the well-to-do had faucet water in their homes; the rest were supplied by twenty thousand water carriers, each bearing two buckets, sometimes up seven flights of stairs. Water closets in the home, and bathrooms with running hot and cold water, were privileges of the very rich. Thousands of shops, marked with their picturesque emblems, maintained their own chaos of discordant and suspected weights and measures till the Revolution established the metric system. There were honest shopkeepers in *maisons de confiance*, but the majority had a reputation for short measures, rigged prices, and shoddy goods.[61] Some shops were assuming a specious splendor for the carriage trade. Poor people bought chiefly from peddlers, who laboriously toted their wares in pails or baskets on their backs, and contributed to the music of the streets with their traditional, unintelligible, welcome cries, from "Baked potatoes!" to "Death on rats!" Rats contested with humanity the housing facilities of the city, and men, women, and children rivaled the rats in the race for food. Said Montesquieu's Persian visitor:

> The houses are so high that one would suppose they were inhabited only by astrologers. You may imagine that a town built in the air, with six or seven houses the one on the top of the other, is densely populated, and that when all the inhabitants come down into the street there is a pretty crush. I have been here a month, and I have not yet seen a single person walking at a foot-pace. There is no one in the world like a Frenchman to get over the ground. He runs and flies.[62]

Add the beggars, the vagabonds, the pickpockets, the street singers, the organ players, the medicine mountebanks. All in all, a populace with a hundred human faults, never to be trusted, always alert for gain, heartily and profusely profane; but, given a little food and wine, the kindest, jolliest, brightest populace in the world.

3. The Bourgeoisie

Between the lowly and the great, hated by the one and scorned by the other, the middle class—doctors, professors, administrators, manufacturers, merchants, financiers—subtly, patiently made its way to wealth and power. The manufacturers took economic risks, and demanded commensurate rewards. They complained that they were harassed in a hundred ways by governmental regulations, and by guild control of markets and skills. The merchants who distributed the product raged against a thousand tolls impeding the movement of goods; at almost every river, canal, and crossroads the noble or ecclesiastical lord of the domain had an agent exacting a fee for permission to proceed. The seigneur explained that these tolls were a reasonable reimbursement for his expense in keeping roads, bridges, and ferries in service and repair. A royal edict of 1724 suppressed twelve hundred such tolls, but hundreds remained, and played their part in earning bourgeois support of the Revolution.

French commerce, hampered inland, was spreading overseas. Marseilles, a free port, dominated European trade with Turkey and the East. The Compagnie des Indes, reconstituted in 1723, extended its markets and political influence in the Caribbean, the Mississippi Valley, and parts of India. Bordeaux, chief outlet for the Atlantic trade, raised its maritime commerce from 40 million livres in 1724 to 250 million in 1788. Over three hundred vessels sailed to America from Bordeaux and Nantes every year, many of them carrying slaves to work the sugar plantations in the Antilles and Louisiana.[63] Sugar from French America was now outselling English sugar from Jamaica and Barbados in European markets;[64] this may have been a motive for the Seven Years' War. The total foreign trade of France rose from 215 million livres in 1715 to 600 million in 1750.[65] Voltaire estimated that the number of trading vessels in French service had increased from three hundred in 1715 to eighteen hundred in 1738.[66]

The rising profits from maritime commerce were the chief stimulus to the conquest of colonies. The zeal of French merchants and missionaries had won for France most of Canada and the Mississippi basin, and some Caribbean isles. England challenged these French possessions as enclosing and endangering its colonies in America; war would decide that issue. A like rivalry divided the French and the English in India. At Pondicherry, on the east coast south of Madras, the French had established themselves in 1683, and in 1688 they received from the Mogul Emperor full control of Chandernagor, north of Calcutta. Under the energetic lead of Joseph Dupleix these two ports captured so much trade and wealth that the English East India Company, which had set up strongholds at Madras (1639), Bombay (1668), and Calcutta (1686), felt itself compelled to fight the French for the disintegrating Mogul realm.

When England and France found themselves on opposite sides in the War of the Austrian Succession (1744), Mahé de La Bourdonnais, who had made a record of enterprising administration in the French islands of Mauritius and Bourbon in the Indian Ocean, proposed to the Versailles government a plan "to ruin the commerce and colonies of the English in India."[67] With a French squadron, and the jealous consent of Dupleix, he attacked Madras and soon compelled its surrender (1746). On his own responsibility he signed an agreement with the English authorities to restore Madras to them for an indemnity of £420,000. Dupleix refused to sanction this arrangement; La Bourdonnais persisted; he sailed on a Dutch ship to Europe, was captured by an English ship, was released on parole, entered Paris, and was sent to the Bastille on a charge of insubordination and treason. He demanded trial; after two years of imprisonment he was tried, and acquitted (1751); he died in 1753. Meanwhile a powerful British fleet besieged Pondicherry (August, 1748); Dupleix defended it with such spirit and skill that the siege was abandoned (October). Seven days later the news reached India that the Treaty of Aix-la-Chapelle had returned Madras to England. The French government, knowing that the inferiority of its navy doomed it to defeat in India, refused to support Dupleix's schemes of conquest; it sent him only minor forces and funds, and finally recalled him to France (1754). He lived long enough to see the utter rout of the French by the English in the India phase of the Seven Years' War.

At the top of the Third Estate were the financiers. They could be old-fashioned small-scale moneylenders, or full-scale bankers handling deposits, loans, and investments, or "tax farmers" serving as revenue agents for the state. The restrictions laid by the Catholic Church upon the charging of interest had now very little effect; John Law found half of France eager to trade in stocks and bonds. Paris opened its Bourse in 1724.

Some financiers were richer than most nobles. Paris-Montmartel had 100 million livres, Lenormant de Tournehem 20 million, Samuel Bernard 33 million.[68] Bernard married his daughters into the aristocracy by giving each of them a dowry of 800,000 livres.[69] He was a gentleman and a patriot; in 1715 he himself fixed the tax on his property at nine million livres, so revealing a wealth that he might have partly concealed;[70] and when he died (1739) the examination of his accounts disclosed the great extent of his secret charities.[71] The four brothers Paris developed their banking firm into a political power. Voltaire learned from them much of his financial cunning, and shocked Europe by being both a philosopher and a millionaire.

The best-hated financiers in eighteenth-century France were the "farmers general." The *ferme générale* had been organized in 1697 to collect indirect taxes—chiefly on subsidies, registrations, drafts, salt, and tobacco. In order to spend these revenues before they were collected, the government farmed them out to some individual who paid it a stipulated sum for the right to gather them over a period of six years. The increase in taxes, wealth, and inflation is reflected in the rising price paid for this lucrative lease: 80 million livres in 1726, 92 million in 1744, 152 million in 1774; no government has ever been at a loss for ways to spend its people's money. The lessee delegated the collection of the taxes to forty or more "farmers general" (*fermiers généraux*), each of whom paid a million or more livres as advance security, and licked his fingers as the revenues passed through them; so the profits of the forty farmers general for 1726–30 exceeded 156 million livres.[72] Many of such collectors bought estates and titles, built costly palaces, and lived in a pompous luxury that aroused the ire of aristocracy and clergy. Some of them collected art and artists, poets and mistresses, and opened their homes as havens or salons to the intelligentsia. Helvétius, most amiable of the *philosophes*, was one of the most generous of the *fermiers généraux*. Rousseau was long the guest of Mme. d'Épinay, a farmer general's wife; Rameau and Vanloo enjoyed the hospitality of Alexandre de La Popelinière, chief Maecenas among the financiers. The upper bourgeoisie, anxious for social recognition, revenged themselves for ecclesiastical censures and titled contempt by supporting the philosophers against the Church, and later against the nobility. Perhaps it was the financiers who financed the Revolution.

IV. THE GOVERNMENT

The middle classes were now powerful in the state, for they filled all but those lofty ministries that needed the aura of a family tree. They were the bureaucracy. Their wits having been sharpened by natural selection in the economic arena, they proved more skillful and competent than the unprodded and lackadaisical scions of the vegetating nobility. The *noblesse de robe* in the *parlements* and the magistracies really belonged to the bourgeoisie in origin and character. The middle class governed the communes, the forty provinces, the commissaries of war, supplies, and communications, the care of mines, roads, streets, bridges, rivers, canals, and ports. In the army the generals were nobles, but they followed campaigns planned for them by middle-class strategists in Paris.[73] The bourgeois form of the French state in the nineteenth century was already prefigured in the eighteenth.

The administration of France was generally acknowledged to be the best in Europe, but it had mortal defects. It was so centralized, pervasive, and detailed that it checked local initiative and vitality, and wasted much time in the transmission of orders and reports. Compared with England, France was a stifling despotism. No meetings of the people were permitted, no popular suffrage was taken except in minor local affairs, no Parliament checked the king. Louis XV improved the government by neglecting it, but he delegated to his ministers such royal powers as the issuance of *lettres de cachet*, and this authority was often abused. Sometimes, it is true, such "secret letters" served to accelerate governmental action by evading technical details of administrative procedure ("red tape"). One *lettre de cachet* of Louis XIV established the Comédie-Française in 1680. Some *lettres* saved the reputation of a family by summarily imprisoning a miscreant member without a public trial that would have bared private woes; some, as in Voltaire's second sojourn in the Bastille, prevented a forgivable fool from completing his folly. In several cases they were issued at the request of a desperate parent (like the elder Mirabeau) to discipline an unruly son. Usually, in such instances, incarceration was genteel and brief. But there were many cases of flagrant cruelty, as when the poet Desforges was confined for six years (1750–56) in an iron cage for denouncing the government's expulsion of the Young Pretender from France.[74] If we may believe the generally accurate Grimm, the government was so grateful to Maurice de Saxe for his victories on the battlefield that it sent a *lettre de cachet* to the poet Charles Favart commanding him to add his wife to the list of Saxe's concubines.[75] Any offense to a noble by a commoner, any major criticism of the government, might bring a *lettre de cachet* and imprisonment without trial or stated cause. Such arbitrary orders created a mounting resentment as the century progressed.

French law was as retarded as French administration was advanced. It varied from province to province, recalling their former isolation and autonomy; there were 350 different bodies of law in different regions of France. Colbert had made an unsuccessful attempt to systematize and define French law in the Ordonnance Criminelle of 1670, but even his code mingled confusedly medieval and modern, Germanic and Roman, canon and civil legislation. New laws were made on the need of the moment by the king, usually at the urging of his ministers, with only a hurried inquiry into their consistency with existing laws. It was difficult for the citizen to discover what the law was in his particular place and case.

Criminal law was enforced in the counties by the *maréchaussée*, or mounted police, and in the larger cities by municipal police. Those in Paris had been well organized and trained by Marc René de Voyer d'Argenson, who not only fathered famous sons, but, as lieutenant general of police from 1697 to 1718, earned the nickname "Damné" because he looked like the Devil. In any case he was a terror to the criminals of Paris, for he knew their haunts and ways; and yet (Saint-Simon assures us) he "was full of humanity"[76]–a Joubert before *Les Misérables*.

An arrested person was confined, before his trial, under conditions hardly different from those designed for punishment. He might, like Jean Calas, spend months in chains and mental torture, in filth and daily danger of disease. If he tried to escape his property was confiscated. If charged with a major crime he was not allowed to communicate with a lawyer. There was no right of habeas corpus, no trial by jury. Witnesses were questioned separately and privately. If the judge believed the suspected man guilty, but had insufficient evidence to convict him, he was authorized to use torture to elicit a confession. Such judicial torture declined in frequency and severity under Louis XV, but it remained a part of French legal procedure until 1780.

Penalties ranged from fines to dismemberment. The pillory was favored for punishing dishonesty in business. Thieves and other petty criminals were flogged as they were drawn at a cart-tail through the streets. Theft by domestics might be punished with death, but employers rarely invoked this law. Condemnation to the galleys was officially ended in 1748. Death was the statutory penalty for a great variety of offenses, including sorcery, blasphemy, incest, homosexuality, and bestiality. Decapitation and burning at the stake were no longer used, but execution could be enhanced by "drawing and quartering" the condemned, or by breaking his limbs with an iron bar as he lay bound to a wheel. "A capital execution," we are told, "was always looked forward to with delight by the people, especially in Paris."[77]

The judiciary was almost as complicated as the law. In the countryside there were thousands of feudal courts administering local law, and presided over by judges appointed by the proprietary seigneur; these courts could deal only with petty cases, could impose no penalty beyond a small fine, and were subject to appeal; but the peasant found it difficult and expensive to win a suit against a lord. Above these seignorial courts were those of the territorial *bailli* and *séné-chal*. Many towns had communal courts. Over all these lower tribunals were presidial courts administering royal law. The king might appoint special courts for special purposes. The Church tried its clergy by its own canon law in ecclesiastical courts. Lawyers swarmed in and around the various courts, profiting from a French passion for litigation. Thirteen major cities had *parlements* composed of judges acting as supreme courts for these cities and their environs; the Paris Parlement so served nearly a third of France. Each *parlement* claimed that until it had passed upon, accepted, and registered it, no edict of king or government became law. The royal Council of State never admitted this claim, but often allowed the *parlements* the right of remonstrance. The drearier part of French history revolved around these contested claims of *parlements* and king.

Between the Paris Parlement and the king stood the ministries and the court. All the ministers together constituted the Conseil d'État, or Council of State. The court consisted of the ministers plus those nobles or clergymen or distinguished commoners who had been presented to the king, plus the aides and servants of these courtiers. Strict protocol marked out each courtier's status, qualifications, precedence, privileges, and duties, and an elaborate and detailed code of etiquette eased the friction and burdened the lives of several hundred proud and jealous individuals. Lavish ceremonies alleviated the monotony of court routine, and provided the mystic ambience indispensable to royal government. The favorite amusements at court were gossip, eating, gambling, hunting, and adultery. "In France," reported the Neapolitan ambassador, "nine tenths of the people die of hunger, one tenth of indigestion."[78] Enormous sums were lost and won at play. To pay their debts courtiers sold their influence to the highest bidder; no one could obtain an office or a perquisite without a substantial fee to some member of the court. Nearly every husband at court had a mistress, and nearly every wife a lover. No one grudged the King his concubines; the nobles merely complained that in Mme. de Pompadour he had taken a commoner to his bed when they would have felt honored to have him deflower their daughters.

Though Louis XV had officially come of age in 1723, he was then only thirteen years old, and he turned over the administration to Louis Henri, Duc de Bourbon. The Comte de Toulouse, legitimized offspring of Louis XIV, had been considered for the post, but had been rejected as "too honest to make a good minister."[79] "Monsieur le Duc" himself was a man of good will. He did his best to alleviate the poverty of the people; he thought to do this by an officially fixed scale of prices and wages, but the law of supply and demand defeated his hopes. He dared to lay an income tax of two per cent upon all classes; the clergy protested, and conspired for his fall.[80] He allowed too much influence to his mistress, the Marquise de Prie. She was clever, but her intelligence fell short of her beauty. She maneuvered the marriage of Louis XV to Marie Leszczyńska, hoping to keep the young Queen in tutelage; however, Marie soon lost her influence. Mme. de Prie favored Voltaire, alienated the clergy, and led the Duke to attack the episcopal tutor who had recommended him to the King as chief minister. But the King admired and trusted his tutor beyond any other man in the state.

André Hercule de Fleury had been made bishop of Fréjus in 1698, royal tutor in 1715. Soon he gained a dominant influence over the boy's mind. The bishop was tall, handsome, pliant, gracious; a bit lazy, and never pushing his fortune, but he arrived. Michelet and Sainte-Beuve believed that Fleury, as preceptor, had weakened the young monarch's character with carefree indulgence, and had trained him to favor the Jesuits;[81] but Voltaire, no friend of the clergy, thought highly of Fleury both as tutor and as minister:

> Fleury applied himself to mold the mind of his pupil to business, secrecy, and probity, and preserved, amid the hurry and agitation of the court, during the minority [of the King], the good graces of the Regent and the esteem of the public. He never made a merit of his own services, nor complained of others, and never engaged in cabals or intrigues of the court. . . . He privately endeavored to make himself acquainted with the affairs of the kingdom at home, and its interests

abroad. In a word, the circumspection of his conduct and the amiability of his disposition made all France wish to see him at the head of the administration.[82]

When Fleury learned that his continuing influence in the determination of policy had provoked the Duc de Bourbon to recommend his dismissal from the court, he made no attempt to maintain his place, but quietly withdrew to the monastery of the Sulpicians at Issy, a suburb of Paris (December 18, 1725). The King ordered the Duke to ask Fleury to return. Fleury did. On June 11 Louis XV, responding to the evident desire of the court, the clergy, and the public,[83] abruptly commanded Bourbon "to retire to Chantilly and remain there till further orders." Mme. de Prie was banished to her château in Normandy, where, bored to death, she poisoned herself (1727).

Fleury, still advancing by retreating, took no official position; on the contrary he persuaded the King to declare that henceforth he himself would rule. But Louis preferred to hunt or gamble, and Fleury became prime minister in all but name (June 11, 1726). He was now seventy-three years old. Many ambitious souls looked for his early death, but he ruled France for seventeen years.

He did not forget that he was a priest. On October 8 he revoked the two per cent tax so far as it concerned the clergy; they responded with a *don gratuit* of five million livres to the state. Fleury asked their support to his request for a cardinal's hat, which he needed for precedence over the dukes in the Council of State; it was given him (November 5), and now he made no effort to conceal the fact that he was ruling France.

He astonished the court by remaining as modest in power as he had been in preparation. He lived with an almost parsimonious simplicity, satisfied with the reality, without the appurtenances, of power. "His exaltation," wrote Voltaire, "made no change in his manners, and everyone was surprised to find in a prime minister the most engaging, and at the same time the most disinterested, courtier."[84] "He was the first of our ministers," said Henri Martin, "who lived without luxury and died poor."[85] "He was perfectly honest, and never abused his position."[86] He was "infinitely more tolerant than his entourage."[87] He dealt amiably with Voltaire, and winked at the private practice of Protestant rites; but he gave no toleration to the Jansenists.

He attended in his leisurely way not only to the formation of policy but to the administration of the government. He chose his aides with discerning judgment, and managed them with both firmness and courtesy. Under him Henri François d'Aguesseau continued with his long task (1727–51) of reforming and codifying the law, and Philibert Orry restored order and stability to the finances of the state. Avoiding war until he was forced to it by the dynastic ambitions of the ruling family, Fleury gave France long periods of peace that allowed her to reinvigorate her economic life. His success seemed to justify in advance the arguments soon to be voiced by the physiocrats, that to govern little is to govern well. He promised to halt inflation, and kept his word. Internal and foreign commerce expanded rapidly; revenues rose. Spending the revenues with resolute economy, checking the cost of court festivities, he was able to remove from all classes (1727) the two per cent income tax, and to lower the taille that fell so heavily upon the peasantry. He returned to the cities and towns the right to elect their own officials. Under the example of his personal rectitude the morals of the court reluctantly improved.

Against these credits some major debits raise their heads. He allowed the farmers general to continue their collection of taxes without ministerial interference. To further the vast plan of road building conceived by the intendants he established the *corvée* that put the peasants to work with no reward but food. He founded military schools for the sons of the aristocracy, but he economized imprudently by neglecting the repair and extension of the navy; soon French commerce and colonies were at the mercy of English fleets. He trusted too fondly to his ability to keep the peace with England.

So long as Robert Walpole ruled England, the Cardinal's pacific policy prospered. The two men, though poles apart in morals and character, agreed on the desirability of peace. In 1733, however, his advisers on foreign affairs persuaded him into a halfhearted attempt to replace the King's father-in-law, Stanislas Leszczyński, upon the throne of Poland. But Leszczyński proposed to reform the Polish constitution and set up a strong government; Russia and Austria preferred a Poland hamstrung by the *liberum veto;* in the War of the Polish Succession (1733–38) they chased Leszczyński from Warsaw and then from Danzig; Fleury, averse to a major conflict, advised Stanislas to retire to Nancy and Lunéville as titular "king of Lorraine." It was not all a disaster; Leszczyński and the Powers agreed that on his death Lorraine, which was predominantly French, should revert to France. It so transpired in 1766.

Fleury, eighty-eight years old, strove with all his waning energy to keep France out of the War of the Austrian Succession (1740). A woman overruled him. Félicité de Nesle, Marquise de Vintimille, who for the time being was sharing the King's bed, listened in rapture to Charles Auguste Fouquet, Comte de Belle-Isle, grandson of the artistic embezzler, Nicolas Fouquet, whom Louis XIV had so profitably deposed. Belle-Isle told her that Fleury was an old fool; that now, when Frederick II of Prussia was attacking the young Maria Theresa of Austria, a golden opportunity had come for dismembering her empire; France must join Frederick and share the spoils. The charming mistress sang these strains to her royal lover; she urged him to take the reins from the Cardinal's timid hands, and make France glorious again. Fleury pleaded with him that both honor and interest forbade Belle-Isle's scheme; England would not let Austria be destroyed to make France so dangerously great; France would have to fight England too; and France was doing so well in peace! On June 7, 1741, Louis declared war on Austria. On November 25 Belle-Isle captured Prague, and nearly all France agreed with him that Fleury was an old fool.

After a year of war the shifty Frederick, deserting France, signed a secret truce with Austria. The Austrian armies, so released, moved into Bohemia and began to encircle Prague; it was only a matter of time before Belle-Isle and his twenty thousand men, already harassed by a hostile population, would be compelled to surrender. On July 11, 1742, Fleury sent to the Austrian commander, Count von Königsegg, a humiliating appeal for mild terms to the French garrison. "Many people know," he wrote, "how opposed I was to the resolutions we took, and that I was in a way forced to consent."[88] Königsegg sent the letter to Maria Theresa, who at once gave it to the world. A French army was sent to rescue Belle-Isle; it never reached him. In December Belle-Isle, leaving six thousand sick or wounded men behind, led his main force out of Prague to the frontier at Eger; but the flight took place in wintry weather over a hundred miles of mountainous or marshy terrain covered with snow or ice and infested with enemy raiders; of the fourteen thousand men who began that march twelve hundred died on the way. France applauded the brilliant salvage of a humiliating reverse. Fleury gave up his ministry, retired to Issy, and died (January 29, 1743), ninety years old.

The King announced that henceforth he would be his own prime minister.

V. LOUIS XV

How does it feel to be king from the age of five? The boy who was destined to rule France for fifty-nine years was hardly noticed in his early childhood; he was weak, and was expected to die soon. Then suddenly, in 1712, both his parents, the Duke and Duchess of Burgundy, were carried off by smallpox, and the boy was heir to the throne. Three years later he was king.

Every precaution was taken to unfit him for rule. His governess, Mme. de Ventadour, worried tremulously about the boy's health, and shielded him from any hardening weather. A Jesuit confessor infused into him an awesome reverence for the Church. Fleury, as tutor, was complaisant and indulgent, and seems to have thought that it would be a blessing for France to have a do-nothing king. The lad's governor, Maréchal de Villeroi, administered an opposite poison: leading him to a window of the Tuileries to receive the plaudits of a multitude gathered to acclaim him, "Look, *mon maître*," he said, "all that crowd, all those people, are yours; all belong to you; you are their master."[89] Omnipotence married incompetence.

Spoiled by adoration, selfish in power, lazy and willful, Louis developed into a bored and taciturn youth, forgivably shunning the surveillance of his guardians—and later the ceremonies and servility of the court—to seek an outlet in wood carving, needlework, milking cows, playing with dogs.[90] The elements of cruelty that lurk in all of us were allowed in him to come through his timidity to the surface; it is related that in his boyhood he took pleasure in hurting, even killing, animals.[91] In mature years he sublimated this into hunting, but it may have entered into his callous use and quick discarding of the young women trained in the Parc aux Cerfs for a stay in his bed. And yet a certain shy sensitivity and considerateness marked his treatment of his friends.

He had a good mind, which might have excelled if supported by character. He astonished all by his retentive memory and ready wit. He naturally preferred games to study, but he absorbed some real instruction in Latin, mathematics, history, botany, and military arts. He grew up to be tall, slender but broad-shouldered, with fine complexion and curly golden hair; Maréchal de Richelieu called him "the handsomest lad in his dominions."[92] The museum at Versailles preserves Vanloo's portrait of him at thirteen, with sword and armor hardly befitting the boyish face. René Louis d'Argenson compared him to Eros. Women fell in love with him at first sight. When he took sick (1722), all France prayed for him; when he recovered, France wept with joy. This people which had suffered so much from its kings rejoiced in the hope that soon the youth would marry and beget a son to continue his noble house.

Indeed, he had already been affianced (1721), aged eleven, to María Ana Victoria, aged two, daughter of Philip V of Spain; she had been delivered to Paris, and was now waiting for nubility. But Mme. de Prie thought she could ensure her continuing influence by having this tentative union annulled, and marrying Louis to Marie Leszczyńska, daughter of the deposed King of Poland. She had her way. The Infanta was sent back to Spain (1725)—an insult never forgiven by the Spanish court. Stanislas was in refuge at Wissembourg in Alsace when he received the French King's request for his daughter's hand. Entering the room where she and her mother were at work, he said, "Let us fall on our knees and thank God." "My dear father," exclaimed Marie joyfully, "are you recalled to the throne of Poland?" "God has done us a more astounding grace," Stanislas replied; "you are made Queen of France."[93] Marie had never dreamed of elevation to the greatest throne in Europe; she had seen pictures of Louis XV as of someone unattainably exalted, handsome, and powerful. The French treasury sent her dresses, petticoats, shoes, gloves, jewelry; it promised her 250,000 livres upon her reaching Versailles, and a life annuity of twenty thousand gold crowns. She took it all in a daze, and thanked God for her good fortune. She was married to the King by proxy at Strasbourg (August 15, 1725); she went merrily through days of tribulation on storm-drenched roads to Paris; she was married to the King in person at Fontainebleau on September 5. He was fifteen, she was twenty-two. She was not beautiful, she was only good.

Louis, who had as yet shown no interest in women, awoke at the touch of his modest bride. He embraced her with an ardor that surprised his entourage; and for some time their life was an idyl of love and happiness. She won the respect and loyalty of the people, but she was never popular. She was kind, affectionate, tender, and not lacking in playful wit; nevertheless Versailles missed in her the alert mind and vivacious speech that had become obligatory in ladies of the court. She was shocked by the morals of the aristocracy, but she made no other criticism than to give an example of a faithful wife, eager to please her husband and to give him an heir. In twelve years she bore ten children, and in her off years she suffered miscarriages. The royal appetite became a problem for the Queen; she begged the King to be continent at least on the festivals of the major saints. Then, through her labors and duties, she developed a scrofulous fistula, and the King's ardor sought other channels. Her gratitude to Mme. de Prie and the Duc de Bourbon was a misfortune; she listened too patiently when, in the royal presence, the Duke denounced Fleury; when Fleury came to power he sent her daughters to a distant convent on grounds of economy, and his continuing influence weighted the scales against her. As the King grew colder she retired to an inner circle of her friends, played cards, wove tapestry, tried painting, and found solace in practices of piety and charity. "She lived a convent life amid the fevers and frivolities of the court."[94]

The King had to be amused, and Mme. de Prie had chosen for him an unamusing wife. But not until seven years after his marriage did he take a mistress; then he took four in succession, yet with a certain fidelity, for they were all sisters. None was very comely, but all were lively and amusing, and all but one were experts in coquetry. Louise de Nesle, Comtesse de Mailly, had the honor of being apparently the first to seduce the King (1732). Like Louise de La Vallière, she sincerely loved her royal master; she sought neither riches nor power, but only to make him happy. When her sister Félicité, fresh from a convent, competed for the King's bed, Louise shared Louis with her (1739) in a heterodox *ménage à quatre*—for he still visited the Queen. The complication troubled the conscience of the King; for a time he avoided the Eucharist, having heard terrible stories of men who had dropped dead on taking the Host into a sinful mouth.[95] This second siren, according to one of her sisters, "had the figure of a grenadier, the neck of a crane, and the smell of a monkey";[96] she managed nevertheless to become pregnant. To preserve the proprieties Louis found a husband for her, making her the Marquise de Vintimille. In 1740 Mme. de Mailly withdrew to a convent; she left it a year later to tend her victorious rival, who was dying in childbirth (1741). The King wept, Mme. de Mailly wept with him; he found comfort in her arms; she became mistress again.

A third sister, Adélaïde de Nesle, fat and ugly, was clever and witty; she amused the King with her mimicry and repartee; he enjoyed her, found a husband for her, and passed on. A fourth sister, Mme. de Flavacourt, resisted him and befriended the Queen. But a fifth sister, ablest of them all, Marie Anne de Nesle de La Tournelle, persuaded Mme. de Mailly to present her to the King. She not only conquered him (1742), but insisted on being sole mistress; the amiable Mailly was sent away penniless, falling in a day from royalty to piety; so one Nesle drove out another. Some time later she had to disturb a number of worshipers to reach her chair in Notre-Dame. One of these muttered, "A lot of fuss over a whore." "Sir," she said, "since you know me so well, grant me the favor of praying God for me."[97] God must have found it easy to forgive her.

The new Nesle was the most beautiful of the sorority. Nattier's portrait of her—fair of face, swelling bosom, graceful figure, swirling silk revealing pretty feet—explains the King's precipitance. To all this she added a wit as sparkling as her eyes. Unlike La Mailly, she craved riches and power. She reckoned her curves were worth the duchy of Châteauroux, which brought 85,000 francs a year; she received it and its title of duchess (1743), and for a year she entered into history.

A strong faction at court favored her, for it hoped to use her influence in winning the King to an active martial policy, in which the primacy of government would return from the bourgeois bureaucracy to the military nobility. Louis at times labored dutifully in council with his ministers; he more often delegated his authority and tasks to them, seldom met with them, rarely contradicted them, occasionally signed conflicting decrees proposed by rival aides with conflicting policies. He fled from the irksome etiquette of the court to his dogs, his horses, and the hunt; when he did not hunt the court said, "Today the King does nothing." Though he did not lack courage, he had no taste for war; he preferred a bed to a trench.

In bed and boudoir his voluptuous Duchess, reviving Agnès Sorel, urged him to play an active part in war against England and Austria. She pictured Louis XIV leading his army to glory at Mons and Namur, and asked why

Louis XV, as handsome and brave as his great-grandfather, should not likewise shine in armor at the head of his troops. She had her way, and died in victory. For a moment the *roi fainéant* awoke from his lethargy. Perhaps it was at her prompting that when the end had come at last to the pacific Fleury, Louis announced that he would rule as well as reign. On April 26, 1744, France resumed active war against Austria; on May 22 alliance was renewed with Frederick of Prussia, who sent his thanks to Mme. de Châteauroux. Louis proceeded in royal fanfare to the front, followed a day later by his mistress and other ladies of the court, all attended by their wonted luxuries. The main French army, led by the King but directed in tactics by Adrien Maurice de Noailles and Maurice de Saxe, won easy victories at Courtrai, Menin, Ypres, and Furnes. Louis XIV and the *grand siècle* seemed reborn.

Amid the festivities word came that a French force, badly supported by its Bavarian allies, had allowed an Austro-Hungarian army to occupy parts of Alsace and Lorraine; Stanislas, never rid of misfortune, had to flee from Lunéville. Louis left Flanders and hurried to Metz, hoping to inspire the defeated army by his presence. But there, as the result of unwonted excitement, varied labors, indigestion, and midsummer heat, he fell seriously sick, and worsened so rapidly that by August 11 he was thought to be in danger of death. His mistress had followed him, and now superintended his care; the bishop of Soissons refused to allow him the last sacrament until the Duchess had been dismissed; Louis yielded and banished her to 150 miles from the court (August 14, 1744). The populace hooted her as she left the city.

Meanwhile Marie Leszczyńska had traveled in haste across France to be at the bedside of her husband; en route her cortege met the carriages of Châteauroux and her party. The King embraced the Queen, and said, "I have caused you much sorrow, which you do not deserve; I beg you to forgive me for it." She answered, "Do you not know that you never need pardon from me? God alone has been offended." When the King began to mend she wrote to Mme. de Maurepas that she was "the happiest of mortals." All France went wild with joy at the King's recovery and repentance; in Paris the citizens embraced one another in the streets; some embraced the horse of the courier who had brought the good news. A poet called the King "Louis le Bien-Aimé," Louis the Well Beloved; the nation echoed the phrase. Louis, hearing of it, wondered, "What have I done to make them love me so much?"[98] He had served as a father image for his people.

Frederick saved Alsace for France by invading Bohemia; the Austro-Hungarian army left Alsace to rescue Prague. Louis, still weak, joined his army advancing into Germany, and saw it take Freiburg-im-Breisgau. In

November he returned to Versailles. He recalled Mme. de Châteauroux to favor, and exiled the bishop of Soissons; but on December 8, after many days of fever and delirium, the mistress died. She was buried at night to spare her corpse the insults of the crowd. Resentful of the clergy, the King avoided the sacraments at Christmas, and waited for another love.

For a time the nation forgot the sins of Le Bien-Aimé in the triumphs of its army, and a German Protestant general was the hero of France. Maurice de Saxe was the son of Augustus the Strong, Elector of Saxony and King of Poland. His mother was the Countess Maria Aurora von Königsmarck, distinguished among that monarch's mistresses for such beauty and wit that Voltaire called her "the most famous woman of two centuries."[99] At eighteen Maurice married Johanna Victoria, Countess von Loeben, whose morals were as wicked as his father's; he dissipated her fortune, denounced her adulteries, and divorced her (1721). After displaying his courage in many campaigns, he went to Paris to study mathematics; and in 1720 he obtained a commission in the French army. After surviving all the efforts of his ex-wife to have him poisoned, he found a devoted mistress in Adrienne Lecouvreur, then (1721) dominating the Comédie-Française. He left France in 1725 to carve out a kingdom for himself in Kurland (now part of Latvia). The great tragedienne, though suffering deeply the loss of her lover, gave him, toward the expenses of his enterprise, all her silver and jewels, forty thousand livres in all. With this and seven thousand thalers raised by his mother, he went to Kurland, and was elected to the ducal throne (1726). But both Catherine I of Russia and his own father supported the Polish Diet in opposing his accession, and a Polish army drove the otherwise invincible soldier out of Kurland. Returning to Paris (1728), he found that the great actress had waited for him faithfully, hoping now to be his sole love. But he had inherited the morals and instability of his father; he accepted her as merely *prima inter pares* among his mistresses.

Despicable in morals, using one woman after another without returning their devotion, he became on the battlefield an incomparable genius of strategy, bold in conception, alert to every danger and opportunity. Frederick the Great, his only rival in that age, said of him that he "could give lessons to any general in Europe."[100] In the spring of 1745, having been appointed commander in chief of the French army, he was ordered to the front. He was near death in Paris at the time, exhausted with excesses and suffering agonies from dropsy. Voltaire asked him how, in such a condition, he could think of taking the field. Maurice replied, *"Il ne s'agit pas de vivre, mais de partir"* (The important point is not to live but to set out).[101] On May 11, with 52,000 men, he fought the English and the Dutch, 46,000 strong, at Fontenoy. Louis XV and the Dauphin watched the famous battle from a nearby hill. Maurice, too dropsical to ride a horse, directed the action from a wicker chair. Voltaire tells us, in what may have developed as a patriotic legend,[102] that when the hostile masses of infantry came face to face within musket range, Lord Charles Hay, captain of the English Guards, called out, "Gentlemen of the French Guards, give fire," and that the Comte d'Antroche replied for the French, "Gentlemen, we never fire first; do you begin."[103] Courtesy or stratagem, it was costly; nine officers and 434 foot men were killed, thirty officers and 430 soldiers were wounded, by that first volley;[104] the French infantry faltered, turned, and fled. Maurice sent word to the King to withdraw; Louis refused, even when the retreating soldiers reached him; and perhaps his resolution shamed them. Then Maurice mounted a horse, reordered his forces, and let loose upon the enemy the "Maison du Roi," the household troops of the King. Seeing their King in danger of capture or death, and inspired by the reckless ubiquity of Maréchal de Saxe under fire, the French renewed the battle; nobles and commoners on both sides became heroes in the anesthesia of fury and glory; finally the English fell back in disorder, and Maurice sent word to the King that the bitter engagement had been won. The English and Dutch had lost 7,500 men, the French 7,200. Louis bent his head in shame as the survivors cheered him. "See, my son," he told the Dauphin, "what a victory costs. Learn to be chary of the blood of your subjects."[105] While the King and his entourage returned to Versailles, Maurice went on to take Ghent, Bruges, Audenaarde, Ostend, Brussels; for a time all Flanders was French.

Frederick canceled the results of Fontenoy by signing a separate peace with Austria (December, 1745); France was left to fight alone on half a dozen fronts from Flanders to Italy. By the Treaty of Aix-la-Chapelle (1748) she relinquished Flanders, and had to be content with obtaining the duchies of Parma, Piacenza, and Guastalla for Louis' new son-in-law, the Infante Don Felipe of Spain. Maurice of Saxony lived on till 1750, loaded with riches, honors, and disease, and finding time, between mistresses, to write some philosophical *Rêveries:*

> What a spectacle is presented today by the nations! We see some men living in leisure, pleasure, and wealth at the expense of the multitude, which can subsist only by providing ever new pleasures for these few. This assemblage of oppressors and oppressed constitutes what we call a society.[106]

Another of the exalted few dared dream of a kindlier regime. René Louis de Voyer, Marquis d'Argenson, who for three years (1744–47) served Louis XV as minister of foreign affairs, composed in 1739, but dared not publish, *Considérations sur le gouvernement de la France* (1765). Those who till the land, he wrote, are the most valuable part of the population, and should be freed from all feudal dues and obligations; indeed, the state should lend money to small farmers to help them finance their future crops.[107] Trade is vital to a nation's prosperity and should be freed from all internal tolls, even, wherever possible, from all import or export dues. Nobles are the least precious element in the state; they are incompetent as administrators, and in the economy they are the drones of the hive; they should abdicate. "If anyone should say that these principles favor democracy and look to the destruction of the nobility, he would not be mistaken." Legislation should aim at the greatest possible equality. The communes should be governed by locally elected officials, but the central and absolute power should reside in a king, for only an absolute monarchy can protect the people from oppression by the strong.[108] D'Argenson anticipated the *philosophes* in hoping for reform through an enlightened king, and told the nobility what it recognized only on August 4, 1789, when it surrendered its feudal privileges. He was a stage on the way of France to Rousseau and Revolution.

In 1747 Louis yielded to the urging of Noailles, Maurepas, and Pompadour, and dismissed d'Argenson. The Marquis lost his faith in kings. In 1753 he predicted 1789:

> The evil resulting from our absolute monarchical government is persuading all France and all Europe that it is the worst of governments. . . . This opinion advances, rises, grows stronger, and may lead to national revolution. . . . Everything is preparing the way for civil war. . . . The minds of men are turning to discontent and disobedience, and everything seems moving toward a great revolution, in both religion and government.[109]

Or, as the King's new mistress was to put it, "*Après moi le déluge.*"

VI. MME. DE POMPADOUR

She was one of the most remarkable women in history, dowered with such beauty and grace as blinded most men to her sins, and yet with such powers of mind that for a brilliant decade she governed France, protected Voltaire, saved Diderot's *Encyclopédie*, and led the *philosophes* to claim her as one of their own. It is difficult to look at Boucher's portrait of her (in the Wallace Collection) without losing the impartiality of the historian in the infatuation of the man. Was she one of nature's masterpieces—or just one of Boucher's?

She was already thirty-eight when he painted her, and her fragile health was failing. He did not debase her with the superficial sensuality of his rosy nudes. Instead he pictured the classic features of her face, the grace of her figure, the artistry of her dress, the smooth delicacy of her hands, the "pompadour" of her light-brown hair. Perhaps he enhanced these charms by his imagination and skill, but even he did not transmit her gay laughter and gentle spirit, much less her subtle and penetrating intelligence, her quiet force of character, the tenacity of her sometimes ruthless will.

She had been beautiful almost from her birth. But she had not chosen her parents well, and she had to struggle throughout her life against aristocratic scorn of her middle-class origin. Her father was a provision merchant, François Poisson, who could never live down his name—Mr. Fish. Accused of malversation, he was sentenced to be hanged; he fled to Hamburg, maneuvered a pardon, and returned to Paris (1741). The mother, a daughter of the *entrepreneur des provisions des Invalides*, engaged in gallantries while her husband languished in Hamburg; she enjoyed a long liaison with a rich farmer general, Charles François Lenormant de Tournehem, who paid for the education of the pretty girl born to Mme. Poisson in 1721.

Jeanne Antoinette Poisson had the best available tutors—Jélyotte, the great baritone, for singing, Crébillon *père* for elocution; in time she rivaled the stars of the stage in singing, dancing, and acting; "her voice in itself was a seduction."[110] She learned to draw and engrave, and played the harpsichord well enough to win the enthusiastic praise of Mme. de Mailly. When Jeanne was nine an old woman (whom she later rewarded for prescience) predicted that she would someday be "a mistress to the King."[111] At fifteen her beauty and accomplishments were such that her mother called her "*un morceau de roi*," a morsel for a king, and thought it would be a pity not to make her a queen.[112] But the royal tidbit had already begun to cough blood.

When she was twenty M. de Tournehem persuaded her to marry his nephew, Charles Guillaume Lenormant d'Étioles, son of the treasurer of the mint. The husband fell in love with his wife, and displayed her proudly in the salons. At Mme. de Tencin's she met Montesquieu, Fontenelle, Duclos, Marivaux, and added the art of conversation to her other charms. Soon she herself was entertaining, with Fontenelle, Montesquieu, and Voltaire on her line. She was happy, bore two children, and vowed that "no one in the world but the King himself would make her unfaithful to her husband."[113] What foresight!

Her mother thought that the exception could be arranged. She saw to it that Jeanne should go riding in a handsome phaeton in the Sénart woods, where Louis hunted. Repeatedly he saw her unforgettable face. The royal valets were bribed to praise her beauty to the King. On February 28, 1745, she attended a masked ball given in the Hôtel de Ville for the marriage of the Dauphin. She spoke to the King; he asked her to remove her mask for a moment; she did, and danced away. In April he saw her at a comedy played by an Italian troupe at Versailles. A few days later he sent her an invitation to supper. "Amuse him," her mother advised. Jeanne amused

Louis with surrender. He offered her an apartment at Versailles; she accepted. M. de Tournehem urged the husband to take the matter philosophically: "Do not incur ridicule by growing angry like a bourgeois, or by making a scene."[114] The King made M. d'Étioles a farmer general; he resigned himself to be a tax collector. The mother rejoiced in her daughter's elevation, and died. In September Jeanne received a handsome property, became the Marquise de Pompadour, and was presented as such to the court and the Queen, whom she mollified with a modest confusion. The Queen forgave her as a necessary evil, and invited her to dinner. The Dauphin, however, called her "Madame Whore." The court resented the intrusion of a bourgeoise into the King's bed and purse, and did not fail to notice her occasional relapses into middle-class words and ways. Paris enjoyed epigrams and lampoons about "the King's grisette." She suffered her unpopularity in silence until she could consolidate her victory.

Seeing in Louis a god of boredom, to whom, having everything, everything had lost its savor, she made herself the genius of entertainment. She diverted him with dances, comedies, concerts, operas, supper parties, excursions, hunts; and in the intervals she delighted him with her vivacity, her intelligent conversation, and her wit. She set up the "Théâtre des Petits Appartements" at Versailles, and persuaded the court, as in the days of Louis XIV, to take parts on the stage; she herself acted in Molière's comedies, and so well that the King pronounced her "the most charming woman in France."[115] Soon the nobles competed for roles; the dour Dauphin himself accepted a part opposite "Madame Whore," and condescended to be courteous to her in the world of make-believe. When the King fell into religious moods she soothed him with religious music, which she sang so entrancingly that he forgot his fear of hell. He became dependent upon her for his interest in life; he ate with her, played, danced, drove, hunted with her, spent nearly every night with her. Within a few years she was physically exhausted.

The court complained that she distracted the King from his duties as a ruler, and that she was a heavy burden on the revenues. She adorned her figure with the most costly costumes and gems. Her boudoir sparkled with toiletware of crystal, silver, and gold. Her rooms were embellished with lacquered or satinwood or buhlwork furniture, and the choicest potteries of Dresden, Sèvres, China, and Japan; they were lighted with stately chandeliers of silver and glass, which were reflected in great mirrors on the walls; the ceilings were painted by Boucher and Vanloo with voluptuous goddesses of love. Feeling imprisoned even amid this luxury, she drew immense sums from the King or the treasury to build or furnish palaces, whose lavish equipment and extensive gardens she excused as required for entertaining majesty. She had an estate and the Maison Crécy at Dreux; she

raised the sumptuous Château de Bellevue on the banks of the Seine between Sèvres and Meudon; she put up pretty "hermitages" in the woods of
Versailles, Fontainebleau, and Compiègne. She took over the Hôtel de
Pontchartrain as her Paris residence, and then moved to the palace of the
Comte d'Évreux in the Rue du Faubourg St.-Honoré. Altogether the
charming lady seems to have spent 36,327,268 livres,[116] part of which took
the form of art that remained in the possession of France. Her household
expenses ran to 33,000 livres per year.[117] France condemned her as costing
more than a war.

She gathered power as well as wealth. She became the main channel
through which appointments, pensions, pardons, and other blessings flowed
from the King. She secured gifts, titles, sinecures for her relatives. For her
little daughter, Alexandrine, whom she called "Fanfan," she judged nothing
too good; she dreamed of marrying her to a son of Louis XV by Mme. de
Vintimille; but Fanfan died at nine, breaking Pompadour's heart. Her
brother Abel, handsome and well-mannered, earned his own favor with
the King, who called him *petit-frère*, brother-in-law, and often invited him
to supper. Pompadour made him Marquis de Marigny, and appointed him
directeur général des bâtiments—commissioner of buildings. He performed
his functions with such industry and competence that nearly everyone was
pleased. Pompadour offered to make him a duke; he refused.

Partly through him, but much more in her own person, she had a pervasive influence upon French—even European—art. She failed in her efforts
to be an artist herself, but she loved art with a sincere devotion, and everything that she touched took on beauty. The minor arts smiled bewitchingly
under her encouragement. She convinced Louis XV that France could make
her own porcelain, instead of importing it from China and Dresden at a
cost of 500,000 livres per year. She persevered until the government undertook to finance the porcelain works at Sèvres. Furniture, dinner services,
clocks, fans, couches, vases, bottles, boxes, cameos, mirrors, assumed a fragile loveliness to meet her refined and exacting taste; she became the Queen
of Rococo.[118] Much of her extravagant expenditure went to support painters, sculptors, engravers, cabinetmakers, and architects. She gave commissions to Boucher, Oudry, La Tour, and a hundred other artists. She inspired
Vanloo and Chardin to paint scenes of common life, ending the hackneyed
repetition of subjects from ancient or medieval legend or history. She bore
with smiling tolerance the grumblings and insolence of La Tour when he
came to paint her portrait. Her name was given to fans, hairdos, dresses,
dishes, sofas, beds, chairs, ribbons, and the "Pompadour rose" of her favored
porcelain. Now, rather than under Louis XIV, the influence of France upon
European civilization reached its highest point.

She was probably the most cultured woman of her time. She had a library of 3,500 volumes, 738 of them on history, 215 on philosophy, many on art, some on politics or law, several romances of love. Apparently, besides amusing the King, fending off her enemies, and helping to govern France, she found time to read good books, for she herself wrote excellent French, in letters rich in substance as well as charm. She begged her lover to rival his great-grandfather in the patronage of literature, but his piety and parsimony held him back. When she tried to shame him by noting that Frederick the Great had given d'Alembert a pension of twelve hundred livres, he answered, "There are so many more *beaux-esprits* . . . here than in Prussia, I should be forced to have a very large dinner table to assemble them all"; and he began to count them on his fingers—"Maupertuis, Fontenelle, Lamotte, Voltaire, Fréron, Piron, Destouches, Montesquieu, Cardinal de Polignac." People around him added, "D'Alembert, Clairaut, Crébillon *fils*, Prévost . . ." "Well," sighed the King, "for twenty-five years all *that* might have been dining or supping with me!"[119]

So Pompadour took his place as patron. She brought Voltaire to court, gave him commissions, tried to protect him from his *faux-pas*. She helped Montesquieu, Marmontel, Duclos, Buffon, Rousseau; she eased Voltaire and Duclos into the French Academy. When she heard that Crébillon *père* was living in poverty she secured a pension for him, gave him an apartment in the Louvre, supported a revival of his *Catilina*, and had the royal printing office issue an elegant edition of the old man's plays. She chose as her personal physician François Quesnay, protagonist of the physiocrats, and assigned him a suite of rooms directly under her own at Versailles. There she entertained Diderot, d'Alembert, Duclos, Hélvetius, Turgot, and others whose ideas would have startled the King; and (Marmontel reports) "not being able to invite that group of philosophers to her salon, she would come down herself to see them at table and talk with them."[120]

Naturally the clergy, and the party of the *dévots* at court, led by the Dauphin, looked with shocked consternation at this coddling of infidels. Moreover, Pompadour was known to favor the taxation of ecclesiastical property, even its secularization, if this should prove the only escape from the bankruptcy of the state.[121] The Jesuits advised the King's confessor to refuse him the sacraments so long as he kept this dangerous mistress.[122] The King's children defended the clergy, and the eldest daughter, Henriette, whom he loved best, used her influence to divorce him from Pompadour. Every Easter was a crisis for the lovers. In 1751 Louis expressed a longing for the Eucharist. In an effort to calm him and appease his confessor, Father Pérusseau, the Marquise took to religious observances, went daily to Mass, prayed with high visibility, and assured the confessor that her relations with the King were now platonically pure. Unconvinced, the priest demanded her departure from the court as a condition precedent to the King's admission to the Sacrament. Pérusseau died, but his successor, Père Desmarets, was equally firm. She stood her ground, but continued her outward piety. She never forgave the Jesuits for not taking her "conversion" seriously; perhaps her resentment played a minor part in their expulsion from France in 1762.

She was probably telling the truth in claiming that she no longer had sexual relations with Louis; d'Argenson, one of her enemies, confirmed this.[123] She had already confided to her intimates her increasing difficulty in rising to the royal heats;[124] and she confessed that on one occasion her lack of enthusiasm had cooled the King into an angry impotence.[125] She drugged herself with love philters,[126] with little result but damage to her health. Her foes at court became aware of the situation, and renewed their plots to supplant her. In 1753 d'Argenson arranged to have the voluptuous Mme. de Choiseul-Romanet slip into the King's arms, but she demanded rewards that were thought incommensurate with her sacrifice, and Pompadour was soon able to have her dismissed. It was now that the harassed *maîtresse-en-titre* resigned herself to the abomination of the Parc aux Cerfs.

In this "Stag Park," at the farther end of Versailles, a small lodging was equipped to house one or two young women, with their attendants, until such time as Louis received them in his private apartments or came to their cottage, usually in the guise of a Polish count. Gossip said that the girls were many; legend added that some were only nine or ten years old. Apparently there were never more than two at a time,[127] but a succession of them was brought and trained to give the King the *droit du seigneur*. When one of them became pregnant she received from 10,000 to 100,000 livres to help her find a husband in the provinces, and the children so born were given a pension of some 11,000 livres per year. Mme. de Pompadour knew of this incredible seraglio, and held her peace. Unwilling to be displaced by some noble mistress who would doubtless exile her from the court, perhaps from Paris, she preferred that the King's depraved tastes should be sated by young women of lower estate and moderate ambitions; and in this she herself sank to her lowest estate. "It is his heart that I grudge," she told Mme. du Hausset, "and all these young women, who have no education, will not rob me of that."[128]

The court was not audibly shocked by the new arrangements; several courtiers themselves maintained cottages for their mistresses in that same Parc aux Cerfs.[129] But Pompadour's enemies presumed that her reign had now come to an end. They were mistaken; the King remained her devoted friend long after she had ceased to be his concubine. In 1752 he had officially accorded her the status of duchess. In 1756, over the Queen's protests, he gave her the high post of *dame du palais de la reine*. She attended the Queen, assisted her at dinner, accompanied her to Mass. As her new position required her residence at court, the Jesuits withdrew their demand for her expulsion; the excommunication under which she had long lived was annulled, and she was admitted to the sacraments. The King's daughters, so long hostile to her, came to visit her at Choisy.

Louis spent hours with her almost every day, still taking pleasure in the intelligence of her conversation, and the charm of her unfailing grace. He continued to respect, and often to follow, her advice on appointments, domestic measures, even foreign policy. She gave orders to ministers, received ambassadors, chose generals. Sometimes she spoke of the King and herself as sharing the government: "*nous*" (we); "*nous verrons*" (we shall see). Place seekers crowded her anteroom; she received them courteously, and could say no graciously. Her foes admitted the surprising extent of her political knowledge, the skill of her diplomatic address, the frequent justice of her views.[130] She had long since pointed to the incompetence of French generals as a source of France's military decline; in 1750 she proposed to Louis the establishment of an École Militaire, where the sons of officers slain or impoverished in the service of the state should receive instruction in the art and science of war. The King agreed, but was slow in providing funds; Pompadour transferred to the enterprise her own income for one year, and raised additional money through a lottery and a tax on playing cards; at last (1758) the school was opened, as an adjunct to the Hôtel des Invalides.

Now this bewitching minister without portfolio advised a daring revision of foreign policy for France. Probably the initiative in this fateful "reversal of alliances" was taken by Count von Kaunitz, the Austrian ambassador at Paris; it was furthered by the reluctant condescension of the pious Empress Maria Theresa, who addressed Pompadour as "*ma bonne amie*" and "*ma cousine*," and by Frederick the Great's insulting reference to the Marquise as "*Cotillon Quatre*," Petticoat Four, at the French court. Mme. de Châteauroux and the Marquis d'Argenson had directed foreign policy toward friendship with Prussia. Kaunitz and Pompadour pointed out that the new Prussia—strengthened by victory in the War of the Austrian Succession, armed with 150,000 trained soldiers, and led by an able, ambitious, and unscrupulous general and king who had twice betrayed France by signing a separate peace—would soon be a greater danger than Austria, which had now lost Silesia, and could no longer expect support from a Spain under Bourbon rule; the old Hapsburg encirclement of France was gone. The argument took on sharper point when (January 16, 1756) Prussia signed an alliance with England—France's historic enemy. The French Council of State replied by signing an alliance with Austria (May 1). The Marquise de Pompadour, now again spitting blood, still but thirty-five years old, and with but eight years of life left in her, had played her part in setting the stage for the Seven Years' War.

CHAPTER VIII

Morals and Manners

I. EDUCATION

ONE of the many basic conflicts fought in eighteenth-century France was the effort of the Church to retain—and the effort of the *philosophes* and others to end—ecclesiastical control over education. The contest culminated in the expulsion of the Jesuits from France in 1762, the nationalization of French schools, and the triumph of secularized education in the Revolution. In the first half of the century the controversy was only beginning to take form.

The great majority of the peasants could not read. In many rural communities, even up to 1789, the municipal authorities "could hardly write."[1] Most parishes, however, had a *petite école* where the priest or his appointee taught reading, writing, and catechism, chiefly to boys, for a small fee paid by the parents per pupil.[2] Children whose parents could not afford to pay were admitted gratis if they applied. Attendance was legally required by the edicts of 1694 and 1724, but these were not enforced.[3] Many peasant fathers kept their children from school, partly through need of them on the farm, partly because they feared that education would be a troublesome superfluity in those destined to till the land. Education could not guarantee a rise in status, for class barriers were almost insurmountable in the first half of the century. In the villages and small towns those who had learned to read seldom read anything other than what concerned their daily work. Everyone knew the catechism, but only in the cities was there any knowledge of literature, science, or history.

In the middle and upper classes most education was carried on at home by governesses, then by tutors, finally by dancing masters; these last were expected to teach to both sexes the difficult arts of sitting, standing, walking, talking, and gesturing, with courtesy and grace. Some girls received private lessons in Latin; nearly all above the poor learned to sing and to play the harpsichord. The higher education of girls was carried on in convents, where they progressed in religion, embroidery, music, dancing, and the proper conduct of a young woman and a wife.

Secondary education for boys was almost wholly in the hands of Jesuits, though the Oratorians and the Benedictines shared in the work. Skeptics like Voltaire and Helvétius were among the many distinguished graduates of the Jesuit College of Louis-le-Grand, where Père Charles Porée, professor of "rhetoric" (i.e., language, literature, and speech) left loving memories among his students. The curriculum in the Jesuit schools had hardly changed in two centuries. Though it continued to emphasize religion and the formation of character, the material was largely classical. The authors of ancient Rome were studied in the original, and for five or six years the young scholars lived in intimacy with pagan thought; no wonder their Christian faith suffered some questioning. Furthermore, the Jesuits "spared no efforts to develop the intelligence and zeal of their students."[4] These were encouraged to debate, to speak in public, and to act in plays; they were taught rules for the arrangement and expression of ideas; part of the clarity of French literature was a product of Jesuit colleges. Finally, the student received rigorous courses in logic, metaphysics, and ethics, partly through Aristotle, partly through the Scholastic philosophers; and here again, though the conclusions were orthodox, the habit of reasoning remained—became, indeed, the outstanding mark of this specifically "Age of Reason." Flogging was also a part of the curriculum, even for students of philosophy, and with no distinction of rank; the future Marquis d'Argenson and the Duc de Boufflers were flogged before their classes for having shot peas at their reverend professors.[5]

Already there were complaints that the curriculum paid little attention to the advances of knowledge, that the instruction was too theoretical, giving no preparation for practical life, and that the insistent religious indoctrination warped or closed the mind. In a once famous *Traité des études* (1726–28) Charles Rollin, rector of the University of Paris, defended the classical curriculum and the stress on religion. The chief goal of education, he held, is to make men better. Good teachers "have little regard for the sciences where these do not conduce to virtue; they set no store by the deepest erudition when it is not accompanied by probity. They prefer an honest man to a man of learning."[6] But, said Rollin, it is difficult to form moral character without basing it on religious belief. Hence "the aim of our labors, the end of all our teaching, should be religion."[7] The *philosophes* would soon call this in question; the debate on the necessity of religion for morality would continue throughout the eighteenth century, and through the next. It is alive today.

II. MORALS

Rollin's argument seemed to be borne out by the class differences in morality. The peasants, who clung to their religion, lived a relatively moral life; this, however, may have been due to the fact that the family was the unit of agricultural production, the father was also the employer, and family discipline was rooted in an economic discipline enforced by the sequence of the seasons and the demands of the soil. In the middle classes too religion actively survived, and supported parental authority as the basis of social order. The conception of the nation as an association of families through generations of time gave the strength of solidarity and tradition to middle-class morality. The bourgeois wife was a model of industry, piety, and motherhood. She took childbearing in her stride, and was soon at her work again. She was content with her home and her neighborly associations, and rarely touched that gilded world in which fidelity was smiled at as passé; we seldom hear of adultery in the middle-class wife. Father and mother alike set an example of steady habits, religious observance, and mutual affection. This was the life that Chardin lovingly commemorated in such pictures as *Le Bénédicité*.

All classes practiced charity and hospitality. The Church collected and distributed alms. The antireligious *philosophes* preached *bienfaisance*, which they based on love of humanity rather than of God; modern humanitarianism was the child of both religion and philosophy. Monasteries handed out food to the hungry, and nuns tended the sick; hospitals, almshouses, orphanages, and homes of refuge were maintained by state, ecclesiastical, or guild funds. Some bishops were worldly wastrels, but some, like the bishops of Auxerre, Mirepoix, Boulogne, and Marseilles, gave their wealth and their lives to charity. State officials were not mere place seekers and sinecure parasites; the provosts of Paris distributed food, firewood, and money to the poor, and at Reims a municipal councilor gave 500,000 livres to charity. Louis XV had strains of sympathy and timid tenderness. When 600,000 livres were allotted for fireworks to celebrate the birth of the new Duke of Burgundy (1751), he canceled the display and ordered the sum to be divided as dowries for the six hundred poorest girls of Paris; and other cities followed his example. The Queen lived frugally, and spent most of her income on good works. The Duc d'Orléans, son of the riotous Regent, gave most of his fortune to charity. The seamier side of the story appears in the corruption and negligence that marred the management of charitable institutions. There were several cases in which hospital directors pocketed money sent them for the care of the sick or the poor.

Social morality reflected the nature of man—selfish and generous, brutal and kind, mingling etiquette and carnage on the battlefield. In the lower and upper classes men and women gambled irresponsibly, sometimes losing the fortunes of their families; and cheating was frequent.[8] In France, as in England, the government profited from this gambling propensity by establishing a national lottery. The most immoral feature of French life was the heartless extravagance of the court aristocracy living on revenues from peasant poverty. The bedsheets of the Duchesse de La Ferté, lavish with lace, cost 40,000 crowns; the pearls of Mme. d'Egmont were worth 400,-000.⁹ Dishonesty in office was normal. Offices continued to be sold, and were used by the purchasers for illegal reimbursement. A large part of the money collected in taxes never reached the treasury. Amid this corruption patriotism flourished; the Frenchman never ceased to love France, the Parisian could not long live outside Paris. And almost every Frenchman was brave. At the siege of Mahón, to stop drunkenness among his troops, the Maréchal de Richelieu decreed: "Anyone among you who in future is found drunk will not have the honor of taking part in the assault"; drinking almost stopped.¹⁰ Dueling persisted despite all prohibitions. "In France," said Lord Chesterfield, "a man is dishonored by not resenting an affront, and utterly ruined by resenting it."¹¹

Homosexual acts were punishable with burning at the stake, but this law was enforced only among the poor, as upon a mulcherd in 1724. The Abbé Desfontaines, who had taught in a Jesuit college for fifteen years, was arrested on such a charge in 1725. He appealed to Voltaire for help; Voltaire rose from a sickbed, rode to Fontainebleau, and persuaded Fleury and Mme. de Prie to secure a pardon;¹² for the next twenty years Desfontaines was one of Voltaire's most active enemies. Some of the King's pages were deviates; one of them, La Trémouille, appears to have made the sixteen-year-old ruler his Ganymede.¹³

Prostitution was popular among the poor and the rich. In the towns employers paid their female help less than the cost of necessaries, and allowed them to supplement their daily labor with nocturnal solicitation.¹⁴ A contemporary scribe reckoned the prostitutes in Paris at forty thousand; another estimate said sixty thousand.¹⁵ Public opinion, except in the middle classes, was lenient to such women; it knew that many nobles, clerics, and other pillars of society helped to create the demand that generated this supply; and it had the decency to condemn the poor vendor less than the affluent purchaser. The police looked the other way except when some private or public complaint was made against the *filles;* then a wholesale arrest would be made to clear the skirts of the government; the women would be herded before some judge, who would condemn them to jail or hospital; they would be shaved and disciplined, and soon released, and their hair would grow again. If they gave too much trouble, or offended a man of power, they could be sent to Louisiana. Insolent courtesans displayed their carriages and jewels on the Cours-la-Reine in Paris or on the promenade at Longchamp.¹⁶ If they secured membership, even as supernumeraries, in the Comédie-Française or the Opéra, they were usually immune to arrest for selling their charms. Some of them rose to be artists' models or the kept women of nobles or financiers. Some captured husbands, titles, fortunes; one became the Baronne de Saint-Chamond.

Love marriages, without parental consent, were increasing in number and in literature, and they were recognized as legal if sworn to before a notary. But in the great majority of cases, even in the peasantry, marriages were still arranged by the parents as a union of properties and families rather than as a union of persons. The family, not the individual, was the unit of society; hence the continuity of the family and its property was held more important than the passing pleasures or tender sentiments of precipitate youth. Moreover, said a peasant to his daughter, "chance is less blind than love."[17]

The legal age of marriage was fourteen for boys, thirteen for girls, but they might be legally betrothed from the age of seven, which medieval philosophy had fixed as beginning the "age of reason." The hounds of desire were so hot in the chase that parents married off their daughters as soon as practicable to avoid untimely deflowering; so the Marquise de Sauveboeuf was a widow at thirteen. Girls in the middle and upper classes were kept in convents until their mates had been chosen; then they were hurried from nunnery to matrimony, and had to be well guarded on the way. In this immoral regime nearly all women were virgins at marriage.

Since the French aristocracy disdained commerce and industry, and feudal revenues seldom paid for court residence and display, the nobility resigned itself to mating its land-rich, money-poor sons with land-poor, money-rich daughters of the upper bourgeoisie. When the son of the Duchesse de Chaulnes objected to marrying the richly dowered daughter of the merchant Bonnier, the mother explained to him that "to marry advantageously beneath oneself is merely taking dung to manure one's acres."[18] Usually, in such unions, the titled son, while using his wife's livres, periodically reminded her of her lowly origin, and soon took a mistress to certify his scorn. This too was remembered when the middle classes aided the Revolution.

No social stigma, in the aristocracy, was attached to adultery; it was accepted as a pleasant substitute for the divorce that the national religion forbade. A husband serving in the army or the provinces might take a mistress without giving his wife an acceptable reason for complaint. He or she might be separated by attendance at court or duties on the manor; again he might take a mistress. Since marriage was contracted with no pretense that sentiment could override property, many noble couples lived much of their lives apart, mutually licensing each other's sins, provided these were gracefully veiled and, in the woman's case, confined to one man at a time. Montesquieu made his Persian traveler report that in Paris "a husband who would wish to have sole possession of his wife would be regarded as a disturber of public happiness, and as a fool who should wish to enjoy the light of the sun to the exclusion of other men."[19] The Duc de Lauzun, who for ten years had not seen his wife, was asked what he would say if his wife sent him word that she was pregnant; he answered like an eighteenth-century gentleman: "I would write and tell her that I was delighted that Heaven had blessed our union; be careful of your health; I will call and pay my respects this evening."[20] Jealousy was bad form.

The champion adulterer and model of fashion in this age was Louis François Armand de Vignerot du Plessis, Duc de Richelieu, grandnephew of the austere Cardinal. A dozen titled ladies fell in turn into his bed, drawn by his rank, his wealth, and his reputation. When his ten-year-old son was rebuked for slow progress in Latin, he retorted, "My father never knew Latin, and yet he had the fairest women in France."[21] This did not prevent the Duke's election to the French Academy twenty-three years before his friend and creditor Voltaire, who was two years his senior. Public opinion frowned, however, when he served as procurer of concubines for the King. Mme. Geoffrin barred him from her circle as an "*épluchure* [select assemblage] *des grands vices*."[22] He lived to the age of ninety-two, escaping the Revolution by one year.

Such being the relations of spouses, we can imagine the fate of their children. In the nobility they were frankly treated as impediments. They were dismissed at birth to wet nurses; they were brought up by governesses and tutors; they only intermittently saw their parents. Talleyrand said he had never slept under the same roof as his father and mother. Parents thought it wise to maintain a respectful distance between themselves and their progeny; intimacy was exceptional, familiarity was unheard of. The son always addressed his father as "monsieur"; the daughter kissed her mother's hand. When the children grew up they were sent off to the army, to the Church, or to a nunnery. As in England, nearly all the property went to the eldest son.

This way of life continued in the court nobility till the accession of Louis XVI in 1774. It revealed in another aspect the loss of religious belief in the upper classes; the Christian conception of marriage, like the medieval ideal of chivalry, was quite abandoned; the pursuit of pleasure was more nakedly "pagan" than at any time since Imperial and decadent Rome. Many works on morality were published in eighteenth-century France, but books of deliberate indecency abounded, and circulated widely, though clandestinely. "The French," wrote Frederick the Great, "and above all the inhabitants of Paris, were now sybarites enervated by pleasure and ease."[23] The Marquis d'Argenson, about 1749, saw in the decline of moral sensibility another omen of national disaster:

The heart is a faculty of which we despoil ourselves every day by giving it no exercise, while the mind is continually sharpened and refined. We become more and more intellectual. . . . I predict that this realm will perish from the extinction of the faculties that derive from the heart. We have no more friends; we no longer love our mistresses; how shall we love our country? . . . Men lose daily some part of that fine quality which we call sensibility. Love, and the need to love, disappear. . . . Calculations of interest absorb us continually; everything is a commerce of intrigue. . . . The interior fire goes out for lack of nourishment; a paralysis creeps over the heart.[24]

It is the voice of Pascal speaking for Port-Royal, the voice of Rousseau a generation before Jean Jacques, the voice of sensitive spirits in any age of intellectual ferment and liberation. We shall hear it again.

III. MANNERS

Never was a reckless morality so gilded with refinement of manners, elegance of dress and speech, variety of pleasures, the charm of women, the flowery politeness of correspondence, the brilliance of intellect and wit. "Never before had there been in France, nor was there in contemporary Europe, nor . . . has there ever been in the world since, a society so polished, so intelligent, so delightful, as French society of the eighteenth century."[25] The French, said Hume in 1741, "have in a great measure perfected that art, the most useful and agreeable of any, *l'art de vivre*, the art of society and conversation."[26] It was toward the end of this period that the word *civilization* came into use. It did not appear in Johnson's *Dictionary* in 1755, nor in the *Grand Vocabulaire* published in thirty volumes in Paris in 1768.

The French felt especially civilized in their dress. Men quite rivaled women in the care they took with their clothes. In the upper classes fashion required them to wear a large three-cornered hat, with feathers and gold braid; but as this disturbed their wigs they usually wore it under the arm. Wigs were smaller now than under the Great King, but they were more general, even among artisans. There were twelve hundred wig shops in Paris, with six thousand employees. Hair and wig were powdered. Male hair was usually long, caught behind the neck by a ribbon or in a bag. A long coat of fancy coloring and material—generally of velvet—covered the inner costume, which showed a vest open at the throat, a fluffy silk shirt, a wide cravat, and sleeves spreading into ornate ruffles at the wrists. Knee breeches (*culottes*) were colored; stockings were of white silk, shoes were buckled with silver clasps. Courtiers, as a distinguishing mark, wore shoes with red heels. Some of them used whalebones to keep their coattails in proper spread; some wore diamonds in their buttonholes; all carried a sword, and some a cane. The wearing of a sword was forbidden to servants, apprentices, and musicians.[27] The bourgeois dressed simply, in coat and *culottes* of plain dark cloth, with stockings of black or gray wool, and shoes with thick soles and low heels. Artisans and household help took on the discarded garments of the rich; the elder Mirabeau grumbled that he could not tell a blacksmith from a lord.

Women still enjoyed the freedom of their legs within the spacious sanctum of their farthingales. The clergy denounced as "she-monkeys" and "clerks of the Devil" the women who wore such hoopskirts, but the ladies loved them for the majesty they gave to their figures even when *enceintes*. Mme. de Créqui tells us, "I could not whisper to Mme. d'Egmont, because our hoops prevented our being near together."[28] Milady's high-heeled shoes —of colored leather set off with embroidery of silver or gold—made her feet entrancing if unseen; her bootmakers rose into the upper bourgeoisie by such artistry; romances were written about a pretty foot, which was usually a pretty shoe. Almost as exciting were the flowered heelless "mules" which Milady wore at home. Useful also were the flounces, ribbons, fans, and *pretintailles*, or ornamental "pretties," that caught the male's roving eye or disguised the female's roving form. Corsets of whalebone molded that form to fashionable shape. Enough of the bosom was shown to certify a cozy amplitude. Coiffures were low and simple; the tower hairdo waited till 1763. Cosmetics doctored hands, arms, face, and hair; but men fell little short of women in using perfume. Every ladylike face was painted and powdered, and strategically patched with beauty-spot *mouches* (flies) made of black silk and cut in the shape of hearts, teardrops, moons, comets, or stars. A great lady would wear seven or eight of these pasted on the forehead, on the temples, near the eyes, and at the corners of the mouth; she carried a patch-box with additional *mouches* in case any should fall off. A rich lady's boudoir table shone with *nécessaires*—boxes of gold or silver or lapis lazuli designed to hold toiletries. Costly jewels sparkled on arms, throat, and ears, and in the hair. Favored males were admitted to the boudoir to converse with Milady as her maids equipped her for the campaigns of the day. In the aristocracy men were slaves to women, women were slaves to fashion, and fashion was determined by couturiers. Attempts to control fashion or dress by sumptuary laws were abandoned in France after 1704. Western Europe generally followed French fashions, but there was also a reverse flow: so the marriage of Louis XV with Marie Leszczyńska brought in styles *à la Polonaise;* the war against Austria-Hungary introduced *hongrelines;* and the marriage of the Dauphin to the Infanta María Teresa Rafaela (1745) restored the mantilla to popularity in France.

Meals were not as ornate as dress, but they required as subtle and varied a science, as delicate an art. French cooking was already the model and peril of Christendom. Voltaire warned his countrymen in 1749 that their heavy repasts would "eventually numb all the faculties of the mind";[29] he gave a good example of simple diet and nimble wits. The higher the class, the more was eaten; so a typical dinner at the table of Louis XV included soup, a roast of beef, a cut of veal, some chicken, a partridge, a pigeon, fruit, and preserves.[30] "There are very few peasants," Voltaire tells us, "who eat meat more than once a month."[31] Vegetables were a luxury in the city, for it was difficult to keep them fresh. Eels were in fashion. Some *grands seigneurs* spent 500,000 livres a year on their cuisine; one spent 72,000 on a dinner given to the King and the court. In great houses the maître d'hôtel was a person of impressive majesty; he was richly clad, wore a sword, and flashed a diamond ring. Women cooks were contemned. Cooks were ambitious to invent new dishes to immortalize their masters; so France ate *filet de volaille à la Bellevue* (Pompadour's favorite palace), *poulets à la Villeroi*, and *sauce mayonnaise* which commemorated the victory of Richelieu at Mahón.[32] The main meal was taken at three or four in the afternoon; supper was added at nine or ten.

Coffee now rivaled wine as a drink. Michelet must have loved coffee, for he thought that its mounting influx from Arabia, India, the island of Bourbon, and the Caribbean contributed to the exhilaration of spirit that marked the Enlightenment.[33] Every apothecary sold coffee in grain or in a drink at the counter. There were three hundred cafés in Paris in 1715, six hundred in 1750, and a proportionate number in the provincial towns. At the Café Procope—called also the Cave, because it was always kept dark—Diderot spilled ideas and Voltaire came in disguise to hear comments on his latest play. Such coffeehouses were the salons of the commoners, where men might play chess or checkers or dominoes, and, above all, talk; for men had grown lonelier as city crowds had increased.

Clubs were private cafés, restricted in membership and tending to specific interests. So the Abbé Alari established (c. 1721) the Club de l'Entresol (a mezzanine in the abbé's home) where some twenty statesmen, magistrates, and men of letters gathered to discuss the problems of the day, including religion and politics. Bolingbroke gave it its name, and so brought the word *club* into the French language. There the Abbé de Saint-Pierre expounded his plans for social reforms and perpetual peace; some of these worried Cardinal Fleury, who ordered the disbandment of the club in 1731. Three years later Jacobite refugees from England founded in Paris the first French Freemasonry lodge. Montesquieu joined it, and several members of the high nobility. It served as a refuge for deists and as a center of political intrigue; it became a channel of English influence, and prepared the way for the *philosophes*.

Bored with the round of domestic toil, men and women flocked to the promenades, dance halls, theaters, concerts, and opera; the rich took to the hunt, the bourgeoisie to *fêtes champêtres*. The Bois de Boulogne, the Champs-Élysées, the Jardins des Tuileries, the Luxembourg Gardens, and the Jardin des Plantes—or "Jardin du Roi," as it was then called—were favorite resorts for carriage rides, walks, lovers' haunts, and Easter parades. If people stayed home they amused themselves with indoor games, dances, chamber concerts, and private theatricals. Everyone danced. Ballet had become a complex and royal art, in which the King himself occasionally pranced a part. Ballet dancers like La Camargo and La Gaussin were the toast of the town and the delicacies of millionaires.

IV. MUSIC

Music in France had declined since Lully had outdone Molière in amusing the Great King. There was not here the same madness about music that made Italy forget its political subjection, nor that laborious devotion to compositional technique which was creating the massive Masses and prolonged Passions of Bach's Germany. French music was in transition from classic form to baroque decoration to rococo grace, from complex counterpoint mutilating words to fluent melodies and tender themes congenial to French character. Popular composers still issued amorous, satirical, or melancholy songs deifying lasses, defying kings, deprecating virginity and delay. Patronage of music was spreading from kings requiring majesty to financiers apologizing for their fortunes with concerts, dramas, and poetry open to the influential few. Rousseau's opera *Les Muses galantes* was produced in the home of the farmer general La Popelinière. Some rich men had orchestras of their own. Performances open to the public for an admission charge were regularly offered in Paris by the Concerts Spirituels, organized in 1725; and other cities followed suit. Opera was presented in the Palais-Royal, usually in late afternoon, concluding by 8:30 P.M.; then the audience, in evening dress, promenaded in the Tuileries Gardens, and singers and instrumentalists entertained them in the open air; this was one of many charming features of Paris life.

We perceive in reading Diderot's *Le Neveu de Rameau* how many composers and executants were then the rage who are forgotten now. Only one French composer in this period left behind him works that still cling to life. Jean Philippe Rameau had every impulse to music. His father was organist in the Church of St.-Étienne at Dijon. Enthusiastic biographers assure us that Jean at seven could read at sight any music placed before him. At college he so absorbed himself in music that the Jesuit fathers expelled him; thereafter he hardly ever opened a book except of or on music. Soon he was so proficient on organ, harpsichord, and violin that Dijon had nothing more to teach him. When he strayed into love, his father, thinking this a waste of talent, sent him to Italy to study its secrets of melody (1701).

Back in France, Jean served as organist in Clermont-Ferrand, succeeded his father in Dijon (1709–14), returned to Clermont as organist of the cathedral (1716), and settled in Paris in 1721. There, in 1722, aged thirty-nine, he wrote the outstanding work of musical theory in eighteenth-century France—*Traité de l'harmonie réduite à ses principes naturels*. Rameau argued that in a proper musical composition there is always, whether scored or not, a "fundamental base" from which all chords above it can be derived; that all chords can be deduced from the harmonic series of partial tones; and that these chords may be inverted without losing their identity. Rameau wrote in a style intelligible only to the most obdurate musicians, but his ideas pleased the mathematician d'Alembert, who gave them a more lucid exposition in 1752. Today the laws of chordal association formulated by Rameau are accepted as the theoretical foundation of musical composition.[34]

Opposed by the critics, Rameau fought back with compositions and expositions until he was finally revered for having reduced music to law as Newton had reduced the stars.[35] In 1726, aged forty-three, he married Marie Mangot, aged eighteen. In 1727 he put to music Voltaire's lyric drama *Samson*, but its production was forbidden on the ground that Biblical stories should not be reduced to opera. Rameau had to butter his bread by serving as organist in the Church of St.-Croix-de-la-Bretonnerie. He was fifty before he conquered the operatic stage.

In that year (1733) Abbé Pellegrin offered him a libretto, *Hippolyte et Aricie*, founded on Racine's *Phèdre*, but he exacted from Rameau a bill for five hundred livres as security in case the opera should fail. When it was rehearsed the abbé was so delighted with the music that he tore up the bill at the end of the first act. The public performance at the Académie de Musique surprised the audience with bold departures from the modes that had become a sacred tradition since Lully. Critics protested Rameau's novel rhythms, heretical modulations, and orchestral elaborations; even the orchestra resented the music. For a time Rameau thought of abandoning all attempts at opera, but his next effort, *Les Indes galantes* (1735), won the audience by its flow of melody, and his *Castor et Pollux* (1737) was one of the great triumphs in French operatic history.

Success spoiled him. He boasted that he could turn any libretto into a good opera, and that he could set a newspaper to music.[36] He produced a long succession of indifferent operas. When the managers of the Académie de Musique tired of him, he composed pieces for the harpsichord, violin, or flute. Louis XV—or Mme. de Pompadour—came to his aid by engaging him to write the music for Voltaire's *La Princesse de Navarre*, which had a re-assuring success at Versailles (1745). He was restored to favor at the Académie, and wrote more operas. As Paris became familiar with his style it forgot Lully, and acclaimed Rameau as the unrivaled monarch of the musical world.

Then in 1752 he found himself faced with a new challenge. Virtuosos and composers had come in from Italy, and a noisy war began between French and Italian music, which would culminate in the seventies with Piccini versus Gluck. An Italian troupe presented at the Paris Opéra, as an intermezzo, Pergolesi's *La serva padrona*, one of the classics of comic opera. The friends of French music countered with pamphlets and Rameau. The court divided into two camps; Mme. de Pompadour supported French music, the Queen defended the Italian; Grimm attacked all French opera (1752), and Rousseau declared French music impossible. The final sentence of Rousseau's *Lettre sur la musique française* (1753) was characteristic of his emotional unbalance:

> I believe I have made it evident that there is neither measure nor melody in French music, because the language does not allow them; that French singing is only a continued barking and complaining, unbearable to any unprepossessed ear; that its harmony is rough [*brute*], without expression, and feeling only what it has learned from its teacher; that French arias are not arias, that French recitative is no recitative. Whence I concluded that the French have no music, and cannot have any, or that if ever they have any, it will be so much the worse for them.

The partisans of French music retaliated with twenty-five pamphlets, and burned Rousseau in effigy at the Opéra door.[37] Rameau was unwillingly used as the *pièce de résistance* in this *Guerre des Bouffons*, or War of Buffoons. When it subsided, and he was pronounced victor, he acknowledged that French music had still much to learn from the Italian; and were he not so old, he said, he would go back to Italy to study the methods of Pergolesi and other Italian masters.

He was now at the height of his popularity, but he had many enemies, old and new. He added to them with a pamphlet exposing the errors in the articles on music in the *Encyclopédie*. Rousseau, who had written most of the articles, turned upon him with hatred; and Diderot, father of the *Encyclopédie*, abused the old composer with respectful discrimination in *Le Neveu de Rameau*, which Diderot had the grace not to publish:

> The famous musician who delivered us from the plainsong of Lully that we had intoned for over a century, and who wrote so much visionary gibberish and apocalyptic truth about the theory of music—writings which neither he nor anyone else ever understood. We have from him a number of operas in which one finds harmony, snatches of song, disconnected ideas, clatter, flights, triumphal processions, spears, apotheoses, . . . and dance tunes that will last for all time.[38]

When, in 1760, aged seventy-seven, Rameau appeared in a box at the revival of his opera *Dardanus*, he received an ovation that almost rivaled that which would be given to Voltaire eighteen years later. The King gave him a patent of nobility, and Dijon, proud of its son, exempted him and his family from municipal taxes to the end of time. At the height of his glory he caught typhoid fever, wasted away quickly, and died, September 12, 1764. Paris accorded him a ceremonial interment in the Church of St.-Eustache, and many towns in France held services in his honor.

V. THE SALONS

Paris was the cultural capital of the world rather than of France. "Those who live a hundred leagues from the capital," said Duclos, "are a hundred years away from it in ways of conduct and thought."[39] Probably never in history had a city so hummed with varied life. Polite society and advanced literature were bound in an intoxicating intimacy. The fear of hell had gone from the educated Parisians, and had left them unprecedentedly gay, careless in their new confidence that there was no omnipotent ogre in the skies eavesdropping on their sins. From that emancipation of the mind no somber aftermath had yet come of a world shorn of divinity and moral goal and shivering in the chill of insignificance. Conversation was brilliant, wit frolicked and crackled, and often lapsed into superficial badinage; thought then stayed on the surface of things, as if in fear of finding nothing beneath; and scandal gossip ran quickly from club to club, from home to home. But often conversation dared to play on dangerous heights of politics, religion, and philosophy where it would seldom venture to move today.

This society was brilliant because women were its life. They were the deities it worshiped, and they set its tone. Somehow, despite custom and hindrances, they caught enough education to talk intelligently with the intellectual lions they loved to entertain. They rivaled the men in attending the lectures of scientists.[40] As men lived less in the camp, more in the capital and at the court, they became increasingly sensitive to the intangible charms of woman—grace of movement, melody of voice, vivacity of spirit, brightness of eyes, delicacy of tact, tenderness of solicitude, kindness of soul. These qualities had made women lovable in every civilization; but probably in no other culture had nature, training, dress, jewelry, and cosmetics made them such bewitching contraptions as in eighteenth-century France. All these allurements, however, could not explain the power of women. Intelligence in the handling of men was needed, and the intelligence of women matched and sometimes overreached the intellect of men. Women knew men better than men knew women; men came forward too precipitately for ideas to mature into understanding, while the modest retreat required even of receptive women gave them time to observe, experiment, and plan their campaigns.

As male sensitivity widened and deepened, feminine influence grew. Bravery on the battlefield looked for reward in the salon as well as in the boudoir and the court; poets were thrilled to find pretty and patient ears; philosophers were exalted to win a gracious hearing from women of refinement and rank; even the most learned savant discovered an intellectual stimulus in soft bosoms and rustling silk. So, before their "emancipation," women exercised a sovereignty that gave its distinctive character to the age. "Women ruled then," Mme. Vigée-Lebrun later recalled; "the Revolution has dethroned them."[41] They not only taught manners to men, they advanced or demoted them in political, even in academic life. So Mme. de Tencin secured the election of Marivaux, instead of Voltaire, to the Immortals in 1742. *Cherchez la femme* was the technique of success; find the woman whom the man loves, and you find the way to your man.

Claudine Alexandrine de Tencin was, after Pompadour, the most interesting of these women who swayed the powers of France in the first half of the eighteenth century. We have seen her escaping from a convent and generating d'Alembert. In Paris she took a home in the Rue St.-Honoré, where she entertained a succession of lovers, including Bolingbroke, Richelieu, Fontenelle (silent but virile at seventy), sundry abbés, and the head of the Paris police. Gossip added her brother to the list, but probably she loved Pierre only as a fond sister resolved to make him a cardinal, if not prime minister. Through him and others she proposed to be a power in the life of France.

First, she gathered money. She invested in Law's System, but sold in good time. She accepted the guardianship of Charles Joseph de La Fresnai's fortune, then refused to return it to him; he killed himself in her rooms, leaving a will denouncing her as a thief (1726); she was sent to the Bastille, but her friends secured her release; she kept most of the money, and outfaced and outlived all the gossip of the city and the court.

About 1728 she added a salon to her bed as a steppingstone to power. On Tuesday evenings she entertained for dinner a number of distinguished men, whom she called her *bêtes*, or menagerie: Fontenelle, Montesquieu, Marivaux, Prévost, Helvétius, Astruc, Marmontel, Hénault, Duclos, Mably, Condorcet, and occasionally Chesterfield. The assemblage was usually all male; Tencin brooked no rivals at her table. But she gave her "beasts" free rein, and took no offense at their evident rejection of Christianity. All ranks were leveled there; count and commoner met on one level. Here, tradition would later say, was the most brilliant and searching conversation in all that century of boundless talk.[42]

Through her guests, her lovers, and her confessors she pulled strings that ran from Versailles to Rome. Her brother was not ambitious; he longed for the quiet simplicity of provincial life; but she saw to it that he was made archbishop, then cardinal, at last a minister in the Council of State. She helped to make Mme. de Châteauroux the King's mistress, and prodded her to prod him to lead his army in war. She saw in the lethargy of Louis a source and omen of political decay, and perhaps she was right in thinking that if she were prime minister the government would take on more direction and vitality. In her salon men boldly discussed the degeneration of the monarchy and the possibility of revolution.

In her old age she lost memory of her sins, allied herself with the Jesuits, campaigned against the Jansenists, and corresponded intimately with Pope Benedict XIV, who sent her his portrait in recognition of her services to the Church. The kindness that had often graced her faults found many outlets. When Montesquieu's *Spirit of Laws* (1748) was received at first with public indifference she bought up almost the whole first edition, and distributed it gratis among her many friends. She took young Marmontel in tow and mothered him with advice—above all, to attach himself in friendship to women rather than to men as a means of rising in the world.[43] She herself, in these years of her decline, became an author, covering the indiscretion with anonymity; her two romances were compared by friendly critics with Mme. de La Fayette's *Princesse de Clèves*.

La Tencin died in 1749, aged sixty-eight. "Where shall I dine on Tuesdays now?" old Fontenelle wondered, and then answered himself cheerfully, "Very well; I shall dine at Madame Geoffrin's."[44] Perhaps we shall meet him there.

Almost as old as Tencin's salon, almost as lasting as Geoffrin's, was Mme. du Deffand's. Orphaned at six (1703), Marie de Vichy-Chamrond was placed in a convent of some educational repute. She began to reason at an unseemly age, asking questions alarmingly skeptical; the abbess, at a loss, turned her over to the learned preacher Massillon, who, unable to explain the unintelligible, gave her up as beyond salvation. At twenty-one she became Marquise du Deffand through a marriage of convenience; she soon found her husband intolerably prosaic, and separated from him by an agreement that left her well financed. In Paris and Versailles she gambled passionately—"I thought of nothing else"; but after three months and painful losses "I was horrified at myself and cured myself of that folly." She did a brief stint as mistress to the Regent,[45] then passed over to his enemy, the Duchesse du Maine. At Sceaux she met Charles Hénault, president of the Chambre des Enquêtes (Court of Inquiry); he became her lover, and then subsided into her lifelong friend.

After living for some time with her brother she moved into that same house in the Rue de Beaune where Voltaire was to die. Already famous for her beauty, her sparkling eyes, and her merciless wit, she attracted to her table (1739 f.) a group of celebrities who came to constitute a salon almost as notable as Tencin's: Hénault, Montesquieu, Voltaire, Mme. du Châtelet, Diderot, d'Alembert, Marmontel, Mme. de Staal de Launay . . . In 1747, now fifty and slightly subdued, she took a handsome apartment in the convent of St.-Joseph in the Rue St.-Dominique. It was the custom for convents to let rooms to spinsters, widows, or women separated from their mates; usually such accommodations were in buildings outside the nunnery proper, but in the case of this wealthy skeptic the suite was within the convent walls; indeed, it was the very apartment that had lodged the sinful founder of that convent, Mme. de Montespan. The Marquise's salon followed her to her new home, but perhaps the environment frightened the *philosophes;* Diderot came no more, Marmontel seldom, Grimm now and then; soon d'Alembert would break away. Most of the new company at St.-Joseph's were scions of the old aristocracy—Marshals Luxembourg and Mirepoix and their wives, the Dukes and Duchesses de Boufflers and de Choiseul, the Duchesses d'Aiguillon, de Gramont, and de Villeroi, and Mme. du Deffand's childhood and lifelong friend Pont-de-Veyle. They met at six, dined at nine, played cards, gambled, dissected current politics, literature, and art, and departed toward 2 A.M. Distinguished foreigners, coming to Paris, angled for an invitation to this *bureau d'esprit* of the nobility. Lord Bath reported in 1751: "I recall an evening when the talk turned on the history of England. How surprised and confused I was to find that the company knew all our history better than we knew it ourselves!"[46]

Du Deffand had the best mind and the worst character among the *salonnières*. She was proud, cynical, and more openly selfish than we usually allow ourselves to appear; when Helvétius' *De l'Esprit* labored La Rochefoucauld's point that all human motives are egoistic, she remarked, "Bah!

he has only revealed everyone's secret."[47] She could be spitefully satirical, as in describing Mme. du Châtelet. She had seen all but the simple and tender sides of French life, and assumed that the poor shared, as far as their means allowed, all the vices of the rich. She put no more stock in the utopian aspirations of the philosophers than in the comforting myths of the ancient faith; she shunned conclusions and preferred good manners. She despised Diderot as a boor, liked and then hated d'Alembert, and admired Voltaire because he was a seigneur of manners as well as of the mind. She met him in 1721. When he fled from Paris she began with him in 1736 a correspondence that is one of the classics of French literature. Her letters equaled his in subtlety, penetration, finesse, and art, but fell short of his amiability, ease, and grace.

At fifty-five she began to lose her sight. She consulted every specialist, then every quack. When, after three years of struggle, she became completely blind (1754), she notified her friends that if they continued to attend her soirees they must put up with a blind old woman. They came nevertheless, and Voltaire, from Geneva, assured her that her wit was even brighter than her eyes had been; he encouraged her to go on living if only to enrage those who paid her annuities. She found in Julie de Lespinasse a pretty, vivacious, and charming young woman who helped her to receive and entertain; and now she presided at her dinners like some blind Homer over a round table of sages and bards. She moved with dignity and defiance through another twenty-six years. Her too we hope to meet again.

It was a brilliant age because the women in it were brilliant, combining brains with beauty beyond any precedent. It was because of them that French writers warmed thought with feeling and graced philosophy with wit. How could Voltaire have become Voltaire without them? Even blunt and cloudy Diderot confessed: "Women accustom us to discuss with charm and clearness the dryest and thorniest subjects. We talk to them unceasingly; we wish them to listen; we are afraid of tiring or boring them. Hence we develop a particular method of explaining ourselves easily, and this method passes from conversation into style."[48] Because of women French prose became brighter than poetry, and the French language took on a suave charm, an elegance of phrase, a courtesy of speech, that made it delectable and supreme. And because of women French art passed from the massive *bizarreries* of baroque to a refinement of form and taste that embellished every aspect of French life.

CHAPTER IX

The Worship of Beauty

I. THE TRIUMPH OF ROCOCO

IN this age between the Regency and the Seven Years' War—the age of *le style Louis Quinze*—women challenged the gods for adoration, and the pursuit of beauty rivaled the devotions of piety and the passions of war. In art and music, as in science and philosophy, the supernatural receded before the natural. The ascendancy of a woman over a sensual and sensitive king gave new prestige to delicacy and sentiment; the hedonistic orientation of life that had begun under Philippe d'Orléans reached its fullest expression under Pompadour. Beauty became more than ever a matter of "tactile values"; it was something pleasant to touch as well as to behold, from Sèvres porcelains to Boucher's nudes. The sublime gave place to the delightful, the dignified to the graceful, the grandeur of size to the charm of elegance. Rococo was the art of an epicurean moneyed minority eager to enjoy every pleasure before the disappearance of its fragile world in an anticipated deluge of change. In that frankly earthly style lines gamboled, colors softened, flowers had no thorns, subjects shunned tragedy to stress the bright potentialities of life. Rococo was the last stage of baroque, of the rebellion of imagination against reality, of freedom against order and rules. Yet it was not disorderly license; its products still had logic and structure, giving form to significance; but it abhorred straight lines and sharp angles, it shied away from symmetry, and found it painful to leave any piece of furniture uncarved. Despite its coquettish prettiness, rococo produced thousands of objects unsurpassed in finish and elegance. And for half a century it made the minor arts the major art of France.

Never before, so far as we know, had there been such activity, rarely such excellence, in the once lesser fields of aesthetic enterprise. In this period the artist and the artisan were again made one, as in medieval Europe, and those who could beautify the intimate appurtenances of life were honored with the painters, sculptors, and architects of the age.

Never before had furniture been so exquisite. In this "style of Louis Fifteenth" it was no longer so monumental as under the Great King; it was designed for comfort rather than for dignity; it was more fitted to feminine contours and finery than to majesty and display. Sofas took on a diversity of shapes to suit attitudes and moods; "today," Voltaire wrote, "social behavior is easier than in the past," and "ladies can be seen reading on sofas or daybeds without causing embarrassment to their friends and acquaintances."[1] Beds were crowned with delicate canopies, their panels were painted or upholstered, their posts were handsomely carved. New types of furniture were developed to meet the needs of a generation that preferred Venus to Mars. The large, deep-cushioned, upholstered armchair (*fauteuil* or *bergère*), the tapestried sofa, the chaise-longue, the writing table (*escritoire*), the desk (or *secrétaire*), the commode, the footrest, the console, the chiffonier, the buffet—these took now the forms, often the names, that they have in essence retained to our time. Carving and other ornamentation were profuse to an extent that provoked a reaction in the second half of the century. The "buhlwork" introduced by André Charles Boulle under Louis XIV—an inlay of furniture with metal or shell—was carried on by his sons as cabinetmakers to Louis XV; and a dozen variations of marquetry broke up the surface of painted, veneered, or lacquered wood. Voltaire ranked some lacquerwork of eighteenth-century France as equal to any that had come from China or Japan. Craftsmen like Cressent, Oppenordt, Oeben, Caffiéri, and Meissonier achieved such pre-eminence in the design or adornment of furniture that cabinetmakers came from abroad to study their techniques, and then spread French styles from London to St. Petersburg. Juste Aurèle Meissonier included in one mind a dozen arts: he built houses, decorated their interiors, fashioned furniture, molded candlesticks and silverware, designed snuffboxes and watch cases, organized *pompes funèbres* or *galantes*, and wrote several works to transmit his skills; he was almost the *uomo universale* of his time.

As the ceremonious publicity of the seventeenth century was replaced by the intimacies of life under Louis XV, interior decoration passed from splendor to refinement; and here again the age marked a zenith. Furniture, carpets, upholstery, *objets d'art*, clocks, mirrors, panels, tapestries, drapes, paintings, ceilings, chandeliers, even bookcases were brought into gratifying harmonies of color and style. Sometimes, we may suspect, books were bought for the color and texture of their bindings as well as for their contents; but we can understand that pleasure too, and we gaze with envy at personal libraries housed behind glass in handsome cases set into the wall. Dining rooms were rare in France before 1750; dining tables were usually made to be easily multiplied and removed, for dinner guests might be incalculably numerous. Chimneypieces were no longer the massive monuments that had come down from the Middle Ages to Louis XIV, but they were richly embellished, and now and then (a rare instance of poor taste in this period) female figures were used as caryatids upholding the mantelpiece. Heating was almost entirely by open fireplaces, protected by ornamental screens, but here and there we find in France a stove faced, as in Germany, with decorated faïence. Lighting was by candles in a hundred different fixtures, culminating in immense and glittering chandeliers of rock crystal, glass, or bronze. We marvel at the amount of reading that was done by candlelight; but perhaps the difficulties diminished the production and consumption of trash.

Wall panels, lightly colored and delicately adorned, replaced tapestries as the century advanced, and in this period the art of tapestry had its final flowering. In almost every variety of textiles—from damasks, embroideries, and brocade to immense carpets and drapes—France now challenged the finest weaves of the Orient. Amiens specialized in pictured velvets; Lyons, Tours, and Nîmes were famous for decorated silks; in Lyons Jean Pillement, Jean Baptiste Huet, and others made wall hangings stamped and sewn with Chinese or Turkish motifs and scenes that captivated Pompadour. Tapestries were woven in the nationalized factories of Paris and Beauvais, and in private shops at Aubusson and Lille. They had by this time lost their utilitarian function of protecting against damp and drafts; they were purely decorative, and were often reduced in size to suit the tendency to smaller rooms. The weavers at Les Gobelins and Beauvais followed designs prepared, and the colors prescribed, by the leading painters of the age. Especially beautiful were the fifteen tapestries woven by the Gobelins (1717) after cartoons provided by Charles Antoine Coypel to illustrate *Don Quixote*. The Beauvais weavers, as we shall see, produced some fine tapestries after designs by Boucher. The Savonneries—originally soap works—were reorganized in 1712 as the "Royal Factory for the Manufacture of Carpets in the Persian and Near-Eastern Styles"; soon they were weaving massive carpets distinguished by careful drawing, varied colors, and soft velvet pile; these are the finest pile carpets of eighteenth-century France. It was the tapestry factories that made the painstaking upholstery for the chairs of the well-to-do. Many humble fingers must have been worn to calluses to prevent the same on thriving fundaments.

French potters were entering upon an adventurous age. The wars of Louis XIV gave them an opportunity: the old King melted his silver to finance his armies; he replaced his silverware with faïence, and bade his subjects do likewise; soon the faïence factories at Rouen, Lille, Sceaux, Strasbourg, Moustiers-Ste.-Marie, and Marseilles were meeting this new demand; and after the death of Louis XIV the taste for dishes and other objects in faïence encouraged the potters to produce some of the finest wares of the kind in European history. Artists as famous as Boucher, Falconet, and Pajou painted scenes or molded forms for French faïence.

Meanwhile France was moving toward the production of porcelain. Soft-paste varieties had long since been made in Europe—as far back as 1581 in

Florence, 1673 in Rouen. These, however, were imitations of Chinese exemplars; they were made not from the hard-paste kaolin, or china-stone
clay, as fused at high temperatures in the Far East, but from softer clays
fired at low temperatures and covered with a glossy "frit." Even so, these
pâte-tendre porcelains—especially those fired at Chantilly, Vincennes, and
Mennecy-Villeroi (near Paris)—were very beautiful. Hard-paste porcelain
continued to be imported from China or Dresden. In 1749 Mme. de Pompadour coaxed 100,000 livres from Louis XV, and 250,000 from private
sources, to expand the production of soft-paste wares at Vincennes. In 1756
she had Vincennes' hundred artisans moved to a more commodious building
at Sèvres (between Paris and Versailles), and there, in 1769, France began
to make true hard-paste porcelain.

Goldsmiths and silversmiths had the advantage that the French monarchy
used their products as a national reserve, transferring bullion into extravagant forms of beauty that could be readily fused in emergency. Under
Louis XV the middle classes enlarged the demand for silverware as utensils
and decoration. Almost every type of cutlery now used took its present
form in eighteenth-century France: oyster forks, ice spoons, sugar spoons,
hunting services, traveling services, folding knives and forks; add exqui-
sitely carved or molded salt cellars, teapots, ewers, jugs, toilet articles, candlesticks . . . ; in this field the Louis Quinze is "the purest of all French
styles."[2] The goldsmiths and silversmiths made also the little boxes that men
as well as women carried to hold snuff or pills or cosmetics or sweets, and
a hundred types of containers for the toilet table and the boudoir. The
Prince de Conti had a collection of eight hundred boxes, all of different
form, all of precious metal, and all of fine workmanship. Many other materials were used for similar purposes—agate, mother-of-pearl, lapis lazuli . . .
The cutting and setting of jewelry were the privilege of the 350 master
craftsmen of the goldsmiths' guild.

Metalwork bore the mark of the age in its delicate pattern and finish.
Andirons took fabulous forms in intricate designs, usually of fantastic animals. Gilt bronze was used to make or decorate andirons, torches, candela-
bras, or chandeliers, or to mount clocks, barometers, porcelain, or jade; the
eighteenth century was the heyday of modern bronze. Clocks could be
monsters—watches could be gems—of bronze, enamel, silver, or gold, chased
in the most exquisite style. Torches were in some cases masterpieces of
sculpture, like that which Falconet made for Versailles. Miniatures and medallions were among the temptations of the time. One family, the Roettiers,
produced within a century five *graveurs de médailles*, all so distinguished
for their work that they were welcomed into the Académie Royale des
Beaux-Arts along with the greatest painters and sculptors. It was in the little
things of life that the eighteenth century displayed its most careless wealth

and most careful art. "Those who have not lived before 1789," said Talley-rand, "will never know how sweet life could be"[3]—if one could choose his class and dodge the guillotine.

II. ARCHITECTURE

Architecture almost ignored rococo. Styles change less readily in building than in decoration, for the requirements of stability are less fluid than the tides of taste. The Académie Royale de l'Architecture, organized by Colbert in 1671, was now led by inheritors of the Louis XIV traditions. Robert de Cotte contin-ued the work of Jules Hardouin-Mansard, who had completed the Palace of Versailles; Germain Boffrand was a pupil of Mansard; Jacques Jules Gabriel and his son Jacques Ange were collateral descendants of Mansard; so the stream of talent obdurately dug its bed. These men preserved the baroque, even the semi-classical, exteriors of the *grand siècle* with columns, capitals, architraves, and cupolas; but many of their constructions allowed a frolic of rococo within.

The decline of faith left little stimulus for new churches; two old ones, how-ever, had their façades renewed. Robert de Cotte faced St.-Roch with classical columns and pediment (1736), and Jean Nicolas Servandoni provided St.-Sulpice (1733–45) with a massive two-storied portico of Doric and Ionic colonnades in somber Palladian style. But it was secular architecture that expressed the spirit of the age. Several of the palaces built in this period later became national ministries or foreign embassies: so the Hôtel de Matignon (1721) became the Austrian embassy, and then the home of the prime minister; the Palais-Bourbon (1722–50) was partly incorporated into the Chambre des Députés; the Hôtel de Soubise (remodeled in 1742) became the Archives Nationales.

Under the Marquis de Marigny as commissioner of buildings a large number of architects, sculptors, painters, and decorators prospered; he found lodgings and commissions for them, and saw that they were adequately paid. His favorite architect was Jacques Ange Gabriel, who accepted wholeheartedly the classical tradition. After the Peace of Aix-la-Chapelle (1748) Edme Bouchardon was engaged to cast an equestrian statue of Louis XV, and Gabriel was asked to de-sign the entourage for this monument. Around an open space between the Jar-dins des Tuileries and the Champs-Élysées he placed a ring of balustrades and sunken gardens; on the north side he raised the present Hotel Crillon and the present Ministry of the Marine, both in purely classic form; and to adorn the square he set up four mythological figures, which the Parisians soon named after the royal mistresses—Mailly, Vintimille, Châteauroux, and Pompadour. The square was named Place Louis Quinze; now we call it Place de la Concorde. It is a comfort to know that there were traffic jams there two hundred years ago. This same James Angel Gabriel in 1752 built the perfectly proportioned École Militaire, whose Corinthian columns are as graceful as any in the Roman Forum.

It was not only Paris that had its face remodeled in this reign. At Chantilly the Duc de Bourbon engaged Jean Aubert to set up for his horses and dogs stables so palatial as to invite contrast with the cottages of the peasants. In Lorraine Stanislas Leszczyński made Nancy one of the fairest cities in France. There Boffrand finished the cathedral that had been begun by his master Jules Hardouin-Mansard. Emmanuel Héré de Corny laid out (1750–57) the "New City" at Nancy: a rococo Hôtel de Ville, or City Hall; the Place Stanislas, leading through a public garden and a triumphal arch to the Place de la Carrière and the Palais du Gouvernement; and Jean Lamour guarded this Place Stanislas with iron grilles (1751–55) that are the finest of their kind in modern art. Lyons now gave itself the Place Louis-le-Grand; Nantes, Rouen, Reims, and Bordeaux each opened a Place Royale; Toulouse raised a noble Capitole; Rouen provided lovely fountains; stately bridges beautified Sens, Nantes, and Blois; and Montpellier spread out its promenade. Between 1730 and 1760 Jean Jacques Gabriel transformed Bordeaux into a modern city with open squares, wide avenues, airy parks, a handsome waterfront, and public buildings in majestic Renaissance style.

Finally French architecture crossed frontiers; French architects were commissioned to build in Switzerland, Germany, Denmark, Russia, Italy, Spain. By the middle of the century, when France was declining in military power and political prestige, she reached the height of her influence in manners and art.

III. SCULPTURE

Sculpture in this period was fighting an angry struggle for recognition as a major art. Its function had long been mainly decorative; but whereas under Louis XIV it had commissions to adorn great palaces and extensive gardens, it was less favored now that the royal passion for building had exhausted itself and France. The rich were hiding in smaller structures, and heroic statuary found no place in drawing rooms and boudoirs. Sculptors complained that the Académie Royale de Peinture et de Sculpture gave most of its prizes to painters; Pigalle proposed that there be a royal sculptor as well as a royal painter, and personally campaigned for the order of St.-Michel to break down the tradition that only painters received this reward. Reluctantly the sculptors turned to decorating homes with small pieces, vases, and reliefs, and sought to rival the portrait painters by giving to decaying, paying flesh the illusion of lasting bronze or stone. Some of them, entering more intimately into the home, adopted the elegance, naturalness, and playfulness of rococo, while still favoring the sobriety of classic lines.

As with painters and artisans, the sculptor's art tended to run in families. Nicolas Coustou helped his teacher, Antoine Coysevox, to decorate the royal palaces at Marly and Versailles; he designed the great figures, symbolizing French rivers, that are now in the Hôtel de Ville at Lyons; his *Descent from the Cross* is still in Notre-Dame-de-Paris; and his *Berger Chasseur* is one of a dozen masterly statues that face time and weather in the Gardens of the Tuileries. Nicolas' younger brother, Guillaume Coustou I, turned Marie Leszczyńska into marble as Juno,[4] and carved the powerful *Horses of Marly* (1740–45)—

originally for that palace, but now rebelling against the bridle at the west and east approaches to the Place de la Concorde. Guillaume's son, Guillaume Coustou II, made for the Dauphin the tomb in the cathedral of Sens.

Nancy gave birth to another artistic dynasty. Jacob Sigisbert Adam transmitted sculpture and architecture to three sons. Lambert Sigisbert Adam, after ten years of tutelage in Rome, went up to Paris, where he collaborated with his younger brother, Nicolas Sébastien, in designing the Neptune and Amphitrite Fountain in the gardens of Versailles. Then he moved to Potsdam and carved for Frederick the Great, as gifts from Louis XV, two marble groups—*Hunting* and *Fishing*—for the grounds of Sanssouci. Nicolas Sébastien returned to Nancy and designed the tomb of Katharin Opalinska in the Church of Notre-Dame-de-Bon-Secours. A third brother, François Balthasar Gaspard, helped to decorate Stanislas' capital.

A third family of sculptors began with Filippo Caffieri, who left Italy in 1660 to work with his son François Charles for Louis XIV. Another son, Jacques Caffiéri, brought the genius of the line to its peak, surpassing all his contemporaries as a worker in bronze. Nearly all the royal palaces competed for his time. At Versailles he and his son Philippe adorned the chimneypiece in the apartment of the Dauphin, and made the rococo bronze pedestal for the King's famous astronomical clock. The bronze mounts that Jacques made for furniture are now treasured beyond the furniture itself.[5]

Edme Bouchardon, whom Voltaire called "our Pheidias,"[6] accepted completely the classical principles proclaimed by his patron the Comte de Caylus. For many years he labored in rivalry with Pigalle, until Pigalle thought himself surpassed; Diderot quoted the younger sculptor as saying that he had "never entered Bouchardon's studio without coming out with a sense of discouragement that lasted entire weeks."[7] Diderot thought that Bouchardon's *Amour* (*Cupid*)[8] was destined to immortality, but it hardly catches the fire of love. Better is the fountain that the sculptor carved for the Rue de Grenelle in Paris— a masterpiece of classic dignity and strength. In 1749 the city commissioned him to execute an equestrian statue of Louis XV. He worked on it nine years, cast it in 1758, but did not live to see it set up. Dying (1762), he asked the municipal authorities to let Pigalle finish the enterprise; so their long rivalry ended in a gesture of admiration and trust. The statue was erected in the Place Louis Quinze, and was demolished as a hated emblem by the Revolution (1792).

Jean Baptiste Lemoyne rejected classical restraints as sentencing sculpture to death. Why should not marble or bronze, as well as pictorial tempera or oil, express movement, feeling, laughter, joy, and grief—as, indeed, Hellenistic statuary had dared to do? In that spirit Lemoyne designed the tombs of Cardinal Fleury and the painter Pierre Mignard for the Church of St.-Roch. So, in the *Montesquieu* that he carved for Bordeaux, he showed the author of *The Spirit of Laws* as a quizzical, melancholy skeptic, a cross between a Roman senator and a provincial philosopher smiling at Parisian ways. That fleeting smile became almost the identifying signature of the many portrait busts that Lemoyne made, by order of the King, to commemorate divers worthies of France. This lively expressionistic style triumphed over the classicism of Bouchardon and passed down to Pigalle, Pajou, Houdon, and Falconet in one of the great ages of sculpture in France.

IV. PAINTING

The commanding artists were now the painters, and the dominance of Boucher reflected again the influence of women on the arts. The Marquise de Pompadour felt that painters had dallied long enough with Roman heroes, Christian martyrs, and Greek gods; let them see the loveliness of living women in the finery of their costume or the rosiness of their flesh; let them catch in line and color the unprecedented elegance of the age in features, manners, dress, and all the accessories of an affluent minority life. Woman, once a sin, proclaimed herself still a sin, but only to be more tempting; she revenged herself on those frightened centuries in which she had been humiliated by the Church as the mother and agent of damnation, and had been admitted to a eunuch-conceived Paradise only through the virginity of the Mother of God. Nothing could more boldly announce the decline of religion in France than the displacement of the Virgin in French art.

The King, the aristocracy, and the financiers replaced the Church in patronage. In Paris the painters' Académie de St.-Luc served as a rival and prod to the conservative Académie Royale des Beaux-Arts; and in the provinces additional academies sprang up at Lyons, Nancy, Metz, Marseilles, Toulouse, Bordeaux, Clermont-Ferrand, Pau, Dijon, and Reims. Besides the annual Prix de Rome a dozen competitions and prizes kept the art world in movement and ferment; and sometimes the King or another patron would console losers by buying their entries or pensioning them for a stay in Italy.

Artists displayed their paintings in the streets; on some religious festivals they pinned them to the hangings that the pious draped from their windows on processional routes. To discourage what seemed to established artists an unseemly procedure, the Académie des Beaux-Arts, after an interruption of thirty-three years, resumed in 1737, in the Salon Carré of the Louvre, the public exhibition of contemporary paintings and sculpture. This annual—or, after 1751, biennial—"Salon" became, in late August and through September, an exciting event in the artistic and social life of Paris, and in the literary world. The war between conservatives in the Academy and rebels in or out of it made art a battle rivaling sex and war in the gossip of the capital; devotees of chaste line and corrective discipline scorned, and were scorned by, protagonists of color, experiment, innovation, liberty. Art criticism became a flourishing enterprise. The *Réflexions sur la peinture*

(1747) of Comte de Caylus were read to a full concourse of the Académie; Grimm reported the exhibitions to the clients of his letters; and Diderot came out of his war on Christianity to emerge as the most controversial art critic of the time. Engravers like Jacques Le Blon and Laurent Cars spread the flutter by disseminating prints of famous works, by illustrating books, and by producing masterpieces of their own. Engraving in color began with Le Blon in 1720.

Never, except in religious art, had artists won so keen a public, or so wide a patronage. Now the painter addressed himself to the world.

1. In the Antechamber

So many painters rose to prominence in this period that merely to mention them would dam our stream. We shall look more carefully at Boucher, Chardin, and La Tour, but there are others who would be shocked to be ignored.

There was the brilliant but lackadaisical Jean Francois de Troy, too handsome to be great; everybody loved him, and he agreed sufficiently to use his own features as those of Christ in *The Agony in the Garden*.[9] He judged it more pleasant to seduce women than to picture them, and left behind him many broken hearts and blemished works. — François (not to be confused with the sculptor Jean Baptiste) Lemoyne decorated the vault of the Salon d'Hercule at Versailles with 142 vast figures, and transmitted to his pupil Boucher the art of replacing the "brown sauce" of Rembrandt with Pompadour rose. — Charles Antoine Coypel, son and grandson of painters, anticipated Chardin in genre; we have met him as painter to the Regent; in 1747 he was *premier peintre* to Louis XV. Frederick was glad to have his *Lady before a Mirror* for the Palace of Sanssouci, and the Louvre still displays his Gobelin tapestry of *L'Amour et Psyché*, a rich assemblage of flesh and drapery.

Jean Marc Nattier was the vogue in portraiture, for he knew how to redeem with pose, color, and the play of light the defects with which birth or life had flawed his sitters; all but one of the ladies he painted were pleased to find themselves, on his canvases, as alluring as they had always believed themselves to be. His *Madame de Pompadour* hangs in Versailles— lovely tinted hair, and gentle eyes hardly revealing her will to power. Royalty competed for Nattier: he showed Marie Leszczyńska as a modest bourgeoise setting out for a rural holiday,[10] and did full justice to the beauty of the Queen's daughter Adélaïde.[11] When Peter the Great came to Paris, Nattier made portraits of him and his Czarina; Peter invited him to move to Russia; Nattier refused; Peter carried off the portraits without bothering to pay. — Jacques André Aved, born in Flanders, brought to Paris some Flemish realism, picturing people as they were; the elder Mirabeau must have been alarmed to see himself as Aved saw him,[12] but it is one of the great portraits of the century.

To all these gentlemen of the antechamber—even to Boucher and Chardin—Grimm and Diderot preferred Carle Vanloo. He came of a long line of pictorial Vanloos, of whom we know nine by name. Born at Nice in 1705, he was taken by his painter brother Jean Baptiste to Rome, where he studied with both the chisel and the brush. At Paris he won the Prix de Rome (1724); he spent another session in Italy, and returned to France. He pleased the Academy, and angered Boucher, by following all the academic rules. As he had never spared time from his art to learn reading or writing, good manners or polite discourse, Pompadour shunned him with a pretty shiver as a *"bête à faire peur"*—a "frightful beast";[13] nevertheless she commissioned him to paint *A Spanish Conversation*. For a while he accepted the mood of the time, and pictured women dressed in ideal contours; but he soon sobered down to an exemplary family life, proud of his accomplished wife and fond of his daughter Caroline. In 1753 he shared with Boucher in decorating the gorgeous Salle du Conseil in the Palace of Fontainebleau. He climbed to such affectionate fame that when he appeared in his seat at the Comédie-Française after an almost mortal illness, the entire audience rose and applauded, revealing the close relation of art and letters in that tensely cultural age.

Jean Baptiste Oudry recorded the royal hunts in engravings, paintings, and tapestries. The Queen chose him as her teacher, and marveled to watch him work. Some of his engravings provided excellent guides for tapestry weavers; soon Oudry was appointed director of the royal factory at Beauvais. He found there nothing but chaos and decadence; he reorganized the operations with a firm hand, infected the workers with his enthusiasm, and designed for them a series of tapestries illustrating with delectable animals the fables of La Fontaine. There too he made the cartoon for the dazzling assemblage of women and beasts that hangs in the Louvre as the Diana Portiere. The weavers at Les Gobelins become jealous of these Beauvais successes; they persuaded the King to transfer Oudry to the older factory; and there Oudry wore himself out in a long struggle to have the weavers accept the colors that he prescribed. Meanwhile he contributed, both in Beauvais and in Paris, to train the varied talents of the most distinctive, brilliant, and berated artist of mid-century France.

2. Boucher: 1703–70

Listen to Diderot contemplating Boucher's nudes:

> What colors! what variety! what wealth of objects and ideas! This man has all but truth. . . . The degradation of taste, of color, of composition, of character, of expression, has followed step by step the debasement of morals. . . . What should this man paint save what he conceives in his imagination? And what can he conceive who spends his life in the company of women of the town? . . . This man takes the brush only to show me buttocks and breasts. He knows not what grace is. . . . Delicacy, honesty, innocence, and simplicity have become strangers to him. He has never seen nature for an instant; at least not the nature which interests my soul, yours, that of any wellborn child, that of any woman who has feeling. He is without taste. . . . And it is at that moment, forsooth, that he is made first painter to the King [1765].[14]

Boucher presumably never saw this critique, since it was directed to Grimm's foreign clientele. Let us look at him without malice aforethought.

He was a child of Paris, of its code and ways. His father was a designer who kept an art shop near the Louvre, and taught François the rudiments of painting and sculpture. As the boy showed a facile talent, he was apprenticed to the engraver Laurent Cars, then to the painter François Lemoyne. Being engaged to paint scenery for the Opéra, he fell in with a succession of actresses and chorus girls; he imitated, so far as his means allowed, all the dissipations of the Regency.[15] Once, he tells us, he experienced an idyllic love for a pretty *fruitière*, Rosette; she seemed to him simplicity and purity incarnate; he took her as model for a Madonna into which he poured all that remained of his boyhood piety. But while this work was still unfinished he relapsed into promiscuity. When he tried to finish it his inspiration had vanished, and Rosette too. He never recaptured that moment of tender imagination.[16]

His skill developed rapidly under the tutelage of Lemoyne. In that atelier he learned something of Correggio's flair for feminine figures of classic features and supple grace. At the Luxembourg Palace he studied the resplendent canvases in which Rubens had turned the life of Marie de Médicis into an epic of color and *noblesses de robes*. In 1723, aged twenty, he won the Prix de Rome, entitling him to three years' board and lodging in Paris, a pension of three hundred livres, and four years in Rome. We get a picture of student life in the Paris of the Regency when we are told that his companions carried the victor on their shoulders around the Place du Louvre.

In 1727 he accompanied Carle Vanloo to Italy. The director of the Académie Royale de France in Rome reported that he had found for "a young man named Boucher . . . a little hole of a room, and I have packed him in there. I am afraid it is really no more than a hole, but at least he will be under cover."[17] The "modest youth," as the director described him, did not always have to sleep there, for he found many beds open to him in Rome. It is significant of changing taste that he showed no liking for the work of Raphael or Michelangelo, but struck up a friendship with Tiepolo.

Returning to Paris (1731), he continued to burn the candle at both ends. He was seldom content with any but a firsthand knowledge of his models. Nevertheless he found time to paint some outstanding pictures—e.g., *L'En-lèvement d'Europe* (*The Rape of Europa*), one of his countless expositions of the female form. In 1733 he thought he had discovered Venus herself in his model Jeanne Buseaux, and, though he felt that "marriage is scarcely in my line,"[18] he took her as his wife. He was briefly faithful to her, and she repaid him in kind. Probably she posed for his painting *Renaud et Armide*,[19] which won him full membership in the Académie des Beaux-Arts (1734). Louis XV now commissioned him to paint cheerful scenes in the bedroom of the still loved Queen. With the reopening of the Salon in 1737 his work found wider fame and patronage; thereafter he knew no poverty, and soon no rival.

His specialty was nudes. Until his marriage he had seldom lingered long enough with one woman to discover much more of her than her skin; but he had found that surface endlessly interesting, and seemed resolved to portray it in every nook and cranny, every form and pose, from hair of blond silk to feet that never knew a shoe. Boucher was rococo in the flesh.

But he was more than that. Though later critics condemned his art as technically defective, he was actually a master craftsman in composition, color, and line; however he sometimes scrimped his art in hurry for a fee. Many contemporaries acclaimed the fresh plein-air spirit of his pictures, the fertility of his imagination, the easy grace of his line; and the hostile Diderot thought that "no one understands as Boucher does the art of light and shade."[20] Hardly any branch of painting eluded his skill. Those of us who know only some of his paintings and tapestries are surprised to learn that "the popularity of Boucher was due as much to his drawings as to his paintings."[21] His drawings became precious items in his lifetime; illustrious collectors competed for them; they were bought like easel pictures, and were hung on bedroom or boudoir walls. They were marvels of economy— a dimple made with a dot, a smile dashed off with a line, and all the sheen and rustle of silken skirts emerging miraculously from a bit of chalk.

Surely not for the pelf involved, but because of the genius and imagination swelling in him, lighting his eyes, driving his hands, Boucher worked ten hours a day in his studio, leaving his mark on almost everything that he touched. Besides a thousand pictures, he painted fans, ostrich eggs, pottery, medallions, screens, furniture, carriages, stage scenery, the walls and ceiling of a theater; all alert Paris came to see the décor he provided as background for Noverre's ballet *Les Fêtes chinoises* (1754). He had only a minor interest in landscapes, being Aphrodite's ambassador to the Louvre; yet he enshrined his human forms in woods and fields, by sparkling waters or shady ruins, under white clouds in a blue sky, and a warm sun abetting and approving the heat of the blood. One would have thought genre pictures quite uncongenial to him; nevertheless he painted *A Family Scene*, and—as if to free himself from the thralldom of beauty—he represented farmyards, barns, dovecotes, wheelbarrows, back-yard debris, donkeys ambling under a load of clattering pans. To round out his repertoire he became the greatest tapestry designer of the century.

In 1736 Oudry invited him to Beauvais to design for the weavers there. He began with fourteen drawings of Italian village scenes;[22] they proved so successful that they were woven at least a dozen times before his death. He proceeded to a more typical theme, *The Story of Psyche*—five hangings modeled by Mme. Boucher; these tapestries are among the choice masterpieces of eighteenth-century art. He crowned his work with six tapestries called *The Noble Pastoral*;[23] one of these, *The Bird Catchers* (*La Pipée aux Oiseaux*) shows as charming a pair of lovers as ever evolved from silk or wool. Critics have complained that with Oudry and Boucher tapestry became too much like painting, and lost its distinguishing virtues. Louis XV hardly minded, for when Oudry died (1755) he promoted Boucher to head Les Gobelins.

Meanwhile the triumphant artist had won the ardent patronage of Pompadour. For her he decorated the palace of Bellevue, and designed its furniture. For the theater with which she strove to entertain the King he painted the scenery and devised the costumes. He made several portraits of her, so appealing in beauty and grace that all judgment hesitates before them. The charge that Boucher never got beyond the flesh is silenced here; he has made us see not so much the physical charms of the mistress as the qualities of intelligence and tenderness that endeared her to the King, the cultural interest that made her the goddess of the *philosophes*, and the feminine artistry of dress that daily clothed with new allure the body's fading charms. Through these portraits, and La Tour's, she could quietly remind the King of the beauty that was gone and the subtler bewitchments that remained. Perhaps, too, she used Boucher's sensual pictures to please the royal lust. No wonder she made Boucher her favorite, secured him an apartment in the Louvre, took lessons from him in engraving, discussed with him her plans for decorating her palaces and promoting the arts. For her he painted

(1753) two of his greatest pictures, *Le Lever du Soleil* (*Sunrise*) and *Le Coucher du Soleil* (*Sunset*)[24]—in both of which, of course, the sun is outshone by human forms.

He survived Pompadour, survived the disastrous war with England and Frederick, and continued prosperous to the end of his sixty-seven years. Commissions flowed in; he became wealthy, but worked as zealously as ever, and he redeemed his wealth with generosity. He was now a benevolent satyr, untiringly sensual, but ever gay and kind, "obliging and disinterested, . . . incapable of base jealousies, . . . immune from any low appetite for money gains."[25] He worked too fast to reach the highest excellence; he indulged his imagination so freely that he lost touch with reality. He told Reynolds that he needed no models, and preferred to paint from memory, but his memory idealized. Uncorrected by reality, he became careless in his drawing and exaggerated in color; he almost invited the harsh criticisms that came upon him in his later years. Grimm, Diderot, and others accused him of mistaking prettiness for beauty, of reducing art from dignity to specious and superficial decoration, and of lowering the moral tone of the time by idealizing physical charms. Diderot denounced his "simperings, affectations, . . . beauty spots, rouge, gewgaws, . . . frivolous women, libidinous satyrs, bastard infants of Bacchus and Silenus."[26] Dying at work in his studio, Boucher left unfinished on his easel *The Toilette of Venus*—as if to defy Diderot. And Diderot, hearing that the artist was dead, had a twitch of remorse. "I have spoken too much evil of Boucher," he said; "I retract."[27] Let us leave the matter there.

3. Chardin: 1699–1779

How different from Boucher's was the world of Chardin—what a contrast in conceptions of beauty, in character and wit! Here was almost a class war, a revolt of the middle-middle class against the wasteful epicureanism of the financiers, the aristocracy, and the court. Jean Baptiste Siméon Chardin was born bourgeois, remained contentedly bourgeois, and painted bourgeois life affectionately to the end. His father was a master cabinetmaker, high in his guild, owner of a home in the Rue de Seine on the Left Bank. Because he supposed that Jean would succeed him in his trade, he gave him little schooling, much manual training. Chardin later regretted this scantiness of education, but it kept him from treading again the old tracks in art, and turned his face and brush to the objects around him in the workshop and the home. He liked to draw, and soon itched to paint. The father let him enroll in the studio of Pierre Jacques Cazes, then a painter for the court.

The youth was unhappy there; the classical models he was told to copy seemed absurdly remote from the life he knew. When a surgeon friend of his father asked him to paint a sign proclaiming the barber-surgeon's trade and displaying its instruments, Jean, perhaps remembering Watteau's emblem for Gersaint, painted a vast signboard showing a man wounded in a duel, attended by a surgeon and assistant; but for good measure Chardin added a water carrier, a constable, some night watchmen, a carriage, a woman gazing from its window, a crowd of onlookers peering over heads —and all in an éclat of bustle and gestures and excitement. The surgeon was displeased, and proposed to discard the sign, but it won so much attention and approval from passers-by that he let it remain over his door. We hear no more of Chardin till in 1728 his paintings of a fish (*La Raie*) and a sideboard with silver and fruit (*Le Buffet*) drew special praise in an open-air exhibition in the Place Dauphine. Some members of the Academy invited him to apply for membership; he arranged to have a few of his paintings displayed there anonymously; they were acclaimed as masterpieces, ascribed to Flemings; he confessed his authorship; he was reproved for the ruse, but was admitted (1728).

In 1731 he became the fiancé of Marguerite Sainctar, whose parents promised a good dowry. During the engagement these parents suffered heavy losses and died, leaving Marguerite penniless; Chardin married her nevertheless. Chardin *père* gave them rooms on the third floor of a house that he had recently bought at the corner of the Rue du Four and the Rue Princesse. There the artist pitched his studio, which was also his kitchen; for he had now definitely chosen to paint still life and genre. The vegetables, fruit, fish, bread, and meat that littered the room became in turn the models for his brush and the menu of his meals.

Chardin was charmed by the changing shapes and colors of ordinary things. He saw in them qualities of texture and light rarely noticed by incurious eyes. The cheeks of an apple were to him as romantic as a maiden's blush, and the gleam of a knife on the green of a tablecloth challenged him to catch it in its flight and fix it in his art. He rendered these lowly objects with such fidelity and insight, such mastery of color and contour, light and shade, as few painters have displayed. We look at these *natures mortes* and perceive that they are alive, that we never saw them properly before, never realized the complexity and uniqueness of their forms, nor the nuances of their tints. Chardin found poetry not only in a vase of flowers or a cluster of grapes, but in an old worn caldron, a nut, an orange rind, a crumbling crust of bread. There had always been poetry in them, as the Flemish and the Dutch had known; but who in the France of Boucher and Pompadour had ever suspected it? The beauty of these objects, of course, was in the eye of the beholder, or rather in his soul; it was Chardin's intense feeling, as well as his intent vision—and his poverty—that made a lyric of the larder, an epic of a menu.

Everyone knows the story—or legend?—of how he was prodded into painting human forms. One day he heard his friend Aved refuse a commission of four hundred livres to paint a portrait; Chardin, accustomed to small fees, marveled at the refusal; Aved answered, "You think a portrait is as easy to paint as a sausage?"[28] It was a cruel jibe, but useful; Chardin had confined his subjects too narrowly, and would soon have satiated his clients with dishes and food. He resolved to paint figures, and discovered in himself a genius of sympathetic portrayal that he had allowed to sleep. Meeting the challenge head on, he painted a portrait of Aved himself as *Le Souffleur* (*The Blower*).[29] He bettered this with *Le Château de Cartes* (*The House of Cards*); but here too the excellence was in the clothing rather than the face. In *L'Enfant au Toton* (*The Child with a Top*) Chardin struck his second stride: the hands a bit awkward, but the face revealing a sympathetic understanding. This tender empathy found outlets in his pictures of girls, as in the two masterpieces in the Rothschild Collection: a girl playing badminton, another "amusing herself with her luncheon."

In women Chardin saw not the rosy lures that had aroused Boucher but the wifely and maternal virtues that made the family the prop and savior of the state. With Chardin the middle-class woman entered French art, and had her due. He knew her and loved her in all her engaging services: bringing food from the market, drawing water, peeling turnips, winding wool, caring for the sick, warning the schoolboy against truancy, or (in the most famous of Chardin's pictures, *Le Bénédicité*[30]) holding up the meal until the youngest daughter, with little hands joined, has murmured grace. He saw woman always in her house dress, without frills, never idle, serving her husband or her children from dawn and the morning prayers till they are all safely tucked in bed. Through Chardin we see a Paris saner than the court, still clinging to the old morality, and to the religious faith that gave it a mystical support. It is the most wholesome art in all of art's history.

These now universally acclaimed pictures found a very limited market, and brought Chardin just enough francs to maintain him in contented simplicity. He could not haggle with customers; he let his pictures go for almost any offered fee; and as he worked slowly and laboriously, he wore himself out in relative poverty, while Boucher used himself up in affluence. When his first wife died, after only four years of marriage, he let his rooms and affairs fall into a baccalaureate disorder. His friends prevailed upon him to remarry, if only to have a woman's deft and patient hand restore some order to his ménage. He hesitated for nine years, then took to wife the widow Marguerite Pouget, in literally a marriage of convenience. She brought him a moderate dowry, including a house that she owned at 13

Rue Princesse. He moved into it, and his poverty ended. She was a good woman and a solicitous wife. He learned to love her gratefully.

To further finance him the King gave him (1752) a pension of five hundred livres, and the Academy (1754) appointed him its treasurer. Soon afterward it engaged him to place the pictures submitted to its Salons; he was thoroughly unsuited to this task, but his wife helped him. In 1756 a friendly engraver, Charles Nicolas Cochin II, persuaded Marigny to give Chardin a comfortable apartment in the Louvre. It was this same Cochin who, anxious to draw Chardin away from culinary repetitions, secured for him a commission to paint three *dessus-de-porte* pictures—to be placed "over the door"—for some rooms in Marigny's château. Chardin laboriously produced (1765) *Attributs des Arts, Attributs des Sciences,* and *Attributs de la Musique.*[31] A further commission resulted in two similar tableaux for Pompadour's palace of Bellevue. Unfortunately the five thousand livres pledged for these five pictures were not paid till 1771.

Meanwhile the aging artist was losing his skill. In 1767 Diderot, who in 1759 had hailed his work as the soul of "nature and truth," said sadly, "Chardin is an excellent genre painter, but he is passing."[32] La Tour's pastels were capturing the fancy of Paris. In a burst of rivalry Chardin himself took chalk and paper, and astonished La Tour by turning out two pastel portraits of himself which are among the most arresting and most finished products in the Louvre. One showed him with an old double-knotted coif on his head, spectacles crowning the end of his nose, cravat wound warmly about his neck; the other revealed the same garb, the same face full of wonder and character, plus a visor to shade his ailing eyes. Still more remarkable was the pastel portrait that he made of his second wife, now sixty-eight years old, a lovely and kindly face, drawn with skill and love. This is the picture that we would choose as the chef-d'oeuvre of Chardin.

It was a triumphant close to a unique and honorable life. We need not picture Chardin as a man immune to human faults; indeed, he too, pierced by the nettles of life and jealousy, could react with touching choler and prickly speech. But when he died (1779) not a soul in the envious, slanderous world of Parisian art and wit could find a hostile word to say of him. Even that decaying regime seemed to realize that Chardin had revealed, with a technique that none surpassed in his time, the France that was the real and still healthy France, that hidden world of simple labor and family loyalty that would survive—and would enable France to survive—a century of chaos and revolution. He was, said Diderot, "the greatest magician that we have had."[33]

4. La Tour: 1704–88

The veering vanes of taste today award the palm for eighteenth-century French painting not to Boucher, nor to Chardin, but to Maurice Quentin de La Tour. As a "character" he is the most interesting of the three, for he mingled his vices and virtues with impish insouciance, drove the whole cowering world into a corner, and, like Diogenes, told a king to get out of his way. He was a moneygrubber of consummate rapacity, bumptious, impudent, arrogant; a bitter enemy and incalculable friend, as vain as an old man concealing or boasting his years. He was an honest, straightforward curmudgeon, a lavish philanthropist, a genial boor, a fire-eating patriot, a scorner of titles, refusing a royal offer of nobility. But all this is irrelevant; he was the greatest draftsman of his time, and the greatest pastel painter in the history of France.

Louis XV, sitting to La Tour for a portrait, was piqued by his frequent praise of foreigners. "I thought you were a Frenchman," said the King. "No, Sire," answered the artist, "I am a Picard, from Saint-Quentin."[34] He was born there to a prosperous musician, who proposed to make him an engineer. The boy preferred to draw pictures; the father reproved him; Maurice, aged fifteen, fled to Paris, then to Reims, then to Cambrai, painting portraits here and there. At Cambrai an English diplomat invited him to London as his guest. Maurice went, made money and merry, returned to Paris, and posed as an English painter. Rosalba Carriera was in Paris in 1721; her pastel portraits were sought for by every notable from the Regent to the newest *nouveau riche*. La Tour found that such drawing with colored crayons suited his hectic temperament better than the patient elaboration of oil. Through years of trial and error he learned to achieve with chalk such shades and subtleties of color and expression as no other portraitist of the time could match.

When he exhibited some of his portrayals in the Salon of 1737 the oil painters began to fear this crayon competition. His three pastels were the talk of the Salon of 1740; his portrait of Président de Rieux, in the black robe and red gown of a magistrate, was the triumph of the Salon of 1741; his portrait of the Turkish ambassador was besieged with admiring spectators in 1742. Soon all the fashionable world demanded transfiguration into chalk. La Tour's encounter with the King became historic. The artist began by objecting to the room chosen, which admitted light from every side. "What do you expect me to do in this lantern?" grumbled La Tour. "I particularly chose this sequestered room," replied the King, "so that we should not be interrupted." "I did not know, Sire," said La Tour, "that you were not the master in your own house." On another occasion he expressed regret that France had no adequate fleet; the King slyly countered, "And what about Vernet?"—who was painting seascapes crowded with ships.[35] When La Tour found the Dauphin misinformed on some affair, La Tour told him blandly, "You see how easily people of your kind allow yourselves to be taken in by swindlers."[36]

Despite his distressing candor, the Academy in 1746 admitted him to full membership—which was a certificate of mastery. But in 1749, prodded by the oil painters, it resolved to accept no more works in pastel. In 1753 a painter complained that "M. de La Tour has so developed the art of pastel that he may provoke a distaste for oil painting."[37] La Tour fought back with invectives and chef-d'oeuvres.

He had a rival in pastel; Jean Baptiste Perronneau was preferred by Lemoyne, Oudry, and other Academicians. La Tour asked him to paint a portrait of La Tour; Perronneau complied and produced a masterpiece. La Tour paid him handsomely, but then painted himself in one of the most revealing self-portraits known. He arranged with Chardin to have the two portraits exhibited side by side in the Salon of 1751. Everyone agreed that the *autoritratto* excelled Perronneau's portrait. La Tour's *La Tour* still smiles in victory in the Louvre.

There, too, is the portrait with which he challenged Boucher—the one pastel that he exhibited in 1755. He almost lost the opportunity. When an invitation came to paint the most famous woman of the reign, he replied, "Kindly inform Madame de Pompadour that I do not go out to paint." It was his way of luring fortune by retreat. His friends begged him to yield; he sent word that he would come, but on condition that no one should interrupt the sitting. Arriving, he removed his gaiters, unbuckled his shoes, discarded his wig and his collar, covered his head with a taffeta cap, and began to paint. Suddenly the door opened; the King entered. La Tour protested, "You gave me your promise, madame, that your door would remain closed." The King laughed, and begged him to resume work. La Tour refused. "It is impossible for me to obey your Majesty. I shall return when Madame is alone. . . . I do not like to be interrupted." The King withdrew, and La Tour completed the sitting.

Of the two most famous portraits of Pompadour, La Tour's is profounder than Boucher's; less brilliant in color, less exquisite in finish and detail, but more mature in expression and interpretation. La Tour pictured the Marquise, doubtless at her own suggestion, as the patroness of art, music, letters, and philosophy. On a nearby sofa a guitar; in her hand some sheets of music; on the table a globe, a portfolio of her own engravings, Voltaire's *Henriade*, Montesquieu's *Esprit des lois*, and Volume IV of Diderot's *Encyclopédie*.

When La Tour had finished the portrait he asked for a fee of 48,000 livres. Madame, extravagant though she was, thought this a bit *de trop;* she sent him 24,000 livres in gold. La Tour proposed to send the money back. Chardin asked him whether he knew the cost of the paintings in Notre-Dame, which included masterpieces by Le Brun and Le Sueur. "No," La Tour admitted. Chardin calculated their total cost at 12,600 livres. La Tour, readjusting his perspective, accepted the 24,000 livres. In general he charged for his portraits according to the wealth of the sitters; if they objected he sent them away unportrayed. Probably he made exceptions for Voltaire, Rousseau, and d'Alembert, for he warmly admired the *philosophes,* and frankly avowed his own loss of religious belief.

Perhaps because of his high fees he was in universal demand. Through him we know the leading personalities of the age; he became a pantheon in pastel. He drew lovely portraits of the Queen, of the young Dauphin and the demure Dauphine,[38] and of La Camargo, prima ballerina; he managed to make Rousseau look amiable and sane;[39] in one of his finest works he pictured Maurice de Saxe, the handsome victor over armies and women;[40] he caught the full fire of life in the eyes of his friend the painter Jean Restout;[41] and he dressed himself in silk and lace and wig for the self-portrait that now hangs in Amiens. Despite his rough manners, his lawless caprices, and his unpredictable moods he was welcomed in aristocratic homes, in M. de La Popelinière's circle at Passy, in Mme. Geoffrin's salon. He was on terms of friendship with the leading writers of his time, even with the painters and sculptors who envied his success—Vanloo, Chardin, Greuze, Pigalle, Pajou. The King gave him a superfluous pension, and a lodging in the Louvre. The man must have been lovable after all.

He never married, but he did not scatter his seed as widely as Boucher. He had a mistress, Mlle. Fel, whose singing helped to make the success of Rousseau's opera *Le Devin du village;* Grimm sickened with unrequited love for her, but she gave herself wholeheartedly to La Tour. He remembered her accommodations so gratefully that in his eightieth year he still drank to her memory. Her devotion was one of his consolations when age stiffened his fingers and dulled his eyes. He paid for the *hybris* of his zenith with the long humiliation of his decline; he outlived his genius, and had to hear critics speak of it as dead.

Nearing eighty, he left his apartment in the Louvre to live in the fresher air of Auteuil; and finally he returned to the city of his birth. St.-Quentin received the prodigal son with salvos of gunfire, ringing of bells, and popular acclaim. In that quiet town he lived four years more, his proud reason fading into a mild and harmless insanity, mumbling a pantheistic philosophy, praying to God and the sun, and dreaming hopefully of revolution. He died a year before its coming, kissing the hands of his servants in his final agony.

CHAPTER X

The Play of the Mind

I. THE WORD INDUSTRY

THE French language had now become the second tongue of every educated European, the accepted medium of international diplomacy. Frederick the Great used it regularly, except to his troops; Gibbon wrote his first book in French, and for a time thought of writing in French his history of declining Rome. In 1784 the Berlin Academy announced a prize competition for an essay explaining the causes of this pre-eminence, and issued its own publications in French. The chief causes were the political supremacy of France under Louiv XIV, the spread of the French language by French troops in the Netherlands, Germany, Austria, and Spain, the unquestioned superiority of French literature on the Continent (England had reservations), the popularity of Parisian society as the finishing school of the European elite, the desire to replace Latin with a more modern and flexible speech in the commerce of nations, and the purification and standardization of the French language by the French Academy through its Dictionary. Nowhere had any vernacular reached such precision and variety, such point and charm of phrase, such elegance and clarity of style. There were some losses in this victory: French prose sacrificed the simple directness of Montaigne, the rough and hearty vitality of Rabelais; French poetry languished in the prison of Boileau's rules. The Academy itself, until Duclos aroused it after his election in 1746, had slipped into dreamy formalism and cautious mediocrity.

The relative freedom of thought and speech under the Regency had encouraged the multiplication of authors, publishers, and libraries. Printer-publisher-booksellers lurked everywhere, even though, as the century advanced, their trade became perilous; in Paris alone there were 360, nearly all of them poor. Many towns now had circulating libraries, and many libraries maintained reading rooms open to the public for an admission fee of forty sous. Authorship seldom sufficed as a way of life; it was usually appended to some other occupation; so the elder Crébillon was a notary's clerk, and Rousseau copied music. A few famous writers could sell their product at a good price; Marivaux, ruined by the collapse of Law's System, retrieved his finances with his plays and *Marianne*, and Rousseau, usually poor, received five thousand livres for *Émile*. The only copyright available was the *privilège du roi*, or royal permission to publish; this protected the author against the pirating of his book in France, but not against its piratical printing abroad; it was granted only to manuscripts guaranteed by official censors to contain nothing offensive to Church or state. New ideas could surmount that barrier only through disguising their subject matter or their heresies. This ruse failing, an author might send his manuscript to Amsterdam, The Hague, Geneva, or some other foreign city, to be printed there in French, distributed abroad, and circulated clandestinely in France.

The expansion of the middle class, the spread of education, and the gathering of intellect in Paris were generating an audience eager for books, and a swarm of authors rose to saturate this demand. The weakening of the state under Louis XV, and the decline of religious belief, stimulated the oral and written discussion of political and philosophical issues. The aristocracy, resenting both the monarchy that had shorn it of power and the Church that was supporting the monarchy, offered an interested hearing to criticism of the government and the creed; and the upper middle class joined in this receptivity, hoping for a change that would give them social equality with the nobility.

In this new atmosphere authors attained a status rarely accorded them either before or after the eighteenth century. They were welcomed in the salons, where they held forth with all the facility of their eloquence; they were received in titled homes so long as they stepped upon no titled toes; they were entertained and sometimes housed by financiers like La Popelinière. Despite their poverty they became a force in the state. "Of all empires," said Duclos in 1751, "that of the men of mind [*gens d'esprit*], without being visible, is most widely spread. Men of power can command, but men of intellect govern; for in the long run . . . public opinion sooner or later overcomes or upsets every form of despotism."[1] (The technique of forming public opinion by money or government had not yet been perfected in 1751.)

Cheered on by a widening audience, stimulated by hundreds of alert competitors, liberated by the decline of dogma, spurred by the vanity of print, French writers now launched upon the inky sea such a flotilla of letters, pamphlets, brochures, diatribes, essays, memoirs, histories, novels, dramas, poems, theologies, philosophies, and pornography as finally broke through all the chains of censorship, swept away all resistance, and transformed the mind, the faith, and the government of France and, in some measure, of the world. Never in literature had there been such subtle wit, such delicate pleasantry, such coarse buffoonery, such lethal ridicule. Every orthodoxy of Church or state trembled under the assault of these sharply pointed, sometimes poisoned, usually nameless, pens.

Even private correspondence became a public art. Men and women revised, rewrote, polished their letters in the hope that these would shine before more eyes than two; and sometimes they succeeded so well that their
letters became *belles-lettres*, literature. Loving conversation, they talked on
paper to absent friends or enemies with all the naturalness of face-to-face
speech, all the sparkle and vitality of exchanges across the table in salons.
Such letters were no mere trivia of personal news; they were in many cases
discourses on politics, literature, or art. Sometimes they were in verse—*vers
de société*—bubbling with the rhymes that come so readily in French, and
warm with the hope of praise. So Voltaire delighted his friends with epistolary poems poured from the cornucopia of his agile mind and facile art.

The age of oratory was ending, for eighteenth-century France feared to
be bored, even by a Bossuet; it would return with the Revolution. Memoirs
were still in fashion, for, being letters to posterity, they kept some of the
charm of correspondence. It was at the end of this period, in 1755, that the
Mémoires of the Baronne de Staal de Launay, who had died in 1750, at last
reached print, recalling the days of the Regency and the *soirées de Sceaux;*
here, said Grimm, was a lady who rivaled Voltaire himself in the excellence
of her prose.[2]

II. THE STAGE

The theaters surpassed the salons in the place they held in the life and
affection of Paris. "The theater," said Voltaire to Marmontel in 1745, "is
the most enchanting of all careers. It is there that in one day you may obtain glory and fortune. One successful piece renders a man at the same time
rich and celebrated."[3] There were good theaters in the provinces, there
were private theatricals in rich homes, there were dramatic performances
before King and court at Versailles; but it was in Paris that the enthusiasm
for plays became a fever of controversy and delight. The highest standards
of subject and performance were maintained by the Comédie-Française in
the Théâtre-Français; but larger audiences flocked to the Théâtre des Italiens and the Opéra-Comique.

All these theaters, and the Opéra in the Palais-Royal, were spacious el-
lipses, with several tiers of boxes or seats for the perfumed few; less aromatic
spectators stood in the "parterre" (i.e., on the ground), which we misname
the orchestra; no seats were placed there till the Revolution. As many as
150 extra-paying fops or devotees sat on the stage, surrounding the action
on three sides. Voltaire denounced this custom as hampering the players
and destroying the illusion. "Hence it arises that most of our plays are nothing but long discourses; all theatrical action is lost, or, if practiced, appears

ridiculous."[4] How, he asked, could a dramatist represent on such a stage such a scene as Brutus and then Antony addressing the Roman populace after Caesar's assassination? How could the poor Ghost in *Hamlet* peek through these privileged anatomies? Hardly any of Shakespeare's plays could be presented under such conditions.[5] Voltaire's vigorous protests, seconded by Diderot and others, finally had effect, and by 1759 the stages of the French theaters were cleared.

Voltaire had less success in his campaign to improve the theological status of actors. Socially their condition had improved; they were received in aristocratic homes, and in many cases they played at royal command. But the Church still condemned the theater as a school for scandal, held all actors to be *ipso facto* excommunicated, and forbade their burial in consecrated ground—which included every cemetery in Paris. Voltaire pointed the contradiction:

> Actors are paid wages by the King, and excommunicated by the Church; they are ordered by the King to play every evening, and forbidden to play at all by the ritual. If they do not play they are put into prison [as happened when His Majesty's Players went on strike]; if they play they are [at death] cast into the sewers. We delight to live with them, and object to be buried with them; we admit them to our tables, and close our cemeteries to them.[6]

Adrienne Lecouvreur, the greatest French actress of her time, illustrated these antitheses in her life and death. Born near Reims in 1692, she came to Paris at the age of ten. Living near the Théâtre-Français, she found her way into it frequently, and imitated at home the tragediennes whom she admired from the parterre. At fourteen she organized a company of amateurs, which performed on private stages. The actor Le Grand gave her lessons, and secured a place for her in a troupe acting in Strasbourg. For years, like Molière, she played in the provinces, passing from role to role, and doubtless from one romance to another. Longing for love, she found only lechers; two of them in succession left her pregnant and refused her marriage; at eighteen she bore a daughter, at twenty-four another. By 1715 she was back in Paris, for young Voltaire met her there and then, and was for a time something more than a friend.[7] In 1717 she was the leading lady at the Théâtre-Français, the haunt and aspiration of her youth.

Like many famous actresses, she was not particularly beautiful; she was rather stout, and her features were irregular. But she had an indescribable grace in carriage and manners, a seductive music in her voice, a light of fire and feeling in her dark eyes, a mobile and noble expression in her face; her every action expressed personality. She refused to follow the oratorical style of speech that had been made traditional in French acting by the long, rectangular form of the early theaters; she resolved to act her part and speak her lines as naturally on the boards as in real life, except for the distinct articulation and added volume of voice needed to carry her words to the farthest auditors. In her brief career she accomplished a revolution in histrionic art. This was founded also in her depth of feeling, her capacity to convey the passion and tenderness of love, the full pathos or terror of a tragic scene. She excelled in the difficult art of listening actively and expressively while others spoke.

Old men praised her, youths lost their hearts and wits over her. Young Charles Augustin de Ferriol, Comte d'Argental, who was to be the "angel" and agent of Voltaire, developed for her an ardor that alarmed his mother, who, fearing that he would propose marriage and be accepted, vowed to send him to the colonies. When Adrienne heard of this she wrote to Mme. de Ferriol (March 22, 1721) assuring her that she would discourage the youth's addresses:

> I will write to him whatever you please. I will never see him again if you desire it. But do not threaten to send him to the end of the world. He can be useful to his country; he can be the delight of his friends; he will crown you with satisfaction and fame; you have only to guide his talents and let his virtues act.[8]

She was right; d'Argental rose to be a councilor of the Parlement of Paris. In his eighty-fifth year, going through the papers his mother had left, he came upon this letter, of which he had known nothing before.

Adrienne in her turn experienced all the rapture and desolation of love and rejection. Often to her performances came the young Prince Maurice of Saxony, not yet swollen with victories, but so handsome and romantic that when he pledged her his lifelong devotion she thought that this was the hero she had long awaited. (When it comes to pledging lifelong devotion men have as many lives as a cat.) She accepted him as her lover (1721), and for a time they lived in such cooing fidelity that Paris compared them to La Fontaine's amorous turtledoves. But the young soldier, already a *maréchal de camp*, dreamed of kingdoms; we have seen him running off to Kurland to seek a crown, half financed by Adrienne's savings.

She consoled herself in his absence by establishing a salon. It was not without intellectual profit that she had learned the elegance of Racine and the ideas of Molière; she had become one of the best-educated women in France. Her friends were not casual admirers, but men and women who liked her mind. Fontenelle, Voltaire, d'Argental, the Comte de Caylus came regularly to her dinners; and some titled ladies were glad to join that sparkling company.

In 1728 the defeated soldier of fortune returned to Paris. Absence had cooled his glands; he discovered that Adrienne was four years his senior, being now thirty-six; and a dozen rich women were offering to share his bed. One of them was almost as royal as himself, Louise de Lorraine, Duchesse de Bouillon, granddaughter of Poland's noble hero Jan Sobieski. She paraded Maurice so boldly in her box at the Théâtre-Français that Adrienne faced that box when, with some emphasis, she recited angry lines from Racine's *Phèdre:*

> *Je ne suis point de ces femmes hardies*
> *Qui, portant dans le crime une tranquille paix,*
> *Ont su se faire un front qui ne rougit jamais*[9]

—"I am not one of those brazen women who, bringing into crime a [show of] tranquil peace, have learned to put on a front that never blushes with shame."

In July, 1729, Siméon Bouret, abbé and painter of miniatures, informed Mlle. Lecouvreur that two masked agents of a court lady had proposed to him to give the actress some poisoned pills, for which service he was to receive 6,600 livres. Adrienne notified the police. They arrested the abbé and questioned him severely, but he persisted in his story. She wrote a characteristic letter to the *lieutenant* of police, asking him to free the abbé:

> I have talked with him and made him talk often and for a long time, and he always answered connectedly and intelligently. It is not that I wish what he said to be true; I have a hundred times more reason to wish he may be crazy. Ah, would to God I had only to solicit his pardon! But if he is innocent, think, monsieur, what an interest I ought to take in his fate, and how cruel this uncertainty is to me. Do not consider my profession or my birth; deign to see my soul, which is sincere and laid bare in this letter.[10]

The Duc de Bouillon, however, insisted that the abbé should be detained. He was released several months later, still adhering to his story. We do not yet know if it was true.

In February, 1730, Mlle. Lecouvreur began to suffer from a diarrhea that grew daily worse. She continued her roles at the theater, but early in March she had to be carried from the theater in a faint. On March 15, with her last strength, she played Jocaste in Voltaire's *Oedipe*. On the seventeenth she took to her bed, bleeding mortally from severe inflammation of the bowels. The Maréchal no longer came to her; only Voltaire and d'Argental attended her in this tragic and humiliating end. She died on March 20 in Voltaire's arms.*

---

* In 1849 Eugène Scribe and Ernest Legouvé produced in Paris their successful but not quite accurate drama, *Adrienne Lecouvreur;* and in 1902 Francesco Cilèa composed an opera on the same theme.

Since she had refused the last rites of the Church,[11] canon law forbade her burial in consecrated ground. A friend engaged two torchbearers to take her body in a hackney coach and bury her clandestinely on the banks of the Seine, in what became the Rue de Bourgogne. (In that same year 1730 Anne Oldfield, an English actress, was buried with public honors in Westminster Abbey.) Voltaire wrote (1730) a poem, *La Mort de Mademoiselle Lecouvreur*, passionately denouncing the indignity of this burial.

> *Tous les coeurs sont émus de ma douleur mortelle,*
> *J'entends de tous côtés les beaux-arts éperdus*
> *S'écrier en pleurant, "Melpomène n'est plus!"*
> 　　*Que direz-vous, race future,*
> *Lorsque vous apprendrez la flétrissante injure*
> *Qu' à ces arts désolés font des hommes cruels?*
> 　　*Ils privent de la sépulture*
> *Celle qui dans la Grèce aurait eu des autels.*
> *Je les ai vus soumis, autour d'elles empressés;*
> *Sitôt qu'elle n'est plus, elle est donc criminelle!*
> *Elle a charmé le monde, et vous l'en punissez!*
> *Non, ces bords désormais ne seront plus profanes;*
> *Ils contiennent ta cendre, et ce triste tombeau,*
> *Honoré par nos chants, consacré par tes mânes,*
> 　　*Est pour nous un temple nouveau!**

The greatest dramatist of this period was, of course, Voltaire. He had many rivals, among them Prosper Jolyot de Crébillon, an old survival who should have been long since dead. From 1705 to 1711 Crébillon had produced successful plays; then, convinced by the decided failure of his *Xerxès* (1714) and *Sémiramis* (1717) that he was through, he had retired from authorship, and fallen into a poverty consoled in his garret by his tender collection of ten dogs, fifteen cats, and some ravens. In 1745 Mme. de Pompadour rescued him with a pension and a sinecure, and arranged for an edition of his collected works to be published by the government press. He came to Versailles to thank her; ill, she received him while she remained in her bed; as he bent to kiss her hand Louis XV entered. "Madame," cried the septuagenarian, "I am undone; the King has surprised us together."[12] Louis enjoyed this flash of wit, and joined Pompadour in urging him to complete

---

* "All hearts are moved like mine by mortal grief. I hear on every side the distracted arts cry out in tears, 'Melpomene [Muse of tragedy] is no more!' What will you say, you of tomorrow, when you learn the withering injury done by heartless men to these desolated arts? They deprive of burial her who in Greece would have had altars. I have seen them adoring her, crowding about her; hardly is she dead when she becomes a criminal! She charmed the world, and you punish her! No! those banks will never henceforth be profane; they hold your ashes; and this sad tomb will be for us a new temple, honored in our chants, and consecrated by your shades."

his abandoned play on Catiline. She and the court attended and applauded the première (1748), and Crébillon again thrilled with fame and francs. In 1754, aged eighty, he produced his last play. He survived eight years more, happy with his animals.

Voltaire did not enjoy this appearance of a competitor from the grave. But he had also to face, in comedy, the rivalry of the versatile and effervescent Marivaux. Pierre Carlet de Chamblain de Marivaux became a satirist when, by chance, he saw his seventeen-year-old sweetheart practicing her seductive charms before a mirror. His heart was only momentarily sprained, for his father was the rich director of the mint at Riom, and many a young lady yearned to be Pierre's wife. He married for love, and surprised Paris by leading a life of sexual sobriety. He joined the salon of Mme. de Tencin, and may have learned there the gay wit, elegant phrasing, and subtle feeling that went into the *marivaudage* of his plays.

His first success was *Arlequin poli par l'amour*, which ran for twelve successive nights at the Théâtre des Italiens in 1720. Just as he was sipping his royalties he lost most of his money in the crash of Law's bank. We are told that he retrieved his fortune with his pen,[13] writing a long succession of comedies that amused Paris with their graceful badinage and clever plots. The most famous of them, *Le Jeu de l'amour et du hasard* (*The Game of Love and Chance*), turned on the simultaneous but unconcerted resolve of two couples to test the devotion of their as-yet-unseen fiancé(e)s by an exchange of garb and manner between master and man, mistress and maid, developing through a concatenation of coincidences as absurd as Desdemona's handkerchief. The women of Paris were better pleased than the men with the love tangles in these plays, and their tender sentiment. Here too, as in Versailles and the salons, as in Watteau and Boucher, woman ruled, and had the deciding word; and the analysis of feeling replaced the problems of politics and the heroics of war. The masculine comedy of Molière gave way before the feminine comedy that ruled the French stage (barring Beaumarchais) to the days of Scribe, Dumas *fils*, and Sardou.

III. THE FRENCH NOVEL

It was this same Marivaux who gave a new form to the novel in France. In 1731 he published Part I of *La Vie de Marianne*. It was well received; he continued to offer further installments until 1741, when there were eleven; he left it unfinished (though he survived till 1763) because his aim had been not so much to tell a tale as to analyze character, particularly in woman, especially in love. Nothing could be more arresting than the opening scene: a band of robbers hold up a stagecoach, and kill everybody in it except Marianne, who survives to tell the story in her old age. The heroine and supposed author keeps her intriguing anonymity to the end; she transmits the manuscript to a friend with the caution, "Do not forget that you have promised never to say who I am; I wish to be known only to you."[14]

As her parents were among the casualties, Marianne is brought up by a charitable bourgeoise, becomes a salesgirl in a lingerie shop, and swells into charms that arouse M. de Climal. He brings her small gifts, then costly gifts, and soon asks for her person as his reward. She rejects him, and sends back his presents after some hesitations which Marivaux describes with delicate understanding. We should have said that meanwhile she had met Climal's nephew, M. de Valville, who has less money than his uncle, but also less years. Valville, however, keeps Marianne in suspense for a thousand pages, and goes off with another woman; at which point Marivaux's story ends.

This was the outstanding psychological novel of eighteenth-century France, to be rivaled only by Choderlos de Laclos' *Liaisons dangereuses* (1782). It recalled Mme. de La Fayette's *Princesse de Clèves* (1678), hardly equaled it in delicacy of feeling or beauty of style, but surpassed it in the dissection of motive and sentiment. Here is a woman who, like Richardson's Pamela, preserves her honor, but for its marketable worth; she knows that women have only frail and perishable values to offer for the monogamous support of the polygamous male. It is a subtler picture than Richardson's. *Pamela* (1740) was begun nine years after *Marianne*, and may have been influenced by it; in return Richardson's *Clarissa* (1747) helped Rousseau's *La Nouvelle Héloïse*.

Marivaux reflected the sturdy and cautious morals of the middle class; Crébillon *fils* found his interest in the reckless license of the aristocracy. Known as "Crébillon *le gai*" in contrast to his father, "Crébillon *le tragique*" (who called his son the worst of his many productions), Claude Prosper Jolyot de Crébillon grew up in the Paris of the Regency, whose morals quite outweighed his Jesuit education. For several years he shared his father's garret, ravens, dogs, and cats. In 1734, aged twenty-seven, he achieved fame by his novel *L'Écumoire—The Surface-Skimmer;* this might have been the title of all his heroes and books, for in them love, as Chamfort put it, is merely the "contact of two skins."[15] The story was laid in Japan, but it was so transparent a satire on Church and state in France, and on the tiny Duchesse du Maine ("the Fairy Cucumber"), that Cardinal Fleury banished him from Paris for five years.

Returning, the author issued in 1740 his most notorious novel, *Le Sopha*, which earned him a briefer banishment. The scene was Agra, but the morals were Parisian. The "sultan" is bored, and calls for stories. The young courtier Amanzei obliges by telling how, in a previous incarnation, he had been a sofa; and he recalls some of the sins that had tested his springs. The succession of adulteries is increasingly detailed. Crébillon took special delight in the story of Almahide and Mochles, who, after verbose boasting of their chastity, confess that their thoughts are as unchaste as other people's conduct; they conclude that there could be no greater guilt in the action than in the thought; whereupon they suit the deed to the word. This, however, was an exceptional case; Crébillon's women usually require some financial *quid* for their *quo;* so Amina counted her quid carefully, and "complied with her lover's desire only after she had made quite sure that he had not blundered in his arithmetic."[16]

The book had its calculated success, and found readers in many languages, all addicted to irregular conjugations. Laurence Sterne confessed to having been influenced by the novels of Crébillon; Horace Walpole preferred them to Fielding's; the virtuous Thomas Gray's conception of Paradise was "to read eternally new romances by Marivaux and Crébillon."[17] Lady Henrietta Stafford rushed over from England, became Crébillon's mistress, the mother of his child, then his wife; we are told that he "made her a model husband."[18] In 1752 he joined Alexis Piron and Charles Collé in founding the Caveau (Cave), a club for gay wits notable for irreverence and pranks. In 1759, by a *reductio ad absurdum*, he was appointed royal censor of literature; and when, after irritating delays, his father died (1762), the son inherited his pension. All's well that ends well.

Crébillon's books lost their popularity long before his death, but meanwhile a learned cleric had written a novel that still lives and moves today. The life of Antoine François Prévost d'Exiles, known as the Abbé Prévost, was as varied and troubled as the careers that came from his pen. Born in Artois in 1697, educated by the Jesuits, he became a novice in the Jesuit order (1713), left it to join the army, worked his way up to a commission, fell in love, suffered a broken heart, and became a Benedictine monk (1719) and priest (1726). Thenceforth, marvelous to relate, he supported himself almost entirely by his pen.

Even before abandoning monastic life he had begun a romance, *Mémoires et aventures d'un homme de qualité*, of which the first four volumes were published at Paris in 1728. After a year in England he moved to Holland. In 1730 he began to publish a second romance, *Le Philosophe anglais, ou Histoire de Monsieur Cleveland, fils naturel de Cromwell*; this— one of the earliest historical novels—he drew out to eight volumes in the next nine years. In 1731 he published at Amsterdam Volumes V–VII of the *Mémoires*; Volume VII was separately published at Paris (1731) as *Les Aventures du chevalier des Grieux et de Manon Lescaut, par Monsieur D.* It was forbidden by the French government, and entered at once upon its still continuing popularity. "Paris," we are told, "went wild over it; . . . people rushed for the book as if to a fire."[19]

The story of Manon is enclosed in a clumsy mechanism of make-believe. Twelve prostitutes are in a vehicle en route to Le Havre for deportation to America. The Marquis ——, the nameless "man of quality" who is supposed to author all seven volumes of the *Mémoires*, is struck by the beauty of one of the girls, whose face is later described as one "that could bring back the world to idolatry."[20] He sees also the desolate Chevalier des Grieux, who gazes in tears at his former mistress, Manon, and mourns that he is too bankrupt to follow her into exile. The Marquis, doubly touched, gives Des Grieux four louis d'or, which enabled the Chevalier to accompany Manon to Louisiana. Two years later the Marquis sees him at Calais, and takes him home. The remainder of the little volume is Des Grieux's account of his romance.

He was an exemplary, wellborn youth, who excelled in everything at college in Amiens. His parents intended him for the order of the Knights of Malta, and in their fond hopes "they already had me wearing the Cross."[21] But Manon passed by, and all was changed. She was then fifteen; he was seventeen, and "had never given a thought to the difference of the sexes." This arrested development was at once accelerated. Manon tells him that she has been sent to Amiens, against her will, to become a nun. He offers to rescue her; they elope to Paris. Their mutual admiration seemed a sufficient covenant; "we dispensed with the rites of the Church, and found ourselves man and wife without having given it a thought." His brother discovers him, has him arrested, and takes him back to the father, who informs him that Manon has already become the mistress of the banker Monsieur B. Des Grieux proposes to go and kill B.; the father locks up his son. A friend, Tiburge, comes, confirms the claim that Manon is B.'s mistress, and urges Des Grieux to take holy orders. The youth enters the Seminary of St.-Sulpice, and becomes an abbé. "I thought myself absolutely purged from the wickedness of love." Two years later he comes up for public examination and disputation at the Sorbonne. Manon is in the audience; she makes her way to him, confesses her infidelity, but swears that she has sinned with B. only to raise money for Des Grieux. They elope again.

They take a house in suburban Chaillot. They live expensively on the sixty thousand francs received by Manon from Monsieur B.; Des Grieux, dis-abbéed and re-chevaliered, hopes to win forgiveness and francs from his father, or to inherit property on his father's death. They are robbed, and find themselves suddenly penniless. "I realized then that one can love money without being a miser. . . . I knew Manon; . . . however faithful and fond she might be in good fortune, one could not count on her in want. She cared too much for pleasure and plenty to sacrifice them for me."[22] And he loves her more than honor. He lets her brothers teach him how to cheat at cards. He wins a small fortune, but is robbed again. Manon leaves him for a wealthy old voluptuary, explaining in a note, "I am working to make my Chevalier rich and happy." He joins with her in a plot to get money out of the old man; they succeed, abscond, are arrested. She is committed to the common hospital as a prostitute, he is sent to a monastery. From this he escapes by shooting dead the porter who guards the gate. He borrows money and bribes the hospital attendants to let Manon escape. She vows eternal love.

When their funds are exhausted she allows a moneyed heir to set her up as mistress. She is again arrested, and Des Grieux's father persuades the authorities to deport her. Des Grieux attempts to rescue her en route; failing, he embarks with her to New Orleans. There she learns to bear poverty, and to give Des Grieux complete fidelity. They return to the practices of religion. But the colonial governor's son falls in love with her. As she and Des Grieux have still neglected to secure a legal marriage, the governor exercises his right to assign her to any colonist; he bids her accept his son. Des Grieux kills the son in a duel. He and Manon escape from New Orleans into the wilderness, on foot. After weary miles she faints, and dies. "For two days and two nights I stayed with my lips pressed to the face and hands of my dear Manon." He digs her grave there with his hands, buries her, and lies down on the grave to die. But his good friend Tiburge, who meanwhile has come from France, finds him, and takes him back to Calais, to the Marquis, to tell his tale.

Manon Lescaut became the fountainhead of a Mississippi of *romans larmoyants*, romances wet with tears. Every woman, even if she is not "at heart a rake," weeps over Manon's grave and Des Grieux's grief, forgiving her financial stratagems and his caitiff crimes. Prévost struck a new note by endowing his hero and heroine with so many faults; he made them real by baring Manon's supreme love of pleasure, and her lover's capacity for parasitism, cheating, theft, and homicide; she is an old type of heroine, he is assuredly a new type of hero. The book might have reached a starker power had he been left to die on Manon's grave.

Perhaps Prévost told the story with such feeling because he had himself all the ardor of Des Grieux. It was an autobiography before the event. But he was no parasitic idler. He translated the three enormous novels of Richardson into French, and these translations inaugurated in France that craze for Richardson which found such diverse expression in Rousseau and Diderot. He translated Middleton's *Life of Cicero*, and Hume's *History of England*. He wrote several minor novels, and many volumes of the *Histoire générale des voyages*. In 1733, at Amsterdam, he fell in love with another man's mistress. Learning that the Benedictines had secured an order for his imprisonment, he fled to England, taking the lady with him. In London he earned his bread by tutoring. On December 15 he was arrested on a charge

Fig. 46—Unknown artist of the French 18th-century school: *Voltaire*. Château de Versailles

FIG. 47—ENGRAVING AFTER A PAINTING BY DEVERIA: *Montesquieu.* (Bettmann Archive)
PAGE 340

FIG. 48—NICOLAS DE LARGILLIÈRE: *Madame du Châtelet.* Gallery of Fine Arts, Columbus, Ohio (Bettmann Archive) PAGE 365

FIG. 50—MATTHÄUS DANIEL
PÖPPELMANN: *The Zwinger
Palace*, Dresden (Bettmann
Archive)   PAGE 399

FIG. 51 — JOHANN MICHAEL
FISCHER: *The Abbey Church
(Klosterkirche) of the Benedictine Monastery at Otto-
beuren*. (Bettmann Archive)
          PAGE 406

FIG. 52—BALTHASAR NEUMANN: *Staircase of the Prince-Bishop's Residenz*, Würzburg. From Werner Weisbach, *Die Kunst des Barock* (Berlin: Propyläen-Verlag, 1924)   PAGE 405

FIG. 53—JAKOB PRANDTAUER: *The Cloister at Melk.* (Bettmann Archive)
PAGE 432

Fig. 54—Lorenzo Mattielli: *Neptune Fountain*, Dresden (Bettmann Archive)

Fig. 55—Balthasar Permoser: *St. Ambrose*. Museum, Bautzen, Germany
(Bettmann Archive)   PAGE 405

FIG. 56—E. G. HAUSSMANN: *Johann Sebastian Bach*. Thomasschule, Leipzig (Bettmann Archive)   PAGE 412

FIG. 57—ENGRAVING AFTER A PAINTING BY ANTOINE PESNE: *Frederick the Great as a Child of Three, with His Sister Wilhelmine*. Formerly in the Berlin Museum (Bettmann Archive)   PAGES 404, 439

FIG. 58—ENGRAVING AFTER A PAINT-
ING BY CARLE VANLOO: *Frederick
the Great*. (Bettmann Archive)
PAGE 439

FIG. 59—GEORG WENZESLAUS VON
KNOBELSDORFF: *Sanssouci Palace*,
Potsdam (Bettmann Archive)
PAGE 406

Fig. 60—Johann Lukas von Hildebrandt: *Upper Belvedere Palace*, Vienna (Bettmann Archive) PAGE 433

Fig. 61—Johann Bernhard Fischer von Erlach and others: *Schönbrunn Palace*, Vienna. Photograph courtesy of the Austrian State Tourist Office PAGE 433

Fig. 62—*Maria Theresa Monument*, Vienna. Photograph by O. V. W. Hubmann, courtesy of the Austrian State Tourist Office

F<small>IG</small>. 63–J<small>OHANN</small> B<small>ERNHARD</small> F<small>ISCHER</small> <small>VON</small> E<small>RLACH</small> <small>AND</small> <small>HIS</small> <small>SON</small> J<small>OSEF</small> E<small>MANUEL</small>: *Karls-kirche* (*Church of St. Charles*), Vienna (Bettmann Archive)   <small>PAGE</small> 432

FIG. 64—GEORG RAPHAEL DONNER: *Andromeda Fountain*, Vienna (Bettmann Archive)

FIG. 65—JOHANN BERNHARD FISCHER VON ERLACH AND HIS SON JOSEF EMANUEL: *Central Hall, National Library*, Vienna (Bettmann Archive)   PAGE 433

Fig. 66—Daniel Gran: *Cupola Frescoes in the National Library*, Vienna (Bettmann Archive)

Fig. 67—Georg Wenzeslaus von Knobelsdorff: *The Golden Gallery in the Schloss Charlottenburg.* From Max Osborn, *Die Kunst des Rokoko* (Berlin: Propyläen-Verlag, 1926)

PAGE 404

by one of his pupils that he had forged a note for fifty pounds—a crime for which the statutory penalty was death. He was soon released, for reasons unknown. He returned to France (1734) and rejoined the Benedictine order. In 1753 he was appointed to the Priory of St.-Georges-de-Gennes.

His death, ten years later, led to a legend told as fact by his grandniece to Sainte-Beuve: that Prévost was stricken with apoplexy while walking in the woods of Chantilly; that a doctor, thinking him dead, cut him open to find the cause of his death; that Prévost was still alive, but that the post-mortem killed him.[23] The story is now generally rejected.[24]

Prévost's influence was immense. It shared in shaping Rousseau's *La Nouvelle Héloïse*; it moved the tough-minded, tenderhearted Diderot to write sentimental *drames larmoyants*; it took a completely idealistic turn in Bernardin de Saint-Pierre's *Paul et Virginie*; it reappeared in the *Dame aux camélias* (1848) of Dumas *fils*; it played a part in the Romantic movement till Flaubert introduced *Madame Bovary* (1857); and Manon still lives and dies in opera.

IV. MINOR SAGES

Another abbé returns to our story, and this time we must give him his due. We have seen Charles Irénée Castel, Abbé de Saint-Pierre, shocking the diplomats at Utrecht (1712) with *Mémoire pour rendre la paix perpétuelle*, which was to fascinate both Rousseau and Kant. And we have seen him proposing to the Club de l'Entresol a medley of ideas and reforms so advanced that Cardinal Fleury felt inspired to close the club and save the state (1731). What were these ideas?

Like so many rebels, his mind was sharpened by a Jesuit education. It did not take him long to shed the popular faith; and though he continued to profess Catholicism, he did it some sly damage by his *Discourse against Mohammedanism*, in which his arguments, like Voltaire's in *Mahomet*, could readily be applied to orthodox Christianity. His *Physical Explanation* of "the pretended miracles told by Protestants, schismatics, and Mohammedans" was obviously intended to question Catholic miracles as well.

In 1717, and again in 1729, he republished in expanded form his *Projet de paix perpétuelle*. He pleaded with the sovereigns of Europe, including the Sultan, to enter into a sacred pact that would mutually guarantee their present possessions, would renounce war as a means of settling international disputes, and would submit these to a European Union armed with force to compel the acceptance of its decisions. He drew up a model charter for the Union, with rules of procedure for its assembly, and specified the financial contributions to be made to the Union by each member state. He could not be expected to foresee that the Congress of Vienna (1815) would form on these lines a Holy Alliance to perpetuate monarchical and feudal institutions, and suppress all revolutionary movements.

No difficulties could shake the confidence of the resilient abbé. He adopted with religious ardor the rising faith in progress; and in *Observations on the Continuous Progress of Universal Reason* (1737) he proclaimed, long before Condorcet, the indefinite perfectibility of mankind through the agency of reason in scientists and governments. After all, he mused, the human race, on accepted authority, is not more than seven or eight thousand years old; therefore it is only "in the infancy of reason"; what may we not expect of its virile youth six thousand years hence, and of its glorious flowering in the maturity of mankind a hundred thousand years from now?[25]

Saint-Pierre foresaw our modern problem: that while science and knowledge have made immense advances, there has been no commensurate progress in morals or politics; knowledge implements vice as much as it enlightens morality. How could the growth of knowledge be turned to the improvement of conduct in individuals and nations? In *A Project to Perfect the Governments of States* (1737) Saint-Pierre proposed the formation of a Political Academy, to be composed of the wisest men in the land, and to act as an advisory body to the ministers of state in matters of social or moral reform. He made many specific proposals: universal education under governmental (not ecclesiastical) control, religious toleration, marriage of the clergy, the unification of French laws, the promotion of public welfare by the state, and the enlargement of national revenues by progressive taxes on incomes and inheritances.[26] The abbé in 1725 added to the French language the word *bienfaisance*, beneficence, to distinguish the humanitarianism that he preferred to the condescending charities of the Old Regime. And long before Helvétius and Bentham he laid down the utilitarian principle that "the value of a book, of a regulation, of an institution, or of any public work is proportioned to the number and grandeur of the actual pleasures it produces, and of the future pleasures which it is calculated to procure for the greatest number of men."[27] Most of the basic ideas of the *philosophes* appeared as a prelude in Saint-Pierre, even to the hope for an enlightened king as an agent of reform. With all his simplicity, naïveté, and prolixity he was one of the seminal minds of the Enlightenment.

Charles Pinot Duclos must have scorned him as a visionary quite uncongenial to a realistic mind. Born at Dinan in Brittany, he kept to the end the sturdy, cautious, obstinate character of the Breton. Son of a well-to-do bourgeois, and of a mother who died at 101, he had in him the iron to survive his wild youth in the Paris of the Regency. He received his higher education from the Jesuits and the *filles de joie*, sowing wild oats lavishly and sharpening his wit in the cafés. Soon his reputation for repartee gave him access to society and the salons. He added to his fame with a novel, *Histoire de la baronne de Luz* (1741), which was almost an indictment of God. The Baroness repels all other assaults upon her marital fidelity, but yields herself to a corrupt magistrate to save the life of her husband, implicated in a conspiracy against the King. She is twice raped. In hysterical anger she cries out, "Cruel Heaven! In what way have I deserved your hatred? Can it be that virtue is hateful to you?"[28]

Despite the tenor and eroticism of this book Duclos was elected to the Academy in 1746 through the influence of Mme. de Pompadour. He entered vigorously into its operations, reorganized it, and brought it into vitalizing touch with the literature and philosophy of the time. In 1751 he succeeded Voltaire as historiographer to the King; in 1754 he maneuvered the election of d'Alembert to the Academy; in 1755 he was elected its permanent secretary, and remained its dominating spirit till his death. He won the Academy to liberal ideas, but he deplored the precipitancy of d'Holbach, Helvétius, and Diderot. "This band of little atheists," he said, "will end by driving me back to the confessional."

We remember him chiefly for his *Considérations sur les moeurs de ce siècle* (1750),* a work of calm and often penetrating analysis of French morals and character. Written before he was forty-five, it begins with the solemnity of a senile sage: "I have lived; I wish to be useful to those who shall live." He regrets that "the most civilized peoples are not also the most virtuous."

> The happiest epoch would be that in which virtue would not be considered a merit. When it begins to be remarked, manners are already altered; and if it becomes an object of ridicule, that is the last stage of corruption.[29]

"The great defect of the Frenchman," in his judgment, "is to have always a youthful character; thereby he is often amiable, rarely stable; he has almost no age of maturity, but passes from youth to decrepitude. . . . The Frenchman is the child of Europe"[30]—just as Paris is its playground. Duclos does not entirely sympathize with the Age of Reason, which he feels swirling around him: "I am not sure that I have too high an opinion of my century, but it seems to me that a certain fermentation of reason tends to develop everywhere."[31]

---

* This was followed in 1751 by *Mémoires pour servir de suite aux Considérations*. Duclos' *Mémoires secrets sur les règnes de Louis XIV et de Louis XV* was not published till 1791. Part of this was translated into English as *Secret Memoirs of the Regency*.

We declaim a great deal in these days against prejudices; perhaps we
have too much destroyed them. Prejudice is a kind of common law
among men. . . . In this matter I cannot avoid blaming those writers
who, . . . wishing to attack a superstition (a motive that could be
praiseworthy and useful if the discussion were kept on a philosophical
plane), sap the foundations of morality and weaken the bonds of society. . . . The sad effect which they produce on their readers is to
make, of the young, bad citizens and scandalous criminals, and to engender unhappiness in old age.[32]

Grimm, the Parisian correspondent of foreign dignitaries, was one of
many who resented these delicate aspersions on philosophy by one who had
sampled many bosoms—"When one has a cold heart and a spoiled taste, he
should not write on morals and the arts";[33] but Grimm had been Duclos'
rival for the favors of Mme. d'Épinay. The *Mémoires* of that tender lady
picture Duclos as rough and tyrannical in possession, and coarsely bitter in
defeat; but Grimm edited those *Mémoires*. If we may believe these hot and
tearful pages, Madame drove Duclos from her home as a treacherous satyr.
The learned Academician wandered to other beds and other lands, and so,
at sixty-seven, to death.

Luc de Clapiers, Marquis de Vauvenargues, was more lovable. At the age
of eighteen he joined the army, drunk with Plutarch and with ambition to
earn glory in the service of the King. He took part in the disastrous adventure of Maréchal de Belle-Isle in the Bohemian campaign of 1741–43; in the
bitter retreat from Prague his legs were frozen; he fought at Dettingen
(1743), but his health was so impaired that he was soon afterward retired
from the army. He sought employment as a diplomat, and through Voltaire's help was on the point of securing it, when an attack of smallpox disfigured his face. His eyesight began to fail, and a chronic consumptive
cough disabled him from active life.

Books became his consolation. After all, he said, "the best things are the
most common; you can purchase the mind of Voltaire for a crown."[34] He
warned against judging books by their weight; "even the best authors talk
too much," and many are ponderously obscure; "clearness is the ornament
of deep thought."[35] The volume that he himself sent to the press in 1746 was
a seventy-five-page *Introduction à la connoissance de l'esprit humain*, followed by 607 *réflexions et maximes* in 115 pages. A year later, in a dingy
Paris hotel, he died, aged thirty-two, the Mozart and Keats of French
philosophy.

"Philosophy," said Vauvenargues, "has its fashions, like dress, music, and
architecture."[36] His own ideas took little color from his time. Only a few

years before Rousseau's idealization of nature and equality, he pictured "nature" as a brutal struggle for power, and equality as a delusion.

> Among kings, among peoples, among individuals, the stronger gives himself rights over the weaker, and the same rule is followed by animals and inanimate beings, so that everything in the universe is executed by violence; and this order, which we blame with some semblance of justice, is the most general law, the most immutable, and the most important in nature.[37]

All men are born unfree and unequal.

> It is not true that equality is a law of nature. Nature has made nothing equal; her sovereign law is subordination and dependence. . . . He who is born to obey will obey even on the throne.[38]

As for free will, that too is a myth. "The will is never the first cause of an action, it is the last spring." If you give the classic instance of free will, that you can choose odd or even "at will," Vauvenargues replies: "If I choose even, it is because the necessity of making a choice offers itself to my thought at the instant that 'even' is present to it."[39] The belief in God, however, is indispensable; only through that faith, Vauvenargues felt, could life and history have any meaning other than everlasting strife and final defeat.[40] The most individual feature of Vauvenargues' philosophy is his defense of the passions. They must not be destroyed, for they are the root of personality, genius, and all vigor of thought.

> The mind is the eye of the soul, but not its force. Its force is in the heart; that is to say, in the passions. The most enlightened reason does not give us the power to act and to will. . . .[41] Great thoughts come from the heart. . . . Perhaps we owe to the passions the greatest accomplishments of the intellect. . . .[42] Reason and feeling advise and supplement each other turn by turn. Whoever consults only one of them, and renounces the other, foolishly deprives himself of a part of the resources given us for our conduct.[43]

Vauvenargues admitted the pervasiveness of self-love, but refused to consider it a vice, since it is the first necessity of nature's first law, self-preservation. Neither is ambition a vice, it is a necessary spur; "the love of glory makes great careers of nations."[44] He adds that "one is not born to glory if he does not recognize the value of time."[45] There are real vices, however, which must be controlled by laws and moral codes; and "the science of government lies in guiding them [vices] to the public good."[46] There are real virtues too, and "the first days of spring have less grace and charm than the growth of virtue in a youth."[47]

Despite his concessions to Hobbes and La Rochefoucauld, and despite his own experience of evil in life, Vauvenargues kept his faith in mankind. Said his friend Marmontel:

> He knew the world and did not despise it. Friend of men, he ranked vice among the misfortunes [rather than among the crimes] of men, and pity held in his heart the place of indignation and hatred. . . . He never humiliated anyone. . . . An unalterable serenity concealed his pains from the eyes of his friends. To sustain adversity one needed only his example; seeing the equanimity of his spirit, we did not dare be unhappy before him.[48]

Voltaire described him as "the most unfortunate of men, and the most tranquil."[49]

One of the most gracious aspects of French literature in the eighteenth century is the warm sympathy and friendly aid that Voltaire, apostle of reason, extended to Vauvenargues, defender of Pascal and the "heart." The youthful philosopher confessed his admiration for "a man who honors our century, and who is not less great, nor less celebrated, than his predecessors."[50] And the older man wrote to him in a moment of modesty: "If you had been born a few years earlier, my writings would have had more worth."[51] The most eloquent passage in all the hundred volumes of Voltaire is his funeral eulogy of Vauvenargues.[52]

V. MONTESQUIEU: 1689–1755

1. Persian Letters

Voltaire found it harder to like Montesquieu, for *The Spirit of Laws* (1748) was generally rated the greatest intellectual production of the age. It appeared when its author was fifty-nine; it was the fruit of fifty years of experience, forty years of study, twenty of composition.

Charles Louis de Secondat, Baron de La Brède et de Montesquieu, was born at La Brède, near Bordeaux in the country of Montaigne, on January 18, 1689. He boasted good-humoredly of descent from those Goths who, after conquering the Roman Empire, "established everywhere monarchy and liberty."[53] In any case he belonged to the nobility, both of sword and of robe: his father was chief justice at Guienne, and his mother brought as her dowry the castle and domain of La Brède. At the moment of his birth a beggar presented himself at the castle gate; he was brought in and fed, and was made the godfather of the child, allegedly in the hope that Charles would never forget the poor.[54] The boy's first three years were spent at nurse among the village peasants. At eleven he was sent to the college of the Oratorians at Juilly, twenty miles from Paris. At sixteen he returned to Bordeaux to study law; at nineteen he received his law degree.

The death of his father (1713) left him, at twenty-four, considerable property and moderate wealth; he was to speak frequently of "my domain" and "my vassals,"[55] and we shall find him firmly upholding feudalism. A year later he was admitted to the Bordeaux Parlement as a councilor and magistrate. In 1716 his uncle, who had bought the presidency of the Parlement, bequeathed to him his fortune and his office. Later Montesquieu would defend "the sale of employments" as "good in monarchical states, because it makes it the profession of persons of family to undertake tasks which they would not assume from disinterested motives alone."[56] While retaining the presidency of the Parlement, he spent most of his time in study. He made experiments, presented papers on physics and physiology to the Academy of Bordeaux, and planned a "geological history of the earth." He never wrote it, but the material he gathered for it forced its way into *The Spirit of Laws*.

He was thirty-two when he caught the mood and ear of Regency Paris with the most brilliant of his books. He did not give his name to the *Lettres persanes* (1721), for it contained passages hardly becoming a magistrate. Probably he took its scheme from *L'Espion du Grand Seigneur* (1684) of Giovanni Marana, in which an imaginary Turkish spy reported to the sultan, with some fetching ribaldry, the absurd beliefs and behavior of the Christians of Europe, and the delightful or murderous contrasts between Christian professions and practices. A similar device of picturing Occidental civilization as seen through Oriental eyes had been used in Addison's *Spectator*; Charles Dufresny, in *Amusements sérieux et comiques*, had conceived the comments of a Siamese in Paris; Nicolas Gueudeville had shown French customs as seen by an American Indian. Antoine Galland's translation of the *Arabian Nights—Mille et une Nuits* (1704–17)—had sharpened French interest in Mohammedan life; so had the travelogues of Jean (Sir John) Chardin and Jean Tavernier. From March to July, 1721, the Turkish ambassador treated Paris to the exotic charm of his dress and ways. Paris was ready for the *Lettres persanes*. Eight editions were sold out within a year.

Montesquieu presented the letters as written by Rica and Usbek, two Persians traveling in France, and by their correspondents in Isfahan. The letters did not merely expose the foibles and prejudices of the French; they revealed also, through the writers themselves, the absurdities of Oriental conduct and creeds; laughing at these faults, the reader was compelled to accept with good grace the ridicule of his own. It was done with so light a touch—who could take offense at these unconscious epigrams, these rapier thrusts with politely buttoned foils? Moreover, certain of the letters contained alluring confidences from Usbek's seraglio in Isfahan. Zachi, his favorite, writes to tell him how painfully she misses his passion; and Rica describes a Mohammedan lady's conception of Paradise as a place where every good woman has a harem of handsome and virile men. Here Montesquieu let himself go into details in the reckless style of the Regency.

Only during that interregnum could the political and religious heresies of the *Lettres* have escaped official rebuke. The old King was dead, the new one was a boy, the Regent was tolerant and gay; now Montesquieu could make his Persians laugh at a "magician" ruler who made people believe that paper was money (Law's System had just crashed).[57] He could expose the corruption of the court, the idleness of spendthrift nobles, the maladministration of state finances. He could praise the ancient republics of Greece and Rome, and the modern republics of Holland and Switzerland. "Monarchy," says Usbek, "is an abnormal condition which always degenerates into despotism."[58] (See below for a different view.)

In Letters XI–XIV Usbek illustrates the nature of man and the problem of government by telling of the Troglodytes, whom he conceives to be Arabian descendants of the Troglodytai described by Herodotus[59] and Aristotle[60] as bestial tribes living in Africa.* Usbek's Troglodytes, resenting governmental interference, killed thinking magistrates, and lived in a paradise of *laissez-faire*. Every seller took advantage of the consumer's need, and raised the price of the product. When a strong man stole the wife of a weak man there was no law or magistrate to appeal to. Murder, rape, and robbery went unpunished except by private violence. When the inhabitants of the highlands suffered from drought, the lowlanders let them starve; when the lowlanders suffered from flood the highlanders let them starve. Soon the tribe died out. Two families survived by emigration; they practiced mutual aid, raised their children in religion and virtue, and "looked upon themselves as one single family; their flocks were almost always intermixed."[61] But as they increased in number they found their customs inadequate to govern them; they chose a king, and submitted to laws. Usbek's conclusion: government is necessary, but fails in its function if it is not based on virtue in ruler and ruled.

The religious heresies in the *Persian Letters* were more startling than the political. Rica observes that Negroes conceive God as black and the Devil as white; he suggests (like Xenophanes) that if triangles confabulated a theology, God would have three sides and sharp points. Usbek marvels at

---

* The word originally meant cave dwellers; literally, those who dig holes and live in them, like our political opponents.

the power of another magician, called pope, who persuades people to believe that bread is not bread, and wine is not wine, "and a thousand things
of a like nature."[62] He laughs at the conflict between Jesuits and Jansenists.
He is horrified by the Spanish and Portuguese Inquisition, where "der-
vishes [Dominican monks] cause men to be burned as they would burn
straw."[63] He smiles at rosaries and scapulars. He wonders how long the
Catholic countries can survive in competition with Protestant peoples, for
he thinks that the prohibition of divorce, and the celibacy of nuns and
monks, will retard the growth of population in France, Italy and Spain
(*cf.* twentieth-century Ireland); at this rate, Usbek calculates, Catholicism
in Europe cannot last five hundred years more.[64]* Moreover, these idle and
supposedly continent monks "hold in their hands almost all the wealth of
the state. They are a miserly crew, always getting and never giving; they
are continually hoarding their income to acquire capital. All this wealth
falls as it were into a palsy; it is not circulated; it is not employed in trade,
industry, or manufactures."[66] Usbek is troubled by the thought that Europe's benighted infidels, who worship Christ instead of Allah and Mo-
hammed, seem all destined to hell, but he has some hope that ultimately
they will accept Islam and be saved.[67]

Usbek, in a transparent parable, considers the Revocation (1685) of
Henry IV's tolerant Edict of Nantes:

> You know, Mirza, that some ministers of Shah Suleiman [Louis
> XIV] formed the design of obliging all the Armenians of Persia [the
> Huguenots] to quit the kingdom or become Mohammedans [Catho-
> lics], in the belief that our empire will continue polluted as long as it
> retains within its bosom these infidels. . . . The persecution of the
> Ghebers by our zealous Mohammedans has obliged them to fly in
> crowds into the Indies, and has deprived Persia of that people which
> labored so heartily. . . . Only one thing remained for bigotry to do,
> and that was to destroy industry, with the result that the Empire
> [France in 1713] fell of itself, carrying along with it that very religion
> which they wished to advance.
>
> If unbiased discussion were possible, I am not sure, Mirza, that it
> would not be a good thing for a state to have several religions. . . .
> History is full of religious wars; but . . . it is not the multiplicity of
> religions which has produced wars; it is the intolerant spirit animating
> that one which believed itself in the ascendant.[68]

The ideas of the *Persian Letters* seem trite to us now, but when they
were expressed they were for the author a matter of life and death, at least

---

* Montesquieu thought, in 1721, that the population of Europe was hardly a tenth of
what it had been under the Roman Empire,[65] that it would continue to decrease, and that
Negroes would soon die out in America. *Caveat vates.*

of imprisonment or banishment; they are trite now because the fight for freedom to express ideas was won. Because the *Lettres persanes* opened a way, Voltaire was able, thirteen years later, to issue his *Lettres sur les Anglais*, putting an English torch to French debris; these two books announced the Enlightenment. Montesquieu and his liberty survived his book because he was a noble and the Regent was tolerant. Even so he did not dare acknowledge his authorship, for there were some disapproving voices amid the general acclaim. D'Argenson, who himself would later criticize the government, thought "these are reflections of a kind which a witty man can easily make, but which a prudent man ought never allow to be printed." And the cautious Marivaux added: "A man must be sparing of his wit on such subjects." Montesquieu recalled: "When I had in some degree gained the esteem of the public, that of the official classes was lost, and I met with a thousand slights."[69]

Nevertheless he came to Paris to sip his fame in society and the salons. Mme. de Tencin, the Marquise de Lambert and the Marquise du Deffand all opened their hearths. Having left his wife behind at La Brède, he had no difficulty falling in love with the ladies of Paris. He aimed high—at Marie Anne de Bourbon, sister of the Duc de Bourbon who became prime minister in 1723. For her, we are told, he composed a little prose poem, *Le Temple de Gnide* (1725), ecstatic with love. He anointed its wantonness by pretending that it was a translation from the Greek, and so obtained royal permission to print it. He pulled wires—especially those of Mme. de Prie—to secure admission to the Academy; the King objected that he was not a resident of Paris; he hurried to Bordeaux, resigned his presidency of its Parlement (1726), returned to Paris, and joined the Forty Immortals in 1728.

In April he set out on a tour that took three years and covered parts of Italy, Austria, Hungary, Switzerland, the Rhineland, Holland, and England. He remained in England eighteen months (November, 1729, to August, 1731). There he formed a friendship with Chesterfield and other notables, was elected to the Royal Society of London and initiated into Freemasonry, was received by George II and Queen Caroline, attended Parliament, and fell in love with what he thought was the British constitution. Like Voltaire he went back to France strong in the admiration for liberty, yet sobered by contact with the problems of government. He retired to La Brède, transformed his park into an English garden, and, except for occasional trips to Paris, gave himself up to the researches and writings that occupied the rest of his life.

2. Why Rome Fell

In 1734 he issued, unsigned but acknowledged, *Considérations sur les causes de la grandeur des Romains et de leur décadence*. He had submitted the manuscript to a Jesuit scholar, and had consented to eliminate passages that might give umbrage to the Church. The book did not and could not repeat the success of the *Lettres persanes;* it contained no indecencies, it dealt with a remote and complex subject, it was relatively conservative in politics and theology. Radicals did not relish the emphasis on moral decay as a cause of national decline, and they were not ready to appreciate the terse wisdom of such sentences as: "Those who have ceased to fear power can still respect authority."[70] Today the little treatise is looked upon as a pioneer attempt at a philosophy of history, and as a classic of French prose, recalling Bossuet but adding brilliance to gravity.

The subject invited the historian-philosopher, for it involved the whole gamut of a great civilization from birth to death, and exposed in broad scope and illuminating detail one of the basic processes of history—the dissolution that seems fated to follow any full evolution in individuals, religions, and states. Already there was a suspicion that France, after the collapse of *le grand siècle*, had entered upon a long period of decay in empire, morals, literature, and art; the profane trinity of Voltaire, Diderot, and Rousseau had not yet appeared to challenge the intellectual supremacy of the seventeenth century. But the rising courage of the new age showed in the fact that Montesquieu, in explaining the course of history, considered only earthly causes, and quietly set aside, except for incidental obeisance, the Providence which, in Bossuet's *Discours sur l'histoire universelle* (1681), had guided all events to divinely determined results. Montesquieu proposed to seek laws in history as Newton had sought them in space:

> It is not Fortune who governs the world, as we see from the history of the Romans. . . . There are general causes, moral or physical, which operate in every monarchy, raise it, maintain it, or overthrow it. All that occurs is subject to these causes; and if a particular cause, like the accidental result of a battle, has ruined a state, there was a general cause which made the downfall of this state ensue from a single battle. In a word, the principal movement [*l'allure principale*] draws with it all the particular occurrences.[71]

Consequently Montesquieu reduced the role of the individual in history. The individual, however great his genius, is but an instrument of the "general movement"; his importance is due not to his surpassing ability so much as to his falling in with what Hegel was to call the *Zeitgeist*, or spirit of the time. "If Caesar and Pompey had thought like Cato [had striven to preserve the powers of the Roman Senate], others would have come to the same ideas [to subordinate the Senate] as those of Caesar and Pompey, and the Republic, destined to perish [from internal causes] would have been led to ruin by some other hand."[72]

But this "destiny" was no mystical guidance or metaphysical force; it was a complex of factors producing the "principal movement"; and the main function of the philosophical historian, in Montesquieu's view, is to ferret out each such factor, analyze it, and show its operation and relations. So the decline of Rome (he thought) was due first of all to a change from a republic—in which there had been a division and balance of powers—to an empire better fitted to govern dependencies, but so centering all rule in one city and one man as to destroy the liberty and vigor of the citizens and the provinces. To this prime cause were added other factors in the course of time: the spread of supine servility among the masses; the desire of the poor to be supported by the state; the weakening of character by wealth, luxury, and license; the influx of aliens unformed by Roman traditions and ready to sell their votes to the highest bidder; the corruption of central and provincial administrators; the depreciation of currency; the excess of taxation; the abandonment of farms; the sapping of martial virility by new religions and a long peace; the failure of military discipline; the ascendancy of the army over the civilian government; the preference of the army for making or unmaking emperors in Rome rather than for defending the frontiers from barbarian invasion . . . Perhaps in reaction against the supernatural emphasis in Bossuet, Montesquieu made little account of those changes in religion which Gibbon was to stress as a main cause of the imperial collapse.

But always Montesquieu came back to what he considered the prime factor in Rome's decadence—the passage from republic to monarchy. By their republican maxims the Romans conquered a hundred peoples; but by the time they had accomplished this the republic could not subsist; and the maxims of the new government, contrary to those of the republic, caused the decline.[73] However, when we go back to Chapter VI, and examine the *maximes*, or methods, by which the Roman Republic conquered "all the peoples," we find a strange assortment: deceit, broken treaties, force, severe punishments, division of the enemy for piecemeal conquest (*divide et impera*), forcible reshuffling of populations, subverting resistant governments by subsidizing internal revolts, and other procedures familiar to statesmen. "The Romans used their allies to destroy an enemy, and then soon destroyed the destroyers."[74] Apparently forgetting this description of republican maxims, or swallowing Machiavelli at one gulp, Montesquieu, in

Chapter XVIII, held up the Republic as an ideal of greatness, and deplored the Empire as a gay landslide to dissolution. Yet he recognized the corruption of politics in the Republic, and the political splendor of the Empire under "the wisdom of Nerva, the glory of Trajan, the valor of Hadrian, and the virtue of the two Antonines";[75] here Montesquieu gave a lead to Gibbon and Renan in naming that period the noblest and happiest in the history of government. In those philosopher-kings too Montesquieu found the ethics of the Stoics, which he clearly preferred to the Christian. His admiration for the Romans of the Republic passed down to the French enthusiasts of the Revolution, and shared in changing French government, martial methods, and art.

The book had some faults of a scholarship made hasty by the press of time and the call of a larger task. Montesquieu was sometimes uncritical in his use of classical texts; so, for example, he took as history Livy's chapters on Rome's beginnings, whereas Valla, Glareanus, Vico, and Pouilly had already rejected that account as legend. He underestimated the economic factors behind the politics of the Gracchi and Caesar. But against these shortcomings a larger view ranges the eloquence, vigor, and concentration of the style, the depth and originality of the thought, the bold attempt to see in one perspective the rise and fall of a complete civilization, and to elevate history from a record of details to the analysis of institutions and the logic of events. Here was a challenge to historians, which Voltaire and Gibbon would seek to meet; and here was that longing for a philosophy of history which Montesquieu himself, after a generation of labor, would try to satisfy with *The Spirit of Laws*.

3. *The Spirit of Laws*

Fourteen years passed between the *Considérations* and *L'Esprit des lois*. Montesquieu had begun his chef-d'oeuvre about 1729, aged forty; the essay on Rome was a by-product and interruption. In 1747, aged fifty-six, he grew tired of the toil, and was tempted to abandon it: "Often have I begun this work, and often have I laid it aside. I have a thousand times cast to the winds the leaves that I had written."[76] He appealed to the Muses to sustain him: "I am running a long course, I am weighed down with sadness and weariness. Pour into my soul the persuasive charm that once I knew, but which now flies from me. You are never so divine as when you lead us *through pleasure* to wisdom and truth."[77] They must have responded, for he carried on. When at last the task was done, he confessed his hesitations and his pride:

I have followed my object without forming a plan; I have known neither rule nor exceptions; I have found the truth only to lose it again. But when I once discovered my principles, everything I sought for came to me; and in the course of twenty years I have seen my work begun, growing up, advancing toward completion, and finished. . . . If this work meets with success I shall owe it chiefly to the grandeur and majesty of the subject. However, I do not think that I have been totally deficient in genius. . . . When I have seen what so many great men in both France and Germany have written [on this subject] before me, I have been lost in admiration, but I have not lost my courage; I have said with Correggio, "And I too am a painter."[78]

He showed the manuscript to Helvétius, Hénault, and Fontenelle. Fontenelle thought the treatise lacked *le bon genre* of French style;[79] Helvétius begged the author not to ruin his reputation as a liberal by publishing a book so lenient to many conservative beliefs.[80] Montesquieu judged these cautions irrelevant, and proceeded to print. Fearing the French censorship, he sent the manuscript to Geneva; it was published there in 1748 in two volumes, unsigned. When the French clergy had ferreted out its heresies they condemned it, and a government order forbade its distribution in France. In 1750 Malesherbes—future savior of the *Encyclopédie*—became censor, removed the prohibition, and the book rapidly made its way. Twenty-two editions were printed in two years, and soon the work was translated into all the languages of Christian Europe.

Titles in Montesquieu's time were honestly, often laboriously, explanatory. So he called his book *On the Spirit of Laws, or On the Relations Which Must Exist between the Laws and the Constitution of Each Government, the Manners, Climate, Religion, Commerce, etc*. It was an essay on the relations between physical forces and social forms, and on the interrelations among the components of civilization. It tried to lay the foundations for what we should now call "scientific" sociology: to make possible —after the manner of research in the natural sciences—verifiable conclusions illuminating present society and conditionally predicting the future. It was, of course, too much for one man to accomplish in the brevity of life and the existing state of ethnology, jurisprudence, and historiography.

More specifically, Montesquieu's thesis was that "the spirit of laws"—i.e., their origin, character, and tendency—is determined first by the climate and soil of the habitat, and then by the physiology, economy, government, religion, morals, and manners of the people. He began with a broad definition: "Laws, in their most general signification, are the necessary relations arising from the nature of things"; obviously he wished to bring the "natural laws" of the physical world, and the assumed regularities in history, under one general concept. Following Grotius, Pufendorf, and other predecessors, he distinguished several kinds of laws: (1) natural law, which he defined as "human reason so far as it governs all the peoples of the earth"[81]— i.e., the "natural rights" of all men as beings endowed with reason; (2) the law of nations in their relations with one another; (3) political law, governing the relations between the individual and the state; and (4) civil law— the relations of individuals with one another.

In the early stages of human society, Montesquieu thought, the basic determinant of laws is the physical character of the terrain. Is it jungle, desert, or arable? Is it inland or coastal? Is it mountainous or plain? What is the quality of the soil, and the nature of the food it yields? In a word, climate is the first, and at first the most powerful, factor in determining a people's economy, its laws, and its "national character." (Bodin in the sixteenth century anticipated, and Buckle in the nineteenth followed, Montesquieu in this initial emphasis.) For example, consider the climatic, and consequent human, differences between north and south:

> People are more vigorous in cold climates. . . . This superiority of strength must produce various effects: for instance, a greater boldness, i.e., more courage; a greater sense of superiority, i.e., less desire of revenge; a greater sense of security, i.e., more frankness, less suspicion, policy, and cunning. . . . I have been at the opera in England and in Italy, where I have seen the same pieces and the same performers; and yet the same music produced such different effects on the two nations; one is so cold and phlegmatic, and the other so lively and enraptured. . . . If we travel toward the north we meet with people who have few vices, many virtues. . . . If we draw near the south we fancy ourselves entirely removed from the verge of morality; here the strongest passions are productive of all manner of crimes, each man endeavoring, let the means be what they will, to indulge his inordinate desires. . . .
> In warm countries the aqueous part of the blood loses itself greatly by perspiration; it must therefore be supplied by a like liquid. Water is there of admirable uses; strong liquors would congeal the globules of the blood which remains after the transuding of the aqueous humor. In cold countries the aqueous part of the blood is very little evacuated by perspiration. They must therefore make use of spirituous liquors, without which the blood would congeal. . . . The law of Mohammed, which prohibits the drinking of wine, is therefore fitted to the climate of Arabia. . . . The law which forbade the Carthaginians to drink wine was a law of the climate. Such a law would be improper for cold countries, where the climate seems to force them to a kind of national intemperance. . . . Drunkenness predominates . . . in proportion to the coldness and humidity of the climate.[82]

Or consider the relations between climate and marriage:

Women, in hot countries, are marriageable at eight, nine, or ten years of age. . . . They are old at twenty; their reason, therefore, never accompanies their beauty. When beauty demands the empire, the want of reason forbids the claim; when reason is obtained, beauty is no more. These women ought then to be in a state of dependency, for reason cannot procure in old age that empire which even youth and beauty could not give. It is therefore extremely natural that in these places a man, when no law opposes it, should leave one wife to take another, and that polygamy should be introduced.

In temperate climates, where the charms of women are best preserved, where they arrive later at maturity, and have children at a more advanced stage of life, the old age of their husbands in some degree follows theirs; and as they have more reason and knowledge at the time of marriage [than their semitropical analogues] . . . it must naturally introduce a kind of equality between the sexes, and in consequence of this, the law of having only one wife. . . . That is the reason why Mohammedanism [with polygamy] was so easily established in Asia, and with such difficulty extended in Europe; why Christianity is maintained in Europe, and has been destroyed in Asia; and, in fine, why the Mohammedans have made such progress in China, and the Christians so little.[83]

At this point Montesquieu realizes that he has replaced Bossuet's Providence with climate, and hastens to add, for God's sake, a saving caution: "Human reasons, however, are subordinate to that Supreme Cause who does whatever He pleases, and renders everything subordinate to His will." Some Jesuits thought that they saw Montesquieu's tongue in his cheek.

He soon resumed his reckless generalizations. In the "East" (Turkey, Persia, India, China, Japan) the climate compels the seclusion of women, for "the hot airs inflame the passions," and would endanger polygamy as well as monogamy if the sexes were as free to mingle as "in our northern countries, where the manners of women are naturally good, where all the passions are calm, where love rules over the heart with so regular and gentle an empire that the least degree of prudence is sufficient to conduct it."[84] "It is a happiness to live in those climates which permit such freedom of converse, where the sex which has most charms seems to embellish society, and where wives, reserving themselves for the pleasure of one, contribute to the amusement of all."[85]

Customs are more directly the result of climate than laws are, for laws must sometimes seek to counter the effects of climate. As civilization advances, climatic factors are and must be more and more controlled by moral or legal restraints, as in the Oriental seclusion of women. And the wisest legislators aim to balance "physical causes." Customs are a function of place and time; none is in itself right or wrong or best. By and large, custom is the best law, since it is a natural adaptation of character to situation. We must move slowly in trying to change a custom. Usually a custom refuses to be changed by a law.[86]

Since habitat determines custom, which determines national character, the form of government will vary with the complex of all three. In general it will depend upon the extent of the area ruled: a republic comports with a small territory, whose leading citizens can assemble in one place for deliberation or action; if the area expands it will require more laws and wars, and will submit to monarchical rule. Monarchy passes into despotism when it governs too much terrain; for only despotic power can keep under subjection the local rulers of distant provinces.[87] A monarchy must rest on "honor"; i.e., its population must be ranged in ranks, and its citizens must be zealous for distinction and preference. A republic must rest on a wide dissemination of "virtue," which Montesquieu defines in his own way as "the love of one's country—i.e., the love of equality."[88]

A republic may be either an aristocracy or a democracy, according as it is ruled by only a part of the citizenry or by all. Montesquieu admires Venice as an aristocratic republic, and the ancient city-states as democracies; he knows but ignores the fact that in these the enfranchised citizens were only a minority. He praises the rule established by William Penn in America, and, still more enthusiastically, the theocratic communism organized by the Jesuits in Paraguay.[89] To be real, however, an honest democracy must provide economic as well as political equality; it should regulate inheritances and dowries, and progressively tax wealth.[90] The best republics are those in which the people, recognizing their incapacity to wisely determine policy, accept the policies adopted by the representatives whom they have chosen.

> A democracy should aim at equality, but it can be ruined by a spirit of extreme equality, when each citizen would fain be on a level with those whom he has chosen to command him. . . . Where this is the case virtue can no longer subsist in the republic. The people are desirous of exercising the functions of the magistrates, who cease to be revered. The deliberations of the senate are slighted; all respect is then laid aside for the senators, and consequently for old age. If there is no more respect for old age, there will be none presently for parents; deference to husbands will be likewise thrown off, and submission to masters. This license will soon become general. . . . The people fall into this misfortune when those in whom they confided, desirous of concealing their corruption, endeavor to corrupt them. . . . The people will divide the public money among themselves, and, having

added the administration of affairs to their indolence, will be for blend-
ing their poverty with the amusement of luxury.[91]

And so, says the Baron, echoing Plato across two thousand years, democracy falls into chaos, invites dictatorship, and disappears.

There are many passages in Montesquieu that favor an aristocratic republic, but he so feared the despotism that he thought potential in democracy that he was willing to put up with monarchy if it ruled by established
laws. The shortest chapter in his book is on despotism, and consists of three
lines: "When the savages of Louisiana desire fruit, they cut the tree to the
root and gather the fruit. This is a symbol of despotic government";[92] i.e.,
the despot cuts down the ablest families to safeguard his power. The examples Montesquieu gave were safely Oriental, but he was apparently fearful
that the Bourbon monarchy was tending toward despotism, now that Cardinal Richelieu and Louis XIV had destroyed the political power of the
aristocracy. He spoke of the Cardinal as "bewitched with the love of despotic power."[93] As a French noble he strongly resented the reduction of his
class to mere courtiers of the king. He believed that "intermediate, subordinate, and dependent powers" were necessary to a healthy monarchy; and
by these powers he meant the landed nobility and the hereditary magis-
tracy, to both of which he belonged. So he defended feudalism at great
length (173 pages), sacrificing the unity and symmetry of his book. Alone
among the philosophers of eighteenth-century France he spoke with respect
of the Middle Ages, and made *Gothic* a term of praise. In the conflict that
continued throughout the reign of Louis XV between the monarch and
the *parlements* the embattled magistrates found an arsenal of argument in
L'Esprit des lois.

Montesquieu's resentment of absolute monarchy as the vestibule to despotism led him to favor a "mixed government" of monarchy, aristocracy,
and democracy—king, nobles, and Parlement or States-General. Hence his
most famous and influential proposal: the separation of the legislative, executive, and judicial powers in a government.[94] The legislature should make
the laws but should not administer them; the executive should administer
them but not make them; the judiciary should limit itself to interpreting
them. The executive should not appoint or control the judges. Ideally, the
legislature would consist of two independent chambers, one representing
the upper classes, the other the commonalty. Here again the Baron speaks:

> In such a state there are always persons distinguished by their birth,
> riches, or honors. Were they to be confounded with the common peo-
> ple, and to have only the weight of a single vote like the rest, the
> common liberty would be their slavery, and they would have no inter-

est in supporting it, as most of the popular resolutions would be against them. The share they have, therefore, ought to be proportioned to their other advantages in the state; which happens only where they form a body that has a right to check the licentiousness of the people, as the people have a right to oppose any encroachment upon their liberty. The legislative power is therefore committed to the body of the nobles, and to that which represents the people, each having its assemblies and deliberations apart, each its separate interest and views.[95]

Each of the three powers in the government, and each of the two chambers in the legislature, should serve as a check and balance against the others. By this complex way the liberties of the citizen will be reconciled with the wisdom, justice, and vigor of the government.

These ideas on mixed government had come down from Aristotle, but the plan for a separation of powers had developed in Montesquieu's mind from his study of Harrington, Algernon Sidney, and Locke, and from his experience in England. He thought he had found there, however imperfect, his ideal of a monarchy checked by democracy in the House of Commons, this checked by aristocracy in the House of Lords; and he supposed that the courts of England were an independent check on Parliament and the king. He idealized what he had seen in England under the chaperonage of Chesterfield and other nobles; but like Voltaire he used this idealization as a spur to France. He must have known that the English courts were not quite independent of Parliament, but he thought it good that France should contemplate the right of the accused in England to an early examination or release on bail, to be tried by a jury of his own class, to challenge his accusers, and to be exempt from torture. But also he thought that "the nobility ought not to be cited before the ordinary court of judicature, but before that part of the legislature which is composed of their own body"; they too should have the right of "being judged by their peers."[96]

Montesquieu, like nearly all of us, became increasingly conservative with age. Conservatism is a function and obligation of old age, as radicalism is a useful function of youth, and moderation a gift and service of middle age; so we have a mixed constitution of a nation's mind, with a division and mutual checking of powers. With all his laud of liberty as the true end of government, Montesquieu defined liberty as "a right of doing whatever the laws permit. If a citizen could do what they forbid he would no longer be possessed of liberty, because all his fellow citizens would have the same power."[97] And he agreed with his fellow Gascon, Montaigne, in deprecating revolutions:

When the form of government has been long established, and affairs have reached a fixed condition, it is almost always prudent to leave them there; because the reasons—often complicated or unknown—which have allowed such a state to subsist will still maintain it.[98]

He rejected the idea of equality in property or power, but he felt like the Gracchi about the concentration of land ownership.

> With land sufficient to nourish a nation . . . the common people have scarcely enough to nourish a family. . . . The clergy, the prince, the cities, the great men, and some of the principal citizens insensibly become proprietors of all the land which lies uncultivated. The families who are ruined have left their fields, and the laboring man is destitute. In this situation they [the ruling classes] . . . should distribute land to all the families that are in want, and procure them materials for clearing and cultivating it. This distribution ought to be continued as long as there is a man to receive it.[99]

He condemned the farming of tax collecting to private financiers. He denounced slavery with moral fervor and bitter irony.[100] He acknowledged the occasional necessity of war, and stretched the concept of defense to sanction pre-emptive war:

> With a state the right of natural defense carries along with it sometimes the necessity of attacking; as, for instance, when one sees that a continuance of peace will enable another to destroy her, and that to attack that nation instantly is the only way to prevent her own destruction.[101]

But he deprecated the competitive amassing of armament:

> A new distemper has spread itself over Europe, infecting our princes, and inducing them to keep up an exorbitant number of troops. It has its redoublings, and of necessity becomes contagious. For as soon as one prince augments his forces, the rest, of course, do the same; so that nothing is gained thereby, but the public ruin.[102]

Though he esteemed patriotism so highly as to identify it with virtue, he had moments in which he dreamed of a larger ethic:

> If I knew of something that was useful to myself but injurious to my family, I would cast it from my mind. If I knew of something which was useful to my family but not to my country, I would try to forget it. If I knew of something that was useful to my country but injurious to Europe and the human race, I should regard it as a crime.[103]

His ultimate ethic and secret religion were those of the ancient Stoics:

Never were any principles more worthy of human nature, and more proper to form the good man. . . . If I could for a moment cease to think that I am a Christian, I should . . . rank the destruction of the sect of Zeno among the misfortunes that have befallen the human race. . . . It was this sect alone that made citizens, this alone that made great men, this alone great emperors. Laying aside for a moment revealed truths, let us search through all nature, and we shall not find a nobler object than the Antonines, not even Julian himself (a commendation thus wrested from me will not render me an accomplice of his apostasy). No, there has not been a prince, since his reign, more worthy to govern mankind.[104]

Visibly Montesquieu took care, in *L'Esprit des lois,* to make his peace with Christianity. He acknowledged God—"for what greater absurdity could there be than a blind fatality which had brought forth intelligent beings?"[105] But he conceived this Supreme Intelligence as expressed in the laws of nature, and never interfering with them. "For Montesquieu," said Faguet, "God is the Spirit of Laws."[106] He accepted supernatural beliefs as a necessary support of a moral code uncongenial to the nature of man. "It is proper there should be some sacred books to serve for a rule, as the Koran among the Arabs, the books of Zoroaster among the Persians, the Veda among the Indians, and the classics among the Chinese. The religious code supplements the civil, and fixes [limits] the extent of arbitrary sway."[107] State and Church should act as checks and balances to each other, but should always remain separate; "this great distinction [is] the basis of the tranquillity of nations."[108] Montesquieu defended religion against Bayle,[109] but he subjected it, like everything else, to the influence of climate and national character:

A moderate government is most agreeable to the Christian religion, and a despotic government to the Mohammedan. . . . When a religion adapted to the climate of one country clashes too much with the climate of another, it cannot be there established, and, if introduced, it will be discarded.[110] . . . The Catholic religion is most agreeable to monarchy, and the Protestant to a republic. . . . When the Christian religion . . . became unhappily divided into Catholic and Protestant, the people of the north embraced the Protestant, and those of the south still adhered to the Catholic. The reason is plain: the people of the north have, and will forever have, a spirit of liberty and independence, which the people of the south have not; and therefore a religion which has no visible head is more agreeable.[111]

While conceding the benefits of religion in gross, he berated it in detail. He condemned the wealth of the clergy in France,[112] and wrote "a most humble remonstrance to the Inquisitors of Spain and Portugal" to stop roasting heretics; he warned them that "if anyone in times to come shall dare to assert that, in the age in which we live, the people of Europe were civilized, you will be cited to prove that they were barbarians."[113] As a patriotic Gallican he laughed at papal infallibility, and insisted that the Church should be subject to the civil power. As to religious toleration he took a middle view: "When the state is at liberty to receive or reject a new religion, it ought to be rejected; when it is received it ought to be tolerated."[114] With all his obeisance to the censor he remained a rationalist. "Reason is the most perfect, the most noble, the most beautiful of all our faculties [*la raison est le plus parfait, le plus noble, et le plus exquis de tous les sens*]."[115] What better motto could the Age of Reason display?

4. Aftermath

The Spirit of Laws was soon recognized as a major event in French literature, but it met with criticism from both right and left. The Jansenists and the Jesuits, normally at odds, united in condemning the book as a subtle repudiation of Christianity. Said the Jansenist *Ecclesiastical News:* "The parentheses that the author inserts to inform us that he is a Christian give slight assurance of his Catholicism; the author would laugh at our simplicity if we should take him for what he is not"; and the reviewer ended with an appeal to the secular authorities to take action against the book.[116] The Jesuits accused Montesquieu of following the philosophy of Spinoza and Hobbes; in assuming laws in history as in natural science, he left no room for freedom of the will. Father Berthier, in the Jesuit *Journal de Trévoux*, argued that truth and justice are absolute, not relative to place or time, and that laws should be based on God-given universal principles, rather than on diversities of climate, soil, custom, or national character.[117] Montesquieu thought it wise to issue (1750) a *Défense de l'Esprit des lois*, in which he disclaimed atheism, materialism, and determinism, and reaffirmed his Christianity. The clergy remained unconvinced.

Meanwhile the rising *philosophes* were also displeased. They considered *The Spirit of Laws* as almost a manual of conservatism; they resented its occasional piety, the moderation of its proposed reforms, and its halfhearted conception of religious toleration.[118] Helvétius wrote to Montesquieu chiding him with laying too much emphasis on the dangers and difficulties of social change.[119] Voltaire, who was preparing his own philosophy of history in the *Essai sur les moeurs*, was not enthusiastic over Montesquieu's achievement. He had not forgotten that Monsieur le Président had opposed his admission to the Academy with the words, "It would be a disgrace to

the Academy if Voltaire were a member, and it will one day be his disgrace
that he was not one."[120] Under the circumstances Voltaire's criticism was
restrained, and was dammed with considerable praise. He argued that Montesquieu had exaggerated the influence of climate; he noted that Christianity had originated in hot Judea and was still flourishing in chilly Norway;
and he thought it more likely that England had gone Protestant because
Anne Boleyn was beautiful than because Henry VIII was cold.[121] If, as
Montesquieu had suggested, the spirit of liberty rose chiefly in mountain
regions, how explain the sturdy Dutch Republic, or the *liberum veto* of
the Polish lords? In his *Philosophical Dictionary* (1764) Voltaire filled
pages with examples indicating that "climate has some influence, government a hundred times more, religion and government combined more
still."[122]

> We might ask those who maintain that climate does everything
> [Montesquieu had not claimed this], why the Emperor Julian, in his
> *Misopogon*, says that what pleased him in the Parisians was the gravity
> of their character and the severity of their manners; and why these
> Parisians, without the slightest change of climate, are now like playful
> children, whom the government punishes and smiles at at the same mo-
> ment, and who themselves, the moment after, also smile and sing lam-
> poons upon their masters.[123]

Voltaire found it

> melancholy that in so many citations and so many maxims the con-
> trary of what is asserted should be almost always the truth. . . . "Peo-
> ple of warm climates are timid, like old men; those of cold countries
> are courageous, like young ones"? We should take great care how
> general propositions escape us. No one has ever been able to make a
> Laplander or an Eskimo warlike, while the Arabs in fourscore years
> conquered a territory which exceeded that of the whole Roman Em-
> pire.[124]

And then the praise:

> After thus convincing ourselves that errors abound in *The Spirit of
> Laws*, . . . that this work wants method, and possesses neither plan
> nor order, it is proper to ask what really forms its merit and has led to
> its great reputation. In the first place, it is written with great wit, whilst
> the authors of all the other books on this subject are tedious. It was on
> this account that a lady [Mme. du Deffand], who possessed as much
> wit as Montesquieu, observed that his book was *l'esprit sur les lois* [wit
> about laws]; it can never be more correctly defined. A still stronger

reason is that the book exhibits grand views, attacks tyranny, superstition, and grinding taxation. . . . Montesquieu was almost always in error with the learned, because he was not learned; but he was almost always right against the fanatics and the promoters of slavery. Europe owes him eternal gratitude.[125]

And he added, elsewhere: "Humanity had lost its title deeds [to freedom], and Montesquieu recovered them."[126]

Later criticism has largely agreed with Voltaire, while checking his own exaggerations.[127] It is true that *The Spirit of Laws* was poorly constructed, with little logic in the arrangement and sequence of the topics, and frequent forgetting of the unifying theme. In his zeal to be a scientist, to accumulate and interpret facts, Montesquieu ceased at times to be an artist; he lost the whole in the parts instead of co-ordinating the parts into a harmonious whole. He had gathered his data over half a lifetime; he wrote his book during twenty years; its sporadic composition injured its unity. He generalized too readily from a few instances, and did not look about him for contrary instances—e.g., Catholic Ireland in the cold and "therefore" Protestant north. He gave away his method when he said: "I have laid down the first principles, and have found that the particular cases follow naturally from them; that the histories of all nations are only consequences of them"; this is the danger of approaching history with a philosophy to be proved by it. In gathering his data Montesquieu accepted too readily the unverified accounts of travelers, and sometimes he took fables and legends for history. Even his direct observation could be faulty; he thought he saw a separation of powers in the English government, when the legislative was visibly absorbing the executive.

Against these faults there must have been great virtues to give the book its acclaim and influence. Voltaire rightly signalized the style. This too, however, suffered from fragmentation. Montesquieu indulged a liking for short chapters, perhaps as a means of emphasis, as in the "chapter" on despotism; the result is unpleasantly staccato, obstructing the flow of thought. Part of this fragmentation may have been due to progressive weakening of his eyes, compelling him to dictate instead of writing. When he let himself go and spoke out, he achieved, with crisp and pithy sentences, some of the brilliance that had brightened the *Lettres persanes*. Voltaire thought there were more epigrams in *L'Esprit des lois* than befitted a work on law. ("In Venice," said Montesquieu, "they are so habituated to parsimony that none but courtesans can make them part with their money."[128]) It is nevertheless a magistral style, moderate and calm. It is occasionally obscure, but it repays unraveling.

Montesquieu was modest and right in ascribing part of the value of the book to its subject and aim. To find laws in laws, some system in their variation in place and time, to enlighten rulers and reformers by considering the sources and limits of legislation in view of the nature and place of states and men—this was a majestic enterprise, whose scope made faults forgivable. Herbert Spencer failed in the same enterprise[129] 148 years later, despite a corps of research aides, and because of a similar passion for generalization; but both attempts were increments of wisdom. Montesquieu's achievement was the greater. He had predecessors;* he did not inaugurate, but he powerfully advanced the historical method for the comparative study of institutions. He anticipated Voltaire in establishing a philosophy of history independent of supernatural causes; and he achieved a breadth and impartiality of view never reached by Voltaire. Burke called Montesquieu "the greatest genius which has enlightened this age";[130] Taine considered him "the best instructed, the most sagacious, and the best balanced of all the spirits of the time."[131] Horace Walpole thought *The Spirit of Laws* "the best book that ever was written."[132] Perhaps not, but it was the greatest book of the generation.

It exhausted its author. He wrote to a friend in 1749: "I confess that this work has nearly killed me. I shall rest; I shall toil no more."[133] He continued to study nevertheless. "Study has been for me," he said, "the sovereign remedy against all the disappointments of life. I have never known any trouble that an hour's reading would not dissipate."[134]

He visited Paris occasionally, and enjoyed his fame, which at that time (1748) equaled Voltaire's. "*The Spirit of Laws*," said Raynal, "has turned the heads of the whole French people. We find this work in the libraries of our scholars and on the dressing tables of our ladies and our fashionable young men."[135] He was again welcomed in the salons, and he was received at court. But for the most part he stayed at La Brède, content to be a *grand seigneur*. His book so pleased the English that they sent in large orders for the wine grown on his lands. In his last years he became almost blind. "It seems to me," he said, "that the little light left to me is but the dawning of the day when my eyes will close forever."[136] In 1754 he went to Paris to end the lease on his house there; but on that visit he developed pneumonia and died, February 10, 1755, aged sixty-six. He had received the last rites of the Catholic Church, but the agnostic Diderot was the only man of letters who attended his funeral.[137] His influence spread over centuries. "In the forty years since the publication of *The Spirit of Laws*," wrote Gibbon, "no work has been more read and criticized, and the spirit of inquiry which it has excited is not the least of our obligations to the author."[138] Gibbon,

* Hippocrates' *Airs, Waters, and Places*; Aristotle's *Constitutions of Athens*; Machiavelli's *Discorsi*; Bodin's *Methodus ad facilem historiarum cognitionem*; Grotius' *De Jure Belli et Pacis*; Vico's *Scienza nuova*; Pufendorf's *De Jure Naturae et Gentium*; etc.

Blackstone, and Burke were among the English writers who profited from *The Spirit of Laws* and *The Greatness and Decadence of the Romans.* Frederick the Great thumbed *L'Esprit des lois* only next to *The Prince;* Catherine the Great thought it should be "the breviary of sovereigns,"[139] and made extracts from it for the men whom she appointed to revise Russia's laws.[140] The framers of the American Constitution took from Montesquieu not only the separation of governmental powers but the exclusion of cabinet members from Congress; and their writings were interspersed with quotations from his work. *The Spirit of Laws* became almost the bible of the moderate leaders in the French Revolution, and from *The Greatness and Decadence* came, in part, their admiration for the Roman Republic. "All the great modern ideas," said Faguet, "have their commencement in Montesquieu."[141] For a generation it was Montesquieu, not Voltaire, who was the voice and hero of the mind of France.

CHAPTER XI

Voltaire in France

I. IN PARIS: 1729–34

ON returning from England, late in 1728 or early in 1729, Voltaire took an inconspicuous lodging in St.-Germain-en-Laye, eleven miles northwest of Paris. He mobilized his friends to secure informal annulment of his exile from France and then from the capital. They succeeded, even to getting his royal pension restored; by April he was again bobbing about Paris. At one gathering he heard the mathematician La Condamine calculate that anyone who should buy all the tickets in a lottery just issued by the city of Paris would make a fortune. Voltaire rushed off, borrowed money from his banker friends, bought all the tickets, and won as predicted. The Comptroller General refused to pay; Voltaire took the matter to the courts, won his case, and was paid.[1] Later in this year 1729 he traveled 150 miles—in two nights and a day—from Paris to Nancy to buy shares in the public funds of the Duke of Lorraine; this venture too brought him substantial gains. Voltaire the poet and philosopher was supported by Voltaire the financier.

In 1730 we see him back in Paris, feverish with enterprise. He had usually several literary irons in the fire, passing from one to another as if finding refreshment in the change without losing time. Now he was writing *Letters on the English*, and a *History of Charles XII*, and *The Death of Mademoiselle Lecouvreur*, and the beginnings of *La Pucelle* (*The Maid*). One day in 1730 the guests of the Duc de Richelieu, discussing Jeanne d'Arc, suggested to Voltaire that he write her history. Jeanne had not yet been accepted as the uncanonized patron saint of France; to the freethinker Voltaire the supernatural elements in her legend seemed to invite a humorous treatment; Richelieu dared him try it; Voltaire composed the proem that day. His plaint for Lecouvreur was not yet published, but his bumbling friend Nicolas Thieriot recited it too widely, and theological hornets resumed their buzzing around Voltaire's head. As if hungry for enemies he staged on December 11 the story of Lucius Junius Brutus, who, in Livy's account, had expelled King Tarquinius and shared in setting up the Roman Republic; the play denied the inviolability of kings, and proclaimed the right of the people to change their rulers. The actors complained that there was no love theme in the plot; Paris agreed that this was an absurd innovation; after fifteen performances it was withdrawn. Sixty-two years later it was revived with great success, for Paris was in a mood to guillotine Louis XVI.

Meanwhile he had secured the royal *privilège* to publish his *Histoire de Charles XII, roi de Suède*. Here was a subject that could hardly offend Louis XV or the Church, and it should please the Queen by its very favorable treatment of her father, Stanislas. An edition of 2,600 copies was printed when, without a word of warning, the royal permission was suddenly withdrawn, and the whole edition was confiscated except a copy in Voltaire's possession. He protested to the Keeper of the Seals; he was informed that a change in foreign policy made it necessary to please Charles's opponent and victim, Augustus "the Strong," who was still king of Poland. Voltaire resolved to ignore the prohibition. He moved in disguise to Rouen, lived there for five months as an "English lord," and directed the secret printing of his history. By October, 1731, it was circulating freely and selling like fiction.

Some critics claimed there was too much fiction in it; a learned historian has called it "a romance," vivid in narrative, inaccurate in detail.[2] Yet Voltaire had prepared the book with scholarly care. He had not only examined masses of state papers, but he had gone out of his way to consult men who could give him firsthand information: ex-King Stanislas, the Maréchal de Saxe, the Duchess of Marlborough, Bolingbroke, Axel Sparre (who had been at the battle of Narva), Fonseca (a Portuguese physician who had served in Turkey during Charles's stay there), and Baron Fabrice (former secretary to Charles). Moreover, Voltaire had lived for a while with Baron von Görtz, Charles's favorite minister; the execution of von Görtz in 1719 may have turned Voltaire to study the "Lion of the North." In 1740 Joran Nordberg, who had served Charles as chaplain, published memoirs in which he pointed out inaccuracies in Voltaire's narrative; Voltaire incorporated these corrections in subsequent editions. There were other flaws, especially in the detailed descriptions of battles. Later critics[3] argued that Voltaire had overrated Charles as "perhaps the most extraordinary man who has ever been on earth, who united in himself all the great qualities of his ancestors, and who had no other defect or unhappiness except to have them all in excess."[4] The last word may redeem the hypertrophe. Voltaire explained that Charles "carried all the heroic virtues to that excess at which they become faults"; he listed these as prodigality, rashness, cruelty, tyranny, and inability to forgive; he showed how these faults in her King had injured Sweden; and he concluded that Charles "was an extraordinary rather than a great man."[5] In any case the book was a work not only of scholarship but of art—of structure, form, color, and style. Soon all educated Europe was reading *Charles XII*, and Voltaire's reputation achieved a spread and depth that it had not had before.

After his return from Rouen (August 5, 1731), Voltaire became the house guest of the Comtesse de Fontaine-Martel in her mansion near the Palais-Royal. She found him such pleasant company that she continued to lodge and feed him till May, 1733. He presided with incomparable vivacity at her literary suppers, and staged plays, preferably his own, in her private theater. During that stay he wrote the libretto for Rameau's *Samson* (1732). It was presumably from the Comtesse's box at the Théâtre-Français that he saw the failure of his *Ériphile* (1732), and the rapturous success of his romantic tragedy *Zaïre* (August 13, 1732). He wrote to a friend:

> Never piece was so well played as *Zaïre* at the fourth representation. I wished you there; you would have seen that the public did not hate your friend. I appeared in a box, and the whole pit clapped me. I blushed, I hid myself, but I should be a hypocrite if I did not confess to you that I was sensibly touched.[6]

Of all his dramas this remained to the end his favorite. They are all dead now, slain by changing fashions of mood and style; but we should exhume at least one of them, for they played a fond and exciting role in his life. Zaïre is a Christian captured in her infancy by the Moslems during the Crusades, and brought up in the Islamic faith; she knows little of France except that it is the land of her birth. She is now a beauty in the seraglio of the Sultan Orosmane at Jerusalem. He has fallen in love with her, she with him; and when the play opens she is about to become his wife. Another Christian captive, Fatima, reproaches her for forgetting that she was once a Christian. In Zaïre's reply Voltaire expresses the geographical determination of religious belief:

> Our thoughts, our manners, our religion, all
> Are formed by custom, and the powerful bent
> Of early years. Born on the banks of Ganges
> Zaïre had worshiped pagan deities;
> At Paris I had been a Christian; here
> I am a happy Mussulman. We know
> But what we learn; the instructing parent's hand
> Graves in our feeble hearts those characters
> Which time retouches, and examples fix
> So deeply in the mind, that nought but God
> Can e'er efface.[7]

Voltaire depicts Orosmane with evident predilection as a man with all the virtues except patience. The Christians are shocked to see that a Moslem can be as decent as any Christian, and the Sultan is surprised to find that a Christian can be good. He refuses to keep a harem and pledges himself to monogamy. But Voltaire is just to his Christian characters too; he writes gracious lines on the beauty of the truly Christian life. One Christian, Nerestam, also captured in infancy, grows up with Zaïre; he is freed on his pledge to return with ransoms for ten Christian captives. He goes, returns, devotes his private fortune to make up the required sum. Orosmane rewards him by liberating not ten but a hundred Christians. Nerestam grieves that these do not include either Zaïre or Lusignan, once (1186–87) the Christian king of Jerusalem. Zaïre pleads with Orosmane for Lusignan's release; it is granted; the aged King identifies Zaïre as his daughter and Nerestam as his son. She is torn between her love for the generous Sultan and the demand of loyalty to her father, her brother, and their faith. Lusignan appeals to her to abandon Orosmane and Islam:

> Oh, think on the pure blood
> Within thy veins, the blood of twenty kings,
> All Christians like myself, the blood of heroes,
> Defenders of the faith, the blood of martyrs!
> Thou art a stranger to thy mother's fate;
> Thou dost not know that in the very moment
> That gave thee birth I saw her massacred
> By those barbarians whose detested faith
> Thou hast embraced. Thy brothers, the dear martyrs,
> Stretch forth their hands from heaven, and wish to embrace
> A sister; oh, remember them! That God,
> Whom thou betrayest, for us and for mankind
> Even in this place expired. . . .

> Behold the sacred mountain where
> Thy Saviour bled; the tomb whence he arose
> Victorious; in each path where'er thou treadest
> Shalt thou behold the footsteps of thy God;
> Wilt thou renounce thy Maker?. . .
> ZAÏRE.   Dear author of my life,
> My father, speak: What must I do?
> LUSIGNAN.   Remove
> At once my shame and sorrow with a word,
> And say thou art a Christian
> ZAÏRE.   Then, my lord,
> I am a Christian. . . .
> LUSIGNAN. Swear thou wilt keep the fatal secret.
> ZAÏRE. I swear.[8]

When Nerestam learns that she still intends to marry Orosmane he is tempted to kill her. He relents, but insists that she accept baptism; she agrees. He sends her a note appointing time and place for the ceremony; Orosmane, not knowing that Nerestam is her brother, mistakes the message for a love note. He comes upon Zaïre as she keeps the appointment, stabs her, finds out that the supposed lovers are brother and sister, and kills himself.

It is a plot cleverly conceived, consistently and dramatically developed, told in flowing melodious verse; and though the sentimental passages now seem overdone, we can understand why Paris took Zaïre and Orosmane to its heart, and why the good sad Queen wept when the play was performed for the court at Fontainebleau. Soon it was translated and produced in England, Italy, and Germany. Now Voltaire was hailed as the greatest living French poet, fit successor to Corneille and Racine. This did not rejoice Jean Baptiste Rousseau, French poet surviving in exile at Brussels; he judged Zaïre "trivial and flat, . . . an odious mélange of piety and libertinage." Voltaire retorted with a long discourse in verse, Le Temple de goût (The Temple of Taste), pillorying Rousseau and exalting Molière.

His head was in the stars, but he did not cease to work. In the winter of 1732–33 he studied mathematics and Newton with his future victim Maupertuis, rewrote Ériphile, revised Zaïre and Charles XII, collected materials for Le Siècle de Louis XIV, put the finishing touches on his Lettres sur les Anglais, produced a new play, Adélaïde, and wrote innumerable trifles—letters, compliments, invitations, epigrams, amorous ditties—all agleam with wit in smoothly polished verse. When his landlady bountiful, Mme. de Fontaine-Martel, died, he moved to a house on the Rue du Long-Point, and engaged in the business of exporting wheat. Then, mingling commerce with romance, he met (1733) Gabrielle Émilie Le Tonnelier de Breteuil, Marquise du Châtelet. With that unique and enterprising woman his life was to be mingled till her death.

She was now twenty-six (he thirty-eight), and she already had a varied career behind her. Daughter of the Baron de Breteuil, she received an unusual education. At twelve she knew Latin and Italian, sang well, played the spinet; at fifteen she began to translate the Aeneid into French verse; then she added English, and studied mathematics with Maupertuis. At nineteen she married the thirty-year-old Marquis Florent Claude du Châtelet-Lomont. She gave him three children, but otherwise they did not see very much of each other; he was usually with his regiment; she remained near the court, gambling for high stakes and experimenting with love. When her first paramour left her she took poison, but was forcibly saved by an emetic. She bore with experienced composure her desertion by a second gallant, the Duc de Richelieu, for all France knew his mobility.

Meeting the Marquise at dinner, Voltaire was not disturbed but rather delighted with her ability to converse on mathematics, astronomy, and Latin poetry. Her physical allure was not irresistible. Other women described her with relish. Hear Mme. du Deffand: "A woman big and dry, without hips, a shallow chest, . . . big arms, big legs, enormous feet, very small head, sharp features, pointed nose, two [!] small eyes of marine green, dark complexion, . . . bad teeth."[9] The Marquise de Créqui concurred: "She was a giantess . . . of wonderful strength, and was, besides, a marvel of awkwardness. She had a skin like a nutmeg grater, and altogether she resembled an ugly grenadier. And yet Voltaire spoke of her beauty!"[10] And handsome Saint-Lambert made clandestine love to her when she was forty-two. We cannot trust these sisterly verdicts; *femina feminae felis*. We gather from her portraits that Émilie was tall and masculine, with high forehead, proud look, features not unattractive, and we are comforted to be told that she had a "bust voluptuous but firm."[11]

Perhaps she had just enough of the man in her to complement the woman in Voltaire. However, she used every feminine device to round out her rather angular charms—cosmetics, perfume, jewels, lace. Voltaire smiled at her love of ornament, but he admired her enthusiasm for science and philosophy. Here was a woman who, even in the hum and froth of Paris and Versailles, could retire from the gambling table to study Newton and Locke. She not only read Newton, she understood him; it was she who translated the *Principia* into French. Voltaire found it convenient to have the same woman as his fellow student and his mistress. Already in 1734 he counted himself her accepted lover: "God! what pleasures I taste in your arms! How fortunate I am that I can admire her whom I love!"[12]

II. LETTERS ON THE ENGLISH

In 1733 and 1734, after much tribulation, he published his first contribution to the Enlightenment. It took the form of twenty-four letters addressed from England to Thieriot. These, translated into English, were issued in London (1733) as *Letters concerning the English Nation*. But to print the originals in France was to risk the liberty of both author and printer. Voltaire eliminated some passages, and tried to get governmental permission to publish the rest. Refused, he again resorted to clandestine publication in Rouen. He warned Jore, the printer, not to let any of this impression circulate for the present, but early in 1734 several copies, entitled *Lettres philosophiques*, reached Paris. A pirate publisher secured a copy, and printed a large edition without Voltaire's knowledge. Meanwhile he and Madame du Châtelet had gone to the Château of Montjeu, near Autun, 190 miles from Paris, to attend the wedding of Richelieu.

The book began with four letters on the English Quakers. These, Voltaire pointed out, had no ecclesiastical organization, no priests, and no sacraments; yet they practiced the precepts of Christ more faithfully than any other Christians he had ever known. He described or imagined a visit to one of them:

"My dear sir," I said, "have you been baptized?"

"No," replied the Quaker, "nor have my brethren."

"How now, *morbleu*!" I cried, "then you are not Christians?"

"My son," he answered, in a mild and quiet voice, "do not swear. We are Christians, and try to be good Christians; but we do not think that Christianity consists in throwing cold water, with a little salt, upon the head."

"Eh, *ventrebleu*!" I protested, "not to speak of this impiety, have you forgotten that Jesus Christ was baptized by John?"

"My friend, no more oaths. . . . Christ received baptism from John, but he himself never baptized anyone. We are the disciples not of John but of Christ."

"Alas, my poor man," I said, "how you would be burned in the land of the Inquisition! . . ."

"Are you circumcised?" he asked.

I replied that I had not that honor.

"Very well, then," he said; "you are a Christian without being circumcised, and I am a Christian without being baptized."

Baptism, like circumcision, said the Quaker, was a pre-Christian custom, superseded by the new Gospel of Christ. And he (or Voltaire) added a word on war:

"We shall never go to war; not because we fear death, . . . but because we are not wolves or tigers or bulldogs but men, Christians. Our God, who bade us love our enemies, . . . surely does not want us to cross the sea to cut the throats of our brothers merely because murderers dressed in red, with hats two feet high, recruit citizens while making a noise with two sticks on the stretched skin of an ass. And when, after victory, all London is brilliant with illuminations, and the sky is aflame with fireworks, and the air resounds with thanksgivings, with church bells, organs, and cannon, we mourn in silence over the slaughter that caused such public joy.[13]

France had almost destroyed itself to compel all Frenchmen to one faith; Voltaire dilated on the comparative toleration of religious differences in

England. "This is a land of sects. An Englishman, like a free man, goes to heaven by whatever route he chooses."[14] Voltaire contrasted the morals of the English clergy with those of their French compeers, and congratulated the English on having no abbés. "When they learn that in France young men, known for their debauches and raised to the prelacy by intrigues, compose tender songs, give long and exquisite dinners almost every day, . . . and call themselves the successors of the Apostles, they thank God that they are Protestants."[15]

Letter VIII turned the Voltairean stiletto upon French government.

> Only the English nation has managed to regulate the power of kings by resisting them, . . . and has finally established this wise government in which the prince, all powerful to do good, has his hands tied against doing evil. [Here Voltaire echoes a famous sentence from Fénelon's *Télémaque*.] . . . To establish liberty in England has been costly, no doubt; the idol of despotism has been drowned in seas of blood; but the English do not think they have purchased good laws too dearly. Other nations have had no less troublous times, but the blood they have shed for the cause of their liberty has only cemented their servitude.[16]

In England the right of habeas corpus forbids imprisonment without stated cause, and requires an open trial by jury; in France you have *lettres de cachet*. Voltaire noted, praised, and exaggerated, fourteen years before Montesquieu, a certain "separation of powers" in the English government, and the working harmony between king, lords, and commons. He pointed out that in England no tax could be levied without consent of Parliament, and that "no man is exempt from paying certain taxes . . . because he is a noble or a priest."[17] In England the younger sons of the nobility enter into commerce and the professions; in France

> the merchant so often hears his profession spoken of with disdain that he is foolish enough to blush for it. I do not know, however, which is more useful to a state—a well-powdered nobleman who knows exactly the time when the King gets up or goes to bed, and gives himself an air of grandeur while playing the role of a slave, . . . or a businessman who [like Voltaire's London host Falkener] enriches his country, dispatches from his office orders to Surat and Cairo, and contributes to the happiness of the world.[18]

Finally, in a passage that laid down a program for France, Voltaire claimed that

> the English constitution has, in fact, arrived at the point of excellence, in consequence of which all men are restored to those *natural rights*

which in nearly all monarchies they are deprived of. These rights are entire liberty of person and property; freedom of the press; the right of being tried in all criminal cases by a jury of independent men; the right of being tried only according to the strict letter of the law; the right of every man to profess, unmolested, what religion he chooses.[19]

Voltaire must have known that only a part of the population enjoyed these "natural rights"; that liberty of person was not secure from the press gang; that there were limits to freedom of speech in religion and politics; that Dissenters and Catholics were excluded from public office; that judges could be bribed to override the law. He was writing no dispassionate description of English realities; he was using England as a whip to stir up revolt in France against oppression by state or Church. The fact that nearly all these rights are now taken for granted in civilized countries illuminates the achievement of the eighteenth century.

Just as important in its effect on modern thought was Voltaire's praise of Bacon, Locke, and Newton. He applied to the impeached Bacon Bolingbroke's judgment on Marlborough: "He was so great a man that I do not recollect whether he had any faults or not."[20] "This great man," he added, "is the father of experimental philosophy"—not by the experiments that Bacon made, but by his powerful appeals for the advancement of scientific research. Here was the thought that would lead Diderot and d'Alembert to name Bacon as the chief inspiration of their *Encyclopédie*.

To Locke Voltaire devoted nearly all of Letter XIII. He found in him not only a science of the mind instead of a mythology of the soul, but an implicit philosophy that, by tracing all knowledge to sensation, turned European thought from divine revelation to human experience as the exclusive source and basis of truth. And he welcomed Locke's suggestion that conceivably matter might be enabled to think. This sentence especially stuck in the throat of the French censors, and had much to do with their condemnation of the book; they seemed to foresee in it the materialism of La Mettrie and Diderot. Voltaire refused to commit himself to materialism, but he revised Descartes' "I think, therefore I am" into "I am a body and I think; I know no more."

Letter XIV advised the French to free themselves from Descartes and study Newton. "Public opinion in England on these two thinkers is that the first was a dreamer and the other a sage." Voltaire honored Descartes' contribution to geometry, but he could not assimilate the whirlpools of the Cartesian cosmology. He admitted that there was something dreamy, or at least soporific, in Newton's essays on ancient chronology and the Apocalypse; Newton wrote these, Voltaire amiably suggested, "to console mankind for his otherwise too great superiority over them."[21] He himself as yet found Newton very difficult, but the assemblage of men prominent in government as well as in science at Newton's funeral had left upon him an impression that determined him to study the *Principia* and make himself an apostle of Newton to France. Here too he sowed the seed of the *Encyclopédie* and the Enlightenment.

Finally, he shocked religious thought in France by subjecting the *Pensées* of Pascal to a hostile critique. He had not intended to include this in the *Lettres;* it had nothing to do with England, but he had sent it from England to Thieriot in 1728; the piratical publisher appended it as Letter xxv; and the result was that the Jansenists—who worshiped Pascal and controlled the Parlement of Paris—now exceeded the Jesuits (who had no love for Pascal) in denouncing Voltaire. Voltaire was constitutionally incapable of agreeing with Pascal: he was at this stage (except in his plays) a militant rationalist who had not yet found a place for feeling in his philosophy. Still young, exuberant, enjoying life amid his heroic tribulations, he reacted against Pascal's despondent pessimism: "I shall dare to take the part of the human race against this sublime misanthrope."[22] He rejected Pascal's "wager" (that it is wiser to bet on God's existence than against it) as "indecent and childish; . . . the interest I have to believe a thing is no proof that such a thing exists."[23] (Pascal had not offered the wager as a proof.) He admitted that we cannot explain the universe or know the destiny of man, but he doubted if we can deduce from this ignorance the truth of the Apostles' Creed. Nor had he at this bouncing age any sympathy with Pascal's longing for repose; man, he proclaimed, "is born for action. . . . Not to be employed, and not to exist, are one and the same thing with regard to man."[24]

These *Remarques sur les Pensées de Pascal* are not Voltaire at his best. He had not prepared them for publication, he had no chance to revise them; and later events—like the Lisbon earthquake—removed the youthful bloom from his optimism. Despite this unconsidered appendage the *Lettres philosophiques* were a milestone in French literature and thought. Here for the first time appeared the short, sharp sentences, the unmistakable clarity, the gay wit and deflating irony, that were henceforth to be a literary signature overriding all cautious denials of authorship; this book and the *Lettres persanes* set the tone of French prose from the Regency to the Revolution. Moreover, it constituted one of the strongest links in that junction of the French and British intellects which Buckle rated "by far the most important fact in the history of the eighteenth century."[25] It was a declaration of war and a map of campaign. Rousseau said of these letters that they played a large part in the awakening of his mind; there must have been thousands of young Frenchmen who owed the book a similar debt. Lafayette said it made him a republican at the age of nine. Heine thought "it was not necessary for the censor to condemn this book; it would have been read without that."[26]

Church and state, King and Parlement, felt that they could not bear in silence so many wounds. The printer was sent to the Bastille, and a *lettre de cachet* was issued for the arrest of Voltaire wherever found. On May 11, 1734, an agent of police appeared at Montjeu with a warrant, but Voltaire, warned probably by Maupertuis and d'Argental, had left five days before, and was already beyond the frontier of France. On June 10, by an order of the Parlement, all discoverable copies of the book were burned by the public hangman in the courtyard of the Palais de Justice as "scandalous, contrary to religion, good morals, and the respect due to authority."

Before learning of Voltaire's safe arrival in Lorraine, the Marquise du Châtelet wrote to a friend: "To know that he, with such health and imagination as he has, is in a prison . . . I do not find in myself constancy enough to support the idea." She and the Duchesse de Richelieu enlisted the aid of titled women to obtain a pardon. The Keeper of the Seals agreed to have the order of arrest rescinded if Voltaire would disavow authorship of the book; he knew quite well that Voltaire was the author, but lent himself to the ruse; he was one of a succession of governmental officials who tempered censorship now and then by looking the other way. Voltaire readily agreed to disclaim authorship; this would be a white lie eminently forgivable; besides, the book that he was to disavow had been distributed without his consent. To the Duchesse d'Aiguillon he wrote:

> They say I must retract. Very willingly. I will declare that Pascal is always right; . . . that all priests are gentle and disinterested; . . . that monks are neither proud nor given to intrigue nor stinking; that the Holy Inquisition is the triumph of humanity and tolerance.[27]

The order of arrest was withdrawn, with the proviso that Voltaire should remain at a respectful distance from Paris. He passed from château to château near the border, and was welcomed by the nobles, who were not very pious and not at all fond of a centralized and absolute monarchy. He received an invitation to reside at the court of Holstein, with a pension of ten thousand francs a year; he refused it.[28] In July he retired to the château of Mme. du Châtelet at Cirey in Champagne. There, as the paying guest of his mistress and her husband, he entered upon the happiest years of his life.

III. IDYL IN CIREY: 1734-44

Cirey is now a village of 230 inhabitants in the *département* of Haute-Marne in northeastern France, only a few miles from Lorraine. Mme. Denis, Voltaire's niece, described it in 1738 as "a frightful solitude . . . four leagues from any habitation, in a country where one sees only mountains and uncultivated land."[29] Perhaps Voltaire loved it for this isolation—a quiet spot where he could study science, write history and philosophy, and be forgotten by the French government, or, if harassed by it, could escape in an hour's dash into Lorraine.

The château was a dilapidated relic of the thirteenth century, rarely used by the Du Châtelets, and long since unfit for civilized living. The Marquis had little interest or funds to repair it; Voltaire lent him forty thousand francs for this purpose at five per cent interest, which the Marquis was not called upon to pay. A few rooms were made habitable; Voltaire moved in, ordered the construction of a new wing, and superintended the rehabilitation of the rest. In November the Marquise arrived with two hundred parcels of baggage, revised Voltaire's repairs to her taste, and settled down—she who had spent most of her adult years at or near the court—to a life of study and bigamous devotion. The amiable Marquis stayed with her and Voltaire, on and off, till 1740, gracefully keeping a separate apartment and separate mealtimes; thereafter he spent most of his time with his regiment. France marveled less at the husband's complaisance than at the lovers' fidelity.

In December Madame returned to Paris, attended the Duchesse de Richelieu in her confinement, and persuaded the government to cancel the exclusion of Voltaire from the capital (March 2, 1735). He came to Paris, and stayed there a few weeks with his mistress. But his past pursued him. Parts of his scandalous *Pucelle* were going the rounds; he himself could not resist reading juicy passages to his friends; and now his anti-Christian *Epistle to Urania*, written fifteen years before, was issued by a pirate publisher. He denied its authorship as a matter of course, but it had the earmarks of his style and thought, and no one believed his denial. Again he fled to Lorraine, and thence cautiously back to Cirey. He received indirect assurances from the government that if he remained there, and gave no further offense, he would not be molested. Mme. du Châtelet rejoined him, bringing her daughter, her son, and their tutor; her third child had died. Now at last this philosophic honeymoon began.

Each of the philosophers had a separate suite of rooms, at opposite ends of the château. Voltaire's was composed of anteroom, study-library, and bedroom. The walls were hung with red velvet tapestries or with pictures; of these he accumulated a costly collection, including a Titian and several Teniers; and there were statues of Venus, Cupid, and Hercules, and a large portrait of their new friend the Crown Prince Frederick of Prussia. There was such cleanliness in these rooms, according to Mme. de Graffigny, that "one could kiss the floor."[30] The Marquise's apartment was in different taste, light yellow and pale blue, with paintings by Veronese and Watteau, picture ceiling, marble floor, and a hundred little boxes, bottles, rings, gems, and toilet articles lying about in her pretty boudoir. Between the two suites ran a large hall fitted up as a laboratory for physics and chemistry, with air pumps, thermometers, furnaces, crucibles, telescope, microscopes, prisms, compasses, scales. There were several guest rooms, not so well equipped. Despite tapestries, the woodland winds still slipped through cracks, windows, and doors; in winter it took thirty-six fireplaces, burning six cords of wood per day, to keep the château tolerably warm. We can imagine the number of servants. Add a theater, for Voltaire loved to act, especially in his own plays; the Marquise, he assures us, was an excellent actress; guests, tutor, and servants rounded out the cast. Sometimes operas were sung there, for Madame (on the same authority) had a *"voix divine."* Also there were puppet shows and magic-lantern shows, which Voltaire accompanied with commentaries that exhausted the company with laughter.

But play was an incident, work was the order of the day. The lovers sometimes collaborated in the laboratory, but usually they worked in their separate quarters, hardly seeing each other during the day except at the main meal, which came toward noon. The Marquis quit the table before the conversation began; Voltaire, too, often left the others to entertain themselves, and stole back to his study. He had his own silver service there, for he sometimes ate alone. We rightly think of him as a vivacious talker; he could be the life of any gathering; but he hated small talk. "It is frightful," he said, "the time we spend in talk. We ought not to lose a minute. The greatest expenditure we can make is of time."[31] Occasionally he hunted venison for exercise.

We must not picture the philosophic mates as angels. Madame could be harsh, overbearing, even cruel. She was a bit straitened in purse, severe and parsimonious with her servants, and she protested when Voltaire paid his more. She had no physical modesty; she thought nothing of completely disrobing in the presence of their secretary Longchamp, or of having him pour warm water upon her as she lay in the bath.[32] She secretly read some of the letters written by or to her guests; but of this we have only the testimony of another woman.[33] As for Voltaire, he had a hundred faults, which will appear in due course. He was as vain as a poet and could pout like a child; he took offense readily and had many a quarrel with his lady. These, however, were but passing clouds that accentuated the sunshine of their days. Voltaire soon recovered his spirits and good cheer, and never tired of telling his friends how happy he was, and how he loved Madame, in his own passionless way. He wrote to her a hundred little poems of affection, each a cameo of compact art. One such literary gem accompanied a ring into which his portrait had been engraved:

Barier grave ces traits destinés pour vos yeux;
Avec quelque plaisir daignez les reconnaître!
Les vôtres dans mon coeur furent gravés bien mieux,
Mais ce fut par un plus grand maître.[34]*

And she, for her part, said, "I could not be away from him for two hours without pain."[35]

Of the two she was the more deeply devoted to science. She exercised the unwritten law of feminine domain by hiding the half-finished manuscript of Voltaire's *Siècle de Louis XIV*, and sternly directing him to science as the proper study of modern man. Mme. de Graffigny, who was their guest in 1738, described her as more assiduous in her scientific pursuits than Voltaire, as spending most of the day and much of the night at her desk, sometimes till five or seven o'clock in the morning.[36] Maupertuis came occasionally to Cirey to continue her lessons in mathematics and physics; perhaps those visits, and Madame's open admiration for Maupertuis' intellectual attainments, stirred in the sensitive Voltaire a jealousy that prepared him for his bout with Maupertuis in Berlin.

Was she a real scholar or did she put on science as a fashionable dress? Mme. du Deffand and several other ladies thought that her studies were a pose. The Marquise de Créqui alleged that "algebra and geometry had the effect of making her half crazy, while her pedantry on the subject of her learning made her insupportable. In reality she muddled up everything that she had learned."[37] But hear Mme. de Graffigny describe a session at Cirey:

> This morning the lady of the house read us a geometrical calculation
> of an English dreamer. . . . The book was in Latin, and she read it to
> us in French. She hesitated a moment at each period, and I supposed it
> was to understand the mathematical calculations. But no; she translated
> easily the mathematical terms; the numbers, the extravagances, nothing
> stopped her. Is not that really astonishing?[38]

Voltaire assured Thieriot that Mme. du Châtelet understood English well, knew all the philosophical works of Cicero, and was deeply interested in mathematics and metaphysics.[39] She once bettered the physicist and Academician de Mairan in a discussion of kinetic energy.[40] She read Cicero and Virgil in Latin, Ariosto and Tasso in Italian, Locke and Newton in English. When Algarotti visited Cirey she conversed with him in Italian. She wrote, but did not publish, a six-volume *Examen de Genèse*, based on the work of English deists, and exposing the contradictions, improbabilities, immoralities, and injustices of the Bible. Her *Traité de la bonheur* was an

---

* "Barier engraves these features for your eyes; do look upon them with some pleasure. Your own are graved more deeply in my heart, but by a greater master still."

original discourse on the foundations of happiness; these, she thought, were health, love, virtue, rational self-indulgence, and the pursuit of knowledge. She translated Newton's *Principia* from Latin into French; edited by Clairaut, it was published in 1756, six years after her death. She composed an *Exposition abrégée du système du monde*, which was published in 1759, and which Voltaire, perhaps gallantly, pronounced superior to his *Éléments de la philosophie de Newton* (1738).[41] When the Académie des Sciences offered (1738) a prize for the best essay on the nature and diffusion of fire, and Voltaire entered the competition, she secretly wrote and submitted her own essay, incognito; she wrote it at night to conceal it from Voltaire, "since in my essay I opposed nearly all of his ideas."[42] Neither won the prize, which went to Euler, but her paper, as well as Voltaire's, was printed by the Academy. Each praised the other's work in an ecstasy of *amor intellectualis*.

For his own essay Voltaire carried on many experiments, some in his laboratory, some in a foundry at neighboring Chaumont.[43] He studied calcination, and came close to discovering oxygen.[44] In May, 1737, we find him writing to the Abbé Moussinot in Paris, asking for a chemist to come and live at Cirey for a hundred écus per year and board; but the chemist must also know how to say Mass on Sundays and holydays in the chapel of the château.[45] As for himself, he believed now only in science. "That which our eyes and mathematics demonstrate to us," he wrote in 1741, "we must hold to be true. In all the rest we must say only, 'I do not know.' "[46] Philosophy at this time meant to him only a summary of science.

It was in this sense that he used the term in his *Éléments de la philosophie de Newton*. He sought the royal privilege for its publication, but was refused. An edition appeared in Amsterdam (1738) without his consent; his own edition came out there in 1741. It was a substantial volume of 440 pages, a splendid example of what the French, with no derogatory intent, call *vulgarisation*—that is, an attempt to make the difficult and recondite more widely understood. The printer added a subtitle: *Mis à la portée de tout le monde*—"brought within the comprehension of everyone"; the Abbé Desfontaines, in a hostile review, altered this to *Mis à la porte de tout le monde*—"shown the door by everyone." On the contrary, nearly everyone praised it; even the Jesuits were generous to it in their *Journal de Trévoux*.[47] Now the Newtonian cosmology of gravitation finally ousted Descartes' vortices from the French mind. Voltaire included an exposition of Newton's optics; he verified the experiments in his own laboratory, and contrived others of his own. He went out of his way to stress the consistency of Newton's philosophy with belief in God; at the same time he emphasized the universality of law in the physical world.

Despite these efforts Voltaire had neither the spirit nor the limitations of a scientist. It is said that he failed as a scientist; we should rather say that he was too rich and varied a personality to give himself fully and finally to science. He used science as a liberation of the mind; that done, he passed on to poetry, drama, philosophy in its largest sense, and humanitarian involvement in the basic affairs of his time. "We should introduce into our existence all imaginable modes, and open every door of the soul to all sorts of knowledge and feeling. So long as these do not go in pell-mell, there is plenty of room for everything."[48] So he wrote at this time (1734) a *Discours sur l'homme*, largely echoing Pope's *Essay on Man*, even to sanctioning the quite un-Voltairean idea that "all is right."[49] He composed in these years most of *La Pucelle d'Orléans*, perhaps as a relief from Newton. And he expounded his own philosophy in a *Traité de métaphysique* which he judiciously refrained from publishing.

It was as unique as all his productions. He began by imagining himself to be a visitor from Jupiter or Mars; so, he thought, he could not be expected to reconcile his views with the Bible. Landing among the Kaffirs of South Africa, he concludes that man is an animal with black skin and wooly hair. Passing to India, he finds men with yellow skin and straight hair; he concludes that man is a genus composed of several distinct species, not all derived from one ancestor.[50] He judges from the appearances of order in the world, and of purposeful design of organs in animals, that there is an intelligent deity designing the whole. He sees no evidence of an immortal soul in man, but he feels that his will is free. Long before Hume and Adam Smith, he derives the moral sense from fellow feeling, sym-pathy. Long before Helvétius and Bentham, he defines virtue and vice as "that which is useful or injurious to the society."[51] We shall look at the *Traité* again later on.

How different from this treatise was Voltaire's rollicking versification of Jeanne d'Arc's history! If we open that mock epic today we must remember that French speech and French literature were freer then than in the first half of the twentieth century. We have seen an example in the *Lettres persanes* of the magistrate Montesquieu; Diderot was even freer, not only in *Les Bijoux indiscrets* but in *Jacques le fataliste*. Compared with these *La Pucelle*, as finally published by Voltaire in 1756, is innocuously mild; presumably the privately circulated original was more Rabelaisian. The grave Condorcet defended the poem, and we are told that Malesherbes, a high official in the French government, learned it by heart.[52] A sedulous search has found some mildly sensual passages in the twenty-one cantos; they are as forgivable as similar pictures in Ariosto; and they are redeemed by many passages of graphic description and vigorous narrative. Like many Frenchmen of his time, Voltaire thought of Jeanne as a healthy and simple peasant girl, probably of bastard birth, given to superstitions and hearing "voices";

and he suspected that France would have been saved from the Goddams (Jeanne's name for the English invaders) even if she had never been born. Otherwise, and allowing for some historical blunders, he told the story faithfully, merely salting it with humor.

> Turning his head toward the dauntless Joan,
> Thus spake the King, in a majestic tone
> Which any might have feared but her alone:
> "Joan, hear me: if thou art a maid, avow."
> She answered: "Oh, great Sire, give orders now
> That doctors sage, with spectacles on nose,
> Who, versed in female mysteries, can depose;
> That clerks, apothecaries, matrons tried
> Be called at once the matter to decide;
> Let them all scrutinize, and let them see."
> By this sage answer Charles knew she must be
> Inspired and blessed with sweet virginity.
> "Good," said the King, "since you know so well,
> Daughter of heaven, I prithee, instant tell
> What with my fair one passed last night in bed?
> Speak free." "Why, nothing happened," Joan said.
> Surprised, the King knelt down and cried aloud,
> "A miracle!" then crossed himself and bowed.[53]

Voltaire amused his guests by reading a canto or two of *La Pucelle* to warm a winter evening. Usually Mme. du Châtelet kept the swelling manuscript under lock and key, but Voltaire carelessly allowed some parts of it to circulate among his friends. Parts were copied, and went the rounds of impolite society more widely than was wise. The fear that the French government would prosecute him—not for the obscenity of the poem but for its incidental satire of monks, Jesuits, prelates, popes, and the Inquisition—became one of the haunting worries of Voltaire's life.

He was more serious with *Alzire*, which had a happy première at the Théâtre-Français on January 27, 1736. It made theatrical history by dressing the actors in the costumes of the indicated time and place the Spanish conquest and spoliation of Peru. Alvarez, the Spanish governor of the fallen state, pleads with the victors to abate their cruelty and greed:

> We are the scourge
> Of this new world, vain, covetous, unjust. . . .
> We alone
> Are the barbarians here; the simple savage,
> Tho' fierce by nature, is in courage equal,
> In goodness our superior.[54]

Paris acclaimed the piece for twenty successive nights, paying 53,640 livres. Voltaire gave his share of the receipts to the players.

On August 8, 1736, he received his first letter from Frederick of Prussia; so began a remarkable correspondence and a tragic friendship. In this same year he published a poem, *Le Mondain* (*The Worldly Man*), which reads like an answer, by anticipation, to Rousseau's *Discourse on the Arts and Sciences* (1750). Voltaire had no patience with the visionaries who were idealizing the "friendly and flowing savage," or were recommending a "return to nature" as an escape from the strains, hypocrisies, and artifices of modern life. He himself was quite comfortable amid his tribulations, and he thought he ought to say a good word for civilization. He saw no virtue in poverty, and no harmony between bugs and love. Primitive men may have been communists, but only because they had nothing; and if they were sober it was only because they had no wine. "For my part I thank the wise nature that for my happiness gave me birth in this age so decried by our melancholy critics. This profane time is just right for my ways. I love luxury, even a soft life [*mollesse*], all the pleasures, the arts in their variety, cleanliness, taste, and ornaments." All this seemed to him clearly preferable to the Garden of Eden. "My dear father Adam, confess that you and Madame Eve had long nails black with dirt, and that your hair was a bit out of order. . . . In vain have scholars sought to locate the Garden of Eden; . . . the terrestrial paradise is where I am."

The ecclesiastics did not like this picture of Adam and Eve; they insisted that the Book of Genesis was good history, and they did not agree with Voltaire about Adam's nails and Eve's hair. Again the word went forth for the arrest of the impious devil of Cirey. Again friends warned him, and he decided to travel. On December 21, 1736, he left Cirey and Émilie, and made his way to Brussels, disguised as the merchant Revol. His admirers there laughed at his disguise, and, in his honor, staged *Alzire*. Jean Baptiste Rousseau warned the Bruxellois that Voltaire had come to preach atheism. Voltaire moved on to Leiden, where crowds collected to see him, and to Amsterdam, where he supervised the printing of his book on Newton. The Marquise began to fear that he would never return. "Two weeks ago," she wrote to d'Argental, "I was in torture if I let two hours pass without seeing him; I wrote to him from my room to his; now two weeks have gone by, and I don't know where he is or what he is doing. . . . I am in a terrible state."[55] At last he returned (March, 1737), vowing that only his love for her could keep him in a France that so hounded him.

In May, 1739, the lovers went to Brussels, where Voltaire used his legal and other wits to defend the Marquise in a suit affecting her property. Then, with her husband, they went on to Paris, where Voltaire offered two plays, *Mahomet* and *Mérope*, to the Comédie-Française, and Madame saw through the press her three-volume *Institutions de physique*. In these "lessons" she played truant from both Voltaire and Newton by favoring the monadic philosophy of Leibniz. In September they returned to Cirey, and soon afterward to Brussels for a long stay. Thence, in September, 1740, Voltaire hurried to Cleves for his first meeting with Frederick—now king —who refused to include Émilie in his invitation. In November he traveled 350 painful miles to Berlin, hoping to play diplomat for Cardinal Fleury; more of this later. Émilie meanwhile went to Fontainebleau, where she labored to secure permission for Voltaire to reside in Paris; apparently Cirey had become a bore. On November 23 she wrote to d'Argental:

> I have been cruelly rewarded for all that I have done at Fontainebleau. I have adjusted the most difficult matters; I have obtained for M. de Voltaire the right to return to his country openly; I won him the good will of the ministry, and paved his way for acceptance by the Academies; in a word, I have given him back in three weeks all that he has taken pains to lose in six years.
>
> And do you know how he repays such zealous devotion? He informs me dryly that he has gone to Berlin, knowing perfectly well that he is piercing my heart, and leaves me in a state of indescribable torture. . . . A fever has seized me, and I hope soon to end my life. . . . And would you believe that the thought that is uppermost in my mind, when I feel that my grief will kill me, is the terrible sorrow my death would bring to M. de Voltaire? . . . I cannot bear the idea that the memory of me will one day cause him unhappiness. All those who have loved him must refrain from reproaching him.

Voltaire tore himself away from Potsdam and royal adulation to rejoin his mistress. On the way back he sent to Frederick a letter that gives his side of the matter:

> I abandon a great monarch who cultivates and honors an art which I idolize, and I go to join a person who reads nothing but the metaphysics of Christian Wolff [the expositor of Leibniz]. I tear myself from the most amiable court in Europe for a lawsuit. I did not leave your adorable court to sigh like an idiot at a woman's knees. But, Sire, that woman abandoned for me everything for which other women abandon their friends. There is no sort of obligation which I am not under to her. . . . Love is often ridiculous, but pure friendship has rights more binding than a king's commands.[56]

He was reunited with Émilie at Brussels, which, because of her prolonged lawsuit, became their second home. In May, 1741, they attended the première of *Mahomet* at Lille, and received an ovation. They returned to Brussels elated, but sombered by a growing consciousness that their idyl was over. Her love was still strong, even if possession was its soul, but Voltaire's fire was escaping through his pen. In July, 1741, he apologized to her for his failing ardor:

> *Si vous voulez que j'aime encore,*
> *Rendez-moi l'âge des amours;*
> *Au crépuscule de mes jours*
> *Réjoignez, s'il se peut, l'aurore.*
> *On meurt deux fois, je le vois bien:*
> *Cesser d'aimer et d'être aimable*
> *C'est une mort insupportable;*
> *Cesser de vivre, ce n'est rien.*[57]*

In August, 1742, they went to Paris to assist at the presentation of *Mahomet* at the Théâtre-Français. Voltaire sought from Cardinal Fleury an official permit for the performance; the Cardinal consented. The Paris première (August 19) was the literary event of the year; magistrates, priests, and poets were numerous in the packed audience. All seemed satisfied except some of the clergy, who claimed that the play was "a bloody satire against the Christian religion." Fréron, Desfontaines, and others joined in the complaint; and though the Cardinal felt that these critics were injuring their own cause, he sent private advice to Voltaire to withdraw the play. This was done after the fourth performance before a full house. Voltaire and Emilie returned in angry frustration to Brussels.

Was *Mahomet* anti-Christian? Not quite. It was against fanaticism and bigotry, but it portrayed the Prophet in a hostile light that should have pleased all Christians innocent of history. Voltaire pictured Mahomet as a conscious deceiver who foists his new religion upon a credulous people, uses their faith as a spur to war, and conquers Mecca by ordering his fanatical devotee, Séide, to assassinate the resisting sheik Zopir. When Séide hesitates, Mahomet reproves him in terms that seemed to some auditors a reflection on the Christian priesthood:

> And dost thou pause? Presumptuous youth, 'tis impious
> But to deliberate. Far from Mahomet
> Be all who for themselves shall dare to judge. . . .
>   Those who reason are not oft
> Prone to believe. Thy part is to obey.
> Have I not told thee what the will of Heaven
> Determines? . . .

---

* "If you wish me still to love, bring me back the age of loves; in the twilight of my days revive, if it is possible, the dawn. We die twice, I see it well. To cease to love and be lovable is a death unbearable; to cease to live is nothing."

> Knowest thou holy Abram here
> Was born, that here his sacred ashes rest—
> He who, obedient to the voice of God,
> Stifled the cries of nature, and gave up
> His darling child? The same all-powerful Being
> Requires of thee a sacrifice; to thee
> He calls for blood; and darest thou hesitate
> When God commands? . . .
>   Strike, then, and by the blood
> Of Zopir merit life eternal.[58]

Séide kills the old man, who, dying, recognizes him as his own son. This, of course, was an attack upon the use of religion to sanction murder and foment war. Voltaire meant it so, and in a letter to Frederick he gave, as examples of pious crimes, the assassination of William of Orange and of Henry III and Henry IV of France. But he denied that the play was an attack upon religion; it was a plea to make Christianity Christian.

Cardinal Fleury consoled him by commissioning him (September, 1742) to try his hand at turning the policy of Frederick to friendship with France. Voltaire, proud to be a diplomat, visited the King at Aachen; Frederick saw through his purposes, and answered his politics with poetry. Voltaire returned to Paris, Émilie, and the drama. On February 20, 1743, his greataest play, *Mérope*, was produced by the Comédie-Française with a success that for a while silenced his enemies.

Several plays had already been written on the theme; Euripides had used it in a drama of which only fragments remain. In a preliminary letter Voltaire acknowledged his special indebtedness to Marchese Francesco Scipione di Maffei of Verona, who had produced a *Merope* in 1713. It was a distinction of these plays that their interest turned on parental rather than sexual love. At the final curtain, we are told, most of the audience was in tears. For the first time in the history of the French theater there were calls for the author to show himself on the stage. According to the accepted account he complied, creating a precedent which Lessing deplored; according to other sources Voltaire refused to go on the stage, though urged to do so by the two duchesses in whose box he sat; he merely stood up for a moment and acknowledged the applause.[59] Frederick gave it as his judgment that *Mérope* was "one of the finest tragedies ever written."[60] Gibbon thought the final act equal to anything in Racine.[61]

The success of *Mérope* was alloyed for Voltaire by the failure, soon afterward, of his candidacy for a seat in the Academy. He campaigned for it eagerly, even to proclaiming himself "a true Catholic" and the author of "many pages sanctified by religion."[62] Louis XV at first favored him, but was deterred by his new minister Maurepas, who protested that it would be unseemly to let so profane a spirit succeed to the seat vacated by the death of Cardinal Fleury. The seat was given to the bishop of Mirepoix. Frederick urged Voltaire to abandon a country that so little honored its geniuses, and come and live with him in Potsdam. Mme. du Châtelet objected. The French government advised him to accept the invitation for a time, and to serve as its secret agent in Berlin. Longing to play politics, Voltaire agreed, and undertook again the racking ride across France, Belgium, and Germany. He spent six weeks (August 30 to October 12, 1743) in the enterprise. Frederick again laughed at his politics and praised his poetry. Voltaire returned to Émilie at Brussels. In April, 1744, they resumed their residence at Cirey, and tried to revive their dying love.

In her *Traité de la bonheur* the Marquise thought that "of all the passions the desire for knowledge is the one which contributes most to happiness, for it is the one which makes us least dependent upon each other." Nevertheless she called love

> the greatest of the good things that are within our grasp, the only one to which even the pleasure of study should be sacrificed. The ideal would be two individuals who would be so attracted to each other that their passions would never cool or become surfeited. But one cannot hope for such harmony of two persons; it would be too perfect. A heart which would be capable of such love, a soul which would be so steadfast and so affectionate, is perhaps born once in a century.[63]

In a touching letter she summed up her surrender of this hope:

> I was happy for ten years in the love of the one who had conquered my soul, and those ten years I spent in perfect communion with him. . . . When age and illness had reduced his affection, a long time passed before I noticed it; I loved for two; I spent my whole life with him, and my trusting heart enjoyed the ecstasy of love, and the illusion of believing itself to be loved. . . . I have lost this happy state.[64]

What was it that had turned Voltaire from love to a kind of intermittent fidelity? He seems to have been sincere in pleading the decline of his physical powers; yet we shall find him, within a year, "sighing like an idiot at a woman's knees." The truth was that he had exhausted one phase of his life and interest—Mme. de Châtelet and science. The isolation of Cirey would have palled much sooner on an average mind; it was a blessing only when the police pursued him and science called. But now he had tasted again the pleasures of Paris and premières; he was even playing a part in national politics. If only from a distance he felt the glamour of the court. His friend the Marquis d'Argenson had become chief minister, his friend and debtor the

Duc de Richelieu was first chamberlain to the King, and Louis himself had relented. In 1745 the Dauphin was to marry the Infanta María Teresa Rafaela; a lordly festival must be prepared; Richelieu commissioned Voltaire to write a play for the occasion. But Rameau was to write the music; poet and composer had to work together; Voltaire must come to Paris. In September, 1744, the lovers bade goodbye to Cirey and moved to the capital.

IV. THE COURTIER: 1745–48

He was now fifty years old. He had for a long time been dying annually; "it is most certain," he wrote to Thieriot in 1735, "that I have but a few years to live."[65] He had then lived forty-one years; he was to live forty-three more. How did he manage this? When he fell seriously ill at Châlons-sur-Marne in 1748, and a physician prescribed some drugs, Voltaire "told me," his secretary reported, "that he would follow none of these directions, for he knew how to manage himself as well in sickness as in health, and he would continue to be his own doctor, as he had always been." In such crises he fasted for a while, then ate a little broth, toast, weak tea, barley and water. Secretary Longchamp adds:

> Thus it was that M. de Voltaire cured himself of a malady which probably would have had grave consequences if he had delivered himself up to the Aesculapius of Châlons. His principle was that our health depends upon ourselves; that its three pivots are sobriety, temperance in all things, and moderate exercise; that in almost all diseases which are not the result of serious accidents, or of radical vitiation of the internal organs, it suffices to aid nature, which is endeavoring to restore us; that it is necessary to confine ourselves to a diet more or less strict and prolonged, suitable liquid nourishment, and other simple means. In this manner I always saw him regulate his conduct as long as I lived with him.[66]

He was as skilled as a banker in the management and investment of his funds. He was an importer, a poet, a contractor, a dramatist, a capitalist, a philosopher, a moneylender, pensioner, and heir. His friend d'Argenson helped him to make a fortune in military supplies.[67] He had inherited part of his father's wealth; in 1745 the death of his brother Armand left to him the income of the remainder. He made large loans to the Duc de Richelieu, the Duc de Villars, the Prince de Guise, and others. He had much trouble recapturing the principal, but he compensated himself with interest.[68] In 1735 Richelieu owed him 46,417 livres, on which the Duke paid four thousand livres per year.[69] In the case of the unreliable M. de Brézé, Voltaire asked ten per cent. Much of his money he invested in bonds of the city of Paris at five or six per cent. He had often to instruct his agent to dun his debtors: "It is necessary, my friend, to ask, to ask again, to press, to see, to importune—but not to persecute—my debtors for my annuities and arrears."[70] His secretary calculated in 1749 that Voltaire's income was eighty thousand livres per year.[71] He was not a moneygrubber or a miser. He repeatedly gave money or other assistance to young students, and lent a helping hand or voice to Vauvenargues, Marmontel, La Harpe; we have seen him surrendering to the actors the proceeds of his plays. When he lost forty thousand livres through the bankruptcy of a farmer general to whom he had lent that sum, he took it calmly, using the wise words taught him in his youth: "The Lord gave, the Lord has taken away; blessed be the name of the Lord."

If he had had less money to take care of, and more flesh on his bones, he might have been less sensitive, nervous, and irritable. He was generous and considerate, usually cheerful, good-humored, vivacious; he was capable of warm and steadfast friendship, and quick to forgive an injury that did not hurt his pride; but he could not with patience bear criticism or hostility ("I envy the beasts two things," he said: "their ignorance of evils to come, and their ignorance of what is said of them"[72]). His sharp wit aroused many enemies. Fréron, Piron, Desfontaines attacked him or his ideas with a violence far greater than came from the clergy; we shall listen to them by and by. Voltaire returned blow for blow, despite Mme. du Châtelet's counsel to be silent. He called them hot names, marshaled his friends to war against them; the Marquise was hard put to it to keep him from rushing to Paris to whip or challenge Desfontaines; he even thought of invoking the censorship to suppress the more virulent of his foes. He had all the defects of his qualities, and a few more.

He found in Rameau a man as proud and irritable as himself; their cooperation was a trial for both; but at last the libretto and the music were complete, the players and musicians were rehearsed; *La Princesse de Navarre* went off well (February 23, 1745). A month later Voltaire was given a room in the palace, near what he described in his very private correspondence as "the most stinking *merde*-hole in Versailles." The Marquise du Châtelet resumed at court the place that she had sacrificed for Voltaire; she had now the dizzy privilege of sitting in the presence of the Queen. The rise of Mme. de Pompadour favored Voltaire; he had known her when she was Mme. d'Étioles, had visited her home, had written trivia in her praise. At her urging the King appointed him (April 1) royal historiographer, with a salary of two thousand livres per year.

He was soon required to earn his fee. On May 11, 1745, the French de-

feated the English at Fontenoy; d'Argenson asked for a commemorative
ode; Voltaire in three days turned out 350 lines; they went through five
editions in two weeks; for a moment the King liked Voltaire, and Voltaire
was a poet of war. To further celebrate the victory Voltaire and Rameau
were commissioned to compose a festival opera. *Le Temple de la gloire*,
performed before the court in December, showed Trajan (i.e., Louis XV)
returning in triumph from battle. Voltaire was given a seat at the King's
table that evening, and ate ambrosia; but he asked Richelieu, too eagerly,
"Trajan est-il content?" (Is Trajan content?); Louis overheard him, thought
him a bit forward, spoke no word to him.

Drunk with a mixture of fame and royalty, Voltaire began another campaign for admission to the Academy. He left no stone unturned. On August 17, 1745, he sent a copy of *Mahomet* to Benedict XIV, asking might
he dedicate it to him. The amiable Pope replied (September 19):

> This day sevennight I was favored with your excellent tragedy of
> *Mahomet*, which I have read with great pleasure. . . . I have the high-
> est esteem for your merit, which is so universally acknowledged. . . .
> I have the highest opinion of your honor and sincerity.
>
> I . . . here give you my apostolical benediction.[73]

Voltaire was so delighted with this accolade that he wrote to the Pope a letter of fervent appreciation, ending: "With the utmost respect and gratitude I kiss your sacred feet."[74] He proclaimed to Paris his attachment to the
Catholic faith and his admiration for the Jesuits. He multiplied his praises
of Pompadour and the King. Pompadour pleaded for him, the King consented, and at last, May 9, 1746, the Academy admitted the leading poet
and dramatist of the age. To make his cup run over, he was appointed (December 22) *gentilhomme ordinaire de la chambre*—"gentleman in ordinary
of the chamber," privileged to wait upon the King.

Probably it was in these days of success and satisfaction that he composed his tale *Babouc, ou le Monde comme il va*. Babouc, a gentleman of
Scythia, sets out to see the world, and especially how things are in Persia
(i.e., France). He is shocked by the wars, the political corruption, the purchase of offices, the farming of taxes, and the wealth of the "Magi" (the
clergy). But he is entertained by a lady (Pompadour) whose beauty, culture, and courtesy reconcile him to "civilization." He notes here and there
actions of generosity, instances of honesty. He visits the Prime Minister (a
memory of Fleury) and finds him laboring earnestly to save Persia from
chaos and defeat. He concludes that matters are as good as they can be in
the current condition of human nature and education, and that "the world
as it goes" does not yet deserve destruction; reform is better than revolu-

tion. As for himself, however, he will imitate the "truly wise," who "live among themselves in retirement and tranquillity."[75] Was Voltaire already lonesome for Cirey?

In any case he was not fashioned for a courtier. With incredible tactlessness he celebrated the success of the French at Bergen op Zoom with a poem in which he spoke of Louis as flying from the victory to the arms of Pompadour, and charged both of them to keep what they had conquered. The Queen was outraged; so were her children; half the court denounced the poet's impudence. Meanwhile Mme. du Châtelet had relapsed into gambling; in one evening she lost 84,000 francs. Voltaire, on her shoulder, warned her in English that she was playing with cheats; some of the players understood and protested. News of this scandalous candor ran through the court, leaving the poet scarcely a friend in Versailles or Fontainebleau. Voltaire and Émilie fled to Sceaux (1747) and the still surviving Duchesse du Maine. There he remained for two months in a remote apartment hidden from public view. And there he tried to forget his plight by writing some of those delightful *contes* or *romans* which helped to make him the most popular author in all the literature of France. Apparently he read them, of an evening, to the intimate guests who constituted the Duchess's private court. Hence their brevity, their gay satire and bubbling wit.

The longest of these stories written in the years 1746–50 was *Zadig, or The Mystery of Fate.* Zadig is an amiable, rich, well-educated young Babylonian, "as wise as it is possible for a man to be. . . . Instructed in the sciences of the ancient Chaldeans, he understood the principles of natural philosophy, . . . and knew as much of metaphysics as has ever been known in any age, that is, little or nothing at all."[76] He is about to marry the lovely Semina when he is attacked by brigands, and suffers a wound that develops into an abscess in the left eye. The famous physician Hermes is brought in from Memphis: he examines the wound, and announces that Zadig will lose the eye. "Had it been the right eye, I could easily have cured it, but the wounds of the left eye are incurable." Semina, declaring that she has an unconquerable aversion to one-eyed men, abandons Zadig and marries his rival. In two days the abscess breaks of its own accord; soon the eye is completely cured; Hermes writes a book to prove that this is impossible. Zadig pleases King Moabdar with his wise counsels, and Queen Astarte with his good looks; she falls in love with him; he flees to a distant city. On the way he sees a man beating a woman; he responds bravely to her cries for help; he interferes, is murderously assailed, and slays the man; the woman rails at him for having killed her lover. Zadig proceeds, and is sold into slavery. . . . Zadig "then imagined men as in fact they are, insects devouring one another on a drop of mud."

Memnon the Philosopher told the story of a man who "one day con-

ceived the insane idea of becoming wholly reasonable." He finds himself
in a hopeless and besieged minority, encounters a hundred calamities, and
decides that the earth is an insane asylum to which the other planets deport
their lunatics.[77]

The Travels of Scarmentado takes a young Cretan to country after country, opening up ever new vistas of fanaticism, chicanery, cruelty, or ignorance. In France the provinces are devastated by religious wars; in England
Queen Mary burns five hundred Protestants, in Spain the people sniff with
relish the odor of roasted heretics. In Turkey Scarmentado narrowly escapes circumcision; in Persia he gets involved in the conflict between the
Sunna and Shi'a sects of Islam; in China he is denounced by the Jesuits as
a distinguished Dominican. At last he returns to Crete. "As I had now seen
all that was rare, good, or beautiful on earth, I resolved for the future to
see nothing but my own home. I took a wife, and soon suspected that she
deceived me; but notwithstanding this doubt, I still found that of all conditions of life this was much the happiest."[78]

Micromégas developed the ideas of relativity exploited by Swift in *The
Travels of Lemuel Gulliver*. "Mr. Micromegas," as befitted an inhabitant of
the great star Sirius, is "120,000 royal feet" tall, and fifty thousand around
the waist; his nose is 6,333 feet long from stem to stern. In his 670th year
he travels to polish his education. Roaming about space, he alights upon
the planet Saturn; he laughs at the pygmy stature—only six thousand feet
or so—of its people, and wonders how these underprivileged Saturnians,
with only seventy-two senses, can ever know reality. "To what age do you
commonly live?" he asks an inhabitant. "Alas," cries the Saturnian, "few,
very few on this globe outlive five hundred revolutions around the sun
[these, according to our way of reckoning, amount to about fifteen thousand years]. So, you see, we in a manner begin to die the very moment we
are born. . . . Scarce do we learn a little when death intervenes before
we can profit by experience."[79] The Sirian invites the Saturnian to join him
in visiting other stars. They stumble upon the planet Earth; the Sirian wets
his feet, the Saturnian is nearly drowned, as they walk through the Mediterranean. Reaching soil, they see masses of the tiny inhabitants moving
about in great excitement. When the Sirian discovers that a hundred thousand of these earthlings, covered with hats, are slaying or being slain by an
equal number covered with turbans, in a dispute [the Crusades] over "a
pitiful molehill [Palestine] no longer than his heel," he cries out indig-
nantly, "Miscreants! . . . I have a good mind to take two or three steps
and trample the whole nest of such ridiculous assassins under my feet."[80]

All this was general and genial, and might have passed without a stir. But
in 1748 Voltaire troubled the winds of Paris with a little pamphlet called
The Voice of the Sage and the People, which attacked the French Church

at a very sensitive point—its property. "In France, where reason becomes more developed every day, reason teaches us that the Church ought to contribute to the expenses of the nation in proportion to its revenues, and that the body set apart to teach justice ought to begin by being an example of it." He claimed that monasteries were wasting the seed of men and the resources of the land in vain idleness. He accused "superstition" of assassinating rulers and shedding streams of blood in persecution and war, and reminded sovereigns that no philosopher had ever raised his hand against his king. If kings would unite with reason and divorce themselves from superstition, how much happier the world would be![81] Rarely has so short an essay roused so long a storm. Fifteen counter-*Voices* were published to answer the anonymous "Sage."

During Voltaire's hibernation at Sceaux, Mme. du Châtelet paid her gambling debts and quieted the resentment of the winners at Voltaire's description of them. She brought him back to Paris, where he supervised the publication of his novelettes. Uncomfortable nevertheless, he thought it wise to accept the invitation of Stanislas Leszczyński to visit his court at Lunéville—some eighteen miles from Nancy, the capital of Lorraine. After a laborious journey the tired lovers reached Lunéville (1748); but a fortnight later a letter from d'Argental informed Voltaire that the actors of the Comédie-Française were ready to go into rehearsal of his play *Sémiramis*, and needed him to coach them in the interpretation of his lines. This play meant much to him. Pompadour, in the goodness of her sinful soul, had brought the impoverished Crébillon *père* back to the stage, and had given a lead to the applause; Marivaux had dared to rank the old man's dramas above Voltaire's; the thin-skinned poet had resolved to prove his superiority by writing plays on the same themes that Crébillon had used. So he hurried back to Paris, leaving Émilie in perilous freedom at Lunéville, and on August 29, 1748, *Sémiramis* had a successful première. After the second performance he hastened in disguise to the Café Procope and listened to the comments of those who had seen his play. There were some favorable judgments, which he accepted as his due, and some unfavorable, which pained him all the more because he had to bear them in silence. He profited from the criticisms to revise the play; it had a good run; and now it ranks among his best.

He hastened back through September storms halfway across France to Lunéville, nearly dying en route at Châlons. When Frederick urged him to continue on to Potsdam he excused himself on the ground that his illnesses had made him lose half his hearing and several teeth, so that he would be merely carrying a corpse to Berlin. Frederick replied: "Come without teeth, without ears, if you cannot come otherwise, so long as that indefinable something which makes you think, and inspires you so beautifully, comes with you."[82] Voltaire chose to stay with Émilie.

V. LIEBESTOD

Good "King" Stanislas loved literature, had read Voltaire, was infected with Enlightenment. In 1749 he would publish his own manifesto, *The Christian Philosopher*, which his daughter the Queen of France would read with sad displeasure. She warned him that his ideas smelled strongly of Voltaire's; but the old man relished the ideas as well as the wit of Voltaire; and as he too had a mistress (the Marquise de Boufflers), he saw no contradiction in making the poet a favorite at his court. Moreover, he appointed Émilie's broad-minded husband grand marshal of his household at two thousand crowns a year.

Another officer of Stanislas' court was Marquis Jean François de Saint-Lambert, captain of the guards. Mme. du Châtelet had first met him in 1747, when he was thirty-one and she forty-one; it was a dangerous age for a woman whose lover had become only a devoted friend. By the spring of 1748 she was writing to the handsome officer love letters of almost girlish abandon. "Come to me as soon as you are dressed." "I shall fly to you as soon as I have supped." Saint-Lambert responded gallantly. Sometime in October Voltaire surprised them in a dark alcove conversing amorously. Only the greatest philosopher can accept cuckoldom graciously. Voltaire did not at once rise to the occasion; he reproached them volubly, but retired to his room when Saint-Lambert offered to give him "satisfaction"—i.e., to kill him at dawn. Émilie came to Voltaire at two o'clock in the morning. She assured him of her eternal love, but gently reminded him that "for a long time you have complained . . . that your strength abandons you. . . . Ought you to be offended that it is one of your friends who supplies your place?" She embraced him, called him the old pet names. His anger melted. "Ah, madame," he said, "you are always right. But since things must be as they are, at least let them not pass before my eyes." The next evening Saint-Lambert called upon Voltaire and apologized for his challenge. Voltaire embraced him. "My child," he told him, "I have forgotten all. It was I who was in the wrong. You are in the happy age of love and delight; enjoy those moments, too brief. An old invalid like me is not made for these pleasures." The next night all three supped together.[83]

This *ménage à trois* continued until December, when Madame decided she must go to Cirey to arrange her finances. Voltaire accompanied her. Frederick renewed his invitation; Voltaire was now inclined to accept it.

But soon after her arrival at Cirey the Marquise confided to him that she was pregnant, and that, at her age, now forty-three, she did not expect to survive childbirth. Voltaire sent word to Frederick not to expect him, and asked Saint-Lambert to come to Cirey. There the three lovers devised a plan to secure the legality of the child. Madame urged her husband to come home to accelerate some business. He was not disturbed to find two lovers supplementing him; he enjoyed the hospitality they gave him. The Marquise put on all her charms of dress and caress. He drank, and consented to make love. Some weeks later she told him that she had indications of pregnancy. He embraced her with pride and joy; he proclaimed the expected event to all and sundry, and everyone offered him congratulations; but Voltaire and Saint-Lambert agreed to "class the child among Mme. du Châtelet's miscellaneous works [*œuvres mêlées*]."[84] The Marquis and Saint-Lambert returned to their posts.

In February, 1749, Émilie and Voltaire moved to Paris. There she worked on her translation of the *Principia*, aided by Clairaut. Two letters to Saint-Lambert (May 18 and 20) reveal her character:

> No, it is not possible for my heart to express to you how it adores you. Do not reproach me for my Newton; I am sufficiently punished for it. Never have I made a greater sacrifice to reason than in remaining here to finish it. . . . I get up at nine, sometimes at eight; I work till three; then I take my coffee; I resume work at four; at ten I stop. . . . I talk till midnight with M. de Voltaire, who comes to supper with me; at midnight I go to work again, and continue till five in the morning. . . . I finish the book for reason and honor, but I love only you.[85]

On June 10 Frederick, thinking Voltaire freed by Saint-Lambert from further responsibility for Mme. du Châtelet, urgently renewed his invitation to Potsdam. Voltaire replied: "Not even Frederick the Great . . . can prevent me from carrying out a duty from which nothing can dispense me. . . . I will not leave a woman who may die in September. Her lying-in has every likelihood of being very dangerous; but if she escapes I promise you, Sire, that I will come and pay my court in October."[86]

In July he took her to Lunéville, where she could have proper medical attendance. The fear of death troubled her—to be taken off just when she had found love again, just when her years of study were to be crowned with the publication of her book. On September 4 she gave birth to a daughter. On September 10, after much suffering, she died. Voltaire, overcome with grief, stumbled out of her room, fell, and remained unconscious for some time. Saint-Lambert helped to revive him. "Ah, my friend," said Voltaire, "it is you who have killed her. . . . Oh, my God, monsieur, what could have induced you to get her into that condition?" Three days later he asked Longchamp for the ring that had been removed from the dead woman's hand. It had once held his own portrait; Longchamp found in it Saint-Lambert's. "Such are women," exclaimed Voltaire. "I took Richelieu out of that ring. Saint-Lambert expelled me. That is the order of nature; one nail drives out another. So go the affairs of this world."[87] Madame was buried at Lunéville with the highest honors of Stanislas' court, and was soon followed by her child.

Voltaire and the Marquis retired to Cirey. Thence Voltaire replied to some letters of condolence from Paris:

> You make my consolation, my dear angels; you make me love the unhappy remainder of my life. . . . I will confess to you that a house which she inhabited, although overwhelming me with grief, is not disagreeable to me. . . . I do not fly from that which speaks to me of her. I love Cirey; . . . the places which she embellished are dear to me. I have not lost a mistress, I have lost half of myself, a soul for whom mine was made, a friend of twenty years, whom I knew in her infancy. The most tender father loves not otherwise his only daughter. I love to find again everywhere the idea of her. I love to talk with her husband, with her son.[88]

And yet he knew that he would waste away if he remained a widower in isolated Cirey. He sent his books, scientific apparatus, and art collection to Paris, and followed them on September 25, 1749. On October 12 he established himself in the capital, in a spacious mansion in the Rue Traversière.

VI. MME. DENIS

He easily persuaded his niece to come and play hostess for him, since she had for some time been his paramour.

Born (1712) Marie Louise Mignot, she was the daughter of Voltaire's sister Catherine. When Catherine died (1726), Voltaire assumed the protection of her children. In 1738, aged twenty-six but graced with a handsome dowry from her uncle, Marie Louise married Captain Nicolas Charles Denis, a minor official in the government. Six years later Denis died, just about the time that Voltaire and the Marquise removed to Paris. The widow sought comfort in Voltaire's arms, and he found new warmth in hers. Apparently his avuncular affection was soon transformed into something quite uncanonical. In a letter of March 23, 1745, he addressed his niece as "my beloved."[89]* This could have been a term of innocent affection, but in December, two years before the Marquise met Saint-Lambert, Voltaire sent to the merry widow a letter which must be quoted verbatim to be believed:

> *Vi baccio mille volte. La mia anima baccia la vostra, mio cazzo, mio cuore sono innamorati di voi. Baccio il vostro gentil culo e tutta la vostra persona.*[90]†

Mme. Denis modestly crossed out some of these words, but presumably she responded amorously, for Voltaire wrote to her from Versailles on December 27, 1745:

> My dear one, . . . you tell me that my letter gave pleasure even to your senses. Mine are like yours; I could not read the delicious words you wrote without feeling inflamed to the depths of my being. I paid your letter the tribute I should like to pay to the whole of your person. . . . I will love you until death.[92]

In three letters of 1746: "I count on kissing my beloved a thousand times."[93] "I should like to live at your feet and die in your arms."[94] "When shall I be able to live with you, forgotten by the whole world?"[95] And on July 27, 1748:

> *Je ne viendrais que pour vous e se il povero stato della mia salute me lo permesse mi gitturai alle vostre genochia e baccarei tutte la vostra Belta. In tanto io figo mille baccii alle tonde poppe, alle transportatrici natiche, a tutta la vostra persona che m'ha fatto tante volte rizzare e m'ha annegato in un fiume di delizie.*[96]‡

There is a dangerous age in men as well as in women; it lasts longer, and commits incredible follies. Voltaire was the most brilliant man of his cen-

---

* This and the subsequent excerpts are taken from manuscript letters discovered by Theodore Besterman in 1957, and purchased by the Pierpont Morgan Library of New York from the descendants of Mme. Denis. Dr. Besterman, director of the Institut et Musée Voltaire at Les Délices, Geneva, published the text with a French translation as *Lettres d'amour de Voltaire à sa nièce* (Paris, 1957), and with an English translation as *The Love Letters of Voltaire to His Niece* (London, 1958). All but four of the 142 letters are in Voltaire's hand. Some of them are in Italian, which Mme. Denis could understand. The letters range from 1742 to 1750, but only three are definitely dated, so that their exact chronology is not certain. The dates given in our text are those assigned by Dr. Besterman.

† "I kiss you a thousand times. My soul kisses yours; my *cazzo*, my heart are enamored of you. I kiss your pretty bottom and all your person."[91]

‡ Translation by Dr. Besterman: "I shall be coming [to Paris] only for you, and if my miserable condition permits, I will throw myself at your knees and kiss all your beauties. In the meantime I press a thousand kisses on your round breasts, on your ravishing bottom, on all your person, which has so often given me erections and plunged me into a flood of delight."[97]

tury, but we should not rank him among the wise. A hundred times he fell into such foolishness, indiscretions, extremes, and childish tantrums as rejoiced his enemies and grieved his friends. Now, forgetting that *verba volant* but *scripta manent*, he put himself at the mercy of a niece who apparently was fond of him, but who loved his money with an expansive embrace; we shall find her using her power over him, and aggrandizing her fortune, to the day of his death. She was not a bad woman in terms of the time. But perhaps she went beyond the code of her age in taking a succession of lovers—Baculard d'Arnaud, Marmontel, the Marquis de Ximénès—to second her uncle's attentions.[98] Marmontel described her favorably in 1747: "That lady was agreeable with all her ugliness; and her easy and unaffected character had imbibed a tincture of that of her uncle. She had much of his taste, his gaiety, his exquisite politeness; so that her society was liked and courted."[99]

On the day of Mme. du Châtelet's death Voltaire wrote to his niece:

> My dear child, I have just lost a friend of twenty years. For a long time now, you know, I have not looked upon Madame du Chastellet [*sic*] as a woman, and I am sure that you will enter into my cruel grief. It is frightful to have seen her die in such circumstances and for such a reason. I am not leaving Monsieur du Chastellet in our mutual sorrow. . . . From Cirey I shall come to Paris to embrace you, and to seek in you my one consolation, the only hope of my life.[100]

During the eight months that he now spent in the capital he received new urgings from Frederick, and he was in a mood to accept. Frederick offered him the post of chamberlain, free lodgings, and a salary of 5,000 thalers.[101] Voltaire, who was a financier as well as a philosopher, asked the Prussian King to advance him, as a loan, sufficient funds to defray the cost of the journey. Frederick complied, but with sly reproof likened the poet to Horace, who thought it wise to "mix the useful with the agreeable."[102] Voltaire asked permission from the French King for his departure; Louis readily agreed, saying to his intimates, "This will make one madman the more at the court of Prussia, and one less at Versailles."[103]

On June 10, 1750, Voltaire left Paris for Berlin.

BOOK III

MIDDLE EUROPE

1713–56

CHAPTER XII

The Germany of Bach

1715–56

I. THE GERMAN SCENE

IT was not to be expected that Voltaire, as he passed through Germany, could discipline his volatile Parisian mind to an appreciation of German bodies, features, manners, speech, Gothic letters, music, and art. He had probably never heard of Johann Sebastian Bach, who died on July 18, 1750, eighteen days after Voltaire reached Berlin. And presumably he had not seen Hume's description of Germany in 1748 as "a fine country, full of industrious honest people; were it united it would be the greatest power . . . in the world."[1]

It was fortunate for France and England that these virile folk, numbering then some twenty millions, were still divided into more than three hundred practically independent states, each with its sovereign prince, its own court, policy, army, coinage, religion, and dress; all in various stages of economic and cultural development; the whole agreeing only in language, music, and art. Sixty-three of the principalities—including Cologne, Hildesheim, Mainz, Trier, Speyer, Würzburg—were ruled by archbishops, bishops, or abbots. Fifty-one cities—chiefly Hamburg, Bremen, Magdeburg, Augsburg, Nuremberg, Ulm, and Frankfurt-am-Main—were "free," i.e., loosely subject, like the princes, to the head of the Holy Roman Empire.

Outside of Saxony and Bavaria, most of the German land was cultivated by serfs legally bound to the soil they tilled, and subject to nearly all the old feudal dues. As late as 1750, of the eight thousand peasants in the bishopric of Hildesheim 4,500 were serfs.[2] Class divisions were sharp, but they were so mortised in time that the commonalty accepted them with very little complaint; and they were mitigated by a greater survival and honoring of seignorial obligations to protect the peasant in misfortune, to care for him in sickness and old age, to look after widows and orphans, and to maintain order and peace.[3] The *Junker* landlords in Prussia distinguished themselves by competent management of their domains, and their quick adoption of improved agricultural techniques.

Now that Germany had had sixty-seven years to recover from the Thirty Years' War, industry and commerce were reviving. The Leipziger Messe was the best-attended fair in Europe; it surpassed the Frankfurt fair even in the sale of books. Frankfurt and Hamburg reached in this century a degree of mercantile activity equaled only by Paris, Marseilles, London, Genoa, Venice, and Constantinople. The merchant princes of Hamburg used their wealth not merely for luxury and display, but for the enthusiastic patronage of opera, poetry, and drama; here Handel had his first triumphs, Klopstock found shelter, and Lessing wrote his *Hamburgische Dramaturgie*—essays on the Hamburg theater. The German cities were then, as now, the best-administered in Europe.[4]

Whereas in France and England the king had succeeded in bringing the nobles into subservience to the central government, the electors, princes, dukes, counts, bishops, or abbots who ruled the German states had deprived the emperor of any real power over their domains, and had brought the lower nobility into attendance at the princely courts. Aside from the free cities, these courts (*Residenzen*) were the centers of cultural as well as political life in Germany. The wealth of the landowners was drawn to them, and was spent in immense palaces, sumptuous expenditure, and magnificent uniforms that in many cases were half the man and most of his authority. So Eberhard Ludwig, Duke of Württemberg, commissioned J. F. Nette and Donato Frizoni to build for him (1704–33) at Ludwigsburg (near Stuttgart) an alternative *Residenz* so lordly in design and decoration, and so replete with elegant furniture and objects of art, as must have cost his subjects many thalers and arduous days. The great *Schloss*, or castle, at Heidelberg, begun in the thirteenth century, added in 1751 a cellar vat with a capacity for brewing 49,000 gallons of beer at a time. At Mannheim Duke Charles Theodore, during his long rule as Elector Palatine (1733–99), spent 35 million florins on artistic and scientific institutions, museums, and libraries, and in support of architects, sculptors, painters, actors, and musicians.[5] Hanover was not large or magnificent, but it had a resplendent opera house, luring Handel. Germany was as mad about music as Mother Italy herself.

Munich too had a great opera house, financed by a tax on playing cards. But the duke-electors of Bavaria made their capital famous also for architecture. When his duchy was overrun by Austrians in the War of the Spanish Succession, Maximilian Emanuel had found refuge in Paris and Versailles; when he returned to Munich (1714) he brought with him a flair for art and the rococo style. With him came a young French architect, François de Cuvilliés, who built for the next Elector, Charles Albert, in the park of Nymphenburg, that masterpiece of German rococo, the little palace called the Amalienburg (1734–39). Simple without, it is a wilderness of ornament within: a domed and dazzling Hall of Mirrors (Spiegelsaal), with silvered stucco carved in latticework and arabesques; and a Yellow Room (Gelbes Zimmer) where the gilt stucco baffles the eye that tries to follow its intricate design. In the same overwhelming style Josef Effner began and Cuvilliés completed the Empire Rooms (Reichen Zimmer) in the ducal residence at Munich. Cuvilliés had left France at the age of twenty, before acquiring the full discipline of French taste; unchecked by him, the German artists elaborated the stucco with amateur abandon, achieving retail perfection within gross exaggeration. The Empire Rooms were shattered in the Second World War.

Frederick Augustus I "the Strong," Elector of Saxony (r. 1694–1733), was not to be outdone by any *Münchner* duke. Despite passing to Warsaw (1697) as King Augustus II of Poland, he found time to tax the Saxons sufficiently to make Dresden "the Florence on the Elbe," leading all German cities in expenditure on art. "The town is the neatest I have seen in Germany," reported Lady Mary Montagu in 1716; "most of the houses are new built; the Elector's palace very handsome."[6] Augustus collected pictures almost as avidly as concubines; his son, Elector Frederick Augustus II (r. 1733–63), poured out money on horses and pictures, and, said Winckelmann, "brought the arts to Germany."[7] In 1743 this younger Augustus sent Algarotti to Italy with ducats to buy paintings; soon afterward the Elector bought for 100,000 sequins ($500,000?) the collection of Duke Francesco III of Modena; and in 1754 he bought Raphael's *Sistine Madonna* for twenty thousand ducats, a then unprecedented price. So the great Gemäldegalerie of Dresden took form.

A handsome opera house rose in Dresden in 1718; its company must have excelled, for Handel raided it for his English ventures in 1719; and under Johann Hasse its orchestra was among the best in Europe.[8] It was in Dresden that Meissen porcelain was born—but that must have a story of its own. In the architecture of the Saxon capital the great name was Matthäus Daniel Pöppelmann. For Augustus *der Starke* he built in 1711–22 the famous Zwinger Palace as a festival center for the court: a brilliant baroque complex of columns, arches, lovely mullioned windows, balconies, and crowning cupola. The Zwinger was destroyed by bombing in 1945, but the magnificent gate has been rebuilt on the original design. For the same inexhaustible Elector the Roman architect Gaetano Chiaveri raised in Italian baroque the Hofkirche, or Court Church (1738–51); this too was largely ruined and successfully restored. History is a contest between art and war, and art plays the part of Sisyphus.

II. GERMAN LIFE

Germany was now leading Europe in elementary education. In 1717 King Frederick William I of Prussia made primary education compulsory in his kingdom, and during the next twenty years he founded 1,700 schools to instruct and indoctrinate the young. These schools were usually taught by laymen; the role of religion in education was diminishing. Stress was laid on obedience and industry, and flogging was *de rigueur*. One schoolmaster reckoned that in fifty-one years of teaching he had given 124,000 lashes with a whip, 136,715 slaps with the hand, 911,527 blows with a stick, and 1,115,800 boxes on the ear. In 1747 Julius Hecker, a Protestant clergyman, established in Berlin the first *Real-schule*, so named because it added mathematics and industrial courses to Latin, German, and French; soon most German cities had similar institutions.

In the universities the study of Greek rose to new prominence, laying the foundations for later German supremacy in Hellenic scholarship. Additional universities rose at Göttingen (1737) and Erlangen (1743). Financed by the Elector of Hanover (become King of England), Göttingen followed the University of Halle in according freedom of teaching to its professors, and expanding instruction in natural science, social studies, and law. University students now discarded the academic gown, wore cloak, sword, and spurs, fought duels, and took instruction from the looser ladies of the town. Except in philosophy and theology, German was the language of education.

Nevertheless the German language was now in bad repute, for the aristocracy was adopting French. Voltaire wrote from Berlin (November 24, 1750): "I find myself here in France; no one talks anything but French. German is for the soldiers and the horses; it is needed only on the road."[9] The German theater presented comedies in German, tragedies in French—usually from the French repertoire. Germany was then the least nationalistic of European states, because it was not yet a state.

German literature suffered from this lack of national consciousness. The most influential German author of the age, Johann Christoph Gottsched, who gathered about him a literary circle that made Leipzig "a little Paris," used German in his writings, but he imported his principles from Boileau, denounced baroque art as a glittering chaos, and called for a return to the classical rules of composition and style as practiced in the France of Louis XIV. Two Swiss critics, Bodmer and Breitinger, attacked Gottsched's admiration of order and rule; poetry, they felt, took its power from forces of feeling and passion deeper than reason; even in Racine a world of emotion and violence welled up through the classic form. "The best writings," Bodmer urged, "are not the result of rules; . . . the rules are derived from the writings."[10]

Christian Gellert, who exceeded all German writers in popularity, agreed with Bodmer, Breitinger, and Pascal that feeling is the heart of thought and the life of poetry. He deserved his Christian name; he was so respected for the purity of his life and the gentleness of his ways that kings and princes attended his lectures on philosophy and ethics at the University of Leipzig, and women came to kiss his hands. He was a man of unashamed sentiment, who mourned the dead at Rossbach instead of celebrating Frederick's victory; yet Frederick, the greatest realist of the age, called him "*le plus raissonable de tous les savans allemans*"—the most reasonable of all German savants.[11] Frederick, however, probably preferred Ewald Christian von Kleist, the virile young poet who died

for him in the battle of Kunersdorf (1759). The King's judgment of German
literature was harsh but hopeful: "We have no good writers whatever; perhaps
they will arise when I am walking in the Elysian Fields. . . . You will laugh
at me for the pains I have taken to impart some notions of taste and Attic salt
to a nation which has hitherto known nothing but how to eat, drink, and
fight."[12] Meanwhile Kant, Klopstock, Wieland, Lessing, Herder, Schiller, and
Goethe had been born.

One German of the time won Frederick's active sympathy. Christian von
Wolff, son of a tanner, rose to be professor at Halle. Taking all knowledge
as his specialty, he tried to systematize it on the basis of Leibniz' philosophy.
Though Mme. du Châtelet called him *"un grand bavard,"* a great babbler,
he pledged himself to reason, and in his stumbling way began the *Aufklärung*, the German Enlightenment. He broke precedent by teaching science
and philosophy in German. Just to list his sixty-seven books would clog our
course. He began with a four-volume treatise on "all the mathematical sciences" (1710); he translated these volumes into Latin (1713); he added a
mathematical dictionary (1716) to facilitate the transition to German. He
proceeded with seven works (1712-25) on logic, metaphysics, ethics, politics, physics, teleology, and biology, each title beginning bravely with the
words *Vernünftige Gedanke*, "reasonable thoughts," as if to fly the flag of
reason at his mast. Aspiring to a European audience, he covered the same vast
area in eight Latin treatises, of which the most influential were the *Psychologia empirica* (1732), the *Psychologia rationalis* (1734), and the *Theologia
naturalis* (1736). After surviving all these pitfalls he explored the philosophy of law (1740-49); and to crown the edifice he wrote an autobiography.

The systematic march of his scholastic style makes him hard reading in
our hectic age, but now and then he touched vital spots. He rejected Locke's
derivation of all knowledge from sensation, and served as a bridge from
Leibniz to Kant by insisting on the active role of the mind in the formation
of ideas. Body and mind, action and idea, are two parallel processes, neither
influencing the other. The external world operates mechanically; it shows
many evidences of purposive design, but there are no miracles in it; and
even the operations of the mind are subject to a determinism of cause and
effect. Ethics should seek a moral code independent of religious belief; it
should not rely on God to terrify men into morality. The function of the
state is not to dominate the individual, but to widen the opportunities for
his development.[13] The ethics of Confucius are especially to be praised, for
they based morality not on supernatural revelation but on human reason.[14]
"The ancient emperors and kings of China were men of a philosophical
turn, . . . and to their care it is owing that their form of government is of
all the best."[15]

Despite Wolff's earnest avowals of Christian belief, many Germans thought his philosophy dangerously heterodox. Some members of the Halle faculty warned Frederick William I that if Wolff's determinism were to be accepted, no soldier who deserted could be punished, and the whole structure of the state would collapse.[16] The frightened King ordered the philosopher to leave Prussia in forty-eight hours on "pain of immediate death." He fled to Marburg and its university, where the students hailed him as the apostle and martyr of reason. Within sixteen years (1721–37) over two hundred books or pamphlets were published attacking or defending him. One of the first official acts of Frederick the Great after his accession (1740) was his warm invitation to the exile to return to Prussia and Halle. Wolff came, and in 1743 he was made chancellor of the university. He grew more orthodox as he aged, and died (1754) with all the piety of an orthodox Christian.

His influence was far greater than one would judge from his present paltry fame. France made him an honorary member of her Académie des Sciences; the Imperial Academy of St. Petersburg named him professor emeritus; the English and the Italians translated him assiduously; the King of Naples made the Wolffian system obligatory in his universities. The younger generation of Germans called him the Sage, and felt that he had taught Germany to think. The old Scholastic methods of teaching declined, academic freedom increased. Martin Knutzen took the Wolffian philosophy to the University of Königsberg, where he taught Immanuel Kant.

The development of science and philosophy, and the disillusioning consequences of Biblical research, shared with powerful secularizing forces in weakening the influence of religion on German life. Deistic ideas, coming in from England through translations and through the connection of England with Hanover, spread among the upper classes, but their effect was negligible compared with the result of the subordination of the Church—Catholic as well as Protestant—to the state. The Reformation had for a time strengthened religious belief; the Thirty Years' War had injured it; now the subservience of the clergy to the ruling princes deprived them of the godly aura that had sanctified their power. Appointments to ecclesiastical office were dictated by the prince or the local feudal lord. The nobility, as in England, affected religion as a matter of political utility and social form. The Lutheran and Calvinist clergy lost status, and Catholicism slowly gained ground. In this period the Protestant states of Saxony, Württemberg, and Hesse passed under Catholic rulers; and the agnostic Frederick had to conciliate Catholic Silesia.

Only one religious movement prospered in Protestant areas—that of the Unitas Fratrum, the Moravian Brethren. In 1722 some of its members, oppressed in Moravia, migrated to Saxony and found refuge on the estate of

Count Nikolaus Ludwig von Zinzendorf. Himself a godson of Philipp Jakob Spener, the young Count saw in the refugees a chance to revive the spirit of Pietism. He built for them on his lands the village of Herrnhut ("the Lord's hill"), and spent nearly all his fortune in printing Bibles, catechisms, hymnbooks, and other literature for their use. His travels in America (1741–42), England (1750), and elsewhere helped to establish colonies of the Unitas Fratrum in every continent; indeed, it was the Moravian Brethren who inaugurated the modern missionary activity in the Protestant churches.[17] Peter Böhler's meeting with John Wesley in 1735 brought a strong influence of the Brethren into the Methodist movement. In America they settled near Bethlehem, Pennsylvania, and in Salem, North Carolina. They kept their faith and discipline almost untouched by winds of doctrine and fashions of dress, perhaps at the cost of some hardness of spirit in their family relations; but the skeptic must respect the strength and sincerity of their belief, and its exceptional accord with their moral life.

Morals in this age were generally more wholesome in Germany than in France, except where imitation of France passed from language to lechery. In the middle classes family life was subject to an almost fanatical discipline; fathers habitually whipped their daughters, sometimes their wives.[18] Frederick William I kept the court of Berlin in fearsome order, but his daughter described the Saxon court at Dresden as quite up to that of Louis XV in adultery. Augustus the Strong, we are assured on dubious authority, had 354 "natural" children, some of whom forgot their common parentage in incestuous beds. Augustus himself was alleged to have taken, as one of his mistresses, his bastard daughter Countess Orczelska,[19] who later taught the *ars amoris* to Frederick the Great. In the early eighteenth century the faculty of law at the University of Halle issued a pronouncement defending princely concubinage.[20]

Manners were strict, but laid no claim to Gallic grace or conversational charm. The nobles, shorn of political power, warmed themselves with uniforms and titles. "I have known," wrote Lord Chesterfield in 1748, "many a letter returned unopened because one title in twenty had been omitted in the direction."[21] Oliver Goldsmith's judgment was patriotically harsh: "Let the Germans have their due; if they are dull, no nation alive assumes a more laudable solemnity, or better understands the decorum of stupidity";[22] and Frederick the Great agreed with him.[23] Eating continued to be a popular way of spending the day. Furniture took over the styles of carving and marquetry then flourishing in France, but there was nothing in France or England quite as jolly as the gaily colored ceramic stoves that roused the envy of Lady Mary Montagu.[24] German gardens were Italianate, but German houses, with their half-timbered fronts, mullioned windows, and protective eaves, gave to German towns a colorful charm revealing a keen, however unformulated, aesthetic sense. And indeed it was a German, Alexander Baumgarten, who in his *Aesthetic* (1750) established the modern use of that term, and announced a theory of beauty and art as a part and problem of philosophy.

III. GERMAN ART

Pottery was here a major art, for in this period the Germans showed Europe how to make porcelain. Augustus the Strong hired Johann Friedrich Böttger to transmute base metals into gold; Böttger failed; but with Spinoza's old friend Walter von Tschirnhaus he established a faïence factory in Dresden, and made experiments that at last succeeded in producing the first European hard-paste porcelain. In 1710 he moved the manufacture to Meissen, fourteen miles from Dresden, and there he continued to refine his methods and products till his death (1719). Meissen porcelain was painted in rich colors on a white background with delicate designs of flowers, birds, genre, landscapes, marine views, and exotic snatches from Oriental dress and life. Under Johann Joachim Kändler the process was further improved; sculpture in porcelain was added to painting under glaze; fantastic figurines preserved the persons of German folklore and comedy; and imaginative masterpieces like the "Swan Service" of Kändler and Eberlein showed that art could rival in brightness and smoothness the varied armory of woman. Soon all aristocratic Europe, even in France, was adorning its rooms with humorously satirical figures in Meissen porcelain. The town retained its leadership in the art till 1758, when it was sacked by the Prussian army in the Seven Years' War.

From Augsburg, Nuremberg, Bayreuth, and other centers the German potters poured into German homes a baroque profusion of ceramic products, from the loveliest faïence and porcelain to jolly jugs that made even beer drinking an aesthetic experience. Through most of the eighteenth century Germany led Europe not only in porcelain but in glass.[25] Nor were the German ironworkers anywhere surpassed in this age; at Augsburg, Ebrach, and elsewhere they made wrought-iron gates rivaling those that Jean Lamour was raising at Nancy. The German goldsmiths were excelled only by the very best in Paris. German engravers (Knobelsdorff, Glume, Rugendas, Ridinger, Georg Kilian, Georg Schmidt) cut or burned exquisite designs into copper plates.[26]

German painters in this period did not win the international renown still awarded to Watteau, Boucher, La Tour, and Chardin. It is part of our unavoidable parochialism that non-Germans are not acquainted with the paintings of Cosmas Asam, Balthasar Denner, Johann Fiedler, Johann Thiele, Johann Ziesenis, Georg de Marées; let us at least recite their names. Better known to us than these is a French artist domiciled in Germany, Antoine Pesne, who became court painter to Frederick William I and Frederick the Great. His masterpiece pictures Frederick as a still innocent child of three, with his six-year-old sister Wilhelmine;[27] if this had been painted in Paris all the world would have heard of it.

One family garnered fame in three fields—painting, sculpture, and architecture. Cosmas Damian Asam, in the Church of St. Emmeram in Regensburg, pictured the assumption of St. Benedict into Paradise, giving him the help of a lofty launching pad. Cosmas joined his brother Egid in designing the interior of the Church of St. Nepomuk in Munich—architecture overlaid with sculpture in wildest baroque. Egid carved in stucco *The Assumption of Mary* for an abbey church at Rohr in Bavaria. A fine Italian hand showed in the imposing Neptune Fountain set up in Dresden by Lorenzo Mattielli; this was a famous feature in the splendor of the Saxon capital. Balthasar Permoser spoiled his sculptured *Apotheosis of Prince Eugene*[28] with a confusion of symbolical figures; he decorated with a like extravagance the pavilion of the Dresden Zwinger; he achieved an almost Michelangelic dignity and force in the *Apostles* grouped around the pulpit of the Hofkirche in Dresden; and his linden-wood *St. Ambrose* in that church ranks near the top of European sculpture in the first half of the eighteenth century. Georg Ebenhecht imagined a slim German beauty in the lovely *Bacchus and Ariadne* that he carved for the park at Sanssouci. German parks and gardens abounded in sculpture; a connoisseur of baroque estimated that "there is a bigger proportion of good garden statues in Germany than in the whole of the rest of Europe put together."[29]

But it was only in architecture that German artists caught the eye of European artists in this age. Johann Balthasar Neumann left his mark in a dozen places. His masterpiece was the *Residenz* of the Prince-Bishop of Würzburg; others collaborated in the design and execution (1719–44), but his was the guiding hand. The Venetian Room and the Mirror Room, resplendent in their decoration, were shattered in the Second World War, but four rooms remain to attest the splendor of the interior; and the lordly staircase, known to all the art world for its ceiling frescoes by Tiepolo, was one of several such structures that helped to give Neumann his preeminence among the architects of his time. Quite different, but almost as fine, was the staircase he built for the episcopal palace in Bruchsal—another casualty of the national suicide. Perhaps more beautiful than either was the double staircase made by him for the Augustusburg at Brühl, near Cologne. Staircases were his passion; he lavished his art on still another in a monastery at Ebrach. Interrupting his ascents and descents, he built the *Wallfahrtskirche* (pilgrimage church) of Vierzehnheiligen on the Main; he decorated in ornate baroque the Paulinuskirche in Trier and the Kreuzbergkirche near Bonn; and to the cathedral at Würzburg he added a chapel whose exterior is as nearly perfect as baroque can be.

Ecclesiastical architecture now specialized in massive monasteries. The Kloster Ettal, a Benedictine cloister which Emperor Louis of Bavaria founded in 1330 in a picturesque valley near Oberammergau, was restored in 1718 by Enrico Zuccalli, and was crowned with a graceful dome. The abbey church was destroyed by fire in 1744; it was rebuilt in 1752 by Josef Schmuzer; the interior was elaborately adorned in gold-and-white rococo style, with frescoes by Johann Zeiller and Martin Knoller; sumptuous side altars were added in 1757, and an organ celebrated for its handsome case. The most impressive of these prayerful monuments is the incredibly rich *Klosterkirche*, or cloister church, of the Benedictine monastery at Otto-beuren, southeast of Memmingen. Here Johann Michael Fischer organized the ensemble, Johann Christian contributed the gilt carvings, and Martin Hörmann provided the choir stalls—the pride of German wood carving in this century. Fischer worked intermittently on this enterprise from 1737 till his death in 1766.

The ruling classes were as loath as the monks to wait for a heaven beyond the grave. Some stately town halls were erected, as at Lüneburg and Bamberg; but the major efforts of secular architecture were devoted to castles and palaces. Karlsruhe had, as *Residenz* of the Margrave of Baden-Durlach, a unique *Schloss* in the shape of a fan—the ribs radiating out from a garden handle into the city streets. This palace, like much of the city, was laid in ruins by the Second World War; the great Schloss Berlin, built by Andreas Schlüter and his successors (1699–1720), fell in the same tragedy; still another victim was the Schloss Monbijou, near the Spandau Gate of Berlin; the castle at Brühl, designed for the Archbishop of Cologne, was partly destroyed; the Schloss Bruchsal was a total loss. At Munich Josef Effner raised the Preysing Palace, and at Trier Johann Seitz housed the ruling Archbishop in the Kurfürstliches Palais (Electoral Palace)—a model of modest beauty. For the Bishop-Elector of Mainz Maximilian von Welsch and Johann Dientzenhofer put up near Pommersfelden another great castle, the Schloss Weissenstein, in which Johann Lukas von Hildebrandt installed a famous double staircase where dignitaries could go up and down without collision.

Frederick the Great capped the secular architecture of Germany in the eighteenth century by commissioning Georg von Knobelsdorff and others to build at Potsdam (sixteen miles out of Berlin), on a design laid out by the King himself, three palaces that in their ensemble almost rivaled Versailles: the Stadtschloss, or State House (1745–51), the Neues Palais (1755), and Frederick's summer residence, which he spelled "Schloss Sanssouci." From the River Havel a broad avenue of gently rising steps led in five stages through a terraced park to this "Castle without Care," whose mullioned windows and central dome took some hints from Dresden's Zwinger

Palace. One wing contained an extensive art gallery; under the dome ran a circle of handsome Corinthian columns; and a *Bibliothek* adorned with rococo scrollwork and gleaming with glass-enclosed books offered a retreat from politics and generals. It was chiefly in Sanssouci that Voltaire met his match in the philosopher-king who could govern a state, defy the church, design a building, sketch a portrait, write passable poetry and excellent history, win a war against half of Europe, compose music, conduct an orchestra, and play the flute.

IV. GERMAN MUSIC

From the birth of Handel and Bach in 1685 to the death of Brahms in 1897 German music was supreme; at any time in those 212 years the greatest living composer, except in opera, was a German.[30] Two musical forms, the oratorio and the fugue, attained their highest development in the work of Germans in the first half of the eighteenth century; and some would add that the Roman Catholic Mass received its final expression at the hands of a German Protestant. The age of painting ended; the age of music began.

Music was part of the religion, as religion was so great a part of music, in every German home. There was hardly a family, except in the poorest class, that could not sing part song, hardly an individual who could not play one or more instruments. Hundreds of amateur groups called *Liebhaber* performed cantatas that professional singers now consider discouragingly difficult.[31] Manuals of music were as popular as the Bible. Music was taught with reading and writing in the common schools. Musical criticism was further advanced than in any other country but Italy, and the leading musical critic of the century was a German.

Johann Mattheson was probably more famous and unpopular among German musicians than any German composer. His vanity clouded his achievements. He knew the classical and the modern literary languages, he wrote on law and politics, he played the organ and the harpsichord so well that he could turn down a dozen invitations to exalted posts. He was an elegant dancer, an accomplished man of the world. He was an expert fencer, who nearly killed Handel in a duel. He sang successfully in the Hamburg Opera; composed operas, cantatas, Passions, oratorios, sonatas, and suites; and developed the cantata form before Bach. For nine years he served as *Kapellmeister* for the Duke of Holstein; then, becoming deaf, he resigned himself to writing. He published eighty-eight books, eight of them on music, and added a treatise on tobacco. He founded and edited (1722-25) *Critica musica*, the earliest known critical discussion of past and current compositions, and compiled a biographical dictionary of contemporary musicians. He died at eighty-three (1764), having powerfully stimulated the musical world.

Musical instruments were in continuous evolution and change, but the organ was still their unchallenged chief. Usually it had three or four manuals or keyboards, plus a pedal board of two and a half octaves, plus a variety of stops that could imitate almost any other instrument. No finer organs have been built than those made by Andreas Silbermann of Strasbourg and Gottfried Silbermann of Freiberg. But string instruments were mounting in popularity. The clavichord (that is, key and string) used a manual of keys to manipulate levers armed with little "tangents" of brass to strike the strings; this instrument was already three centuries old, perhaps more. In the harpsichord (which the French called *clavecin*, and the Italians *clavi-* or *gravicembalo*) the strings were *plucked* by a tongue of quill or leather attached to levers moved by (usually) a double manual of keys, aided by two pedals and three or four stops. The term *clavier* was applied in Germany to any keyboard instrument—clavichord, harpsichord, or piano—and to the manuals of an organ. The harpsichord was essentially a harp in which the fingers plucked the strings through the media of keys, levers, and plectra. It produced sounds of a delicate charm, but since the plectrum rebounded as soon as it had struck the string, this instrument had no means of holding a note or varying its intensity. To get two degrees of tone it had to resort to a double manual—the upper one for *piano* (soft), the lower for *forte* (loud). The pianoforte grew out of efforts to overcome these limitations.

In or before 1709 Bartolommeo Cristofori made at Florence four *gravicembali col piano e forte*—"clavichords with soft and loud." In these the plucking plectrum was replaced by a little leather hammer whose contact with the string could be continued by keeping the key depressed, while the loudness of the note could be determined by the force with which the finger struck the key. In 1711 Scipione di Maffei described the new instrument in his *Giornale dei letterati d'Italia;* in 1725 this essay appeared at Dresden in a German version; in 1726 Gottfried Silbermann, inspired by this translation,[32] built two pianofortes on Cristofori's principles. About 1733 he showed an improved model to Johann Sebastian Bach, who pronounced it too weak in the upper register, and requiring too heavy a touch. Silbermann admitted these defects and labored to remove them. He succeeded so well that Frederick the Great bought fifteen of his pianofortes. Bach played one of these when he visited Frederick in 1747; he liked it, but judged himself too old to adopt the new instrument; he continued through his remaining three years to prefer the organ and the harpsichord.

The orchestra was used mainly in the service of opera or choir; music was seldom composed for it alone except in the form of overtures. Oboes and bassoons were more numerous than in our orchestras today; the wood-winds dominated the strings. Public concerts were as yet rare in Germany; music was almost entirely confined to the church, the opera, the home, or the streets. Semipublic concerts of chamber music were given in Leipzig from 1743 in the homes of prosperous merchants; larger and larger quarters were taken, the performers were increased to sixteen, and in 1746 a Leipzig directory announced that "on Thursdays a Collegium Musicum, under the direction of the worshipful Company of Merchants and other persons, is held from five to eight o'clock at the Three Swans [an inn]"; these concerts, it added, "are fashionably frequented, and are admired with much attention."[33] From this Collegium Musicum evolved in 1781 the Grosses Konzert in the Leipzig Gewandhaus (Drapers' Hall)—the oldest concert series now in existence.

Only a small minority of musical compositions were written for instruments alone; but some of these productions shared in developing the symphony. At Mannheim a school of composers and performers—many of them from Austria, Italy, or Bohemia—took a leading part in this development. There the Elector Palatine Charles Theodore (r. 1733-99), a patron of all the arts, gathered an orchestra that was generally reputed to be the best in Europe. For that group Johann Stamitz, a virtuoso of the violin, composed true symphonies: orchestral compositions divided into three or more movements, of which at least the first followed "sonata form"—exposition of contrasted themes, their "free elaboration," and their recapitulation. Following the lead of Neapolitan composers, the new form took normally the sequence of fast, slow, and fast movements—allegro, andante, allegro; and from the dance it sometimes added a minuet. So the age of polyphonic music, based on one motif and culminating in J. S. Bach, passed into the symphonic age of Haydn, Mozart, and Beethoven.

The human voice remained the most magical of instruments. Karl Philipp Emanuel Bach, Karl Heinrich Graun, and others put to music the passionate love poems of Johann Christian Günther; and Johann Ernst Bach of Weimar found inspiration for several fine lieder in the poetry of Christian Gellert. Opera flourished in Germany now, but it was predominantly Italian in form, importing its compositions and singers from Italy. Every major court had its opera hall, usually open only to the elite. Hamburg, controlled by its merchants, was an exception: it offered German opera, opened the performances to the paying public, and recruited its divas from the market place. In Hamburg Reinhard Keiser ruled the Gänsemarkt (Goosemarket) Theater for forty years. During his reign he composed 116 operas, mostly Italian in text and style, but some of them German. For in 1728 Mattheson's *Musikalischer Patriot* raised a battle cry against the Italian invaders: "Out, barbarians! [*Fuori barbari!*] Let the [operatic] calling be forbidden to the aliens who encompass us from east to west; let them be sent back again across their savage Alps to purify themselves in the furnace of Etna!"[34] But the lure of Italian voices and melodies proved irresistible. Even in Hamburg the rage for Neapolitan operas stifled native productions. Keiser surrendered and moved to Copenhagen; the Hamburg theater closed in 1739 after sixty years of existence; and when it reopened in 1741 it was frankly devoted to Italian opera. When Frederick restored opera to Berlin (1742), he chose German composers but Italian performers. "A German singer!" he exclaimed. "I would as soon hear my horse neigh."[35]

Germany produced in this age one operatic composer of the first rank, Johann Adolf Hasse, but he too wooed Italy. For ten years he studied there with Alessandro Scarlatti and Niccolò Porpora; he married the Italian singer Faustina Bordoni (1730); he wrote the music for Italian librettos by Apostolo Zeno, Metastasio, and others. His early operas were so enthusiastically received in Naples and Venice that Italy called him *"il caro Sassone,"* the lovable Saxon. When he returned to Germany he passionately defended Italian opera. Most Germans agreed with him, and honored him above the absent Handel and far above the obscure Bach; Burney ranked him and Gluck as the Raphael and Michelangelo of music in German lands.[36] No one, not even the Italians, equaled the richness of his hundred operas in melodic or dramatic invention. In 1731 he and his wife, the greatest diva of her time, were invited to Dresden by Augustus the Strong; Faustina captured the capital with her voice, Hasse with his compositions. In 1760 he lost most of his property, including his collected manuscripts, in the bombardment of Dresden by Frederick the Great. The ruined city gave up opera, and Hasse and his wife moved to Vienna, where, by now seventy-four, he competed with Gluck. In 1771, at the marriage of the Archduke Ferdinand in Milan, he shared the musical program with the fourteen-year-old Mozart. "This boy," he is reported to have said, "will throw us all into the shade."[37] Soon afterward he and Faustina went to spend their remaining years in Venice. There they both died in 1783, he aged eighty-four, she ninety. The harmony of their lives surpassed the melody of their songs.

While Italian music triumphed in the opera houses of Germany, church music flourished despite Frederick's ridicule of it as "old-fashioned" and "debased."[38] We shall see Catholic music prospering in Vienna; and in the north the surviving fervor of Protestantism inspired a multitude of cantatas, chorales, and Passions, as if a hundred composers were preparing the way and the forms for Bach. Organ music predominated, but many church orchestras included violins and violoncellos. The influence of opera appeared not only in the enlargement of church orchestras and choirs, but also in the increasingly dramatic character of church compositions.

The most famous composer of religious music in Bach's Germany was

Georg Philipp Telemann, who was born four years before Bach (1681) and died seventeen years after him (1767). Mattheson considered Telemann superior to all his German contemporaries in musical composition; Bach, with one exception, may have agreed, for he transcribed whole cantatas by his rival. Telemann was a child prodigy. At an early age he learned Latin and Greek, the violin and the flute; at eleven he began to compose; at twelve he wrote an opera, which was performed in a theater with himself singing one of the roles. At twelve he composed a cantata, and conducted it standing on a bench so that the players could see him.

He grew into a robust and jolly Teuton, bubbling with humor and melody. In 1701, passing through Halle, he met the sixteen-year-old Handel, and loved him at first sight. He went on to Leipzig to study law, but relapsed into music as organist for the Neuekirche (1704). A year later he accepted the post of *Kapellmeister* in Sorau; then to Eisenach, where he met Bach; in 1714 he served as godfather to Johann Sebastian's son Karl Philipp Emanuel. In 1711 his young wife died, taking his heart with her, he said; but three years later he married again. In 1721 he advanced to Hamburg, where he served as *Kapellmeister* for six churches, directed musical instruction in the *Gymnasium*, took charge of the Hamburg Opera, edited a journal of music, and organized a series of public concerts which continued into our own time. Everything prospered with Telemann, except that his wife preferred Swedish officers.

His productivity rivaled any man's in that age of musical giants. For all the Sundays and feast days of thirty-nine years he composed sacred music—Passions, cantatas, oratorios, anthems and motets; he added operas, comic operas, concertos, trios, serenades; Handel said that Telemann could compose a motet in eight parts as quickly as one writes a letter.[39] He took his style from France, as Hasse took his from Italy, but he added his own peculiar verve. In 1765, aged eighty-four, he wrote a cantata, *Ino*, which Romain Rolland thought equal to the similar productions of Handel, Gluck, and Beethoven. But Telemann was the victim of his own fertility. He composed too rapidly for perfection, and did not have the patience to revise, or the courage to destroy, the imperfect products of his genius; a critic accused him of "incredible immoderation."[40] Today he is almost forgotten; but now and then he comes to us as a disembodied spirit through the air, and we find all his resurrected utterances beautiful.[41]

Frederick was not alone in preferring Karl Heinrich Graun to Telemann and Bach. Karl first reached fame by his soprano voice; this failing, he turned to composition, and at the age of fifteen he wrote a *Grosse Passionskantata* (1716) which was performed in the Kreuzschule at Dresden. After a period as *Kapellmeister* at Brunswick he was engaged by Frederick (1735) to direct music at Rheinsberg. He continued during his remaining fourteen years to serve the Prussian court, for even his religious music pleased the skeptical King. *Der Tod Jesu,* a Passion first performed in the Berlin cathedral in 1755, achieved a renown in Germany rivaled only by that of Handel's *Messiah* in England and Ireland; it was repeated annually in Holy Week till our own time. All Protestant Germany joined Frederick in mourning Graun's comparatively early death.

Meanwhile half a hundred Bachs had laid the seed and scene for their most famous heir. Johann Sebastian himself drew up his family tree in *Ursprung der musikalisch Bachischen Familie,* which reached print in 1917; the meticulous Spitta has devoted 180 pages to charting that Orphean stream. The towns of Thuringia were sprinkled with Bachs, traceable as far back as 1509. The oldest *musikalischer* Bach, with whom Johann Sebastian began his list, was his great-great-grandfather Veit Bach (d. 1619). From him descended four lines of Bachs, many of them prominent as musicians; these were so numerous that they formed a kind of guild, which met periodically to exchange notes. One of them, Johann Ambrosius Bach, received from his father the violin technique which he transmitted to his children. In 1671 he succeeded his cousin as *Hofmusikus,* court musician, at Eisenach. In 1668 he had married Elisabeth Lammerhirt, daughter of a furrier who became a town councilor. By her he had two daughters and six sons. The oldest son, Johann Christoph Bach, rose to be organist at Ohrdruf. Another, Johann Jakob Bach, joined the Swedish army as oboist. The youngest was

V. JOHANN SEBASTIAN BACH: 1685–1750

1. Chronology

He was born on March 21, 1685, at Eisenach, in the duchy of Saxe-Weimar. In the Cottahaus on the Lutherplatz the great reformer had lived as a boy; on a hill overlooking the town stood the Wartburg, the castle where Luther hid from Charles V (1521) and translated the New Testament; Bach's works are the Reformation put to music.

His mother died when he was nine; his father died eight months later; Johann Sebastian and his brother Johann Jakob were taken into the family of their brother Johann Christoph. In the *Gymnasium* at Eisenach Sebastian learned much catechism and some Latin; in the *Lyceum* at neighboring Ohrdruf he studied Latin, Greek, history, and music. He stood high in his classes, and was rapidly advanced. His father had taught him the violin, his brother Christoph taught him the clavier. He took eagerly to these musical studies, as if music ran in his blood. He copied note for note a large number of musical compositions not regulary available to him; so, some think, began the impairment of his sight.

At the age of fifteen, to relieve the pressure on Johann Christoph's growing family, Sebastian set forth to earn his own living. He found employment as a soprano singer in the school of the Convent of St. Michael at Lüneburg; when his voice changed he was kept as a violinist in the orchestra. From Lüneburg he visited Hamburg, twenty-eight miles away, perhaps to attend the opera, certainly to hear the recitals of Johann Adam Reinken, the seventy-seven-year-old organist of the Katharinenkirche. Opera did not attract him, but the art of the organ appealed to his robust spirit; in that towering instrument he felt a challenge to all his energy and skill. By 1703 he was already so accomplished that the Neuekirche at Arnstadt (near Erfurt) engaged him to play, three times a week, the great organ recently installed there, which continued in service till 1863. Free to use the instrument for his studies, he now composed his first significant works.

Ambition kept him always alert to improve his art. He knew that at Lübeck, fifty miles away, the most renowned organist in Germany, Dietrich Buxtehude, would give a series of recitals between Martinmas and Christmas in the Marienkirche. He asked his church's consistory for a month's leave of absence; it was granted; he delegated his duties and fees to his cousin Johann Ernst, and set out on foot (October, 1705) for Lübeck. We have seen Handel and Mattheson making a similar pilgrimage. Bach was not tempted to marry Buxtehude's daughter as the price of inheriting his post; he wanted only to study the master's organ technique. This or something else must have fascinated him, for he did not get back to Arnstadt till the middle of February. On February 21, 1706, the consistory reproved him for extending his leave, and for introducing "many *wunderliche* variations" in his preludes to the congregational hymns. On November 11 he was admonished for failure to train the choir adequately, and for privately allowing "a stranger maiden to sing in the church." (Women were not yet permitted to sing in church.) The alien lass was Maria Barbara Bach, his cousin. He made what excuses he could, but in June, 1707, he resigned, and accepted the post of organist in the Church of St. Blasius at Mühlhausen. His yearly salary, exceptionally good for the time and place, was to be eighty-five gulden, thirteen bushels of corn, two cords of wood, six trusses of brushwood, and three pounds of fish.[42] On October 17 he made Maria Barbara his wife.

But Mühlhausen proved as uncomfortable as Arnstadt. Part of the city had burned down; the harassed citizens were in no mood for wonderful variations; the congregation was torn between orthodox Lutherans who loved to sing and Pietists who thought that music was next to godlessness.

The choir was in chaos, and Bach could transform chaos into order only with notes, not with men. When he received an invitation to become organist and director of the orchestra at the court of Duke Wilhelm Ernst of Saxe-Weimar he humbly begged his Mühlhausen employers to dismiss him.[43] In June, 1708, he moved to his new post.

At Weimar he was well paid—156 gulden a year, raised to 225 in 1713; now he could feed the brood that Maria Barbara was hatching. He was not quite content, for he was subordinate to a *Kapellmeister*, Johann Drese; but he profited from the friendship of Johann Gottfried Walther, organist in the town church, author of the first German dictionary of music (1732), and composer of chorales hardly inferior to Bach's. Perhaps through the learned Walther he undertook now a careful study of French and Italian music. He liked Frescobaldi and Corelli, but was especially charmed by the violin concertos of Vivaldi; he transcribed nine of these for other instruments. Sometimes he incorporated bits of the transcriptions into his own compositions. We can feel the influence of Vivaldi in the Brandenburg Concertos, but we feel in them, too, a deeper spirit and richer art.

His chief duty at Weimar was to serve as organist in the Schlosskirche, or Castle Church. There he had at his disposal an organ small but fully equipped. For that instrument he composed many of his greatest organ pieces: the Passacaglia and Fugue in C Minor, the best of the toccatas, most of the major preludes and fugues, and the *Orgelbüchlein*, or *Little Book for the Organ*. His fame thus far was as an organist, not as a composer. Observers, including the critical Mattheson, marveled at his agility with keys, pedals, and stops; one declared that Bach's feet "flew over the pedal board as if they had wings."[44] He was invited to perform in Halle, Cassel, and other cities. At Cassel (1714) the future Frederick I of Sweden was so impressed that he took from his finger a diamond ring and gave it to Bach. In 1717, at Dresden, Bach met Jean Louis Marchand, who as organist to Louis XV had achieved an international renown. Someone proposed a contest between the two. They agreed to meet in the home of Count von Flemming; each was to play at sight any organ composition placed before him. Bach appeared at the appointed hour; Marchand, for reasons now unknown, left Dresden before that time, giving Bach an unpleasant victory by default.

Despite his industry and his growing fame, he was passed over when the Weimar *Kapellmeister* died; the office was transmitted to the dead man's son. Bach was in a mood to try another court. Prince Leopold of Anhalt-Cöthen offered him the post of *Kapellmeister*. The new Duke of Saxe-Weimar, Wilhelm Augustus, refused to let his organist go; Bach insisted; the Duke imprisoned him (April 6, 1717); Bach persisted; the Duke released him (December 2); Bach hurried with his family to Cöthen. As

Prince Leopold was a Calvinist, and disapproved of church music, Bach's function was to direct the court orchestra, in which the Prince himself played the viola da gamba. Consequently it was in this period (1717–23) that Bach composed much of his chamber music, including the French and English suites. In 1721 he dispatched to Margrave Christian Ludwig of Brandenburg the concertos that bear that name.

Those were mostly happy years, for Prince Leopold loved him, took him along on various journeys, proudly displayed Bach's talent, and remained his friend when history parted their ways. But on July 7, 1720, Maria Barbara died, after giving Bach seven children, of whom four survived. He mourned her for seventeen months; then he took as his second wife Anna Magdalena Wülcken, daughter of a trumpeter in his orchestra. He was now thirty-six, she was only twenty; yet she acquitted herself well of the task assigned to her—to be a faithful mother to his children. Moreover she knew music, aided him in his composition, copied his manuscripts, and sang for him in what he called "a very clear soprano."[45] She bore him thirteen children, but seven died before reaching the age of five; there were many heartbreaks in that wonderful family. As his children grew in number and years, the problem of their education disturbed him. He was a hearty Lutheran; he disliked the gloomy Calvinism that reigned in Cöthen; he refused to send his offspring to the local school, which taught the Calvinist creed. Besides, his beloved Prince married (1721) a young princess whose demands upon Leopold lessened his interest in music. Once again Bach thought it time for a change. He was a restless spirit, but his restlessness made him; if he had remained at Cöthen we should never have heard of him.

In June, 1722, Johann Kuhnau died, after filling for twenty years the post of cantor in the Thomasschule at Leipzig. This was a public school with seven grades and eight teachers, giving instruction especially in Latin, music, and Lutheran theology. The students and graduates, under the direction of the cantor, were expected to provide the music for the churches of the city. The cantor was subject to the rector of the school and to the municipal council, which paid the salaries.

The council asked Telemann to take the vacated post, for it favored the Italian style which characterized Telemann's compositions, but Telemann declined. It then offered the place to Christoph Graupner, *Kappellmeister* at Darmstadt, but Graupner's employer refused to release him from his contract. On February 7, 1723, Bach presented himself as a candidate, and submitted to various tests of his competence. No one doubted his ability as an organist, but some members of the council thought the style of his compositions unduly conservative.[46] One proposed that "as the best musicians are not available, we must take a man of moderate ability."[47] Bach was engaged (April 22, 1723) on condition that he would teach Latin as well as music, that he would lead a modest and retired (*eingezogen*) life, subscribe to the Lutheran doctrine, show the council "all due respect and obedience," and never leave the city without the burgomaster's permission. On May 30 he was installed with his family in the residential wing of the school, and began his official tasks. He stayed at that burdensome post till his death.

Henceforth most of his compositions, except the Mass in B Minor, were composed for use in the two main churches of Leipzig—St. Thomas' and St. Nicholas'. Church services on Sunday began at 7 A.M. with an organ prelude; then the minister intoned the Introit, the choir sang the Kyrie, the minister and the choir—and sometimes the congregation—sang the Gloria in German, the worshipers sang a hymn, the minister chanted the Gospel and the Credo, the organist "preludized," the choir sang a cantata, the congregation sang the hymn "Wir glauben all' in einem Gott" (We All Believe in One God); the minister preached for an hour, prayed, and blessed; there followed Holy Communion, and another hymn. This service concluded at ten in winter, at eleven in summer. At eleven the students and faculty ate dinner in the school. At 1:15 P.M. the choir returned to the church for vespers, prayers, hymns, a sermon, and the German form of the Magnificat. On Good Friday the choir sang the Passion. To perform the music for all these services Bach trained two choirs, each of some twelve members, and an orchestra of some eighteen pieces. Soloists were part of the choir, and sang with it before and after their arias and recitatives.

For his complex services at Leipzig Bach received a salary averaging seven hundred thalers per year. This included his share of the students' tuition fees, and his honorariums for providing music at weddings and funerals. The year 1729, which gave us *The Passion according to St. Matthew*, was reckoned by Bach as a bad year, for the weather was so good that there was a dearth of deaths.[48] Occasionally he earned some extra thalers by conducting public concerts for the Collegium Musicum. He tried to improve his income by claiming control over the music in the Paulinerkirche attached to the University of Leipzig; some competitors objected, and for two years he carried on a controversy with the university authorities, achieving at last a compromise unsatisfactory to everybody concerned.

He fought another long battle with the municipal council, which appointed students to the Thomasschule; the councilors tended to send him scholars chosen through political influence rather than for musical capacity; he could make neither treble nor bass out of such newcomers, and on August 23, 1730, he lodged a formal protest with the council. It retorted that he was an incompetent teacher and a poor disciplinarian, that he lost his temper in scolding the students, that disorder was rife in the choirs and the school.[49] Bach wrote to a friend at Lüneburg for help in finding another post. None being open to him, he appealed (July 27, 1733) to Augustus

III, the new King of Poland, to give him a court position and title that might shield him from the "undeserved affronts" that he received. Augustus took three years to comply; finally (November 19, 1736) he conferred upon Bach the title of *königlicher Hofkomponist*—composer for the royal court. Meanwhile the new director of the Tomasschule, Johann August Ernesti, contested with Bach the right to appoint, discipline, and flog the choir prefects. The dispute dragged on for months; Bach twice ejected Ernesti's appointee from the organ gallery; at last the King confirmed Bach's authority.

So his life as cantor in Leipzig was not a happy one. His spirit and energy were absorbed in his compositions and their performance; little remained for pedagogy or diplomacy. He found some consolation in his spreading fame as composer and organist. He accepted invitations to play at Weimar, Cassel, Naumburg, and Dresden; he received fees for these incidental performances, and for testing organs. In 1740 his son Karl Philipp Emanuel was engaged as cembalist in the chapel orchestra of Frederick the Great; in 1741 Bach visited Berlin; in 1747 Frederick invited him to come and try the pianofortes recently bought from Gottfried Silbermann. The King was astonished by "old Bach's" improvisations; he challenged him to extemporize a fugue in six parts, and was delighted with the response. Returning to Leipzig, Bach composed a trio for flute, violin, and clavier, and sent it, with some other pieces, as a *Musical Offering—Musikalisches Opfer*—dedicated to the royal flutist as "a sovereign admired in music as in all other sciences of war and peace."[50] Aside from such exciting interludes, he gave himself with exhausting devotion to his duties as cantor, to his love for his wife and children, and to the expression of his art and soul in his works.

2. Compositions

a. Instrumental

How shall we be excused for venturing, without professional competence, to survey the magnitude and variety of Bach's production? Nothing is possible here except a catalogue graced with affection.

First of all, then, the organ works, for the organ remained his abiding love; there he was unmatched except by Handel, who was lost beyond the seas. Sometimes Bach would pull out all its stops, just to test its lungs and feel its power. On it he disported himself as with an instrument completely under his control, subject to all his fantasies. But in his imperious fashion he set a limit to the willfulness of performers by specifying, through underlying numerals, the chords to be used with the written bass notes; this is the "figured" or "thorough" bass that indicated the *continuo* by which the organ or harpsichord should accompany other instruments or the voice.

During his stay at Weimar Bach prepared for his oldest son and other students a "little organ book"—*Orgelbüchlein*—composed of forty-five chorale preludes and dedicated "to the Highest God alone for His honor, and to my neighbor that he may teach himself thereby." The function of a chorale prelude was to serve as an instrumental preface to a congregational hymn, to outline its theme and set its mood. The preludes were arranged to form fit sequences for Christmas, Passion Week, and Easter; these events of the ecclesiastical year remained to the end the proccupation of Bach's organ and vocal music. And here at the outset, in the chorale "Alle Menschen müssen sterben"—All Men Must Die—we meet one of Bach's recurrent subjects, always tempered with the resolution to face death with faith in Christ's resurrection as a promise of our own. Years later we shall hear the same note in the somber chorale "Komm, süsser Tod"— Come, Sweet Death. Along with this enveloping piety there is in these preludes, and generally in Bach's instrumental compositions, a healthy humor; sometimes he runs friskily over the keys in a merriment of variations that recalls the complaints of the Arnstadt Consistory.

Altogether Bach left 143 chorale preludes, which students of music rank the most characteristic and technically perfect of his works. They are his lyrics, as the Masses and Passions are his epics. He ran the gamut of musical forms, omitting opera as alien to his place, his temperament, and his conception of music as primarily an offering to God. To give his art freer range he added a fugue to the prelude, letting a theme in the bass run after the same theme in the treble, or vice versa, in an intricate game that delighted his contrapuntal soul. So the Prelude and Fugue in E Minor begins with inviting simplicity, then soars to an almost frightening complexity of richness and power. The Prelude and Fugue in D Minor is already Bach at his best in structure, technical workmanship, thematic development, imaginative exuberance, and massive force. Perhaps finer still is the Passacaglia and Fugue in C Minor. The Spaniards gave the name *pasacalle* to a tune played by a musician "passing along a street"; in Italy it became a dance form; in Bach it is a majestic flow of harmony, at once simple, meditative, and profound.

For the organ or the clavichord Bach wrote a dozen toccatas—i.e., pieces that could exercise the "touch" of a performer. Usually they included rapid runs over the keyboard, brave fortissimi, delicate pianissimi, and a fugue of notes playfully treading upon one another's heels. In this group the Toccata and Fugue in D Minor has won the widest audience, partly through orchestral transcriptions more congenial than the organ to the modern unecclesiastical ear. Of the seven toccatas for clavichord or harpsichord, the Toccata in C Minor is again Bach in all his confident mastery of technique—a frolic of counterpoint followed by an adagio of serene and stately loveliness.

It is difficult for us, with underprivileged fingers and half-illiterate ears, to appreciate the pleasure that Bach took and gave in his compositions for the clavier—which for him usually meant the clavichord. First of all, we should have to understand the principles of structure that he followed in developing a few notes of theme or motive into a complex but orderly elaboration—like the arabesque which, in a Persian carpet or a mosque mihrab, wanders from its base in seeming abandon, yet always with a logic that adds an intellectual satisfaction to the sensual enjoyment of the form. And again, we should have to borrow Bach's manual magic, for he invented a playing technique that called for the full use of all the fingers (including the thumb) of each hand, whereas his predecessors had seldom used or required more than the middle three in their compositions for the clavier. Even in the position of the hand he caused a revolution. Players had tended to keep the hand flat in striking the keys; Bach taught his pupils to curve the hand, so that all the finger tips would strike the keys at the same level. Without that technique Liszt would have been impossible.

Finally, adopting a system proposed by Andreas Werckmeister in 1691, Bach demanded that the strings in the instruments be tuned to equal "temperament"—i.e., that the octave be divided into twelve exactly equal semitones, so that no dissonance might occur in modulation. In many cases he insisted on himself tuning the clavichord that he was to play.[51] So he wrote *Das wohltemperirte Klavier*, or *The Well-tempered* [properly tuned] *Clavichord* (Part I, 1722; Part II, 1744): forty-eight preludes and fugues—two for each major and minor key—"for the use and practice of young musicians who desire to learn, as well as for those who are already skilled in this study, by way of amusement," as the original title read. The pieces are of great technical interest to musicians, but many of them, too, can convey to us Bach's gay caprice or meditative feeling; so Gounod adopted the Prelude in C Major, in a corrupted form, as the obbligato for his "Ave Maria." Some profound spirits, like Albert Schweitzer, have found in these preludes and fugues a "world of peace" amid the turmoil of human strife.[52]

Endless in fertility, Bach issued in 1731 the first part of the *Klavierübung*, which he described as "exercises consisting of preludes, *allemandes*, courantes, sarabands, *gigues*, minuets, and other *galanteries*, composed for the mental recreation of art lovers."[53] In later years he added three further installments, so that this *Clavier Practice* finally included several of his most famous compositions: "inventions," "partitas," sinfonie, the "Goldberg Variations," the "Italian Concerto," and some new chorale preludes for the organ. The "inventions," said the manuscript, were offered as "an honest guide by which lovers of the clavier . . . are shown a plain way . . . not

only to acquire good ideas (*inventiones*), but also to work them out themselves, . . . to acquire a *cantabile* style of playing, and . . . to gain a
strong predilection for composition."[54] By these examples the student could
see how a theme or motive, once found, might be elaborated, usually by
counterpoint, through a logical development to a unifying conclusion.
Bach played with his themes like a jolly juggler, throwing them into the air,
turning them inside out, tumbling them upside down, then setting them
soundly on their feet again. Notes and themes were not only his meat and
drink and atmosphere, they were also his relaxation and his holidays.

The partitas were similar diversions. The Italians had applied the term
partita to a dance composition in several diverse parts. So the Partitas in
D Minor and B Major used five dance forms: the *allemande*, or German
dance, the French courante, the saraband, the minuet, and the *gigue*. The
influence of Italian performers appears here, even to the crossing of hands,
a favorite device with Domenico Scarlatti. These pieces seem slight to us
now; we must remember that they were composed not for the mighty
pianoforte but for the frail clavichord; if we do not ask too much of them
they can still give us a unique delight.

More difficult of digestion are the "Goldberg Variations." Johann The-
ophilus Goldberg was clavichord player for Count Hermann Kayserling,
the Russian envoy at the Dresden court. When the Count visited Leipzig
he brought Goldberg along to soothe him to sleep with music. On these
occasions Goldberg cultivated the acquaintance of Bach, eager to learn his
keyboard technique. Kayserling expressed the wish that Bach would write
some clavichord pieces of a character "that would brighten him up a little
on his sleepless nights."[55] Bach obliged with the "Aria with Thirty Variations," which has proved to be a specific for insomnia. Kayserling rewarded
him with a golden goblet containing a hundred louis d'or. It was probably
he who secured for Bach the appointment as court composer to the Saxon
Elector-King.

Bach's art was in these variations, but hardly his heart. With more feeling and pleasure he dedicated to the clavier seven toccatas, many sonatas, a
wonderfully lively and lovely "Chromatic Fantasy and Fugue" in D minor,
and an "Italian Concerto" in which, with amazing vitality and spirit, he
tried to transfer to the keyboard the effects of a small orchestra.

One form found its way into nearly all his orchestral compositions—the
fugue. The fugue, like most musical forms, had come from Italy; the Germans followed it with an impassioned pursuit that dominated their music
till Haydn. Bach experimented with it in *Die Kunst der Fuge:* he took a
single theme and built from it fourteen fugues and four canons in a contrapuntal labyrinth illustrating every type of fugal technique. He left the
manuscript unfinished at his death; his son Karl Philipp Emanuel published

it (1752); only thirty copies were sold. The age of polyphony and the fugue was dying with its greatest master; counterpoint was giving place to harmony.

He was not as fond of the violin as of the organ and clavichord. He had begun as a violinist, and he sometimes played the viola in the ensembles that he at the same time conducted; but as no contemporary and no son mention his violin playing, we may assume that he was not at his best on that instrument. Yet he must have been proficient, since he composed for the violin and the viola music of extreme difficulty, which presumably he was ready to play himself. All the Western musical world knows the *chaconne* with which he concluded a Partita in D Minor for solo violin; it is a *tour de technique* that every violinist used to look to as his supreme challenge. To some of us it is distasteful showmanship of prestidigitation—a horse torturing a cat at several removes. To Bach it was a daring attempt to achieve on the violin the polyphonic depth and force of the organ. When Busoni transcribed the piece for the piano the polyphony became more natural, and the result was magnificent. (We must not be supercilious about transcriptions, for then we should have to condemn Bach himself.)

When we come to Bach's compositions for his dainty orchestras, even the unprofessional ear finds a dozen odes to joy. The *Musikalisches Opfer* must have delighted Frederick the Great with its sparkling melodies, and startled him with its meditative, half-Oriental strains. In addition to the partitas or suites in the *Klavierübung* Bach wrote fifteen suites for dances. Six were called English, for reasons now unknown; six were more understandably called French, since they followed French models and used French terms, including *suite* itself. In some of them technique predominates; then even the string instruments emit chiefly wind. Yet the simplest soul amongst us can feel the solemn beauty of the famous "Arioso," or "Air for G String," which forms the second movement of Suite No. 3. These compositions were almost forgotten after Bach's death, until Mendelssohn played parts of them to Goethe in 1830, and persuaded the Gewandhaus Orchestra of Leipzig to revive them in 1838.

Bach adopted the concerto form as practiced by Vivaldi, and used it in a dozen varieties of instrumental combinations. For one who was born andante the stately slow movement makes the violin Concerto in D Minor particularly pleasant, and it is again the adagio of the violin Concerto No. 2 in E that moves us with its somber depth and meditative tenderness. Perhaps the most delectable of these pieces is the Concerto in D Minor for Two Violins; the *vivace* is all design without color, like a winter elm; but the largo is an ethereal snatch of pure beauty—beauty standing in its own right, without "program" or any intellectual alloy.

The Brandenburg Concertos have their own special history. On March

23, 1721, Bach sent them to an otherwise forgotten prince with the following letter in French, phrased in the manner of the time:

> To His Royal Highness, Christian Ludwig, Margrave of Branden-
> burg:
>
> Monseigneur:
>
> As I had the honor of playing before your Royal Highness a couple of years ago, and as I observed that you took some pleasure in the small talent that Heaven had given me for music, and in taking leave of me your Royal Highness honored me with a command to send you some pieces of my composition, I now, according to your gracious orders, take the liberty of presenting my very humble respects to your Royal Highness, with the present concertos, . . . humbly praying you not to judge their imperfection by the severity of the fine and delicate taste that everyone knows you to have for music, but rather to consider benignly the profound respect and very humble obedience to which they are meant to testify. For the rest, Monseigneur, I very humbly beg your Royal Highness to have the goodness to continue your graces toward me, and to be convinced that I have nothing so much at heart as the wish to be employed in matters more worthy of you and your service, for, with zeal unequaled, Monseigneur, I am your Royal Highness's most humble and most obedient servant,
>
> Jean Sebastien Bach.[56]

We do not know whether the Margrave acknowledged or rewarded the gift; probably he did, for he was devoted to music, and maintained an excellent orchestra. At his death (1734) the six concertos, in Bach's most careful and elegant hand, were listed among 127 concertos in an inventory found by Spitta in the royal archives at Berlin. In the inventory each of the 127 concertos was valued at four groschen ($1.60?).

The Brandenburg Concertos follow the form of the Italian *concerto grosso*—compositions in several movements, played by a small group of predominating instruments (the *concertino*) accompanied by and contrasted with an orchestra of strings (the *ripieno* or *tutti*). Handel and the Italians used two violins and a violoncello for the *concertino;* Bach varied this with his usual audacity, putting forward a violin, an oboe, a trumpet, and a flute as the leading instruments in the second concerto, a violin and two flutes in the fourth, and a clavichord, a violin, and a flute in the fifth; and he developed the structure into a complex interplay of *concertino* with *ripieno* in a lively debate—of separation, opposition, interpenetration, union —whose art and logic only the professional musician can understand and enjoy. The rest of us may find some passages wearisomely repetitious, reminiscent of a village orchestra beating time for a dance; but even we can feel the charm and delicacy of the dialogue, and find in the slow movements a calming peace more congenial to aging hearts and laggard feet than in the vivacious roulette of the allegros. And yet the second concerto begins with a captivating allegro; the fourth is made delightful by a frolicsome flute; and the fifth is Bach *in excelsis*.

b. Vocal

When Bach composed for the voice he could not lay aside all the arts and legerdemain that he had developed on the keyboard, or the tantalizing feats that he demanded of his orchestras; he wrote for voices as if they were instruments of almost limitless dexterity and range, and he made only a grudging concession to the singer's desire to breathe. He followed the custom of his time in stretching one syllable over half a dozen notes (*"Kyrie ele-e-e-e-e-eison"*); such proliferation is no longer in style. Nevertheless it is through his production for the voice that Bach achieved his present repute as the greatest composer in history.

His trustful faith in the Lutheran creed gave him as warm an inspiration as any that Palestrina had found in the Catholic Mass. He wrote some twenty-four hymns and six motets; it was in hearing one of these six— "Singet dem Herrn"—that Mozart first felt the depth of Bach. For the congregations and his choirs he wrote powerful chorales that would have rejoiced Luther's kindred heart: "An Wasserflüssen Babylons" (By the Waters of Babylon), "Wenn wir in höchsten Nöten sind" (When we Are in Direst Need), "Schmücke dich, o liebe Seele" (Make Yourself Beautiful, Beloved Soul); this last so affected Mendelssohn that he told Schumann, "If life were to deprive me of hope and faith, this one chorale would bring them back."[57]

For the feasts of Christmas, Easter, and the Ascension Bach composed oratorios—massive songs for choruses, soloists, organ, or orchestra. The *Weihnachts Oratorium*, as he called the first, was performed in the Thomaskirche in six parts in six days between Christmas and Epiphany, 1734–35. Assuming full right to his own property, he took some seventeen arias or choruses from his earlier works, and wove them into a two-hour story of the birth of Christ. Some of the self-plagiarisms hardly harmonized with the new text, but one could forgive many faults in a composition that presented, almost at the outset, the chorus "How Shall I Fitly Meet Thee?"

Essentially the oratorios were combinations of cantatas. The cantata itself was a chorale interspersed with arias. Since the Lutheran service frequently invited cantatas, Bach composed about three hundred, of which some two hundred survive. Their intimate connection with the Lutheran ritual has limited their audience in our time, but many of the airs embedded in them have a beauty transcending any theology. At Weimar, in his twenty-sixth year (1711), Bach wrote his first outstanding cantata, "Actus tragicus," mourning the tragedy of death but rejoicing in the hope of resurrection. In 1714–17 he commemorated the divisions of the ecclesiastical year with some of his finest cantatas: for the first Sunday in Advent, 1714, "Nun komm, du Heiden Heiland" (Now Come, Thou Saviour of the Heathen); for Easter of 1715, "Der Himmel lacht, die Erde jubilieret" (The Heavens Laugh, the Earth Rejoices), in which he used three trumpets, a kettledrum, three oboes, two violins, two violas, two violoncellos, a bassoon, and a keyboard *continuo* to help the chorus, and persuade the congregation, to shake with joy over the triumph of Christ; for the fourth Sunday in Advent, 1715, "Herz und Mund und Tat und Leben" (Heart and Mouth and Deed and Life), with the familiar lilting chorale and oboe obbligato, "Jesu, Joy of Man's Desiring"; and for the sixteenth Sunday after Trinity, 1715, "Komm, du süsse Todesstunde" (Come, Thou Sweet Hour of Death). At Leipzig he composed another paean to Christ's resurrection—"Christ lag in Todesbanden" (Christ Lay in Death's Dark Prison). And for the bicentennial (1730) of the Augsburg Confession he put Luther's hymn "Ein' feste Burg ist unser Gott" into the form of a cantata as powerful as the hymn, but perhaps too wildly furious to be a fit expression of faith.

Religious though he was, and wedded to piety by his tasks, Bach had in him a healthy sense of earthly joys, and could laugh as heartily as he could mourn. Secular elements crept into his religious compositions; so some strains from the operas of his time have been detected in the B-Minor Mass.[58] He did not hesitate to lavish the resources of his art upon purely secular cantatas, of which twenty-one exist. He composed a "Hunt Cantata," a "Coffee Cantata," a "Wedding Cantata," and seven cantatas for civic ceremonies. In 1725, for the birthday of Professor August Müller of Leipzig University, he wrote a full-length cantata, "Der zufriedengestellte Aeolus," celebrating, perhaps with a sly metaphor, the liberation of the winds. In 1742 he gave his music to a frankly burlesque "Peasants' Cantata," with boisterous villagers dancing, drinking, and making love. After 1740 church music ceased to predominate in Leipzig, and public concerts increasingly presented secular compositions.

Before religious music entered into its decline Bach carried it to heights never reached before in Protestant lands. Among the many survivals of Catholic liturgy in the Lutheran service was the singing of the Magnificat on the Feast of the Visitation (July 2). This commemorated the visit of Mary to her cousin Elizabeth, when, according to the Gospel of St. Luke (i, 46–55), the Virgin uttered her incomparable song of thanksgiving:

Magnificat anima mea dominum,
Et exsultavit spiritus meus in Deo salutari meo,
Quia respexit humilitatem ancillae suae;
Ecce enim ex hoc beatam me dicent omnes generationes

—"My soul doth magnify the Lord, and my spirit hath rejoiced in God my Saviour, for He hath regarded the low estate of His handmaiden; behold, henceforth all generations will call me blessed." Bach twice set these and subsequent lines to music; in the present form probably for the Christmas service at Leipzig in 1723. Here religion, poetry, and music all reach the same summit in a noble unity.

Six years later he touched those heights again and again in *The Passion according to St. Matthew*. To set to music the story of Christ's sufferings and death had for centuries been part of Catholic ritual. Many Protestant composers in Germany had adapted the cantata form to this purpose; two of them had already used the Gospel of St. Matthew as their text.[59] Bach wrote at least three Passions, following severally the narratives of John (1723), Matthew (1729), and Mark (1731). Of this last only fragments remain. The *Johannespassion* suffers from an illogical sequence of scenes and mingling of events, and from a Teutonic tendency to thunderous declamations; but the later parts subside to a tenderness and delicacy of feeling, a somber depth of contemplation, as moving as anything in music. The aria "Es ist vollbracht" (It Is Accomplished) is a profound rendering of the crucial event in the Christian story; there could be no greater test of a composer or a painter.

On Good Friday afternoon, April 15, 1729, in the Thomaskirche at Leipzig, Bach produced the greatest of his compositions. In this *Matthäuspassion* he had the advantage of a good German libretto, based on Matthew's relatively full account, and arranged by a local litterateur, Christian Friedrich Henrici, pennamed "Picander." Bach himself seems to have written the text for several of the choruses. Some have thought these choruses an unwarranted interruption of the Gospel narrative; but, like the chorus in a Greek play, they add to the drama by comment and interpretation, and their somber harmonies both express and purge our emotions—which are two functions of the highest art. Whereas so much of Bach's music is the proclamation of skill or power, nearly all the *Passion according to St. Matthew* is the voice of sorrow, gratitude, or love—in the tender somber refrain of the recurring chorale, in the delicacy of the arias, in the haunting melodies of flutes singing as if from another world, in the reverent restraint of accompaniments winding around the words and amid the voices like some gold-and-silver illumination of a medieval missal. Here Bach opens to us depths of feeling and significance revealed elsewhere only in the original narrative itself. For to us in Western civilization this remains the most moving of all tragedies, since it does not merely represent the crucifixion of a noble idealist by our fellow men, but symbolizes also his daily crucifixion in Christendom, and the slow death, in many of us, of the faith that loved him as its God.

Bach almost succeeded in touching again, in the B-Minor Mass, the heights of emotion and artistry reached in the *Matthäuspassion*. But he could not feel so fully in harmony with his new enterprise. The Gospel Passion was the root and pivot of the Protestant creed, and Bach was irrevocably immersed in that creed. The Mass, however, was a Roman Catholic development; the Credo itself voiced unmistakable commitment to *"unam sanctam catholicam et apostolicam ecclesiam."* Though the Lutheran ritual still retained much of the Roman Catholic Mass, this much was an uncomfortable vestige which had already discarded the Agnus Dei. In Bach's time and churches the Mass was being part by part replaced by cantatas, and Latin remnants were being progressively eliminated from the liturgy. Bach's Passions were sung in German; he had inserted four German hymns among the Latin verses of his Magnificat; but the Mass was so traditionally Latin that any German interpolations risked the reproach of incongruity. He had risked this challenge by writing four partial Masses with such German adjuncts, to an unsatisfactory result. He studied with care the Catholic Masses composed by Palestrina and other Italians. His connection with the Dresden court suggested that he might please the Catholic Elector-King by composing a Catholic Mass. When he sent to Augustus III (1733) an appeal for a court post and title, he included a Kyrie and a Gloria, which later became parts of the B-Minor Mass. The King apparently took no notice of them. Bach performed them in the churches of Leipzig; they were favorably received; and he proceeded (1733–38) to add a Credo, a Sanctus, an Osanna, a Benedictus, an Agnus Dei, and a "Dona nobis pacem." When the whole was complete it was a Mass in Catholic form. Probably Bach hoped that Augustus III would have it performed in Poland, but this was not to be; it has never been sung in a Catholic church. Bach presented it piecemeal, on divers occasions, in the Thomaskirche or the Nikolaikirche of Leipzig.

Shall we expose the hesitant reservations with which we admire this massive Mass in B Minor? Bach's power overrides in many numbers the humility that should infuse an address to the Deity; sometimes it seems that he must have thought God hard of hearing, as having been so long silent in so many languages. The Kyrie drags along its rumbling and confused immensity, until at last we too cry *"Eleison*—have mercy!" The Gloria is often exquisite in its orchestral accompaniment, and moves on to a lovely aria, the "Qui sedes ad dexteram Patris"; but then it becomes raucous with horns in the "Quoniam tu solus sanctus," and treats the "Cum Sancto Spiritu" with such staccato thunder as must have made the Holy Spirit tremble lest this mighty Teuton should take heaven by storm. Strange to say, the Credo —whose doctrinal niceties, dividing Christendom, do not naturally lend themselves to music—produces the supreme moments of the B-Minor Mass: the "Et incarnatus est" and the Crucifixus, where Bach catches again the hushed reverence of the *St. Matthew Passion*. Then the "Et resurrexit" brings out all the impatient fortissimi of trumpets and drums to shout and roar with jubilation over Christ's conquest of death. The Benedictus calms us with its delicate tenor aria and its heavenly violin solo; the orchestral accompaniment to the Agnus Dei is profoundly beautiful; but the "Dona nobis pacem" is a proof of power rather than a gift of peace.——These are frank reactions of no critical worth. Only those can fully appreciate the B-Minor Mass who, to a Christian rearing that has not lost its emotional overtones, add the technical competence to discern and enjoy the structure, tonalities, and workmanship of the composition, the variety of resources used, the complexity of the orchestration, and the adaptation of musical motives to the ideas of the text.

Some professional musicians criticized Bach in his lifetime. In 1737 Johann Adolf Scheibe (later *Kapellmeister* to the King of Denmark) published an anonymous letter praising Bach as an organist, but suggesting that "this great man would be the admiration of all nations if he had more amenity, and if his works were not made unnatural by their turgid and confused character, and their beauty obscured by too much art."[60] A year later Scheibe renewed the attack: "Bach's church pieces are constantly more artificial and tedious, and by no means so full of impressive conviction, or of such intellectual reflection, as the works of Telemann and Graun."[61] Scheibe had tried to obtain the post of organist at Leipzig; Bach had commented unfavorably on his test performance, and had satirized him in a cantata; there may have been some spite in Scheibe's critique. But Spitta, the most zealous of Bach's admirers, tells us that many of Scheibe's contemporaries shared his views.[62] Some of the critics may have represented the reaction of the new generation in Germany against the contrapuntal music that had reached in Bach an excellence beyond which nothing seemed possible except imitations; the twentieth century has seen a similar reaction against the symphony.

Scheibe would probably have preferred Handel to Bach. But Handel was so lost to England that Germans must have found it difficult to compare him with Bach. When this was done it was always to place Handel first.[63] Beethoven expressed the German view when he said, "Handel is the greatest of us all";[64] but that was before Bach had been quite resurrected from oblivion. It is a pity that these two giants—the chief glories of music and of Germany in the first half of the eighteenth century—never met; they might have influenced each other beneficently. Both men stemmed from the organ, and were recognized as the greatest organists of their time; Bach continued to favor that instrument, while Handel, moving among divas and *castrati*, gave supremacy to the voice. Handel wedded Italian melody to German counterpoint, and opened a road to the future; Bach was the completion and perfection of the polyphonic, fugal, contrapuntal past. Even his sons felt that no further movement was open on that line.

Nevertheless there was something healthy in that old music, which men like Mendelssohn would recall with longing; for it was still infused with trustful faith, not yet disturbed by doubts that would reach to the heart of the consoling creed. It was the voice of a culture "in form," as the consistency and culmination of a tradition and an art. It reflected the ornamental elaboration of baroque, and of a now unchallenged aristocracy. Germany had not yet entered its *Aufklärung*, nor heard any chanticleers of revolution. Lessing was still young; nearly every German took for granted the Nicene Creed; only Prince Frederick of Prussia preferred Voltaire. Soon the magnificent structure of inherited beliefs and ways was to be shaken almost to collapse by the agitations of innovating minds; that old ordered peace, that stability of classes, that marvelous and unquestioning faith, which had written the music of Bach, would pass away; and all things, even music, would change, always excepting man.

3. Coda

His isolation and domestication in Leipzig enabled him to inherit the past without resentment or revolt. His religious faith was, next to his music, his comfort and refuge. He had eighty-three volumes of theology, exegesis, or homilies in his library. To his masculine and orthodox Lutheranism he added some tinge of mysticism, perhaps from the Pietist movement of his time—even though he opposed Pietism as hostile to any church music but hymns. Most of his music was a form of worship. Usually he began to compose by praying "*Jesu juva*" (Jesus help me). He prefaced or ended nearly all his works by dedicating them to the honor and glory of God. He defined music as "*eine wohlklingende Harmonie zur Ehre Gottes und zulässigen Ergötzung des Gemüths*"—"an agreeable harmony for the honor of God and the permissible delight of the soul."[65]

The portraits that survive show him in his later years as a typical German, broad-shouldered, stout, with full and ruddy face and majestic nose; add arched eyebrows that gave him an imperious, half-irritated, half-challenging look. He had a temper, and fought stoutly for his place and views;

otherwise he was an amiable and kindly bear, who could unbend his dignity in humor when opposition ceased. He took no part in the social life of Leipzig, but he did not stint in hospitality to his friends, among whom he numbered many rivals like Hasse and Graun.[66] He was a family man, doubly absorbed in his work and his home. He trained all his ten surviving children to music, and provided them with instruments; his house contained five claviers, a lute, a viola da gamba, and several violins, violas, and violoncellos. As early as 1730 he wrote to a friend: "I can already form a concert, both vocal and instrumental, from my own family."[67] We may see later how his sons carried on his art and surpassed his fame.

In his final years his eyesight failed. In 1749 he consented to an operation by the same doctor who had treated Handel with apparent success; this time it failed, and left him totally blind. Thereafter he lived in a darkened room, for the light that he could not see hurt his eyes. Like the deaf Beethoven, he continued to compose despite his affliction; now he dictated to a son-in-law the chorale prelude "Wenn wir in höchsten Nöten sind." He had long prepared himself for death, had disciplined himself to accept it as, in its due time, a gift of the gods: so he composed the moving "Komm, Süsser Tod":

> Come, kindly Death, blessed repose,
> Come, for my life is dreary,
> And I of earth am weary.
> Come, for I wait for thee,
> Come soon and calm thou me;
> Gently mine eyelids close;
> Come, blest repose.[68]

On July 18, 1750, his eyesight seemed miraculously restored; his family gathered around in joy. But suddenly, on July 28, he died of an apoplectic stroke. In the hopeful language of the time, "he fell calmly and blessedly asleep in God."[69]

After his death he was almost forgotten. Part of this oblivescence was due to the confinement of Bach to Leipzig, part to the difficulty of his vocal compositions, part to the decline of taste for religious music and contrapuntal forms. Johann Hiller, who in 1789 occupied Bach's place as cantor of the Thomasschule, sought "to inspire the pupils with abhorrence of the crudities of Bach."[70] The name Bach, in the second half of the eighteenth century, meant Karl Philipp Emanuel, who regretted the old-fashioned character of his father's music.[71] By 1800 all memory of Johann Sebastian Bach seemed to have disappeared.

Only his sons remembered his work. Two of them described it to Johann Nicolaus Forkel, director of music at the University of Göttingen. Forkel studied several of the compositions, became enthusiastic, and published in 1802 an eighty-nine-page biography which declared that

> the works that Johann Sebastian Bach has left us are a priceless national heritage, of a kind that no other race possesses. . . . The preservation of the memory of this great man is not merely a concern of art, it is a concern of the nation. . . . This man, the greatest musical poet and the greatest musical theoretician that has ever existed, and that probably will ever exist, was a German. Be proud of him, O Fatherland![72]

This appeal to patriotism opened Bach's grave. Karl Zelter, director of the Singakademie in Berlin, bought the manuscript of the *Matthäuspassion*. Felix Mendelssohn, Zelter's pupil, prevailed upon him to let him conduct, at the Singakademie, the first non-church performance of the composition (March 11, 1829). A friend of Mendelssohn remarked that the *St. Matthew Passion* had come to light almost exactly a hundred years after its first presentation, and that a twenty-year-old Jew was accountable for its resurrection.[73] All the performers gave their services free. Mendelssohn added to the revival by including other works of Bach in his recitals. In 1830 he was for a time the guest of Goethe, who kept him busy playing Bach.

The revival fell in with the Romantic movement, and with the renewal of religious faith after the Napoleonic Wars. Rationalism had had its day; it had been associated with the murderous Revolution, and with that terrible "Son of the Revolution" who had so often humiliated Germany on the battlefield; now Germany was victorious, and even Hegel joined in acclaiming Bach as a hero of the nation. In 1837 Robert Schumann appealed for the complete publication of Bach's works; in 1850 the Bachgesellschaft was formed; Bach manuscripts were collected from every source; in 1851 the first volume was issued, in 1900 the forty-sixth and last. Brahms said that the two greatest events in German history during his lifetime were the foundation of the German Empire and the complete publication of Bach.[74] Today these compositions are more frequently performed than those of any other composer, and the ranking of Bach as "the greatest musical poet that has ever existed" is accepted throughout the Western world.

FIG. 68—GEORG RAPHAEL DONNER: *St. Martin and the Beggar*, Pressburg (now Brati-slava) Cathedral (Bettmann Archive)

Fig. 69—*Voltaire's Villa Les Délices*, Geneva, now the Institut et Musée Voltaire (Photograph by Jean Arlaud)

Fig. 70—Georg Raphael Donner: Marble relief, *Hagar in the Wilderness*, Barockmuseum, Vienna
PAGE 434

123.

FIG. 71–JACQUES ANDRÉ NAIGEON: *Pierre Simon Laplace.*
From E. T. Bell, *Men of Mathematics* (New York: Simon
and Schuster, 1937)   PAGE 546

FIG. 72–JAMES SHARPLES: *Joseph
Priestley*. National Portrait Gallery, London (Bettmann Archive)   PAGE 526

FIG. 73–UNKNOWN ARTIST: *Leonard Euler*. From E. T. Bell, *Men
of Mathematics* (Simon and
Schuster, 1937)   PAGE 509

FIG. 74—ENGRAVING FROM A BUST IN THE LIBRARY OF THE INSTITUT DE FRANCE: *Joseph Louis Lagrange*. (Bettmann Archive)

PAGE 510

FIG. 75—LEMUEL FRANCIS ABBOTT: *William Herschel*. National Portrait Gallery, London (Bettmann Archive)   PAGE 541

FIG. 76—ENGRAVING AFTER A PAINTING BY HUBERT DROUAIS IN THE INSTITUT DE FRANCE: *Georges Louis Leclerc de Buffon*. (Bettmann Archive)   PAGE 569

FIG. 77—JACQUES LOUIS DAVID: *Lavoisier and His Wife*. Rockefeller Foundation, New York (Bettmann Archive)   PAGE 531

FIG. 80—M. HOFFMAN: *Carl Linnaeus in Lapp Dress.*
(Bettmann Archive)   PAGE 561

FIG. 81—SIR JOSHUA REYNOLDS: *John Hunter*. Royal College of Surgeons of England, London

PAGE 587

Fig. 82—Giulio Monteverde: *Edward Jenner Vaccinating a Child*. Palazzo Bianco, Genoa (Bettmann Archive)

FIG. 83—UNKNOWN ARTIST: *Julien Offroy de La Mettrie*. From La Mettrie, *Man A Machine* (Chicago: Open Court Publishing Co., 1912) PAGE 617

FIG. 84—EBERLEIN: *Albrecht von Haller*. (Bettmann Archive) PAGES 477, 588

Fig. 89—Charles Nicolas Cochin II: *Frontispiece of the "Encyclopédie."*
Albertina Museum, Vienna   PAGE 635

FIG. 90—JEAN ANTOINE HOUDON: *Voltaire in Old Age*. Château de Versailles (Bettmann Archive)

CHAPTER XIII

Frederick the Great and Maria Theresa

I. IMPERIAL PRELUDE: 1711–40

VOLTAIRE was apparently the first to dub Frederick "Great" ("*Fréd-éric le Grand*"), so early as 1742;[1] the phrase was part of a mutual-admiration pact with still ten years to run. But if history may join Whitman in blowing bugles for the defeated it might as justly call Maria Theresa great, for she was one of several queens who in modern times have surpassed and shamed most kings.

Let us approach her through her background. Six years before her birth her Hapsburg father succeeded (1711) as Charles VI to the throne of the "Holy Roman Empire." Voltaire thought it none of the three, but it was still an empire, dressed in the dignity of nine centuries. Governed loosely from Vienna, it included Austria, Hungary, Bohemia (Czechoslovakia), Styria, Carinthia, Carniola, and the Tirol; and in 1715 it extended its power over the former Spanish Netherlands, which we know as Belgium. The German states were only formally subject to the emperor, but the German free cities acknowledged his authority in their external affairs. Bohemia was now in decline, disordered by religious intolerance and exploited by absentee landlords mostly of alien speech. Hungary had suffered from being the chief area of contention between Christians and Turks; a dozen armies had crossed and consumed it; population had fallen, local government was in chaos; a numerous and martial nobility, now only partly Magyar, refused to pay Imperial taxes, and hated Austrian rule. None but nobles and the Church owned land in Hungary; they divided it into enormous estates tilled by serfs, and drew from them the revenues with which they built great monasteries, castles, and palaces, and patronized music and art. Some nobles owned fifty thousand acres each; the Esterházy family held seven million.[2]

Austria itself, as chief beneficiary of the Empire, was prospering. Whereas Hungary had some two millions population, Austria had approximately 6,100,000 in 1754, expanding to 8,500,000 in 1800. Here, too, the land was owned by nobles or clergy and tilled by serfs; serfdom survived there till 1848. As in England, the estates were kept intact by primogeniture, the bequest of the whole to the oldest son; younger sons were cared for by

appointment to posts in the army, the Church, or the administration; so the
court of the Emperor Charles VI numbered forty thousand souls. There
was no rich middle class in Austria to challenge the omnipotence of the
aristocracy, or dilute its blue blood. Marriages were matters of protocol.
Mistresses and lovers were allowed by unwritten law, but only within the
class. Lady Mary Montagu wrote from Vienna in 1716, presumably with
the exaggerations of a traveler:

> 'Tis the established custom for every lady to have two husbands, one
> that bears the name, and another that performs the duties. And these
> engagements are so well known that it would be a downright affront,
> and publicly resented, if you invited a woman of quality to dinner
> without at the same time inviting her two attendants, . . . lover and
> husband, between whom she always sits in state with great gravity. . .
> A woman looks out for a lover as soon as she is married, as part of her
> equipage.[3]

The aristocracy, throughout what was now being transformed into an
Austro-Hungarian empire, worked hand in hand with the Church. The
nobles probably took the Catholic theology with a grain of salt; several of
them were Freemasons;[4] but they contributed gratefully to a religion that
so graciously helped their serfs and undowered daughters to reconcile
themselves hopefully to their earthly lot. Diversity of creeds would have
confused this operation by leading to debate and doubt; religious toleration
was obviously bad politics. Archbishop Firmian of Salzburg made life so
uncomfortable for the Protestants in his archdiocese that thirty thousand
of them migrated, mostly to Prussia (1722–23),[5] where they strengthened
Austria's rising enemy. Similar migrations or expulsions from Bohemia
shared in the economic decline of that once proudly independent state, and
contributed to the advance of Protestant Germany.

Rich and poor joined in financing the ecclesiastical architecture of the
age. In Prague the greatest of Czech architects, Kilian Ignaz Dientzenhofer, completed in massive grandeur the Church of St. Nicholas, which
Christoph Dientzenhofer had begun. Johann Bernhard Fischer von Erlach,
the greatest of Austrian architects, left his mark in Salzburg, Prague, and
Rome, and, with his son Josef Emanuel, raised a baroque masterpiece in the
Church of St. Charles at Vienna. Magnificent monasteries proclaimed the
glory of God and the comforts of celibacy. There was the Benedictine
abbey at Melk on the Danube, where Jakob Prandtauer and his aides spread[6]
a complex of buildings, towers, and dome, with an interior of stately arches,
perfect pillars, and gorgeous decoration. There was the old convent of the
Augustinian canons at Dürnstein, rebuilt[7] in sumptuous baroque by Josef
Munggenast; note that its chief glories, the main portal and the west tower,

were the product of Matthias Steindl, a sculptor who took up architecture at the age of seventy-eight. There were the Benedictine abbey church and library at Altenburg (also by Munggenast[8]), famous for luxuriant ornament. There was the twelfth-century abbey of the Cistercian friars at Zwettl, where Munggenast and Steindl raised a new façade, tower, and library;[9] the glorious choir, however, was the achievement of Meister Johann in 1343–48; here the old Gothic displayed its superiority over the new baroque. There was Stams Abbey in the Tirol, rebuilt[10] by Georg Gumpp, and distinguished by the iron grilles and stucco decoration of its "Prelates' Staircase"; here the Hapsburg princes were buried. There was the abbey church at Herzogenburg, the chef-d'oeuvre in the brief life (1724–48) of Josef Munggenast's son Franz. And there was the abbey church at Wilhering, which has been judged "the loveliest rococo building in Austria."[11] We remark, in passing, the superb organs in these churches, as at Herzogenburg and Wilhering, and the handsome libraries; typical is the *Bibliotheksaal* of the Benedictine monastery at Admont, housing 94,000 volumes and 1,100 manuscripts in a shrine of baroque embellishment. The monks of Austria were at the height of their glory in this age of waning faith.

The nobles kept pace with them. In Austria and Hungary, as in Germany, every prince hungered for a Versailles; and though he could not rival that unconscionable splendor he gathered sufficient spoils to build a *palais* (as he called it) whose every aspect should mirror his transcendence. Prince Eugene of Savoy raised a summer palace on two levels of his estate outside Vienna: a "Lower Belvedere" (now the Barockmuseum), and an "Upper Belvedere" handsomely designed by Johann Lukas von Hildebrandt. Johann Bernhard Fischer von Erlach designed the Prince's Winter Palace (now the Finance Ministry). He also drew up plans for the palace and gardens of Schönbrunn to rival Versailles, but the actual construction, begun in 1696, abandoned or reduced these plans as it proceeded. Fischer von Erlach and his son Josef Emanuel designed the Imperial—now the National—Library, which a specialist in baroque art considers to have the finest interior of any library in the world.[12] In 1726 Charles VI opened this treasure to the public; in 1737 he bought for it Eugene of Savoy's immense collection of manuscripts and books. Vienna was by far the most beautiful city in the Germanic realm.

Most Austrian architecture was adorned with sculpture. We note with shamefaced ignorance the wood *Crucifixion* by Andrä Thamasch in Stams Abbey, and Balthasar Moll's marble figure of the Emperor Francis I in the Barockmuseum at Vienna; and we can at a distance feel the dedication of Josef Stammel, who gave most of his life to decorating with statuary the Abbey of Admont. But how shall we be pardoned for coming so late to recognize Georg Raphael Donner as second only to Bernini among the sculptors of this age? Born in Esslingen in Lower Austria (1693), he learned his art from Giovanni Giuliani; through this Italian tutelage he acquired the classic bent that enabled him to chasten the exuberance of Austrian baroque. His marble *Apotheosis of Charles VI*,[13] however, still suffers from the fancifulness of baroque—the Emperor is raised to heaven by an angel with charming legs and effulgent breasts; nevertheless we are grateful to art for restoring to the seraphim—whom philosophy had thought bodiless—something tangible. Almost worthy of Renaissance Italy is Donner's *St. Martin and the Beggar* in the cathedral at Pressburg (Bratislava); and his marble relief *Hagar in the Wilderness*[14] has a smooth classic grace. He reached his peak in the figures that he cast in lead for two great fountains in Vienna: the Providence Fountain in the Neuer Markt, representing the rivers of Austria, and the Andromeda Fountain, rivaling the *fonti* of Rome. Just a year before his death in 1741 he cast for the cathedral of Gurk a group representing the lamentation of Mary over the corpse of Christ; this would have made Raphael rejoice that Donner had taken his name.

Neither the painters nor the poets produced in this age in Austria or its dependencies any works that attracted the attention of the outside world, except, perhaps, the frescoes that Daniel Gran painted within the cupola of the great library in Vienna. But in music Vienna was the acknowledged center of the Western world. Charles VI loved music only next to his daughters and his throne. He himself composed an opera, accompanied Farinelli on the harpsichord, and conducted rehearsals. He brought to Vienna the best vocalists, instrumentalists, actors, and scene painters, regardless of cost; on one occasion he spent, in Lady Mary's estimate, thirty thousand pounds to stage one opera.[15] His chapel choir numbered 135 singers and players. Music became imperial, or at least noble: in some operas all the participants—soloists, chorus, ballet, orchestra—were members of the aristocracy. In one such performance the principal role was sung by the Archduchess Maria Theresa.[16]

The greatest librettists of the time accepted the call to Vienna. Apostolo Zeno came from Venice in 1718, served as court poet to Charles VI, and in 1730 retired amiably in favor of Pietro Trapassi, the Neapolitan who had been renamed Metastasio. During the next ten years Metastasio wrote—always in Italian—such stirring poetic dramas that the leading composers of Western Europe were happy to set them to music. No one rivaled him in adapting poetry to the demands of opera—i.e., in adjusting the theme, action, and feeling of his text to provide the requisite solos, duets, recitatives, choruses, ballets, and spectacles; but in return he exacted from the composers the harmonious accordance of the music with the play. His success was so great that Voltaire worried that opera might drive drama from the stage; "*ce beau monstre*," he said, "*étouffe Melpomène* [the Muse of tragedy]."[17]

Over all this music, art, and multilingual court and empire Charles VI presided with lavish hand, kind heart, and martial grief. His generals could not follow his baton; they gave him tragedies when he called for odes to joy. While Eugene of Savoy, who had shared with Marlborough in beating back the armies of Louis XIV, still retained his vigor of mind and command, matters military went well for Austria: she took Belgrade from the Turks, Sardinia from Savoy, and Milan, Naples, and the Spanish Netherlands from Spain. Eugene was promoted to be not only generalissimo of all Austrian armies, but also first minister and director of diplomacy; in effect he ruled everything but opera. But then, in the normal disintegration of our flesh, he grew weak not only in body but in mind. In the War of the Polish Succession (1733–35) Austria slipped into conflict with France, Spain, and Savoy (now known as the "small kingdom of Sardinia"); she lost Lorraine, Naples, and Sicily (1735–38). An alliance with Russia brought on another war with Turkey; Bosnia, Serbia, and Wallachia were lost; Belgrade became Turkish again (1739). The Emperor could not supply the talents missing in his aides. As Frederick the Great saw him,

> Charles VI had received from nature the qualities that make a good citizen, but none of those that make a great man. He was generous, but without discernment; of a spirit limited and without penetration; he had application, but without genius. He worked hard but accomplished little. He knew German law well, and several languages; he excelled above all in Latin. He was a good father, a good husband, but bigoted and superstitious like all the princes of the House of Austria.[18]

His consolation and pride were in his eldest daughter, Maria Theresa, and his heart was set on having her inherit his throne. However, his father, Leopold I, had laid down (1703) a "Pactum Mutuae Successionis," by which the principle of male primogeniture was to govern the succession; in default of a male heir, the crown should pass to the daughters of his son Joseph (b. 1678), and, next in line, to the daughters of his son Charles (b. 1685). The death of Joseph I in 1711 without male heir (but with two surviving daughters) left the crown to Charles. In 1713, in a "Pragmatic Sanction" delivered to his Privy Council, Charles declared his will that his throne and his undivided dominions should pass at his death to his eldest surviving son, and, should no son survive, to his eldest daughter. His only son was born and died in 1716. After waiting four years in vain for another son, Charles appealed to the European powers to avert a war of succession by accepting and collectively guaranteeing the order of succession that he had laid down. In the course of the next eight years his Pragmatic Sanction was officially accepted by Spain, Russia, Prussia, England, Holland, Denmark, Scandinavia, and France.

But there were difficulties, which made much history. Saxony and Bavaria had princes who had married the daughters of Charles's brother Joseph, and who now claimed the succession to the Imperial throne by virtue of the Pactum of Leopold I. Frederick William I of Prussia consented on the understanding that Charles would support his claim to a part of the duchies of Jülich and Berg. Charles apparently agreed to this condition, but soon gave contrary promises to Frederick William's competitors. The Prussian King thereupon allied himself with the Emperor's enemies.[19]

In 1736 Maria Theresa, in her eighteenth year, married Francis Stephen, Duke of Lorraine, later (1737) Grand Duke of Tuscany. On October 20, 1740, Charles VI died, ending the male line of the Hapsburgs, and Maria Theresa mounted the throne as archduchess of Austria and queen of Bohemia and Hungary. Her husband became coruler, but, as he showed little concern or capacity for affairs of state, the full burden of government fell upon the young Queen. She had in 1740 all the charms of womanhood as well as of royalty: fine features, brilliant blue eyes, rich blond hair, grace of manners and movement, the zest of health, the animation of youth.[20] Her intelligence and her character were superior to these charms, yet they seemed inadequate to the problems that encompassed her. She was now four months pregnant with the child who was to succeed her as the "enlightened despot" Joseph II. Her right to the throne was challenged by both Charles Albert, Elector of Bavaria, and Frederick Augustus II, Elector of Saxony, and a strong faction in Vienna favored the Bavarian cause. There was no assurance that Hungary would acknowledge her as its queen; she was not so crowned till June 24, 1741. The Imperial treasury contained only 100,000 florins, which the Empress Dowager, widow of Charles VI, claimed as her own. The army was in disorder, and its generals were incompetent. The Council of State was manned by old men who had lost the ability to organize or command. Rumors circulated that the Turks would soon again march upon Vienna.[21] Philip V of Spain demanded Hungary and Bohemia, the King of Sardinia demanded Lombardy, as the price of recognition.[22] Frederick II, who had become king of Prussia only five months before Maria Theresa's accession, sent an offer to recognize and defend her, and promote her husband's election as emperor, if she would cede to him the greater part of Silesia. She rejected the offer, remembering her father's hope that the realm would remain undivided and unimpaired. On December 23, 1740, Frederick invaded Silesia, and the twenty-three-year-old Queen found herself at war with the strongest power in Germany, and with the man who was to be the greatest general of his time.

II. PRUSSIAN PRELUDE: 1713–40

1. Frederick William I

The Hohenzollern family had succeeded in graduating the electorate of Brandenburg into the kingdom of Prussia in 1701; the Elector had become King Frederick I, and, dying, had bequeathed his realm to his son Frederick William I (r. 1713–40). Through his wife, Sophia Dorothea, the new monarch was son-in-law to George I, who in 1714 mounted the throne of England. The Prussian dominions included East Prussia, Lower Pomerania, the Mark of Brandenburg (centering around Berlin), the district of Cleves in western Germany, and the county of Mark and city of Ravensberg in Westphalia: a loose assortment of lands running interruptedly from the Vistula to the Elbe, and united only by the forces of the King. In 1740 this "Prussia" had some 3,300,000 population, which grew to 5,800,000 by the end of the century. The social structure was mainly feudal: a peasantry paying taxes and feudal dues, a weak middle class, a nobility demanding exemption from taxes as the price of providing military support to the king. It was in part to free himself from dependence upon these nobles that Frederick William I organized a standing army that was to determine for half a century the political history of Central Europe.

Frederick William was quite as unusual a ruler as his more famous son, whose victories were in great part due to his father's army. Neither father nor son was charming; neither appeased the world with good looks or a gracious smile; both fronted it with an air of stern command, wielding regiments. The father was short and stout, with a florid face under a cocked hat, eyes penetrating all pretense, voice announcing will, jaws ready to masticate all opposition. A hearty appetite, and no gourmet, he sent the French cook packing, and ate peasant's food; he consumed much in little time with little ceremony, having work to do. He thought of himself as both the master and the servant of the state. He labored dutifully, angrily, at administration, finding much awry and vowing to beat it into shape. He cut in half the number of pompous commissioners whose conflicting authority had obstructed the business of government. He sold the jewels, horses, and fine furniture bequeathed to him, reduced the royal household to the simplicity of a burgher's home, gathered taxes wherever they could be made to grow, and left to Frederick II a treasury temptingly full.

He required everyone to work as hard as himself. He ordered municipal officials to censor the morals of the population, to preach industry and thrift, and to discipline tramps with hard labor. Commerce and manufactures were kept under state control, but they were encouraged by the improvement of canals and roads. In 1722 the watchful King decreed universal compulsory education; every parish must maintain a school; by 1750 Prussia led all Europe in both primary and secondary education.[23] and the seed was sown for the age of Kant and Goethe.

Finding that pious persons worked more steadily than skeptics, Frederick William supported the Pietist movement. Catholics were grudgingly tolerated. Calvinists were told to stop preaching their predestinarian gloom. Lutherans were ordered to use German instead of Latin in their liturgy, and to abandon surplices, stoles, and the elevation of the Sacrament, as papistical vestiges. When the Archbishop of Salzburg forced fifteen thousand Protestants to emigrate, Frederick William welcomed them, advanced them money for their five-hundred-mile journey, leased them lands (not of the best), provided them with tools and seed on loan, and exempted them from taxation till their soil grew profits. Another fifteen thousand immigrants were brought in from Switzerland and German states. Prussia, ruined by the Thirty Years' War, was restored to economic life.

Behind this royal activity the dominant passion was to make the nation secure in a warring world. When Frederick William came to power the Great Northern War was still on, involving Sweden, Russia, Poland, Denmark, Saxony, soon England; the obvious lesson was that in a world of nationalized robbery a strong army was indispensable even for peace. Anxious to get Stettin as a port for the commerce of Berlin, the Prussian King bought it for 400,000 thalers from the powers that had seized it from Charles XII. Charles, returning from Turkey, refused to recognize this sale of stolen goods; Frederick William offered to return it to Sweden for a return of his 400,000 thalers; Charles had no money, but insisted on regaining Stettin; Prussia declared war on him (1715) and joined his enemies in besieging Stralsund. Charles, half the world against him, fled to Sweden and death; Frederick William returned to Berlin with Stettin in his pocket and triumph in his eyes.

Thereafter his first administrative concern was his army. He was not quite a militarist, certainly not a warrior; he never again waged war, but he was resolved that no one should with impunity make war upon him; this builder of the most famous army of that century was "one of the most pacific of princes."[24] "My maxim," he said, "is to injure no one, but not to let myself be slighted."[25] So he gathered soldiers, and sought with passion the tallest he could find; to win his good will one had only to send him a man at least six feet tall. The King paid well for them, and his heart warmed at their height. He was no madder than his fellow kings, except about inches. France in 1713 had 160,000 regular troops, Russia 130,000, Austria 90,000.[26] To bring the Prussian army up to 80,000 men in a country with a population of only three millions, Frederick William enlisted men from abroad and conscripted men at home. The peasants and the townsmen resisted impressment; they were taken by ruse or force; in one case a recruiting officer invaded a church and carried off the tallest and strongest men, notwithstanding their prayers.[27] (Let us remember that we too conscript.) Once the men were enrolled they were cared for well, but were subjected to ruthless discipline and arduous drill; flogging was the penalty for even minor offenses.

Conscription was applied to the aristocracy too; every able-bodied noble had to serve as an officer as long as he could physically bear the strain. These officers underwent a special training, and were especially honored by the King. They became a ruling caste, which looked down upon merchants, teachers, clergymen, and the middle classes generally as weakling inferiors, and often treated them with swashbuckling insolence or brutality. Meanwhile they drilled the infantry, artillery, and cavalry in such precise formations and flexible movements as probably no other modern army has ever known. The King himself took part in these military maneuvers, and supervised in loving detail the training of his troops. When Frederick II came to the throne he found under his command a force of men ready for stratagems and spoils, and overriding in a moment all the lessons of peace that the Prince had learned from philosophy.

2. Der junge Fritz

The "great Drill-Sergeant of the Prussian Nation" (as Carlyle called Frederick William I[28]) had ten children, of whom the eldest was Wilhelmine. The memoirs which she left at her death (1758) are our most immediate and intimate source for the early history of her brother. Perhaps she detailed with selective emphasis the cruelty of her governess, the hard selfishness of her mother, the brutality of her father, his despotic orders for her marriage, his harsh treatment of the Fritz whom she loved as the pride and solace of her life.[29] "There never was such love as ours for one another. . . . I loved my brother so passionately that I always tried to give him pleasure."[30]

Frederick, born January 24, 1712, was three years her junior. Neither his mother nor his father was pleased with him. They strove to make him a general and a king; he gave every sign of becoming a poet and a musician. We have Frederick William's instructions to the instructors of his son:

> Impress my son with a proper love and fear of God, as the foundation and sole pillar of our temporal and eternal welfare. No false religions, or sects of atheist, Arian, Socinian, or whatever name the poison-

ous things have which can so easily corrupt a young mind, are to be ever named in his hearing [Frederick became all of these]. On the other hand, a proper abhorrence of papistry, and insight into its baselessness and absurdity, are to be communicated to him. . . .

Let the Prince learn French and German, . . . no Latin. . . . Let him learn arithmetic, mathematics, artillery, economy, to the very bottom. . . . History in particular. . . . With increasing years you will more and more . . . go upon fortification, the formation of a camp, and the other sciences of war; that the Prince may, from youth upwards, be trained to act as officer and general. . . . Stamp into my son a true love for the profession of soldier; and impress upon him that as there is nothing in the world which can bring a prince renown and honor like the sword, so he would be a despised creature before all men if he did not love it and seek his sole glory therein.[31]

Had the father lived long enough, he would have been proud of his son as soldier and general; but in those apprentice years everything seemed to go wrong. The boy was bright, but he never bothered to spell. He despised the German language, loved the language, literature, music, and art of France; he liked to write French verses, and continued that diversion to the end of his life. The old King fumed when he saw his son with French books, and still more when he found him playing the flute. Johann Quantz, flutist at the court of Saxony, came to Berlin to teach the boy clandestinely at the mother's request. Hearing the King approach, Quantz hid in a closet, and Frederick quickly changed from French robe to military coat; but the sire flew into a rage at the French books lying about. He ordered the servants to send these to a bookseller; better to sell them than to burn them. The servants did neither; they hid the books, and soon returned them to the Prince.

The old man did his angry loving best to make the boy a warrior. He took him along on hunts, hardened him with outdoor life, accustomed him to danger and rough riding, made him subsist on scrimped food and short sleep, put him in charge of a regiment, taught him to drill his men, to mount a battery, and to fire cannon. Frederick learned all this, and showed courage enough; but the father saw with rising anger that the youth, now sixteen, was developing a suspicious intimacy with two young officers, Captain von Katte and Lieutenant Keith. Katte had read and traveled widely, and, though smallpox had marked him, his "refinement of mind and manners," said Wilhelmine, made him "a most agreeable companion. . . . He boasted of being an *esprit fort* [freethinker]. It was Katte's influence that destroyed all religious belief in my brother."[32]

To these unorthodox developments in his oldest son Frederick William could find no other response than rage and violence. He was accustomed to use his cane upon his servants; he threatened to use it against his son. Meanwhile Wilhelmine was resisting his plans to marry her to some potential political ally; son and daughter seemed fated to disappoint all his hopes. "The King's anger against my brother and myself reached such a pitch that, with the exception of the hours for our meals, we were banished from his presence." At one meeting the King

> threw his plate at my brother's head, who could have been struck had he not gotten out of the way; a second he threw at me, which I also happily escaped; then torrents of abuse followed. . . . As my brother and I passed near him to leave the room, he hit out at us with his crutch. He never saw my brother without threatening him with his stick. Fritz often said to me that he would bear all ill treatment save blows, and that if it came to these he would run away.[33]

We can understand something of the anger felt by the aging King. He had looked forward to leaving his reorganized realm to a son who would continue to foster the army, economize expenditures, build industries, and administer the state with conscience and application; he could not be expected to foresee that this son would do all these and more. In Friedrich he found only an insolent and effeminate youth who curled his hair like a Frenchman instead of cutting it off like a Prussian soldier;[34] who hated soldiers and hunting, laughed at religion, wrote French poems, and played the flute. What future could Prussia have under such a weakling? Even the boy's occasional pleas for forgiveness could be interpreted as cowardice. Once, after boxing his son's ears, the King said to others that had he been treated so by his father he would have shot himself, but that Friedrich had no sense of honor, and would put up with anything.[35]

At Potsdam in the spring of 1730, if we may believe Frederick's report to Wilhelmine, the King tried to kill him.

> He sent for me one morning. As I entered the room he seized me by the hair and threw me to the ground. After having beaten me with his fists he dragged me to the window and tied the curtain cord around my throat. I had fortunately time to get up and seize his hands, but as he pulled with all his might at the cord around my throat, I felt I was being strangled, and screamed for help. A page rushed to my assistance, and had to use force to free me.[36]

Friedrich, now eighteen, confided to Wilhelmine that he was planning to escape to England with Katte and Keith. She pleaded with him not to go; he persisted. She kept his secret fearfully, but the King, who surrounded his son with spies, learned of the plot, and arrested son and daughter, Katte and Keith (August, 1730). Wilhelmine was soon released, and Keith escaped to England, but Friedrich and Katte were court-martialed and were condemned to death (October 30). Katte was executed in the yard of the fortress at Cüstrin (now Kostrzyn in Poland), and Friedrich, on his father's orders, was forced to witness the execution from the windows of his cell (November 6). The King thought of having his son beheaded, and making the next-older son crown prince; but, fearing international repercussions, he reconciled himself to letting Friedrich live.

From November, 1730, till February, 1732, the Prince remained in Cüstrin, at first in close confinement, then restricted to the town, always under close surveillance; but, says Wilhelmine, "all Berlin sent him provisions, and even the greatest delicacies."[37] On August 15, 1731, after a year of separation, the King came to see his son, berated him at length, and told him that if the plot to escape had succeeded "I would have cast your sister for life into a place where she never would have seen sun or moon again."[38] Friedrich knelt and asked forgiveness; the old man broke down, wept, and embraced him; Friedrich kissed his father's feet.[39] He was released, and was sent on a tour of the Prussian provinces to study their economy and administration. Those years of filial strife changed and hardened his character.

Meanwhile Wilhelmine, glad to leave the paternal roof, accepted the hand of Crown Prince Henry of Bayreuth. After their marriage in Berlin (November 30, 1731) she went south, to become (1734) the margravine of Bayreuth, and to make her court hum with culture. It was during her sway there that the princely residence, the Schloss der Eremitage, was transformed into one of the loveliest châteaux in Germany.

Friedrich too had to be married, willy-nilly. He resented the necessity, and threatened: "If the King absolutely will have it, I will marry to obey him; after that I will shove my wife into a corner and live after my own fancy."[40] So he took to the altar (June 12, 1733) Elisabeth Christina, "Serene Princess" of Brunswick-Bevern, he twenty-one, she eighteen, "very handsome," said Friedrich's mother to Wilhelmine, but "as stupid as a bundle of straw—I cannot understand how your brother will get on with such a goose."[41] Though in later years Frederick learned to esteem her highly, in this period he left her mostly to her own resources. They went to live at Rheinsberg, a few miles north of Berlin. There the bachelor husband built himself a tower of refuge, performed experiments in physics and chemistry, gathered scientists, scholars, and musicians around him, and corresponded with Wolff, Fontenelle, Maupertuis, and Voltaire.

3. The Prince and the Philosopher: 1736–40

His correspondence with Voltaire is among the most revealing documents of that time: a brilliant literary expression of two pre-eminent personalities, in which the art of the older man fades before the realism of the maturing youth. Voltaire was now forty-two, Frederick was twenty-four. Voltaire was the acknowledged head of French writers, yet it almost turned his head to receive, from a crown prince soon to be king, the following letter, written from Berlin on August 8, 1736, and sent by private messenger to the poet at Cirey:

> MONSIEUR:
>
> Although I have not the satisfaction of knowing you personally, you are not the less known to me through your works. They are treasures of the mind, if I may so express myself; and they reveal to the reader new beauties at every fresh perusal. . . . If ever the dispute on the comparative merits of the Moderns and the Ancients should be revived, the modern great men will owe it to you, and to you only, that the scale is turned in their favor. . . . Never before did poet put metaphysics into rhythmic cadence; to you the honor was reserved of doing it first.

Frederick, perhaps because of his little Latin, had obviously not yet encountered Lucretius. But he had read Wolff, and he dispatched to Voltaire a

> copy of the Accusation and Defense of M. Wolff, the most celebrated philosopher of our days; who, for having carried light into the darkest places of metaphysics, is cruelly accused of irreligion and atheism. . . . I am getting a translation made of Wolff's *Treatise on God, the Soul and the World.* . . . I will send it to you. . . .
>
> The kindness and assistance you afford to all who devote themselves to the arts and sciences make me hope that you will not exclude me from the number of those whom you find worthy of your instructions. . . .

Apparently Frederick had heard some rumor of *La Pucelle:*

> Monsieur, there is nothing I wish so much as to possess all your writings. . . . If there be among your manuscripts any that you wish to conceal from the eyes of the public, I engage to keep them in the profoundest secrecy. . . .
>
> Nature, when she pleases, forms a great soul endowed with faculties that can advance the arts and sciences; and it is the part of princes to recompense his noble toil. Ah, would Glory but make use of me to crown your success! . . .
>
> If my destiny refuse me the happiness of being able to possess you, may I at least hope one day to see the man whom I have admired so long now from afar; and to assure you, by word of mouth, that I am—

with all the esteem and consideration due to those who, following the torch of truth for guide, consecrate their labors to the Public—monsieur, your affectionate friend,

FRÉDÉRIC, P. R. OF PRUSSIA.[42]

We can imagine the satisfaction with which Voltaire, never too old to be vain, read this letter, sipping its honey before the already jealous Marquise. Soon after its receipt he replied, August 26, 1736:

MONSEIGNEUR:

A man must be devoid of all feeling who would not be infinitely moved by the letter with which your Royal Highness has deigned to honor me. My self-love is only too much flattered by it; but my love of mankind, which I have always nourished in my heart, and which, I venture to say, forms the basis of my character, has given me a very much purer pleasure—to see that there is now in the world a Prince who thinks as a man, a *Philosopher* Prince, who will make men happy.

Permit me to say, there is not a man on earth but owes you thanks for the care you take to cultivate by sound philosophy a soul that is born for command. Good kings there never were except those that had begun by seeking to instruct themselves; by knowing good men from bad, by loving what is true, by detesting persecution and superstition. A prince persisting in such thoughts might bring back the Golden Age to his country! Why do so few princes seek this glory? . . . Because they think more of their royalty than of mankind. Precisely the reverse is your case; and *unless, one day, the tumult of business and the wickedness of men alters so divine a character,** you will be worshiped by your people, and loved by the whole world. Philosophers worthy of the name will flock to your state; thinkers will crowd around your throne. . . . The illustrious Queen Christina left her kingdom to go in search of the arts; so reign, Monseigneur, and the arts will come to seek you. . . .

I cannot sufficiently thank your Royal Highness for the gift of that little book about Monsieur Wolff. I respect metaphysical ideas; they are rays of light amid deep night. More, I think, is not to be hoped from metaphysics. It does not seem likely that the first principles of things will ever be known. The mice that must be in some little holes of an immense building know not whether it is eternal, or who the architect is, or why he built it. Such mice are we; and the Divine Architect who built the universe has never, that I know of, told his secret to one of us. . . .

I shall obey your commands as to sending those unpublished pieces. You shall be my public, Monseigneur, your criticisms will be my reward; it is a price few sovereigns can pay. I am sure of your secrecy.

---

* Italics added.

. . . I should indeed consider it a precious happiness to come to pay my court to your Royal Highness. . . . But the friendship which keeps me in this retirement does not permit my leaving it. Without doubt you think with Julian, that great and much calumniated man, who said, "Friends should always be preferred to kings."

In whatever corner of the world I may end my life, be assured, Monseigneur, my wishes will continually be for you—that is to say, for a whole people's happiness. My heart will rank itself among your subjects; your glory will ever be dear to me. I shall wish that you may always be like yourself, and that other kings may be like you.—I am, with profound respect, your Royal Highness's most humble

VOLTAIRE[43]

The correspondence between the greatest king and the greatest writer of the time continued, with bitter interruptions, for forty-two years. Almost every word of it repays reading, for it is not often that we are privileged to hear the private and considered conversation of two such men. We resist with difficulty the temptation to quote the illuminating judgments, the strokes of wit, in those letters; but some passages help us to visualize the rival giants of sword and pen.*

They agree, at first, in mutual admiration. Frederick expresses astonishment that France has not recognized "the treasure enclosed in its heart," that it allows Voltaire to "live solitary in the deserts of Champagne. . . . Henceforth Cirey shall be my Delphi, and your letters my oracles."[44] "Leave your ungrateful country, and come to a land where you will be adored."[45] Voltaire throws the bouquets back: "You think like Trajan, you write like Pliny, you use French like our best writers. . . . Under your auspices Berlin will be the Athens of Germany, perhaps of Europe."[46] They agree on deism; they affirm belief in God, they confess that they know nothing about Him, they detest the clergy who base their power on pretended access to the Deity.[47] But Frederick is an outright materialist ("What is certain is that I am matter, and that I think"[48]) and determinist; Voltaire is not yet ready to give up free will.[49] Frederick counsels "a profound silence with regard to the Christian fables, which are canonized by their antiquity and the credulity of absurd and insipid people."[50] Voltaire loses no opportunity to indoctrinate his royal pupil with a love of humanity, and a hatred of superstition, fanaticism, and war. Frederick does not take humanity very seriously: "Nature naturally produces thieves, the envious, forgers, murderers; they cover the face of the earth; and without the laws which repress vice each individual would abandon himself to the instincts of nature, and would think only of himself.[51] . . . Men are nat-

---

* The subsequent references are to the English translation, here warmly recommended, by Richard Aldington: *The Letters of Voltaire and Frederick the Great* (New York, 1927).

urally inclined to evil, and they are good only in proportion to the extent that education and experience have modified their impetuosity."[52]

Two events marked the last years of Frederick's tutelage. In 1738 he joined the Freemasons.[53] In 1739, apparently in the warmth of Voltaire's influence, he wrote a small book, *Réfutation du Prince de Machiavel*, which took the Italian philosopher to task for apparently justifying any means that a ruler might think necessary to the preservation or strengthening of his state. No, countered the new Prince; the only true principle of government is the loyalty, justice, and honor of the sovereign. The royal philosopher expressed his scorn for kings who preferred "the fatal glory of conquerors to that won by kindness, justice, and clemency"; he wondered what could induce a man to aggrandize himself through the misery and destruction of other men."[54] Frederick proceeded:

> Machiavelli has not understood the true nature of the sovereign. . . . Far from being the absolute master of those who are under his rule, he is only the first of their servants [*le premier domestique*], and should be the instrument of their welfare, as they are the instrument of his glory.[55]

And, probably again following Voltaire, Frederick praised the English constitution:

> It seems to me that if a form of government may be held up as a model for our days, it is the English. There Parliament is the supreme judge of both the people and the king, while the king has full power of doing good, but none of doing evil.[56]

We find no sign of insincerity in these professions; they are repeated time and again in Frederick's letters of this period. He sent the manuscript to Voltaire (January, 1740), who begged permission to have it published. The proud author shyly consented. Voltaire wrote a preface, took the manuscript to The Hague, saw it through the press, and corrected the proofs. Toward the end of September it burst upon the world, anonymous, under the title *L'Anti-Machiavel*. The secret of its authorship was soon revealed, and readers joined Voltaire in hailing the advent of a philosopher-king.

Frederick William I remained almost to the end the gnarled oak that he had so long been, scolding, denouncing, laying down the law in his striking way. Only when the court preacher told him that he was dying and must forgive his enemies if he wished pardon from God, did he reluctantly make his peace with the world. In his last moments he sent for Friedrich, embraced him, and wept; perhaps after all this willful youth had in him the makings of a king? "Am I not happy," he asked the generals around his bed, "to have such a son to leave behind me?"[57] And the son may have understood better now the old man's feeling that a monarch must have some iron in his blood.

On May 31, 1740, Frederick William I, worn out at fifty-one, yielded up his life and his throne. Anti-Machiavel was king.

III. THE NEW MACHIAVELLI

Frederick II was twenty-eight years old at his accession. As painted by Antoine Pesne a year before, he was still the musician and philosopher despite his shining armor: handsome and kindly features, big blue-gray eyes, lofty brow; "a natural and charming manner," reported the French ambassador, "a soft and ingratiating voice."[58] He was still the pupil of Voltaire. To him he wrote, after six days of rule:

> My lot is changed. I have witnessed the last moments of a king, his agony, his death. On coming to the throne I had no need of that lesson to be disgusted with the vanity of human grandeur. . . . I beg you will see in me nothing but a zealous citizen, a rather skeptical philosopher, and a really faithful friend. For God's sake, write to me as a man, and, like me, scorn titles, names, and all exterior pomp.[59]

And three weeks later, again to Voltaire:

> The infinite amount of work which has fallen to my lot scarcely leaves time for my real grief. I feel that since losing my father I owe myself wholly to my country. With this view I have worked to the limit of my capacity to make the promptest arrangements, and those most suitable to the public good.[60]

It was true. On the second day of his reign, judging from the cold spring that the harvest would be late and poor, he ordered that the public granaries be opened, and that grain be sold to the poor at reasonable rates. On the third day he abolished throughout Prussia the use of torture in criminal trials—twenty-four years before Beccaria's epochal treatise; we should add that judicial torture, though permitted by law, had in practice become obsolete under Frederick William I, and that Frederick for a moment relapsed into its use in one case in 1752.[61] In 1757 he commissioned Samuel von Cocceji, chief of the Prussian judiciary, to supervise an extensive reform of Prussian law.

The influence of philosophy appeared in other actions of this first month.

On June 22 Frederick issued a simple order: "All religions must be tolerated, and the government must see to it that none of them makes unjust encroachments on any other, for in this country every man must get to heaven in his own way."[62] He issued no official order about freedom of the press, but in practice he allowed it, telling his ministers, "*La presse est libre.*" He bore with contemptuous silence a thousand diatribes that were published against him.[63] Once, seeing a lampoon against him posted in the street, he had it removed to a position where it could be more easily read. "My people and I," he said, "have come to an agreement that satisfies us both: they are to say what they please, and I am to do what I please."[64] But the freedom was by no means complete; as Frederick became more and more the Great he allowed no public criticism of his military measures or his tax decrees. He remained an absolute monarch, though he tried to keep his measures consistent with the laws.

He made no attempt to change the structure of Prussian society or government. The administrative boards and agencies remained as before, except that Frederick kept a closer eye on them and joined more assiduously in their work; he became a member of his own bureaucracy. "He begins his government," said the French ambassador, "in a highly satisfactory way: everywhere traits of benevolence, sympathy for his subjects."[65] This did not extend to mitigating serfdom; the Prussian peasant continued to be worse off than the French. The nobles retained their privileges.

The influence of Voltaire joined with the tradition of Leibniz in bringing about a vigorous revival of the Berlin Academy of Sciences. Founded by Frederick I (1701), it had been neglected by Frederick William I. Frederick II now made it the most prominent in Europe. We have seen that he recalled Wolff from exile; Wolff wanted to head the Academy, but he was too old, weak in the legs, and a bit stooping to orthodoxy; Frederick wanted an *esprit fort*, a man abreast of the latest in science, and unimpeded by theology. At Voltaire's suggestion (later mourned) he invited (June, 1740) Pierre Louis Moreau de Maupertuis, now in the summer of life, and fresh from a famous expedition to Lapland to measure a degree of latitude. Maupertuis came and received lavish support; he built a great laboratory, and performed experiments sometimes in the presence of the King and the court. Goldsmith, who must have known the Royal Society of London, judged the Berliner Akademie der Weissenschaften to "excel any other now subsisting."[66]

All this warmed the heart of Voltaire. When Frederick had occasion to visit Cleves he invited his philosopher to meet him; Voltaire, then at Brussels, tore himself away from his fretful Marquise, and traveled 150 miles to the Schloss Moyland; there the new Plato saw his Dionysius for the first time, and spent three days (September 11 to 14, 1740) in ecstasy, spoiled only by the presence of Algarotti and Maupertuis. To M. de Cideville, in a letter of October 18, he gave his view of Frederick:

> It was there I saw one of the most amiable men in the world, who forms the charm of society, who would be everywhere sought after if he were not king; a philosopher without austerity, full of sweetness, complaisance, and obliging ways; not remembering that he is a king when he meets his friends. . . . I needed an effort of memory to recollect that I here saw sitting at the foot of my bed a sovereign who had an army of 100,000 men.[67]

And Frederick was equally pleased. To his aide Jordan he wrote, on September 24:

> I have seen that Voltaire whom I was so curious to know; but I saw him with the quartan fever hanging on me, and my mind as unstrung as my body. . . . He has the eloquence of Cicero, the mildness of Pliny, the wisdom of Agrippa; he combines, in short, what is to be collected of virtues and talents from three of the greatest men of antiquity. His intellect is at work incessantly; every drop of ink is an extract of wit from his pen. . . . La Châtelet is lucky to have him; for of the good things he flings out at random a person who had no faculty but memory might make a brilliant book.[68]

On returning to Berlin Frederick noted that he had an army of 100,000 men. On October 20 Charles VI died, and a young woman with a second-class army became head of the Austro-Hungarian empire. On that very day Frederick sent an ominous letter to Voltaire: "The death of the Emperor alters all my pacific ideas, and I think that in June it will be rather a matter of cannon and powder, soldiers and trenches, than of actresses, balls, and stages; so that I am obliged to cancel the bargain we were about to make."[69]

Voltaire's heart ached. Was his pupil a warmonger like any other king? Taking advantage of Frederick's invitation to visit him in Berlin, he decided to see what he could do for peace. At the same time he might repair his fences at Versailles, for Cardinal Fleury, still at the helm in France, also wanted peace. On November 2 he wrote to the Cardinal, offering his services as a secret agent of France in an effort to win Frederick back to philosophy. Fleury accepted the offer, but gently reproved the new diplomat for his impetuous sallies against religion: "You have been young, and perhaps a little too long [*Vous avez été jeune, et peut-être un peu trop long-temps*]."[70] In another letter of the same date (November 14) the amiable Cardinal acknowledged receipt of the *Anti-Machiavel* from Mme. du Châtelet, and praised it with judicious suspicion of its authorship:

Whoever may be the author of this work, if he is not a prince he deserves to be one; and the little that I have read of it is so wise, so reasonable, and expresses principles so admirable, that the author would be worthy to command other men, provided he has the courage to put them in practice. If he was born a prince, he contracts a very solemn engagement with the public; and the Emperor Antoninus would not have acquired the immortal glory which he retains, age after age, if he had not sustained by the justice of his government the exquisite morality of which he had given such instructive lessons to all sovereigns. . . . I should be infinitely touched if his Prussian Majesty could find in my conduct some conformity with his principles, but I can at least assure you that I regard his as the outline of the most perfect and glorious government.[71]

Voltaire, having arranged that all his traveling expenses should be paid by Frederick, crossed Germany for the first time, and spent almost two weeks with the King at Rheinsberg, Potsdam, and Berlin (November 20 to December 2). He made the mistake of showing to Frederick the Cardinal's letter about the *Anti-Machiavel;* Frederick saw at once that Voltaire was playing diplomat; he translated Fleury's beautiful commendation into an appeal for co-operation with France; and he was irked to find himself hampered by his essay in philosophy. He exchanged verses and repartee with Voltaire, treated him to performances on the flute, and sent him away with nothing more definite than thanks for the quinine with which the poet had mitigated the royal ague. To Jordan, on November 28, Frederick wrote, not naming but meaning Voltaire: "Thy Miser shall drink to the lees of his insatiable desire to enrich himself; he shall have three thousand thalers. This is paying dear for a fool [*c'est bien payer pour un fou*]; never did court jester have such wages before."[72] Apparently the sum included both Voltaire's traveling expenses—which Frederick had probably volunteered to remit—and the cost of publishing the *Anti-Machiavel*, which Voltaire had advanced out of his own pocket. When money comes in, love goes out; Frederick did not relish paying the expenses of a French agent, or the costs of a book which he would gladly have paid the world to forget.

The influence of Frederick William now outweighed the teachings of the philosopher. As the opportunities of power and the responsibilities of rule replaced the music and poetry of his princely years, Frederick grew colder and harder; even the maltreatment which his father had lavished upon him had toughened his skin and his temperament. Every day he saw those 100,000 giants his father had left him; every day he had to feed them. What sense was there in letting them rust and rot in peace? Was there not some wrong that these giants could right? Certainly. There was Silesia, separated from Austria by Bohemia, and much closer to Berlin than to

Vienna; the great River Oder ran down from Prussia to Silesia's capital, Breslau, only 183 miles southeast of Berlin; what were the Austrians doing there? The house of Brandenburg had claims in Silesia—to the former principalities of Jägerndorf, Ratibor, Oppeln, Liegnitz, Brieg, Wohlau; all these had been taken by Austria, or had been ceded to it by arrangements never satisfactory to Prussia. Now that the Austrian succession was in dispute, and Maria Theresa was young and weak, and an infant Czar, Ivan VI, was on the Russian throne—now was the time to urge those old claims, to rectify those old mistakes, and to give Prussia some greater geographical unity and base.

On November 1 Frederick asked Podewils, one of his councilors, "I give you a problem to solve: When one has the advantage, should one make use of it or not? I am ready with my troops and with everything else. If I do not use them now I keep in my hands a powerful but useless instrument. If I use my army it will be said that I have had the skill to take advantage of the superiority which I have over my neighbor." Podewils suggested that this would be considered immoral; Frederick countered, When had kings been deterred by morality?[73] Could he afford to practice the Ten Commandments in that den of wolves known as the Great Powers? But had not Frederick William pledged Prussian support to the Pragmatic Sanction that guaranteed to Maria Theresa the dominions bequeathed to her by her father? That pledge, however, had been conditional on Imperial support of Prussian claims in Jülich and Berg; the support had not been given; on the contrary, it had gone to Prussia's rivals. Now that galling affront could be avenged.

In December Frederick sent an envoy to Maria Theresa to offer her his protection if she would recognize his claims to a part of Silesia. Expecting that the offer would be rejected, he ordered a part of his army, thirty thousand men, to advance. It crossed the border into Silesia December 23, two days before Frederick's envoy reached Vienna. So began the First Silesian War (1740–42), the first phase of

IV. THE WAR OF THE AUSTRIAN SUCCESSION: 1740–48

We shall not follow Frederick in all his military moves; this is a history of civilization. We are interested, however, in the nature of man and the conduct of states as revealed by the words and actions of Frederick, and the shifting policies of the Powers. Probably in no recorded war were the realities of power politics so visibly bared.

The Prussian army moved almost unresisted through Silesia. The Protestant half of the population, which had suffered some persecution under

Austrian rule, welcomed Frederick as a liberator;[74] to the Catholics he pledged—and gave—full freedom to practice their faith. On January 3, 1741, he took peaceful possession of Breslau; "no house," he assures us, "was pillaged, no citizen was insulted, and Prussian discipline shone in all its splendor";[75] it was the most genteel appropriation. Maria Theresa ordered Marshal Neipperg to collect an army in Moravia and cross into Silesia. On April 10 this army engaged Frederick's main Silesian force at Mollwitz, twenty miles southeast of Breslau. Neipperg had 8,600 cavalry, 11,400 infantry, eighteen guns; Frederick had 4,000 cavalry, 16,000 infantry, sixty guns; these differences determined the phases and issues of the battle. The Austrian horsemen overwhelmed the Prussian cavalry, which turned and fled. Marshal Schwerin persuaded Frederick to join in the flight, lest he be captured and held for a ruinous ransom. But after the King and his cavalry had gone, the Prussian infantry withstood all attacks of horse or foot; and the Prussian artillery, reloading their guns with iron ramrods, so damaged the Austrians that Neipperg ordered retreat. Frederick, called back to the scene, was delighted and ashamed to find the battle won. He felt that he had been guilty not only of cowardice but of defective strategy; he had scattered his thirty thousand men through Silesia before consolidating his conquest; and only the courage and training of his infantry had saved the day. "He reflected a great deal," said his *Memoirs*, "on the faults he had committed, and tried to correct them in the sequel."[76] He was never wanting again in bravery, and rarely in tactics or strategy.

The news of her army's defeat reached Maria Theresa as she was recuperating from the birth of her child. In the weakened condition of her forces and her finances her only hope seemed to lie in aid from abroad. She appealed to the many powers that had pledged their support to the Pragmatic Sanction of her rule. England responded cautiously; it needed a strong Austria as a foil to France, but George II feared for his Hanoverian principality if he warred against neighboring Prussia. Parliament voted a subsidy of £300,000 to Maria Theresa, but British envoys urged her to cede Lower (northern) Silesia to Frederick as a price of peace. Frederick was willing, the Queen refused. Poland, Savoy, and the Dutch Republic promised help, but were so slow in sending it that they counted for little in the result.

Every coalition begets its opposite. France, watching the *rapprochement* of her ancient enemies, England and Austria, hurried to form an alliance with Bavaria, Prussia, and Bourbon Spain. We have seen that France had her own Machiavelli, Belle-Isle, who proposed a gem of political brigandage. France, which had pledged to support the Pragmatic Sanction, was to take swift advantage of Maria Theresa's plight: Charles Albert of Bavaria was to be upheld in his claim, through his wife, to the Imperial

throne; France was to offer him money and troops to join in attacking
Austria; if the plan prospered, Maria Theresa was to be restricted to Hun-
gary, Lower Austria, and the Austrian Netherlands; Charles was to be em-
peror, ruling Bavaria, Upper Austria, the Tirol, Bohemia, and part of
Swabia; the second son of the King of Spain was to have the Milanese.
Fleury opposed the scheme, Belle-Isle prevailed, and was sent off to win
Frederick to the conspiracy. France and Bavaria signed their alliance at
Nymphenburg on May 18, 1741. Frederick was reluctant to join; he could
not afford to let France become so strong; he still hoped to come to an arrangement with Maria Theresa; but when she offered him only negligible
concessions, he signed at Breslau on June 5 an alliance with France, Bavaria,
and Spain; if the Austrian dominions were to be divided he wished to share
in the spoils. Each signatory pledged his government to make no secret
separate peace. France guaranteed Frederick's possession of Breslau and
Lower Silesia, promised to prod Sweden into a holding war with Russia,
and agreed to send a French army to prevent England's Hanoverian forces
from entering the game.

Left almost friendless, Maria Theresa resolved to appeal to the martial
lords of Hungary. Those lords, or their ancestors, had suffered much under
Austrian rule; Leopold I had deprived them of their old constitution and
traditional rights; they had little reason to love or succor his granddaughter.
But when she appeared before them in their Diet at Pressburg (September
11, 1741), they were moved by her beauty and tears. She addressed them
in Latin, confessed herself abandoned by her allies, and declared that her
honor and her throne now depended upon the valor and chivalry of
Hungarian knights and arms. That the nobles cried out, "*Moriamur pro
rege nostro*"[77]—"Let us die for our King!" (for so they called the Queen)
—is a fine story now relegated to legend;[78] they bargained considerably,
and drew from her many political concessions; but when, on September
21, her husband Francis Stephen came, with a nurse holding up to them
the six-month-old Joseph, they responded gallantly, and many cried out,
"*Vitam et sanguinem!*"—vowing their lives and blood.[79] A levy en masse
was voted, calling all men to arms, and after many delays a Hungarian
force rode westward to the defense of the Queen.

It would have been too late to save Vienna if Charles Albert had continued his march upon that capital. But meanwhile (September 19) Saxony
had joined the alliance against Austria; Charles Albert feared that Augustus
III would seize Bohemia; Fleury advised the Bavarian to take Bohemia before the Saxons could get to it. Frederick urged Charles to continue on to
Vienna; Charles, financed by France, obeyed France. Frederick, fearing
that a France dominant in both Bavaria and Bohemia would be too strong
for Prussia's security, signed a secret truce with Austria (October 9, 1741);

Maria Theresa, anxious to save Bohemia, provisionally ceded to him Lower Silesia.

Three armies now converged upon Prague: one under Charles Albert, a French force under Belle-Isle, and twenty thousand Saxons. Poorly garrisoned, the Bohemian capital fell at the first assault (November 25). The victory was a disaster for Charles. Absorbed in the Bohemian campaign, he had left his electorate of Bavaria with only minor defenses, never dreaming that Maria Theresa, harassed on so many sides, would be able to take the offensive. But the Queen showed a resilience that dismayed her enemies. She called back ten thousand Austrian troops from Italy; Hungarian regiments were arriving in Vienna; these two armies she placed under Count Ludwig von Khevenhüller, who had learned the art of war under Eugene of Savoy. Ably led, they invaded Bavaria and overran it almost unresisted; on February 12, 1742, they took Munich, its capital. On that same day, at Frankfurt-am-Main, Charles Albert was crowned emperor of the Holy Roman Empire as Charles VII.

Meanwhile Frederick, shifting with every turn in the winds of power, had re-entered the war. He had made the truce conditional on secrecy; Maria Theresa revealed it to France; Frederick overheard these diplomatic whisperings, and hastened to rejoin his allies (December, 1741). He concerted with them a plan by which he would lead an army through Moravia into Lower Austria; he was to be met there by Saxon and Franco-Bavarian forces; together they were to march upon Vienna. But he was now operating amid an actively hostile population, and Hungarian cavalrymen were raiding his lines of communication with Silesia. He turned back and entered Bohemia. There, near Chotusitz, his rear guard was attacked by an Austrian army under Prince Charles Alexander of Lorraine (May 17, 1742). The Prince, brother-in-law to Maria Theresa, was a youth of thirty years, one of the most brilliant and gallant of his line, but he could not match Frederick in the tactics of battle. Each had some twenty-eight thousand men. Frederick's advance guard returned to the scene just in time; he directed its full force against an exposed flank of the Austrians; they fell back in orderly retreat. Both armies suffered heavy losses, but the result convinced Maria Theresa that she could not deal with all her foes at once. She accepted the advice of the English envoys to make a definite peace with Frederick; and this time, by the Treaty of Berlin (July 28, 1742), she ceded to him nearly all of Silesia. So ended the First Silesian War.

The Austrian armies of Khevenhüller and Prince Charles Alexander now moved into Bohemia. The French garrison in Prague faced encirclement and starvation. To prevent this *reductio ad absurdum* of Belle-Isle's dreams, France ordered Marshal Maillebois to lead into Bohemia the army that had been holding the forces of George II in Hanover. So freed, England entered actively into the war, advanced £500,000 to Maria Theresa, and dispatched sixteen thousand troops to Austrian Flanders; and the United Provinces contributed 840,000 florins. The Queen transmuted the money into armies. One of these blocked Maillebois' advance toward Bohemia. Austrian forces, repeatedly augmented, converged upon Prague. Belle-Isle and most of his men escaped to Eger, at great cost. Maria Theresa came up from Vienna to Prague, and there at last (May 12, 1743) she was crowned queen of Bohemia.

Everywhere now she seemed triumphant. In that same May the United Provinces voted her twenty thousand troops. A month later her English allies defeated her French foes at Dettingen. Control of the Mediterranean by the English navy advanced her cause in Italy; on September 13 Charles Emmanuel I, King of Sardinia, joined in alliance with Austria and England; he received a slice of Lombardy from Austria and a pledge of £200,000 a year from England, in return for 45,000 troops; so soldiers were bought in gross, kings in retail. Maria Theresa, as intransigent in victory as she had been heroic in adversity, dreamed now not only of regaining Silesia but of absorbing into her empire Bavaria, Alsace, and Lorraine.

Frederick for a while played with peace. He opened a new opera house in Berlin, wrote poetry, fingered the flute. He renewed his invitations to Voltaire; Voltaire answered that he was still loyal to Émilie. But at this juncture the French ministry, alarmed to find France at war with England, Austria, the Dutch Republic, and Savoy-Sardinia, bethought itself that Frederick's genius and giants would be a welcome aid; that his violations of his treaties with France could be forgiven if he would violate his treaty with Austria; and that he might be persuaded to see, in Austria's resurrected might, a threat to his hold on Silesia, even on Prussia. Who could best explain this to him? Why not try Voltaire, already holding an invitation from Frederick, and always itching to play politics?

So Voltaire the pacifist again bounced and swayed across Germany, and spent six weeks there (August 30 to October 12, 1743) trying to persuade Frederick to war. The King would not commit himself; he sent the philosopher away with nothing but compliments. But as the campaigns of 1744 proceeded he began to fear for his own security and the permanence of his gains. On August 15 he opened the Second Silesian War.

He proposed to begin by conquering Bohemia. As Saxony lay between Berlin and Prague, he marched his troops through Dresden, infuriating the absent Augustus III. By September 2 his eighty thousand men were at the gates of Prague; on September 16 the Austrian garrison surrendered. Leaving five thousand men to hold the Bohemian capital, Frederick moved south, again threatening Vienna. Maria Theresa reacted defiantly; she rode in haste to Pressburg and asked the Hungarian Diet for another levy of troops; it gathered 44,000 for her, and soon added thirty thousand more. She ordered Prince Charles to abandon his attack upon Alsace and lead the main Austrian army eastward to intercept the Prussians. Frederick expected the French to pursue the Austrians; they did not. He tried to force a battle with Charles; the Prince avoided it, but seconded the efforts of raiders to cut the Prussian lines of communication with Silesia and Berlin. History repeated itself; Frederick found his army isolated amid a population fervently Catholic and resourcefully hostile. Hungarian troops were coming to join Prince Charles. Word came that Saxony had openly entered the war on Austria's side. Fearing to be cut off from his own capital and from his sources of supply. Frederick retreated northward, cursing the French who had failed him again; he ordered the Prussian garrison to abandon Prague; and on December 13 he returned to Berlin, not so proud as before, and having learned that the deceiver may be deceived.

The current ran strongly against him. On January 8, 1745, England, the United Provinces, and Poland-Saxony signed at Warsaw a pact with Austria that pledged all signatories to restore to each of them all that it had possessed in 1739—therefore to regain Silesia for Maria Theresa. Augustus III promised thirty thousand men in return for £150,000 from England and Holland—five pounds per soul. On January 20 Charles VII, so briefly emperor, died, aged forty-eight. In his last moments he expressed his sorrow for having ruined his country by aspiring to the Imperial and Bohemian thrones; he begged his son Maximilian Joseph to forgo such pretenses, and make peace with the house of Austria. The new Elector, despite French protests, followed this advice; on April 22 he resigned all claims to empire, and agreed to support Duke Francis Stephen for the Imperial crown. Austrian troops were withdrawn from Bavaria.

The Queen now thought not merely of regaining Silesia but of dismembering Prussia as a guarantee against the ambitions of Frederick.[80] She was temporarily disconcerted by the French victory over her English allies at Fontenoy (May 11, 1745); but in that month she sent her main army into Silesia, and ordered it to seek battle. Reinforced by a Saxon contingent, the Austrians encountered Frederick at Hohenfriedberg (June 4, 1745). Here his skill in tactics saved him; he deployed his cavalry to capture a hill from which his artillery could rake the enemy infantry. After seven hours of slaughter the Austrians and Saxons withdrew, leaving four thousand killed and seven thousand prisoners. This was the decisive battle of the Silesian Wars.

England again bent her diplomacy to peace. The Jacobite invasion of 1745 compelled her to withdraw her best troops from Flanders; Maréchal de Saxe took town after town for France, even the main English base at Ostend; George II feared that the victorious French would reach his beloved Hanover. The British Parliament, which had deposed Walpole for loving peace, was now weary of a war that had cost not only thousands of replaceable men but millions of precious pounds; English envoys pleaded with Maria Theresa to come to terms with Frederick in order that Austrian and English forces might concentrate upon a France reinvigorated by a general whose victories almost equaled his amours. The Queen refused. England threatened to withdraw all aid, end all subsidies; she still refused. England invited Frederick to a conference at Hanover; there it signed with his representatives a separate peace (August 26, 1745); England accepted the terms of the Treaty of Berlin, which confirmed Prussian possession of Silesia; Frederick agreed to support the election of Duke Francis Stephen as emperor. On October 4, at Frankfurt, Francis was crowned emperor and Maria Theresa became empress.

She bade her generals continue the war. They fought the Prussians at Soor in Bohemia (September 30) and at Hennersdorf (November 24); the Austrians, numerically superior, were twice defeated. Meanwhile a Prussian army under Leopold of Anhalt-Dessau advanced into Saxony, and at Kesselsdorf (December 15) overwhelmed the forces protecting Dresden. Frederick, coming up after the victory, entered Dresden unresisted and magnanimous; he forbade pillage, and reassured the children of Augustus III, who had fled to Prague. He offered to withdraw from Saxony if the Elector-King would join England in recognizing Frederick's possession of Silesia, and abandon all aid to Maria Theresa; Augustus consented. Abandoned by both England and Saxony, Maria Theresa signed the Treaty of Dresden (December 25, 1745), ceding Silesia and the county of Glatz to Prussia. So ended the Second Silesian War.

The War of the Austrian Succession had now lost meaning, but it went on; France fought Austria and England for dominance in Flanders; France and Spain fought Austria and Sardinia for dominance in Italy. The victories of the Austrians in Italy were counterbalanced by those of the French in the Netherlands. At last financial exhaustion, rather than any distaste for massacre, persuaded the contestants to peace. By the Treaty of Aix-la-Chapelle, after negotiations that dragged on from April to November, 1748, the War of the Austrian Succession came to a sorry end. Frederick's seizure of Silesia was confirmed, and was the only appreciable gain that any of the powers could show for eight years of competitive destruction. France, despite Saxe's victories, restored the southern Netherlands to Austria; it recognized the Hanoverian dynasty in England, and agreed to expel the Young Pretender from French soil.

The powers rested for eight years, until the labor of women in childbirth could replenish the regiments for another round in the game of kings.

V. FREDERICK AT HOME: 1745-50

The tired victor returned to Berlin (December 28, 1745) vowing "from this day Peace to the end of my life!"[81] All Europe outside of (and some souls in) Prussia denounced him as a treacherous, and admired him as a successful, thief. Voltaire reproved his slaughter and called him "Great."[82] Frederick in 1742 had replied to the poet's protests:

> You ask me for how long my colleagues have agreed to ruin the earth. To this I answer that I have not the slightest knowledge, but that it is now the fashion to make war, and I presume it will last a long time. The Abbé de Saint-Pierre, who distinguishes me sufficiently to honor me with his correspondence, has sent me a beautiful book on the way to re-establish peace in Europe and retain it forever. . . . For the success of the plan all that is lacking is the consent of Europe and a few similar trifles.[83]

To Europe he made his defense in his posthumous *Histoire de mon temps*, adopting Machiavelli's principle that the interest of the state over-rides the rules of private morality:

> Perhaps posterity will see with surprise, in these memoirs, accounts of treaties made and broken. Though there are many precedents for such actions, they would not justify the author of this work if he had no better reasons to excuse his conduct. The interest of the state must serve as the rule for sovereigns. Alliances may be broken for any one of these reasons: (1) when an ally fails to keep his engagements; (2) when an ally plans to deceive you, and when you have no other recourse but to anticipate him; (3) when a major force [*force majeure*] lies upon you and compels you to break your agreements; (4) when you have no means for continuing the war. . . . It seems clear and evident to me that a private individual must scrupulously keep his word. . . . If he is deceived he can ask for the protection of the laws. . . . But to what tribunal can a sovereign have recourse if another prince violates engagements made to him? The word of an individual involves the misfortune of only one man; that of a sovereign may bring a general calamity to whole nations. All this can be reduced to one question: Is it better that the people should perish than that the prince should violate a treaty? What imbecile would hesitate to decide this question?[84]

Frederick agreed with Christian theology that man is by nature wicked. When Sulzer, a school inspector, expressed the opinion that "the inborn inclination of men is rather to good than to evil," the King answered, "*Ach, mein lieber Sulzer, er kennt nicht diese verdammte Rasse* [you don't know this damned race]."[85] Frederick did not merely accept La Rochefoucauld's analysis of human nature as completely egoistic; he believed that man would recognize no restraints on the pursuit of his own interest if he were not checked by fear of the police. Since the state is the individual multiplied, and is deterred in its collective egoism by no international police, it can be checked only by fear of the power of other states. Hence the first duty of "the first servant of the state" (as Frederick called himself) is to organize the power of the nation for defense, which includes pre-emptive offense—to do unto others what they are planning to do unto you. So to Frederick, as to his father, the army was the foundation of the state. He established a carefully supervised and planned economy; he fostered manufactures and commerce; he sent agents throughout Europe to import skilled workers, inventors, industries; but he felt that all this would in the end be of no avail unless he kept his troops the best-drilled, best-disciplined, and most reliable army in Europe.

Having such an army, and a well-organized police, he saw no need for religion as an aid to social order. When Prince William of Brunswick asked did he not think religion to be one of the best props of a ruler's authority, he answered: "I find order and the laws sufficient. . . . Countries have been admirably governed when your religion had no existence."[86] But he accepted whatever help religion could give him in inculcating moral sentiments that contributed to "order." He protected all the religions in his realm, but he insisted on naming the Catholic bishops, especially in Silesia. (Catholic kings also insisted on naming the Catholic bishops, and the English kings named the Anglican bishops.) Everybody—including Greek Catholics, Mohammedans, Unitarians, atheists—was to be free to worship as he liked, or not at all. There was, however, one limitation: when religious controversy became too abusive or violent Frederick put a damper upon it, as upon any threat to internal peace. In his later years he was less tolerant of attacks upon his government than of attacks upon God.

What was he like, this terror of Europe and idol of philosophers? Five feet six inches tall, he had no commanding height. Rather stout in his youth, he was now, after ten years of rule and war, slender, nervous, taut, a wire of electric sensitivity and energy; eyes sharp with a penetrating and skeptical intelligence. He was capable of humor, and his wit was as keen as Voltaire's. As a man uncrossed he could be quite amiable; as a king he was severe, and seldom tempered justice with mercy; he could talk philosophy with his associates while calmly watching soldiers suffering the knout. His cynicism had a biting tongue that sometimes cut his friends. He was usually parsimonious, occasionally generous. Accustomed to being obeyed, he became dictatorial, seldom brooking remonstrance, rarely seeking advice, never taking it. He was loyal to his intimates, but contemptuous of mankind. He spoke seldom to his wife, kept her in financial straits, tore up before her face the note in which she had humbly stated her wants.[87] He was normally kind and affectionate to his sister Wilhelmine, but she too sometimes found him coldly reserved.[88] Other women, except for visiting princesses, he kept at a distance; he had no taste for feminine graces and charms of body or character, and he abominated the light chatter of salons. He preferred philosophers and handsome youths; often he took one of the latter to his rooms after dinner.[89] Perhaps he liked dogs still better. In his later years his best-loved companions were his greyhounds; they slept in his bed; he had monuments raised over their graves, and gave orders that he should be buried near them.[90] He found it difficult to be at once a successful commander and a lovable man.

In 1747 he suffered an apoplectic stroke and remained unconscious for half an hour.[91] Thereafter he countered his unsteady health with steady habits and a frugal regimen. He slept on a thin mattress on a simple folding bed, and wooed sleep by reading. In these middle years he was content with five or six hours of sleep per day. He rose at three, four, or five in the summer, later in winter. He had but one servant to attend him—chiefly to light his fire and shave him; he scorned kings who had to be helped to put on their clothes. He was not noted for cleanliness of person or elegance of dress; he spent half the day in his dressing gown, half in the uniform of a guardsman. His breakfast began with several glasses of water; then followed several cups of coffee, then some cakes, then much fruit. After breakfast he played the flute, pondering politics and philosophy while puffing. Every day, about eleven, he attended the drill and parade of his troops. His main meal, at noon, was usually mixed with conferences. In the afternoon he became an author, spending an hour or two in writing poetry or history; we shall find him an excellent historian of his family and his times. After several hours given to administration, he relaxed with scientists, artists, poets, and musicians. At seven in the evening he might take part as flutist in a concert. At eight-thirty came his famous suppers, usually (after May, 1747) at Sanssouci. To these he invited his closest associates, distinguished visitors, and the leading lights of the Berlin Academy. He bade them be at their ease, forget that he was king, and discourse without fear, which they did on every subject but politics. Frederick himself talked abundantly, learnedly, brilliantly. "His conversation," said the Prince de Ligne, "was encyclopedic; the fine arts, war, medicine, literature, religion, philosophy, morals, history, and legislation passed, turn by turn, in review."[92] Only one added ornament was needed to make this a feast of the mind. He came on July 10, 1750.

VI. VOLTAIRE IN GERMANY: 1750–54

Even he was satisfied with his reception. Frederick put on Gallic manners to greet him. "He took my hand to kiss it," Voltaire reported to Richelieu. "I kissed his, and made myself his slave."[93] He was given an elegant apartment in the Palace of Sanssouci, just over the royal suite. The King's horses, coaches, coachmen, and cuisine were placed at his command. A dozen servants fussed around him; a hundred princes, princesses, nobles, the Queen herself, paid court to him. He was officially a chamberlain to the King at twenty thousand francs a year, but his chief chore was to correct the French of Frederick's poetry and speech. He was second only to the King at the suppers. A German visitor thought their exchanges "a thousand times more interesting than any book."[94] "Never in any place in the world," Voltaire later recalled, "was there greater freedom of conversation concerning the superstitions of mankind."[95]

He was ecstatic. To d'Argental he wrote (September, 1750):

> I find a port after thirty years of storms. I find the protection of a king, the conversation of a philosopher, the agreeable qualities of an amiable man, all united in one who for sixteen years has wished to console me for my misfortunes, make me secure against my enemies. . . . Here I am sure of a destiny forever tranquil. If one can be sure of anything it is of the character of the King of Prussia.[96]

He wrote to Mme. Denis asking her to come and live with him in his paradise. She wisely preferred Paris and younger gallants. She warned him against staying long in Berlin. Friendship with a king (she wrote) is always precarious; he changes his mind and his favorites; one must be always on one's guard not to cross the royal mood or will. Sooner or later Voltaire would find himself a servant and a prisoner rather than a friend.[97]

The foolish philosopher sent the letter to Frederick, who, reluctant to lose his prize, wrote to him in reply (August 23):

> I have seen the letter which your niece writes you from Paris. The affection which she has for you wins my esteem. If I were Mme. Denis I should think as she does; but being what I am, I think otherwise. I should be in despair to be the cause of my enemy's unhappiness; how, then, could I wish the misfortune of a man whom I esteem, whom I love, and who sacrifices to me his country and all that is dearest to humanity? No, my dear Voltaire, if I could foresee that your removal hither would turn the least in the world to your disadvantage, I should

be the first to dissuade you from it. I should prefer your happiness to my extreme pleasure in possessing you. But you are a philosopher; I am one also; what is then more natural, more simple, more according to the order of things, than that philosophers made to live together, united by the same studies, by the same tastes, and by a similar way of thinking, should give one another that satisfaction? . . . I am firmly persuaded that you will be very happy here; that you will be regarded as the father of letters and of people of taste; and that you will find in me all the consolations which a man of your merit can expect from one who esteems him. Good night.[98]

It took the older philosopher only four months to ruin his paradise. Voltaire was a millionaire, but he could not with equanimity miss an opportunity to swell his hoard. The state bank of Saxony had issued notes called *Steuerscheine* (revenue certificates), which had fallen to half their original worth. In the Treaty of Dresden Frederick had required that all such notes that had been bought by Prussians should be redeemed, at maturity, at their face value in gold. Some wily Prussians bought *Steuerscheine* at a low price in Holland and then had them redeemed in full in Prussia. In May, 1748, in justice to Saxony, Frederick forbade such importation. On November 23, 1750, Voltaire summoned to him at Potsdam a Jewish banker, Abraham Hirsch. According to Hirsch, Voltaire asked him to go to Dresden and buy for him 18,430 écus' worth of *Steuerscheine* at thirty-five per cent of their face value. Hirsch claimed to have warned Voltaire that these bank notes could not be legally brought into Prussia; Voltaire (said Hirsch) promised him protection, and gave him letters of exchange on Paris and Leipzig. As security for these sums Hirsch left with Voltaire some diamonds that had been appraised at 18,430 écus. After his agent's departure (December 2) Voltaire regretted the arrangement, and Hirsch, arrived in Dresden, decided not to go through with the transaction; Voltaire stopped payment on the letters of exchange, and the banker returned to Berlin. According to Hirsch, Voltaire sought to bribe him to silence by buying three thousand écus' worth of the diamonds. A dispute arose over the appraisal; Voltaire flew at Hirsch's throat and knocked him down;[99] not receiving further satisfaction, he had Hirsch arrested, and brought the dispute to public trial (December 30). Hirsch exposed Voltaire's plan for buying Saxon bonds; Voltaire denied it, saying he had sent Hirsch to Dresden to buy furs. Nobody believed him.

Frederick, learning of the mess, dispatched an angry letter from Potsdam to Voltaire at Berlin (February 24, 1751):

I was glad to receive you in my house; I esteemed your genius, your talents and acquirements; and I had reason to think that a man of your age, wearied with fencing against authors and exposing himself to the storm, came hither to take refuge as in a safe harbor.

But, on arriving, you exacted of me, in a rather singular manner, not to take Fréron to write news from Paris, and I had the weakness . . . to grant you this, though it is not for you to decide what persons I should take into my service. Baculard d'Arnault [Baculard d'Arnaud, a French poet at Frederick's court] had given you offense, a generous man would have pardoned him; a vindictive man hunts down those whom he takes to hating. . . . Though to me d'Arnault had done nothing, it was on your account that he had to go. . . . You have had the most villainous affair in the world with a Jew. It has made a frightful scandal all over town. And that *Steuerschein* business is so well known in Saxony that they have made grievous complaints of it to me.

For my own part I have preserved peace in my house till your arrival; and I warn you that if you have the passion of intriguing and caballing, you have applied to the wrong hand. I like peaceable, composed people, who do not put into their conduct the passions of tragic drama. In case you can resolve to live like a philosopher, I shall be glad to see you; but if you abandon yourself to all the violences of your passions, and get into quarrels with all the world, you will do me no good by coming hither, and you may as well stay in Berlin.

The trial court declared in favor of Voltaire. He sent humble apologies to the King; Frederick granted him pardon, but advised him to "have no more quarrels, neither with the Old Testament nor with the New."[100] Henceforth Voltaire was lodged not in Sanssouci but in a pleasant rural lodge nearby called "the Marquisat." The King sent him assurances of renewed esteem, but Voltaire's foolishness did not extend to trusting them. The royal poet sent him poems with requests to polish the French; Voltaire labored over them to weariness, and offended the author by making incisive alterations.

Voltaire now composed his poem *Sur la Loi naturelle;* it sought to find God in nature, chiefly along the lines of Alexander Pope. Of far greater import was *Le Siècle de Louis XIV*, which in these worrisome months he brought to finished form, and published in Berlin (1751). He was anxious to have it printed before some necessity should drive him from Germany, for only under Frederick could it be safe from censorship. "You know very well," he wrote to Richelieu on August 31, "that there is not one little censor of books [in Paris] who would not have made a merit and duty out of mutilating or suppressing my work."[101] The sale of the book was forbidden in France; booksellers in Holland and England issued pirated editions, for which they paid Voltaire nothing; noting this, we may better understand his love of money. He had to fight "rogue booksellers"[102] as well as ecclesiastics and governments.

The Age of Louis XIV was the most thoroughly and conscientiously prepared of Voltaire's works. He had planned it in 1732, begun it in 1734 put it aside in 1738, resumed it in 1750. For it he read two hundred volumes and reams of unpublished memoirs, consulted scores of survivors from *le grand siècle*, studied the original papers of protagonists like Louvois and Colbert, secured from the Duc de Noailles the manuscripts left by Louis XIV, and found important documents, hitherto unused, in the archives of the Louvre.[103] He weighed conflicting evidence with discretion and care, and achieved a high degree of accuracy. With Mme. du Châtelet he had tried to be a scientist, and had failed; now he turned to writing history, and there his success was a revolution.

Long ago, in a letter of January 18, 1739, he had expressed his aim: "My chief object is not political and military history, it is the history of the arts, of commerce, of civilization—in a word, of the human mind." And, still better, in a letter written to Thieriot in 1736:

> When I asked for anecdotes on the age of Louis XIV it was less on the King himself than on the arts that flourished in his reign. I should prefer details about Racine and Boileau, Quinault, Lully, Molière, Le Brun, Bossuet, Poussin, Descartes, and others, rather than about the battle of Steenkerke. Nothing but a name remains of those who commanded battalions and fleets; nothing results to the human race from a hundred battles gained; but the great men of whom I have spoken prepared pure and durable delights for generations unborn. A canal that connects two seas, a picture by Poussin, a beautiful tragedy, a discovered truth, are things a thousand times more precious than all the annals of the court, all the narratives of war. You know that with me great men rank first, "heroes" last. I call great men all those who have excelled in the useful and the agreeable. The ravagers of provinces are mere heroes.[104]

Possibly Voltaire would have promoted martial heroes from last place if their victories had saved civilization from barbarism; but it was natural that the philosopher who knew no weapon but words would enjoy raising aloft the men of his own kind; and his name illustrates his thesis by remaining, after two centuries, the most prominent in our memory of his age. Originally he had proposed to give all the book to cultural history; then Mme. du Châtelet suggested to him a "general history" of the nations; consequently he added chapters on politics, war, and the court to make the volume a homogeneous continuation of the larger *Essai sur l'histoire générale* that was taking form under his pen. This may be the reason why the cultural history is not integrated into the rest of the volume: the first half of the book is devoted to political and military history; then follow sections on manners ("characteristics and anecdotes"), government, commerce, science, literature, art, and religion.

The hunted scribe looked back with admiration to the reign under which poets (if they behaved) were honored by the King; perhaps his emphasis on the support of literature and art by Louis XIV was a flank attack upon Louis XV's comparative indifference to such patronage. Now that the grandeur of the former age stood out in gilded retrospect, and its despotism and dragonnades were shunted from memory, Voltaire idealized the Sun King somewhat, and thrilled to the victories of French generals—though he stigmatized the devastation of the Palatinate. But criticism hides its head before this first modern attempt at integral history. Perceptive contemporaries realized that here was a new start—history as the biography of civilization, history as transformed by art and perspective into literature and philosophy. Within a year of its publication the Earl of Chesterfield wrote to his son:

> Voltaire has sent me from Berlin his *Histoire du siècle de Louis XIV*. It came at a very proper time; Lord Bolingbroke had just taught me how history should be read; Voltaire shows me how it should be written. . . . It is the history of the human understanding, written by a man of genius for the use of intelligent men. . . . Free from religious, philosophical, political, and national prejudices beyond any historian I have ever met with, he relates all those matters as truly and as impartially as certain regards, which must always be observed, will allow him.[105]

Amid his literary labors Voltaire fretted over his insecurity at Frederick's court. One day in August, 1751, La Mettrie, the jolly materialist who often read to the King, reported to Voltaire their host's remark: "I need him [Voltaire] another year at most [as polisher of the royal French]; one squeezes the orange, and throws away the peel."[106] Some have doubted the authenticity of the remark; it was not like Frederick to be so confidential, and it was not impossible for La Mettrie to wish Voltaire off the scene. "I have done all that I could not to believe La Mettrie," Voltaire wrote to Mme. Denis on September 2; "but still, I don't know." And to her on October 29: "I keep dreaming about that orange peel. . . . He who was falling from a bell tower and, finding himself at ease in the air, said, 'Good, provided this lasts,' resembles me quite."[107]

There was another Frenchman in Germany who entered into the comedy. Of two Frenchmen in the same court, said Frederick, one must perish.[108] Maupertuis, head of the Berlin Academy, was next in honor to Voltaire alone among the guests at Sanssouci; each was irked by that proximity; and perhaps Voltaire had not forgotten that Mme. du Châtelet had been fond of Maupertuis. In April, 1751, Voltaire gave a dinner party; Maupertuis was invited and came. "Your book *Sur le Bonheur* has given me great pleasure," said Voltaire, "a few obscurities excepted, of which we will talk together some evening." "Obscurities? There may be such for you, monsieur," scowled Maupertuis. Voltaire laid a hand on the scientist's shoulder. "Monsieur le Président," he said, "I esteem you; you are brave, you want war. We will have it, but meanwhile let us eat the King's roast meat."[109] "Maupertuis," he wrote to d'Argental (May 4), "is not of very engaging ways. He takes my dimensions harshly with his quadrant; it is said that there enters something of envy into his data. . . . A somewhat surly gentleman, not too sociable." And on July 24, 1752, to niece Denis: "Maupertuis has discreetly set the rumor going that I found the King's *Works* very bad; that I said to someone, on verses of the King coming in, 'Will he never tire, then, of sending me his dirty linen to wash?' "[110] It is not certain that Maupertuis had conveyed this rumor to Frederick; Voltaire thought it certain, and resolved on war.

One of Maupertuis' contributions to science was the "principle of least action"—that all effects in the world of motion tend to be achieved by the least force sufficient for the result. Samuel Koenig, who owed his membership in the Berlin Academy to Maupertuis, came upon what purported to be a copy of an unpublished letter of Leibniz, in which this principle seemed to be anticipated. He wrote an article about his discovery, but before publishing it he submitted it to Maupertuis, offering to suppress it if the president objected. Maupertuis, perhaps after too hurried a perusal, consented to the publication. Koenig had the article printed in the March, 1751, issue of the Leipzig *Acta eruditorum*. It caused a stir. Maupertuis asked Koenig to submit Leibniz' letter to the Academy; Koenig replied that he had seen only a copy of it among the papers of his friend Henzi, who had been hanged in 1749; he had made a copy of this copy, and now sent it to Maupertuis, who again demanded the original. Koenig confessed that this could not now be found, since Henzi's papers had been scattered after his death. Maupertuis submitted the matter to the Academy (October 7, 1751); the secretary sent to Koenig a peremptory order to produce the original. He could not. On April 13, 1752, the Academy pronounced the supposed letter of Leibniz a forgery. Maupertuis did not attend this session, being ill with consumptive spitting of blood.[111] Koenig sent in his resignation from the Academy, and issued an *Appeal to the Public* (September, 1752).

Koenig had once spent two years at Cirey as the guest of Voltaire and Mme. du Châtelet. Voltaire decided to strike a blow for his former friend at a present enemy. In the quarterly review *Bibliothèque raisonnée* for

September 18 there appeared a "Réponse d'un académicien de Berlin à un académicien de Paris," restating the case for Koenig, and concluding that

> the Sieur Maupertuis has been convicted, in the face of Scientific Europe, not only of plagiarism and blunder, but of having abused his place to suppress free discussion, and to persecute an honest man. . . . Several members of our Academy have protested against so crying a procedure, and would leave the Academy, were it not for fear of displeasing the King.[112]

The article was unsigned, but Frederick knew Voltaire's feline touch. Instead of hurling a royal thunderbolt, he wrote a reply in which the "Réponse" was described as "malicious, cowardly, and infamous," and its author was branded "a shameless impostor," an "ugly brigand," a "concocter of stupid libels."[113] This too was anonymous, but the title page bore the Prussian arms with the eagle, the scepter, and the crown.

Voltaire's pride was piqued. He could never let an enemy have the last word, and perhaps he had made up his mind to break with the King. "I have no scepter," he wrote to Mme. Denis (October 18, 1752), "but I have a pen." He took full advantage of the fact that Maupertuis had just published (Dresden, 1752) a series of *Lettres* in which it was suggested that a hole be bored into the earth, if possible to the center, in order to study its composition; that one of the Pyramids of Egypt be blown up, to discover the secrets of their purpose and design; that a city be built where only Latin would be spoken, so that students might go there for a year or two and learn that language as they had learned their own; that a doctor be paid only after curing the patient; that an adequate dose of opium might enable a man to foresee the future; and that proper care of the body might enable us to prolong life indefinitely.[114] Voltaire seized upon these *Lettres* as easy game, carefully ignoring any item of good sense in them and any hints of humor, and tossed the rest joyously upon the horns of his wit. So, in November, 1752, he composed his famous *Diatribe of Dr. Akakia, Physician and Ordinary to the Pope.*

Diatribe then meant a dissertation; *akakia* is Greek for "guileless simplicity." The supposed physician began in apparent innocence by doubting that so great a man as the president of the Berlin Academy had written so absurd a book. After all, "nothing is more common in the present age than for young and ignorant authors to usher into the world, under well-known names, works unworthy of the supposed writers." These *Lettres* must be such an imposture; it was impossible that the learned president should have written such nonsense. Dr. Akakia protested especially against paying physicians only for cures—a proposal that might have struck a sympathetic chord in Voltaire's aching breast, but: "Does a client deprive a lawyer of his just fee because he has lost his cause? A physician promises his assistance, not a cure. He does all that lies in his power, and is paid accordingly." How would a member of the Academy like it if a certain number of ducats were to be subtracted from his annual salary for every error he has made, for every absurdity that he has uttered, during the year? And the doctor proceeded to detail what Voltaire considered to be errors or absurdities in Maupertuis' works.[115]

It was not so brilliant a satire as commonly supposed; much of it is repetitious, and some of the fault-finding is trivial and ungenerous; we conceal our venom more politely in these days. But Voltaire was so pleased with his performance that he could not resist the added delight of seeing it in print. He sent a manuscript of it to a printer in The Hague. Meanwhile he showed another manuscript to the King. Frederick, who privately agreed that Maupertuis was sometimes insufferably conceited, enjoyed the skit (or so we are told), but forbade Voltaire to publish it; obviously, the dignity and prestige of the Berlin Academy were involved. Voltaire allowed him to keep the manuscript, but the satire was nevertheless published in Holland. Soon thirty thousand copies were flying about Paris, Brussels, The Hague, Berlin. One reached Frederick. He expressed his anger in such terms that Voltaire fled to a private lodging in the capital. On December 24, 1752, he saw from his window the public burning of the *Diatribe* by the official executioner of the state. On January 1, 1753, he remitted to Frederick his gold key as a chamberlain, and his Cross of Merit.

Now he was really ill. Erysipelas burned his brow, dysentery tortured his bowels, fever consumed him. He took to his bed on February 2 and stayed there for two weeks, having, said a visitor, "all the appearance of a skeleton."[116] Frederick, relenting, sent his own physician to attend the poet. When he improved, Voltaire wrote to the King asking permission to visit Plombières, whose waters might heal his erysipelas. Frederick bade his secretary reply (March 16) "that he can leave this service whenever he wishes; that he has no need to employ the pretext of the waters of Plombières; but that he will have the goodness, before setting out, to return to me . . . the volume of poems that I confided to him."[117] On the eighteenth the King invited Voltaire to reoccupy his old apartment in Sanssouci. Voltaire came, remained eight days, and apparently made his peace with the King—but kept the royal poems. On March 26 he bade Frederick au revoir, both pretending that the separation was to be temporary. "Take care of your health above all," said the King, "and don't forget that I expect to see you again after the waters. . . . Bon voyage!"[118] They never saw each other again.

So ended this historic friendship, but the ridiculous enmities went on.

Voltaire, with secretary and baggage, rolled on in his own coach to safety in Saxon Leipzig. There, pleading weakness, he tarried three weeks, adding to the *Diatribe*. On April 6 he received a letter from Maupertuis:

> The gazettes say you are detained sick at Leipzig; private informa-
> tion assures me that you are stopping there only to have new libels
> printed. . . . I have never done anything against you, never written
> anything, never said anything. I have ever found it unworthy of me to
> reply one word to the impertinences which you have hitherto spread
> abroad . . . But if it is true that your intention is to attack me again,
> and to attack me by personalities, . . . I declare to you that . . . my
> health is sufficiently good to find you wherever you may be, and to
> wreak upon you vengeance the most complete.[119]

Voltaire nevertheless printed the embellished *Diatribe*, and with it Maupertuis' letter. The pamphlet, now swollen to fifty pages, became the gossip
of palaces and courts in Germany and France. Wilhelmine wrote from
Bayreuth to Frederick (April 24, 1753) confessing that she had not been
able to keep from laughing over the piece. Maupertuis did not carry out
his threat, nor did he, as some supposed, die of unimplemented rage and
grief; he survived *Dr. Akakia* by six years, and died at Basel in 1759 of
tuberculosis.

On April 19 Voltaire moved on to Gotha. There he put up at the public
inn, but the Duke and Duchess of Saxe-Gotha soon persuaded him to come
and stay in their palace. As the little court went in for culture, the Duchess
gathered notables and literati, and Voltaire read to them from his works,
even from the rollicking *La Pucelle*. Then on to Frankfurt-am-Main,
where Nemesis overtook him.

Seeing that Voltaire continued the war against Maupertuis, Frederick
wondered whether the irresponsible poet might give to the world the poems
that Frederick had composed, and of which a privately printed copy was
still in Voltaire's possession—poems some risqué, some ridiculing Christianity, some speaking with more wit than respect of living sovereigns, and
therefore liable to alienate useful powers. He sent to Freytag, Prussian
resident at Frankfurt, orders to detain Voltaire until the impish skeleton
should surrender the royal poems and various decorations given him by the
King during the honeymoon. Frankfurt was a "free city," but so dependent
upon Frederick's good will that it did not dare interfere with these orders;
moreover, Voltaire was still technically in the service of, and on a leave of
absence from, the Prussian King. On June 1 Freytag went to the Golden
Lion, where Voltaire had arrived the night before, and politely asked for
the insignia and the poetry. Voltaire allowed the resident to examine his
luggage and take the royal decorations; but as for the royal poems, they

were probably in a box that had been forwarded to Hamburg. Freytag
ordered him kept under watch until the box could be brought from Hamburg. On June 9 the fuming philosopher was consoled by the arrival of
Mme. Denis, who helped him express his rage. She was appalled by his
emaciation. "I knew that man [Frederick] would be the death of you!" On
June 18 the box arrived; the volume of poetry was found and surrendered;
but on the same day a new directive from Potsdam ordered Freytag to
maintain the *status quo* till further orders came. Voltaire, his patience quite
at an end, tried to escape; on June 20, leaving his baggage with his niece,
he and his secretary secretly fled from Frankfurt.

Before they could reach the limits of the municipal jurisdiction they
were overtaken by Freytag, who brought them to the city and lodged them
as prisoners in the Goat Inn, for (according to Freytag) "the landlord of
the Golden Lion was unwilling to have Voltaire any longer in his house, on
account of his incredible parsimony."[120] All of Voltaire's money was now
taken from him by his captors; also his watch, some jewels that he wore,
and his snuffbox—which was soon restored to him on his plea that it was
indispensable to his life. On June 21 a letter arrived from Frederick ordering Voltaire's release, but Freytag thought that strict duty required him to
send the King notice that Voltaire had tried to escape; should he still be
allowed to go? On July 5 Frederick answered yes; after thirty-five days
of detention Voltaire was freed. On July 7 he left Frankfurt for Mainz.
Mme. Denis returned to Paris, hoping to secure permission for Voltaire to
enter France.

The news of his arrest had spread, and now, wherever he went, he was
feted and acclaimed, for Frederick was not popular except with Wilhelmine, and Voltaire was still, with all his deviltry, the greatest living poet,
dramatist, and historian. After three weeks in Mainz he moved on, with
the suite of a prince, to Mannheim and Strasbourg (August 15 to October
2), where he feasted his soul with the thought that he was on French soil.
Then on to Colmar (October 2), where Wilhelmine, en route to Montpellier, visited and comforted him "with bounties." His strength revived
enough to inspire some gallant letters to Mme. Denis, who had complained
of a swelling in her thighs:

> Eh, *mon Dieu*, my dear child, what are your legs and mine trying to
> say? If they were together they would be well [*elles se porteraient
> bien*]. . . . Your thighs were not made to suffer. These lovely thighs
> so soon to be kissed are now shamefully treated [*Queste belle cossie
> tantot bacciate sono oggi indignamente trattate*].[121]

In a humbler mood he wrote to Mme. de Pompadour invoking her influence with Louis XV to allow him to return to Paris. But meanwhile a pirate

printer in The Hague published a garbled *Abrégé de l'histoire générale*, an abridgment of Voltaire's unfinished *Essai sur l'histoire générale*, or *Essai sur les moeurs;* it contained some sharp animadversions on Christianity; it sold rapidly in Paris; Louis XV informed Pompadour, "I do not wish Voltaire to come to Paris."[122] The Jesuits in Colmar called for his expulsion from that city. He tried to appease his ecclesiastical enemies by taking the Sacrament at Easter; the sole result was that his friends joined with the Jesuits in calling him a hypocrite. "Behold Voltaire, who knows not where to lay his head," commented Montesquieu, and he added, *"Le bon esprit* is worth more than *le bel esprit.*"[123]

The homeless philosopher desperately thought of leaving Europe and settling in Philadelphia; he admired the spirit of Penn and the work of Franklin, who had just united lightning and electricity; "if the sea did not make me unsupportably sick, it is among the Quakers of Pennsylvania that I would finish the remainder of my life."[124] On June 8, 1754, he left Colmar, and found asylum in the Benedictine Abbey of Senones in Lorraine. There the learned Dom Augustin Calmet was abbot and the library had twelve thousand volumes; for three weeks, amid the monks, Voltaire found peace. On July 2 he moved on to Plombières, and at last drank its waters. Mme. Denis joined him there, and henceforth remained the mistress at least of his household. He resumed his wandering, went back to Colmar, found it uncomfortable, passed on to Dijon for a night, then to Lyons for a month (November 11 to December 10). For a week he was the guest of his old friend and debtor the Duc de Richelieu; then, perhaps fearing to compromise him, he moved to the Palais-Royal Hotel. He attended the Academy of Lyons, and received all its honors. Some of his plays were produced in the local theater, and his spirit was heartened by the applause. He thought of settling in Lyons, but Archbishop Tencin objected,[125] and Voltaire departed. He knew that at any moment he might be arrested if he remained in France.

Late in 1754, or early in 1755, he crossed over the Jura Mountains into Switzerland.

CHAPTER XIV

Switzerland and Voltaire

1715–58

I. LES DÉLICES

ON the Lyons road, just outside the gates of Geneva but within its jurisdiction, Voltaire at last found a place where he could lie down in security and peace, a spacious villa called St.-Jean, with terraced gardens descending to the Rhone. As the laws of the republic forbade the sale of land to any but Swiss Protestants, he provided the 87,000 francs that bought the property (February, 1755) through the agency of Labat de Grandcour and Jean Robert Tronchin.* With all the enthusiasm of a city dweller he bought chickens and a cow, sowed a vegetable garden, and planted trees; it had taken him sixty years to learn that "*il faut cultiver notre jardin.*" Now, he thought, he could forget Frederick, Louis XV, the Parlement of Paris, the bishops, the Jesuits; only his colic and his headaches remained. He was so pleased with his new home that he named it Les Délices (delights).† "I am so happy," he wrote to Thieriot, "that I am ashamed."[1]

As his clever investments were bringing him a lordly income, he indulged himself in lordly luxuries. He kept six horses, four carriages, a coachman, a postilion, two lackeys, a valet, a French cook, a secretary, and a monkey —with whom he liked to compare *homo sapiens*. Over this establishment reigned Mme. Denis, whom Mme. d'Épinay, visiting Les Délices in 1757, described as

> a fat little woman, as round as a ball, about fifty years of age; . . . ugly and good, untruthful without meaning it, and without malice. She has no intellect, and yet seems to have some; she . . . writes verses, argues rationally and irrationally; . . . without too great pretentiousness, and above all without offending anyone. . . . She adores her uncle, both as uncle and as a man; Voltaire loves her, laughs at her, and worships her. In a word, this house is a refuge for an assemblage of contraries, and a delightful spectacle for lookers-on.[2]

---

* There were many Tronchins, chiefly: (1) Jean Robert, banker and *procureur général* of Geneva; (2) Jakob, councilor; (3) François, author and painter; (4) Théodore, physician. "Tronchin" will mean Théodore unless otherwise stated.

† It is still there (1965), much reduced in area, but maintained by the city of Geneva as the Institut et Musée Voltaire.

Another visitor, the rising poet Marmontel, described the new seigneur: "He was in bed when we arrived. He held out his arms, embraced me, and wept for joy. . . . 'You find me at the point of death,' he said; 'come and restore me to life, or receive my last sigh'. . . . A moment later he said, 'I will rise and dine with you.' "[3]

There was one drawback at Les Délices—it was cold in winter. Voltaire, having no flesh, needed heat. Near Lausanne he found a little hermitage, Monrion, whose position sheltered it from the north wind; he bought it, and spent there some winter months in 1755–57. In Lausanne itself he bought (June, 1757), on the Rue du Grand Chêne, a "house which would be called a palace in Italy," with fifteen windows looking down upon the lake.* There, without any protest from the clergy, he staged plays, usually his own. "Tranquillity is a fine thing," he wrote, "but ennui . . . belongs to the same family. To repulse the ugly relation I have set up a theater."[4]

And so, oscillating between Geneva and Lausanne, he became acquainted with Switzerland.

II. THE CANTONS

"By what wonderful policy," asked Samuel Johnson in 1742, "or by what happy conciliation of interests, is it brought to pass that in a body made up of different communities and different religions there should be no vivid commotions, though the people are so warlike that to nominate and raise an army is the same?"[5]

This fascinating complex of three peoples, four languages, and two faiths had remained at peace with the outside world since 1515. By a kind of honor among thieves the powers refrained from attacking it; it was too tiny a prize (227 miles in its greatest length, 137 in its greatest breadth), too poor in natural resources, too mountainous in terrain, and its people were discouragingly brave. The Swiss continued to produce the best soldiers in Europe, but as these were costly to maintain they were leased to divers governments at so much a head. In 1748 there were sixty thousand such *Reisläufer* in foreign service. In some countries they became a permanent part of the military establishment; they were the favorite and most trusted guards of the popes and the French kings; all the world knows how the Swiss Guards died to a man in defense of Louis XVI on August 10, 1792.

In 1715 thirteen cantons constituted the Swiss Confederation: Appenzell, Basel, Glarus, Schaffhausen, and Zurich, which were predominantly German and Protestant; Lucerne, Schwyz, Solothurn, Unterwalden, Uri, and Zug, which were German and Catholic; Bern, which was both German and French, Protestant and Catholic; and Fribourg, which was French and

---

* It is now (1965) an art gallery, with some minor relics of Voltaire.

Catholic. In 1803 the Confederation admitted Aargau, St. Gallen, and Thurgau (German and Protestant), Ticino (Italian and Catholic), and Vaud (French and Protestant). In 1815 three new cantons were added: Geneva (French and Protestant, now rapidly becoming Catholic), Valais (French, German, and Catholic), and the region known to the French as Grisons and to the Germans as Graubünden (chiefly Protestant, and speaking German or Romansh, a vestigial Latin).

Switzerland was republican, but not democratic in our current sense. In each canton a minority of the adult male population, usually the old established families, elected a Great Council or General Council of some two hundred members, and a Small Council of from twenty-four to sixty-four members. The Small Council appointed a still smaller Privy Council, and a burgomaster who served as chief executive officer. There was no separation of powers; the Small Council was also the supreme court. The rural cantons (Uri, Schwyz, Unterwalden, Glarus, Zug, Appenzell) limited the suffrage to indigenous families; other residents, no matter how long domiciled, were ruled as a subject class.[6] Such oligarchies were general in Switzerland. Lucerne limited eligibility for office to twenty-nine families, allowing a new family to enter the circle only when one of the old families died out.[7] In Bern 243 families were eligible to hold office, but of these some sixty-eight regularly held the government. In 1789 the Russian historian Nikolai Karamzin remarked that the citizens of Zurich were "as proud of their title as a king of his crown," since "for more than 150 years no foreigner has obtained the right of citizenship."[8] (We must remind ourselves that nearly all democracies are oligarchies; minorities can be organized for action and power, majorities cannot.)

The cantonal government tended to an authoritarian paternalism. The councils in Zurich issued laws regulating meals, drinking, smoking, driving, weddings, clothing, personal adornment, the dressing of the hair, the wages of labor, the quality of products, the prices of necessaries; these ordinances were relics of old communal or guild rules; and, indeed, in Zurich the masters of the twelve guilds automatically became members of the Small Council, so that this canton was in considerable measure a corporative state. Toward the end of the century Goethe wrote that the shores of the Lake of Zurich gave "a charming and ideal conception of the finest and highest civilization."[9]

The "Town and Republic" of Bern was the largest and strongest of the cantons. It embraced a third of Switzerland, it had the most prosperous economy, and its government was generally admired as provident and competent; Montesquieu compared it with Rome in the best days of the Republic. William Coxe, a British clergyman and learned historian, described the city as he saw it on September 16, 1779:

I was much struck, on entering into Bern, with its singular neatness and beauty. The principal streets are broad and long, not straight but gently curved; the houses are almost uniform, built of a grayish stone upon arcades. Through the middle of the streets runs a lively stream of the clearest water in a stone channel, while several fountains are not less ornamental to the place than beneficial to the inhabitants. The river Aar almost surrounds the town, winding its course over a rocky bed much below the level of the streets. . . . The adjacent country is richly cultivated, and agreeably diversified with hills, lawns, woods, and water; . . . and an abrupt chain of rugged and snow-capped alps bounds the distant horizon.[10]

The great failure of the Bernese patriciate was in its treatment of Vaud. This earthly paradise ran along the Swiss side of the Lake of Geneva from the outskirts of the city of Geneva to Lausanne (its capital), and reached northward to the Lake of Neuchâtel. On those lovely shores and grape-vined hills Voltaire and Gibbon enjoyed a highly civilized life, and Rousseau grew up and suffered, and placed his Julie's virtuous household (at Clarens, near Vevey). The region passed under Bern's control in 1536; its citizens lost eligibility to office, fretted under distant rule, and frequently revolted, but in vain.

The cantons were watchfully jealous of their autonomy. Each considered itself a sovereign state, free to make war and peace and enter into foreign alliances; so the Catholic cantons associated themselves with France throughout the reign of Louis XV. To reduce strife among the cantons each sent delegates to a Swiss Diet meeting in Zurich. But this federal congress had very limited powers: it could not impose its decisions upon any unwilling canton; its resolutions, to be valid, required the consent of all. Free trade was accepted in principle, but was violated by intercantonal tariff wars. There was no common currency, no joint administration of intercantonal roads.

The economic life flourished despite natural obstacles and legislative barriers. Serfdom had disappeared except in a few districts along the German or Austrian border; nearly all peasants owned the soil they tilled. In the "Forest Cantons" (Uri, Schwyz, Unterwalden, and Lucerne) the peasants were poor because of geographical conditions; around Zurich they prospered; in the Bernese several peasants accumulated fortunes through careful and resolute husbandry. Long winters and difficulties of transport forced many Swiss to combine agriculture and industry; the same family that spun cotton or made watches planted gardens or cultivated the vine. Fribourg was already famous for its Gruyère cheese, Zurich for its lace, St. Gallen for its cotton, Geneva for watches, Neuchâtel for lace, all Switzerland for wines. Swiss finance was even then the envy of Europe, and Swiss merchants were active everywhere. Basel throve on trade with France and Germany, Zurich on trade with Germany and Austria. Basel, Geneva, and Lausanne rivaled Amsterdam and The Hague as centers of publishing. After Haller and Rousseau had celebrated the gleaming beauty of Swiss lakes and the imposing majesty of the Swiss Alps, tourism provided a growing support for the federal economy.

The level of morals was probably higher in Switzerland than in any other European land except Scandinavia, where similar conditions produced similar results. The peasant family was a model of industry, sobriety, unity, and thrift. In the cities there was some corruption of politics and selling of offices, but even there the austerity generated by a hard climate, a mountainous terrain, and a Protestant ethic made for moral stability. Dress was modest in the rich as well as in the poor. In Switzerland sumptuary laws were still severe and well observed.[11]

Religion was half the government and half the strife. Regular attendance at church was obligatory, and the towns were too small to let rebels find refuge in the anonymity of the crowd. Sunday was a day of almost unrelieved piety; we are told that in Zurich the taverns trembled with psalms on the Sabbath.[12] But the rival religions—Calvinist and Catholic—gave the worst example of behavior, for they liberated hatred and chained the mind. Some Catholic cantons forbade any but Catholic worship, some Protestant cantons forbade any but the Protestant.[13] Separation from the state church and the formation of independent sects were prohibited by law. In Lucerne in 1747 Jacob Schmidlin was tortured and then strangled for trying to organize a Pietist movement independent of the Church. An oath of Calvinist orthodoxy was required for eligibility to hold political, ecclesiastical, or educational positions in the Protestant cantons.[14] Censorship was severe by both Church and state. In the Forest Cantons the poverty of the peasants, storms, landslides, avalanches, blights, floods, and awe of the encompassing mountains combined to generate a superstitious fear of evil spirits in glowering peaks and whirling winds. To frustrate their supernatural foes the harassed rustics begged for priestly exorcisms and ceremonious blessings of their flocks. Burning for witchcraft ended in Geneva in 1652, in Bern in 1680, in Zurich in 1701, in the Catholic cantons in 1752; but in Glarus a woman was beheaded in 1782 on a charge of having bewitched a child.[15]

Light was opened into this darkness by state schools and public libraries. The University of Basel was in decline through religious fanaticism; it hardly appreciated the achievements of Johann, Jakob, and Daniel Bernoulli, and made Leonhard Euler flee to more hospitable halls. Even so, Switzerland produced scholars, poets, and scientists in full proportion to its population. We have mentioned the Zurich savants Johann Jakob Bodmer and Johann Jakob Breitinger; they had a lasting influence on German literature by countering Gottsched's idolatry of Boileau and classic formulas; they defended the rights of feeling, of the mystical, even the irrational, in literature and life; they extolled English over French poetry, and introduced Shakespeare and Milton to readers of German; they resurrected the *Nibelungenlied* (1751) and the minnesingers. Their doctrine passed down to Lessing, Klopstock, Schiller, and the young Goethe, and opened the way for the Romantic movement in Germany and the revival of interest in the Middle Ages. A Zurich poet, Salomon Gessner, followed this lead, and issued *Idyllen* (1756)—idyls of such pastoral charm that all Europe translated them, and poets like Wieland and Goethe made pilgrimages to his door.

Next to Jean Jacques Rousseau, the most memorable Swiss of the eighteenth century was Albrecht von Haller of Bern, at once the greatest poet and the greatest scientist of his land and time. In Bern, Tübingen, Leiden, London, Paris and Basel he studied law, medicine, physiology, botany, and mathematics. Returning to Bern, he discovered the Alps, felt their beauty, grandeur, and lines, and broke into poetry. So, aged twenty-one (1729), he issued a volume of lyrics, *Die Alpen*, which the enthusiastic Coxe thought "as sublime and immortal as the mountains which are the subject of his song."[16] The book anticipated Rousseau in almost everything. It invited the world to admire the Alps both for their inspiring elevation and as a testimonial to God; it denounced cities as dens of luxury and irreligion leading to physical and moral decay; it lauded the peasants and mountaineers for their hardy frames, sturdy faith, and frugal ways; and it summoned men, women, and children to leave the towns and come out to live in the open air a simpler, saner, healthier life.

But it was as a scientist that Haller won a European renown. In 1736 George II offered him the professorship of botany, medicine, and surgery in the University of Göttingen. There he taught for seventeen years, with such distinction that Oxford and Halle invited him, and Frederick the Great wanted him to succeed Maupertuis as head of the Berlin Academy, Catherine II tried to lure him to St. Petersburg, and Göttingen wished to make him chancellor. Instead he retired to Bern, served as health officer, economist, and head of his canton, and industriously prepared one of the century's scientific masterpieces, *Elementa Physiologiae Corporis humani*, which we shall meet again.

Through all these years and sciences he maintained a devout orthodoxy in religion and a strict integrity of morals. When Voltaire came to live in Switzerland it seemed to Haller that Satan had set up his standard in Geneva and Lausanne. Casanova, who rivaled Haller in the appreciation of beauty, visited both Haller and Voltaire in 1760. Let us enjoy once more Casanova's account of the double adventure:

> Haller was a big man, six feet tall, and broad in proportion—a physical and intellectual colossus. He received me with great affability, and opened his mind, answering all my questions precisely and modestly. . . . When I told him I was looking forward to seeing M. de Voltaire, he said I was quite right to do so, and he added, without bitterness: "Monsieur de Voltaire is a man who deserves to be known, although, contrary to the laws of physics, many people have found him greater at a distance."

A few days later Casanova saw Voltaire at Les Délices.

> "Monsieur de Voltaire," said I, "this is the proudest day of my life. I have been your pupil for twenty years, and my heart rejoices to see my master."
> He asked me where I last came from.
> "From Roche. I did not want to leave Switzerland without having seen Haller. . . . I kept you to the last as a *bonne bouche*."
> "Were you pleased with Haller?"
> "I spent three of the happiest days of my life with him."
> "I congratulate you."
> "I am glad you do him justice. I am sorry he is not so fair toward you."
> "Ah ha! Perhaps we are both of us mistaken."[17]

In 1775, as his final word to the world, Haller published *Letters concerning Several Late Attempts of Freethinking . . . against Revelation*, an earnest effort to offset Voltaire's *Questions sur l'Encyclopédie*. He wrote a touching letter to the dreadful heretic, inviting him (then eighty-one) to recapture "that tranquillity which flies at the approach of genius," but comes to a trusting faith; "then the most celebrated man in Europe would be also the most happy."[18] Haller himself never achieved tranquillity. He was impatient in sickness, being extremely sensitive to pain; "in his later years he took to opium, which, operating as a temporary palliative, only increased his natural impatience."[19] He suffered from fear of hell, and reproached himself for having given so much to "my plants and other buffooneries."[20] He achieved tranquillity on December 12, 1777.

III. GENEVA

Geneva was not in this century a canton in the federation; it was a separate republic—city and hinterland—with French speech and Calvinist faith. In his article on Geneva in the *Encyclopédie*, d'Alembert described it admiringly as he had seen it in 1756:

> It is remarkable that a city having hardly 24,000 inhabitants, and with a territory containing less than thirty villages, has kept its independence, and is among the most flourishing communities in Europe. Rich by its freedom and its commerce, it sees all around it on fire, without ever feeling the effect. The crises that agitate Europe are for it only a spectacle, which it enjoys without taking part in it. Attached to France by freedom and trade, to England by commerce and religion, Geneva pronounces with justice on the wars that these powerful nations wage against each other, but it is too wise to take sides. It judges all the sovereigns of Europe without flattery, injury, or fear.[21]

The emigration of the Huguenots from France was a boon to Geneva; they brought their savings and their skill, and made the city the watchmaking capital of the world. Mme. d'Épinay reckoned six thousand in the jewelry trade.[22] Swiss bankers had a reputation for wisdom and integrity; so Jacques Necker and Albert Gallatin, both Genevans, became respectively finance minister to Louis XVI and treasury secretary of the United States under Jefferson.

Government in Geneva, as elsewhere, was a class privilege. Only those male inhabitants who had been born in Geneva of citizen parents and grandparents were eligible for public office. Below this patrician class came the bourgeoisie—manufacturers, merchants, shopkeepers, guild masters, and members of the professions. Annually, in the Cathedral of St.-Pierre, the patricians and the bourgeoisie, seldom over fifteen hundred in number,[23] assembled to elect a Grand Conseil, or Great Council, of two hundred members, and a Petit Conseil of twenty-five. These councils chose four syndics, each for a year, as the executive heads of the state. Quite unfranchised were a third class, the *habitants*, residents of foreign parentage, and a fourth class, the *natifs*, born in Geneva of non-native Genevans. The *natifs*, forming three fourths of the population, had no civic rights except that of paying taxes; they could not engage in business or the professions, nor could they hold office in the army or mastership in a guild. The political history of the little republic revolved around the struggles of the bourgeoisie to be admitted to office, and of the lower classes to be allowed to vote. In 1737 the burghers took up arms against the patriciate, and forced it to accept a new constitution: all voters were made eligible for election to the Grand Conseil; this was to have the final decision over war and peace, alliances and taxes, although legislation could be proposed only by the Petit Conseil; and the *natifs*, though still voteless, were admitted to some professions. The

government continued to be oligarchic, but it was competently administered, and relatively immune to corruption.

Next in influence to the patriciate was the Consistory of the Calvinist
clergy. It regulated education, morals, and marriage, and allowed no secular interference with its authority. There were no bishops here, and no
monks. The philosopher d'Alembert praised the morals of the Genevan
clergy, and described the city as an island of decency and sobriety, which
he contrasted with the moral riot of upper-class France. Mme. d'Épinay,
after several liaisons, applauded the "strict manners of . . . a free people,
enemy of luxury."[24] According to the clergy, however, Genevan youth
was going to the devil in cabarets, and family prayers were being
scrimped; people gossiped in church, and some blasé worshipers in the rear
puffed at their pipes to help the sermon go down.[25] The preachers complained that they could inflict only spiritual penalties, and that their exhortations were increasingly ignored.

Voltaire was delighted to find that several members of the Genevan
clergy were rather advanced in their theology. They came to enjoy his
hospitality at Les Délices, and privately confessed that they retained little
of Calvin's dour creed. One of them, Jacques Vernes, advised in his *Instruction chrétienne* (1754) that religion be based on reason when addressing
adults, but that "for the common people . . . it will be useful to explain
these truths by some popular means, with proofs fit to . . . make a greater
impression upon the minds of the multitude."[26] Voltaire wrote to Cideville
(April 12, 1756): "Geneva is no longer the Geneva of Calvin—far from it;
it is a land full of philosophers. The 'reasonable Christianity' of Locke is
the religion of nearly all the ministers; and the adoration of a Supreme
Being, joined to a system of morality, is the religion of nearly all the magistrates."[27] In the *Essai sur les moeurs* (1756), after denouncing Calvin's role
in the execution of Servetus, Voltaire added: "It seems that today an
amende honorable is made to the ashes of Servetus; the learned pastors of
the Protestant churches . . . have embraced his [Unitarian] sentiments."[28]
D'Alembert, after visiting Geneva and Les Délices (1756), talking with
some ministers, and comparing notes with Voltaire, wrote for Volume VII
(1757) of the *Encyclopédie* an article on Geneva in which he lauded the
liberalism of its clergy:

> Several of them do not believe in the divinity of Jesus Christ, of
> which their leader Calvin was so zealous a defender and for which he
> had Servetus burned. . . . Hell, one of the principal points in our be-
> lief, is today no longer one for many of Geneva's ministers; it would,
> according to them, insult the Divinity to imagine that this Being, full of
> goodness and justice, was capable of punishing our faults by an eternity
> of torments. . . . They believe that there are punishments in another

life, but for a time; thus purgatory, which was one of the principal causes of the separation of the Protestants from the Roman Church, is today the only punishment many of them admit after death; here is a new touch to add to the history of human contradictions.

To sum up in a word, many of Geneva's pastors have no religion other than a complete Socinianism, rejecting all those things which are called mysteries, and imagining that the first principle of a true religion is to propose nothing to belief which offends reason. . . . Religion has been practically reduced to the adoration of a single God, at least among all those not of the common classes.[29]

When the Genevan clergy read this article they were unanimously alarmed—the conservatives to find such heretics in Calvinist pulpits, the liberals to find their private heresies so publicly exposed. The Company of Pastors examined the suspects; they warmly repudiated d'Alembert's allegations, and the Company issued a formal reaffirmation of Calvinist orthodoxy.[30]

Calvin himself was part cause of the unseemly enlightenment praised by d'Alembert, for the academy that he had founded was now one of the finest educational establishments in Europe. It taught Calvinism, but not too intensely; it gave excellent courses in classical literature, and it trained good teachers for Geneva's schools—with all expenses borne by the state. A library of 25,000 volumes lent books to the public. D'Alembert found "the people much better educated than elsewhere."[31] Coxe was astonished to hear tradesmen discoursing intelligently on literature and politics. Geneva, in this century, contributed to science the work of Charles Bonnet in physiology and psychology, and of Horace de Saussure in meteorology and geology. In art it literally gave Jean Étienne Liotard to the world: after studying in Geneva and Paris he went to Rome, where he portrayed Clement XII and many cardinals; then to Constantinople, where he lived and worked for five years, then to Vienna, Paris, England, and Holland, buttering his bread with portraits, pastels, enamels, engravings and paintings on glass. He drew a remarkably honest portrait of himself in old age,[32] looking more simian than Voltaire.

Geneva did not do well in literature. Alert censorship of print stifled literary ambition and originality. The drama was outlawed as a nursery of scandal. When Voltaire in 1755 first staged a play—Zaïre—in the drawing room at Les Délices, the clergy grumbled, but tolerated the crime as the private foible of a distinguished guest. When, however, Voltaire organized a company of actors from among the young people of Geneva, and projected a series of dramatic performances, the Consistory (July 31, 1755) called upon the Grand Conseil to enforce "the decrees of 1732 and 1739 forbidding all representations of plays, as well public as private," and it bade the pastors to forbid their parishioners to "play parts in tragedies in the home of the Sieur de Voltaire." Voltaire professed repentance, but staged plays in his winter home at Lausanne. Probably at his suggestion, d'Alembert introduced into the aforesaid article on Geneva a plea for removal of the prohibition:

> It is not because Geneva disapproves of dramas [*spectacles*] in themselves, but because (they say) it fears the taste for finery, dissipation, and libertinage which theatrical companies spread among the young. However, would it not be possible to remedy these disadvantages by laws severe and well enforced? . . . Literature would progress without increasing immorality, and Geneva would unite the wisdom of Sparta with the culture of Athens.

The Consistory made no response to this appeal, but Jean Jacques Rousseau (as we shall see) replied to it in a famous *Lettre à M. d'Alembert sur les spectacles* (1758). After buying the seigniory of Ferney Voltaire bypassed the prohibition by building a theater at Châtelaine, on French soil but close to the Genevan border. There he produced plays, and secured for the opening Paris' leading actor, Henri Louis Lekain. The Geneva pastors forbade attendance, but the performances were so popular that on those occasions when Lekain was to appear the pit was filled hours before the program began. The old warrior at last won his campaign; in 1766 the Grand Conseil ended the Genevan prohibition of plays.

IV. THE NEW HISTORY

An eyewitness of Lekain's performance in Voltaire's *Sémiramis* described the author's appearance there:

> Not the least part of the exhibition was Voltaire himself, seated against a first wing, in view of all the audience, applauding like one possessed, now with his cane, now by exclamations—"It could not be better! . . . Ah, mon Dieu, how well that was done!" . . . So little was he able to control his enthusiasm that when Lekain left the stage . . . he ran after him . . . A more comic incongruity could not be imagined, for Voltaire resembled one of those old men of comedy—his stockings rolled upon his knees, and dressed in the costume of the "good old times," unable to sustain himself on his trembling limbs except with the aid of a cane. All the marks of old age are imprinted upon his countenance; his cheeks are hollow and wrinkled, his nose prolonged, his eyes almost extinguished.[33]

Amid theatricals, politics, visitors, and gardening, he found time to complete and publish at Les Délices two major works, one notorious for alleged indecency, the other marking a new epoch in the writing of history.

La Pucelle had been with him, as a literary recreation, ever since 1730. Apparently he had no intention of publishing it, for it not only made fun of the heroic Maid of Orléans, but satirized the creed, crimes, rites, and dignitaries of the Catholic Church. Friends and enemies added to the circulating manuscripts bits of obscenity and hilarity that even Voltaire would not have put upon paper. Now, in 1755, just as he was finding peace in Geneva, there appeared in Basel a pirated and garbled version of the poem. This was banned by the Pope, was burned by the Paris Parlement, and was confiscated by the Geneva police; a Paris printer was sent to the galleys for reissuing it in 1757. Voltaire denied authorship; he sent to Richelieu, Mme. de Pompadour, and some government officials copies of a relatively decent text; in 1762 he published this, and suffered no molestation for it. He tried to atone to Jeanne d'Arc by giving a fairer and soberer account of her in his *Essai sur les moeurs*.[34]

That *Essai* was intended as his chef-d'oeuvre, and was also in one sense a monument to the mistress whose memory he revered. He had accepted as a challenge the contempt that Mme. du Châtelet had poured upon such modern historians as she knew:

> What does it matter to me, a Frenchwoman living on my estate, to know that Egil succeeded Haquin in Sweden, and that Ottoman was the son of Ortogrul? I have read with pleasure the history of the Greeks and the Romans; they offered me certain great pictures which attracted me. But I have never yet been able to finish any long history of our modern nations. I can see scarcely anything in them but confusion: a host of minute events without connection or sequence, a thousand battles which settled nothing. . . . I renounced a study which overwhelms the mind without illuminating it.[35]

Voltaire agreed with her, but he knew that this was only history *as written*. He mourned the diverse transmogrifications of the past by current prejudices; in this sense "history . . . is nothing but a pack of tricks that we play upon the dead."[36]* And yet to ignore history would be to endlessly repeat its errors, massacres, and crimes. There are three avenues to that large and tolerant perspective which is philosophy: one is the study of men in life through experience; another, the study of things in space through science; a third, the study of events in time through history. Vol-

---

* It was apparently Fénelon, not Voltaire, who said that "*l'histoire n'est qu'une fable convenue*" (history is nothing but a fable agreed upon).[37] The agreement is not evident.

taire had attempted the second by studying Newton; now he turned to the third. As early as 1738 he laid down a new principle: *"Il faut écrire l'histoire en philosophe"*—one must write history as a philosopher.[38] So he suggested to the Marquise:

> If amid so much material rude and unformed you should choose wherewith to construct an edifice for your own use; if, while leaving out all the details of warfare, . . . all the petty negotiations which have been only useless knavery; . . . if, while preserving those details that paint manners, you should form out of that chaos a general and well-defined picture; if you should discover in events *the history of the human mind*, would you believe you had lost your time?[39]

He worked on the project intermittently for twenty years, reading voraciously, making references, gathering notes. In 1739 he drew up for Mme. du Châtelet an *Abrégé de l'histoire générale;* in 1745–46 parts of this were printed in *Le Mercure de France;* in 1750 he issued his *History of the Crusades;* in 1753, at The Hague, the *Abrégé* appeared in two volumes, in 1754 in three; finally at Geneva in 1756 the full text was published in seven volumes as *Essai sur l'histoire générale;* this contained *Le Siècle de Louis XIV* and some preliminary chapters on Oriental civilizations. In 1762 he added a *Précis du siècle de Louis XV.* The edition of 1769 established *Essai sur les moeurs et l'esprit des nations depuis Charlemagne jusqu'à nos jours* as the definitive title. The word *moeurs* meant not only manners and morals but customs, ideas, beliefs, and laws. Voltaire did not always cover all these topics, nor did he record the history of scholarship, science, philosophy, or art; but in the large his book was a brave approach to a history of civilization from the earliest times to his own. The Oriental portions were sketchy preludes; the fuller account began with Charlemagne, where Bossuet's *Discours sur l'histoire universelle* (1679) had left off. "I want to know," wrote Voltaire, "what were the steps by which men passed from barbarism to civilization"—by which he meant the passage from the Middle Ages to "modern" times.[40]

He gave credit to Bossuet for attempting a "universal history," but he protested against conceiving this as a history of the Jews and the Christians, and of Greece and Rome chiefly in relation to Christianity. He pounced upon the bishop's neglect of China and India, and his conception of the Arabs as mere barbarian heretics. He recognized the philosophic endeavor of his predecessor in seeking a unifying theme or process in history, but he could not agree that history can be explained as the operation of Providence, or by seeing the hand of God in every major event. He saw history rather as the slow and fumbling advance of man, through natural causes and human effort, from ignorance to knowledge, from miracles to science, from superstition to reason. He could see no Providential design in the maelstrom of events. Perhaps in reaction to Bossuet he made organized religion the villain in his story, since it seemed to him generally allied with obscurantism, given to oppression, and fomenting war. In his eagerness to discourage fanaticism and persecution Voltaire weighted his narrative as heavily in one direction as Bossuet had in the other.

In his new cosmopolitan perspective, made possible by the progress of geography through the reports of explorers, missionaries, merchants, and travelers, Europe assumed a more modest position in the panorama of history. Voltaire was impressed by "the collection of astronomical observations made during nineteen hundred successive years in Babylonia, and transferred by Alexander to Greece";[41] he concluded that there must have been, along the Tigris and Euphrates, a widespread and developed civilization, usually passed over with a sentence or two in such histories as Bossuet's. Still more was he moved by the antiquity, extent, and excellence of civilization in China; this, he thought, "places the Chinese above all the other nations of the world. . . . Yet this nation and India, the most ancient of extant states, . . . which had invented nearly all the arts almost before we possessed any of them, have always been omitted, down to our own time, in our pretended universal histories."[42] It pleased the anti-Christian warrior to find and to present so many great cultures so long antedating Christianity, quite unacquainted with the Bible, and yet producing artists, poets, scientists, sages, and saints generations before the birth of Christ. It delighted the irate, moneylending anti-Semite to reduce Judea to a very small role in history.

He made some efforts to be fair to the Christians. In his pages not all the popes are bad, not all the monks are parasites. He had a good word for popes like Alexander III, "who abolished vassalage, . . . restored the rights of the people, and chastised the wickedness of crowned heads";[43] and he admired the "consummate courage" of Julius II, and "the grandeur of his views."[44] He sympathized with the efforts of the papacy to establish a moral power checking the wars of states and the injustices of kings. He admitted that the bishops of the Church, after the fall of the Western Roman Empire, were the ablest governors in that disintegrating, reintegrating age. Moreover,

> in those barbaric times, when the peoples were so wretched, it was a great consolation to find in the cloisters a secure retreat against tyranny.[45] . . . It cannot be denied that there were great virtues in the cloister; there was hardly a monastery which did not contain admirable beings who did honor to human nature. Too many writers have made it a pleasure to search out the disorders and vices with which these refuges of piety were sometimes stained.[46]

But by and large Voltaire, caught with the embattled Encyclopedists in a war against the Catholic Church in France, emphasized the faults of Christianity in history. He minimized the persecution of Christians by Rome, and anticipated Gibbon in reckoning this as far less frequent and murderous than the persecution of heretics by the Church. He gave another lead to Gibbon in arguing that the new religion had weakened the Roman state. He thought that priests had usurped power by propagating absurd doctrines among ignorant and credulous people, and by using the hypnotic power of ritual to deaden the mind and strengthen these delusions. He charged that popes had extended their sway, and had amassed wealth, by using documents such as the "Donation of Constantine," now generally admitted to be spurious. He declared that the Spanish Inquisition and the massacre of the heretical Albigenses were the vilest events in history.

The Middle Ages in Christendom seemed to him a desolate interlude between Julian and Rabelais; but he was among the first to recognize the debt of European thought to Arab science, medicine, and philosophy. He praised Louis IX as the ideal of a Christian king, but he saw no nobility in Charlemagne, no sense in Scholasticism, no grandeur in the Gothic cathedrals, which he dismissed as "a fantastic compound of rudeness and filigree." His hunted spirit could not be expected to appreciate the work of the Christian creed and priesthood in forming character and morals, preserving communal order and peace, promoting nearly all the arts, inspiring majestic music, embellishing the life of the poor with ceremony, festival, song, and hope. He was a man at war, and a man cannot fight well unless he has learned to hate. Only the victor can appreciate his enemy.

Was he correct in his facts? Usually, but of course he made mistakes. The Abbé Nonnotte published two volumes, *Erreurs de Voltaire*, and added some of his own.[47] Robertson, himself a great historian, was impressed by Voltaire's general accuracy in so wide a field.[48] Covering so many subjects in so many countries through so many centuries, Voltaire made no pretense of confining himself to original documents or contemporary sources, but he used his secondary authorities with discrimination and judicious weighing of the evidence. He made it a rule to question any testimony that seemed to contradict "common sense" or the general experience of mankind. Doubtless he would have confessed today that the incredibilities of one age may be accepted routine in the next, but he laid it down as a guiding principle that "incredulity is the foundation of all knowledge."[49] So he anticipated Barthold Niebuhr in rejecting the early chapters of Livy as legendary; he laughed Romulus, Remus, and their *alma mater* wolf out of court; he suspected Tacitus of vengeful exaggerations in describing the vices of Tiberius, Claudius, Nero, and Caligula; he doubted

Herodotus and Suetonius as retailers of hearsay, and he thought Plutarch too fond of anecdotes to be entirely reliable; but he accepted Thucydides, Xenophon, and Polybius as trustworthy historians. He was skeptical of monkish chronicles, but he praised Du Cange and the "careful" Tillemont and the "profound" Mabillon. He refused to continue the ancient custom of imaginary speeches, or the modern custom of historical "portraits." He subordinated the individual in the general stream of ideas and events, and the only heroes he worshiped were those of the mind.

In the *Essai* and elsewhere Voltaire suggested rather than formulated his philosophy of history. He wrote a "Philosophie de l'histoire," and prefixed it to an edition of the *Essai* in 1765. He had an aversion to "systems" of thought, to all attempts to squeeze the universe into a formula; he knew that facts have sworn eternal enmity to generalizations; and perhaps he felt that any philosophy of history should follow and derive from, rather than precede and decide, the recital of events. Some wide conclusions, however, emerged from his narrative: that civilization preceded "Adam" and "the Creation" by many thousands of years; that human nature is fundamentally the same in all ages and lands, but is diversely modified by different customs; that climate, government, and religion are the basic determinants of these variations; that the "empire of custom is far larger than that of nature";[50] that chance and accident (within the universal rule of natural laws) play an important role in generating events; that history is made less by the genius of individuals than by the instinctive operations of human multitudes upon their environment; that in this way are produced, bit by bit, the manners, morals, economies, laws, sciences, and arts that make a civilization and produce the spirit of the times. "My principal end is always to observe the spirit of the times, since it is that which directs the great events of the world."[51]

All in all, as Voltaire saw it in his "Récapitulation," history (as generally written) was a bitter and tragic story.

> I have now gone through the immense scene of revolutions that the world has experienced since the time of Charlemagne; and to what have they tended? To desolation, and the loss of millions of lives! Every great event has been a capital misfortune. History has kept no account of times of peace and tranquillity; it relates only ravages and disasters. . . . All history, in short, is little else than a long succession of useless cruelties, . . . a collection of crimes, follies, and misfortunes, among which we have now and then met with a few virtues, and some happy times, as we see sometimes a few scattered huts in a barren desert. . . . As nature has placed in the heart of man interest, pride, and all the passions, it is no wonder that . . . we meet with almost a continuous succession of crimes and disasters.[52]

This is a very dyspeptic picture, as if composed amid those fretful days in Berlin, or amid the indignities and frustrations of Frankfurt. The picture might have been brighter if Voltaire had spent more of his pages in reporting the history of literature, science, philosophy, and art. As the picture stands, one wonders why Voltaire went to so much trouble to depict it at such length. He would have answered: to shock the reader into conscience and thought, and to stir governments to remold education and legislation to form better men. We cannot change human nature, but we can modify its operations by saner customs and wiser laws. If ideas have changed the world, why may not better ideas make a better world? So, in the end, Voltaire moderated his pessimism with hope for the dissemination of reason as a patient agent in the progress of mankind.

The faults of the *Essai sur les moeurs* were soon pointed out. Not only Nonnotte but Larcher, Guénée, and many others pounced upon its errors of fact, and the Jesuits had no trouble in exposing its distorting bias. Montesquieu agreed with them in this regard; "Voltaire," he said, "is like the monks who write not for the sake of the subject that they treat, but for the glory of their order; he writes for his convent."[53] Voltaire replied to his critics that he had stressed the sins of Christianity because others were still defending them; he quoted contemporary authors who commended the crusades against the Albigenses, the execution of Huss, even the Massacre of St. Bartholomew; the world surely needed a history that would brand these actions as crimes against humanity and morality.[54] — Perhaps, with all his illuminating conception of how history should be written, Voltaire mistook the function of the historian; he sat in judgment on each person and event, and passed sentence on them like some Committee of Public Safety pledged to protect and advance the intellectual revolution. And he judged men not in terms of their own disordered time and restricted knowledge, but in the light of the wider knowledge that had come since their death. Written sporadically over a score of years, amid so many distracting enterprises and tribulations, the *Essai* lacked continuity of narrative and unity of form, and it did not quite integrate its parts into a consistent whole.

But the merits of the *Essai* were numberless. Its range of knowledge was immense, and testified to sedulous research. Its bright style, weighted with philosophy and lightened with humor, raised it far above most works of history between Tacitus and Gibbon. Its general spirit alleviated its bias; the book is still warm with love of liberty, toleration, justice, and reason. Here again, after so many lifeless, credulous chronicles, historiography became an art. In one generation three more histories transformed past events into literature and philosophy: Hume's *History of England*, Robertson's *History of the Reign of the Emperor Charles V*, Gibbon's *Decline and Fall of the Roman Empire*—all of them indebted to the spirit, and in part to the example, of Voltaire. Michelet wrote gratefully of the *Essai* as "this *History* which made all historiography, which begot all of us, critics and narrators alike."[55] And what are we doing here but walking in the path of Voltaire?

When the Seven Years' War ranged France against Frederick, Voltaire's latent love of his country rose again, perhaps mingled with old memories of Frankfurt and a new distrust of Geneva. After d'Alembert's article, and the retreat of the Geneva clergy from the audacities to which it had pledged them, Voltaire felt as unsafe in Switzerland as in France. When could he return to his native soil?

For once fortune favored him. The Duc de Choiseul, who enjoyed the exile's books, became minister of foreign affairs in 1758; Mme. de Pompadour, though in physical decline, was at the height of her influence, and had forgiven Voltaire's gaucheries; now the French government, while the King dallied in his seraglio, could wink at the terrible heretic's re-entry into France. In October, 1758, he moved three and a half miles out of Switzerland, and became the patriarch of Ferney. He was sixty-four and still near death; but he ranged himself against the strongest power in Europe in the most basic conflict of the century.

BOOK IV

THE ADVANCEMENT OF LEARNING

1715–89

CHAPTER XV

The Scholars

I. THE INTELLECTUAL ENVIRONMENT

THE growth of knowledge was impeded by inertia, superstition, persecution, censorship, and ecclesiastical control of education. These obstacles were weaker than before, but they were still far stronger than in an
industrial civilization where the competition of individuals, groups, and
nations compels men to search for new ideas and ways, new means for old
ends. Most men in the eighteenth century moved in a slowly changing
milieu where traditional responses and ideas usually sufficed for the needs
of life. When novel situations and events did not readily lend themselves
to natural explanations, the common mind ascribed them to supernatural
causes, and rested.

A thousand superstitions survived side by side with the rising enlightenment. Highborn ladies trembled at unfavorable horoscopes, or believed
that a drowned child could be revived if a poor woman would light a
candle and set it afloat in a cup to set fire to a bridge on the Seine. The
Princesse de Conti promised the Abbé Leroux a sumptuous equipage if he
would find her the philosopher's stone. Julie de Lespinasse, after living for
years with the skeptical scientist d'Alembert, kept her faith in lucky and
unlucky days. Fortunetellers lived on the credit given to their clairvoyance;
so Mme. de Pompadour, the Abbé de Bernis, and the Duc de Choiseul
secretly consulted Mme. Bontemps, who read the future in coffee grounds.[1]
According to Montesquieu, Paris swarmed with magicians and other impostors who offered to ensure worldly success or eternal youth. The
Comte de Saint-Germain persuaded Louis XV that the sick finances of
France could be restored by secret methods of manufacturing diamonds
and gold.[2] The Duc de Richelieu played with black magic—invoking
Satan's aid. The old Prince of Anhalt-Dessau, who won many battles for
Prussia, did not believe in God, but if he met three old women on his way
to hunt he would return home; it was "a bad time."[3] Thousands of people
wore amulets or talismans to avert evils. A thousand magical prescriptions
served as popular medicine. Religious relics could cure almost any ailment,
and relics of Christ or the saints could be found anywhere—a bit of his
raiment at Trier, his cloak at Turin and Laon, one of the nails of the True

Cross in the Abbey of St.-Denis. In England the cause of the Stuart Pretenders was advanced by the widely held notion that they could by their touch cure scrofula—a power denied to the Hanoverian kings because they were "usurpers" not blessed by divine right. Most peasants were sure that they heard elves or fairies in the woods. The belief in ghosts was declining; but the learned Benedictine Dom Augustin Calmet wrote a history of vampires—corpses that went out of their graves at night to suck the blood of the living; this book was published with the approval of the Sorbonne.[4]

The worst superstition of all, the belief in witchcraft, disappeared in this century, except for some local vestiges. In 1736 the "divines of the Associated Presbyteries" of Scotland passed a resolution reaffirming their belief in witchcraft;[5] and as late as 1765 the most famous of English jurists, Sir William Blackstone, wrote in his *Commentaries:* "To deny the possibility, nay, actual existence, of witchcraft and sorcery is flatly to contradict the revealed word of God; . . . the thing itself is a truth to which every nation in the world hath in its turn borne testimony." Despite Blackstone and the Bible the English law that had made witchcraft a felony was repealed in 1736. No execution for witchcraft is recorded in France after 1718, none in Scotland after 1722; an execution in Switzerland in 1782 is the last recorded on the European Continent.[6] Gradually the increase of wealth and towns, the spread of education, the experiments of scientists, the appeals of scholars and philosophers reduced the role of devils and ghosts in human life and thought, and judges, defying popular fanaticism, refused to hear accusations of sorcery. Europe began to forget that it had sacrificed 100,000 men, women, and girls to just one of its superstitions.[7]

Meanwhile persecution of dissent by Church and state, by Catholics and Protestants, exerted its terrors to keep from the public mind any ideas that might disturb vested beliefs and powers. The Catholic Church claimed to have been established by the Son of God, therefore to be the depository and sole authorized interpreter of divine truth, therefore to have the right to suppress heresy. It concluded that outside the Church no one could be saved from eternal damnation. Had not Christ said, "He that believeth and is baptized shall be saved; he that believeth not shall be condemned"?[8] So the Fourth Lateran Ecumenical Council, in 1215, had made it part of the *fides definita*—required every Catholic to believe—that "there is one universal Church of the faithful, outside which no one at all can be saved."*

---

* *Una est fidelium universalis Ecclesia, extra quam nullus omnino salvatur.* Pope Pius IX reaffirmed the doctrine in his encyclical of August 10, 1863: "The Catholic dogma is well known, namely, that no one can be saved outside the Catholic Church [*Notissimum est catholicum dogma neminem scilicet extra catholicam ecclesiam posse salvari*]." (*Catholic Encyclopedia*, III, 753b.) It is fair to add that recent Catholic theology softens the dogma. "The doctrine . . . summed up in the phrase *Extra Ecclesiam nulla salus* . . . does not mean that none can be saved except those who are in visible communion with the Church.

Louis XV accepted this doctrine as logically derived from Scriptural texts, and as useful in molding a unified national mind. In 1732 the public exercise of Protestant worship in France was forbidden on pain of torture, the galleys, or death.[9] The Catholic population was more tolerant than its leaders; it condemned these savage penalties, and the edict was so laxly enforced that in 1744 the Huguenots of France dared to hold a national synod. But in 1767 the Sorbonne, the Faculty of Theology at the University of Paris, reiterated the old claim: "The prince has received the temporal sword in order to repress such doctrines as materialism, atheism, and deism, which cut the bonds of society and instigate crime, and also to crush every teaching threatening to shake the foundations of the Catholic faith."[10] In Spain and Portugal this policy was strictly enforced; in Italy, more leniently. In Russia the Orthodox Church required similar unanimity.

Many Protestant states agreed with the Catholics on the necessity of persecution. In Denmark and Sweden the laws demanded adherence to the Lutheran faith; in practice other Protestants, and even Catholics, were unmolested, though they remained ineligible to hold public office. In Switzerland each canton was free to choose its own faith and enforce it. In Germany the rule that the people must follow the religion of the prince was increasingly ignored. In the United Provinces Protestant ecclesiastics rejected toleration as an invitation to religious indifference, but the laity refused to follow the clergy in this matter, and relative freedom from persecution made Holland a refuge for unorthodox ideas and publications. In England the laws allowed religious dissent, but they harassed Dissenters with social and political disabilities. Samuel Johnson declared in 1763 that "false doctrine should be checked on its first appearance; the civil power should unite with the Church in punishing those who dared to attack the established religion."[11] The British government occasionally burned books, or pilloried authors, that had questioned the fundamentals of the Christian faith; so Woolston was fined and jailed in 1730, and in 1762 Peter Annet was sentenced to the pillory, then to a year's imprisonment with hard labor, for his attacks on Christianity. The laws against Catholics were loosely administered in England, but in Ireland they were enforced with rigor until Lord Chesterfield, as lord lieutenant in 1745, refused to apply them; and in the second half of the eighteenth century some of the severe regulations were repealed. In general the theory of persecution was maintained by both the Catholic and the Protestant clergy till 1789, except where Catholics or

---

The Catholic Church has ever taught that nothing else is needed to obtain justification than an act of perfect charity and of contrition. Whoever, under the impulse of actual grace, elicits these acts receives immediately the gift of sanctifying grace, and is numbered among the children of God. Should he die in these dispositions he will assuredly attain heaven." (*Ibid.*, 752b.)

Protestants were in the minority, but the practice of persecution declined as a new public opinion took form with the development of religious doubt. The instinct to persecute passed from religion to politics as the state replaced the Church as the guardian of unanimity and order and as the object of heretical dissent.

Censorship of speech and press was generally more relaxed in Protestant than in Catholic countries; it was mildest in Holland and England. It was strict in most of the Swiss cantons. The city fathers of Geneva burned a few unorthodox books, but seldom took action against the authors themselves. In Germany censorship was handicapped by the multiplicity of states, each with its own official creed; a writer could move across a frontier from an unfriendly to a friendly or indifferent environment. In Prussia censorship was practically abolished by Frederick the Great, but was restored by his successor in 1786. Denmark, except for a brief interlude under Struensee, maintained censorship of books till 1849. Sweden forbade the publication of material critical of Lutheranism or the government; in 1764 the University of Uppsala issued a list of forbidden books; but in 1766 Sweden established full freedom of the press.

In France censorship had broadened from precedent to precedent since Francis I, and was renewed by an edict of 1723: "No publishers or others may print or reprint, anywhere in the kingdom, any books without having obtained permission in advance by letters sealed with the Great Seal." In 1741 there were seventy-six official censors. Before giving a book the *permission et privilège du roi* the censor was required to testify that the book contained nothing contrary to religion, public order, or sound morality. Even after being published with the royal imprimatur a book might be condemned by the Paris Parlement or the Sorbonne. In the first half of the eighteenth century the royal censorship was only loosely enforced. Thousands of books appeared without the *privilège* and with impunity; in many cases, especially when Malesherbes was chief censor (1750–63), an author received *permission tacite*—an informal pledge that the book in question might be printed without fear of prosecution. A book published without the permission of the government might be burned by the public executioner, while the author remained free; and if he was sent to the Bastille it was usually for a brief and genteel imprisonment.[12]

This era of relative toleration ended with the attempt of Damiens to assassinate Louis XV (January 5, 1757). In April a savage edict decreed death for "all those who shall be convicted of having written or printed any works intended to attack religion, to assail the royal authority, or to disturb the order and tranquillity of the realm." In 1764 another decree forbade the publication of works on the finances of the state. Books, pamphlets, even prefaces to plays, were subjected to the most detailed scrutiny and control. Sentences varying from the pillory and flogging to nine years in the galleys were imposed for buying or selling copies of Voltaire's *La Pucelle* or his *Dictionnaire philosophique*. In 1762 d'Alembert wrote to Voltaire: "You cannot imagine what degree of fury the Inquisition has reached [in France]. The inspectors of thought . . . delete from all books such words as *superstition, indulgence, persecution*."[13] Hatred grew tense on both sides of the conflict between religion and philosophy; what had begun as a campaign against superstition rose to the pitch of a war against Christianity. Revolution came in France, and not in eighteenth-century England, partly because censorship by state or Church, which was mild in England, was so strong in France that the imprisoned mind could expand only by the violent destruction of its bonds.

The *philosophes* (i.e., those French philosophers who joined in the attack upon Christianity) protested against the censorship as condemning French thought to sterility. But they themselves sometimes asked the censor to check their opponents. So d'Alembert begged Malesherbes to suppress Fréron's *antiphilosophe* periodical, *L'Année littéraire;* Malesherbes, though pro-*philosophes*, refused.[14] Voltaire asked the Queen to prohibit the performance of a parody on his play *Sémiramis;* she would not, but Pompadour did.[15]

Meanwhile the *philosophes* contrived a variety of ways to elude the censorship. They sent their manuscripts to foreign publishers, usually to Amsterdam, The Hague, or Geneva; thence their books, in French, were imported wholesale into France; almost every day forbidden books arrived by boat at Bordeaux or other points on the French coast or frontier. Disguised with innocent titles, they were peddled from street to street, from town to town. Some nobles not overfriendly to the centralized monarchy allowed such volumes to be sold in their territory.[16] Voltaire's correspondence, which unified the philosophic campaign, escaped much of the censorship because his friend Damilaville for a time held a post in the finance administration, and was able to countersign with the seal of the comptroller general the letters and packages of Voltaire and his associates.[17] Many government officials, some clergymen, read with pleasure the books that the government or the clergy had condemned. French authors of foreign-published volumes rarely put their names on the title page, and when they were accused of authorship they lied with a stout conscience; this was part of the game, sanctioned by the laws of war. Voltaire not only denied the authorship of several of his books, he sometimes foisted them upon dead people, and he confused the scent by issuing criticisms or denunciations of his own works. The game included devices of form or tricks of expression that helped to form the subtlety of French prose: double meanings, dialogues, allegories, stories, irony, transparent exaggeration, and, all in all, such delicate wit as no other literature has ever matched. The Abbé Galiani defined eloquence as the art of saying something without being sent to the Bastille.

Only second to the censorship as an obstacle to free thought was the control of education by the clergy. In France the local curés taught or supervised the parish schools; secondary education was in the hands of the Jesuits, the Oratorians, or the Christian Brothers. All Europe acclaimed the Jesuits as teachers of classical languages and literatures, but they were less helpful in science. Many of the *philosophes* had had their wits sharpened by a Jesuit education. The University of Paris was dominated by priests far more conservative than the Jesuits. The University of Orléans, famous for law, and the University of Montpellier, famous for medicine, were relatively secular. It is significant that neither Montesquieu, Voltaire, Diderot, Maupertuis, Helvétius, nor Buffon attended a university. The French mind, struggling to free itself from theological leading strings, flowered not in universities but in academies and salons.

Learned academies had sprung up in this century in Berlin (1701), Uppsala (1710), St. Petersburg (1724), and Copenhagen (1743). In 1739 Linnaeus and five other Swedish scholars formed the Collegium Curiosum; in 1741 this was incorporated as the Kongliga Svenska Vetenskaps-academien, which became the Swedish Royal Academy. In France there were provincial academies in Orléans, Bordeaux, Toulouse, Auxerre, Metz, Besançon, Dijon, Lyons, Caen, Rouen, Montauban, Angers, Nancy, Aix-en-Provence. The academies steered clear of heresy, but they encouraged science and experiment, and they tolerated and stimulated discussion; it was the prize competitions offered by the Dijon Academy in 1749 and 1754 that started Rousseau on his way toward the French Revolution. In Paris the French Academy of moribund Immortals was awakened from dogmatic slumbers by the election of Duclos (1746) and d'Alembert (1754); and the rise of Duclos to the strategic post of "permanent secretary" (1755) marked the capture of the Academy by the *philosophes*.

Learned journals added to the intellectual stimulation. One of the best was the *Mémoires pour servir à l'histoire des sciences et des beaux-arts*, edited by the Jesuits from 1701 to 1762, and known as the *Journal de Trévoux* from their publishing house at Trévoux, near Lyons; this was the most erudite and liberal of the religious publications. There were seventy-three periodicals in Paris alone, led by the *Mercure de France* and the *Journal des savants*. Two of Voltaire's most effective and persistent enemies edited influential journals: Desfontaines founded the *Nouvelles littéraires* in 1721, and Fréron published the *Année littéraire* from 1754 to 1774. Germany followed suit with *Briefe die neueste Literatur betreffend*, which numbered Lessing and Moses Mendelssohn among its frequent contributors. In Italy the *Giornale dei letterati* covered science, literature, and art, while *Caffè* was a journal of opinion on the style of *The Spectator*. In Sweden Olof von Dalin made *Svenska Argus* a messenger of the Enlightenment. As nearly all these periodicals used the vernacular and were independent of ecclesiastical control, they were a rising leaven in the ferment of their time.

Typical of the eighteenth century, as of our own, was a spreading eagerness for knowledge—precisely that intellectual lust which the Middle Ages had condemned as a sin of foolish pride. Authors responded with a zeal to make knowledge more widely available and intelligible. "Outlines" abounded; books like *Mathematics Made Easy*, *The Essential Bayle*, *L'Esprit de Montaigne*, and *L'Esprit de Fontenelle* strove to put science, literature, and philosophy *à la portée de tout le monde*—within the comprehension of all the world. More and more professors taught in the vernaculars, reaching audiences incapable of Latin. Libraries and museums were expanding, and were opening their treasures to students. In 1753 Sir Hans Sloane bequeathed to the British nation his collection of fifty thousand books, several thousand manuscripts, and a great number of pictures, coins, and antiquities; Parliament voted twenty thousand pounds to his heirs in recompense, and the collection became the nucleus of the British Museum. The Harleian and Cottonian collections of manuscripts, and the accumulated libraries of the kings of England were added; and in 1759 the great museum was opened to the public. In 1928 it had 3,200,000 printed volumes and 56,000 manuscripts on its fifty-five miles of shelves.

Finally, encyclopedias took form to gather, order, and transmit the new stores of knowledge to all who could read and think. There had been such works in the Middle Ages, as by Isidore, Bishop (c.600–636) of Seville, and Vincent of Beauvais (c.1190–c.1264). In the seventeenth century there had been Johann Heinrich Alsted's *Encyclopaedia* (1630) and Louis Moreri's *Grand Dictionnaire historique* (1674). Bayle's *Dictionnaire historique et critique* (1697) was rather an assemblage of disturbing facts and suggestive theories than an encyclopedia, but it had more influence on the mind of educated Europe than any similar work before Diderot's. At London, in 1728, Ephraim Chambers published in two volumes a *Cyclopoedia, or an Universal Dictionary of Arts and Sciences;* it omitted history, biography, and geography, but by its system of cross references, and in other ways, it gave a lead to the epochal *Encyclopédie* (1751 f.) of Diderot and d'Alembert. In 1771 there appeared in three volumes the first edition of the *Encyclopaedia Britannica, or Dictionary of Arts and Sciences,* "by a society of gentlemen in Scotland, printed in Edinburgh." A second edition (1778) ran to ten volumes, and advanced upon its predecessors by including history and biography. So it has grown, from edition to edition, through two hundred years. How many of us have foraged in that harvest ten times a day, and pilfered from that treasury!

By 1789 the middle classes in Western Europe were as well informed as the aristocracy and the clergy. Print had made its way. That, after all, was the basic revolution.

II. THE SCHOLARLY REVELATION

Classical scholarship was in modest decline from its peak under the Scaligers, Casaubon, Salmasius, and Bentley; but Nicolas Fréret upheld their tradition of scholarly devotion and far-reaching results. Admitted to the Académie Royale des Inscriptions et Belles-Lettres at the age of twenty-six, he read to it in that year (1714) a paper, *Sur l'Origine des Francs*, which upset the proud legend that the Franks were "free" men coming from Greece or Troy; rather, they were South German barbarians. The Abbé Vertot denounced Fréret to the government as a libeler of the monarchy; the young scholar was sent to the Bastille for a short stay; thereafter he confined his researches to other lands than France. He drew up 1,375 maps illustrating ancient geography. He gathered illuminating data on the history of classic science and art, and on the origins of the Greek mythology. His eight volumes on ancient chronology corrected the epochal work of Joseph Justus Scaliger, and established Chinese chronology on lines accepted today; this was one of a thousand scholarly pinpricks that punctured the Biblical conception of history.

A similar blow was struck at classic fables when Pouilly read before the same Academy (1722) a paper questioning Livy's account of early Roman history. Lorenzo Valla had suggested such doubts on this point about 1440; Vico had developed them in 1721; but Pouilly's wide research definitely discredited as legends the stories of Romulus and Remus, of the Horatii and the Curiatii; the way was made straight for the work of Barthold Niebuhr in the nineteenth century. Not quite within the temporal bounds of this chapter, but belonging to the eighteenth century, were the *Prolegomena ad Homerum* (1795), in which Friedrich Wolf disintegrated Homer into a whole school and dynasty of singers; and Richard Porson's meticulous editions of Aeschylus and Euripides; and Joseph Eckhel's *Doctrina Numorum veterum* (1792–98), which founded the science of numismatics.

It was not till the discovery of Herculaneum that the world of classical scholarship felt again the ecstasy of such a revelation as had come through the humanists of the Renaissance. In 1738 some workmen preparing the foundations of a hunting lodge for King Charles IV of Naples unearthed by accident the ruins of Herculaneum; in 1748 a first inspection revealed some of the astonishing structures of Pompeii, also buried by the eruption of Vesuvius in A.D. 79; and in 1752 the majestic temples built by Greek colonists at Paestum were recovered from the jungle growth of darkened centuries. The master engraver Piranesi described the excavated temples, palaces, and statues of Pompeii in etchings whose prints found eager purchasers everywhere in Europe. The result of these discoveries was a fervent revival of interest in ancient art, a strong impetus to the neoclassical movement led by Winckelmann, and an immense addition to modern knowledge of ancient ways.

We must pause to acknowledge the debt of scholarship to monks who used their libraries and manuscript collections to make researches and compile records extremely helpful to the modern mind. The Benedictines of St.-Maur continued their old devotion to historical studies. Dom Bernard de Montfaucon founded the science of paleography with his *Palaeographica graeca* (1708); he illuminated ancient history by means of ancient art in his *Antiquité expliquée et représentée en figures* (ten volumes, 1719–24), and he turned his painstaking studies to his own country in five folio volumes, *Les Monuments de la monarchie française* (1729–33). Dom Antoine Rivet de la Grange began in 1733 the Benedictine *Histoire littéraire de la France*, which served as progenitor and storehouse for all later histories of early French literature. The greatest of these eighteenth-century Benedictine scholars was Dom Augustin Calmet, whose monastery at Senones gave Voltaire asylum in 1754; Voltaire never ceased to profit, and sometimes he pilfered, from Calmet's *Commentaire littéral sur tous les livres de l'Ancien et du Nouveau Testament* (1707–16). Despite certain shortcomings,[18] these twenty-four volumes were acclaimed as a monument of erudition. Calmet wrote several other works of Biblical exegesis, followed Bossuet in composing an *Histoire universelle* (1735), and spent nearly all his waking hours in study and prayer. "Who is Madame de Pompadour?" he asked Voltaire in happy ignorance.[19] He refused a bishopric, and wrote his own epitaph: "*Hic jacet qui multum legit, scripsit, oravit; utinam bene! Amen*" (Here lies one who read much, wrote much, prayed much; may it have been well! Amen).[20]

Some bold laics joined in Biblical criticism. The physician Jean Astruc, assuming the Mosaic author of the Pentateuch, studied its sources in his *Conjectures sur les mémoires originaux dont il paraît que Moïse s'est servi pour composer le livre de la Genèse* (1753); here for the first time it was pointed out that the use of two different names for God, Yahveh and Elohim, indicated two original stories of the Creation, loosely and repetitiously combined in the Book of Genesis. Other Biblical students tried to calculate, on the basis of the Pentateuch, the date of the Creation, and arrived at two hundred diverse results. Orientalists disturbed the orthodox by quoting Egyptian chronology that claimed to go back thirteen thousand years, and Chinese calculations that Chinese civilization had lasted ninety thousand years. No one believed the Indian

Brahmins who held that the world had existed through 326,669 ages, each of which had contained many centuries.[21]

The most audacious and far-reaching contribution to Biblical studies in the eighteenth century was made by a German professor of Oriental languages in the Hamburg Academy. Hermann Reimarus left at his death in 1768 a four-thousand-page manuscript on which he had labored for twenty years—"Schutzschrift für die vernünftigen Verehrer Gottes" (Apology for the Rational Worshipers of God). No one dared publish it until Lessing issued (1774–78) seven portions of it as "fragments of an anonymous work [*Fragmente eines Ungenannten*] found at Wolfenbüttel" (where Lessing was librarian). Nearly all literate Germany except Frederick the Great rose in protest; even the liberal scholar Johann Semler called Lessing mad to serve as godfather to so devastating a criticism of orthodox beliefs. For in the seventh fragment, *Von dem Zwecke Jesu und Seine Jünge* (*On the Aim of Jesus and His Disciples*), Reimarus not only rejected the miracles and resurrection of Christ, but pictured him as an earnest, lovable, deluded young Jew who was faithful to Judaism to the end, accepted the belief of some Jews that the world was soon to be destroyed, and based his ethical principles on this premise as a preparation for the event. Reimarus thought that Jesus interpreted the phrase "Kingdom of Heaven" in the sense then current among his people, as a coming kingdom of the Jews liberated from Rome.[22] His despondent cry on the Cross, "My God, my God, why hast Thou abandoned me?," was a confession of his humanity and his defeat. After his disappearance some of the Apostles transferred this promised kingdom to a life after death. In this sense it was not Christ but the Apostles who inaugurated Christianity. All in all, says Reimarus' erudite interpreter, Albert Schweitzer, "his work is perhaps the most splendid achievement in the whole course of the historical investigation of the life of Jesus, for he was the first to grasp the fact that the world of thought in which Jesus moved was essentially eschatological"—based on the theory of an imminent end of the world.[23]

From the study of Jewish antiquities scholars passed timidly to Oriental peoples that had rejected Christ or never heard his name. Galland's French translation of the *Arabian Nights* (1704–17), de Reland's *Religion des Mahométans* (1721), Burigny's *Histoire de la philosophie païenne* (1724), Boulainvilliers' *Vie de Mahomet* (1730), and Sale's English translation of the Koran (1734) revealed Islam as not a world of barbarism but as the domain of a powerful rival creed, and of a moral order that seemed to work despite its concessions to the natural polygamy of mankind. Abraham Hyacinthe Anquetil-Duperron opened another realm by translating the Scriptures of the Parsees. He was attracted by reading in a Paris library some extracts from the Zend-Avesta; he abandoned his preparation for the priest-hood, and resolved to explore at first hand the sacred books of the East. Too poor to buy passage, he enlisted, aged twenty-three (1754), as a soldier in a French expedition to India. Arrived at Pondicherry, he quickly learned to read modern Persian; at Chandernagor he took up Sanskrit; at Surat he persuaded a Parsee priest to teach him Pahlavi and Zend. In 1762 he returned to Paris with 180 Oriental manuscripts and set himself to trans-late them; meanwhile he lived on bread, cheese, and water, and avoided marriage as an impossible expense. In 1771 he published his French version of the Zend-Avesta, and fragments of other books of the Parsees; and in 1804 he issued *Les Oupanichads.* Slowly the awareness of non-Christian re-ligions and moral codes shared in undermining the dogmatism of European faiths.

Of these ethnic revelations the most influential was the opening up of Chinese history and philosophy by European missionaries, travelers, and scholars. It had begun with Marco Polo's return to Venice in 1295; it was advanced by French and English translations (1588) of the Jesuit Father Juan Gonzales de Mendoza's *Historia del reino de la China* (Lisbon, 1584), and with Hakluyt's English translation, in his *Voyages* (1589–1600), of a Latin treatise, *Of the Kingdom of China* (Macao, 1590). The new influ-ence appeared in Montaigne's essay "Of Experience" (1591?): "China, in whose realm the government and the arts, without any knowledge of our own institutions, surpass these in many points of excellence."[24] In 1615 the Jesuit Nicolas Trigault published his account *De christiana expeditione apud Sinas;* it was soon translated into French, and into English in *Purchas his Pilgrimes* (1625). Trigault and others lauded the Chinese system of making specific and detailed education a prerequisite for public office, of admitting all classes of the male population to examination for office, and of submitting all governmental agencies to periodical inspection. Another Jesuit, the amazing polymath Athanasius Kircher, published in 1670 a veri-table encyclopedia, *China illustrata,* in which he praised the Chinese gov-ernment as administered by philosopher-kings.[25]

The Jesuits gave generous commendation to Chinese religion and philos-ophy. Trigault reported that the educated Chinese conceived God as the soul of the world, and the world as his body; Spinoza, who held a similar view, could have read this idea in a book published in Amsterdam in 1649; his Latin teacher Frans van den Enden had this book in his library.[26] In 1622 the Jesuits published a Latin translation of Confucius as *Sapientia sinica;* in a further summary, *Confucius Sinarum philosophus* (1687), they called the Confucian ethics "the excellentest morality that ever was taught, a morality which might be said to proceed from the school of Jesus Christ."[27] In *Mémoires de la Chine* (1696) the Jesuit Louis Le Comte wrote

that the Chinese people had "for two thousand years preserved the knowledge of the true God," and had "practiced the purest moral code while
Europe was yet steeped in error and corruption";[28] this book was condemned by the Sorbonne. In 1697 Leibniz, cautious politically but alert to
every breeze in the intellectual atmosphere, published his *Novissima Sinaica*
("the latest news from China"). He rated Europe as excelling China in
science and philosophy, yet

> who would formerly have believed that there is a people that surpasses
> us in its principles of civil life? And this, nevertheless, we now experi-
> ence in the case of the Chinese . . . in ethics and politics. For it is
> impossible to describe how beautifully everything in the laws of the
> Chinese, more than in those of other peoples, is directed to the achieve-
> ment of public tranquillity. . . . The state of our affairs, as corruptions
> spread among us without measure, seems to me such that it would ap-
> pear almost necessary that Chinese missionaries should be sent to us to
> teach us the use and practice of natural religion, just as we send mis-
> sionaries to them to teach them revealed religion. And so I believe that
> if a wise man were chosen to pass judgment . . . upon the excellence
> of peoples, he would award the golden apple to the Chinese—except
> that we should have the better of them in one supreme but superhuman
> thing, namely, the divine gift of the Christian religion.[29]

Leibniz urged the academies of Europe to gather information about
China, and he helped persuade the French government to send accomplished Jesuit scholars to join the mission in China and make factual reports. In 1735 Jean Baptiste du Halde summarized these and other data in
his *Description . . . de l'empire de la Chine;* a year later this was translated into English; in both France and England it had wide influence.
Du Halde was the first to give Mencius a European reputation. By the
middle of the eighteenth century Bossuet's *Histoire universelle* had been
discredited by the revelation of old, extensive, and enlightened cultures
which his "universal" history had almost ignored; and the way was open
for Voltaire's larger perspective of the story of civilization.

The results of these enthusiastic exaggerations appeared in European
customs, arts, manners, literature, and philosophy. In 1739 the Marquis
d'Argens published a series of *Lettres chinoises* by an imaginary Chinese,
criticizing European institutions and ways; in 1757 Horace Walpole
amused England with a "Letter from Xo Ho, a Chinese Philosopher"; in
1760 Goldsmith used the same device in his *Citizen of the World*. When
the Emperor Joseph II in person plowed a piece of land, he was imitating
a custom of the Chinese emperors.[30] When the fine ladies of Paris opened
their parasols against the sun, they were displaying a pretty contraption

introduced into France from China by the Jesuits;[31] toward the end of the eighteenth century the umbrella evolved from the parasol. Chinese porcelain and Japanese lacquer had in the seventeenth century become prized possessions in European homes; Chinese wallpaper, in which the small units, properly placed, made a single large pictorial pattern, captured English fancy toward 1700; Chinese furniture entered English homes about 1750. All through the eighteenth century the taste for *chinoiseries*—articles of Chinese make or style—characterized English and French decoration, ran through Italy and Germany, entered into rococo ornament, and became so compulsive a fashion that a dozen satirists rose to challenge its tyranny. Chinese silk became a symbol of status; Chinese gardens spread over Western Europe; Chinese firecrackers burned European thumbs.[32] Gozzi's *Turandot* was a Chinese fantasy. A dozen plays with a Chinese background appeared on the English stage; and Voltaire developed his *Orphelin de la Chine* from a Chinese drama in the third volume of Du Halde.[33]

Chinese influence on Western thought was keenest in France, where the *esprits forts* seized upon it as another weapon against Christianity. They rejoiced to find that Confucius was a freethinker rather than a displaced Jesuit. They proclaimed that the Confucian ethic proved the practicability of a moral code independent of supernatural religion.[34] Bayle pointed out (1685) that a Chinese emperor was giving free scope to Catholic missionaries while Louis XIV, revoking Henry IV's tolerant Edict of Nantes, was enforcing religious conformity through the barbarous violence of dragonnades. Misinterpreting the Confucians as atheists, Bayle cited them as disproving the argument from universal consent for the existence of God.[35] Montesquieu stood his ground against the Oriental tide, called the Chinese emperors despots, denounced dishonest Chinese merchants, exposed the poverty of the Chinese masses, and predicted tragic results from overpopulation in China.[36] Quesnay tried to answer Montesquieu in *Le Despotisme de la Chine* (1767), praised it as "enlightened despotism," and cited Chinese models for needed reforms in French economy and government. Turgot, skeptical of the Chinese utopia, commissioned two Chinese Catholic priests in France to go to China and seek factual answers to fifty-two questions; their report encouraged a more realistic appraisal of good and bad in Chinese life.[37]

Voltaire read extensively and eagerly on China. He gave Chinese civilization the first three chapters in his *Essai sur les moeurs;* and in his *Dictionnaire philosophique* he called China "the finest, the most ancient, the most extensive, the most populous and well-regulated kingdom on earth."[38] His admiration for Chinese government shared in inclining him to the belief that the best hope for social reform lay in *despotisme éclairé,* by which he meant enlightened monarchy. Like several other Frenchmen, and like the German philosopher Wolff, he was ready to canonize Confucius, who "had taught the Chinese people the principles of virtue five hundred years before the founding of Christianity."[39] Voltaire, famous for his good manners, thought the decorum, self-restraint, and quiet peaceableness of the Chinese a model for his excitable countrymen,[40] and perhaps for himself. When two poems by the current Chinese Emperor, Ch'ien Lung (r. 1736–96), were translated into French, Voltaire responded in verse. The Emperor sent him a porcelain vase.

European acquaintance with alien faiths and institutions was a powerful factor in weakening Christian theology. The news from Persia, India, Egypt, China, and America led to an endless series of embarrassing questions. How, asked Montesquieu, could one choose the true religion out of two thousand different faiths?[41] How, asked a hundred others, could the world have been created in 4004 B.C. when in 4000 B.C. China already had a developed civilization? Why had China no record or tradition of Noah's Flood, which, according to the Bible, had covered the whole earth? Why had God confined his Scriptural revelation to a small nation in western Asia if he had intended it for mankind? How could anyone believe that outside the Church there would be no salvation?—were all those billions who had lived in India, China, and Japan now roasting in hell? The theologians struggled to answer these and similar questions with a mountain of distinctions and explanations, but the structure of dogma nevertheless showed new cracks day by day, often as the result of missionary reports; sometimes it seemed that the Jesuits in China had been converted to Confucius instead of converting the Chinese to Christ.

And was it not by the science they brought, rather than by the theology they taught, that those cultured Jesuits had won so many friends among the Chinese?

CHAPTER XVI

The Scientific Advance*

1715-89

I. THE EXPANDING QUEST

SCIENCE too was offering a new revelation. The growth of science— of its pursuit, its methods, its findings, its successful predictions and productions, its power, and its prestige—is the positive side of that basic modern development whose negative side is the decline of supernatural belief. Two priesthoods came into conflict: the one devoted to the molding of character through religion, the other to the education of the intellect through science. The first priesthood predominates in ages of poverty or disaster, when men are grateful for spiritual comfort and moral order; the second in ages of progressive wealth, when men incline to limit their hopes to the earth.

It is customary to rank the eighteenth century below the seventeenth in scientific achievements; and certainly there are no figures here that tower like Galileo or Newton, no accomplishments commensurate with the enlargement of the known universe or the cosmic extension of gravitation, or the formulation of calculus, or the discovery of the circulation of the blood. And yet, what a galaxy of stars brightens the scientific scene in the eighteenth century!—Euler and Lagrange in mathematics, Herschel and Laplace in astronomy, d'Alembert, Franklin, Galvani, and Volta in physics, Priestley and Lavoisier in chemistry, Linnaeus in botany, Buffon and Lamarck in biology, Haller in physiology, John Hunter in anatomy, Condillac in psychology, Jenner and Boerhaave in medicine. The multiplying academies gave more and more of their time and funds to scientific research. The universities increasingly admitted science to their curriculums; between 1702 and 1750 Cambridge established chairs in anatomy, astronomy, botany, chemistry, geology, and "experimental philosophy"—i.e., physics. Scientific method became more rigorously experimental. The nationalistic animosity that had tarnished the International of the Mind in the controversy between Newton and Leibniz subsided, and the new priesthood joined hands across frontiers, theologies, and wars to explore the expanding unknown. Recruits came from every class, from the impoverished Priestley

---

* This chapter is especially indebted to A. Wolf's *History of Science, Technology, and Philosophy in the 18th Century.*

and the foundling d'Alembert to the titled Buffon and the millionaire Lavoisier. Kings and princes entered the quest: George III took up botany,
John V astronomy, Louis XVI physics. Amateurs like Montesquieu and
Voltaire, women like Mme. du Châtelet and the actress Mlle. Clairon labored or played in laboratories, and Jesuit scientists like Boscovich strove
to unite the old faith and the new.

Not till our own explosive times did science enjoy such popularity and
honor. The éclat of Newton's discoveries in mathematics, mechanics, and
astronomy had raised the heads of scientists everywhere in Europe. They
could not rise to be master of the mint, but on the Continent, after 1750,
they were welcomed in scented society and rubbed wigs with lords and
dukes. In Paris the lecture halls of science were crowded by eager listen-
ers of all sexes and ranks. Goldsmith, visiting Paris in 1755, reported, "I
have seen as bright a circle of beauty at the chemical lectures of Rouelle as
gracing the court of Versailles."[1] Fashionable women kept books of science
on their dressing tables, and, like Mme. de Pompadour, had their portraits
painted with squares and telescopes at their feet. People lost interest in
theology, they sloughed off the other world while cherishing their superstitions. Science became the mode and mood of an age that moved in a
complex stream of hectic change to its catastrophic end.

II. MATHEMATICS

1. Euler

Change was now slow in mathematics because so much had already been
done in that field through five millenniums that Newton seemed to have
left no other regions to conquer. For a while, after his death (1727), a reaction set in against the assumptions and abstruseness of calculus. Bishop
Berkeley, in a vigorous critique (*The Analyst*, 1734), assailed these as
quite equaling the mysteries of metaphysics and theology, and taunted the
followers of science with "submitting to authority, taking things on trust,
and believing points inconceivable," precisely as had been charged against
the followers of religious faith. Mathematicians have been as hard put to
answer him on this head as materialists have been to refute his idealism.

However, mathematics built bridges, and the pursuit of numbers continued. In England Abraham Demoivre, Nicholas Saunderson, and Brook
Taylor, and in Scotland Colin Maclaurin, developed the Newtonian form
of calculus. Demoivre advanced the mathematics of chance and of life annuities; being of French birth and English residence, he was chosen by the
Royal Society of London (1712) to arbitrate the rival claims of Newton

and Leibniz to the invention of infinitesimal calculus. Saunderson became blind at the age of one; he learned to carry on long and complicated mathematical problems mentally; he was appointed professor of mathematics at Cambridge at the age of twenty-nine (1711), and wrote an *Algebra* that won international acclaim; we shall see how his career fascinated Diderot. Taylor left his name on a basic theorem of calculus, and Maclaurin showed that a liquid mass rotating on its axis would take an ellipsoidal form.

In Basel the Bernoulli family continued through three generations to produce distinguished scientists. Protestant in faith, the family had fled from Antwerp (1583) to avoid the atrocities of Alva. Two of seven Bernoulli mathematicians belong to the age of Louis XIV; a third, Johann I (1667–1748), overspread two reigns. Daniel (1700–82) became professor of mathematics at St. Petersburg at the age of twenty-five, but returned eight years later to teach anatomy, botany, physics, and finally philosophy in the University of Basel; he left works on calculus, acoustics, and astronomy, and almost founded mathematical physics. His brother Johann II (1710–90) taught rhetoric and mathematics, and left his mark on the theory of heat and light. Daniel won prizes of the Académie des Sciences ten times, Johann thrice. Of Johann's sons, Johann III (1744–1807) became astronomer royal at the Berlin Academy, and Jakob II (1758?–89) taught physics at Basel, mathematics at St. Petersburg. This remarkable family spanned the curriculum, the century, and the Continent.

Leonhard Euler, pupil of Johann Bernoulli I and friendly rival of Daniel, stands out as the most versatile and prolific mathematician of his time. Born at Basel in 1707, dying at St. Petersburg in 1783, eminent in mathematics, mechanics, optics, acoustics, hydrodynamics, astronomy, chemistry, and medicine, and knowing half the *Aeneid* by heart, he illustrated the uses of diversity and the scope of the human mind. In three major treatises on calculus he freed the new science from the geometric placenta in which it had been born, and established it as algebraic calculus—"analysis." To these classics he added works on algebra, mechanics, astronomy, and music; however, his *Tentamen novae Theoriae Musicae* (1729) "contained too much geometry for musicians, and too much music for geometers."[2] With all his science he retained his religious faith to the end.

When Daniel Bernoulli moved to St. Petersburg he promised to get Leonhard a post in the Academy there. The youth went, aged twenty; and when Daniel left Russia (1733) Euler succeeded him as head of the mathematical section. He astonished his fellow Academicians by computing in three days astronomical tables that were expected to require several months. On this and other tasks he worked so intensely, night and day and by poor light, that in 1735 he lost the sight of his right eye. He married, and began at once to add and multiply, while death subtracted; of his thirteen children eight died young. His own life was not safe in a capital racked with political intrigue and assassinations. In 1741 he accepted an invitation from Frederick the Great to join the Berlin Academy; there, in 1759, he succeeded Maupertuis in charge of mathematics. Frederick's mother liked him, but found him strangely reticent. "Why don't you speak to me?" she asked. "Madame," he replied, "I come from a country where if you speak you are hanged."[3] The Russians, however, could be gentlemen. They continued his salary for a long time after his departure; and when a Russian army, invading Brandenburg, pillaged Euler's farm, the general indemnified him handsomely, and the Empress Elizabeth Petrovna added to the sum.

The history of science honors Euler first for his work in calculus, and especially for his systematic treatment of the calculus of variations. He advanced both geometry and trigonometry as branches of analysis. He was the first to distinctly conceive the notion of a mathematical function, which is now the heart of mathematics. In mechanics he formulated the general equations that still bear his name. In optics he was the first to apply calculus to the vibrations of light, and to formulate the curve of vibration as dependent upon elasticity and density. He deduced the laws of refraction analytically, and made those studies in the dispersion of light that prepared for the construction of achromatic lenses. He shared in the international enterprise of finding longitude at sea by charting the position of the planets and the phases of the moon; his approximate solution helped John Harrison to draw up successful lunar tables for the British Admiralty.

In 1766 Catherine the Great asked Euler to return to St. Petersburg. He did, and she treated him royally. Soon after his arrival he became totally blind. His memory was so accurate, and his speed of calculation so great, that he continued to produce almost as actively as before. Now he dictated his *Complete Introduction to Algebra* to a young tailor who, when this began, knew nothing of mathematics beyond simple reckoning; this book gave to algebra the form that it retained to our time. In 1771 a fire destroyed Euler's home; the blind mathematician was saved from the flames by a fellow Swiss from Basel, Peter Grimm, who carried him on his shoulders to safety. Euler died in 1783, aged seventy-six, from a stroke suffered while playing with a grandson.

2. Lagrange

Only one man surpassed him in his century and science, and that was his protégé. Joseph Louis Lagrange was one of eleven children born to a French couple domiciled in Turin; of these eleven he alone survived infancy. He was turned from the classics to science by reading a memoir ad-

dressed by Halley to the Royal Society of London; at once he devoted himself to mathematics, and soon with such success that at the age of eighteen
he was professor of geometry at the Turin Artillery Academy. From his
students, nearly all older than himself, he organized a research society that
grew into the Turin Academy of Science. At nineteen he sent to Euler a
new method for treating the calculus of variations; Euler replied that this
procedure solved difficulties which he himself had been unable to overcome. The kindly Swiss delayed making public his own results, "so as not
to deprive you of any part of the glory which is your due."[4] Lagrange announced his method in the first volume issued by the Turin Academy
(1759). Euler, in his own memoir on the calculus of variations, gave the
younger man full credit; and in that year 1759 he had him elected a foreign member of the Berlin Academy, at the age of twenty-three. When
Euler left Prussia he recommended Lagrange as his successor at the Academy; d'Alembert warmly seconded the proposal; and in 1766 Lagrange
moved to Berlin. He greeted Frederick II as "the greatest king in Europe";
Frederick welcomed him as "the greatest mathematician in Europe."[5] This
was premature, but it soon became true. The friendly relations among the
leading mathematicians of the eighteenth century—Euler, Lagrange, Clairaut, d'Alembert, and Legendre—form a pleasant episode in the history of
science.

During his twenty years at Berlin Lagrange gradually put together his
masterpiece, *Mécanique analytique*. Incidentally to this basic enterprise he
delved into astronomy, and offered a theory of Jupiter's satellites and an
explanation of lunar librations—alterations in the visible portions of the
moon. In 1786 Frederick the Great died, and was succeeded by Frederick
William II, who cared little for science. Lagrange accepted an invitation
from Louis XVI to join the Académie des Sciences; he was given comfortable
quarters in the Louvre, and became a special favorite of Marie Antoinette,
who did what she could to lighten his frequent spells of melancholy. He
brought with him the manuscript of *Mécanique analytique*, but he could
find no publisher for so difficult a printing problem in a city seething with
revolution. His friends Adrien Legendre and the Abbé Marie finally prevailed upon a printer to undertake the task, but only after the abbé had
promised to buy all copies unsold after a stated date. When the book that
summed up his life work was placed in Lagrange's hands (1788), he did
not care to look at it; he was in one of those periodic depressions in which
he lost all interest in mathematics, even in life. For two years the book remained unopened on his desk.

The *Mécanique analytique* is rated by general consent as the summit of
eighteenth-century mathematics. Second only to the *Principia* in their
field, it advanced upon Newton's book by using "analysis"—algebraic cal-

culus—instead of geometry in the discovery and exposition of solutions; said the preface, "No diagrams will be found in this work." By this method Lagrange reduced mechanics to general formulas—the calculus of variations —from which specific equations could be derived for each particular problem; these general equations still dominate mechanics, and bear his name. Ernst Mach described them as one of the greatest contributions ever made to the economy of thought.[6] They raised Alfred North Whitehead to religious ecstasy: "The beauty and almost divine simplicity of these equations is such that these formulae are worthy to rank with those mysterious symbols which in ancient times were held directly to indicate the Supreme Reason at the base of all things."[7]

When the Revolution broke out with the fall of the Bastille (July 14, 1789), Lagrange, as a favorite of royalty, was advised to return to Berlin; he refused. He had always sympathized with the oppressed, but he had no faith in the ability of revolution to escape the results of the natural inequality of men. He was horrified by the massacres of September, 1792, and the execution of his friend Lavoisier, but his moody silence saved him from the guillotine. When the École Normale was opened (1795) Lagrange was put in charge of mathematics; when that school was closed and the École Polytechnique was established (1797), he was its first professor; the mathematical basis and bent of French education are part of Lagrange's enduring influence.

In 1791 a committee was appointed to devise a new system of weights and measures; Lagrange, Lavoisier, and Laplace were among its first members; two of this trinity were "purged" after three months, and Lagrange became the leading spirit in formulating the metric system. The committee chose as the basis of length a quadrant of the earth—a quarter of the great circle passing around the earth at sea level through the poles; one ten-millionth of this was taken as the new unit of length, and was called a *mètre* —a meter. A subcommittee chose as the new unit of weight a gram: the weight of distilled water, at zero temperature centigrade, occupying a cube each side of which measured one centimeter—one hundredth of a meter. In this way all lengths and weights were based upon one physical constant, and upon the number ten. There were still many defenders of the duodecimal system, which took twelve as its base, as in England and generally in our measurement of time. Lagrange stood firmly for ten, and had his way. The metric system was adopted by the French government on November 25, 1792, and remains, with some modifications, as perhaps the most lasting result of the French Revolution.

Romance brightened Lagrange's advancing age. When he was fifty-six a girl of seventeen, daughter of his friend the astronomer Lemonnier, insisted on marrying him and devoting herself to mitigating his hypochondria. Lagrange yielded, and became so grateful for her love that he accompanied her to balls and musicales. He had learned to like music—which is a trick that mathematics plays upon the ear—because "it isolates me. I hear the first three measures; at the fourth I distinguish nothing; I give myself up to my thoughts; nothing interrupts me; and it is thus that I solve more than one difficult problem."[8]

As the fever of revolution subsided, France complimented itself on having exempted the supreme mathematician of the age from the guillotine. In 1796 Talleyrand was sent to Turin to wait in state upon Lagrange's father and tell him, "Your son, whom Piedmont is proud to have produced, and France to possess, has done honor to all mankind by his genius."[9] Napoleon, between campaigns, liked to talk with the mathematician-become-philosopher.

The old man's interest in mathematics revived when (1810–13) he revised and enlarged the *Mécanique analytique* for its second edition. But as usual he worked too hard and fast; spells of dizziness weakened him; once his wife found him unconscious on the floor, his head bleeding from a cut caused by his fall against the edge of a table. He realized that his physical resources were running out, but he accepted this gradual disintegration as normal and reasonable. To Monge and others who attended him he said:

> "I was very ill yesterday, my friends. I felt I was going to die. My body grew weaker little by little; my intellectual and physical faculties were extinguished insensibly. I observed the well-graduated progression of the diminution of my strength, and I came to the end without sorrow, without regrets, and by a very gentle decline. Death is not to be dreaded, and when it comes without pain it is a last function which is not unpleasant. . . . Death is the absolute repose of the body."[10]

He died on April 10, 1813, aged seventy-five, mourning only that he had to leave his faithful wife to the hazards of that age, when it seemed that all the world was in arms against France.

His friends Gaspard Monge and Adrien Legendre carried into the nineteenth century those mathematical researches which provided the foundations of industrial advance. The work of Legendre (1752–1833) belongs to the post-Revolution age; we merely salute him on our way. Monge was the son of a peddler and knife-grinder; our notion of French poverty is checked when we see this simple workingman sending three sons through college. Gaspard took all available prizes in school. At fourteen he built a fire engine; at sixteen he declined the invitation of his Jesuit teachers to join their order; instead he became professor of physics and mathematics in the École Militaire at Mézières. There he formulated the principles of descriptive geometry—a system of presenting three-dimensional figures on one descriptive plane. The procedure proved so useful in designing fortifications and other constructions that for fifteen years the French army forbade him to divulge it publicly. Then (1794) he was allowed to teach it at the École Normale in Paris. Lagrange, attending his lecture there, marveled like Molière's Jourdain: "Before hearing Monge, I did not know that I knew descriptive geometry."[11] Monge served the embattled republic well, and rose to be minister of the marine. Napoleon entrusted many confidential missions to him. After the restoration of the Bourbons Monge was reduced to insecurity and poverty. When he died (1818) his students at the École Polytechnique were forbidden to attend his funeral. The next morning they marched in a body to the cemetery and laid a wreath upon his grave.

III. PHYSICS

1. Matter, Motion, Heat, and Light

Mathematics grew because it was the basic and indispensable tool of all science, reducing experience and experiment to quantitative formulations that made possible precise prediction and practical control. The first step was to apply it to matter in general: to discover the regularities and establish the "laws" of energy, motion, heat, sound, light, magnetism, electricity; here were mysteries enough waiting to be explored.

Pierre Louis Moreau de Maupertuis abandoned a career in the French army to devote himself to science. He preceded Voltaire in introducing Newton to France, and in appreciating and instructing Mme. du Châtelet. In 1736, as we shall see, he directed an expedition to Lapland to measure a degree of the meridian. In 1740 he accepted an invitation to visit Frederick II; he followed Frederick into the battle of Mollwitz (1741), was captured by the Austrians, but was soon released. In 1745 he joined the Academy of Sciences at Berlin, and a year later he became its president. To the Paris Académie des Sciences in 1744, and to the Berlin Academy in 1746, he expounded his principle of least action: "Whenever any change occurs in nature, the quantity of action employed for this change is always the least possible." This, he thought, proved a rational order in nature, and therefore the existence of a rational God.[12] Euler and Lagrange developed the principle, and in our own time it played a part in the quantum theory. In an *Essai de cosmologie* (1750) Maupertuis revived an indestructible heresy: while still recognizing design in nature, he confessed to seeing in it also signs of stupidity or evil, as if a demon were competing with a benevolent deity in the management of the cosmos.[13] Maupertuis might have agreed with his merciless enemy Voltaire that St. Augustine should have remained a Manichaean.

We have noted the birth of d'Alembert as the unpremeditated issue of a passing contact between an artilleryman and an ex-nun. The Paris police found him, a few hours old, on the steps of the Church of St.-Jean-le-Rond (1717); they had him baptized Jean Baptiste Le Rond, and sent him to a nurse in the country. His father, the Chevalier Destouches, claimed him, gave him (for reasons unknown to us) the name d'Arembert, and paid Mme. Rousseau, a glazier's wife, to adopt the child. She proved a model stepmother, and Jean a model and precocious boy. When he was seven the father proudly displayed him to the mother, Mme. de Tencin, but she decided that her career as mistress and *salonnière* would be impeded by accepting him. She contributed nothing to his support, so far as we know, but the Chevalier, before dying in 1726, left him an annuity of twelve hundred livres.

Jean studied at the Collège des Quatre-Nations, then at the University of Paris, where he received the degree in law. There, about 1738, he changed his name from d'Arembert to d'Alembert. Tiring of law, he turned to medicine; but an incidental interest in mathematics became a passion: "mathematics," he said, "was for me my mistress."[14] He continued till he was forty-eight to live with Mme. Rousseau, looking upon her gratefully as his only mother. She thought it disgraceful that a man should so abandon himself to study and show no economic itch. "You will never be anything better than a philosopher," she mourned, adding, "And what is a philosopher? 'Tis a madman who torments himself all his life so that people may talk about him when he is dead."[15]

Probably his inspiring motives were not a desire for posthumous fame but a proud rivalry with established savants, and that beaver instinct which takes delight in building, in forging order upon a chaos of materials or ideas. In any case he began at twenty-two to submit papers to the Académie des Sciences: one on integral calculus (1739), another on the refraction of light (1741); this gave the earliest explanation of the bending of light rays in passing from one fluid to another of greater density; for this the Académie admitted him to "adjoint" membership. Two years later he published his main scientific work, *Traité de dynamique*, which sought to reduce to mathematical equations all problems of matter in motion; this anticipated by forty-two years Lagrange's superior *Mécanique analytique*; it keeps historical significance because it formulated the basic theorem now known as "D'Alembert's principle," too technical for our general digestion, but immensely helpful in mechanical calculations. He applied it in a *Traité de l'équilibre et du mouvement des fluides* (1744);

this so impressed the Académie that it awarded him a pension of five hundred livres, which must have appeased Mme. Rousseau.

Partly from his principle, partly from an original equation in calculus, d'Alembert arrived at a formula for the motion of winds. He dedicated his *Réflexions sur la cause générale des vents* (1747) to Frederick the Great, who responded by inviting him to settle in Berlin; d'Alembert refused, showing at thirty more wisdom than Voltaire was to show at fifty-six. In an *Essai d'une nouvelle théorie de la résistance des fluides* (1752) he tried to find mechanical formulas for the resistance of water to a body moving on it; he failed, but in 1775, under a commission from Turgot, he and Condorcet and the Abbé Bossut made experiments that helped to determine the laws of fluid resistance to surface-moving bodies. Late in life he studied the motion of vibrating chords, and issued (1779) *Éléments de musique théorique et pratique*, following and modifying the system of Rameau; this book won the praise of the famous musicologist Charles Burney. All in all, d'Alembert had one of the keenest minds of the century.

When Maupertuis resigned as president of the Berlin Academy Frederick the Great offered the post to d'Alembert. The mathematician-physicist-astronomer-encyclopedist was poor, but he courteously refused; he cherished his freedom, his friends, and Paris. Frederick respected his motives, and, with the permission of Louis XV, sent him a modest pension of twelve hundred livres. In 1762 Catherine the Great invited him to Russia and the Academy of St. Petersburg; he declined, for he was now in love. Perhaps informed of this, Catherine persisted, bade him come "*avec tous vos amis,*" with all his friends, and offered him a salary of 100,000 francs a year. She took his refusals graciously, and continued to correspond with him, discussing with him her mode and problems of government. In 1763 Frederick urged him at least to visit Potsdam; d'Alembert went, and dined with the King for two months. He again declined the presidency of the Berlin Academy; instead he induced Frederick to raise the salary of Euler, who had a large family.[16] We hope to meet d'Alembert again.

The amazing Bernoullis made some incidental contributions to mechanics. Johann I formulated (1717) the principle of virtual velocities: "In all equilibrium of forces whatsoever, in whatever manner they are applied, and in whatever directions they act upon one another, whether directly or indirectly, the sum of the positive energies will be equal to the sum of the negative energies taken positively." Johann and his son Daniel (1735) proclaimed that the sum of *vis viva* (living force) in the world is always constant; this principle was reformulated in the nineteenth century as the conservation of energy. Daniel applied the conception to good effect in his *Hydrodynamics* (1738), a modern classic in an especially difficult field. In that volume he founded the kinetic theory of gases: a gas is composed of tiny particles moving about with great rapidity, and exerting pressure upon the container by their repeated impacts; heat increases the velocity of the particles and therefore the pressure of the gas; and the lessening of the volume (as Boyle had shown) proportionately increases the pressure.

In the physics of heat the great name for the eighteenth century is Joseph Black. Born in Bordeaux to a Scot born in Belfast, he studied chemistry in the University of Glasgow, and at the age of twenty-six (1754) made experiments in what we would now call oxidation or corrosion; these indicated the action of a gas distinct from common air; he detected this in the balance, and called it "fixed air" (now called carbon dioxide); Black had come close to the discovery of oxygen. In 1756, as lecturer in chemistry, anatomy, and medicine at the university, he began observations that led him to his theory of "latent heat": when a substance is in process of changing from a solid to a liquid state, or from a liquid to a gas, the changing substance absorbs from the atmosphere an amount of heat not detectable as a change of temperature; and this latent heat is given back to the atmosphere when a gas changes into a liquid or a liquid into a solid. James Watt applied this theory in his improvement of the steam engine. Black, like nearly all predecessors of Priestley, thought of heat as a material substance ("caloric") added to or subtracted from matter rising or falling in warmth; not until 1798 did Benjamin Thompson, Count Rumford, show that heat is not a substance but a mode of motion, now conceived as an accelerated motion of a body's constituent parts.

Meanwhile Johan Carl Wilcke of Stockholm, independently of Black, arrived at a similar theory of latent heat (1772). In a series of experiments reported in 1777 the Swedish scientist introduced the term "radiant heat"—the invisible heat given off by hot materials; he distinguished it from light, described its lines of motion and its reflection and concentration by mirrors, and prepared for the later correlation of both heat and light as kindred forms of radiation. Wilcke, Black, Lavoisier, Laplace, and other investigators determined the approximate value of "absolute zero" (the lowest temperature possible in principle). The British adopted as the unit of heat that quantity which raises the temperature of a pound of water one degree Fahrenheit; the French, and the Continent in general, preferred to use that quantity of heat which raises the temperature of a kilogram of water one degree centigrade.

The eighteenth century made little progress in the theory of light, because nearly all physicists accepted Newton's "corpuscular hypothesis"—that light is the emission of particles from the object to the eye. Euler led a minority that defended a wave theory. Following Huygens, he assumed that the "empty" space between the heavenly bodies, and between other visible objects, is filled with "ether," a material too fine to be perceived by our senses or our instruments, but strongly suggested by the phenomena of gravity, magnetism, and electricity. Light, in Euler's view, is an undulation in the ether, just as sound is an undulation in the air. He distinguished colors as due to different periods of vibration in light waves, and anticipated the current assignment of blue light to the shortest period of vibration, and red light to the longest. — Pierre Bouguer verified by experiment what Kepler had worked out theoretically, that the intensity of light varies inversely as the square of the distance from its source. Johann Lambert devised ways of measuring the intensity of light, and reported that the brightness of the sun is 277,000 times that of the moon; this, like our childhood theology, we must take on faith.

2. Electricity

The most brilliant advances in eighteenth-century physics were in the field of electricity. Frictional electricity had long been known; Thales of Miletus (600 B.C.) was familiar with the power of amber, jet, and a few other substances, when rubbed, to attract light objects like feathers or straw. William Gilbert, physician to Queen Elizabeth, called this attractive power "electron" (from the Greek ēlektron, amber) and, in Latin, vis electrica. The next step was to find a way to conduct and use this static electricity. Guericke and Hauksbee had sought such means in the seventeenth century; it remained for Stephen Gray to make the decisive discovery (1729).

Gray was an old irascible pensioner in a London almshouse. Having "electrified," by rubbing, a glass tube corked at both ends, he found that the corks, as well as the tube, would attract a feather. He inserted one end of a wooden rod into one of the corks, and the other end into an ivory ball; when he rubbed the tube the ball, as well as the tube and the corks, attracted a feather; the vis electrica had been conducted along the rod. Using packthread or strong twine instead of the rod, he was able to conduct the electricity through a distance of 765 feet. When he used hair, silk, resin, or glass as a connection there was no conduction; in this way Gray remarked the difference between conductors and non-conductors, and he discovered that non-conductors could be used for the preservation or storage of electric charges. When he suspended 666 feet of conductive packthread from a long succession of inclined poles, and sent the electric "virtue" (as he called it) through that distance, he in effect anticipated the telegraph.

France took up the quest. Jean Desaguliers, continuing (1736) Gray's experiments, divided substances into conductors and non-conductors (which he called "electrics per se"), and found that the latter could be changed into conductors by being moistened with water. Charles Du Fay carried on researches which he reported to the Académie des Sciences in 1733–37; and in a modest letter to the Royal Society of London (1734) he formulated his most important conclusion:

> Chance has thrown in my way another Principle: . . . that there are two distinct electricities, very different from each other; one of which

I call *vitreous electricity*, and the other *resinous electricity*. The first is
that of glass, rock crystal, precious stones, hair of animals, wool, and
many other bodies. The second is that of amber, copal, gum-lack, silk,
thread, paper, and a vast number of other substances. The character of
these two electricities is that a body of the vitreous electricity . . . repels all such as are of the same electricity, and, on the contrary, attracts
all those of the resinous electricity.[17]

So, Du Fay found, two bodies electrified by contact with the same electrified body repel each other; every schoolboy can recall his astonishment
at seeing two pith balls, suspended by non-conductors from the same
point and lying in contact with each other, suddenly spring apart when
touched by the same electrified glass rod. Later experiments showed that
"vitreous" bodies may develop "resinous" electricity, and "resinous" bodies
may develop "vitreous" electricity. Franklin therefore replaced Du Fay's
terms with *positive* and *negative*. Du Fay amused his contemporaries by
suspending a man by non-conductive cords, charging him with electricity
by contact with an electrified body, and then drawing sparks from his
body, with no harm to the hanging man.*

The scene moved to Germany. About 1742 Georg Bose in some part
anticipated Franklin by suggesting that the aurora borealis is of electrical
origin. In 1744 Christian Ludolff, at the Berlin Academy, showed that an
electric spark can ignite an inflammable fluid. Bose exploded gunpowder
in this way, inaugurating the use of electricity in blasting, firing cannon,
and a hundred other ways. In the same year Gottlieb Kratzenstein began
the employment of electricity in dealing with diseases. In October, 1745,
E. G. von Kleist, a Pomeranian clergyman, discovered that an electrical
charge could be stored in a glass tube by filling this with a liquid into which
he had inserted a nail connected with a machine producing frictional electricity; when the connection was severed, the liquid retained its charge
for several hours. A few months later Pieter van Musschenbroek, professor
at Leiden, without any knowledge of Kleist's experiments, made the same
discovery, and received from a charged but disconnected bowl a shock
that for a moment seemed mortal; he took two days to recover. Further experiments at Leiden showed that a heavier charge could be stored in an
empty bottle if its lower interior and exterior surfaces had been coated

---

* Now began a century of electrical tricks. Georg Bose, a professor in the University of
Leipzig, invited several friends to dinner; secretly he insulated the table, but connected
various objects on it with an electricity-producing machine hidden in the next room; when
the guests were about to eat he signaled an aide to start the machine; sparks flew out from
dishes, viands, flowers. He introduced to the company an attractive young woman whose
shoes insulated her from the floor, but whose person had been charged with electricity; he
invited the guests to kiss her; the gallants received shocks which, reported the professor,
nearly "knocked their teeth out."[18]

with tinfoil. Daniel Gralath conceived the idea of binding several such "Leiden jars" together, and found that their discharge would kill small animals.

In 1746 Louis Guillaume in Paris and in 1747 William Watson in London demonstrated what Watson was the first to call a "circuit." Watson laid a wire some twelve hundred feet long across Westminster Bridge; on one side of the Thames a man held one end of the wire and touched the water; on the other side a second man held the wire and a Leiden jar; when a third man touched the jar with one hand and with the other grasped a wire that extended into the river, the "circuit" was closed, and all three men received a shock. In 1747 Grummert of Dresden noted that sparks could be made for some distance through a partial vacuum, giving out considerable light.

This year 1747 brings us to Benjamin Franklin, who then began the electrical experiments that made his name and honor oscillate between science and politics. Here was one of the great minds and hearts of history, whose creative curiosity ranged from such proposals as daylight-saving time, rocking chairs and bifocal glasses to lightning rods and the one-fluid theory of electricity. A leading scientist of our century, Sir Joseph Thomson, confessed that he was "struck by the similarity between some of the views which we are led to take by the results of the most recent researches with those enunciated by Franklin in the very infancy of the subject."[19]

One of Franklin's first discoveries was the effect of pointed bodies in "drawing off and throwing off the electrical fire."[20] He found that "a long, slender shaft-bodkin" could attract a flow of electricity from an electrified ball six or eight inches distant, whereas a blunt body had to be brought within an inch of the ball to produce the same effect. Franklin spoke of electricity as fire, but this fire, he thought, was the result of a disturbance between the equilibrium of the "positive" and "negative" fiery *fluids* which he conceived electricity to be. All bodies, in his view, contained such electrical fluid: a "plus" body, containing more than its normal amount, is positively electrified, and tends to discharge its surplus into a body containing a normal amount or less; a "minus" body, containing less than its normal amount, is negatively electrified, and will draw electricity from a body containing a normal amount or more. On this basis Franklin developed a battery composed of eleven large glass plates covered with sheets of lead, which were electrified to a high excess; when this structure was brought into contact with bodies less heavily charged, it released part of its charge with a force that (said Franklin) "knew no bounds," sometimes exceeding "the greatest known effects of common lightning."[21]

Several investigators—Wall, Newton, Hauksbee, Gray, and others—had noted the resemblance between electric sparks and lightning; Franklin proved their identity. In 1750 he sent to the Royal Society of London a letter reading in part:

> May not the knowledge of this power of points be of use to mankind in preserving houses, churches, ships, etc., from the stroke of lightning, by directing us to fix on the highest parts of the edifices upright rods of iron made sharp as a needle, and gilt to prevent rusting, and from the foot of these rods a wire drawn down the outside of the building into the grounds, or round one of the shrouds of a ship down her side till it reaches the water? Would not these pointed rods probably draw the electrical fire silently out of a cloud before it came nigh enough to strike, and thereby secure us from that most sudden and terrible mischief?[22]

He went on to describe an experiment by which this could be tested. The Royal Society rejected the proposal as visionary, and refused to publish Franklin's letter. Two French scientists, de Lor and d'Alibard, put Franklin's theory to trial by erecting in a garden at Marly (1752) a pointed iron rod fifty feet high; they instructed a guard to touch the rod with an insulated brass wire if, in their absence, thunder clouds should pass overhead. The clouds came, the guard touched the rod not only with wire but also with his hand; sparks flew and crackled, and the guard was severely shocked. De Lor and d'Alibard confirmed the guard's report by further tests, and informed the Académie des Sciences, "Franklin's idea is no longer a conjecture but a reality."

Franklin himself was not satisfied; he wished to make the identity of lightning and electricity evident by "extracting" lightning with something sent up into the storm cloud itself. In June, 1752, as a thunderstorm began, he sent up, on strong twine, a kite made of silk (as better fitted than paper to bear wind and moisture without tearing); a sharply pointed wire projected some twelve inches from the top of the kite; and at the observer's end of the twine a key was fastened with a silk ribbon. In sending to England (October 19) directions for repeating the experiment, Franklin indicated the results:

> When the rain has wet the kite twine so that it can conduct the electric fire freely, you will find it stream out plentifully from the key at the approach of your knuckle, and with this key a phial [or Leiden jar] may be charged; and from electric fire thus obtained spirits may be kindled, and all other electric experiments [may be] performed which are usually done by the help of a rubbed glass globe or tube; and therefore the sameness of the electrical matter with that of lightning completely demonstrated.[23]

The experiment was repeated in France (1753) with a larger kite and a 780-foot cord twisted around an iron wire, ending at the observer in a metal tube which, in action, emitted sparks eight inches long. Professor G. W. Richman of St. Petersburg, making a similar test, was killed by the shock (1753). Franklin's publications, sent to England in 1751–54, won him election to the repentant Royal Society, and its Copley Medal. Their translation into French evoked a complimentary letter from Louis XV, and enthusiastic praise from Diderot, who called them models of scientific reporting. Those translations prepared for the favorable reception given to Franklin when he came to France to seek aid for the American colonies in their revolution. When, with the help of France, that revolution succeeded, d'Alembert (or Turgot) summed up Franklin's achievement in a compact line worthy of Virgil or Lucretius:

Eripuit coelo fulmen sceptrumque tyrannis

—"he snatched the lightning from the sky, and the scepter from the tyrants."

All Europe was alive, after 1750, with electrical theories and experiments. John Canton (1753) and the versatile Wilcke (1757) led the way in studying electrostatic induction, by which an uncharged conductor becomes electrified when placed near a charged body. Wilcke proved that most substances can be charged with positive (or negative) electricity if rubbed with a body less (or more) highly charged than themselves. Working with Wilcke at Berlin, Aepinus (Franz Ulrich Hoch) showed that two metal plates separated only by a layer of air acted like a Leiden jar. Joseph Priestley sought to measure the strength of an electric charge, and the maximum width across which the spark of a given charge would pass. He reported that when a spark crossed a gap even as wide as two inches between two metal rods in a vacuum, a "thin blue or purple light" appeared in the gap. But Priestley's most brilliant contribution to electrical theory was the suggestion that the laws of electricity might be like those of gravitation, and that the force exerted upon each other by separate electric charges would vary inversely as the square of the distance between their source. Henry Cavendish (who, like Priestley, is remembered chiefly for his work in chemistry) tested Priestley's suggestion in a series of patient experiments; he arrived at a slight but important modification, which James Clerk Maxwell further refined in 1878; as such the law is received today. Charles Augustin de Coulomb, after valuable work on the tension of beams and the resistance of metals to torsion, submitted to the Académie des Sciences reports of experiments (1785–89) which applied the torsion balance (a needle supported on a fine fiber) to the measurement of magnetic influences and electrical charges; in both cases he substantially verified the law of inverse squares.

Two Italians, like Coulomb, left their names in the terminology of electricity. Luigi Galvani, professor of anatomy at Bologna, discovered not only that muscular contractions could be produced in dead animals by direct electrical contact (this had long been known), but that such contractions occurred when the leg of a dead frog, connected with the earth, was brought near a machine that was discharging an electric spark. Similar convulsions were produced in frogs' legs—likewise grounded, and tied to long iron wires—when lightning flashed into the room. Galvani was surprised to find that he could make a frog's leg contract without any use or presence of electrical apparatus, merely by bringing the nerve and muscle of the leg into contact with two different metals. He concluded that there was a natural electricity in the animal organism.

Alessandro Volta, professor of physics at Pavia, repeated these experiments, and at first agreed with his countryman's theory of animal electricity. But his further researches modified his views. Repeating an experience reported by J. G. Sulzer about 1750, Volta found that if he placed a piece of tin on the tip of his tongue, and a piece of silver on the back of his tongue, he felt a strong sour taste whenever he connected the two metals with a wire. By connecting his forehead and his palate with these two different metals he obtained a sensation of light. In 1792 he announced his conclusion that the metals themselves, and not the animal tissue, produced the electricity merely by their interaction with each other and their contact with a moist substance, preferably a solution of salt. Further experiments proved that the contact of two different metals caused them to be electrically charged—one positively, the other negatively—without the mediation of any moist substance, animal or not; but such direct contact produced only an interchange of charges, not an outflow of current. To produce a current Volta made a "Voltaic pile" by superimposing several layers, each composed of two connected plates of different metal and one plate of moist paper or wood. So was formed, in the last year of the eighteenth century, the first electrical-current battery. The way was opened for electricity to remake the face and night of the world.

IV. CHEMISTRY

1. The Pursuit of Oxygen

"Physics and mathematics," wrote Edward Gibbon in 1761, "are now on the throne. They see their sisters prostrate before them, chained to their car, or at most adorning their triumph. Perhaps their own fall is not far distant."[24] It was an unlucky prediction; physics is now the queen of the sciences, mathematics is her helpmate, and no man can tell what will come of their union.

Nevertheless, amid all the victories of seventeenth-century mathematics, physics, and astronomy, a young science had emerged from the swaddling clothes of alchemy. A tragic error almost stifled it in its infancy. Following a theory proposed by Johann Becher in 1669, Georg Stahl, professor of medicine and chemistry at Halle, interpreted combustion as the liberation of "phlogiston" from the burning material into the air. (*Phlogiston* was Greek for *inflammable; phlox* was Greek for *flame*, and is our word for a plant whose flowers are sometimes flaming red.) By 1750 most chemists in Western Europe accepted this theory of heat or fire as a substance detached from burning matter. But no one could explain why, if this was so, metals weighed more after burning than before.

Our current explanation of combustion was prepared by the work of Hales, Black, and Scheele on the chemistry of the air. Stephen Hales paved the way by devising a "pneumatic trough," or air receptacle, into which gases could be collected in a closed vessel over water. He pointed out that gases (which he called "airs") were contained in many solids, and he described air as "a fine elastic fluid, with particles *of a very different nature* floating in it."[25] The decomposition of air and water into diverse substances put an end to the agelong conception of air, water, fire, and earth as the four fundamental elements. In the next generation the experiments of Joseph Black (1756) proved that one constituent of air was what, after Hales, he called "fixed air"—i.e., air contained in, and removable from, solid or liquid substances; we now term it carbon dioxide, or "carbonic-acid gas." Black further cleared the way to the discovery of oxygen by showing experimentally that this gas is contained in human exhalations. But he still believed in phlogiston, and oxygen, hydrogen, and nitrogen were still mysteries.

Sweden contributed lavishly to eighteenth-century chemistry. Torbern Olof Bergman, whom we shall meet again as a pioneer in physical geography, was primarily a chemist, famous and loved as a professor of that science in the University of Uppsala. He was the first to obtain nickel in a pure state and the first to show the importance of carbon in determining the physical properties of carbon-iron compounds. In his relatively short life of forty-nine years he studied, with over thirty thousand experiments, the chemical affinities of fifty-nine substances, and reported his findings in *Elective Attractions* (1775). He died before completing this task, but meanwhile he had passed on to Scheele his devotion to chemical research.

English historians of science now gallantly concede that a Swedish chemist, Karl Wilhelm Scheele, anticipated (1772) Priestley's discovery (1774) of what Lavoisier (1779) was the first to call oxygen. Scheele lived most of his forty-three years in poverty. Beginning as an apprentice to an apothecary in Göteborg, he rose no higher than to be a pharmacist in the modest town of Köping. His teacher, Torbern Bergman, obtained a small pension for him from the Stockholm Academy of Science; Scheele spent eighty per cent of it on chemical experiments. He performed most of these at night after the day's work, and with the simplest laboratory equipment; hence his early death. Yet he covered nearly the whole field of the new science, and defined it with his usual simplicity: "The object and chief business of chemistry is skillfully to separate substances into their constituents, to discover their properties, and to compound them in different ways."[26]

In 1775 he sent to the printer a manuscript entitled *Chemical Treatise on Air and Fire;* its publication was delayed till 1777, but nearly all the experiments it described had been carried out before 1773. Scheele, while holding till his death the belief in phlogiston, laid down the basic proposition that unpolluted atmosphere is composed of two gases: one of these he named "fire-air" (our oxygen), as the main support of fire; the other he called "vitiated air" (our nitrogen), as air that has lost "fire-air." He prepared oxygen in several ways. In one method he mixed concentrated sulfuric acid with finely ground manganese, heated the mixture in a retort, and collected the resultant gas in a bladder that had been pressed nearly free of air. He found that when the gas so produced was played over a lighted candle, this "began to burn with a larger flame, and emitted such a bright light that it dazed the eyes."[27] He concluded that "fire-air" was the gas that supported fire. "There is little doubt but that he obtained the gas two years before Priestley."[28]

This was but a fraction of Scheele's achievement. His record as a discoverer of new substances is probably unequaled.[29] He was the first to isolate chlorine, barium, manganese, and such new compounds as ammonia, glycerine, and hydrofluoric, tannic, benzoic, oxalic, malic, and tartaric acids. His discovery that chlorine would bleach cloth, vegetables, and flowers was put to commercial uses by Berthollet in France and James Watt in England. In further researches Scheele discovered uric acid by analyzing stone in the bladder (1776). In 1777 he prepared sulfuretted hydrogen, and in 1778 molybdic acid; in 1780 he proved that the acidity of sour milk is due to lactic acid; in 1781 he obtained tungstic acid from calcium tungstate (now known as scheelite); in 1783 he discovered prussic (hydrocyanic) acid, without realizing its poisonous character. He produced also arsine gas (a deadly compound of arsenic), and the arsenic pigment now known as Scheele's green.[30] He helped to make photography possible by showing that sunlight reduces chloride of silver to silver, and that the diverse rays that compose white light have different effects upon silver salts. The incredibly fruitful labor of this brief life proved of endless importance in the industrial developments of the nineteenth century.

2. Priestley

Joseph Priestley, rather than Scheele, for a long time received the credit for the discovery of oxygen because he discovered it independently of Scheele, and announced his discovery in 1775, two years before Scheele's retarded publication. We honor him nevertheless because his researches enabled Lavoisier to give chemistry its modern form; because he was among the pioneers in the scientific study of electricity; and because he contributed so boldly to British thought on religion and government that a fanatical mob burned down his house in Birmingham, and induced him to seek refuge in America. He touched the history of civilization at many points, and is one of its most inspiring characters.

He was born in Yorkshire in 1733, son of a Dissenter cloth-dresser. He studied voraciously in science, philosophy, theology, and languages; he learned Latin, Greek, French, German, Italian, Arabic, even some Syriac and Chaldee. He set up as a Dissenting preacher in Suffolk, but an impediment in his speech lessened the appeal of his eloquence. At twenty-five he organized a private school, whose curriculum he enlivened with experiments in physics and chemistry. At twenty-eight he became tutor in a Dissenting academy at Warrington; there he taught five languages and yet found time for researches that won him a fellowship in the Royal Society (1766). In that year he met Franklin in London, and was encouraged by him to write *The History and Present State of Electricity* (1767), an admirable survey of the whole subject up to his own time. In 1767 he was appointed pastor of Mill Hill Chapel at Leeds. He recalled later that "it was in consequence of living for some time in the neighborhood of a public brewery that I was induced to make experiments in fixed air"[31]—the brewery mash emitted carbonic-acid gas. He dissolved this in water, and liked its bubbling tang; this was the first "soda water."

In 1772 he was relieved of economic worry by appointment to the post of librarian to Lord Shelburne. In the house provided for him at Colne he performed the experiments that won him international renown. He improved upon Hales's pneumatic trough by collecting over mercury, instead of over water, the gases generated by diverse mixtures. So in 1772 he isolated nitric oxide, nitrous oxide ("laughing gas"), and hydrogen chloride; in 1773 ammonia (independently of Scheele); in 1774 sulfur dioxide; in 1776 nitrogen peroxide. On March 15, 1775, he communicated to the Royal Society a letter announcing his discovery of oxygen. In Volume II of his *Experiments and Observations on Different Kinds of Air* (1775) he described his method. Using a strong burning lens, he said,

I proceeded . . . to examine, by the help of it, what kind of air a great variety of substances would yield [when so heated], putting them into . . . vessels . . . filled with quicksilver and kept inverted in a basin of the same. With this apparatus, . . . on the first of August, 1774, I endeavored to extract air from *mercurius calcinatus per se* [mercuric oxide]; and I presently found that, by means of this lens, air was expelled from it very readily. . . . What surprised me, more than I can well express, was that a candle burned in this air with a remarkably vigorous flame.[32]

Noting, like Scheele, that a mouse lived much longer in this "dephlogisticated air" (as he called oxygen) than in the ordinary atmosphere, he thought he might safely sample the new air himself.

My reader will not wonder that, after having ascertained the superior goodness of dephlogisticated air by mice living in it, and the other tests above mentioned, I should have the curiosity to taste it by myself. I have gratified that curiosity by breathing it, drawing it through a glass siphon; and by this means I reduced a large jar full of it to the standard of common air. The feeling of it to my lungs was not sensibly different from common air, but I fancied that my breast felt peculiarly light for some time afterward. Who can tell but that, in time, this pure air may become a fashionable article of luxury? Hitherto only two mice and I have had the privilege of breathing it.[33]

He predicted some forms of this future luxury:

From the greater strength and vivacity of the flame of a candle in this pure air, it may be conjectured that it might be peculiarly salutary to the lungs in certain morbid cases, when the common air would not be sufficient to carry off the phlogistic putrid effluvium [carbon dioxide] fast enough. But perhaps we may also infer from these experiments that though pure dephlogisticated air [oxygen] might be very useful as a *medicine*, it might not be so proper for us in the usual healthy state of the body; for as a candle burns out faster in dephlogisticated air than in common air, so we might, as may be said, *live out too fast*, and the animal power be too soon exhausted, in this pure kind of air.[34]

Priestley's experimental work was brilliant with fruitful hypotheses and alert perceptions, but his theoretical interpretations were mostly traditional. Like Stahl and Scheele, he supposed that in combustion a substance, phlogiston, was emitted by the burning material; this substance, in his view, united with one constituent of the atmosphere to form "vitiated air," or "phlogisticated air" (our nitrogen); the other constituent was in his nomenclature "dephlogisticated air," which Lavoisier was to name oxygen. While Lavoisier argued that a material in process of combustion absorbed oxygen from the air instead of expelling phlogiston into it, Priestley to the end of his life retained the old conception.

In 1774 he traveled with Lord Shelburne on the Continent, and told him of the oxygen experiments. In 1780 Shelburne retired him with an annuity of £150. Priestley settled in Birmingham as junior minister of a large Dissenting congregation known as the New Meeting Society. He joined James Watt, Josiah Wedgwood, Erasmus Darwin, Matthew Boulton, and others in a "Lunar Society" that discussed the latest ideas in science, technology, and philosophy. He was popular with nearly all classes, admired for his cheerful spirit, his modesty and generosity, and "the unspotted purity of his life."[35] But some of his neighbors questioned his Christianity. In *Disquisitions relating to Matter and Spirit* (1777) he reduced everything, even the soul, to matter. This, he insisted, was perfectly orthodox,

> it being well known to the learned . . . that what the ancients meant by an immaterial being was only a *finer kind* of what we should now call matter; something like air or breath, which first supplied a name for the *soul*. . . . Consequently the ancients did not exclude from mind the property of *extension* and local pressure. It had, in their idea, some common properties with matter, was capable of being united with it, of acting and being acted upon by it. . . . It was therefore seen that . . . the power of sensation or thought . . . might be imparted to the very grossest matter, . . . and that the *soul* and *body*, being in reality the same kind of substance, must die together.[36]

In a further publication of the same year, *The Doctrine of Philosophical Necessity Illustrated*, Priestley, following Hartley and Hume, enthusiastically denied the freedom of the will. And in a *History of the Corruptions of Christianity* (1782), he rejected miracles, the Fall, the Atonement, and the Trinity; all these doctrines he considered to be "corruptions" developed in the evolution of Christianity; they were not to be found in the teachings of Christ or the twelve Apostles. All that was left of Christianity in Priestley was the belief in God, based on the evidences of divine design. Not quite reconciled to mortality, he suggested that at the Last Day God would re-create all the dead. His real hope, however, was not in a heaven above but in a utopia that would be built on this earth by the victory of science over superstition and ignorance. Seldom has the eighteenth-century religion of progress been more fervently expressed:

> All knowledge will be subdivided and extended; and knowledge, as Lord Bacon observes, being power, the human powers will in fact be

increased; nature, including both its materials and its laws, will be more at our command; men will make their situation in this world abundantly more easy and comfortable; they will probably prolong their existence on it, and will daily grow more happy, each in himself, and more able (and, I believe, more disposed) to communicate happiness to others. Thus, whatever was the beginning of this world, the end will be glorious and paradisaical beyond what our imaginations can now conceive.[37] . . . Happy are they who contribute to diffuse the pure light of this everlasting gospel.[38]

Part of this glorious progress, in Priestley's vision, was to be political, and would be based upon a simple humanitarian principle: "The good and happiness of the . . . majority of the members of any state is the great standard by which everything relating to that state must finally be determined";[39] here Bentham, according to Bentham, found one source of his utilitarian philosophy. The only just government, said Priestley, is one that aims at the happiness of its citizens, and it is quite consistent with Christianity that an obviously unjust government should be overthrown by the people. To St. Paul's caution that "the powers that be are ordained of God" Priestley replied that "for the same reason the powers which will be will be ordained of God also."[40]

It was natural that such a rebel should sympathize with the colonies in their protest against taxation without representation. Still more warmly did he acclaim the French Revolution. When Burke denounced it Priestley defended it; Burke, in Parliament, branded him as a heretic. Some of Priestley's friends shared his radical views. On July 14, 1791, the "Constitutional Society of Birmingham" met in the Royal Hotel to celebrate the anniversary of the fall of the Bastille. Priestley did not attend. A crowd gathered before the hotel, listened to its leaders' attacks upon heretics and traitors, and stoned the hotel windows; the banqueters fled. The crowd moved on to Priestley's house, and joyously burned it down, including his laboratory and instruments, his library and manuscripts. Then for three days it ranged through Birmingham, swearing to kill all "philosophers"; terrified citizens scrawled on their windowpanes, "No philosophers here." Priestley fled to Dudley, then to London. Thence on July 19 he addressed a letter to the people of Birmingham:

My Late Townsmen and Neighbors,

After living with you eleven years, in which you had uniform experience of my peaceful behavior in my attention to the quiet duties of my profession, and those of philosophy, I was far from expecting the injuries which I and my friends have lately received from you. . . . Happily the minds of Englishmen have a horror of *murder* and therefore you did not, I hope, think of that. . . . But what is the value of life when everything is done to make it wretched? . . .

You have destroyed the most truly valuable and useful apparatus of philosophical instruments. . . . You have destroyed a library . . . which no money can repurchase except in a long course of time. But what I feel far more, you have destroyed manuscripts which have been the result of the laborious study of many years, and which I shall never be able to recompose; and this has been done to one who never did, or imagined, you any harm.

You are mistaken if you imagine that this conduct of yours has any tendency to serve your cause, or to prejudice ours. . . . Should you destroy myself as well as my house, library, and apparatus, ten more persons, of equal or superior spirit and ability, would instantly spring up. If those ten were destroyed, an hundred would appear. . . .

In this business we are the sheep and you the wolves. We will persevere in our character, and hope you will change yours. At all events, we return you blessings for curses, and pray that you may soon return to that industry, and those sober manners, for which the inhabitants of Birmingham were formerly distinguished.

I am, your sincere well-wisher,
J. PRIESTLEY.[41]

Nevertheless he sued the city for damages, estimating his loss at £4,500; Charles James Fox helped his suit; Birmingham awarded him £2,502. He tried to establish a new domicile in England, but churchmen, royalists, and his fellows in the Royal Society shunned him.[42] The French Académie des Sciences, through its secretary, Condorcet, sent him an offer of a home and laboratory in France. On April 8, 1794, aged sixty-one, he emigrated to America. He made his new home in the town of Northumberland, in Franklin's Pennsylvania, on the banks of that lovely Susquehanna River about which Coleridge and Southey were soon to dream. He resumed his experiments, and discovered the composition of carbon monoxide. He was welcomed by learned societies, and was offered the chair in chemistry at the University of Pennsylvania. In 1796 he delivered before the Universalists of Philadelphia a series of discourses on "The Evidences of Christianity"; his audience included Vice-President John Adams and many members of Congress. From those meetings a Unitarian Society took form. Two years later Timothy Pickering, Secretary of State under President Adams, proposed to deport Priestley as an undesirable alien. The election of Jefferson (1800) ended Priestley's insecurity, and he was allowed four years of peace. In 1803 he wrote his last scientific paper, still defending phlogiston. He died at Northumberland on February 6, 1804. In 1943 the Pennsylvania legislature designated his home as a national memorial.

While Thomas Paine took up Priestley's campaign as a rebel Christian, Henry Cavendish pursued the chemistry of gases. Son of a lord, nephew of a duke, Cavendish at forty inherited one of the greatest fortunes in England. Timid, hesitant in speech, careless of dress, he lived as a recluse in his laboratory at Clapham Common, London, and made no overtures to fame. His research was distinguished by meticulous measuring and weighing of all materials before and after an experiment; these measurements enabled Lavoisier to formulate the principle that in chemical changes the amount of matter remains constant.

In 1766 Cavendish reported to the Royal Society his experiments on "factitious air"—i.e., gas derived from solids. By dissolving zinc or tin in acids he produced what he called "inflammable air"; he identified this with phlogiston; we now call it hydrogen; Cavendish was the first to recognize this as a distinct element, and to determine its specific gravity. In 1783, following up an experiment by Priestley, he found that when an electric spark was passed through a mixture of common air and "inflammable air," part of the mixture was condensed into dew; he concluded from this electrolysis that water is composed of 2.014 volumes of "inflammable air" to one volume of Priestley's "dephlogisticated air"—or, as we now say, H_2O; this was the first definite proof that water is a compound, not an element. (James Watt independently suggested the same composition of water in that same year 1783.) Again applying an electric spark to a mixture of hydrogen with common air, Cavendish obtained nitric acid, and concluded that pure air is composed of oxygen and nitrogen. (Daniel Rutherford of Edinburgh had discovered nitrogen as a distinct element in 1772.) Cavendish admitted a small residue which he could not explain, but which he calculated to be 0.83 per cent of the original amount. This remained a mystery till 1894, when Rayleigh and Ramsay isolated this part, now called argon, as a separate element, and found it to be by weight 0.94 per cent common air. Cavendish's scales were justified.

3. Lavoisier

Meanwhile, across the Channel, a group of enthusiastic researchers gave France the lead in the new science, and gave chemistry essentially the form that it has today. At their source stood Guillaume Rouelle, distinguished for his work on the chemistry of salts, but best known for the lecture courses in which he taught chemistry to rich and poor, to Diderot and Rousseau, and to the greatest chemist of them all.

Antoine Lavoisier had the advantage or handicap of being born to wealth

(1743). His father, an advocate in the Paris Parlement, gave the boy all the education then available, and bequeathed to him, then twenty-three years old, 300,000 livres. Such a fortune could have aborted a literary career, but it was a help in a science that demanded expensive apparatus and long years of preparation. Sent to a law school, Antoine escaped from it into mathematics and astronomy, and attended Rouelle's lectures in the auditorium of the Jardin du Roi. Nevertheless he completed his law studies, and then accompanied Jean Guettard in making mineralogical tours and maps of France. In 1768 he was elected to the Académie des Sciences, which at that time included Buffon, Quesnay, Turgot, and Condorcet. A year later he joined the farmers general in their unpopular business of collecting excise taxes to reimburse themselves for their advances to the government. He paid 520,000 livres for a third interest in one of the sixty shares of the *ferme générale;* in 1770 he raised this to a full share. In 1771 he married Marie Paulze, daughter of a rich farmer general. He spent part of his time now in traveling through the provinces, collecting revenue, tax data, and geological specimens. His wealth financed a great laboratory and costly experiments,* but it brought him to the guillotine.

He took an active part in public affairs. Appointed (1775) *régisseur des poudres,* commissioner of gunpowder, he increased the production and improved the quality of that explosive, making possible its large-scale export to the American colonies and the victories of the French Revolutionary armies. "French gunpowder," said Lavoisier in 1789, "has become the best in Europe. . . . One can say with truth that to it North America owes its liberty."[43] He served on a variety of official boards, national or municipal, and met with versatile intelligence diverse problems of taxation, coinage, banking, scientific agriculture, and public charity. As a member of the provincial assembly at Orléans (1787) he labored to better economic and social conditions. During the critical food shortage of 1788 he advanced his own money to several towns for the purchase of grain. He was a public-spirited man who kept on making money.

Amid all these activities he did not cease to be a scientist. His laboratory became the most complex and extensive before the nineteenth century: 250 instruments, thirteen thousand glass containers, thousands of chemical preparations, and three precision balances that later helped to determine the gram as the unit of weight in the metric system. Weighing and measuring were half the secret of Lavoisier's discoveries; through them he changed chemistry from a qualitative theory to a quantitative science. It was by

---

* In one of his early experiments he burned two diamonds to prove that the sole product of their combustion was carbon dioxide. As this was also the only product of completely burned charcoal, Lavoisier in this way proved the chemical identity of charcoal and diamonds as forms of pure carbon.

careful weighing that he proved Stahl's phlogiston to be an encumbering myth. That myth had assumed the existence of a mysterious substance which in combustion left the burning material and entered the air. On November 1, 1772, Lavoisier submitted to the Académie des Sciences a note that read:

> About eight days ago I discovered that sulfur in burning, far from losing weight, rather gains it; that is to say, that from a pound of sulfur may be obtained more than a pound of vitriolic acid, allowance being made for the moisture of the air. It is the same in the case of phosphorus. The gain in weight comes from the prodigious quantity of air which is fixed [i.e., absorbed by the burning matter] during the combustion, and combines with the [vitriolic] vapors. This discovery, which I have established by experiments that I consider decisive, has made me believe that what is observed in the combustion of sulfur and phosphorus may equally well take place in the case of all those bodies which gain weight on combustion or calcination.[44]

Instead of the burning material giving something to the air, it took something *from* the air. What was this something?

In the fall of 1774 Lavoisier published an account of further experiments. He put a weighed quantity of tin into a weighed flask large enough to contain considerable air; he sealed the flask, and heated the whole till the tin had been well oxidized. Having allowed the system to cool, he found that its weight remained unchanged. But when he broke the seal air rushed into the flask, indicating that a partial vacuum had been created in the flask. How? Lavoisier saw no other explanation except that the burning tin had absorbed into itself a part of the air. What was this something?

In October, 1774, Lavoisier met Priestley in Paris. Priestley told him of the experiments he had made in August, which Priestley still interpreted as showing an escape of phlogiston from the burned substance into the air. On April 26, 1775, Lavoisier read to the Académie a memoir reporting the experiments that had led him to view combustion as the absorption, by a burning substance, of a mysterious element from the air, which he provisionally called *air éminemment pur*. Like Priestley, he had discovered oxygen; unlike Priestley, he had overthrown the phlogiston myth. Not till 1779 did he coin, for the combustible element in the air, the name *oxygène*, from Greek words meaning "acid-generator," for Lavoisier mistakenly believed that oxygen was an indispensable constituent of all acids.

Like Priestley, Lavoisier observed that the kind of air absorbed by metals in combustion is also the kind that best supports animal life. On May 3, 1777, he presented to the Académie a paper "On the Respiration of Animals." "Five sixths of the air we breathe," he reported, "is incapable of supporting the respiration of animals, or ignition and combustion; . . . one fifth only of the volume of atmospheric air is respirable." He added that "an air which has for some time served to support this vital function has much in common with that in which metals have been calcined [oxidized]; knowledge of the one [process] may naturally be applied to the other." Lavoisier thereupon founded organic analysis by describing respiration as the combination of oxygen with organic matter. In this process he noted a liberation of heat, as in combustion; and he further confirmed the analogy of respiration and combustion by showing that carbon dioxide and water are given off (as in respiration) by the burning of such organic substances as sugar, oil, and wax. The science of physiology was now revolutionized by the spreading interpretation of organic processes in physicochemical terms.

The multiplication of experiments, the growth of chemical knowledge, and the abandonment of the phlogiston theory required a new formulation, and a new nomenclature, for the burgeoning science. The Académie des Sciences appointed Lavoisier, Guyton de Morveau, Fourcroy, and Berthollet to attempt this task. In 1787 they published *Méthode d'une nomenclature chimique*. Old-fashioned names like *powder of algaroth*, *butter of arsenic*, and *flowers of zinc* were discarded; *dephlogisticated air* became *oxygen; phlogisticated air* became *azote*, then *nitrogen; inflammable gas* became *hydrogen; fixed air* became *carbon acid gas; calcination* became *oxidation*, compounds were named from their components. A table of "simple substances" listed thirty-two elements known to Lavoisier; chemists now list ninety-eight. Most of the terms adopted in the *Méthode* are standard in chemical terminology today. Lavoisier presented the new nomenclature, and summed up the new science, in his *Traité élémentaire de chimie*; this appeared in 1789, and marked another revolution—the end of Stahl's phlogiston and Aristotle's elements.

Lavoisier himself was a victim of the French Revolution. He had shared in the efforts to avoid it, and in the evils that brought it on. In the decade that prepared it he served zealously on commissions to study and correct abuses in prisons and hospitals. To Comptroller General Laurent de Villedeuil he presented (1787) a memoir listing nine factors in the exploitation of the peasantry. His words were especially honorable coming from a millionaire owner of land:

> Let us be bold enough to say that . . . until the reign of Louis XVI the people counted for nothing in France; it was only the power, the authority, and the wealth of the state that were considered; the happiness of the people, the liberty and well-being of the individual, were words that never fell upon the ears of our former rulers, who were not

aware that the real object of government must be to increase the sum total of enjoyment, happiness, and welfare of all its subjects. . . . The unfortunate farmer groans in his cottage, unrepresented and unde- fended, his interests cared for by none of the great departments of the national administration.[45]

Lavoisier was chosen to represent the Third Estate at the provincial as- sembly that met at Orléans in 1787. There he offered a measure for abolish- ing the *corvée* and for maintaining the roads not by the forced labor of the peasantry but by taxes levied on *all* classes; the nobility and the clergy de- feated this proposal. He recommended a system of social security by which all Frenchmen who so wished would contribute to support their old age; this too was defeated. In a memoir addressed to the government in 1785 he laid down the principle that the coming States-General should have full legislative power, the king to be merely its executive agent; that it should be convoked regularly; that taxation should be universal, and the press free:[46] Lavoisier was unquestionably one of the most enlightened members of the French bourgeoisie, and probably his proposals expressed part of its political strategy.

He was also one of the leading members of the *ferme générale*, which was the object of almost universal resentment. From 1768 to 1786 his profits as a farmer general had averaged 66,667 livres per year, an annual rate of 8.28 per cent; he may have been right in considering this a reasonable return for the labor and risks involved. It was at his suggestion that chief minister Calonne, in 1783–87, built a wall around Paris to check the smugglers who were evading tolls; the wall and the new customshouses and barriers cost thirty million livres, and evoked widespread condemnation; the Duc de Nivernois proclaimed that the originator of the scheme should be hanged.

Lavoisier supported the Revolution in 1789, when it was still under con- trol by the middle classes. A year later he felt that it was moving toward ex- cess, violence, and war, and he pleaded for restraint. In November some employees of the *ferme générale* published a pamphlet accusing the *ferme* of embezzling their pension fund. "Tremble," they wrote, "you who have sucked the blood of the unfortunate."[47] In 1791 Marat began a personal campaign against Lavoisier. The "Friend of the People" had published in 1780 *Recherches physiques sur le feu*, in which he claimed to have made visible the secret element in fire; Lavoisier had refused to take the claim seriously; Marat had not forgotten. In his periodical, *Ami du peuple*, January 27, 1791, Marat denounced the chemist-financier as a charlatan with a fat income, a man "whose only claim to public recognition is that he put Paris in prison by cutting off the fresh air with a wall that cost the poor 33 mil- lion livres. . . . Would to Heaven that he had been strung up to the lamp-post."[48] On March 20, 1791, the Constituent Assembly abolished the *ferme générale*.

Next to be attacked was the Académie des Sciences, for all institutions surviving from the Old Regime were suspected of counterrevolutionary sympathies. Lavoisier defended the Académie, and became the chief target. On August 8, 1793, the Académie was ordered to disband. At its last meeting the roster was signed by, among others, Lagrange, Lavoisier, Lalande, Lamarck, Berthollet, and Monge. Each now went his own way, hoping that the guillotine would not find him.

In the same month Lavoisier, inspired by the ideas of Condorcet, submitted to the Convention a plan for a national system of schools. Primary education was to be free for both sexes "as a duty that society owes to the child." Secondary education, also open to both sexes, was to be expanded by the establishment of technical colleges throughout France. A month later his rooms were ransacked by governmental agents; among the letters found there, from Lavoisier's friends, were some that condemned the Revolution and spoke hopefully of foreign armies that would soon overthrow it; other letters showed Lavoisier and his wife planning to escape to Scotland.[49] On November 24, 1793, thirty-two former farmers general, including Lavoisier, were arrested. His wife moved every influence to effect his release; she failed, but was allowed to visit him. In prison he continued to work on his exposition of the new chemistry. The financiers were accused of having charged excessive interest, of having adulterated tobacco with water, and of absorbing 130 million livres in illegal profits. On May 5, 1794, they were summoned before the Revolutionary Tribunal. Eight were acquitted; twenty-four, including Lavoisier, were condemned to death. When the presiding judge was asked to commute the sentence on the ground that Lavoisier and some others were savants of value to the state, he was reported to have answered, "The Republic has no need of savants"; but there is no convincing evidence for this tale.[50] Lavoisier was guillotined on the very day of the sentence, May 8, 1794, on what is now the Place de la Concorde. Lagrange is said to have commented, "It took only a moment to cut off his head, and a hundred years may not give us another like it."[51]

All the property of Lavoisier and his widow was confiscated to help repay the Republic for the 130,000,000 livres allegedly owed by the *ferme générale* to the state. Mme. Lavoisier, penniless, was supported by an old servant of the family. In 1795 the French government repudiated the condemnation of Lavoisier; her property was restored to Mme. Lavoisier, who survived till 1836. In October, 1795, the Lycée des Arts held a funeral service in Lavoisier's memory, with Lagrange delivering the eulogy. A bust was unveiled bearing the inscription "Victim of tyranny, respected friend of the arts, he continues to live; through his genius he still serves humanity."[52]

V. ASTRONOMY

1. Instrumental Prelude

How far did the findings of mathematics, physics, and chemistry illuminate the sky? Of all the audacities of science the most daring is the attempt to fling its measuring rods around the stars, to subject those scintillating beauties to nocturnal spying, to analyze their constituents across a billion miles, and to confine their motions to man-made logic and laws. Mind and the heavens are the poles of our wonder and study, and the greatest wonder is mind legislating for the firmament.

The farseeing instruments had been invented, the major discoveries had been made; the eighteenth century undertook to improve the instruments (Graham, Hadley, Dollond), extend the discoveries (Bradley and Herschel), apply the latest mathematics to the stars (d'Alembert and Clairaut), and organize the results in a new system of cosmic dynamics (Laplace).

The telescope was bettered and enlarged. "Equatorial telescopes" were made which turned on two axes—one parallel, the other perpendicular, to the plane of the axis of the earth; this choice of axes enabled the observer to keep a celestial object in view long enough for detailed study and micrometric measurement. Newton had been discouraged from use of the refracting telescope by the belief that light, in being refracted by lenses, must necessarily be broken up into colors, so confusing observation; he gave up the problem of making a color-free refraction, and turned to the reflecting telescope. In 1733 Chester Moor Hall, a "gentleman amateur," solved the problem by combining lenses of different refractive media, neutralizing the diversity of color. He did not publish his discovery, and John Dollond had to work out independently the principles and construction of the achromatic telescope, which he announced in the *Philosophical Transactions* of the Royal Society of London in 1758.

In 1725 George Graham, a Quaker watchmaker, made for Edmund Halley at Greenwich Observatory a mural quadrant—a mechanical quarter-circle graduated into degrees and minutes, and fixed on a wall so as to catch the transit of a star across the meridian. For Halley, James Bradley, and Pierre Lemonnier, Graham made transit instruments combining telescope, axis, clock, and chronograph, to mark such transits with greater accuracy than before. In 1730 Thomas Godfrey, a member of Franklin's intellectual circle in Philadelphia, described to his friends an instrument for measuring angles and altitudes by means of double reflection through opposed mirrors seen in a telescope; but he did not publish it till 1734. In 1730 John Hadley built a similar instrument, an octant—a graduated arc of an eighth of a circle; in 1757 this was enlarged to a sixth. By enabling a navigator to see at once, in the reflecting telescope, both the horizon and the sun (or a star), Hadley's "sextant" allowed a more precise measurement of the angle separating the objects. This, combined with Harrison's marine chronometer, made navigation an almost exact science.

To determine the position of a ship at sea the navigator had to determine the longitude and latitude. To find the longitude he had to ascertain his time at the place and moment by astronomical observation, and to compare this local time with a clock set to keep standard (Greenwich) time wherever the clock might be. The problem was to construct a chronometer that would not be affected by changes of temperature or the motions of the ship. In 1714 the British government offered twenty thousand pounds for a method of finding longitude within half a degree. John Harrison, a Yorkshire clockmaker, submitted to George Graham (1728) plans for a marine chronometer; Graham advanced the money to construct it; completed in 1735, it used two massive and opposed balances instead of a pendulum; four balance springs, moving contrary to one another, compensated for the motions of the vessel; and a manifold of brass and steel rods, expanding with heat and contracting with cold, and connected with the springs, neutralized the variations in temperature. The Board of Longitude sent Harrison with his chronometer on a test voyage to Lisbon. The results encouraged the Board to provide funds for a second, third, and fourth improvement. This fourth chronometer, only five inches wide, was tried on a voyage to the West Indies (1759); on that trip the clock lost no more than five seconds additional to its normal and precalculated loss (when stationary on land) of eighty seconds per thirty days. After some disputes Harrison received the full award of twenty thousand pounds. With this and other marine instruments, the British navy was now (at the height of the Seven Years' War, 1756–63) equipped to rule the waves.

2. Astronomic Theory

The British and French competed ardently in studying astronomy; this was no remote or "pure" science for them; it entered into the struggle for mastery of the seas, and therefore of the whole colonial and commercial world. Germany and Russia through Euler, Italy through Boscovich, contributed to the contest without sharing in the spoils.

Euler, Clairaut, and d'Alembert aided navigation by their studies of the moon, tabulating its changes of place and phase in relation to the sun and the earth, and its effects upon tides. From Euler's records Johann Tobias Mayer, at the University of Göttingen, drew up lunar tables which won a gift from the British Board of Longitude. In 1738 the Paris Académie des Sciences offered a prize for a theory of tides. Four authors received awards: Daniel Bernoulli,

Euler, Colin Maclaurin, and A. Cavallieri. All but the last based their explanations upon Newton's, adding the rotation of the earth to the attraction of the sun and the moon as a factor in determining tides. The Académie on several occasions invited essays on the perturbations of the planets—their real or apparent deviations from elliptical orbits. Clairaut's essay won the prize in 1747, Euler's in 1756.

Ruggiero Giuseppe Boscovich honored his Jesuit order by illuminating discoveries in astronomy and physics. Born in Ragusa, he entered the novitiate at Rome at fourteen, astonished his teachers at the Collegium Romanum by his precocity in science, and was appointed to the chair of mathematics there at twenty-nine. From that time onward he issued sixty-six publications. He shared in determining the general orbit of comets, and gave the first geometric solution for finding the orbit and equator of a planet. In his treatise *De materiae divisibilitate* (1748) he expounded his view of matter as composed of points, or fields, of force, each a center alternately of repulsion and attraction—a theory recalling Leibniz' monads and prefiguring the atomic hypotheses of our time. The versatile Jesuit organized practical enterprises—surveying and mapping the Papal States, damming the lakes that threatened to submerge Lucca, making plans to drain the Pontine Marshes, and helping to design the Brera Observatory at Milan. At his urging, in 1757, Pope Benedict XIV abrogated the decree of the Index Expurgatorius against the Copernican system. He was given membership in the Paris Académie des Sciences and the London Royal Society. In 1761–62 he was received with honors in France, England, Poland, and Turkey. In 1772 he accepted appointment by Louis XV as director of optics in the French navy. He returned to Italy in 1783, and died at Milan in 1787, at the age of seventy-six. He left behind him several volumes of poetry.

The most brilliant luminary among British astronomers in the first half of the eighteenth century was James Bradley. His uncle, James Pound, a rector at Wanstead in Essex, was an amateur astronomer, with an observatory of his own; there the boy learned that there was a science as well as an aesthetic of the stars. After taking his M.A. at Oxford, Bradley hurried back to Wanstead, made original observations, reported them to the Royal Society, and was elected to its membership at the age of twenty-six (1718). Three years later he became Savilian professor of astronomy at Oxford. When the great Halley died, in 1742, Bradley was appointed to succeed him at Greenwich as astronomer royal. In that post he remained till his death (1762).

His first major enterprise was to determine the annual parallax of a star—i.e., the difference in its apparent direction as seen (1) from a point on the surface of the earth, and (2) from an imaginary point at the center of the sun.

If, as Copernicus had supposed, the earth revolved in orbit around the sun, such a difference should exist; none had been demonstrated; if it could be proved it would corroborate Copernicus. The omniventurous Robert Hooke had tried (1669) to show such a parallax in the case of the star gamma Draconis; he had failed. Samuel Molyneux, a moneyed amateur, resumed the attempt in 1725 at Kew; Bradley joined him there; their results only partly confirmed the Copernican hypothesis. Bradley returned to Wanstead, and engaged George Graham to construct for him a "zenith sector" telescope enabling him to observe not one star but two hundred stars in their transit across the meridian. After thirteen months of observation and calculation, Bradley was able to show an annual cycle of alternating southward and northward deviations in the apparent position of the same star; and he explained this alternation as due to the earth's orbital motion. This discovery of the "aberration of light" (1729) explained hundreds of hitherto puzzling observations and deviations; it made a revolutionary distinction between the observed position and the "real," or calculated, position of any star; it agreed handsomely with Copernicus, since it depended upon the revolution of the earth around the sun. Its effect upon astronomy was so illuminating that a French astronomer-historian, Joseph Delambre, proposed to rank Bradley with Kepler, even with Hipparchus himself.[53]

Bradley went on to his second major discovery: the "nutation"—literally the nodding—of the earth's axis of rotation, like the axial vacillation of a spinning top. The stars whose apparent motions had been described as performing an annual cycle, due to the revolution of the earth around the sun, did not, in Bradley's observations, return, after a year, to precisely the same apparent positions as before. It occurred to him that the discrepancy might be due to a slight bending of the earth's axis by periodic changes in the relation between the moon's orbit around the earth and the earth's orbit around the sun. He studied these changes through nineteen years (1728–47); at the end of the nineteenth year he found that the stars had returned to exactly the same apparent positions they had had at the beginning of the first year. He felt certain now that the nutation of the earth's axis was due to the orbital motion of the moon, and its action upon the equatorial parts of the earth. His report of these findings was an exciting event in the proceedings of the Royal Society for 1748. Patience has its heroes as well as war.

During Bradley's tenure as astronomer royal, Britain submitted to a painful operation: after 170 years of resistance it accepted the Gregorian calendar, but obstinately named it the Reformed calendar. An act of Parliament (1750) ordered that the eleven days following the second of September, 1752, were to be omitted from the "New Style"; that September 3 was to be called September 14; and that the legal year should thereafter begin not on March 25 but on January 1. This involved complications in business dealings and ecclesiastical holydays; it stirred many protests, and angry Britons demanded, "Give us back our eleven days!"[54]—but in the end science triumphed over bookkeeping and theology.

3. Herschel

English astronomy reached its peak when William Herschel added Uranus to the planets and abandoned his career as a musician. His father* was a musician in the Hanoverian army; the son, born in Hanover in 1738 and named Friedrich Wilhelm, adopted his father's profession, and served as musician in the first campaign of the Seven Years' War; but his health was so delicate (he lived to be almost eighty-four) that he was released. In 1757 he was sent to England to seek his fortune in music. At Bath, which then rivaled London as a center of fashionable society, he rose from oboist to conductor to organist in the Octagon Chapel. He composed, taught music, and sometimes gave thirty-five lessons in a week. At night he unbent by studying calculus; thence he passed to optics, finally to astronomy. He brought over from Germany his brother Jacob and, in 1772, his sister Caroline, who managed their household, learned to keep astronomical records, and at last became an astronomer in her own right.

Fired with ambition to chart the skies, Herschel, helped by his brother, made his own telescope. He ground and polished the lenses himself, and on one occasion he continued this operation uninterrupted for sixteen hours, Caroline feeding him as he worked, or relieving the tedium by reading to him from Cervantes, Fielding, or Sterne. This was the first of several telescopes made by Herschel or under his supervision. In 1774, aged thirty-six, he made his first observation, but for many years yet he could give to astronomy only such time as was left him by his work as a musician. Four times he studied every part of the heavens. In the second of these cosmic tours, on March 14, 1781, he made his epochal discovery, whose importance he vastly underestimated:

> In examining the small stars in the neighborhood of H. Geminorum I perceived one that appeared visibly larger than the rest. Being struck with its uncommon appearance, I compared it to H. Geminorum and the small star in the quartile between Auriga and Gemini; and finding it so much larger than either of them, I suspected it to be a comet.[55]

---

* The name Herschel is typically Jewish, and the astronomer's first biographer, E. S. Holden, thought that the father, who was named Isaac, was Jewish. The evidence is inconclusive. The boy received Christian baptism at an early age. Cf. *The Jewish Encyclopedia*, VI, 362d, and Cecil Roth, *The Jewish Contributions to Civilization*, 189.

It was not a comet; continued scrutiny soon showed that it revolved around the sun in an almost circular orbit, nineteen times greater than the orbit of the earth, and twice that of Saturn; it was a new planet, the first so recognized in the written records of astronomy. All the learned world acclaimed the discovery, which doubled the diameter of the solar system as previously known. The Royal Society awarded Herschel a fellowship and the Copley Medal; George III persuaded him to give up his career as a musician and become astronomer to the King. Herschel named the new planet Georgium Sidus (Star of the Georges); but astronomers later agreed to call it Uranus, taking it away from the Hanoverian kings and surrendering it, like nearly all its fellows, to the pagan gods.

In 1781 William and Caroline moved to Slough, a pretty town on the way from London to Windsor. His modest salary of two hundred pounds a year could not support him, his sister, and his instruments; he added to it by making and selling telescopes. For himself he built them even larger, until in 1785 he made one forty feet long, with a mirror four feet in diameter. Fanny Burney, daughter of the musician-historian whom we have often quoted, wrote in her diary under December 30, 1786:

> This morning my dear father carried me [i.e., drove her, for she was thirty-six] to Dr. Herschel. This great and very extraordinary man received us with almost open arms. . . . By the invitation of Mr. Herschel I took a walk . . . through his telescope! and it held me quite upright, and without the least inconvenience; so would it have done had I been dressed in feathers and a bell-hoop—such is its circumference.[56]

In 1787 Herschel discovered two satellites of Uranus, which he named Oberon and Titania; in 1789 he found the sixth and seventh satellites of Saturn. In 1788 he married a wealthy widow; he no longer had to worry about money, but he continued his investigations with undiminished fervor. Usually he worked all through those nights when the stars were out and were not dimmed by too bright a moon. Most of his observations were made in the open air from a platform reached by a fifty-foot ladder. Sometimes the cold was so severe that the ink froze in the bottle that Caroline took with her to record his findings.

Carrying on more systematically, and with better telescopes, the work of Charles Messier and Nicolas de Lacaille in locating and listing nebulae and star clusters, Herschel submitted to the Royal Society (1782–1802) catalogues of 2,500 nebulae and clusters, and 848 double stars. Of these 848 he had himself discovered 227. He suggested that they might be paired in mutual gravitation and revolution—an illuminating application of Newton's theory to interstellar relations. In many cases what had looked like one star turned out to be a cluster of individual stars, and some of these clusters, seen in the larger telescopes, proved to be separate stars at vastly different distances from the earth. The Milky Way, in the new magnification, was transformed from a cloud of glowing matter into an immense aggregation and succession of single luminaries. Now the sky, which had seemed to be merely studded with stars, appeared to be crowded with them almost as thickly as drops of water in the rain. And whereas the unaided human eye had seen only stars of the first to the sixth magnitude, Herschel's telescopes revealed additional stars 1,342 times fainter than the brightest. Like Galileo, Herschel had immensely expanded the known universe. If Pascal had trembled before the "infinity" of the heavens known to his time, what would he have felt before this endless depth beyond depth of stars beyond counting, some, said Herschel, "11,750,000,000,000,000,000,000,000 miles" from the earth?[57] Many of the stars were suns with planets revolving about them. Our own sun and its planets and their satellites were collectively reduced to a speck in a cosmos of light.

One of Herschel's most brilliant suggestions related to the motion of our solar system through space. Previous observations had indicated that certain associated stars had, in recorded time, decreased or increased their divergence from each other. He wondered might not this variation be due to the motion of the solar system away from the converging—or toward the diverging—stars, as two lamps on opposite sides of a street will seem to converge or diverge as we leave or approach them. He concluded that the solar system as a whole was moving away from certain stars, and toward a star in the constellation Hercules. He published his hypothesis in 1783; a few months later Pierre Prévost announced a similar theory. The rival groups of astronomers, English and French, were in eager competition and close accord.

A contemporary described Herschel, in his eighty-second year, as "a great, simple, good old man. His simplicity, his kindness, his anecdotes, his readiness to explain his own sublime conceptions of the universe, are indescribably charming."[58] In all his work Caroline shared with a devotion as beautiful as in any romance. Not only did she keep careful records of his observations, and make complicated mathematical calculations to guide him, but she herself discovered three nebulae and eight comets. After William's death (1822) she returned to live with her relatives in Hanover; there she kept up her studies, and catalogued still further the findings of her brother. In 1828 she received the gold medal of the Astronomical Society, and in 1846 a medal from the King of Prussia. She died in 1848, in her ninety-eighth year.

4. Some French Astronomers

Around the Paris Observatory (completed in 1671) there gathered a galaxy of stargazers, in which the Cassini family formed through four generations a successive constellation. Giovanni Domenico Cassini directed the Observatory from 1671 to 1712. Dying, he was succeeded as director by his son Jacques, who was succeeded (1756) by *his* son César François Cassini de Thury, who in turn was succeeded (1784) by his son Jacques Dominique, who died as the Comte de Cassini in 1845 at the age of ninety-seven. Here was a family worthy to be named with the Bernoullis and the Bachs.

Jean Le Rond d'Alembert had no family, either before or after, but he gathered sciences around him as one would gather children. Applying his mathematics to astronomy, he reduced to law Newton's theory of the precession of the equinoxes, and Bradley's hypothesis of the axial nutation of the earth. "The discovery of these results," said Laplace, "was in Newton's time beyond the means of analysis and mechanics. . . . The honor of doing this was reserved to d'Alembert. A year and a half after the publication in which Bradley presented his discovery, d'Alembert offered his treatise [*Recherches sur la précession des équinoxes* (1749)], a work as remarkable in the history of celestial mechanics and dynamics as that of Bradley in the annals of astronomy."[59]

It is a blot on d'Alembert's record that he did not enjoy the successes of his rivals—but which of us has risen to such saintly delight? He criticized with special zeal the work of Alexis Clairaut. At ten Alexis knew infinitesimal calculus; at twelve he submitted his first paper to the Académie des Sciences; at eighteen he published a book containing such important additions to geometry as won him adjoint membership in the Académie (1731), at an age six years younger than d'Alembert was to be on receiving the same honor in 1741. Clairaut was among the scientists chosen to accompany Maupertuis on the expedition to Lapland (1736) for measuring an arc of the meridian. Returning, he presented to the Académie memoirs on geometry, algebra, conic sections, and calculus. He published in 1743 his *Théorie de la figure de la terre*, which calculated, by "Clairaut's theorem," and more precisely than Newton or Maclaurin had done, the form that a rotating body mechanically assumes from the natural gravitation of its parts. His interest in Newton brought him into touch with Mme. du Châtelet; he helped her with her translation of the *Principia*, and shared with Voltaire the honor of converting French scientists from Descartes' vortices to Newton's gravitation.

In 1746–49 Euler, Clairaut, and d'Alembert worked independently to find, by the new methods of calculus, the apogee of the moon—its moment of maximum distance from the earth; Euler and Clairaut published approximately the same results; d'Alembert followed with a still more accurate computation. A prize offered by the Academy of St. Petersburg for charting the moon's motion was won by Clairaut, who published his results in *Théorie de la lune* (1752). Next he applied his mathematics to the perturbations of the earth due to Venus and the moon; from these variations he estimated the mass of Venus to be 66.7 per cent, and that of the moon as 1.49 per cent, that of the earth; our current figures are 81.5 and 1.82 per cent.

In 1757 the astronomers of Europe began to look out for the return of the comet that Halley had predicted. To guide their observations Clairaut undertook to compute the perturbations the comet would have suffered in passing by Saturn and Jupiter. He calculated that these and other experiences had retarded it by 618 days, and advised the Académie des Sciences that the comet would be at perihelion (its point nearest the sun) about April 13, 1759. An amateur watcher discerned it on Christmas Day, 1758; it passed perihelion on March 12, 1759, thirty-two days earlier than Clairaut's reckoning. Even so the event was a triumph for science and a transient blow to superstition.* Clairaut presented his studies on the subject in *Théorie du mouvement des comètes* (1760). His successes, and his great personal charm, made him a prize catch for the rival salons. He attended them frequently, and died at fifty-two (1765). "No French savant of this age merited a higher renown."[60]

There were many more whom history should commemorate, though it would spoil the story to tell all. There was Joseph Delisle, who studied the spots and corona of the sun, and founded the St. Petersburg Observatory; and Nicolas de Lacaille, who went to the Cape of Good Hope for the Académie des Sciences, spent ten years (1750–60) charting southern skies, and died of overwork at forty-nine; and Pierre Lemonnier, who went with Maupertuis to Lapland at twenty-one, carried on studies of the moon through fifty years, analyzed the motions of Jupiter and Saturn, and observed and recorded Uranus (1768–69) long before Herschel discovered it to be a planet (1781). And Joseph de Lalande, whose *Traité de l'astronomie* (1764) surveyed every branch of the science, taught it at the Collège de France for forty-six years, and established in 1802 the Lalande Prize, which is still given annually for the best contribution to astronomy. And Jean Baptiste Delambre, who determined the orbit of Uranus, succeeded Lalande at the Collège, and added to Lalande's ecumenical exposition a history of astronomy in six painstaking volumes (1817–27).

---

* Halley's comet is expected again in 1986.

5. *Laplace*

He was born (1749) Pierre Simon Laplace, of a middle-class family in Normandy, and became the Marquis Pierre Simon de Laplace. He made his first mark by his pious theological essays in school, and became the most confirmed atheist of Napoleonic France. At the age of eighteen he was sent to Paris with a letter of introduction to d'Alembert. D'Alembert, who received many such letters and discounted their encomiums, refused to see him. Resolute, Laplace addressed to him a letter on the general principles of mechanics. D'Alembert responded: "Monsieur, you see that I paid little attention to recommendations. You need none; you have introduced yourself better. That is enough for me. My support is your due."[61] Soon, through d'Alembert's influence, Laplace was appointed teacher of mathematics at the École Militaire. In a later letter to d'Alembert he analyzed his own passion for mathematics:

I have always cultivated mathematics by taste rather than from desire for a vain reputation. My greatest amusement is to study the march of the inventors, to see their genius at grips with the obstacles they have encountered and overcome. I then put myself in their place, and ask myself how I should have gone about surmounting these same obstacles; and although this substitution in the great majority of instances has been humiliating to my self-love, nevertheless the pleasure of rejoicing in their success has amply repaid me for this little humiliation. If I am fortunate enough to add something to their works, I attribute all the merit to their first efforts.[62]

We detect some pride in this conscious modesty. In any case Laplace's ambition was grandly immodest, for he undertook to reduce the entire universe to one mathematical system by applying to all celestial bodies and phenomena the Newtonian theory of gravitation. Newton had left the cosmos in a precarious condition: it was, he thought, subject to irregularities that mounted in time, so that God had to intervene now and then to set it right again. Many scientists, like Euler, were not convinced that the world was a mechanism. Laplace proposed to prove it mechanically.

He began (1773) with a paper showing that the variations in the mean distances of each planet from the sun were subject to nearly precise mathematical formulation, and were therefore periodic and mechanical; for this paper the Académie des Sciences elected him to associate membership at the age of twenty-four. Henceforth Laplace, with a unity, direction, and persistence of purpose characteristic of great men, devoted his life to reducing one after another operation of the universe to mathematical equations. "All the effects of nature," he wrote, "are only the mathematical consequences of a small number of immutable laws."[63]

Though his major works did not appear till after the Revolution, their preparation had begun long before. His *Exposition du système du monde* (1796) was a popular and nonmechanical introduction to his views, notable for its lucid and fluent style, and embodying his famous hypothesis (anticipated by Kant in 1755) as to the origin of the solar system. Laplace proposed to explain the revolution and rotation of the planets and their satellites by postulating a primeval nebula of hot gases, or other minute particles, enveloping the sun and extending to the farthest reaches of the solar system. This nebula, rotating with the sun, gradually cooled, and contracted into rings perhaps like those now seen around Saturn. Further cooling and contraction condensed these rings into planets, which then, by a similar process, evolved their own satellites; and a like condensation of nebulae may have produced the stars. Laplace assumed that all planets and satellites revolved in the same direction, and practically in the same plane; he did not know, at the time, that the satellites of Uranus move in a contrary direction. This "nebular hypothesis" is now rejected as an explanation of the solar system, but is widely accepted as explaining the condensation of stars out of nebulae. Laplace expounded it only in his popular work, and did not take it too seriously. "These conjectures on the formation of the stars and the solar system . . . I present with all the distrust [*défiance*] which everything that is not a result of observation or of calculation ought to inspire."[64]

Laplace summed up his observations, equations, and theories—and nearly all the starry science of his time—in the five stately volumes of his *Mécanique céleste* (1799–1825), which Jean Baptiste Fourier called the *Almagest* of modern astronomy. He stated his aim with sublime simplicity: "given the eighteen known bodies of the solar system, and their positions and motions at any time, to deduce from their mutual gravitation, by . . . mathematical calculation, their positions and motions at any other time; and to show that these agree with those actually observed." To realize his plan Laplace had to study the perturbations caused by the cross-influences of the members—sun, planets, and satellites—of the solar system, and reduce these to periodic and predictable regularity. All these perturbations, he believed, could be explained by the mathematics of gravitation. In this attempt to prove the stability and self-sufficiency of the solar system, and of the rest of the world, Laplace assumed a completely mechanistic view, and gave a classic expression to the deterministic philosophy:

> We ought to regard the present state of the universe as the effect of its antecedent state, and as the cause of the state that is to follow. An intelligence knowing all the forces acting in nature at a given instant,

as well as the momentary positions of all things in the universe, would be able to comprehend in one single formula the motions of the largest bodies as well as of the lightest atoms in the world, provided that its intellect were sufficiently powerful to subject all data to analysis; to it nothing would be uncertain, the future as well as the past would be present to its eyes. [*Cf.* the Scholastic conception of God.] The perfection that the human mind has been able to give to astronomy affords a feeble outline of such an intelligence. Discoveries in mechanics and geometry, coupled with those in universal gravitation, have brought the mind within reach of comprehending in the same analytical formulas the past and the future state of the system of the world. All the mind's efforts in the search for truth tend to approximate to the intelligence we have just imagined, although it will forever remain infinitely remote from such an intelligence.[65]

When Napoleon asked Laplace why his *Mécanique céleste* had made no mention of God, the scientist is said to have replied, "*Je n'avais pas besoin de cette hypothèse-là*" (I had no need of that hypothesis).[66] But Laplace had his modest moments. In his *Théorie analytique des probabilités* (1812) —which is the basis of nearly all later work in that field—he deprived science of all certainty:

> Strictly speaking, one may even say that nearly all our knowledge is problematical; and in the small number of things which we are able to know with certainty, even in the mathematical sciences themselves, induction and analogy, the principal means for discovering truth, are based on probabilities.[67]*

In addition to his epochal and widely influential formulation of astronomical discoveries and hypotheses to his date, Laplace made specific contributions. He illuminated nearly every department of physics with the "Laplace equations" for a "potential," which made it easier to ascertain the intensity of energy, or the velocity of motion, at any point in a field of lines of force. He calculated the earth's dynamical ellipticity from those perturbations of the moon which were ascribed to the oblate form of our globe. He developed an analytical theory of the tides, and from their phenomena he deduced the mass of the moon. He found an improved method for determining the orbit of comets. He discovered the numerical relations between the movements of Jupiter's satellites. He computed with characteristic precision the secular (century-long) acceleration of the moon's mean motion.

---

* "Even in the classical [Newtonian] mechanics Laplace's proof of the stability of the solar system is no longer considered conclusive. . . . No rigorous answer has been given."— Florian Cajori in notes to Newton's *Mathematical Principles of Natural Philosophy*, p. 678.

His studies of the moon provided the basis for the improved tables of lunar motions drawn up in 1812 by his pupil Jean Charles Burckhardt. And finally he rose from science to philosophy—from knowledge to wisdom— in a flight of eloquence worthy of Buffon:

> Astronomy, by the dignity of its object matter and the perfection of its theories, is the fairest monument of the human spirit, the noblest testimony of human intelligence. Seduced by self-love and the illusions of his senses, man for a long time regarded himself as the center in the movement of the stars, and his vain arrogance was punished by the terrors that these inspired. Then he saw himself on a planet almost imperceptible in the solar system, whose vast extent is itself but an insensible point in the immensity of space. The sublime results to which this discovery has led him are well fitted to console him for the rank that it assigns to the earth, in showing him his own grandeur in the extreme minuteness of the base from which he measures the stars. Let him preserve with care, and augment, the results of these noble sciences, which are the delight of thinking beings. Those sciences have rendered important services to navigation and geography, but their greatest blessing has been to dissipate the fears produced by celestial phenomena, and to destroy the errors born from ignorance of our true relations with nature, errors and fears that will readily be reborn if the torch of science is ever extinguished.[68]

Laplace found it easier to adjust his life to the convulsions of French politics than his mathematics to the irregularities of the stars. When the Revolution came he weathered it by being more valuable alive than dead: with Lagrange he was employed to manufacture saltpeter for gunpowder and to calculate trajectories for cannon balls. He was made a member of the commission for weights and measures that formulated the metric system. In 1785 he had examined and passed, as a candidate for an artillery corps, the sixteen-year-old Bonaparte; in 1798 General Bonaparte took him to Egypt to study the stars from the Pyramids. In 1799 the First Consul appointed him minister of the interior; after six weeks he dismissed him because "Laplace sought subtleties everywhere, . . . and carried the spirit of the infinitely small into administration."[69] To console him Bonaparte nominated him to the new Senate, and made him a count. Now, in the gold and lace of his rank, his portrait was painted by Jacques André Naigeon: a handsome and noble face, eyes saddened as if with the consciousness that death mocks all majesty, that astronomy is a groping in the dark, and that science is a speck of light in a sea of night. On his deathbed (1827) all vanity left him, and almost his last words were: "That which we know is but a little thing; that which we do not know is immense."[70]

VI. ABOUT THE EARTH

Four sciences studied the earth: meteorology explored its envelope of weather; geodesy estimated its size, shape, density, and such distances as involved its surface curvature; geology delved into its composition, depths, and history; geography charted its lands and seas.

1. Meteorology

Besides the simple rain gauge, the science of weather used four measuring instruments: the thermometer for temperature, the barometer for atmospheric pressure, the anemometer for winds, the hygrometer for moisture in the air.

In or before 1721 Gabriel Daniel Fahrenheit, a German instrument maker in Amsterdam, developed the thermometer, which Galileo had invented in 1603; Fahrenheit used mercury instead of water as the expanding-contracting fluid, and divided the scale into degrees based upon the freezing point of water (32°) and the oral temperature of the normal human body (98.6°). In 1730 René de Réaumur reported to the Académie des Sciences "rules for constructing thermometers with comparable gradations"; he took the freezing point of water as zero, and its boiling point as 80°, and he graduated the scale to make the degrees correspond to equal increments in the rise or fall of the thermometric fluid, for which he used alcohol. Anders Celsius of Uppsala, about 1742, improved Réaumur's thermometer by returning to the use of mercury, and dividing the scale into a hundred "centigrade" degrees between the freezing and the boiling points of water. By determining these points more precisely, Jean André Deluc of Geneva, in 1772, gave the rival thermometers essentially the form they have today: the Fahrenheit form for English-speaking peoples, the centigrade form for others.

The barometer had been invented by Torricelli in 1643, but its readings of atmospheric pressure were made uncertain by factors for which he had not allowed: the quality of the mercury, the bore of the tube, and the temperature of the air. Various researches, culminating in the experiments and calculations of Deluc (1717–1817), remedied these defects, and brought the mercury barometer into its current form.

Divers crude anemometers were made in the seventeenth century. At his death in 1721 Pierre Huet, the scholarly bishop of Avranches, left a design for an anemometer (the word was apparently his invention) that would measure the force of the wind by funneling it into a tube where its pressure would raise a column of mercury. This was improved by the "wind gauge" (1775) of the Scottish physician James Lind. John Smeaton devised (c. 1750) a mechanism for measuring wind velocity. The best eighteenth-century instrument for measuring moisture was the hygrometer of the versatile Genevan Horace de Saussure (1783), which was based upon the expansion and contraction of a human hair by changes in humidity. William Cullen provided a basis for another type of hygrometer by noting the cooling effect of fluids in evaporation.

With these and other instruments, such as the magnetic needle, science strove to detect regularities in the vagaries of weather. The first requisite was reliable records. Some had been kept for France by the Académie des Sciences since 1688. From 1717 to 1727 a Breslau physician kept daily records of weather reports which he had solicited from many parts of Germany; and in 1724 the Royal Society of London began to compile meteorological reports not only from Britain but also from the Continent, India, and North America. A still wider and more systematic co-ordination of daily reports was organized in 1780 by J. J. Hemmer at Mannheim, under the patronage of the Elector Palatine Charles Theodore; but this was abandoned (1792) during the wars of the French Revolution.

One meteorological phenomenon that sparked much speculation was the aurora borealis. Edmund Halley carefully studied the outbursts of these "northern lights" on March 16–17, 1716, and ascribed them to magnetic influences emanating from the earth. In 1741 Hjorter and other Scandinavian observers noted that irregular variations of the compass needle occurred at the time of the displays. In 1793 John Dalton, the chemist, pointed out that the streamers of the lights are parallel to the dipping needle, and that their vertex, or point of convergence, lies in the magnetic meridian. The eighteenth century, therefore, recognized the electrical nature of the phenomenon, which is now interpreted as an electrical discharge in the earth's atmosphere, due to ionization caused by particles shot out from the sun.

The literature of meteorology in the eighteenth century began with Christian von Wolff's *Aerometricae elementa* (1709), which summed up the known data to date, and suggested some new instruments. D'Alembert attempted a mathematical formulation of wind motions in *Réflexions sur la cause générale des vents*, which won a prize offered by the Berlin Academy in 1747. The outstanding treatise in this period was the massive *Traité de météorologie* (1774) by Louis Cotte, a priest of Montmorency. Cotte gathered and tabulated the results of his own and other observations, described instruments, and applied his findings to agriculture; he gave the flowering and maturation time of various crops, the dates at which swallows came and went, and when the nightingale could be expected to sing; he regarded the winds as the chief causes of changes in the weather; and finally he offered tentative formulas for weather forecasts. Jean Deluc's *Recherches sur les modifications de l'atmosphère* (1772) extended the experiments of Pascal (1648) and Halley (1686) on the relations between altitude and atmospheric pressure, and formulated the law that "at a certain temperature the differences between the logarithms of the heights of the mercury [in the barometer] give immediately, in thousandths of a fathom, the difference in heights of the places where the barometer was observed."[71] By attaching a level to his barometer, Deluc was able to estimate barometrically the altitude of various landmarks; so he calculated the height of Mont Blanc as 14,346 feet above sea level. Horace de Saussure, after ascending the mountain and taking barometric readings at its peak (1787), obtained a measurement of 15,700 feet.

2. Geodesy

Geodesy literally meant "dividing the earth." To do this neatly it was necessary to know the shape of the globe. By 1700 there was general agreement that the earth was not quite spherical but ellipsoidal—flattened a bit at its extremities. Newton thought it was flattened at the poles; the Cassinis held that it was flattened at the equator. To decide this international issue the Académie des Sciences sent out two expeditions. One, led by Charles de La Condamine, Pierre Bouguer, and Louis Godin, went (1735) to what was then Peru (now Ecuador) to measure a degree of astronomic latitude on an arc of the meridian near the equator.* They found that the distance between one degree of astronomic latitude and the next, on the meridian passing over their place of observation, was 362,800 feet. In 1736 a similar expedition was sent to Lapland, under Maupertuis and Clairaut, to measure a degree of astronomic latitude on an arc of the meridian at a place as near as practicable to the Arctic Circle. It reported that the length of a degree there was 367,100 feet—a little more than sixty-nine miles. These findings indicated that the length of a degree of astronomic latitude increased slightly as the observer moved from the equator toward the pole; and the increase was interpreted as due to the polar flattening of the earth. The Académie des Sciences conceded that Newton had been vindicated. The measurements taken in these expeditions were later made the basis for determining a meter, the metric system, and the precise astronomical time of various localities on the earth.

Bouguer, noting some deflections of the plumb line in the Peruvian observations, ascribed them to the attractive force of the nearby Mt. Chimborazo. By measuring the deflection he estimated the density of the mountain, and on that basis he tried to calculate the density of the earth. Nevil Maskelyne, astronomer royal to George III, pursued the quest (1774–78) by dropping a plumb line now on one side, now on the other, of a granite

---

* Astronomic latitude is the angular distance between the equator and the plumb-line direction of gravity at any given place. The meridian of a place is the great circle that passes directly over it from pole to pole.

mountain in Scotland. In both cases the line was deflected some twelve angular seconds toward the mountain. Maskelyne concluded that the density of the earth would bear the same ratio to the density of the mountain as the gravitational force of the earth bore to the twelve seconds' deviation. On this basis Charles Hutton calculated the earth's density to be approximately 4.5 times that of water—a figure now generally accepted, which Newton had reached, by a typically brilliant conjecture, a century before.

3. Geology

The study of the origin, age, and constitution of the earth, of its crust and subsurface, of its earthquakes, volcanoes, craters, and fossils, was still hampered by theological taboos. Fossils were generally explained as the relics of marine organisms left on land by the waters receding after Noah's Flood, which was believed to have covered the globe. In 1721 Antonio Vallisnieri, in his treatise *Dei corpi marini che sui monti si trovano*, pointed out that a temporary flood could not account for so widespread a deposit of marine formations. Anton Moro, in his volume *De' crostacei e degli altri marini corpi che si trovano su' monti* (Venice, 1740), suggested that the fossils had been thrown up by volcanic eruptions from the sea. Originally the earth had been covered with water; subterranean fires forced up the underlying land above the subsiding sea, and created mountains and continents.

Benoît de Maillet left at his death (1738) a manuscript which came to print in 1748 as *Telliamed, ou Entretiens d'un philosophe indien avec un missionaire français*. His views were put into the mouth of a Hindu sage, but it soon appeared that "Telliamed" was "de Maillet" reversed; and the storm evoked by the book might have reconciled the author to his timely death. In his theory land, mountains, and fossils had been formed not by volcanic eruptions but by the gradual subsidence of the waters that had once covered the earth. All land plants and animals, Maillet suggested, had evolved from corresponding marine organisms; indeed, men and women were evolved from mermen and mermaids who, like the frog, had lost their tails. The recession of the waters was caused by evaporation, which reduced the sea level by some three feet every thousand years. Eventually, Maillet warned, the oceans will quite dry up, and subterranean fires will come to the surface and consume all living things.

A year after *Telliamed* Georges Louis de Buffon issued the first of his two magistral contributions to a young science still swaddled in unverifiable speculation. His *Théorie de la terre* (1749) was written at forty-two, his *Époques de la nature* (1778) was written at seventy-one. He began with

Cartesian caution, by postulating an initial push given to the world by God; thereafter the *Théorie* offered a purely natural explanation of cosmic events. Anticipating by two centuries the latest theory of cosmogony, Buffon suggested that the planets had originated as fragments detached from the sun by the impact or gravitational pull of some powerful comet; hence all the planets were at first molten and luminous masses, like the sun today, but they gradually cooled and darkened in the cold of space. The "days" allowed for the Creation in the Book of Genesis must be interpreted as epochs. Of these we may distinguish seven:

1. The earth took its spheroidal shape as the result of its rotation, and slowly its surface cooled (3,000 years).
2. The earth congealed into a solid body (32,000 years).
3. Its envelope of vapors condensed to form a universal ocean (25,000 years).
4. The waters of this ocean subsided by disappearing through crevices in the crust of the earth, leaving vegetation on the surface, and fossils at various heights on the land (10,000 years).
5. Land animals appeared (5,000 years).
6. The sinking of the ocean divided the Western from the Eastern Hemisphere, Greenland from Europe, Newfoundland from Spain, and left many islands apparently rising from the sea (5,000 years).
7. The development of man (5,000 years).

Adding these seven ages together, Buffon noted that they came to 85,000 years. He would marvel at the superior imagination of current geologists, who allow the earth a history of four billion years.

Buffon founded paleontology by studying fossil bones and deducing from them the successive epochs of organic life. The first lines of his *Époques de la nature* display his perspective and his style:

> *Comme dans l'histoire civile on consulte les titres, on recherche les médailles, on déchiffre les inscriptions antiques, pour déterminer les époques des révolutions humaines et constater les dates des événements moraux, de même, dans l'histoire naturelle, il faut fouiller les archives du monde, tirer des entrailles de la terre les vieux monuments, receuillir leur débris, et rassembler en un corps de preuves tous les indices des changements physiques qui peuvent nous faire remonter aux différents âges de la nature. C'est le seul moyen de fixer quelques points dans l'immensité de l'espace, et de placer un certain nombre de pierres numéraires sur la route éternelle du temps. Le passé est comme la distance; notre vue y décroit, et s'y perdrait de même si l'histoire et la chro-*

nologie n'eussent placer des fanaux, des flambeaux, aux points les plus obscurs.[72]*

And then, having come to paleontology only in his advanced years, he wrote:

> With sorrow I leave these fascinating objects, these precious monuments of ancient nature, which my own old age gives me no time to examine sufficiently to draw from them the conclusions which I envision, but which, founded only on hypothesis, should have no place in this work, wherein I have made it a law to present only truths based on facts. After me others will come.[73]

The *Époques de la nature* was one of the epochal books of the eighteenth century. Buffon lavished upon it all his artistry of style, even (if we believe him) to rewriting some parts of it seventeen times.[74] And he poured into it all the power of his imagination, so that he seemed to be describing, across a chasm of sixty thousand years, the constructions of his thought as if they were events unrolling before his eyes.† Grimm hailed the book as "one of the most sublime poems that philosophy has ever dared to inspire," and Cuvier pronounced it "the most celebrated of all the works of Buffon, in a style truly sublime."[76]

Meanwhile humbler students sought to chart the distribution of minerals in the soil. Jean Guettard won the praise of the Académie des Sciences by his *Mémoire et carte minéralogique* (1746). While making this first attempt at a geological survey, he discovered extinct volcanoes in France; he explained surrounding deposits as solidified lava, and hot springs as the last stages of these volcanic forces. The Lisbon earthquake stimulated John Mitchell to prepare an *Essay on the Causes and Phenomena of Earthquakes* (1760); he suggested that they were due to the sudden contact of subterranean fire and water, producing expansive evaporation; this found some outlet through volcanoes and craters, but when such escapes were not available they produced tremors in the surface of the earth; these earth waves,

---

* "Just as, in civil history, we examine titles, study coins and medallions, decipher ancient inscriptions, to determine the epochs of human revolutions and fix dates of events in the history of society, even so, in natural history, we must exhume the archives of the world, draw from the bowels of the earth old monuments, collect their remains, and gather into a body of evidence all the indications of physical change that can enable us to go back to the different ages of nature. This is the sole means of fixing some points in the immensity of space, and of placing a certain number of milestones on the eternal route of time. The past is like distance: our view decreases, and would be quite lost if history and chronology had not placed beacons and flares at the obscurest points."

† Sainte-Beuve phrased this brilliantly: " 'Where were you,' said God to Job, 'when I laid the foundations of the earth?' M. de Buffon seems to say to us, without excitement, 'I was there.' "[75]

Mitchell suggested, can be plotted to find the focus of the quake. So geology, still young, gave birth to the science of seismology.

Stratigraphy too became a specialty: men puzzled over the origin, composition, and sequence of the strata in the crust of the earth. Coal mines offered an opening to such studies; so John Strachey gave to the Royal Society (1719) "A Curious Description of the Strata Observed in the Coalmines of Mendip in Somersetshire." In 1762 Georg Christian Füchsel issued the first detailed geological map, describing the nine "formations" in the soil of Thuringia, and establishing the conception of a formation as a succession of strata collectively representing a geological epoch.

Rival theories fought over the causes of such formations. Abraham Werner, who for forty-two years (1775–1817) taught at the Freiberg School of mines, made his professorial chair the popular seat of the "Neptunist" view: continents, mountains, rocks, and strata had all been produced by the action of water, by the subsidence—sometimes slow, sometimes catastrophic—of a once universal ocean; rocks were the precipitation or sedimentation of minerals left dry by the receding sea; strata were the periods and deposits of this recession.

James Hutton added fire to water in explaining the vicissitudes of the earth. Born in Edinburgh in 1726, he became one of that remarkable group—Hume, John Home, Lord Kames, Adam Smith, Robertson, Hutcheson, Maskelyne, Maclaurin, John Playfair, Joseph Black—that constituted the Scottish Enlightenment. He passed from medicine to chemistry to geology, and soon concluded that many times the six thousand years allowed by the theologians would be required for the history of our globe. He noted that wind and water are slowly eroding mountains and depositing them into the plains, and that thousands of rivulets carry off material into rivers, which then carry it into the sea; let this process continue indefinitely, and the grasping figures or raging claws of the oceans could swallow whole continents. Nearly all geological formations might have resulted from such slow natural operations as one might see in any eroding farm or encroaching sea, or any river digging its own bed with patient pertinacity, leaving the record of its falling levels on the strata of rocks and soil. Such gradual changes, Hutton felt, were the basic causes of terrestrial transformations. "In interpreting nature," he held, "no powers are to be employed that are not natural to the globe, no action to be admitted except those of which we know the principle, and no extraordinary events to be alleged in order to explain a common appearance."[77]

But if such erosion has been going on for thousands of millenniums, why are any continents left? Because, said Hutton, the eroded material, accumulating at the bottom of the sea, is subject to pressure and heat; it fuses, consolidates, expands, mounts, emerges from the waters to form islands,

mountains, continents. That there is subterranean heat is evidenced by volcanoes. Geological history, then, is a circulatory process, a vast systole and
diastole which repeatedly pours continents into seas, and from those seas
raises up new continents. Later students named Hutton's theory "vulcan-
ism," from its dependence upon the effects of heat, or "plutonism," from
the ancient god of the nether world.

Hutton himself hesitated to publish his views, for he knew that they
would be opposed not only by believers in the literal infallibility of the
Bible, but quite as sharply by the "Neptunists," who found an enthusiastic
defender in Robert Jameson, professor of natural philosophy in the University of Edinburgh. Hutton confined himself at first to expounding his
theory to a few friends; then, at their urging, he read two papers on the
subject to the recently established Royal Society of Edinburgh in 1785.
Criticism was polite until 1793, when a Dublin mineralogist attacked Hutton in terms that stirred his ire. He replied by publishing one of the classics
of geology, *Theory of the Earth* (1795). Two years later he died. Through
John Playfair's lucid *Illustrations of Huttonian Theory* (1802), the conception of great changes produced by slow processes passed into other
sciences, and prepared Europe for Darwin's application of it to the origin
of species and the descent of man.

4. Geography

But the surface of the earth is more fascinating than its bowels. The
progressive exhibition of the diversities of mankind in race, institutions,
morals, and creeds was a powerful factor in broadening the borders of the
modern mind. Exploration proceeded ever more curiously and acquisitively
into the unknown; not for science's sake but to find raw materials, gold, silver, precious stones, food, markets, colonies, and to chart the seas for safer
navigation in peace and war. Even the voyage of the mutinous *Bounty*
(1789) had for its original object the transplantation of the breadfruit tree
from the South Seas to the West Indies. The French, the Dutch, and the
English competed most eagerly in the game, knowing that the mastery of
the world was at stake.

One of the most venturesome explorations originated in the mind of
Peter the Great, who, shortly before his death in 1725, commissioned Vitus
Bering, a Danish captain in the Russian navy, to explore the northeastern
coast of Siberia. The Academy of St. Petersburg appointed an astronomer,
a naturalist, and an historian to accompany the expedition. Proceeding over-
land to Kamchatka, Bering sailed (1728) to 67° north latitude, discovered
the strait that bears his name, and then returned to St. Petersburg. On a sec-

ond expedition he built a fleet at Okhotsk, and sailed eastward till he sighted North America (1741); so a Dane discovered that continent from the west as the Norse Leif Ericson had discovered it from the east. On the voyage back Bering's ship lost its bearings in a heavy fog, and the crew spent six months on a previously uninhabited island near Kamchatka. On that island, which also carries his name, the great Dane died of scurvy (1741) at the age of sixty. Another vessel in the expedition discovered the Aleutian Islands. Russia took possession of Alaska, and missionaries were sent out to acquaint the Eskimos with Christian theology.

The advance of Russia into America stirred other nations to explore the Pacific. As part of a war with Spain (1740) England dispatched a fleet under George Anson to harass the Spanish settlements in South America. Scurvy decimated his crews, and storms off Cape Horn wrecked some of his ships; but he forced his way into the South Pacific, stopped at the Juan Fernández Islands, and found proof that Alexander Selkirk (Defoe's Robinson Crusoe) had been there (1704–9); then he crossed the Pacific, captured a Spanish galleon near the Philippines, took its treasure of gold and silver ($1,500,000), crossed the Indian Ocean, rounded the Cape of Good Hope, eluded the Spanish and French fleets that sought to intercept him, and reached England June 15, 1744, after a voyage of three years and nine months. The prize bullion was transported from Spithead to London in thirty-two wagons to the accompaniment of martial music. All England acclaimed Anson, and four editions of his narrative were bought up in one year.

In 1763 the French government sent out a similar expedition under Louis Antoine de Bougainville, with instructions to establish a French settlement in the Falkland Islands; their position three hundred miles east of the Strait of Magellan gave them military value for control of the passage from the Atlantic to the Pacific. He accomplished his mission and returned to France. In 1765 he sailed again, passed through the strait into the Pacific, reached Tahiti (1768)—which Samuel Wallis had discovered a year before —took possession of it for France, discovered the Samoa group and the New Hebrides Islands, rounded the Cape of Good Hope, and reached France in 1769, bringing from the Pacific tropics the bougainvillaea vine. His account of his voyage stressed the pleasant climate of Tahiti and the happy health, good nature, and easy morals of the natives. We shall find Diderot commenting enviously on this report in his *Supplément au Voyage de Bougainville*.

In 1764 the British government commissioned Captain John Byron to pick up some useful territory in the South Seas. He landed at Fort Egmont in the Falkland Islands and took possession of the islands for England, not knowing that the French were already there. Spain claimed prior possession, France yielded to her, Spain yielded to England (1771), Argentina claims them today. Byron continued around the globe, but left no further mark on history. In an earlier voyage, as midshipman under Anson, he had been shipwrecked on the Chile coast (1741); his account of this was used by his grandson Lord Byron in *Don Juan*.

For English-speaking peoples the outstanding explorer of the eighteenth century was Captain James Cook. Son of a farm laborer, he was apprenticed at twelve to a haberdasher. Finding insufficient adventure in lingerie, he joined the navy, served as "marine surveyor" along the coasts of Newfoundland and Labrador, and acquired a reputation as mathematician, astronomer, and navigator. In 1768, aged forty, he was chosen to lead an expedition for noting the transit of Venus, and making geographical researches, in the South Pacific. He sailed August 25 on the *Endeavour*, accompanied by several scientists, one of whom, Sir Joseph Banks, had equipped the vessel out of his own funds.* The transit was observed at Tahiti June 3, 1769. Thence Cook sailed in quest of a great continent (Terra Australis) supposed by some geographers to be hiding in the southern seas. He found none, but he explored the Society Islands and the coasts of New Zealand, charting them carefully. He went on to Australia (then known as New Holland), took possession of the eastern coast for Great Britain, sailed around Africa, and reached England on June 12, 1771.

On July 13, 1772, with the *Resolution* and the *Endeavour*, he set out again to find the imaginary southern continent. He searched the sea eastward and southward between the Cape of Good Hope and New Zealand, and crossed the Antarctic Circle to 71° south latitude without seeing land; then the mounting danger from ice floes compelled him to turn back. He visited Easter Island, and wrote a description of its gigantic statues. He charted the Marquesas and Tonga Islands, and called the latter "Friendly" because of the gentleness of the natives. He discovered New Caledonia, Norfolk Island, and the Isle of Pines (Kunie). He traversed the South Pacific eastward to Cape Horn, continued over the South Atlantic to the Cape of Good Hope, sailed north to England, and reached port July 25, 1775, after a voyage of over sixty thousand miles and 1,107 days.

His third expedition sought a water route from Alaska across North America to the Atlantic. He left Plymouth July 12, 1776, with the *Resolution* and the *Discovery*, sailed around the Cape of Good Hope, touched again at Tahiti, proceeded northeast, and chanced upon his greatest discovery, the Hawaiian Islands (February, 1778). These had been seen by the Spanish navigator Juan Gaetano in 1555, but they had been forgotten by Europe for over two centuries. After continuing northeast, Cook reached

---

* He served as president of the Royal Society of London from 1778 to 1820, and bequeathed his library and collections to the British Museum.

what is now the state of Oregon, and surveyed the North American coast up to and beyond Bering Strait to the northern limits of Alaska. At 70° 41′ north latitude his advance was barred by a wall of ice rising twelve feet above the sea and stretching as far as the crow's-nest eye could reach. Defeated in his search for a Northeast Passage across America, Cook returned to Hawaii. There, where previously he had received a friendly welcome, he met his end. The natives were kind but thievish; they stole one of the *Discovery*'s boats; Cook led a group of his men to recapture it; they succeeded, but Cook, who insisted on being the last to leave the shore, was surrounded by the angry natives, and was beaten to death (February 14, 1779), aged fifty-one. England honors him as the greatest and noblest of her maritime explorers, an accomplished scientist, a fearless captain loved by all his crews.

Almost as heroic was the expedition led by Jean François de Galaup, Comte de La Pérouse, commissioned by the French government to follow up Cook's discoveries. He sailed in 1785 around South America and up to Alaska, crossed to Asia, and was the first European to pass through the strait (which till lately bore his name) between Russian Sakhalin and Japanese Hokkaido. Turning south, he explored the coast of Australia and reached the Santa Cruz Islands. There, apparently, he was shipwrecked (1788), for he was never heard of again.

Land exploration was also a challenge to the lust for adventure and gain. In 1716 a Jesuit missionary reached Lhasa, the "Forbidden City" of Tibet. Carsten Niebuhr explored and described Arabia, Palestine, Syria, Asia Minor, and Persia (1761). James Bruce traveled through East Africa and rediscovered the source of the Blue Nile (1768). In North America French explorers founded New Orleans (1718) and moved north along the Mississippi to the Missouri; in Canada they struggled to reach the Pacific, but the Rocky Mountains proved insurmountable. Meanwhile English settlers pushed inland to the Ohio River, and Spanish friars led the way from Mexico through California to Monterey, and up the Colorado River basin into Utah; soon North America would be one of the prizes in the Seven Years' War. In South America La Condamine, after measuring a degree of latitude at the equator, led an expedition from the sources of the Amazon near Quito to its mouth at the Atlantic, four thousand miles away.

The mapmakers could never quite keep up with the explorers. Through half a century (1744–93) César François Cassini and his son Jacques Dominique issued in 184 successive sheets a map of France thirty-six feet long by thirty-six feet wide, showing in unprecedented detail all roads, rivers, abbeys, farms, mills, even wayside crosses and gallows. Torbern Olof Bergman, not content with being one of the greatest chemists of the eighteenth century, published in 1766 a *Werlds Beskribning*, or world description, summarizing the meteorology, geology, and physical geography of his time. He suggested that many islands were peaks of mountain ranges now mostly submerged; so the West Indies might be the remains of a range that had connected Florida with South America. Horace de Saussure, after twenty-four years as professor of philosophy at the University of Geneva, made famous ascents of Mont Blanc (1787) and the Klein Matterhorn (1792), and composed voluminous studies of Swiss mountains in their atmospheric conditions, formations, strata, fossils, and plants, making a marvelous mixture of meteorology, geology, geography, and botany. Let us remember, when we are told that history is the Newgate Calendar of nations, that it is also the record of a thousand forms of heroism and nobility.

VII. BOTANY

1. Linnaeus

And so we come to life! Now that the compound microscope had been developed, it was possible to examine more minutely the structure of plants, even to the secrets of their sex. Botany graduated from its servitude to medicine, and Linnaeus mapped the teeming world of life with the care and devotion of a scientific saint.

His father, Nils Linné, was pastor of a Lutheran flock at Stenbrohult in Sweden. The son of a clergyman has especial difficulty in preserving his piety, but Carl managed it, and found, especially in the plant world, endless reasons for thankfulness to the Creator. And indeed there are moments when life appears so beautiful that only an ingrate could be an atheist.

Nils was an enthusiastic gardener, who loved to secure choice trees and rare flowers and set them in the soil around his rectory as a living litany of praise. These were Carl's toys and intimates in boyhood, so that (he tells us) he grew up with "an unquenchable love for plants."[78] Many a day he played truant from school to collect specimens in woods and fields. The father longed to make him a clergyman, for the lad was the soul of goodness, and might teach more by deed than by creed; but Carl took to medicine as the only career in which he could both botanize and eat. So in 1727, aged twenty, he was enrolled as a medical student in the University of Lund. A year later, with glowing recommendations from his teachers, he was sent to the University of Uppsala. As one of five children he could not receive much financial aid from his parents. Too poor to have his shoes repaired, he put paper in them to cover the holes and keep out some of the cold. With such incentives to study, he advanced rapidly in both botany and medicine. In 1731 he was appointed deputy lecturer in botany, and tutor in the home of Professor Rudbeck, who had twenty-four children; "now, through the grace of God," he wrote, "I have an income."[79]

When the Vetenskapssocietet (Scientific Society) of Uppsala decided to send an expedition to study the flora of Lapland, Linnaeus was chosen as leader. He and his young associates set out on May 12, 1732. He described the departure in his naturally flowery style:

> The sky was bright and genial; a gentle breeze from the west lent a refreshing coolness to the air. . . . The buds of the birch trees were beginning to burst into leaf; the foliage on most trees was fairly advanced; only the elm and the ash remained bare. The lark was singing far on high. After a mile or so we came to the entrance of a forest; there the lark left us, but on the crest of the pine the blackbird poured forth his song of love.[80]

This is typical of Linnaeus; he was ever alert, with every sense, to the sights, sounds, and fragrances of nature, and never admitted any distinction between botany and poetry. He led his troop over 1,440 miles of Lapland, through a hundred dangers and hardships, and brought them back safely to Uppsala on September 10.

Still almost penniless, he tried to support himself by lecturing, but a rival had the lectures prohibited on the ground that Linnaeus had not yet completed the medical course or taken his degree. Meanwhile Carl had fallen in love with "Lisa"—Sarah Elisabeth Moraea, daughter of a local physician. She offered him her savings, he added his own, and, so financed, he set out for Holland (1735). At the University of Harderwijk he passed his examinations and received his medical degree. A year later, at Leiden, he met the great Boerhaave, and almost forgot Lisa. Inspired and helped by that nobleman of science, Linnaeus issued one of the classics of botany, *Systema Naturae*. It ran through twelve editions in his lifetime; in the first it consisted of only fourteen folio sheets; in the twelfth it ran to 2,300 pages, in three volumes octavo. Near Amsterdam he replenished his funds by reorganizing and cataloguing the botanical collection of George Cliffort, a director of the East India Company. With incredible industry he brought out in 1736 *Bibilotheca botanica*, and in 1737 *Genera Plantarum*. In 1738 he went to Paris to study the Jardin du Roi. There, without introducing himself, he joined a group of students to whom Bernard de Jussieu was lecturing in Latin on exotic plants. One plant puzzled the professor; Linnaeus ventured to suggest, "*Haec planta faciem americanam habet*" (This plant has an American appearance). Jussieu looked at him, and surmised, "You are Linnaeus." Carl confessed, and Jussieu, with the fine brotherhood of science, gave him an unstinted welcome.[81] Linnaeus was offered professorships in Paris, Leiden, and Göttingen, but he thought it time to return to Lisa

(1739). Such long betrothals were not then unusual, and in many cases they probably contributed to stability of morals and maturity of character. They married, and Carl settled down as a physician in Stockholm.

For a time, like any young doctor, he waited in vain for patients. One day in a tavern he heard a youth complain that no one had been able to cure him of gonorrhea. Linnaeus cured him, and soon other young men who had been too anxious to prove their manhood came for similar relief. The doctor's practice spread to lung ailments. Count Carl Gustav Tessin, speaker of the House of Nobles in the Riksdag, became acquainted with him, and secured him appointment as physician to the Admiralty (1739). In that year Linnaeus helped to found the Royal Academy of Science, and became its first president. In the fall of 1741 he was chosen professor of anatomy at Uppsala; soon he exchanged this chair for that of botany, materia medica, and "natural history" (geology and biology); at last he was the right man in the right place. He communicated his enthusiasm for botany to his students; he worked with them in informal intimacy, and he was never so happy as when he led them on some natural-history foray.

> We made frequent excursions in search of plants, insects, and birds. On Wednesday and Saturday of each week we herborized from dawn till dark. Then the pupils returned to town wearing flowers in their hats, and escorted their professor to his garden, preceded by rustic musicians. That was the last degree of magnificence in our pleasant science.[82]

He sent some of his students to various quarters of the world to secure exotic plants; for these young explorers (some of whom sacrificed their lives in their quest) he secured free passage on the ships of the Dutch East India Company. He stimulated them with the hope of adding their names to plants in the great system of nomenclature that he was preparing. They noted that he gave the name *camellia* to the flowering shrub that had been found in the Philippines by the Jesuit George Kamel.

In the *Systema naturae*, the *Genera Plantarum*, the *Classes Plantarum* (1738), the *Philosophia botanica* (1751), and the *Species Plantarum* (1753) he built up his monumental classification. In this task he had several predecessors, especially Bauhin and Tournefort; and Rivinus had already (1690) suggested a binomial method of naming plants. Despite these labors Linnaeus found the collections of his time in a state of disorder that seriously hampered the scientific study of plants. Hundreds of new varieties had been discovered, to which botanists had given conflicting names. Linnaeus undertook to classify all known plants first by their class, then in the class by their order, in the order by their genus, in the genus by their species; so he arrived at a Latin name internationally acceptable. As the basis of his classification he took the presence and character, or the absence, of distinctively reproductive organs; so he divided plants into "phanerogams," those having visible organs of reproduction (their flowers), and "cryptogams," in which (as in mosses and ferns) there are no flowers producing seeds, and the reproductive structures are hidden or inconspicuous.

Some timid souls objected that this emphasis on sex would dangerously influence the imagination of youth.[83] Hardier critics, in the course of the next hundred years, pointed out more basic defects in Linnaeus' classification. He was so interested in finding nooks and names for plants that for a time he diverted botany from the study of plant functions and forms. Since a transformation of species would have confused his system, and would have contradicted the Book of Genesis, he laid down the principle that all species had been directly created by God and had remained unchanged throughout their history. Later (1762) he modified this orthodox attitude by suggesting that new species might arise by the hybrid crossing of kindred types.[84] Though he treated man (whom he trustfully called "homo sapiens") as part of the animal kingdom, and classified him as a species in the order of primates, along with the ape, his system impeded the development of evolutionary ideas.

Buffon criticized the Linnaean classification on the ground that genera and species are not objective things but are merely names for convenient mental divisions of a complex reality in which all classes, at their edges, melt into one another; nothing exists, outside the mind, except individuals; here was the old medieval debate between realism and nominalism. Linnaeus (proving himself human) replied that Buffon's eloquence must not be allowed to deceive the world; and he refused to eat in a room where Buffon's portrait was hung along with his own.[85] In a more genial moment he admitted that his arrangement was imperfect, that classification of plants by sexual apparatus left many loose ends; and in *Philosophia botanica* he proposed a "natural" system based upon the form and development of the organs of a plant. His nomenclature, as distinct from his classification, proved to be a great convenience, both in botany and in zoology, and with some modifications it still prevails.

In his old age Linnaeus was honored by all Europe as the prince of botanists. In 1761 he was knighted by the King, and became Carl von Linné. Ten years later he received a love letter from the second most famous author of the century, Jean Jacques Rousseau, who had translated the *Philosophia botanica*, and had found in botanizing a cure for philosophy: "Accept, kind sir, the homage of a very ignorant but very zealous disciple of yours, who owes in great part to meditation on your writings the tranquillity he enjoys . . . I honor you, and I love you with all my heart."[86]

Linnaeus, like Rousseau and Voltaire, died in 1778. His library and botanical collections were bought from his widow by James Edward Smith, who joined others (1788) in founding the Linnaean Society of London to care for the "Linnaean treasure." From that center a long series of publications spread the work of the botanist throughout Europe and America. Goethe named, as the greatest influences in his mental life, Shakespeare, Spinoza, and Linnaeus.[87]

2. In the Vineyard

Hundreds of devotees carried on the botanic quest. In France we find one of those virile families where a common dedication unites the members across the centuries. Antoine de Jussieu, coming up to Paris from Lyons, rose in 1708 to be director of the Jardin du Roi. His younger brother Bernard was a lecturer and "demonstrator" there; we have seen him welcoming Linnaeus. Another brother, Joseph, went to South America with La Condamine, and sent the *Heliotropium peruvianum* for transplantation in Europe. A nephew, Antoine Laurent de Jussieu, published in 1789 the work that began to replace the Linnaean system: *Genera plantarum secundum ordines naturales disposita*. He classified plants morphologically (according to their forms) by the presence, absence, or number of cotyledons (seed leaves): those plants that had none he called acotyledons; those with one only, monocotyledons; those with two, dicotyledons. His son Adrien carried on their work into the nineteenth century. In 1824 Augustin de Candolle, building upon the labors of the Jussieus, outlined the classification that is received today.

The sexuality of plants had been discovered by Nehemiah Grew in or before 1682, and had been confirmed by Camerarius in 1691. Cotton Mather reported from Boston to the Royal Society of London (1716) a demonstration of hybridization by wind pollination:

> My neighbor planted a row of hills in his field with our Indian corn, but such a grain as was colored *red* and *blue;* the rest of the field he planted with corn of the most usual color, which is *yellow.* To the most *windward side* this row infected four of the next neighboring rows, . . . to render them colored like what grew on itself. But on the *leeward side* no less than seven or eight rows were so colored, and some smaller impression was made on those that were yet further distant.[88]

In 1717 Richard Bradley proved the necessity of fertilization by an experiment with tulips. From twelve of these, "in perfect health," he removed all pollen; "these bore no seed all that summer, while . . . every one of four hundred plants which I had let alone produced seed."[89] He studied cross-fertilization, and foresaw some fascinating results. "By this knowledge we may alter the property and taste of any fruit by impregnating the one with the farina [pollen] of another of the same class" but of a different variety or species. Moreover, "a curious person may by this knowledge produce such rare kinds of plants as have not yet been heard of"; and he told how Thomas Fairchild had grown a new variety "from the seed of a carnation that had been impregnated by the farina of the sweet William." He found such interspecies hybrids to be sterile, and compared them with mules.

Philip Miller, in 1721, gave the first known account of plant fertilization by bees. He removed the "apices" of certain flowers before they could "cast their dust"; yet the seed of these apparently emasculated flowers ripened normally. Friends questioned his report; he repeated the same experiment more carefully, with the same result.

> About two days after, as I was sitting in my garden, I perceived in a bed of tulips near me some bees very busy in the middle of the flowers; on viewing them I saw them come out with their legs and bellies loaded with dust, and one of them flew into a tulip that I had castrated; upon which I took my microscope, and examined the tulip he flew into, and found he had left dust enough to impregnate the tulip; which, when I told my friends, . . . reconciled them again. . . . Unless there be provision to keep out insects, plants may be impregnated by insects much smaller than bees.[90]

Josef Kölreuter, professor of natural history at Karlsruhe, made a special study (1760 f.) of cross-fertilization and the physiochemistry of pollination. His sixty-five experiments had immense influence on agriculture in several continents. He concluded that crossing is fruitful only in closely related plants; but when it is successful the hybrids grow more rapidly, flower sooner, last longer, and produce young shoots more abundantly than the original varieties, and are not weakened by developing seed. Konrad Sprengel showed (1793) that cross-fertilization—usually by insects, less often by wind—is common within a species; and he argued, with warm teleological conviction, that the form and arrangement of parts in many flowers is designed to prevent self-fertilization. Johann Hedwig opened up a new field of research by studying the reproductive process in cryptogams (1782). Between 1788 and 1791 Joseph Gärtner of Württemberg issued, in two installments, his encyclopedic survey of the fruit and seeds of plants; this became the groundwork of nineteenth-century botany.

In 1759 Caspar Friedrich Wolff, in his *Theoria Generationis*, enunciated a theory of plant development usually ascribed to Goethe:

In the entire plant, whose parts we wonder at as being at first glance so extraordinarily diverse, I finally perceive and recognize nothing beyond leaves and stem, for the root may be regarded as a stem. . . . All parts of the plant, except the stem, are modified leaves.[91]

Meanwhile a major figure in eighteenth-century science, Stephen Hales, explored the mystery of plant nutrition. He was another of those many Anglican clergymen who found no hindrance in their flexible theology to the pursuit of science or scholarship. Though accepting divine design, he made no use of this in his scientific inquiries. In 1727 he published his results in one of the classics of botany, *Vegetable Staticks, . . . an Essay towards a Natural History of Vegetation.* His preface explained:

About twenty years since, I made several haemostatical experiments on dogs, and six years afterwards repeated the same on horses and other animals, in order to find out the force of the blood in the arteries [our "systolic blood pressure"]. . . . At which time I wished I could have made the like experiments to discover the force of the sap in vegetables; but despaired of ever effecting it till, about seven years since, I hit upon it while I was endeavoring by several ways to stop the bleeding of an old stem of a vine.[92]

Harvey's discovery of the circulation of the blood in animals had led botanists to assume a similar circulatory movement of liquids in plants. Hales disproved this supposition by experiments that showed a tree absorbing water at its branches' ends as well as by its roots; water moved inward from branches to trunk as well as from trunk to branches; and he was able to measure the absorption. Sap, however, moved up from roots to leaves through the pressure of sap expanding in the roots. The leaves absorbed nourishment from the air.

At this point the ingenious Priestley illuminated the problem by one of the most brilliant discoveries of the century—the nutritive absorption, by the chlorophyll of plants in sunlight, of carbon dioxide exhaled by animals. He described this part of his work in the first volume (1774) of his *Experiments and Observations:*

I took a quantity of air, made thoroughly noxious by mice breathing and dying in it, and divided it into two parts; one of which I put into a phial immersed in water; and in the other [which was] contained in a glass jar standing in water, I put a sprig of mint. This was about the beginning of August, 1771, and after eight or nine days I found that a mouse lived perfectly well in that part of the air in which the sprig of mint had grown, but died the moment it was put into the other part of the same original quantity of air, and which I had kept in the very same exposure, but without any plant growing in it.

After several similar experiments Priestley concluded that

the injury which is continually done to the atmosphere by the respiration of such a number of animals, and the putrefaction of such masses of both vegetable and animal matter, is in part at least repaired by the vegetable creation. And notwithstanding the prodigious mass of air that is corrupted daily by the abovementioned causes, yet, if we consider the immense profusion of vegetables upon the face of the earth, . . . it can hardly be thought but that it may be a sufficient counterbalance to it, and that the remedy is adequate to the evil.[93]

In 1764 the Dutch biologist Jan Ingenhousz, domiciled in London, became acquainted with Priestley. He was impressed by the theory that plants purified the air by absorbing, and thriving on, the carbon dioxide exhaled by animals. But Ingenhousz found that plants do not perform this function in the dark. In *Experiments on Vegetables* (1779) he showed that plants as well as animals exhale carbon dioxide, and that their green leaves and shoots absorb this, and exhale oxygen, only in clear daylight. So we remove flowers from hospital rooms at night.

The light of the sun, and not the warmth, is the chief reason, if not the only one, which makes the plants yield their dephlogisticated air [i.e., oxygen]. . . . A plant . . . not capable . . . of going in search of its food must find, within . . . the space it occupies, everything which is wanted for itself. . . . The tree spreads through the air those numberless fans, disposing them . . . to incumber each other as little as possible in pumping from the surrounding air all that they can absorb from it, and to present . . . this substance . . . to the direct rays of the sun, on purpose to receive the benefit which that great luminary can give it.[94]

This, of course, was only a partial picture of plant nutrition. Jean Senebier, a Geneva pastor, showed (1800) that only the green parts of plants are able to decompose the carbon dioxide of the air into carbon and oxygen. In 1804 Nicolas Théodore de Saussure, son of the Alpine explorer, studied the contribution of the soil, in water and salts, to the nourishment of plants. All these studies had vital results in the epochal development of soil fertility and agricultural production in the nineteenth and twentieth centuries. Here the vision and patience of scientists enriched the table of almost every family in Christendom.

VIII. ZOOLOGY

1. Buffon

The greatest naturalist of the eighteenth century was born at Montbard in Burgundy (1707) to a councilor of the Dijon Parlement. Dijon was then an independent center of French culture; it was a competition proposed by the Dijon Academy that gave an opening to Rousseau's revolt against civilization and Voltaire. Georges Louis Leclerc de Buffon studied at the Jesuit college in Dijon. There he became attached to a young Englishman, Lord Kingston, with whom, after graduation, he traveled in Italy and England. In 1732 he fell heir to a considerable property, bringing him some 300,000 livres a year; now he was free to abandon the law, for which his father had intended him, and to indulge his interest in science. On a hill at the end of his garden at Montbard, two hundred yards from his house, he built a study in an old tower called the Tour de St.-Louis. Here he secluded himself from six o'clock every morning, and here he wrote most of his books. Excited by the story of how Archimedes burned a hostile fleet in the harbor of Syracuse by a series of burning mirrors, he made eight experiments, combining at last 154 mirrors, and thereby setting fire to planks of wood 150 feet away.[95] For a time he hesitated between "natural history" and astronomy; in 1735 he translated Hales's *Vegetable Staticks*, and grounded himself in botany; but in 1740 he translated Newton's *Fluxions*, and felt the seduction of mathematics; Euclid joined Archimedes in his pantheon.

In 1739 he was appointed director (*intendant*) of the Jardin du Roi, and he moved to Paris. Only then did he make biology his main enterprise. Under his supervision the royal botanical garden was enriched with hundreds of new plants from every quarter of the earth. Buffon admitted to the Jardin all interested students, and made it a school of botany. Later, leaving it in good hands, he returned to Montbard and his Tour de St.-Louis, and began to organize his observations into the most famous scientific book of the century.

The first three volumes of the *Histoire naturelle, générale et particulière*, were published in 1749. Paris was in a mood to learn science, and now that it found geology and biology dressed in stately, lucid prose, and illustrated with alluring plates, it made these volumes almost as popular as Montesquieu's *L'Esprit des lois*, which had appeared only a year before. Aided in botany by the brothers Antoine and Bernard de Jussieu, and in zoology by Louis Daubenton, Guéneau de Montbéliard, and others, Buffon proceeded to add volume upon volume to his opus; twelve more were sent forth by 1767; nine more, on birds, in 1770-83; five on minerals in 1783-88; seven on other topics in 1774-89. After his death (1788) his unpublished manuscripts were edited and issued in eight volumes (1788-1804) by Étienne de La-cépède. All in all, the *Histoire naturelle* finally comprised forty-four volumes, which had consumed more than one life in their preparation, and over half a century in their publication. Day after day Buffon rose early, walked to his tower, and advanced step by step to his goal. Having survived some sexual escapades in his youth, he seems to have put women out of his life until 1752, when, aged forty-five, he married Marie de Saint-Belon. Though he made no pretense to marital fidelity,[96] he learned to love his wife, as many Frenchmen do after adultery, and her death in 1769 darkened his remaining years.

The *Histoire naturelle* undertook to describe the heavens, the earth, and the whole known world of plants and animals, including man. Buffon sought to reduce all this wilderness of facts to an order and law through the conceptions of universal continuity and necessity. We have noted his theory of the planets as fragments broken from the sun by collision with a comet, and his "epochs of nature" as stages in the evolution of the globe. In the world of plants he rejected Linnaeus' classification by sexual organs as too arbitrary, inadequate, and rigid. He accepted the Linnaean nomenclature reluctantly, and on condition that the names be placed on the underside of the labels attached to the plants in the Jardin.[97] His own classification of animals was absurd, but confessedly provisional; he arranged them by their utility to man, and so began with the horse; later, prodded by Daubenton, he adopted a classification by distinctive characteristics. His professional critics laughed at his classifications, and questioned his generalizations, but his readers rejoiced in his vivid descriptions and the lordly breadth of his views.

He helped to establish anthropology by studying the variations of the human species under the influence of climate, soil, institutions, and beliefs; such forces, he thought, have varied the color and features of races, and have generated diversity of manners, tastes, and ideas. One of his boldest hypotheses was that there are no fixed and unchangeable species in nature, that one species melts into the next, and that science, if matured, could ascend step by step from supposedly lifeless minerals to man himself. He saw only a difference of degree between the inorganic and the organic.

He noted that new varieties of animals have been formed by artificial selection, and argued that similar results could be produced in nature by geographical migration and segregation. He anticipated Malthus by observing that the limitless fertility of plant and animal species repeatedly places an intolerable burden upon the fertility of the soil, leading to the elimination of many individuals and species in the struggle for existence.

> Species less perfect, more delicate, heavier, less active, less well armed, have already disappeared, or will disappear.[98] . . . Many species have been perfected, or made degenerate, by great changes in land or sea, by the favors or disfavors of Nature, by food, by the prolonged influences of climate, contrary or favorable . . . [and] are no longer what they formerly were.[99]

Though he conceded a soul to man, he recognized in the human body the same sensory organs, nerves, muscles, and bones as in the higher beasts. Consequently he reduced "romantic love" to the same physiological basis as in the sexual magnetism of animals; indeed, he reserved the poetry of love to his eloquent descriptions of matings and parentage in birds. "Why," he asked, "does love make all other beings happy, but bring so much unhappiness to man? It is because only the physical part of this passion is good; the moral elements in it are worth nothing."[100] (Mme. de Pompadour reproved him for this passage, but quite amiably.)[101] Man, Buffon concluded, "is an animal in every *material* point."[102] And

> if we once admit that there are families of plants and animals, so that the ass may be of the family of the horse, and that one might differ from another only by degeneration from a common ancestor, . . . we might be driven to admit that the ape is of the family of man, that he is but a degenerate man, and that he and man have had a common ancestor. . . . If the point were once gained that among animals and vegetables there had been . . . even a single species which had been produced in the course of direct descent from another species, . . . then there is no further limit to be set to the power of Nature, and we should not be wrong in supposing that with sufficient time she could have evolved all other organic forms from one primordial type.

Then, suddenly remembering Genesis and the Sorbonne, Buffon added: "But no! It is certain from divine revelation that all animals have alike been favored with the grace of an act of direct creation, and that the first pair of every species issued full-formed from the hands of the Creator."[103]

Nevertheless the Syndic of the Sorbonne, or Faculty of Theology at the University of Paris, notified Buffon (June 15, 1751) that some parts of his *Histoire naturelle* contradicted the teachings of religion, and must be withdrawn—especially his ideas on the great age of the earth, the derivation of the planets from the sun, and the assertion that truth is derived only from science. The author smilingly apologized:

I declare that I had no intention of contradicting the text of Scrip-
ture; that I believe most firmly all that is therein related about creation,
both as to the order of time and as to matter of fact. I abandon everything in my book respecting the formation of the earth, and generally
all that may be contrary to the narrative of Moses.[104]

Probably Buffon, aristocrat, felt that it would be bad manners to quarrel
publicly with the faith of the people, and that an unmollified Sorbonne
might interfere with his great plan; in any case his work, if completed,
would be an illuminating commentary on his apology. The educated classes
saw the smile in his retraction, and noted that his later volumes continued
his heresies. But Buffon would not join Voltaire and Diderot in their attack
upon Christianity. He rejected the claim of La Mettrie and other materialists to have reduced life and thought to matter in mechanical motion. "Organization, life, soul, are our real and proper existence; matter is only a
foreign envelope whose connection with the soul is unknown, and whose
presence is an obstacle."[105]

The *philosophes*, however, welcomed him as a powerful ally. They noted
that his enthusiasm and apostrophes were directed to an impersonal Nature,
creative and fecund, rather than to a personal deity. God, in Buffon as in
Voltaire, sowed the seeds of life, and then allowed natural causes to do all
the rest. Buffon rejected design in nature, and inclined to a Spinozistic
pantheism. Like Turgenev he saw reality as a vast cosmic laboratory in
which nature, through spacious eons, experimented with one form, organ,
or species after another. In this vision he came to a conclusion apparently
contradicting his criticism of Linnaeus; now it was the individual that
seemed unreal, and the species was the relatively lasting reality. But the
contradiction could be resolved: species, genus, family, and class are still
only ideas, constructed by the mind to give some manageable order to our
experience of the confusing profusion of organisms; individuals remain the
sole living realities; but their existence is so brief that to the philosopher
they appear as merely flickering impressions of some larger and more lasting form. In this sense Plato was right: *man* is real, *men* are fleeting moments in the phantasmagoria of life.

Buffon's readers enjoyed these dizzy visions, but his critics complained
that he lost himself too recklessly in generalizations, sometimes sacrificing
accuracy in details. Voltaire laughed at his acceptance of spontaneous generation; Linnaeus scorned his work on plants; Réaumur had no respect for
Buffon on bees; and zoologists were amused by his classification of animals
according to their usefulness for man. But everyone applauded his style.

For Buffon belongs to literature as well as to science, and only integrated
history can do him justice. Rarely had a scientist expressed himself with
such stately eloquence. Rousseau, himself a master of style, said of Buffon:

"As a writer I know none his equal. His is the first pen of his century."[106]
Here the judicious Grimm, though Rousseau's foe, agreed with him: "One
is justly surprised to read discourses of a hundred pages written, from the
first line to the last, always with the same nobility of style and the same
fire, adorned with the most brilliant and the most natural coloring."[107]
Buffon wrote as a man freed from want and dowered with time; there was
nothing hurried in his work, as often in Voltaire; he labored as carefully
with his words as with his specimens. As he saw a Leibnizian law of continuity in things, so he established one in style, smoothing every transition,
and ordering all ideas in a sequence that made his language flow like a
broad, deep stream. Whereas the secret of Voltaire's style was the quick
and lucid expression of incisive thought, Buffon's method was a leisurely
ordering of spacious ideas vitalized with feeling. He felt the majesty of
nature, and made his science a song of praise.

He was quite conscious of his literary flair. He delighted to read to his
visitors melodious passages from his volumes; and when he was elected to
the French Academy he took as his theme, on the day of his reception
(August 25, 1753), not some marvel of science, but an analysis of style.
That illustrious *Discours*, as Cuvier said, "gave at once the precept and the
example,"[108] for it was itself a gem of style. From all but the French it is
hidden in the mountain of his works, and little of it has come to us but its
famous, pithy, cryptic judgment that "the style is the man." Therefore let
us spread it out here, and look at it leisurely. Its brilliance is dulled in translation, but even so, and though cruelly syncopated for our ignoble haste,
it can adorn any page. After some introductory compliments to an audience
that included many masters of style, Buffon proceeded:

> It is only in enlightened ages that men have written and spoken well.
> True eloquence . . . is quite different from that natural facility of
> speech which is . . . given to all whose passions are strong, . . . and
> whose imagination is quick. . . . But in those few men whose head is
> steady, whose taste is delicate, and whose sense is exquisite—and who,
> like you, messieurs, count for little the tone, the gestures, and the
> empty sound of words—there must be substance, thought, and reason;
> there must be the art of presenting these, of defining and ordering
> them; it is not enough to strike the ears and catch the eyes; one must
> act upon the soul and touch the heart while speaking to the mind. . . .
> The more substance and force we give to our thought by meditation,
> the easier it will be to realize them in expression.
>
> All this is not yet style, but is its base; it sustains style, directs it,
> regulates its movement, and submits it to laws. Without this the best
> writer loses himself, his pen wanders without a guide, and throws out
> at hazard formless sketches and discordant figures. However brilliant

the colors that he uses, whatever beauties he scatters in the details, he will be choked by the mass of his ideas; he will not make us feel; his work will have no structure. . . . It is for this reason that those who write as they speak, however well they speak, write badly; and those who abandon themselves to the first fire of their imagination take a tone which they cannot sustain. . . .

Why are the works of Nature so perfect? It is because each work is a whole, because Nature works on an eternal plan which she never forgets. She prepares in silence the germs of her production, she sketches by a single stroke the primitive form of every living thing; she develops it, she perfects it by a continuous movement and in a pre-scribed time. . . . The mind of man can create nothing, produce nothing, except after having been enriched by experience and medita-tion; its experiences are the seeds of its productions. But if he imitates Nature in his procedure and his labor, if he raises himself by contem-plation to the most sublime truths, if he reunites them, links them on a chain, forms of them a whole, a thought-out system, then he will establish, upon unshakable foundations, immortal monuments.

It is for lack of plan, for not having sufficiently reflected on his purpose, that even a man of thought finds himself confused, and knows not where to begin to write; he perceives at the same time a great num-ber of ideas; and since he has neither compared nor arranged them in order, nothing determines him to prefer some to others; he remains perplexed. But when he has made a plan, when once he has assembled and placed in order all the essential thoughts on his subject, he will perceive at once and with ease at what point he should take up his pen; he will feel his ideas ripening in his mind; he will hurry to bring them to light, he will find pleasure in writing, his ideas will follow one another readily, his style will be natural and easy; a certain warmth will arise from this pleasure, will spread over his work, and give life to his expression; animation will mount, the tone will be elevated, objects will take color, and feeling, joined to light, will increase and spread, will pass from that which we say to that which we are about to say; the style will become interesting and luminous. . . .

Only those works that are well written will pass down to posterity. The quantity of knowledge, the singularity of the facts, even the novelty of discoveries, will not be sure guarantees of immortality; if the works that contain them are concerned with petty objects, or if they are written without taste or nobility, . . . they will perish; for the knowledge, the facts, the discoveries are easily removed and carried off, and even gain by being placed in more able hands. Those things are outside the man, but the style is the man himself [*le style est l'homme même*]; the style cannot be stolen, transported, or altered; if it is elevated, noble, and sublime, the author will be admired equally in all times, for only truth is durable and everlasting.[109]

"This discourse," said Villemain, "so admired at the time, seems to surpass all that had yet been thought on the subject; and we cite it even today as a universal rule."[110] Perhaps some deductions must be made. Buffon's description holds better for prose than for poetry. It does more justice to the "classic" than to the "romantic" style; it is in the tradition of Boileau, and rightly elevates reason; but it leaves too little room for the Rousseaus, the Chateaubriands, and the Hugos of French prose, or for the enticing confusion of Rabelais and Montaigne, or for the moving, artless simplicity of the New Testament. It could with difficulty explain why Rousseau's *Confessions,* so poor in reason, so rich in feeling, remains one of the greatest books of the eighteenth century. Truth can be a fact of feeling as well as a structure of reason or a perfection of form.

Buffon's style was the man, a robe of dignity for an aristocratic soul. Only in the absorption of his studies did Buffon forget that he was a seigneur as well as a scientist and scribe. He took in his stride the multiplying honors that crowned his old age. Louis XV made him Comte de Buffon in 1771, and invited him to Fontainebleau. The learned academies of Europe and America offered him honorary membership. He contemplated without qualm the statue that his son raised to him in the Jardin du Roi. His tower at Montbard became in his lifetime a goal of pilgrimage rivaling Voltaire's Ferney; there Rousseau came, knelt at the threshold, and kissed the floor.[111] Prince Henry of Prussia called; and though Catherine the Great could not manage this, she sent him word that she counted him second only to Newton.

Even in old age he was stately and handsome—"the body of an athlete," said Voltaire, "and the soul of a sage";[112] looking, said Hume, not like a man of letters but like a marshal of France.[113] The people of Montbard adored him. Buffon was fully aware of all this, he prided himself on his fitness and appearance, and had his hair dressed and powdered twice a day.[114] He enjoyed good health till he was seventy-two. Then he began to suffer from stone, but he continued to work, and refused to permit an operation. He survived nine years more, and died in 1788. Twenty thousand people attended his funeral. Hardly a year after his death his remains were exhumed, and were scattered to the winds, and his monument was razed to the ground, by revolutionists who could not forgive him for having been a nobleman; and his son was guillotined.[115]

2. Toward Evolution

Led by such a master of perspective, patience, and prose, biology began to lure more and more students from the mathematics and physics that in the seventeenth century had held most scientists in thrall. Diderot, moved by all the currents of his time, felt something of this change. "At this moment," he wrote in 1754, "we touch upon a great revolution in the sciences. From the inclination that the best minds seem now to have for moral philosophy, literature, natural history, and experimental physics, I dare predict that before another hundred years have passed we shall not count three great mathematicians [*géomètres*] in Europe."[116] (The year 1859 saw the climax of modern biology.)

The new science was discouraged by its initial problem—the origin of life. Many attempts were made to show that life could be generated spontaneously from nonliving matter. The multitude of micro-organisms found by the microscope in a drop of water gave new vigor to the old theory of abiogenesis despite Redi's apparent disproof of it in 1668. In 1748 John Needham, an English Catholic priest resident on the Continent, revived the theory by repeating Redi's experiments with different results. He boiled some mutton gravy in flasks, which he immediately corked and sealed. On opening the flasks a few days later he found them teeming with organisms. Arguing that any living germs in the broth must have been killed by boiling, and that the flasks had been firmly sealed with mastic, Needham concluded that new organisms had been spontaneously generated in the liquid. Buffon was impressed, but in 1765 Spallanzani, then a professor at Modena, repeated Needham's experiments to a contrary conclusion. He found that boiling an infusion for two minutes did not destroy all germs, but that boiling it for forty-five minutes did, and that in this case no organisms appeared. The controversy continued until Schwann and Pasteur apparently disposed of it in the nineteenth century.

Mysteries almost as baffling surrounded the processes of reproduction. James Logan, Charles Bonnet, and Caspar Wolff puzzled over the roles of the male and female elements in reproduction, and asked how the combined elements can—as they seem to—contain in themselves the predetermination of all the parts and structures in the mature form. Bonnet proposed a fantastic theory of *emboîtement*, or "incapsulation": the female contains the germs of all her children, these germs contain the germs of the grandchildren, and so on until imagination rebels; science too can run to mythology. Wolff, whose name adorns the Wolffian ducts, defended Harvey's theory of "epigenesis": each embryo is created anew by the parental elements. Wolff anticipated von Baer's germ-layer theory of organ formation in *De Formatione Intestinorum* (1768), which von Baer described as "the greatest masterpiece of scientific observation that we possess."[117]

Is the regeneration of tissue a form of reproduction? Abraham Trembley, of Geneva, astonished the learned world in 1744 by experiments that revealed the regenerative obstinacy of the fresh-water polyp: he cut one into four longitudinal strips, each of which grew into a complete and normal organism. He hesitated whether to call the polyp a plant or an animal; it seemed rooted like a plant, but it grabbed and digested food like an animal; speculative souls hailed it as bridging the gap between the plant and animal worlds in the "great chain of being."[118] Trembley concluded, as biologists now do, that it is an animal. Its squirming, groping tentacles led Réaumur to call it "polyp," or many-footed. We know it also as the hydra, from the legendary monster with nine heads; as soon as Heracles cut off one of these, two heads grew in its place. In literature the hydra has served as a simile with a hundred thousand lives.

René Antoine de Réaumur was second only to Buffon in the biology of this age, and far superior to him in accuracy of observation. Educated as a physician, he abandoned practice as soon as he was financially independent, and gave himself to scientific research. He seemed at home in a dozen fields. In 1710 he was commissioned to survey and describe the industries and industrial arts of France; he did this with characteristic thoroughness, and made recommendations that led to the establishment of new industries and the revival of ailing ones. He devised the method of tinning iron that is still employed, and investigated the chemical differences between iron and steel. These and other contributions to metallurgy won him a pension of twelve thousand livres from the government; he gave the money to the Académie des Sciences. We have seen his work on the thermometer.

Meanwhile he was enriching biology. In 1712 he showed that the lobster could regenerate an amputated limb. In 1715 he correctly described the electric shock emitted by the torpedo fish. Between 1734 and 1742 he published his masterpiece, *Mémoires pour servir à l'histoire des insectes*— six volumes painstakingly illustrated, and written in a style of charm and animation that made insects almost as interesting as the lovers in the romances of Crébillon *fils*. Like Fabre in our time, he became fascinated by all

> that relates to the character and manners, so to speak, and to the liveli-
> hood, of so many little animals. I have observed their different ways of
> life, how they get their nourishment, the ruses which some of them use
> to seize their prey, the precautions which others take to keep themselves
> safe from enemies, . . . the choice of places where to lay their eggs
> so that the young, hatching out, will find suitable food from the mo-
> ment of their birth.[119]

Réaumur agreed with Voltaire that the behavior and structure of organisms could not be explained without assuming a power of design in nature; his volumes served as ammunition to those who opposed the atheistic current that soon flowed in France. Diderot ridiculed him for spending so much time on bugs,[120] but it was such careful work that laid the factual foundations of modern biology.

What must Diderot have said when he heard that Réaumur's friend Charles Bonnet had demonstrated virgin birth—parthenogenesis—in the animal kingdom? By isolating newborn aphids (the tree lice that love our orange trees) he had found that a female of the species can reproduce fertile offspring without having received the male element usually required; apparently the purpose of sex was not merely reproduction, but the enrichment of the offspring through contribution of diverse qualities from two parents differently endowed. These experiments, reported to the Académie des Sciences in 1740, were described in Bonnet's *Traité d'insectologie* (1745). In *Recherches sur . . . des plantes* (1754) Bonnet suggested that some plants have powers of sensation, even of discrimination and selection, therefore of judgment—the essence of intelligence.

It was this same Geneva-born Bonnet who seems to have first applied the term *evolution* to biology;[121] however, he meant by it the chain of beings from atoms to man. The idea of evolution as the natural development of new species from old ones appeared repeatedly in eighteenth-century science and philosophy. So Benoît de Maillet suggested in his posthumous *Telliamed* (1748) that all land animals evolved from kindred marine organisms through transformation of species by the changed environment; in this way birds had originated from flying fish, lions from sea lions, men from mermen. Three years later Maupertuis' *Système de la nature* not only classed apes and men as allied species,[122] but anticipated in outline Darwin's theory of the evolution of new species through the environmental selection of fortuitous variations favorable to survival. Said the unfortunate scientist who was soon to fall on the point of Voltaire's pen:

> The elementary particles which form the embryo are each drawn from the corresponding structure of the parent, and conserve a sort of recollection of their previous form. . . . We can thus readily explain how new species are formed, . . . by supposing that the elementary particles may not always retain the order which they present in the parents, but may fortuitously produce differences which, multiplying and accumulating, have resulted in the infinite variety of species which we see at the present time.[123]

In this manner, given sufficient time, a single prototype (Maupertuis thought) could have produced all living forms—a proposition tentatively entertained by Buffon, and warmly applauded by Diderot.

Jean Baptiste Robinet returned, in *De la Nature* (1761), to the older idea of evolution as a "ladder of beings" (*échelle des êtres*): all nature is a series of efforts to produce even more perfect beings; in conformity with

Leibniz' law of continuity (which admitted no break between the lowest and the highest beings), all forms, even stones, are experiments whereby Nature works her way upward through minerals, plants, and beasts to man. Man himself is only a stage in the great enterprise: beings more perfect will someday replace him.[124]

James Burnett, Lord Monboddo, a Scottish judge, was a Darwinian nearly a century before Darwin. In *The Origin and Progress of Language* (1773-92) he pictured prehistoric man as having no language and no social organization, and as in no way distinguished, in mental attainments or way of life, from the apes; man and the orangutan (as Edward Tyson had said in 1699) are of the same genus; the orangutan (by which Monboddo meant the gorilla or the chimpanzee) is a man who failed to develop. Only through language and social organization did prehistoric man become primitive man. Human history is not a decline from primeval perfection, as in Genesis, but a slow and painful ascent.[125]

The poet Goethe touched the history of science at several points. In 1786 he discovered the intermaxillary bone, and in 1790 he suggested that the skull is composed of modified vertebrae. Independently of Caspar Wolff he reached the theory that all parts of a plant are modifications of leaves; and he held that all plants descended by general metamorphosis from one archetype which he called *Urpflanze*.

Last in the line of eighteenth-century Darwinians is the great Darwin's grandfather. Erasmus Darwin was quite as interesting a personality as Charles. Born in 1731, educated at Cambridge and Edinburgh, he settled down to the practice of medicine in Nottingham, then in Lichfield, then in Derby, where he died in 1802. From Lichfield he rode regularly to Birmingham, fifteen miles away, to attend the dinners of the "Lunar Society," of which he was the moving spirit, and of which Priestley became the most famous member. A bright and amiable personality shines out in the older Darwin's letter to Matthew Boulton apologizing for having missed a meeting:

> I am sorry the infernal divinities who visit mankind with diseases . . . should have prevented my seeing all your great men at Soho [Birmingham] today. Lord! what inventions, what wit, what rhetoric —metaphysical, mechanical, and pyrotechnical—will be on the wing, bandied like a shuttlecock from one to another of your troop of philosophers! while poor I, . . . imprisoned in a post-chaise, am joggled, and jostled, and bumped, and bruised along the King's highroad to make war upon a stomach-ache or a fever.[126]

Amid this busy life he wrote a substantial *Zoonomia* (1794-96), mingling medicine and philosophy, and several volumes of science poetry:

Botanic Garden (1788), *Loves of the Plants* (1788), and *The Temple of Nature* (1802). The last book expressed his evolutionary ideas. It began by affirming abiogenesis as the most probable theory of the origin of life:

> Hence without parents, by spontaneous birth,
> Rise the first specks of animated earth. . . .
> Organic life beneath the shoreless waves
> Was born and nursed in ocean's pearly caves;
> First, forms minute, unseen by spheric glass,
> Move on the mud, or pierce the watery mass;
> These, as successive generations bloom,
> New powers acquire, and larger limbs assume;
> Whence countless groups of vegetation spring,
> And breathing realms of fin and feet and wing.[127]

So life evolved from marine forms to amphibians in the ooze, and to the numberless species of sea and land and air. The poet quoted Buffon and Helvétius on features of the human anatomy indicating that man formerly walked on four feet and is not yet fully adjusted to an erect posture. One species of ape emerged to a higher state by using the forefeet as hands, and developing the thumb as a useful counterforce to the fingers. In all the stages of evolution there is a struggle among animals for food and mates, and among plants for soil, moisture, light, and air. In this struggle (said Erasmus Darwin) evolution took place by the development of organs through efforts to meet new needs (not by the natural selection of chance variations favorable to survival, as Charles Darwin was to say); so plants grow through efforts to get air and light. In *Zoonomia* the doctor foreshadowed Lamarck: "All animals undergo transformations which are in part produced by their own exertions, in response to pleasures and pains, and many of these acquired forms or propensities are transmitted to their posterity."[128] So the snout of the pig was developed for foraging, the trunk of the elephant to reach down for food, the rough tongue of cattle to pull up blades of grass, the beak of the bird to snatch up seeds. To which the doctor added a theory of protective coloration: "There are organs developed for protective purposes, diversifying both the form and color of the body for concealment and for combat."[129] And he concluded with a majestic glance over eons:

> From thus meditating upon the minute portions of times in which many of the above changes have been produced, would it be too bold to imagine, in the great length of time since the earth began to exist, perhaps millions of years before the commencement of the history of mankind, that all warm-blooded animals have arisen from one living filament, which the first great Cause imbued with animality, with

the power of acquiring new parts, attended by new propensities, directed by irritations, sensations, volitions, and associations, and thus possessing the faculty of continuing to improve by its own inherent activity, and of delivering down those improvements by generation to posterity, world without end?[130]

"It is curious," wrote Charles Darwin, "how largely my grandfather . . . anticipated the views and erroneous grounds of opinion of Lamarck in his *Zoonomia.*"[131] Perhaps the grandfather would not admit that he was on the wrong track. In any case he had expounded a theory that is not yet dead, and in his genial way he had struck a blow for evolution.

IX. PSYCHOLOGY

From minerals to plants to animals to man the scientific quest advanced. Armed with the microscope, and spurred on by the needs of physicians, a growing fraternity of students peered into the human body, and found its organs and functions indisputably similar to those of the higher beasts. But there still seemed to be a break in the chain of being: nearly everyone agreed that the mind of man differed in kind, as well as degree, from the mind of animals.

In 1749 David Hartley, an English clergyman turned physician, ventured into the gap by founding physiological psychology. For sixteen years (1730-46) he gathered data; then, in 1749, he published his *Observations on Man*. Ambitious to find a principle governing the relations of ideas as Newton had proposed a principle governing the relations of bodies, Hartley applied the association of ideas to the explanation not only of imagination and memory, as Hobbes and Locke had done, but also of emotion, reason, action, and the moral sense. He pictured sensation as first a vibration in the particles of a nerve stimulated by an external object, and then as the transmission of this vibration along the nerve to the brain, like "the free propagation of sounds along the surface of water."[132] The brain is a mass of nerve fibrils whose vibrations are the correlates of memories; one or more of these fibrils is agitated by an incoming vibration associated with it in past experience; this reverberation is the physiological concomitant of an idea. For every mental state there is a corporeal correlate, and for every bodily operation there is a mental or neural accompaniment; the association of ideas is the mental side of the association of nerve vibrations aroused by their contiguity or succession in past experience. Hartley's physiological picture was, of course, highly simplified, and never touched the mystery of consciousness; but it shared in reconciling a small minority of Englishmen to the mortality of their minds.

Another clergyman, Étienne Bonnot de Condillac, approached the problems of mind from a purely psychological side. Born at Grenoble (1714), he was educated at a Jesuit seminary in Paris, and was ordained a priest. Admitted to the salons of Mme. de Tencin and Mme. Geoffrin, he met Rousseau and Diderot, lost religious ardor, abandoned all sacerdotal functions, and gave himself to the game of ideas. He studied the historic systems of philosophy, and rejected them in a *Traité des systèmes* (1749), which voiced the spirit of the *philosophes*: all these proud structures of co-ordinated half-truths are fanciful proliferations from our fragmentary knowledge of the universe; it is better to examine a part of experience inductively than to reason deductively about the whole.

In an *Essai sur l'origine des connaissances humaines* (1746) Condillac had followed Locke's analysis of mental operations; but in his most successful production, *Traité des sensations* (1754), he accepted a more radical view—that the "reflection" in which Locke had recognized a second source of ideas is itself only a combination of sensations, which are the sole source of all mental states. An external world exists, for our most basic sense, that of touch, encounters resistance; nevertheless, all that we know is our sensations and the ideas that they generate.

Condillac illustrated this proposition with a famous comparison. Perhaps he took it from Buffon, but he ascribed it to his late *inspiratrice* Mlle. Ferrand, who had left him an obliging legacy. He pictured a marble statue "organized internally like ourselves, but animated by a mind shorn of all ideas,"[133] possessing only one sense, that of smell, and capable of distinguishing between pleasure and pain. He proposed to show how from the sensations of this statue all forms of thought could be derived. "Judgment, reflection, desires, passions, etc., are merely sensations variously transformed."[134] Attention is born with the first sensation. Judgment comes with the second, which begets comparison with the first. Memory is a past sensation revived by a present sensation or by another memory. Imagination is a memory vividly revived, or a group of memories projected or combined. Desire or aversion is the active memory of a pleasant or disagreeable sensation. Reflection is the alternation of memories and desires. Will is a strong desire accompanied by an assumption that the object is attainable. Personality, the ego, the self, does not exist at the outset; it takes form as the total collection of the individual's memories and desires.[135] In this way, from merely the sense of smell—or from any other one sense— nearly all operations of the mind can be deduced. Add four other senses, and the statue develops a complex mind.

All this was an interesting tour de force, and it made considerable noise among the intellectuals of Paris. But critics had no difficulty in showing that Condillac's method was as deductive and hypothetical as anything in the systems of philosophy; that he quite ignored the problem of consciousness; and that he had not explained how the original sensitivity had arisen. A sensitive statue, even if it only smells, is no statue, unless it be that dignitary whom Turgenev described as posing as proudly as if he were his own monument raised by public subscription.

In 1767 Condillac was appointed tutor to the future Duke of Parma. He spent the next nine years in Italy, and composed for his pupil seventeen volumes which were published in 1769-73 as *Cours d'études*, or *Course of Studies*. These volumes are of a high order, but the two on history deserve a special salute because they included the history of ideas, manners, economic systems, morals, arts, sciences, amusements, roads—altogether a fuller record of "civilization" than Voltaire had given in the *Essai sur les moeurs*. In 1780, at the request of Prince Ignacy Potocki, Condillac drew up a *Logique* for the schools of Lithuania; this too was of exceptional excellence. In that year he died.

His influence survived for a century, appearing as late as 1870 in Taine's *De l'Intelligence*. Condillac's psychology was standard in the educational system established by the National Convention that governed France from 1792 to 1795. Anatomists like Vicq-d'Azyr, chemists like Lavoisier, astronomers like Laplace, biologists like Lamarck, alienists like Pinel, psychologists like Bonnet and Cabanis, acknowledged his lead. Pierre Jean Georges Cabanis, in 1796, described the brain as "a special organ whose particular function it is to produce thought, just as the stomach and the intestines have the special function of carrying on the work of digestion, and the liver that of filtering bile."[136] The *philosophes* who surrounded Condillac ignored his professions of faith in God, free will, and an immaterial, immortal soul; they claimed that a naturalistic, semimaterialistic, hedonistic philosophy logically followed from his reduction of all knowledge to sensation, and of all motives to pleasure and pain. Rousseau and Helvétius concluded that if the mind of man at birth is mere receptivity, education can mold intelligence and character with little regard to hereditary differences of mental capacity. Here was the psychological ground of many radical political philosophies.

The reaction against materialistic psychology came in France only after Napoleon had clipped the claws of the Revolution and had signed the Concordat of 1801 with the Church. It came earlier in Germany, where the antisensationist tradition of Leibniz was still strong. Men like Johann Nicolaus Tetens, professor at the University of Rostock, attacked the school of Condillac as mere theoreticians rather than scientists. All this talk of "vibrations" and "nerve fluid" was pure hypothesis; had anyone seen these things? Tetens argued that a scientific psychology would seek direct observation of mental processes; it would make introspection its major instrument, and would thereby build up a psychology on a truly inductive basis. It would soon find that the "laws of association" formulated by Hobbes, Locke, and Hartley do not correspond with our actual experience; that imagination often revives or combines ideas in quite a different order from that in which sensation gave them; and that links in the chain of association sometimes drop out in a very fanciful way. Desire seems to be the immanent reality of an organism, and hardly conforms to mechanical laws. Mind is an active, forming force, not a "blank paper" upon which sensation writes its will.

So the stage was set for Immanuel Kant.

X. THE IMPACT OF SCIENCE UPON CIVILIZATION

If this chapter, however inadequate, has wound itself out to an abnormal length, it is not only because we have recognized the scientists as well as their science as belonging to history, it is also because the evolution of ideas is our basic interest, and because ideas played a role in the eighteenth century next only to the nature of man himself. If the achievements of science in that revolutionary era were not as startling as those of the preceding century from Galileo and Descartes to Newton and Leibniz, they entered more powerfully into almost every phase of European history. Through Voltaire and a hundred lesser exegetes the results of research were spread in the middle and upper classes; the new sciences of chemistry, geology, and zoology joined in the slow but profound impress of expanding knowledge upon the literate mind; and the effects were endless.

The influence of science, strange to say, was least and last upon technology. Man's ways of sowing and reaping, mining and manufacturing, building and transporting, had been formed through centuries of trial and error, and traditions and inertia only reluctantly accepted improvements suggested by laboratory experiments; not till the end of this era did science accelerate the Industrial Revolution. Even so, the first stages of that revolution owed a great deal to chemical researches on dyes; the use of chlorine for bleaching textiles was established by Berthollet (1788), and the industrial manufacture of soda and sal ammoniac was introduced by James Hutton and Nicolas Leblanc. The study of gases by Boyle and Mariotte, and of heat by Black, shared in the development of the steam engine—which, however, was due chiefly to mechanics on the scene. As the century proceeded, a closer rapport grew between practical men seeking production and scientists seeking truth; the Académie des Sciences sent investigators into fields, factories, and workshops, and issued twenty volumes of *Descriptions des arts et métiers* (1761–81). In return the burgeoning industries began to call upon science for data and experiments; so Coulomb reduced to reliable formulas the tension of beams, and the problems of the steam engine stimulated science to new researches in the relation between force and heat. In the nineteenth century these liaisons were to transform the economic and physical world.

The major impact of science was naturally upon philosophy, for philosophy, which is the quest of wisdom, must build upon science, which is the pursuit of knowledge. At every step science seemed to enlarge the world in complexity and scope, and new perspectives had to be formed. It was no small adjustment that the human mind had to make after discovering that man was not the center of the universe but an atom and moment in the baffling immensities of space and time; that adjustment has not yet been made. By a proud response as old as Copernicus man was almost overcome by the grandeur of his discovery of his littleness; the pride of science obscured the modesty of philosophy; men conceived new utopias in terms of science, and the idea of progress offered a new religion to the modern soul.

The effect of science upon religion—or rather upon Christianity—seemed lethal. Doubtless men would continue to form or favor conceptions of the world that would give hope and consolation, meaning and dignity, to harassed, fleeting lives; but how could the Christian epos of creation, original sin, and divine redemption stand up in a perspective that reduced the earth to a speck among a million stars? What was man that the God of such a universe should be mindful of him? How could the poetry of Genesis survive the explorations of geology? And what of the dozen or more religions in regions now opened up by geography?—were they clearly inferior to Christianity in their doctrines or their moral codes and results? How could the miracles of Christ, not to mention those widely ascribed to saints and Satan, be reconciled with the apparent reign of universal law? How could the soul or mind of man be immortal when it seemed so dependent upon the nerves and other tissues visibly doomed to decay? What must happen to the religion so challenged by a science daily growing in scope, achievements, and prestige? And what must happen to a civilization based upon a moral code based upon that religion?

CHAPTER XVII

Medicine

1715–89

I. ANATOMY AND PHYSIOLOGY

A ND there was the impact of science upon medicine. The healing art
was bound up with the improvement of the microscope and the thermometer, with the rise of chemistry and biology, and, above all, with the
advancing knowledge of human and animal anatomy and physiology. Most
of the researches in anatomy and physiology were the work of the doctors
themselves.

Giovanni Battista Morgagni was typical of the many physicians who
made medicine a science by keeping clinical records of the cases that came
under their care. Seven hundred such cases were scrutinized by him in
his devoted career as practitioner and professor of medicine at Padua. In
his eightieth year (1761) he reported his observations in the form of seventy letters that founded pathological anatomy: *De sedibus et causis mor-
borum per anatomen indagatis* (*On the Seats and Causes of Diseases as
Investigated by Anatomy*). Here he gave classical descriptions of heart
block, yellow atrophy of the liver, and tuberculosis of the kidney; he identified the clinical features of pneumonia with solidifications of the lungs;
and he added significantly to cardiology. "The section on aneurysm [ab-
normal blood-filled dilation] of the aorta," said Sir William Osler, "remains one of the best ever written"; and "what could be more correct than
his account of angina pectoris?"[1] Now, more clearly than ever before, the
seat of each illness was localized in morbid alterations of specific organs.
Impressed by Morgagni's work, the hospitals—with no protest from Church
or state—provided him and his assistants with cadavers from all classes of
the community, even nobles and ecclesiastics; many individuals, in the
wish to advance science, expressed a desire to have their bodies examined
by Morgagni after their death.[2] He made experiments on animals, again
without protest from the Church. He continued to teach till his ninetieth
year. In 1764, aged eighty-two, he was reported to be "as hale as a man
of fifty, and still working without spectacles."[3] His students proudly proclaimed him "*anatomicorum totius Europae princeps.*" In 1931 his native
Forlì raised a monument to him in the piazza that bears his name.

His pupil Antonio Scarpa became professor of anatomy at Modena at the age of twenty. When, aged thirty-six (1783), he was promoted to the chair of anatomy at Pavia, he joined Spallanzani and Volta in making that university one of the greatest in Europe. His anatomical studies of the ear, the nose, the feet, and the nerves won him international renown; his *Osservazioni sulle principali malattie degli occhi* (1801) continued for several decades to be the standard text of ophthalmology. Just a year younger than Scarpa, Félix Vicq-d'Azyr studied the comparative anatomy of birds, quadrupeds, and man; his results showed a remarkable and detailed similarity in the structure of the limbs in men and beasts, and shared in putting man in his biological place. He died at forty-six (1794), without having completed a work which had already brought the anatomy of the brain to its eighteenth-century peak.

In Great Britain two Hunters, born in Scotland, added brilliance to the Scottish Enlightenment by their work in anatomy and surgery. William's lectures revolutionized the teaching of anatomy in London, where that subject had long been hampered by restriction on the availability of cadavers. He won fame by his epochal discovery (1758) of the absorbent function of the lymphatics, by his classic *Anatomy of the Gravid Uterus* (1774), and by his volcanic temper, which he explained on the ground that, being an anatomist, he was accustomed to "the passive submission of dead bodies."[4] He died in 1783, aged sixty-five, from exhaustion incurred in a lecture. He bequeathed his extensive anatomical collection to Glasgow, where it is still maintained as the Hunterian Museum.

John Hunter was born ten years after his brother, and died ten years after his brother's death. At twenty-one (1749) he had acquired sufficient knowledge to take charge of William's class in practical anatomy. While with his brother, he solved the problem of the descent of the testes in the foetus, traced the placental circulation and the ramifications of nasal and olfactory nerves, discovered the tear ducts, and took a leading part in exposing the functions of the lymphatic ducts. At twenty-seven he entered Oxford; however, finding Latin and Greek deader than cadavers, he left college and joined the army as a surgeon. In active service abroad he learned much about gunshot wounds; at his death he left a classic treatise on that subject. Back in England, he practiced and taught surgery, and continued his investigations of anatomy and physiology. In 1767 he met with an accident that ruptured his "tendon of Achilles" (which binds the muscles of the calf of the leg to the heel); from observations then made on himself, and from experiments on dogs, he found successful surgery for club feet and other deformities involving tendons. Having inadvertently inoculated himself with syphilis, he delayed its treatment in order to study the disease at first hand;[5] however, he made the mistake of identifying syphilis with gonorrhea. He proved by experiment that digestion does not take place in snakes and lizards during hibernation. In his house at Brompton he gathered for his researches a weird menagerie of pheasants, partridges, toads, fish, geese, hedgehogs, silkworms, bees, hornets, wasps, an eagle, two leopards, and a bull. He nearly lost his life wrestling with the bull and recapturing escaped leopards. He anatomized over five hundred species of animals. He studied the effects of various toxins, and admitted in 1780 that he had "poisoned some thousands of animals."

In 1785 he sat for his portrait to Reynolds, but at first proved too restless; Sir Joshua was about to abandon the sitting, when Hunter fell into a deep and motionless reverie which enabled the artist to make the sketch for the portrait now in the Royal College of Surgeons. Like his brother, John was of an irritable and imperious temper. Finding himself subject to angina pectoris, he said, "My life is in the hands of any rascal who chooses to annoy and tease me."[6] Contradicted by one of his colleagues, he fell into a rage, and died within a few minutes (1793). He was buried in Westminster Abbey, next to the remains of Ben Jonson. His collection of thirteen thousand specimens was acquired by the Corporation of Surgeons through a governmental grant, and became in 1836 the Hunterian Museum of London. The "Hunterian oration" delivered in his memory is an annual event in the English medical world.

In physiology the great name of this period was Albrecht von Haller. We have met him as a poet in his youth; in his later years he placed himself at the head of his kind by his *Elementa physiologiae Corporis humani*, which appeared in eight volumes between 1757 and 1766. They not only recorded all the current lore of human anatomy and physiology, but included his own discoveries on the role of the bile in the digestion of fats, and on the irritability or contractility of muscle fibers independently of nerves and even when separated from the body. Diderot concluded from these and similar experiments, "If life remains in organs severed from the body, where is the soul? What happens to its unity? . . . to its indivisibility?"[7] He argued from such evidence that all physiological processes are mechanical. Haller disagreed; the irritability of organic tissue, he felt, indicated a vital principle absent in inorganic substances and incompatible with a mechanistic philosophy. Further studies by Haller showed that "the structure of the bones of quadrupeds is essentially the same as that of birds," and that "the bones in man are not different in any part of their structure from those of quadrupeds."[8] In 1755 he made the first recorded observation of atherosclerosis, the accumulation of mushy fat in the walls of the blood vessels. "When we open the pages of Haller," said Sir William Foster, "we feel that we have passed into modern times."[9]

Other investigations lent support to a mechanistic view. Robert Whytt showed (1751) that reflex actions need involve only a small segment of the spinal cord. The work of Priestley, Lavoisier, Laplace, and Lagrange seemed to reduce respiration to chemical processes analogous to combustion. Réaumur's experiments (1752) proved that digestion results from the chemical action of gastric juices; Spallanzani showed (1782) that this action of the digestive juices upon food could go on even outside the stomach; and John Hunter discovered that after death these juices begin to digest the stomach wall itself.

Spallanzani was one of the major figures in eighteenth-century physiology. We have seen his experiments on "spontaneous" generation. His interest in digestion knew no bounds. He discovered the digestive function of saliva. He experimented on himself by stimulated vomiting, and by swallowing bags and tubes, which he patiently recovered from his stools. He was the first to show that the systolic contraction of the heart sends blood into the smallest capillaries. He showed that perspiration is not akin to respiration, but can, up to a certain point, take the place of breathing. Though an abbot, he became an authority on fertilization. He found that when the male organs of a frog were covered with waxed linen the female remained unfertilized after mating; but when he collected the male fluid from the linen, and placed it in contact with the female eggs, these became fertilized. He obtained artificial fertilization in mammals by injecting the sperm of a dog into the uterus of a bitch.[10] The twentieth century finally appreciated the scope and significance of his indefatigable experiments, and recognized him as one of the elect in the priesthood of science.

II. THE INGENUITY OF DISEASE

Did the growth of knowledge defeat the resourcefulness of disease? Hardly. Voltaire estimated the average longevity of human life in his time at twenty-two years.[11] The slums of the growing cities made for a high rate of infantile mortality, sometimes reaching fifty per cent.[12] In London fifty-eight per cent of all children died before their fifth birthday.[13] The abandonment of infants was widely practiced. In the eight years 1771–77 nearly 32,000 children were admitted to the Paris Foundling Hospital— eighty-nine per day; of these babies 25,476 (eighty per cent) died before completing their first year. A contribution to infant mortality was made in the eighteenth century by the spread of dry-nursing—the replacement of the breast of mother or wet nurse by the bottle. Sir Hans Sloane reckoned the death rate of bottle-fed infants as three times that of the breast-fed. The new method became especially popular in the upper classes of France, until Rousseau's *Émile* (1762) made breast feeding fashionable.

Abortion and contraception continued. The linen sheath, recommended by Fallopio in 1564 to prevent venereal infection, was used in the eighteenth century to prevent conception.[14] Dr. Jean Astruc, in *De Morbis venereis* (1736), mentioned debauchees who "have been employing for some time sacs made of fine, seamless membrane in the form of a sheath, . . . called in English 'condum.' "[15] A Mrs. Phillips in 1776 issued handbills in London announcing that her shop had a full supply of such "implements of safety, which secure the health of her customers."[16] Despite these "machines," as they were called, venereal disease took its toll in every class. Lord Chesterfield warned his son to be careful, for though "in love a man may lose his heart with dignity, . . . if he loses his nose he loses his character into the bargain."[17]

We who live after Jenner can hardly imagine what a curse smallpox was before he converted the Western world to vaccination. Voltaire calculated that "in a hundred persons that come into the world, at least sixty contract smallpox; of these sixty, twenty die . . . and twenty more keep very disagreeable marks of this cruel disorder as long as they live."[18] Between 1712 and 1715 three heirs to the French throne died of smallpox. The Prince de Ligne thought that 200,000 inmates of nunneries and monasteries had sought refuge there from the humiliation of smallpox disfigurement.[19] The disease reached epidemic proportions in Paris in 1719, in Sweden in 1749–65, in Vienna in 1763 and 1767, in Tuscany in 1764, in London in 1766 and 1770.

Epidemics in general were now less severe than in earlier centuries, but they remained among the hazards of life. They were more formidable in the countryside than in the cities, despite urban slums, for the peasants could seldom afford medical care. Epidemics of typhus, typhoid fever, and smallpox killed eighty thousand persons in Brittany in the one year 1741.[20] In 1709 bubonic plague carried off 300,000 persons in Prussia; it reappeared with less intensity in the Ukraine in 1737, in Messina in 1743, in Moscow in 1789. Scarlet fever, malaria (*mal aria*, bad air), dysentery, were common, especially in the lower classes, where they were favored by poverty of public sanitation and personal hygiene. Epidemics of contagious puerperal fever occurred in Paris, Dublin, Aberdeen, Thurgau, and Bern. Influenza, which the French called *la grippe* (adhesion), reached the epidemic stage at various times in Italy, Sweden, and Germany. Occasionally it led to infantile poliomyelitis, as in the boy who became Sir Walter Scott. Pneumonia, diphtheria, and erysipelas now and then neared epidemic proportions. Whooping cough, which seems so minor now, was widespread and dangerous, especially in northern Europe; in Sweden forty thousand children died of it between 1749 and 1764. Yellow fever came in from America, and rose to epidemic form at Lisbon in 1723. To these and a hundred other ailments the ladies of the upper classes added "the vapors"—a confused mixture of nervous exhaustion, hypochondria, insomnia, and boredom, rising at times to hysteria.

Against such public enemies the governments provided some measures of sanitation. But offal was still for the most part emptied into the streets. Water closets appeared in Paris at the beginning of the century, but only in a few houses; they were almost entirely lacking elsewhere on the Continent. Bathrooms were a luxury of the rich. Public baths were probably less numerous than in the Renaissance. Hygiene made more progress in armies and navies than in cities. Sir John Pringle advanced military medicine (1774), and James Lind of Scotland revolutionized naval hygiene (1757). In Anson's expedition of 1740 some seventy-five per cent of the crews were at times disabled by scurvy. In an epochal treatise on that disease (1754) Lind pointed out that orange or lemon juice had been used in treating it by the Dutch in 1565 and by Sir Richard Hawkins in 1593; through Lind's influence this preventive was introduced in the British navy (1757). In Cook's second voyage, lasting over three years (1772–75), only one case of scurvy proved fatal. In 1795 the use of citrus juices or fruits was made obligatory in the British navy (hence the name "limey" for a British sailor or soldier); thereafter naval scurvy disappeared.

It was a milestone in eighteenth-century humanitarianism when Victor Riqueti, Marquis de Mirabeau, laid down the principle (1756) that the health of the people is a responsibility of the state. Johann Peter Frank, who began life as a poor child abandoned at a street door, proposed a complete system of public medical service in his *System einer vollständigen medizinischen Polizei* (1777–78). These four volumes, the "noble monument of a lifelong devotion to humanity,"[21] described the measures that should be taken by any civilized community to dispose of waste, to guard the purity of water and food, to maintain hygiene in schools and factories, and to protect the health of women in industry; for good measure the doctor prescribed the taxation of bachelors, gave advice on conjugal hygiene, and demanded the education of children in the principles of health. Napoleon was one of those who appreciated Frank's ideas; he begged Frank to come and serve Paris; Frank remained in Vienna.

Hospitals lagged far behind the need for institutional care of disease. Their number grew, but their quality declined. England in particular multiplied its hospitals in the eighteenth century, but all of them were maintained by private contributions, none by state endowment.[22] In Paris the leading hospital, the Hôtel-Dieu, received 251,178 patients in the eleven years from 1737 to 1748; of these, 61,091 died. The demands on this "Mansion of God" led to its putting three, four, five, even six persons in the same bed; "the dying and those on the road to recovery lay next to each other; . . . the air was tainted with the emanations from so many diseased bodies."[23] It was one of the many beneficent acts of Louis XVI that in 1781 he decreed that "henceforward 2,500 patients should have a separate bed, that five hundred should sleep in double beds divided with a partition," and that there should be special rooms for the convalescent.[24] Nevertheless, seven years later the hospital had single beds for only 486 patients; 1,220 beds held four or more patients, and eight hundred patients lay on straw.[25] In Frankfurt-am-Main and other cities the air in the hospitals was so fetid that "physicians declined hospital service as equivalent to a sentence of death."[26]

III. TREATMENT

A few doctors dared to undermine their income by spreading a knowledge of preventive medicine. Dr. John Arbuthnot of London, in an *Essay concerning the Nature of Ailments* (1731), argued that diet would do almost all that medicine could accomplish. He anticipated later complaints in a treatise, *The Cost of Preserving Health* (1744). The instruction of medical students improved slowly, with the Italian universities (Padua, Bologna, Pavia, Rome) still in the lead, and with Vienna, Paris, and Montpellier following; but even in these there were only four or five professors. Each teacher collected fees for his own course, and issued tickets of admission, sometimes on the back of playing cards.[27] Certain hospitals now began to teach clinical medicine. Legal practice of medicine, or of midwifery, required a diploma from an accredited institution.

Just as Georg Stahl's theory of fire as "phlogiston" dominated chemistry in the century before Lavoisier, so his concept of "animism" dominated medicine. Rejecting Descartes' view of the body as a mechanism, Stahl pictured the soul as an immaterial principle of life molding the body as its instrument. Consequently (he held) nature, in the form of this life force, is the chief agent in curing disease; sickness is an effort of the *anima* to re-establish the normal tone, operation, and harmony of disordered organs; heightened temperature and quickened pulse are means that nature uses to overcome disease; a wise doctor will rely chiefly on such processes of auto-detoxication, and will be reluctant to administer drugs. Stahl left unanswered the question of the cause that produced the disorder. One answer was given by Marcus Antonius Plenciz, who in 1762 revived Athanasius Kircher's conception of disease as due to infection by a microorganism; for each disease, said Plenciz, there is a particular invading organism, with a definite period of incubation. This remarkable prevision of the germ theory left no mark on eighteenth-century therapy, and had to be revived a second time in the nineteenth century.

Some new methods of diagnosis were advanced. Stephen Hales advocated the measurement of blood pressure; Leopold Auenbrugger introduced percussion of the chest as a way of detecting fluid in the thorax. Two Scots, George Martine and James Currie, developed the use of the clinical thermometer.

Drugs, surgery, and quackery competed for the money of the patient. Bloodletting was still the standard panacea; one physician calculated in 1754 that forty thousand deaths were caused each year in France by excessive withdrawal of blood.[28] Toward the end of the century protests mounted, and found an effective voice in Wolstein's *Annotations regarding Venesection* (1791). Drugs multiplied. The official London Pharmacopoeia of 1746 discarded prescriptions made of spider webs, unicorn horns, and virgin's milk, but it retained theriac, crab's eyes, wood lice, vipers, and pearls as forming curative mixtures. The Pharmacopoeia of 1721 gave official standing to paregoric (containing opium), ipecac, tartar emetic, spirit of *sal volatile*, and other new drugs; the edition of 1746 added valerian, sweet spirits of niter, and "balsam" (tincture of benzoin); the edition of 1788 sanctioned arnica, sarsaparilla, cascarilla, magnesia, tincture of opium . . . Castor oil came into use in modern Europe about 1764, arsenic toward 1786; colchicum was introduced for gout in 1763. William Withering, a Shropshire lad, learned from an old granddame that foxglove (digitalis) is good for dropsy; he earned a niche in medical history by discovering its usefulness in ailments of the heart (1783). Many reputable physicians made and sold their own drugs, and charged rather for their prescriptions than for their visits. "Proprietary medicines"—from secret and patented formulas—made some individuals rich. So England absorbed tons of "Stoughton's Elixir," "Betton's British Oils," "Hooper's Female Pills," and Ching's "Worm Lozenges."

Quacks were an appealing element in the medical scene. "Count" Alessandro di Cagliostro, whose real name was Giuseppe Balsamo, sold an elixir of long life to wealthy ninnies in several lands. "Chevalier" Taylor, armed with his cataract needle, proposed to cure any disorder of the eyes; Gibbon and Handel heard him hopefully. Joanna Stevens persuaded Parliament to pay her five thousand pounds for divulging the secret of her cure for the stone; when her recipe was published (1739) it proved to be a compound of eggshells, snails, seeds and soap; and in each of the cases which she claimed to have cured, stone was found in the bladder after death.

The most famous quack of the eighteenth century was Franz Anton Mesmer. The thesis that earned him a doctor's degree at Vienna (1766) renewed the old claim of astrological influences on man; these he explained by magnetic waves. For a time he tried to cure diseases by stroking the affected parts with magnets; later, having met a priest who seemed to cure merely by laying on of hands, he discarded magnets, but announced that an occult force dwelt within him, which could be transmitted to others under financial stimulation. He opened an office in Vienna, where he treated patients by touching them—as kings had done for scrofula, and as faith healers do today. The police declared him a charlatan, and ordered him to leave Vienna within forty-eight hours. He moved to Paris (1778), and began afresh by publishing a *Mémoire sur la découverte du magnétisme animal* (1779). Patients came to him to be "mesmerized"; he touched them with a wand, or stared into their eyes until he produced a semihypnotic submission to his suggestions; in this hypnotizing process his ugliness was a terrifying asset. He set up magnetic tubs (*baquets*) containing a mixture based on hydrogen sulfide, and provided with iron projections which the patients touched as they joined hands with one another; to make the cure more certain Mesmer himself touched each in turn. His patients included the Marquis de Lafayette, the Duchesse de Bourbon, the Princesse de Lamballe, and other persons prominent at court. Louis XVI offered him ten thousand francs if he would reveal his secret and establish a Magnetic Institute open to all; he refused. Within six months he took in 350,000 francs.[29] In 1784 the Académie des Sciences appointed a committee, including Lavoisier and Franklin, to investigate Mesmer's methods. Its report admitted some of his claims and cures (especially of minor nervous ailments), but rejected his theory of animal magnetism. The French Revolutionary government denounced him as an impostor, confiscated his tempting fortune, and banished him from France. He died in Switzerland in 1815.

In London James Graham opened (1780) a "Temple of Health" on Mesmer's principles, but with improvements. He provided a magical wedding bed for married couples, which was guaranteed to ensure beautiful offspring; he rented it at a hundred pounds per night.[30] His assistant as "Goddess of Health" in his procedures was Emma Lyon, destined, as Lady Hamilton, to hypnotize Lord Nelson himself.

Confused by the proliferation of quacks and their miraculous cures, both the public and the medical profession took nearly all of the eighteenth century to accept prophylactic inoculation as a legitimate form of therapy. The transfer of weakened virus from a smallpox-infected human being to another person to make him immune to smallpox had been practiced by the ancient Chinese.[31] For the same purpose Circassian women pricked the body with needles touched with smallpox fluids. In 1714 a communication from Dr. Emanuel Timoni, read before the Royal Society of London, described "the procuring of the smallpox by incision or inoculation, as it has for a long time been practiced in Constantinople."[32] In a letter sent from Constantinople on April 1, 1717, Lady Mary Wortley Montagu wrote:

> The smallpox, so fatal and so general amongst us [British], is here [made] entirely harmless by the invention of ingrafting. . . . Every year thousands undergo this operation . . . There is no example of anyone that has died of it. You may believe that I am very well satisfied of the safety of the experiment, since I intend to try it on my dear little son.[33]

The boy, six years old, was inoculated in March, 1718, by Dr. Charles Maitland, an English physician then in Turkey.

In 1721 a smallpox epidemic spread through London, proving especially fatal to children. Lady Mary, who had returned from Turkey, commissioned Dr. Maitland, also repatriated, to inoculate her four-year-old daughter. Three prominent doctors were invited to see how little the future Lady Bute was disturbed by the results. They were impressed, and one of them had his son inoculated. Lady Mary propagated the idea at court. Princess Caroline agreed to have it tested on six criminals who had been condemned to be hanged; they submitted on a promise of freedom if they survived; one suffered a mild attack of the disease; the others showed no ill effects; all six were released. In 1722 the Princess had the operation performed on the orphan children of St. James's Parish, with complete success; in April she had it performed on two of her daughters. Acceptance of inoculation spread among the British aristocracy, but the death of two inoculated persons in their households arrested the movement and gave a hold to the opposition. One critic complained that "an experiment practiced only by a few Ignorant Women . . . should on a sudden, and upon slender Experience, so far obtain in one of the Politest Nations in the World as to be received into the Royal Palace."[34] Lady Mary felt the stab, and published an anonymous "Plain Account of the Inoculating of the Small Pox by a Turkey Merchant." Most English physicians rejected inoculation as unsafe, but in 1760 Robert and Daniel Sutton introduced inoculation by puncture, and reported that in 30,000 cases they had had 1,200 fatalities—four per cent. As late as 1772 Edward Massey, an English clergyman, preached against "the dangerous and sinful practice of inoculation," and stood stoutly by the old theological view that diseases are sent by Providence for the punishment of sin.[35] (Perhaps, like many old religious doctrines, this could be profanely rephrased: disease is often a punishment for ignorance or negligence.)

Other countries took up the idea. In America Dr. Zabdiel Boylston, during the sixth epidemic of smallpox in Boston, inoculated his son (1721), and performed 246 additional inoculations despite an excited opposition that threatened to hang him. Most of the Puritan clergy defended him and shared the obloquy brought upon him.[36] Benjamin Franklin and Benjamin Rush gave their influential support to the inoculation movement in Philadelphia. In France the Regent Philippe d'Orléans, with his usual courage, led the way by having his two children inoculated. The Faculty of Medicine at the University of Paris opposed the practice till 1763. Voltaire, in his *Lettres sur les Anglais*, praised Lady Mary's campaign, noted the universality of the practice among the Circassians, and ascribed it to the monetary value of beauty: "The Circassians are poor, but have handsome daughters, who accordingly are the principal article of their foreign trade. It is they who furnish beauties for the seraglios of the Grand Seigneur and the sufi of Persia, and others who are rich enough to purchase and maintain these precious commodities."[37] An Italian physician, Angelo Gatti, spread the inoculation experiment in France, and Théodore Tronchin in Switzerland. Catherine the Great and Grand Duke Paul of Russia had themselves inoculated on the urging of Voltaire (1768); and in that year Jan Ingenhousz inoculated three of the imperial family in Vienna.

All these experiments, using smallpox serum from a human being, left much dissatisfaction, for the rate of mortality from inoculation, though down to four per cent, was still disagreeably high. An English surgeon, Edward Jenner, noticed that dairymaids who had contracted cowpox (a relatively mild disease) rarely contracted the often fatal smallpox. About 1778 he conceived the idea of conferring immunity to smallpox by inoculating with a vaccine made from a pox-infected cow (*vacca* is Latin for *cow*). This had already been done by a Dorset farmer, Benjamin Jesty, in 1774–89, without attracting the attention of the medical world. In May, 1796, Jenner performed vaccination by inoculating James Phipps with cowpox pus. In July he inoculated the same boy with smallpox virus. The boy did not develop smallpox. Jenner concluded that cowpox vaccine gave immunity to smallpox. In 1798 he published his epochal *Inquiry into the Cause and Effects of the Variolae Vaccinae* (*variola* was the medical name for smallpox), reporting his twenty-three cases, all successful. Subsequent experiments were so convincing that in 1802 and 1807 Parliament granted Jenner thirty thousand pounds to extend his work and improve his procedure. Smallpox, which for centuries had been one of the major scourges of human life, thereafter rapidly diminished its incidence, until today its occurrence in Europe and America is almost always due to the infection of unvaccinated persons by the importation of the virus from countries where inoculation is not practiced.

IV. SPECIALISTS

The medical art was becoming so complex with increasing medical science that it budded specialties. Gynecology was not yet a separate devotion, but obstetrics was now a distinct skill, and passed more and more into male hands. Feminine modesty still preferred trained midwives where these were available, but several royal mothers in childbirth set the example of accepting the ministrations of men. William Smellie led the way in England with his studies in the mechanism of labor and the use of the forceps—studies brought together, after thirty years of experience, in his classic *Midwifery* (1752).

Ophthalmology made a significant advance with operations for cataract by William Cheselden (1728) and Jacques Daviel; the latter originated (1752) the modern treatment of cataract by extraction of the lens. In 1760 the first bifocal spectacles were made, for Benjamin Franklin and apparently at his suggestion. We shall find Diderot studying the psychology of blind persons, and suggesting that they might be taught to read by touch; perhaps in collusion with him Rousseau (it is said) proposed embossed printing for the blind.[38]

Otology progressed through the use of the catheter for cleansing the Eustachian tube (1724), through the first successful operation for mastoid (1736), and through the discovery of an elastic fluid in the labyrinth of the ear (1742). Giacomo Rodríguez Pereira of Spain, having fallen in love with a deaf-and-dumb girl, devoted himself to developing a sign language using only one hand; the Abbé Charles Michel de l'Épée improved silent chatter with an ambidextrous alphabet, and dedicated his life to the education—even to the maintenance—of his pupils.

The treatment of the insane became more humane with the decline of the old theological view—held by Bossuet and Wesley—that insanity was a diabolical possession allowed by God as a punishment for guilt inherited or acquired. In the Narrenthurm (Fools' Tower) at Vienna the inmates were on view to paying sightseers like animals in a menagerie. The Bethlehem ("Bedlam") Hospital for Lunatics was one of the showplaces of London, where, for a fee, the public might gaze upon madcaps tied by chain and iron collar to the wall. In the Hôtel-Dieu at Paris the insane were treated with cruelty or negligence by underpaid and overworked attendants. Still worse were private asylums, which could be persuaded to accept for incarceration sane persons delivered to them by hostile relatives.[39] Various drugs or devices were used to cure or quiet the victims—opium, camphor, belladonna, bleedings, enemas, or a mustard plaster on the head. Some specialists thought that a sudden douche of cold water could mitigate melancholia; others recommended marriage as a cure for insanity. The first modern move toward a saner treatment of insanity was made by the Quakers of Pennsylvania, who established asylums where the condition was treated as a disease. In 1774 Grand Duke Leopold I of Tuscany founded in Florence the Ospedale Bonifazio, where, under the direction of Vincenzo Chiarugi, a scientific approach to the problem was inaugurated. In 1788 the French government appointed a commission to reform the care of the insane. The chairman, Philippe Pinel, had begun as a divinity student, had changed to philosophy, and had imbibed the humanitarian ethics of Voltaire, Diderot, and Rousseau. In 1791 he published his *Traité médico-philosophique sur l'aliénation mentale*, a milestone in modern medicine. In 1792 he was made medical director of the Bicêtre, one of the largest asylums in France; two years later he was advanced to the still larger Salpêtrière. After many appeals to the Revolutionary government he received permission to strike off the chains from his patients, to release them from their cells, and to give them fresh air, sunlight, exercise, and progressive mental tasks. This was one of many triumphs of secular humanitarianism in the most agnostic of centuries.

V. SURGERY

Next to the development of inoculation into vaccination, the most substantial advance in eighteenth-century medicine was in surgery. The old tie with the barber's art survived till 1745 in England, but in France it was ended by Louis XIV. (The barber's red-and-white-striped pole, symbolizing a bloody bandage, still recalls his surgical past.)

In 1724 Louis XV sanctioned the creation of five chairs of surgery in the Collège de St.-Côme at Paris. The Faculty of Medicine at the University of Paris protested against exalting surgery to such dignity; the physicians, decked out in their red scholastic robes and preceded by a beadle and an usher, marched to St.-Côme, where a lecture on surgery was in process; finding the door locked, they tried to break it open, and shouted imprecations against surgeons as upstart barbers; but the crowd that had assembled turned upon the physicians and drove them away. In 1731 Georges Maréchal and François de La Peyronie secured a royal charter to found the Académie de Chirurgie (Academy of Surgery); and in 1743 the King issued an ordinance freeing the surgeons of France from union with the barbers' guild, and requiring a college degree as prerequisite to surgical practice. Henceforth a surgeon could look a physician in the face.

A similar development took place in England. In 1745 the surgeons were formally separated from the barbers, and it was made a penal offense to practice surgery in or near London without examination and licensing by a committee of master surgeons; the Royal College of Surgeons, however, was not officially chartered till 1800. In Germany, before Frederick the Great, surgery was mainly in the hands of barbers, executioners, and strolling unlicensed practitioners who set bones, couched cataracts, bound up hernias, and cut out stones. In the army—which was Prussia's pride—the surgeon was called *Feldscherer*, field cutter, because his functions included serving as barber to the officers. But a Collegium Medico-Chirurgicum was opened in Berlin in 1724.

Most of the great surgeons of the eighteenth century were French. Jean Louis Petit invented the screw tourniquet, and made improvements in amputations and herniotomy. Diderot, in *The Dream of d'Alembert*, made the famous physician Théophile de Bordeu describe an operation on the brain by La Peyronie. Jean André Venel of Geneva founded surgical orthopedics (1780). In England William Cheselden developed the lateral operation for stone (1727) to a point hardly improved upon since,[40] and boasted of having performed one lithotomy in fifty-four seconds. English surgery became a science when John Hunter established it on the basis of sound anatomy and physiology. He experimented on animals to find substitutes for operations often fatal in man. In 1786, having discovered, in the case of a buck, that collateral blood vessels can continue the circulation when passage through a main trunk is arrested, he saved the life of a man suffering an aneurysm of the leg by tying the artery above the swelling and relying upon the surrounding parts of the body to absorb the contents of the tumor. This operation has saved countless limbs and lives.

John Hunter's name stands high also in the development of dentistry. In seventeenth-century England this art was mostly left to tooth pullers, who cried out their arrival and displayed strings of teeth as their coat of arms. In 1728 Pierre Fauchard proclaimed dentistry a branch of surgery, in his treatise *Le Chirugien dentiste*. But Hunter was the first to apply scientific methods to the study of teeth. He introduced their classification as cuspids, bicuspids, molars, and incisors; he devised appliances for correcting malocclusion; and he was the first to recommend complete removal of the pulp before filling a tooth. He summed up his views in his *Natural History of the Human Teeth* (1771).

Most minor operations were performed without anesthesia. The ancients had used various soporific potions—"nepenthe," opium, henbane, mandrake, hemlock, etc.; God himself, said the Book of Genesis, put Adam into "a deep sleep" before taking out a rib. Dioscorides, in the first century of the Christian Era, prescribed mandragora wine in surgical operations.[41] India used *Cannabis indica* (Indian hemp). Surgical sleeping draughts were mentioned by Origen in the second century, and by St. Hilary of Poitiers in the fourth. Most of the old soporifics continued in use in the Middle Ages; so the famous medical school of Salerno advocated a "sleeping sponge." In modern Europe the favorite anesthetic was drunkenness. Only in 1799 did Sir Humphry Davy discover the anesthetic properties of nitrous oxide ("laughing gas"). The anesthetic possibilities of ether were discovered in 1839 by Dr. Crawford Long of Danielsville, Georgia.

VI. THE PHYSICIANS

The growth of wealth, the rise of the middle classes in number and purse, and the progress of medical science and education gave a higher status and income to physicians than they had usually known before. La Mettrie, himself a physician, rejoiced: "Everything gives way to the great art of the healer. The doctor is the one philosopher who deserves well of his country. . . . The mere sight of him restores our calm, . . . and breeds fresh hope."[42] Voltaire was critical of medicines—"regimen is superior to medicine"; and of most doctors—"out of every hundred physicians ninety-eight are charlatans"; but he added: "Men who are occupied in the restoration of health to other men, by the joint exercise of skill and humanity, are above all the great of the earth. They even partake of divinity, since to preserve and renew is almost as noble as to create."[43] Diderot praised the Faculty of Medicine in the University of Paris[44] whose Faculty of Theology was the bane of his life. "There are no books I read more gladly," he said, "than books about medicine, no men whose conversation is more interesting to me than that of doctors—but only when I am well."[45] He made Dr. de Bordeu the central character in Le Rêve d'Alembert. The profession was satirized as usual, as in the plays of Goldoni, the pictures of Chodowiecki, the Ferdinand Count Fathom of Smollett, and the delectable caricatures of Thomas Rowlandson.

Better fees and incomes raised physicians to better status. Most of them, in England, charged a guinea for a visit. Some of them earned six thousand pounds a year. Sir Hans Sloane, the first physician to be made a baronet, became president of the Royal Society, and Josef von Quarin was made a baron by Joseph II of Austria. Physicians were welcomed in the best clubs of London, in the best salons of Paris. They no longer wore the lugubrious soutane, or black robe; they dressed in the best fashion of the upper middle class. In England they displayed a coat of red satin or brocade, knee breeches, buckled shoes, goldheaded cane, and sometimes a sword; in France they dressed with the pomp of a high ecclesiastic.

Some physicians call for special remembrance. Simon André Tissot was famous in Lausanne as a leading advocate of inoculation and an authority on epilepsy; he labored not only to heal the sick but also to keep the well well; his *Avis au peuple sur la santé*, or *Advice to the People on Health* (1760), ran through ten editions in six years, and was translated into every major language of Europe. Leopold Auenbrugger was chief in a circle of great doctors who gave honor to Vienna under Maria Theresa; he was loved for his modesty, honesty, and charity, "a noble example of the substantial worth and charm of old-fashioned German character at its very best."[46] Not quite so popular was Dr. Joseph Ignace Guillotin, who served as a deputy in the States-General of 1789, upheld capital punishment, and proposed the use of a beheading machine that would avoid the misstrokes of executioners. And Théodore Tronchin was the most famous physician in Switzerland.

He was a favorite pupil of Boerhaave at Leiden, practiced twenty years in Amsterdam, married the granddaughter of Jan de Witt, moved back to his native Geneva, and there introduced inoculation (1749) by beginning on himself and his children. In 1756 the Duc d'Orléans invited him to Paris to inoculate his son the Duc de Chartres and his daughter the current Mlle. de Montpensier. Paris marveled at such courage; but when the patients came through with no perceivable harm, the elite world flocked to Tronchin's lodgings in the Palais-Royal, eager to be made immune to a disease that had long maintained a high rate of mortality in France.

His success gave weight to his views on other matters. He preceded Rousseau in urging mothers to nurse their children. He told his patients to take less medicine and more exercise in the open air, to eat simple foods, to bathe more frequently, to wash in cold water, discard their wigs, night-caps, and bed curtains, and retire and rise at an early hour. He startled the court at Versailles by ordering the windows of the palace—which had always remained closed—to be opened at least part of every day, even in winter. His ideas became fashionable. Highborn ladies took walks in the early morning hours, clad, for ventilation's sake, in short skirts that were soon named *tronchines*.[47]

When Voltaire settled in Geneva he put himself under Tronchin's care. "He is a man six feet tall," said Voltaire, "wise as Aesculapius, and as handsome as Apollo."[48] Tronchin did not reciprocate these compliments, but, as Voltaire said of himself and Haller, perhaps they were both mistaken. Mme. d'Épinay, who had come all the way from Paris to Geneva to take treatment from Tronchin, gave a very flattering picture of him:

> I am going to spend two or three days at Voltaire's house with M. Tronchin. Really, I discover every day new features in Tronchin which inspire me with boundless respect and regard for him. His charity, his distinterestedness, his affection and care for his wife, are

unexampled. Now that I know her, I declare to you that she is the sulkiest and most unendurable woman in existence.[49]

But who can trust one woman on another?

It was not an especially great century in the history of medicine; the medical scene was still darkened with mysticism, quackery, and theories that should already have been shamed by experience. But the progress of anatomy and physiology had now placed medicine upon a sounder basis than before; medical education was more thorough and more widely available; unlicensed practice was fading away; specialties were increasing knowledge and improving care; surgery was liberated; miraculous cures were losing repute; and the triumphs of medicine were playing their quiet part in that basic conflict between faith and reason which was taking the forefront in the life of the mind.

BOOK V

THE ATTACK UPON CHRISTIANITY

1730–74

CHAPTER XVIII

The Atheists

1730–51

I. THE PHILOSOPHIC ECSTASY

LET us define our terms. By *philosopher* we shall mean anyone who tries to arrive at reasoned opinions on any subject whatever as seen in a large perspective. More specifically, in these chapters, we shall apply the term to those who seek a rational view of the origin, nature, significance, and destiny of the universe, life, or man. Philosophy must not be understood as in opposition to religion, and any large perspective of human life must make room for religion. But since many philosophers in eighteenth-century France were hostile to Christianity as they knew it, the word *philosophe* took on an anti-Christian connotation;* and usually, in our use of the French term, it will carry that implication. So we shall call La Mettrie, Voltaire, Diderot, d'Alembert, Grimm, Helvétius, and d'Holbach *philosophes;* but we shall not so term Rousseau—though we should call him a philosopher, if only because he gave a *reasoned* argument in defense of feeling and faith. We must also allow for the fact that a *philosophe* might oppose all the religions around him, and yet, like Voltaire, consistently and to the end profess belief in God. The debate that agitated the intellectual classes in the half century before the Revolution was not quite a conflict between religion and philosophy; it was primarily a conflict between the *philosophes* and Catholic Christianity as it then existed in France. It was the pent-up wrath of the French mind after centuries in which religion had sullied its services with obscurantism, persecution, and massacre. The reaction went to extremes, but so had the Massacre of St. Bartholomew (1572), the assassination of Henry IV (1610), and the dragonnades of the Revocation (1685).

Never had there been such a multitude of philosophers. Helvétius remarked "the taste of our age for philosophy,"[2] and d'Alembert wrote:

---

* Guillaume François Berthier, the brilliant Jesuit who edited the *Journal de Trévoux*, noted in the issue of July, 1759: "The custom has been established to call *philosophe* those who attack revealed religion, and 'persecutor' those who battle for its defense."[1]

> Our century has called itself the century of philosophy par excellence. . . . From the principles of the profane sciences to the foundations of revelation, from metaphysics to questions of taste, from music to morals, . . . from the rights of princes to those of peoples, . . . everything has been discussed, analyzed, disputed. . . . One cannot deny that philosophy among us has shown progress. Natural science from day to day accumulates new riches. . . . Nearly all fields of knowledge have assumed new forms.[3]

The French philosophers were a new breed. First of all, they were clear. They were not solemn recluses, talking to themselves or their like in esoteric gibberish. They were men of letters, who knew how to make thoughts shine through words. They turned their backs on metaphysics as a hopeless quest, and on systems of philosophy as pretentious vanities. They wrote not long convoluted treatises, laboriously evolving the world from one idea, but relatively short essays, diverting dialogues, novels sometimes spiced with obscenity, satires that could slay with laughter, epigrams that could crush with a line. These philosophers attuned their speech to the men and women of the salons; in many cases they addressed their works to distinguished ladies; such books were bound to be intelligible, and might make atheism charming. So philosophy became a social force, moving out of the schools into society and government. It took part in the conflict of powers; it was in the news. And since all educated Europe looked to France for the latest notions, the works of the French philosophers reached into England, Italy, Spain, Portugal, Germany, Sweden, and Russia, and became European events. Frederick the Great and Catherine the Great were proud to be *philosophes*, and perhaps they were not disturbed when French conservatives predicted that the freethinkers of France were undermining her morals, unity, and power.

Gutenberg was having his effect: print was spreading science, history, Biblical criticism, the pagan classics; the philosophers could now speak to a larger and better-prepared audience than ever before. They did not disdain to come down from their towers and "popularize" knowledge. Not that they put much trust in the "common man" as they knew him in that age; but they were confident that the dissemination of "truth" would improve the conduct and happiness of mankind. D'Alembert regarded "the art of instructing and enlightening men" as "the noblest portion and gift within human reach."[4] *Sapere aude*—"to dare to know"—became the motto of this *éclaircissement*, or enlightenment, this Age of Reason triumphant and fulfilled.

For now the faith in reason, which had had its chanticleer in Francis Bacon a century before, became the foundation and instrument of "liberal" thought—i.e., in this aspect, thought liberated from the myths of the Bible and the dogmas of the Church. Reason appeared in all the glory of a new revelation; it claimed authority henceforth in every field, and proposed to re-form education, religion, morals, literature, economy, and government in its own bright image. The *philosophes* admitted the frailty of reason, as of everything human; they knew that it could be deceived by bad logic or a mistaken interpretation of experience; and they did not have to wait for Schopenhauer to tell them that reason is usually the servant of desire, the handmaiden of the will. Hume, who dominated this Age of Reason in Britain, was the strongest critic that reason ever encountered, possibly excepting Kant. Voltaire time and again acknowledged the limits of reason, and Diderot agreed with Rousseau that feeling is more basic than reason. Nearly all the philosophers of the Enlightenment recognized that the majority of men, even in the most civilized nation, are too pressed by economic necessities and toil to have time for the development of reason, and that the masses of mankind are moved far more by passion and prejudice than by reason. Even so, the hope remained that reason could be spread, and could be freed from narrow selfishness and interested indoctrination.

And so, despite their periods of pessimism, a spirit of optimism prevailed among the *philosophes*. Never had men been so confident that they could remold, if not themselves, at least society. Despite the disasters of the Seven Years' War, despite the loss of Canada and India to England, there rose in the second half of the eighteenth century an *élan* of the mind that seemed to make old and ailing France young and strong again. Not since the days of the Greek Sophists had there been so many ideas in the air, or so invigorating a spirit of inquiry and debate; no wonder Duclos sensed around him "a certain fermentation of reason tending to develop everywhere."[5] And because Paris was now the intellectual capital of Europe, the Enlightenment became as wide a movement as the Renaissance and the Reformation. Indeed, it seemed the logical culmination of the earlier movements. The Renaissance had gone back beyond Christianity to explore the pagan mind; the Reformation had broken the bonds of doctrinal authority, and, almost despite itself, had let loose the play of reason. Now those two preludes to modernity could complete themselves. Man could at last liberate himself from medieval dogmas and Oriental myths; he could shrug off that bewildering, terrifying theology, and stand up free, free to doubt, to inquire, to think, to gather knowledge and spread it, free to build a new religion around the altar of reason and the service of mankind. It was a noble intoxication.

II. THE BACKGROUND OF REVOLT

But how had all this come about? Why had so many philosophers, especially in France, turned against Christianity, which, after all, had mingled hope with its terrors, charity with its crimes, beauty with its sins?

In England the revolt, as expressed by the deists, had met with a relatively tolerant hearing, even from the Established Church; and perhaps for that reason the fire of revolt had died down. Moreover, the Church in England was subject to the state, and no longer made any active pretense to be a rival independent power. But in France the Church was a powerful organization owning a large share of the national wealth and soil, and yet bound by supreme allegiance to a foreign power. It seemed to be draining more wealth from secular into ecclesiastical hands through its role in the making of wills and the guidance of bequests; it refused to pay taxes beyond its occasional "gratuitous gift"; it held thousands of peasants in practical serfdom on its lands; it maintained monks in what seemed to be fruitless idleness. It had repeatedly profited from false documents and bogus miracles. It controlled nearly all schools and universities, through which it inoculated the minds of the young with stupefying absurdities. It denounced as heresy any teaching contrary to its own, and used the state to enforce its censorship over speech and press. It had done its best to choke the intellectual development of France. It had urged Louis XIV into the inhuman persecution of the Huguenots, and the heartless destruction of Port-Royal. It had been guilty of barbarous campaigns against the Albigenses, and of sanctioning massacres like that of St. Bartholomew's Day; it had fomented religious wars that had almost ruined France. And amid all these crimes against the human spirit it had pretended, and had made millions of simple people believe, that it was above and beyond reason and questioning, that it had inherited a divine revelation, that it was the infallible and divinely inspired vicegerent of God, and that its crimes were as much the will of God as were its charities.

The Church offered many answers to this indictment; we shall hear them in due course. Meanwhile these proliferating charges moved thousands of minds to resentment and protest, and finally to an impassioned hostility. Skeptics multiplied to the point where they ceased to fear the clergy, and openly harassed them with difficult questions. When, about 1730, Father Tournemine, at the Collège Louis-le-Grand, invited unbelievers to meet him, "his room," we are told, "was soon filled with freethinkers, deists, materialists; he converted hardly any."[6] The clergy were appalled at the number of Frenchmen and Frenchwomen who died rejecting the sacraments of the Church. Mme. de Prie threatened to have her servants throw through the window the curé who importuned her to accept extreme unction.[7] A priest complained that "the moment we appear we are forced into discussion. We are called upon to prove, for example, the utility of prayer to a man who does not believe in God, and the necessity of fasting to a man who has all his life denied the immortality of the soul. The effort is very irksome, while those who laugh are not on our side."[8]

Barbier remarked in 1751, "We may see in this country a revolution in favor of Protestantism."[9] He was mistaken. The expulsion of the Huguenots had left no halfway house between Catholicism and unbelief. French liberal thought skipped the Reformation, and went at one leap from the Renaissance to the Enlightenment. So in France it was not to the Jansenists or to the few surviving Protestants that the French mind turned in its rebellion; it was to Montaigne, Descartes, Gassendi, Bayle, and Montesquieu. When the French freethinkers went back to Descartes they rejected nearly all of him but his "methodic doubt" and his mechanistic interpretation of the objective world. Bayle was honored as the subtlest of reasoners, whose doubts had generated a thousand doubts more; his *Dictionnaire* was an inexhaustible armory for the enemies of the Church.

The example of England was an emboldening inspiration to the freethinkers of France. First, Francis Bacon, whose call to inductive science seemed to promise so much more fruit than Descartes' magical deduction of God and immortality from the existence of Descartes. Then Hobbes, whose blunt materialism never ceased to agitate Diderot. Then Newton, who seemed to have reduced God to a button-presser in the world machine; the French did not yet know that Newton was more prolific in theology than in science. Then the English deists, who had given courage and impetus to Voltaire. And finally Locke, for the French skeptics thought that all religion collapsed before the proposition that all ideas are derived from sensation. If sensation is a product of external forces, mind is a product of experience, not a deathless gift of an invisible God. And if experience creates character, character can be changed by altering educational methods and content, and reforming social institutions. From these two propositions men like Diderot, Helvétius, and d'Holbach drew revolutionary conclusions. "Can there be anything more splendid," asked Voltaire, with Locke in mind, "than to put the whole world into commotion by a few arguments?"[10] (Voltaire died before 1789.)

Hear again the alert Marquis d'Argenson, writing in 1753:

> It would be a mistake to attribute the loss of religion in France to the English philosophy, which has not gained more than a hundred *philosophes* or so in Paris, instead of setting it down to the hatred against the priests, which goes to the very last extreme.

And he added, after that prediction of revolution which we have already quoted:

> It [the revolution] will be a very different thing from the rude Reformation—a medley of superstition and freedom that came to us from Germany in the sixteenth century. As our nation and our century are enlightened in so very different a fashion, they will go whither they ought to go: they will expel the priests, abolish the priesthood, and get rid of all revelation and all mystery. . . .
> One may not speak in behalf of the clergy in social circles; one is scoffed at and regarded as a "familiar" [spy] of the Inquisition. . . .
> The priests remark that this year there is a diminution of more than one third in the number of communicants. The college of the Jesuits is being deserted; 120 boarders have been withdrawn from these so greatly defamed monks.[11]

There were other intellectual influences that weakened the medieval creed. The *philosophes* joined with the orthodox in rejecting Spinoza, for the great Jew had been labeled atheist, and it was dangerous to speak of him without denouncing him, as Hume and Voltaire took care to do; but clandestinely Spinoza was being read; his *Tractatus theologico-politicus* was stirring up Biblical criticism; and M. le Comte de Boulainvilliers expounded Spinoza under the pretense of refuting him. Hume himself, influenced by France, was influencing France. Freemasons were establishing lodges in France, and were privately enjoying their deistic heresies. Exploration, history, and the comparative study of religions were adding fire to the crucible in which Christianity was being tried as never before. Every science, in its growth, was raising the respect for reason, the belief in universal law, the disbelief in miracles, including the greatest and most frequent miracle of all—the daily transformation of bread and wine, by fifty thousand simple priests, into the body and blood of Christ.

Social forces entered into the decay of dogma. Every increase in wealth was accelerating the race for pleasure, and was making the restraints of Christian morality more and more irksome in a Paris where the Most Christian King kept a stud of mistresses, and the Virgin Mary had been displaced by Mme. de Pompadour. And even the moral laxity of the age was turned into an indictment of Christianity: how was it that after seventeen hundred years of Christian domination the morals of Europe were no better than those of American savages or the "heathen Chinee"?

Every class but the peasantry included a skeptical minority. The governmental bureaucracy resented the independence and the tax immunity of the Church; the old association between the Church and its "secular arm," the state, was breaking down. There were freethinkers like Malesherbes in the department of censorship, actively protecting Diderot and the *Encyclopédie;* and much closer to the King was Mme. de Pompadour, who hated the Jesuits and was counted by Voltaire as "one of us." The aristocracy thought of the Church as supporting a Bourbon dynasty that had deposed the aristocracy from rule; they were not averse to weakening the clergy; many nobles enjoyed the irreverencies of Voltaire. The upper middle class smiled its favor upon the intellectuals who were battling the clergy; it had never forgiven the Church for condemning interest and favoring landowners over moneyed men; if these supercilious bishops were taken down a peg the bourgeoisie would move up in the scale of repute and power; so financiers like La Popelinière, Helvétius, and d'Holbach opened their homes and purses, even, in some cases, their hearts, to the crusade against the Church. The lawyers had long since been envious of the clergy; they looked forward to the time when they could rule the state, as they were already ruling the *parlements.* In 1747 a police report alleged that there was hardly an officer of the Paris Parlement who had not an irreligious publication or manuscript in his home.[12] The cafés of Paris hummed with atheism; lampoons of the clergy were the feast of urban wits, who referred to God as "Monsieur de l'Être," Mr. Being. Even in the provinces anticlerical literature circulated widely; some traveling salesmen profitably peddled from door to door a brochure entitled *The Three Most Famous Impostors: Moses, Jesus, and Mahomet.** And was not the clergy itself infected with religious doubt—even, here and there, with out-and-out atheism? Consider, for example,

III. JEAN MESLIER: 1678–1733

He was the parish priest of Etrépigny in Champagne. Every year he gave to the poor whatever remained of his salary after paying the cost of his abstemious life. After thirty years of quiet and exemplary ministry he died, aged fifty-five, bequeathing all his possessions to the people of his parish, and leaving three manuscript copies of a treatise which he entitled "My Testament." One copy was addressed to his parishioners; this was surely the strangest bequest in history. On the enclosing envelope he begged their pardon for having served error and prejudice through all his career. Apparently he had lost his religious faith before ordination. 'If I embraced a profession so directly opposed to my sentiments, it was not through cupidity; I obeyed my parents."[13] Voltaire published parts of the *Testament* in 1762; d'Holbach and Diderot issued a summary of it in 1772 as *Le Bon Sens du curé Meslier;* the full text was not printed till 1861–64;

---

* The manuscript is in the Bibliothèque Nationale.

it is now long since out of print, and rarely accessible. In all the campaign against Christianity, from Bayle to the Revolution, there was no attack so thoroughgoing, so merciless, as that of this village priest.

He seems to have begun his doubts by studying the Bible. The result showed that the Church had been only moderately wise in keeping the Bible from the common people; she should have kept it from the clergy too. Father John found many difficulties in Holy Writ. Why was the genealogy of Christ in the Gospel of St. Matthew so different from that in Luke, if both were authored by God? Why did both of these genealogies end with Joseph, who was soon to be excused from begetting Jesus? Why should the Son of God be complimented on being the Son of David, who was an arrant adulterer? Did the Old Testament prophecies apply to Christ, or were those applications mere tours de theological force? Were the miracles of the New Testament pious frauds, or were they natural operations misunderstood? Should one believe such stories, or follow reason? Jean voted for reason:

> I will not sacrifice my reason, because this reason alone enables me to distinguish between good and evil, the true and the false. . . . I will not give up experience, because it is a much better guide than imagination, or than the authority of the guides whom they wish to give me. . . . I will not distrust my senses. I do not ignore the fact that they can sometimes lead me into error; but on the other hand I know that they do not deceive me always; . . . my senses suffice to rectify the hasty judgments which they induced me to form.[14]

Meslier saw no warrant in reason for believing in free will or the immortality of the soul. He thought that we should be grateful that we are all allowed an eternal sleep after the turmoil of "this world, which causes more trouble than pleasure to the majority of you. . . . Return peaceably to the universal home from which you come, . . . and pass by without murmuring, like all the beings that surround you."[15] To those who defended the conception of heaven as a consolation, he replied that on their own allegations only a minority ever reached that goal, while the majority went to hell; how, then, could the idea of immortality be a consolation? "The belief which delivers me from overwhelming fears . . . appears to me more desirable than the uncertainty in which I am left through belief in a God who, master of his favors, gives them but to his favorites, and permits all the others to render themselves worthy of eternal punishments." How could any civilized person believe in a god who would condemn his creatures to everlasting hell?

> Is there in nature a man so cruel as to wish in cold blood to torment, I do not say--his fellow beings, but any sentient being whatever?

> Conclude, then, O theologians, that according to your own principles
> your God is infinitely more wicked than the most wicked of men.
> . . . The priests have made of God such a malicious, ferocious being . . .
> that there are few men in the world who do not wish that God did not
> exist. . . . What morals would we have if we should imitate this
> God![16]

Voltaire thought this was a bit extreme, and in publishing the *Testament*
he did his best to soften the priest's atheism into deism; but Meslier was
quite uncompromising. The Christian God, he argued, is the author of all
evil, for, since he is omnipotent, nothing can happen without his consent.
If he gives us life, he also causes death; if he grants us health and riches, he
sends us, in recompense, poverty, famine, disasters, and war.[17] There are
in the world many indications of intelligent design, but are there not quite
as many signs that this Divine Providence, if it exists, is capable of the
most devilish mischief?

> All the books are filled with the most flattering praises of Provi-
> dence, whose attentive care is extolled. . . . However, if we examine
> all parts of this globe, we see the uncivilized as well as the civilized
> man in a perpetual struggle with Providence; he is compelled to ward
> off the blows which it sends in the form of hurricanes, tempests,
> frost, hail, inundations, sterility, and the diverse accidents which so
> often render all man's labors useless. In a word, I see the human race
> continually occupied in protecting itself from the wicked tricks of
> this Providence, which is said to be busy with the care of their
> happiness.[18]

After all, was there ever a stranger and more incredible God than this?
For thousands of years he kept himself hidden from mankind, and heard
without any clear and visible response the prayers and praises of billions
of men. He is supposed to be infinitely wise, but his empire is ridden with
disorder and destruction. He is supposed to be good, but he punishes like
an inhuman fiend. He is supposed to be just, and he lets the wicked prosper
and his saints be tortured to death. He is continually occupied in creating
and destroying.[19]

Instead of holding, like Voltaire, that belief in God is natural and universal, Meslier contended that such a belief is unnatural, and has to be
infused into the adolescent mind.

> All children are atheists—they have no idea of God. . . . Men be-
> lieve in God only upon the word of those who have no more idea of
> him than they themselves. Our nurses are our first theologians; they
> talk to children about God as they talk to them of werewolves. . . .

Very few people would have a god if care had not been taken to give them one.[20]

And whereas most atheists professed admiration for Jesus, Meslier included Christ too in his passionate demolition of religious faith. First of all, what sane man could believe that "God, with the view of reconciling himself with mankind, . . . would sacrifice his own innocent and sinless son?"[21] As for Jesus himself,

> We see in him . . . a fanatic, a misanthrope, who, preaching to the wretched, advises them to be poor, to combat and extinguish nature, to hate pleasure, to seek sufferings, and to despise themselves. He tells them to leave father, mother, all the ties of life, in order to follow him. What beautiful morality! . . . It must be divine, because it is impracticable for men.[22]

Meslier moves on to complete materialism. It is not necessary to go beyond matter and ask who created it; the puzzle of origins would be merely put back a step to the child's natural question, "Who made God?" "I say to you that matter acts of itself. . . . Leave to theologians their 'First Cause'; nature has no need of this in order to produce all the effects which you see."[23] If you must worship something, worship the sun, as many peoples do, for the sun is the real creator of our life and health and light and warmth and joy. But alas, mourns Meslier, "if religion were clear, it would have fewer attractions for the ignorant. They need obscurity, mysteries, fables, miracles, incredible things.[24] . . . Priests and legislators, by inventing religions and forging mysteries, . . . have served them to their taste. In this way they attract enthusiasts, women, and the illiterate."[25]

All in all, in Meslier's view, religion has been part of a conspiracy between Church and state to frighten people into a convenient obedience to absolute rule.[26] The priests "took great care to make their God a terrible, capricious, and changeable tyrant; it was necessary for them that he should be thus that he might lend himself to their various interests."[27] In this conspiracy the priests are more to blame than the kings, for they capture control of the prince in his childhood and then through the confessional; they mold him to superstition, they warp and stunt his reason, they lead him on to religious intolerance and brutal persecution.[28] In this way,

> theological disputes . . . have unsettled empires, caused revolutions, ruined sovereigns, devastated the whole of Europe. These despicable quarrels could not be extinguished even in rivers of blood. . . . The votaries of a religion which preaches . . . charity, harmony, and peace have shown themselves more ferocious than cannibals or savages every time that their instructors have excited them to the destruction

of their brethren. There is no crime which men have not committed in
the idea of pleasing the deity or appeasing his wrath,[29] . . . or to sanction the knaveries of impostors on account of a being who exists only in
their imagination.[30]

This gigantic and self-perpetuating conspiracy of Church and state
against man and reason is defended on the ground that a supernatural religion, and even a religion of terror, is an indispensable aid in the task of
forming men to morality.

But is it true that this dogma [of heaven and hell] renders men . . .
more virtuous? The nations where this fiction is established, are they
remarkable for the morality of their conduct?[31] . . . To disabuse us
. . . it is sufficient to open the eyes and to consider what are the
morals of the most religious people. We see haughty tyrants, courtiers,
countless extortioners, unscrupulous magistrates, impostors, adulterers,
libertines, prostitutes, thieves, and rogues of all kinds, who have never
doubted the existence of a vindictive God, or the punishments of hell,
or the joys of Paradise.[32]

No; theological ideas, though professed by nearly all men, have very little
effect upon their conduct. God is far away, but temptation is near. "Whom
does the idea of God overawe? A few weak men disappointed and disgusted with this world; some persons whose passions are already extin-
guished by age, infirmities, or reverses of fortune."[33] It is not the Church
but the state that produces order and trains citizens to obey laws. "Social
restraints [are] more powerful than religion in making men behave."[34] In
the long run the best morality is one founded upon reason and intelligence:

To discern the true principles of morality men have no need of
theology, of revelation, or of gods; they need but common sense. They
have only to look within themselves, to reflect upon their own nature,
to consult their obvious interests, to consider the object of society and
of each of its members; and they will easily understand that virtue is
an advantage, and that vice is an injury, to beings of their species.
. . . Men are unhappy only because they are ignorant; they are
ignorant only because everything conspires to prevent them from
being enlightened; and they are wicked only because their reason is
not sufficiently developed.[35]

Philosophers could build a natural and effective morality if they were
not frightened into a hypocritical orthodoxy by fear of powerful priests.

From the most remote periods theology alone regulated the march
of philosophy. What aid has theology given it? It changed it into an

unintelligible jargon, . . . with words void of sense, better suited to obscure than to enlighten. . . . How Descartes, Malebranche, Leibniz, and many others have been compelled to invent hypotheses and evasions in order to reconcile their discoveries with the reveries and the blunders which religion had rendered sacred! With what precautions have not the greatest philosophers guarded themselves, even at the risk of being absurd . . . and unintelligible, whenever their ideas did not correspond with the principles of theology! Vigilant priests were always ready to extinguish systems which could not be made to tally with their interests. . . . All that the most enlightened men could do was to speak and write with hidden meaning; and often, by a cowardly complaisance, to shamefully ally falsehood with truth. . . . How could modern philosophers, who, threatened with the most cruel persecution, were called upon to renounce reason and to submit to faith—that is, to priestly authority—how could men thus fettered give free flight to their genius, . . . or hasten human progress?[36]

Some philosophers have had the courage to accept experience and reason as their guides, and to shake off the chains of superstition—Leucippus, Democritus, Epicurus, Strabo. "But their systems, too simple, too sensible, and too stripped of wonders for the lovers of fancy, were obliged to yield to the fabulous conjectures of Plato, Socrates, and Zeno. Among the moderns, Hobbes, Spinoza, Bayle, and others have followed the path of Epicurus."[37]

Meslier mourned the loss to mankind from this domination of philosophy by theology. He pleaded for freedom of thought as the basic right that "alone can give to men humaneness and grandeur of soul."[38]

> It is only by showing them the truth that they can know their best interests and the real motives that will lead them to happiness. Long enough have the instructors of the people fixed their eyes upon heaven; let them at last bring them back to earth. Tired of an incomprehensible theology, of ridiculous fables, of impenetrable mysteries, of puerile ceremonies, let the human mind occupy itself with natural things, intelligible objects, sensible truths, and useful knowledge.[39]

Let thought and speech and print be free, let education be secular and unconstrained, and men will move day by day toward utopia. The existing social order is iniquitous; it makes a small minority idly rich and corrupt with luxury, at the cost of keeping millions of men in a degrading poverty and ignorance. The root of the evil is the institution of property. Property is theft, and education, religion, and law are adjusted to protect and sanctify this theft.[40] A revolution to overthrow this conspiracy of the few against the many would be quite justified. "Where," Meslier cried out in his final fury, "where are the Jacques Clément [who killed Henry III] and the Ravaillac [assassin of Henry IV] of our France? Are there men still alive in our days to stun and stab all these detestable monsters, enemies of the human race, and by these means deliver the people from tyranny?"[41] Let the nation appropriate all property; let every man be put to moderate work; let the product be equally shared. Let men and women mate as they wish and part when they please; let their children be brought up together in communal schools. There would then be an end to domestic strife, to class war, and poverty; then Christianity would at last be real![42]

Having said all this, Jean Meslier concluded his *Testament* with a defiance to all who, as he knew, would execrate him.

> Let them think and judge and say and do what they will; . . . I shall pay little heed. . . . Even now I have almost ceased to heed what happens in the world. The dead, whose company I am now about to join, have no more troubles, and disquiet themselves no more. So I am putting *finis* to all this. Even now I am little more than nothing. Soon I shall be nothing indeed.[43]

Was there ever a testament like this in the history of mankind? Picture the lonely priest, shorn of all faith and hope, living out his silenced life in a village where probably every soul but his own would have been horrified to learn his secret thoughts. So he talked freely only to his manuscript; and there, recklessly and without any wide knowledge of the nature of man, he poured out his resentment in the most complete antireligious declaration that even this age would ever know. All the campaign of Voltaire against *l'infâme* was here, all the materialism of La Mettrie, the atheism of d'Holbach, the devastating phantasies of Diderot, even the communism of Babeuf. Hesitantly issued by Voltaire, joyfully published by d'Holbach, the *Testament* of Jean Meslier entered into the ferment of the French mind, and shared in preparing the collapse of the Old Regime and the ecstasies of the Revolution.

IV. IS MAN A MACHINE?

Yes, said Julien Offroy de La Mettrie. Born in St.-Malo (1709) to a prosperous merchant, he received abundant education, and decided to be a poet. His father recommended the ecclesiastical profession as less perilous; he sent Julien to a college at Plessis, where the boy became an ardent Jansenist. But a doctor friend of the father thought (as Frederick the Great put it) that "a mediocre physician would be better paid for his remedies than a good priest for his absolutions."[44] So Julien turned his zeal to anatomy and medicine, received the doctor's degree at Reims, studied under Boerhaave at Leiden, wrote several medical treatises, served as surgeon in the French army, and saw "one per cent glory and ninety-nine per cent diarrhea"[45] on the fields of Dettingen and Fontenoy. Himself bedded with violent fever, he claimed, on recovery, that the clearness of his thinking had varied with the height of his fever; from this he concluded that thought is a function of the brain. He published these and allied ideas in 1745 in *Histoire naturelle de l'âme*.

We cannot know what the soul is (ran the argument), and we do not know what matter is; we do know, however, that we never find a soul without a body. To study the soul we must study the body, and to study the body we must investigate the laws of matter. Matter is not mere extension, it is also a capacity for motion; it contains an active principle, which takes more and more complex forms in different bodies. We do not know that matter has of itself the power to feel, but we see evidences of that power in even the lowest animals. It is more logical to believe that this sensitivity is a development from some kindred potentiality in matter than to ascribe it to some mysterious soul infused into bodies by a supernatural agency. So the "active principle" in matter evolves through plants and animals until in man it enables the heart to beat, the stomach to digest, and the brain to think. This is the natural history of the soul.

The chaplain in La Mettrie's regiment trembled at this conclusion. He sounded an alarm, and the medicophilosopher was dismissed from his post as surgeon. His fellow physicians might have come to his aid, but he had written about the same time a little book, *The Politics of Physicians*, satirizing their intrigues in competition for lucrative posts. They joined in denouncing him; he found both his practice and his reputation ruined. He fled to Leiden, wrote another attack upon the medical profession, and turned to philosophy.

So at Leiden in 1748 he issued *L'Homme machine*. By the term *machine* La Mettrie means a body whose actions are due entirely to physical or chemical causes and processes. That the animal body is a machine in this sense is clear to him from a hundred phenomena: the flesh of animals continues to palpitate, and their intestines continue peristalsis, for some time after death; muscles separated from the body contract when stimulated, and so forth. Animals, then, are machines; and if so, why not men, whose bones, muscles, tendons, and nerves are so remarkably similar to those of the higher animals? The mind obviously depends upon the physicochemical operations of the body. Opium, coffee, wine, and diverse drugs do not merely affect the body, they can alter the stream and character of thought, the mood and force of the will. Change a few fibers in Fontenelle's brain, and you make him an idiot.[46] Bodily disease can weaken the mind; "the soul gains vigor with the body, and acquires keenness as the body gains strength."[47] Diet influences character; so "the English, who eat meat red and bloody, and not as well done as ours, seem to share more or less in the savagery due to this kind of food."[48] "Should we, then, be astonished that the philosophers have always had in mind the health of the body in order to preserve the health of the soul?" and "that Pythagoras gave rules for diet as carefully as Plato forbade wine?"[49] And La Mettrie concludes:

> Since all the faculties of the soul depend to such a degree on the proper organization of the brain and of the whole body, . . . they are apparently but this organization itself; the soul is clearly an enlightened machine . . . *Soul* is therefore but an empty word, of which no one has any idea, and which an enlightened man should use only to signify the part in us that thinks.[50]

In *L'Homme plante* (1748) La Mettrie developed the "great chain of being" into a theory of evolution. He lost some of his confidence when he tried to bridge the apparent gap between the inorganic and the organic; suddenly he forgot mechanism, and slipped into vitalism: he supposed certain *semences*, seeds, which enabled matter to beget life.[51] After that he found it easy to follow Lucretius: "The first generations must have been quite imperfect; . . . perfection could not have been the work of a day in nature, any more than in art."[52] To diminish the gap between animals and men, La Mettrie argues, against Descartes, that some animals reason:

> Let us observe the ape, the beaver, the elephant, etc., in their operation. If it is clear that these activities cannot be performed without intelligence, why refuse intelligence to these animals? And if you grant them a soul, you are lost. . . . Who does not see that the soul of an animal must be either mortal or immortal, whichever ours is?[53]

There is no great difference between the simplest man and the most intelligent animal. "Imbeciles . . . are animals with human faces, as the intelligent ape is a little man in another shape."[54] La Mettrie adds, with his peculiar humor, that "the entire realm of man" is "but a composite of different monkeys, at whose head Pope has placed Newton."[55] Man ceased to be a monkey only when he invented specific sounds as convenient expressions for specific ideas; he became man through language.[56]

Did La Mettrie admit a God as Prime Mover of the world machine? Voltaire and Diderot had defended the argument from design; La Mettrie rejected it scornfully:

> All reasoning based on final causes is frivolous. . . . Nature makes silk the way the *Bourgeois Gentilhomme* speaks prose—without know-

ing it. It is as blind when it gives life as it is innocent when it destroys it. . . . Having, without seeing, made eyes that see, it has made, without thinking, a machine that thinks.[57]

La Mettrie was not explicitly an atheist; he affected rather to discard the question of God as unimportant; "it does not matter, for our peace of mind, whether matter is eternal or has been created, whether there is or is not a God."[58] But he quoted a probably fictitious "friend" as holding that "the universe will never be happy unless it is atheistic"; for then there will be no more theological disputes, no ecclesiastical persecutions, no more religious wars, and man will express his natural instincts with no sense of sin.[59] As for himself, La Mettrie was content with materialism. He ended his *L'Homme machine* on a defiant note: "Such is my system—or rather the truth, unless I am much deceived. It is short and simple. Dispute it now who will."[60] Perhaps as a parting jest he dedicated his agnostic manifesto to the pious poet and physiologist Albrecht von Haller, who rejected the dedication with horror in a letter to the *Journal des savants* for May, 1749:

> The anonymous author of *L'Homme machine* having dedicated to me a work as dangerous as it is unusual, I feel that I owe it to God, to religion, and to myself to make the following statement: . . . I declare that the book in question is completely alien to my sentiments. I regard its dedication to myself as an outrage, exceeding in cruelty all those which its anonymous author has inflicted on so many worthy people; and I beg the . . . public to be assured that I have never had anything to do with the author, . . . that I do not know him, . . . and that I should look upon any consonance of views between us as one of the most unmitigated calamities that could possibly befall me.[61]

La Mettrie continued to print the dedication in later editions of his book.

L'Homme machine was widely reviewed and unanimously refuted. It was a simple matter to criticize the disorderly composition of the little volume, to condemn its self-assurance, and to expose careless errors of fact. It was not at all obvious that "the soul and the body fall asleep together";[62] some authors are more brilliant in their dreams than on the page. A sick body may house a good mind, as with Pope and Scarron; and our rare-meat lovers will not admit that they are still in the hunting stage. La Mettrie himself, who was up to every prank, published a pretended critique of his book in an anonymous *L'Homme plus qu'une machine* (*Man More Than a Machine*)—probably as a means of drawing attention to his major work.

On the other hand, he may have been really impressed by antimechanistic arguments. We know that he was interested in Trembley's demonstration (1744) of the fresh-water polyp's regenerative powers, which did not easily accord with mechanistic theory. Georg Stahl, of phlogiston fame, had boldly inverted the physiological thesis by declaring (1707) that instead of the body determining the ideas and volitions of the soul, it was the soul—the inherent animating principle—that determined the growth and action of the organs. Théophile de Bordeu—physician to d'Alembert— held that physiological processes, even of the simplest digestion, are incapable of mechanistic or purely chemical explanations.[63] And Jean Baptiste Robinet offered a cosmic vitalism that endowed all matter with life and sensitivity. La Mettrie was apparently willing to accept this solution of the problem of matter versus life.

Meanwhile he proceeded to deduce a hedonistic ethic from his materialistic philosophy. In three separate works—*Discours sur le bonheur, La Volupté (Pleasure)*, and *L'Art de jouir (The Art of Enjoyment)*—he proclaimed self-love to be the highest virtue, and sense pleasure the supreme good. He resented the theological denigration of the pleasures of life, and questioned the alleged superiority of intellectual pleasure; all pleasures, he thought, are really sensual; hence simple people, who do not bother with intellect, are happier than philosophers. Let no man (said La Mettrie) repent his indulgence in sensual delights if these involved no harm to others. Nor should the criminal be held morally responsible for his crimes; he is the product of heredity and environment, over which he had no control. He should be treated not with sermons but with medicine; with a firmness that protects society, but also with a humaneness that recognizes universal determinism. "It would be desirable to have for judges none but the most skillful physicians."[64]

These pronouncements marked the victory of Epicurus (misunderstood) over Zeno in eighteenth-century France: the Stoic philosophy of the classic age of Louis XIV surrendered, in the Enlightenment, to the Epicurean vindication of pleasure, the universalization of matter, and the banishment of the gods. No wonder La Mettrie's books were widely sold to a public disillusioned of theology and tired of classic formalism and moral restraint. Polite society, however, shied away from him as an intellectual maverick who had incontinently revealed too many upper-class tenets. The clergy attacked him as an emissary of Satan; the theologians of Leiden prodded the Dutch government into ordering him out of the country. The freethinking Frederick the Great invited him to Prussia (February, 1748), gave him a pension, and enrolled him in the Berlin Academy of Sciences. La Mettrie resumed the practice of medicine, and wrote, on asthma and dysentery, treatises that the King considered the best of their kind. Voltaire, after rubbing elbows with La Mettrie at Frederick's court, wrote to Mme. Denis (November 6, 1750):

There is here too gay a man; it is La Mettrie. His ideas are fireworks always in the form of skyrockets. His chatter is amusing for half a quarter of an hour, and mortally tiresome thereafter. He has just made, without knowing it, a bad book, . . . in which he proscribes virtue and remorse, eulogizes the vices, and invites his readers to disorderly living—all without bad intention. There are in his work a thousand brilliant touches, and not half a page of reason; they are like flashes of lightning in the night. . . . God keep me from taking him for my doctor! He would give me corrosive sublimate instead of rhubarb, very innocently, and then begin to laugh. This strange doctor is the King's reader, and the best of it is that he is at present reading to him the *History of the Church*. He goes over hundreds of pages of it, and there are places where monarch and reader are ready to choke with laughter.[65]

La Mettrie had described death as the conclusion of a farce ("*la farce est jouée*"); on November 11, 1751, aged forty-two, he offered himself as an example. At a dinner given by a patient whom he had cured of a serious ailment, he gorged himself with a *pâté* of pheasant, was seized with a violent fever, and died. For once, said Voltaire, the patient had killed his doctor.[66] The King wrote for the funeral a handsome eulogy, and Voltaire breathed relief. The dead man's ideas passed down to Diderot and d'Holbach, and entered into the spirit of the age.

CHAPTER XIX

Diderot and the *Encyclopédie*

1713–68

I. SHIFTLESS YEARS: 1713–48

HE was born on October 5, 1713, at Langres in Champagne, thirty-eight miles from Dijon. His father, Didier Diderot, was a cutler specializing in surgical instruments; the family had been engaged in cutlery for two hundred years past. Denis did not inherit his forebears' contented stability of occupation and belief, but he never ceased to reverence his father's simple honesty and quiet charity. "My son, my son," so Denis quoted him, "an excellent pillow is that of reason, but I find that my head rests still more softly on that of religion and the laws";[1] here in one sentence were the two voices of eighteenth-century France. Another son became a priest, and a sworn enemy to Denis. A sister entered a convent.

Denis himself verged on priesthood. From his eighth to his fifteenth year he attended a Jesuit school in Langres; at twelve he was tonsured, wore a black cassock, practiced asceticism, and resolved to become a Jesuit. Later he explained this as an exuberance of his fluids: he had mistaken "the first stimuli of a developing sexuality for the voice of God."[2] Didier rejoiced at his son's new vocation, and gladly escorted him to Paris (1729) to enroll him in the Jesuit Collège Louis-le-Grand. There, in 1732, the youth received the master's degree. But, as in many cases, the Jesuits lost a novice by sharpening a mind. Denis discovered that Paris had even more brothels than churches. He dropped his cassock and piety and became a lawyer's apprentice. Soon he discarded the law and entered upon a decade of transient occupations and garret poverty. After long patience his father cut off his allowance, but his mother sent him secret subsidies. Denis borrowed money, and sometimes repaid. He tutored boys in mathematics, wrote sermons for priests, and served as a bookseller's hack. Meanwhile he continued his studies of mathematics, Latin, Greek, and English, and picked up considerable Italian. He was lawless, but he was avid of knowledge and life. He never learned discipline, but he learned nearly everything else.

Purse empty, glands full, he fell in love and decided to marry. Antoinette Champion was his senior by three years and eight months, but she was a woman. She reproached him with his libertine youth; he assured her that this was a prelude to marital fidelity; he would be her faithful mate forever. "It is to you that my last love letters are addressed, and may heaven punish me as the most wicked of all men, the most traitorous of all men, if ever in my life I write one to anyone else."[3] His finest letters violated this vow. Antoinette's mother, yielding to her daughter's tears and the suitor's fluent tongue, agreed to the marriage on condition that he secure his father's consent. Diderot gathered sufficient funds to pay the coach fare to Langres, 180 miles away.

Arrived, he impressed his father by receiving there the proofs of his translation from the English of a history of Greece. Didier offered to support him in any career Denis should choose; but some choice must be made. The youth announced his eagerness to marry; the father upbraided him as a shiftless ingrate; the son answered insolently, and vowed to marry with or without paternal consent or coin. Didier had him imprisoned in a local monastery. Denis escaped, walked ninety miles to Troyes, caught a coach there, and returned to Paris.

But Mme. Champion was resolute; her daughter should not marry a man severed from parents and patrimony. Diderot, living almost penniless in a dingy room, fell seriously sick. Antoinette heard of this, rushed to him, and dragged her mother with her; the mother's resistance broke down. Together they nursed the ailing philosopher; and on November 6, 1743, "Nanette" and her "Ninot" (as they called each other) were united at midnight in a little church that thrived on clandestine marriages. Nine months later they rejoiced in the birth of a daughter, who, six weeks later, died. Three other children came, of whom only one survived childhood. Antoinette proved to be a faithful wife but an inadequate companion, quite unable to follow her husband's intellectual flights, and volubly discontent with the petty income he made as a translator. He returned to his baccalaureate cafés, living on coffee, playing chess. By 1746 he had taken a mistress, Mme. de Puisieux. For her he wrote his *Pensées philosophiques*, and *Les Bijoux indiscrets*, and the *Lettre sur les aveugles*.

He had long since succumbed to the fascination of philosophy—which draws us ever onward because it never answers the questions that we never cease to ask. Like most freethinkers of that century, he was shaken to his intellectual roots by reading Montaigne and Bayle, finding on nearly every page of the *Essais* and the *Dictionnaire* some arresting thought. Perhaps through Montaigne's rich references to the pagan classics, he was drawn to further study of the Greek and Roman philosophers—especially to Democritus, Epicurus, and Lucretius; he himself was the "laughing philosopher" of his age, a materialist bubbling with spirit. He could not afford to visit England, like Voltaire and Montesquieu, but he learned to read

English readily, even to enjoy its poets and dramatists; we shall see him responding to the sentiment of Thomson, and defending, like Lillo, the drama of middle-class life. He was stirred by Francis Bacon's call to the conquest of nature by organized scientific research, and proceeded to exalt experiment as the supreme tool of reason. He attended—now in these formative years and again in preparing the *Encyclopédie*—lectures on biology, physiology, and medicine; for three years he followed the *conférences* of Rouelle on chemistry, taking 1,258 folio pages of notes. He studied anatomy and physics, and kept abreast of the mathematics of his time. He went on from Bacon to Hobbes and Locke and the English deists. He translated (1745) Shaftesbury's *Inquiry concerning Virtue and Merit*, adding "reflections" of his own. He continued through all vacillations to believe with Shaftesbury that the good, the true, and the beautiful are near allied, and that a moral code based on reason rather than religion can adequately serve social order.

Bursting with all this stimulation, and with his own expansive imagination, he issued anonymously in 1746 his *Pensées philosophiques*. It was sufficiently radical to be attributed to La Mettrie, and eloquent enough to be ascribed to Voltaire; perhaps it owed something to both. It began with a defense of the "passions." Here the intrepid reasoner, agreeing with his friend Rousseau, argued that no harm would be done if philosophy should "say a word in favor of reason's rivals, since it is only the passions [*les grandes passions*] that can raise the soul to great things. Without the passions there would be nothing sublime, either in morals or in works; the arts would return to their infancy, and virtue would be limited to petty deeds."[4] But passions without order would be destructive; some harmony must be established among them; a way must be found by which one may check the other. Hence we need reason, and must make this our supreme guide. Here was an early attempt of the Enlightenment to reconcile reason with feeling, Voltaire with Rousseau.

Like Voltaire, Diderot was in this first period of his development a deist. The evidences of design compel belief in an intelligent deity. Mechanism can explain matter and motion but not life or thought. The future atheist challenged the atheist to explain the marvels of insect life recently displayed in the researches of Réaumur and Bonnet.

> Have you ever noticed in the reasoning or actions of any man more intelligence, order, sagacity, consistency, than in the mechanism of an insect? Is not the Divinity as clearly imprinted in the eye of a gnat as the faculty of thought is in the works of the great Newton? . . . Just think that I objected to you only the wing of the butterfly and the eye of a gnat, when I could have crushed you with the weight of the universe![5]

Nevertheless Diderot rejected with scorn the God revealed in the Bible; that deity seemed to him a monster of cruelty, and the Church that spread this conception was denounced by him as a fountainhead of ignorance, intolerance, and persecution. Could anything be more absurd than a God who makes God die on the Cross in order to appease the anger of God against a woman and a man four thousand years dead? And "if," as some theologians reckoned, "there are a thousand damned for every soul saved, then the Devil wins the argument, and without abandoning his son to death." Diderot recognized no other divine revelation than nature itself, and he pleaded with his readers to rise to a conception of deity worthy of the universe that science had revealed. "*Élargissez Dieu!*" he demanded. "Enlarge and liberate God!"[6]

The Parlement of Paris ordered the book to be burned by the public executioner on the charge of "presenting to restless and bold minds the most absurd and most criminal thoughts of which the depravity of human nature is capable, and of placing all religions, by an affected uncertainty, nearly on the same level in order to end up by not recognizing any."[7] Advertised by the burning (July 7, 1746), the little volume found an unexpected number of readers. It was translated into German and Italian; and when it was whispered about that Diderot was the author, he rose at once to a place near Voltaire. He received fifty louis from the publisher; these he turned over to his mistress, who needed new clothes.

As Mme. de Puisieux' wants expanded, Diderot wrote another book (1747). The parish priest heard of it, and begged the police to protect Christianity from this second assault. They surprised the author in his home and confiscated the manuscript; or, some say, they contented themselves with his promise not to publish it. In any case the *Promenade du sceptique* remained unprinted till 1830. It could not add to his fame, but it relieved his feelings. Using the philosopher's favorite dodge, the dialogue, he allowed a deist, a pantheist, and an atheist to expound their views of divinity. The deist repeats with vigor the argument from design; Diderot was not yet convinced that the remarkable adaptation of means to ends in organisms could be explained by a blind process of fortuitous evolution. The atheist insists that matter and motion, physics and chemistry, are a better explanation of the universe than a deity who merely postpones the problem of origin. The pantheist, who has the last word, holds that mind and matter are co-eternal, that together they constitute the universe, and that this cosmic unity is God. Perhaps Diderot had been reading Spinoza.

The year 1748 was exciting and laborious. Antoinette had borne a son, and Mme. de Puisieux was demanding the emoluments of adultery. Probably to raise money quickly, Diderot now wrote a licentious novel, *Les Bijoux indiscrets*. According to his daughter, the future Mme. de Vandeul (whose *Mémoires pour servir à l'histoire de la vie et des ouvrages de Diderot* cannot be trusted without corroboration), he had remarked to his mistress that writing a novel was a comparatively simple matter. She challenged the statement; he wagered that he could turn out a successful novel in a fortnight. Obviously imitating the younger Crébillon's *Le Sopha* (1740), where a sofa recounted the amours under which it had groaned, Diderot imagined a sultan's magic ring which, when pointed to the "indiscreet jewels" of a woman's person, caused them to confess their experiences. As the ring was turned upon thirty ladies, the interest of the two volumes seldom flagged. The author mingled with the ribaldry some provocative remarks on music, literature, and the theater, and added a dream in which the sultan sees a child called "Experiment" grow larger and stronger until it destroys an old temple called "Hypothesis." Despite these intrusions of philosophy, the book realized its aim: it made money. The publisher Laurent Durand paid Diderot twelve hundred livres for the manuscript, and though the volumes could be sold only "under the counter," they proved remunerative. Six French editions were printed in 1748; ten editions appeared in France between 1920 and 1960. "*Les Bijoux . . .* is Diderot's most published work."[8]

He varied his mood by composing scientific treatises. He valued highly his *Mémoires sur différents sujets de mathématique* (1748), which contained learned and original discourses on acoustics, tension, air resistance, and "a project for a new organ" that anyone could play. Some of the essays won high praise from *The Gentleman's Magazine* and the *Journal des savants*, even from the Jesuit *Journal de Trévoux*, which invited more of such researches "on the part of a man as clever and able as M. Diderot seems to be, of whom we should also observe that his style is as elegant, trenchant, and unaffected as it is lively and ingenious."[9] Diderot continued throughout his life to make such desultory sallies into physical science, but he leaned increasingly to problems of psychology and philosophy. And in almost every field he was the most original thinker of his time.

II. THE BLIND, THE DEAF, AND THE DUMB: 1749–51

He was especially attracted by a question which the Irishman William Molyneux had raised about 1692: Will a man born blind who has learned to distinguish a cube from a sphere by touch, be able, if his sight is restored, to differentiate at once a cube from a sphere, or will he require, before he can make this distinction, some experience of the relations between forms touched and the same forms seen? The latter answer had been given by Molyneux and his friend Locke. In 1728 Willian Cheselden op-

erated successfully upon a fourteen-year-old boy who had been blind from
birth; the boy had to be trained before he could differentiate forms by
sight alone. Diderot noted also the career of Nicholas Saunderson, who
had lost his sight at the age of one and had never recovered it, but, by making for himself a kind of mathematical Braille, had acquired such profi-
ciency as to be appointed professor of mathematics at Cambridge.

Early in 1749 Réaumur invited a select group to see what would happen
when the bandages were removed from the eyes of a woman who had undergone an operation to cure her congenital blindness. Diderot was piqued
that neither he nor any other of the *philosophes* had been included in the
invitation, and with his usual recklessness he suggested that Réaumur had
arranged to have the unveiling take place before "certain eyes of no consequence."[10] According to Diderot's daughter this phrase offended Mme.
Dupré de Saint-Maur, who prided herself on her eyes, and who was the
current mistress of the current *directeur de la librairie*, or chief censor of
publications, the Comte d'Argenson (Marc Pierre, younger brother of René
Louis, the Marquis).

On June 9 Durand published Diderot's *Lettre sur les aveugles à l'usage
de ceux qui voient* (*Letter on the Blind for the Use of Those Who See*).
It took the form of a letter addressed to Mme. de Puisieux. It began with
an account of the visit that Diderot and some friends had made to a blind
winegrower. They were struck by the sense of order shown by the blind
man—a sense so sure that his wife relied on him at night to put back in its
proper place everything disturbed during the day. All his surviving senses
were keener than those of normal men. "The smoothness of the flesh has
[for him] no less subtle nuances than the sound of the voice, and there is
no fear that he will mistake another woman for his wife, unless he gains by
the exchange."[11] He could not understand how one could know a face
without touching it. His sense of beauty was confined to tactile values,
pleasantness of voice, and utility. He had no shame in nudity, since he
thought of clothing as a protection against weather, not as a concealment
of the body from others' eyes. Theft he considered a major crime, because
he was so helpless against it.

Diderot concluded that our ideas of right and wrong are derived not
from God but from our sensory experience. Even the idea of God has to
be learned, and it too, like morality, is relative and diverse. The existence
of God is doubtful, for the argument from design has lost much of its
force. Yes, there are evidences of design in many organisms and organs, as
in the fly and the eye; but there is no sign of design in the universe as a
whole, for some parts are hindrances—if not fatal enemies—to other parts;
almost every organism is bound to be eaten by another. The eye seems
a wonderful instance of adjustment of means to ends, but there are gross

imperfections in it (as Helmholtz would later point out in detail). There is a creative spontaneity in nature, but it is half blind, and runs to much disorder and waste. Pretending to quote from a "Life and Character of Dr. Nicholas Saunderson" by William Inchlif (who apparently never existed), Diderot made the blind professor say, "Why talk to me of all that fine spectacle which has never been made for me? . . . If you want me to believe in God you must make me touch him."[12] In the imaginary biography Saunderson rejected God,* and attributed the order of the universe to a natural selection of organs and organisms by the survival of the fittest.

> All defective combinations of matter have disappeared, and only those remained in which the mechanism implied no important contradiction, and which could subsist by their own means and reproduce themselves. . . . Even now the order of the world is not so perfect but that monstrous products appear from time to time. . . . What is this world? A composite subject to revolutions all of which indicate a persistent tendency to destruction, a rapid succession of beings that follow each other, push each other, and disappear.[13]

Diderot concluded with agnosticism: "Alas, madame, when we put human knowledge in the balance of Montaigne, we shall not be far from accepting his motto. For what do we know? Of the nature of matter, nothing. Of the nature of mind or thought, still less, nothing whatever."[14]

All in all, this *Lettre sur les aveugles* is one of the outstanding productions of the French Enlightenment. It is fascinating as a narrative, brilliantly perceptive as psychology, imaginatively suggestive as philosophy, tiresome only toward the end of its sixty pages. It contains some indelicacies, hardly in place in an epistle supposedly addressed to a lady; but perhaps Mme. de Puisieux was accustomed to Diderot's mixture of plebeian frankness with erudite discourse. For good measure the essay included a detailed proposal for what later took the name of Louis Braille.[15]

Voltaire, who was then (1749) in Paris, wrote to Diderot an enthusiastic commendation of the *Lettre*:

> I have read with extreme pleasure your book, which says much and suggests more. For a long time I have esteemed you as much as I despise the stupid barbarians who condemn what they do not understand. . . .
> But I confess that I am not at all of the opinion of Saunderson, who denies a God because he was born blind. Perhaps I am mistaken, but in his place I should have recognized a very intelligent Being, who had given me so many supplements to sight. . . .

---

* According to his friends Saunderson died a pious death. The Royal Society of London resented Diderot's ascription of atheism to one of its members; and it never admitted him to corresponding membership.

I desire passionately to converse with you, no matter whether you think you are one of his works or whether you think you are a nicely organized portion of an eternal and necessary matter. Before my departure from Lunéville I should like you to give me the honor of taking a philosophical dinner with me, at my house, together with several sages.

Diderot replied (June 11):

The moment when I received your letter, *monsieur et cher maître*, was one of the happiest of my life.

Saunderson's opinion is no more mine than yours. . . . I believe in God, but I get along very well with atheists. . . . It is very important not to mistake hemlock for parsley, but not at all important whether or not you believe in God. The world, said Montaigne, is a ball that he has abandoned to the philosophers to bat around . . .[16]

Before anything could come of this correspondence Diderot was arrested. The government, angered by public criticism of the humiliating Peace of Aix-la-Chapelle, put several of its critics in jail, and thought it time to check Diderot. Whether the atheism lurking in the *Lettre* had brought protests from the clergy, or whether Mme. Dupré de Saint-Maur, resenting Diderot's remark about "inconsequential eyes," had prodded her lover to action, we do not know. In any case the Comte d'Argenson sent a *lettre de cachet* (July 23, 1749) to the Marquis du Châtelet, governor of the Fortress of Vincennes: "Receive in the Château de Vincennes the man Diderot, and hold him there until a further order from me."[17] Early the next morning the police knocked at Diderot's door. They searched his rooms and found two or three unbound copies of the *Lettre sur les aveugles*, plus boxes of material that Diderot was preparing for the epochal *Encyclopédie*. They carried him off to Vincennes (on the outskirts of Paris), where he was lodged solitary in a cell of the gloomy castle. He was allowed to keep with him a book which he had had in his pocket when arrested—*Paradise Lost*. He now had leisure to read it carefully. He annotated it in no orthodox spirit, and used its vacant pages for writing down some thoughts on less godly topics. He made ink by scraping slate from the walls, grinding it, and mixing it with wine. A toothpick served him for a pen.

Meanwhile his wife, left desolate with her three-year-old son, hurried to Police Lieutenant General Berryer, and implored him to release her husband. She disclaimed any knowledge of his writings. "All I know is that his writings must resemble his conduct. He esteems honor a thousand times dearer than life, and his works reflect the virtues he practices."[18]

If Antoinette knew nothing about Mme. de Puisieux, the police did. More effective was a plea from the men who had already engaged Diderot to edit an encyclopedia; they assured the Comte d'Argenson that the enterprise could not proceed without his prisoner. On July 31 Berryer sent for Diderot and questioned him. He denied authorship of the *Lettre*, of the *Pensées*, of the *Bijoux indiscrets*. Berryer knew that he was lying, and sent him back to Vincennes.

In August—just a month before her death—Mme. du Châtelet, presumably at Voltaire's urging, wrote from Lunéville to her kinsman the governor of Vincennes, and begged him at least to mitigate the conditions of Diderot's imprisonment. About August 10 Berryer offered to let the prisoner enjoy the freedom and comforts of the castle's great hall, with permission to receive books and visitors, if he would make an honest confession. On August 13 the chastened philosopher addressed to Berryer the following document:

> I admit to you . . . that the *Pensées*, the *Bijoux*, and the *Lettre sur les aveugles* are debaucheries of the mind that escaped from me; but I can . . . promise you on my honor (and I do have honor) that they will be the last, and that they are the only ones. . . . As for those who have taken part in the publication of these works, nothing will be hidden from you. I shall depose verbally, in the depths [secrecy] of your heart, the names both of the publishers and of the printers.[19]

On August 20 he was released from his cell, was promoted to a comfortable room, and was allowed to receive visitors and to walk in the gardens of the château. On the twenty-first he signed a promise not to leave the building or its grounds without official permission. His wife came to comfort and upbraid him, and his old love for her revived. D'Alembert came, and Rousseau, and Mme. de Puisieux. The entrepreneurs of the *Encyclopédie* brought him manuscripts, and he resumed his editorial work. Learning that his brother had told his father of his arrest, he wrote to the ailing cutler, claimed that his incarceration was due to a woman's spite, and asked for financial aid. The father answered in a letter (September 3, 1749) that reveals the human side of the conflict between religion and the *philosophes*:

> MY SON:
>
> I have received the two letters which you wrote to me recently, informing me of your detention and its cause. I cannot help saying that there surely must have been other reasons than those given in one of your letters. . . .

Since nothing happens without God's consent, I do not know which is better for your moral well-being: that your imprisonment should be ended, or that it should be prolonged for several months during which you could seriously reflect on yourself. Remember that if the Lord has given you talents, it was not for you to work to weaken the doctrines of our Holy Religion. . . .

I have given you sufficient proof of my love. In giving you an education it was in the hope that you would make good use of it, and not that its results should throw me, as they have done, into the most bitter sorrow and chagrin on learning of your disgrace. . . .

Forgive, and I shall forgive you. I know, my son, that no one is exempt from calumny, and that they may impute to you works in which you have had no share. . . .

You will never receive any consideration from me until you have informed me, truly and unequivocally, whether you are married, as they have written to me from Paris, and whether you have two children. If this marriage is legitimate and the thing is done, I am satisfied. I hope you will not refuse your sister the pleasure of bringing them up, and me the pleasure of seeing them under my eyes.

You ask for money. What! A man like you, who is working on immense projects, . . . can need money? And you have just spent a month in a place where it cost you nothing to live! . . .

Remember your poor mother. In the reproaches that she made to you she told you several times that you were blind. Give me proofs to the contrary. Once again, and above all, be faithful in the execution of your promises.

You will find enclosed a draft for 150 livres, . . . which you will spend as you see fit.

I await impatiently the happy day which will calm my worries by informing me that you are free. As soon as I find out I will go render thanks to the Lord.

Meanwhile, my son, with all the love that I owe to you,

Your affectionate father,
DIDEROT[20]

We do not have Denis' answer; he would have been hard put to equal that letter in nobility.

He was released on November 3, 1749, after three and a half months of imprisonment. He went home happy to his wife and child, and for a time he forgot Mme. de Puisieux. But on June 30, 1750, his son, aged four, died of a violent fever. A third child, born soon afterward, was badly injured at its baptism, being dropped to the floor of the church by an attendant; it died before the year was out. Three births, three deaths. Diderot went back to his evenings at the Café Procope. About 1750 Rousseau introduced him to Friedrich Melchior Grimm, and there began a triune friendship of some importance to literature. This was the year in which Voltaire abandoned France for Berlin, Rousseau wrote his prize-winning essay on civilization as a disease, and Diderot's prospectus announced the *Encyclopédie*.

While working on the first volume of this project he digressed into another psychological inquiry, whose results he published (1751) in a *Lettre sur les sourds et muets à l'usage de ceux qui entendent et qui parlent (Letter on the Deaf and Dumb, for the Use of Those Who Hear and Who Speak)*. Not yet having forgotten Vincennes, he avoided heresy, and received from the censor (now the kindly Malesherbes) "tacit permission" to publish the essay in France without his name and without fear of prosecution. Diderot proposed to ask questions of a deaf-mute, to observe the gestures with which the deaf-mute answered, and to illuminate thereby the origin of language through gestures. A great actor (for Diderot was already pregnant with his *Paradox of the Actor*) sometimes conveys a thought or a feeling more effectively through a gesture or a facial expression than through words. The first words were probably vocal gestures—sounds illustrative of the idea in mind. In poets the word chosen has not only an intellectual denotation, or meaning, but also a symbolic connotation, or nuance; it has visual implications (e.g., compare *see* and *gaze*) or overtones of sound (compare *say* and *murmur*); hence real poetry is untranslatable.

As usual in Diderot, the discourse is vacillating and disorderly, but rich in suggestive asides. "My idea would be to decompose a man, so to speak, and to consider what he derives from each of his senses" (Condillac later [1754] built his *Traité des sensations* around this notion). Or again, contrast poetry with painting: the poet can narrate events, the painter can show only one moment: his picture is a gesture, which tries to express at once past, present, and future; here was one germ of Lessing's *Laokoon* (1766).

But by this time the first volume of the *Encyclopédie* was ready for publication.

III. HISTORY OF A BOOK: 1746-65

The *Encyclopédie*, said the Roman Catholic critic Brunetière, "is the great affair of its time, the goal to which everything preceding it was tending, the origin of everything that has followed it, and consequently the true center for any history of ideas in the eighteenth century."[21] "It belonged only to a philosophical century to attempt an encyclopedia," said Diderot.[22] The work of Bacon, Descartes, Hobbes, Locke, Berkeley, Spinoza, Bayle, and Leibniz in philosophy; the advances made in science by Copernicus, Vesalius, Kepler, Galileo, Descartes, Huygens, and Newton; the exploration of the earth by navigators, missionaries, and travelers, and the rediscovery of the past by scholars and historians: all this mounting knowledge and speculation waited to be put in order for public accessibility and use.

Chambers' *Cyclopoedia, or an Universal Dictionary of Arts and Sciences* (1728) seemed at first to meet this need. In 1743 a Paris publisher, André François Le Breton, proposed to have it translated into French, with changes and additions suited to French needs. The project grew until it aimed at ten volumes. To meet the expense Le Breton took into partnership, for this undertaking, three other publishers—Briasson, David, and Durand. They engaged the Abbé de Gua de Malves as editor, obtained a license to print with the *privilège du roi*, and issued (1745) a tentative prospectus. In December they or Gua de Malves enlisted the aid of Diderot and d'Alembert. In 1747 Gua de Malves withdrew, and on October 16 the publishers appointed Diderot editor in chief, with a salary of 144 livres per month, and asked d'Alembert to take charge of the articles on mathematics.

As the work proceeded Diderot became increasingly dissatisfied with the Chambers text. We can measure this by his giving fifty-six columns to anatomy, which in Chambers had received one, and fourteen columns to agriculture, which in Chambers had rated thirty-six lines. Finally he recommended that Chambers' book be put aside, and that an entirely new encyclopedia be prepared. (Malves may have already suggested this.) The publishers agreed, and Diderot (not yet the heretical author of the *Letter on the Blind*) persuaded the earnestly orthodox Chancellor d'Aguesseau to extend the *privilège du roi* to the extended enterprise (April, 1748).

But how was this to be financed? Le Breton reckoned it would cost two million livres; actually it cost less—some 1,140,000; even so there must have been many doubts about securing sufficient subscribers to warrant going to press. Diderot had already commissioned many articles—and secured some—for the first volumes when his imprisonment at Vincennes interrupted the work. Released, he gave all his time to it, and in November, 1750, the publishers sent out eight thousand copies of a prospectus written by Diderot. (In 1950 the French government reprinted this in national commemoration of the event.) It announced that a company of well-known men of letters, experts, and specialists proposed to gather existing knowledge of the arts and sciences into an orderly whole, alphabetically arranged, and fitted with cross references that would facilitate use by scholars and students. "The word *encyclopédie*," said the prospectus, "signifies the interrelationship of the sciences"; literally it meant instruction, or learning, gathered in a circle. Not only had knowledge grown immensely, said Diderot, but the need for its dissemination was urgent; it would be of no use if not shared. All this, according to the prospectus, was to be compressed into eight volumes of text and two of plates. Subscriptions were solicited at 280 livres for the set, payable in nine installments. The whole was to be completed in two years. In our hindsight this prospectus appears as one of the first announcements that the reign of science had begun, and that a new faith had been offered for the salvation of mankind.

The response to the prospectus was inspiring, especially from the upper middle class. After Mme. Geoffrin's death it was disclosed that she and her husband had contributed over 500,000 livres to the expenses of the *Encyclopédie*.[23] With this work in France, and Johnson's *Dictionary* (1755) in England, European literature declared its independence of aristocrats and servile dedications, and addressed itself to the larger public whose eye and voice it proposed to be. The *Encyclopédie* was the most famous of all experiments in the popularization of knowledge.[24]

The first volume appeared on June 28, 1751. It contained 914 large double-columned folio pages. The frontispiece, engraved by Charles Cochin, was typical of the eighteenth century: it showed humanity groping for knowledge, which was represented by a beautiful woman in diaphanous gauze. The title was impressive: *Encyclopédie, ou Dictionnaire raisonné des sciences, des arts, et des métiers, par une Société de gens de lettres. Mise en ordre et publiée par M. Diderot, . . . et quant à la partie mathématique par M. d'Alembert. : . . . Avec approbation et privilège du Roi.* The volume was judiciously dedicated to "*Monseigneur le comte d'Argenson, ministre et secrétaire d'état et de guerre.*" It was not encyclopedic in our present sense: it did not propose to include biographies or history; but some biographies, strangely enough, were given under the birthplace of the person. On the other hand, it was in part a dictionary, defining many terms, listing synonyms, and giving grammatical rules.

The most memorable part of Volume I was the "Discours préliminaire." D'Alembert was chosen to write this because he was known both as a leading scientist and as a master of French prose. Despite these distinctions he was living in stoic poverty in Paris. When Voltaire described the majestic view from Les Délices, d'Alembert replied: "You write to me from your bed, whence you command ten leagues of lake, and I answer you from my hole, whence I command a patch of sky three ells long."[25] He was an agnostic, but he had not joined in any public criticism of the Church. In the "Discours" he tried to disarm ecclesiastical opposition:

> The nature of man is an impenetrable mystery when one is enlightened by reason alone. We can say the same of our existence present and future, of the essence of the Being to whom we owe it, and of the kind of worship he requires from us. Hence nothing is

more necessary to us than a revealed religion which instructs us in such diverse subjects.[26]

He apologized to Voltaire for these obeisances: "Such phrases as these are notarial style, and serve only as passports for the truths that we wish to establish. . . . Time will teach men to distinguish what we have thought from what we have said."[27]

Following a proposal by Francis Bacon, the "Discours préliminaire" classified all knowledge according to the mental faculty involved. So history came under "Memory," science under "Philosophy," and theology under "Reason"; literature and art came under "Imagination." Diderot and d'Alembert were quite proud of this scheme, and made from it, as a folded insert after the "Discours," a chart of knowledge which evoked great admiration in its day. Next to Bacon's, the strongest influence in the *Encyclopédie* was that of Locke. "It is to sensations that we owe all our ideas," said the "Discours." From this statement the editors hoped, in the course of the eight volumes, to deduce an entire philosophy: a natural religion that would reduce God to an initial push, a natural psychology that would make mind a function of the body, and a natural ethic that would define virtue in terms of man's duties to man rather than to God. This program was cautiously implied in the "Discours."

From these first principles d'Alembert passed on to survey the history of science and philosophy. He praised the ancients, deprecated the Middle Ages, and rejoiced in the Renaissance.

> We should be unjust if we failed to recognize our debt to Italy. It is from her that we have received the sciences which later produced such abundant fruit in all Europe; it is to her above all that we owe the *beaux-arts* and good taste of which she has furnished us with so great a number of inimitable models.[28]

The heroes of modern thought came in for laurels:

> At the head of these illustrious personages should be placed the immortal Chancellor of England, Francis Bacon, whose works, so justly esteemed, . . . deserve our study even more than our praise. When we consider the sane and spacious views of this great man, the multitude of subjects surveyed by his mind, the boldness of his style—which everywhere combined the most sublime images with the most rigorous precision—we are tempted to regard him as the greatest, the most universal, and the most eloquent of philosophers.[29]

D'Alembert proceeded to show how the profound genius of Descartes, so fertile in mathematics, had been hampered in philosophy by religious persecution:

Descartes at least dared to show to alert minds how to free themselves from the yoke of Scholasticism, opinion, authority— in a word,
from prejudice and barbarism; and by this revolt, of which we today
gather the fruits, he rendered to philosophy a service perhaps more
difficult than all those that it owes to his renowned successors. We
may regard him as the chief of a sworn band, who had the courage to
lead a revolt against a despotic and arbitrary power, and who, by his
inspiring resolution, raised the foundations of a government more just
and benevolent than any that he could live to see established. If he
finished by thinking to explain everything, he at least began by doubting all; and the weapons that we must use to combat him are not the
less his own because we turn them against him.

After discussing Newton, Locke, and Leibniz, d'Alembert concluded
with an expression of faith in the beneficent effects of knowledge growing and spreading. "Our century believes itself destined to change the laws in
every kind."[30] Warmed with that hope, d'Alembert made his "Discours"
one of the masterpieces of eighteenth-century French prose. Buffon and
Montesquieu joined in praising those introductory pages; Raynal rated
them as "one of the most philosophical, logical, luminous, exact, compact,
and best-written pieces that we have in our language."[31]

Volume I was not visibly antireligious. The articles on Christian doctrine and ritual were almost orthodox; several of them pointed out difficulties, but they usually ended with a solemn obeisance to the Church.
Quite often there were heretical asides and incidental attacks upon superstition and fanaticism, but these were hidden in articles on apparently innocent subjects like the Scythian lamb or the eagle; so the piece headed
"Agnus scythicus" expanded into a treatise on evidence which left the belief in miracles in an unhappy state; and the article "Aigle," after discussing popular credulity, concluded with transparent irony: "Happy the
people whose religion asks it to believe only things true, holy, and sublime,
and to imitate only virtuous actions. Such a religion is ours, in which the
philosopher has only to follow his reason to arrive at the feet of our altars."[32] Slyly, here and there, the bubbles of myth and legend were pricked,
and a spirit of rationalist humanism emerged.

Nevertheless the Jesuits gave the volume a friendly reception. Guillaume
François Berthier, the learned editor of the *Journal de Trévoux*, politely
objected to the stress laid upon heretical philosophers in the "Discours
préliminaire"; he pointed out inaccuracies and plagiarisms, and asked for
stricter censorship of future volumes; but he praised the *Encyclopédie* as a
"very lofty, very solid enterprise, whose editors, when it is completed, will
justly be able to apply to themselves the Horatian claim, *Exegi monumentum
aere perennius*." And he added: "No one is more disposed to recognize the

fine sections of the *Encyclopédie;* we shall review them with complaisance in our extracts to come."[33]

Another priest was not so lenient. Jean François Boyer, former bishop of Mirepoix, complained to the King that the authors had deceived the censors. Louis sent him to Malesherbes, who had recently become chief censor of publication (*directeur de la librairie*). Malesherbes promised that future volumes would be more carefully screened; but during his tenure of various governmental offices he used all his influence to protect the *philosophes.* It was fortunate for the rebels that this Chrétien Guillaume de Malesherbes, who had been made a skeptic by reading Bayle, and who had written a book, *La Liberté de la presse,* was censor of publications from 1750 to 1763—the most critical period in the lives of Voltaire, Diderot, Helvétius, and Rousseau. "In a century in which every citizen can speak to the entire nation by means of print," Malesherbes wrote, "those who have the talent for instructing men or the gift of moving them —in a word, men of letters—are, amid a dispersed people, what the orators of Rome and Athens were in the midst of a people assembled."[34] He fostered the intellectual movement by granting *permission tacite* to books that could not, even in his regime, receive the *approbation et privilège du roi.* For in his view "a man who had read only the books that . . . appeared with the express consent of the government . . . would be behind his contemporaries by almost a century."[35]

This happy moment for the *Encyclopédie* was ended by one of the most curious incidents in the history of the Enlightenment. On November 18, 1751, Jean Martin de Prades, seeking a degree at the Sorbonne, offered to the theologians an apparently innocuous thesis—"*Quel est celui sur la face duquel Dieu a répandu le souffle de la vie?*" (Who is he over whose face God spread the breath of life?) While the examining pundits nodded or slept, the young abbé, in excellent Latin, exposed chronological conflicts in the Bible, reduced the miracles of Christ to a level with those of Aesculapius, and replaced revelation with a natural and liberal theology. The Sorbonne accepted the thesis and granted the degree. The Jansenists, now controlling the Parlement of Paris, denounced the Sorbonne; a rumor went about that Diderot had had a hand in the thesis; the Sorbonne revoked the degree, and ordered the abbé's arrest. De Prades fled to Prussia, where he was lodged by Voltaire until he succeeded La Mettrie as reader to Frederick the Great.

The guardians of orthodoxy were shocked to find that this same Prades had contributed the article "Certitude" to Volume II of the *Encyclopédie,* which appeared in January, 1752. This article also had a tang of Diderot in it. The outcry against the undertaking mounted. Berthier, while praising the volume for its many contributions to knowledge, rebuked the editors for a piece in which it was said that most men honor literature as they do religion—i.e., "as something they can neither know nor practice nor love." Such a statement, said the Jesuit, deserved "the greatest attention on the part of the authors and the editors of the *Encyclopédie*, in order that henceforth nothing similar be inserted in it."[36] On January 31 Christophe de Beaumont, archbishop of Paris, condemned the *Encyclopédie* as a subtle attack upon religion; and on February 7 a decree of the Council of State forbade any further sale or publication of the work. On that day the Marquis d'Argenson wrote in his journal:

> This morning appeared an *arrêt du conseil* which had not been foreseen: it suppressed the *Dictionnaire encyclopédique*, with some appalling allegations, such as revolt against God and the royal authority, [and] corruption of morals . . . It is said on this score that the authors of this dictionary . . . must shortly be put to death.[37]

It was not as bad as that. Diderot was not arrested, but nearly all the material that he had gathered was confiscated by the government. Voltaire wrote from Potsdam urging Diderot to transfer the enterprise to Berlin, where it could proceed under Frederick's protection; but Diderot was helpless without his material, and Le Breton was hopeful that the government, after the storm had subsided, would modify its prohibition. Malesherbes, the Marquis d'Argenson, and Mme. de Pompadour supported Le Breton's appeal to the Council; and in the spring of 1752 it consented to the publication of further volumes with "tacit permission." Mme. de Pompadour advised d'Alembert and Diderot to resume their work, "observing a necessary reserve in all things touching religion and authority."[38] To appease the clergy, Malesherbes agreed that all future volumes should be censored by three theologians chosen by ex-bishop Boyer.

Volumes III to VI appeared at yearly intervals, 1753–56, all subjected to strict censorship. The furor had given the *Encyclopédie* wide publicity and had made it the symbol of liberal ideas; the number of subscribers rose to 3,100 with Volume III, 4,200 with Volume IV.

D'Alembert emerged from the ordeal somewhat shaken. To secure his personal safety he stipulated that henceforth he would be responsible only for the mathematical articles. Diderot, however, was for fighting the censorship. On October 12, 1752, he published, ostensibly at Berlin and in the name of de Prades, a *Suite de l'apologie* [Continuation of the Defense] *de M. l'abbé de Prades*. Referring to a recent episcopal denunciation of the Sorbonne thesis, he spoke out angrily:

> I know nothing so indecent, and so injurious to religion, as these vague declamations against reason on the part of some theologians.

One would say, to hear them, that men cannot enter into the bosom of Christianity except as a flock of beasts enters a stable, and that one has to renounce common sense to embrace our religion or to persist in it. To establish such principles, I repeat, is to reduce man to the level of the brute, and place falsehood and truth on an equal footing.[39]

He continued in Volume III the indirect attacks upon Christianity, usually covering them with professions of orthodoxy. His article "Sacred Chronology" exposed again contradictions in the Old Testament, and cast doubts upon the accuracy of Biblical texts. His article on the Chaldeans stressed their achievements in astronomy, but lamented their subjection to priests. "It is to dishonor reason to put it in bonds as the Chaldeans did. Man is born to think for himself." The article "Chaos" listed difficulties in the idea of creation, and detailed—in pretending to refute—the arguments for the eternity of matter. Mingled with such controversial pieces were his excellent articles on commerce, competition, composition (in painting), and *comédiens*—which meant actors. Diderot explained that he was neither a painter nor a connoisseur of paintings, but he had been compelled to write on the subject because the "vaunted amateur" whom he had commissioned to write on pictorial composition had submitted a worthless fragment. Diderot's article expressed some of the ideas that later enlivened his *Salons*. The article "Comédiens" carried on Voltaire's campaign for the civil rights of actors.

Volume III won much praise, tempered by criticism from the Jesuits and Élie Fréron's *Année litteraire*. New contributors raised the prestige of the work: Duclos began to take part with Volume IV, Voltaire and Turgot with Volume V, Necker and Quesnay with Volume VI. During the first four years of the undertaking Voltaire had been absorbed or embroiled in Germany; now (1755), settled in Geneva, he sent in the articles "Élégance," "Éloquence," and "Esprit" (Intelligence)—all graced with elegance, eloquence, and *esprit*. Diderot himself wrote for Volume VI an article, "Encyclopedia," which some scholars have rated the best piece in the whole work. It was certainly one of the longest, running to 34,000 words. He told of the difficulties the enterprise had faced, not only from forces aiming at its destruction, but also from restricted funds inadequate to pay contributors and printers, and from the human frailties of authors harassed in health and cramped for time. He admitted the many defects of the first five volumes, which had been produced in haste and trepidation; he promised improvement, and with some feeling he made his own act of faith:

The end of an encyclopedia is to assemble the knowledge scattered over the earth, to expound it to contemporaries, and to transmit it to posterity, to the end that the labors of past centuries should not be useless to those who are to come, and that our successors, becoming better instructed, may become at the same time more virtuous and happy, and that we may not die without having deserved well of the human race.

He thought of the *Encyclopédie* as a blow for posterity, and trusted that posterity would vindicate him. He imagined "some great revolution that has suspended the progress of the sciences and the work of the [industrial] arts, and has replunged into darkness a part of the world," and he warmed himself with hopes of the "gratitude such a generation will have for men who feared and foresaw this ravage, and gave a shelter to the knowledge accumulated by past ages." "Posterity," he said, "is for the philosopher what the 'other world' is for the man of religion."[40]

Volume VII, published in the fall of 1757, brought another crisis, worse than any before it. Quesnay and Turgot contributed famous expositions of physiocratic *laissez-faire* economics. Louis de Jaucourt, who was now one of the most frequent contributors, authored an insultingly brief article, "France," in which most of the nine hundred words went not to the history but to the faults of France: the dangerously extreme inequality of wealth, the poverty of the peasants, the hypertrophy of Paris, and the depopulation of the provinces. And in an article "Government" Jaucourt wrote: "The people's greatest good is its liberty. . . . Without liberty happiness is banished from states." Voltaire wrote for this volume an ostentatiously learned article on fornication. But the *pièce de résistance*—at least the piece that *aroused* most resistance—was that article on Geneva which we have already encountered in its Swiss milieu. D'Alembert forgot his "notarial" caution and his resolve to confine himself to mathematics. He brought both Geneva and Paris down upon his head by representing the Calvinist clergy as discarding the divinity of Christ.

Grimm at once saw that this article was a tactless blunder, and reported that it was creating an uproar. A Jesuit denounced the volume in a sermon delivered at Versailles before the King. "It is asserted," d'Alembert wrote to Voltaire, "that I praise the ministers of Geneva in a fashion prejudicial to the Catholic Church."[41] On January 5, 1757, an attempt had been made to assassinate the King. He responded by reviving an old law that condemned to death the authors, publishers, and sellers of books that attacked religion or disturbed the state. Several writers were imprisoned. None suffered death, but the sensitive d'Alembert was understandably frightened. Shrinking from the turmoil, he severed his connection with the *Encyclopédie* (January 1, 1758). For a moment he lost perspective; he accused Mme. de Pompadour of favoring the *antiphilosophes*, and asked Malesherbes to suppress their leader Fréron. Voltaire urged him not to resign; d'Alembert replied (January 20): "You do not know the position we are in, and the fury of the authorities against us. . . . I doubt that Diderot will continue without me; but I know that if he does he is preparing for himself trials and tribulations for ten years."[42] Eight days later his terror had increased. "If they [the enemies] print such things today by express order of those in authority, it is not to rest there; it means a heaping of fagots around the seventh volume, and to throw us into the flames for an eighth."[43] Voltaire yielded to d'Alembert, and counseled Diderot to abandon the *Encyclopédie*, since, if it continued at all, it would be under a censorship nullifying the value of the work as a means of checking the power of the Church over the French mind.[44] Turgot, Marmontel, Duclos, and Morellet refused to contribute further articles. Diderot himself for a time lost heart. "There is hardly a day," he wrote, "but I am tempted to go and live in obscurity and tranquillity in the depths of my province of Champagne."[45] But he would not surrender. "To abandon the work," he wrote to Voltaire (February, 1758), "is to turn one's back on the breach, and do what the rascals who persecute us desire. If you but knew with what joy they learned of d'Alembert's desertion, and what maneuvers they undertake to prevent him from returning!"

At their assembly in 1758 the bishops of France offered an unusually large *don gratuit* to the King, and begged him to end the "tacit permission" that allowed the *Encyclopédie* to be published in France. Abraham de Chaumeix began in 1758 to issue a series of volumes called *Préjugés légitimes contre l'Encyclopédie*. The publication of Helvétius' radical *De l'Esprit* (July 27, 1758) roused further protests; the *Encyclopédie* was involved in that storm because Diderot was widely rumored to have close connections with Helvétius. To make the situation more desperate Rousseau, who had been contributing articles on music to the *Encyclopédie*, refused further participation; and on October 22, 1758, his *Lettre à M. d'Alembert sur les spectacles* made public his break with the *philosophes*. The camp of the Encyclopedists seemed irrevocably broken up. On January 23, 1759, the King's attorney, Omer de Fleury, warned the Parlement of Paris that "there is a project formed, a society organized, to propagate materialism, to destroy religion, to inspire a spirit of independence, and to nourish the corruption of morals."[46] Finally, on March 8, an order of the Council of State completely outlawed the *Encyclopédie;* no new volume was to be printed, and none of the existing volumes was to be sold. The decree explained: "The advantages to be derived from a work of this sort, in respect to progress in the arts and sciences, can never compensate for the irreparable damage that results from it in regard to morality and religion."[47]

The edict threatened not only the personal security of the *philosophes* but the financial solvency of the publishers. Many subscribers had paid for future volumes; how could these advances be refunded? Most of that money had been spent in publishing Volumes I–VII and preparing Volume VIII, which was ready for distribution when the royal decree fell. Diderot persuaded the publishers not to give up. Perhaps this ukase too would be modified in time; if not, the remaining volumes could be printed abroad. At the request of the publishers Diderot secluded himself in his home and toiled on Volume IX. Meanwhile Malesherbes and others labored to appease the government.

At this juncture—in the summer of 1759—there appeared in Paris a surreptitious and anonymous pamphlet entitled *Mémorandum pour Abraham Chaumeix*, a piece at once dull and violent, attacking with the crudest insults not only the government, the Parlement, the Jesuits, and the Jansenists, but Christ himself and his mother. Diderot reported that "the work is being attributed to me, and that almost with unanimity."[48] He went to Malesherbes, to the lieutenant general of the police and to the advocate general of the Parlement, and swore that he had nothing to do with this explosion of street-corner atheism. His friends believed him, but advised him to leave Paris. He refused; such flight, he argued, would be a confession of guilt. Malesherbes warned him that the police were planning to raid his rooms and confiscate his papers; he must hide these at once. "But where?" asked the harassed rebel; how could he in a few hours find hiding places for all the materials that he had accumulated? "Send them to me," said Malesherbes; "no one will come here to look for them."[49] Meanwhile the police discovered the printers of the scandalous pamphlet, and concluded that Diderot had had no connection with it. No order for the seizure of his papers was issued. He was relieved, but verged on a nervous breakdown. D'Holbach, his rich friend, took him away on a vacation to various places near Paris. "I carried everywhere with me," Diderot wrote, "stumbling steps and a melancholy soul."[50]

Back in Paris, he signed with the publishers a new contract to prepare nine additional volumes of the *Encyclopédie*, for 25,000 livres. D'Alembert offered to resume responsibility for mathematical articles; Diderot rebuked him for desertion in the face of the enemy, but accepted his contributions. Voltaire too rejoined the fold. Diderot hoped to finish the seventeenth and final volume in 1760, but in September, 1761, he wrote: "The terrible revision is over. I have spent twenty-five days in succession at it, at the rate of ten hours a day."[51] Ten days later he was still immured in his room, examining plates. Volumes VIII–XVII were printed in Paris in quick succession, but were marked as published in Neuchâtel; Sartine, the new lieutenant general of the Paris police, winked at the deception;[52] and the expulsion of the Jesuits in 1762 eased the way.* In September, 1762, Catherine the Great offered to complete the *Encyclopédie* under governmental protection at St. Petersburg; a similar offer came from Frederick the Great through Voltaire; perhaps these proposals persuaded the French officials to allow the printing in Paris. The final volume of text appeared in 1765; eleven volumes of plates were added between 1765 and 1772. A five-volume *Supplément* and a two-volume *Table générale* (index) were issued between 1776 and 1780. Diderot was asked to edit these, but he was worn out, and refused. The most important publishing enterprise of the century had consumed him, but had made him as immortal as the vicissitudes of civilization will permit.

IV. THE *ENCYCLOPÉDIE* ITSELF

Nearly all its contents have been superseded by the intellectual revolution which it helped to foment; they engage our interest only as events in the history of ideas, and as weapons used by the *philosophes* in their conflict with the only Christianity that they knew. The attack, as we have seen, was seldom direct. The articles "Jesus" and "Christianity," both by Diderot, were essentially orthodox; the second was praised by an Italian abbé. Several priests contributed articles; so the Abbé Yvon wrote "Atheists." The *Encyclopédie* supported not atheism but deism. However, the cross references were sometimes seductive; appended to an orthodox article, they often pointed to other articles that suggested doubts; so the exemplary piece on God referred to the article "Demonstration," which laid down principles of evidence lethal to miracles and myths. Sometimes the least reasonable elements in the Christian creed were expounded with apparent acceptance, but in a way to evoke questioning. Chinese or Mohammedan doctrines similar to those of Christianity were rejected as irrational. The article "Priests," probably by d'Holbach, was outspoken in hostility, for the *philosophes* hated the clergy as foes of free thought and as prods to persecution. The author pretended to be writing of pagan priests:

> Superstition having multiplied the ceremonies of the diverse cults, the persons conducting the ceremonies soon formed a separate order.

---

* The pleasant story that Mme. de Pompadour induced Louis XV to withdraw his opposition to the publication of Volumes VIII–XVII by showing him the article on gunpowder is now generally rejected as a fancy of Voltaire's.[53] The story is given in Vol. XLVIII of Beuchot's edition of Voltaire's works, and also in the Goncourts' *Madame de Pompadour*, p. 147.

The people believed that these persons were entirely devoted to the divinity; hence the priests shared in the respect given to the divinity. Vulgar occupations appeared to be beneath them, and the people believed themselves obliged to provide for their subsistence . . . as depositories and interpreters of the divine will, and as mediators between gods and men. . . .

To more surely establish their domination, the priests depicted the gods as cruel, vindictive, implacable. They introduced ceremonies, initiations, mysteries, whose atrocity could nourish in men that somber melancholy so favorable to the empire of fanaticism. Then human blood flowed in great streams over the altars; the people, cowed with fear and stupefied with superstition, thought no price too high to pay for the good will of the gods. Mothers delivered without a tear their tender infants to the devouring flames; thousands of victims fell under the sacrificial knife. . . .

It was difficult for men so reverenced to remain long within the borders of subordination necessary to social order. The priesthood, drunk with power, often disputed the rights of the kings. . . . Fanaticism and superstition held the knife suspended over the heads of sovereigns; thrones were shaken whenever kings wished to repress or punish holy men, whose interests were confounded with those of the gods. . . . To wish to limit their power was to sap the foundations of religion.[54]

Generally the war on the old faith took the form of praising the new beliefs and methods of science and philosophy; to replace religion with science, and priests with philosophers, at least in the educated classes, was the dream of the *philosophes*. The sciences received lengthy expositions; for example, fifty-six columns were given to "Anatomy." Under "Geology" there were long articles on minerals, metals, strata, fossils, glaciers, mines, earthquakes, volcanoes, and precious stones. Philosophy, in the new view, was to be based entirely on science; it would build no "systems," it would shun metaphysics, it would not pontificate on the origin and destiny of the world. The article "École" made a frontal assault upon the Scholastic philosophers as men who had abandoned the search for knowledge, had surrendered to theology, and had lost themselves safely in logical cobwebs and metaphysical clouds.

Diderot contributed a remarkable series of articles on the history of philosophy; they leaned heavily on Johann Jakob Brucker's *Historia critica Philosophiae* (1742–44), but they showed original research in French thought. The essays on the Eleatics and Epicurus expounded materialism; other articles extolled Bruno and Hobbes. In Diderot philosophy became a religion. "Reason is for the philosopher what grace is for the Christian."[55] "Let us hasten to render philosophy popular," he cried;[56] and in the article

"Encyclopedia" he wrote like an apostle: "Today, when philosophy advances with giant steps, when it submits to its empire all the objects of its interest, when its voice is the dominant voice, and it begins to break the yoke of authority and tradition, to hold to the laws of reason . . ." Here was the brave new faith, with a youthful confidence not often to be found again. Perhaps with an eye to his imperial protectress in Russia he added, like Plato: "Unite a ruler [Catherine II] with a philosopher of this kind [Diderot], and you will have a perfect sovereign."[57]

If such a philosopher could replace the priest as guide-confessor to a king, he would counsel, first of all, a spread of freedom, especially to speech and press. "No man has received from nature the right of commanding others";[58] so much for the divine right of kings. And as for revolution:

> Power acquired by violence is only a usurpation, and lasts only as long as the force of him who commands prevails over that of those who obey. . . . If these in turn become stronger and shake off their yoke, they do so with as much right and justice as did the former who had imposed it upon them. The same law that made the authority unmakes it; it is the law of the stronger. . . . Therefore true and legitimate power necessarily has limits. . . . The prince holds from his subjects themselves the authority that he has over them; and this authority is limited by the laws of nature and of the state. . . . It is not the state which belongs to the prince, but rather the prince who belongs to the state.[59]

The *Encyclopédie* was not socialistic, nor democratic; it accepted monarchy, and rejected that notion of equality which Rousseau expounded so forcefully in 1755. Jaucourt's article "Natural Equality" advocated equality before the law, but added: "I know too well the necessity of different conditions, grades, honors, distinctions, prerogatives, subordinations, which must rule under all governments."[60] Diderot at this time considered private property the indispensable basis of civilization.[61] The article "Man," however, had a communistic moment: "The net profit of a society, if equally distributed, may be preferable to a larger profit if this is distributed unequally and has the effect of dividing the people into classes." And—talking of almshouses—"it would be of far more value to work for the prevention of misery than to multiply places of refuge for the miserable."[62]

A philosophical king would periodically examine the title deeds to feudal domains, and would abolish feudal privileges no longer merited by seignorial services to the peasantry or the state.[63] He would find a humane substitute for the forced labor of the *corvée*, and he would forbid the trade in slaves. He would, so far as his power extended, put an end to wars of dynastic rivalry or greed. He would seek to cleanse the trial courts of corruption, to end the sale of offices, and to mitigate the ferocity of the penal code; at the very least he would put an end to judicial torture. And instead of lending his aid to the perpetuation of superstition he would dedicate his labors to advancing that golden age in which statesmanship would ally itself with science in an unremitting war upon ignorance, illness, and poverty.

By and large the economic ideas of the *Encyclopédie* were those of the middle class to which most of the *philosophes* belonged. Often they were the views of the physiocrats who, under the lead of Quesnay and Mirabeau *père*, dominated economic theory in midcentury France. Free enterprise—and therefore free commerce and free competition—were held vital to free men; hence guilds, as impediments to all these, were condemned. These ideas were destined to take the stage of history in the ministry of Turgot (1774).

The *Encyclopédie* gave alert and enthusiastic attention to the industrial technology that was beginning to transform the economic face of England and France. The mechanical arts, Diderot maintained, should be honored as the application of science, and surely the application is as precious as the theory. "What absurdity in our judgments! We exhort men to occupy themselves usefully, and we despise useful men."[64] He hoped to make the *Encyclopédie* a treasury of technology so thorough that if the mechanical arts were by some tragedy destroyed they could be rebuilt from one surviving set of its volumes. He himself wrote long and painstaking articles on steel, agriculture, needles, bronze, the boring machine ("Alésoir"), shirts, stockings, shoes, bread. He admired the genius of inventors and the skills of artisans; he went in person, or sent his agents, to farms, shops, and factories to study new processes and products; and he supervised the engravings, numbering almost a thousand, that made the eleven volumes of plates the marvel of their kind in their age; to those volumes the government was proud to extend the *approbation et privilège du roi*. Here were fifty-five plates on the textile industry, eleven on minting, ten on military technics, five on making gunpowder, three on the manufacture of pins; the last were a source for Adam Smith's famous passage on the division of labor into "eighteen distinct operations" in producing a pin.[65] To get this knowledge, said Diderot,

> we turned to the ablest artisans in Paris and throughout the kingdom. We took the trouble . . . to ask them questions, to write at their dictation, . . . to get from them the terms used in their trades, . . . to rectify, in long and frequent interviews with one group of workmen, what others had imperfectly, obscurely, or sometimes inaccurately explained. . . . We have sent engravers into the shops, who have drawn designs of the machines and tools, omitting nothing that could make them clear to the eyes.[66]

When, in 1773, the Ottoman Sultan asked Baron de Tott to manufacture cannon for the forts of the Dardanelles, the Baron used the *Encyclopédie* article on cannon as one of his constant guides.[67]

After his work on the text was completed, Diderot suffered a mortification that almost broke his spirit. Happening to examine an article, he discovered that many parts of the proofsheets that he had corrected and approved had been omitted in print. A survey of other articles showed a similar bowdlerization in Volumes IX to XVII. The omissions were usually of passages that might have further aroused the clergy or the Parlement; and the deletions had been made with no regard for the logic or continuity of what remained. Le Breton confessed that he had performed the surgery to save the *Encyclopédie* from further tribulation, and himself from bankruptcy. Grimm reported the results:

> The discovery threw Diderot into a frenzy which I shall never forget. "For years," he cried to Le Breton, "you have been basely cheating me. You have massacred . . . the work of twenty good men who have devoted their time, their talents, their vigils, from love of right and truth, in the simple hope of seeing their ideas given to the public, and reaping from them a little consideration richly earned. . . . You will henceforth be cited as a man who has been guilty of an act of treachery, an act of vile hardihood, to which nothing that has ever happened in this world can be compared." [68]

He never forgave Le Breton.

Looking back upon the great enterprise, we see it to have been, by its history as well as its contents, the outstanding achievement of the French Enlightenment. And as Diderot's part in it was central and indispensable, his stature rises to a place only after Voltaire's and Rousseau's in the intellectual panorama of eighteenth-century France. His industry as editor was pervasive and exhausting. He made the cross references, corrected errors, read the proofs. He ran about Paris seeking and prodding contributors. He himself wrote hundreds of articles when contributors could not be found or when they proved incompetent. He was the last resort when all others had failed. So we find him writing on philosophy, canvas, Christianity, boa constrictors, beauty, playing cards, breweries, and consecrated bread. His article "Intolerance" anticipated Voltaire's treatise, and may have suggested several of its ideas. Many of his pieces were studded with errors, and some of them were indiscriminately hostile and unjust, like that on the Jesuits. But he was a man in a hurry, embattled and pursued, and fighting back with every weapon he could find.

Now that the excitement of battle has subsided, we can recognize the shortcomings of the *Encyclopédie*. There were a thousand errors of fact.

There were careless repetitions and flagrant omissions. There were substantial plagiarisms, as Jesuit scholars pointed out; some articles were "a mosaic of borrowings."[69] Berthier, in three issues of the *Journal de Trévoux*, showed, with exact references and parallel quotations, over a hundred plagiarisms in Volume I. Most of these thefts were brief and unimportant, as in definitions, but several extended to three or four columns copied almost word for word.

There were serious intellectual defects in the *Encyclopédie*. The contributors had too simple a view of human nature, too sanguine an estimate of the honesty of reason, too vague an understanding of its frailty, too optimistic a prospect of how men would use the knowledge that science was giving them. The *philosophes* in general, and Diderot in particular, lacked historical sense; they seldom paused to inquire how the beliefs they combated had arisen, and what human needs, rather than priestly inventions, had given them birth and permanence. They were quite blind to the immense contribution of religion to social order, to moral character, to music and art, to the mitigation of poverty and suffering. Their antireligious bias was so strong that they could never lay claim to that impartiality which we should now consider essential to a good encyclopedia. Though some Jesuits, like Berthier, were often fair in their criticism, most of the *Encyclopédie*'s critics were as partial as the *philosophes*.

Diderot felt keenly the factual faults of the work. He wrote in 1755: "The first edition of an encyclopedia cannot but be a very ill-formed and incomplete compilation";[70] and he expected that it would soon be superseded. Even so the bulky product found its way into the centers of thought on the Continent. The twenty-eight volumes were thrice reprinted in Switzerland, twice in Italy, once in Germany, once in Russia. Pirated editions came back into France to spread the influence of the contraband ideas. All in all, there were forty-three editions in twenty-five years—a remarkable record for so costly a set. Families read its articles together in the evening; eager groups were formed to study it; Thomas Jefferson advised James Madison to buy it. Now the gospel of reason as against mythology, of knowledge as against dogma, of progress through education as against the resigned contemplation of death, all passed like a pollen-laden wind over Europe, disturbing every tradition, stimulating thought, at last fomenting revolt. The *Encyclopédie* was the revolution before the Revolution.

CHAPTER XX

Diderot Proteus

1758–73

I. THE PANTHEIST

WE call him Proteus because, like the sea god in Homer, he "tried to escape his captors by assuming all sorts of shapes."[1] Voltaire called him Pantophilus because Diderot was in love with every branch of science, literature, philosophy, and art. In each of these fields he had intimate knowledge; to each he made suggestive contributions. Ideas were his meat and drink. He gathered them, savored and sampled them, and poured them out in a profuse chaos whenever he found a blank sheet or a willing ear. "I throw my ideas upon paper, and they become what they may"[2]—perhaps foes. He never co-ordinated them, never bothered with consistency; we can quote him in almost any direction, but his composite direction was unmistakable. He was more original than Voltaire, perhaps because he had never accepted classic norms, and could let himself go without well-bred restraints. He followed every theory wherever it led him, sometimes to its depths, sometimes to its dregs. He saw every point of view except those of the priest and the saint, because he had no certainties.

> As for me, I concern myself more with forming than with dissipating clouds, with suspending judgment rather than with judging. . . . I do not decide, I ask questions.[3] . . . I let my mind rove wantonly, give it free rein to follow any idea, wise or mad, that may come uppermost; I chase it as do young libertines on the track of a courtesan whose face is windblown and smiling, whose eyes sparkle, and whose nose turns up. . . . My ideas are my trollops.[4]

Diderot had an intellectual imagination; he visioned ideas, philosophies, personalities, as others vision forms and scenes. Who else in his time could have conceived the scandalous, unmoral, shiftless, fascinating "nephew of Rameau"? After creating a character, he let it develop as of its own accord; he let it lead him on as if the character were the author, and the author the puppet. He imagined himself in the place of a young unwilling nun, and made her so real that skeptical Frenchmen worried over her woes. He experimented mentally with ideas, entertained them for a time, imagined their consequences in logic or action, then tossed them aside. There was hardly an idea of that time that did not enter his head. He was not only and literally a walking encyclopedia, he was a moving laboratory, and his ideas wandered with his feet.

So in *Pensées sur l'interprétation de la nature*, which he published in 1754—anonymously, but with *permission tacite* from the benevolent Malesherbes—he played with ideas of monism, materialism, mechanism, vitalism, and evolution. Still under Bacon's spell, he took from him the title, the aphoristic form, and the summons to scientists to labor in concert for the conquest of nature through experiment and reason. He was inspired, too, by Maupertuis' *Système universel de la nature* (1751), and Buffon's *Histoire naturelle* (1749 f.); he agreed with Maupertuis that all matter might be alive, and with Buffon that biology was now ready to speak to philosophy. He welcomed in both authors the emerging hypothesis of evolution.

He began with a proud design: "It is nature that I wish to describe [*écrire*]; nature is the only book for the philosopher."[5] He conceived of nature as a half-blind, half-intelligent power operating upon matter, making matter live, making life take a million experimental forms, improving this organ, discarding that one, giving birth and death creatively. In that cosmic laboratory thousands of species have appeared and disappeared.

> Just as in the animal and plant kingdoms an individual begins, . . . grows, endures, perishes, and passes away, could it not be likewise with entire species? If faith did not teach us that animals come from the hands of the Creator such as we see them, and if it were allowed to have the least doubt of their commencement and their end, might not the philosopher, abandoned to his conjectures, suppose that animality had from all eternity its particular elements, scattered and confounded in the mass of matter; that these elements happened to unite, since it was possible for this to happen; that the embryo formed from these elements passed through an infinity of organizations and developments; that it acquired in succession movement, sensation, ideas, thought, reflection, consciousness, feelings, passions, signs, gestures, articulate sounds, language, laws, sciences, and arts; that millions of years passed between these developments; that perhaps it [the organism] has still further developments to undergo, other additions to receive, now unknown to us; . . . that it may lose these faculties as it acquired them; that it may forever disappear from nature, or, rather, continue to exist under a form, and with faculties, quite other than those which we notice in it in this moment of time?[6]

Nature in Diderot is everything; she is his God; but of her essence we know only her confused abundance and restless change. Nature is matter alive. Everything is matter, but matter contains in itself the *élan* of life and the potentiality of thought. Man is not a machine, but neither is he an immaterial spirit; body and soul are one organism, and die together. "Everything destroys itself and perishes; nothing remains but the world; nothing endures but time."[7] Nature is neutral: she makes no distinction between good and evil, great and small, sinner and saint. She cares for the species rather than for the individual; let the individual mature and reproduce, then let him die; and every species too will die. Nature is wise in a myriad subtle details, which seem to show design; she gives organisms instincts that enable them to live and make live; but also she is blind, destroying philosophers and fools alike with one belch of fire, one heave of her shoulders through the crust of the earth. We shall never be able to understand Nature, or to ferret out her purpose or meaning, if she have any; for we ourselves, in all our bloody and majestic history, are among her transient and infinitesimal sports.

II. *THE DREAM OF D'ALEMBERT*

Diderot continued his speculations on nature in one of the strangest productions in French literature—*Le Rêve d'Alembert*. It was characteristic of him to present his thoughts in the form of a dream, to foist the dream upon his friend, and to make two famous contemporaries—Julie de Lespinasse and Dr. Théophile de Bordeu—the speakers in the dialogue. "I put my ideas into the mouth of a man who dreams," Diderot told his mistress; "it is often necessary to give wisdom the air of foolishness in order to procure it entry."[8] Under these disguises he let his philosophical imagination run wild, careless of personal peril and social effects. He was quite pleased with the result; he described it to Sophie Volland as "the maddest and deepest thing ever written; there are five or six pages that will make your sister's hair stand on end";[9] yet he assured her that it contained "not a single improper word."[10] He wrote it in 1769, read parts of it to friends, and thought of having it printed—presumably abroad and unsigned; but Mlle. de Lespinasse protested, for reasons that will soon be obvious. In a heroic gesture he threw the manuscript into the fire, probably knowing that there was another copy; in any case, the work was printed in 1830.

It is a tripartite affair. In the preliminary "conversation" ("Entretien entre d'Alembert et Diderot") the mathematician objects to his friend's vitalistic materialism as no more acceptable than the Schoolmen's conception of God. "Between you and the animal," Diderot tells him, "there is no difference but one of organism" (degree of organic development), and likewise between animal and plant; consequently everything in man must have its seed or its analogy in plants. And in matter too? asks d'Alembert. Yes, Diderot replies; for "how do you know that feeling is essentially incompatible with matter—you who do not know the essence of anything, neither of matter nor of feeling? . . . There is not more than one substance in the universe, in man, in animals."[11]

The second part of the trilogy shows Dr. Bordeu and Mlle. de Lespinasse at the bedside of d'Alembert, who is asleep after his argumentative evening with Diderot. (Mademoiselle, already famous for her salon, was living with d'Alembert in a kind of Platonic cohabitation.) She reports to the doctor that her friend has had a wild dream, and has talked so strangely in his sleep that she took notes. For example, d'Alembert to Diderot: "Stop a moment, philosopher. I can easily comprehend an aggregate . . . of little feeling beings, but an animal? A whole . . . with consciousness of its own unity? I do not see it; no, I do not see it."[12] The dreamer dreams that Diderot, dodging the question, takes his stand on spontaneous generation: "When I have seen passive matter become a state of feeling, nothing can astonish me further."[13] If (Diderot continues) all existing species should pass away, they or other animal forms would in the amplitude of time be produced by the fermentation of the earth and the air. Bordeu and Mademoiselle take up the discussion, but are interrupted by a sudden cry from the dreaming man, who now talks like Diderot:

> Why am I what I am? Because it was inevitable that I should be. . . . If everything is a general flux, . . . what will not be produced here or elsewhere by the passing and vicissitudes of some millions of centuries? Who can tell what the thinking and feeling being is on Saturn? . . . Might the feeling and thinking being on Saturn have more senses than we? Ah, if so, the Saturnian is unfortunate, [for] the more the senses, the more the needs.[14]

"He is right," Bordeu comments Lamarckianly; "organs produce needs, and, reciprocally, needs produce organs."

D'Alembert wakes for a moment, finds Bordeu kissing Lespinasse, protests, is told to go back to sleep, and obeys. Now the doctor and the *salonnière* forget him, and pursue the train of ideas started by the dream. Bordeu notes the birth of human freaks, and challenges the believers in divine design to explain them. Mademoiselle has a bright *aperçu:* "Perhaps man is only the freak of a woman, or woman of a man."[15] The doctor enlarges on this Diderotically: "The only difference between them is that one has a bag hanging outside, and the other has it tucked away inside." D'Alembert wakes and protests, "I think you are talking filth to Mademoiselle de Lespinasse." Bordeu rises to keep an appointment with another patient; d'Alembert begs him to stay long enough to explain: "How comes it that I have remained myself to myself and to others through all the vicissitudes I have undergone in the course of my life, and when perhaps I possess no longer a single one of the molecules I brought with me at birth?" The doctor replies, "Memory, and . . . the slowness of the changes"; and Mademoiselle offers a striking analogy: "The spirit of a monastery is conserved because the monastery repeoples itself bit by bit, and when a new monk enters he finds a hundred old ones who lead him on to think and feel like them."[16]

Bordeu thenceforth dominates the discussion. He differentiates "romantic" from "classic" genius as the senses dominating, or being dominated by, conscious mind. He thinks Lespinasse an obvious example of the first, and blandly informs her, "You will divide your time between laughter and tears, and never be more than a child." He gives a physiological explanation of dreams:

> Sleep is a state in which there is no more ensemble [no more co-ordination of the senses by consciousness or purpose]. All concerted action, all discipline, ceases. The master [the conscious self] is abandoned to the discretion of his vassals [the senses]. . . . Is the optic thread [nerves] agitated? Then the origin of the network [the brain] sees. If the auditory thread demands, it hears. Action and reaction [sensation and response] are the only things which subsist between them. This is consequent on . . . the law of continuity and habit. If the action begins by the voluptuous end which nature has destined for the pleasure of love and the propagation of the species, the effect . . . on the origin of the bundle will be to reveal the image of the beloved. If this image, on the other hand, is first of all revealed to the origin of the bundle, the tension of the voluptuous end, the effervescence and effusion of the seminal fluid, will be the effect of the reaction. . . . In the waking state the network obeys the impressions made by an external object. Asleep, it is from the exercise of its own feeling that everything passing within itself emanates. There is nothing to distract in a dream; hence its vivacity.[17]

Perhaps feeling that the patient he had intended to visit would be more readily cured by nature than by medicine, Bordeu forgets him, and proceeds to expound determinism, and to describe "self-respect, shame, and remorse" as "puerilities founded on the ignorance and vanity of a person who imputes to himself the merit and demerit of an inevitable instant."[18]

Diderot became so enamored of Bordeu as his mouthpiece that in Part III, "Suite de l'entretien" (Continuation of the Conversation) he left d'Alembert out altogether. So freed, the doctor denounces chastity as unnatural, and approves of onanism as the necessary relief of congested vesicles. "Nature tolerates nothing useless. And then can I be blameworthy in helping her when she calls for my aid by the least equivocal of symptoms? Let us never provoke her, but occasionally lend her a hand."[19] The doctor ends by recommending experiments in the reproductive mingling of different species, possibly producing thereby a type of man-animal that might contentedly act as servant to man. Mademoiselle, anticipating Anatole France and the penguins, wonders, should these half-men be baptized?

> BORDEU (about to leave). Have you seen in the zoological gardens, in a glass cage, an orangutan with the look of St. John preaching in the desert?
> MADEMOISELLE. Yes, I have.
> BORDEU (going). The Cardinal de Polignac said to it one day, "Speak, and I baptize thee."[20]

In *Éléments de physiologie* (c. 1774) Diderot rounded out his theory of evolution with some musing on the "missing link":

> It is necessary to begin by classifying beings, from the inert molecule (if there is one) to the active molecule, to the microscopic animal, to the . . . plant, to the animal, to man. . . . One mustn't believe the chain of being to be interrupted by the diversity of forms; the form is only a mask which deceives, and a missing link exists perhaps in an unknown being which the progress of comparative anatomy has not yet been able to assign to its true place.[21]

III. DIDEROT ON CHRISTIANITY

He had promised Sophie Volland that there would be nothing in *The Dream of d'Alembert* about religion; actually, of course, the trilogy expressed a philosophy that quite dispensed with deity. Publicly he remained a deist, keeping God as Prime Mover only, and denying providence, or divine design. Theoretically he was an agnostic, disclaiming any knowledge of, or interest in, anything beyond the world of the senses and the sciences. Sometimes he spoke vaguely of a cosmic consciousness, which stumbled along through endless time, making experiments, producing now sterile freaks or lucky accidents—hardly a God to receive a prayer. In another mood he could become violently antagonistic. He told of the misanthrope who, in revenge upon life, propagated the idea of God; the idea spread, and soon "men fell to quarreling, hating, and cutting one another's throats; and they have been doing the same thing ever since that abominable name was pronounced." And Diderot added, in cautious ecstasy, "I would sacrifice my life, perhaps, if I could annihilate forever the notion of God."[22] Yet the same muddleheaded genius felt the amazing order and grandeur of the cosmos; he wrote to Mlle. Volland: "Atheism is close to being a kind of superstition, as puerile as the other"; and he added: "I am maddened at being entangled in a devilish philosophy that my mind cannot help approving and my heart refuting."[23] In his later years he admitted the difficulty of deriving the organic from the inorganic, or thought from sensation.[24]

But he never relented in his war on Christianity. A passionate paragraph in a private letter sums up his case against it:

> The Christian religion is to my mind the most absurd and atrocious in its dogmas: the most unintelligible, the most metaphysical, the most entangled and obscure, and consequently the most subject to divisions, sects, schisms, heresies; the most mischievous for the public tranquillity, the most dangerous to sovereigns by its hierarchic order, its persecutions, its discipline; the most flat, the most dreary, the most Gothic and most gloomy in its ceremonies; the most puerile and unsociable in its morality; . . . the most intolerant of all.[25]

In *Promenade du sceptique* (1747) he had acknowledged the services of the Church in training character and forming morals; in later years he thought that while discouraging petty crime the Christian religion had fomented greater ones: "Sooner or later a moment comes when the notion which had prevented a man from stealing a shilling will cause 100,000 men to be slaughtered. Fine compensation!"[26] However, "our religious opinions have little influence on our morals";[27] men fear present laws more than a distant hell and an invisible God. Even a priest "hardly relies upon praying to the gods except when he is little concerned about the matter."[28] In 1783 Diderot predicted that belief in God, and submission to kings, would be everywhere at an end within a few years;[29] the prediction seemed verified in France in 1792; but Diderot also predicted that "the belief in the existence of God will remain forever."[30]

Like most of those who have lost their faith in Catholic doctrine, this same Diderot who thought Christian ceremonies dreary and gloomy remained sensitive to the beauty and solemnity of Catholic ritual, and he defended it against Protestant critics in his *Salon of 1765:*

> Those absurd rigorists do not know the effect of outward ceremonies upon the people. They have never seen our Adoration of the Cross on Good Friday, the enthusiasm of the multitude at the procession of Corpus Christi, an enthusiasm by which I am sometimes carried away. I have never seen that long file of priests in sacerdotal vest-

ments, those young acolytes in white albs, . . . strewing flowers before the Holy Sacrament, that crowd preceding and following them in
religious silence, so many men prostrate on the ground, I have never
heard that grave, pathetic chant sung by the priests and affectionately
answered by numberless men, women, girls, and children, without
being stirred in my inmost heart, and without tears coming into my
eyes.[31]

But after wiping his eyes he resumed the attack. In the *Entretien d'un
philosophe avec la maréchale de——*(1776), he imagined a skeptic, whom
he named Crudeli (Italian for *cruel*), talking with a titled lady who "held
that the man who denies the Blessed Trinity is a ruffian who will end on
the gallows." She is surprised to find that M. Crudeli, who is an atheist,
is not also a sensualist and a thief. "I think that if I had nothing to fear
or hope after death I should allow myself a good many little pleasures here
below." Crudeli asks, "What are those things?" "They are only for my
confessor's ears. . . . But what motive can an unbeliever have for being
good, unless he is mad?" She retreats a little before his arguments, then
takes a new line of defense: "We must have something with which to
frighten off those actions which escape the severity of the laws." And besides, "if you destroy religion, what will you put in its place?" Crudeli
answers, "Suppose I had nothing to put in its place, there would always be
one terrible prejudice less." He pictures Mohammedans on a Christian-
killing rampage, and Christians burning Mohammedans and Jews.

> MARÉCHALE. Suppose everything that you believe false should be true,
>   and you were damned. It is a terrible thing to be damned—to
>   burn through eternity.
> CRUDELI. La Fontaine thought we should be as comfortable as fishes in
>   water.
> MARÉCHALE. Yes, yes, but your La Fontaine became very serious at
>   the end, and I expect the same of you.
> CRUDELI. I can answer for nothing when my brain has softened.

The most anticlerical of the *philosophes* kept a special bitterness for
what seemed to him the waste of human seed and energy in monasteries
and nunneries. One of his angriest pages excoriated parents who condemned unwilling daughters to convent life; and his technically most finished production is an imaginary re-creation of such a nun's career. *La
Religieuse (The Nun)* was written in 1760 as the result of a prank by
which Grimm and Diderot hoped to bring back to their company the
Marquis de Croixmare from Caen to Paris. About this time Diderot was
aroused by a nun's appeal to the Parlement of Paris to release her from
the vows that (she claimed) her parents had constrained her to take. The

kindly Marquis wrote to the Parlement in her behalf, but in vain. We know nothing more of this nun, but Diderot reconstructed her history with such realistic fancy that she will live for centuries. He supposed that she had escaped from her convent, and he sent to Croixmare, as if from her pen, a series of letters describing her conventual experiences and asking his help in beginning a new life. The Marquis answered; Diderot replied in her name; and this correspondence continued through four months and 150 pages.

Diderot pictured Suzanne persecuted by a harsh abbess, imprisoned, stripped, tortured, starved. She complains to a priest, who secures her transfer to another convent; there, however, the abbess is a Lesbian who overwhelms her with love and solicits her co-operation. Diderot probably exaggerated the cruelties of abbesses and the griefs of nuns, but he made all the priests in his story amiable and benevolent, and he treated the Lesbian theme with a delicacy rare in his works. The Marquis was moved, and came to Paris. The hoax was revealed to him; he forgave it. The strange device had produced a remarkable study in psychology, perhaps influenced by Richardson's *Clarissa*; never had a skeptic entered so vividly into the feelings of a reluctant saint. A visitor who came upon the author during the composition of these letters found him, says Grimm, "plunged in grief . . . and tears."[32] Diderot confessed that he was weeping over his own tale, for tears came to him as readily as to Rousseau. He was forgivably proud of his epistolary novel, of its verisimilitude, sentiment, and style; he revised it carefully, and bequeathed it for publication after his death. It saw the light in 1796, under the Revolution. In 1865 *La Religieuse* was publicly burned by order of the Tribunal of the Seine.[33]

Published with it in 1796, burned with it in 1865, was *Jacques le fataliste et son maître*, which Diderot, with the pathos of nearness, considered his greatest work.[34] It may be so, but it is also the most absurd. Infatuated with *Tristram Shandy* (1760-67), he adopted Sterne's trick of composing a story largely of interruptions, intruding upon it whimsically now and then to talk to the reader about the characters and the plot. He began and ended the book with passages and incidents copied directly from Sterne,[35] and he bettered Sterne's example of startling the reader with an occasional indecency. The two characters that carry the story reflect Cervantes' device of contrasting master and man in temperament and philosophy. The master rejects, Jacques professes, fatalism; "Everything . . . that happens down here," he says, "is written up yonder."[36] Jacques "believed that a man wended his way just as necessarily to glory or ignominy as a ball . . . would follow the slope of the mountain" down which it rolled. "His [former] captain had filled Jacques' head with all these ideas drained out of Spinoza, whom he knew by heart"[37]—a rare captain.

Midway in the story Diderot tarries to tell, with verve and skill, the story of the Marquise de la Pommeraye, mistress of the Marquis des Arcis. Suspecting that he has tired of her, she resolves to find out by hinting that their liaison has become a bore. She is deeply offended by his admission that he is willing to relapse from a lover into a friend. She plans a unique revenge. She finds a pretty prostitute, finances her rehabilitation, teaches her grammar, manners, and an impressive piety, introduces her to the Marquis as a lady of lineage, trains her to arouse his humors and reject his advances, guides her in the art of eliciting a proposal of marriage. Some months after the marriage Mme. de la Pommeraye reveals to the Marquis the past of his mate. But the Marquise's revenge is spoiled by an anomalous development. The reformed sinner has learned to love her Marquis; in shame and tears she confesses her deception, and proposes to disappear from his life. Meanwhile she has been so faithful and affectionate a wife that the Marquis has discovered more happiness in marriage than ever in adultery. He forgives her, and refuses to let her go; he lives with her in brave content, and Mme. de la Pommeraye eats her heart out in defeat.

This intermezzo is by all means the most striking part of *Jacques le fataliste;* it has the close texture, the subtle touches of psychological realism, the concentrated feeling quietly expressed, which are missing in the novel as a whole. Schiller recognized it as a gem of literary art, and translated it into German in 1785.

IV. *THE NEPHEW OF RAMEAU*

Le Neveu de Rameau, and not *Jacques le fataliste*, is Diderot's greatest single book—"the classical work," Goethe called it, "of an outstanding man."[38] Written in 1761, this too was left unpublished, for it is by all means the most scandalous, as well as the most original, of Diderot's productions. Apparently he thought it too indigestible to be offered even to his friends. After his death a copy of the text found its way into a Germany throbbing with *Sturm und Drang*. Schiller was shocked and excited by it, and passed it on to Goethe, who, at the height of his fame (1805), translated it into German. This translation entered France, and was retranslated into French (1821). Another copy was published in 1823, but it had come to the printer bowdlerized by Diderot's daughter. The original manuscript was not discovered till 1891, in a bookstall on the quays of the Seine. That manuscript is now in the J. Pierpont Morgan Library in New York.

Diderot chose, as the mouthpiece of ideas too bizarre for even Diderot to express in the first person, Jean François Rameau, nephew of the famous composer Jean Philippe Rameau (d. 1764), who was still alive when the unpublishable dialogue was written. Diderot knew music well; he talked familiarly of Locatelli, Pergolesi, Jommelli, Galuppi, Leo, Vinci, Tartini, and Hasse, and rightly predicted that in violin playing the difficult would soon displace the beautiful.[39]

The nephew composed music, and had some success as a music teacher; but he was harassed by the handicap of his name, and jealous of his uncle's superiority; he gave up the battle, and sank into the Bohemian shiftlessness and self-indulgent amoralism described by Diderot. Many other traits attributed to him in the dialogue are confirmed by contemporary reports,[40] but history gives no support to Diderot's characterization of him as a pander who proposed to market the beauty of his wife. When that wife died Jean François lost all self-respect; his sarcastic and unchastened tongue made him a social outcast; at last he was excluded from the home of the rich M. Bertin, on whom he had for years depended for his dinners; and he had to seek associates in the Café de la Régence and other outposts of advanced and penniless ideas.

Diderot begins (note how he weaves his books into his life):

> Let the weather be fair or overcast, it is my habit, about five o'clock in the afternoon, to go walking toward the Palais-Royal. It is I whom you can see always alone, dreaming on d'Argenson's bench. I discuss with myself politics, love, taste, philosophy. I abandon my mind to all its libertinage. . . . When the weather is too cold or wet I take refuge in the Café de la Régence, where I watch the chess games. . . . One afternoon I was there, looking around, talking little, hearing as little as I could, when I was approached by one of the most bizarre persons in the land.[41]

There follows a remarkable character portait: a man who has drunk the dregs of life and bitterly recalls the wine; formerly moneyed and comfortable, with the prettiest wife in Paris; received *once* in every fashionable home;[42] abreast of all the culture in France; sunk now into poverty and degradation, living on merciful dinners and forgotten loans, seeing nothing in life but struggle and defeat, rejecting all religion as a beautiful and terrible lie, viewing all morality as timidity and sham, and yet keeping enough of his past to clothe his disillusionment in educated eloquence and rational dress. He has a sharp and bitter humor: "Madame So-and-So has been delivered of twins; each father will have one"; or, of a new opera: "It has some pretty passages; too bad this is not the first time they have been composed."[43] His deepest tragedy is that he believes in nothing. He has heard Rousseauian mouthings about nature—how much better it is than civilization; but he observes that "in nature all species devour one another," and the sublime end of every organism is to be eaten. He sees the

same anthropophagy in the economic world, except that there men consume one another by due process of law. All morality, he thinks, is a hoax
that the clever play upon the simple, or that the simple play upon themselves. See that pious woman coming from church with modest downcast
eyes; "her imagination at night rehearses the scenes of the [licentious]
Portier des Chartrains and the [libidinous] postures of Aretino."[44] The wise
man, thinks the nephew, will laugh at the Ten Commandments, and enjoy
all the sins judiciously. "Hurrah for wisdom and philosophy!—the wisdom
of Solomon: to drink good wines, gorge on choice foods, tumble pretty
women, sleep on downy beds; outside of that, all is vanity."[45] After this,
what was left for the Nietzsches and Baudelaires to say?

Diderot ends this *danse macabre* of ideas by calling the nephew "a do-
nothing, a glutton, a coward, a spirit of mud"—to which Rameau replies,
"I believe you are right."[46] A mean thought comes to us: How could
Diderot have drawn this character so vividly if he had not found him lurking in himself? He protests against the idea. He admits that he is no saint.

> I do not condemn the pleasure of the senses. I too have a palate
> that relishes delicate dishes and delicious wines. I have a heart and
> eyes, and I like to see a beautiful woman, I like to feel under my
> hand the firmness and roundness of her throat [*gorge*], to press her lips
> to mine, to draw pleasure from her eyes, and to expire in her arms.
> Sometimes, with my friends, a little debauch, even a bit tumultuous,
> does not displease me. But—I will not conceal it from you—it seems
> to me infinitely sweeter to have helped the unfortunate, . . . to have
> given salutary counsel, to have read an agreeable book, to take a walk
> with a man or a woman dear to me, to have given some instructive
> hours to my children, to have written a good page, to fulfill the
> duties of my place, to say to my beloved tender and sweet words that
> bring her arms around my neck. . . .
>
> A man of my acquaintance grew to wealth in Cartagena; he was a
> younger son in a country where custom transmits all property to the
> eldest. Word reached him in Colombia that his older brother, a spoiled
> brat, had despoiled his too indulgent father and mother of all that they
> possessed, and had expelled them from their château; and that these
> good people were now languishing in poverty in a provincial town.
> What did this younger son do, who, so badly treated by his parents,
> had gone so far abroad to seek his fortune? He sent them help, he
> hastened to arrange his affairs and return, opulent, to his father and
> mother; he restored them to their home, he provided dowries to get his
> sisters married. Ah, my dear Rameau, this man regards those months as
> the happiest in his life. He spoke of them to me with tears in his eyes.
> And I, in telling you his story, I feel my heart troubled with joy, with
> a pleasure that can find no words.[47]

V. ETHICS AND POLITICS

There were in Diderot at least two characters, as in us all: a private self, preserving secretly all the impulses of human nature as found in primitive, savage, even animal, life; and a public self reluctantly accepting education, discipline, and morality as the price to be paid for protection by social order. There were still other selves in him: the Diderot who had not forgotten his youth, his Bohemian liberties and loves, his freedom from responsibilities except to the police; and there was the paterfamilias who, if allowed a mistress capable of understanding his language and ideas, could be also, intermittently, a fairly good husband, a doting father, a half-domesticated animal, a man with some appreciation of money, morality, and law.

This Jekyll and Hyde produced, between 1770 and 1772, two dialogues illustrating the vacillation of his views. In *Entretien d'un père avec ses enfants* he drew a loving picture of his father gently expounding "the danger of those who put themselves above the law." But two years later he wrote the most radical of all his works. Louis Antoine de Bougainville had just (1771) published his *Voyage autour du monde*, recounting his experiences in Tahiti and other South Pacific isles. Diderot seized upon parts of the narrative as illustrating certain superiorities of savagery to civilization. To elucidate these he composed (1772), with his usual verve, imagination, and partiality, a *Supplément au Voyage de Bougainville*, which saw the light only in 1796. He took up an old Tahitian mentioned by Bougainville, and fancied him making a farewell address to the admiral of the departing French:

> And you, chief of the brigands who obey you, quickly push off your vessel from our shore. We are innocent, we are happy; all you can do for us is to spoil our happiness. We follow the pure instinct of nature; you have sought to efface its character from our souls. Here all things belong to all men; you have preached some strange distinction between "thine" and "mine." Our daughters and our wives were held in common by us all; you have shared this privilege with us, and . . . have inflamed them with frenzies unknown before. . . . You have slaughtered each other for them; they have come back stained with your blood.
>
> We are free, and behold, you have planted in our earth the title of our future slavery. . . . On this metal blade you have written, *This country is ours.* . . . And why? Because you have set foot here? If a Tahitian disembarked one day upon your shores, and graved upon one of your stones . . . *This country belongs to the inhabitants of Tahiti,* what would you think of such a proceeding? . . .

He whom you wish to seize like an animal, the Tahitian, is your brother. . . . What right have you over him that he has not over you? You came. Did we fall upon you? Did we pillage your ships? . . . No. We respected our image in you. Leave us our customs, they are wiser and more honorable than yours. We have no wish to barter what you call our ignorance against your useless knowledge.[48]

The Nestor of Tahiti goes on to remind the Europeans how cordial was the welcome they had received; how they were housed and fed and loved. For (Diderot supposed) there was no Sixth Commandment in the island, and no jealousy; the native women could not understand the ship's chaplain when he spoke of sin and shame; they gave the ultimate hospitality to the sailors. With what result? Syphilis, unknown to the islanders before, was now appearing in the native women, and was being communicated to the native men. The old man begs the visitors to leave the island and never return.

Diderot added a "Conversation of the Chaplain and Orou"—a native who had learned Spanish. Orou, on whose hut the chaplain has been billeted, offers him the choice of his wife and daughters as his bedmate. The chaplain explains that his moral code forbids him to accept such a favor, but one of the girls touches him and he becomes a man. He spends the next three days explaining Christian ethics to Orou, and the next three nights sleeping in turn with a second daughter and a third daughter, and "the fourth night, as in honor bound, he consecrated to the wife of his host."[49] His efforts to convert Orou to Christianity provide Diderot with a joyful page:

> CHAPLAIN. What is marriage with you?
> OROU. Agreement to share the same hut and sleep in the same bed as long as we wish to do so.
> CHAPLAIN. And when you wish no longer?
> OROU. We separate.
> CHAPLAIN. And what happens to the children?

This is no problem, says Orou; the lady returns with them to her father; she is soon courted by another man, who is glad to accept her children, for children are economic assets in an agricultural society.

> CHAPLAIN. Can a father sleep with his daughter, a mother with her son, a brother with his sister, a husband with another man's wife?
> OROU. Why not?
> CHAPLAIN. I suppose, however, that even here a son does not often sleep with his mother.
> OROU. Not unless he has a great deal of respect for her.[50]

The chaplain comes away almost won to "Tahitian" ways; he admits that he "was tempted to throw his clothes into the ship and pass the rest of his life among" these "children of nature." Diderot concludes almost as his former friend Rousseau had argued in his *Discourse on the Arts and Sciences* (1750) and his *Discourse on the Origin of Inequality* (1755):

> Would you like an abridged account of almost all our wretchedness? Here it is. There existed a natural man. There was introduced into this man an artificial man; and a civil war, enduring throughout life, arose. . . . Sometimes the natural man is stronger, sometimes he is struck down by the moral and artificial man. In either case the poor monster is pulled about, pinched with tweezers, tortured, stretched on the wheel, . . . ceaselessly unhappy.[51]

Diderot, of course, was very poorly informed about the Tahitians. Bougainville himself had described them as ridden with superstitions and taboos, terrified by imaginary evil spirits, and subject to priests, not to mention a variety of insects and diseases. Diderot, restless in monogamy, was in no mood to understand why the necessities of social order had placed so many restraints upon the lawless sexual instincts of mankind. He was one more example of the individual intellect imagining itself wiser than the customs of the race.

There is an amusing contrast between the ethical philosophy of Diderot the writer and that of Diderot the man. Theoretically, at times, his moral ideas verged upon anarchism. In those moments he described human nature as basically good, and on this assumption he proposed to "follow nature"— i.e., instinct. Only through instinct, he felt, could the individual free himself from the bonds that religion and society lay upon him with their thousand conventions, prohibitions, and laws. In this mood he described coitus as "the sovereign happiness";[52] he defined love as "the voluptuous rubbing of two membranes," and "the voluptuous loss of a few drops of liquid";[53] and he assured his mistress that adultery "is a fault less reprehensible than the slightest lie."[54] He was a philosopher longing to live like a rooster.

As his experience of life widened he reversed almost all his ethical views. Veering from Rousseau toward Voltaire, he took an increasingly gloomy view of man as bad by nature as well as through social deterioration. "Nothing shows so well how detestable human nature is as the facility with which people consent to the most wicked acts when [as in a crowd] . . . nobody is personally responsible for the evil that is done."[55] "Believe me," says Jacques the Fatalist, "we never pity anyone but ourselves."[56] Now Diderot cancels his earlier exaggerations with new ones: "The natural man" would "twist his father's neck and sleep with his mother were it not for the development of his reason by education."[57] As his sexual needs diminished, Diderot came to agree with Epicurus that "the pleasures of the soul" are more steadily satisfying than physical delights.[58] "Is there," he asks, "only physical pleasure in possessing a beautiful woman? Is there only physical pain in losing her by death or inconstancy? Is not the distinction between physical and moral as solid as that between the animalcule that feels and the animal that reasons?"[59]

Now that he had arrived at the biological conception of virtue as any quality that makes for survival, he came vaguely to understand that the highest virtues are those that make for the survival of the group, since social organization is the chief means of individual survival. Diderot recognized, in the nephew of Rameau, what happens to one who tries to cast off the restraints imposed upon the individual for the preservation of the group; such a man becomes a derelict without faith, food, mate, or hope. So Diderot concludes his dream of Tahiti with a tardy council of moderation: "We will preach against insensate laws until they are reformed. But meanwhile we will submit to them. He who of his own authority infringes a bad law authorizes everyone else to infringe a good one. It is less inconvenient to be mad among madmen than to be wise all alone."[60]

When his daughter Angélique developed the charms of young womanhood, Diderot began to worry about her morals. He watched over her virginity as a precious and marketable asset, and after he had seen her safely married he warned her against adultery; the very suspicion of infidelity on her part, he told her, would crush him with grief and make him die of shame.[61] In his art criticisms he denounced Boucher as corrupt, and exalted modesty and other Christian virtues as pictured by Greuze and Chardin; in his plays he preached the old virtues like any settled and prosperous bourgeois. Diderot amused himself with such pieces of reckless humor as the *Supplément au Voyage de Bougainville*, and with anarchistic revels of imagination at the dinners of d'Holbach; but when he came home he insisted upon all the middle-class virtues, and tried to practice them if only he might be allowed a little adultery.

His political ideas were as confused as his views of morality, and with his good-humored candor he admitted it. He did not agree with Voltaire that an enlightened monarch would prove the best available instrument of reform; he condemned Frederick the Great as a tyrant, and he tried to convert Catherine the Great to democratic ideas. He accepted constitutional monarchy, but proposed a national assembly—chosen by property owners as having a stake in good and economical government.[62] (When he wrote this, none but the propertied middle class could be imagined as a possible substitute for the aristocracy in the government of France.) He dreamed of a benign society in which both liberty and equality (those natural enemies) would be assured to all, but he doubted if any reforms would be effective until widespread education should have raised the average intelligence of the people.*

His economic ideas were radical in theory, moderate in application. Even in old age he clung to an anarchistic communism as his ideal. "I am convinced that there cannot be any real happiness for mankind except in a social state in which there would be no king, no magistrate, no priest, no laws, no thine or mine, no ownership of property, no vices or virtues";[65] but he confessed that this prospect is *diablement idéal*."[66] "What a devilish social economy we have!" exclaimed the nephew of Rameau. "There are some men who are gorged with everything, while others, who have stomachs just as importunate, haven't a bite to put between their teeth."[67] Diderot knew, in his sober moments, that inequality of possessions will continue as long as inequality of ability remains. He dismissed socialism as impracticable because as yet there was only a small, disorganized, and hardly conscious proletariat; but he hoped that the status of these workers would soon be raised. When it came to practical reforms, he stood with the physiocrats on the side of nascent capitalism. He declared the rights of property to be sacred and absolute, condemned any infringement of those rights by the state, and joined with Quesnay, Turgot, and Voltaire in calling for the liberation of industry and commerce from governmental controls.[68] He favored state subsidies to agriculture as that part of the economy that was most vital and yet most at the mercy of the rest.[69] Like all of us, he grew more conservative as his years and his income increased.

VI. DIDEROT ON ART

All this rambling invasion of theology, ethics, politics, and economics constituted merely a few sides of Diderot's polymorphous interest and activity; there were many more. Who would have thought that this burly Jack-of-all-ideas would become, overnight, the leading art critic of his age?

In 1759 his friend Grimm, busy with war and Mme. d'Épinay, asked Diderot to substitute for him in reporting to the clientele of his *Correspondance* the biennial exhibitions of paintings and sculpture in the Louvre.

---

* The often quoted, often mangled lines,

> *Et ses mains ourdiraient les entrailles du prêtre*
> *Au défaut d'un cordon pour étrangler les rois*[63]

—"and his hands would twist the entrails of the priest for lack of a rope to strangle the kings"—were put by Diderot into the mouth of a fanatic in his play *Les Éleuthéromanes, ou les furieux de la liberté (The Freedom Maniacs, or the Madmen of Liberty)*; they cannot be taken as Diderot's view, for he explicitly condemned regicide: "Let the people never see royal blood flow for any cause whatever."[64] The lines could have had no influence on the fate of Louis XVI, for they were not published till 1795.

Diderot reported the Salons between 1759 and 1771, and those of 1775 and 1781, sometimes at great length, for in these notes he let himself wander freely over almost every phase of human life. Nothing so fresh and intimate had ever appeared in art criticism before. Some of his critiques were cast in the form of conversations with painters at the exhibition itself; some were introduced as a personal communication to Grimm—as in 1761:

> Here, my friend, are the ideas that have passed through my head
> on seeing the pictures exhibited in this year's Salon. I throw them upon
> the paper without much care to select them or to express them. . . .
> The only thought I have had in mind is to spare you some moments
> that you will employ better.[70]

He went at his new task with ebullient delight. He thanked Grimm for compelling him to look at the exhibited art not with the "superficial and distracted gaze" of the passing crowd, but with the resolve to study each canvas or marble until he really felt its artistry and significance. He had no technical preparation, but he talked with the artists themselves—Chardin, La Tour, Cochin, Falconet . . . ; he studied their method of composition, brushwork, and coloring. "I opened my soul to the effects [produced by the artist's labor]; I conceived the magic of the light and the shade; I understood color; I acquired the feeling of the flesh."[71]

He became in the end a competent critic of technique. But, disclaiming all technical knowledge, he proposed merely to say what each work meant to him. First he described the subject or story in some detail, since most of Grimm's clientele would never see the pieces in question; some clients, however, bought pictures on Diderot's recommendation. Often he would imagine, and graphically recount, the living drama of which the artist represented only the concentrated, telling moment; at times he turned art into literature; and at last he could boast: "Chardin, La Grenée, Greuze, and others . . . have assured me that I was the only literary man whose images could pass upon the canvas almost as they had succeeded one another in my head."[72]

He expressed his preferences and prejudices with unabashed candor. After denouncing almost everything in contemporary French civilization, he defended French painters with patriotic ardor. He called Hogarth a liar and an ignoramus for saying that France had no colorist. "Chardin," he retorted, "is perhaps one of the greatest colorists in all painting."[73] He was severe on Nattier. He railed at Boucher's nudes, but enjoyed them. After criticizing the defects in one nude he added: "All the same, let me have her just as she is, and I do not think I shall waste time complaining that her hair is too dark." A picture of Joseph rejecting the advances of Potiphar's wife angered him. "I can't imagine what he could have wanted. I wouldn't have asked for any better, and I have often settled for less."[74] He sympathized with artists who painted nudes, and especially with sculptors who modeled them; after all, "what can you do in statuary with buttons and pants?"[75] He liked Greuze's pictures of girlish innocence; he fully shared Greuze's sentimentality; he particularly appreciated the portraits of Greuze's wife, who had been Diderot's mistress in his youth. He relished the wild landscapes in Dutch and Flemish art, and found "more poetry in a single tree which has suffered the buffets of the years and seasons, than in all the façade of a palace. A palace must be in ruins to be an object of interest."[76] He rejected the classic emphasis on rationality, order, and harmony, and exalted creative imagination above analytical reason. He called for "compositions terrible or sensuous, which . . . carry love or terror to the depths of your heart, dissolve your senses, and purge your soul; there is something in that which no rules can achieve."[77] He despised the notion of "art for art's sake"; art, he thought, had a moral task: "to honor virtue and expose vice."[78]

To his observations on the Salon of 1765 Diderot felt confident enough to add an "Essai sur la peinture." Like Plato and Aristotle he found the essence of beauty in the harmonious relation of parts in a whole; but he suggested that there must also be a harmony of the object with its environment and with its intended purpose. Ideally, he thought beauty might be defined as complete adaptation to function; so a healthy and intelligent man should seem beautiful. Art should select, in a scene, the features that point its significance, and should eliminate irrelevant elements; it need not be a slavish imitation of the objective and indiscriminate reality. Yet the artist must study the natural object rather than ancient models or formal rules; better one Teniers than a dozen fanciful Watteaus. Diderot felt a certain discord between reason and art; he recognized that Boileau's classical precepts had crippled French poetry. Here he left Voltaire and sided with Rousseau: art must above all be the voice and product of feeling. Therefore he exalted color, while Reynolds in the same decade was extolling design. "Design gives form to beings," Diderot conceded, "but color gives them life."[79] Goethe found many things in this essay that seemed to him wrong, but he translated portions of it, and described it to Schiller as "a magnificent work; it speaks even more usefully to the poet than to the painter, though for the painter too it is a torch of powerful illumination."[80]

VII. DIDEROT AND THE THEATER

"When I was young," Diderot wrote, "I hesitated between the Sorbonne [priesthood] and the stage."[81] And in 1774: "For some thirty years I have

against my taste made the *Encyclopédie*, and written only two plays."[82]
He attached more importance to his plays than to his novels; and as most
of his novels were published only after his death, his plays had the greater
influence on his fame and his life. And they constituted almost a revolution in the history of the French theater.

He had read with emotion the novels of Richardson; in 1761 he wrote an
Éloge de Richardson, rising to lyric praise of the Englishman for his evoca-
tion of feeling, his inculcation of virtue, his courage in picturing middle-
class life as worthy of serious art. Moreover, Diderot had been impressed
by George Lillo's *The London Merchant* (1731), which had successfully
brought the sentiments and tribulations of the business class to the English
stage. He called the play "sublime," even compared it with Sophocles; why
should not broken hearts be worthy of tragic drama despite their lack of
pedigree? When Diderot took to composing plays in the *genre sérieux* he
startled French conventions by using middle-class characters and writing
in prose. So in 1757 he sent to stage and press *Le Fils naturel, ou les
épreuves de la vertu*. It had no success on the boards; it was acted twice in
the provinces (1757), not till 1771 in Paris, and then, apparently, only
once. But in its printed form it became a *cause célèbre*.

The story was interesting enough. The virtuous, prosperous bastard
Dorval finds himself falling in love with Rosalie, the betrothed of his host,
Clairville. He perceives that she returns his affection; he resolves to absent
himself rather than ruin the nuptials of his friend. As he is about to leave
he sees Clairville attacked by armed assailants; he fights them and saves
his friend's life. When he learns that Rosalie's merchant father has lost his
fortune and can give her no dowry, he secretly makes up her loss. The
bankrupt merchant turns out to be Dorval's father as well as Rosalie's; she
reconciles herself to being his sister; she marries Clairville; Dorval marries
Clairville's sister Constance, and the play ends with everyone bathed in
tears of joy. This was Diderot's contribution to what critics had already
termed *la comédie larmoyante*—the drama of tears.*

What gave the play a place in French history was a series of dialogues
published with it, and later entitled *Entretiens sur Le Fils naturel*. The
tradition of the French theater was that serious (as distinguished from
comic) drama should concern itself only with personages of the nobility,
and should be written in verse. Diderot now expounded his view that serious drama should not be afraid to use bourgeois characters and occupations, and scenes from domestic life, presented with realism and in prose.
He proposed to show that the phrase *bourgeois gentilhomme* (middle-class
gentleman) was not the laughable contradiction-in-terms that Molière had

---

* *Comédie* and *comédien* meant drama and actor rather than comedy and comedian. Any
play with a happy ending was called a *comédie*.

taken it to be, but a development of the new society in which the bourgeoisie was rising in wealth, status, and power. The dramatist, he argued, should
present not so much studies in character as conditions of actual life—e.g.,
in the family, in the army, in politics, in the professions, even in industry.
And as the middle classes were a chief repository of virtue in France,
Diderot insisted that one function of the new *drame* (as he called it) should
be "to inspire men with love of virtue and abhorrence of vice." He branded
a merely entertaining art as an idle-class luxury; every art should have a
social function and use; and what better aim could the theater have than to
make virtue charming?

The play and its accompanying pronunciamento divided intellectual
Paris into hostile camps. Palissot and other *antiphilosophes* ridiculed Diderot's ideas. Fréron did not merely criticize the play as dull didacticism
wet with sentiment and unreal virtue, but he showed, in successive issues
of his *Année littéraire*, a suspicious similarity between the first half of *Le
Fils naturel* and the comedy *Il vero amico (The True Friend)* which Goldoni had staged at Venice in 1750. Diderot confessed:

> I took possession of it as if it were a piece of property belonging to
> me. Goldoni has not been more scrupulous. He laid hold of *L'Avare*
> [Molière's *The Miser*] without anyone taking it into his head to find
> that bad; and no one among us has dreamed of accusing Molière or
> Corneille of plagiarism for having tacitly borrowed the idea of some
> play either from an Italian author or from the Spanish theater.[83]

Of course this was true of Corneille's *Le Cid* and Molière's *Le Festin de
pierre (Don Juan)*.

Encouraged by friends, defiant of his enemies, and amid the direst
troubles of the *Encyclopédie*, Diderot wrote and published (1758) another
play, *Le Père de famille*, and added to it a provocative "Discours sur la
poésie dramatique"—a title reminiscent of the one that Dryden had used
for a similar essay ninety years before. *The Family Father* was produced
in Toulouse and Marseilles in 1760, and at the Théâtre-Français in Paris in
February, 1761; there it ran for seven nights, which was considered a moderate success. Voltaire allowed performances of his tragedy *Tancrède* to be
postponed to permit this run, and he wrote to his new rival: "Oh, my dear
brother Diderot! I yield you my place with all my heart, and I should like
to crown you with laurel." Diderot replied: "Thank you, my dear master.
I know how much you must have desired the success of your disciple, and
I am touched by it. My affection and homage to the end of my life."[84] The
play was successfully revived at the Théâtre-Français in 1769, and became
a minor element in the triumph of the *philosophes*.

The plot was partly autobiographical. The father is a loving reminiscence

of Didier Diderot, except that he preaches far more than that good man
had been reported to do. The son, Saint-Albin (a fond portrait of Denis
Diderot), seeks parental permission to marry Sophie, a girl of the working
class. The father consents to see her, likes her, but refuses to let his son
marry so poor a lass. After five acts, and by a coincidence that has served
a thousand dramas, the young lady turns out to be a daughter of excellent
family; the father relents; all is well. Fréron could be pardoned for calling
the plot melodramatic, mechanical, and absurd. One critic pointed out that
this ode to virtue was dedicated to Grimm, who had shared a prostitute
with Rousseau and was now the lover of Mme. d'Épinay, and that Diderot
had named the heroine after his mistress Sophie Volland. Voltaire, while
complimenting the author on the "tender and virtuous things" in the play,
wrote to Mme. du Deffand: "Have you had *Le Père de famille* read to you?
Isn't it ludicrous? In faith, our century is a poor one compared to that of
Louis XIV."[85]

Diderot, however, felt that the seventeenth-century French drama had
been a thoroughly unnatural form—in its pompous, declamatory style, in
its straitlaced unities of action, place, and time, and in its supine imitation
of ancient classics rather than of living realities. His plays, unashamedly sentimental, were omens of the Romantic reaction against the intellectualism
and emotional restraint of the classic age. Diderot's influence was felt also
in the increasing realism of scenic sets, in the historic veracity of the actors'
dress, in the nationalism of their delivery; and it shared with Voltaire's
campaign in clearing the French stage of spectators. "Every improvement
in the art of production for the past 150 years," said Gustave Lanson, "has
sprung from Diderot"[87]—except that scenery now tends to be more imaginative than realistic. Germany too responded to Diderot, whom Sainte-
Beuve called "the most German of Frenchman." Lessing translated *Le
Père de famille* and the dramatic discourses, and declared that "no more
philosophical mind than Diderot's has occupied itself with the theater since
Aristotle."[88]

He had his say also on the histrionic art. In a challenging essay, *Paradoxe
sur le comédien* (1778), he argued that to move an audience the actor must
not surrender himself to the emotion he expresses, but must remain completely self-possessed. This, of course, flew in the face of Horace's advice
to poets, "*Si vis me flere, primum tibi flendum est*" (If you wish me to
weep you must first weep yourself). No, said Diderot; the actor

> must have in himself an unmoved and disinterested onlooker. He must
> have penetration and no sensibility . . . If the actor were full, really
> full, of feeling, how could he play the same part twice running with
> the same spirit and success? Full of fire at the first performance, he

would be worn out, or cold as marble, at the third. . . . Fill the front of the theater with tearful creatures, but I will have none of them on the boards.[89]

(A counsel hardly followed by those who acted Diderot's plays.)

It was a paradox in Diderot himself, for in 1757 he had written: "Poets [and] actors . . . feel intensely, and reflect little."[90] Now he reversed himself, perhaps after watching David Garrick, in Paris (1763, 1770), simulate diverse emotions in quick succession and at will. Or he might have found his paradox in Hamlet's bidding to the players at Elsinore: "In the very torrent, tempest, and (as I may say) whirlwind of passion, acquire and beget a temperance that may give it smoothness."[91] Sir Henry Irving rejected Diderot's analysis, but a modern critic believes that "it has remained to this day the most significant attempt to deal with the problem of acting."[92] Actors may be emotional in life, but not on the stage. (Perhaps their self-control on the stage leads to their emotional release in life; hence many sins must be forgiven them.) They must study the indicated feeling in its causes, and express it in their gestures and speech, but they must "remember" it "in tranquillity."[93] Diderot struck the balance in a letter to Mlle. Jodin: "An actor who has nothing but sense and judgment is cold; one who has nothing but verve and sensibility is mad."[94]

Looking back upon this disorderly review of Diderot's chaotic mind, we forgive his confusion in the literally magnanimous profusion of his ideas and the scope of his interests. Nothing human was alien to him except religion, and even there, as we have seen, he was not immune to religious feeling. It was characteristic of him to begin with mathematics and physics, and end with drama and music. He could not be a great scientist, being too impatient for research and experiment; he leaped too buoyantly to generalizations, but these were almost always illuminating. He knew enough about music to write a method of clavecin instruction and a treatise on harmony. He composed the most influential plays, and the best novels, of his time; in the short story he excelled all his contemporaries except Voltaire; and he surpassed Voltaire himself in giving to the short story that concentration of thought and action which determined the form into our own day. Addicted to conversation and trained in the salons, he developed the dialogue to a brilliance and vitality seldom equaled before or since. And he wrote philosophy not in a secret language for ivory towers, but as a living debate, on living themes, among men willingly caught in the stream of the world.

VIII. DIDEROT

Behind this kaleidoscopic mind was a man of many virtues and almost every fault, each taking its turn on the stage of his life. When Michel Vanloo painted him Diderot protested that the face in the picture showed only a fleeting part of him, merely one expression of but one mood.

> I had a hundred different expressions in a day, according to the mood that was on me. I was serene, sad, dreamy, tender, violent, passionate, eager. The outward signs of my many and varying states of mind chased one another so rapidly across my face that the painter's eye caught a different me from moment to moment, and never got one right.[95]

Gradually, however, those many faces merged into a composite mold, and left him the rugged physiognomy that we see in the portrait by Greuze: as somber as Caesar, worn out by his passionate encounters with an army of ideas and enemies, and by attempts to express in static words the fluent nuances of his yes-and-no's. High brow receding on a half-bald head; large rustic ears and big bent nose, firm mouth and fighting chin, brown eyes heavy and sad, as if recalling unrecallable errors, or realizing the indestructibility of superstition, or noting the high birth rate of simplicity. Usually in public he wore a wig, but when he lost himself in the ecstasy of monologue he might remove it, play with it, or rest it on his lap. He was absorbed in being, and had no time for seeming.

He yielded to no one in appreciation of his character. He admitted, "I get excited for a moment"; but "a moment later I am myself again, the frank, gentle, just, indulgent, honest, charitable, obliging man. Continue, if you please, this eulogy, for it isn't complete. I haven't said anything about my intelligence." He doubted if any man alive was more honest than he, and he was sure that even the "pillars of the Church" would rely upon his word. "What beautiful souls yours, mine, and his are!" he wrote to his mistress, letting Grimm into the trinity. He spoke with rapture about his books and plays, confident of their immortality. He thought his morals excellent, and indeed he had only one mistress at a time. He spoke of himself as "the philosopher," and acknowledged his likeness to Socrates. "What does it matter," he asked, "whether I owe my estimable qualities to nature or experience, so long as they are solid, and vanity never spoils them?"[96]

Actually he had most of the virtues with which he credited himself. He was honest in the sense of candid, though he had done a deal of lying in his youth. There was no pose or affectation in him. He was gentle except in speech, where he was often wild and sometimes so coarse that Mme.

Geoffrin had to call him to order and decency. He certainly had courage, for he continued to fight when so many friends deserted him, when even Voltaire advised him to quit. He was just, except to piety and Rousseau; we may see later that he did not sufficiently allow for Jean Jacques' sensibility. He was unquestionably generous, always ready to aid those who appealed to him, and more lavish in praise of others than of himself. He spent many days substituting for Grimm in the *Correspondance*, or putting into effective shape the literary efforts of his friends. He helped a long succession of poor people with gifts out of his modest income. When a needy scribe showed him a satire on Diderot and asked him to revise it, saying that he needed bread, Diderot revised and improved it, and suggested that he dedicate it to the current Duc d'Orléans, "who does me the honor to hate me." It was so done, and the Duke sent the young author twenty-five louis.[97] He was lenient in his criticisms of books and paintings (excepting Boucher's), saying that he preferred to point to the good rather than belabor the bad.[98] He was the most good-humored of the *philosophes*. Rousseau till 1758, and Grimm to the end, corroborated Diderot's estimate of his own character. They spoke of him, said Mme. d'Épinay, with "the greatest veneration"; they admired his genius, but "his character was the object of their particular enthusiasm. M. Grimm says that he is the most perfect mortal he knows."[99] To such friends his faults were those of a child naïvely frank. They reckoned him profounder than Voltaire.

He was assuredly richer than Voltaire in ideas, for there were no checks and balances in his constitution. He was more imaginative, less rational, more impetuous, never mature. "Diderot," said Voltaire, "is too hot an oven; everything that is baked in it gets burned";[100] even so, many things came out half baked. He was as keen as Rousseau in sensibility, as tender in his sentiments, as ready to weep over the loveliness of nature and the tragedies of life. He made his *religieuse* say, and it probably expressed himself, "For a tender soul the shedding of tears is a delicious condition."[101] His visitors sometimes found him in tears—or in a rage—over a book. Perhaps his friendship with Rousseau was based upon a community of sentiment, the same exaltation of feeling, the same love of nature, the same romantic conception of genius as instinct, passion, and imagination, the same enthusiasm for the novels of Richardson. He longed to warn Clarissa against Lovelace, and when he read of cruel kings he could easily imagine himself "using a dagger with marvelous facility."[102] Voltaire + Rousseau = Diderot; neither of those two could forgive him for including them both while remaining unique and himself.

His habits expressed the ambivalence of his qualities. He liked good food to the point of gourmandizing and gallstones, but he was alive to all the cultural offerings of his time. He hated and ridiculed travel,[103] but he crossed Europe to slap the thighs of Catherine the Great. He wept over beautiful poetry, and indulged in coarse obscenity. He despised money, and talked of poverty as the inspiring friend of philosophers; but when his father died he went to Langres (1759) and was glad to get his third of the patrimony, so that by 1760 he had an income of four thousand livres per year. "I need a carriage," he said, "a comfortable apartment [it was a duplex], fine linen, a perfumed woman, and I could easily put up with the other curses of our civilized state"; here the Voltaire in him checked and laughed at the Rousseau.

His wife was too busy with frustrated motherhood and unperfumed housework to provide a fit and necessary audience for his proliferating ideas. Like Milton he cried out for divorce on grounds of intellectual incompatibility. Not allowed this, he did what the French still do—he took a mistress. There was, briefly, Mlle. Babuti, who became Mme. Greuze. Then Mme. de Puisieux, who held him for a decade. In 1755 he found just what he needed: a young woman who for eighteen years gave him love, fidelity, and understanding. Louise Henriette Volland (whom he rechristened Sophie because she seemed to him the soul of wisdom) was already thirty-eight when they first met—unmarried, plump, shortsighted; he described her as wearing spectacles on a rather "dried-up" face, and he had to scold her, now and then, for rivaling his appetite. But she had gathered books instead of lovers; she had read widely, even in politics and philosophy; she talked well, and listened better. Diderot found her legs too thick, but he was grateful for her ears, and loved her mind and heart.

> Ah, Grimm [he wrote], what a woman! How tender she is, how sweet, how honest, delicate, sensible! She reflects . . . We don't know any more than she does in customs, morals, feelings, in an infinity of important things. She has her judgment, views, ideas, her own way of thinking, formed according to reason, truth, and common sense; neither public opinion nor authorities, nor anything, can subjugate them.[104]

This could not all be infatuation, for the objective Dr. Tronchin saw in her "the soul of an eagle in a house of gauze";[105] that is, she loved fine clothes and intellectual flights.

To her, through twenty years, Diderot wrote his finest letters, which remain among the literary treasures of the eighteenth century. He could write to her frankly about everything; he could send her his bawdy stories and his latest speculations; he would write to her as he would talk "if I were at your side, an arm on the back of your chair."[106] In his relationship with her he realized, as never before, the part that feeling and sentiment can play in life. Now he could hardly believe in determinism; it seemed incredible that their complex exchange of devotion and ideas could be the physicochemical result of some primeval nebula. Sometimes, in such a mood, he could even speak of God. He told Sophie how, walking in the countryside with Grimm, he plucked a blade of wheat and fell into thought over the mystery of growth. "What are you doing?" asked Grimm. "I am listening." "Who is talking to you?" "God."[107]

After some twelve years of his liaison with Sophie Volland his love subsided, his letters grew shorter, his protestations of fidelity more forced. In 1769, aged fifty-seven, he succeeded his dead friend Damilaville as the lover of Mme. de Meaux, aged fifty-four. A year later a younger gallant displaced Diderot. Meanwhile Denis continued to assure Sophie of his "eternal love."

Through all the wanderings of his heart and mind his wife, Antoinette, bore with him faithfully, scolded him incontinently, and sought consolation in religion and cards. They quarreled almost daily, and time did not bridge the gap between the man with a thousand ideas and the woman with one God. When his friends came to visit him they never stopped to greet her. When she discovered his affair with Sophie she burst into a fury which seemed to him quite unproportioned to so common a diversion. For a while he had his meals served to him in his study. "She is beginning to feel the effects of this little divorce," he wrote to Grimm. "The exhaustion of her funds, which is not distant, will bring reconciliation."[108] She fell sick, he relented, and tended her with grumbling care. She responded with such sweetness that he thought she must be dying; however, he described her illness jokingly in a letter to Sophie. When his friend Suard proposed to marry, Diderot advised him to drown himself instead. (Suard's marriage was one of the happiest in that unhappy age.)

Probably Diderot would have fled from his home had he not so loved his domestic comforts and his pretty daughter. Antoinette was forty-three when (1753) she bore her fourth child. As Marie Angélique grew up through all the charms of girlhood, Diderot concentrated all his tenderness upon her. He joined her in her games; we picture the topheavy philosopher playing hopscotch with her, and hide-and-seek, and blindman's buff. "I was crazy about my little girl. What a lovely character! What a woman I could make of her if her mother would let me!" He took care to preach to her all the Christian virtues, and as she neared nubility he gave her explicit instructions on guarding herself against the wolves of Paris. What did their proposals mean? "They mean: 'Mademoiselle, out of complacence for me, will you dishonor yourself, lose all social status, banish yourself from society, have yourself locked up in a convent, and make your father and mother die of grief?' "[109] So, like any French father, he saved up money to provide her dowry, and negotiated with divers families to get her a

husband in due time. He made the choice, Antoinette disapproved, Angélique approved, and was married (1772). Diderot wept at losing her, and
wept still more when he saw her happiness in marriage. He helped the
young couple generously, saying, "Isn't it better to help them at a difficult
moment than to wait until they no longer need anything?" The son-in-law
became a successful manufacturer, whose descendants, after the restoration
of the Bourbon monarchy (1814), became cautious conservatives.

As Diderot matured through parentage he began to understand his father
better, and to honor the code of morals that helped a man to bring up a
good family. But much of the Bohemian remained in him. Though he loved
his den, his old clothes and slippers, and liked to toast his toes before a
fire, he absented himself from such felicity now and then, as when he spent
a month with d'Holbach at Grandval. He still frequented the cafés, and
was a familiar figure in some salons. Mme. Geoffrin loved him despite his
rough speech, and in a burst of maternal affection she sent him a new desk,
cozy armchairs of leather, a great clock of gold and bronze, and a luxurious
dressing gown. He thanked her, and sadly let his old furniture be taken
away: but he expressed tender regrets for his discarded *robe de chambre:*

> Why did I not keep it? It was just made for me, and I was made for
> it. It followed every fold in my body without inconveniencing me.
> It was picturesque and handsome. The new robe, stiff and starched,
> makes a mannequin of me. There was no call to which its good nature
> did not lend itself. . . . If a book was covered with dust, one of its
> flaps was ready as a duster. When the ink on my pen was thick and
> would not flow, its side was ready. You could see, traced in long black
> stripes, the frequent services it had rendered me. These long stripes an-
> nounced the man of letters, the writer, the toiler. At present I look like
> one of the idle rich; no one recognizes me. . . . I was absolute master
> of my old dressing gown; I have become the slave of the new one.[110]

He counted his friendships the chief solace and inspiration of his life.
His association with Grimm was closer and more permanent than any of
his loves. In 1772, when they had known each other for twenty-two years,
he wrote to him: "My tender, my only friend, you have always been, you
will always be, my dear and only friend."[111] Yet there were times when he
was keenly hurt by Grimm's coldness and seeming indifference. The German exploited Diderot's good nature, often delegating to him the writing
of his *Correspondance*; Diderot substituted for him not only in reporting
the Salon exhibitions but in reviewing the latest books; and sometimes he
worked through the night to meet the deadline that Grimm had laid
down.[112] Grimm offered to pay him; Diderot refused to be paid. It is sad
to relate that when (1773) Stanislas II Poniatowski, King of Poland, hear-

ing that Diderot was planning to visit St. Petersburg, proposed to invite him to stop in Warsaw, Grimm advised the King that there would be no profit in making the philosopher's acquaintance. "Instead of utilizing his time to share the glory of genius with Voltaire, Diderot wastes it writing scrap for these [*Correspondance*] sheets, or giving it away to all who are bold enough to ask for it. I dare say to your Majesty that he will die unknown."[113]

Probably Diderot's happiest hours (aside from those he spent with Angélique) were when he took the floor at the dinners of d'Holbach or Mme. Geoffrin, and sailed forth rudderless on a stream of eloquence on any subject whatever. He was not at his best in polite gatherings where wit, rather than ideas, was in demand. Mme. Geoffrin herself was frightened by his enthusiasms, and her counsels of moderation and decency weighted his flights. But at the Baron's table, where, as Hume was assured, "seventeen atheists" assembled, he could let himself go; and then (nearly all agreed) there was nothing so fascinating, so absorbing, in all the brilliant conversation of Paris. "He who has known Diderot only in his writings," said Marmontel, "has not known him at all. . . . I have experienced few greater intellectual pleasures."[114] Henri Meister, who often heard him, described him in an apt comparison:

> When I recall Diderot, the immense variety of his ideas, the amazing multiplicity of his knowledge, the rapid flight, the warmth, the impetuous tumult of his imagination, all the charm and all the disorder of his conversation, I venture to liken his character to nature herself, exactly as he used to conceive her—rich, fertile, abounding in germs of every sort, gentle and fierce, simple and majestic, worthy and sublime, but without any dominating principle, without a master, and without a God.[115]

Or hear a firsthand report on Diderot's conversation, by Proteus himself:

> I seemed extraordinary to them, inspired, divine. Grimm hardly had eyes enough to see me, nor ears enough to hear me. Everybody was astonished. I myself felt a contentment within me that I can't express. It was like a fire burning in my depths that seared my breast, spread over them, and set fire to them. It was an evening of enthusiasm, for which I was the hearth.[116]

His contemporary reputation was greater among those who knew him than among those who had merely read his published works, which were chiefly the *Encyclopédie* and his plays; the best of them—*La Religieuse, Jacques le fataliste, Le Rêve d'Alembert, Le Neveu de Rameau*—were still unprinted at his death. Partly for this reason, partly because of the radicalism of his ideas on religion and sex, he failed—and never tried—to win admission to the Academy. To his friends, however, he was *le philosophe*—*the* philosopher, leader of the rebel tribe. Rousseau, even after coming to hate him as a secret enemy, wrote in the *Confessions*: "At the distance of some centuries Diderot will seem a prodigious man. People will look from afar at that universal head with mingled admiration and astonishment, as we look today at the heads of Plato and Aristotle."[117]

Goethe, Schiller, Lessing were fascinated by Diderot's writings; Stendhal, Balzac, Delacroix joined in the admiration; Comte rated him the supreme genius of that exciting age;[118] Michelet called him "the true Prometheus," and said that one could draw upon Diderot's works for a hundred years and infinite riches would still be left.[119] Or shall we hear Mme. Geoffrin, who knew him well but had not read his books? "He is a good and honest man," she wrote, "but he is so wrongheaded, and is so badly balanced, that he sees and hears nothing as it is; he is always like a man who dreams, and who believes his dreams to be real."[120]

He was good and bad, honest and dishonest, wrongheaded and intuitive, badly balanced and brilliantly creative, a dreamer, warrior, and seer, whose stature in history seems to grow as his time recedes, until today some think him "the most interesting and provocative figure of the French eighteenth century."[121] Let us leave the matter there until we meet him again—face to face with an empress, and then in the rendezvous of the *philosophes* with death.

CHAPTER XXI

The Spreading Campaign

1758–74

I. HELVÉTIUS: 1715–71

1. Development

THE family was of Swiss-Germanic origin, like those virile stocks that make Bern and Zurich proud and prosperous today. One member, in Neuchâtel, took the name Schweitzer—i.e., Swiss; another, who removed to the Netherlands, bore the name Helvetius—i.e., Swiss. This second branch moved to Paris about 1680. There Jean Claude Adrien Helvétius became physician to Queen Marie Leszczyńska. Of his twenty children the one who here concerns us was born January 26, 1715. Claude Adrien was reared in the odor of medicine, which left some trace in his philosophy. After studying under the Jesuits at the Collège Louis-le-Grand he was apprenticed to a tax collector. Soon he was rich; at the age of twenty-three he had an income of 360,000 livres per year.[1] He was handsome, a good fencer, dancer, and shot, a favorite with courtiers and courtesans. He was appointed maître d'hôtel—master of the household—to the Queen. He was thoroughly unprepared to become a philosopher—except of the kind that is too clever to write books.

But in 1738 he met Voltaire, was awed by his mind and fame, and began to dream of authorship; would it not be a novel distinction to be at once a financier and a philosopher? He spent some time at Bordeaux as the guest of Montesquieu, and then in Burgundy with Buffon; these were formative influences. He became a close friend with another millionaire, Baron d'Holbach, the archmaterialist of the age. At the Baron's dinners, and in the salon of Mme. de Graffigny, he met Diderot, Grimm, Rousseau, Duclos, Galiani, Marmontel, Turgot. He was transformed.

In 1751 he made two fateful decisions. He abandoned his lucrative post as a farmer general of taxes, retired to a feudal estate at Voré-au-Perche, and devoted himself to writing a book that would move the world. In the same year, aged thirty-six, he married Anne Catherine de Ligniville d'Autricourt, a countess of the Holy Roman Empire, aged thirty-two, one of the most beautiful and accomplished women in France. He took her at once to Voré, for fear, said Grimm, that Paris would tarnish her. There—or was it in Paris?—Fontenelle, nearing one hundred, entered the dressing room of the lovely Countess and found her in almost complete dishabille. "*Ah, madame*," he cried, in gay retreat, "*si je n'avais que quatre-vingts ans* [if only I were but eighty years old]!"[2]

The happy couple maintained also a house in Paris, and there Helvétius' hospitality, graced by his wife's charms, drew to them such intellectual lions as Diderot, d'Holbach, Fontenelle, Buffon, d'Alembert, Turgot, Galiani, Morellet, Condorcet, and Hume. "You should see," said Marmontel, "how agreeable his home became for literary men."[3] At those dinners Helvétius tried to guide the conversation to the themes on which he planned to write; he invited criticism of his ideas, and showed himself a good listener; Morellet complained that Helvétius "was always composing his book in company."[4]

After seven years of incubation the beloved volume came forth, July 15, 1758, as *De l'Esprit (On Intelligence)*. To the surprise of the friends who had seen it in manuscript, it appeared with the precious "privilege of the King." Malesherbes had delegated to Jean Pierre Tercier the task of censoring it; Tercier reported: "I have found nothing in it which in my judgment ought to prevent its publication."[5] On August 6 the advocate general of the Paris Parlement branded the book a mass of heresies; on August 10 the Council of State revoked the privilege to print; soon Tercier was ousted from his lucrative posts. The amiable author protested that he had made no attack upon Christianity. "Of what impiety can they accuse me? I have in no part of this work denied the Trinity, or the divinity of Jesus, or the immortality of the soul, or the resurrection of the dead, or any other article of the papal creed; I have not therefore in any way attacked religion."[6] Voltaire, fearing that Helvétius would be sent to the Bastille, advised him to travel. But Helvétius was too comfortable at home to sacrifice so much for a book. He issued a retraction in the form of a letter to a priest; and when the government declared this inadequate he signed an apology "so humiliating," wrote Grimm, "that one would not have been astonished to see a man take refuge with the Hottentots rather than put his name to such avowals."[7] Mme. Helvétius came to Versailles to intercede for her husband; the government contented itself with ordering him to retire to his estate for two years. The penalty might have been more severe had not the King remembered that his own life had once been saved by Helvétius' father, then physician to the Queen. On January 3, 1759, Pope Clement XIII condemned the book as scandalous and licentious; and in February it was publicly burned by order of the Parlement. We have seen how this "fuss over an omelet," as Voltaire called it, shared with d'Alembert's article on Geneva in leading to the suppression of the *Encyclopédie*. With all this advertising *De l'Esprit* became the most widely read of all the volumes that played a part in the campaign against Christianity. Twenty editions appeared in French within six months, and it was soon translated into English and German. Today only a few scholars know of it, and it is almost impossible to obtain.

Helvétius published no more, but he continued to write. Leisurely but angrily he restated and amplified his views in the treatise *De l'Homme* (*On Man*), which attacked priests as venal peddlers of hope and fear, perpetuators of ignorance, and murderers of thought. In these two books we find all the ideals of that ambitious time: liberty, equality, and fraternity: liberty of speech, press, assembly, and worship, equality for both sexes and all classes in educational opportunity and before the law, and an almost socialistic advocacy of the "welfare state" as a compensatory protection of the simple poor against the clever rich—all capped with a semireligious faith in the indefinite perfectibility of mankind. Here again, if we listen well, is the voice of the Revolution.

2. Philosophy

Like nearly all the *philosophes*, Helvétius begins with Locke: all ideas are derived from sensation, therefore from the experience of the individual. All mental states are combinations of sensations felt at present, or revived from the past through memory, or projected into the future through imagination. Judgment is the sensation of differences among sensations; and reason is a combination of judgments.

Mind and soul are not the same: mind is an assemblage or sequence of mental states; soul is the sensitivity of the organism, the capacity to receive sensations. All sensation is physical, all soul is a power in matter. "All the phenomena of medicine and natural history evidently prove that this power . . . begins with the formation of the bodily organs, lasts as long as they last, and is destroyed with their dissolution."[8] Animals have souls. Man became superior to the beasts through the development of upright stature, which gradually turned his forefeet into hands capable of grasping (*com-pre-hend*-ing) and manipulating objects.

Having begun with Locke, Helvétius proceeds with Hobbes. All action is desire responding to sensations present or recalled. Desire is the memory of the pleasure that attended certain sensations. Passion is a persisting desire, and varies in intensity according to the pain or pleasure remembered and expected. The passions often lead us into error because they fix our attention upon some particular part of an object or a situation, not allowing us to view it on every side.[9] (In this sense intelligence is the delay of reaction to allow wider perception and fuller response.) Nevertheless passions are to character what motion is to matter; they supply the drive, even the drive for knowledge. "The mental achievement of a person varies with the intensity of his passions. The man of genius is a man of strong passions; the stupid man is devoid of them."[10] The basic passion is love of power, and this is basic because it enlarges our ability to realize our desires.

Up to this point Helvétius' work deserved Voltaire's description of it as an "omelet"—a mingling of ideas long current in the philosophical world. But now he advanced to his most distinctive propositions. Since all ideas come from the individual's experiences, diversity in the ideas and character of individuals and nations depends upon differences in individual or national environment. All men at birth have an equal aptitude for understanding and judgment; there are no inborn superiorities of mind. "All are endowed with a strength and power of attention sufficient to raise them to the rank of illustrious men" if environment, education, and circumstance favor them; "the inequality of their capacity is always the effect of the difference of situation in which chance has placed them."[11]

> At the moment the child is delivered from the womb . . . he enters life without ideas and without passions. The only one he feels is that of hunger. It is not in the cradle [not from heredity] that we received the passions of pride, avarice, ambition, the desire for esteem and glory. These factious passions, generated amid towns and cities, presuppose conventions and laws already established among men. . . . Such passions would be unknown to him who was carried by a storm, at the moment of his birth, to a desert waste, and, like Romulus, nourished by a wolf. . . . The love of glory is an acquisition, and therefore the effect of instruction.[12]

Even the genius is the product of environment—i.e., of experience plus circumstance. The genius adds the last step in an invention to many steps taken before him, and this final step is due to circumstance. "Every new idea is the gift of chance"—i.e., to "a series of effects of which we do not perceive the cause."[13]

> Whence proceeds the extreme inequality of understanding? Because nobody perceives precisely the same objects, nor is precisely in the same situation, nor has received the same education; and because chance, which presides over our instruction, does not conduct all men to mines equally rich and fruitful. It is therefore to education—taken in the fullest extent that we can give to this term, and in which the idea of chance is also included, that we are to refer the inequality of understanding.[14]

Probably this psychological analysis—especially generous in a millionaire —was derived from a political attitude. Conservatives stress the differences and influence of heredity, and the need for caution in changing institutions rooted in natural and native inequalities of ability and character. Reformers stress the differences and influence of environment, by which inequalities of ability, power, and wealth seem due to chance—to the accidents of birth and the privileges of condition rather than to innate merit; inequality can therefore be reduced by equalizing education and bettering the environment. Helvétius applies his theory of natural equality to races as well as to individuals: all races would have reached equal development if their environmental opportunities had been equal. Consequently national pride, like pride of person or class, has no warrant in reality. "The liberty of which the English are so proud . . . is less the reward of their courage than the gift of fortune"—i.e., of the protective Channel and seas. (Internal liberty, other things equal, varies inversely as external danger.)

Obviously, on these premises, the road of progress follows the improvement of education, society, and government. "Education is capable of effecting everything"; does it not teach the bear to dance?[15] All progress, even in morals, depends upon the spread of knowledge and the training of intelligence; "destroy ignorance, and you will destroy all the seeds of moral evil."[16] To approach this goal the entire educational system of France must be rebuilt; it must be freed from the Church and assigned to the state; and it must be provided for all persons, of either sex and any age. The teaching of Latin and Greek must be replaced by education in science and technics, and new stress must be laid upon forming healthy bodies and "wise and virtuous minds."[17]

Here Helvétius, while not denying any Christian dogma, enters upon a passionate plea for the curtailment of ecclesiastical power in France. He attacks the Church from a social rather than a theological standpoint. He denounces the Catholic glorification of celibacy and poverty, but rejoices that very few Christians take these ideas seriously; "a secret incredulity frequently opposes the pernicious effect of religious principles."[18] Catholic control of education, he charges, not only retards the technical advance of a nation by slighting science, but it enables the clergy to form the mind of the child to priestly domination.[19]

> The desire of the clergy in all times has been to be powerful and opulent. By what method can it satisfy this desire? By selling hope and fear. The priests, wholesale dealers in these commodities, were sensible that this sale would be assured and lucrative.[20] . . . The power of the priest depends upon the superstitions and stupid credulity of the people. It is of little worth to him that they be learned; the less they know, the more docile they will be to his dictates.[21] . . .

In every religion the first objective of the priests is to stifle the curiosity of men, to prevent the examination of every dogma whose absurdity is too palpable to be concealed.[22] . . . Man is born ignorant, but he is not born a fool; and it is not without labor that he is made one. That he should be made such, and be able to extinguish in himself his natural light, much art and method must be employed; instruction must heap upon him error upon error.[23] . . . There is nothing which the sacerdotal power cannot execute by the aid of superstition. For by that it robs the magistrates of their authority and kings of their legitimate power; thereby it subdues the people, and acquires a power over them which is frequently superior to the laws; and thereby it finally corrupts the very principles of morality.[24]

Helvétius adds eight chapters on toleration.

Religious intolerance is the daughter of sacerdotal ambition and stupid credulity.[25] . . . If I believe my nurse and my tutor, every other religion is false, mine alone is the truth. But is it acknowledged as such by the universe? No: the earth still groans under the multitude of temples consecrated to error.[26] . . . What does the history of religions teach us? That they have everywhere lighted up the torch of intolerance, strewed the plains with corpses, imbrued the fields with blood, burned cities, and laid waste empires.[27] . . . Are not the Turks, whose religion is a religion of blood, more tolerant than we? We see Christian churches at Constantinople, but there are no mosques in Paris.[28] . . . Toleration subjects the priest to the prince; intolerance subjects the prince to the priest.[29]

Helvétius is inclined to make one exception in favor of intolerance:

There is one cause in which toleration can be detrimental to a people, and that is when it tolerates a religion that is intolerant, such as the Catholic. This religion, becoming the most powerful in a state, will always shed the blood of its stupid protectors. . . . Let not the insinuating manner of the Catholics impose upon the Protestants. The same priests who in Prussia regard intolerance as an abomination and an infraction of natural and divine law look on tolerance in France as a crime and a heresy. What renders the same man so different in different countries? His weakness in Prussia and his power in France. When we consider the conduct of Catholic Christians they at first, when feeble, appear to be lambs; but when strong they are tigers.[30]

Helvétius had a good word to say, now and then, for Christianity, especially for Protestantism. He was not an atheist, but he abhorred the Biblical conception of God as "resembling an Oriental tyrant, . . . punishing slight faults with eternal torments."[31] He hoped for a "universal religion" which, under state control, would promote a "natural morality" free from rewards and punishments after death.[32] He put human reason above all human claims to a divine revelation. "An honest man will always obey his reason in preference to revelation; for it is, he will say, more certain that God is the author of human reason . . . than that he is the author of a particular book."[33]

But are not supernatural beliefs, and a divine sanction, necessary to the efficacy of a moral code? Not at all, says Helvétius.

> It is not on religion . . . but on legislation alone that the vices, the virtues, the power, and the felicity of the people depend. . . . Every crime not punished by the laws is daily committed; what stronger proof can there be of the inutility of religion? . . . Whence arises the present security of Paris? From the devotion of its inhabitants? No, . . . from the regularity and vigil of the police. . . . At what period did Constantinople become the sink of all the vices? At the very time the Christian religion was established. . . . The most Christian kings have not been the greatest monarchs. Few of them have displayed the virtues of Titus, Trajan, or Antoninus. What pious prince can be compared with these?[34]

Hence it seemed to Helvétius that the task of philosophy was to devise and promote a morality independent of religious belief. From this point of view he wrote what one student has called "the most scientific examination of social ethics to appear from the pen of any *philosophe*."[35] He was resolved neither to berate nor to idealize human nature; he would take it as he found it, with all its selfishness, and try to build upon it a natural ethic. By nature man is neither good nor bad; he is a creature trying to preserve himself in a world where every organism will sooner or later be eaten by another.[36] The picture that Rousseau had recently given of primitive society seemed to Helvétius a jejune imagination; Hobbes was nearer the truth in describing the "state of nature" as a war of each against all.[37] The terms *good* and *bad*, as applied to men, have sense only in society; all goodness is social virtue, and is a product of social training for social ends.

> Unhappy is the prince who confides in the original goodness of character. M. Rousseau supposes its existence, experience denies it; whoever consults this will learn that the child kills flies, beats his dog, strangles his sparrow—that the child . . . has all the vices of the man. The man in power [freed from social restraints] is often unjust; the sturdy child is the same; when he is not checked by the presence of his mates he appropriates by force, like the man in power, the sweetmeat or plaything of his companion.[38]

Obviously, then, there is no innate moral sense; all judgments of right and wrong are developed during the experience of the individual from the teachings and compulsions of his family, his community, his government, and his church. When the individual is freed from these compulsions—as in absolute rule, war, or a crowd—he tends to revert to lawlessness and immorality; and in "most nations morality is now nothing more than a collection of the . . . precepts dictated by the powerful to secure their authority and to be unjust with impunity." But morality properly understood is "the science of the means invented by men to live together in the happiest manner. . . . If those in power do not oppose its progress, this science will advance in proportion as the people acquire new knowledge."[39]

Helvétius is a frank hedonist: the goal of life is happiness here on earth, happiness is a continuity of pleasure, and all pleasure is basically sensual or physiological.[40] "The activity of the mind and the acquisition of knowledge" are the most permanently satisfying pleasures,[41] but they too are fundamentally physical. Asceticism is foolish, sexual pleasure is quite legitimate if it injures no one. Virtue is not obedience to the laws of God, it is behavior that gives the greatest pleasure to the greatest number. Here Helvétius clearly formulates the utilitarian ethics already (1725) suggested by Hutcheson and later (1789) expounded by Bentham.

> To be virtuous it is necessary to unite nobleness of soul with an enlightened understanding. Whoever combines these gifts conducts himself by the compass of public utility. This utility is the principle of all human virtues, and the foundation of all legislation . . . All laws should follow a single principle, the utility of the public—i.e., of the greatest number of the persons under the same government . . . This principle contains all morality and legislation.[42]

Nevertheless, in Helvétius' view all actions, however moral and virtuous, are egoistic. They are not necessarily selfish; many actions are altruistic in the sense that they are intended to benefit others, sometimes at great cost to the agent; but even these actions are egoistic in the sense that they are motivated by the impulse to self-satisfaction; we are altruistic because, by instinct or training, we can take great pleasure in pleasing others; so the mother may sacrifice herself for her child, as the hero for his country. When we do good to others it is because we consciously or unconsciously remember with pleasure the returned love, or the social approval, that followed similar actions in the past; in this way certain altruistic deeds may become habitual, and we may feel discomfort or fear if we do not perform them. Religious asceticism or devotion may appear to be highly virtuous, but it is only a long-term investment in celestial securities. "If a hermit or a monk imposes upon himself the law of silence, flogs himself every night,

lives on pulse and water, sleeps on straw, . . . he thinks by virtue of emaciation to gain a fortune in heaven."[43] If a cruel action is not condemned by
the local community, these holy men will commit it without shame or recourse, as in burning heretics.[44] Even friendship is egoistic: it is an exchange
of services, if only of ears; where such exchange ceases, friendship fades;
"nothing is more uncommon than a friendship of long standing."[45] "Ultimately it is always ourselves that we love in others."[46]

Whereas La Rochefoucauld, in similarly reducing all motives to self-
love, deplored it as a vice, Helvétius accepts it as a virtue insofar as it makes
for self-preservation. In any case it is a universal fact of life; and "to be
offended by the operations of self-love is to complain of the showers of
spring, the heats of summer, . . . the frosts of winter."[47] It is precisely upon
the universality of self-love that he proposes to establish a "scientific"
morality. Education and legislation can mold character and habit into
finding discomfort in unsocial actions, and pleasure in virtue—i.e., in action
beneficial to the group. The philosopher should study human behavior and
social needs with a view to discovering what forms of conduct are most
beneficial to the largest number of people, and he should plead with educators and legislators to provide inducements and deterrents that, by appealing to self-love, will encourage social behavior. What benefits would accrue
to mankind from such an entente between philosophers and kings! "The
virtues and happiness of a people come not from the sanctity of their religion, but from the wisdom of their laws."[48]

So, as the summit of his philosophy, Helvétius turned to study legislation
and government. Politically he is the most radical of the *philosophes*. He
does not share Voltaire's faith in "enlightened despots"; such rulers would
tend to suppress any opinions but their own, which might be mistaken and
injurious. He quotes Frederick the Great as saying to the Berlin Academy,
"Nothing is better than an arbitrary government under princes just,
humane, and virtuous; but nothing is worse under the common race of
kings."[49] A limited or constitutional monarchy like England's is good;
better is a federation of democratic republics pledged to united action
against an aggressor.[50] Theoretically aristocracy is unjust, since superior
ability is a product of chance; but complete democracy is undesirable as
long as the poor are uneducated and propertyless; consequently a wise
legislator will aim to spread education and property.

This millionaire financier deplores the concentration of wealth and its
facilitation by a money economy.

> The almost universal unhappiness of men and nations arises from the
> imperfections of their laws, and the too unequal partition of their
> riches. There are in most kingdoms only two classes of citizens, one
> of which wants necessaries while the other riots in superfluities.[51] . . .

> If the corruption of the people in power is never more manifest than in the ages of the greatest luxury, it is because in those ages the riches of a nation are collected into the smallest number of hands.[52]

The replacement of land with money as the symbol and fulcrum of power engenders such a race for riches as disturbs all social stability, sharpens the class war, and leads to a ruinous inflation.

> In a nation gradually increasing in wealth and money—especially paper money—the cost of commodities and labor will continually rise. . . . As labor becomes very dear in a rich nation, that nation will import more from other nations than it will export to them. If all other factors remain the same, . . . the money of the rich nation will insensibly pass to the poorer nation, which, becoming opulent in turn, will ruin itself in the same way.[53]

Is there any escape from the concentration of wealth and the scramble for money?

> One would be to multiply the number of proprietors by making a new distribution of the land. . . . When a man's lands exceed a certain number of acres, they should be taxed at a rate exceeding the rent. . . . Such a redistribution is made almost impossible in a money economy, . . . [but] if wisely conceived it could be executed by continual and insensible alterations.[54]

Diminish the riches of some, augment those of others, and put the poor in such a state of ease that they may by seven or eight hours per day abundantly provide for the wants of themselves and their families. Then a people will become as happy as the nature of man will allow.[55]

3. Influence

Here, in two books and one man, are almost all the ideas that made the French Revolution, and almost all the ideas that agitate nations today. No wonder educated Frenchmen, in the third quarter of the eighteenth century, ranked Helvétius as almost the equal of Voltaire, Rousseau, and Diderot, and gave his first book such popularity and acclaim as was hardly accorded to any other volume of the age. "No book," said Brunetière, "has made more noise in its time, or spread abroad more ideas destined to make their way in the world."[56] Brissot reported in 1775 that "the system of Helvétius has the greatest vogue"; Turgot, while opposing it, complained that it was praised "with a kind of fury"; another described it as "found on every toilette table."[57] All critics commended the clarity of its style, the force of its epigrams, and the evident humanitarianism of a man who, having everything, advocated a redistribution of wealth.

However, the *philosophes* themselves criticized his "system" as based on erroneous conceptions. Voltaire defended the claims of heredity; all men are not at birth equal in potential excellence of mind and character; geniuses, he thought, are born, not made.[58] Diderot agreed with Voltaire. In a *Réfutation de l'ouvrage d'Helvétius intitulé L'Homme* (written in 1775, but not published till a hundred years later) he argued that sensations are transformed differently in different individuals by inherited differences in the structure of the brain.[59]

> Man is not born blank. True, he is born without ideas and without directed passions; but from the first moment of his life he is endowed with a predisposition to conceive, compare, and retain some ideas with more relish than others; and with dominant tendencies later resulting in actual passions.[60]

Here Diderot, who had begun with Locke, turned back to Leibniz and held out a hand to Kant. The influence of environment and schooling, in Diderot's view, is always limited by heredity. "We cannot give what nature has refused; perhaps we destroy what she gives. . . . Education improves her gifts."[61] He resented the reduction of intellectual delights to sensual pleasure, and joined in the general outcry against Helvétius' notion that all altruism is egoism unconscious or concealed.

Mme. du Deffand was one of the few who agreed on this point with Helvétius. "This man," she said, "has revealed everybody's secret [*C'est un homme qui a dit le secret de tout le monde*]."[62] Adam Smith, following his friend Hume, insisted that altruism was founded upon feelings of sympathy as innate as egoism; but in *The Wealth of Nations* he based his economic theory on the universality of self-love. Mme. Roland, in the ecstasies of the Revolution, was repelled by Helvétius. "I felt myself impelled by a generosity which he never recognized. . . . I confronted his theories with the great . . . heroes that history has immortalized."[63]

These problems cannot be solved in a paragraph. It seems clear that differences in hereditary or congenital constitution substantially affect the operation of environment and education; how else shall we explain the quite diverse character and development of brothers despite the similarity of origin and opportunities? And yet Helvétius was on the right track: within the limits decreed by heredity, immense changes can be effected in the behavior of individuals and groups by differences in environment, education, and legislation; how else shall we explain the emergence of man from barbarism to civilization? — Perhaps we should admit to Helvétius that no one consciously acts in a way more painful than its alternative. But certain social instincts—maternal love, gregariousness, love of approval—though they cannot rival the individualistic instincts in total force, are strong enough to generate altruistic actions before any conscious weighing of pleasure, pain, or result. Each of us is an ego, but some of us spread our egos to include our family, community, country, or mankind. In this sense the largest egos are the best.

In any case many men were moved to thought and action by Helvétius' ideas. It was probably under his influence that La Chalotais began his campaign to replace the schools of village priests, and the Jesuit colleges, with a system of education controlled by the state. The public schools of America go back to the proposals of Condorcet, who called himself a disciple of Helvétius.[64] Beccaria testified that the works of Helvétius inspired him to write his historic plea for the reform of penal law and policy. Bentham declared: "I owe to Helvétius' *De l'Esprit* a great part of my ideas"—including the utilitarian principle of seeking in morality and in legislation the greatest happiness of the greatest number.[65] The National Convention of 1792 certified its sense of Helvétius' influence on the Revolution by giving his daughters the title *filles de la nation*. William Godwin based his *Enquiry concerning Political Justice* (1793) upon the teachings of Helvétius; and Godwin's wife, Mary Wollstonecraft, was led to compose her epochal *Rights of Woman* (1792) partly by Helvétius' claim that the intellectual inequalities between the sexes were largely due to inequalities of education and opportunity.[66]

Many of Helvétius' contemporaries contrasted his theory of universal egoism with the kindness of his character and the benevolence of his life. Marmontel wrote of him: "There could not be a better man; liberal and generous without ostentation, and beneficent from the goodness of his heart."[67] Grimm, seldom lavish in praise, described Helvétius as a "true gentleman," just, indulgent, free from all ill-humor, a good husband, a good father, a good friend, a good man.[68] True of himself were the words that Helvétius wrote in *De l'Esprit*:

> In order to love mankind we must expect little from them. . . . Every man, so long as his passions do not obscure his reason, will always be more indulgent in proportion as he is more enlightened. . . . If the great man is always the most indulgent, . . . if he pours over the faults of others the lenient balm of pity, and is slow in discovering those faults, it is because the elevation of his mind will not permit him to expatiate upon the vices and follies of individual persons, but only upon those of mankind in general.[69]

At Voré and in Paris he lived with his wife and children an idyl of devotion and happiness. In 1764 he traveled in England and Germany, met Hume and Gibbon and Frederick the Great. In 1770 he shared in financing Pigalle's statue of Voltaire. He died in 1771, with d'Holbach and other friends at his bedside. His widow, loving his memory, refused all suitors for her hand, including Benjamin Franklin. She survived her husband by twenty-nine years, passed through the Revolution safely, and died in 1800, aged eighty-one.

II. AUXILIARIES

A very swarm of minor *philosophes,* in the third quarter of the eighteenth century, joined in the attack upon Christianity. They labored with all the industry and enthusiasm of early Christians spreading the new Gospel, or of Spanish Christians expelling Moors. They poured forth a stream of tracts and treatises, and when their own profusion ebbed they translated all the antireligious literature they could find, from Lucretius to Hobbes. They devised a new calendar of saints and martyrs, canonizing Julian the Apostate and idolizing Pomponazzi, Bruno, Campanella, Vanini, Bayle, and other victims of persecution. They condemned the Jews not for charging interest on loans but for having begotten Christianity. They dethroned Jehovah as a monster of cruelty, a god of war, the first of the genocides. They laughed at original sin, and the God who had to send himself down to earth as his son, to be scourged and crucified to appease the anger of himself as Father piqued by a woman's desire for apples or knowledge. They branded the Crusades as a land-grabbing, commerce-cornering expedition. They scorned the Middle Ages as all Dark Ages, and looked down upon the Gothic cathedrals as barbarous and grotesque. D'Alembert noted about him "a certain exaltation of ideas," a "fermentation," a "general effervescence of minds, . . . [which] with a kind of violence has swept along with it everything that stood in its way."[70]

There was Jacques André Naigeon, whom Sainte-Beuve described as "a fanatical beadle of atheism";[71] he came to live and work with d'Holbach as translator and editor; together they published in ten years thirty books, large or small, original or imported, all against Christianity; "it is raining bombs in the house of the Lord," said Diderot.[72] There was Nicolas Boulanger, another friend of d'Holbach, who labored in the cause till his death (1759), and left behind him a manuscript entitled *Antiquité dévoilée (Antiquity Unveiled).* D'Holbach kept this in storage till 1765, when the chief minister was Choiseul, friendly to the *philosophes;* then he sent it to the press with a flaming introduction by Diderot. Religion, said Boulanger, arose through primitive man's fears of floods and other apparently super-natural catastrophes; it was organized by priests and kings in a conspiracy to sanctify tyranny in return for tyrannical enforcement of orthodox belief; and mankind would never escape from that dark conspiracy except by following the light of reason in defiance of priests and kings.[73]

More important was André Morellet, another Jesuit product, one more abbé wandering in rebel ranks. Born in 1727, he lived long enough to be described by Mme. Necker as "a bear" who nevertheless "had candor, probity, and a thousand good qualities, and enough religion to suspect that there may be a God, and sometimes to admit it to his friends, relying on their discretion not to reveal his credulity."[74] Under Diderot's tutelage he wrote some articles for the *Encyclopédie*. At d'Holbach's dinners he displayed so mordant a wit that Voltaire called him the Abbé Mord-les—"the Reverend Mr. Bite-Them"; but Marmontel wrote that he had "profound ideas . . . and a heart as upright as it is sound."[75] In 1762 he pubilshed a *Manuel des Inquisiteurs*, composed of selections from the *Directorium Inquisitorum* of Nicolás Eymerico, who had zealously served as Grand Inquisitor from 1356 to 1399. Frenchmen had almost forgotten the Spanish Inquisition; Morellet refreshed their memory by merely quoting the procedures and penalties of that institution in its heyday. Malesherbes gave Morellet governmental permission to print the book, for, he said, the penal code of France was still practically identical with that of the Inquisitors.[76] Morellet could hardly believe it, but in the year that saw his book go to press Jean Calas was broken on the wheel by the Parlement of Toulouse.

Of another abbé, Guillaume Raynal, the usually calm Grimm reported in his *Correspondance* for 1772: "Since Montesquieu's *Esprit des lois* our literature perhaps has produced no monument that is worthier to pass to the remotest posterity, and to consecrate the progress of our enlightenment, than Raynal's *Philosophical and Political History of European Settlements and Commerce in the Two Indies*."[77] Probably Grimm was especially well disposed to the author because it was Raynal who had inaugurated in 1753, and bequeathed to Grimm in 1755, the *Correspondance littéraire* which ever since had buttered Grimm's bread; moreover, Grimm's friend Diderot had had a hand in preparing Raynal's immortal and now unopened book. Grimm's judgment seemed confirmed by the immediate popularity of the *Histoire philosophique et politique des établissements et du commerce des Européens dans les deux Indes*, published in 1772. Forty editions were sold out before 1789; there were uncounted pirated editions and translations; Franklin, Gibbon, and Robertson praised it; Toussaint L'Ouverture found in it the inspiration for his slave-liberating devotion and campaign (1791). An erudite critic thought it had more influence upon the French Revolution than even the *Social Contract* of Rousseau.[78]

Raynal had entered Paris as a poor priest. A legend that reveals the gay mood of the rebels ascribed his escape from starvation to the fact that the Abbé Prévost had received twenty sous to say a Mass for a dead soul; that Prévost had paid the Abbé de Laporte fifteen sous to say it in his stead; and that Laporte had paid Raynal eight sous to say it in *his* stead.[79] Raynal was glad to eat at the tables of Helvétius and d'Holbach; he proved to be pleasant company, and seems to have secured the aid of several authors besides Diderot in collecting material, even in writing sections of his book. Rousseau, who quarreled with all and sundry, found Raynal unquarrelable, and thanked him, in the *Confessions*, for unswerving friendship and financial aid.[80]

Raynal must have made money somehow, for he is said to have bribed the censor for permission to issue his book.[81] Twenty years of labor had gone into its preparation. It detailed and denounced the greed, treachery, and violence of the Europeans in dealing with the natives of the East and West Indies, and it warned the white man of the terrible revenge that the colored races might take if ever they came to power.[82] It was the first French indictment of colonial exploitation; it was among the first books to stress the importance of commerce in determining modern history; it contributed, in passing, to the idealization of Indian natives, and to the cult of Chinese civilization by European liberals. Running through the diffuse volumes were the dominant themes of the Enlightenment: hatred of superstition and priestcraft, and resentment of state-and-Church tyranny over life and thought. Raynal passionately subscribed to the view that Catholicism was an imposture by which prelates and rulers had joined forces to support each other through myths, miracles, propaganda, oppression, and massacre. He appealed to the rulers of Europe to dissociate themselves from all ecclesiastical ties, to allow freedom of speech and publication, and to prepare the way for democratic government. He did not spare Protestantism; this too, he said, had been guilty of intolerance; and he described the fanaticism of the Puritans in New England, the "witch" persecution in Salem.

Despite its long preparation, Raynal's book was ultimately condemned to oblivion by its faults. Careless in its facts, it mistook legends for history, neglected dates, gave no references to authorities, confused its materials, and engaged (or allowed Diderot to engage) in oratorical effusions and emotional appeals hardly becoming in a work of history. But those were no times for calm impartiality; a book was a weapon, and could not be dulled by presenting opposed sides; literature was war. The French government so assumed; the Parlement of Paris ordered the book to be burned, and Raynal was ordered to leave France. He fled to the Netherlands, but thought it safe to return in 1784 under the mildest of Bourbon kings.

He was one of the few *philosophes* to see and survive the Revolution. He was shocked by its violence and its use of all the old machinery of intolerance. On May 31, 1791, aged seventy-eight, he addressed to the Constituent Assembly a letter warning it against excesses. "I have long dared to tell kings of their duties," he wrote; "let me today tell the people of its errors." He pointed out that the tyranny of the populace could be as cruel and unjust as the despotism of monarchs. He defended the right of the clergy to preach religion, so long as the opponents of priestcraft were left free to speak their minds; he protested against the laws enforcing a state religion, and against the outrages of the mob upon priests. Robespierre persuaded the Assembly to let the old man escape the guillotine, but Raynal's property was confiscated by the government, and he died in destitution (1796) amid the triumphs and terrors of the Revolution.

III. D'HOLBACH

1. The Amiable Atheist

The best-beloved of all the *philosophes* in Paris was a German, born (1723) at Edesheim in the episcopal principality of Speyer. He was baptized as Paul Heinrich Dietrich von Holbach, and was reared as a Roman Catholic. His grandfather had made a fortune by introducing ipecac from Holland to Versailles. At Leiden Paul studied science and learned English. After the Peace of Aix-la-Chapelle (1748) he settled in Paris, became a French subject, married into a family of financiers, and achieved nobility by investing 110,000 livres at five per cent in the "Company of Secretaries of the King." He was called "Baron" by his circle because he owned an estate in Westphalia, which brought him sixty thousand livres per year. Altogether he had an annual income of 200,000 livres—"a fortune," said Morellet, "which no one has ever used more nobly, nor with greater benefit to science and art."[83] He played Maecenas to Marivaux and other authors; he collected a large library, paintings, drawings, and natural-history specimens.

His home became, as one wit put it, "the Café d'Europe"; his dinners and salon in Paris or at his country villa, Grandval, made him, in Horace Walpole's phrase, the "maître d'hôtel of philosophy." On Thursdays and Sundays Mme. d'Holbach prepared the table for twelve guests, not always the same, but most frequently the leaders of the anti-Christian war: Diderot, Helvétius, d'Alembert, Raynal, Boulanger, Morellet, Saint-Lambert, Marmontel; sometimes Buffon, Turgot, and Quesnay. Rousseau came, too, but shuddered at the atheism bubbling around him. There Diderot was at his wildest, and the Abbé Galiani kept philosophy on the ground by puncturing theory with wit. The "Synagogue," as the Baron called these gatherings, met at two o'clock, talked, ate, and talked till seven or eight; those were the days when conversation was unwritten literature, not a chaos of interruptions and trivialities. No topics were barred there; "that was the place," said Morellet, "to hear the freest, most animated, and most instructive conversation that ever was . . . in regard to philosophy, religion, and government; light pleasantries had no place there. . . . It was there, above all, that Diderot lighted our minds and warmed our souls."[84] Diderot himself reported to Mlle. Volland that they talked "of art, poetry, the philosophy of love, . . . the sentiment of immortality, of men, gods, and kings, of space and time, of death and life."[85] "Sometimes," said Marmontel, "I thought I heard the disciples of Pythagoras or Plato."[86] Or,

> when the fine weather came, we sometimes exchanged these dinners for philosophical walks . . . along the banks of the Seine; the repast on those days was a large dinner of fish; and we went by turns to the places most celebrated for the supply of that article, commonly to St.-Cloud. We went down early in a boat, breathing the air of the river, and we returned in the evening through the Bois de Boulogne.[87]

D'Holbach's salon became so famous that foreigners visiting Paris pulled wires to get an invitation. So, at divers times, came Hume, Sterne, Garrick, Horace Walpole, Franklin, Priestley, Adam Smith, Beccaria. They were somewhat disturbed by the number of atheists they found there; how many times have we heard the story (told by Diderot to Romilly) that when Hume doubted the actual existence of atheists, the Baron assured him, "Here you are at table with seventeen."[88] Gibbon related that the *philosophes* of Paris "laughed at the cautious skepticism of Hume, preached the tenets of atheism with the bigotry of dogmatists, and damned all believers with ridicule and contempt."[89] Priestley also reported that "all the philosophical persons to whom I was introduced at Paris [were] unbelievers in Christianity, and even professed atheists."[90] However, Morellet noted, "a goodly number of us were theists, and not ashamed of it; and we defended ourselves vigorously against the atheists, though we loved them for being such good company."[91] Walpole found d'Holbach's "pigeon house of philosophers" offensive to his English taste. He was so disgusted by perceiving that Raynal knew more than he about English commerce and colonies that he pretended to be deaf. Hume's own account was perhaps too accommodating: "The men of letters here [in Paris] are really very agreeable; all of them men of the world, living in entire, or almost entire, harmony among themselves, and quite irreproachable in their morals.

It would give you great satisfaction to find that there is not a single deist among them."[92] The evidence is rather confusing.

But all agreed that the Baron and his wife were perfect hosts and lovable characters. Mme. d'Holbach, according to Grimm, lived only for her husband; once she had welcomed and nourished his guests, she retired to a corner with her knitting and took no further part in the conversation.[93] She died in 1754, in the prime of her life; for a time d'Holbach remained "in a state of utter despair."[94] Two years later he married her sister, who proved equally devoted. He was so unassuming in his manners, so amiable in argument, so secret in his beneficence,[95] that hardly anyone suspected him of writing so powerful a defense of atheism as the *Système de la nature*. "I never saw a man more simply simple," said his *salonnière* rival, Mme. Geoffrin.[96] Rousseau, who learned to hate nearly all the *philosophes*, retained such admiration for d'Holbach's character that he used him as a model for the virtuous agnostic Wolmar in *La Nouvelle Héloïse*. Grimm, who analyzed everyone but Rousseau with calm objectivity, wrote:

> It was natural for Baron d'Holbach to believe in the empire of reason, for his passions (and we always judge others by ourselves) were such as in all cases to give the ascendancy to virtue and correct principles. It was impossible for him to hate anyone; yet he could not, without an effort, dissemble his professed horror of priests. . . . Whenever he spoke of these his naturally good temper forsook him.[97]

So d'Holbach warmly supported the *Encyclopédie*, contributed money and articles to it, and gave Diderot comfort and courage when even d'Alembert and Voltaire were deserting the enterprise. His articles were mostly on natural science, for in that field the Baron was probably the best-informed of all the *philosophes*. "I have never met with a man more learned," wrote Grimm in 1789, "and I have never seen anyone who cared so little to pass for learned in the eyes of the world."[98] He translated many scientific treatises from the German, aided by Naigeon. For this work he was made a member of the academies of Berlin and St. Petersburg. He never sought admission to the French Academy.

Fascinated by science, and expecting from it a rapid betterment of human life, d'Holbach looked with unrelenting hostility upon the Church, whose control of education seemed to bar the way to the development of scientific knowledge. He lost no chance of attacking the clergy. He wrote the articles "Prêtres" and "Théocratie" for the *Encyclopédie*. From 1766 onward he organized with Naigeon a veritable factory of anti-Christian literature. In quick succession appeared *Le Tableau des saints, De l'Imposture sacerdotale, Prêtres démasqués, De la Cruauté religieuse, L'Enfer détruit;* here was a new apostle of glad tidings—hell had been destroyed.

In 1761 there issued from what some called "this laboratory of atheism" a volume entitled *Christianisme dévoilé* (*Christianity Exposed*), written chiefly by d'Holbach but ascribed on the title page to "the late M. Boulanger." For selling this book a peddler was branded and sent to the galleys for five years; for buying and reselling it a boy was branded and sent to the galleys for nine years.[99] It was a frontal assault upon the alliance of Church and state, and quite anticipated Marx's description of religion as the "opium of the people."

> Religion is the art of intoxicating men with enthusiasm [this word in the eighteenth century meant religious fervor], to prevent them from dealing with the evils with which their governors oppress them. . . . The art of reigning has become nothing more than that of profiting from the errors and abjection of mind and soul into which superstition has plunged the nations. . . . By means of threatening men with invisible powers, they [Church and state] force them to suffer in silence the miseries with which visible powers afflict them. They are made to hope that if they agree to being unhappy in this world, they will be happy in the next.[100]

D'Holbach thought this union of Church and state the fundamental evil in France. "It is as a citizen that I attack religion, because it seems to me harmful to the happiness of the state, hostile to the mind of man, and contrary to sound morality."[101]

> Instead of morality the Christian is taught the miraculous fables and inconceivable dogmas of a religion thoroughly hostile to right reason. From his very first step in his studies he is taught to distrust the evidence of his senses, to subdue his reason, . . . and to rely blindly on the authority of his master. . . . Those who have shaken themselves free from these notions find themselves powerless against errors sucked in with their mother's milk.[102]

To rest morality upon religious beliefs, d'Holbach argued, is a risky procedure, for such beliefs are subject to change, and their fall may damage the moral code allied with them.

> Everyone who has discovered the weakness or falsity of the evidence upon which his religion is based . . . will be tempted to believe that the morality is as chimerical as the religion it is founded on. . . . That is how it is that the words *infidel* and *libertine* have become synonymous. There would be no such disadvantage if a natural morality were taught instead of a theological. Instead of prohibiting debauchery, crime, and vice because God and religion forbid them, we ought

to say that all excess is harmful to man's conservation, makes him despicable in the eyes of society, is forbidden by reason, . . . and is forbidden by nature, which wants him to work for his lasting happiness.[103]

It is hard to understand how a man so burdened with money should have found time or urge to write so many books. In 1767 he sent forth a *Théologie portative* earnestly making fun of Christian doctrines and reducing all theology to the ecclesiastical will to power. In 1768 he published *La Contagion sacrée, ou histoire naturelle de la superstition*, ostensibly translated "from the English of Jean Trenchard"; and in the same year he issued *Lettres à Eugénie, ou préservatif contre les préjugés*, which pretended to be by an Epicurean philosopher in Sceaux. In 1769 came an *Essai sur les préjugés, par M. du Marsais*, explaining that the only cure for the evils of religion was the spread of education and philosophy. And in 1770 the busy Baron published his chef-d'oeuvre, the most powerful single volume issued in the campaign against Christianity.

2. *The System of Nature*

Système de la nature, ou des lois du monde physique et du monde moral was printed professedly in London, actually in Amsterdam, in two large volumes, and bore, as the name of the author, "M. Mirabaud." This man, now ten years dead, had been secretary to the French Academy. An introduction gave a sketch of his life and works. No one believed that the good and exemplary Mirabaud had written so scandalous a book.

The quadrennial Assembly of the Clergy (1770), after voting a grant of money to the King, appealed to him to suppress the anti-Christian literature that was circulating in France. Louis XV ordered his prosecutor to act at once. The Parlement of Paris condemned seven books, among them d'Holbach's *Christianisme dévoilé* and the *Système de la nature*, as "impious, blasphemous, and seditious, tending to destroy all idea of divinity, to rouse the people to revolt against religion and government, to overthrow all the principles of public security and morality, and to turn subjects away from obedience to their sovereign." The books were to be burned, the authors were to be arrested and severely punished. Morellet tells us that ten men knew that d'Holbach was the author, and that they kept the secret for twenty years. The "Synagogue" continued its meetings, and to some of them Mme. d'Holbach invited Canon Bergier, who had just received a pension from the clergy for his scholarly articles defending the Catholic Church. Many suspected Diderot of having written parts of the book. It was, as a whole, too orderly and solemn to have come from his pen, but he may have contributed the flowery apostrophe to Nature at the end. In any case, Diderot felt unsafe in Paris, and thought it wise to visit Langres.

The *Système*, smuggled in from Holland, was bought eagerly by a wide public, including, says Voltaire, "scholars, the ignorant, and women."[104] Diderot was delighted with it. "What I like," he said, "is a philosophy clear, definite, and frank, such as you have in the *System of Nature*. The author is not an atheist on one page and a deist on another. His philosophy is all of one piece"[105]—quite unlike Diderot's. What he really liked was that d'Holbach was an atheist on every page. And yet the book was infused with an almost religious devotion to the happiness of mankind. D'Holbach, seeing so much misery in a world ruled by kings and priests, concluded that men would be happier if they turned their backs upon priests and kings, and followed scientists and philosophers. The opening sentences of the book announce its spirit and theme:

> The source of man's unhappiness is his ignorance of nature. The pertinacity with which he clings to blind opinions imbibed in his infancy, . . . [and] the consequent prejudice that warps his mind, . . . appear to doom him to continual error. . . . He takes the tone of his ideas on the authority of others, who are themselves in error, or who have an interest in deceiving him. To remove this Cimmerian darkness, . . . to guide him out of this Cretan labyrinth, requires the clue of Ariadne, with all the love she could bestow on Theseus. . . . It exacts a most undaunted courage, . . . a persevering resolution. . . .
>
> The most important of our duties, then, is to seek means by which we may destroy delusions that can never do more than mislead us. The remedies for these evils must be sought in Nature herself. It is only in the abundance of her resources that we can rationally expect to find antidotes to the mischief brought upon us by an ill-directed, an overpowering enthusiasm. It is time these remedies were sought; it is time to look the evil boldly in the face, to examine its foundations, to scrutinize its superstructure. Reason, with its faithful guide experience, must attack in their entrenchments those prejudices of which the human race has been too long the victim. . . .
>
> Let us try to inspire man with courage, with respect for his reason, with an inextinguishable love for truth, to the end that he may learn to consult his experience, and no longer be the dupe of an imagination led astray by authority; . . . that he may learn to found his morals on his nature, on his wants, on the real advantage of society; that he may dare to love himself; that he may become a virtuous and rational being, in which case he cannot fail to be happy.[106]

Having so stated his program, d'Holbach proceeds systematically to reject all supernatural beings and considerations; to accept nature with all its beauty, cruelty, limitation, and possibilities; to reduce all reality to matter and motion; and to build upon this materialistic basis a system of morality which he hopes would be capable of transforming savages into citizens, of forming individual character and social order, and of giving a reasonable happiness even to a life inevitably destined to death.

He begins and ends with nature, but he disclaims any attempt to personify it; he defines it as "the great whole that results from the assemblage of matter under its various combinations"; it is d'Holbach's affectionate name for the universe. Matter he defines cautiously as "in general all that affects our senses in any fashion whatever."

> Everything in the universe is in motion; the essence of matter is to act; if we consider it attentively, we shall discover that no particle of it enjoys absolute repose. . . . All that appears to us to be at rest does not remain even for one instant in the same state. All beings are continually breeding, increasing, decreasing, and dispersing. . . . The hardest stones, by degrees, give way to the touch of air.[107]

The whole offers to our contemplation "nothing but an immense, uninterrupted succession of causes and effects."[108] The more our knowledge grows, the more overwhelming is the evidence that the universe acts only through natural causes. It may be difficult to understand how "inanimate matter can pass into life," but it is even more difficult to believe that life is a special creation of some mysterious entity external to the material universe. It is difficult to understand how matter can come to feel, but other properties of matter, like "gravity, magnetism, elasticity, electricity," are "not less inexplicable than feeling."[109]

Man too is "a being purely physical," subject to the same laws that govern the rest of the world. How could a physical body and an immaterial mind act upon each other? The "soul" is merely the total organization and activity of the body, and can have no separate existence. "To say that the soul will feel, think, enjoy, and suffer after the death of the body is to pretend that a clock shivered into a thousand pieces will continue to strike the hour . . . and mark the progress of time."[110] The conception of mind and soul as immaterial entities has retarded our treatment of mental diseases; when we consider mind as a function of the body we enable medical science to cure many mental disorders by attacking their physical causes.*[111]

---

* "It is certainly true as a historical fact," said John Morley, "that the rational treatment of insane persons, and the rational view of certain kinds of crime, were due to men like Pinel, trained in the materialistic school of the eighteenth century. And it was clearly impossible that the great and humane reforms in this field could have taken place before the decisive decay of theology."[112]

Being a function of the body, mind is subject to the universal rule of natural causes and effects. Chapter XI of the *Système* is the most eloquent defense of determinism in all the range of French philosophy:

> Man's life is a line that nature commands him to describe upon the surface of the earth, without his being able to swerve from it even for an instant. He is born without his consent; his organization in no wise depends upon himself; his ideas come to him involuntarily; his habits are in the power of those who cause him to contract them. He is unceasingly modified by causes, visible or concealed, over which he has no control, which necessarily regulate his mode of existence, give a color to his thinking, and determine his manner of acting. He is good or bad, happy or miserable, wise or foolish, reasonable or irrational, without his will counting for anything in these various states.[113]

This determinism seems to imply fatalism, and d'Holbach, unlike most determinists, frankly accepts the implication. The condition of the universe at any moment is determined by its condition at the preceding moment, and this was determined by its predecessor, and so on as far in the past as you like, so that any moment in the history of the universe may be taken as determining all later moments, as far in the future as you like. This apparent subjection of man—of every genius or saint in every conception or prayer—to some primeval gas does not deter d'Holbach; he accepts his fate with stoic pride:

> Man is the work of Nature; he exists in Nature; he is submitted to her laws. He cannot deliver himself from them, nor can he step beyond them, even in thought. . . . Instead, therefore, of seeking outside the world. . . . for beings who can procure him a happiness denied him by Nature, let man study this Nature, let him learn her laws, contemplate her forces, observe the immutable rules by which she acts; let him apply these discoveries to his own felicity, and submit in silence to her mandates, which nothing can alter; let him cheerfully consent to ignore causes hidden from him by an impenetrable veil; let him without murmuring yield to the decrees of a universal necessity which can never be brought within his comprehension, nor ever emancipate him from those laws that are imposed upon him by his essence.[114]

Does this fatalism warrant us in concluding that there is no use in our trying to avoid evil, dishonor, sickness, or death, and that we may as well cease all effort, all ambition or aspiration, and let events take their course? D'Holbach replies that even here we have no choice: heredity and environment have already determined whether we shall subside into apathy or respond actively to the needs and challenges of life. And he anticipates the objection that determinism, by appearing to excuse crime, may increase it. Determinism does not suggest that crime should not be punished; on the contrary it will lead the legislator, the teacher, and public opinion to provide, by laws or morals, better deterrents to crime and more inducements to social behavior; these deterrents and inducements will enter into the environmental factors molding the conduct of men. But determinism does warrant us in considering crime, and all unsocial behavior, as a mental imbalance due to heredity, environment, or circumstance; therefore we must deal with such behavior as we treat disease; we must abandon the use of torture and extreme penalties, for these increase the opposition between the individual and society, and accustom people to violence and cruelty rather than deter them from crime.

In this philosophy, of course, there is no room for God. D'Holbach's unflagging antipathy, not only to theism but to deism and pantheism as well, led his contemporaries to call him "the personal enemy of the Almighty."[115] "If we go back to the beginning we can always find that ignorance and fear have created gods; fancy, enthusiasm, or deceit has adorned or disfigured them; weakness worships them, credulity keeps them alive, custom respects them, tyranny supports them to . . . serve its own ends."[116] He raises against theism all the old arguments, and grows as hot as Helvétius against the Biblical conception of God.[117] The majestic order and regularity of the universe do not suggest to him any supreme intelligence; they are due to natural causes operating mechanically, and require no attribution to a deity who would himself be more inexplicable than the world. Order and disorder, like good and evil, beauty and ugliness, are subjective conceptions, derived from the pleasure or displeasure that our perceptions give us; but man is not "the measure of all things"; his satisfactions are no objective standard to apply to the universe; Nature proceeds without regard to what we, from our infinitesimal point in space, consider good or bad, ugly or beautiful. From the point of view of the whole "there is no such thing as real evil. Insects find a safe retreat in the ruins of the palace that crushes men in its fall."[118] We must learn to regard Nature, with her sublimities and catastrophes, as imperturbably neutral.

> All that has been said in the course of this work proves clearly that everything is necessary, that everything is always in order relative to Nature, where all beings do nothing more than follow the laws that are imposed on their respective classes. . . . Nature distributes with the same hand that which is called order and that which is called disorder, that which is called pleasure and that which is called pain; in short she diffuses, by the necessity of her existence, both evil and good. . . . Let not man, therefore, either praise her bounty or tax her with malice; let him not imagine that his vociferations or supplications can

ever arrest her colossal power, always acting after immutable laws. . . . When he suffers let him not seek a remedy by recurring to chimeras that his own distempered imagination has created; let him draw from the stores of Nature the remedies which she offers for the evils she brings upon him; let him search in her bosom for those salutary productions to which she has given birth.[119]

D'Holbach comes close to reintroducing God in the form of Nature. After vowing not to personify it he tends to deify her, speaks of her omnipotence, her will, her plan, her bounty; he thinks of her as man's best guide, and lets Diderot (?) write a sophomoric apostrophe to her as the concluding paragraph of a powerful book: "O Nature, sovereign of all beings! and ye, her adorable daughters, Virtue, Reason, and Truth, remain forever our only divinities! It is to you that belong the praises of the human race; to you appertains the homage of the earth," and so on. Such pantheistic piety is hardly in key with d'Holbach's view of nature as handing out good and evil impartially: "Winds, tempests, hurricanes, volcanoes, wars, plagues, famine, diseases, death are as necessary to her eternal march as the [not everywhere!] beneficent heat of the sun."[120] We are reminded of Calvin's God, stingy with heaven and lavish of hell.

In his characteristic mood d'Holbach repudiates not only the idea of God but the very word. "The words *God* and *create* . . . ought to be banished from the language of all those who desire to speak to be understood. These are abstract words, invented by ignorance; they are only calculated to satisfy men lacking in experience, men too idle or too timid to study nature and its ways."[121] He rejects deism as a compromise with superstition,[122] and makes a veritable religion of atheism:

> The friend of mankind cannot be a friend of God, who at all times has been a real scourge to the earth. The apostle of nature will not be the instrument of deceitful chimeras, by which the world is made an abode of illusions; the adorer of truth will not compromise with falsehood. . . . He knows that the happiness of the human race imperiously exacts that the dark, unsteady edifice of superstition shall be razed to its foundations, in order to elevate on its ruins a temple to nature suitable to peace—a fane sacred to virtue. . . . If his efforts should be in vain; if he cannot inspire with courage beings too much accustomed to tremble, he will at least applaud himself for having dared the attempt. Nevertheless he will not judge his efforts fruitless if he has been able to make only a single mortal happy, if his principles have calmed the transports of one honest mind. . . . At least he will have the advantage of having banished from his own mind the importunate terror of superstition, . . . of having trodden underfoot those chimeras with which the unfortunate are tormented. Thus,

escaped from the peril of the storm, he will calmly contemplate, from the summit of his rock, those tremendous hurricanes which superstition excites; and he will hold forth a succoring hand to those who shall be willing to accept it.[123]

3. Morals and the State

But is atheism compatible with popular morality? Can the powerful egoistic impulses of common men be controlled by a moral code shorn of all religious devotion and support? D'Holbach faced this question in the *Système de la nature*, and returned to it in 1776 with a three-volume *Morale universelle*. First of all, he doubts if religion, all in all, has made for morality:

> In spite of a hell so horrid even in description, what crowds of abandoned criminals fill our cities! . . . Are condemned thieves and murderers either atheists or skeptics? Those wretches believe in a God . . . Does the most religious father, in advising his son, speak to him of a vindictive God? . . . His constitution destroyed by debauchery, his fortune ruined by gambling, the contempt of society—these are the motives that the father employs.[124]

And even supposing that religion sometimes helps morality, does this balance the harm that religion causes?

> Against one timid man whom this idea [of hell] restrains, there are thousands upon whom it operates to no effect; there are millions whom it makes irrational, whom it turns into savage persecutors, whom it converts into wicked . . . fanatics; there are millions whose minds it disturbs, and whom it diverts from their duty to society.[125]

And consider the hypocrisy forced upon skeptics by the social pressure of religion:

> Those who wish to form an idea of the shackles imposed by theology upon the genius of philosophers born under the "Christian Dispensation," let them read the metaphysical romances of Leibniz, Descartes, Malebranche, Cudworth, etc., and coolly examine the ingenious but rhapsodical systems entitled "the pre-established harmony" of "occasional causes." [126]

Moreover, by concentrating human thought upon individual salvation in another world, Christianity deadened civic feeling in this one, leaving men insensitive to the misery of their fellows, and to the injustices committed by oppressive groups and governments.

D'Holbach rejects the Christian-Voltairean idea that man is born with a sense of right and wrong. Conscience is the voice not of God but of the policeman; it is the deposit of a thousand exhortations, commands, and reproofs falling upon the individual in his growth. "We may define conscience as our knowledge of the effects which our actions produce upon our fellow men, and, in reaction, upon ourselves."[127] Such conscience can be a false guide, for it may have been formed by a slanted education, by misunderstood experience, by erroneous reasoning, or by a corrupt public opinion. There is no vice or crime that cannot be made to seem a virtue by indoctrination or evil example; so adultery, however forbidden by religion, has become a proud achievement, sycophancy is *de rigueur* at court, rape and rapine, among soldiers, are considered legitimate rewards of risking life and limb. "We see rich men who suffer no pricks of conscience over wealth acquired at the expense of their fellow citizens," and "zealots whose conscience, blinded by false ideas, . . . urges them to exterminate without remorse those who have different opinions than their own." The best that we can hope for is a conscience formed by a better education, by an acquired habit of looking forward to the effects of our actions upon others and ourselves, and by a healthier public opinion which an intelligent individual will hesitate to offend.[128]

D'Holbach agrees with Christianity that man is by nature inclined to "sin"—i.e., to behavior injurious to the group; but he rejects as ridiculous the notion that this "sinful nature" is an inheritance from the "sin of our first parents." He accepts egoism as fundamental in human conduct, and, like Helvétius, he proposes to found his moral code upon it by making social behavior advantageous to the individual. "Morals would be a vain science if it did not incontestably prove to man that his interest consists in being virtuous."[129] Something can be achieved by an education that explains the dependence of individual welfare upon the welfare of the group, and a considerable degree of "altruism" can be evoked by appealing to the natural desire for social approval, distinction, and rewards. So d'Holbach formulates his ethic as "the Code of Nature":

> Live for yourself and your fellow creature. I [Nature] approve of your pleasures while they injure neither you nor others, whom I have rendered necessary to your happiness. . . . Be just, since justice supports the human race. Be good, since your goodness will attract every heart to you. Be indulgent, since you live among beings weak like yourself. Be modest, as your pride will hurt the self-love of everyone around you. Pardon injuries, do good to him who injures you, that you may . . . gain his friendship. Be moderate, temperate, and chaste, since

lechery, intemperance, and excess will destroy you and make you contemptible.[130]

If government cared more actively for the health, protection, and education of the people, there would be far less crime;[131] when one has much to lose he does not readily risk it in unsocial conduct. If education trained pupils to reason, instead of frightening them with irrational beliefs that soon lose their force, men would be morally improved by increased ability to apply experience to action, foreseeing, in the light of the past, the future effects of present deeds. In the long run intelligence is the highest virtue, and such virtue is the best road to happiness.

In *Système de la nature*, *Système social* (1772, three volumes), *Politique naturelle* (1772, two volumes), and *Éthocratie* (1776) the indefatigable millionaire took up the problems of society and government. In these books the attack passes from the Church to the state. D'Holbach agrees with Locke and Marx that labor is the source of all wealth, but, like Locke, he justifies private property as the right of a man to the product of his labor. Himself a noble, he would do away with hereditary aristocracy:

> A body of men that can lay claim to wealth and honor solely though the title of birth must of necessity serve as a discouragement to the other classes of citizens. Those who have only ancestors have no right to reward. . . . Hereditary nobility can only be regarded as a pernicious abuse, fit only for favoring the indolence . . . and incompetence of one class to the detriment of all.[132] . . . Old title deeds, ancient documents, preserved in medieval castles—are they to confer upon their inheritors a claim to the most exalted posts in Church and state, in the courts of justice, or in the army, regardless of whether these inheritors possess the talents necessary for the proper accomplishment of such duties?[133]

As for the clergy, let them shift for themselves. Church and state should be strictly separate; religious groups should be treated as voluntary associations, enjoying toleration but no state support; and a wise government will prevent any one religion from intolerance or persecution.[134]

Himself a *rentier*, d'Holbach criticizes the idle *rentiers* of the middle class, and he has a baron's scorn of businessmen. "There is no more dangerous creature alive then the businessman seeking his prey."[135] The greed of commerce is now replacing dynastic ambitions as a cause of war:

> States are ready to cut each other's throats [for] some heaps of sand. Entire nations become the dupes of avaricious businessmen, who beguile them with the hope of wealth, the fruit of which they gather

only for themselves. Countries are depopulated, taxation is piled up, peoples are impoverished, to satisfy the greed of a small group.

He strikes a passing blow at Britain, which had just taken India and Canada:

> There is one people who in the transports of their greed seem to have formed the extravagant project of usurping the commerce of the world and making themselves owners of the seas—an iniquitous and mad project whose execution . . . would hastily bring to certain ruin the nation that is guided by this frenzy. . . . The day will come when Indians, having learned the art of war from Europeans, will hurl them from their shores.[136]

D'Holbach is inclined to the physiocratic gospel of *laissez-faire*:

> The government should do nothing for the merchant except to leave him alone. No regulations can guide him in his enterprises so well as his own interest. . . . The state owes commerce nothing but protection. Among commercial nations those that allow their subjects the most unlimited liberty may be sure of soon excelling all others.[137]

But then, too, he advises governments to prevent a dangerous concentration of wealth. He quotes with relish St. Jerome's swift barb, *"Dives aut iniquus est, aut iniqui haeres"* (The rich man is either a scoundrel or a scoundrel's heir).[138]

> In almost all nations three quarters of the subjects possess nothing. . . . When a small number of men absorb all the property and wealth in a state, they become the masters of that state. . . . Governments seem to have altogether neglected this important truth.[139] . . . When the public will or law ceases to keep the balance even between the different members of society, the laziness of some, aided by force, fraud, and seduction, succeeds in appropriating the fruit of the labor of others.[140]

Nearly all kings, in d'Holbach's opinion, ally themselves with the clever minority in exploiting the majority. He seems to be thinking of Louis XV.

> On the face of this globe we see only unjust sovereigns, enervated by luxury, corrupted by flattery, depraved by licentiousness, made wicked by impurity, devoid of talents, without morals, . . . and incapable of exerting an energy for the benefit of the states they govern. They are consequently but little occupied with the welfare of their people, and indifferent to their duties, of which, indeed, they are often

ignorant. Stimulated by the desire . . . to feed their insatiable ambition, they engage in useless, depopulating wars, and never occupy their minds with those objects which are the most important to the happiness of their nation.[141]

Obviously thinking of the French government, d'Holbach lashes out at the farming of tax collections to private financiers:

> The despot addresses himself to a class of citizens who furnish him with the means for his avidity in exchange for the right to extort with impunity from all others. . . . In his blindness he does not see that the taxes on his subjects are often doubled; that the sums that go to enrich the extortioners are lost to himself; and that the army of subordinate *publicani* is subsidized at a pure loss, to make war on the nation. . . . These brigands, grown rich, arouse the jealousy of the nobility and the envy of their fellow citizens. . . . Wealth becomes the one and only motive, . . . the thirst for gold lays hold of every heart.[142]

At times the comfortable aristocrat talks like the angriest of unplaced youths: "Are nations to work without respite to satisfy the vanity, the luxury, the greed of a pack of useless and corrupt bloodsuckers?"[143] In this mood he echoes the *Contrat Social* of his former friend Rousseau:

> Man is wicked not because he is born so but because he is rendered so. The great and powerful crush with impunity the indigent and unhappy. These, at the risk of their lives, seek to retaliate the evil they have received; they attack either openly or secretly a country that to them is a stepmother, who gives all to some of her children, and deprives the others of everything. . . .
> Man is almost everywhere a slave. It follows of necessity that he is base, selfish, dissimulating, without honor; in a word, that he has the vices of the state of which he is a member. Everywhere he is deceived, encouraged in ignorance, and prevented from using his reason; of course he must everywhere be stupid, irrational, and wicked; everywhere he sees vice and crime applauded and honored; he concludes that vice is good, and that virtue is only a useless self-sacrifice. . . . If governments were enlightened, and seriously occupied themselves with the instruction and welfare of the people, and if laws were equitable, . . . it would not be necessary to seek in another life for financial chimeras which always prove abortive against the infuriate passions and real wants of man.[144]

How can this exploitation be stopped? The first step is to abolish absolute monarchy. "Absolute power must necessarily corrupt in heart and mind whoever holds it.[145] . . . The power of the king should always be subordinate to the representatives of the people; and these representatives should depend continuously on the will of their constituents";[146] here is a call for the summoning of the fateful States-General of 1789. Since every government derives its powers from the consent of the governed, "the society may at any time revoke these powers if the government ceases to represent the general will";[147] here is the voice of Rousseau and revolution.

But revolutions, sometimes at great cost, destroy the past in order to rebuild it under another phrase and form.

> Not through dangerous convulsions, not through conflict, regicide, and useless crimes, can the wounds of the nation be healed. These violent remedies are always more cruel than the evils they are intended to cure. . . . The voice of reason is neither seditious nor bloodthirsty. The reforms which it proposes may be slow, but therefore all the better planned.[148]

Men are imperfect, and cannot make perfect states; utopias are chimeras "incompatible with the nature of a being whose feeble machine is subject to derangement, and whose ardent imagination will not always submit to the guidance of reason. . . . The perfecting of politics can only be the slow fruit of the experience of centuries."[149] Progress is not a straight line, and it is a long one; many generations of education and experiment will be needed to clarify the causes and cures of social ills. Democracy is an ideal, possible only in small states and with widespread popular intelligence; it would be unwise in the France of Louis XVI. Perhaps this new king, so good and well-intentioned, will engage great talents to reform the state. So, in the end, d'Holbach contents himself with a constitutional monarchy, and he dedicates his *Éthocratie* to Louis as "a just, human, beneficent king, . . . father of his people, protector of the poor."[150] In that desperate hope the aging *philosophe* hung up his arms.

4. D'Holbach and His Critics

The *Système de la nature* is the most thorough and forthright exposition of materialism and atheism in all the history of philosophy. The endless hesitations, contradictions, and subtleties of Voltaire, the vague enthusiasms and ambivalent lucubrations of Diderot, the confusing repudiations of Rousseau by Jean Jacques, are here replaced by a careful consistency of ideas, and a forceful expression in a style sometimes heavy, occasionally flowery, often eloquent, always direct and clear. Yet, realizing that seven hundred such pages would be too much for the general digestion, and anxious to reach a wider audience, d'Holbach expounded his views again, in a simpler forum, in *Le Bon Sens, ou idées opposées aux idées surnaturelles* (1772). Seldom has a writer been so assiduous in spreading such unpopular convictions.

That he was heard far and wide is proved by the reaction of Frederick the Great to the *Système de la nature.* He who had so courted the *philosophes,* and had been lauded as their patron and ideal, turned against them when he saw one of their leaders attacking absolute monarchy as well as Christianity. It had been to his advantage to have the Catholic powers weakened in their internal unity by the campaign against the Church; but to find that rebel ecstasy daring now to insult kings as well as God stirred him to resentment, perhaps to fear. The same pen that had once written *Anti-Machiavel* now composed a *Réfutation du Système de la nature.* This man d'Holbach was going too far and too fast. "When one speaks in public," Frederick suggested, "he should consider the delicacy of superstitious ears; he should not shock anybody; he should wait till the time is sufficiently enlightened to let him think out loud."[15ʰ]

Apparently at Frederick's suggestion, but probably still more through fear that the extreme radicalism of d'Holbach would alienate all but atheists and revolutionaries from the philosophic camp, Voltaire, like a general reproving a presumptuous lieutenant, inserted into the article "Dieu" in his *Dictionnaire philosophique* several pages criticizing d'Holbach's chef-d'oeuvre. He began:

> The author has had the advantage of being read by both learned and ignorant, and by women. His style, then, has merits which that of Spinoza lacked. He is often luminous, sometimes eloquent, although, like all the rest, he may be charged with repetitions, declamations, and self-contradictions. But as regards profundity he is very often to be distrusted both in physics and in morals. The interest of mankind is here involved; we will therefore examine whether his doctrine is true and useful.

Voltaire would not agree that the order which we ascribe to the universe, and the disorder which we may think to find in it, are subjective concepts and prejudices; he argued that the order is overwhelmingly obvious, and that disorder is sometimes painfully clear.

> What, is not a child born blind or without legs, or a monstrous freak, contrary to the nature of the species? Is it not the ordinary regularity of nature that makes order, and the irregularity that constitutes disorder? Is it not a great derangement, a dreadful disorder, when nature gives a child hunger and a closed esophagus? Evacuations

of every kind are necessary, yet the excretory channels are frequently without openings, which it is necessary to remedy. . . . The origin of the disorder remains to be discovered, but the disorder is real.

As to matter having the power to generate life and mind, Voltaire, though he too had once inclined to that view, preferred a modest agnosticism to d'Holbach's confident assumptions:

"Experience [he quotes from the *Système*] proves to us that the matter which we regard as inert and dead assumes action, life, and intelligence when it is combined in a certain way." But this is precisely the difficulty. How does a living germ arise? About this the author and the reader are alike ignorant. Hence, are not the *System of Nature*, and all the [philosophical] systems in the world, so many dreams? "It would be necessary [says d'Holbach] to define the vital principle, which I deem impossible." Is not this definition very easy? . . . Is not life organization with feeling? But that these two properties can arise solely from matter in motion it is impossible to prove; and if it is impossible to prove, why affirm it? . . . Many readers will feel indignant at the decisive tone assumed when nothing is explained. . . . When you venture to affirm that there is no God, or that matter acts of itself by an eternal necessity, you must demonstrate this like a proposition in Euclid; otherwise you rest your system on a "perhaps." What a foundation for a belief that is of the greatest importance to the human race!

D'Holbach had supported abiogenesis by referring to the experiments (1748) of the English Jesuit Needham, who believed that he had produced new organisms out of nonliving matter. Voltaire, alert to the latest developments in science, referred to the experiments (1765) of Spallanzani as having shown the error of Needham's procedure and conclusions. D'Holbach had seen no design in nature; Voltaire sees much. He argues that the development of intelligence in man indicates an intelligence in or behind the universe. Finally he returns to his famous proposition that "if God did not exist it would be necessary to invent him"; that without belief in a Supreme Being, in his intelligence and his justice, life with its mysteries and miseries would be unbearable. He joins d'Holbach in scorning superstition, but he defends religion as the simple adoration of a deity. He concludes amiably:

I am persuaded that you are in a great error, but I am equally convinced that you are honest in your self-delusion. You would have men virtuous even without a God, although you have unfortunately said that "so soon as vice renders man happy he must love vice"—a frightful proposition, which your friends should have prevailed upon you to erase. Everywhere else you inspire probity. This philosophical dispute will only be between you and a few philosophers scattered over Europe, and the rest of the world will not even hear of it. The people do not read us. . . . You are wrong, but we owe respect to your genius and your virtue.[152]

We do not know if Voltaire had his heart in this refutation. We note his light remark, when he heard that Frederick also had written against the *Système de la nature*, "God had on his side the two least superstitious men in all Europe—which ought to have pleased him immensely."[153] He asked the Duc de Richelieu to let Louis XV know that the unwilling exile of Ferney had written an answer to the audacious book that was the talk of Paris.

D'Holbach's friends published Voltaire's critique as a means of advertising the Baron's ideas. Young rebels took up materialism as a badge of bravery in the war against Catholicism. D'Holbach's philosophy entered into the spirit of the French Revolution before and after Robespierre—who preferred Rousseau; we hear echoes of the *Système* in Camille Desmoulins, Marat, and Danton.[154] "D'Holbach, more than Voltaire, more than Diderot," said Faguet, "is the father of all the philosophy and all the antireligious polemics of the end of the eighteenth and the first half of the nineteenth century."[155] During the Directory a minister sent copies of a book by d'Holbach to all departmental heads in an attempt to check the Catholic revival.[156] In England we feel d'Holbach's influence in the materialism of Priestley (1777); Godwin's *Enquiry concerning Political Justice* stemmed from d'Holbach, Helvétius, and Rousseau in that order of influence;[157] and the enthusiastic atheism of Godwin's son-in-law, Shelley, dated from his reading of the *Système de la nature*, which he began to translate as a means of enlisting the Oxford dons in the campaign against religion.[158] In Germany it was d'Holbach's materialism, as well as Hume's skepticism, that aroused Kant from his "dogmatic slumber." Perhaps Marx, through devious channels, inherited his materialist tradition from d'Holbach.

Long before the Baron wrote, Berkeley had made the most damaging point about materialism: mind is the only reality directly known; matter (since d'Holbach defined it as "all that affects our senses") is known only indirectly, through mind; and it seems unreasonable to reduce the directly to the indirectly known. We are not so clear about matter as we used to be; we are as much mystified by the atom as by mind; both are being resolved into forms of energy that we cannot understand. And it is as difficult now as in the days of Locke and Voltaire to imagine how "matter" can become idea, much less consciousness. The mechanistic interpretation of life proved fruitful in physiology, but the possibility still remains that organs (matter) may be products and instruments of desire (mind), like the muscles of an athlete. Mechanism, determinism, even "natural law," may be summary simplifications, logically irrefutable because they are tools invented by the mind for the convenient handling of phenomena, events, and things. These tools have become inextricable elements in scientific thought, but they are unsatisfactory when applied to the mind that fashioned them. We do not know that the world is logical.

CHAPTER XXII

Voltaire and Christianity

1734–78

I. VOLTAIRE AND GOD

WE may study later the nonreligious activities, opinions, and interests of that consuming fire called Voltaire, burning fitfully at Ferney; here we summarize only his views on religion and his war against Christianity. We shall say nothing about him that has not been said a hundred times before; and he said nothing about Christianity that had not been said before. It is only that when he said it the words passed like a flame through Europe, and became a force molding his time, and ours.

It was natural that he should question the Christian creed, for a religion is intended to quiet rather than excite the intellect, and Voltaire was intellect incarnate, unquiet and unappeased. We have seen him in his career joining the skeptical wits of the Temple, nourishing his doubts among the deists of England, pursuing science at Cirey, and exchanging infidelities with Frederick in Germany. Yet, until he was fifty-six, he kept his unbelief as an incidental expression or private sport, and made no open war upon the Church. On the contrary, he publicly and repeatedly defended the fundamentals of the Christian faith—a just God, free will, and immortality. Unless we account him a liar (which he often was), he retained till death his belief in God and in the value of religion. We may quote him to almost any purpose, for, like every living thing, he grew and changed and decayed; which of us retained at fifty the views he held at twenty, or, at seventy, the views he held at fifty? Voltaire contradicted himself endlessly because he lived long and wrote much; his opinions were the fluent vision of his mounting years.[1]

At Cirey, about 1734, he tried to formulate his ideas on first and last things in a *Traité de métaphysique*. Years before Paley made the comparison familiar to Englishmen, Voltaire submitted that it was as logical to postulate an intelligent mind in the universe as to suppose that a watchmaker had made a watch; in either case he saw evidence of design in the adaptation of specific means to particular ends. But just as the watch, though designed by intelligence, operates according to fixed laws, so does the universe; there are no miracles. Yet somehow he could not throw off the feeling that the human will is in some mysterious way and modest degree free, though he knew well that free volitions acting upon a mechanical world must upset its mechanism. Mind is a form and function of matter; "we ought to judge," said Voltaire, following Locke, "that it is quite possible for God to add thought to matter";[2] that matter should think is no greater miracle than it would be for an immaterial mind to act upon a material body. The soul is merely the life of the body, and dies with it. There is no other divine revelation than nature itself; this is enough, and inexhaustible. There may be some good in religion, but an intelligent man does not need it as a support to morality; too often, in history, it has been used by priests to bemuse the public mind while kings picked the public pocket. Virtue should be defined in terms of social good rather than obedience to God, and it should not depend upon rewards and punishments after death.

Voltaire read these seventy-five pages to Mme. du Châtelet, who apparently discouraged their publication. He seems to have agreed with her; he put the manuscript aside, and it was never printed during his lifetime. Moreover, he became convinced that any rational metaphysics—any attempt by reason to explain the origin, nature, or destiny of the world and man—would be forever beyond human power. He read the philosophers, but he did not admire their systems. "In metaphysics and morals," he thought, "the ancients have said everything. We always encounter or repeat them. All modern books of this description are merely repetitions."[3] He must have been impressed by Spinoza's system, for he labored to refute it.

Despite his disclaimers, he could not still his interest in the insoluble. From time to time, during the years 1734–56, he delved into metaphysics and theology. He continued to the end of his life to rest his belief in God upon the argument from design, though he ridiculed the excesses of teleology. "I may not believe that noses were made as convenient bridges for spectacles, but I am convinced that they were made to smell with."[4] And: "To affirm that the eye is not made to see, nor the ear to hear, nor the stomach to digest—is not this the most monstrous absurdity?"[5] When a young author knocked at the door of Les Délices (1757), and introduced himself to Voltaire as "a young atheist ready to serve" him, Voltaire replied, "And I have the honor to be a deist employer; but though our professions are so opposed, I will give you supper today and work tomorrow; I can make use of your arms, though not of your head."[6] He called himself a deist, but he was rather a theist: that is, his God was not an impersonal force more or less identical with nature, but a conscious intelligence designing and ruling the world. Generally, after 1750, he called himself a theist;[7]

and in the *Philosophical Dictionary*, in the article "Theism," he wrote in terms that could justify Condorcet's description of Voltaire as "a deeply religious man":

> The theist is a man firmly persuaded of the existence of a Supreme Being equally good and powerful, who has formed all . . . existences; who punishes crimes without cruelty, and rewards virtuous actions with kindness. The theist does not know how God punishes, how he rewards, how he pardons, for he is not presumptuous enough to flatter himself that he understands how God acts; but he knows that God acts, and that God is just. The difficulties opposed to a Providence do not stagger him in his faith, for they are only great difficulties, not proofs; he submits himself to that Providence, although he perceives only some of its effects and some appearances; and, judging of the things he does not see by those he sees, he thinks that this Providence pervades all places and all ages.
>
> United in this principle with all the rest of the universe, he does not join any of the sects, who all contradict themselves. His religion is the most ancient and the most extended, for the simple adoration of a God has preceded all the systems in the world. . . . He believes that religion consists neither in the opinions of incomprehensible metaphysics nor in vain decorations, but in adoration and justice. To do good is his worship; to submit himself to God is his doctrine. . . . He laughs at Loreto and Mecca, but he succors the indigent and defends the oppressed.[8]

Was Voltaire sincere in these professions? Some students ascribe them to caution, or to a desire to move to atheism one step at a time,[9] or to a hope that religious faith inculcated in his servants would lessen pilferage; and there are passages in Voltaire that seem to justify this interpretation. ("If you have but a village to govern, it must have a religion."[10]) One of his most quoted remarks appears to reduce religion to a public utility; but the context of that line puts it in a fairer light. It occurs in the *Epistle to the Author of "The Three Impostors"*:

> *Si Dieu n'existait pas il faudrait l'inventer,*
> *Mais toute la nature nous crie qu'il existe.*[11]

—"If God did not exist, it would be necessary to invent him, *but all nature cries out to us that he does exist,*" and the entire poem is a plea for belief. Voltaire returns to the theistic argument again and again, as if to answer his own doubts. In his final decade he wrote as often against atheism as against orthodoxy. Meanwhile he made war upon the popular conception of the deity as a God of Vengeance damning most of mankind to an everlasting hell. "The human race would be too unhappy if it were as common to commit atrocities as to believe in them."[12] "If God made man in his own image, we have well repaid him"[13]—by making him in ours; nothing could better reveal man's conception of himself than his conception of God.

Voltaire struggled to reconcile his theism with the existence of evil. In these efforts at theodicy he came close to the optimism of Leibniz (which he was to ridicule in *Candide*): what is evil from the standpoint of the part may be good, or at least not evil, in the perspective of the whole; this is not the best conceivable, but the best possible, world.[14] "When everything is counted and weighed up," he wrote to Frederick in 1738, "I think there are infinitely more enjoyments than bitterness in this life"[15]—but this was written in his hale and middle years. He did not believe that man is wicked by nature; on the contrary, he held that man has an innate sense of justice, and a *bienveillance naturelle*—a natural feeling of good will toward other men.[16] There are countless varieties and contradictions in the moral ideas and customs of mankind, but all peoples, Voltaire thought, condemn parricide and fratricide.[17]

In 1752, at Potsdam, he composed a poem, *La Loi naturelle* (published in 1756), which summarized his "natural religion." As it took the form of a letter to the skeptical Frederick II, it could hardly have been an attempt to please the pious; but it comes closer to piety and orthodoxy than anything else that Voltaire ever printed. It not only affirms faith in God the Creator, but describes man's moral sense as infused into him by the Deity;[18] here he speaks like Rousseau, and anticipates the enthusiasm of Kant for the categorical imperative of conscience. He defines his religion in one line: *"Adore un Dieu, sois juste, et chéris ta patrie."*[19] He surveys the varieties of religious belief, laments their hatreds and fanaticisms, and pleads for mutual toleration among the creeds. He ends with a prayer that any saint might have signed. The Paris Parlement ordered the poem to be publicly burned (January 23, 1759), probably because some lines in it condemned Jansenism.

We may conclude that until 1751—until he was fifty-seven years old—Voltaire refrained from any outright and public attack upon Christianity or the Catholic Church. What was it that aroused him to open war, precisely at an age when most rebels have subsided into peace? It was the suppression of the *Encyclopédie*, the orthodox explanations of the Lisbon earthquake, and the ferocious executions of Jean Calas and the Chevalier de La Barre.

II. VOLTAIRE AND THE *ENCYCLOPÉDIE*

He was in Potsdam when the first volume of the *Encyclopédie* was published (1751). He must have read with warm pleasure the lines by which d'Alembert had paid homage to him in the "Discours préliminaire": "May I not . . . render to this rare genius the tribute and eulogy that he merits, which he has so frequently received from his compatriots, from foreigners, and from his enemies, and to which posterity will add full measure when he can no longer enjoy the praise?" Voltaire returned the compliment in a letter of September 5, 1752, to d'Alembert: "You and M. Diderot are accomplishing a work which will be the glory of France and the shame of those who persecute you. . . . Of eloquent philosophers I recognize only you and him." He pledged his support, and lost no opportunity to call attention to the enterprise as "an immense and immortal work, which accuses the shortness of human life."[20]

However busy with his own major compositions—*Le Siècle de Louis XIV* and *Essai sur les moeurs*—and embroiled with Hirsch, Maupertuis, and Frederick, Voltaire found time to send to d'Alembert (1753) some brief articles "only as material which you will arrange at your pleasure in the immortal edifice which you are raising. Add, shorten; I give you my pebbles to insert into some corner of the wall." [21] He invoked the aid of influential friends to protect the editors. In 1755 he wrote to d'Alembert: "As long as I have a breath of life I am at the service of the illustrious authors of the *Encylopédie*. I consider myself greatly honored to be able to contribute, even feebly, to the greatest and handsomest monument of the nation and of literature."[22] With that letter he enclosed articles on fire, force, fornication, French, genius, and taste (*goût*). Examining the first five volumes, he found much to praise, something to deplore. He asked the editors to require clearness and brevity of all contributors, and he cautioned d'Alembert (whom he mistakenly supposed to be chief editor): "You are poorly seconded; there are bad soldiers in the army of a great general. . . . I am sorry to see that the writer of the article "Enfer" declares that hell was a point in the doctrine of Moses; now, by all the devils, that is not true." [23]

Soon he sent in several minor articles, and a major disquisition on history. He persuaded a learned priest of Lausanne, Antoine Noé de Polier, to write for the *Encyclopédie* the articles "Magi," "Magic," "Magician," and "Messiah," all quietly heretical. We have seen how Voltaire had some responsibility for d'Alembert's article on Geneva (1757); he weathered the ensuing storm by inviting the betrayed clergymen to dinner. When disaster threatened the great enterprise (January, 1758) he wrote to Diderot:

> Go on, brave Diderot, intrepid d'Alembert; . . . fall upon the
> knaves, destroy their empty declamations, their miserable sophistries,
> their historical lies, their contradictions and absurdities beyond num-
> ber; do not let men of intelligence become the slaves of those who

have none. The new generation will owe to you both reason and liberty.[24]

Diderot made no answer, d'Alembert insisted on withdrawing; Voltaire himself, losing courage, and offended by Diderot's silence, decided to abandon ship. On February 6 or 7 he wrote again to Diderot, asking him to restore to him his yet unpublished contributions. Diderot replied that the manuscripts were with d'Alembert; but that if Voltaire should repeat the request for their return he would "never forget the injury." On February 26 Voltaire wrote to d'Argental: "I love M. Diderot, I respect him, and I am angry." But to the same on March 12: "If you see this good man Diderot, tell the poor slave that I pardon him with as full a heart as I pity him."[25] In May d'Alembert sent the demanded articles to Voltaire; in June d'Alembert resumed work for the *Encyclopédie;* Voltaire again submitted the articles, but asked that they be published, if at all, without his name. He proposed that the enterprise be moved to another country, where it would suffer less emasculation by censorship actual or feared; Diderot thought the proposal impracticable. Voltaire lost faith in the value of a massive and expensive encyclopedia as a vehicle of liberal propaganda. On June 26, 1758, he notified Diderot that other preoccupations would make it impossible for him to contribute further material; besides, as matters now stood between the editors, the government, and the Church, "one is obliged to lie, and we are persecuted if we have not lied enough."[26] The furor created by Helvétius' *De l'Esprit* (July) frightened the aging rebel into writing an answer to that book. On November 16 he informed Diderot that he had bought a house at Ferney, and intended henceforth to live quietly as a country gentleman.

Was he deceiving himself, or was he planning to resume the war by other means?

III. THE THEOLOGY OF EARTHQUAKES

While the *Encyclopédie* was in the throes of repeated deaths and resurrections, the Lisbon earthquake sent its tremors throughout European philosophy. At 9:40 A.M. on All Saints' Day, November 1, 1755, the earth shrugged its shoulders in Portugal and North Africa; in six minutes thirty churches and a thousand houses were demolished, fifteen thousand people were killed, and fifteen thousand more were fatally injured, in one of the most picturesque capitals in the world. There was nothing unprecedented in such wholesale slaughter, but there were some attendant circumstances that troubled the theologians. Why had the Great Inscrutable chosen so Catholic a city, so holy a festival, and such an hour—when nearly all pious citizens were attending Mass? And why had he spared, amid the general ruin, the house of Sebastião de Carvalho e Mello—the future Marquês de Pombal—the ruling minister who was in all Europe the most fervent enemy of the Jesuits?

A Portuguese Jesuit, Malagrida, explained that the quake, and the calamitous tidal wave that had followed it, were God's punishment for the vice that had prospered in Lisbon;[27] but were the sinners the only ones that went to pray in the churches on that awful morning? Why had so many holy priests and dedicated nuns perished in the quake and the conflagration? The Moslems would have hailed the catastrophe as Allah's revenge upon the Portuguese Inquisition, but the quake had destroyed the great Mosque of Al-Mansur in Rabat. Some Protestant dominies in London ascribed the disaster to divine reprobation of Catholic crimes against humanity; but on November 19 of the same year an earthquake damaged fifteen hundred houses in Boston, Massachusetts, home of the Pilgrims and the Puritans. William Warburton announced that the massacre in Lisbon "displayed God's glory in its fairest colors."[28] John Wesley preached a sermon on "The Cause and Cure of Earthquakes"; "sin," he said, "is the moral cause of earthquakes, whatever their natural cause may be; . . . they are the effect of that curse which was brought upon the earth by the original transgression" of Adam and Eve.[29]

Voltaire fumed at these explanations, but he himself could find none to reconcile the event with his faith in a just God. Where now was Leibniz' "best of all possible worlds"? Or Pope's "Whatever is, is right"—or his pretense that "all partial evil" is "universal good"?[30] In an angry reaction against his own early optimism Voltaire composed (1756) his greatest poem—"On the Lisbon Disaster, or An Examination of the Axiom 'All Is Well.'" Here is our chance to sample at once his thought and his verse.

> *O malheureux mortels! O terre déplorable!*
> *O de tous les mortels assemblage effroyable!*
> *D'inutiles douleurs éternel entretien!*
> *Philosophes trompés qui criez, "Tout est bien."*
> *Accourez, contemplez ces ruines affreuses,*
> *Ces débris, ces lambeaux, ces cendres malheureuses,*
> *Ces femmes, ces enfants l'un sur l'autre entassés,*
> *Sous ce marbre rompus ces membres dispersés;*
> *Cent mille infortunés que la terre dévore,*
> *Qui, sanglants, déchirés, et palpitants encore,*
> *Enterrés sous leurs toits, terminent sans secours*
> *Dans l'horreur des tourments leurs lamentables jours!*
> *Aux cris demi-formés de leurs cendres fumantes,*

Direz-vous, "C'est l'effet des éternelles lois
Qui d'un Dieu libre et bon nécessitent le choix?"
Direz-vous, en voyant cet amas de victimes,
"Dieu est vengé, leur mort est le prix de leurs crimes?"*

But what crime, what fault had those infants committed who lay crushed and bloody on their mothers' breasts? Had London or Paris less vice than Lisbon? Yet Lisbon is shattered, and Paris dances.

Could not an omniscient God have made a world without such meaningless suffering? "I respect my God, but I love mankind."

The poet looks upon the world of life, and sees everywhere, in a thousand forms, a struggle for existence, in which every organism, sooner or later, is slain. This bitter summary of biology demands a literal translation:

> The ferocious vulture darts upon its timid prey, and feasts with joy upon the bleeding limbs. All seems well for him; but soon an eagle with sharply cutting beak devours the vulture in its turn. Man reaches the lordly eagle with a deadly shot; and man lies in the dust on the battlefield, bloody, pierced with blows, amid a mound of dying men; there he serves as the frightful food of voracious birds. Thus all the world in all its members groans, all born for suffering and for mutual death. And in this fatal chaos you will compose, from the misery of each part, the happiness of the whole! What happiness? Oh, weak and miserable mortal! You cry out in mournful tones that "all is well"; the universe gives you the lie, and your own heart refutes a hundred times the error of your mind. The elements, and animals, and men—all are in war. Let us confess it: evil strides the earth.

How does this scene of universal strife and ignominious, agonizing death comport with the belief in a good God? He exists, but he is a baffling

---

* Oh, miserable mortals, grieving earth!
 Oh, frightful gathering of all mankind!
 Eternal host of useless sufferings!
 Ye silly sages who cry, "All is well,"
 Come, contemplate these ruins horrible,
 This wreck, these shreds and ashes of your race;
 Women and children heaped in common death,
 These scattered members under broken shafts;
 A hundred thousand luckless by the earth
 Devoured, who, bleeding, torn, and still alive,
 Buried beneath their roofs, end without help
 Their lamentable days in torment vile!
 To their expiring and half-formed cries,
 The smoking cinders of this ghoulish scene,
 Say you, "This follows from eternal laws
 Binding the choice of God both free and good"?
 Will you, before this mass of victims, say,
 "God is revenged, their death repays their crimes"?

mystery. He sends his son to redeem mankind, yet the earth and man remain the same despite his sacrifice.

> What can the farthest-reaching mind say of this? Nothing; the book
> of fate is closed to our view. Man, a stranger to himself, is unknown
> to man. What am I? Where am I? Whither do I go? Whence did I
> come? Atoms tormented on this heap of mud, which death engulfs,
> and with which fate plays; yet thinking atoms, atoms whose eyes,
> guided by thought, have measured the skies. We throw our minds
> across the infinite, yet cannot for one moment see and know ourselves.

This, of course, is the note that Pascal had sounded a hundred years before, in prose greater than Voltaire's verse. Voltaire had once rejected Pascal; now he echoes his pessimism. From the same premises Pascal had concluded, Let us surrender ourselves to Christian faith and hope. Originally Voltaire ended his poem with a somber, stoic couplet:

> *Que faut-il, O mortels? Mortels, il faut souffrir,*
> *Se soumettre en silence, adorer, et mourir*

—"What must we do, O mortals? Mortals, we must suffer, submit in silence, adore, and die." His friends protested that such a hopeless ending was unbearable. He changed the final line to read:

> *Se soumettre, adorer, espérer, et mourir*

—"Submit, adore, hope, and die." No one was satisfied; he gave in, and added twenty-nine lines, yielding himself to Providence, and trusting that "only God is right."

Nevertheless the poem shocked not only the orthodox, but the *philosophes* as well; such a despondent tone seemed to take all the wind out of philosophic sails. Rousseau sent to Voltaire a long and eloquent letter explaining that all human ills are the result of human faults; the Lisbon earthquake was a just punishment of man for abandoning a natural life and living in cities; if men had kept to the simple life of scattered villages and modest homes, there would have been relatively few victims. We must put our faith in the goodness of God, said Jean Jacques, for that is the sole alternative to a suicidal pessimism; we must continue to believe, with Leibniz, that since God has created this world, everything in it, in the long run and the long view, must be right. Some printer secured a copy of this letter and published it; it was widely acclaimed as an able reply to Voltaire's poem. Voltaire kept his peace for an unusually long time. When he dealt again with optimism it was in his most perfect production, a book that in a generation went around the world, and that is now the most living relic and symbol of Voltaire.

IV. *CANDIDE*

It was published early in 1759 as *Candide, ou l'optimisme*, purportedly "translated from the German of Dr. Ralph, with additions found in the pocket of the Doctor when he died at Minden." The Great Council of Geneva almost at once (March 5) ordered it to be burned. Of course Voltaire denied his authorship; "people must have lost their senses," he wrote to a friendly pastor in Geneva, "to attribute to me that pack of nonsense. I have, thank God, better occupations."[31] But France was unanimous: no other man could have written *Candide*. Here was that deceptively simple, smoothly flowing, lightly prancing, impishly ironic prose that only he could write; here and there a little obscenity, a little scatology; everywhere a playful, darting, lethal irreverence; if the style is the man, this had to be Voltaire.

It begins innocently, but soon betrays the master's twinkling eye:

> In the country of Westphalia, in the castle of the most noble Baron Thunder-ten-tronckh, lived a youth whom nature had endowed with a most sweet disposition. . . . He had a solid judgment joined to the most unaffected simplicity; and for that reason, I believe, he was named Candide. The old servants of the house suspected him to have been the son of the Baron's sister, by a good and honorable gentleman of the neighborhood, whom that demoiselle refused to marry, because he could produce no more than seventy-one quarterings;

he was inadmissible in marriage, though adequate in bed. The handsome young bastard is tutored by Professor Pangloss (All-tongue), who

> could prove to admiration that there is no effect without a cause, and that in this best of all possible worlds the Baron's castle was the most magnificent of all castles, and Milady the best of possible baronesses [despite her 350 pounds]. It is demonstrable, said he, that things cannot be otherwise than as they are; for, as all things have been created for some end, they must necessarily have been created for the best end. Observe, for instance, the nose is formed for spectacles, therefore we wear spectacles. The legs are visibly designed for stockings; accordingly we wear stockings. . . . They who assert that everything is right do not express themselves correctly; they should say that everything is *best*.

Candide "listened attentively, and believed implicitly," for Mlle. Cuné-gonde, the Baron's daughter, was obviously the best and most beautiful creature that could possibly have been created. She invites him to fall in love with her; he falls; the Baron gives him several "*grands coups de pied dans le derrière*," and puts him out of the castle.

Candide wanders, and is captured by recruiters who impress him into the Bulgarian (with Voltairean reminiscences of the Prussian) army. "There he was made to wheel about to the right, to the left, to draw his rammer, to return his rammer, to present, to fire, to march, and they gave him thirty blows with a cane." He sees battle, deserts, and comes upon Pangloss, who is now minus the end of his nose, and will soon lose an eye and an ear, as the result of excessive propinquity with the pretty wench Pacquette, "who was infected with an ailment which she had received from a learned Cordelier [Franciscan friar], who . . . had it from an old countess, who had received it from a captain of cavalry, who owed it to a marquise, who had it from a page, who had it from a Jesuit, who had received it from one of the companions of Christopher Columbus."[32]

Candide and Pangloss are shipwrecked near Lisbon, and reach shore just in time for the earthquake. They survive, but are arrested as heretics by the Inquisition; Pangloss is hanged; Candide escapes through the aid of Cunégonde, who, having been raped by soldiers, and then sold to a Jew, had recently been sold to a leading Inquisitor. Candide and Cunégonde flee with the help of an old lady, who silences their complaints by telling how she came near being eaten at the siege of Azor by the starving Turks among whom she had fallen; but, by the mercy of half-blind fate, they began by merely cutting off one buttock of each available woman; the siege ended before any further samplings; "now," concludes the old woman, "stop bemoaning your misery, and rejoice that you can sit on two buttocks."

They cross the Atlantic in hopes that the New World will be less cruel than the Old. In Buenos Aires the commandant appropriates Cunégonde to himself. Candide is banished; he enters the Jesuit colony in Paraguay, finds there Cunégonde's brother, who attacks him for daring to think of marry-ing her; Candide kills him, and resumes his desolate wandering. In a se-cluded Peruvian valley he comes upon El Dorado, a land where gold is so abundant that no one values it; a land without money or prisons, or lawyers, or priests, or economic strife; its happy people live to two hundred years, and have no religion except a simple worship of one God. Candide picks up some gold and moves on, still hungering for Cunégonde. He sails back to Europe, and reaches Portsmouth in time to see Admiral Byng shot for losing a battle; in this country, says Candide's new friend Martin, it is considered wise to kill an admiral now and then, "*pour en-courager les autres*"—to encourage the others.[33]

Learning that Cunégonde is in Venice, Candide takes ship to Italy. In Venice he is depressed by learning about the miseries of the prostitutes. He hears gondoliers singing, and concludes that he has found some happy men, but Martin checks him:

"You do not see them at home with their wives and their brats [*marmots d'enfants*]. The doge has his griefs, the gondoliers have theirs. It is true that, all in all, the lot of a gondolier is preferable to that of a doge; but I believe the difference is so trifling that it is not worth the trouble of examining it."[34]

Cunégonde is not in Venice, she is in Constantinople. Candide hurries there, finds that she is now an old and ugly slave; nevertheless he frees her and marries her. Pangloss, having been insufficiently hanged by the Inquisition, rejoins his pupil and resumes his defense of optimism. They meet an almost happy man, who entertains them with home-grown fruits and nuts. "You must have a large estate," Candide inquires. "I have only twenty acres," replies the Turk; "I cultivate them with my children; our labor keeps away three great evils—boredom, vice, and need."[35] Candide decides to do likewise; he, Cunégonde, and their friends till a plot of ground and grow their own food; the one-buttock woman, a reformed prostitute, and her friend the friar put their hands to various tasks; they labor, are tired, eat, are a bit bored, but moderately content. Pangloss argues that this must be the best of all possible worlds, since their sufferings have brought them to this peace. That was well said, replies Candide, *"mais il faut cultiver notre jardin"*—we must cultivate our garden. The little novel ends.

Voltaire had managed to put into small compass, within the frame of a story of adventure and love, a telling satire of Leibniz' theodicy, Pope's optimism, religious abuses, monastic amours, class prejudices, political corruption, legal chicanery, judicial venality, the barbarity of the penal code, the injustice of slavery, and the destructiveness of war; *Candide* was composed while the Seven Years' War dragged through its hither and thither of victory, devastation, and death. Flaubert called Voltaire's masterpiece *"le résumé de toutes ses oeuvres,"* the summary of all his works.[36] It had the defect of most satires, absurd exaggeration; but Voltaire knew quite well that few men ever encounter so bitter a concatenation of catastrophes as Candide's. He must have known, too, that though it is good to cultivate one's garden, to do well one's individual and immediate task, it is also good to have larger interests than one's field. He cultivated well his garden at Ferney, but he cried out to all Europe against the execution of Calas.

V. THE CONSCIENCE OF EUROPE

Jean Calas was one of a small group of Huguenots—Calvinist Protestants —left in Toulouse after a century of persecution, confiscation of property, and compulsory conversion to Catholicism. The law of France not only excluded Protestants from public office, it declared them ineligible to be lawyers, or physicians, or apothecaries, or midwives, or booksellers, or goldsmiths, or grocers. If they had not been baptized they had no civil rights whatever. If they had not been married by a Catholic priest they were held to be living in concubinage, and their children were accounted illegitimate.[37] Protestant services were forbidden; men found at such services were to be sent to the galleys for life; women so found were condemned to life imprisonment; and the officiating clergyman was put to death. These laws were not strictly enforced in or near Paris; the severity of their enforcement varied with distance from the capital.

Southern France was especially intense in its religious hatreds; there the struggle between Catholics and Huguenots had been most merciless; each side had committed atrocities that were yet warm in transmitted memories. In Toulouse, in 1562, the victorious Catholics had slain three thousand Huguenots, and the Parlement of Toulouse had condemned two hundred more to torture and death.[38] Every year the Catholics of Toulouse commemorated that slaughter with grateful ceremonies and a religious procession. The guilds of craftsmen, the various grades of nobles and clergy, the "companies" of White Penitents, Black Penitents, and Gray Penitents marched solemnly through the city, carrying awesome relics—the skull of the first bishop of Toulouse, a piece of the Virgin's dress, and bones of children killed in Herod's legendary "slaughter of the innocents." It was unfortunate for Calas that the approaching year was the bicentenary of the events of 1562.

The Parlement of Toulouse, which was as powerful in Languedoc as that of Paris was in central France, was now predominantly Jansenist—i.e., Catholic with a strong infusion of Calvinistic rigor and gloom. It lost no chance to prove itself more inflexibly Catholic than the Jesuits. On March 2, 1761, it condemned to death the Huguenot Pastor Rochette for conducting Protestant services, and it decreed death for three "gentlemen of the Comte de Foix" who had tried to free Rochette from the gendarmes.[39] On March 22 it ordered the torture and execution of a Huguenot shopkeeper on the charge that he had killed a son who had proposed to become a Catholic.

It should be said, in fairness to fanatics, that Calvin's *Institutes of the Christian Religion* gave some ground for their belief that Calvinists considered it permissible for a father to kill a disobedient child. In times when law was still weak, and the family was the chief—almost the only—source of discipline, many societies gave the father the right of life and death over his children. Something of this patriarchal code may have been in Calvin's mind when he wrote: "The Lord commands all those who are disobedient to their parents to be put to death."[40] Calvin referred to Deuteronomy xxi, 17–21, and Matthew xv, 4–6; those passages, however, merely allow the parents to accuse their son before "the elders of the city," who then may condemn him to death; and doubtless this is what Calvin meant. But the excited Catholics of southern France suspected that Huguenot parents, unable to appeal to the "elders of the city," would take that old law into their own hands.

It is against this dark background that we must see the case of Jean Calas.

He was a *marchand d'indiennes*—dealer in linens—who kept a store on the main street of Toulouse, where he had lived for forty years. He and his wife had four sons and two daughters. For thirty years they had kept a Catholic, Jeanne Vignière, as governess of their children, even after she had converted one son, Louis, to Catholicism. Louis now lived as an apprentice in another street, and received a regular allowance from his father. Donat, the youngest son, was apprenticed at Nîmes. Two other sons, Pierre and Marc Antoine, lived with their parents. Marc Antoine, the oldest, had studied law, but when he was prepared to practice he found the profession closed to all but Catholics. He tried to conceal his Protestantism, and to secure a certificate of Catholicism; his deceit was discovered, and he faced a choice of abandoning Protestantism or letting his years of law study go to waste. He took to brooding, gambling, and drink. He liked to declaim Hamlet's soliloquy on suicide.[41]

On October 13, 1761, the Calas family gathered in their rooms over the store. Gaubert Lavaysse, a friend of Marc Antoine, had just arrived from Bordeaux; he accepted the father's invitation to stay for dinner. After the meal Marc Antoine went down to the shop. Wondering why he did not return, Pierre and Lavaysse descended, and found him hanging from a bar that he had placed between two doorposts. They took him down, called the father, and sent for a doctor. They tried to revive him, but the doctor pronounced him dead.

At this point the father made a tragic error. He knew that a law then in force required that a suicide be drawn naked through the streets, be pelted by the populace with mud and stones, and then be hanged; and all his property was to be forfeited to the state. The father begged, and persuaded, his family to report the case as a natural death.[42] Meanwhile the cries of Pierre and the arrival of the doctor had brought a crowd to the door of the shop. An officer came up, heard the story told him, saw the rope and the mark it had left on the dead man's neck, and ordered the family, Lavaysse, and Jeanne Vignière to the Hôtel de Ville. There they were locked up in separate cells. On the next day each of them was questioned. All abandoned the claim of a natural death, and testified to a suicide. The commandant of police refused to believe them, and charged them with having killed Marc Antoine to prevent his becoming a convert. The accusation was taken up by the populace and by many members of the Toulouse Parlement. A frenzy of revenge closed the minds of the people.

It seems incredible to us now that anyone should believe in the murder of a son by his father to prevent a change of faith; but that is because we are thinking as individuals, and after two centuries of decline in religious faith. The people of Toulouse thought en masse, as a crowd; and crowds can feel but they cannot think. The frenzy was fed by a ceremony which the White Penitents staged in their chapel; over an empty coffin a skeleton was suspended, holding in one hand an inscription, "Abjuration of Heresy," and in the other a palm branch, symbolizing martyrdom; below was the name "Marc Antoine Calas." Assuming that the youth was not a suicide, they buried the corpse with great pomp in the Church of St. Stephen. A part of the clergy protested in vain against this anticipation of a verdict of murder.[43]

The trial of the Calas family took place before the twelve judges of the municipal court of Toulouse. An admonition was sent out, to be read on three successive Sundays in every church, summoning to the witness stand all who knew anything about the death. Several persons appeared. A barber testified that he had heard a cry from the Calas house on the fatal evening: "Ah, *mon Dieu*, they are strangling me!" Others claimed to have heard such cries. On November 10, 1761, the municipal court pronounced Jean Calas, his wife, and Pierre guilty, and sentenced them to be hanged; it condemned Lavaysse to the galleys, and Jeanne Vignière to five years' imprisonment. The Catholic governess had sworn to the innocence of her Protestant employers.

The decision was appealed to the Parlement of Toulouse, which appointed a panel of thirteen judges. Sixty-three additional witnesses were heard. All the hostile evidence was hearsay. The trial dragged on for three months, during which the Calas family and Lavaysse were kept in separate confinement. The final decision condemned only the father. No one explained how a man sixty-four years old, unaided, could have overcome and strangled his mature son. The court hoped that Calas, under torture, would confess. He was subjected to the *question ordinaire:* his arms and legs were stretched until they were pulled from their sockets. He was repeatedly exhorted to confess; he repeatedly affirmed that Marc Antoine had committed suicide. After half an hour's rest he was put to the *question extraordinaire;* fifteen pints of water were poured down his throat; he still protested his innocence; fifteen further pints were forced into him, swelling his body to twice its normal size; he still maintained his innocence. He was allowed to expel the water. Then he was taken to a public square before the cathedral; he was laid upon a cross; an executioner, with eleven blows of an iron bar, broke each of his limbs in two places; the old man, calling upon Jesus Christ, proclaimed his innocence. After two hours of agony he was strangled. The corpse was bound to a stake and burned (March 10, 1762).[44]

The other prisoners were freed, but the property of Calas was confiscated by the state. The widow and Pierre crept into hidden retirement at Montauban. The two daughters were sent to separate convents. Donat, finding his position at Nîmes endangered, fled to Geneva. Voltaire, hearing of the tragedy on March 22, invited Donat to meet him at Les Délices. "I asked him," wrote Voltaire to Damilaville, "if his father and mother were of violent character. He told me that they had never beaten any of their children, and that there were no parents more tender and indulgent."[45] Voltaire consulted two Genevan merchants who had lodged with Calas at Toulouse; they confirmed Donat's statement. He wrote to friends in Languedoc; "both Catholics and Protestants replied to me that the guilt of the family was beyond reasonable doubt."[46] Voltaire communicated with the widow; she sent him a statement so manifestly sincere that he was moved to action. He appealed to Cardinal de Bernis, to d'Argental, to the Duchesse d'Enville, to the Marquise de Nicolaï, to the Duc de Villars, to the Duc de Richelieu, to beg the King's ministers, Choiseul and Saint-Florentin, to order an investigation of the trial. He took Donat Calas into his family, brought Pierre Calas to Geneva, and persuaded Mme. Calas to take lodging in Paris, where she could be available for examination. He engaged lawyers to advise him on the legal technicalities of the case. He published a pamphlet, *Original Documents concerning the Death of Sieur Calas,*[47] and followed this up with further publications. He appealed to other authors to lend their pens to the effort to rouse the conscience of Europe. He wrote to Damilaville: "Cry out yourself, and let others cry out; cry out for the Calas family and against fanaticism."[48] And to d'Alembert: "Shout everywhere, I beg you, for the Calas family against fanaticism, for it is *l'infâme* that has caused their misery."[49] He solicited funds to help him bear the expense of the campaign, which he had thus far paid himself. Contributions came from a hundred quarters, including the Queen of England, the Empress of Russia, the King of Poland. A prominent Paris lawyer, Élie de Beaumont, agreed, without fee, to prepare the case for presentation to the Council of State. The daughters of Calas were moved to Paris to join their mother. One of them brought a letter from a Catholic nun appealing for the Calas family.[50] On March 7, 1763, mother and daughters were given audience by the King's ministers. The verdict was unanimous that the case be examined. All relevant documents were ordered from Toulouse.

But the Toulouse magistrates found a hundred devices for delay in gathering and remitting the papers. It was during that summer that Voltaire wrote and sent forth his epochal *Traité sur la tolérance*. To widen its appeal he adopted a tone of surprising moderation. Concealing his authorship, he spoke as a man of Christian piety, a believer in immortality; he praised the bishops of France as "gentlemen who think and act with a nobility that befits their birth";[51] he pretended to accept the principle, "Out of the Church there is no salvation."[52] The treatise was addressed not to philosophers but to the Catholic clergy itself. Even so, it had its audacities, for often he forgot his audience.

He began with an account of the trial and execution of Calas. He reviewed the history of toleration, exaggerating it in the case of Greece and Rome. He anticipated Gibbon by arguing that Roman persecution of Christians was immeasurably surpassed by Christian persecution of heretics, who were "hanged, drowned, broken on the wheel, or burned, for the love of God."[53] He defended the Reformation as a justified revolt against the sale of indulgences by a papacy lately disgraced through the amours of Pope Alexander VI and the murders perpetrated by the Pope's son Caesar Borgia. He expressed his shock at reading a recent attempt to justify the Massacre of St. Bartholomew.* He admitted that Protestants too had been intolerant.† Nevertheless he recommended that Protestant worship be allowed in France, and that the banished Huguenots be allowed to return.

> They ask only the protection of natural law, the validity of their marriages, security as to the condition of their children, the right to inherit from their fathers, and the enfranchisement of their persons. They ask not for public chapels, or the right to municipal offices and dignities.[55]

Despite this strategic limitation, Voltaire defined toleration:

> Do I propose, then, that every citizen shall be free to follow his own reason, and believe whatever his enlightened or deluded reason

---

* This was in an *Apologie de Louis XIV* (1762), by the Abbé de Caveyrac. Many Catholic clergymen condemned this book.[54]

† "The Lutheran and Calvinist preachers would probably be as little inclined to pity, as obdurate and intolerant, as they upbraid their antagonists with being. The barbarous law whereby any Roman Catholic is forbidden to reside more than three days in certain countries is not yet revoked."—*Essay on Free Toleration*, in *Works*, XXIa, 257. Cf. Voltaire's denunciation of the intolerant Huguenot Jurieu in the article "David" in the *Dictionnaire philosophique*.

shall dictate to him? Certainly, provided he does not disturb the public order. . . . If you insist that it is a crime not to believe in the dominant religion, you condemn the first Christians, your forefathers; and you justify those whom you reproach with persecuting them. . . . For a government to have the right to punish the errors of men it is necessary that their errors should take the form of crime. They do not take the form of crime unless they disturb society. They disturb society when they engender fanaticism. Hence men must avoid fanaticism in order to deserve toleration.[56]

Voltaire concluded with an address to the Deity:

Thou hast not given us hearts to hate, nor hands to kill, one another. Grant that we may aid one another to support the burden of this painful and transitory life! May the trifling differences in the garments that cover our frail bodies, in the mode of expressing our . . . thoughts, in our ridiculous customs and imperfect laws . . . —in a word, may the slight variations that are found amongst the atoms called men not be used by us as signals of mutual hatred and persecution! . . . May all men remember that they are brothers![57]

We do not know what share this appeal had in leading to the edict of toleration issued by Louis XVI in 1787; nor whether it reached or moved the ministers of Louis XV. In any case, after delays that tried the souls of the Calas family and their defenders, the King's Council, on March 9, 1765, declared the condemnation of Jean Calas annulled, and pronounced him innocent; and Choiseul obtained from the King a grant of thirty thousand livres as compensation to the widow and her children for the loss of their property. When the news of the verdict reached Ferney, Voltaire wept with joy.

Meanwhile (March 19, 1764) a municipal court at Mazamet, in south-central France, ordered Pierre Paul Sirven and his wife to be hanged on the charge of murdering their daughter Élisabeth to prevent her conversion to Catholicism. The judgment decreed that the two surviving daughters must witness the execution of their parents.[58] The ceremony had to be performed in effigy, for the family had fled to Geneva (April, 1762), and had told their story to Voltaire.

Sirven was a Protestant living in Castres, some forty miles east of Toulouse. On March 6, 1760, the youngest daughter, Élisabeth, disappeared. The parents sought for her in vain. The bishop of Castres summoned them, and informed them that he had sent the girl to a convent after she had confided to him her desire to become a Catholic. French law, established under Louis XIV, allowed Catholic authorities to remove from the parents, if necessary by force, any child above the age of seven who asked for conversion. In the convent Élisabeth had delusions, spoke to angels, tore the clothes from her body, and begged to be flogged. The nuns, at a loss for ways to handle her, notified the bishop, who ordered her restored to her parents.

In July, 1761, the family moved to St.-Abby, fifty miles from Castres. There, one night in December, Élisabeth left her room, and did not return. On January 3 her corpse was found in a well. The people of St.-Abby were not inclined to charge the Sirvens with murder. Of forty-five witnesses called before the local court, all without exception expressed the opinion that the girl had committed suicide, or had fallen into the well by accident. The local prosecutor, Trinquier, sent notice of the case to the prosecutor general in Toulouse, who instructed him to proceed on the assumption that Sirven was guilty. This seemed improbable, for Sirven had been out of town on the night of Élisabeth's disappearance. His wife was old and weak. One of the daughters was pregnant. It was hardly likely that these women could have pushed the girl into a well without a cry being heard. But on January 20 Trinquier ordered Sirven's arrest.

Sirven knew that some two months previously the municipal court of Toulouse had condemned Jean Calas to death on a similar charge, and on dubious evidence. Ultimately his own case, if he submitted to arrest and trial, would come before the Parlement of Toulouse. Having no confidence in these courts, he led his wife and daughters, in midwinter, across France and over the Cévennes Mountains to Geneva, hoping that the defender of Calas would come to his aid.

Voltaire, still immersed in his campaign for Calas, thought it unwise to confuse the French mind with two causes at once. He contributed to the support of the family, whose property had been confiscated. But when the Toulouse authorities dragged their feet in responding to the demand for the Calas documents, Voltaire resumed the attack by beginning a campaign for Sirven. Again he appealed for help and funds; contributions came from Frederick II of Prussia and Christian VII of Denmark, and again from Catherine II of Russia and Stanislas Poniatowski, King of Poland. The Mazamet court refused Voltaire's request for a copy of the trial record. We must not detail the struggle in this case; it went on till finally, in 1771, the Parlement of Toulouse reversed the verdict of the lower court, pronounced the Sirvens innocent, and restored their property. "It took two hours to condemn this man to death," said Voltaire, "and nine years to render justice to his innocence."[59]

Amid these labors he was alarmed to learn that he himself was involved in a case that had flared up at Abbeville on the Channel Coast. On the night of August 8–9, 1765, a wooden crucifix on the Pont-Neuf over the Somme was mutilated, and a crucifix in the Cemetery of St.-Catherine was smeared with ordure. When these profanations were discovered the clergy and people of the town were horrified. The bishop of Amiens came to Abbeville and, barefoot, led a procession which nearly all the population followed, begging forgiveness of God. A *monitoire* was read in all the churches decreeing severe penalties for all who could shed light on the mystery and failed to come forward. Magistrate Duval heard seventy-seven witnesses. Some of them testified that they had noticed three young men pass a Corpus Christi procession without either bending a knee or removing their hats. Others alleged that a band of youths in Abbeville, including Duval's son, made a practice of burlesquing religious ceremonies and singing licentious songs.[60] On August 26 warrants were issued for Gaillard d'Étallonde, for Chevalier Jean François Lefebre de La Barre, and for a youth of seventeen known to history only as Moisnel. D'Étallonde fled to Prussia, Moisnel and La Barre were arrested. Moisnel won partial pardon by confessing that he and the others were guilty of the acts alleged. He accused La Barre of having spat upon pictures of the saints, of having sung an obscene litany called "La Madeleine," of having lent him the *Dictionnaire philosophique* and *Epître à Uranie* of Voltaire; and he claimed to have seen d'Étallonde strike the crucifix on the bridge and sully the cross in the cemetery.

La Barre was the grandson of an impoverished general. He confessed to being a heretic. A witness reported that La Barre, on being asked why he had not removed his hat before the Corpus Christi procession, had replied that he "regarded the Host as a piece of wax," and could not understand why anyone would adore a God of dough. La Barre admitted that he might have said something of the kind; he had (he said) heard other young men express such sentiments, and thought he might harmlessly hold them, too. His library was examined; among his books were Voltaire's *Dictionnaire*, Helvétius' *De l'Esprit*, and other volumes satirizing religion. At first he disclaimed all knowledge of d'Étallonde's desecrations, but when he learned that Moisnel had revealed them, he confessed that it was true. The final indictment charged La Barre with "uttering blasphemies against God, the Holy Eucharist, the Holy Virgin, the religion and commandments of God and of the Church; singing two songs filled with execrable and abominable blasphemies, . . . rendering marks of adoration and respect to infamous books; profaning the sign of the cross, the mystery of the consecration of the wine, and the benedictions in use in churches and among Christians."[61]

On February 28, 1766, the Abbeville court pronounced sentence. La Barre, and d'Étallonde if apprehended, were to be put to the torture to elicit the names of accomplices; they were to do public penance before the principal church of the city; their tongues were to be torn out by the roots, they were then to be beheaded, and their bodies were to be burned to ashes. The *Dictionnaire philosophique* of Voltaire was to be thrown into the same fire. The sentence was appealed to the Parlement of Paris. Some members pleaded for mitigation; Councilor Pasquier replied that a signal and frightening punishment was needed to stem the tide of godlessness that was threatening all moral and social stability; the real criminal, he argued, was Voltaire, but as that source of the evil was beyond reach of the Parlement, his disciple should suffer in his stead. Two members voted to commute the sentence; fifteen voted for its full execution. On July 1, 1766, it was carried out, except that there was no tearing out of the tongue. La Barre bore his fate without implicating any of his friends. The executioner severed the head with a well-directed blow, to the applause of the crowd.[62]

Voltaire was shocked by the severity of the punishment; this, he felt, was a barbarity worthy of the Spanish Inquisition at its worst. The bishop of Annecy wrote to the French court demanding that all the penalties prescribed in the Revocation of the Edict of Nantes be applied to Voltaire. "That rascally bishop," wrote Voltaire to d'Alembert, "still swears . . . that he will have me burned in this world or the other. . . . To escape being burned I am laying in a supply of holy water."[63] Fearing that he might be summoned before the Parlement of Dijon, he took the opportunity to try the medicinal waters at Rolle in Switzerland. Then he returned to Ferney, and resumed his efforts for Sirven.

Now he proposed to d'Alembert and Diderot that he and they and other *philosophes* leave benighted France and settle in Cleves under the protection of Frederick the Great. Neither they nor Frederick enthused over the plan. Frederick agreed that the punishment of La Barre was extreme; for his part he would rather have condemned the youth to read the entire *Summa theologica* of Thomas Aquinas; this, he thought, would be a fate worse than death. Frederick proceeded to give Voltaire a bit of advice:

> The scene which has occurred at Abbeville is tragic, but was there not some fault in those who were punished? Should we directly attack the prejudices that time has consecrated in the mind of nations? And if we wish to enjoy liberty of thought, must we insult established belief? A man who does not wish to make a disturbance is rarely persecuted. Remember Fontenelle's saying: "If my hand were full of truths, I should think more than once before opening it."[64]

As to the proposed colony of *philosophes* at Cleves, Frederick offered protection, but on condition that they keep the peace and respect the faith of the people. He added:

The average man does not deserve to be enlightened. . . . If the philosophers were to form a government, the people, after 150 years, would forge some new superstition, and would either pray to little idols, or to the graves in which the great men were buried, or invoke the sun, or commit some similar nonsense. Superstition is a weakness of the human mind, which is inseparably tied up with it; it has always existed, and always will.[65]

Voltaire persisted in his campaign. He sent forth a simple *Narrative of the Death of the Chevalier de La Barre*. He wrote to his royal friends asking them to intercede with Louis XV to have the dead youth in some way rehabilitated; and when these efforts failed he sent to Louis XVI (1775) a letter entitled "The Cry of Innocent Blood." The judgment against La Barre was never reversed, but Voltaire had the satisfaction of seeing Turgot revise the criminal code that had sanctioned the execution of a youth for offenses that seemed to merit something less than decapitation. With an energy remarkable at his age, Voltaire continued to the end of his life to lead the crusade against the excesses of Church and state. In 1764 he secured the liberation of Claude Chaumont, who had been condemned to the galleys for attending Protestant services. When Comte Thomas de Lally, the French commander who had been defeated by the English in India, was beheaded in Paris (1766) on charges of treason and cowardice, Voltaire, appealed to by Lally's son, wrote a 300-page volume, *Historical Fragments on India*, exonerating the Count; and he urged Mme. du Barry to intercede with Louis XV. The sentence was annulled in 1778, shortly before Voltaire's death.

These labors exhausted the octogenarian warrior, but they made him the hero of liberal France. Diderot remarked, in *Le Neveu de Rameau*, "[Voltaire's] *Mahomet* is a sublime work, but I would like better to have vindicated Calas."[66] Pomaret, a Protestant minister in Geneva, said to Voltaire: "You seem to attack Christianity, and yet you do the work of a Christian."[67] And Frederick, after all his cautions, joined in the tributes to the man who had made himself the conscience of Europe: "How splendid it is that a philosopher makes his voice heard from his refuge, and that the human race, whose spokesman he is, forces the judges to revise an unjust sentence. If nothing else spoke in favor of M. de Voltaire, this alone would be enough to earn him a place among the benefactors of mankind."[68]

VI. *ÉCRASEZ L'INFÂME!*

It was in the ardor of these struggles that Voltaire's opposition to Christianity became a hatred that almost consumed a decade of his life (1759–

69). He had begun with a youthful scorn of the miracles, mysteries, and myths that comforted the people; and he passed on to a mocking skepticism of those Christian doctrines, like the Trinity, the Incarnation, and the Atonement, which St. Thomas Aquinas had frankly confessed to be beyond the reach of reason. But these moods of rebellion were natural in an active mind feeling the sap of growth; Voltaire might have passed through them to the man of the world's genial connivance at beliefs so dear to the masses and so useful as an aid to social order and moral discipline. In the first half of the eighteenth century the French clergy were relatively tolerant, and the hierarchy shared in the advancing Enlightenment. But the growth of unbelief, and the acclaim that greeted the *Encyclopédie*, frightened them, and they seized upon the terror inspired in the King by Damiens' attempt at assassination (1757) to draw from the state an edict (1759) making any attack upon the Church a crime to be punished with death. The *philosophes* saw in this a declaration of war, and felt that henceforth they need spare no feelings, no traditions, in attacking what seemed to them a murderous absurdity. Behind the beauty and poetry of religion they saw propaganda conscripting art; behind the support that Christianity had given to morality they saw a thousand heretics burned at the stake, the Albigensians crushed out in a homicidal crusade, Spain and Portugal darkened with autos-da-fé, France torn apart by rival mythologies, and all the future of the human spirit subject in every land to the repeated resurrection of superstition, priestcraft, and persecution. They would fight such a medieval reaction with the last years of their life.

Three events made the year 1762 a turning point in the irrepressible conflict. In March the execution of Jean Calas seemed to announce the return of France to the Middle Ages and the Inquisition. The trial, torture, and murder were all conducted by the "secular arm," but against the background of popular fanaticism engendered by religious indoctrination, ceremony, and hate. In May Rousseau's *Émile* gave to the world the "Profession of Faith of the Savoyard Vicar," which, though written by an opponent of the *philosophes*, swept away from Christianity almost everything but belief in God and the ethics of Christ. The burning of the book on June 11 in Paris and on June 19 in Geneva seemed to unite Catholicism and Calvinism in a conspiracy against the human mind. In August the condemnation of the Jesuits by the Paris Parlement was apparently a triumph for the *philosophes*, but it was also a victory for the Jansenists who controlled the Parlements of Paris, Toulouse, and Rouen; and the actions of the *parlements* in the cases of Calas and La Barre made it clear that the Jansenists were as bitter enemies of intellectual freedom as any in the history of France. Meanwhile the hostility between the *parlements* and the court, and the growing ascendancy (1758–70) of the semi-Voltairean

Choiseul in the government, gave the *philosophes* an opportunity to fight back with less than their usual danger from state censors and the police. The stage was set for the climax of the attack upon Christianity.

Now Voltaire spread and shouted the watchword of his ire, "*Écrasez l'infâme!* Crush the infamy!" He had begun to use the phrase in 1759; henceforth he repeated it a hundred times and in a dozen forms; occasionally he used it as a signature.[69] A fresh vitality came to the sixty-eight-year-old Voltaire as he likened himself to Cato Senex crying out, at the end of his speeches to the Roman Senate, "*Delenda est Carthago! Deleatur Carthago!*" "I have the colic," he wrote, "I suffer much; but when I attack *l'infâme* my pain is relieved."[70] With almost youthful enthusiasm, with incredible confidence, he set himself and a few hesitant aides to assail the most powerful institution in the history of mankind.

What did he mean by "the infamy"? Did he propose to crush superstition, fanaticism, obscurantism, and persecution? Or was he undertaking to destroy the Catholic Church, or all forms of Christianity, or all religion itself? Hardly the last, for we find him again and again, even amid the campaign, professing his theistic faith, sometimes in terms warm with Voltairean piety. In the *Dictionnaire philosophique* he defined religion indirectly: "Almost everything that goes beyond the adoration of a Supreme Being, and of submitting one's heart to his eternal orders, is superstition."[71] This would seem to reject all forms of Christianity except Unitarianism. Voltaire repudiated nearly all the distinctive doctrines of traditional Christianity—original sin, Trinity, Incarnation, Atonement, Eucharist; he ridiculed the "sacrifice" of God to God on the Cross, or by the priest in the Mass. Consequently he rejected most forms of Protestantism too; he reckoned Calvinism to be as obscurantist as Catholicism, and shocked the Genevan pastors by calling Calvin "*atroce.*" He thought he could live contentedly under the Established Church as he had seen it in England. He wrote to d'Alembert "I hope you will destroy *l'infâme;* that is the great point. It must be reduced to the state it has in England; and you will reach this end if you wish. This is the greatest service which we can render to the human race."[72] We may conclude that by *l'infâme* he meant not religion in general, but religion as organized to propagate superstition and mythology, to control education, and to oppose dissent with censorship and persecution. And such was Christianity as Voltaire saw it in history and in France.

So he burned all his bridges behind him, and called his cohorts to war. "To overturn the columns only five or six *philosophes* are needed who understand one another. . . . The vine of truth has been cultivated by the d'Alemberts, the Diderots, the Bolingbrokes, and the Humes,"[73] but too sporadically, and without consistent plan. Now they must unite, and he takes it for granted that he will be their general. He advises them on tactics: "Strike, and hide your hand. . . . I hope that every year each of our fraternity will aim some arrows at the monster, without its learning from whose hand they came."[74] Let the brothers insinuate themselves into the academies, into posts of authority, if possible into the ministry. They need not convert the masses, they need only convert those men of initiative and power who lead the masses; see how one man, Peter the Great, changed the soul and face of Russia. And so Voltaire tried to enlist Frederick in the cause (January 5, 1767):

> Sire, you are perfectly right: a wise and courageous prince, with money, troops, and laws, can quite well govern men without the aid of religion, which was made only to deceive them. . . . Your Majesty will do the human race an eternal service by extirpating this infamous superstition. I do not say among the rabble, who are not worthy of being enlightened, and who are apt for every yoke; I say among honest people, among men who think, among those who wish to think. . . . 'Tis for you to feed their minds. . . . My one regret in dying is that I cannot aid you in this noble enterprise.[75]

Frederick smiled at the old man's naïveté, but Voltaire persisted, and not without some effect, as we may later see, on the cabinet ministers of France, Portugal, and Spain.

He welcomed lesser aides. He wrote apostolic exhortations to Bordes in Lyons, to Servan in Grenoble, to Pierre Rousseau in Bouillon, to Audibert in Marseilles, to Ribaute in Montauban, to the Marquis d'Argence in Charente, to the Abbé Audra in Toulouse. All these and others he called "*les frères*," the brethren; to them he sent material and appeals, prodding them lest they sleep on their arms.

> Attack, brothers, skillfully, all of you, *l'infâme*. What interests me is the propagation of the faith and of truth, the progress of philosophy, the suppression of *l'infâme*.

> Drink to my health with brother Plato [Diderot], and *écrasez l'infâme*.

> I embrace all my brethren. My health is pitiable. *Écrasez l'infâme*.

> I embrace my brethren in Confucius, . . . in Lucretius, in Cicero, in Socrates, in Marcus Aurelius, in Julian, and in the communion of all our patriarchs.

> My tender benediction to all the brethren. *Orate fratres, et vigilate* [pray, brothers, and watch]. *Écrasez l'infâme*.[76]

Now books became weapons, and literature became war. Not only did Diderot, d'Alembert, Helvétius, d'Holbach, Raynal, Morellet, and a dozen others bring their pens to the battle, but Voltaire himself, always dying, became a veritable armory of anticlerical missiles. Within a decade he sent forth some thirty booklets. He had no belief in the efficacy of large volumes.

> What harm can a book [the *Encyclopédie*] do that costs a hundred crowns? . . . Twenty volumes folio will never create a revolution. It is the little portable volumes of thirty sous that are to be feared. If the Gospel had cost 1200 sesterces the Christian religion would never have been established.[77]

So he poured forth not merely histories and plays but pamphlets, stories, sermons, "instructions," catechisms, diatribes, dialogues, letters, short critiques of the Bible or of Church history, anything that could circulate easily and prick the *infâme*. People called these productions *petits pâtés*—cookies, easy to digest. Long ago Frederick had written to him:

> I imagine that somewhere in France there is a select society of superior and equal geniuses who all work together and publish their writings under the name of Voltaire. . . . If this supposition is true I shall become a Trinitarian, and shall begin to see daylight in this mystery which the Christians have hitherto believed without understanding.[78]

But now Voltaire did not write in the name of Voltaire. He used over a hundred different pseudonyms; and sometimes, in his impish humor, he ascribed his anti-Christian blasts to "the Archbishop of Canterbury" or "the Archbishop of Paris," or an abbé, a pastor, or a monk. To throw the hounds of heaven off his trail he dedicated one of his pellets to himself. He knew printers in Paris, Amsterdam, the Hague, London, and Berlin; he used them in his campaign. Through Damilaville and others he had his brochures given free to booksellers, who sold them at low price and calculated risk. The seed went forth.

He published now (1762) that *Sermon des cinquantes*, or *Sermon of the Fifty*, which he had written at least ten years before and had read to Frederick at Potsdam. It was his first direct attack upon Christianity. It began quite innocently:

> Fifty persons, educated, pious, and reasonable [the Quakers in London?], assembled every Sunday in a populous commercial city. They prayed, and one of them pronounced a discourse; then they dined;

then they took up a collection for the poor. Each presided in turn, led the prayer, and pronounced the sermon. This is one of the prayers, and one of the sermons. . . .

God of all the globes and stars, . . . keep us from all superstition. If we insult you by unworthy sacrifices, abolish these infamous mysteries. If we dishonor the Divinity by absurd fables, may these fables perish forever. . . . Let men live and die in the worship of one sole God, . . . a God who could neither be born nor die.[79]

The sermon argued that the God revealed in the Old Testament is a boastful, jealous, angry, cruel, homicidal God, whom no sane person could worship, and that David was a scoundrel, a lecher, and a murderer. How could anyone believe such a book to be the word of God? And how from the Gospels could have come the incredible theology of Christianity, the easy, daily feat of turning a wafer into the body and blood of Christ, the innumerable relics, the sale of indulgences, the hatreds and holocausts of the religious wars?

We are told that the people need mysteries, and must be deceived. My brethren, dare anyone commit this outrage on humanity? Have not our fathers [the Reformers] taken from the people their transubstantiation, auricular confession, indulgences, exorcisms, false miracles, and ridiculous statues? Are not our people now accustomed to doing without these superstitions? We must have the courage to go a few steps further. The people are not so weak in mind as is supposed; they will easily admit a wise and simple cult of one God. . . . We seek not to despoil the clergy of what the liberality of their followers has given them; we wish them—since most of them secretly laugh at the falsehoods they teach—to join us in preaching the truth. . . . What incalculable good would be done by that happy change![80]

All this is tiresome to us today, but it was revolutionary material in eighteenth-century France. No wonder Voltaire sent it forth under the pretense that it had been written by La Mettrie, who was safely dead.

In 1763 the warrior diverted himself with dramas, a worthless short story called "Blanc et noir," and a little *Catéchisme de l'honnête homme* retailing his "natural religion." But 1764 was a major year: Voltaire kept his printers busy with *L'Évangile de la raison*, and *Examen de la religion* (a modified edition of Jean Meslier's fiery *Testament*), and one of his most important publications: *Dictionnaire philosophique portatif*. It was not the immense tome of 824 large double-column pages that we have in one form today, or the five or eight volumes that it fills in his collected works; it was a small book, easy to hold or to conceal. The brevity of its articles, the simplicity and clarity of its style, carried it to a million readers in a dozen lands.

It is a remarkable production for one man. There are probably a thousand errors in it, but the vast accumulation of data, the erudition in almost every field, make the book one of the miracles in the history of literature. What industry, loquacity, pertinacity! Voltaire gossips; he has something to say on nearly everything, and almost always something of still-living interest. There are here many bits of frivolity, triviality, or superficiality; there are some foolish remarks ("The intellect of Europe has made greater progress in the last one hundred years than in the whole world before since the days of Brahma and Zoroaster");[81] but no man can be wise through a thousand pages, and no other man has ever been brilliant so long. Even etymologies are given, for Voltaire, like every curious reader, was attracted by the tribulations that words have suffered in their travels through time and space. And here, in the article "Abuse of Words"—and again in the article "Miracles"—is the famous Voltairean imperative "Define your terms!"

Essentially the book aimed to serve as an arsenal of arguments against Christianity as Voltaire knew it. Here once more are the incredibilities, absurdities, and scandals of the Bible, not only in the article "Contradictions," but on almost every page. Who gave the Church the authority to pronounce "canonical" and God-inspired four of the fifty gospels that were written in the century after the death of Jesus? What a revealing oversight it was to speak of the Virgin Birth of Jesus and yet trace his genealogy to that rascal David through the allegedly *fainéant* Joseph! Why did Christianity reject the Mosaic Law despite Christ's repeated confirmation of it? Was Paul, who rejected that Law (because of a little piece of skin) a greater authority than Christ?

The city fathers of Geneva did not like the *Dictionnaire philosophique;* on September 24, 1763, the Council of Twenty-five ordered the executioner to burn every copy that he could find. The Parlement of Paris ordered a similar bonfire in 1765; we have seen the fate of the book in Abbeville (1766). Voltaire assured the Genevan authorities that the *Dictionary* was the work of a corps of writers entirely unknown to him. Meanwhile he prepared supplementary articles for the four further editions that were secretly printed before the end of 1765, and he poured new material into the five additional editions that appeared before his death in 1778. He arranged with the conniving booksellers of Geneva to supply them with as many free copies as they could distribute, and with salesmen to leave copies at private doors.[82]

He continued the war with intensified passion in the years 1765–67. In 1764 he had finally abandoned his house at Les Délices in a Geneva too hot for his heresies; for almost three years he hardly stirred from his property at Ferney; and nearly every month he sent to some printer a new pamphlet against *l'infâme*. *Les Questions de Zapata* (March, 1767) pretended to be the queries put to a committee of theologians by a professor of theology at the University of Salamanca in 1629. Zapata confessed to doubts about the Star of Bethlehem, the supposed census of "the whole earth" by Augustus, the slaughter of the innocents, and the temptation of Jesus by Satan on a hill whence one could see all the kingdoms of the earth." Where was that wonderful hill? Why had not Christ kept his promise to "come in a cloud, with power and great glory," to establish the "kingdom of God" before "this generation shall pass away?"[83] What had detained him? "Was the fog too thick?"[84] "What must I do with those who dare to doubt? . . . Must I, for their edification, have the ordinary and extraordinary question [torture] put to them?" Or "would it not be better to avoid these labyrinths, and simply preach virtue?"[85] The conclusion:

> Zapata, receiving no answer, took to preaching God in all simplicity. He announced to men the common father, the rewarder, the punisher, the pardoner. He extricated the truth from the lies, and separated religion from fanaticism; he taught and practiced virtue. He was gentle, kindly, and modest, and he was burned at Valladolid in the year of grace 1631.[86]

In May, 1767, Voltaire returned to the attack more vigorously in a work of 105 pages, *Examen important de milord Bolingbroke;* here he put his arguments into the mouth of the dead Englishman, but Bolingbroke would probably have accepted the imposition. In the same year Voltaire published *L'Ingénu,* a delightful 100-page story of an unbelievably virtuous Huron Indian brought to France from America, and confused by European customs and Christian theology. In 1769 came *Le Cri des nations*—an appeal to Catholic Europe to throw off the alleged sovereignty of popes over kings and states. Again in that year he sallied forth with a studious but impassioned *Histoire du Parlement,* condemning that body as a conspiracy of Jansenist reactionaries. And in 1770–72 he issued nine volumes as *Questions sur l'Encyclopédie,* a mélange of articles constituting another one-man encyclopedia, even more pointedly anti-Catholic than the *Portatif.*

Usually he disguised his publications with deceptive titles: *Homily on the Interpretation of the Old Testament, Epistle to the Romans, Sermons of the Rev. Jacques Rossetes, Homily of Pastor Bourne, Counsels to the Fathers of Families.* The educated public of France guessed that Voltaire had written them, for he could not disguise his style, but no one proved it. This exciting game became the talk of Paris and Geneva, and its echoes were heard in London, Amsterdam, Berlin, even in Vienna. Never in history had a writer played such hide-and-seek with such powerful enemies, and with such success. A hundred opponents tried to answer him; he rebutted them all, fighting back roughly, sometimes coarsely or unfairly; *c'était la guerre*. And he enjoyed it. In the ardor of battle he forgot to die.

Indeed, a strange new optimism came upon him, he who had seemed, after the Lisbon earthquake and *Candide*, to advise surrender to the evils of life as invincible. He dreamed of "philosophy" victorious over a Church entrenched in the needs of the people. If twelve unlettered fishermen had established Christianity, why could not twelve *philosophes* shake it out of its dogmas and Inquisitions? "Live happy and *écrasez l'infâme*," he wrote to one of the "brothers," and he assured them, "We will crush it!"[87] Were not a king, an empress, a royal mistress, and many other prominent persons openly or secretly on his side? He courted the court by attacking the Parlement of Paris; he enjoyed the favor of Mme. de Pompadour, and later of Mme. du Barry; he even hoped for the connivance of Louis XV. He wrote to d'Alembert in 1767: "Let us bless this happy revolution which has been produced in the minds of all honest men in the last fifteen or twenty years; it has surpassed my hopes."[88] Had he not foretold it? Had he not written to Helvétius, in 1760: "This century begins to see the triumph of reason"?[89]

VII. RELIGION AND REASON

He was not so simple as to imagine that religion had been invented by priests. On the contrary he wrote, in the *Dictionnaire philosophique:*

> The idea of a god is derived from feeling, and that natural logic which unfolds itself with age, even in the rudest of mankind. Astonishing effects of nature were beheld—harvests and barrenness, fair weather and storms, benefits and scourges; and the hand of a [supernatural] master was felt. . . . The first sovereigns in their time used these notions to cement their power.[90]

Each group singled out one of the supernatural powers as its tutelary deity, and gave him adoration and sacrifices in the hope that he would protect the group against the power and gods of other groups. Priests had been produced by these beliefs, but the interpretations and rituals were the work of the priests. In the course of time priests played upon human fear to extend their power. They committed all kinds of knavery, extending at last to the murder of "heretics," the assassination of whole groups, and the near-ruin of nations. Voltaire concluded: "I hated priests, I hate them, I shall hate them till doomsday."[91]

He found much that he could accept in non-Christian religions, especially in Confucianism (which was not a religion); but very little in Christian theology pleased him. "I have two hundred volumes on this subject,
and, what is worse, I have read them. It is like going the rounds of a lunatic
asylum."[92] He added little to previous Biblical criticism; his function was to
spread it, and the effect is with us still. With more audacity than most of
his predecessors, he emphasized again and again the absurdity of Noah's
Deluge, the passage of the Red Sea, the slaughter of the innocents, and
so forth; and he never tired of denouncing the story and theory of "original sin." He quoted with indignation St. Augustine's dictum, "The Catholic faith teaches that all men are born so guilty that even infants are certainly damned when they die without having been regenerated in Jesus."[93]
(We are now informed that such infants go to a pleasantly warm place
called Limbo, next door to hell.)

As to Jesus, Voltaire vacillated. From the natural piety of childhood he
passed to youthful irreverencies, even to accepting the story of Mary's
affair with a Roman soldier; and at one time he thought of Jesus as a deluded fanatic—"*un fou.*"[94] As he matured he learned to admire the ethical
precepts of Jesus; we shall be saved by practicing those principles, he said,
rather than by believing that Christ was God. He made much fun of the
Trinity in *The Atheist and the Sage*. The atheist asks, "Do you believe
that Jesus Christ has one nature, one person, and one will, or two natures,
two persons, and two wills, or one will, one nature, and two persons, or two
wills, two persons, and one nature, or—" but the sage bids him forget such
puzzles and be a good Christian.[95] Voltaire points out that Christ, unlike St.
Paul and subsequent Christians, remained faithful to Judaism, despite his
criticism of the Pharisees:

> This Eternal God, having made himself a Jew, adheres to the Jewish
> religion during the whole of his life. He performs its functions, he
> frequents the Jewish Temple, he announces nothing contrary to
> Jewish Law. All his disciples are Jews and observe the Jewish cere-
> monies. It is certainly not he who established the Christian religion.
> . . . There is not a single dogma [characteristic] of Christianity that
> was preached by Jesus Chirst.[96]

Jesus, in Voltaire's view, accepted the belief of many pious Jews before
him that the world as they knew it was coming to an end, and would soon
be replaced by the "Kingdom of Heaven"—i.e., the direct rule of God on
earth. (Modern criticism accepts this view.)

In his final years Voltaire responded more and more warmly to the
story of Christ. He began to call him "my brother," "my master."[97] He
pictured himself as transported in a dream into a desert covered with heaps

of bones; here the remains of 300,000 massacred Jews, there four mounds of Christians "strangled because of metaphysical disputes"; and piles of gold and silver topped with the croziers and crowns of disintegrated prelates and kings. Then his guiding angel took him into a green valley, where lived the great sages; there he saw Numa Pompilius, Pythagoras, Zoroaster, Thales, Socrates . . . Finally

> I advanced with my guide into a grove higher than that in which the sages of antiquity tasted a pleasant repose. I saw a man of sweet and simple aspect, who seemed to me some thirty-five years old; his feet and hands swollen and bleeding, his side pierced, his flesh torn with blows of a whip. There was no comparison between the sufferings of this sage and those of Socrates.

Voltaire asked him the cause of his death. Jesus replied, "Priests and judges." Had he intended to found a new religion? No. Was he responsible for those mountains of bones, those masses of royal or sacerdotal gold? No; "I and mine lived in the humblest poverty." Then in what did true religion consist? "Have I not told you before? Love God, and love your neighbor as yourself." "If this is the case," said Voltaire, "I take you for my sole master." "He made me a sign that filled me with consolation. The vision disappeared, and I was left with my conscience at peace."[98]

But that was a later mood. In his war years Voltaire saw the history of Christianity as predominantly a misfortune for mankind. The mysticism of Paul, the fables of Gospels canonical or apocryphal, the legends of martyrs and miracles, and the strategy of priestcraft combined with the hopeful credulity of the poor to produce the Christian Church. Then the Fathers of the Church formulated the doctrine in eloquence capable of satisfying middle-class minds. Bit by bit the light of classic culture was dimmed by the spread of childish imaginations and pious frauds, until darkness settled for centuries upon the European mind. Meditative men, lazy men, men shrinking from the challenges and responsibilities of life, crept into monasteries and infected one another with neurotic dreams of women, devils, and gods. Learned councils assembled to debate whether one absurdity or another should become part of the infallible creed. The Church, basing its power on the popular appetite for consolatory myths, became stronger than the state basing its authority on organized force; the power of the sword became dependent upon the power of the word; popes deposed emperors, and absolved nations from loyalty to their kings.

In Voltaire's view the Protestant Reformation was only a halting step toward reason. He applauded the revolt against monastic mendicants, indulgence peddlers, and moneygrubbing ecclesiastics who in some cases "absorbed the whole revenue of a province;" in northern Europe the "people adopted a cheaper religion."[99] But he was revolted by the emphasis placed by Luther and Calvin on predestination;[100] imagine a ruler who condemned two thirds of his subjects to everlasting fire! Or consider the various Christian interpretations of the Eucharist: the Catholics profess that they eat God and not bread, the Lutherans eat both God and bread, the Calvinists eat bread but not God; "if anyone told us of a like extravagance or madness among Hottentots and Kaffirs, we should think we were being imposed upon."[101] The advance of reason is leaving such controversies far behind; "were Luther and Calvin to return to the world, they would make no more noise than the Scotists and the Thomists."[102] If Protestants continue to preach such a theology the educated classes will abandon them, while the masses will prefer the fragrant and colorful faith of Rome. Already, Voltaire surmised, "Calvinism and Lutheranism are in danger in Germany; that country is full of great bishoprics, sovereign abbacies and canonries, all proper for making conversions."[103]

Should religion, then, be altogether abandoned by reasonable men? No; a religion preaching God and virtue, and no other dogmas, would be of real service to mankind. In earlier years Voltaire had thought that "those who would need the help of religion to be good men are to be pitied," and that a society might live with a natural morality independent of supernatural beliefs.[104] But as he enlarged his experience of human passions he came to admit that no moral code could successfully withstand the primitive force of the individualistic instincts unless it was buttressed by popular belief that the code had its source and sanction in an all-seeing, rewarding, and punishing God. After agreeing with Locke that there are no innate ideas, he fell back upon Leibniz' contention that the moral sense is inborn, and he defined it as a sentiment of justice placed in us by God. "Laws watch over known crimes, religion over secret crimes."[105] Says the sage in *The Atheist and the Sage*:

> I will presume (God forbid it!) that all Englishmen are atheists. I will allow that there may be some peaceable citizens, quiet by nature, rich enough to be honest, regulated by honor, and so attentive to demeanor that they contrive to live together in society. . . . But the poor and needy atheist, sure of impunity, would be a fool if he did not assassinate or steal to get money. Then would all the bonds of society be sundered. All secret crimes would inundate the world, and, like locusts, though at first imperceptible, would overspread the earth. . . . Who would restrain great kings? . . . An atheist king is more dangerous than a fanatical Ravaillac. . . . Atheism abounded in Italy in the fifteenth century. What was the consequence? It was as com-

mon a matter to poison another as to invite him to supper. . . . Faith, then, in a God who rewards good actions, punishes the bad, and forgives lesser faults, is most useful to mankind.[106]

Finally Voltaire inclined to see some sense in the doctrine of hell:

> To those philosophers who in their writings deny a hell, I will say: "Gentlemen, we do not pass our days with Cicero, Atticus, Marcus Aurelius, Epictetus, . . . nor with the too scrupulously virtuous Spinoza, who, although laboring under poverty and destitution, gave back to the children of the Grand Pensionary de Witt an allowance of 300 florins which had been granted him by that great statesman— whose heart, it may be remembered, the Hollanders devoured. . . . In a word, gentlemen, all men are not philosophers. We are obliged to hold intercourse and transact business and mix up in life with knaves possessing little or no reflection, with a vast number of persons addicted to brutality, intoxication, and rapine. You may, if you please, preach to them that the soul of man is mortal. As for myself, I shall be sure to thunder in their ears that if they rob me they will inevitably be damned.[107]

We conclude that the Devil can quote Voltaire to his purpose. After appealing for a religion freed from fables,[108] the great skeptic ended preaching the worst fable of all. He had asked for a religion confined to the inculcation of morality;[109] now he admitted that common men cannot be kept from crime except by a religion of heaven and hell. The Church could claim that he had come to Canossa.

At the age of seventy-two he rephrased his faith under the chastened title *The Ignorant Philosopher* (1766). He confesses at the outset that he does not know what matter or mind is, nor how he thinks, nor how his thought can move his arm.[110] He asks himself a question that apparently never occurred to him before: "Is it necessary for me to know?" But he adds: "I cannot divest myself of a desire of being instructed; my baffled curiosity is ever insatiable."[111] He is now convinced that the will is not free; "the ignoramus who thinks thus did not always think so, but he is at length compelled to yield."[112] "Is there a God?" Yes, as the Intelligence behind "the order, the prodigious art, and the mechanical and geometrical laws that reign in the universe";[113] but this Supreme Intelligence is known to us only in his existence, not in his nature. "Miserable mortal! If I cannot understand my own intelligence, if I cannot know by what I am animated, how can I have any acquaintance with that ineffable intelligence which visibly presides over the universe? . . . But we are his work."[114] Voltaire is inclined to believe that there was never a creation in time, that the world has always existed, "has ever issued from that primitive and necessary cause, as light emanates from the sun," and that "nature has always been animated."[115] He still believes that there is design in the universe, a Providence that guides the whole but lets the part—including each human individual—shift for itself.[116] And he concludes: "If you tell me that I have taught you nothing, remember that I set out by informing you that I am ignorant."[117]

The perplexed philosopher began to envy those who had never thought but had only believed and hoped. And yet he came back to Socrates' view that a life without thought is unworthy of a man. He expressed his hovering between these views of life in *L'Histoire d'un bon Brahmin* (1761):

> In my travels I once happened to meet with an aged Brahmin. This man had great understanding, great learning, . . . and great wealth. . . .
>
> "I wish," he said to me one day, "I had never been born."
>
> "Why so?" I asked.
>
> "Because I have been studying these forty years, and I find it has been so much time lost. Though I teach others, I know nothing . . . I exist in time, without knowing what time is. I am placed, as our wise men say, in the confines between two eternities, and yet have no idea of eternity. I am composed of matter. I think, but I have never been able to satisfy myself what it is that produces thought. . . . I do not know why I exist, and yet I am applied to every day for a solution of the enigma. I must return an answer, but I can say nothing satisfactory on the subject. I talk a great deal, and when I have done speaking I remain confounded, and ashamed of what I have said." . . .
>
> The condition in which I saw this good man gave me real concern. . . . The same day I had a conversation with an old woman, his neighbor. I asked her if she had ever been unhappy for not understanding how her soul was made. She did not comprehend my question. She had not, for the briefest moment in her life, had a thought about these subjects with which the good Brahmin had so tormented himself. She believed from the bottom of her heart in the metamorphoses of her god Vishnu, and, provided she could get some of the sacred water of the Ganges in which to make her ablutions, she thought herself the happiest of women.
>
> Struck with the happiness of this poor creature, I returned to my philosopher, whom I thus addressed:
>
> "Are you not ashamed to be thus miserable when, not fifty yards from you, there is an old automaton who thinks of nothing and lives contented?"
>
> "You are right," he replied. "I have said to myself a thousand times that I should be happy if I were as ignorant as my old neighbors, and yet it is a happiness I do not desire."

The reply of the Brahmin made a greater impression upon me than anything that had passed. . . . I concluded that although we may set a great value upon happiness, we set a still greater value upon reason. But after mature reflection . . . I still thought there was great madness in preferring reason to happiness.[118]

VIII. VOLTAIRE *BIGOT*

In a similar mood Pascal had chosen to submit his logic-ridden intellect to the Catholic Church as an organization that through long experience had found a combination of doctrine and ritual helpful to morality and comforting to wonder and grief. Voltaire did not go so far, but in his seventies he moved confusedly in that direction.

He began by reconciling himself to the general desirability of some religion. When Boswell asked him (December 29, 1764), "Would you have no public worship?" Voltaire answered, "Yes, with all my heart. Let us meet four times a year in a great temple, with music, and thank God for all his gifts. There is one sun, there is one God; let us have one religion; then all mankind will be brethren."[119] The sun offered him, so to speak, a halfway house to God. In May, 1774, aged eighty, he rose before dawn, and climbed with a friend to see the sunrise from a nearby hill; perhaps he had been reading Rousseau. Reaching the top exhausted, and overwhelmed by the glory of the triumphant sun, he knelt and cried, "O mighty God, I believe!" But, the Voltaire in him rebounding, he said as he rose to his feet, "As to Monsieur the Son and Madame his mother, that is another matter!"[120]

Gradually he went further, and consented to allow a clergy, which would teach morality to the people and offer prayers to God.[121] He acknowledged that the bishops in France and England had done some good in organizing social order; but cardinals were too expensive, and should be dispensed with. He had a tender regard for the simple parish priest who kept the village register, helped the poor, and made peace in troubled families; these curés should be more respected, better paid, less exploited by their ecclesiastical superiors.[122] In generous moments the old penitent was willing to increase the religious assemblies from four times a year to once a month, even once a week.[123] There should be prayers and thanksgiving, acts of adoration, and lessons in morality; but no "sacrifice," no prayers of petition, and let the sermons be short! If you must have religious pictures or statues, let them commemorate not dubious saints but the heroes of humanity, like Henry IV (saving his mistresses). And no supernatural dogmas except the existence of a just God. The ecclesiastical organization should be subject to the state; the clergy should be trained and paid by the government.

Monasteries and convents might remain, but only as refuges for the old or sick. Like so many skeptics, Voltaire had a tender regard for the nuns who came out of their convents to help the sick and the poor. Seeing the Sisters of Charity in the hospitals of Paris, he had written, in the *Essai sur les moeurs:* "There is not, on all the earth, anything to equal the sacrifice of beauty, youth, and often high birth, which the gentle sex offers gladly in order to solace, in the hospitals, the welter of human suffering. . . . The nations separated from the Roman faith have but imperfectly copied so noble a charity."[124]

As "all the world knows," Voltaire built near his mansion at Ferney a little church over whose portal he proudly inscribed the words "*Deo erexit Voltaire*." "This," he claimed, "is the only church in the world dedicated to God alone; all the others are dedicated to saints."[125] He asked Rome to send him some sacred relics for his chapel; the Pope sent him a haircloth of St. Francis of Assisi. On the altar Voltaire placed a life-size gilded-metal statue of Christ, not as the crucified, but as a sage. There, from 1760 onward, he attended Mass every Sunday; he had himself censered as seigneur of the village; and at Easter, in 1768, he went to Communion.[126] He sent his servants to church regularly, and paid to have their children taught the catechism.[127]

Much of this piety may have been designed to give his villagers a good example, to encourage them in beliefs that might lessen their crimes and safeguard his property. He made sure that the court at Versailles should hear of his exemplary behavior, and perhaps he hoped that this would facilitate his campaigns for the Calas, the Sirvens, and La Barre, and his own return to Paris; and indeed the King and the Queen were pleased to hear of his reform. The Abbé de La Bletterie approved of Voltaire's taking the Sacrament, but remarked, on seeing the communicant's emaciation, that Voltaire had forgotten to have himself buried; to which Voltaire, bowing courteously, replied, "After you, monsieur."[128] On March 31, 1769, he summoned a notary and signed, before several witnesses, an affirmation that he wished to die in the Catholic religion.[129] The *frères* in Paris laughed at him; he bore their gibes good-humoredly.

After 1768 he adopted the monastic custom of having devotional works read to him at mealtime; for this purpose he preferred the sermons of Massillon; he could appreciate literature even when it came in a cassock. He had shared in the campaign against the Jesuits, but in 1770 he joined a lay association of the Capuchin friars, and received from the head of that order the title *père temporal des capucins de Gex*—the little county in which he was a feudal lord. He was quite proud of this honor, wrote a dozen letters about it, signed some letters "Frère Voltaire, *capucin indigne*." Frederick hailed him as a new saint of the Church, but informed him that the ecclesiastical authorities in Rome had in that same year burned some of the "unworthy Capuchin's" works.[130] It is difficult now to discern whether this rapprochement with the Church was sincere, or whether it was a peace offering to Versailles, or whether it was motived by fear lest his corpse be forbidden burial in consecrated ground—which included all the cemeteries in France. Perhaps all three motives played a part in the divine comedy.

In these final years, 1770–78, he devoted his pen rather to repudiating atheism then to attacking Christianity. Into the article "God" in the *Dictionnaire philosophique* he inserted two sections in refutation of d'Holbach's *Système de la nature*. In 1772 he composed a vigorous essay, *Il faut prendre un Parti* (*We Must Take Sides*), in which he argued for "God and toleration." He confessed to Mme. Necker, to the Duchesse de Choiseul, to Prince Frederick William of Prussia, his fear that the movement for religious toleration would be defeated by the advocacy of atheism. He regretted that his criticism of d'Holbach was endangering the solidarity of the *frères*, but he persisted: "I have no doubt that the author, and three supporters of this book, will become my implacable enemies for having spoken my thoughts; and I have declared to them that I will speak out as long as I breathe, without fearing either the fanatics of atheism or the fanatics of superstition."[131] The *holbachiens* retorted that the rich seigneur was playing politics with Versailles, and was using God to police his servants and peasants at Ferney.

In the last decade of his life the men whom he had once hailed and spurred on as brothers in the campaign against *l'infâme* looked upon him as a lost leader. Diderot had never loved him, had never taken to corresponding with him, had resented Voltaire's evident assumption that d'Alembert was the chief and soul of the *Encyclopédie*. Diderot applauded the defense of Calas, but he let slip a jealous line: "This man is never more than the second in all genres."[132] Voltaire did not share Diderot's revolutionary politics, nor his liking for the bourgeois drama of sentiment; the bourgeois become aristocrat could not relish the bourgeois contentedly bourgeois. Neither Diderot nor d'Holbach made the pilgrimage of devotion to Ferney. Grimm commented with undue severity on Voltaire's criticism of Hobbes and Spinoza: "The 'Ignorant Philosopher' has with difficulty skimmed the surface of these matters."[133] And now the atheists of Paris, growing in number and pride, turned their backs upon Voltaire. So early as 1765, even amid the battle against *l'infâme*, one of them dismissed him with scorn: "*Il est un bigot, c'est un déiste.*"[134]

Buffeted from both sides, the frail patriarch began, toward 1770, to lose faith in the prospects of victory. He called himself a "great destroyer" who had built nothing.[135] His new religion of "God and tolerance," he feared, would come only when rulers would accept the Abbé de Saint-Pierre's "project for perpetual peace"—i.e., probably never at all. He had long suspected the frailty of philosophy and the unattractiveness of reason. "No philosopher has influenced the manners of even the street he lived in."[136] He surrendered the masses to "superstition" or mythology. He hoped to win some "forty thousand sages" in France, and the educated strata of the middle class; but even this hope began to fade in the twilight of his years. "To enlighten the young, bit by bit"—this was all the dream that was left to him as he prepared, aged eighty-four, to see Paris and die. Perhaps, in the marvelous welcome that he was destined to receive there, his faith and hope in man would return.

Was he a philosopher? Yes, though he made no system, vacillated on everything, and too often remained on the surface of things. He was not a philosopher if the word means the maker of a system of unified and consistent thought about the world and man. He turned away from systems as the impudent sallies of the minuscle into the infinite. But he was a philosopher if that means a mind seriously occupied with the basic problems of nature, morals, government, life, and destiny. He was not considered profound, but perhaps that was because he was uncertain and clear. His ideas were seldom original, but in philosophy nearly all original ideas are foolish, and lack of originality is a sign of wisdom. Certainly the form that he gave to his ideas was original; Voltaire is without question the most brilliant writer that ever lived. Was he second in every field, as Diderot charged? Second in philosophy to Diderot, yes, and in drama to Corneille and Racine; but he was first and best in his time in his conception and writing of history, in the grace of his poetry, in the charm and wit of his prose, in the range of his thought and his influence. His spirit moved like a flame over the continent and the century, and stirs a million souls in every generation.

Perhaps he hated too much, but we must remember the provocation; we must imagine ourselves back in an age when men were burned at the stake, or broken on the wheel, for deviating from orthodoxy. We can appreciate Christianity better today than he could then, because he fought with some success to moderate its dogmas and violence. We can feel the power and splendor of the Old Testament, the beauty and elevation of the New, because we are free to think of them as the labor and inspiration of fallible men. We can be grateful for the ethics of Christ, because he no longer threatens us with hell, nor curses the men and cities that will not hear him.[137] We can feel the nobility of St. Francis of Assisi, because we are no longer asked to believe that St. Francis Xavier was heard in several languages while he spoke in one. We can feel the poetry and drama of religious ritual now that the transient triumph of toleration leaves us free to worship or abstain. We can accept a hundred legends as profound symbols or illuminating allegories, because we are no longer required to accept their literal truth. We have learned to sympathize with that which we once loved and had to leave, as we retain a tender memory for the loves of our youth. And to whom, more than to any other one man, do we owe this precious and epochal liberation? To Voltaire.

CHAPTER XXIII

The Triumph of the *Philosophes*

1715–89

I. THE CLERGY FIGHTS BACK

THERE was much to be said for Christianity, and its defenders said it with vigor, sometimes with blind misjudging of the age, sometimes with the grace and clarity that France expects even of theology. There were ecclesiastics who still insisted that any deviation from defined Catholic doctrine should be punished by the state, and that the Massacre of St. Bartholomew was as legitimate as surgery.[1] But there were others who took up the gage like gentlemen, and allowed the enemy to choose the weapon—reason. It was a gallant gesture, for when a religion consents to reason it begins to die.

Some nine hundred works in defense of Christianity were published in France between 1715 and 1789, ninety in one year (1770) alone.[2] Diderot's *Pensées philosophiques*, Helvétius' *De l'Esprit*, Rousseau's *Émile*, drew ten refutations each. The Abbé Houteville, in *La Religion chrétienne prouvée par les faits* (1722), contended (like Archbishop Whately a century later) that the miracles proving the divinity of Christianity were as reliably attested as the accepted events of secular history. The Abbé Guyon spread through two volumes his satirical *Oracle des nouveaux philosophes* (1759–60). The Abbé Pluche spread out the *Spectacle de la nature* in eight volumes (1739–46); it went through eighteen costly editions; it displayed the wonders of science, and the evidences of design in nature, to manifest the existence of a Deity supreme in intelligence and power. If the human mind finds some puzzles in the immense scene, let it be modest; we must not reject God because we cannot understand him; meanwhile let us be grateful for the splendor and glory of his works. The Abbé Gauchat in fifteen volumes of *Lettres critiques* (1755–63) attacked the evolutionary hypotheses of Buffon, Diderot, and others with a reckless argument: "If men were once fishes, . . . one of two things followed: either man does not have a spiritual and immortal soul or fishes also have such a soul—two equally impious suppositions";[3] the *philosophes* gladly agreed. The Abbé Sigorgne, in

La Philosophie chrétienne (1765), stressed the necessity of religion as a support for morality; purely secular restraints merely sharpen the wits of criminals who no longer believe in the all-seeing eye of God. In 1767 the Abbé Mayeul Chandon published a *Dictionnaire antiphilosophique* which went through seven editions. In 1770 Père Nonotte, "an ex-Jesuit with the vast erudition of the members of this order,"[4] issued his massive *Erreurs de Voltaire;* this book sold out four editions in its first year, six in eight years; as late as 1857 Flaubert listed it as part of the reading of Emma Bovary. The Abbé Guénée defended the Bible with "spirit, taste, urbanity, and learning" in *Lettres de quelques Juifs* (1776), letters purporting to come from learned Jews; Voltaire admitted that Guénée "bites to the blood."[5] Catholic apologists, lay and clerical, directed a monthly barrage against the *philosophes* in *La Religion vengée;* and in 1771 they began to publish an *Encyclopédie méthodique* vaster even then Diderot's, and attacking every weak point in that citadel of doubt.

The materialists encountered an able opponent in Nicolas Sylvestre Bergier, a parish priest in the diocese of Besançon. His *Déisme réfuté par lui-même* (1765) was "the answer of a real curé to the Savoyard Vicar of Rousseau's imagination."[6] For his *Certitude des preuves du Christianisme* (1767) he received a letter of praise from the Pope. At the age of fifty-one (1769) he was elevated to a canonry in Notre-Dame-de-Paris, and became confessor to the daughters of Louis XV. In that year he published an *Apologie de la religion chrétienne contre l'auteur du Christianisme dévoilé* —a blast against d'Holbach. Pleased, the Assembly of the Clergy voted him (1770) an annual pension of two thousand livres to give him more leisure to defend the faith. Within a year he issued a two-volume *Examen du matérialisme*, a reply to d'Holbach's *Système de la nature*. He pointed out again that mind is the only reality immediately known to us; why should it be reduced to something else known only through mind?[7] He charged d'Holbach with several inconsistencies: (1) the Baron pronounced God to be unknowable, but then applied to matter those qualities of infinity and eternity which he had found unintelligible in our concept of the Deity; (2) he accepted determinism, and yet exhorted men to reform their conduct; (3) he attributed religion (a) to the ignorance of primitive man, (b) to the chicanery of priests, (c) to the cunning of lawmakers—let him make up his mind. The abbé put aside the criticism of the Old Testament by explaining that the human amanuenses of God had used Oriental metaphors; therefore the Bible must not always be taken literally. The New Testament is the essence of Christianity; the divinity of the religion is proved by the life and miracles of Christ; however, the authority of the Church rests not on the Bible only, but on the Apostolic Succession of her bishops and their traditions of the faith. In *Examen de la religion chrétienne* (1771) Bergier stressed the argument that atheism, despite the exceptional individualities signalized by Bayle, would ruin morality.

The finest figure among the clerical defenders of Catholicism in eighteenth-century France was Guillaume François Berthier.[8] Entering at the age of twelve (1714) the Jesuit college at Bourges, he distinguished himself by a keenness of mind that did no visible harm to his piety. At seventeen he expressed to his parents his desire to join the Society of Jesus; they bade him think it over for a year; he did, and persisted. In his novitiate at Paris he read, studied, and prayed so assiduously that he seldom gave more than five hours a day to sleep. He developed so rapidly that at nineteen he was appointed to teach the humanities at the Collège de Blois. After seven years there, and another year of novitiate, he was sent to Rennes, then to Rouen, as professor of philosophy. In 1745 the Jesuits made him editor of their *Journal de Trévoux*, which was then published in Paris. Under his leadership this periodical became one of the most respected voices of educated France.

He wrote most of the *Journal* himself. He lived in a small cell, never heated, and worked every hour of the waking day. His door was open to all who came; his mind was open on every subject but the faith that warmed his life. La Harpe, a pupil of Voltaire, described Berthier as "that man universally admired by scholars for his vast knowledge, and by all Europe for his modest virtues."[9] He had the charm of French courtesy, even in controversy; he attacked ideas, not characters, and praised the talents of his opponents.[10] Nevertheless, he defended religious intolerance. Believing that the Catholic Church had been founded by Christ the Son of God, he held it a Christian duty to prevent, by any peaceful means, the dissemination of religious error; in a Christian nation anti-Christian propaganda should be banned as injurious to moral conduct and the stability of the state. He thought "it would be wrong to confound Catholic intolerance with zeal for persecution,"[11] but he offered no promise that persecution would not be resumed. In 1759 he retorted the charge of intolerance upon the *philosophes*: "Unbelievers, you accuse us of a fanaticism which we do not have a semblance of possessing, while the hatred which animates you against our religion inspires in you a fanaticism whose too apparent excesses are inconceivable."[12]

He did not admit the universal finality of reason. Even on Locke's sensationist terms, reason can reach only as far as the senses; beyond these limits there are realities that must forever remain mysteries to finite minds; therefore the "true philosopher limits his search where he cannot reasonably penetrate."[13] To seek to subject the universe, or the traditional and general beliefs of mankind, to the test of individual reason is a form of intellectual pride; a modest man will accept the creed of his fellow men, even if he cannot understand it. In a rare mean moment Berthier suggested that many unbelievers reject religion because it interferes with their pleasures. If such *libertins* should prevail, he predicted, the moral code would collapse, passion would be loosed, and civilization would disappear in a morass of self-seeking, sensualism, deceit, and crime. If there is no free will, there is no moral responsibility; "since it [determinism] does not admit any law binding the conscience, the only guilty person will be the one who does not succeed."[14] Morality would then be merely a calculus of expediency; no sense of justice would restrain the clever minority from abusing the simplicity of the majority; no ruler would feel any other obligation to his people than to keep his exploitation of them this side of revolution.[15]

Berthier, as we have seen, welcomed and commended the first volume of the *Encyclopédie*. He exposed its inaccuracies and plagiarisms with incontestable scholarship; so he showed that the article "Agir" (To Act), by the Abbé Yvon, extending to three columns in folio, was taken "completely and word for word from Father Buffier's *Traité des vérités premières*."[16] He praised the article on Arab philosophy, but expressed dismay at finding in the article "Athée" the arguments for atheism laid out at the same length, and with the same force, as those against it, leaving the existence of God in serious doubt. When, in Volume II, the anti-Christian bent became more evident, he attacked it with verve and skill. He pointed out that the *Encyclopédie* derived the authority of a government from the consent of the governed; this, said Berthier, is a view dangerous to hereditary monarchy. He may have been instrumental in having the *Encylopédie* repressed.[17]

In the *Journal de Trévoux* for April, 1757, he examined Voltaire's *Essai sur les moeurs*. "It is sad for us to find here a living author whose talents we admire, [but who] abuses them in the most essential matters." He saw in Voltaire's work an attempt "to destroy the Church and religion, to elevate upon their ruins a philosophic structure, a temple dedicated to license of thought, and vowed to independence from all authority, to reduce and restrict worship and morality to a philosophy purely human and secular." He charged Voltaire with a bias that disgraced the historian, with an almost complete blindness to the virtues and services of Christianity, and a passionate resolve to find every possible fault in its teachings and career. Voltaire, he said, pretended to believe in God, but the effect of his writings was to promote atheism. When, in the same issue, Berthier turned to Voltaire's *La Pucelle*, he lost his temper and cried out:

> Never has hell vomited up a more deadly plague. . . . Voluptuousness here impudently displays the most lewd pictures; obscenity borrows the language of the market place; . . . the basest buffoonery

seasons its impiety. . . . The odor given off by these verses is enough
to infect and corrupt every age and condition in society.[18]

Voltaire did not hurry to reply. He still entertained an affectionate remembrance of his Jesuit teachers, still had on the walls of his study at
Ferney a portrait of the kindly and devoted Father Porée.[19] But when the
French government suppressed the *Encyclopédie* he yielded to d'Alembert's urging, and took up arms against Berthier. He accused him of opposing the *Encyclopédie* because it competed with the *Dictionnaire de Trévoux*, which he supposed to be a Jesuit product (it was so only in part, and
unofficially); and he invited the Society of Jesus to dissociate itself from
this "gazetteer" of Trévoux. "What an employment for a priest, . . . to
sell every month, from a bookstore, an anthology of slander and rash judgments!"[20] Berthier answered (July, 1759) that the editors of the *Journal de
Trévoux* had no connection with the editors of the *Dictionnaire de Trévoux*; he confessed that being a "gazetteer" was "neither beautiful nor
agreeable," but he upheld the right of a priest to use a periodical to praise
good works and censure bad. He regretted that Voltaire had stooped to
personalities and charges of venality; and he ended by expressing the hope
that "this man of fine talents" would, in "the remaining moments which
Providence is allowing him," return to "that holy religion—not only the
natural but the Christian and the Catholic—in which he was born."[21] In
November Voltaire (doubtless remembering Swift's imaginary burial of
John Partridge) issued a solemn *Relation de la maladie, la confession, la
mort, et l'apparition du jésuite Berthier*, telling how the editor had died of
a fit of yawning over the *Journal de Trévoux*. He excused his method of
controversy in a letter to Mme. d'Épinay: "We must render *l'infâme* and
its defenders ridiculous."[22]

In 1762 the *parlements* of France ordered the suppression of the Jesuits.
Glad to end his travail as editor, Berthier went to a Trappist monastery for
a silent and meditative retreat. He asked to be admitted to that order, but
the general of the Jesuits refused to release him. He was engaged by Louis
XV to tutor the royal children, but when the King (1764) signed the
decree expelling all Jesuits from France, Berthier emigrated to Germany.
In 1776 he was allowed to return. He lived in retirement with his brother
in Bourges, and died there, aged seventy-eight, in 1782. He was a good man.

II. THE *ANTIPHILOSOPHES*

The war became bloodier when cassocks and courtesies were discarded
and the journalists set their sights on the *philosophes;* now all the wit and
vocabulary of Paris were brought to bear and to kill. We have seen how

Voltaire in 1725 went to some trouble to save Pierre Desfontaines from the statutory punishment for homosexual acts, which was death. Desfontaines never forgave him. In 1735 he began a periodical publication, *Observations sur les écrits modernes,* which continued till 1743. In its pages he made himself the defender of all the virtues, chastity in particular; he attacked with indignation any sign of lax morality, or of imperfect orthodoxy, in the literature of the day. He became the bitterest enemy of Voltaire. When he died (1745) he bequeathed his crusade to his friend Fréron.

Élie Catherine Fréron was the ablest, bravest, and most learned of the *antiphilosophes.* He was scholar enough to write an *Histoire de Marie Stuart* (1742) and an eight-volume *Histoire de l'empire d'Allemagne* (1771). He was poet enough to compose an "Ode sur la bataille de Fontenoy" (1745), which Voltaire must have viewed as insolent competition with his own ode as royal historiographer. He founded in 1745 a periodical, *Lettres sur quelques écrits de cette âge,* which more than once drew blood from Voltaire. Fréron had his years of poverty en route to a coach-and-four; once he suffered six weeks of imprisonment in the Bastille for criticizing an influential abbé; but he fought for thirty years his lusty battle for the past. He harbored some intelligible resentment against Voltaire for dissuading Frederick from hiring him as Paris correspondent.[23] In 1754 he founded a new review, *Année litteraire,* which he edited and mostly wrote, and published every ten days until 1774.

Fréron admired the religious conservatism of Bossuet, and the stately ways and style of the seventeenth century; he felt that the *philosophes* had a culpably superficial understanding of social organization, the supports of morality, and the consolations of faith.

> Never was there an age more fertile than ours in seditious writers, who . . . concentrate all their powers on attacking the Godhead. They call themselves apostles of humanity, never realizing that it ill befits a citizen, and does a grave disservice to mankind, to rob them of the only hopes which offer them some mitigation of their life's ills. They do not understand that they are upsetting the social order, inciting the poor against the rich, the weak against the strong, and putting arms into millions of hands hitherto restrained from violence by their moral and religious sense quite as much as by the law.[24]

This attack upon religion, Fréron predicted, would loosen all the foundations of the state. He anticipated by a generation the warnings of Edmund Burke.

> Is not the fanaticism of your irreligion more absurd and more dangerous than the fanaticism of superstition? Begin by tolerating

the faith of your fathers. You talk of nothing but tolerance, and never was a sect more intolerant. . . . As for me, I hold to no cabal of *bel esprit*, and to no party except that of religion, morality, and honor.[25]

Fréron was an acute critic. He lost no chance to puncture the sensitive vanity of the *philosophes*. He made fun of their dogmaticism, and of Voltaire's seignorial pretensions as "Comte de Tournay." When they replied by calling him a rascal and a bigot, he retaliated by calling Diderot a hypocrite, Grimm a sycophant of foreign notables, and the whole infidel group "knaves, crooks, puppies, and scoundrels."[26] He accused the Encyclopedists of stealing illustrations from Réaumur's book on ants; they denied the charge; the Académie des Sciences supported their denial; later facts substantiated the charge.[27] He did not do so well *in re* Calas; he suggested that the evidence indicated Calas' guilt, and he wrote that Voltaire, in defending Calas, "was not so much carried away by the feeling of humanity as by the urge to recall public attention to his existence," and "to make people talk about him."[28] Mlle. Clairon, a leading *tragédienne*, liked and visited Voltaire; Fréron sedulously praised her rival, and dropped hints about the immoral private life of a certain actress. The actors resented his allegations as undue interference with their personal affairs; the Duc de Richelieu, no persecutor of adultery, persuaded Louis XV to order Fréron back to the Bastille, but the Queen secured his pardon "for his piety and zeal in combating the *philosophes*."[29] When Turgot, friend of the *philosophes*, rose to power, the *privilège* of the *Année litteraire* was withdrawn (1774). Fréron comforted himself with good food, and died of a hearty meal (1776). His widow asked Voltaire to adopt his daughter, but Voltaire thought that this would be carrying gallantry to extremes.

Almost as damaging to the *philosophes* as Fréron's thirty volumes was one word—the last in the title of Jacob Nicolas Moreau's satire, *Nouveau Mémoire pour servir à l'histoire des cacouacs* (1757). The Cacouacs, said Moreau, were a species of barely human animals who carried a pouch of poison under their tongues; when they spoke, this venom mingled with their words and polluted all the surrounding air. The clever author quoted passages from Diderot, d'Alembert, Voltaire, and Rousseau; he argued that these men were veritable poisoners of the breath of life, and he charged them with doing evil "precisely for the pleasure of doing evil."[30] He called them atheists, anarchists, immoralists, egoists; but it was the term *cacouac* that pained them most keenly; it suggested the cacophony of quacking ducks, the bedlam of insane prattlers, sometimes (as the word intended) the odor of latrines. Voltaire struggled to reply, but who can refute a smell?

The conservatives took courage and multiplied their blows. In 1757 they won an ambitious and vivacious recruit. Charles Palissot de Monteney had visited Voltaire at Les Délices (1754), with an introduction by Thieriot as "a disciple formed by your works."[31] A year later he staged at Nancy a comedy genially satirizing Rousseau. In Paris he cultivated the young and devout Princesse de Robecq, who was at least the friend of the Duc de Choiseul. Diderot, adept in *faux-pas*, had censured her morals in the preface to his *Fils naturel*. Perhaps to placate her, Palissot published (1757) *Petites Lettres sur de grands philosophes*, severely criticizing Diderot but praising Voltaire. And on May 2, 1760, under the patronage of Mlle. de Robecq, he offered at the Théâtre-Français the outstanding comedy of the season, *Les Philosophes*. This was to Helvétius, Diderot, and Rousseau what the *Clouds* of Aristophanes had been to Socrates 2,183 years before. Helvétius was portrayed as the philosopher-pedant Valère, who explains the altruism of egoism to the bluestocking Cidalise; the audience at once recognized in this lady Mme. Geoffrin, whose salon was frequented by the *philosophes*. Diderot was portrayed as Dortidius. In the servant Crispin, who moved across the stage on all fours, munching lettuce, the Parisians saw a caricature of Jean Jacques Rousseau, who had in 1750 denounced civilization and idealized a "state of nature." It was crude but legitimate satire, and everyone but the victims enjoyed it. Mlle. de Robecq had packed the house with her friends, other *dévots*, and several members of the hierarchy. The Princess herself, though dying of tuberculosis, insisted on gracing the première with her feverish beauty; at the end of the second act she had Palissot summoned to her box, and publicly embraced him; then, coughing blood, she was carried home.[32] In twenty-nine days *Les Philosophes* was played fourteen times.

Meanwhile a loftier figure had joined in the attack upon the unbelievers. Jean Jacques Le Franc, Marquis de Pompignan, a provincial magistrate, wrote poems and plays significant enough to win him election to the Academy. In his speech of acceptance he denounced

> this deceptive philosophy, which calls itself the organ of truth and serves as an instrument of calumny. It vaunts its own moderation and modesty, and swells with importance and pride. Its followers, bold and haughty with the pen, tremble basely in their lives. There is nothing sure in their principles, no consolation in their ethics, no rule for the present, no goal for the future.[33]

Louis XV praised the speech. Voltaire made fun of it in an anonymous seven-page pamphlet entitled *Les Quand*, each paragraph beginning with the word *quand—when*. For example:

> *When* one has the honor to be received into an honorable society
> of men of letters, it is not necessary that his reception speech be a
> satire on men of letters; this is to insult the society and the pub-
> lic. . . .
> *When* one is scarcely a man of letters at all, and not in the least a
> philosopher, it does not become him to say that our nation has only
> a false literature and a vain philosophy . . .

and so forth, not very brilliantly. But then Morellet followed with a broad-
sheet of *ifs* (*Les Si*), and, soon afterward, one of *wherefores* (*Les Pour-
quoi*); and Voltaire added successive sheets of *tos, thats, whos, yesses, noes,*
and *whys*. Pompignan fled from this hurricane to his native Montauban,
and never appeared in the Academy again. But in 1772 he returned to the
conflict with *La Religion vengée de l'incrédulité par l'incrédulité même*.
Materialism, he urged, left no real sanction for morality; if there is no God
everything is permitted; all we need do is to elude the police. And if there
is no heaven, "how," asked the Marquis, "will you persuade men that they
should be satisfied with the position of subordination that the republic
allots them?"[34]

The Abbé Galiani, coming from Naples to Paris in 1761, and for eight
years shining in the salons, told the *philosophes*—who loved him—that the
plea of some of them to "follow nature" was a counsel of madness that
would reduce civilized men to brutality and savagery;[35] that the evidences of
design in the universe were overwhelming;[36] and that skepticism led to intellectual emptiness and spiritual despair:

> By dint of enlightening ourselves we have found more void than
> fullness. . . . This void, persisting in our souls and our imagination,
> is the true cause of our melancholy.[37] . . . After all is said and done, in-
> credulity is the greatest effort the spirit of man may make against his
> own instincts and tastes. . . . Men need certainty. . . . The ma-
> jority of men, and especially of women (whose imagination is double
> ours) . . . could not be agnostic; and those capable of agnosticism
> would be able to sustain the effort only at the height of their souls'
> youth and strength. If the soul grows old, some belief reappears.[38]
> . . . Agnosticism is a reasoned despair [*un désespoir raisonné*].[39]

Against the brilliant Galiani, the learned Bergier, the courteous Berthier,
the industrious Fréron, the titled Pompignan, the tantalizing Palissot, and
the cackling Moreau the *philosophes* used every weapon of intellectual
war, from reason and ridicule to censorship and vituperation. Voltaire gave
up his peace, risked his security, to answer, often with more wit than argument, every assailant of *philosophie* and *raison*. "Send me the names of

these miserable fellows," he wrote to Diderot, "and I will treat them as they deserve."[40]

It was difficult to get at Moreau, for he was librarian and historiographer to the Queen. But Pompignan could be pilloried with particles, and Palissot could be punctured with puns. So Marmontel wrote, quite untranslatably:

Cet homme avait nom Pali.	This man had once the name Pali.
On dit d'abord Palis fade,	At first they called him Palis Dull,
Puis Palis fou, Palis flat;	Then Palis Low and Palis Fool,
Palis froid et Palis fat;	Palis Vain and Palis Cool.
Pour couronner la tirade	To top all the tirade
En fin de turlupinade,	And end the pasquinade,
On rencontra le vrai mot:	The fit word came at once—
On le nomma Palis-sot.	They named him Palis Dunce.
M'abaissant jusqu'à toi,	To come down to your level
Je joue avec le mot;	I with the word must revel.
Réfléchis, si tu peux,	Reflect, if you can use that tool,
Mais n'écris pas . . . lis . . . sot.	But write not; rather read, you fool.

Diderot postponed his revenge till he retailed Pallissot's debauchery in *Le Neveu de Rameau;*[41] it was hardly worthy of a philosopher, but he had the decency not to publish it, and it did not see French print till after its victim's death. Morellet, however, sent forth at once a stinging satire, lampooning not only Palissot but his *protectrice*, Mlle. de Robecq. Her friends at court had Morellet committed to the Bastille (June 11, 1760), and she made matters worse for him by dying (June 26). Rousseau secured his release, but henceforth dissociated himself from the *philosophes*. Palissot tarnished his triumph with dissipation. In 1778 he turned with the Voltairean tide, and rejoined the *philosophes*.

Their heaviest blows fell upon Fréron. Diderot described him, in *Le Neveu*,[42] as one of a group of literary hacks who lived by eating at the table of the millionaire Bertin. Voltaire devoted one of his cleverest quips to Fréron:

> *L'autre jour, au fond d'un vallon,*
> *Un serpent piqua Jean Fréron.*
> *Que pensez-vous qu'il arriva?*
> *Ce fut le serpent qui creva.* *

Typical of the grossness that often interrupted the good manners of Voltaire and the eighteenth century was his description of Fréron as "*le ver*

---

* "The other day, down in a valley, a serpent stung John Fréron. What think you happened then? It was the serpent that died."

sorti du cul de Desfontaines" (the worm that came out of Desfontaines' behind).[43] But the grand attack came in Voltaire's play *L'Écossaise* (*The Lady from Scotland*), which opened at the Théâtre-Français on July 26, 1760. It burlesqued Palissot's *Les Philosophes* with obvious exaggerations by ascribing to his victims the responsibility for the defeats of the French armies in war and the collapse of the state finances. Fréron was pictured as a Grub Street scribbler who manufactured infamy at one pistole per paragraph. Among the terms applied to him in Voltaire's play were *scoundrel, toad, hound, spy, lizard, snake,* and *heart of filth*.[44] Voltaire followed custom by packing the house with friends of himself or the *frères*. The play rivaled Palissot's in popularity, appearing sixteen times in five weeks. Fréron rode out the storm by attending the première with his pretty wife and conspicuously leading the applause. Voltaire recognized the mettle of his antagonist. When a visitor asked whom he should consult in Paris on the merits of new books, Voltaire replied, "Apply to that villain Fréron; . . . he is the only man who has taste. I am obliged to confess it, though I love him not."[45]

III. THE FALL OF THE JESUITS

The sudden collapse of the Society of Jesus, though it was effected rather by the Parlement of Paris than by the *philosophes*, revealed the temper of the times. Called by its founder the "Company of Jesus," approved by Pope Paul III in 1540 as Societas Jesu, "a mendicant order of clerks regular" (i.e., a body of religious following a defined rule and living on alms), these "Jesuits," as their critics called them, became within a century the most powerful group of ecclesiastics in the Catholic Church. By 1575 they had established twelve colleges in France alone; soon they dominated the education of French youth. For two hundred years the kings of France chose Jesuits as their confessors; other Catholic rulers followed suit; and by this and other means the Society of Jesus intimately influenced the history of Europe.

Almost from their beginnings in Paris they were opposed by the Parlement and the Sorbonne. In 1594 the Parlement accused them of instigating the attempt of Jean Châtel upon the life of Henry IV, and in 1610 it charged them with having stirred Ravaillac to murder the King. The Parlement gave force to its accusations by referring to the *De rege* of the Spanish Jesuit Mariana, who had defended, under certain conditions, the morality of regicide. But the Society grew in number and power. It dominated the religious policies of Louis XIV, and led him to attack the Jansenists of Port-Royal as Calvinists in a Catholic disguise. The *Provincial Letters* then written by Pascal (1656 f.) were still remembered by the educated minority in France. Nevertheless, in 1749 the Society had 3,350 members in France, of whom 1,763 were priests. They stood out among the French clergy as the best scholars, the subtlest theologians, the most eloquent preachers, the most devoted, industrious, and successful defenders of the Church. They contributed to a score of sciences, and influenced the forms of art. They were, by general consent, the best educators in Europe. They were distinguished by the austerity of their morals, and yet they used every device of casuistry to lighten the demands of Christian ethics upon common men; even so they never condoned the adulteries of the nobles or the kings. By their arduous preparation and their patient persistence they made themselves a power over the policies of sovereigns and the minds of men. At times it seemed that all Europe would yield to the tenacity of their united and disciplined will.

Their power almost ruined them. It became too evident to the kings that the "Ultramontanism" of the Jesuits, if unchecked, would make all secular rulers the vassals of the popes, and would restore the authority of Imperial Rome. Though closer than any other group to royal ears, they defended the right of the people to overthrow the king. Though they were relatively liberal in theology and morals, and strove to reconcile science and the Church, they cultivated popular piety by supporting the claim of Marguerite Marie Alacoque that Christ had revealed to her his Sacred Heart burning with love for mankind. They trained the intellects of Descartes, Molière, Voltaire, and Diderot, only to see these brilliant men turn against them and the whole system of Jesuit education.

It was charged that the curriculum of their schools clung too long to Latin; that it discouraged the growth of knowledge by excluding any but traditional ideas; that it appealed too much to memory and to passive obedience; that the unchanging *ratio studiorum* had lost touch with the needs of the time for a greater utilization of science and a more realistic view of human life. So d'Alembert, in the article "Collège" in the *Encyclopédie*, deplored the six years spent by Jesuit pupils in acquiring a dead language; he recommended more attention to English and Italian, to history and science and modern philosophy; he appealed to the government to take control of education and establish a new curriculum in new schools. In 1762 Rousseau published his *Émile*, announcing a revolution in education.

The *philosophes*, however, were a minor factor in the decline of the Jesuits in France. A kind of mutual truce dulled the mutual hostility: the unbelievers respected the learning and character of the Jesuits, and these, by patient handling, hoped to bring the errant skeptics back into the orthodox fold. Voltaire found it hard to make war against his former teachers. He had submitted his *Henriade* to Father Porée with a request for the correction of any passages injurious to religion.[46] In the *Temple de goût* he had praised the Jesuits for their appreciation of literature, and for their large use of mathematics in the education of youth. The *Journal de Trévoux* responded with favorable reviews of the *Henriade, Charles XII*, and the *Philosophie de Newton*. This *entente demi-cordiale* ended when Voltaire joined Frederick in Potsdam; the Jesuit leaders then abandoned him as a lost soul, but as late as 1757 some of them attempted a reconciliation between Voltaire and the Society.[47] At Ferney (1758 f.) Voltaire maintained friendly relations with the local Jesuits; several of them enjoyed his hospitality; meanwhile he had attacked the Church on a hundred pages of the *Essai sur les moeurs*, and he was writing anti-Christian articles for the *Dictionnaire philosophique*. When he heard of the attack upon the Jesuits of Portugal (1757 f.) by the chief minister, Carvalho, and the burning of the Jesuit Malagrida (1764), he denounced Carvalho's charges as unjust, and condemned the execution as an atrocity.[48] But all through those years he himself was at war with the Church, and the writings of his "brethren," Diderot, d'Alembert, and Morellet, were contributing to the weakening of the Jesuits in France.

Perhaps the Masonic lodges, generally dedicated to deism, shared in the sapping operation. But the strongest influences in the tragedy were personal and class antagonisms. Mme. de Pompadour could not forget that the Jesuits had opposed every step in her rise, had denied absolution to the King as long as he kept her, and had refused to take seriously her sudden conversion to piety. Cardinal de Bernis, long a favorite of the Marquise, later declared that the suppression of the Society in France was due mainly to the unwillingness of the Jesuit confessors to grant absolution to La Pompadour despite her assurances that her relations with Louis XV were no longer physical.[49] The King echoed her resentment. Why were these priests, so lenient to others, so hard on the woman who had brightened his weary, isolated life? Why were they increasing in corporate wealth while he was struggling to raise funds for his army and navy in a disastrous war—and for the robes of his mistress and the pensions of her understudies in the Parc aux Cerfs? Damiens had tried to kill the King; the Jesuits had no demonstrable connection with the attempt; but Damiens had had a Jesuit confessor; and had not some dead Jesuit defended regicide? The King began to listen to Choiseul and other semi-Voltaireans in his ministry, who argued that the time had come to free the state from tutelage to the Church, to build a social and moral order independent of an obscurantist clergy and a medieval theology. If little Portugal, darkly superstitious, had dared to expel the Jesuits, why could not enlightened France?

Stricken by these diverse enmities, and widely suspected of having bound France to Austria in the Seven Years' War, the Jesuits suffered a strangely sudden unpopularity. After the defeat of the French by Frederick at Rossbach (1757), and the fortunes of France had apparently reached nadir, and crippled soldiers became a frequent sight in Paris, the Jesuits became a target for jokes, rumors, slanders running even to suggestions of pederasty.[50] They were accused of worldliness, of heresy, of coveting wealth, of being the secret agents of foreign powers. Many of the secular clergy criticized their theology as too liberal, their casuistry as demoralizing, their politics as the betrayal of France to Rome. In 1759 d'Alembert wrote to Voltaire: "Brother Berthier and his accomplices dare not appear on the streets these days for fear that people will throw Portuguese oranges at their heads."[51]

The most powerful of all the forces that were converging upon the Jesuits was the hostility of the Paris Parlement. That assemblage was composed of lawyers or magistrates belonging to the *noblesse de robe*, encased in gowns as awesome as the cassocks of the priests. This second aristocracy, well organized and eloquently vocal, was rapidly rising in power, and eager to challenge the authority of the clergy. Moreover, the Parlement was predominantly Jansenist. Despite all the suppression that Jansenism had suffered, that austere doctrine, the gloomy outcome of Paul's hardening of Christ's more gentle Christianity, had captured large sections of the French middle class, and most thoroughly those legal minds that felt its logic and saw in it a stance of strength against the Jesuits. Now, it was precisely the Jesuits who had urged Louis XIV to pursue the Jansenists to the complete destruction of Port-Royal, and to the bitter compulsion to accept the reluctant papal bull that had made Jansenism a heresy more disabling than atheism. If only some opportunity would come to retaliate those injuries, to avenge that persecution!

The Jesuits gave the Parlement that opportunity. They had for generations past engaged in industry and commerce as a means of financing their seminaries, colleges, missions, and politics. In Rome they held a monopoly in several lines of production or trade; in Angers, France, they ran a sugar refinery;[52] they maintained trading posts in many foreign lands, as in Goa; in Spanish and Portuguese America they were among the richest entrepreneurs.[53] Private enterprise complained of this competition, and even good Catholics wondered why an order vowed to poverty should accumulate such wealth. One of their most active businessmen was Father Antoine de La Valette, superior-general of the Jesuits in the Antilles. In the name of the Society he managed extensive plantations in the West Indies. He employed thousands of Negro slaves,[54] and exported sugar and coffee to Europe. In 1755 he borrowed large sums from banks in Marseilles; to repay these loans he sent a shipment of merchandise to France; the vessel, with a cargo valued at two million francs ($5,000,000?), was seized by English men-of-war (1755) in the preliminaries to the Seven Years' War. Hoping to recoup these losses, La Valette borrowed more; he failed and declared bankruptcy, owing 2,400,000 francs. His creditors demanded payment, and asked the Society to acknowledge responsibility for the debts of La Valette. The Jesuit leaders refused, alleging that he had acted as an individual, and not in the name of their order. The bankers sued the Society. Father Frey, political expert of the Society in France, advised it to lay the matter before the Parlement. It was so done (March, 1761), and the fate of the order lay in the hands of its strongest enemy. Meanwhile a Jesuit sent a secret paper to the King, recommending dismissal of Choiseul from the ministry as a man hostile to the Society and religion. Choiseul defended himself successfully.

Parlement seized the opportunity to examine the constitutions and other documents revealing the organization and activities of the Society. On May 8 it gave judgment in favor of the plaintiff, and ordered the Society to pay all of La Valette's debts. The Jesuits began to make arrangements with the principal creditors.[55] But on July 8 the Abbé Terray presented to the Parlement a report "on the moral and practical doctrine of the . . . Society of Jesus." On the basis of this report the Parlement issued (August 6) two decrees. One condemned to the fire a large number of Jesuit publications of the preceding two centuries as "teaching murderous and abominable" principles against the security of citizens and sovereigns; it forbade further additions to the membership of the Society in France; and ordered that by April 1, 1762, all Jesuit schools in France be closed except such as should receive letters of permission from the Parlement. The other decree offered to receive complaints against abuses of authority in or by the Society. The King (August 29) suspended the execution of these decrees; Parlement consented to hold them in abeyance till April 1. The harassed King tried for a compromise. In January, 1762, he sent to Clement XIII, and to Lorenzo Ricci, general of the Jesuits, a proposal that henceforth all the general's powers for France should be delegated to five provincial vicars sworn to obey the laws of France and the Gallican Articles of 1682, which in effect freed the French Church from submission to the pope; furthermore, the Jesuit colleges in France should be subject to inspection by the *parlements*. Both the Pope and Ricci rejected this proposal with a defiant response: *"Sint ut sunt, aut non sint"* (Let them [the Jesuits] be as they are, or not at all).[56] In behalf of the Society Clement appealed to the French clergy directly, which violated French law; the French clergy refused to accept the brief, and remitted it to the King, who returned it to the Pope.

The provincial *parlements* now entered the drama. Various reports filed with them added to the charges against the Jesuits. The Parlement of

Rennes in Brittany was impressed by the *Comptes rendus des constitutions des Jésuites* presented to it in 1761–62 by its *procureur général*, Louis René de La Chalotais. This charged the Society with heresy, idolatry, illegal operations, and the inculcation of regicide; it contended that every Jesuit had to swear absolute obedience to the pope and to the general of the order, who resided in Rome; that therefore the Society was by its very constitution a threat to France and the King; and it urged that the education of children should be the exclusive right of the state. On February 15, 1762, the Parlement of Rouen ordered all Jesuits in Normandy to vacate their houses and colleges, to remove all foreign directors, and to accept the Gallican Articles. Similar decrees were issued by the Parlements of Rennes, Aix-en-Provence, Pau, Toulouse, Perpignan, and Bordeaux. On April 1 the Parlement of Paris ordered the enforcement of its decrees, and transferred to other administrators the Jesuit schools within its jurisdiction.

The secular clergy, though traditionally jealous of the Jesuits, tried to save them. An assembly of French bishops (May 1) appealed to the King in behalf of the order as

> an institution useful to the state, . . . a society of religious who were so praiseworthy for the integrity of their morals, the austerity of their discipline, the vastness of their labors and their erudition, and for the countless services they have rendered to the Church. . . . Everything, Sire, pleads with you in favor of the Jesuits: religion claims them as its defenders, the Church as her ministers, Christians as the guardians of their conscience; a great number of your subjects who have been their pupils intercede with you for their old masters; all the youth of the kingdom pray for those who are to form their minds and their hearts. Do not, Sire, turn a deaf ear to our united supplication.[57]

The Queen, her daughters, the Dauphin, and the others of the *dévot* party at the court added their pleas for the Jesuits, but Choiseul and Pompadour now definitely advised the King to yield to the Parlement and close the Jesuit schools. Louis was reminded that he must soon raise new taxes, and that these would require the assent of the Parlement. While he vacillated between opposed counsels the Parlement took decisive steps. On August 6, 1762, it declared that the Society of Jesus was inconsistent with the laws of France, that the oaths of the members overrode their loyalty to the King, and that the subjection of the Society to an alien authority made it a foreign body within a supposedly sovereign state; therefore the Parlement ordered the Society dissolved in France, and bade the Jesuits vacate, within eight days, all their French property, which was declared forfeited to the King.

The King delayed by eight months the full execution of this decree.

Two *parlements*—Besançon and Douai—refused to obey the decrees; three —Dijon, Grenoble, Metz—temporized. But the Paris Parlement insisted, and finally, in November, 1764, Louis ordered the complete suppression of the Society of Jesus in France. The confiscated property amounted to 58 million francs,[58] and may have helped to reconcile the King to the dissolution. A small pension was allowed to the ex-Jesuits, and for a time they were permitted to stay in France; but in 1767 the Paris Parlement decreed that all former Jesuits must leave France. Only a few renounced their order and remained.

The expulsion was agreeable to the nobility, the middle class, the literati, and the Jansenists, but was unpopular with the rest of the population. Christophe de Beaumont, archbishop of Paris, vigorously condemned the actions of the Parlement. An assembly of the French clergy (1765) unanimously expressed grief over the dissolution of the Society, and pleaded for its restoration. Pope Clement XIII, in the bull *Apostolicum*, proclaimed the innocence of the Jesuits; the bull was burned in the streets of several cities by the public executioner, on the ground that the popes had no legal right to interfere with French affairs.[59] The *philosophes* at first hailed the expulsion as an inspiring victory for liberal thought, and d'Alembert noted with pleasure the comment of the Biblical scholar Jean Astruc that "it was not the Jansenists but the *Encyclopédie* that killed the Jesuits."[60] The number of free-thought publications now rapidly increased; it was in the decade after the expulsion that d'Holbach and his aides carried the anti-Christian campaign to the point of atheism.

On second thought, however, the *philosophes* perceived that the victory belonged less to them than to the Jansenists and the *parlements*, and that it left free thought facing an enemy far more intolerant than the Jesuits.[61] In his *Histoire de la destruction des Jésuites* (1765) d'Alembert expressed only a tempered elation over their fate:

> It is certain that the greater part of them, who had no voice in affairs, . . . should not have suffered for the faults of their superiors, if such a distinction were practicable. There were thousands of innocents whom we have regretfully confused with some twenty guilty individuals. . . . The destruction of the Society will redound to the great advantage of reason, provided Jansenist intolerance does not succeed to Jesuit intolerance. . . . If we had to choose between these two sects we should prefer the Society of Jesus as the less tyrannical. The Jesuits—accommodating people provided one did not declare himself their enemy—allowed one to think as he pleased. The Jansenists want everyone to think as they do. If they were masters they would exercise the most violent inquisition over minds, speech, and morals.[62]

As if to illustrate these views, the Jansenist Parlement of Paris, in the same year of 1762 in which it ordered the dissolution of the Society of Jesus, also ordered the public burning of Rousseau's relatively pious *Émile;* the Jansenist Parlement of Toulouse, in that year, broke Jean Calas on the wheel; the Paris Parlement, in 1765, burned Voltaire's *Dictionnaire philosophique,* and, a year later, confirmed the sentence of torture and execution laid upon the young Chevalier de La Barre by the court of Abbeville.

On September 25, 1762, d'Alembert had written to Voltaire: "Do you know what I heard about you yesterday? That you begin to pity the Jesuits, and are tempted to write in their favor."[63] There had always been a fund of pity in Voltaire, and now that the battle against the Society seemed thoroughly won he could hear some voices of reproach from his dead teachers. He took into his home at Ferney one of the ex-Jesuits, Père Adam, who handled his charities and regularly beat him at chess. Voltaire warned La Chalotais: "Beware lest one day Jansenism do as much harm as the Jesuits have done. . . . What will it serve me to be delivered from the foxes if they deliver me to the wolves?"[64] He feared that the Jansenists, like the Puritans in seventeenth-century England, would close the theaters, and the theater was almost his favorite passion. So he wrote to d'Alembert: "The Jesuits were necessary; they were a diversion; we made fun of them, and we are going to be crushed by pedants."[65] He was ready to pardon the Jesuits if only because they had loved the classics and the drama.[66]

His friend and enemy Frederick the Great joined in these sentiments. "Why," Frederick asked the Prince de Ligne in 1764,

> why have they destroyed those repositories of the graces of Athens and Rome, those excellent professors of the humanities, and perhaps of humanity, the Jesuits? Education will suffer. . . . But as my brothers the Kings, most Catholic, most Christian, most faithful and apostolic, have tumbled them out, I, most heretical, gather as many as I can; I preserve the breed.[67]

When d'Alembert warned Frederick that he would regret this amiability, and reminded him that the Jesuits had opposed his conquest of Silesia, the King reproved the philosopher:

> You need not be alarmed for my safety; I have nothing to fear from the Jesuits. They can teach the youth of the country, and they are better able to do that than anyone else. It is true that they were on the other side during the war, but as a philosopher you ought not to reproach one for being kind and humane to everyone of the human species, no matter what religion or society he belongs to. Try to be more of a philosopher and less of a metaphysician.[68]

When Pope Clement XIV dissolved the entire Society of Jesus in 1773 Frederick refused to allow the publication of the papal bull in his realm. The Jesuits were maintained in their property and functions in Prussia and Silesia.

Catherine II left undisturbed the Jesuits whom she found in that part of Poland which she appropriated in 1772, and she protected those who later entered Russia. There they labored patiently until their restoration (1814).

IV. EDUCATION AND PROGRESS

But who would educate French youth now that the Jesuits were gone? Here was chaos, but also an opening for a pedagogical revolution.

La Chalotais, still warm with his indictment of the Jesuits, seized the opportunity, and offered to France an *Essai d'éducation nationale* (1763) which the *philosophes* crowned with acclaim. His present plea was that the schools of France should not pass from one religious fraternity to another—for example, to the Christian Brothers or to the Oratorians. He was no atheist; at least he welcomed the support of religion for morality; he would have it taught and honored, but he would not have the clergy control education. He admitted that many ecclesiastics were excellent teachers, unrivaled in patience and devotion, but sooner or later, he argued, their domination of the classroom closed the mind to original thought, and indoctrinated pupils with loyalty to a foreign power. The rules of morality should be taught independently of any religious creed; "the laws of ethics take precedence over all laws, both divine and human, and would subsist even if these laws had never been declared."[69] La Chalotais too wanted indoctrination, but with nationalist ideals;[70] nationalism was to be the new religion. "I demand for the nation an education that will depend upon the state alone."[71] The teachers should be laymen, or, if priests, they should belong to the secular clergy, not to a religious order. The aim of education should be to prepare the individual not for heaven but for life, and not for blind obedience but for competent service in the professions, in administration, and in the industrial arts. French, not Latin, should be the language of instruction; Latin should receive less time, English and German more. The curriculum should include plenty of science, and from the lowest grades; even children of five to ten years of age can absorb the elements of geography, physics, and natural history. History too should have a larger place in school studies; but "what is ordinarily lacking, both to those who write history and to those who read it, is a philosophic mind";[72] here La Chalotais handed Voltaire the palm. In later grades there should be instruction in art and taste. Greater provision should be made for the education of women, but it was unnecessary to educate the poor. The son of a peasant would not learn in school anything better than he would learn in the field, and further education would merely make him discontent in his class.

Helvétius, Turgot, and Condorcet were shocked by this last opinion, but Voltaire applauded it. He wrote to La Chalotais: "I thank you for forbidding laborers to study. I, who cultivate the earth, need manual workers, not tonsured clerics. Send me especially ignorant brothers to drive or harness my coaches."[73] And to Damilaville, who had proposed education for all: "I doubt if those who have only their muscle to live by will ever have time to become educated; they would die of hunger before becoming philosophers. . . . It is not the manual worker whom we must instruct, it is the urban bourgeoisie."[74] In other passages he condescended to favor primary education for all, but hoped that secondary education would be sufficiently restricted to leave a large class of manual workers to do the physical work of society.[75] The first task of education, in Voltaire's view, was to end the ecclesiastical indoctrination which he held responsible for the superstitions of the masses and the fanaticism of the crowd.

Diderot, at the request of Catherine II, drew up in 1773 a *Plan d'une université pour le gouvernement de la Russie*. Like La Chalotais, he denounced the traditional curriculum, in terms that we hear today:

> In the Faculty of Arts there are still taught . . . two dead languages, which are of use to only a small number of citizens, and these languages are studied for six or seven years without being learned. Under the name of rhetoric the art of speaking is taught before the art of thinking; under the name of logic the head is filled with Aristotelian subtleties; . . . under the name of metaphysics trifling and knotty points are discussed, laying the foundation of both skepticism and bigotry; under the name of physics there is an endless dispute about matter and the system of the world, but not a word of natural history [geology and biology], of chemistry, of the movements and gravitation of bodies; there are very few experiments, still less anatomical dissection, and no geography.[76]

Diderot called for state control of education, for lay teachers, and for more science; education should be practical, producing good agronomists, technicians, scientists, and administrators. Latin should be taught only after the age of seventeen; it could be omitted altogether if the student had no prospect of using it; but "it is impossible to be a man of letters without a knowledge of Greek and Latin."[77] Since genius may arise in any class, the schools should be open to all, without charge; and poor children should receive books and food free.[78]

So belabored, the French government struggled to avert the educational interregnum threatened by the expulsion of the Jesuits. The confiscated property of the order was largely applied to a reorganization of the five hundred colleges of France. These were made part of the University of Paris; the Collège Louis-le-Grand became a normal school to train teachers; salaries were established at what seemed a reasonable rate; teachers were exempted from municipal duties, and were promised a pension on completing their term of service. Benedictines, Oratorians, and Christian Brothers were accepted as teachers, but the *philosophes* campaigned against them, and with some effect. Catholic doctrine was still a substantial part of the curriculum, but science and modern philosophy began to displace Aristotle and the Scholastics, and some lay teachers managed to convey the ideas of the *philosophes*.[79] Laboratories were set up in the colleges, with professors of experimental physics, and technical and military schools were opened in Paris and the provinces. There were several warnings that the new curriculum would improve intellect rather than character, would weaken morality and discipline, and lead to revolution.[80]

The *philosophes*, however, pinned all their hopes for the future on the reform of education. Generally they believed that man was by nature good, and that some false or wicked turns of priestcraft or politics had depraved him; all he had to do was to cleanse himself of artifice and go back to "nature"—which no one satisfactorily defined. This, as we shall see, was the essence of Rousseau. We have noted Helvétius' faith that "education can change everything."[81] Even the skeptical Voltaire, in some moods, thought that "we are a species of monkey that can be taught to act reasonably or unreasonably."[82] The belief in the indefinite possibilities of progress through the improvement and extension of education became a sustaining dogma of the new religion. Heaven and utopia are the rival buckets that hover over the well of fate: when one goes down the other goes up; hope draws up one or the other in turn. Perhaps when both buckets come up empty a civilization loses heart and begins to die.

Turgot formulated the new faith in a lecture at the Sorbonne on December 11, 1750, on "The Successive Advances of the Human Mind."

> The human race, viewed from its earliest beginning, presents itself to the eye of the philosopher as a vast whole which, like every individual being, has its time of childhood and progress. . . . Manners become gentler; the mind becomes more enlightened; nations, hitherto living in isolation, draw nearer to one another; trade and political relations link up the various quarters of the globe; and the whole body of mankind, through vicissitudes of calm and tempest, of fair days and foul, continues its onward march, albeit with tardy steps, toward an ever-nearing perfection.[83]

Voltaire hesitantly agreed:

> We may believe that reason and industry will always progress more and more; that the useful arts will be improved; that of the evils which afflict men, prejudices—which are not their least scourge—will gradually disappear among all those who govern nations; and that philosophy, universally diffused, will give some consolation to the human spirit for the calamities which it will experience in all ages.[84]

The dying *philosophe* hailed Turgot's rise to power in 1774, for he had no faith in the masses, and had attached his hopes to the enlightenment of kings. We cannot educate the canaille, as he called the commonalty of mankind; they are worn out with toil before they learn to think; but we can educate a few men who, nearing the top, may educate the monarch. This dream of "enlightened despots" as the leaders of human advance was the precarious *thèse royale* upon which most of the *philosophes* rested their vision of progress. They had many premonitions of revolution, but they feared rather than desired it; they trusted that reason would win the governing class, that ministers and rulers would listen to philosophy, and that they would effect the reforms that would avert revolution and set mankind on the road to happiness. So they hailed the reforms of Frederick II; they forgave the sins of Catherine II; and had they lived they would have rejoiced in Joseph II of Austria. And what is our faith in government but that hope revived?

V. THE NEW MORALITY

A tantalizing problem remained. Could a state survive without a religion to buttress social order with supernatural hopes and fears? Could popular morality be maintained without popular belief in the divine origin of the moral code, and in a God who saw everything, who rewarded and avenged? The *philosophes* (excepting Voltaire) claimed that such motives were not needed for morality; granting that this might be true about the cultured few, was it true about the rest? And was the morality of the cultured few an ethical echo of the faith they had lost, of the religious rearing they had received?

The *philosophes* gambled on the efficacy of a natural ethic. Voltaire had his doubts about it, but Diderot, d'Alembert, Helvétius, d'Holbach, Mably, Turgot, and others argued for a morality that would be independent of theology, and therefore strong enough to survive the vicissitudes of belief. Bayle had led the way by arguing that atheists would be just as moral as believers; but he had defined morality as the habit of conformity with reason, he had assumed that man is a rational animal, and he had left reason undefined. Should society or the individual be judge of what was reasonable? If "society" and the individual disagreed, what but force could decide between them? Would social order be merely a contest between the enforcement and the evasion of the law, and would morality merely calculate the chances of detection? F. V. Toussaint had expounded a natural ethic in *Les Moeurs* (1748); he too had defined virtue as "fidelity in fulfilling the obligations imposed by reason";[85] but how many men could reason, or did reason if they could? And was not character (which determined action) formed before reason developed, and was not reason the harlot of the strongest desire? These were some of the problems that confronted a natural ethic.

Most of the *philosophes* accepted the universality of self-love as the basic source of all conscious action, but they trusted that education, legislation, and reason could turn self-love to mutual co-operation and social order. D'Alembert confidently rested natural morality on

> one single and incontrovertible fact—the need that men have of one another, and the reciprocal obligations which that need imposes. This much being granted, all the moral laws follow from it in orderly and ineluctable sequence. All questions that have to do with morals have a solution ready to hand in the heart of each one of us—a solution which our passions sometimes circumvent, but which they never destroy. And the solution of each particular question leads . . . to the parent stem, and that, of course, is our own self-interest which is the basic principle of all moral obligations.[86]

Some of the *philosophes* recognized that this assumed a general predominance of reason in the generality of men—that is, a self-interest sufficiently "enlightened" to see the results of the ego's choice in a perspective large enough to reconcile the selfishness of the individual with the good of the group. Voltaire did not share this trust in the intelligence of egoism; reasoning seemed to him a very exceptional operation. He preferred to base his ethic on the reality of an altruism independent of self-love, and he derived this altruism from a sense of justice infused into men by God. The *frères* condemned him as surrendering the case to religion.

Having assumed the universality of self-love, the *philosophes* in general concluded that happiness is the supreme good, and that all pleasures are permissible if they do no harm to the group or to the individual himself. Borrowing the methods of the Church, Grimm, d'Holbach, Mably, and Saint-Lambert wrote catechisms expounding the new morality. Saint-Lambert addressed his *Catéchisme universel* to children of twelve or thirteen years:

Q. What is man?

A. A being possessed of feeling and understanding.

Q. That being so, what should he do?

A. Pursue pleasure and avoid pain.

Q. Is this not self-love?

A. It is the necessary effect thereof.

Q. Does self-love exist in all men alike?

A. It does, because all men aim at self-preservation and at attaining happiness.

Q. What do you understand by happiness?

A. A continuous state in which we experience more pleasure than pain.

Q. What must we do to attain this state?

A. Cultivate our reason and act in accord therewith.

Q. What is reason?

A. The knowledge of truths that conduce to our well-being.

Q. Does not self-love always lead us to discover those truths and act in accord with them?

A. No, for all men do not know how self-love should be practiced.

Q. What do you mean by that?

A. I mean that some men love themselves rightly, and others wrongly.

Q. Who are those who love themselves rightly?

A. Those who seek to know one another, and who do not separate their own happiness from the happiness of others.[87]

In their practical ethics the *philosophes* built upon their memories of Christian morality. For the worship of God, Mary, and the saints, which had indirectly aided morality, they substituted direct devotion to mankind. The Abbé de Saint-Pierre had proposed a new word for an old virtue—*bienfaisance*, which we weakly translate as *beneficence*, but which meant active mutual aid, and co-operation with others in common beneficent tasks. Along with this the *philosophes* stressed *humanité*, which meant humaneness, humanitarianism. This had its roots in the second of the two commandments enunciated by Christ. Raynal, when he branded as inhuman the cruelty of Europeans to Negroes and Indians (East and West), must have known that a Spanish bishop, Las Casas, had led the way in such condemnation in 1539. But the fresh enthusiasm for helping the poor, the sick, and the oppressed was due chiefly to the *philosophes*, and above all to Voltaire. To his persistent campaigns was due the reform of law in France. The French clergy had been noted for their charity, but they now had the experience of seeing the practical ethics of Christianity preached with remarkable success by the *philosophes*. Morality grew more independent of religion; in the fields of humaneness, sympathy, toleration, philanthropy, and peace it passed from a theological to a secular basis, and influenced society as seldom before.

Faced with the moral problems generated by war, the *philosophes* avoided pacifism while counseling peace. Voltaire admitted wars of defense, but he argued that war is robbery, that it impoverishes the victorious nation as well as the defeated, that it enriches only a few princes, war contractors, and royal mistresses. He protested Frederick's invasion of Silesia and probably had it in mind when, in a passionate article, "War," in the *Dictionnaire philosophique*, he explained how easily a royal conscience can be reconciled to aggression:

> A genealogist proves to a prince that he descends in a direct line from a count, whose parents made a family compact three or four centuries ago with a house the memory of which does not even exist. That house had distant pretensions to a province. . . . The prince and his council see his right at once. This province, which is some hundred leagues distant from him, in vain protests that it knows him not, that it has no desire to be governed by him, that to give laws to its people he must at least have their consent. . . . He immediately assembles a great number of men who have nothing to lose, dresses them in coarse blue cloth, . . . makes them turn to the right and left, and marches to glory.

Nevertheless, Voltaire advised Catherine II to take up arms and drive the Turks from Europe; he wrote a patriotic elegy for the officers who had died for France in 1741; and he blessed the army of France in its victory at Fontenoy.

The *philosophes* rejected nationalism and patriotism on the ground that these emotions narrowed the conceptions of humanity and moral obligation and made it easier for kings to lead their people into war. The article "Patrie" in the *Dictionnaire philosophique* condemned patriotism as incorporated egotism. Voltaire begged the French to moderate their boasting of superiority in language, literature, art, and war, and reminded them of their faults, crimes, and defects.[88] Montesquieu, Voltaire, Diderot, and d'Alembert in France, like Lessing, Kant, Herder, Goethe, and Schiller in Germany, were "good Europeans," and Frenchmen or Germans afterward. As one religion and one language had promoted cosmopolitanism in Western Europe in the Middle Ages, so cosmopolitanism developed on the Continent as a result of the spread of the French language and culture. Rousseau in 1755 spoke of "those great cosmopolitan minds that make light of the barriers designed to sunder nation from nation, and who, like the Sovereign Power that created them, embrace all mankind within the scope of their benevolence."[89] Elsewhere he wrote, with characteristic exaggeration: "There are no longer Frenchmen or Germans, . . . there are only Europeans."[90] This was true only of the nobility and the intelligentsia, but in those strata the cosmopolitan spirit extended from Paris to Naples and St. Petersburg. Even in wartime aristocrats and literati mingled with others of their class across frontiers; Hume, Horace Walpole, Gibbon, and Adam Smith were welcomed in Parisian society while England and France were at war, and the Prince de Ligne felt at home in almost any European capital. Soldiers too had a bit of this internationalism. "Every German officer," said Duke Ferdinand of Brunswick, "should feel honored to serve under the French flag";[91] an entire regiment in the French army—the Allemands Royaux—was composed of Germans. The Revolution put an end to this cosmopolitan camaraderie of manners and minds; the ascendancy of France faded, and nationalism advanced.

So the intellectual revolt, which in part had risen out of a moral revulsion against the cruelties of gods and priests, passed from a rejection of the old theology to an ethic of universal brotherhood that was derived from the finest aspect of the superseded faith. But the question whether a moral code unsupported by religion could maintain social order remained unsolved. It is still with us; we live in that critical experiment.

VI. RELIGION IN RETREAT

Meanwhile, for the time being, the *philosophes* appeared to have won their war against Christianity. That admirably impartial historian Henri Martin described the people of France in 1762 as "a generation which had no belief in Christianity."[92] In 1770 the *avocat général* Séguier reported:

> The *philosophes* have with one hand sought to shake the throne, and with the other to upset the altars. Their purpose was to change public opinion on civil and religious institutions, and that revolution, so to speak, has been effected. History and poetry, romances and even dictionaries have been infected with the poison of incredulity. Their writings are hardly published before they inundate the provinces like a torrent. The contagion has spread into workshops and cottages.[93]

As if to illustrate this report, Sylvan Maréchal compiled in 1771 a *Dictionnaire des athées*, which he expanded somewhat by including Abélard, Boccaccio, and Bishop Berkeley.[94] In 1775 the Archbishop of Toulouse declared that *"le monstrueux athéisme est devenu l'opinion dominante."*[95] Mme. du Deffand supposed that belief in the Christian miracles was as extinct as belief in the Greek mythology.[96] The Devil survived as an expletive, hell as a jest;[97] and the heaven of theology had been upset in space by the new astronomy, just as it recedes from space with the planetary explorations of our age. De Tocqueville spoke in 1856 of "the universal discredit into which all religious belief fell at the end of the eighteenth century."[98]

All these statements were exaggerated, and were probably made with Paris and the upper and literate classes in mind. Lecky's judgment was more discriminating: "The anti-Christian literature represented the opinions, and met the demands, of the great body of the educated classes; and crowds of administrators in all departments [of the government] connived at, or favored, its circulation."[99] The French masses still cherished the medieval faith as the prop and poetry of their toilsome lives. They accepted not only old miracles but new ones. Peddlers found a profitable market for miracle-working statuettes of the Virgin.[100] Statues and relics were carried in processions to avert or end some public calamity. The churches, even in Paris, were filled on the great festivals of the religious year, and the church bells caroled through the city their reverberating invitations. Religious confraternities numbered many members, at least in the provincial towns. "Frère" Servan, writing from Grenoble to d'Alembert (1767), assured him: "You would be astonished at the progress of philosophy in these barbarous regions"; and at Dijon there were sixty sets of the *Encyclopédie*. But these cases were exceptional; by and large the provincial bourgeoisie remained faithful to the Church.

In Paris the new movement reached every class. The workers were increasingly anticlerical; the cafés had long since dismissed God. A nobleman told how his hairdresser said to him, while powdering his hair: "You see, sir, though I am a miserable scrub, I have no more religion than anyone else."[101] The women of the proletariat carried on the old worship, and fondly fingered their rosaries. Fashionable women, however, followed the philosophic mode, dispensing with religion until they reached desiccation; nearly all of them sent for the priest when they were sure of imminent death. Most of the major salons belonged to the *philosophes*. Mme. du Deffand despised these men, but Mme. Geoffrin let them dominate her dinners; d'Alembert, Turgot, and Condorcet reigned around Mlle. de Lespinasse, and Grimm presided for Mme. d'Épinay. Horace Walpole described the intellectual atmosphere of the salons in 1765:

> There is God and the King to be pulled down; . . . men and women are devoutly employed in the demolition. They think me quite profane for having any belief left.[102] . . . The *philosophes* are insupportable, superficial, overbearing, and fanatic; they preach incessantly, and their avowed doctrine is atheism; you would not believe how openly. Don't wonder, therefore, if I should return a Jesuit.[103]

Nevertheless the Academy chose nine *philosophes* to its membership in the fourteen elections between 1760 and 1770; and in 1772 it made d'Alembert its permanent secretary.

The nobles consumed with anticlerical delight the offerings of the *esprits forts*. "Atheism was universal in high society," reported Lamothe-Langon; "to believe in God was an invitation to ridicule."[104] "After 1771 irreligion prevailed in the aristocracy."[105] The Duchesse d'Enville and the Duchesses de Choiseul, Gramont, Montesson, and Tessé were deists. Men high in the government—Choiseul, Rohan, Maurepas, Beauvau, Chauvelin—mingled amiably with d'Alembert, Turgot, Condorcet. Meanwhile the *philosophes* explained to France that feudalism had outlived its usefulness, that hereditary privileges were injustice fossilized, that a good shoemaker is better than a wastrel lord, and that all power stems from the people.

Even the clergy took the contagion. Chamfort in 1769 measured the degree of sacerdotal unbelief with the grades of the hierarchy: "The priest must believe a little; . . . the vicar can smile at a proposition against religion; the bishop laughs outright; the cardinal adds his own quip."[106] Diderot and d'Holbach numbered several skeptical abbés among their friends. The Abbés Torné, Fauchet, Maury, de Beauvais, and de Boulogne "were among the most outspoken of the *philosophes*."[107] We hear of a "Société de Prêtres Beaux-Esprits"; some of these "witty priests" were deists, some were atheists—Mesliers come to life. Priestley, dining with Turgot in 1774, was informed by the Marquis de Chastellux "that the two gentlemen opposite were the Bishop of Aix and the Archbishop of Toulouse, but 'they are no more believers than you or I.' I assured him that I was a believer, and M. Le Roy, the philosopher, told me that I was the only man of sense he knew that was a Christian."[108]

Even in the monasteries atheism had some friends. Dom Collignon, to avoid scandal, had his two mistresses at his table only when his other guests were trusted friends; he did not allow the Apostles' Creed to interfere with his pleasures, but he considered religion an admirable institution for maintaining morals among commoners.[109] Diderot told (1769) of a day he had passed with two monks:

> One of them read the first draft of a very fresh and very vigorous treatise on atheism, full of new and bold ideas; I learned with edification that this was the current doctrine in their cloisters. For the rest, these two monks were the "big bonnets" of their monasteries. They had intellect, gaiety, good feeling, knowledge.[110]

A fervent Catholic historian tells us that toward the end of the eighteenth century "a sentiment of contempt, exaggerated but universal, had replaced everywhere the profound veneration which the great monasteries had so long inspired in the Catholic world."[111]

The growth of toleration resulted chiefly from the decline of religious belief; it is easier to be tolerant when we are indifferent. Voltaire's success in the cases of Calas and the Sirvens moved several provincial governors to recommend to the central government a mitigation of the laws against Protestants. This was done. The edicts against heresy were not repealed, but they were only mildly enforced; the Huguenots were left in peace, as Voltaire had proposed. The Parlement of Toulouse showed its repentance by extending toleration to a degree that alarmed the King.[112] Some prelates —e.g., Bishop Fitzjames of Soissons in 1757—issued a pastoral letter calling upon all Christians to regard all men as brothers.[113]

Voltaire gave philosophy the credit for this victory. "It seems to me," he wrote to d'Alembert in 1764, "that only the philosophers have in some measure softened the manners of men, and that without them we would have two or three St. Bartholomew Massacres in every century."[114] We must note again that the *philosophes* themselves were sometimes intolerant. D'Alembert and Marmontel exhorted Malesherbes to suppress Fréron (1757),[115] and d'Alembert asked him to prosecute some critics of the *Encyclopédie* (1758). Mme. Helvétius urged him to silence a journal that had vilified her husband's *De l'Esprit* (1758). Voltaire on several occasions begged the authorities to suppress parodies and libels against the philosophic group;[116] and so far as these were real libels—injurious falsehoods—he was justified.

There were other factors besides philosophy in promoting toleration. The Reformation, though it sanctioned intolerance, generated so many sects (several of them strong enough to defend themselves) that intolerance seldom dared go beyond words. The sects had to dispute by argument, and they unwillingly accepted the test—and promoted the prestige—of reason. The memory of the "religious" wars in France, England, and Germany, and of the economic losses thereby incurred, turned many economic and political leaders to toleration. Mercantile centers like Hamburg, Amsterdam, and London found it necessary to put up with the different creeds and customs of their customers. The growing strength of the nationalist state made it more independent of religious unity as a means of maintaining social order. The spread of acquaintance with different civilizations and cults weakened the confidence of each faith in its monopoly of God. Above all, the advances of science made it difficult for religious dogma to proceed to barbarities like the trials of the Inquisition and the executions for witchcraft. The *philosophes* embraced most of these influences in their propaganda for toleration, and could reasonably claim much credit for the victory. It was a measure of their success that whereas in the first half of the eighteenth century Huguenot preachers were still being hanged in France, in 1776 and 1778 a Swiss Protestant was summoned by a Catholic king to save the state.

VII. SUMMING UP

So we end as we began, by perceiving that it was the philosophers and the theologians, not the warriors and diplomats, who were fighting the crucial battle of the eighteenth century, and that we were justified in calling that period the Age of Voltaire. "The philosophers of different nations," said Condorcet, "embracing in their meditations the entire interests of mankind, . . . formed a firm and united phalanx against every description of error and every species of tyranny."[117] It was by no means a united phalanx; we shall see Rousseau leaving the ranks, and Kant striving to reconcile philosophy and religion. But it was truly a struggle for the soul of man, and the results are with us today.

By the time Voltaire left Ferney for his triumph in Paris (1778), the movement that he had led had become the dominant power in European thought. Fréron, its devoted enemy, described it as "the malady and folly of the age."[118] The Jesuits had fled, and the Jansenists were in retreat. The whole tone of French society had changed. Nearly every writer in France followed the line and sought the approval of the *philosophes; philosophie* was in a hundred titles and a thousand mouths; "a word of praise from Voltaire, Diderot, or d'Alembert was more valued than the favor of a prince."[119] The salons and the Academy, sometimes even the King's ministry, were in "philosophic" hands.

Foreign visitors angled for admission to salons where they might meet and hear the famous *philosophes;* returning to their own lands, they spread the new ideas. Hume, though in many of his views he preceded Voltaire, looked up to him as a master; Robertson sent to Ferney his splendid *Charles V;* Chesterfield, Horace Walpole, and Garrick were among a score of Voltaire's English correspondents; Smollett, Franklin, and others joined in preparing an English translation and edition of Voltaire's works in thirty-seven volumes (1762). In America the founders of the new republic were deeply stirred by the writings of the *philosophes.* As to Germany, hear Goethe's remarks to Eckermann in 1820 and 1831:

> You have no idea of the influence which Voltaire and his great contemporaries had in my youth, and how they governed the [mind of the] whole civilized world. . . . It seems to me quite extraordinary to see what men the French had in their literature in the last century.

> I am astonished when I merely look at it. It was the metamorphosis
> of a hundred-year-old literature, which had been growing ever since
> Louis XIV, and now stood in full flower.[120]

Kings and queens joined in acclaiming Voltaire, and proudly listed themselves among his followers. Frederick the Great had been among the first
to sense his importance; now in 1767, after thirty years of knowing him
in all the faults of his character and the brilliance of his mind, he hailed
the triumph of the campaign against *l'infâme:* "The edifice [of supersti-
tion] is sapped to its foundations," and "the nations will write in their annals that Voltaire was the promoter of this revolution that is taking place,
in the eighteenth century, in the human spirit."[121] Catherine II of Russia
and Gustavus III of Sweden joined in this adulation; and though the Emperor Joseph II could not so openly declare himself, he unquestionably
owed to the *philosophes* the spirit of his reforms. Admirers of Voltaire
rose to power in Catholic Milan, Parma, Naples, even Madrid. Grimm
summed up the situation in 1767: "It gives me pleasure to note that an
immense republic of cultivated spirits is being formed in Europe. Enlightenment is spreading on all sides."[122]

Voltaire himself, overcoming the natural pessimism of old age, sounded
a note of victory in 1771:

> Well-constituted minds are now very numerous; they are at the
> head of nations; they influence public manners; and year by year the
> fanaticism that overspread the earth is receding in its detestable usur-
> pations. . . . If religion no longer gives birth to civil wars, it is to
> philosophy alone that we are indebted; theological disputes begin to
> be regarded in much the same manner as the quarrels of Punch and
> Judy at the fair. A usurpation odious and injurious, founded upon
> fraud on one side and stupidity on the other, is being at every instant
> undermined by reason, which is establishing its reign.[123]

Let us give him his due. We may admit, with our hindsight knowledge
of the Revolution's excesses and of the reaction that followed, that the
philosophes (excepting Voltaire) had too sanguine a confidence in human
nature; that they underestimated the force of instincts generated in thousands of years of insecurity, savagery, and barbarism; that they exaggerated
the power of education to develop reason as a sufficient controller of those
instincts; that they were blind to the demands of imagination and sentiment, and deaf to the cry of the defeated for the consolations of belief.
They gave too little weight to traditions and institutions produced by centuries of trial and error, and too great weight to the individual intellect that
at best is the product of a brief and narrow life. But if these were serious

misjudgments, they were rooted not merely in intellectual pride but also in a generous aspiration for human betterment. To the eighteenth-century thinkers—and to the perhaps profounder philosophers of the seventeenth— we owe the relative freedom that we enjoy in our thought and speech and creeds; we owe the multiplication of schools, libraries, and universities; we owe a hundred humane reforms in law and government, in the treatment of crime, sickness, and insanity. To them, and to the followers of Rousseau, we owe the immense stimulation of mind that produced the literature, science, philosophy, and statesmanship of the nineteenth century. Because of them our religions can free themselves more and more from a dulling superstition and a sadistic theology, can turn their backs upon obscurantism and persecution, and can recognize the need for mutual sympathy in the diverse tentatives of our ignorance and our hope. Because of those men we, here and now, can write without fear, though not without reproach. When we cease to honor Voltaire we shall be unworthy of freedom.

Epilogue in Elysium

Persons of the Dialogue: Pope Benedict XIV and Voltaire
Scene: A place in the grateful memory of mankind

BENEDICT. I am happy to see you here, monsieur, for though you did much damage to the Church which I was allowed to head for eighteen years, you did much good in chastising the sins and errors of the Church, and the injustices that shamed all of us in your time.

VOLTAIRE. You are now, as you were in life, the most gracious and forgiving of the popes. If every "servant of the servants of God" had been like you I would have recognized the sins of the Church as the natural property of men, and I would have continued to honor a great institution. You will remember how, for over fifty years, I respected the Jesuits.

BENEDICT. I remember, but I am sorry that you joined in the attack upon them just when they had moderated their political intrigues and were standing up bravely against the licentiousness of the King.

VOLTAIRE. I should have known better than to side with the Jansenists in that argument.

BENEDICT. Well, you see that you too can make mistakes, just like a pope. And now that I have found you in a modest mood, will you let me tell you why I remained faithful to the Church that you abandoned?

VOLTAIRE. That would be most interesting.

BENEDICT. I'm afraid I shall tire you, for I shall have to do most of the talking. But remember how many volumes you wrote.

VOLTAIRE. I often longed to see Rome, and I should have been happy to have you talk to me.

BENEDICT. And I often wished that I might speak with you. I must confess that I enjoyed your wit and your artistry. But it was your brilliance that led you astray. It is difficult to be brilliant and conservative; there is little charm, for active minds, in standing for tradition and authority; it is tempting to be critical, for then you can feel the pleasure of individuality and novelty. But in philosophy it is almost impossible to be original without being wrong. And I should like to talk with you not as a priest or a theologian, but as one philosopher to another.

VOLTAIRE. Thank you. There has been considerable doubt as to my being a philosopher.

BENEDICT. You had the good sense not to fabricate a new system. But you made a fundamental and grievous mistake.

VOLTAIRE. What was that one?

BENEDICT. You thought it possible for one mind, in one lifetime, to acquire such scope of knowledge and depth of understanding as to be fit to sit in judgment upon the wisdom of the race—upon traditions and institutions that have taken form out of the experience of centuries. Tradition is to the group what memory is to the individual; and just as the snapping of memory may bring insanity, so a sudden break with tradition may plunge a whole nation into madness, like France in the Revolution.

VOLTAIRE. France did not go mad; it concentrated into a decade the resentment accumulated during centuries of oppression. Besides, the "race" you speak of is not a mind, it is a collection and succession of fallible individuals; and the wisdom of the race is only the composite of the errors and insights of individuals. What has determined which elements in that flotsam of ideas shall be transmitted to posterity and acquire the aura and moss of time?

BENEDICT. The success or failure of ideas in the experiments of communities and nations has determined the survival of some ideas and the loss of the rest.

VOLTAIRE. I am not so sure. Perhaps prejudice robed in authority determined in many cases what ideas should be preserved, and censorship may have prevented a thousand good ideas from entering into the traditions of the race.

BENEDICT. I suppose my predecessors thought of censorship as a means of preventing the spread of ideas that would destroy the moral basis of social order, and the inspiring beliefs that help humanity to bear the burdens of life. I will admit that our censors made some grave mistakes, as in the case of Galileo—though I think we were more gentle with him than your followers have led many people to believe.

VOLTAIRE. Tradition, then, is capable of being wrong and oppressive, and an impediment to the advancement of understanding. How can man progress if he is forbidden to question tradition?

BENEDICT. Perhaps we should question progress too, but let us put that problem aside for the present. I believe that we should be allowed to question traditions and institutions, but with care that we do not destroy more than we can build, and with caution that the stone that we dislodge shall not prove to be a necessary support to what we wish to preserve, and always with a modest consciousness that the experience of generations may be wiser than the reason of a transitory individual.

VOLTAIRE. And yet reason is the noblest gift that God has given us.

BENEDICT. No; love is. I do not wish to belittle reason, but it should be the servant of love, not of pride.

VOLTAIRE. I often admitted the frailty of reason, I know that it tends to prove anything suggested by our desires; and my distant friend Diderot wrote somewhere that the truths of feeling are more unshakable than the truths of logical demonstration.[1] The true skeptic will doubt reason too. Perhaps I exaggerated reason because that madman Rousseau exaggerated feeling. To subordinate reason to feeling is, to my mind, more disastrous than to subordinate feeling to reason.

BENEDICT. The whole man needs both in their interplay. But now I wonder will you accompany me in a further step? Won't you agree that the clearest and most direct knowledge that we have is the knowledge that we exist, and that we think?

VOLTAIRE. Well?

BENEDICT. So we know thought more immediately than we know anything else?

VOLTAIRE. I wonder. I believe that we know things long before we turn into ourselves and realize that we are thinking.

BENEDICT. But confess that when you look within you perceive a reality entirely different from the matter to which you were sometimes inclined to reduce everything.

VOLTAIRE. I had my doubts about it. But proceed.

BENEDICT. Confess, too, that what you perceive when you look within is some reality of choice, some freedom of will.

VOLTAIRE. You go too fast, Father. I once believed that I enjoyed a moderate degree of freedom, but logic forced me to accept determinism.

BENEDICT. That is, you surrendered what you immediately perceived to what you concluded from a long and precarious process of reasoning.

VOLTAIRE. I couldn't refute that tough little lens-grinder Spinoza. Have you read Spinoza?

BENEDICT. Of course. A pope is not bound by the Index Expurgatorius.

VOLTAIRE. You know that we considered him an atheist.

BENEDICT. We mustn't throw epithets at one another. He was a lovable fellow, but unbearably gloomy. He saw God so universally that he left no room for human personality. He was as religious as Augustine, and as great a saint.

VOLTAIRE. I love you, Benedict; you are kinder to him than I was.

BENEDICT. Let's get on. I ask you to agree that thought, consciousness, and the sense of personality are the realities most directly known to us.

VOLTAIRE. Very well; granted.

BENEDICT. So I feel justified in rejecting materialism, atheism, and determinism. Each of us is a soul. Religion builds on that fact.

VOLTAIRE. Suppose all that; how does it warrant the mass of absurdities that were added, century after century, to the creed of the Church?

BENEDICT. There were many absurdities, I know. Many incredibilities. But the people cry out for them, and in several instances the Church, in accepting such marvels into her creed, yielded to persistent and widespread popular demand. If you take from the people the beliefs we allow them to hold, they will adopt legends and superstitions beyond control. Organized religion does not invent superstition, it checks it. Destroy an organized faith, and it will be replaced by that wilderness of disorderly superstitions that are now arising like maggots in the wounds of Christianity. And even so, there are more incredibilities in science than in religion. Is there anything more incredible than the belief that the condition of some primeval nebula determined and compelled every line in your plays?

VOLTAIRE. But those stories about asbestos saints who couldn't be burned, and a decapitated saint walking with his head in his hand, and Mary lifted up into heaven—I just couldn't stomach them.

BENEDICT. You always had a weak stomach. The people make no difficulty about them, for these stories are part of a creed that gives support and consolation to their lives. That is why they will never listen to you for long, since the breath of their life depends upon not hearing you. So, in the struggle between faith and unbelief, faith always wins. See how Catholicism is winning Western Germany, regaining your infidel France, holding Latin America, and rising to power in North America, even in the land of the Pilgrims and the Puritans.

VOLTAIRE. Sometimes, Father, I think your religion recovers not through the truth of your creed, nor through the attractiveness of your myths, not even through your clever use of drama and art, but through your devilishly subtle encouragement of fertility among your people. I perceive that the birth rate is the chief enemy of philosophy. We breed from the bottom and die at the top; and the fertility of simplicity defeats the activity of intelligence.

BENEDICT. You are mistaken if you think that our birth rate is the secret of our success; something far profounder is involved. Shall I tell you why intelligent people all over the world are returning to religion?

VOLTAIRE. Because they are tired of thinking.

BENEDICT. Not quite. They have discovered that your philosophy has no answer but ignorance and despair. And wise men perceive that all attempts at what your brethren called a natural ethic have failed. You and I probably agree that man is born with individualistic instincts formed in thousands of years of primitive conditions; that his social instincts are relatively weak; and that a strong code of morals and laws is needed to tame this natural anarchist into a normally peaceful citizen. Our theologians called those individualistic instincts original sin, inherited from our "first parents"—that is, from those harassed, lawless men, ever endangered hunters, who had always to be ready to fight and kill for food or mates; who had to be violently acquisitive, and pugnacious, and cruel, because whatever social organization they had was still weak, and they had to depend upon themselves for security in their lives and possessions.

VOLTAIRE. You are not talking like a pope.

BENEDICT. I told you we should talk like philosophers. A pope too can be a philosopher, but he has to express the conclusions of philosophy in terms not only intelligible to the people, but capable of influencing their emotions and conduct. We are convinced—and the world is returning to us because it is learning—that no moral code of confessedly human origin will be sufficiently impressive to control the unsocial impulses of the natural man. Our people are held up in their moral life—though this is uncongenial to the flesh—by a moral code taught them in their formative childhood as part of their religion, and as the word not of man but of God. You wish to keep the morality and discard the theology; but it is the theology that makes the morality sink into the soul. We must make the moral code an inseparable part of that religious belief which is man's most precious possession; for only through such belief does life acquire a meaning and a dignity that can support and ennoble our existence.

VOLTAIRE. So Moses invented those conversations with God?

BENEDICT. No mature mind asks such a question.

VOLTAIRE. You are quite right.

BENEDICT. I forgive your immature sarcasm. Certainly Hammurabi, Lycurgus, and Numa Pompilius were wise in recognizing that morality must be given a religious foundation if it is not to crumble under the persistent attacks of our strongest instincts. You too accepted this when you talked about a rewarding and punishing God. You wanted your servants to have religion, but you thought your friends could get along without it.

VOLTAIRE. I still think that philosophers can dispense with it.

BENEDICT. How naïve you are! Are children capable of philosophy? Can children reason? Society is based upon morality, morality is based upon character, character is formed in childhood and youth long before reason can be a guide. We must infuse morality into the individual when he is young and malleable; then it may be strong enough to withstand his individualistic impulses, even his individualistic reasoning. I'm afraid you began to think too soon. The intellect is a constitutional individualist, and when it is uncontrolled by morality it can tear a society to pieces.

VOLTAIRE. Some of the finest men of my time found reason a sufficient morality.

BENEDICT. That was before the individualistic intellect had time to overcome the effects of religion. A few men, like Spinoza and Bayle, d'Holbach and Helvétius, may have led good lives after abandoning the religion of their fathers; but how do we know that their virtues were not the result of their religious education?

VOLTAIRE. There were hundreds of people among my contemporaries who were contemptible profligates despite religious educations and Catholic orthodoxy, like Cardinal Dubois and Louis XV—

BENEDICT: Of whom you wrote a fulsome eulogy.

VOLTAIRE. Alas, yes. I was like some of your monks; I used pious frauds to obtain what I felt were good ends.

BENEDICT. However, there is no doubt that thousands of people orthodox in faith—even people who attend to all the observances of religion—can become great sinners and passionate criminals. Religion is no infallible cure for crime, it is only a help in the great task of civilizing mankind; we believe that without it men would be far worse than they are.

VOLTAIRE. But that awful doctrine of hell turned God into an ogre more cruel than any despot in history.

BENEDICT. You resent that doctrine, but if you knew men better you would understand that they must be frightened with fears as well as encouraged with hopes. The fear of God is the beginning of wisdom. When your followers lost that fear they began to deteriorate. You were relatively decent in your immorality; there was something beautiful in your long association with Madame du Châtelet; but your relations with your niece were disgraceful. And you found nothing to reproach in the conduct of your lecherous friend the Duc de Richelieu.

VOLTAIRE. How could I reproach him? I would have endangered my loans.

BENEDICT. You did not live long enough to see how atheism came close to making man the most despicable of beasts. Have you read the Marquis de Sade? During the ecstasy of the French Revolution he published three novels[2] in which he explained that if there is no God, everything is permitted except detection by the agents of the law. He pointed out that many wicked people prosper on earth, and many good people suffer; therefore, since there is no heaven or hell, there is no sense in being good to the detriment of our pleasures. He concluded that if the will is not free, there is no moral responsibility; there is no right or wrong, there are only weak and strong. Goodness is weakness, and weakness is evil; even the pleasure of the strong in exploiting the weak is justifiable. Cruelty, he argued, is natural, and often pleasurable. So he approved every form of pleasure, including the most disgusting and degenerate perversions, until at last the *summum bonum* seemed to lie in inflicting or receiving pain as a mode of sexual delight.

VOLTAIRE. That man should have been flogged to within an inch of his life.

BENEDICT. Yes, if you could catch him; but if you couldn't? Think of the countless crimes that are committed every day and are never detected or never punished. You have to have a moral code that will deter a man from crime even when he feels secure from detection. Is it any wonder that the "Age of Voltaire" was one of the most immoral in history? I will not say anything about your own *Pucelle*, but think of the King's Parc aux Cerfs, and the licentious literature that was printed in great quantity, widely sold, and eagerly bought, even by women. This reckless provision of erotic excitement becomes an obscene flood in times and lands of unbelief.

VOLTAIRE. You must know, your Holiness, that the sexual instinct is very strong, even in some popes, and that it will find expression despite every law.

BENEDICT. Because of its strength it needs special controls, and certainly no encouragement. That is why we tried to channel it within orderly marriage, and did all we could to make early marriage possible. In your modern societies you make marriage impossible for all but reckless and improvident men until long after they reach sexual maturity; yet you make continence difficult for them by stimulating their sexual imagination and desire at every turn by literature and the theater, under the shibboleth of freedom for the press and the stage.

VOLTAIRE. Our young people take no lasting harm from their freedom.

BENEDICT. I think you are wrong. A man accustomed to promiscuity before marriage will seldom prove a faithful husband; and a woman who gives herself freely before marriage will only exceptionally make a faithful wife. So you are driven to allow divorce on ever easier conditions. We make marriage a solemn sacrament, a vow of lifelong patience and fidelity; you make marriage a business contract, which either party is free to cancel after a passing quarrel, or in prospect of a younger or richer mate. Every home now has all its doors open, inviting flight, and the institution of marriage falls into a chaos of temporary and experimental unions tragic for women and fatal to moral order.

VOLTAIRE. But, my dear Father, monogamy is unnatural and unbearable.

BENEDICT. All restraint of instinct is unnatural, and yet without many such restraints society is impossible. And I believe that a man or woman with one mate and several children is happier than a man or woman with several mates and one child. How can a man be long happy who, excited by a new face and a pretty form, has divorced the wife who has lost her beauty in bearing and rearing his children?

VOLTAIRE. But by forbidding divorce you have had to tolerate the adultery that is so widespread in Catholic countries.

BENEDICT. Yes, there we are weak and guilty; weak through the growth of unbelief. Perhaps, because it allows an apparently united home for the children, adultery is better than divorce, and involves a less lasting derangement of the family; but I am ashamed that we have found no better solution.

VOLTAIRE. You are an honest man, Father. I would give all that I ever had if I could share your faith and your goodness.

BENEDICT. And yet you are so hard to convince! Sometimes I despair of winning back brilliant men like you, whose pens move a million souls for evil or for good. But some of your followers are opening their eyes to the awful reality. The bubble of progress has exploded in a century that has seen more wholesale murder of men and women, more devastation of cities and desolation of hearts, than any other century in history. Progress in knowledge, science, comforts, and power is only progress in means; if there is no improvement in ends, purposes, or desires, progress is a delusion. Reason improves the instrumentalities, but the ends are determined by instincts formed before birth and established before reason can grow.

VOLTAIRE. I still have faith in human intelligence; we shall improve ends as well as means as we become more secure in our lives.

BENEDICT. Are you becoming more secure? Is violent crime decreasing? Is war less terrible than before? You hope against hope that the destructiveness of your weapons will deter you and your enemies from war; but did the equivalent progress from the arrow to the bomb stop nations from challenging each other to the death?

VOLTAIRE. The education of the human race will take many centuries.

BENEDICT. Meanwhile consider the spiritual devastation that your propaganda has spread, perhaps more tragic than any ruin of cities. Is not atheism the prelude to a profounder pessimism than believers have ever known? And you, rich and famous, did you not often think of suicide?

VOLTAIRE. Yes. I tried to believe in God, but I confess to you that God meant nothing in my life, and that in my secret heart I too felt a void where my childhood faith had been. But probably this feeling belongs only to individuals and generations in transition; the grandchildren of these pessimists will frolic in the freedom of their lives, and have more happiness than poor Christians darkened with fear of hell.

BENEDICT. That fear played only a minor role in the lives of the great majority of the faithful. What inspired them was the feeling that the agony of death was not a meaningless obscenity but the prelude to a larger life, in which all earthly injustices and cruelties would be righted and healed, and they would be united in happiness and peace with those whom they had loved and lost.

VOLTAIRE. Yes, that was a real comfort, however illusory. I didn't feel it, because I hardly knew my mother, I seldom saw my father, and I had no known children.

BENEDICT. You were not a complete man, and so your philosophy was not complete. Did you ever know the life of the poor?

VOLTAIRE. Only from the outside; but I tried to be just and helpful to the poor who lived on my estates.

BENEDICT. Yes, you were a good seigneur. And you saw to it that the consoling faith of your people should be renewed by religious instruction and worship. But meanwhile your desolating gospel of no hope beyond the grave was being spread over France. Have you ever answered de Musset's question?[3] After you or your followers have taught the poor that the only heaven they can ever reach must be created by them on earth, and after they have slaughtered their rulers, and new rulers appear, and poverty remains, together with greater disorder and insecurity than before—what comfort will you then be able to offer to the defeated poor?

VOLTAIRE. I did not recommend slaughtering their rulers; I suspected that the new rulers would be much like the old, but with worse manners.

BENEDICT. I will not say that revolution is never justified. But we have learned, through the experience accumulated and transmitted by our undying hierarchy, that after every overturn there will soon again be masters and men, rich and relatively poor. We are all born unequal, and every new invention, every added complexity of life or thought, increases the gap between the simple and the clever, the weak and the strong. Those hopeful revolutionists talked of liberty, and equality, and fraternity. But these idols never get along together. If you establish liberty you let natural inequalities multiply into artificial inequalities; and to check these you have to restrain liberty; so your utopias of freedom sometimes become straitjackets of despotism, and in the turmoil fraternity becomes only a phrase.

VOLTAIRE. Yes, it is so.

BENEDICT. Well, then, which of us offers the greater consolation to the inevitably defeated majority? Do you think you will be doing a favor to the toilers of France and Italy if you convince them that their wayside shrines, their crosses, religious images, and devout offerings are meaningless mummeries, and that their prayers are addressed to an empty sky? Could there be any greater tragedy than that men should have to believe that there is nothing in life but the struggle for existence, and nothing certain in it but death?

VOLTAIRE. I sympathize with your feeling, Father. I was touched and disturbed by a letter that came to me from Madame de Talmond. I remember it well: "I think, sir, that a philosopher should never write but to endeavor to render mankind less wicked and unhappy than they are. Now, you do quite the contrary. You are always writing against that religion which alone is able to restrain wickedness and to afford consolation in misfortune."[4] But I have my faith, too—that in the long run truth will be a blessing even to the poor.

BENEDICT. Truth is not truth unless it remains true through generations. The past generations belie you, future generations will reproach you. Even the victors in the struggle of life will reprove you for taking from the poor the hopes that reconciled them to their humble place in the inevitable stratification of any society.

VOLTAIRE. I would not lend myself to such a double deception of the poor.

BENEDICT. We do not deceive them. We teach them faith, hope, and charity, and all three are real boons to human life. You made miserable jokes about the Trinity; but have you any notion of the comfort brought to millions and millions of souls by the thought that God himself had come down to this earth to share their sufferings and atone for their sins? You laughed at the Virgin Birth, but is there in all literature a more lovable and inspiring symbol of womanly modesty and maternal love?

VOLTAIRE. It is a beautiful story. If you had read all my ninety-nine volumes you would have noted that I acknowledged the value of consolatory myths.[5]

BENEDICT. We do not admit that they are myths; they are among the profoundest truths. Their effects are among the most certain facts of history. I will not speak of the art and music they have engendered, which are among the richest portions of man's heritage.

VOLTAIRE. The art was excellent, but your Gregorian chant is a gloomy bore.

BENEDICT. If you were profounder you would appreciate the value of our rituals and our sacraments. Our ceremonies bring the worshipers together in a living drama and a unifying brotherhood. Our sacraments are really what we call them—outward signs of an inward grace. It is a comfort to parents to see their child, through baptism and confirmation, accepted into the community and into the inheritance of the ancient faith; so the generations are united into a timeless family, and the individual need not feel alone. It is a boon to the sinner to confess his sins and receive absolution; you say that this merely permits him to sin again; we say that it encourages him to begin a better life, unburdened with the weight of guilt. Are not your psychiatrists struggling to find a substitute for the confessional? And do they create as many neurotics as they cure? Is it not beautiful that in the sacrament of the Eucharist weak man is strengthened and inspired by union with God? Have you ever seen anything lovelier than children going to their First Communion?

VOLTAIRE. I'm still shocked by the idea of eating God. It's a remnant of savage customs.

BENEDICT. Again you confuse the outward sign with the inward grace. There is nothing so shallow as sophistication; it judges everything from the surface, and thinks it is profound. All modern life has been misled by it. In religion the mature mind has passed through three stages: belief, unbelief, and understanding.

VOLTAIRE. You may be right. But that does not justify the hypocrisy of your sinful prelates, or the persecution of honest thought.

BENEDICT. Yes, we have been guilty. The faith is good, but its ministrants are men and women, fallible and sinful.

VOLTAIRE. But if its ministrants are fallible, why do they claim infallibility?

BENEDICT. The Church claims infallibility only for her most official, fundamental, and considered judgments. Somewhere debate has to stop if the mind or the society is to have peace.

VOLTAIRE. And so we come back to the stifling consorship and brutal intolerance that were the bane of my life and the disgrace of ecclesiastical history. I can see the doors of the Inquisition opening again.

BENEDICT. I hope not. It was because the papacy was weak that the Inquisition was so cruel; my predecessors strove to check it.

VOLTAIRE. The popes too were guilty. They looked with equanimity upon the killing of hundreds of Jews during the Crusades, and they conspired with the French state to slaughter the Albigenses. Why should we go back to a faith that, with all its charm, could engender, and can still condone, such savagery?

BENEDICT. We shared in the manners of our time. We share now in the improvement of morals. See our priests; are they not a fine group of men in education, devotion, and conduct?

VOLTAIRE. So I am told, but perhaps that is because they have competition. Who knows what they will be when the higher birth rate of their adherents gives them political supremacy? The Christians of the first three centuries of our era were noted for their superior morals, but you know what they became when they rose to power. They killed a hundred times more people for religious dissent than all the Roman emperors had ever done.

BENEDICT. Our people were then only emerging into education. Let us hope that we shall do better next time.

VOLTAIRE. The Church did do better at times. During the Italian Renaissance some of your predecessors showed an urbane tolerance of unbelief when unbelievers made no attempt to deprive the poor of their consolatory faith. I, for one, do not wish to destroy the faith of the poor. And I assure you that the poor do not read my books.

BENEDICT. Blessed be the poor.

VOLTAIRE. Meanwhile you must forgive me if I and my like continue our efforts to enlighten a minority sufficiently numerous and resolute to prevent any recurrence of ecclesiastical domination over the thought of educated men. History would be worthless to us if it did not teach us to keep on our guard against the natural intolerance of an orthodoxy wielding power. I honor and reverence you, Benedict, but I must remain Voltaire.

BENEDICT. May God forgive you.

VOLTAIRE. Pardon is the word for all.

Bibliographical Guide

to editions referred to in the Notes

ACTON, JOHN EMERICH, LORD, *Lectures on Modern History*. London, 1950.

ALDINGTON, RICHARD, *French Comedies of the Eighteenth Century*. London: Routledge, n.d.

ALDIS, JANET, *Madame Geoffrin: Her Salon and Her Times*. New York, 1905.

ALLEN, B. SPRAGUE, *Tides in English Taste*, 2v. New York, 1958.

ALLEN, ROBERT J., *Life in Eighteenth-Century England*. Boston Museum of Fine Arts, 1941.

ALTAMIRA, RAFAEL, *A History of Spain*. Princeton, N. J., 1955.

ARNOLD, MATTHEW, *Essays in Criticism*. New York: Home Library, n.d.

ASHTON, T. S., *Economic History of England: The Eighteenth Century*. New York, 1959.

AUSUBEL, NATHAN, *Superman: The Life of Frederick the Great*. New York, 1931.

BAEDEKER, KARL, *Austria*. Leipzig, 1926.

BARNES, HARRY ELMER, *Economic History of the Western World*. New York, 1942.

BATIFFOL, LOUIS, ed., *The Great Literary Salons*, tr. Mabel Robinson. New York, 1930.

BEARD, MIRIAM, *History of the Business Man*. New York, 1938.

BEARNE, MRS., *A Court Painter [Boucher] and His Circle*. London, 1913.

BECKER, CARL, *The Heavenly City of the Eighteenth-Century Philosophers*. New Haven, Conn., 1951.

BECKETT, R. B., *Hogarth*. London, 1949.

BELL, E. T., *Men of Mathematics*. New York, 1937.

BENN, ALFRED W., *History of English Rationalism in the Nineteenth Century*, 2v. London, 1906.

BERNAL, J. D., *Science in History*. London, 1957.

BERRY, ARTHUR, *Short History of Astronomy*. New York, 1909.

BERTRAND, JOSEPH, *D'Alembert*. Paris, 1889.

BESANT, SIR WALTER, *London in the Eighteenth Century*. London, 1903.

BESTERMAN, THEODORE, *Studies on Voltaire and the Eighteenth Century*. Geneva, 1955 f.

BLACK, J. B., *The Art of History*. New York, 1926.

BLACKSTONE, SIR WILLIAM, *Commentaries on the Laws of England*, ed. George Chase. New York, 1914.

BLOCK, MAURICE, *François Boucher and the Beauvais Tapestries*. Boston, 1933.

BOCK, ELFRIED, *Geschichte der graphischen Kunst*. Berlin: Propyläen Verlag, 1930.

BOLINGBROKE, HENRY ST. JOHN, VISCOUNT, *On the Spirit of Patriotism; The Idea of a Patriot King*. London, n.d.

BOSWELL, JAMES, *Boswell on the Grand Tour: Germany and Switzerland*. New York, 1955.

——, *Journal of a Tour to the Hebrides*. Everyman's Library.

——, *Life of Samuel Johnson*. Modern Library.

BOTTIGLIA, W. F., *Voltaire's* Candide. Geneva, 1959.

BRANDES, GEORG, *Voltaire*, 2v. New York, 1930.

BRETT, G. S., *History of Psychology*. London, 1953.

BROCKWAY, WALLACE, and WEINSTOCK, HERBERT, *Men of Music*. New York, 1939.

BROCKWAY, WALLACE, and WINER, BART, *A Second Treasury of the World's Great Letters*. New York, 1941.

BRUNETIÈRE, FERDINAND, *Manual of the History of French Literature*, tr. Ralph Derechef. New York, 1898.

BUCKLE, HENRY THOMAS, *Introduction to the History of Civilization in England*, 2v. in 4. New York, 1913.

BUFFON, GEORGES LOUIS LECLERC, COMTE DE, *Oeuvres complètes*, 12v. Paris, 1853 f.

BURKE, EDMUND, *Reflections on the French Revolution, and Other Essays*. Everyman's Library.

BURNEY, CHARLES, *General History of Music*, 2v. New York, 1957.

BURNEY, FANNY, *Diary*. Everyman's Library.

BURTON, JOHN H., *Life and Correspondence of David Hume*, 2v. Edinburgh, 1846.

BURY, J. B., *History of Freedom of Thought*. New York: Home University Library, n.d.

——, *The Idea of Progress*. New York, 1955.

BUTTERFIELD, H., *The Origins of Modern Science*. New York, 1951.

CALVIN, JOHN, *Institutes of the Christian Religion*, 2v. Philadelphia, 1928.

Cambridge History of English Literature, 14v. New York, 1910 f.

Cambridge Modern History, 12v. New York, 1907 f.

CAMPBELL, THOMAS J., *The Jesuits*. New York, 1921.

CARLYLE, THOMAS, *History of Friedrich the Second*, 7v. New York, 1901.

CASANOVA, GIOVANNI JACOPO, *Memoirs*, 2v. London, 1922.

CASSIRER, ERNST, *The Philosophy of the Enlightenment*. Princeton, N.J., 1951.

——, *The Question of Jean Jacques Rousseau*, tr. Peter Gay. New York, 1954.

CASTIGLIONI, ARTURO, *A History of Medicine*. New York, 1941.

Catholic Encyclopedia, 16v. New York, 1912.

CHAMBERS, F. P., *The History of Taste*. New York, 1932.

CHAPONNIÈRE, PAUL, *Chez les Calvinistes*. Paris, 1936.

——, *Genève*. Grenoble, n.d.

CHATEAUBRIAND, VICOMTE FRANÇOIS RENÉ DE, *The Genius of Christianity*. Baltimore: John Murphy, n.d.

CHESTERFIELD, PHILIP DORMER STANHOPE, 4TH EARL OF, *Letters to His Son*. New York, 1901.

CHIDSEY, DONALD BARR, *Marlborough*. New York, 1929.

CHURCHILL, WINSTON S., *History of the English-Speaking Peoples*, 4v. London, 1957.

CLARK, BARRETT H., *Great Short Biographies of the World*. New York, 1928.

CLARK, GEORGE NORMAN, *The Seventeenth Century*. Oxford University Press, 1929.

CLERGUE, HELEN, *The Salon*. New York, 1907.

COBBAN, ALFRED, *History of Modern France*, 2v. Penguin Books, 1957.

———, *In Search of Humanity*. New York, 1960.

COLLINS, JOHN CHURTON, *Bolingbroke, and Voltaire in England*. New York, 1886.

CONDILLAC, ÉTIENNE BONNOT DE, *Traité des sensations*. Paris: Hastier, n.d.

CONDORCET, M. J. A. N. CARITAT, MARQUIS DE, *Esquisse d'un tableau du progrès de l'esprit humain*. Philadelphia, 1796.

COXE, WILLIAM, *History of the House of Austria*, 3v. London, 1847.

———, *Travels in Switzerland*, 1776 f., 3v. London, 1801.

CRAVEN, THOMAS, *Treasury of Art Masterpieces*. New York, 1952.

CRÉBILLON, CLAUDE PROSPER JOLYOT DE (CRÉBILLON *fils*), *Le Sopha*. London, 1927.

CRÉQUI, RENÉE CAROLINE DE FROULLAY, MARQUISE DE, *Souvenirs*. New York, 1904.

CROCKER, LESTER G., *An Age of Crisis: Man and the World in Eighteenth-Century French Thought*. Baltimore, 1959.

———, *The Embattled Philosopher: Life of Denis Diderot*. East Lansing, Mich., 1954.

CRU, ROBERT LOYALTY, *Diderot as a Disciple of English Thought*. New York, 1913.

CUMMING, IAN, *Helvétius*. London, 1955.

DAKIN, DOUGLAS, *Turgot and the Ancien Régime in France*. London, 1939.

D'ALTON, E. A., *History of Ireland*, 6v. Dublin, n.d.

DAVISON, ARCHIBALD, *Bach and Handel*. Cambridge, Mass., 1951.

DEFOE, DANIEL, *Tour through England and Wales*, 2v. Everyman's Library.

DESNOIRESTERRES, GUSTAVE, *Voltaire et la société française au dix-huitième siècle*, 8v. Paris, 1871.

DEUTSCH, OTTO, *Handel*. London, 1955.

DIDEROT, DENIS, *Dialogues*. New York, 1927.

———, *Jacques the Fatalist and His Master*, tr. J. Robert Loy. New York, 1959.

———, *Oeuvres*. Paris: Bibliothèque de la Pléiade, 1935.

———, *The Paradox of Acting*. New York, 1957.

———, *Salons*, 3v. Paris, 1821.

———, *Writings on the Theater*. Cambridge, Eng., 1936.

DILKE, LADY EMILIA, *French Architects and Sculptors of the Eighteenth Century*. London, 1900.

DILLON, EDWARD, *Glass*. New York, 1907.

DOBSON, AUSTIN, *Hogarth*. London, 1883.

DUCLOS, CHARLES PINOT, *Considérations sur les moeurs*. Cambridge, Eng., 1939.

———, *Secret Memoirs of the Regency*. New York, 1910.

DUCROS, LOUIS, *French Society in the Eighteenth Century*. London, 1926.

DU HAUSSET, MADAME, *Memoirs of Madame de Pompadour*. New York, 1928.

DUNNING, W. A., *History of Political Theories*, 3v. New York, 1905 f.
DUPEE, F. W., *Great French Short Novels*. New York, 1952.

ECKERMANN, JOHANN PETER, and SORET, M., *Conversations with Goethe*. London, 1882.
EDWARDS, H. SUTHERLAND, *Idols of the French Stage*, 2v. London, 1889.
ELLIS, HAVELOCK, *The New Spirit*. London: Walter Scott Publishing Co., n.d.
Encyclopaedia Britannica, 14th ed.
Encyclopaedia of Religion and Ethics, ed. James Hastings, 12v. New York, 1928.
ÉPINAY, LOUISE DE LA LIVE D', *Memoirs and Correspondence*, tr. J. H. Freese, 3v. London, 1899.
ERCOLE, LUCIENNE, *Gay Court Life: France in the Eighteenth Century*. New York, 1932.

FAGUET, ÉMILE, *Dix-huitième siècle: Études littéraires*. Paris, n.d.
———, *Literary History of France*. New York, 1907.
FANIEL, STÉPHANE, *French Art of the Eighteenth Century*. New York, 1957.
FAŸ, BERNARD, *La Franc-Maçonnerie et la révolution intellectuelle du dix-huitième siècle*. Paris, 1935.
FELLOWS, OTIS E., and TORREY, NORMAN L., eds., *The Age of Enlightenment*. New York, 1942.
———, *Diderot Studies*, 2v. Syracuse, N.Y., 1949.
FIELDING, HENRY, *Works*, 12v. New York, 1903.
FLINT, ROBERT, *History of the Philosophy of History*. New York, 1894.
FORD, BORIS, ed., *From Dryden to Johnson*. Penguin Books, 1957.
FRANCKE, KUNO, *History of German Literature as Determined by Social Forces*. New York, 1901.
FRANKEL, CHARLES, *The Faith of Reason*. New York, 1948.
FREDERICK II (THE GREAT), *Mémoires*, 2v. Paris, 1866.
FRENCH, SIDNEY J., *Torch and Crucible: The Life and Death of Antoine Lavoisier*. Princeton, N.J., 1941.
FÜLOP-MILLER, RENÉ, *The Power and Secret of the Jesuits*. New York, 1930.
FUNCK-BRENTANO, FRANTZ, *L'Ancien Régime*. Paris, 1926.

GARNETT, RICHARD, *History of Italian Literature*. New York, 1898.
———, and GOSSE, EDMUND, *English Literature, an Illustrated Record*, 4v. New York, 1908.
GARRISON, FIELDING H., *History of Medicine*. Philadelphia, 1929.
GAY, PETER, *Voltaire's Politics*. Princeton, N.J., 1959.
GEORGE, M. DOROTHY, *London Life in the Eighteenth Century*. London, 1925.
GERSHOY, LEO, *From Despotism to Revolution: 1763–89*. New York, 1944.
GIBBON, EDWARD, *Journal and Ephemerides*. New York: Norton, n.d.
———, *Memoirs*. London, 1900.
———, *Miscellaneous Writings*. New York, 1907.
GILBERT, O. P., *The Prince de Ligne*. New York, n.d.
GOLDSMITH, OLIVER, *Miscellaneous Works*. London, 1904.
GONCOURT, EDMOND and JULES DE, *French Eighteenth-Century Painters*. New York, 1948.
———, *Madame de Pompadour*. Paris, n.d.
———, *The Woman of the Eighteenth Century*. New York, 1927.

GOOCH, G. P., *Catherine the Great and Other Studies*. New York, 1954.

GOODWIN, A., *The European Nobility in the Eighteenth Century*. London, 1953.

GOURLIE, NORAH, *The Prince of Botanists: Carl Linnaeus*. London, 1953.

GRIMM, DIDEROT, RAYNAL, et al., *Correspondance littéraire, philosophique, et critique*, 16v. Paris, 1877–82.

GROSSMAN, MORDECAI, *The Philosophy of Helvétius*. New York, 1926.

Grove's Dictionary of Music and Musicians, 5v. New York, 1927 f.

GUIZOT, FRANÇOIS, *History of France*, 8v. London, 1872.

HALSBAND, ROBERT, *Life of Lady Mary Wortley Montagu*. Oxford, Eng., 1957.

HAMPDEN, JOHN, ed., *Eighteenth-Century Plays*. Everyman's Library.

HARDING, T. SWANN, *Fads, Frauds, and Physicians*. New York, 1930.

HAUSER, ARNOLD, *The Social History of Art*, 2v. New York, 1952.

HAVENS, GEORGE, *The Age of Ideas*. New York, 1955.

HAZARD, PAUL, *European Thought in the Eighteenth Century*. New Haven, 1954.

HEARNSHAW, F. J., ed., *Social and Political Ideas of Some English Thinkers of the Augustan Age*. New York, 1950.

——, *Social and Political Ideas of Some Great French Thinkers of the Age of Reason*. New York, 1950.

HELVÉTIUS, CLAUDE ADRIEN, *De l'Esprit, or Essays on the Mind*. London, 1807.

——, *Treatise on Man*, 2v. London, 1810.

HENDEL, CHARLES W., *Citizen of Geneva: Selections from the Letters of Jean-Jacques Rousseau*. Oxford University Press, 1937.

HERBERT, SYDNEY, *The Fall of Feudalism in France*. London, 1921.

HERODOTUS, *History*, ed. Rawlinson, 4v. London, 1862.

HEROLD, J. CHRISTOPHER, *The Swiss without Halos*. New York, 1948.

HIMES, NORMAN, *Medical History of Contraception*. Baltimore, 1936.

HOBHOUSE, LEONARD T., *Morals in Evolution*. New York, 1916.

HOLBACH, BARON PAUL HENRI DIETRICH D', *The System of Nature*, tr. H. O. Robinson, 2v. in 1. Boston, 1868.

HOLZKNECHT, KARL, *The Backgrounds of Shakespeare*. New York, 1950.

HOROWITZ, I. L., *Claude Helvétius*. New York, 1954.

HUME, DAVID, *Dialogues concerning Natural Religion*. New York, 1948.

——, *Enquiries concerning the Human Understanding and concerning the Principles of Morals*. Oxford University Press, 1955.

——, *Essays and Treatises*, 4v. London, 1770.

——, *Essays, Moral and Political*. London: Ward, Locke, & Co., n.d.

——, *History of England*, 5v. Philadelphia: Porter & Coates, n.d.

——, *Treatise of Human Nature*, 2v. Everyman's Library.

HUXLEY, THOMAS H., *Hume*. New York, 1901.

——, *Science and Education*. New York, 1896.

INGE, WILLLIAM R., *Christian Mysticism*. London, 1899.

JAMES, B. B., *Women of England*. Philadelphia, 1908.

JARDINE, SIR WILLIAM, *The Naturalist's Library*. London, n.d.

JAURÈS, JEAN, *Histoire socialiste de la Révolution française*, 8v. Paris, 1922.

JEFFERSON, D. W., ed., *Eighteenth-Century Prose*. Pelican Books, 1956.

JOHNSON, SAMUEL, *Lives of the English Poets*, 2v. Everyman's Library.
——, *The Rambler*. Everyman's Library.

KAVANAGH, JULIA, *Woman in France during the Eighteenth Century*, 2v. New York, 1893.
KÖHLER, CARL, *A History of Costume*. New York, 1928.
KOVEN, ANNA DE, *Horace Walpole and Madame du Deffand*. New York, 1929.
KRUTCH, JOSEPH WOOD, *Samuel Johnson*. New York, 1945.

LA BRUYÈRE and VAUVENARGUES, *Selections*. New York, 1903.
LACROIX, PAUL, *The Eighteenth Century in France*. London: Bickers & Son, n.d.
LA FONTAINERIE, F. DE, *French Liberalism and Education in the Eighteenth Century*. New York, 1932.
LA METTRIE, JULIEN OFFROY DE, *Man a Machine*. Chicago, 1912.
LANFREY, PIERRE, *L'Église et les philosophes au dix-huitième siècle*. Paris, 1857.
LANG, ANDREW, *History of Scotland*, 4v. Edinburgh, 1902.
LÁNG, P. H., *Music in Western Civilization*. New York, 1941.
LANGDON-DAVIES, JOHN, *Short History of Women*. New York, 1927.
LANGE, FRIEDRICH ALBERT, *History of Materialism*, 3v. in 1. New York, 1925.
LANGER, WILLIAM L., *Encyclopedia of World History*. Boston, 1948.
LANSON, GUSTAVE, *Voltaire*. Paris, 1906.
LASKI, HAROLD, *Political Thought in England, Locke to Bentham*. Oxford University Press, 1950.
LEA, HENRY C., *History of the Inquisition in Spain*, 4v. New York, 1906.
——, *Superstition and Force*. Philadelphia, 1892.
LECKY, WILLIAM E., *History of England in the Eighteenth Century*, 8v. London, 1888.
——, *History of the Rise and Influence of the Spirit of Rationalism in Europe*, 2v. London, 1910.
LESAGE, ALAIN RENÉ, *Adventures of Gil Blas*. New York: A. L. Burt, n.d.
LÉVY-BRUHL, LUCIEN, *History of Modern Philosophy in France*. Chicago, 1924.
LEWIS, D. B. WYNDHAM, *Four Favorites*. New York, 1949.
LICHTENBERGER, ANDRÉ, *Le Socialisme et la Révolution française*. Paris, 1899.
LIPSON, E., *Growth of English Society*. London, 1949.
LOCY, W. A., *Biology and Its Makers*. New York, 1915.
——, *Growth of Biology*. New York, 1925.
LOUGH, J., ed., *The* Encyclopédie *of Diderot and d'Alembert: Selected Articles*. Cambridge, Eng., 1954.
LOVEJOY, ARTHUR, *Essays in the History of Ideas*. Baltimore, 1948.
——, *The Great Chain of Being*. Cambridge, Mass., 1953.
LÜTZOW, COUNT FRANZ VON, *Bohemia*. Everyman's Library.

MACAULAY, THOMAS BABINGTON, *Critical, Historical, and Miscellaneous Essays and Poems*, 2v. New York, 1886.
——, *Critical and Historical Essays*, 2v. Everyman's Library.
MACKAY, CHARLES, *Extraordinary Popular Delusions and the Madness of Crowds*. Boston, 1932.
MANDEVILLE, BERNARD, *The Fable of the Bees*. London, 1934.
MANTOUX, PAUL, *The Industrial Revolution in the Eighteenth Century*. London, 1955.

MARIVAUX, PIERRE DE, *La Vie de Marianne*. Paris: Charpentier, n.d.
MARKUN, LEO, *Mrs. Grundy: A History of Four Centuries of Morals*. New York, 1930.
MARMONTEL, JEAN FRANÇOIS, *Memoirs*, 2v. New York, n.d.
MARTIN, HENRI, *Histoire de France*, 16v. Paris, 1865.
MARTIN, KINGSLEY, *The Rise of French Liberal Thought*. New York, 1956.
MASSON, PIERRE, *La Religion de Rousseau*, 3v. Paris, 1916.
MAVERICK, L. A., *China, a Model for Europe*. San Antonio, Tex., 1946.
McCABE, JOSEPH, *Candid History of the Jesuits*. New York, 1913.
McCONNELL, FRANCIS J., *John Wesley*. New York: Abingdon Press, n.d.
McKIE, DOUGLAS, *Antoine Lavoisier*. New York, 1952.
McKINNEY, H. D., and ANDERSON, W. R., *Music in History*. Cincinnati, 1940.
MESLIER, JEAN, *Superstition in All Ages, or Last Will and Testament*, tr. Anna Knoop. New York, 1950.
MICHELET, JULES, *Histoire de France*, 5v. Paris: Hetzel & Cie., n.d.
MITFORD, NANCY, *Madame de Pompadour*. New York, 1953.
———, *Voltaire in Love*. New York, 1958.
MONROE, PAUL, *Text-Book in the History of Education*. New York, 1928.
MONTAGU, LADY MARY WORTLEY, *Letters and Works*, 2v. London, 1893 f.
MONTALEMBERT, CHARLES, COMTE DE, *The Monks of the West*, 2v. Boston: Marlier, Callanan & Co., n.d.
MONTESQUIEU, CHARLES DE SECONDAT, BARON DE, *Grandeur et décadence des Romains*. Paris, 1924.
———, *Persian Letters*. London: Routledge, n.d.
———, *The Spirit of Laws*, 2v. New York, 1899.
MOORE, F. J., *History of Chemistry*. New York, 1918.
MORLEY, JOHN, *Diderot and the Encyclopaedists*, 2v. London, 1923.
———, *Life of Voltaire*, in Voltaire, *Works* (New York, 1927), Vol. XXIb.
MORNET, DANIEL, *Les Origines intellectuelles de la Révolution française*. Paris, 1933.
MOSSNER, ERNEST, *Bishop Butler and the Age of Reason*. New York, 1936.
———, *Life of David Hume*. Austin, Tex., 1954.
MOUSNIER, R., and LABROUSSE, E., *Le Dix-huitième Siècle*. Paris, 1853.
MOWAT, R. B., *The Age of Reason*. Boston, 1934.
MUSSET, ALFRED DE, *Confessions of a Child of the Century*. New York, 1908.

NAGEL, ERNEST, *The Structure of Science*. New York, 1961.
NAVES, RAYMOND, *Voltaire et l'Encyclopédie*. Paris, 1938.
NAWRATH, ALFRED, *Austria*. London, 1956.
New Cambridge Modern History, Vol. VII. Cambridge, Eng., 1957.
NEWTON, ISAAC, *Mathematical Principles of Natural Philosophy*, ed. Florian Cajori. Berkeley, Calif., 1956.
NICOLSON, HAROLD, *The Age of Reason*. London, 1960.
NOYES, ALFRED, *Voltaire*. New York, 1936.
NUSSBAUM, F. L., *History of the Economic Institutions of Modern Europe*. New York, 1937.

OECHSLI, WILHELM, *History of Switzerland*. Cambridge, Eng., 1922.
OGG, DAVID, *Europe in the Seventeenth Century*. London, 1956.
ORTEGA Y GASSET, JOSÉ, *Toward a Philosophy of History*. New York, 1941.

Osborn, Henry Fairfield, *From the Greeks to Darwin.* New York, 1922.
———, *Men of the Old Stone Age.* New York, 1915.
Osler, William, *Evolution of Modern Medicine.* New Haven, 1923.
Oxford History of Music, 7v. London, 1929 f.

Palache, John, *Four Novelists of the Old Regime.* New York, 1926.
Palmer, R. R., *Catholics and Unbelievers in Eighteenth-Century France.* Princeton, N.J., 1939.
Pappas, John N., *Berthier's* Journal de Trévoux *and the Philosophes.* Geneva, 1957.
Parton, James, *Life of Voltaire,* 2v. Boston, 1882.
Pincherle, Marc, *Vivaldi.* New York, 1962.
Pinot, Virgile, *La Chine et la formation de l'esprit philosophique en France, 1640–1740.* Paris, 1932.
Pomeau, René, *La Religion de Voltaire.* Paris, 1958.
Pope, Alexander, *Collected Poems.* Everyman's Library.
Pratt, Waldo Selden, *History of Music.* New York, 1927.
Prévost, Antoine, *Manon Lescaut,* tr. Helen Waddell. New York, 1935.
Putnam, G. H., *The Censorship of the Church of Rome,* 2v. New York, 1906.

Quennell, Marjorie and Charles, *History of Everyday Things in England, 1733–1851.* New York, 1934.
Quennell, Peter, *Caroline of England.* New York, 1940.
———, *Hogarth's Progress.* New York, 1955.

Ranke, Leopold, *History of the Popes,* 3v. London, 1878.
———, *History of the Reformation in Germany.* London, 1905.
Reichwin, A., *China and Europe: Intellectual and Artistic Contacts in the Eighteenth Century.* New York, 1925.
Renard, G., and Weulersee, G., *Life and Work in Modern Europe.* London, 1926.
Richard, Ernst, *History of German Civilization.* New York, 1911.
Richardson, Samuel, *Clarissa.* Modern Library.
———, *Pamela,* 2v. Everyman's Library.
Ridder, André de, *J. B. S. Chardin.* Paris, 1932.
Robertson, John Mackinnon, *Short History of Freethought,* 2v. London, 1914.
Robertson, William, *History of the Reign of the Emperor Charles V,* 2v. London, 1898.
Rogers, James Edwin Thorold, *Economic Interpretation of History.* London, 1891.
Rolland, Romain, *Musical Tour through the Land of the Past.* London, 1922.
Rousseau, Jean Jacques, *Confessions.* London, n.d.
Rowse, A. L., *The Early Churchills.* New York, 1956.

Sade, Marquis de, *Justine.* Paris, 1791.
Sainte-Beuve, Charles Augustin, *English Portraits.* New York, 1875.
———, *Portraits of the Eighteenth Century,* 2v. in 1. New York, 1905.
Saint-Simon, Louis de Rouvroy, Duc de, *Memoirs,* 3v. London, 1901.
Schoenfeld, Hermann, *Women of the Teutonic Nations.* Philadelphia, 1908.

SCHUSTER, M. LINCOLN, *Treasury of the World's Great Letters*. New York, 1940.

SCHWEITZER, ALBERT, *J. S. Bach*, 2v. Leipzig, 1911.

———, *Quest of the Historical Jesus*. London, 1926.

SEDGWICK, W. T., and TYLER, H. W., *Short History of Science*. New York, 1927.

SÉE, HENRI, *Economic and Social Conditions in France during the Eighteenth Century*. New York, 1935.

———, *Les Idées politiques en France au dix-huitième siècle*. Paris, 1920.

SÉGUR, MARQUIS P. M. M. H. DE, *Julie de Lespinasse*. New York, 1927.

SHAFTESBURY, ANTHONY ASHLEY COOPER, 3D EARL OF, *Characteristics*, 2v. London, 1900.

SIGERIST, H. E., *The Great Doctors*. New York, 1933.

SIME, JAMES, *Lessing*, 2v. London, 1879.

SITWELL, SACHEVERELL, *German Baroque Art*. New York, 1928.

SMITH, ADAM, *The Wealth of Nations*, 2v. Everyman's Library.

SMITH, D. E., *History of Mathematics*, 2v. Boston, 1923.

SMITH, PRESERVED, *History of Modern Culture*, 2v. New York, 1930.

SMOLLETT, TOBIAS, *Adventures of Peregrine Pickle*. New York, 1936.

———, *Humphrey Clinker*. Modern Library.

———, *Roderick Random*. Everyman's Library.

———, *Travels through France and Italy*. London, 1919.

SOREL, ALBERT, *Montesquieu*. Chicago, 1888.

SPITTA, PHILIP, *Johann Sebastian Bach*, 3v. in 2. New York, 1951.

STEPHEN, LESLIE, *Alexander Pope*. New York, 1880.

———, *English Literature and Society in the Eighteenth Century*. London, 1904.

———, *History of English Thought in the Eighteenth Century*, 2v. London, 1902.

STRACHEY, LYTTON, *Books and Characters*. New York, 1922.

———, *Portraits in Miniature*. New York, 1931.

STRYIENSKI, CASIMIR, *The Eighteenth Century*. London, 1916.

SUMNER, WILLIAM GRAHAM, *Folkways*. Boston, 1906.

TAINE, HIPPOLYTE, *The Ancient Regime*. New York, 1891.

———, *History of English Literature*. New York, 1873.

TAWNEY, R. H., *Religion and the Rise of Capitalism*. New York, 1926.

TEXTE, JOSEPH, *Jean-Jacques Rousseau and the Cosmopolitan Spirit in Literature*. London, 1899.

THACKERAY, WILLIAM MAKEPEACE, *English Humourists*. Boston: Dana, Estes & Co., n.d.

———, *The Four Georges*. Boston: Dana, Estes & Co., n.d.

THOMPSON, JAMES W., *Economic and Social History of Europe in the Later Middle Ages*. New York, 1931.

THORNTON, J. C., *Table Talk from Ben Jonson to Leigh Hunt*. Everyman's Library.

TIETZE, HANS, *Treasures of the Great National Galleries*. New York, 1954.

TOCQUEVILLE, ALEXIS DE, *L'Ancien Régime*. Oxford, Eng., 1927.

TORREY, NORMAN L., *The Spirit of Voltaire*. New York, 1938.

———, *Voltaire and the English Deists*. New Haven, 1930.

TOTH, KARL, *Woman and Rococo in France*. Philadelphia, 1931.

TOYNBEE, ARNOLD J., *A Study of History*, 10v. Oxford, 1935 f.

———, *A Study of History*, Vols. I–VI, abridged by D. C. Somervell. New York, 1947.

TRAILL, HENRY DUFF, ed., *Social England*, 6v. New York, 1902.

TRATTNER, E. R., *Architects of Ideas*. New York, 1938.

TRAUBEL, HORACE, *With Walt Whitman in Camden*. Boston, 1906.

TREVELYAN, G. M., *England under the Stuarts*. New York, 1933.

———, *English Social History*. London, 1947.

TURBERVILLE, A. S., ed., *Johnson's England*, 2v. Oxford, Eng., 1952.

TURNER, P. M., and BAKER, C. H., *Stories of the French Artists*. New York, 1910.

USHER, ABBOTT P., *History of Mechanical Inventions*. New York, 1929.

VARTANIAN, ARAM, *Diderot and Descartes*. Princeton, N.J., 1953.

VAUVENARGUES, LUC DE CLAPIERS, MARQUIS DE, *Oeuvres choisies*. Paris: Garnier, n.d.

VILLARI, PASQUALE, *Life and Times of Niccolò Machiavelli*, 2v. in 1. New York: Scribner's, n.d.

VOLTAIRE, *Age of Louis XIV*. Everyman's Library.

———, *Age of Louis XV*, 2v. Glasgow, 1771.

———, *Correspondance*, ed. Theodore Besterman, 59v. Geneva, 1950 f.

———, *History of Charles XII*. Everyman's Library.

———, *Lettres d'Alsace à sa nièce Mme Denis*. Paris, 1938.

———, *Lettres d'amour de Voltaire à sa nièce*, ed. Theodore Besterman. Paris, 1957. English edition, *Love Letters of Voltaire to His Niece*, London, 1958.

———, *Notebooks*, ed. Theodore Besterman, 2v. Geneva, 1952.

———, *Oeuvres complètes*. Paris, 1825 f.

———, *Philosophical Dictionary*, in *Works*, Vols. III–VI.

———, *Romans*, 2v. Paris: Flammarion, n.d.

———, *Selected Works*, ed. Joseph McCabe. London, 1911.

———, *Works*, 44v. in 22. New York, 1927.

——— and FREDERICK THE GREAT, *Letters*, tr. Richard Aldington. New York, 1927.

WADE, IRA, *Studies in Voltaire*. Princeton, N.J., 1947.

———, *Voltaire and Madame du Châtelet*. Princeton, N.J., 1941.

WALPOLE, HORACE, *Letters*, ed. Peter Cunningham, 9v. London, 1880.

———, *Memoires of the Last Ten Years of the Reign of George the Second*, 2v. London, 1822.

WALISZEWSKI, K., *The Romance of an Empress: Catherine II of Russia*. New York, 1929.

WEBB, SIDNEY and BEATRICE, *History of Trade Unionism*. New York, 1920.

WEINSTOCK, HERBERT, *Handel*. New York, 1959.

WESLEY, JOHN, *The Heart of Wesley's Journal*. New York, 1942.

WESTERMARCK, EDVARD A., *The Origin and Development of the Moral Ideas*, 2v. London, 1924.

———, *A Short History of Marriage*. New York, 1926.

WHARTON, GRACE and PHILIP, *The Wits and Beaux of Society*, 2v. Philadelphia, 1860.

WHITE, ANDREW, *History of the Warfare of Science with Theology in Christendom*, 2v. New York, 1929.

WHITEHEAD, ALFRED NORTH, *Science in the Modern World*. New York, 1926.

WICKWAR, W. H., *Baron d'Holbach*. London, 1935.

WILENSKI, R. H., *English Painting*. London, 1946.

WILHELMINE, MARGRAVINE OF BAYREUTH, *Memoirs*. London, 1887.

WILLEY, BASIL, *The Eighteenth-Century Background*. London, 1949.

WILLIAMS, HENRY SMITH, *History of Science*, 5v. New York, 1909.

WILSON, ARTHUR M., *Diderot: The Testing Years, 1713–59*. New York, 1957.

WINGFIELD-STRATFORD, ESME, *History of British Civilization*. London, 1948.

WOLF, A., *History of Science, Technology, and Philosophy in the Eighteenth Century*. New York, 1939.

WOODS, GEORGE, WATT, HOMER, and ANDERSON, GEORGE, *The Literature of England*, 2v. Chicago, 1936.

World Christian Handbook. London, 1957.

WORMELEY, KATHARINE PRESCOTT, *Correspondence of Madame, Princess Palatine, . . . Marie Adélaïde de Savoie, . . . and Madame de Maintenon . . .* Boston, 1902.

Notes

APOLOGY

1. Brandes, G., *Voltaire*, I, 4.
2. Cousin, Victor, *Histoire de la philosophie*, in Buckle, H. T., *History of Civilization in England*, I, 519n.
3. Voltaire, *Age of Louis XIV*, 16.

CHAPTER I

1. Brandes, *Voltaire*, I, 30.
2. *Ibid.*, 31; Parton, James, *Life of Voltaire*, I, 26; Campbell, T. J., *The Jesuits*, 354.
3. Desnoiresterres, *Voltaire et la société française au xviiie siècle*, I, 32.
4. *Ibid.*, 17-18.
5. Letter of Feb. 7, 1746, to Father Latour, in Desnoiresterres, I, 24; Brandes, I, 44.
6. Parton, I, 53.
7. Hazard, Paul, *European Thought in the 18th Century*, 129.
8. Parton, I, 66.
9. Desnoiresterres, I, 171.
10. Duclos, C. P., *Secret Memoirs of the Regency*, 6.
11. Saint-Simon, *Memoirs*, II, 329.
12. Duclos, 10.
13. Saint-Simon, II, 326.
14. Desnoiresterres, I, 96.
15. Wormeley, K. P., *Correspondence of Madame, Princess Palatine, . . . Marie Adélaïde de Savoie, . . . and Mme. de Maintenon*, 29.
16. Guizot, F., *History of France*, V, 3.
17. Martin, Henri, *Histoire de France*, XV, 13.
18. Ducros, Louis, *French Society in the 18th Century*, 55.
19. Martin, H., XV, 20-22; Desnoiresterres, I, 164.
20. Stryienski, C., *Eighteenth Century*, 82.
21. Beard, Miriam, *History of the Business Man*, 47.
22. Martin, H., XV, 53.
23. Voltaire, *Works*, XVI, 20.
24. Martin, H., XV, 54.
25. Michelet, J., *Histoire de France*, V, 268.
26. Saint-Simon, II, 232.
27. *Ibid.*, III, 239.
28. Martin, H., XV, 62.
29. Saint-Simon, III, 243.
30. In Lacroix, Paul, *Eighteenth Century in France*, 201.
31. Wormeley, 31.
32. Guizot, V, 42.
33. Duclos, *Secret Memoirs*, 70.
34. Martin, H., XV., 107.
35. Saint-Simon, III, 338.
36. Michelet, V, 133.
37. *Ibid.*, 135.
38. Saint-Simon, III, 69.
39. Voltaire, *Works*, XVIa, 155.
40. Saint-Simon, III, 418.
41. *Cambridge Modern History*, II, 133.
42. Michelet, V, 197; Martin, H., XV, 11n.
43. Duclos, *Secret Memoirs*, 8.
44. Ercole, L., *Gay Court Life in France in the 18th Century*, 18-20.
45. Saint-Simon, III, 69.
46. Ercole, 27.
47. *Ibid.*, 10.
48. Ducros, *French Society*, 56.
49. Ercole, 44.
50. *Camb. Mod. History*, VI, 132.
51. Duclos, *Secret Memoirs*, 131.
52. Ercole, 44.
53. Martin, H., XIV, 552n., and Michelet, V, 160, credit the charge of incest.
54. Martin, XV, 12.
55. Dupuy, *Dialogues sur les plaisirs*, 14, in Crocker, L. G., *Age of Crisis*, 117.
56. Brunetière, F., *Manual of the History of French Literature*, 282.
57. Wormeley, 30.
58. Lacroix, 83.
59. Michelet, V, 251.
60. Martin, H., XV, 339.
61. Batiffol, L., *The Great Literary Salons*, 103.
62. Toth, K., *Woman and Rococo in France*, 107.
63. *Ibid.*
64. Lacroix, 417.
65. Ercole, 56.
66. Louvre.
67. Metropolitan Museum of Art, New York.
68. Louvre.
69. Metropolitan Mus. of Art.
70. Wallace Collection, London.
71. Dresden, Gemäldegalerie.
72. Wallace Collection.
73. There are outstanding collections of Watteau's drawings in the Louvre and in the Pierpont Morgan Library, New York.
74. Goncourt, E. and J. de, *French 18th-Century Painters*, 1.

75. Aldington, R., *French Comedies of the 18th Century*, 103.
76. Sainte-Beuve, *Portraits of the 18th Century*, I, 81.
77. *Ibid.*, 82.
78. Lesage, *Adventures of Gil Blas*, prefatory memoir.
79. Aldington, 131.
80. Lesage, *Gil Blas*, Book VIII, Ch. x.
81. *Gil Blas*, last line.
82. Sainte-Beuve, *Portraits*, I, 104.
83. Saint-Simon, III, 42; *cf.* 91-94.
84. Créqui, Marquise de, *Souvenirs*, 44.
85. Michelet, V, 126.
86. Faguet, Émile, *Literary History of France*, 474.
87. Saint-Simon, III, 376.
88. Duclos, *Secret Memoirs*, 326.
89. Michelet, V, 155; Martin, H., XV, 80.
90. *Ibid.*, 115.
91. Saint-Simon, III, 373.
92. *Ibid.*, 376.
93. 77.
94. In Torrey, N., *The Spirit of Voltaire*, 21.
95. Parton, I, 99.
96. Desnoiresterres, I, 217.
97. Parton, I, 98.
98. Brandes, I, 97.
99. *Ibid.*, 98.
100. 99.
101. Parton, I, 115.
102. Like Desnoiresterres, I, 159, and Brandes, I, 100.
103. Créqui, 149.
104. Desnoiresterres, I, 157.
105. Beard, Miriam, *History of the Business Man*, 463; Brandes, I, 306.
106. Desnoiresterres, I, 190.
107. Parton, I, 154.
108. Desnoiresterres, I, 242; Faguet, *Literary History*, 469, gives a different version: "*Gare que cet écrit in extremis n'aille pas à son addresse.*"
109. Parton, I, 165.
110. Voltaire, *Works*, XXIa, 221.
111. Frederick the Great, *Mémoires*, I, 59.
112. Desnoiresterres, I, 345.
113. Brandes, I, 152.
114. *Ibid.*; Parton, I, 185.
115. Parton, I, 190.

CHAPTER II

1. Shakespeare, *Richard II*, II, i.
2. Defoe, *Tour through England and Wales*, I, 1 and *passim*.
3. Voltaire, *Lettres philosophiques*, No. 9; Ashton, T., *Economic History of England: The 18th Century*, 36.
4. Quennell, M. and C., *History of Every-*

day Things in England, 21; Mantoux, P., *Industrial Revolution in the 18th Century*, 165.
5. Quennell, *Everyday Things*, 12.
6. Trevelyan, G. M., *English Social History*, 379.
7. Besant, Sir Walter, *London in the 18th Century*, 386.
8. Lipson, E., *Growth of English Society*, 212.
9. Nussbaum, *Economic Institutions of Modern Europe*, 252.
10. Jaurès, *Histoire socialiste de la Révolution française*, I, 67.
11. Usher, A., *History of Mechanical Inventions*, 280.
12. Lipson, 196.
13. Ashton, *Economic History*, 220.
14. *Encyclopaedia Britannica*, VI, 544a.
15. Mantoux, 73.
16. Ashton, 201-4.
17. In Tawney, R. H., *Religion and the Rise of Capitalism*, 190.
18. Ashton, 212; Mantoux, 72.
19. Ashton, 203.
20. Webb, S. and B., *History of Trade Unionism*, 31-50.
21. Mantoux, 119.
22. Chesterfield, Earl of, *Letters to His Son*, letter of Sept. 22, 1749.
23. Mantoux, 102; Taine, H., *Ancient Regime*, 33.
24. Beard, M., *Business Man*, 430.
25. Voltaire, *Lettres sur les Anglais*, No. 10, in Mantoux, 138.
26. Hume, David, *Enquiry concerning the Principles of Morals*, 248.
27. In Beard, M., 435.
28. Lecky, W. E., *History of England*, I, 323.
29. Mackay, C., *Extraordinary Popular Delusions*, 50.
30. *Ibid.*, 55.
31. Quennell, P., *Caroline of England*, 71.
32. *Camb. Mod. History*, VI, 181.
33. Mackay, 73.
34. *Ibid.*, 78.
35. Voltaire, *Works*, XIIIa, 23.
36. Ranke, L., *History of the Reformation in Germany*, 468.
37. Rogers, J. E. T., *Economic Interpretation of History*, 157; Ashton, 2; Ogg, David, *Europe in the 17th Century*, 2.
38. Defoe, *Tour*, I, 337.
39. Besant, *London in the 18th Century*, 352.
40. Trevelyan, *English Social History*, 142.
41. Lecky, *History of England*, I, 482-84.
42. *Ibid.*
43. Letter of Mar. 23, 1752.
44. Besant, 380-81.

45. W. R. Brock in *New Camb. Mod. History*, VII, 266.
46. Besant, 238.
47. Lecky, II, 543-45.
48. James, B. B., *Women of England*, 335.
49. Besant, 138.
50. Markun, L., *Mrs. Grundy*, 183.
51. Faÿ, B., *La Franc-Maçonnerie et la révolution intellectuelle du xviiie siècle*, 78-79.
52. Besant, 384.
53. Blackstone, *Commentaries on the Laws of England*, 151n.
54. Congreve, Wm., *Way of the World*, III, iii, in Hampden, J., *Eighteenth-Century Plays*.
55. Gay, John, *Beggar's Opera*, I, v, in Hampden.
56. Halsband, R., *Lady Mary Wortley Montagu*, 14.
57. Langdon-Davies, J., *Short History of Women*, 305.
58. Besant, 459; Lecky, I, 522; Quennell, P., *Caroline of England*, 29.
59. George, M. Dorothy, *London in the 18th Century*, 29.
60. Lecky, I, 477.
61. *Ibid.*, 479; Besant, 297 f.
62. Berkeley, George, *Siris*, in Jefferson, D. W., *Eighteenth-Century Prose*, 122.
63. Besant, 301-2.
64. Turberville, *Johnson's England*, I, 48.
65. Boswell, *Journal of a Tour to the Hebrides*, 84 (Aug. 31, 1773).
66. *Enc. Brit.*, XX, 779d.
67. *Camb. Mod. History*, VI, 187.
68. Ashton, 62-63.
69. Hobhouse, L. T., *Morals in Evolution*, 313.
70. Besant, 342.
71. Lecky, I, 183.
72. *Ibid.*, 367; Barnes, H. E., *Economic History of the Western World*, 256.
73. Westermarck, E. A., *Origin and Development of the Moral Ideas*, II, 558.
74. Turberville, I, 72.
75. Some instances in Thackeray, *The Four Georges*, 42-43.
76. Turberville, I, 312.
77. Fielding, H., *Amelia*, Book I, Ch. ii.
78. Turberville, I, 310.
79. Quennell, M. and C., *Everyday Things*, 9.
80. Lecky, I, 507.
81. Turberville, I, 322.
82. *Ibid.*, 319; Lecky, I, 501-2.
83. Smith, Preserved, *History of Modern Culture*, II, 586.
84. Johnson, S., *The Rambler*, 183.
85. Pope, A., *Imitations of Horace*, Epistle II.
86. James, B. B., *Women of England*, 318.
87. Turberville, I, 341.
88. Thackeray, *Four Georges*, 41.
89. Allen, B. S., *Tides in English Taste*, I, 249.
90. Lecky, I, 552.
91. *Ibid.*, 553-54.
92. Walpole, H., *Letters*, I, 309 (June 29, 1744).
93. Weinstock, H., *Handel*, 228.
94. Allen, B. S., *Tides*, I, 94; Chesterfield, *Letters*, Oct. 19, 1748.
95. Clergue, H., *The Salon*, 4.
96. Chesterfield, *Letters*, June 11, 1750.
97. Sainte-Beuve, *English Portraits*, 25.
98. Wharton, G. and P., *Wits and Beaux of Society*, I, 349.
99. Sainte-Beuve, *English Portraits*, 29.
100. Chesterfield, letter of July 8, 1739.
101. Letter of June, 1752, in *Letters to His Son*, II, 96.
102. Letter of Apr. 19, 1749.
103. Apr. 13, 1752.
104. Nov. 6, 1747.
105. May 16, 1751.
106. May 23, 1751.
107. Sept. 5, 1748.
108. Apr. 15, 1751.
109. In Sainte-Beuve, *English Portraits*, 41.
110. Dec. 25, 1753.
111. May 17, 1748.
112. Nov. 11, 1752.
113. Oct. 9, 1747.
114. Feb. 22, 1748.
115. Oct. 19, 1748.
116. Jan. 8, 1750.
117. Apr. 13, 1752.
118. Dec. 25, 1753.
119. Stephen, Leslie, *English Literature and Society in the 18th Century*, 150.
120. Krutch, J. W., *Samuel Johnson*, 354.
121. Chesterfield, July 25, 1741.
122. Feb. 24, 1747.
123. Krutch, 354.
124. Parton, II, 551.
125. Sainte-Beuve, *English Portraits*, 43.
126. Nicolson, H., *Age of Reason*, 201.
127. In Sainte-Beuve, *English Portraits*, 34.
128. Dec. 2, 1746.
129. Oct. 17, 1768.
130. *Letters*, II, 334.
131. Oct. 11, 1769.
132. Sainte-Beuve, *English Portraits*, 44.
133. *Ibid.*, 45.

CHAPTER III

1. Acton, Lord, *Lectures on Modern History*, 266.
2. Quennell, P., *Caroline*, 22.
3. Halsband, *Lady Mary*, 45.

4. Voltaire, *Works*, XXIb, 70-72; *cf.* Laski, H., *Political Thought in England, Locke to Bentham*, 16.
5. Hauser, *Social History of Art*, II, 261.
6. *New Cambridge Modern History*, VII, 261.
7. Voltaire, XIXb, 29.
8. Chidsey, D. B., *Marlborough*, 291.
9. Rowse, A. L., *The Early Churchills*, 131.
10. Martin, H., XV, 76.
11. Lang, A., *History of Scotland*, IV, 226-27.
12. Collins, J. C., *Bolingbroke, and Voltaire in England*, 117.
13. Churchill, W. S., *History of the English-Speaking Peoples*, III, 91.
14. Schoenfeld, H., *Women of the Teutonic Nations*, 275.
15. Quennell, *Caroline*, 93; Martin, H., XV, 343.
16. Traill, H. D., *Social England*, V, 139.
17. Walpole, H., *Reminiscences*, in *Letters*, introd., *cxxx*.
18. Walpole, H., *Memoires of . . . the Reign of George II*, I, 63.
19. Thackeray, *Four Georges*, 33.
20. Wharton, G. and P., *Wits and Beaux of Society*, I, 276.
21. Lecky, *History of England*, I, 465.
22. Mossner, *Bishop Butler and the Age of Reason*, 4; Quennell, *Caroline*, 134.
23. *Camb. Mod. History*, VI, 77.
24. Voltaire, XIXb, 23.
25. Lecky, I, 520.
26. Quennell, *Caroline*, 252.
27. Lecky, I, 326; *Camb. Mod. History*, VI, 181.
28. Macaulay, T., *Essays*, I, 346.
29. Walpole, *Memoires of the Reign of George II*, II, 273.
30. Mossner, *Bishop Butler*, 5.
31. Beard, M., *History of the Business Man*, 477.
32. Macaulay, *Essays*, I, 348; Lecky, I, 367-72; Koven, A. de, *Horace Walpole and Mme. du Deffand*, 13.
33. Lord Hervey in Jefferson, D. W., *Eighteenth-Century Prose*, 28.
34. Tucker in Lecky, I, 334.
35. Frederick the Great, *Mémoires*, I, 29.
36. Chesterfield, letter of Dec. 12, 1749.
37. In Lovejoy, *Essays*, 177.
38. Collins, J. C., *Bolingbroke*, 166.
39. *Camb. History of English Literature*, IX, 254.
40. Bolingbroke, *On the Spirit of Patriotism*, 28.
41. Collins, J. C., 172.
42. Bolingbroke, 128.
43. Hearnshaw, F. J., *Social and Political Ideas of Some English Thinkers of the Augustan Age*, 215.
44. *Ibid.*
45. Acton, *Lectures*, 273.
46. See *Camb. Mod. History*, VI, 64 f.; Wingfield-Stratford, *History of British Civilization*, 681; Churchill, III, 101.
47. Lecky, I, 385n.; Burke, *Letters on a Regicide Peace*, in *Reflections on the French Revolution*.
48. Altamira, R., *History of Spain*, 435.
49. *Enc. Brit.*, XX, 779c.
50. In Lecky, I, 394.
51. *Ibid.*, 291.
52. *Ibid.*
53. 239.
54. 241.
55. Mantoux, *Industrial Revolution*, 87.
56. Swift, Jonathan, *Short View of the State of Ireland*, in Lecky, II, 208.
57. Lecky, II, 424.
58. *Camb. Mod. History*, VI, 485.
59. D'Alton, E. A., *History of Ireland*, IV, 531.
60. Lecky, II, 199.
61. D'Alton, IV, 472-73.
62. Lecky, II, 217.
63. *Ibid.*
64. Mossner, *Life of Hume*, 234.
65. Lecky, II, 83.
66. Trevelyan, *English Social History*, 444.
67. Robertson, J. M., *Short History of Freethought*, II, 168.
68. Traill, *Social England*, V, 159.
69. Lang, A., *History of Scotland*, IV, 425-27.
70. *Ibid.*, 449.
71. 451.
72. Voltaire, *Age of Louis XV*, II, 14.
73. Lang, A., IV, 512.
74. *Camb. Mod. History*, VI, 117.
75. Lang, A., IV, 519.
76. *Enc. Brit.*, IV., 292d.
77. Voltaire, *Age of Louis XV*, II, 44.
78. Frederick, *Mémoires*, I, 191.
79. Wingfield-Stratford, 682.
80. Lecky, II, 479-80.
81. *Ibid.*, 476.
82. Churchill, III, 112.

CHAPTER IV

1. *Pensées diverses*, in Lecky, II, 531n.
2. Davidson, John, introd. to Montesquieu's *Persian Letters*, xxi.
3. *Ibid.*
4. Hervey, *Memoirs of the Court of George II*, in introd. to Mandeville's *Fable of the Bees*, x.
5. Besant, *London*, 152.
6. *Camb. Mod. History*, VI, 79.

7. Stephen, L., *History of English Thought in the 18th Century*, I, 217.
8. Thackeray, *Four Georges*, 34.
9. Lecky, II, 468.
10. Hume, D., essay "Of National Character."
11. Besant, 153.
12. Lecky, I, 275-76, 303-4.
13. Trevelyan, G. M., *England under the Stuarts*, 342.
14. Robertson, J. M., *History of Freethought*, II, 161; Lecky, I, 313.
15. Voltaire, XIXb, 218.
16. Voltaire, VIa, 288.
17. Woolston, *Discourses*, I, 34, in Stephen, *History of English Thought*, I, 232.
18. Bury, J. B., *History of Freedom of Thought*, 141; Voltaire, *Philosophical Dictionary*, article "Miracles," in *Works*, VIa, 288-93; Robertson, J. M., *Freethought*, II, 157-59; Stephen, *History of English Thought*, I, 228-38.
19. Benn, A. W., *History of English Rationalism in the 19th Century*, I, 145.
20. Tindal, M., *Christianity as Old as the Creation*, 14, in Stephen, *History*, I, 139.
21. Stephen, I, 262; Robertson, II, 158.
22. In Stephen, I, 266.
23. Collins, J. C., *Bolingbroke*, 183.
24. Stephen, I, 178.
25. Torrey, N. L., *Voltaire and the English Deists*, 149.
26. In Hearnshaw, *English Thinkers of the Augustan Age*, 240.
27. Stephen, *History*, I, 180.
28. Collins, J. C., 180.
29. Goldsmith, O., *Life of Bolingbroke*, in Clark, B. H., *Great Short Biographies*, 1057.
30. In Stephen, I, 246.
31. *Ibid.*, 345.
32. 349-52.
33. 356.
34. *Enc. Brit.*, IV, 463b.
35. Mossner, *Bishop Butler and the Age of Reason*, 8.
36. Toynbee, Arnold J., *Study of History*, abridgment of Vols. I-VI by D. C. Somervell, 486.
37. Gibbon, Edward, *Memoirs*, 21.
38. Turberville, *Johnson's England*, I, 33.
39. Inge, *Christian Mysticism*, 283.
40. *Camb. Mod. History*, VI, 81.
41. Gibbon, *Memoirs*, 22.
42. Bearne, *Court Painter*, 198.
43. Voltaire, essay "Epic Poetry."
44. Besant, 149.
45. McConnell, F. J., *John Wesley*, 13.
46. Wesley, John, *Journal*, 94.
47. *Encyclopaedia of Religion and Ethics*, XII, 724d.
48. *Ibid.*, 725a.
49. McConnell, 47.
50. Lecky, II, 554.
51. Wesley, *Journal*, 43; Hastings, XII, 725d.
52. *Enc. Brit.*, XXIII, 576.
53. Lecky, II, 565.
54. *Ibid.*
55. 563.
56. 591-94; Lecky, *History of European Rationalism*, I, 45.
57. Turberville, *Johnson's England*, I, 221.
58. Wesley, *Journal* for 1739, in Lecky, *History of England*, II, 584.
59. *Ibid.*, 583.
60. 590.
61. 636; Toynbee, *Study of History*, IX, 459-60.
62. McConnell, 48.
63. *Ibid.*, 66.
64. Wesley, *Journal*, entry for Mar. 30, 1736.
65. *World Christian Handbook*, 5.
66. *Journal* for Jan. 1, 1790.
67. Shaftesbury, 3d Earl of, *Characteristics*, I, 260.
68. Mandeville, *Fable of the Bees*, 83-85.
69. Hutcheson, F., *Inquiry concerning Moral Good and Evil*, in *Enc. Brit.*, XI, 945c.
70. Buckle, II, 334.
71. *Ibid.*, 336.
72. Hume, D., *Dialogues concerning Natural Religion*, 4.
73. Huxley, T. H., *Hume*, 3.
74. *Ibid.*, 6.
75. Mossner, *Life of Hume*, 51.
76. Huxley, 6.
77. "My Own Life," in Hume, *Dialogues concerning Natural Religion*, 233.
78. Mossner, 82.
79. *Ibid.*, 94.
80. 111.
81. Hume, *Treatise of Human Nature*, Book I, Part II, Sec. 5.
82. *Ibid.*, I, II, 1.
83. I, III, 10 and 7.
84. I, IV, 2 and 6.
85. I, IV, 1.
86. *Ibid.*
87. Appendix.
88. I, IV, 1.
89. I, IV, 7.
90. I, IV, 2.
91. I, IV, 1.
92. II, III, 3.
93. *Ibid.*
94. II, I, 10.
95. II, I, 7.
96. II, I, 8.
97. II, II, 11.

98. "My Own Life," in Hume, *Dialogues concerning Natural Religion*, p. 234.
99. Mossner, p. 129.
100. *Treatise*, III, I, Sec. 1.
101. III, II, 2.
102. III, III, 6.
103. Mossner, p. 213.
104. *Ibid.*, 215-18.
105. Hume, *Enquiry concerning the Human Understanding*, p. 2.
106. *Ibid.*, Part X, Secs. 91-95 and 100-101.
107. XI, 102.
108. *Enquiry concerning the Principles of Morals*, V, I, Secs. 174-75; Appendix II; cf. essay "Of the Dignity and Meanness of Human Nature."
109. *Enquiry concerning . . . Morals*, IX, I, Sec. 226.
110. *Ibid.*, IV, Sec. 166.
111. "My Own Life," *loc. cit.*, p. 236.
112. *Dialogues concerning Natural Religion*, 156.
113. *Ibid.*, 148.
114. 182-83.
115. Essay "On Suicide."
116. *Dialogues*, 210.
117. *Ibid.*, 194.
118. 211.
119. 169.
120. 180.
121. 171.
122. 227.
123. 214.
124. Hume, *Natural History of Religion*, Secs. I, XIII-XV, in Cassirer, E., *Philosophy of the Enlightenment*, p. 181.
125. *Dialogues*, introd., xv.
126. Burton, *Life of Hume*, II, in Lecky, *History of England*, II, 543.
127. *Enquiry concerning . . . Morals*, III, II, Sec. 155.
128. Hume, *History of England*, IV, p. 480.
129. Hume, *Essays Literary, Moral, and Political*, 27, 273.
130. *Ibid.*, 161.
131. Essay "Of National Character."
132. *Enquiry concerning the Human Understanding*, Part VII, Sec. 65.
133. Essay "Of Commerce."
134. Essay "Of Civil Liberty."
135. Essay "Jealousy of Trade."
136. In Black, *Art of History*, p. 80.
137. Mossner, 317.
138. Essay "Of the Study of History."
139. "My Own Life," *loc. cit.*, 236.
140. In Black, 114.
141. Mossner, 318.
142. "My Own Life," *loc. cit.*, 236.
143. *Ibid.*, 237.
144. Mossner, 223.

145. *Ibid.*, 318.
146. 444-45.
147. "My Own Life," *loc. cit.*, 238.
148. *Ibid.*, 239.
149. *Enquiry concerning the Human Understanding*, Part XI, Sec. 108.
150. Mossner, 568.
151. Adam Smith, letter to Wm. Strahan, Nov. 9, 1776, in Hume, *Dialogues*, p. 247.
152. *Treatise of Human Nature*, Book I, Part IV, Sec. 5.
153. Wolf, *History of Science*, 757.
154. Mossner, 478.
155. Hume, *Dialogues*, introd., xxx.
156. Mossner, 588.
157. "My Own Life," *loc. cit.*, 239.
158. Strachey, L., *Portraits in Miniature*, 151.
159. "My Own Life," *loc. cit.*, 244.
160. *Ibid.*, 245.
161. Mossner, 598-600.
162. *Ibid.*, 603.

CHAPTER V

1. Sainte-Beuve, *Portraits of the 18th Century*, I, 132.
2. Buckle, I, 312.
3. Johnson, *Lives of the Poets*, II, 143.
4. Pope, "Epistle to Dr. Arbuthnot," lines 127-28.
5. *Essay on Criticism*, lines 214-15.
6. *Ibid.*, line 298.
7. Lines 631-42.
8. 585-87.
9. Stephen, L., *Alexander Pope*, 45.
10. *Rape of the Lock*, Canto II, lines 105-9.
11. *Ibid.*, III, 16.
12. V, 85-86.
13. See "Windsor Forest," lines 41-42.
14. Pope, "Eloïsa to Abelard," lines 281-92.
15. *Ibid.*, lines 325-28.
16. Stephen, *Pope*, p. 61.
17. *Ibid.*, 64.
18. Johnson, *Lives*, II, 161.
19. Stephen, *Pope*, 64.
20. *Ibid.*, 78.
21. Pope, "Second Epistle of the Second Book of Horace," lines 68-69, in *Collected Poems*, p. 305.
22. Thornton, J. C., *Table Talk from Ben Jonson to Leigh Hunt*, 112.
23. E.g., see Jefferson, *Eighteenth-Century Prose*, 25.
24. Parton, I, 214.
25. Stephen, *Pope*, 91.
26. Boston Museum of Fine Arts.
27. London, National Portrait Gallery.
28. Stephen, *Pope*, 100.

29. See "Farewell to London," in *Poems*, 368, and Strachey, *Portraits*, 14.

30. Garnett and Gosse, *English Literature*, III, 199.

31. Pope, *Dunciad*, Book II, lines 75-76, 102-8, 155-56.

32. *Ibid.*, Book IV, lines 471-82.

33. Robertson, J. M., in Shaftesbury, *Characteristics*, introd., p. *xxv*.

34. Collins, *Bolingbroke*, 158.

35. Stephen, *Pope*, 166.

36. *Essay on Man*, Epistle I, lines 1-16.

37. Milton, *Paradise Lost*, I, line 26.

38. *Essay on Man*, I, 81-84.

39. I, 91-96.

40. End of Epistle I.

41. *Essay on Man*, II, 1-17.

42. *Ibid.*, 217-20.

43. III, 303-6.

44. IV, 35-36.

45. 49-50.

46. Taine, H., *History of English Literature*, Book III, Ch. vii, Sec. 4.

47. Voltaire, *Lettres sur les Anglais*, in *Works*, XIXb, p. 94.

48. Johnson, *Lives*, II, 193.

49. "Epistle to Dr. Arbuthnot," lines 305-29.

50. *Satires*, epilogue, lines 208-9.

51. *Dunciad*, IV, 629-55.

52. Johnson, *Lives*, II, p. 199.

53. Thackeray, *English Humourists*, 213.

54. Walt Whitman, in Traubel, H., *With Walt Whitman in Camden*, 126.

55. Lecky, *History of England*, I, 463.

56. Brandes, *Voltaire*, I, 16.

57. Woods, Watt, and Anderson, *Literature of England*, II, 51.

58. Garnett and Gosse, III, 287; questioned by *Camb. History of English Literature*, X, 147.

59. Arnold, M., *Essays in Criticism*, 317.

60. Johnson, *Lives*, II, 391, 388.

61. Allen, R. J., *Life in 18th-Century England*, 16.

62. Brandes, *Voltaire*, I, 32.

63. Lecky, *History of England*, I, 541.

64. Mossner, *Hume*, 357.

65. *Ibid.*, 360.

66. 379.

67. 364.

68. Pope, "Epitaph on Gay."

69. Gay, John, *Beggar's Opera*, I, v.

70. *Ibid.*, I, viii.

71. III, xi.

72. *Camb. History of English Literature*, X, 3.

73. Richardson, S., *Pamela*, 2.

74. *Ibid.*, 179.

75. Richardson, *Clarissa*, 429-31.

76. *Ibid.*, introd., *viii*.

77. *Ibid., ix*.

78. Montagu, Lady Mary W., *Letters*, II, 232 (Mar. 1, 1752).

79. Rousseau, J. J., letter to Duclos, Nov. 19, 1760.

80. Francke, K., *History of German Literature*, 216.

81. Texte, J., *J. J. Rousseau and the Cosmopolitan Spirit*, 148 f.

82. Fielding, H., introd. to *Amelia*, xxiii; Thackeray, *English Humourists*, 263n.

83. Fielding, *Joseph Andrews*, Book I, Ch. x.

84. Saintsbury, G., introd. to *Pamela*.

85. *Joseph Andrews*, II, xiv.

86. Fielding, *Jonathan Wild*, preface.

87. *Jonathan Wild*, I, i.

88. *Ibid.*, I, v.

89. I, iii.

90. III, vii.

91. IV, xv.

92. Thackeray, *English Humourists*, 266n.

93. Fielding, *Tom Jones*, III, v.

94. *Ibid.*, III, x.

95. XVIII, xii.

96. Besant, *London*, 502 f.; Lecky, *History of England*, I, 487.

97. *Amelia*, IV, ii.

98. *Ibid.*, I, ii.

99. XI, ix.

100. VI, ii.

101. Thackeray, 263.

102. Smollett, T., *Roderick Random*, Ch. xi, pp. 56-58.

103. *Ibid.*, xx, 114.

104. xvii, 95.

105. xxxix, 223.

106. Smollett, *Adventures of Peregrine Pickle*, Ch. ii.

107. *Ibid.*, vi.

108. Thackeray, 254n.

109. *Ibid.*, 255n.

110. 254n.

111. Smollett, *Travels through France and Italy*, xxvii.

112. Thackeray, 256.

113. Smollett, *Humphrey Clinker*, 16 (letter of Apr. 18).

114. *Ibid.*, 142 (letter of June 8).

115. 218-20 (letter of July 4).

116. 225-37 (letter of July 13).

117. Montagu, Lady M. W., *Letters*, I, 173.

118. Halsband, *Lady Mary Wortley Montagu*, 11.

119. Montagu, *Letters*, I, 174 (Apr. 25, 1710).

120. *Ibid.*, 178.

121. 181.

122. Letter of Aug. 16, 1712; Halsband, 25.

123. Pope, *Collected Poems*, 370.

124. Halsband, 58.

125. Pope, letter of Aug. 18, 1716, in Montagu, I, 405-7.
126. Montagu, I, 237 (Sept. 14, 1716).
127. Brockway and Winer, *Second Treasury of the World's Great Letters*, 170.
128. Halsband, 63.
129. Montagu, I, 431, 434.
130. Collection of the Marquess of Bute.
131. Pope, *Poems*, 371.
132. Halsband, 113.
133. *Ibid.*, 130.
134. 141.
135. *Camb. History of English Literature*, IX, 277.
136. Translated from Halsband, 156.
137. *Ibid.*, 157.
138. Walpole, H., *Letters*, I, 57-62 (Sept. 25 and Oct. 2, 1740).
139. Halsband, 204, 218.
140. *Ibid.*, 218.
141. 289.

CHAPTER VI

1. Turberville, *Johnson's England*, II, 75.
2. Allen, B. S., *Tides in English Taste*, I, 73 f.
3. Lecky, *History of England*, I, 530.
4. Tate Gallery, London.
5. Staatsbibliothek, Hamburg.
6. Traill, *Social England*, V, 271.
7. Wilenski, R., *English Painting*, 102.
8. Thackeray, *English Humourists*, 247n.
9. Beckett, R. B., *Hogarth*, 22.
10. Vienna.
11. Collection of Sir Francis Cook.
12. Frick Gallery, New York.
13. Metropolitan Museum of Art, New York.
14. Tate Gallery.
15. *Ibid.*
16. National Gallery, London.
17. Tate Gallery.
18. Thackeray, 247.
19. Quennell, P., *Hogarth's Progress*, 31.
20. Tate Gallery.
21. Thackeray, 245n.; Wilenski, 60.
22. Wilensky, 79 f.; Dobson, *Hogarth*, 23.
23. Wilenski, 72.
24. Beckett, 13.
25. Art Gallery, Birmingham, England.
26. St. Bartholomew's Hospital, London.
27. Collection of Earl of Faversham.
28. Wilenski, 63; Beckett, 18, questions this story.
29. Wilenski, 85.
30. Dobson, 21.
31. Wilenski, 71.
32. Tate Gallery.
33. Wilenski, 68.
34. Craven, Thos., *Treasury of Art Masterpieces*, 210; Quennell, P., *Hogarth*, 7.
35. Wingfield-Stratford, *History of British Civilization*, 777.
36. Dobson, 31.
37. *Grove's Dictionary of Music and Musicians*, II, 406.
38. Weinstock, *Handel*, 55.
39. Brockway and Weinstock, *Men of Music*, 60; Turberville, *Johnson's England*, II, 160.
40. This section is especially indebted to Herbert Weinstock's *Handel*.
41. *Grove's Dictionary*, II, 504.
42. Weinstock, 32; Brockway and Weinstock, 57.
43. *Oxford History of Music*, IV, 80; Weinstock, 38.
44. Mainwaring, John, *Life of Handel*, in Deutsch, Otto, *Handel*, 27.
45. Burney, C., *General History of Music*, II, 662.
46. Weinstock, 60.
47. *Ibid.*, 92.
48. 97.
49. *Oxford History of Music*, IV, 209.
50. Burney, II, 721n.
51. *Ibid.*
52. Weinstock, 115.
53. *Ibid.*, 172.
54. McKinney and Anderson, *Music in History*, 438.
55. Weinstock, 207.
56. Burney, II, 817.
57. Weinstock, 212.
58. Láng, P. H., *Music in Western Civilization*, 522.
59. Brockway and Weinstock, *Men of Music*, 76.
60. *Oxford History of Music*, IV, 84; Weinstock, 225; Brockway and Weinstock, 76.
61. Weinstock, 232.
62. *Ibid.*, 239.
63. 241.
64. Rolland, R., *Musical Tour through the Land of the Past*, 58.
65. *Oxford History of Music*, IV, 198.
66. Weinstock, 77.
67. Brockway and Weinstock, 81.
68. Rolland, 49.
69. Davison, A., *Bach and Handel*, 46.
70. *Ibid.*, 44.
71. Rolland, 67.
72. Weinstock, 303.
73. *Ibid.*, 305.
74. Davison, A., 41.
75. *Oxford History of Music*, IV, 85-89, 93.
76. Burney, II, 1023.

77. Letter to Thieriot in Strachey, *Books and Characters*, 122.
78. E.g., *Works*, XXIa, 211.
79. *Works*, XIXb, 91.
80. Goldsmith, O., *Life of Voltaire*, in *Miscellaneous Works*, 504.
81. Letter of July 19, 1776, in Desnoiresterres, VIII, 108; article "Dramatic Art" quoted in Holzknecht, *Backgrounds of Shakespeare*, 387.
82. Collins, J. C., *Bolingbroke, and Voltaire in England*, 201; Brandes, *Voltaire*, I, 173.
83. Johnson, *Lives of the Poets*, II, 7.
84. *Works*, XIXb, 209.
85. In Buckle, I, 528.
86. *Philosophical Dictionary*, article "Government."
87. Gay, *Voltaire's Politics*, 44.
88. Parton, II, 523.
89. Voltaire, *Correspondance*, ed. Besterman, II, 31.
90. Johnson, *Lives*, II, 176; Collins, J. C., 210.
91. Collins, 230.
92. Brunetière, *Manual of the History of French Literature*, 319.

CHAPTER VII

1. Sée, H., *Economic and Social Conditions in France during the 18th Century*, 87.
2. *Ibid.*, 84.
3. Sumner, W. G., *Folkways*, 165.
4. Sée, 104; Goodwin, A., *The European Nobility in the 18th Century*, 36.
5. Tocqueville, *L'Ancien Régime*, 107.
6. Ducros, L., *French Society in the 18th Century*, 158, 207; Wolf, A., *History of Science . . . and Philosophy in the 18th Century*, 558.
7. Palmer, R. R., *Catholics and Unbelievers in 18th-Century France*, 13n.
8. Lacroix, P., *Eighteenth Century*, 138.
9. *Camb. Mod. History*, VIII, 53.
10. Lacroix, 138.
11. Ducros, 24; Herbert, S., *Fall of Feudalism in France*, xvii.
12. Taine, *Ancient Regime*, 130.
13. Goodwin, *European Nobility*, 31.
14. Jaurès, *Histoire socialiste*, I, 32.
15. Sée, 61.
16. Taine, *Ancient Regime*, 20, 41.
17. Tocqueville, 34.
18. Taine, 15.
19. *Camb. Mod. History*, VIII, 53.
20. *Ibid.*, 52; Sée, 3.
21. Palmer, R. R., 25; Lacroix, 157.

22. Taine, 42 f.
23. Voltaire, *Works*, XVIa, 261.
24. Martin, H., XV, 439.
25. *Ibid.*, 439-40.
26. Lacroix, 157.
27. *Ibid.*, 269.
28. Taine, 34.
29. *Ibid.*, 119-20.
30. Goncourts, *Woman of the 18th Century*, 10, 15; Montalembert, *Monks of the West*, II, 86.
31. Martin, Kingsley, *Rise of French Liberal Thought*, 79.
32. Taine, 62; Michelet, *Histoire de France*, V, 288.
33. Martin, H., XV, 441.
34. *Ibid.*, 442.
35. Taine, 63.
36. Lecky, *History of England*, V, 329.
37. Desnoiresterres, VIII, 248.
38. Lacroix, 270.
39. Guizot, *History of France*, V, 48.
40. Sée, 4.
41. Herbert, *Fall of Feudalism*, 56.
42. Taine, 23-24; Ducros, 256-57.
43. Herbert, 37.
44. Sée, 15.
45. Herbert, 4-5.
46. Sée, 28.
47. Montagu, Lady Mary W., *Letters*, I, 395 (Oct. 10, 1718).
48. Taine, 330.
49. Martin, H., XV, 216.
50. Sée, 38.
51. Voltaire, *Works*, XIXa, 94.
52. *Philosophical Dictionary*, article "Lent."
53. Cobban, *History of Modern France*, 42.
54. Sée, 182.
55. Renard and Weulersee, *Life and Work in Modern Europe*, 193.
56. Mantoux, *Industrial Revolution*, 409.
57. Sée, 165.
58. Taine, 334.
59. Mornet, *Origines intellectuelles de la Révolution française*, 28.
60. Parton, II, 184.
61. Lacroix, 228.
62. *Ibid.*, 311.
63. Nussbaum, *History of the Economic Institutions of Modern Europe*, 124.
64. Jaurès, *Histoire socialiste*, I, 67.
65. Sée, 151-53.
66. Martin, H., XV, 213.
67. *Ibid.*, 305.
68. Sée, 93.
69. Ducros, 160.
70. Toth, *Woman and Rococo in France*, 179.
71. Lacroix, 206.
72. *Ibid.*

73. Goncourts, *Madame de Pompadour*, 5-7.
74. Desnoiresterres, III, 241.
75. Grimm, *Correspondance*, VIII, 231-33, in Buckle, I, 539.
76. Saint-Simon in Lacroix, 302.
77. Lacroix, 299.
78. Ducros, 53.
79. Stryienski, *Eighteenth Century*, 57.
80. Lanfrey, *L'Eglise et les philosophes au xviiie siècle*, 129.
81. Michelet, V, 277; Sainte-Beuve, *Portraits of the 18th Century*, I, 445.
82. Voltaire, *Works*, XVIa, 157.
83. Stryienski, 79.
84. *Works*, XVIa, 158.
85. Martin, H., XV, 256n.
86. Stryienski, 85.
87. Desnoiresterres, II, 336.
88. Martin, H., XV, 251.
89. Saint-Simon, *Memoirs*, III, 283.
90. *Michelet*, V, 248.
91. Martin, H., XV, 116n.; Ercole, *Gay Court Life*, 88.
92. Bearne, *Court Painter*, 85.
93. Guizot, *History of France*, V, 78.
94. Goncourts, *Pompadour*, 9.
95. Michelet, V, 325.
96. Ercole, 167.
97. Lewis, D. B. Wyndham, *Four Favorites*, 42.
98. Stryienski, 140-41.
99. *Webster's Biographical Dictionary*, 833.
100. Brandes, I, 224.
101. Voltaire, *Works*, XVIb, 224.
102. Carlyle, Thos., *History of Friedrich II*, IV, 438; *Enc. Brit.*, IX, 454a.
103. Voltaire, XVIb, 238; Martin, H., XV, 282; Stryienski, 148.
104. Voltaire, XVIb, 239.
105. Stryienski, 149.
106. Martin, H., XV, 431n.
107. Lichtenberger in Martin, K., *Rise of French Liberal Thought*, 238.
108. Martin, H., XV, 356-58.
109. Lecky, *England*, V, 327.
110. Goncourts, *Pompadour*, 12.
111. Michelet, V, 349.
112. Ercole, 197.
113. Goncourts, 117.
114. Ercole, 203.
115. Lewis, *Four Favorites*, 48.
116. Taine, *Ancient Regime*, 82.
117. Goncourts, 71.
118. *Ibid.*, 348.
119. Sainte-Beuve, I, 450.
120. *Ibid.*, 451.
121. Michelet, V, 354.
122. Martin, H., XV, 436.
123. Goncourts, 131.
124. Lewis, 50.
125. Ercole, 209.
126. Toth, 165.
127. Goncourts, 127.
128. Du Hausset, Mme., *Memoirs of Mme. de Pompadour*, 65.
129. Ercole, 220.
130. Goncourts, *Woman of the 18th Century*, 249.

CHAPTER VIII

1. Sée, *Economic and Social Conditions*, 48 f.
2. Funck-Brentano, *L'Ancien Régime*, 422.
3. La Fontainerie, *French Liberalism and Education*, 6.
4. Lacroix, 252.
5. *Ibid.*, 151.
6. 242.
7. 244.
8. Desnoiresterres, III, 133.
9. Créqui, *Souvenirs*, 57, 121.
10. Ducros, *French Society*, 83.
11. Chesterfield, *Letters*, I, 348.
12. Brandes, I, 147.
13. *Ibid.*, 141.
14. Goncourts, *Woman of the 18th Century*, 187.
15. *Ibid.*, 188.
16. Mornet, *Origines intellectuelles de la Révolution française*, 53.
17. Funck-Brentano, 50.
18. Ducros, 61.
19. Quoted in Funck-Brentano, 60.
20. Taine, *Ancient Regime*, 134.
21. Walpole, *Letters*, I, 309 (Oct. 28, 1752).
22. Toth, 135.
23. Frederick the Great, *Mémoires*, I, 25.
24. D'Argenson, *Mémoires*, in Martin, H., XV, 341.
25. Ducros, 342.
26. Mossner, *Hume*, 92.
27. Köhler, Carl, *History of Costume*, 340.
28. Créqui, 123.
29. Lacroix, 370.
30. Ducros, 35.
31. *Philosophical Dictionary*, art. "Lent," in *Works*, VIa, 108.
32. Mousnier and Labrousse, *Dix-huitième Siècle*, 166.
33. Michelet, V, 189.
34. Láng, P. H., *Music in Western Civilization*, 441.
35. Burney, C., *General History of Music*, II, 965, 969.
36. *Grove's Dictionary of Music and Musicians*, IV, 320d.
37. Burney, II, 970.
38. Diderot, *Le Neveu de Rameau*.
39. Duclos, C., *Considérations sur les moeurs*, 13.

40. Goldsmith, O., *Miscellaneous Works*, 430.
41. Mme. Vigée-Lebrun, *Mémoires*, I, 156, in Taine, *Ancient Regime*, 141n.
42. Goncourts, *Woman*, 317.
43. Marmontel, *Memoirs*, I, 181.
44. Batiffol, *Great Literary Salons*, 131.
45. Walpole to Gray, Jan. 25, 1766.
46. Batiffol, 208.
47. Kavanagh, *Woman in France during the 18th Century*, I, 168.
48. Diderot, "On Women," in *Dialogues*, 196.

CHAPTER IX

1. Faniel, S., *French Art of the 18th Century*, 36.
2. *Ibid.*, 91.
3. Funck-Brentano, 180.
4. Louvre.
5. See the great commode in the Wallace Collection.
6. Dilke, Lady E., *French Architects and Sculptors of the 18th Century*, 77.
7. *Ibid.*, 81.
8. Louvre.
9. Turner and Baker, *Stories of the French Artists*, 181.
10. Dijon Museum.
11. Versailles Museum.
12. Louvre.
13. Bearne, *Court Painter*, 164.
14. Diderot, *Salons*, I, 9, 114-19.
15. Bearne, 43.
16. Turner, 193.
17. Goncourts, *French 18th-Century Painters*, 61.
18. Turner, 197.
19. Louvre.
20. Block, *François Boucher and the Beauvais Tapestries*, 26.
21. Goncourts, *French Painters*, 69.
22. Seven are in the Huntington Library and Gallery at San Marino, Calif.
23. *Ibid.*
24. Wallace Collection.
25. Goncourts, *French Painters*, 91.
26. *Ibid.*, 84.
27. Block, 22.
28. Ridder, *Chardin*, 8; Goncourts, *French Painters*, 117.
29. Louvre.
30. Louvre.
31. Louvre.
32. Goncourts, 141-42; Havens, *Age of Ideas*, 321.
33. Diderot, *Salons*, III, 4.
34. Goncourts, 177n.
35. *Ibid.*
36. *Ibid.*

37. *Ibid.*, 164n.
38. Louvre.
39. St.-Quentin Museum.
40. Dresden.
41. St.-Quentin.

CHAPTER X

1. Duclos, *Considérations*, 217.
2. Grimm, *Correspondance*, III, 73.
3. Parton, I, 509.
4. Voltaire, essay "Ancient and Modern Tragedy," in *Works*, XIXa, 134.
5. "Discourse on Tragedy," in *Works*, XIXb, 181 f.
6. Parton, II, 325.
7. Brandes, I, 72.
8. Edwards, H. S., *Idols of the French Stage*, 83; Sainte-Beuve, *Portraits of the 18th Century*, I, 170.
9. Michelet, V, 303.
10. Sainte-Beuve, I, 180.
11. Michelet, V, 304.
12. Mitford, N., *Madame de Pompadour*, 126.
13. Hazard, *European Thought in the 18th Century*, 260.
14. Marivaux, *Vie de Marianne*, 3.
15. Crébillon *fils*, *Le Sopha*, introd.
16. *Le Sopha*, 65.
17. Palache, *Four Novelists of the Old Regime*, 4, 49.
18. Crébillon, *Le Sopha*, introd.
19. Saintsbury, G., introd. to Prévost's *Manon Lescaut*, xliii.
20. *Manon Lescaut*, 220.
21. *Ibid.*, 10.
22. 57.
23. Faguet, E., *Literary History of France*, 489.
24. Saintsbury, introd. to *Manon Lescaut*, ix-xii.
25. Bury, J., *History of the Idea of Progress*, 135-36; Martin, K., 280.
26. Lichtenberger, A., *Le Socialisme et la Révolution française*, 73; Martin, H., XV, 335; Martin, K., 62; Hazard, 197.
27. In Martin, K., 61.
28. In Crocker, *Age of Crisis*, 426-29.
29. Duclos, *Considérations*, 11-12.
30. *Ibid.*, 17, 21.
31. 27.
32. 25.
33. Toth, 38.
34. La Bruyère and Vauvenargues, *Selections*, 189.
35. Vauvenargues, *Oeuvres choisies*, cxv, iv.
36. La Bruyère and Vauvenargues, 179.
37. Vauvenargues, CLXXXVII.
38. *Ibid.*, CLXXXII.

39. Crocker, *Age of Crisis*, 138-39.
40. *Ibid.*, 30.
41. Vauvenargues, CLXIX.
42. La Bruyère and Vauvenargues, 173.
43. Vauvenargues, CL.
44. *Ibid.*, LVII.
45. CLXXX.
46. CLVII.
47. P. 158.
48. P. 173.
49. *Ibid.*
50. 310.
51. Voltaire, letter of Apr. 4, 1744, in Martin, H., XV, 407n.
52. Voltaire, XIXa, 43.
53. Sorel, A., *Montesquieu*, 125.
54. *Ibid.*, 9.
55. 23.
56. Montesquieu, *Spirit of Laws*, Book V, Ch. xix.
57. *Persian Letters*, xxiv.
58. In Sorel, 43.
59. Herodotus, *History*, IV, 183.
60. Aristotle, *Historia animalium*, viii, 12.
61. *Persian Letters*, xii.
62. Letter xxiv.
63. xxix.
64. cxviii.
65. cxiii.
66. cxviii.
67. xxxv.
68. lxxxvi.
69. Sorel, 49.
70. *Grandeur et décadence des Romains*, introd., vi.
71. *Ibid.*, Ch. xviii.
72. Ch. xii.
73. Ch. xviii.
74. Ch. vi.
75. Ch. xv.
76. Quoted in Faguet, *Dix-huitième Siècle*, 195.
77. *Spirit of Laws*, preface.
78. *Ibid.*
79. Palache, 35.
80. Martin, K., 151.
81. *Spirit of Laws*, Book I, Ch. iii.
82. *Ibid.*, XIV, i-x.
83. XVI, i-iii.
84. *Ibid.*, xi.
85. *Ibid.*
86. XIV, v.
87. VIII, xvi-xix.
88. Explanatory notes prefixed by Montesquieu to the second edition.
89. IV, vi.
90. In Sée, H., *Idées politiques en France au xviii* siècle, 46.
91. *Spirit of Laws*, VIII, ii.
92. V, xiii.
93. V, x.

94. XI, vi.
95. *Ibid.*
96. *Ibid.*
97. XI, iii.
98. *Grandeur et décadence*, Ch. vii.
99. *Spirit of Laws*, XXIII, xxviii.
100. XV, v.
101. X, ii.
102. XIII, xvii.
103. *Pensées diverses*, in Hearnshaw, *Great Thinkers of the Age of Reason*, 116.
104. Faguet, *Dix-huitième Siècle*, 173.
105. *Spirit of Laws*, XXIV, x.
106. I, i.
107. XII, xxix.
108. In Havens, *Age of Ideas*, 121.
109. *Spirit of Laws*, XXIV, ii.
110. *Ibid.*, iii and xxvi.
111. XXIV, v.
112. XXV, v.
113. *Ibid.*, xiii.
114. *Ibid.*, x.
115. Quoted in Faguet, 195.
116. Sorel, 166.
117. Pappas, *Berthier's* Journal de Trévoux, 78 f.; Martin, K., 153.
118. Sorel, 163.
119. Martin, K., 168.
120. Sorel, 165.
121. Voltaire, XIXa, 238-39.
122. *Philosophical Dictionary*, art. "Climate," in *Works*, IVa, 204-9.
123. *Ibid.*
124. Art. "Laws," in *Works*, VIa, 104.
125. Art. "Laws, Spirit of," in *Works*, VIa, 106-8.
126. Morley, *Life of Voltaire*, 9.
127. Cf. Macaulay, *Critical . . . Essays and Poems*, I, 226; Dunning, *History of Political Theories*, III, 428-31; Flint, *History of the Philosophy of History*, 272-76; Brunetière, 301; Stephen, L., *English Thought in the 18th Century*, II, 188; Sorel, 139-41.
128. *Spirit of Laws*, VII, iii.
129. Spencer, *Principles of Sociology* (3v., London, 1876-96).
130. Laski, H., *Political Thought in England*, 109.
131. Taine, *Ancient Regime*, 213.
132. Walpole, *Letters*, II, 187 (Jan. 10, 1750).
133. Sainte-Beuve, *Portraits*, I, 146.
134. Hearnshaw, *French Thinkers of the Age of Reason*, 116.
135. Havens, *Age of Ideas*, 127.
136. Sorel, 169.
137. Grimm, *Correspondance*, II, 491.
138. Gibbon, E., *Decline and Fall of the Roman Empire* (1779 ed.), II, 142.
139. Waliszewski, *Romance of an Empress*, 91.

140. Sorel, 171.
141. Faguet, *Dix-huitième Siècle*, 188.

CHAPTER XI

1. Desnoiresterres, I, 410.
2. Bain, R. N., in Voltaire, *Charles XII*, introd., *xxii*.
3. E.g., Buckle, I, 577.
4. Voltaire, *Charles XII*, p. 11.
5. *Ibid.*, 334.
6. Letter of Aug. 25, 1732, in *Works*, XXIa, 216.
7. *Zaïre*, I, i, in *Works*, Xa, 27.
8. *Zaïre*, II, iii.
9. Desnoiresterres, II, 2.
10. Créqui, *Souvenirs*, 35.
11. Brandes, I, 256.
12. *Ibid.*, 345.
13. *Letters on the English*, Letter 1, in *Works*, XIXb, 193-98.
14. Letter v.
15. *Ibid.*
16. Letter VIII, translation in Havens, *Age of Ideas*, 168.
17. *Ibid.*, 169.
18. Letter x.
19. Letter VIII; Hearnshaw, *French Thinkers of the Age of Reason*, 151.
20. *Works*, XIXb, 29.
21. Brandes, I, 203.
22. Voltaire, XIb, 212.
23. *Ibid.*, 219.
24. 235
25. Buckle, I, 517.
26. Parton, I, 225.
27. *Ibid.*, 303.
28. 343.
29. Desnoiresterres, II, 139.
30. Parton, I, 384.
31. Desnoiresterres, II, 239.
32. *Ibid.*, III, 113-15.
33. Françoise de Graffigny, *Vie privée de Voltaire et Mme du Châtelet à Cirey* (Paris, 1820), in Brandes, I, 400.
34. Brandes, I, 354.
35. Pomeau, *La Religion de Voltaire*, 190.
36. Parton, I, 391.
37. Créqui, 35.
38. Parton, I, 389.
39. Wade, Ira, *Voltaire and Mme. du Châtelet*, 14.
40. *Ibid.*
41. 37.
42. Brandes, I, 388.
43. Voltaire, XXIa, 197-201.
44. Desnoiresterres, III, 330.
45. Voltaire, XXIa, 193, 209.
46. Letter of Apr. 15, 1741, in Gay, *Voltaire's Politics*, 26.
47. Brandes, I, 365; Desnoiresterres, II, 53.
48. Voltaire, XXIb, 107.
49. Ia, 299.
50. Voltaire, *Traité de métaphysique (Oeuvres complètes*, XLIII), end of Ch. i.
51. *Ibid.*, p. 187.
52. Taine, *Ancient Regime*, 258.
53. *La Pucelle*, Canto II, in *Works*, XXa, 83 f.
54. Voltaire, *Alzire*, I, i.
55. Brandes, I, 361.
56. Parton, I, 445.
57. Fellows and Torrey, *Age of Enlightenment*, 474.
58. *Mahomet*, III, vi, in *Works*, VIIIb, 55.
59. Brandes, II, 8.
60. Voltaire and Frederick the Great, *Letters*, p. 102.
61. Gibbon, E., *Journal*, 130.
62. Parton, I, 462.
63. Brandes, I, 405.
64. *Ibid.*
65. Mitford, N., *Voltaire in Love*, 75.
66. Parton, I, 542-45.
67. Martin, H., XV, 402.
68. Voltaire, XXIb, 98.
69. XXIa, 190, 193.
70. *Ibid.*, 195.
71. Parton, I, 575.
72. *Ibid.*, 352.
73. Voltaire, VIIIb, 12.
74. *Ibid.*, 14.
75. Voltaire, IIa, 282.
76. Ib, 6.
77. IIb, 41.
78. IIa, 63.
79. IIa, 26.
80. IIa, 44-45.
81. Parton, I, 581-82.
82. Voltaire and Frederick, *Letters*, 188, 191.
83. Longchamp in Parton, I, 553 f.
84. Longchamp in Desnoiresterres, III, 246, and Parton, I, 556.
85. Parton, I, 562.
86. Voltaire and Frederick, *Letters*, 197.
87. Desnoiresterres, III, 390.
88. Parton, I, 571.
89. Voltaire-Frederick *Letters*, 33.
90. Voltaire, *Lettres d'amour à sa nièce*, 53.
91. Voltaire, *Love Letters to His Niece*, 46. Dr. Besterman translates *cazzo* as "prick."
92. *Lettres d'amour*, 57; *Love Letters*, 48.
93. *Lettres d'amour*, 69; *Love Letters*, 54.
94. *Lettres d'amour*, 77; *Love Letters*, 57.
95. *Lettres d'amour*, 77; *Love Letters*, 58.
96. *Lettres d'amour*, 146.
97. *Love Letters*, 103.
98. *Lettres d'amour*, 15.
99. Marmontel, *Memoirs*, I, 121.
100. Mitford, N., *Voltaire in Love*, 303.

101. Nicolson, *Age of Reason*, 110.
102. Voltaire-Frederick *Letters*, 212; Gay, *Voltaire's Politics*, 150.
103. Gay, 151.

CHAPTER XII

1. Mossner, *Hume*, 210.
2. Richard, E., *History of German Civilization*, 326; de Tocqueville, *L'Ancien Régime*, 27; Thompson, J. W., *Economic and Social History of . . . the Later Middle Ages*, 483.
3. Taine, *Ancient Regime*, 28.
4. See Mühlhausen as described in Spitta, *J. S. Bach*, I, 344.
5. Láng, *Music in Western Civilization*, 608.
6. Montagu, Lady Mary W., *Letters*, I, 255 (Nov. 21, 1716).
7 Tietze, *Treasures of the Great National Galleries*, 137.
8. Burney, C., *General History of Music*, II, 943.
9. Desnoiresterres, IV, 160.
10. In Cassirer, *Philosophy of the Enlightenment*, 334.
11. Francke, *History of German Literature*, 223.
12. Ausubel, *Superman: The Life of Frederick the Great*, 756.
13. Wolf, *History of Science . . . and Philosophy*, 778.
14. Hazard, *European Thought in the 18th Century*, 40.
15. Lovejoy, *Essays in the History of Ideas*, 108.
16. *Enc. Brit.*, XXIII, 697c.
17. *Enc. of Religion and Ethics*, VIII, 838b.
18. Schoenfeld, *Women of the Teutonic Nations*, 283.
19. *Ibid.*, 298.
20. Text in Smith, P., *History of Modern Culture*, II, 601.
21. Chesterfield, *Letters*, Sept. 5, 1748.
22. Goldsmith, O., *Inquiry into the Present State of Polite Learning in Europe*, in *Miscellaneous Works*, 426.
23. Frederick the Great, *Mémoires*, I, 63.
24. Montagu, Lady Mary, letter of Dec. 17, 1716.
25. Dillon, E., *Glass*, 5.
26. Bock, E., *Geschichte der Graphischen Kunst*, 477-84.
27. Berlin.
28. Barockmuseum, Vienna.
29. Sitwell, S., *German Baroque Art*, 94.
30. *Oxford History of Music*, IV, 4.
31. Láng, 450.
32. Spitta, *Bach*, II, 46; *Enc. Brit.*, XVII, 896b.

33. Spitta, III, 18.
34. Rolland, *Musical Tour*, 84.
35. *Ibid.*, 211.
36. 207-8.
37. *Grove's Dictionary of Music*, II, 556.
38. Rolland, 211n.
39. *Grove's*, V, 297.
40. Ebeling in Rolland, 119.
41. E.g., Concerto in D for trumpet; Suite in A Minor for flute; Don Quixote Suite.
42. Schweitzer, A., *J. S. Bach*, I, 103-4.
43. Spitta, I, 373.
44. *Grove's*, I, 158. On the Vivaldi transcriptions, see Pincherle, Marc, *Vivaldi*, 230-31.
45. Spitta, II, 147.
46. Láng, 493.
47. *Grove's*, I, 161.
48. Schweitzer, I, 115.
49. Spitta, III, 261-64.
50. *Grove's*, I, 165.
51. Pratt, *History of Music*, 257.
52. Schweitzer, I, 338.
53. *Ibid.*, 321.
54. Spitta, II, 55.
55. Forkel in Schweitzer, I, 323.
56. *Ibid.*, 404.
57. 292.
58. Láng, 499.
59. Davison, A., *Bach and Handel*, 56.
60. Schweitzer, I, 180.
61. Spitta, III, 252.
62. *Ibid.*
63. 263.
64. Weinstock, *Handel*, 4.
65. *Grove's*, I, 167.
66. Rolland, 71.
67. Spitta, II, 147.
68. McKinney and Anderson, *Music in History*, 407.
69. Words of the preacher at Bach's funeral, Spitta, III, 275.
70. Letter of Karl Zelter in Schweitzer, I, 231.
71. *Ibid.*, 230; Rolland, 219; Davison, 11.
72. Schweitzer, I, 238.
73. *Ibid.*, 242.
74. 254.

CHAPTER XIII

1. Carlyle, T., *Friedrich the Second*, IV, 173.
2. Goodwin, *European Nobility*, 129.
3. Montagu, Lady Mary, *Letters*, I, 245.
4. Goodwin, 112.
5. Mowat, R. B., *Age of Reason*, 264; *New Camb. Mod. History*, VII, 402.
6. In 1714-34.
7. 1720-33.

8. 1715–56.
9. 1722–32.
10. 1729–32.
11. Nawrath, *Austria*, 15. The church was built in 1733.
12. Sitwell, *German Baroque Art*, 37; cf. Baedeker, *Austria*, 46.
13. Barockmuseum, Vienna.
14. *Ibid.*
15. Montagu, Lady M., I, 238.
16. Burney, C., II, 942.
17. Garnett, R., *History of Italian Literature*, 315.
18. Frederick, *Mémoires*, I, 14.
19. *Enc. Brit.*, X, 274b.
20. Coxe, Wm., *History of the House of Austria*, III, 241.
21. *Ibid.*, 242.
22. *New Camb. Mod. History*, VII, 407.
23. Monroe, Paul, *History of Education*, 435.
24. Macaulay, *Essays*, II, 121; Acton, *Lectures on Modern History*, 288.
25. *Camb. Mod. History*, VI, 210.
26. *Ibid.*, 213.
27. 214.
28. Carlyle, *Friedrich*, I, 335.
29. Wilhelmine, Margravine, *Memoirs*, 31, 34, 52, 204.
30. *Ibid.*, 13, 63.
31. Carlyle, I, 377.
32. Wilhelmine, 91.
33. *Ibid.*, 84, 91.
34. Carlyle, II, 95.
35. *Camb. Mod. History*, VI, 212.
36. Wilhelmine, 109.
37. *Ibid.*, 164.
38. Carlyle, II, 327.
39. *Ibid.*, 339.
40. 349.
41. Wilhelmine, 230.
42. Carlyle, III, 64-66.
43. *Ibid.*, 66-68.
44. Voltaire-Frederick *Letters*, Nov. 4, 1736.
45. Apr. 7, 1737.
46. Jan. 20, 1737.
47. Frederick to Voltaire, Nov. 4, 1736, Feb. 8, 1737.
48. Dec. 3, 1736.
49. Dec. 25, 1737.
50. June, 1738.
51. Dec. 25, 1737.
52. Mar. 28, 1738.
53. Carlyle, III, 98.
54. Parton, I, 240.
55. Frederick, quoted in Villari, P., *Life and Times of Niccolò Machiavelli*, II, 201.
56. In Francke, *History of German Literature*, 230.
57. Carlyle, III, 142.
58. Valori in Ausubel, 435.
59. Frederick to Voltaire, June 6, 1740.
60. June 27, 1740.
61. Lea, H. C., *Superstition and Force*, 575.
62. Carlyle, III, 161.
63. *Ibid.*, 163.
64. Smith, P., *History of Modern Culture*, II, 571.
65. Carlyle, III, 175.
66. Goldsmith, O., *Miscellaneous Works*, 427.
67. Carlyle, III, 233.
68. *Ibid.*; Desnoiresterres, II, 290.
69. Voltaire-Frederick *Letters*, 143.
70. Fleury to Voltaire, Nov. 14, 1740, in Parton, I, 438.
71. *Ibid.*
72. Carlyle, III, 278.
73. Ausubel, 443.
74. Lützow, Count von, *Bohemia*, 317.
75. Frederick, *Mémoires*, I, 94.
76. *Ibid.*, 103.
77. Coxe, *House of Austria*, III, 270; Macaulay, *Essays*, II, 126.
78. *Enc. Brit.*, XIV, 881d.
79. Carlyle, IV, 70.
80. Coxe, III, 309.
81. Carlyle, V, 36.
82. Voltaire to Frederick, March, 1742, in Voltaire-Frederick *Letters*, 159.
83. Frederick to Voltaire, Feb. 12, 1742.
84. Frederick, *Mémoires*, I, 5.
85. *Enc. Brit.*, IX, 718c.
86. In Robertson, J. M., *Short History of Freethought*, II, 313.
87. Carlyle, V, 201.
88. *Ibid.*, III, 260.
89. Carlyle, V, 197, hotly repudiates any sodomitic implications.
90. *Enc. Brit.*, IX, 718c.
91. Carlyle, V, 65.
92. *Ibid.*, VII, 462; Mowat, *Age of Reason*, 101.
93. Letter of Aug. 31, 1750, in Parton, I, 611.
94. Desnoiresterres, IV, 108.
95. Taine, *Ancient Regime*, 281n.
96. Voltaire, *Works*, XXIa, 221.
97. Parton, I, 610.
98. *Ibid.*
99. Carlyle, V, 137.
100. *Ibid.*, 146.
101. Gay, *Voltaire's Politics*, 154.
102. Voltaire, XXIa, 213.
103. Lanson, *Voltaire*, 112-13.
104. Parton, I, 340.
105. Chesterfield, letter of Apr. 13, 1752.
106. Parton, II, 59.
107. *Ibid.*, 59-60; Desnoiresterres, IV, 196.
108. Morley, *Life of Voltaire*, 184.
109. Carlyle, V, 182.
110. *Ibid.*, 180.
111. 209.

112. 213.
113. 214; Strachey, *Books and Characters*, 191.
114. Voltaire, XIXa, 184f.
115. *Ibid.*
116. Parton, II, 126.
117. *Ibid.*, 103.
118. Carlyle, V, 223.
119. Parton, II, 108.
120. *Ibid.*, 138.
121. Voltaire, *Lettres d'Alsace*, 135-36 (Dec. 14, 1753).
122. Parton, II, 167-69.
123. Montesquieu, letter of Sept. 28, 1753, in Lanfrey, *L'Église et les philosophes*, 162.
124. *Philosophical Dictionary*, article "Quakers."
125. Bertrand, J., *D'Alembert*, 91.

CHAPTER XIV

1. Letter of May 27, 1756, in Chaponnière, *Voltaire chez les Calvinistes*, 18.
2. Épinay, Mme. d', *Memoirs and Correspondence*, III, 178.
3. Marmontel, *Memoirs*, I, 317.
4. Morley, *Life of Voltaire*, 200.
5. Boswell, *Life of Samuel Johnson*, 87.
6. Oechsli, W., *History of Switzerland*, 260.
7. *Ibid.*, 272.
8. In Herold, *The Swiss without Halos*, 161.
9. Oechsli, 264.
10. Coxe, *Travels in Switzerland*, II, 225.
11. *Ibid.*, 179.
12. Oechsli, 265.
13. Coxe, *Travels*, I, 304.
14. Oechsli, 243.
15. *Ibid.*, 245.
16. Coxe, II, 262.
17. Casanova, *Memoirs*, I, 392, 407.
18. Coxe, II, 292.
19. *Ibid.*
20. Francke, *History of German Literature*, 220.
21. Lough, J., *The Encyclopédie*, 56.
22. Épinay, *Memoirs*, III, 199.
23. Coxe, II, 357.
24. Épinay, III, 173-75.
25. Masson, P., *La Religion de Rousseau*, I, 10-11.
26. In Naves, *Voltaire et l'Encyclopédie*, 148.
27. *Ibid.*, 39.
28. 40.
29. Lough, 94.
30. Desnoiresterres, V, 179-81.
31. Lough, 92.
32. Geneva, Musée d'Art et d'Histoire.
33. Jean Gaberel in Parton, II, 228.

34. Voltaire, *Essai sur les moeurs*, Ch. lxviii.
35. Morley, 284.
36. *Ibid.*, 290.
37. Flint, *History of the Philosophy of History*, 254.
38. Letter to Thieriot, Oct. 31, 1738.
39. Parton, I, 465.
40. Buckle, I, 580.
41. *Phil. Dict.*, art. "History," in *Works*, Vb, 64.
42. *Ibid.*
43. Voltaire, *Works*, XVIa, 137.
44. XIVa, 230.
45. *Essai sur les moeurs*, Ch. xx.
46. *Ibid.*, Ch. cxxxix.
47. Lanson, *Voltaire*, 123-24.
48. Robertson, Wm., *History of the Reign of Charles V*, I, 290.
49. "Observations on History," in *Works*, XIXa, 269.
50. *Essai*, Ch. cxcvii.
51. Ch. lxviii.
52. *Works*, XVIa, 133-36, 144.
53. Chateaubriand, *The Genius of Christianity*, III, iii, 6, p. 430.
54. Voltaire, XVIa, 250-51.
55. Michelet, V, 274.

CHAPTER XV

1. Goncourts, *Woman of the 18th Century*, 307 f.
2. Smith, P., *Modern Culture*, II, 543; Nicolson, *Age of Reason*, 294.
3. Frederick to Voltaire, June 29, 1771.
4. Voltaire, *Works*, VIIb, 143.
5. Lecky, *History of Rationalism*, 145.
6. Blackstone, *Commentaries* (Oxford, 1775), IV, 60, in Lea, H. C., *History of the Inquisition in Spain*, IV, 247.
7. Clark, G. N., *The 17th Century*, 246.
8. Voltaire's estimate, in *Works*, XXIa, 250.
9. Mark xvi, 16.
10. Smith, P., *Modern Culture*, II, 555.
11. *Ibid.*, 556.
12. 550.
13. Putnam, G. H., *Censorship of the Church of Rome*, II, 255.
14. Wilson, A., *Diderot*, 121-22.
15. Brandes, II, 107.
16. Bertrand, *D'Alembert*, 92.
17. Brandes, II, 50.
18. Mornet, *Origines intellectuelles de la Révolution française*, 258.
19. *Cf. Catholic Enc.*, III, 189.
20. Voltaire, *Notebooks*, II, 351.
21. Faguet, *Literary History of France*, 361, 516.
22. Smith, P., II, 268.

23. Schweitzer, A., *Quest of the Historical Jesus*, 23.
24. Quoted in Lovejoy, *Essays in the History of Ideas*, 103.
25. *Ibid.*, 103 f.
26. Hsin-hai Chang, in private correspondence with the authors.
27. In Lovejoy, *Essays*, 105.
28. Voltaire, *Age of Louis XIV*, 455.
29. In Lovejoy, 105-6.
30. Maverick, L. A., *China, a Model for Europe*, 126.
31. Fülop-Miller, R., *Power and Secret of the Jesuits*, 485.
32. Reichwin, A., *China and Europe*, 124.
33. Voltaire, *Works*, VIIIa, 176.
34. Pinot, V., *La Chine et la formation de l'esprit philosophique en France*, 425.
35. *Ibid.*, 315, 281.
36. Maverick, 242.
37. *Ibid.*, 113.
38. *Philosophical Dictionary*, art. "Glory," in *Works*, Va, 208.
39. *Works*, XVIa, 119; XVIIIb, 278.
40. XIIIa, 29.
41. Montesquieu, *Persian Letters*, XLVI.

CHAPTER XVI

1. Buckle, I, 660n.
2. Fuss, N., in Smith, D. E., *History of Mathematics*, I, 522.
3. Bell, E. T., *Men of Mathematics*, 148.
4. *Ibid.*, 156.
5. 159.
6. Wolf, *History of Science*, 70.
7. Whitehead, A. N., *Science and the Modern World*, 91.
8. Bell, 170.
9. *Ibid.*
10. 171.
11. 185.
12. Whitehead, 90.
13. In Crocker, *Age of Crisis*, 8.
14. Bertrand, *D'Alembert*, 32.
15. Morley, J., *Diderot*, I, 123.
16. Bertrand, 143, 153, 164; Ségur, *Julie de Lespinasse*, 113-14.
17. Wolf, 217.
18. Williams, *History of Science*, II, 275.
19. Smith, P., *Modern Culture*, II, 73.
20. Williams, II, 286.
21. *Ibid.*, 289.
22. 290.
23. 295; Wolf, 232.
24. Gibbon, *Essai sur l'étude de la littérature*, in *Miscellaneous Writings*, 2.
25. Williams, IV, 11.
26. Scheele, *Treatise on Fire and Air*, in Wolf, 358.
27. *Ibid.*, 359.

28. *Enc. Brit.*, XX, 62c.
29. *Ibid.*, 62b.
30. Moore, F. J., *History of Chemistry*, 37-38.
31. French, S. J., *Torch and Crucible: The Life and Death of Antoine Lavoisier*, 80.
32. In Wolf, 353.
33. Moore, 44.
34. *Ibid.*, 42.
35. Huxley, T. H., *Science and Education*, 23.
36. In Willey, *Eighteenth-Century Background*, 177.
37. Priestley, Jos., *Essay on the First Principles of Government*, in Willey, 195.
38. Priestley, *History of the Corruptions of Christianity*, in Willey, 170.
39. *Essay on the First Principles of Government*, in Huxley, 27.
40. *Ibid.*, in Willey, 197.
41. Schuster, M. Lincoln, *Treasury of the World's Great Letters*, 187.
42. French, S. J., 215.
43. Dakin, *Turgot and the Ancien Régime in France*, 166.
44. Moore, 49.
45. McKie, *Antoine Lavoisier*, 225.
46. *Ibid.*, 293.
47. 325.
48. 319.
49. 412 f.
50. 404.
51. 407.
52. French, 267.
53. Williams, III, 11.
54. Langer, W. L., *Encyclopedia of World History*, 435.
55. Berry, *Short History of Astronomy*, 325.
56. Burney, Fanny, *Diary*, 161 (Dec. 30, 1786).
57. Williams, III, 21.
58. *Enc. Brit.*, XI, 520d.
59. Bertrand, *D'Alembert*, 45.
60. Martin, H., XV, 397.
61. Bell, *Men of Mathematics*, 173.
62. *Ibid.*
63. 172.
64. Laplace, *Système du monde*, V, vi, in Berry, 322.
65. Laplace, *Théorie analytique des probabilités*, preface, in Nagel, *Structure of Science*, 282.
66. Quoted by Cajori in Newton, *Mathematical Principles of Natural Philosophy*, 677.
67. Sedgwick and Tyler, *Short History of Science*, 332.
68. Mousnier and Labrousse, *Dix-huitième Siècle*, 31.

69. In Bell, 182.
70. Berry, 307.
71. Wolf, 299.
72. Buffon, *Oeuvres*, IX, 455.
73. *Ibid.*, 388.
74. XI, 454.
75. Sainte-Beuve, *Portraits of the 18th Century*, II, 269.
76. Buffon, *Oeuvres*, IX, 454.
77. Trattner, *Architects of Ideas*, 66.
78. Gourlie, *Prince of Botanists: Carl Linnaeus*, 3.
79. *Ibid.*, 34.
80. In Hazard, *European Thought in the 18th Century*, 354.
81. Locy, *Biology and Its Makers*, 122.
82. Sainte-Beuve, II, 263.
83. Lecky, *History of . . . Rationalism*, II, 16.
84. Osborn, H. F., *From the Greeks to Darwin*, 130.
85. Bearne, *A Court Painter and his Circle*, 272.
86. Rousseau, letter of Sept. 21, 1771.
87. Gourlie, 270.
88. Wolf, 455.
89. *Ibid.*, 456.
90. 457.
91. *Enc. Brit.*, XVIII 3a.
92. Locy, 399.
93. Wolf, 349.
94. *Ibid.*, 450.
95. Jardine, Wm., *The Naturalist's Library*, 24.
96. *Ibid.*, 321.
97. Sainte-Beuve, II, 264.
98. Osborn, 136.
99. In Butterfield, *Origins of Modern Science*, 175.
100. Buffon, *Discours sur la nature des animaux*, in Martin, H., XVI, 37.
101. Goncourts, *Madame de Pompadour*, 145.
102. Osborn, H. F., *Men of the Old Stone Age*, 3.
103. Osborn, *From the Greeks to Darwin*, 134, and Martin, K., *Rise of French Liberal Thought*, 99-100.
104. In Smith, P., II, 518.
105. In Buffon, *Oeuvres complètes*, I, introd., xxii.
106. Rousseau, letter of Nov. 4, 1764.
107. Sainte-Beuve, II, 208.
108. Buffon, I, introd., xviii.
109. *Ibid.*, XII, 324-30.
110. *Ibid.*, 324n.
111. Hazard, 144.
112. Voltaire, letter to Helvétius, Oct. 27, 1740.
113. Sainte-Beuve, II, 254.

114. Jardine, 32.
115. *Ibid.*, 29.
116. In Fellows and Torrey, *Age of Enlightenment*, 588n.
117. Garrison, F., *History of Medicine*, 334.
118. Lovejoy, A., *The Great Chain of Being*, 233.
119. Réaumur, *Mémoires*, in Smith, P., *Modern Culture*, II, 101.
120. Vartanian, A., *Diderot and Descartes*, 176.
121. Osborn, *From the Greeks to Darwin*, 118.
122. Maupertuis in Crocker, *Age of Crisis*, 81.
123. Osborn, 114-15.
124. *Ibid.*, 122.
125. Lovejoy, *Essays in the History of Ideas*, 147.
126. Turberville, A. S., ed., *Johnson's England*, II, 245.
127. Osborn, 119.
128. *Ibid.*, 145.
129. 146.
130. *Ibid.*
131. 149.
132. Brett, G. S., *History of Psychology*, 423.
133. Condillac, *Traité des sensations*, 38
134. *Ibid.*
135. *Ibid.*, 70.
136. Wolf, 689.

CHAPTER XVII

1. Osler, *Evolution of Modern Medicine*, 187.
2. Sigerist, *Great Doctors*, 235.
3. Castiglioni, A., *History of Medicine*, 602.
4. Williams, H. S., *History of Science*, IV, 78.
5. Garrison, *History of Medicine*, 346.
6. *Ibid.*
7. Vartanian, *Diderot and Descartes*, 270.
8. Wolf, 263.
9. Locy, *Growth of Biology*, 443.
10. Castiglioni, 613.
11. Voltaire, *Philosophical Dictionary*, art. "Good."
12. Garrison, 402.
13. Besant, *London*, 380.
14. Himes, *Medical History of Contraception*, 187.
15. *Ibid.*, 191.
16. 198.
17. Chesterfield, *Letters*, Feb. 5, 1750.
18. Voltaire, *Works*, XIXb, 24.
19. Goncourts, *The Woman of the 18th Century*, 11.

20. Sée, *Economic and Social Conditions in France in the 18th Century*, 42.
21. Garrison, 321.
22. Traill, *Social England*, V, 425.
23. Chamousset in Lacroix, *Eighteenth Century in France*, 272.
24. *Ibid.*
25. Garrison, 400.
26. *Ibid.*
27. Castiglioni, 657.
28. Ducros, *French Society in the 18th Century*, 179.
29. Ercole, *Gay Court Life*, 421.
30. Harding, T. S., *Fads, Frauds, and Physicians*, 151.
31. Castiglioni, 641.
32. Traill, V, 51.
33. Montagu, Lady Mary W., *Letters*, I, 308.
34. Halsband, *Life of Lady Mary Wortley Montagu*, 111.
35. White, A. D., *Warfare of Science with Theology*, II, 55.
36. *Ibid.*, 57; Garrison, 373.
37. Voltaire, *Works*, XIXb, 20.
38. Garrison, 351.
39. Besant, 377-78.
40. Garrison, 343.
41. *Ibid.*, 110.
42. La Mettrie, *Man a Machine*, dedication.
43. *Phil. Dict.*, art. "Physicians."
44. Ford, Boris, ed., *From Dryden to Johnson*, 211.
45. Havens, *The Age of Ideas*, 345.
46. Garrison, 353; Sigerist, 237.
47. Aldis, *Madame Geoffrin*, 191; Herold, *The Swiss without Halos*, 85.
48. Brandes, *Voltaire*, II, 111.
49. Mme. d'Épinay, *Memoirs*, III, 200.

CHAPTER XVIII

1. Pappas, J. N., *Berthier's* Journal de Trévoux *and the Philosophes*, 122.
2. Helvétius, *De l'Esprit*, Eng. translation, 414.
3. D'Alembert, *Mélanges de littérature, d'histoire, et de philosophie* (1759), in Cassirer, *Philosophy of the Enlightenment*, 3; Frankel, *Faith of Reason*, 7-8.
4. In Wolf, 39.
5. Duclos, *Considérations sur les moeurs*, 27.
6. Mornet, *Origines intellectuelles de la Révolution française*, 55.
7. *Ibid.*, 54.
8. Taine, *Ancient Regime*, 288.
9. *Ibid.*
10. In Martin, K., *Rise of French Liberal Thought*, 122.
11. Morley, *Diderot*, I, 169.
12. Mornet, 52.
13. Meslier, Jean, *Superstition in All Ages, or Last Will and Testament*, 30.
14. *Ibid.*, Sec. cxxxv.
15. cviii.
16. lxvi, clxxxii-iii, and clx.
17. clx.
18. lii.
19. ii.
20. xxxii.
21. xc.
22. clx.
23. xl.
24. xii.
25. cxii.
26. clxi.
27. cliii.
28. cxlix.
29. clv.
30. Preface, p. 37.
31. cvii.
32. cxli.
33. clxvi.
34. clxii.
35. Preface, pp. 42-43.
36. cciv.
37. *Ibid.*
38. clv.
39. Preface, p. 41.
40. In Martin, K., 240.
41. *Ibid.*, 242.
42. 241-42.
43. Hazard, *European Thought in the 18th Century*, 56.
44. La Mettrie, *Man a Machine*, 4.
45. Walt Whitman's formula for war.
46. La Mettrie, 99.
47. *Ibid.*, 100.
48. 94.
49. 134.
50. 128.
51. In Fellows and Torrey, *Diderot Studies*, II, 305.
52. *Ibid.*, 316.
53. La Mettrie, 146.
54. *Ibid.*
55. Fellows and Torrey, *Diderot Studies*, II, 316.
56. La Mettrie, 103.
57. Fellows and Torrey, II, 307.
58. La Mettrie, 122.
59. *Ibid.*, 129.
60. 149.
61. In Hazard, 128.
62. La Mettrie, 92.
63. Martin, H., *Histoire de France*, XV, 397.
64. La Mettrie, 119; Lange, F. A., *History of Materialism*, II, 86 f.

65. Parton, *Life of Voltaire*, II, 15.
66. Desnoiresterres, IV, 198-200.

CHAPTER XIX

1. Crocker, L. G., *Embattled Philosopher*, 5.
2. *Ibid.*, 8.
3. 38.
4. Diderot, *Pensées philosophiques*, in Fellows and Torrey, *Age of Enlightenment*, 264.
5. Crocker, 65.
6. Diderot, *pensée* XXVI.
7. In Crocker, 68.
8. Wilson, A. M., *Diderot: The Testing Years*, 86.
9. Cru, R. L., *Diderot as a Disciple of English Thought*, 189; Wilson, A. M., 90.
10. Diderot, *Lettre sur les aveugles*, in *Oeuvres*, 601.
11. *Ibid.*, 608.
12. 629.
13. 631-32.
14. 650.
15. 617-22.
16. Crocker, 102-3.
17. Havens, *Age of Ideas*, 289.
18. Crocker, 77.
19. *Ibid.*, 83.
20. 87.
21. Brunetière, *Évolution des genres dans l'histoire de la littérature* (Paris, 1890), 210, in Wilson, *Diderot*, 169.
22. Diderot, art. "Encyclopedia."
23. Aldis, *Madame Geoffrin*, 91.
24. Hazard, 199.
25. Morley, *Life of Voltaire*, 198.
26. Fellows and Torrey, *Age of Enlightenment*, 316; Lanfrey, *L'Église et les philosophes*, 165.
27. Lévy-Bruhl, *History of Modern Philosophy in France*, 212.
28. Fellows and Torrey, 319.
29. *Ibid.*, 320.
30. Ortega y Gasset, *Toward a Philosophy of History*, 77.
31. Crocker, *Embattled Philos.*, 133.
32. Lough, K., ed., *The* Encyclopédie: *Selected Articles*, 6.
33. Pappas, *Berthier's* Journal de Trévoux, 181-82.
34. Wilson, 162.
35. *Ibid.*, 163.
36. Pappas, 185.
37. Wilson, 160.
38. Robertson, J. M., *Short History of Freethought*, II, 235; Wilson, 165.
39. Wilson, 169.

40. Becker, C., *Heavenly City of the 18th-Century Philosophers*, 119.
41. Wilson, 283.
42. *Ibid.*, 288.
43. Naves, *Voltaire et l'Encyclopédie*, 52.
44. Wilson, 288-89.
45. Fellows and Torrey, *Diderot Studies*, II, 175.
46. Wilson, 312.
47. *Ibid.*
48. 358.
49. 339; Crocker, *Embattled Philos.*, 237.
50. Wilson, 339.
51. Crocker, 239.
52. Green, F. C., in Diderot, *Writings on the Theater*, 12.
53. See Hazard, 202, and Naves, 98.
54. In Lough, *Selected Articles*, 180-83.
55. Diderot, art. "Philosophy."
56. Vartanian, *Diderot and Descartes*, 23.
57. Art. "Philosophy."
58. Art. "Political Authority."
59. *Ibid.*
60. Lough, 43.
61. Morley, *Diderot*, I, 216.
62. *Ibid.*, 172.
63. Article "Privileges."
64. Article "Art."
65. Smith, Adam, *Wealth of Nations*, I, 5.
66. Diderot, Prospectus, in Havens, 307.
67. Wilson, 136.
68. Grimm, *Correspondance*, VII, 146.
69. Lough, introd., XIV.
70. Art. "Encyclopedia."

CHAPTER XX

1. *Enc. Brit.*, XVII, 614.
2. Cru, *Diderot*, 234.
3. *Ibid.*, 395.
4. Dupee, F. W., *Great French Short Novels*, 8.
5. Vartanian, *Diderot and Descartes*, 115.
6. *Pensées sur l'interprétation de la nature*, Sec. LVIII, in Fellows and Torrey, *Age of Enlightenment*, 276, and Wilson, *Diderot*, 194.
7. Faguet, *Dix-huitième siècle*, 334.
8. Letter of Sept. 2, 1769, to Sophie Volland.
9. Letter of Sept. 11, 1769.
10. Letter of Sept. 2, 1769.
11. Diderot, *Dialogues*, 34-35.
12. *Ibid.*, 43.
13. 53.
14. 57.
15. 69.
16. 79-80.
17. 93.
18. 96.
19. 105.

20. 110.
21. Fellows and Torrey, *Diderot Studies*, II, 322.
22. Crocker, *Embattled Philosopher*, 318.
23. *Ibid.*, 320.
24. *Ibid.*, 409; Crocker, *Age of Crisis*, 124.
25. Letter to Damilaville, 1766, in Morley, *Diderot*, I, 20.
26. Cru, 65.
27. Diderot, *Jacques the Fatalist*, 125.
28. Diderot, *Plan for a University*, in La Fontainerie, *French Liberalism and Education in the 18th Century*, 279.
29. *Enc. Brit.*, IV, 419a.
30. Crocker, *Embattled Philos.*, 319.
31. Cru, 417.
32. Grimm, *Correspondance*, 1770, in Diderot, *Oeuvres*, 957-59.
33. Fellows and Torrey, *Diderot Studies*, I, 67.
34. *Ibid.*, 68.
35. These passages are listed in Diderot, *Jacques the Fatalist*, 271-73.
36. *Ibid.*, 8.
37. 166.
38. Crocker, *Embattled Philos.*, 268.
39. *Neveu de Rameau*, in Diderot, *Oeuvres*, 249.
40. Fellows and Torrey, *Diderot Studies*, I, 143 f.
41. *Oeuvres*, 191.
42. G. B. Shaw's phrase.
43. *Oeuvres*, 262, 270.
44. *Ibid.*, 222.
45. 218.
46. 268.
47. 220.
48. *Dialogues*, 119-20.
49. *Ibid.*, 146.
50. 140-41.
51. 154.
52. "Essay on Women," in *Dialogues*, 186.
53. Crocker, *Age of Crisis*, 101.
54. Crocker, *Embattled Philos.*, 340.
55. Crocker, *Age of Crisis*, 209.
56. *Ibid.*, 274.
57. *Neveu de Rameau*, in Crocker, *Age of Crisis*, 209.
58. *Ibid.*, 105.
59. 104.
60. *Supplement to the Voyage of Bougainville*, in *Dialogues*, 157.
61. Crocker, *Embattled Philos.*, 343.
62. Articles "Civil Liberty" and "Representatives."
63. Diderot, *Oeuvres*, Édition Assézat et Tourneux (Paris, 1875-77), IX, 16.
64. *Ibid.*, II, 412, in Morley, *Diderot*, II, 242-43.
65. Cru, 135.
66. Ellis, Havelock, *The New Spirit*, 62.
67. Havens, *Age of Ideas*, 341.
68. Crocker, *Embattled Philos.*, 398.
69. *Ibid.*, 393.
70. Diderot, *Salons*, I, 1.
71. *Ibid.*, 79.
72. Faguet, *Dix-huitième Siècle*, 230.
73. Diderot, *Salons*, I, 188.
74. Crocker, 176.
75. *Ibid.*, 196.
76. Chambers, F. P., *History of Taste*, 146.
77. *Ibid.*, 140 f.
78. Hauser, Arnold, *Social History of Art*, II, 533.
79. *Salons*, I, 418.
80. Morley, *Diderot*, II, 79.
81. Crocker, 19.
82. Cru, 287.
83. Wilson, 273.
84. Crocker, 243.
85. Wilson, 326.
86. Voltaire, *Phil. Dict.*, article "Rhyme."
87. Wilson, 237.
88. Sime, *Lessing*, I, 209.
89. Diderot, *Paradox of Acting*, 14, 18.
90. Cru, 328.
91. *Hamlet*, III, ii.
92. Lee Strasberg, in Diderot, *Paradox of Acting*, introd., x.
93. Wordsworth's phrase.
94. Ellis, *The New Spirit*, 56.
95. Hazard, 383.
96. Crocker, *Embattled Philos.*, 232-33.
97. Michelet, V, 408n.
98. Morley, *Diderot*, I, 30.
99. Mme. d'Épinay, *Memoirs*, II, 73.
100. Taine, *Ancient Regime*, 266.
101. Diderot, *Oeuvres*, 143.
102. Crocker, 26.
103. *Salons*, II, 354.
104. Crocker, 147.
105. *Ibid.*
106. Letter of July 14, 1762.
107. Crocker, 297.
108. *Ibid.*, 213-15.
109. 220.
110. "Regrets sur ma vieille robe de chambre," in *Oeuvres*, 733.
111. Crocker, 301.
112. Morley, I, 262.
113. Crocker, 302.
114. Marmontel, *Memoirs*, I, 360.
115. Morley, *Diderot*, I, 41.
116. Crocker, 292.
117. Wilson, 8.
118. Morley, I, 10.
119. Fellows and Torrey, *Diderot Studies*, I, ix.
120. Letter to King Stanislas Poniatowski in Aldis, *Madame Geoffrin*, 185.
121. Fellows and Torrey, *Diderot Studies*, I, vii.

CHAPTER XXI

1. Cumming, Ian, *Helvétius*, 36.
2. *Ibid.*, 57.
3. Marmontel, *Memoirs*, I, 258.
4. Cumming, 137.
5. Parton, *Voltaire*, II, 302.
6. Helvétius, *Treatise on Man* (*De l'Homme*), Vol. II, p. 480.
7. Grimm, *Corresp.*, II, 262.
8. Helvétius, *Treatise on Man*, Section II, Ch. iii.
9. Helvétius, *De l'Esprit*, p. 11.
10. *Ibid.*, in Grossman, *Philosophy of Helvétius*, 88.
11. Helvétius, *De l'Esprit*, 175, 222, 277.
12. *Treatise on Man*, IV, i.
13. *Ibid.*, III, ii and iv.
14. IV, xxiii.
15. IV, iii and i.
16. VI, i.
17. *De l'Esprit*, p. 489.
18. *Treatise*, VII, iv.
19. *Ibid.*, I, iii.
20. II, xxi.
21. I, ix.
22. II, xxii.
23. I, iii.
24. I, x.
25. VII, i.
26. I, ii.
27. VII, i.
28. *De l'Esprit*, p. 174.
29. *Treatise*, IX, xxxi.
30. *Ibid.*, IV, xxi.
31. I, xiv.
32. I, xiii-xiv.
33. VII, xii.
34. VII, iii and iv.
35. Mordecai Grossman in Horowitz, *Claude Helvétius*, p. 18.
36. *Treatise*, V, iii-x.
37. *Ibid.*, VI, viii.
38. V, iii-iv.
39. V, iii.
40. *De l'Esprit*, p. 279; Cumming, 79.
41. *Treatise*, VI, i.
42. *De l'Esprit*, pp. 6, 17.
43. In Martin, K., p. 180.
44. *Treatise*, II, vii.
45. *De l'Esprit*, p. 269.
46. *Ibid.*, 47; Grossman, *Philosophy of Helvétius*, 96.
47. *De l'Esprit*, 29.
48. *Ibid.*, 184, 144.
49. *Treatise*, IV, ii.
50. Horowitz, p. 100.
51. *Ibid.*, 121.
52. *Treatise*, VI, v and x.
53. *Ibid.*, VI, xv.
54. VI, vii and xi.
55. VIII, iii and v.
56. Brunetière, *Essays in French Literature*, p. 327.
57. Buckle, I, 624n.
58. Cassirer, *Philosophy of the Enlightenment*, 64.
59. Crocker, *Age of Crisis*, 123.
60. In Grossman, *Philosophy of Helvétius*, 147.
61. Crocker, *Embattled Philos.*, 408.
62. Victor Cousin, *Histoire de la philosophie*, III, 201, in Buckle, I, 624n.
63. Morley, *Diderot*, II, 141.
64. Cumming, 218.
65. Morley, II, 142.
66. Grossman, 169.
67. Marmontel, *Memoirs*, I, 258.
68. Cumming, 139.
69. *De l'Esprit*, 87; Morley, II, 157.
70. D'Alembert, *Éléments de philosophie*, in Cassirer, *Enlightenment*, 4.
71. Sainte-Beuve, *Portraits of the 18th Century*, II, 105.
72. Wickwar, *Baron d'Holbach*, 86.
73. *Ibid.*, 59-60; Mornet, *Origines*, 107.
74. Gooch, *Catherine the Great and Other Studies*, 192.
75. Marmontel, *Memoirs*, I, 256.
76. Morley, *Life of Voltaire*, 215.
77. Morley, *Diderot*, II, 193.
78. Robertson, J. M., *Short History of Freethought*, II, 254.
79. Morley, *Diderot*, II, 194.
80. Rousseau, *Confessions*, 139.
81. Robertson, J. M., II, 254.
82. Morley, *Diderot*, II, 215.
83. Wickwar, 22.
84. *Ibid.*, 23, 27.
85. Diderot, letter of May 10, 1759.
86. Marmontel, I, 351.
87. *Ibid.*
88. Wickwar, 39; Burton, *Life of Hume*, II, 220.
89. Gibbon, *Memoirs*, in Mossner, *Life of David Hume*, 485.
90. Priestley, *Memoirs*, I, 74, in Buckle, I, 621n.
91. Wickwar, 25.
92. *Ibid.*, 38.
93. Mme. d'Épinay, *Memoirs*, II, 169.
94. *Ibid.*, 130.
95. Wickwar, 109.
96. Robertson, J. M., II, 272.
97. Grimm, *Corresp.*, Aug. 10, 1789.
98. *Ibid.*
99 Wickwar, 86.
100. D'Holbach, *Le Christianisme dévoilé*, in Pomeau, *La Religion de Voltaire*, 293.
101. Wickwar, 126.
102. *Ibid.*, 135.
103. 127.

104. *Phil. Dict.*, art. "God," Sec. 4.
105. Morley, *Diderot*, II, p. 159.
106. D'Holbach, *System of Nature*, preface, pp. *viii-x*.
107. *Ibid.*, Vol. I, Ch. ii.
108. I, i.
109. I, ii and viii.
110. I, xiii.
111. I, ix.
112. Morley, *Diderot*, II, p. 74.
113. D'Holbach, *System*, I, Ch. xi.
114. *Ibid.*, I, i.
115. Dakin, *Turgot and the Ancien Régime*, p. 16.
116. Martin, K., 175.
117. D'Holbach, *System*, II, Ch. vi.
118. *Ibid.*, II, v.
119. I, xiii.
120. *Ibid.*
121. II, iv.
122. II, v.
123. II, xii.
124. *System*, appendix, Ch. xxiii.
125. *System*, I, xiii.
126. *Ibid.*, I, vii.
127. D'Holbach, *Morale universelle*, Vol. I, Ch. i, in Fellows and Torrey, *Age of Enlightenment*, p. 362.
128. *Ibid.*, 363.
129. *System of Nature*, I, xv.
130. *Ibid.*, appendix, xix.
131. *System*, I, xiv.
132. D'Holbach, *Politique naturelle*, Part IV, Ch. xxvii, in Wickwar, 182.
133. *Éthocratie*, Ch. x, in Hazard, 264.
134. *Politique naturelle*, Part VI, Ch. xiv.
135. Cumming, 112.
136. *Politique naturelle*, in Martin, K., 188.
137. *Ibid.*, 189.
138. Wickwar, 178.
139. Martin, K., 189.
140. Wickwar, 178.
141. *System of Nature*, Vol. I, Ch. xiv.
142. *Politique naturelle*, Part VI, Ch. xxxix, in Wickwar, 212-13.
143. *Système social*, Vol. II, 151, in Cobban, *In Search of Humanity*, 166.
144. *System of Nature*, I, xiv.
145. D'Holbach, *Contagion sacrée*, 145, in Wickwar, 141.
146. In Mornet, *Origines*, 103.
147. *System of Nature*, I, ix.
148. *Système social*, II, ii, in Cassirer, *The Question of Jean-Jacques Rousseau*, 68.
149. *Politique naturelle*, Part I, Ch. vi, in Frankel, *The Faith of Reason*, 71.
150. Mornet, 103.
151. Lanfrey, *L'Église et les philosophes*, 331.
152. *Phil. Dict.*, art. "God."
153. Wickwar, 89.
154. Morley, *Diderot*, 183.

155. Faguet, *Literary History of France*, 497.
156. Wickwar, 111.
157. Hearnshaw, *Social and Political Ideas of . . . the Age of Reason*, 213.
158. Wickwar, 113.

CHAPTER XXII

1. This is what Faguet forgot in one of the most biased essays in French literature; see, e.g., *Dix-huitième Siècle*, 210.
2. Wade, *Studies in Voltaire*, 67.
3. *Phil. Dict.*, art. "Emblems."
4. Noyes, *Voltaire*, 487.
5. *Phil. Dict.*, art, "God."
6. Desnoiresterres, V, 167.
7. Pomeau, *Religion de Voltaire*, 422.
8. Voltaire, *Works*, VIIb, 82.
9. Mornet, *Origines*, 82; Torrey, *Spirit of Voltaire*, 254, 283.
10. *Phil. Dict.*, in *Works*, VIIa, 62.
11. In Pomeau, 400, and Crocker, *Age of Crisis*, 385.
12. Parton, *Voltaire*, II, 432.
13. Pomeau, 159, 183.
14. Lévy-Bruhl, 185-86.
15. Letter of May 20, 1738, in Voltaire and Frederick the Great, *Letters*, 115.
16. Voltaire, *Notebooks*, I, 402.
17. *Traité de métaphysique*, Ch. ix.
18. *La Loi naturelle*, in *Works*, Xb, 25-26.
19. *Ibid.*; Fellows and Torrey, *Age of Enlightenment*, 424.
20. Bottiglia, *Voltaire's* Candide, 108; Mowat, *Age of Reason*, 36.
21. Letter of Oct., 1753, to d'Alembert, in Desnoiresterres, V, 163.
22. In Torrey, *Spirit of Voltaire*, 87.
23. Letters of May 24 and Dec. 22, 1757.
24. Voltaire, *Oeuvres*, ed. Moland, XXXIX, 363. See also Pomeau, 301; Naves, *Voltaire et l'Encyclopédie*, 53.
25. Naves, 54-57.
26. *Ibid.*, 62-63; Pomeau, 302.
27. Campbell, *The Jesuits*, 453.
28. Nicolson, H., *Age of Reason*, 81.
29. In Smith, P., II, 540.
30. Pope, *Essay on Man*.
31. Parton, II, 215.
32. Voltaire, *Romans*, I, 165, 169.
33. *Ibid.*, 233.
34. 237.
35. 257.
36. Bottiglia, 249.
37. Pomeau, 318.
38. Martin, H., *Histoire de France*, IX, 127.
39. Pomeau, 319-21.
40. Calvin, *Institutes of the Christian Religion*, Eng. tr., I, 360.
41. Parton, II, 356.
42. Desnoiresterres, VI, 160.

43. "Essay on toleration," in Voltaire, *Selected Works*, 78; Pomeau, 325.
44. Our account is based upon A. Coquerel's *Jean Calas et sa famille* (Paris, 1858), as summarized in Parton, II, 367.
45. Letter of Mar. 1, 1765.
46. *Ibid.*
47. Text in Parton, II, 356.
48. Letter of Mar. 29, 1762.
49. Letter of Sept., 1762, in Gay, *Voltaire's Politics*, 277.
50. Brandes, *Voltaire*, II, 196.
51. Voltaire, *Selected Works*, 86.
52. *Ibid.*, 113.
53. Parton, II, 433.
54. Mornet, *Origines*, 112.
55. *Selected Works*, 88.
56. *Ibid.*, 100, 108.
57. Voltaire, *Works*, IIb, 277.
58. Brandes, II, 214.
59. Desnoiresterres, VII, 469.
60. Parton, II, 397.
61. *Ibid.*
62. Desnoiresterres, VI, 493.
63. Torrey, *Spirit of Voltaire*, 129.
64. Letter of Frederick the Great, Aug. 7, 1766.
65. Letter of Frederick, Sept., 1766, in Brandes, II, 231.
66. Diderot, *Oeuvres*, 220.
67. Chaponnière, *Voltaire chez les Calvinistes*, 260.
68. In Brandes, II, 232.
69. Voltaire, *Correspondance*, ed. Besterman, Letter 7584.
70. Pomeau, 311.
71. *Phil. Dict.*, art. "Superstition."
72. Letter of June 3, 1760.
73. Letter of Dec. 6, 1757.
74. Pomeau, 213; Bertrand, *D'Alembert*, 118.
75. Voltaire and Frederick, *Letters*, 283.
76. Parton, II, 285.
77. Letter to Damilaville, Apr. 5, 1765.
78. Frederick to Voltaire, Sept. 9, 1739.
79. Voltaire, *Oeuvres complètes*, XLIII, 198-200.
80. *Selected Works*, 59.
81. *Phil. Dict.*, art. "Laws."
82. J. Gaberel in Parton, II, 428.
83. Luke xxi, 27-32.
84. *Questions of Zapata*, No. 58, in *Selected Works*, 34.
85. *Ibid.*, Nos. 65-66.
86. *Ibid.*, No. 66.
87. Parton, 286.
88. Letter of June 4, 1767.
89. *New Camb. Mod. History*, VII, 152.
90. *Phil. Dict.*, art. "God."
91. Letter of Nov. 28, 1752.
92. *Oeuvres complètes*, XLI, 570, in Torrey, *Spirit of Voltaire*, 279.
93. *Phil. Dict.*, art. "Sin."
94. Pomeau, 373.
95. *Works*, Ib, 139.
96. *Phil. Dict.*, art. "Miracles."
97. Pomeau, 348.
98. *Ibid.*, 374.
99. *Phil. Dict.*, art. "Climate."
100. Art. "Grace."
101. *Profession de foi des théistes*, in Black, *Art of History*, 57.
102. *Works*, XIXa, 228.
103. *Ibid.*, 238.
104. *Traité de métaphysique.*
105. Crocker, *Age of Crisis*, 385.
106. *Ibid.*, 190; *cf. Phil. Dict.*, art. "Atheism," and art. "God," Sec. v.
107. Art. "Hell."
108. Art. "Fraud."
109. Art. "Morality."
110. Voltaire, *The Ignorant Philosopher*, Secs. II-III.
111. *Ibid.*, III-IV.
112. XIII.
113. XIV.
114. XVII, XIX.
115. XX.
116. XXIV.
117. LI.
118. *Works*, IIa, 312-16.
119. *Boswell on the Grand Tour: Germany and Switzerland*, 304.
120. Noyes, *Voltaire*, 555; Pomeau, 411.
121. Voltaire, *Oeuvres complètes*, XXVI, 199, in Pomeau, 438.
122. Art. "Curate."
123. Pomeau, 439.
124. *Essai sur les moeurs*, Ch. cxxxix, in Ducros, *French Society in the 18th Century*, 199.
125. Desnoiresterres, VI, 118.
126. *Ibid.*, 63-64; Pomeau, 431.
127. Desnoiresterres, VII, 237.
128. Torrey, *Spirit of Voltaire*, 225.
129. Desnoiresterres, VII, 228.
130. *Ibid.*, 287.
131. Pomeau, 390.
132. Diderot, *Letters to Sophie Volland*, I, 29, in Pomeau, 332.
133. Grimm, *Corresp.*, VII, 51.
134. Walpole, H., in Mossner, *Bishop Butler and the Age of Reason*, 175; *cf.* Mornet, *Origines*, 139, and Morley, *Life of Voltaire*, 88.
135. Letter to Mme. du Deffand, June 1, 1770.
136. *Ignorant Philosopher*, Sec. xxiv.
137. Mark ix, 45-48; Matt. xiii, 40-42; Luke xvi, 23-26.

CHAPTER XXIII

1. Pomeau, 300.
2. Mornet, *Origines*, 206.
3. Gauchat, *Lettres critiques*, XV, 224, in Vartanian, *Diderot and Descartes*, 313.
4. Pomeau, 338.
5. Voltaire, letter of Dec. 8, 1776.
6. Palmer, R.R., *Catholics and Unbelievers*, 96.
7. *Ibid.*, 142.
8. Our account follows John H. Pappas, *Berthier's* Journal de Trévoux *and the Philosophes*.
9. *Ibid.*, 38.
10. 23, 137.
11. 48.
12. 128.
13. 48.
14. 205.
15. *Ibid.*
16. 184.
17. 186.
18. 110.
19. 113.
20. 119.
21. 122.
22. 131.
23. Desnoiresterres, III, 389.
24. Hazard, *Eighteenth Century*, 78.
25. Cornou, *Élie Fréron*, in Martin, K., 96.
26. Crocker, *Embattled Philosopher*, 240.
27. *Ibid.*
28. Brandes, II, 205.
29. *Ibid.*, 206.
30. Noyes, *Voltaire*, 51.
31. *Ibid.*, 71.
32. Lanfrey, 195.
33. In Masson, *La Religion de Rousseau*, III, 31.
34. Crocker, *Age of Crisis*, 382.
35. Lichtenberger, A., *Le Socialisme et la Révolution française*, 6n.
36. Crocker, *Emb. Philosopher*, 305.
37. Toth, *Woman and Rococo*, 224, 234.
38. Goncourts, *Woman of the 18th Century*, 305.
39. Toth, 234.
40. Letter of Jan. 10, 1758, in Naves, 53.
41. *Oeuvres*, 231, 239-40.
42. *Ibid.*, 235, etc.
43. Grimm, II, 373.
44. Palmer, *Catholics and Unbelievers*, 7.
45. Parton, II, 334.
46. Pappas, 85.
47. *Ibid.*, 114.
48. 117.
49. Fülop-Miller, *Power and Secret of the Jesuits*, 374.
50. Gay, *Voltaire's Politics*, 310.
51. Pappas, 129.
52. Beard, Miriam, *History of the Business Man*, 414.
53. Martin, H., *Histoire de France*, XVI, 201.
54. Lanfrey, 267; Campbell, *The Jesuits*, 482.
55. *Ibid.*, 483.
56. *Catholic Encyclopedia*, XIV, 98a; Martin, H., XVI, 211; Ranke, *History of the Popes*, II, 447.
57. Campbell, 487.
58. *Ibid.*, 485.
59. McCabe, *Candid History of the Jesuits*, 251.
60. Robertson, J. M., *History of Freethought*, II, 236.
61. Desnoiresterres, VI, 269.
62. Bertrand, *D'Alembert*, 132.
63. Lanfrey, 269.
64. *Ibid.*, 270.
65. Pappas, 135.
66. Pomeau, 317.
67. Gilbert, *Prince de Ligne*, 138; Carlyle, *Friedrich the Second*, VII, 470.
68. Campbell, *The Jesuits*, 639.
69. La Fontainerie, *French Liberalism and Education in the 18th Century*, 143, 149.
70. Cumming, *Helvétius*, 160.
71. La Fontainerie, 80.
72. *Ibid.*, 117.
73. *Ibid.*, 39; Desnoiresterres, VI, 239.
74. Letter of Apr. 1, 1766.
75. Lanson, *Voltaire*, 183.
76. Smith, P., *Modern Culture*, II, 446.
77. La Fontainerie, 240.
78. Sée, H., *Les idées politiques en France*, 142.
79. Mornet, *Origines*, 177.
80. Lacroix, *Eighteenth Century*, 265.
81. Helvétius, *Treatise on Man*, Vol. II, p. 402.
82. Brunetière, *Manual of French Literature*, 298.
83. Hazard, 369.
84. Bury, *Idea of Progress*, 149.
85. Smith, P., II, 614.
86. D'Alembert, *Éléments de la philosophie*, Ch. iv, in Hazard, 166.
87. Hazard, 169.
88. Voltaire, *Works*, XIXa, 89 f.
89. Hazard, 250.
90. Rousseau, *Sur le gouvernement de Pologne*, in Black, *Art of History*, 20.
91. Source lost.
92. Martin, H., *Histoire de France*, XVI, 212.
93. Bury, *Idea of Progress*, 203; Parton, II, 433.
94. Hazard, 126.

95. Buckle, I, 620.
96. Parton, II, 507.
97. Lecky, *History of . . . Rationalism*, I, 125.
98. Tocqueville, *L'Ancien Régime*, 165.
99. Lecky, *History of England*, V, 336.
100. Mornet, *Origines*, 214-16.
101. La Harpe in Taine, *Ancient Regime*, 400.
102. Walpole, H., letter of Oct. 19, 1765.
103. *Id.*, letter of Nov. 19, 1765.
104. Mornet, 269.
105. *Ibid.*
106. Toth, *Woman and Rococo*, 234.
107. Mornet, 272.
108. Willey, *Eighteenth-Century Background*, 192.
109. Taine, *Ancient Regime*, 293.
110. Robertson, J. M., *History of Freethought*, II, 278.
111. Montalembert, *Monks of the West*, I, 86.
112. Mornet, 141.
113. Voltaire, *Oeuvres complètes*, XLIII, 237.

114. Letter of Nov. 9, 1764.
115. Wilson, *Diderot*, 286; Palmer, *Catholics and Unbelievers*, 17.
116. Torrey, *Spirit of Voltaire*, 133.
117. Condorcet, *Progrès de l'esprit humain*, 251.
118. Mornet, 125.
119. *Ibid.*, 273.
120. Eckermann and Soret, *Conversations with Goethe*, 421, 529.
121. Frederick to Voltaire, May 5, 1767.
122. Grimm, *Corresp.*, Sept. 15, 1767.
123. *Dict. Phil.*, art. "God."

EPILOGUE

1. Crocker, *Embattled Philosopher*, 407.
2. Sade, Marquis de, *Justine* (1791), *Juliette* (1792), *Philosophie dans le boudoir* (1793).
3. Musset, Alfred de, *Confessions of a Child of the Century*, 21 f.
4. Chaponnière, *Geneva*, 231.
5. *Phil. Dict.*, art. "God," Sec. IV; art. "Polytheism."

Index

Dates in parentheses following a name are of birth and death except when preceded by *r.*, when they indicate duration of reign for popes and rulers of states. A single date preceded by *fl.* denotes a *floruit*. A footnote is indicated by an asterisk. Italicized page numbers indicate principal treatment. All dates are A.D. unless otherwise noted.

Frank, Johann Peter (1745–1821), 591

Frankfurt-am-Main, free city of, 397-98, 454, 457, 592; Voltaire's detention at, 469-70, 488, 489

Franklin, Benjamin (1706–90), 132, 507, 537, 596, 597; electrical experiments of, 471, 519, 520-22; in France, 522, 594, 692; and *philosophes*, 693, 694, 784; and Priestley, 526, 530

Frascati, Italy, 109

Frederick I, King of Prussia (r. 1701–13), Elector of Brandenburg as Frederick III (r. 1688–1701), 437, 448

Frederick I, King of Sweden (r. 1720–51) and Landgrave of Hesse-Cassel, 414

Frederick II the Great, King of Prussia (r. 1740–86), 89, 221, 277, 291, 360, 403, 405, 437, *439-60*, 599, 606, 638, 665, 692

AT HOME: accession of, 402, 436, 439, 447; his accomplishments, 407; and Algarotti, 212, 449; his appearance and character, 447, 459-60; as author, 407, 458, 460, 407, 446, 449-50, 452, 458, 460, 711, 713; on Charles VI, 435; and the *Encyclopédie*, 639, 644; on England, 98, 446; the "enlightened despot," 447-48, 459, 688, 711, 776; father's maltreatment of, 439-42, 450; at father's deathbed, 446-47; free press under, 448, 496; French language favored by, 323, 440, 441; on George II, 113; on Germans and German culture, 400-401, 403, 410, 440; and La Mettrie, 465, 617, 621-22; his marriage, 442, 460; and Maupertuis, 442, 448-49, 466-69, 514, 516, 719; as musician, 407, 417, 439, 440, 441, 450, 455, 460; opera and music fostered by, 408, 410-12, 417, 421, 455; as poet, 407, 439, 441, 450, 455, 460, 461, 463, 465, 466; and Mme. de Pompadour, 285; his regimen, 460; religion, contempt for, 402, 410, 428, 440, 441, 445, 502, 617, 715, 718; religious toleration under, 402, 448, 452, 772-73; and Sanssouci, 309, 311, 406-7, 460, 461; science fostered by, 283, 441, 448-49, 460, 477, 510, 511, 514, 516, 621; on superstition, 736; his suppers, 460, 461; and Voltaire, *see* FREDERICK AND VOLTAIRE *below*; and Wilhelmine, 405, 439, 441, 442, 460, 469, 470; and Wolff, 401, 402, 442-44 *passim*, 448

AT WAR: his army, 439, 449, 450, 459, 460; his demand for Silesia rejected, 436, 451; invades and conquers Silesia (1740–41), 109, 271, 436, 451-52, 514, 772, 779; negotiates secret truce with Austria (1741), 272, 453-54; re-enters war, 454; in Second Silesian War (1744–45), 276, 455-57; signs separate peace with Austria in both wars, 278, 454, 457; justifies his actions, 458; and Seven Years' War, 285, 316, 400, 410, 489, 768

FREDERICK AND VOLTAIRE: praises V.'s *Henriade*, 40; beginning of their friendship, 372, 378; his early correspondence with V., as crown prince (1736–40), 378, *442-46*, 718, 740; sends V. his *Anti-Machiavel*, 446; his letters to V. on his accession, 447; V.'s influence on his reign, 447-48, 450; his first meeting with V., at Cleves (1740), 379, 448-49; V. visits him in Berlin (1740) as French agent, 379, 449-50; is dubbed "Great" by V., 431, 458; is reproved by V. for making war, 458, 779; his answer, 458; V.'s second visit as French agent, at Aachen (1742), 381; invites V. to live at Berlin-Potsdam, 382, 445, 455; V.'s third visit as French agent, at Berlin (1743), 382, 455; renews his invitations to V. (1748–50), offers post, 388-90, 393; V. at his court (1750–53), 461 f., 621-22, 715, 718, 740; is dissuaded by V. from hiring Fréron, 463, 760; attacks V. for Hirsch and Maupertuis disputes, 462-63, 467-68, 719; compels V. to return his poems, 469-70; supports V.'s campaigns, 733, 735-36, 739, 744; both answer d'Holbach, 711, 713; on V.'s joining the Capuchins, 751-52; pays tribute to V., 736, 785

Frederick Augustus I, Elector of Saxony (r. 1694–1733), *see* Augustus II the Strong, King of Poland

Frederick Augustus II, Elector of Saxony (r. 1733–63), *see* Augustus III, King of Poland

Frederick Louis, Prince of Wales (1707–51), 81, 94, 99, 100, 179, 235, 236, 241

Frederick William I, King of Prussia (r. 1713–40), 399-400, 402, 403, 405, *437-42*, 447, 448; army of, 437, 438-39, 450, 459; death of, 446-47; and Frederick II, 437, 439-40, 440-42, 450; and Pragmatic Sanction, 436, 451

Frederick William II, King of Prussia (r. 1786–97), 496, 511, 752

Frederick William IV, King of Prussia (r. 1840–61), 543

free donations, *see dons gratuits*

free enterprise, 54, 262, 647

Free Inquiry into the Miraculous Powers . . . in the Christian Church, A (Middleton), 122-23

Freemasonry, 79, 294-95, 344, 432, 446, 610, 767

free trade, 98, 156, 262, 279, 475, 647

free will, doctrine of, 118, 134, 356, 583, 758; rejected, 143, 339, 528, 612; Voltaire on, 445, 715, 716, 748

Freiberg, Saxony, 408

Freiberg School of Mines, 556

Freiburg-im-Breisgau, 276

French Academy (Académie Française, Forty Immortals), 24, 291, 344, 679, 697, 699, 762, 763, 784; d'Alembert and, 337, 498, 782; Buf-

About the Authors

WILL DURANT was born in North Adams, Massachusetts, on November 5, 1885. He was educated in the Catholic parochial schools there and in Kearny, New Jersey, and thereafter in St. Peter's (Jesuit) College, Jersey City, New Jersey, and Columbia University. New York. For a summer he served as a cub reporter on the New York *Journal*, in 1907, but finding the work too strenuous for his temperament, he settled down at Seton Hall College, South Orange, New Jersey, to teach Latin, French, English, and geometry (1907-11). He entered the seminary at Seton Hall in 1909, but withdrew in 1911 for reasons he has described in his book *Transition*. He passed from this quiet seminary to the most radical circles in New York, and became (1911-13) the teacher of the Ferrer Modern School, an experiment in libertarian education. In 1912 he toured Europe at the invitation and expense of Alden Freeman, who had befriended him and now undertook to broaden his borders.

Returning to the Ferrer School, he fell in love with one of his pupils—who had been born Ida Kaufman in Russia on May 10, 1898—resigned his position, and married her (1913). For four years he took graduate work at Columbia University, specializing in biology under Morgan and Calkins and in philosophy under Woodbridge and Dewey. He received the doctorate in philosophy in 1917, and taught philosophy at Columbia University for one year. In 1914, in a Presbyterian church in New York, he began those lectures on history, literature, and philosophy that, continuing twice weekly for thirteen years, provided the initial material for his later works.

The unexpected success of *The Story of Philosophy* (1926) enabled him to retire from teaching in 1927. Thenceforth, except for some incidental essays Mr. and Mrs. Durant gave nearly all their working hours (eight to fourteen daily) to *The Story of Civilization*. To better prepare themselves they toured Europe in 1927, went around the world in 1930 to study Egypt, the Near East, India, China, and Japan, and toured the globe again in 1932 to visit Japan, Manchuria, Siberia, Russia, and Poland. These travels provided the background for *Our Oriental Heritage* (1935) as the first volume in *The Story of Civilization*. Several further visits to Europe prepared for Volume 2, *The Life of Greece* (1939), and Volume 3, *Caesar and Christ* (1944). In 1948, six months in Turkey, Iraq, Iran, Egypt, and Europe provided perspective for Volume 4, *The Age of Faith* (1950). In 1951 Mr. and Mrs. Durant returned to Italy to add to a lifetime of gleanings for Volume 5, *The Renaissance* (1953); and in 1954 further studies in Italy, Switzerland, Germany, France, and England opened new vistas for Volume 6, *The Reformation* (1957).

Mrs. Durant's share in the preparation of these volumes became more and more substantial with each year, until in the case of Volume 7, *The Age of Reason Begins* (1961), it was so great that justice required the union of both names on the title page. And so it was on *The Age of Louis XIV* (1963), *The Age of Voltaire* (1965), and *Rousseau and Revolution* (winner of the Pulitzer Prize in 1968).

The publication of Volume 11, *The Age of Napoleon*, in 1975 concluded five decades of achievement. Ariel Durant died on October 25, 1981, at the age of 83; Will Durant died 13 days later, on November 7, aged 96. Their last published work was *A Dual Autobiography* (1977).